New Media Research Resources

Whether students want to investigate the ideas behind a thought-provoking topic or conduct in-depth research for a paper, our new media research resources online and on CD-ROM can help them refine their research skills, find what they need in the library or on the Web, and then use and document their sources effectively.

DocLinks

bedfordstmartins.com/doclinks

A database of over 750 annotated Web links to primary documents online for the study of American history. Document links include speeches, legislation, United States Supreme Court decisions, treaties, social commentary, newspaper articles, visual artifacts, songs, and poems.

History Links Library

bedfordstmartins.com/historylinks

A database of more than 350 carefully reviewed and annotated American history Web sites containing material on historical archeology, primary documents collections, photograph and illustration galleries, map collections, secondary readings, and audio sources.

Research and Documentation Online

bedfordstmartins.com/resdoc

Diana Hacker, *Prince George's Community College*

This online version of Diana Hacker's popular booklet provides clear advice across the disciplines on how to find, evaluate, and integrate outside material into a paper, how to cite sources correctly, and how to format in MLA, APA, CBE, and *Chicago* styles.

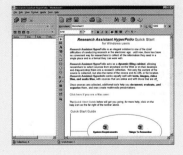

Research Assistant Hyperfolio

Delivered on CD-ROM, this intelligent tool for conducting research helps students collect, evaluate, and cite sources found both online and off.

bedfordstmartins.com/history

PACIFIC OCEAN

CANADA

MEXICO

WASHINGTON

Seattle
Olympia
Spokane
Portland
Salem

OREGON

IDAHO

Boise

NEVADA

Reno
Carson City

Sacramento
San Francisco
Oakland
San Jose

Fresno

CALIFORNIA

Las Vegas

Los Angeles

San Diego

PACIFIC
OCEAN

Great
Falls
Helena

MONTANA

Billings

WYOMING

Great
Salt Lake

Salt
Lake
City

UTAH

Cheyenne

Denver

COLORADO

Colorado
Springs

Santa Fe
Albuquerque

ARIZONA

NEW MEXICO

Phoenix

Tucson

El Paso

NORTH DAKOTA

Bismarck
Fargo

SOUTH DAKOTA

Pierre

NEBRASKA

KANSAS

Wichita

OKLAHOMA

Amarillo

TEXAS

Austin

San
Antonio

ROCKY MOUNTAINS

SIERRA NEVADA

Columbia R.
Columbia R.
Snake R.
Sacramento R.
San Joaquin R.
Green R.
Colorado R.
Missouri R.
Yellowstone R.
North Platte R.
Platte R.
South Platte R.
Arkansas R.
Red R.
Colorado R.
Pecos R.
Rio Grande
Nueces R.

HAWAII

Honolulu

PACIFIC OCEAN

0   50   100 miles
0   50   100 kilometers

160°W   155°W

RUSSIA

ALASKA

BROOKS RANGE

ALASKA RANGE

Anchorage

Juneau

CANADA

Bering Sea

Gulf of Alaska

International Date Line

Yukon R.

0   200   400 miles
0   200   400 kilometers

N
W   E
S

22°N
20°N
25°N
50°N
20°N

70°N

60°N

175°E   175°W   165°W   155°W   145°W   135°W

120°W   115°W   110°W

45°N
40°N
35°N
30°N

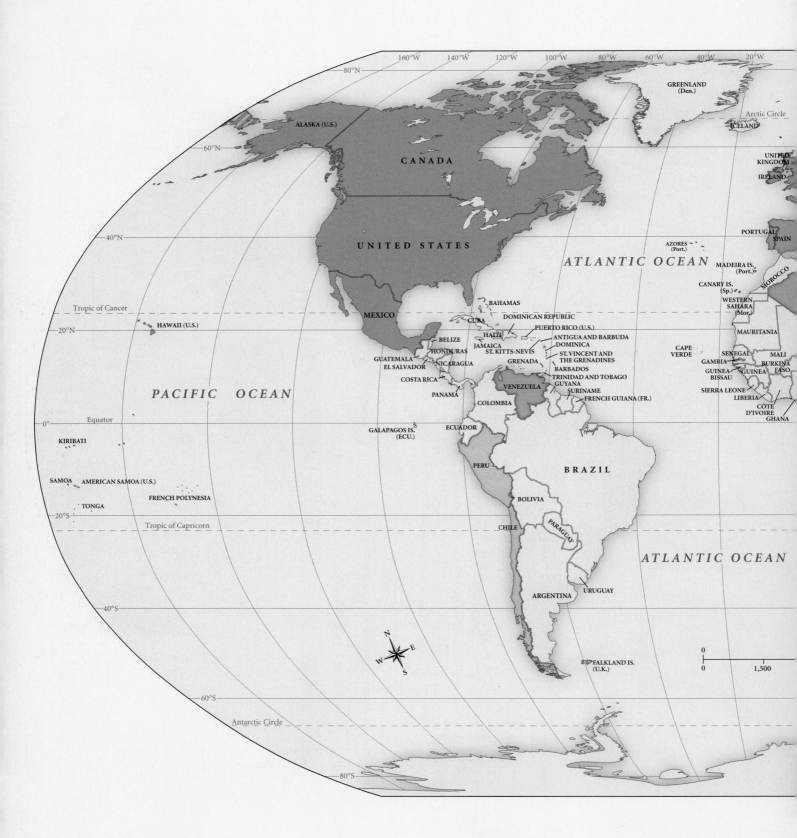

PACIFIC OCEAN

ATLANTIC OCEAN

ATLANTIC OCEAN

ALASKA (U.S.)

CANADA

UNITED STATES

GREENLAND (Den.)

Arctic Circle

ICELAND

UNITED KINGDOM

IRELAND

PORTUGAL

SPAIN

AZORES (Port.)

MADEIRA IS. (Port.)

CANARY IS. (Sp.)

MOROCCO

WESTERN SAHARA (Mor.)

MEXICO

HAWAII (U.S.)

Tropic of Cancer

BAHAMAS

CUBA

DOMINICAN REPUBLIC

PUERTO RICO (U.S.)

HAITI

ANTIGUA AND BARBUDA

JAMAICA

ST. KITTS-NEVIS

DOMINICA

BELIZE

ST. VINCENT AND THE GRENADINES

HONDURAS

GRENADA

GUATEMALA

BARBADOS

EL SALVADOR

TRINIDAD AND TOBAGO

NICARAGUA

GUYANA

COSTA RICA

VENEZUELA

SURINAME

PANAMA

FRENCH GUIANA (FR.)

COLOMBIA

MAURITANIA

CAPE VERDE

SENEGAL

MALI

GAMBIA

BURKINA FASO

GUINEA-BISSAU

GUINEA

SIERRA LEONE

LIBERIA

CÔTE D'IVOIRE

GHANA

GALAPAGOS IS. (ECU.)

ECUADOR

PERU

BRAZIL

KIRIBATI

SAMOA

AMERICAN SAMOA (U.S.)

FRENCH POLYNESIA

TONGA

BOLIVIA

CHILE

PARAGUAY

Tropic of Capricorn

ARGENTINA

URUGUAY

FALKLAND IS. (U.K.)

N
E
S
W

0

0   1,500

Antarctic Circle

Political divisions as of April 2003

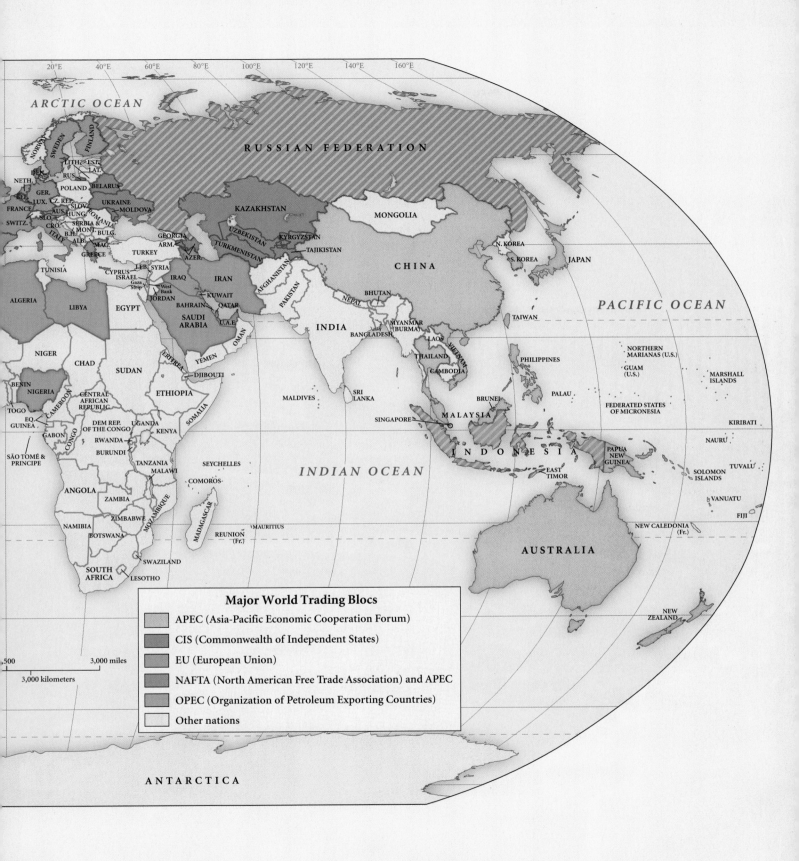

ARCTIC OCEAN

20°E   40°E   60°E   80°E   100°E   120°E   140°E   160°E

RUSSIAN FEDERATION

NORWAY
SWEDEN
FINLAND
DEN.
LITH. EST.
RUS. LAT.
NETH.
GER. POLAND BELARUS
BEL.
LUX. CZ. REP.
FRANCE SLOV. UKRAINE
AUS. HUNG. MOLDOVA
SWITZ. SLO. ROMANIA
ITALY CRO. SERBIA &
B.H. MONT. BULG.
ALB. MAC.
GREECE
TUNISIA TURKEY

KAZAKHSTAN
UZBEKISTAN KYRGYZSTAN
GEORGIA TURKMENISTAN TAJIKISTAN
ARM.
AZER.

MONGOLIA

N. KOREA
S. KOREA JAPAN

CHINA

TAIWAN

PACIFIC OCEAN

CYPRUS LEB. SYRIA
ISRAEL IRAQ IRAN
Gaza West KUWAIT
Strip Bank BAHRAIN QATAR
JORDAN

ALGERIA LIBYA EGYPT
SAUDI
ARABIA U.A.E.
OMAN

AFGHANISTAN
PAKISTAN

NEPAL BHUTAN
INDIA
BANGLADESH MYANMAR
(BURMA)
LAOS
THAILAND VIETNAM
CAMBODIA

PHILIPPINES

NORTHERN
MARIANAS (U.S.)

GUAM
(U.S.)

MARSHALL
ISLANDS

NIGER CHAD SUDAN
ERITREA
YEMEN
DJIBOUTI

BENIN NIGERIA CENTRAL
AFRICAN
REPUBLIC ETHIOPIA
TOGO
EQ.
GUINEA CAMEROON
GABON CONGO DEM. REP.
OF THE CONGO UGANDA
RWANDA KENYA
BURUNDI
SÃO TOMÉ &
PRÍNCIPE

SOMALIA

MALDIVES

SRI
LANKA

BRUNEI
MALAYSIA
SINGAPORE

PALAU

FEDERATED STATES
OF MICRONESIA

KIRIBATI

NAURU

SEYCHELLES

INDONESIA

PAPUA
NEW
GUINEA

TUVALU

TANZANIA
MALAWI
ANGOLA COMOROS
ZAMBIA
MOZAMBIQUE
ZIMBABWE
NAMIBIA MADAGASCAR
BOTSWANA REUNION
(Fr.)
MAURITIUS

EAST
TIMOR

SOLOMON
ISLANDS

VANUATU

FIJI

INDIAN OCEAN

NEW CALEDONIA
(Fr.)

AUSTRALIA

SWAZILAND
SOUTH
AFRICA LESOTHO

NEW
ZEALAND

500   3,000 miles

3,000 kilometers

Major World Trading Blocs

- APEC (Asia-Pacific Economic Cooperation Forum)
- CIS (Commonwealth of Independent States)
- EU (European Union)
- NAFTA (North American Free Trade Association) and APEC
- OPEC (Organization of Petroleum Exporting Countries)
- Other nations

ANTARCTICA

FIFTH EDITION

America's History

Volume 2: Since 1865

James A. Henretta

University of Maryland

David Brody

University of California, Davis

Lynn Dumenil

Occidental College

Susan Ware

Radcliffe Institute for Advanced Study

Bedford / St. Martin's

Boston • New York

For Bedford / St. Martin's

Publisher for History: Patricia A. Rossi
Director of Development for History: Jane Knetzger
Executive Editor for History: Elizabeth M. Welch
Developmental Editors: Jessica N. Angell and William J. Lombardo
Production Editor: Lori Chong Roncka
Production Assistants: Tina Lai, Kristen Merrill
Senior Production Supervisor: Joe Ford
Marketing Manager: Jenna Bookin Barry
Art Director: Donna Lee Dennison
Text Design: Gretchen Tolles for Anna George Design
Cover Design: Billy Boardman and Donna Lee Dennison
Copy Editors: Barbara G. Flanagan; Susan M. Free of Reap 'n Sow
Indexer: EdIndex
Photo Research: Pembroke Herbert/Picture Research Consultants & Archives
Advisory Editor for Cartography: Gerald A. Danzer
Map Development and Coordination: Tina Samaha
Cartography: Mapping Specialists Limited
Composition: TechBooks
Printing and Binding: R.R. Donnelley & Sons Company

President: Joan E. Feinberg
Editorial Director: Denise B. Wydra
Director of Editing, Design, and Production: Marcia Cohen
Managing Editor: Elizabeth M. Schaaf

Library of Congress Control Number: 2003101705

Manufactured in the United States of America.

8   7   6   5   4   3
f   e   d   c   b   a

For information, write: Bedford / St. Martin's, 75 Arlington Street, Boston, MA 02116 (617–399–4000)

ISBN: 0–312–39879–4 (hardcover)
ISBN: 0–312–40934–6 (paperback Vol. 1)
ISBN: 0–312–40958–3 (paperback Vol. 2)

Cover and title page art: Civic Center from Hollywood Freeway, Los Angeles, 1953. Curt Teich Postcard, private collection.

For Emily and Rebecca;
Siena, Cameron, Alex, Lea, and Eleanor;
Norman

In this, the fifth edition, *America's History* makes its debut as a book of the twenty-first century. When we first embarked on this edition, the country was at peace, the economy seemed invincible, and presidential candidate George W. Bush was advocating a "humble" foreign policy and no more "nation-building." The destruction of New York's World Trade Center on September 11, 2001, put an end to most Americans' hopes for a new age of normalcy; instead the nation finds itself plunged into a global war on terrorism, a war without end and without borders. As if on cue, many of our certitudes—about enduring prosperity, about the integrity of our business institutions, about an unsullied Catholic Church, about worldwide enthusiasm for America as global superpower—came crashing down. As the world becomes a threatening place, even those college students who don't think much about America's past or today's news have to wonder: How did that happen?

This question is at the heart of historical inquiry. And in asking it, the student is thinking historically. In *America's History* we aspire to satisfy that student's curiosity. We try to ask the right questions—the big ones and the not-so-big—and then write narrative history that illuminates the answers. The story, we hope, tells not only what happened, but *why*. We exclude no student from our potential audience of readers. How could we, when we hold the conviction that every student, bar none, wants to understand the world in which she lives?

From the very inception of *America's History*, we set out to write a *democratic* history, one that would convey the experiences of ordinary people even as it recorded the accomplishments of the great and powerful. We focus not only on the marvelous diversity of peoples who became American but also on the institutions—political, economic, cultural, and social—that forged a common national identity. And we present these historical trajectories in an integrated way, using each perspective to make better sense of the others. In our discussion of government and politics, diplomacy and war, we show how they affected—and were affected by—ethnic groups and economic conditions, intellectual beliefs and social changes, and the religious and moral values of the times. Just as important, we place the American experience in a global context. We trace aspects of American society to their origins in European and African cultures, consider the American Industrial Revolution within the framework of the world economy, and plot the foreign relations of the United States as part of an ever-shifting international system of imperial expansion, financial exchange, and diplomatic alliances.

In emphasizing the global context, however, we had something more in mind. We wanted to remind students that America never existed alone in the world; that other nations experienced developments comparable to our own; and that, knowing this, we can better understand what was distinctive and particular to the American experience. At opportune junctures, we pause for a comparative discussion, for example about the abolition of slavery in different nineteenth-century plantation economies. This discussion enables us to explain why, in the universal struggle by emancipated slaves for economic freedom, the freedmen of the American South became sharecropping tenants in a market economy and not, as in the Caribbean, gang laborers or subsistence farmers. The operative word is *explain* and, insofar as we can make it so, explaining the past is what we intend *America's History* to do. The challenge is to write a text that has explanatory power and yet is immediately accessible to every student who enrolls in the survey course.

Organization

Accomplishing these goals means first of all grounding *America's History* in a strong conceptual framework and a clear chronology. The nation's history is divided into six **parts**, corresponding to the major phases of American development. Each part begins at a crucial turning point, such as the American Revolution or the cold war, and emphasizes the dynamic forces that unleashed it and that symbolized the era. We want to show how people of all classes and groups make their own history, but also how people's choices are influenced and constrained by circumstances: the customs and institutions inherited from the past and the distribution of power in the present. We are writing narrative history, but harnessed to historical argument, not simply a retelling of "this happened, then that happened."

To aid student comprehension, each part begins with a two-page overview. First, a **thematic timeline** highlights the key developments in politics, the economy, society, culture, and foreign affairs; then these themes are fleshed out in a corresponding **part essay**. Each part essay focuses on the crucial engines of historical change—in some eras primarily economic, in others political or diplomatic—that created new conditions of life and transformed social relations. The part organization, encapsulated in the thematic timelines and opening essays, helps students understand the major themes and periods of American history, to see how bits and pieces of historical data acquire significance as part of a larger pattern of development.

The individual chapters are similarly constructed with student comprehension in mind. A **chapter outline** gives readers an overview of the text discussion, followed by a **thematic introduction** that orients them to the central issues and ideas of the chapter. Then, at the end of the chapter, we reiterate the themes in an **analytic summary** and remind students of important events in a **chapter timeline**. A **new glossary** defines the **key concepts** boldfaced in the text where first mentioned. **Suggested references** for each chapter, now united at the back of the book and expanded to include Web sites, are annotated for students and, in another measure to facilitate research, are divided into sections corresponding to those of the chapter.

Features

The fifth edition of *America's History* contains a wealth of special features, offered not with an eye to embellishing the book but as essential components of the text's pedagogical mission. Each chapter includes two **American Voices**—excerpts from letters, diaries, autobiographies, and public testimony that convey the experience of ordinary Americans in their own words. Exciting new selections include "Red Jacket: A Seneca Chief's Understanding of Religion," "Spotswood Rice: 'Freeing My Children from Slavery,'" and "Susana Archuleta: A Chicana Youth Gets New Deal Work." In keeping with our global focus, **Voices from Abroad** similarly offers first-person testimony by foreign visitors and observers in every chapter. "Louis Antonine De Bougainville: The Defense of Canada," "The Ford Miracle: 'Slaves' to the Assembly Line," and "Fei Xiaotong: America's Crisis of Faith" are a few of the new Voices from Abroad selections in this edition. Recognizing the centrality of technology in American life, we offer in each part two **New Technology** essays in which we describe key technical innovations and their impact on American history. Examples range from the cultivation of corn and the mechanization of spinning to rural electrification and the biotech revolution. We retain our vivid **American Lives** feature—incisive biographies in every chapter of well-known, representative American figures such as founder of the African Methodist Episcopal Church Richard Allen, social reformer Dorothea Dix, newspaperman William Randolph Hearst, and Mexican American labor organizer Bert Corona.

In this fifth edition, we add a new part feature, concluding essays we entitle **Thinking about History**. In these essays we take up a major theme discussed in the preceding chapters and examine how it is currently being reconsidered by historians. The particular dynamic on which we focus is the relationship between past and present. The Thinking about History essay for Part Four, for example, deals with the Great Plains, whose settlement after the Civil War is treated in Chapter 16 as the final stage in the westward movement. This is an unexceptional perspective, with an air of the inevitable about it. But today the Great Plains are emptying out. The attempt at taming this semiarid, fragile land is increasingly seen as an ecological disaster, a terrible misstep in the nation's development. As they assimilate that knowledge, the essay asks, how are scholars rethinking the history of Great Plains settlement? And how, as a result, is that history likely to be rewritten in the future? Other Thinking about History essays deal with the tripartite colonial legacy of slavery, racism, and republicanism; the renewed scholarly debate over federalism prompted by the "Reagan Revolution" of the 1980s; the recent controversy over the words "under God" in the Pledge of Allegiance; and the role of gender in explaining the origins and character of the U.S. welfare system. We offer these new essays in hopes of alerting students to the excitement and vitality of historical inquiry and, just as important, in hopes of revealing that the past they are studying is essential to understanding the world in which they live.

Those aims similarly prompt us to offer at the close of the book an **Epilogue** subtitled "Thinking about Contemporary History." Here, however, the argument moves in a direction opposite to the earlier Thinking about History essays—not how the present influences our reading of the past, but how knowledge of the past enables us to understand the present. While we were preparing the fourth edition, the approach of the millennium suggested to us the idea of a historically reflective Epilogue on America in 2000. The Epilogue in this fifth edition, while also reflective about the uses of history, is more concerned with applying that knowledge to the fraught world that college students currently face, most particularly in the wake of September 11.

We revised with equal care the text's illustration program. *America's History* has always been noted for the rich collection of maps, figures, and pictures that help students so much to visualize the past. There is, however, always room for improvement. **One-quarter of the pictures are new** to this edition, selected to reflect changes in the text and to underscore chapter themes. Most appear in full color, with unusually **substantive captions** that actively engage students with the image and encourage them to analyze artwork as primary sources. A **new design** complements the illustrations while drawing attention to our most significant revision of the text's visual aids: a **thoroughly revised and expanded map program**. To oversee the new map program we have enlisted Professor Gerald A. Danzer of the University of Illinois at Chicago, a specialist in geographic literacy. He has worked assiduously to make our maps better teaching tools, reworking many of them, enhancing the topography, and adding map annotations that call out key points. The map program is also much expanded, with over forty new maps, covering every aspect of American life that can be captured geographically. New maps on the Ice Age, the Columbian Exchange, the National Parks and Forests, the Dust Bowl, public works projects of the New Deal, and nuclear weapons testing consider the environmental ramifications of historical events and policies. Creating new maps is an opportunity to further reinforce for students how America's history is indeed part of a broader global history, and to this end we have added maps on the settling of the Americas, fifteenth-century West Africa and the Mediterranean, European immigration to the United States at the turn of the twentieth century, and the Great Powers in East Asia in 1910. We have added new elections maps and have added map series into the narrative that show change over time, depicting, for example, Eurasian trade systems in 1500, 1650, and 1770.

This new map program is well supported by tools that teach students how to extract as much information from a map as possible and to make connections beyond the map to the narrative. The text's introduction now contains a **map primer** that walks students through a map step-by-step, offering guidance and tips on how to "read" and analyze the map. **Cross-references to online map activities**, which appear at the bottom of a key map in each chapter, encourage students to test and improve upon these skills. A **map workbook**, also written by Professor Danzer, provides skill-building exercises for a map in each chapter, effectively teaching students how to use maps to enrich their understanding of American history.

Taken together, these documents, essays, pictures, and maps offer instructors a trove of teaching materials and supply students with rich fare for experiencing the world of the American past.

Textual Changes

Of all the reasons for a new edition, of course, the most compelling is to improve the text itself—a task we have found to be never finished and yet, to our surprise, always gratifying. In this fifth edition, we are spurred on by a shift in authorial responsibility, which always brings forth much rewriting. Marilynn Johnson retires with this edition, and Lynn Dumenil of Occidental College assumes responsibility for the modern era (Chapters 22–30). Professor Dumenil is not, however, new to this project. She joined us when we undertook a concise version, assuming responsibility for the same set of chapters that are now in her charge for *America's History*. It was an opportune meeting for us because Professor Dumenil's work on the concise version makes her a seasoned practitioner of the arts of concision and clarity that, more than anything else, we hope distinguishes the writing of *America's History*.

Ask students taking the U.S. survey—or their instructors, for that matter—what's the biggest problem with the course and they're likely to answer, "Too much to cover!" They have a point. After all, every passing year brings more American history to write about and read about. Consider the issue from a generational perspective. When the most senior of the authors of *America's History* was taking the U.S. survey in 1948–1949, most of Part Six had not yet happened! The intervening years, moreover, have seen an explosion of research into areas of our past that were invisible to earlier generations of historians—from women's history and gender roles to race and ethnicity to family life, popular culture, and work. No one, of course, would want to go back to the days when American history was essentially a chronicle of politics, diplomacy, and white men. But the inclusive, multifaceted history that we celebrate does make life harder for textbook writers. We have to resist the creep, the extra pages, that bulk up our books as we strive to incorporate what's new in the field and in contemporary America. In the fourth edition, we mounted a counteroffensive, cutting two chapters and reducing chapter length by 10 percent. In this edition, we declare victory, with even leaner chapters, 15 percent shorter than in the previous edition, so that, in effect, three words are doing the work originally of four. Our aim is to achieve a clearer, more sharply delineated narrative. Brevity, we have learned all over again, is the best antidote to imprecise language and murky argument. As textbook authors, we have always contended that if written with enough clarity and skill, the introductory survey can be made accessible to students at all levels without simplifying the story or skimping on explanation. In this fifth edition, we have enlisted the power of brevity to reach that goal.

While streamlining the narrative, we also took full advantage of the opportunity that revision affords to integrate new scholarship into our text. In the first chapter, the collision of societies now encompasses Africa as well as Europe and Native America. Our treatment of Native Americans in the colonial era incorporates recent anthropologically influenced work showing how Indian peoples maintained elements of their traditional culture in the face of European domination. We draw on new work dealing with the role of women and gender in eighteenth-century religion and antebellum politics and recent scholarship on the crisis over slavery after Independence. We offer an expanded treatment of the role of state policy during the antebellum Market Revolution, and we draw on recent Reconstruction scholarship that sees the transition from slavery to freedom as largely a battle over labor systems. We continue to incorporate more about the Far West into the nation's historical narrative, relying on the new western history for insight into the interactions among environment, peoples, and economic development. Advances in gender history enable us to offer a new discussion of bachelorhood and masculinity in the late nineteenth century and to temper our treatment of progressive welfare policy as we become aware of its patriarchal underpinnings. New scholarship on ethnic minorities similarly enables us to amplify our discussion of Native Americans during World War I and the New Deal, Asian Americans during the Great Depression, and black women during the 1920s and the later civil rights struggles. Recent scholarship based on hitherto closed Soviet and U.S. archives continues to inform our treatment of the cold war, and analysis of the turbulent 2000 presidential election and the advent of a new Republican administration bring the book to a thoughtful close. In these ways, and others, we strive to maintain the reputation of *America's History* as a fresh and timely text.

Supplements

Readers of *America's History* often cite its ancillary package as a key to the book's success in the classroom. Hence we have revised and expanded with care our array of print and electronic ancillaries for students and teachers.

For Students

Print Resources

Documents to Accompany *America's History*. Volume 1 by Melvin Yazawa (University of New Mexico), Volume 2 by Kevin Fernlund (University of Missouri, St. Louis). Revised for the fifth edition of *America's History*, this affordable documents collection offers students over 350 primary-source readings on topics covered in the main textbook, arranged to match the book's organization. One-quarter of the documents in the collection are new to this edition, giving emphasis to contested issues in American history that will spark critical thinking and class discussions. More than thirty visuals, meant to be "read" and analyzed like written sources, have been added. With many new documents emphasizing the environment, the West, and America in the context of the larger world, the collection remains a balanced assortment of political, economic, social, and cultural sources. Each document is preceded by a brief introduction and followed by questions for further thought, both of which help students analyze the documents and place them in historical context.

Maps in Context: A Workbook for American History. By Gerald A. Danzer (University of Illinois, Chicago). Published in two volumes and written by an expert in geographic literacy, these skill-building workbooks (approximately 100 pages each) correspond to the organization of *America's History* and offer instructors a powerful tool to help their students understand the essential connections between geography and history. Organized into three sections—Basic Geography, Mapping America's History, and One-Minute Quizzes—*Maps in Context* presents a wealth of in-class or take-home projects and convenient pop quizzes that give students hands-on experience working with maps from all areas of American history.

The Bedford Series in History and Culture. Natalie Zemon Davis (Princeton University); Ernest R. May (Harvard University); David W. Blight (Yale University); and Lynn Hunt (University of California at Los Angeles), advisory editors.

Over 65 American titles in this highly praised series combine first-rate scholarship, historical narrative, and important primary documents for undergraduate courses. Each book is brief, inexpensive, and focused on a specific topic or period. Package discounts are available.

Historians at Work Series. Edward Countryman (Southern Methodist University), advisory editor. Each volume in this series combines the best thinking about an important historical issue with helpful learning aids. Unabridged selections by distinguished historians, each with a differing perspective, provide a unique structure within which to examine a single question. With headnotes and questions to guide their reading and complete, original footnotes, students are able to engage in discussion that captures the intellectual excitement of historical research and interpretation. Package discounts are available.

New Media Resources

Online Study Guide at bedfordstmartins.com /henretta The *Online Study Guide* features up-to-date technology to present students with attractive and highly effective presentations and learning tools with unique self-assessment capabilities. As a student completes a practice test, the *Online Study Guide* immediately assesses his performance, targets the subject areas that need review, and refers the student back to the appropriate portions of the text. Through a series of multiple-choice, fill-in-the-blank, short-answer, and essay questions, students can gauge how well they have mastered the chapter's key events and themes. Multimedia activities on maps, visuals, and primary sources engage all types of learners and encourage critical thinking.

DocLinks at bedfordstmartins.com/doclinks DocLinks is a new, extensive database of over 750 annotated Web links to primary documents online for the study of American history. Links to speeches, legislation, U.S. Supreme Court decisions, narratives and testimony, treaties, essays, political manifestos, visual artifacts, songs, and poems provide students with a comprehensive understanding of critical events and trends in U.S. history and society. Documents are searchable by topic and date and are indexed to the chapters of *America's History*.

History Links Library at bedfordstmartins.com /historylinks Links Library is a searchable database of more than 200 carefully reviewed and annotated links to Web sites on American history. The links can be searched by topic or by specific chapters in *America's History*. Teachers can assign these links as the basis for homework assignments or research projects, or students can use them as a point of departure for their own history research.

Research and Documentation Online at bedfordstmartins.com/resdoc By Diana Hacker (Prince George's Community College). This online version of Hacker's popular booklet provides clear advice across the disciplines on how to integrate outside material into a paper, how to cite sources correctly, and how to format in MLA, APA, *Chicago*, or CBE style.

Research Assistant Hyperfolio. Delivered on CD-ROM, this intelligent tool for conducting research helps students collect, evaluate, and cite sources found both online and off.

After September 11: An Online Reader for Writers

bedfordstmartins.com/september11 This free collection of more than 100 annotated links provides social, political, economic, and cultural commentary based on the terrorist attacks of September 11, 2001, on the United States. Thoughtful discussion questions and ideas for research and writing projects are included.

For Instructors

Print Resources

Instructor's Resource Manual. By Bradley T. Gericke (U.S. Army Command and General Staff College). The *Instructor's Resource Manual*, provided free of charge with adoption of the textbook, offers an extensive collection of tools to aid both the first-time and the experienced teacher in structuring and customizing the American history course. Paralleling the textbook organization, this resource includes instructional objectives, annotated chapter outlines to guide lectures, and a chapter summary for each of the book's chapters. Lecture strategies and ideas for class discussion offer possible approaches to teaching each chapter and to presenting potentially difficult topics. A set of exercises for students includes both discussion questions and writing assignments for maps and special features. The manual also offers instructional objectives for each of the book's six parts to help instructors tie together larger sections of the book and provides critical thinking questions to pair with the part-closing Thinking about History essays. Additionally, each

chapter of the manual gives an outline of supplementary material (books from the Bedford Series in History and Culture, particular selections from *Documents to Accompany America's History*, activities from the *Online Study Guide*) that pertains to the chapter's content.

Transparencies. A newly expanded set of over 150 full-color acetate transparencies, free to adopters, includes all the maps and many images from the text.

New Media Resources

Computerized Test Bank. A fully updated Test Bank CD-ROM offers over 80 exercises for each chapter, allowing instructors to pick and choose from a collection of multiple-choice, fill-in, map, and short and long essay questions. To aid instructors in tailoring their tests to suit their classes, every question is labeled by topic according to chapter headings and includes a textbook page number so instructors can direct students to a particular page for correct answers. Also, the software allows instructors to edit both questions and answers to further customize their tests. Correct answers are included.

Instructor's Resource CD-ROM. This easy-to-operate disc provides instructors with the resources to build engaging multimedia classroom presentations around a variety of art, photos, maps, and figures from the text. These visuals are provided in two formats: chapter-based PowerPoint files that are fully customizable and individual JPEG files.

Map Central at bedfordstmartins.com/mapcentral Map central is a searchable database of over 700 maps from Bedford/St. Martin's history survey texts that can be used to create visually striking classroom lectures.

Using the Bedford Series in the U.S. History Survey

bedfordstmartins.com/usingseries This short online guide by Scott Hovey gives practical suggestions for using the more than 65 volumes from the Bedford Series in History and Culture with *America's History* in the survey classroom. The guide not only supplies links between the text and these supplements but also provides ideas for starting discussions focused on the primary sources featured in the volumes.

Videos and multimedia. A wide assortment of videos and CD-ROMs on various topics in American history is available to qualified adopters.

Book Companion Site at bedfordstmartins.com /henretta The companion Web site for *America's History*, Fifth Edition, uses the dynamic nature of the

Web to extend the goals of the textbook and offers a convenient home base for students and instructors by gathering all the electronic resources for the text at a single Web address.

Acknowledgments

We are very grateful to the following scholars and teachers who reported on their experiences with the third edition or reviewed chapters of the fourth edition. Their comments often challenged us to rethink or justify our interpretations and always provided a check on accuracy down to the smallest detail.

Ruth M. Alexander, *Colorado State University*
Robert J. Allison, *Suffolk University*
Robin F. Bachin, *University of Miami*
Albert I. Berger, *University of North Dakota*
Neal A. Brooks, *Essex Community College (Maryland)*
Thomas Bryan, *Alvin Community College*
Montgomery Buell, *Walla Walla College*
Markus C. Cachia-Riedl, *University of California, Berkeley*
Kay J. Carr, *Southern Illinois University at Carbondale*
William Carrigan, *Rowan University*
Myles L. Clowers, *San Diego City College*
Curtis Cole, *Huron University College*
Rory T. L. Cornish, *University of Louisiana, Monroe*
John P. Daly, *Louisiana Tech University*
Thomas S. Dicke, *Southwest Missouri State University*
Jonathan Earle, *University of Kansas*
Bradley T. Gericke, *United States Military Academy*
Sally Hadden, *Florida State University*
Paul Harvey, *University of Colorado*
Lybeth Hodges, *Texas Women's University*
Nita S. Howard, *Clovis Community College*
Jen A. Huntley-Smith, *University of Nevada—Reno*
Davis D. Joyce, *East Central University (Oklahoma)*
Louisa Kilgroe, *North Carolina State University*
Keith L. King, *Houston Community College Southeast*
Norman D. Love, *El Paso Community College*
John Lyons, *Joliet Junior College*
John R. McKivigan, *West Virginia University*
Samuel T. McSeveney, *Vanderbilt University*
Rick Malmström, *The Ellis School*
M. Catherine Miller, *Texas Tech University*
Carl H. Moneyhon, *University of Arkansas—Little Rock*

Max Page, *Yale University*
Charles K. Piehl, *Mankato State University*
Edwin G. Quattlebaum III, *Phillips Academy*
Dona Reaser, *Columbus State Community College*
Steven D. Reschly, *Truman State University*
Leonard Riforgiato, *Penn State University—Shenango*
Howard B. Rock, *Florida International University*
Neil Sapper, *Amarillo College*
Timothy Shannon, *Gettysburg College*
Peter H. Shattuck, *California State University—Sacramento*
Anthony J. Springer, *Dallas Christian College*
April Summitt, *Andrews University*
Emily J. Teipe, *Fullerton College*
Suzanne R. Thurman, *Mesa State College*
Benson Tong, *Wichita State University*
Diane Tuinstra, *Kansas State University*
Ken L. Weatherbie, *Del Mar College*
Cecil E. Weller Jr., *San Jacinto College South*
Arthur J. Worrall, *Colorado State University*

As the authors of *America's History,* we know better than anyone else how much of this book is the work of other hands and other minds. We are grateful to the many scholars whose books and articles we have enjoyed and used in writing this narrative and to the editors and production staff who have provided invaluable assistance in previous editions of our text. With advice and support from Elizabeth Welch, Gretchen Boger, Louise Townsend, and Amy Langlais, Jessica Angell expertly edited our text. Charles Christensen, Joan Feinberg, Denise Wydra, Tisha Rossi, Jane Knetzger, and Marcia Cohen have been generous in providing the resources we needed to produce the fifth edition. Special thanks are due to many other individuals: Pembroke Herbert and her staff at Picture Research Associates; our project editor, Lori Chong Roncka; William Lombardo and Tina Samaha, who directed our map program, and Professor Gerald A. Danzer, a distinguished geographer and our map consultant; the fine copyeditors who worked closely with us—Barbara Flanagan and Susan M. Free; Anna George and Gretchen Tolles, who crafted our new design; our cover designers, Billy Boardman and Donna Dennison; our marketing manager, Jenna Bookin Barry; and managing editor Elizabeth Schaaf. Bradley T. Gericke diligently wrote many of the supplements for *America's History,* and Jennifer Blanksteen, Corinne McCutchen, Elizabeth Harrison, Coleen O'Hanley, and Stuart Holdsworth were of great assistance in editing and producing them. We also want to express our thanks for the valuable assistance provided by Norman S. Cohen, Michael Cohen, and Patricia Deveneau.

From the very beginning we have considered this book a joint intellectual venture, and with each edition our collaborative effort has grown. We are proud to acknowledge our collective authorship of *America's History.*

Understanding History through Maps:
An Introduction for Students

Maps and historical studies have much in common: both use art and science to create representations of things we cannot experience directly. In the case of maps, most spaces are too vast and too complex to be understood with a single look. History has an additional challenge: the past has forever slipped away and we need devices to help us recover and understand it. Both the cartographer (or mapmaker) and the historian start by gathering facts, but they are quickly overwhelmed with data, and faced with the need to select, shorten, and clarify their portrayals. The cartographer turns to symbols and visual images while the historian depends primarily on words and concepts. Working together, the historian and the cartographer combine their talents to craft a coherent narrative about the past. Their primary subjects—people, places, and times—are intimately connected. Every historical map needs a title and date, both suggested by human experience. Similarly, every historical account happened in a specific location; events, as we say, "take place."

People, places, and times are the building blocks of all history textbooks. The authors of *America's History*, Fifth Edition, selected over 150 maps designed to establish the geographic context of their story. Combined with the illustrations, figures, and narrative, the maps help readers make connections with the past and get a feel for the setting in which events happened. As in all history textbooks, the maps in *America's History* do double duty. First, they function as shorthand geography, giving readers a picture of a place. Second, maps call attention to human events that

The Common Map Projections: Orthographic, Azimuthal Equidistant, Mercator, and Gall-Peters Equal-Area

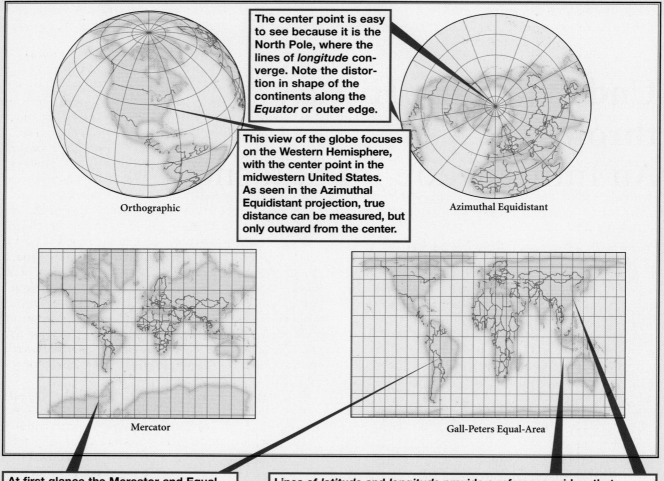

The center point is easy to see because it is the North Pole, where the lines of *longitude* converge. Note the distortion in shape of the continents along the *Equator* or outer edge.

This view of the globe focuses on the Western Hemisphere, with the center point in the midwestern United States. As seen in the Azimuthal Equidistant projection, true distance can be measured, but only outward from the center.

Orthographic

Azimuthal Equidistant

Mercator

Gall-Peters Equal-Area

At first glance the Mercator and Equal-Area projections look similar, but a close examination reveals different degrees of geographic distortion.

Lines of *latitude* and *longitude* provide a reference grid so that points on the map can be easily connected to a global position. Lines of latitude circle the globe east to west and are called *parallels*. Lines of longitude circle the globe north to south and are called *meridians*.

Figure A provides examples of several common map projections: Orthographic, Azimuthal Equidistant, Mercator, and Gall-Peters Equal-Area. All are considered world maps because they seek to depict the entire globe, or as much of it as possible. Because presenting a round image on a flat sheet of paper necessarily distorts area, shape, direction, and distance, over the years cartographers have developed numerous strategies to make their maps. Each projection is useful for a different purpose, and no single projection is the "right" one.

The Orthographic and Azimuthal Equidistant projections show the world as a globe—a three-dimensional object—but the viewer can only see two dimensions of it from any one point in space. The rounded look of the planet is retained, but only half the world can be depicted. The Orthographic projection most resembles a globe. Although it exhibits distortions in shape and area near the edges, the viewer mentally corrects these because of her familiarity with the view. Here, the shape and area of North America is relatively accurate, but to the east, across the Atlantic Ocean, western Europe is not. The Azimuthal Equidistant projection takes the skin off the globe and flattens it out to produce a two-dimensional circle. Like the Orthographic projection, it depicts half the

earth—here, the Northern Hemisphere is shown with the outer edge being the Equator. Its advantage is that it shows correct direction and distance, either of a country or continent, but only measured from the center point (in this case the North Pole). Its disadvantage is that because of the flattening and stretching, it significantly distorts (increases) the size of land forms and bodies of water near the edges.

The Mercator and Gall-Peters Equal-Area projections allow the viewer to see the entire world at a single glance. The Mercator projection accurately depicts the relative size and position of continents, countries, and bodies of water at the Equator, and fairly accurately until 45 degrees north and south latitude. Above and below these latitudes areas become distorted, as you can see from looking at Greenland, which becomes enlarged to look almost as big as North America, and Antarctica, which fills the entire bottom of the map. To correct this distortion problem, geographers developed the Gall-Peters Equal-Area projection. Its great advantage is that it depicts the areas of the continents in accurate proportion. However, its disadvantage is that it significantly distorts their shapes, as shown by the elongated views of Africa and South America.

are historically significant because they help explain change over time. To derive full benefit from the historical maps in *America's History*, readers need to view them with bifocal vision—with one eye on the physical environment and the other on the event or process depicted. A successfully read map mixes the two images, allowing for an appreciation of the human-environmental interaction that is at the root of all our experiences.

Beginning to Read Historical Maps

Readers face three challenges when looking at a map in a history textbook. First, we must discern the event being portrayed. What is the purpose of the map? Second, we must see the geography on the image, to turn the lines and symbols on the map into a picture of the physical environment in which the event took place. What area of the world are we looking at? What did it look like at the time represented? Third, maps place a major demand on our powers of understanding: How did the event and the place interact with each other? What opportunities and constraints did the environment provide? How did topography, climate, resources, or other elements of the geographic situation influence the course of events? Conversely, how did people have an impact on their environment? How did they perceive it and use it? How did a knowledge of, or attitudes toward, the physical environment differ between individuals and groups? Did these attitudes change over time? And, finally, what does it all mean? What does some insight into the experiences of people on earth tell us about who we are and where we have been?

Maps cannot tell us everything about history, and some maps are more complex than others. They have limitations as well as possibilities, and they function best when, as in *America's History*, they are accompanied by graphic aids and are integrated into the narrative flow. Maps also depend on an active reader, one who knows how to use maps and has some facility in integrating all the elements of a textbook into a meaningful educational experience. The ability to understand the strengths and limitations of maps is the core of cartographic literacy.

Developing Cartographic Literacy

The best way to start developing cartographic literacy is to review the three major shortcomings of maps. First, maps change the outer face of a globe, or a portion of it, into a flat surface. This transformation has less effect on maps that have a large scale and hence portray only a small portion of the globe. But on world maps and other small-scale portrayals the distortion created by projecting a sphere onto a plane becomes serious. The process produces exaggerations and inconsistencies of shape, direction, and/or area (Figure A).

Second, maps have a difficult time showing the irregularities on the earth's surface that are important in real life. How are mountains and valleys, plains and plateaus, hills and canyons to be indicated on a flat sheet of paper? Maps, after all, take a vantage point in the sky rather than a view toward the horizon. As Figure B illustrates, to indicate topography the cartographer must use a bag of tricks—symbols, contour lines, and suggestive shading. All of these devices rely on the reader to interpret their meaning and to translate them into landscapes.

The third limitation of maps is that they must be selective. Reducing the size of reality demands simplification, and the cartographer must focus on a few points while excluding the vast majority of details. What should be emphasized? Where should the presentation end? These choices turn any map into a very selective instrument, fashioned for a particular purpose. All maps present an argument advocating a point of view, and good maps raise more questions than they answer. Maps should not be thought of as final steps in the learning process. Instead, consider them as catalysts provided to spur active thought and raise additional issues.

These limitations of maps are directly linked to their strengths and advantages. A world map is the only way we can see all of the earth's surface at a glance. Even a round globe, a much more accurate representation of the planet, can present only a portion of its subject at one time. Paradoxically, if we want to picture the global dimension of something, only a flat world map will do. Maps help us comprehend places we cannot actually see because the distances are too vast. An ocean, a continent, a nation, a state, even a city or a town cannot be taken in by one look. Only its representation on a map enables us to see it whole.

Maps also clarify the world for us. As models of reality, they extract certain features for emphasis to make the world intelligible. Maps are instructional devices, and the cartographer always follows a lesson plan. One way to begin reading a map is to figure out the purpose of the lesson. What is the basic message the map is intended to convey? The title of the map is a good place to start, especially any dates that might be provided. Dates help readers connect the map with the narrative, placing the event described into a sequence of happenings and connecting the incident to other developments occurring at the same time. The alert reader will connect the map's title to its caption. The word *caption* is derived from the same root as the word *capture*. The sentences in every map caption in *America's History* are designed to help the reader seize the purpose of the map—and thus turn it into a valuable possession.

Working with maps also deepens our understanding of the basic themes of geography and how they relate to

FIGURE B

MAP 16.7 The Settlement of the Pacific Slope, 1860–1890

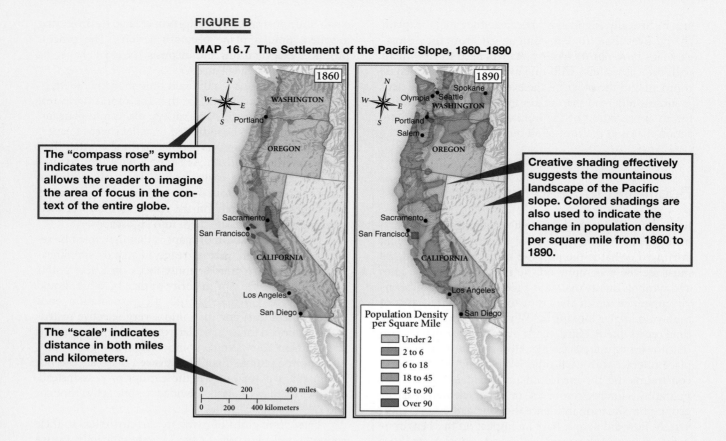

The "compass rose" symbol indicates true north and allows the reader to imagine the area of focus in the context of the entire globe.

The "scale" indicates distance in both miles and kilometers.

Creative shading effectively suggests the mountainous landscape of the Pacific slope. Colored shadings are also used to indicate the change in population density per square mile from 1860 to 1890.

Population Density per Square Mile

- Under 2
- 2 to 6
- 6 to 18
- 18 to 45
- 45 to 90
- Over 90

historical studies. Five of these themes—location, place, region, movement, and interaction—are presented as questions on the following pages, with several maps provided to illustrate how each particular theme might enrich a reader's understanding of the map and the historical situation it depicts. All of the maps reappear later in the text, and all of the questions might be called upon to enhance the value of any individual map. In the end, attention to these basic themes will fortify the reader's cartographic literacy, as well as foster her historical understanding.

Location: Where Is This Place?

"When?" and "Where?" are the first questions asked by historians and cartographers. Every event is connected to a place, and every place needs to be identified by a date. Maps are the best devices to show location, and in the final analysis any place on a map is located in reference to

the earth as a whole. Location depends, in an absolute sense, on a reference to global position, most conveniently cited in terms of latitude and longitude (see Figure A).

In a relative sense, however, location can depend on the distance, direction, or travel time from one place to another. As Figure C indicates, in 1817 Pittsburgh, Pennsylvania, was more than ten days' travel from New York City, a distance of roughly 370 miles. By 1841 improvements in travel made the trip possible in about five or six days. Relative location is also at the heart of Figure D, showing the Japanese relocation camps during World War II. Note that latitude and longitude are not used on this map because absolute location is not the point. Instead, this map is intended to show how far the Japanese Americans were forced to relocate—within the same state, several states away, or halfway across the nation. It is not necessary to show all of the states, since only those west of the Mississippi River were primarily involved. The cartographer assumes that the map reader will realize that a portion of the country is not shown and will, if needed, fill in the missing part from her mental map.

FIGURE C

MAP 10.4 The Speed of News in 1817 and 1841

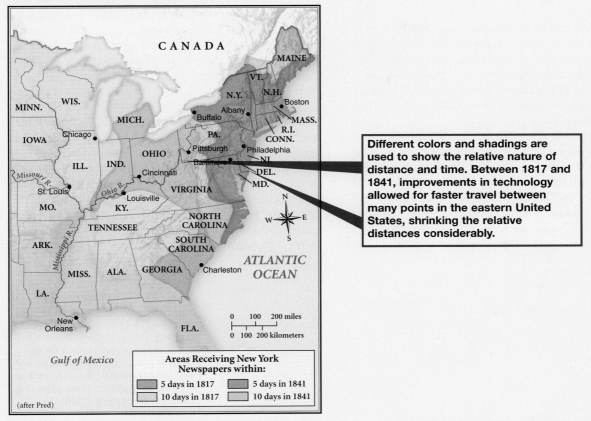

Different colors and shadings are used to show the relative nature of distance and time. Between 1817 and 1841, improvements in technology allowed for faster travel between many points in the eastern United States, shrinking the relative distances considerably.

Areas Receiving New York Newspapers within:

5 days in 1817	5 days in 1841
10 days in 1817	10 days in 1841

(after Pred)

FIGURE D

MAP 26.2 Japanese Relocation Camps

Inset maps allow the cartographer to use a large-scale map to depict the main subject area (here, the continental United States) and still show additional areas relevant to the topic. Alaska and Hawaii were territories, not states, during World War II and are included here because Japanese Americans lived in both.

This national map appears to float free of its location on the planet. Neither oceans nor continents are used to suggest a global position. The boundaries of the United States serve as the boundaries of the map, isolating the nation from its geographical position but allowing for greater focus.

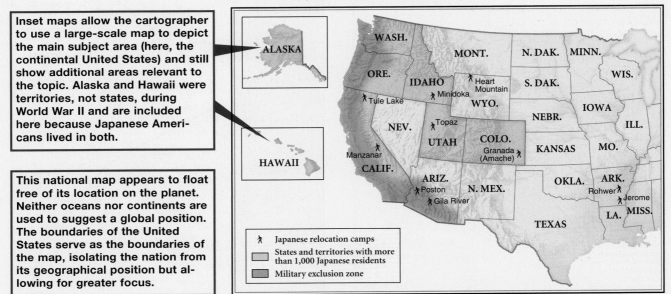

Japanese relocation camps
States and territories with more than 1,000 Japanese residents
Military exclusion zone

Place: How Did This Location Become a Place?

Human activity creates places. Locations exist on their own without the presence of people, but they become places when people use them in some way. As human enterprise thickens and generation after generation use a place, it accumulates artifacts, develops layers of remains, and creates a variety of associations held in a society's history and memory.

Places have two sets of characteristics: physical and human, the products of both nature and culture. A complete physical description of a place would show the topography of the site, identify any bodies of water, and then inventory its climate, minerals, soils, plants, and animals. The human characteristics of a site would start with how people used the land, noting the settlement patterns, buildings and roads, population distribution, economic activities, social organization, language, and culture. The historian takes an additional step and considers how these have changed over time and what that change means. It would take many maps to approach a complete description of a historic place and to unravel all the characteristics and experiences that make it significant. Indeed, the very word *place* suggests a uniqueness that has emerged in large part from a particular history.

Figure E presents a pair of maps that show the settlement pattern of the Barrow plantation in Georgia in 1860 and in 1881. These illustrate how important the date is on any map. The passing of a slave society and the emergence of a sharecropping economy transformed the Barrow landscape. Only the big house remained in place between 1860 and 1881. The tight organization of a controlled society gave way to a dispersed community, but one that gained focal points on a church and a school in addition to the cotton-gin house.

The "key" includes symbols that make the map legible. Each item in the key is represented on the map. A pie chart that shows how ex-slave Handy Barrow made his income is also provided, allowing the map to convey additional information.

FIGURE E

MAP 15.2 The Barrow Plantation, 1860 and 1881

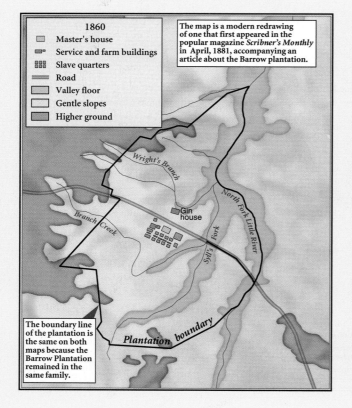

1860
- Master's house
- Service and farm buildings
- Slave quarters
- Road
- Valley floor
- Gentle slopes
- Higher ground

The map is a modern redrawing of one that first appeared in the popular magazine *Scribner's Monthly* in April, 1881, accompanying an article about the Barrow plantation.

The boundary line of the plantation is the same on both maps because the Barrow Plantation remained in the same family.

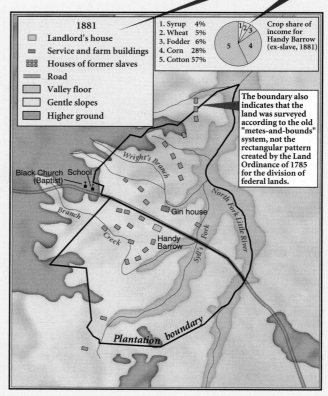

1881
- Landlord's house
- Service and farm buildings
- Houses of former slaves
- Road
- Valley floor
- Gentle slopes
- Higher ground

1. Syrup 4%
2. Wheat 5%
3. Fodder 6%
4. Corn 28%
5. Cotton 57%

Crop share of income for Handy Barrow (ex-slave, 1881)

The boundary also indicates that the land was surveyed according to the old "metes-and-bounds" system, not the rectangular pattern created by the Land Ordinance of 1785 for the division of federal lands.

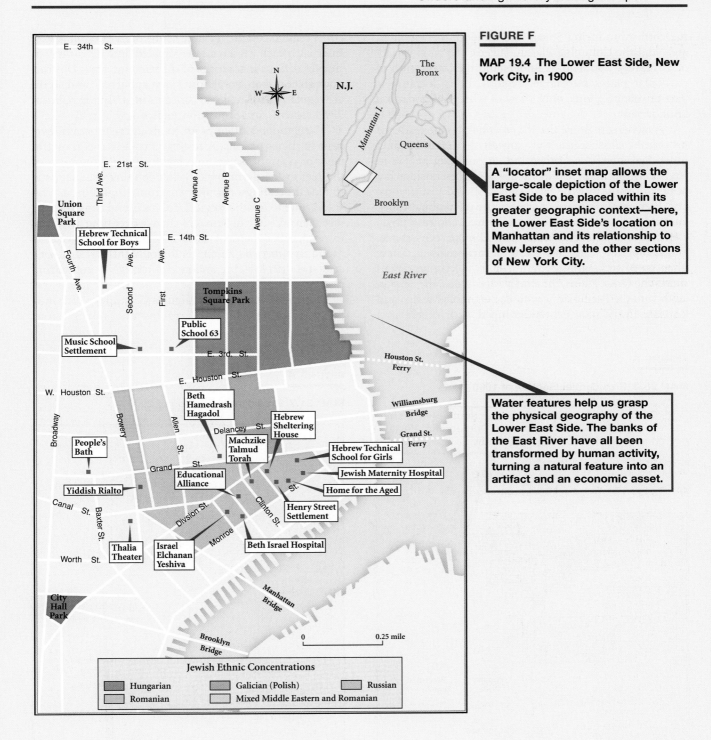

MAP 19.4 The Lower East Side, New York City, in 1900

A "locator" inset map allows the large-scale depiction of the Lower East Side to be placed within its greater geographic context—here, the Lower East Side's location on Manhattan and its relationship to New Jersey and the other sections of New York City.

Water features help us grasp the physical geography of the Lower East Side. The banks of the East River have all been transformed by human activity, turning a natural feature into an artifact and an economic asset.

Figure F maps neighborhood institutions in an urban environment. Again the date is essential to note because the Lower East Side of New York surely had a different mix of institutions in 1850 or 1950 than it did in 1900, the time of the map. In larger terms, the sense of place created here results from its waterfront location, the concentrations of ethnic groups, and the variety of neighborhood institutions.

Region: What Does a Place Have in Common with Its Surroundings?

The concept of place highlights the unique elements of every location. By contrast, the idea of a region highlights elements in common, tying certain places together as a group distinguishable from other places. New England, the cotton-producing South, the Phoenix metropolitan area, and the Columbia Plateau suggest the wide variety of groupings that help us understand the integration of particular places into larger regions. Every location is part of many regions, only a few of which share natural boundaries.

Perceiving regional ties is a great help to the reader of historical maps because they suggest the forces binding individual interests together and encouraging people to act in common. The United States could be considered a political region in which like values, shared institutions, and a common heritage create a sense of national unity. Such a region is a human construction; in contrast, physical characteristics like landforms, climate, ecosystems, and geological structures create natural regions. These often cross national boundaries. Thus the United States shares the Great Plains, the Rocky Mountains, the canyon lands, and the Pacific slope with its neighbors Mexico and Canada. Every state can be grouped with others into

larger regional entities like the Midwest or the Gulf States. Internally each state can be divided into a variety of smaller regions that represent differing interests. Upstate, downstate, urban, rural, inner city, suburban, and so on are regularly used regional concepts in analyzing political developments and historical trends.

Geographers often point to an internal pattern evident in many regions. A historical core marks a central place or point of origin for a region. Toward the edges of the region the dominance of the defining characteristic thins out, creating a periphery or frontier marking a transition zone to another region. To this useful construct the historian adds the dynamic of change over time. One way to engage the maps of the many presidential elections found in *America's History* is to apply the regional concept and then look for evidence of change by comparing maps.

Consider, for example, Figures G and H, which illuminate the importance of regions in thinking about

FIGURE G

MAP 28.3 Presidential Election of 1960

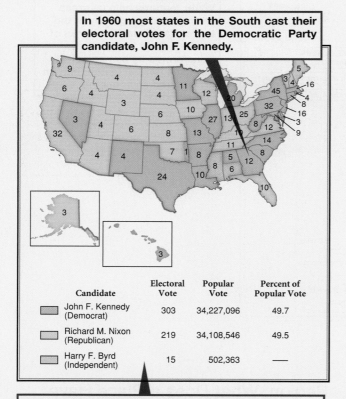

In 1960 most states in the South cast their electoral votes for the Democratic Party candidate, John F. Kennedy.

Candidate	Electoral Vote	Popular Vote	Percent of Popular Vote
John F. Kennedy (Democrat)	303	34,227,096	49.7
Richard M. Nixon (Republican)	219	34,108,546	49.5
Harry F. Byrd (Independent)	15	502,363	—

The presidential election maps in *America's History* allow the reader to quickly see the national distribution of electoral votes on a regional and state basis. Another way to depict election results graphically would be to show the winner of the popular vote per county. By shifting the focus, the results might look very different and raise further questions.

FIGURE H

MAP 31.7 Presidential Election of 2000

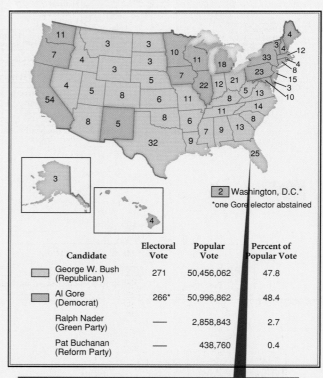

2 Washington, D.C.*
*one Gore elector abstained

Candidate	Electoral Vote	Popular Vote	Percent of Popular Vote
George W. Bush (Republican)	271	50,456,062	47.8
Al Gore (Democrat)	266*	50,996,862	48.4
Ralph Nader (Green Party)	—	2,858,843	2.7
Pat Buchanan (Reform Party)	—	438,760	0.4

Forty years later in the 2000 presidential election, the southern states cast their electoral votes for the Republican Party candidate, George W. Bush. In Alabama, Georgia, Mississippi, North and South Carolina, and Texas, Bush won easily with 55–59 percent of the popular vote; only in Florida was his victory razor-thin.

American politics. In 1960, as Figure G indicates, the South voted solidly Democratic. In 2000, the South voted just as solidly Republican, as shown by Figure H. How can such a fundamental political shift be explained? Understanding regional histories and identities explains a great deal, and presidential election maps like those placed throughout *America's History* are powerful tools that help readers focus on regional patterns and other shifts in voting behavior.

Figure I shows how a particular place—here, the Tennessee Valley—can be considered part of several overlapping regions, the significance of which changes depending on the interest of the viewer. Emerging out of the politics of the New Deal, in the 1930s the Tennessee Valley area became, for the first time, clearly defined. Figure I uses two sets of data to describe the Tennessee Valley Authority: the area served by TVA electric power (an example of a cultural region) and the actual watershed of the river (a natural region).

Movement: What Is Happening Here?

All change involves movement. People move in their daily activities, in seasonal patterns, and in migration to new places of residence. In the process they cross many boundaries. People also use products that move from one place to another through the economic system. An important type of movement is "diffusion," a concept used by geographers to describe the process by which people, animals, goods, services, ideas, and information move from a point of origin to other locations. Diffusion is sometimes a planned, purposeful activity, but it can also be accidental, like the spread of disease. To understand a map fully, the reader must always envision it as one part of a sequence, not unlike a "still" excerpted from a motion picture. To capture all of this activity on a map is a difficult undertaking. To understand the map,

FIGURE I

Map 25.4 The Tennessee Valley Authority, 1933–1952

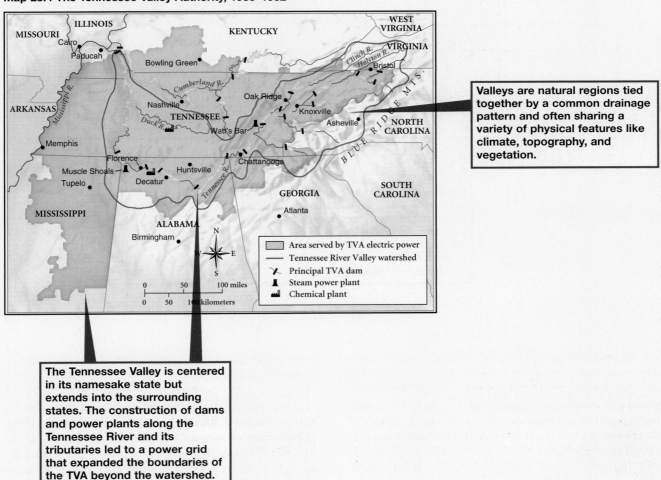

Valleys are natural regions tied together by a common drainage pattern and often sharing a variety of physical features like climate, topography, and vegetation.

The Tennessee Valley is centered in its namesake state but extends into the surrounding states. The construction of dams and power plants along the Tennessee River and its tributaries led to a power grid that expanded the boundaries of the TVA beyond the watershed.

FIGURE J

MAP 8.2 Regional Cultures Move West, 1790–1820

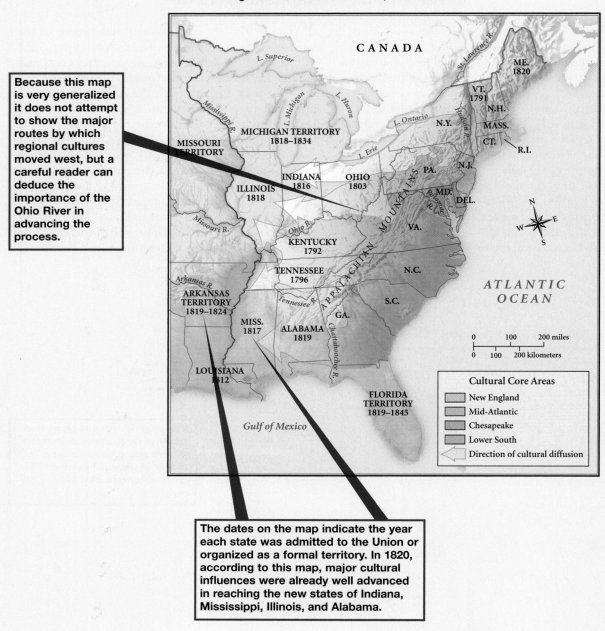

Because this map is very generalized it does not attempt to show the major routes by which regional cultures moved west, but a careful reader can deduce the importance of the Ohio River in advancing the process.

The dates on the map indicate the year each state was admitted to the Union or organized as a formal territory. In 1820, according to this map, major cultural influences were already well advanced in reaching the new states of Indiana, Mississippi, Illinois, and Alabama.

the viewer must perceive that the silent sheet of paper depicts commotion.

Cartographers employ a range of strategies to emphasize movement on maps. One way is to show, usually through color and shading, the routes along which the movement is channeled. Another device, favored in historical cartography to show military campaigns, is to provide dramatic arrows indicating the course of action. Often the width of the arrows represents the size of the army on the march, giving maps with arrows the qualities of graphs and charts.

Figure J uses both arrows and shading to provide a very generalized idea of the way cultural traits such as religious identity, speech patterns, and housing types moved from core areas along the Atlantic coast to the American interior. The large arrows show the general direction of these movements, while the shading indicates the density of the process up to 1820. The large arrows

FIGURE K

MAP 18.2 The Diffusion of the Australian Ballot

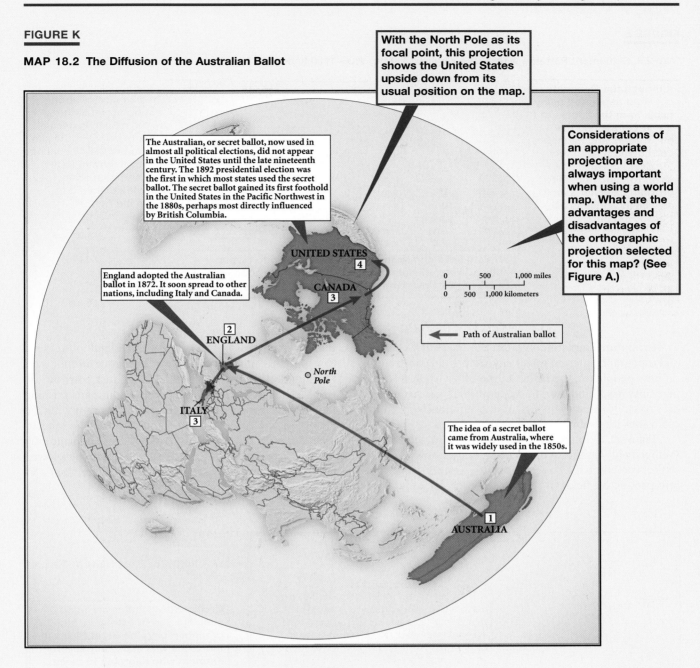

With the North Pole as its focal point, this projection shows the United States upside down from its usual position on the map.

The Australian, or secret ballot, now used in almost all political elections, did not appear in the United States until the late nineteenth century. The 1892 presidential election was the first in which most states used the secret ballot. The secret ballot gained its first foothold in the United States in the Pacific Northwest in the 1880s, perhaps most directly influenced by British Columbia.

Considerations of an appropriate projection are always important when using a world map. What are the advantages and disadvantages of the orthographic projection selected for this map? (See Figure A.)

England adopted the Australian ballot in 1872. It soon spread to other nations, including Italy and Canada.

The idea of a secret ballot came from Australia, where it was widely used in the 1850s.

0   500   1,000 miles
0   500   1,000 kilometers

← Path of Australian ballot

also indicate that the movement continued into the future. A creative use of cartographic symbols makes this example very dynamic.

The diffusion of a key idea in modern democratic governance—the Australian, or secret, ballot—is featured in Figure K. Note that a world map is needed for this process because the practice started in Australia in the 1850s and then spread to England. From there it was adopted in several other countries, including Italy and Canada. By the 1880s the secret ballot had gained a foothold in the United States in the Pacific Northwest. In 1892 most states used the Australian ballot for presidential elections.

Interaction: How Do People and Their Environment Influence Each Other?

The interaction between people and the environment divides into two major categories. First, people change their environment to suit their needs. The pioneer era in American history records the chopping down of great trees, followed by the clearing of land to raise crops and animals largely brought from Europe and Africa. Second, opportunities and constraints of the environment force people to change their behavior and culture as they adapt

FIGURE L

Map 2.6 Settlement Patterns within New England Towns, 1630–1700 (inset)

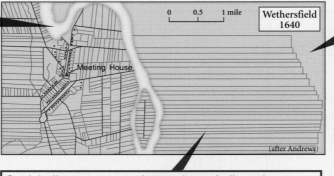

Although the Connecti-cut River separated many fields from the homes of the farmers along the major road, and might be considered a hindrance, the river was also an asset to the community, providing a water supply as well as a means of transportation.

The absence of strong topographical features on the map is important. Settlers selected the site for Wethersfield because the level terrain, fertile soil, and temperate climate combined to make it a fruitful agricultural settlement.

Straight lines on a map almost always indicate human activity. Here, the lots and fields are carefully arranged to take maximum advantage of the site.

to their natural surroundings. On the one hand, climate and topography present major environmental constraints on how people use the land. On the other hand, human ingenuity has found ways to put almost all places to some use, often turning elements of the environment from curiosities into valuable resources.

Figure L, a plan of the agricultural settlement of Wethersfield, Connecticut, in 1640, shows how Puritan settlers carved up the flood plain of the Connecticut River into productive fields. It seems as if every bit of land in

the settlement was put to use, even the island in the river. Contrast this image, spelling out human triumph, with the situation shown in Figure M. The dust bowl on the Great Plains in the 1930s resulted from humans pushing too hard against environmental constraints, removing the grasses of the American West and plowing the land to plant crops. In the extended period of drought beginning in 1930 crops died and winds ripped apart the plowed landscape, blowing the topsoil away in huge clouds of dust.

FIGURE M

MAP 24.3 The Dust Bowl, 1930–1941

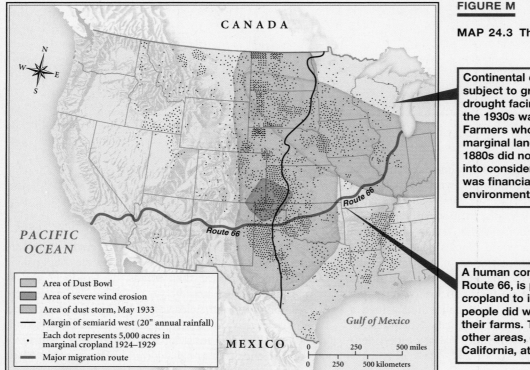

Continental climates are often subject to great extremes, and the drought facing the Great Plains in the 1930s was especially severe. Farmers who migrated to these marginal lands beginning in the 1880s did not take these extremes into consideration, and the result was financial disaster and environmental catastrophe.

A human construction project, Route 66, is placed on this map of cropland to indicate what many people did when they faced ruin on their farms. Thousands moved to other areas, especially southern California, at the end of the road.

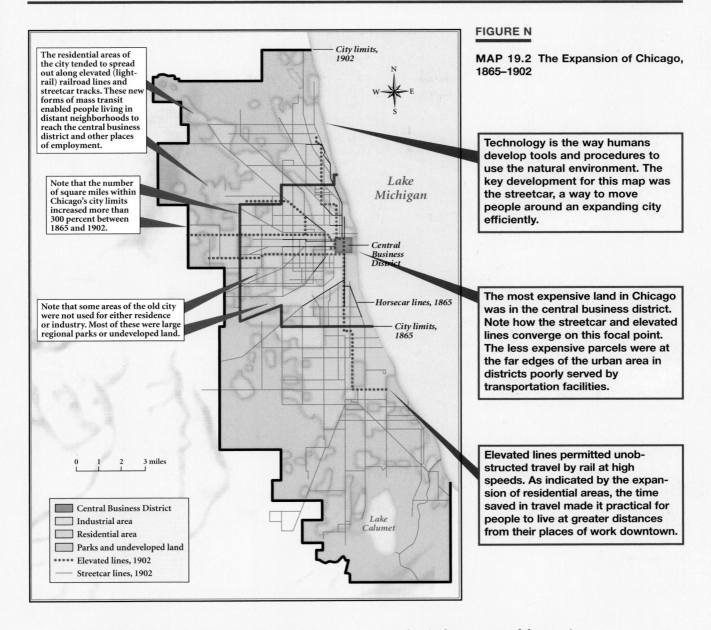

FIGURE N

MAP 19.2 The Expansion of Chicago, 1865–1902

The residential areas of the city tended to spread out along elevated (light-rail) railroad lines and streetcar tracks. These new forms of mass transit enabled people living in distant neighborhoods to reach the central business district and other places of employment.

Note that the number of square miles within Chicago's city limits increased more than 300 percent between 1865 and 1902.

Note that some areas of the old city were not used for either residence or industry. Most of these were large regional parks or undeveloped land.

Technology is the way humans develop tools and procedures to use the natural environment. The key development for this map was the streetcar, a way to move people around an expanding city efficiently.

The most expensive land in Chicago was in the central business district. Note how the streetcar and elevated lines converge on this focal point. The less expensive parcels were at the far edges of the urban area in districts poorly served by transportation facilities.

Elevated lines permitted unobstructed travel by rail at high speeds. As indicated by the expansion of residential areas, the time saved in travel made it practical for people to live at greater distances from their places of work downtown.

City limits, 1902

Lake Michigan

Central Business District

Horsecar lines, 1865

City limits, 1865

Lake Calumet

0 1 2 3 miles

- Central Business District
- Industrial area
- Residential area
- Parks and undeveloped land
- ••••• Elevated lines, 1902
- —— Streetcar lines, 1902

Figure N details the expansion of a major city, showing that human-environmental concerns operate in urban areas as well as in the countryside. In the case of Chicago, a wet, low-lying former lake bed became the site for a metropolis, which numbered about two million residents by 1900. The flat topography enabled the city to be laid out on straight lines but created sanitation and drainage problems, eventually addressed only by major human efforts, which included reversing the flow of the Chicago River.

Conclusion

Every time you encounter a map in *America's History*, ask yourself the following eight questions. With practice, you will improve your cartographic literacy, thereby deepening your historical understanding.

1. What is the purpose of the map?

2. What date is represented on the map and why is this date historically significant?

3. How does the map help explain the narrative?

4. What additional information does the caption provide?

5. What elements are emphasized on the map?

6. How does the map represent the actual landscape?

7. In what ways does the map show change over time?

8. How do the basic themes of geography—location, place, region, movement, and human-environmental interaction—help unlock the theme of the map?

—GERALD A. DANZER,
University of Illinois at Chicago

C O N T E N T S

Chapter 15
Reconstruction, 1865–1877   *429*

PART FOUR
A Maturing Industrial Society, 1877–1914   *454*

Chapter 16
The American West   *457*

Chapter 17
Capital and Labor in the Age of Enterprise, 1877–1900   *485*

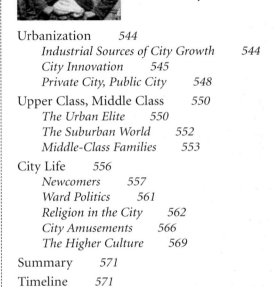

Chapter 18
The Politics of Late-Nineteenth-Century America   *515*

Chapter 19
The Rise of the City   *543*

Chapter 20
The Progressive Era   *573*

PART FIVE

The Modern State and Society, 1914–1945   634

Chapter 24
The Great
Depression   *695*

Chapter 25
The New Deal,
1933–1939   *721*

Chapter 26
The World at War,
1939–1945   *749*

PART SIX
America and the World, 1945 to the Present   780

Chapter 27
Cold War America, 1945–1960   783

Chapter 28
The Affluent Society and the Liberal Consensus, 1945–1965   815

Epilogue:

Thinking about Contemporary History   *939*

An asterisk (∗) indicates a map annotated to highlight key points and to promote map-reading skills.

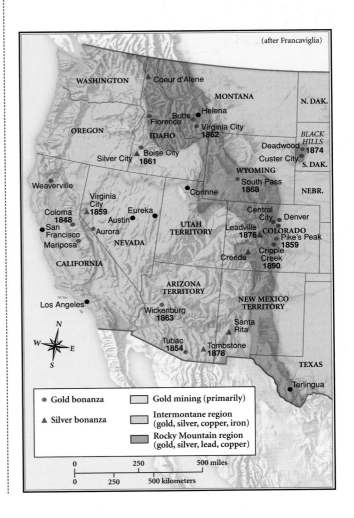

FIGURES AND TABLES

Figures

Tables

JAMES A. HENRETTA is Priscilla Alden Burke Professor of American History at the University of Maryland, College Park. He received his undergraduate education at Swarthmore College and his Ph.D. from Harvard University. He has taught at the University of Sussex, England; Princeton University; UCLA; Boston University; as a Fulbright lecturer in Australia at the University of New England; and at Oxford University as the Harmsworth Professor of American History. His publications include *The Evolution of American Society, 1700–1815: An Interdisciplinary Analysis; "Salutary Neglect": Colonial Administration under the Duke of Newcastle; Evolution and Revolution: American Society, 1600–1820;* and *The Origins of American Capitalism.* Recently he coedited and contributed to a collection of original essays, *Republicanism and Liberalism in America and the German States, 1750–1850,* as part of his larger research project on "The Liberal State in America: New York, 1820–1975." In 2002–2003, he held the John Hope Franklin Fellowship at the National Humanities Center in North Carolina.

DAVID BRODY is Professor Emeritus of History at the University of California, Davis. He received his B.A., M.A., and Ph.D. from Harvard University. He has taught at the University of Warwick in England, at Moscow State University in the former Soviet Union, and at Sydney University in Australia. He is the author of *Steelworkers in America; Workers in Industrial America: Essays on the 20th Century Struggle;* and *In Labor's Cause: Main Themes on the History of the American Worker.* He has been awarded fellowships from the Social Science Research Council, the Guggenheim Foundation, and the National Endowment for the Humanities. He is past president (1991–1992) of the Pacific Coast branch of the American Historical Association. His current research is on labor law and workplace regimes during the Great Depression.

LYNN DUMENIL is Robert Glass Cleland Professor of American History at Occidental College in Los Angeles. She is a graduate of the University of Southern California and received her Ph.D. from the University of California, Berkeley. She has written *The Modern Temper: American Culture and Society in the 1920s* and *Freemasonry and American Culture: 1880–1930.* Her articles and reviews have appeared in the *Journal of American History;* the *Journal of American Ethnic History: Reviews in American History;* and the *American Historical Review.* She has been a historical consultant to several documentary film projects and is on the Pelzer Prize Committee of the Organization of American Historians. Her current work, for which she received a National Endowment for the Humanities Fellowship, is on World War I, citizenship, and the state. In 2001–2002 she was the Bicentennial Fulbright Chair in American Studies at the University of Helsinki.

SUSAN WARE specializes in twentieth-century U.S. history and the history of American women. She is affiliated with the Radcliffe Institute for Advanced Study, Harvard University, where she is editing the next volume of the noted biographical dictionary *Notable American Women.* Ware received her undergraduate degree from Wellesley College and her Ph.D. from Harvard University and from 1986 to 1995 taught in the history department at New York University. Her publications include *Beyond Suffrage: Women in the New Deal; Holding Their Own: American Women in the 1930s; Partner and I: Molly Dewson, Feminism, and New Deal Politics; Modern American Women: A Documentary History; Still Missing: Amelia Earhart and the Search for Modern Feminism;* and *Letter to the World: Seven Women Who Shaped the American Century.* She has served on the national advisory boards of the Franklin and Eleanor Roosevelt Institute and the Schlesinger Library at Radcliffe and has been a historical consultant to numerous documentary film projects. Her most recent project is a biography of radio talk show pioneer Mary Margaret McBride.

America's History

Volume 2: Since 1865

CHAPTER 15

Reconstruction

1865–1877

IN HIS SECOND INAUGURAL ADDRESS, President Lincoln spoke of the need to "bind up the nation's wounds." No one knew better than Lincoln how daunting a task that would be. Foremost, of course, were the terms on which the rebellious states would be restored to the Union. But America's Civil War had opened more fundamental questions. Slavery was finished. That much was certain. But what system of labor should replace plantation slavery? What rights should the freedmen be accorded beyond emancipation? How far should the federal government go to settle these questions? And who should decide—the president or Congress?

◄ *Chloe and Sam* (1882)

After the Civil War the country went through the wrenching peacemaking process known as Reconstruction. The struggle between the victorious North and the vanquished South was fought out on a political landscape, but Thomas Hovenden's heartwarming painting reminds us of the deeper meaning of Reconstruction: that Chloe and Sam, after lives spent in slavery, might end their days in the dignity of freedom.

Thomas Colville Fine Art.

The last speech Lincoln delivered, on April 11, 1865, demonstrated his grasp of these issues. Reconstruction, he said, had to be regarded as a practical, not a theoretical, problem. It could be solved only if Republicans remained united, even if that meant compromising on principled differences dividing them, and only if the defeated South gave its consent, even if that meant forgiveness of the South's transgressions. The speech showed, above all, Lincoln's sense of the fluidity of events, of policy toward the South as an evolving, not a fixed, position.

What course Reconstruction might have taken had Lincoln lived is one of the unanswerable questions of American history. On April 14, 1865—five days after Lee's surrender at Appomattox—Lincoln was shot in the head at Ford's Theatre in Washington by a fanatic actor named John Wilkes Booth. Ironically, Lincoln might have been spared if the war had dragged on longer, for Booth and his Confederate associates had originally plotted to kidnap the president to force a negotiated settlement. After Lee's surrender, Booth became bent on revenge. Without regaining consciousness, Lincoln died on April 15.

With one stroke John Wilkes Booth had sent Lincoln to martyrdom, hardened many Northerners against the South, and handed the presidency to a man utterly lacking in Lincoln's moral sense and political judgment, Vice President Andrew Johnson.

Presidential Reconstruction

The procedure for Reconstruction—how to restore rebellious states to the Union—was not addressed by the Founding Fathers. The Constitution does not say which branch of government handles the readmission of rebellious states or, for that matter, even contemplates the possibility of secession. It was an open question whether, on seceding, the Confederate states had legally left the Union. If so, their reentry surely required legislative action by Congress. If not, if even in defeat they retained their constitutional status, then the terms for restoring them to the Union might be defined as an administrative matter best left to the president. The ensuing battle between the White House and Capitol Hill was one of the fault lines in Reconstruction's stormy history.

Lincoln's Approach

Lincoln, as wartime president, had the elbow room to take the initiative, offering in December 1863 a general amnesty to all but high-ranking Confederates willing to pledge loyalty to the Union. When 10 percent of a state's 1860 voters had taken this oath, the state would be restored to the Union, provided that it abolished slavery. The Confederate states (save those like Louisiana and Tennessee that were under Union control) rebuffed Lincoln's generous offer, ensuring that the war would have to be fought to the bitter end.

What the Ten Percent Plan also revealed was the rocky road that lay ahead for Reconstruction. In Louisiana, for example, the Unionist government restored under Lincoln's offer employed curfew laws to restrict the movements of the freed slaves and vagrancy regulations to force them back to work. But the Louisiana freedmen fought back. Led by the free black community of New Orleans, they began to agitate for political rights. No less than their former masters, ex-slaves intended to be actors in the savage drama of Reconstruction.

With the struggle in Louisiana in mind, congressional Republicans proposed a stricter substitute for Lincoln's Ten Percent Plan. The initiative came from the Radical wing of the party—those bent on a stern peace and full rights for the freedmen—but with broad support among more moderate Republicans. The Wade-Davis Bill, passed on July 2, 1864, laid down, as conditions for the restoration of the rebellious states to the Union, an oath of allegiance by a majority of each state's adult white men, new state governments formed only by those who had never carried arms against the Union, and permanent disfranchisement of Confederate leaders. The Wade-Davis bill served notice that the congressional Republicans were not about to hand over Reconstruction policy to the president.

Rather than openly challenging Congress, Lincoln executed a **pocket veto** of the Wade-Davis bill by not signing it before Congress adjourned. At the same time he initiated informal talks with congressional leaders aimed at finding common ground. Lincoln's successor, however, had no such inclinations. Andrew Johnson held the view that Reconstruction was the president's prerogative, and by an accident of timing he was free to act on his convictions: under leisurely rules that went back to the early republic, the 39th Congress elected back in November 1864 was not scheduled to convene until December 1865.

Johnson's Initiative

Andrew Johnson was a self-made man from the hills of eastern Tennessee. A Jacksonian Democrat, he saw himself as the champion of the common man. He hated what he called the "bloated, corrupt aristocracy" of the Northeast, and he was equally disdainful of the southern planters, whom he blamed for the poverty of the South's small farmers. It was the poor whites that he championed; Johnson, a slave owner himself, had little sympathy for the enslaved blacks. Johnson's political career had taken him to the U.S. Senate, where he remained when the war broke out, loyal to the Union. After federal forces captured Nashville, Johnson became Tennessee's military governor. The Republicans nominated him for vice president in 1864 in an effort to promote wartime unity and to court the support of southern Unionists.

In May 1865, just a month after Lincoln's death, Johnson launched his own Reconstruction plan. He offered amnesty to all Southerners who took an oath of allegiance to the Constitution, except for high-ranking Confederate officials and wealthy planters, whom he held responsible for secession. Such persons could be pardoned only by the president. Johnson appointed provisional governors for the southern states and, as conditions for their restoration, required only that they revoke their ordinances of secession, repudiate their Confederate debts, and ratify the Thirteenth Amendment, which abolished slavery. Within months all the former Confederate

Andrew Johnson

The president was not an easy man. This photograph of Andrew Johnson (1808–1875) conveys some of the prickly qualities that contributed so centrally to his failure to reach an agreement with Republicans on a moderate Reconstruction program.
Library of Congress.

states had met Johnson's requirements and had functioning, elected governments.

At first Republicans responded favorably. The moderates among them were sympathetic to Johnson's argument that it was up to the states, not the federal government, to settle what civil and political rights the freedmen should have. Even the Radicals held their fire. They liked the stern treatment of Confederate leaders, and they hoped that the new southern governments would show good faith by generous treatment of the freed slaves.

Nothing of the sort happened. The South lay in ruins (see Voices from Abroad, "David Macrae: The Devastated South," p. 432). But Southerners held fast to the old order. The newly seated legislatures moved to restore slavery in all but name. They enacted laws—known as **Black Codes**—designed to drive the former slaves back to the plantations and deny them elementary civil rights. The new governments had mostly been formed by southern Unionists, but when it came to racial attitudes, little distinguished these loyalists from the Confederates. The latter, moreover, soon filtered back into the corridors of power. Despite his hard words against them, Johnson forgave ex-Confederate leaders easily, so long as he got the satisfaction of humbling them in their appeals to him for pardons.

His perceived indulgence of their efforts to restore white supremacy emboldened the ex-Confederates. They packed the delegations to the new Congress with

old comrades—nine members of the Confederate Congress, seven former officials of Confederate state governments, four generals and four colonels, and even the vice president of the Confederacy, Alexander Stephens. This was the last straw for the Republicans.

Under the Constitution Congress is "the judge of the Elections, Returns and Qualifications of its own Members" (Article 1, Section 5; see Documents, p. D-8). With this power the Republican majorities in both houses refused to admit the southern delegations when Congress convened in early December 1865, effectively blocking Johnson's Reconstruction program. Seeking to formulate the terms on which the South would be readmitted to Congress, the Republicans established a House-Senate committee—the Joint Committee on Reconstruction—and began public hearings on conditions in the South.

In response the southern states backed away from the most flagrant of the Black Codes, replacing them with regulatory ordinances silent on race yet not different in effect; in practice they applied to blacks, not to whites. On top of that a wave of violence erupted across the South against the freedmen. In Tennessee a Nashville paper reported that white gangs "are riding about whipping, maiming and killing all negroes who do not obey the orders of their former masters, just as if slavery existed." Listening to the testimony of officials, observers, and victims, Republicans concluded that the South had embarked on a concerted effort to circumvent the Thirteenth Amendment. The only possible response was for the federal government to intervene.

Back in March 1865, before adjourning, the 38th Congress had established the Freedmen's Bureau to provide emergency aid to ex-slaves during the transition from war to peace. Now in early 1866, under the leadership of the moderate Republican Senator Lyman Trumbull, Congress voted to extend the Freedmen's Bureau's life, gave it direct funding for the first time, and authorized its agents to investigate mistreatment of blacks.

More extraordinary was Trumbull's proposal for a Civil Rights Act declaring all persons born in the United States to be citizens and granting them—without regard to race—equal rights of contract, access to the courts, and protection of person and property. Trumbull's bill nullified all state laws depriving citizens of these rights, authorized U.S. attorneys to bring enforcement suits in the federal courts, and provided for fines and imprisonment for violators, including public officials. Provoked by an unrepentant South, Republicans of the most moderate persuasion demanded that the federal government assume responsibility for securing the basic civil rights of the freedmen.

Acting on Freedom

While Congress debated, emancipated slaves acted on their own idea of freedom. News that their bondage was

David Macrae

The Devastated South

I*n this excerpt from* The Americans at Home *(1870), an account of his tour of the United States, the Scottish clergyman David Macrae describes the war-stricken South as he found it in 1867–1868.*

I was struck with a remark made by a Southern gentleman in answer to the assertion that Jefferson Davis [the president of the Confederacy] had culpably continued the war for six months after all hope had been abandoned.

"Sir," he said, "Mr. Davis knew the temper of the South as well as any man in it. He knew if there was to be anything worth calling peace, the South must win; or, if she couldn't win, she wanted to be whipped—well whipped—thoroughly whipped."

The further south I went, the oftener these remarks came back upon me. Evidence was everywhere that the South had maintained the desperate conflict until she was utterly exhausted. . . . Almost every man I met at the South, especially in North Carolina, Georgia, and Virginia, seemed to have been in the army; and it was painful to find many who had returned were mutilated, maimed, or broken in health by exposure. When I remarked this to a young Confederate officer in North Carolina, and said I was glad to see that he had escaped unhurt, he said, "Wait till we get to the office, sir, and I will tell you more about that." When we got there, he pulled up one leg of his trousers, and showed me that he had an iron rod there to strengthen his limb, and enable him to walk without limping, half of his foot being off. He showed me on the other leg a deep scar made by a fragment of a shell; and these were two of but seven wounds which had left their marks upon his body. When he heard me speak of relics, he said, "Try to find a North Carolina gentleman without a Yankee mark on him."

Nearly three years had passed when I travelled through the country, and yet we have seen what traces the war had left in such cities as Richmond, Petersburg, and Columbia. The same spectacle met me at Charleston. Churches and houses had been battered down by heavy shot and shell hurled into the city from Federal batteries at a distance of five miles. Even the valley of desolation made by a great fire in 1861, through the very heart of the city, remained unbuilt. There, after the lapse of seven years, stood the blackened ruins of streets and houses waiting for the coming of a better day. . . . Over the country districts the prostration was equally marked. Along the track of Sherman's army especially, the devastation was fearful—farms laid waste, fences burned, bridges destroyed, houses left in ruins, plantations in many cases turned into wilderness again.

The people had shared in the general wreck, and looked poverty-stricken, careworn, and dejected. Ladies who before the war had lived in affluence, with black servants round them to attend to their every wish, were boarding together in half-furnished houses, cooking their own food and washing their own linen, some of them, I was told, so utterly destitute that they did not know when they finished one meal where they were to find the next. . . . Men who had held commanding positions during the war had fallen out of sight and were filling humble situations—struggling, many of them, to earn a bare subsistence. . . . I remember dining with three cultured Southern gentlemen, one a general, the other, I think, a captain, and the third a lieutenant. They were all living together in a plain little wooden house, such as they would formerly have provided for their servants. Two of them were engaged in a railway office, the third was seeking a situation, frequently, in his vain search, passing the large blinded house where he had lived in luxurious ease before the war.

Source: Allan Nevins, ed., *America through British Eyes* (Gloucester, MA: Peter Smith, 1968), 345–47.

over left them exultant and hopeful (see American Voices, "Jourdon Anderson: Relishing Freedom," p. 434). Freedom meant many things—the end of punishment by the lash, the ability to move around, the reuniting of families, the opportunity to begin schools, to form churches and social clubs, and, not least, to engage in politics. Across the South blacks held mass meetings, paraded, and formed organizations. Topmost among

their demands were equality before the law and the right to vote—"an essential and inseparable element of self-government."

Struggling for Economic Independence. First of all, however, came ownership of land, which emancipated blacks believed was the basis for true freedom. During the Civil War they had acted on this assumption whenever

Union armies drew near. In the chaotic final months of the war, as plantation owners fled Union forces, freedmen seized control of land where they could. Most famously, General William T. Sherman reserved large coastal tracts in Georgia and South Carolina—the Sea Islands and abandoned plantations within thirty miles of the coast—for liberated slaves and settled them on forty-acre plots. Sherman only wanted to be rid of the responsibility for the refugees as his army drove across the lower South. But the freedmen assumed that Sherman's order meant that the land would be theirs. When the war ended, resettlement became the responsibility of the Freedmen's Bureau, which was charged with feeding and clothing war refugees, distributing confiscated land to "loyal refugees and freedmen," and regulating labor contracts between freedmen and planters.

Encouraged by the Freedmen's Bureau, blacks across the South occupied confiscated or abandoned land. Many families stayed on their old plantations, awaiting redistribution of the land to them after the war. When the South Carolina planter Thomas Pinckney returned home, his freed slaves told him: "We ain't going nowhere. We are going to work right here on the land where we were born and what belongs to us."

Johnson's amnesty plan, entitling pardoned Confederates to recover property seized during the war, shattered these hopes. In October 1865 Johnson ordered General Oliver O. Howard, head of the Freedmen's Bureau, to tell Sea Islands' blacks that the land they occupied would have to be restored to the white owners. When Howard reluctantly obeyed, the dispossessed farmers protested: "Why do you take away our lands? You take them from us who have always been true, always true to the Government! You give them to our all-time enemies! That is not right!"

In the Sea Islands and elsewhere, former slaves resisted efforts to remove them. Led by black veterans of the Union army, they fought pitched battles with plantation owners and bands of ex-Confederate soldiers. Landowners struck back hard. One black veteran wrote from Maryland: "The returned colard Solgers are in Many cases beten, and their guns taken from them, we darcent walk out of an evening. . . . They beat us badly and Sumtime Shoot us." Often aided by federal troops, the local whites generally prevailed in this land war.

Resisting Wage Labor. As planters prepared for a new growing season, a great battle took shape over the labor system that would replace slavery. Convinced that blacks needed supervision, planters wanted to retain the gang labor of the past, only now with wages replacing the food, clothing, and shelter their slaves had once received. The Freedmen's Bureau, although watchful against exploitative labor contracts, sided with the planters. The main thing, its designers had always felt, was that the bureau not encourage dependency "in the guise of guardianship." Rely upon your "own efforts and exertions," an agent told a large crowd of freedmen in North Carolina, "make contracts with the planters" and "respect the rights of property."

This was advice given with little regard for the world in which those North Carolina freedmen lived. It was not only their unequal bargaining power they worried about, or even that their ex-masters' real desire was to re-enslave them under the guise of "free" contracts. In their eyes the condition of wage labor was itself, by definition, debasing. The rural South was not like the North, where working for wages was the norm and qualified a man as independent. In the South, selling one's labor to another—and in particular, selling one's labor to work another's land—implied not freedom, but dependency. To be a "freeman"—a fully empowered citizen—meant heading a household, owning some property, conducting one's own affairs.

So the issue of wage labor cut to the very core of the former slaves' struggle for freedom. Nothing had been more horrifying than that as slaves their persons had been the property of others. When a master cast his eye on a slave woman, her husband had no recourse, nor, for that matter, was rape of a slave a crime. In a famous oration celebrating the anniversary of emancipation, the Reverend Henry M. Turner spoke bitterly of the time when his people had "no security for domestic happiness," when "our wives were sold and husbands bought, children were begotten and enslaved by their fathers," and "we therefore were polygamists by virtue of our condition." That was why formalizing marriage was so urgent a matter after emancipation and why, when hard-pressed planters demanded that freedwomen go back into the fields, they resisted so resolutely. If the ex-slaves were to be free as white folk, then their wives could not, any more than white wives, labor for others. "I seen on some plantations," one freedman recounted, "where the white men would . . . tell colored men that their wives and children could not live on their places unless they work in the fields. The colored men [answered that] whenever they wanted their wives to work they would tell them themselves; and if he could not rule his own domestic affairs on that place he would leave it and go someplace else."

The reader will see the irony in this definition of freedom: it assumed the wife's subordinate role and designated her labor the husband's property. But if that was the price of freedom, freedwomen were prepared to pay it. Far better to take a chance with their own men than with their ex-masters.

Many freedpeople voted with their feet, abandoning their old plantations and seeking better lives and more freedom in the towns and cities of the South. Those who remained in the countryside refused to work the cotton fields under the hated gang-labor system or negotiated tenaciously over the terms of their labor contracts. Whatever system of labor finally might emerge, it was clear that the freedpeople would never settle for anything resembling the old plantation system.

Jourdon Anderson

Relishing Freedom

Folklorists have recorded the sly ways that slaves found, even in bondage, for "puttin' down" their masters. But only in freedom—and beyond reach in a northern state at that—could Anderson's sarcasm be expressed so openly, with the jest that his family might consider returning if they first received the wages due them, calculated to the dollar, for all those years in slavery. Yet intermixed with the bitterness, and the pride in personal dignity, is an admission of affection for "the dear old home" that helps explain why, even after the horror of bondage, ex-slaves often chose to remain in familiar surroundings and even work for their former masters. Anderson's letter, although probably written or edited by a white friend in Dayton, surely is faithful to what the ex-slave wanted to say.

Dayton, Ohio. August 7, 1865.
To My Old Master, Colonel P. H. Anderson, Big Spring, Tennessee.
Sir:

I got your letter, and was glad to find that you had not forgotten Jourdon, and that you wanted me to come back and live with you again, promising to do better for me than anybody else can. I have often felt uneasy about you. I thought the Yankees would have hung you long before this, for harboring Rebs they found at your house. I suppose they never heard about your going to Colonel Martin's to kill the Union soldier that was left by his company in their stable. Although you shot at me twice before I left you, I did not want to hear of your being hurt, and am glad you are still living. It would do me good to go back to the dear old home again, and see Miss Mary and Miss Martha and Allen, Esther, Green, and Lee. Give my love to them all, and tell them I hope we will meet in the better world, if not in this. I would have gone back to see you all when I was working in the Nashville Hospital, but one of the neighbors told me that Henry intended to shoot me if he ever got a chance.

I want to know particularly what the good chance is you propose to give me. I am doing tolerably well here.

I get twenty-five dollars a month, with victuals and clothing; have a comfortable home for Mandy,—the folks call her Mrs. Anderson,—and the children—Milly, Jane, and Grundy—go to school and are learning well. The teacher says Grundy has a head for a preacher. They go to Sunday school, and Mandy and me attend church regularly. We are kindly treated. Sometimes we overhear others saying, "Them colored people were slaves" down in Tennessee. The children feel hurt when they hear such remarks; but I tell them it was no disgrace in Tennessee to belong to Colonel Anderson. Many darkeys would have been proud, as I used to be, to call you master. Now if you will write and say what wages you will give me, I will be better able to decide whether it would be to my advantage to move back again. . . .

Mandy says she would be afraid to go back without some proof that you were disposed to treat us justly and kindly; and we have concluded to test your sincerity by asking you to send us our wages for the time we served you. This will make us forget and forgive old scores, and rely on your justice and friendship in the future. I served you faithfully for thirty-two years, and Mandy twenty years. At twenty-five dollars a month for me and two dollars a week for Mandy, our earnings would amount to eleven thousand six hundred and eighty dollars. Add to this the interest for the time our wages have been kept back, and deduct what you paid for our clothing, and three doctor's visits to me, and pulling a tooth for Mandy, and the balance will show what we are in justice entitled to. . . .

In answering this letter, please state if there would be any safety for my Milly and Jane, who are now grown up, and both good-looking girls. You know how it was with poor Matilda and Catherine. I would rather stay here and starve—and die, if it come to that—than have my girls brought to shame by the violence and wickedness of their young masters. You will also please state if there has been any schools opened for the colored children in your neighborhood. The great desire of my life now is to give my children an education, and have them form virtuous habits.

Say howdy to George Carter, and thank him for taking the pistol from you when you were shooting at me.

From your old servant,
Jourdon Anderson

Source: Stanley I. Kutler, ed., *Looking for America*, 2nd ed. (New York: W. W. Norton, 1979), 2: 4–6.

Wage Labor of Former Slaves
This photograph, taken in South Carolina shortly after the Civil War, shows former slaves leaving the cotton fields. Ex-slaves were organized into work crews probably not that different from earlier slave gangs, although they now worked for wages and their plug-hatted boss bore little resemblance to the slave drivers of the past.
New-York Historical Society.

The efforts of former slaves to control their own lives challenged deeply entrenched white attitudes. "The destiny of the black race," asserted one Texan, could be summarized "in one sentence—subordination to the white race." Southern whites, a Freedmen's Bureau official observed, could not "conceive of the negro having any rights at all." And when freedmen resisted, white retribution was swift and often terrible. In Pine Bluff, Arkansas, "after some kind of dispute with some freedmen," whites set fire to their cabins and hanged twenty-four of the inhabitants—men, women, and children. The toll of murdered and beaten blacks mounted into untold thousands. The governments established under Johnson's plan only put the stamp of legality on the pervasive efforts to enforce white supremacy. Blacks "would be *just as well* off with no law at all or no Government," concluded a Freedmen's Bureau agent, as with the justice they got under the restored white rule.

In this unequal struggle, blacks turned to Washington. "We stood by the government when it wanted help," a black Mississippian wrote President Johnson. "Now . . . will it stand by us?"

Congress versus President

Andrew Johnson was, alas, not the man to ask. In February 1866 he vetoed the Freedmen's Bureau bill. The bureau, Johnson charged, was an "immense patronage," showering benefits on blacks never granted to "our own people." Republicans could not muster enough votes to override his veto. A month later, further rebuffing his critics, Johnson vetoed Trumbull's civil rights bill, arguing that federal protection of black civil rights constituted "a stride toward centralization." His racism, hitherto muted, now blazed forth. In his view granting blacks the privileges of citizenship was discriminatory, operating "in favor of the colored and against the white race," and threatening all manner of evil consequences, including racial mixing.

Galvanized by Johnson's attack on the civil rights bill, the Republicans went into action. In early April they got the necessary two-thirds majorities in both houses to override a presidential veto. The enactment of the civil rights bill into law was a truly historic event, the first time Congress had prevailed over a presidential veto on a major piece of legislation. Republican resolve was reinforced by news of mounting violence in the South, culminating in three days of rioting in Memphis. Forty-six blacks and two whites were left dead, and hundreds of black homes, churches, and schools were looted and burned. In July an angry Congress renewed the Freedmen's Bureau over a second Johnson veto.

The Fourteenth Amendment.   Eager to consolidate their gains, Republicans moved to enshrine black civil rights in an amendment to the Constitution. The heart of the Fourteenth Amendment was Section 1, which declared that "all persons born or naturalized in the United States" were citizens. No state could abridge "the privileges or immunities of citizens of the United States," deprive "any person of life, liberty, or property, without due process of law," or deny anyone "the equal protection of the laws." These phrases were vague, intentionally so, but they established the constitutionality of the Civil Rights Act and, more important, the basis on which the courts and Congress could establish an enforceable standard of equality before the law in the states.

For the moment, however, the Fourteenth Amendment was most important for its impact on national politics. With the 1866 Congressional elections approaching, Johnson somehow figured he had a winning issue in the Fourteenth Amendment. He urged the states not to ratify it. Months earlier, Johnson had begun to maneuver politically against the Republicans, aiming to build a coalition of white Southerners, northern Democrats, and conservative Republicans under the banner of National Union. Any hope of creating a new party, however, was shattered by Johnson's intemperate behavior and by escalating violence in the South. A dissension-ridden National Union convention in July ended inconclusively, and Johnson's campaign against the Fourteenth Amendment became, effectively, a campaign for the Democratic Party.

Republicans responded furiously, unveiling a practice that would become known as "waving the bloody shirt." The Democrats were traitors, charged Indiana governor Oliver Morton, and their party was "a common sewer and loathesome receptacle, into which is emptied every element of treason North and South, every element of inhumanity and barbarism which has dishonored this age." In late August Johnson embarked on a disastrous "swing around the circle"—a railroad tour from Washington to Chicago and St. Louis and back. It was unprecedented for a president to campaign personally, and Johnson made matters worse by engaging in shouting matches with hecklers and insulting the hostile crowds.

The 1866 Congressional elections inflicted a humiliating defeat on Johnson. The Republicans won a three-to-one majority in Congress, so that, to begin with, the Republicans considered themselves "masters of the situation," free to proceed "entirely regardless of [Johnson's] opinions or wishes." As a referendum on the Fourteenth Amendment, moreover, the election registered overwhelming popular support for the civil rights of the former slaves. The Republican Party emerged with a new sense of unity—a unity coalescing not at the center, but on the left, around the unbending program of the Radical minority.

Radical Republicans. The Radicals represented the abolitionist strain within the Republican Party. Most of them hailed from New England or from the area of the upper Midwest settled by New Englanders. In the Senate they were led by Charles Sumner of Massachusetts; in the House, by Thaddeus Stevens from Pennsylvania. For them Reconstruction was never primarily about restoring the Union but about remaking southern society. "The foundations of their institutions . . . must be broken up and relaid," declared Stevens, "or all our blood and treasure will have been spent in vain."

Only a handful went as far as Stevens in demanding that the plantations be treated as "forfeited estates of the enemy" and broken up into small farms for the former slaves. About the need to guarantee the freedmen's civil and political rights, however, there was agreement. In this endeavor Radicals had no qualms about expanding the powers of the national government. "The power of the great landed aristocracy in those regions, if unrestrained by power from without, would inevitably reassert itself," warned Congressman George Julian. Radicals were aggressively partisan. They regarded the Republican Party as the instrument of the Lord and black votes as the means by which the party would bring regeneration of the South.

At first, in the months after Appomattox, few but the Radicals themselves imagined that so extreme a program had any chance of enactment. Black suffrage especially seemed beyond reach, since the northern states (excepting in New England) denied blacks the vote at this time. And yet as fury mounted against the intransigent South, Republicans became ever more radicalized until, in the wake of the smashing victory of 1866, they embraced the Radicals' vision of a reconstructed South.

Radical Reconstruction

Afterward, thoughtful Southerners admitted that the South had brought radical Reconstruction on itself. "We had, in 1865, a white man's government in Alabama," remarked the man who had been Johnson's provisional governor, "but we lost it." The state's "great blunder" was not to "have at once taken the negro right under the protection of the laws." Remarkably, the South remained defiant even after the 1866 elections. Every state legislature but Tennessee's rejected the Fourteenth Amendment, mostly by virtual acclamation. It was as if they could not imagine that governments installed under the presidential imprimatur and fully functioning might be swept away. But that, in fact, is just what the Republicans intended to do.

Congress Takes Command

The Reconstruction Act of 1867, enacted in March by the Republican Congress, organized the South as a conquered land, dividing it into five military districts, each under the command of a Union general (Map 15.1). The price for reentering the Union was granting the vote to the freedmen and disfranchising those of the South's prewar leadership class who had participated in the rebellion. Each military commander was ordered to register

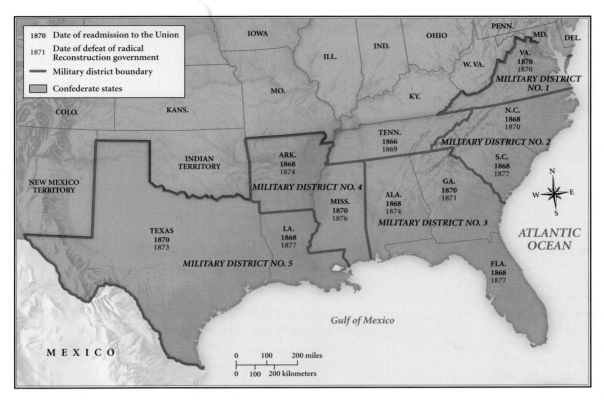

MAP 15.1 Reconstruction

The federal government organized the Confederate states into five military districts during radical Reconstruction. For each state the first date indicates when that state was readmitted to the Union; the second date shows when Radical Republicans lost control of the state government. All the ex-Confederate states rejoined the Union from 1868 to 1870, but the periods of radical rule varied widely. Republicans lasted only a few months in Virginia; they held on until the end of Reconstruction in Louisiana, Florida, and South Carolina.

all eligible adult males (black as well as white), supervise the election of state conventions, and make certain that the new constitutions contained guarantees of black suffrage. Congress would readmit a state to the Union if its voters ratified the constitution, if that document proved acceptable to Congress, and if the new state legislature approved the Fourteenth Amendment (thus insuring the needed ratification by three-fourths of the states). Johnson vetoed the Reconstruction Act, but Congress overrode the veto (Table 15.1).

Impeachment. Republicans also restricted President Johnson's room for maneuver. The Tenure of Office Act, a companion to the Reconstruction Act, required Senate consent for the removal of any official whose appointment had required Senate confirmation. Congress chiefly wanted to protect Secretary of War Edwin M. Stanton, a Lincoln holdover and the only member of Johnson's cabinet who favored radical Reconstruction. In his position Stanton could do much to frustrate Johnson's anticipated efforts to undermine Reconstruction. The law also required the president to issue all orders to the army through its commanding general, Ulysses S. Grant. In effect

Congress was attempting to reconstruct the presidency as well as the South.

Seemingly defeated, Johnson appointed generals recommended by Stanton and Grant to command the five military districts in the South. But he was just biding his time. In August 1867, after Congress had adjourned, he "suspended" Stanton and replaced him with Grant, believing that the general would act like a good soldier and follow orders. Next Johnson replaced four of the commanding generals. Johnson, however, had misjudged Grant, who publicly objected to the president's machinations. When the Senate reconvened in the fall, it overruled Stanton's suspension. Grant, now an open enemy of Johnson's, resigned so that Stanton could resume his office.

On February 21, 1868, Johnson formally dismissed Stanton. The feisty secretary of war, however, barricaded the door of his office and refused to admit the replacement Johnson had appointed. Three days later, House Republicans introduced articles of **impeachment** against the president, employing the power granted the House of Representatives by the Constitution to charge high federal officials with "Treason, Bribery, or other high Crimes and Misdemeanors." The House overwhelmingly approved

TABLE 15.1 Primary Reconstruction Laws and Constitutional Amendments

Law (Date of Congressional Passage)	Key Provisions
Thirteenth Amendment (January 1865*)	Prohibited slavery
Civil Rights Act of 1866 (April 1866)	Defined citizenship rights of freedmen Authorized federal authorities to bring suit against those who violated those rights
Fourteenth Amendment (June 1866†)	Established national citizenship for persons born or naturalized in the United States Prohibited the states from depriving citizens of their civil rights or equal protection under the law Reduced state representation in House of Representatives by the percentage of adult male citizens denied the vote
Reconstruction Act of 1867 (March 1867‡)	Divided the South into five military districts, each under the command of a Union general Established requirements for readmission of ex-Confederate states to the Union
Tenure of Office Act (March 1867)	Required Senate consent for removal of any federal official whose appointment had required Senate confirmation
Fifteenth Amendment (February 1869)	Forbade states to deny citizens the right to vote on the grounds of race, color, or "previous condition of servitude"
Ku Klux Klan Act (April 1871)	Authorized the president to use federal prosecutions and military force to suppress conspiracies to deprive citizens of the right to vote and enjoy the equal protection of the law

*Ratified by three-fourths of all states in December 1868.
†Ratified by three-fourths of all states in July 1868.
‡Ratified by three-fourths of all states in March 1870.

eleven counts of presidential misconduct, nine of which dealt with violations of the Tenure of Office Act.

The case went to the Senate, which acts as the court in impeachment cases, with Chief Justice Salmon P. Chase presiding. After an eleven-week trial, thirty-five senators on May 15 voted for conviction, one vote short of the two-thirds majority required. Seven moderate Republicans broke ranks, voting for acquittal along with twelve Democrats. The dissenting Republicans felt that the Tenure of Office Act was of dubious validity (in fact, the Supreme Court subsequently declared it unconstitutional), that the motives of the impeachers were really political, and that removing a president for defying Congress was too extreme and too threatening to constitutional checks and balances, even for the sake of punishing Johnson.

Despite his acquittal, however, Johnson had been defanged. For the remainder of his term he was powerless to alter the course of Reconstruction.

The Election of 1868. The impeachment controversy made Grant, already the North's war hero, a Republican hero as well, and he easily won the party's presidential nomination in 1868. In the fall campaign he supported

radical Reconstruction, but he also urged reconciliation between the sections. His Democratic opponent Horatio Seymour, a former governor of New York, almost declined the nomination because he doubted that the Democrats could overcome the stigma of their ties with the disloyal South.

As Seymour feared, the Republicans "waved the bloody shirt," stirring up old wartime emotions against the Democrats to great effect. Grant won about the same share of the northern vote (55 percent) that Lincoln had won in 1864 and received 214 of 294 electoral votes. The Republicans also retained two-thirds majorities in both houses of Congress.

The Fifteenth Amendment. In the wake of their smashing victory, the Republicans quickly produced the last major piece of Reconstruction legislation—the Fifteenth Amendment, which forbade either the federal government or the states from denying citizens the right to vote on the basis of race, color, or "previous condition of servitude" (see Documents, p. D-17). The amendment left room for **poll taxes** and property or literacy tests that might be used to discourage blacks from voting, which

Resistance in the South

This engraving, entitled "If He Is a Union Man or Freedman: Verdict, Hang the D——— Yankee and Nigger," appeared in Harper's Weekly on March 23, 1867, just as the Reconstruction Act was being adopted. Thomas Nast's cartoon encapsulated the outrage at the South's murderous intransigence that led even moderate Republicans to support radical Reconstruction.
Library of Congress.

For more help analyzing this image, see the ONLINE STUDY GUIDE at bedfordstmartins.com/henretta.

was necessary because its authors did not want to alienate northern states that already relied on such qualifications to keep immigrants and the "unworthy" poor from the polls. A California senator warned that in his state, with its rabidly anti-Chinese sentiment (see Chapter 16), any restriction on that power would "kill our party as dead as a stone."

Despite grumbling by Radical Republicans, the amendment passed without modification in February 1869. Congress required the states still under federal control—Virginia, Mississippi, Texas, and Georgia—to ratify it as a condition for being readmitted to the Union. A year later the Fifteenth Amendment became part of the Constitution.

Woman Suffrage Denied.   If the Fifteenth Amendment troubled some proponents of black suffrage, this was nothing compared to the outrage felt by women's rights advocates. They had fought the good fight for the abolition

of slavery for so many years, only to be abandoned when the chance finally came to get the vote for women. All it would have taken was one more word in the Fifteenth Amendment so that the protected categories for voting would have read "race, color, *sex*, or previous condition." Leading suffragists such as Susan B. Anthony and Elizabeth Cady Stanton did not want to hear from Radical Republicans that this was "the Negro's hour" and that women would have to wait for another day. How could suffrage be granted to ex-slaves, Stanton demanded to know, but not to them?

In her despair Stanton lashed out in ugly racist terms against "Patrick and Sambo and Hans and Ung Tung," ignorant as they were about the Declaration of Independence, yet entitled to vote, while the best and most accomplished of American women remained voteless. In 1869 the annual meeting of the Equal Rights Association, the champion of both black and woman suffrage, broke up in acrimony, and Stanton and Anthony came out against the Fifteenth Amendment.

At this searing moment a schism opened in the ranks of the women's movement. The majority, led by Lucy Stone and Julia Ward Howe, reconciled themselves to disappointment and accepted the priority of black suffrage. Organized into the American Woman Suffrage Association, these moderates remained allied to the Republican Party, in hopes that once Reconstruction had been settled it would be time for the woman's vote. The Stanton-Anthony group, however, struck out in a new direction. The embittered Stanton declared that woman "must not put her trust in man" in fighting for her rights. The new organization she headed, the New York–based National Woman Suffrage Association, accepted only women, focused exclusively on women's rights, and resolutely took up the battle for a federal woman suffrage amendment.

The fracturing of the women's movement obscured the common ground the two sides shared. Both now realized that a constituency had to be built beyond the narrow confines of abolitionism and evangelical reform. Both elevated suffrage into the preeminent women's issue. And both were energized by a shared anger not evident in earlier times. "If I were to give vent to all my pent-up wrath concerning the subordination of woman," Lydia Maria Child wrote the Republican warhorse Charles Sumner in 1872, "I might frighten *you*. . . . Suffice it, therefore, to say, either the theory of our government is *false*, or women have a right to vote." If radical Reconstruction seemed a barren time for women's rights, in fact it had planted the seeds of the modern feminist movement.

Republican Rule in the South

Between 1868 and 1871 all the southern states met the congressional stipulations and rejoined the Union. Protected by federal troops and encouraged by northern party leaders, state Republican organizations took hold

A Woman Suffrage Quilt

Homemade quilts provided funds and a means of persuasion for the temperance and antislavery movements. Suffragists, however, regarded quilts and needlework as symbols of the domestic subjugation of women, so woman suffrage quilts, such as this one (c. 1860–1880) depicting a women's rights lecture, were rare.
Collections of Mrs. Nancy W. Livingston and Mrs. Elizabeth Livingston Jaeger / Photo courtesy, Los Angeles County Museum of Art.

across the South and won control of the newly established Reconstruction governments. These Republican administrations remained in power for periods ranging from a few months in Virginia to nine years in South Carolina, Louisiana, and Florida (see Map 15.1). Their core support came from African Americans, who constituted a majority of registered voters in Alabama, Florida, South Carolina, and Mississippi.

Carpetbaggers and Scalawags.   Southern white Republicans faced the scorn of Democratic ex-Confederates, who mocked them as **scalawags**—an ancient Scots-Irish term for runty, worthless animals. Whites who had come from the North they denounced as **carpetbaggers**—self-seeking interlopers who carried all their property in cheap suitcases called carpetbags. Such labels glossed over the actual diversity of these white Republicans.

Some carpetbaggers, while motivated by personal profit, also brought capital and skills. Others were Union army veterans taken with the South—its climate, people, and economic opportunities. And interspersed with the self-seekers were many idealists anxious to advance the cause of emancipation.

The scalawags were even more diverse. Some were former slave owners, ex-Whigs and even ex-Democrats, drawn to Republicanism as the best way to attract

northern capital to southern railroads, mines, and factories. In southwest Texas the large population of Germans was strongly Republican. They sent to Congress Edward Degener, an immigrant San Antonio grocer whom Confederate authorities had imprisoned and whose sons had been executed for treason. But most numerous among the scalawags were yeomen farmers from the backcountry districts who wanted to rid the South of its slaveholding aristocracy. Scalawags had generally fought against, or at least refused to support, the Confederacy; they believed that slavery had victimized whites as well as blacks. "Now is the time," a Georgia scalawag wrote, "for every man to come out and speak his principles publickly [*sic*] and vote for liberty as we have been in bondage long enough."

African American Leadership.   The Democrats' scorn for black political leaders as ignorant field hands was just as false as stereotypes about white Republicans. The first African American leaders in the South came from an elite of blacks freed before the Civil War. They were joined by northern blacks who moved south when radical Reconstruction offered the prospect of meaningful freedom. Like their white allies, many were Union army veterans. Some had participated in the antislavery crusade; a number were employed by the Freedmen's Bureau or northern missionary societies. Others had escaped from slavery and were returning home. One of these was Blanche K. Bruce, who had been tutored on the Virginia plantation of his white father. During the war Bruce escaped and established a school for ex-slaves in Missouri. In 1869 he moved to Mississippi, became active in politics, and in 1874 became Mississippi's second black U.S. senator.

As the reconstructed Republican governments of 1867 began to function, this diverse group of ministers, artisans, shopkeepers, and former soldiers reached out to the freedmen. African American speakers, some financed by the Republican Party, fanned out into the old plantation districts and recruited ex-slaves for political roles. Still, few of the new leaders were field hands; most had been preachers or artisans. The literacy of one ex-slave, Thomas Allen, who was a Baptist minister and shoemaker, helped him win election to the Georgia legislature. "In my county," he recalled, "the colored people came to me for instructions, and I gave them the best instructions I could. I took the *New York Tribune* and other papers, and in that way I found out a great deal, and I told them whatever I thought was right."

Although never proportionate to their numbers in the population, black officeholders were prominent across the South. In South Carolina African Americans constituted a majority in the lower house of the legislature in 1868. Three were elected to Congress, another joined the state supreme court. Over the entire course of Reconstruction, twenty African Americans served in

THE FIRST COLORED SENATOR AND REPRESENTATIVES.
In the 41ˢᵗ and 42ⁿᵈ Congress of the United States.

African American Congressional Delegation, 1872

This Currier and Ives lithograph celebrates one of the notable achievements of radical Reconstruction—the representation that ex-slaves won, however briefly, in the U.S. Congress. Hiram Revels of Mississippi, the Senate's first African American member, is seated at the extreme left.

Granger Collection.

state administrations as governor, lieutenant governor, secretary of state, treasurer, or superintendent of education, more than six hundred served as state legislators, and sixteen as congressmen.

The Radical Program. The Republicans who took office had ambitious plans for a reconstructed South. They wanted to end its dependence on cotton agriculture and build an entrepreneurial economy like the North's. They fell far short of achieving this vision but accomplished more than their critics gave them credit for.

The Republicans modernized state constitutions, eliminated property qualification for the vote, and made more offices elective. They attended especially to the personal freedom of the ex-slaves, sweeping out the shadow Black Codes that coerced the freedmen and limited their mobility. Women also benefited from the Republican defense of personal liberty. Nearly all the new constitutions expanded the rights of married women, enabling them to hold property and earnings independent of their husbands—"a wonderful reform," a Georgia woman wrote, for "the cause of Women's Rights." Republican social programs called for hospitals, more humane penitentiaries, and asylums for orphans and the insane. Republican governments built roads in areas where roads had never existed. They poured money into rebuilding the region's railroad network. And they did all this without federal financing.

To pay for their ambitious programs the Republican governments copied taxes that Jacksonian reformers had earlier introduced in the North—in particular, gen-

eral property taxes on both real estate and personal wealth. The goal was to make planters pay their fair share and to broaden the tax base. In many plantation counties, former slaves served as tax assessors and collectors, administering the taxation of their one-time owners.

Higher tax revenues never managed to overtake the burgeoning obligations assumed by the Reconstruction governments. State debts mounted rapidly and, as interest payments on bonds fell into arrears, public credit collapsed. On top of that, much of the spending was wasted or ended in the pockets of state officials. Corruption was endemic to American politics, present in the southern states before the Republicans came on the scene, and rampant everywhere in this era, not least in the Grant administration itself. Still, in the free-spending atmosphere of the southern Republican regimes, corruption was especially luxuriant and damaging to the cause of radical Reconstruction.

Nothing, however, could dim the achievement in public education. Here the South had lagged woefully; only Tennessee had a system of public schooling before the Civil War. Republican state governments vowed to make up for lost time, viewing education as the foundation for a democratic order. African Americans of all ages rushed to attend the newly established schools, even when they had to pay tuition. An elderly man in Mississippi explained his hunger for education: "Ole missus used to read the good book [the Bible] to us . . . on Sunday evenin's, but she mostly read dem places where it says, 'Servants obey your masters.' . . . Now we is free, there's heaps of tings in that old book we is just suffering to learn." By 1875 about half of all the children in Florida, Mississippi, and South Carolina were in school.

The Role of Black Churches. The building of schools was part of a larger effort by African Americans to fortify the institutions that had sustained their spirit during the days before emancipation. Religious belief had struck deep roots in nineteenth-century slave society. Now, in freedom, the African Americans left their old white-dominated congregations, where they had been relegated to segregated balconies and denied any voice in church governance, and built churches of their own. These churches joined together to form African American versions of the Southern Methodist and Southern Baptist denominations, including, most prominently, the National Baptist Convention and the African Methodist Episcopal Church. Everywhere the robust black churches served not only as places of worship but as schools, social centers, and political meeting halls.

Black clerics were community leaders and often, political leaders as well. As Charles H. Pearce, a Methodist minister in Florida, declared, "A man in this State cannot do his whole duty as a minister except he looks out for the political interests of his people." Calling forth the special destiny of the ex-slaves as the new "Children of Israel," black ministers provided a powerful religious underpinning for the Republican politics of their congregations.

The Quest for Land

In the meantime the freedmen were locked in a great economic struggle with their former owners. In 1869 the Republican government of South Carolina had established a land commission empowered to buy property and resell it on easy terms to the landless. In this way about 14,000 black families acquired farms. South Carolina's land distribution plan showed what was possible, but it was the exception and not the rule. Despite a lot of rhetoric, Republican regimes elsewhere did little to help the freedmen fulfill their dreams of becoming independent farmers. Federal efforts proved equally feeble. The Southern Homestead Act of 1866 offered eighty-acre grants to settlers, limited for the first year to freedmen and southern Unionists. The advantage was strictly symbolic, however, since the public land made available to homesteaders was off the beaten track in swampy, infertile parts of the Lower South. Only about a thousand families succeeded.

Sharecropping. There was no reversing President Johnson's order restoring confiscated lands to ex-Confederates. Property rights, it seemed, trumped everything else, even for most Radical Republicans. The Freedman's Bureau, which had earlier championed the land claims of the ex-slaves, now devoted itself to teaching them how to be good agricultural laborers.

While they yearned for farms of their own, most freedmen started out landless and with no option but to work for their former owners. But not, they vowed, under the conditions of slavery—no gang work, no overseers, no fines or punishments, no regulation of their private lives. In certain parts of the agricultural South wage work became the norm—for example, on the great sugar plantations of Louisiana taken over after the war by northern investors. The problem was that cotton planters lacked the money to pay wages, at least not until the crop came in, and sometimes, in lieu of a straight wage, they offered a share of the crop. As a wage,

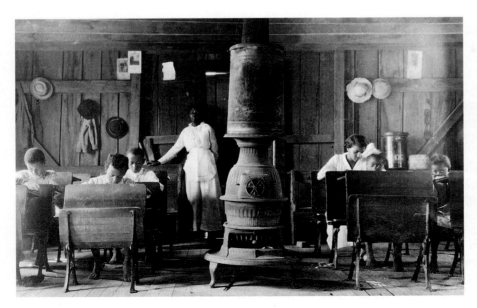

Freedmen's School, c. 1870
This rare photograph shows the interior of one of the 3,000 freedmen's schools established across the South after the Civil War. Although many of these schools were staffed by white missionaries, a main objective of northern educators was to prepare black women to take over the classrooms. The black teacher shown here is surely one of the first. Library of Congress.

this was a bad deal for the freedmen, but if they could be paid in shares for their work, why could they not pay in shares to rent the land they worked?

This form of land tenantry was already familiar in parts of the white South, and the freedmen now seized on it for the independence it offered them. Planters resisted, believing, as one wrote, that "wages are the only successful system of controlling hands." But, in a battle of wills that broke out all across the cotton South, the planters yielded to "the inveterate prejudices of the freedmen, who desire to be masters of their own time."

Thus there sprang up the distinctive laboring system of cotton agriculture—**sharecropping**, in which the freedmen worked as renters, exchanging their labor for the use of land, house, implements, sometimes seed and fertilizer, typically turning over half to two-thirds of their crops to the landlord (Map 15.2). The sharecropping system joined laborers and the owners of land and capital in a common sharing of risks and returns. But it was a very unequal relationship, given the force of southern law and custom on the white landowner's side, and given the sharecroppers' dire economic circumstances. Starting out penniless, they had no way of making it through the first growing season without borrowing for food and supplies.

Country storekeepers stepped in. Bankrolled by their northern suppliers, they "furnished" the sharecropper and took as collateral a **lien** on the crop, effectively assuming ownership of the cropper's share and leaving him only the proceeds that remained after his debts had been paid. Once indebted at one store, the sharecropper was no longer free to shop around and became an easy target for exorbitant prices, unfair interest rates, and crooked bookkeeping. As cotton prices declined during the 1870s, more and more sharecroppers failed to settle accounts and fell into permanent debt.

And if the merchant was also the landowner, or conspired with the landowner, the debt became a pretext for forced labor, or **peonage**, although evidence now suggests that sharecroppers generally managed to pull up stakes and move on once things became hopeless. Sharecroppers always thought twice about moving, however, because part of their "capital" was being known and well reputed in their home communities. Freedmen who lacked that local standing generally found sharecropping hard going and ended up in the ranks of agricultural laborers.

In the face of so much adversity, black families struggled to better themselves. Being that it enabled *family*, struggle was, in truth, the saving advantage of sharecropping because it mobilized husbands and wives in common enterprise while shielding both from personal subordination to whites. Freedwomen were doubly blessed, neither field hands for their ex-masters, nor dependent housewives, but partners laboring side by side with their husbands. The trouble with sharecropping, one planter grumbled, was that "it makes the laborer too independent; he becomes a partner, and has to be consulted." By the end of Reconstruction, about one-quarter of sharecropping families had managed to save enough to rent with cash payments, and eventually black farmers owned about a third of the land they cultivated.

A Comparative Perspective. The battle between planters and freedmen over the land was by no means unique to the American South. Whenever slavery ended—in Haiti after the slave revolt of 1791, in the British Caribbean by abolition in 1833, in Cuba and Brazil by gradual emancipation during the 1880s—a fierce struggle ensued between planters bent on restoring a gang-labor system and ex-slaves bent on gaining economic autonomy. The outcome of this universal

Sharecroppers

This sharecropping family stands proudly in front of their new cabin and young cotton crop, which is planted nearly up to the cabin door. But the presence of the white landlord in the background casts a shadow on them, suggesting their hard struggle for economic freedom. Brown Brothers.

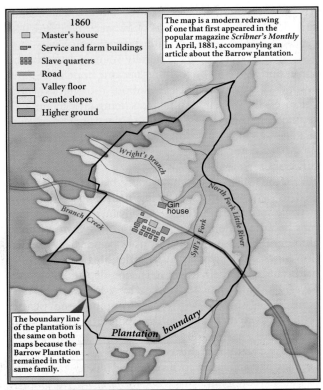

1860

- ☐ Master's house
- ☐▪ Service and farm buildings
- ☷ Slave quarters
- ▭ Road
- Valley floor
- Gentle slopes
- Higher ground

The map is a modern redrawing of one that first appeared in the popular magazine *Scribner's Monthly* in April, 1881, accompanying an article about the Barrow plantation.

Wright's Branch

North Fork Little River

Branch Creek

Gin house

Syll's Fork

The boundary line of the plantation is the same on both maps because the Barrow Plantation remained in the same family.

Plantation boundary

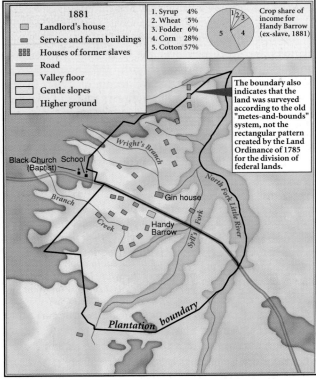

1881

- ☐ Landlord's house
- ☐ Service and farm buildings
- ☷ Houses of former slaves
- ▭ Road
- Valley floor
- Gentle slopes
- Higher ground

1. Syrup 4%
2. Wheat 5%
3. Fodder 6%
4. Corn 28%
5. Cotton 57%

Crop share of income for Handy Barrow (ex-slave, 1881)

The boundary also indicates that the land was surveyed according to the old "metes-and-bounds" system, not the rectangular pattern created by the Land Ordinance of 1785 for the division of federal lands.

Wright's Branch

Black Church (Baptist) School

North Fork Little River

Branch Creek

Gin house

Syll's Fork

Handy Barrow

Plantation boundary

◀ **MAP 15.2 The Barrow Plantation, 1860 and 1881**

Comparing the 1860 map of this central Georgia plantation with the 1881 map reveals the impact of sharecropping on patterns of black residence. In 1860 the slave quarters were clustered near the planter's house. The sharecroppers scattered across the plantation's 2,000 acres, building cabins on the ridges of land between the low-lying streams. The name Barrow was common among the sharecropping families, which means almost certainly that they had been slaves on the Barrow plantation who, years after emancipation, still had not moved on. For all the croppers freedom surely meant not only their individual lots and cabins, but the school and church shown on the map.

so by the importation of indentured servants from India and China. Where land could not be had, as in British Barbados or Antigua, the ex-slaves returned to plantation labor as wage workers, although often in some combination with customary rights to housing and garden plots. The cotton South fit neither of these broad patterns. The freedmen did not get the land, but neither did the planters get field hands. What both got was sharecropping.

The reason for this exceptional outcome was ultimately political. Elsewhere, emancipation almost never meant civil or political equality for the freed slaves. Even in the British islands, where substantial self-government existed, high property qualifications effectively disfranchised the ex-slaves. In the United States, however, hard on the heels of emancipation came civil rights, manhood suffrage and, for a brief era, a real measure of political power for the freedmen. Sharecropping took shape during Reconstruction, and there was no going back afterward.

For the freedmen sharecropping was not the worst choice; it certainly beat laboring for their former owners. But for southern agriculture the costs were devastating. Sharecropping committed the South inflexibly to cotton, despite soil depletion and low prices. Crop diversification declined, costing the South its self-sufficiency in grains and livestock. And with farms leased year-to-year, neither tenant nor owner had much incentive to improve the property. The crop-lien system lined merchants' pockets with unearned profits that might otherwise have gone into agricultural improvement. The result was a stagnant farm economy, blighting the South's future and condemning it to economic backwardness—a kind of retribution, in fact, for the fresh injustices visited on the people it had once enslaved.

The Undoing of Reconstruction

Ex-Confederates were blind to the benefits of radical Reconstruction. Indeed, no amount of achievement could have persuaded them that it was anything but an abomination, undertaken without their consent and intended

conflict depended on the ex-slaves' access to land. Where vacant land existed, as in British Guiana, or where plantations could be seized, as in Haiti, the ex-slaves became subsistence farmers, and insofar as the Caribbean plantation economy survived without the ex-slaves, it did

to deny them their rightful place in southern society. Led by the planters, ex-Confederates staged a massive counterrevolution—one designed to "redeem" the South and restore them to political power under the banner of the Democratic Party. But the **Redeemers** could not have succeeded on their own. They needed the complicity of the North. The undoing of Reconstruction is as much about northern acquiescence as it is about southern resistance.

Counterrevolution

Insofar as they could win at the ballot box, southern Democrats took that route. They worked hard to get ex-Confederates restored to the rolls of registered voters, they appealed to racial solidarity and southern patriotism, and they campaigned against black rule as a threat to white supremacy. But force was equally acceptable. Throughout the Deep South, especially where black voters were heavily concentrated, ex-Confederate planters and their supporters organized secret societies and waged campaigns of terrorism against blacks and their white allies.

The Ku Klux Klan. The most widespread of these groups, the Ku Klux Klan, first appeared in 1866 as a Tennessee social club but quickly became a paramilitary force under the aegis of Nathan Bedford Forrest, the Confederacy's most decorated cavalry general (see American Lives, "Nathan Bedford Forrest: Defender of Southern Honor," p. 446). By 1870 the Klan was operating almost everywhere in the South as a terrorist organization serving the Democratic Party. The Klan murdered and whipped Republican politicians, burned black schools and churches, and attacked party gatherings (see American Voices, "Harriet Hernandes: The Intimidation of Black Voters," p. 448). Such terrorist tactics enabled the Democrats to seize power in Georgia and North Carolina in 1870 and make substantial gains elsewhere. An African American politician in North Carolina wrote, "Our former masters are fast taking the reins of government."

Congress responded by passing enforcement legislation, including the Ku Klux Klan Act of 1871, authorizing President Grant to use federal prosecutions, military force, and martial law to suppress conspiracies to deprive citizens of the right to vote, hold office, serve on juries, and enjoy equal protection of the law. In South Carolina, where the Klan was most deeply entrenched, federal troops occupied nine counties, made hundreds of arrests, and drove as many as 2,000 Klansmen from the state.

The Grant administration's assault on the Klan raised the spirits of southern Republicans, but it also emphasized how dependent they were on the federal government. The potency of the Ku Klux Klan Act, a Mississippi Republican wrote, "derived alone from its

Klan Portrait

Two armed Klansmen pose in their disguises, which they donned not only to hide their identity but also to intimidate their black neighbors. Northern audiences saw a lithograph based on this photograph in Harper's Weekly *on December 28, 1868.*
Rutherford B. Hayes Presidential Center.

source" in the federal government. "No such law could be enforced by state authority, the local power being too weak." If they were to prevail over antiblack terrorism, Republicans needed what one carpetbagger described as "steady, unswerving power from without."

The Failure of Federal Enforcement. But northern Republicans were growing weary of Reconstruction and the endless bloodshed it seemed to produce. Prosecuting Klansmen was an uphill battle. U.S. attorneys usually faced all-white juries, and the Justice Department lacked the resources to handle the cases. After 1872 prosecutions began to drop off, and many Klansmen received hasty pardons; few served significant prison terms.

In a kind of self-fulfilling prophecy, the unwillingness of the Grant administration to shore up Reconstruction guaranteed that it would fail. Republican governments that were denied federal help found themselves overwhelmed by the massive resistance of

Nathan Bedford Forrest: Defender of Southern Honor

Nathan Bedford Forrest in Uniform, c. 1865
Library of Congress.

As a boy Nathan Bedford Forrest had little stake in the old plantation order of the South. His father was a blacksmith who followed the frontier to Tennessee, where Nathan, the oldest of eleven children, was born on July 13, 1821. When he was only sixteen, his father died, leaving Forrest the primary breadwinner. With hardly any schooling, the boy took charge of the family's rented Mississippi farm; he also became an adept horse-trader. At age twenty-one, when his mother remarried, Forrest left for Hernando, Mississippi, where his uncle ran a livery business.

Tall and physically imposing, Forrest was normally soft-spoken, the soul of courtesy, but he had a violent temper. When four men attacked his uncle, Forrest leapt to his defense. The uncle died from a bullet meant for his nephew, but the young Forrest had shown his mettle. Admiring his raw courage, Hernando citizens rewarded Forrest by electing him town constable. Equally implacable in love, Forrest so insistently wooed a young lady from a well-connected local family that at their third meeting she agreed to marry him.

For a hard-driving young man like Forrest, the booming cotton economy offered much opportunity. He took over his uncle's business, ran a stagecoach service, traded livestock and—in due course—slaves. In 1851 ambition took him and his family to Memphis, Tennessee, where he became a well-known slave trader. With his profits he purchased a large plantation in Mississippi. By now he had become a man of substance, a leading Memphis citizen. In the sectional crisis brewing in the late 1850s, Forrest fiercely championed southern rights and, of course, slavery.

When war came in 1861, Forrest immediately organized a Tennessee cavalry regiment. In April 1862 he distinguished himself at the bloody battle of Shiloh, where he was badly wounded. Promoted to brigadier general, he began a brilliant career as a cavalry raider, fighting mostly behind Union lines. His warrior spirit often led him into the thick of battle, oblivious to the fact that he was a general and not a trooper. That same explosiveness ignited one of the war's worst atrocities, the slaughter by his men of black troops at Fort Pillow, Tennessee, on April 12, 1864, evidently because of

rumors that the Fort Pillow garrison had been harassing local whites loyal to the Confederacy.

The Fort Pillow massacre anticipated the civil strife that would consume Tennessee over the next half-decade. The Republican governor William G. Brownlow, a former Confederate prisoner, was not shy about calling his enemies to account. Elected in March 1865, he disfranchised ex-Confederates, leaving political power in the hands of a minority of Unionist whites and freed slaves. Foreshadowing the reaction to radical Reconstruction a few years later, ex-Confederates around the state concluded that they could regain power only by waging a secret campaign of terror against Brownlow's black supporters. This was the genesis, among other things, of the first den of the Ku Klux Klan in Pulaski, Tennessee, sometime in late 1865 or early 1866.

Home safe from the war, Forrest was absorbed by his own damaged fortunes. The wealth represented by his slaves had been wiped out by emancipation, and he was heavily in debt. With the aid of the Freedmen's Bureau, Forrest managed to put his former slaves back to work on his plantation. But flooding over war-damaged levies wiped out his cotton crop. In August 1866 he gave up, surrendering his plantation to his creditors, swept down, like so many others, by the war-devastated economy. In desperation, he considered leading an expedition of former Confederate comrades to seize the riches of Mexico.

A more promising avenue for Forrest's energies, however, had by now opened up. From its obscure beginnings after the war, the Ku Klux Klan proliferated wildly across Tennessee and into neighboring states. What the Klan needed was a tough, respected figure able to impose order on the Invisible Empire and prevent it from spinning out of control—none other than Nathan Bedford Forrest. At a clandestine meeting in Nashville sometime in late 1866, he accepted the job and donned the robes of Grand Wizard, the Klan's highest office. Forrest's activities are mostly unknown because he worked in secrecy, but there is no mystery about why he gravitated to the Klan. For him, the Klan was politics by other means, the vehicle by which disfranchised former Confederates like himself might strike a blow against the despised Republicans who ran Tennessee.

In many towns, including Memphis, the Klan became virtually identical to the Democratic clubs; in fact, Klan members—including Forrest—dominated the state's delegation to the Democratic national convention of 1868. On the ground the Klan unleashed a murderous campaign of terror against Republican sympathizers. Governor Brownlow responded resolutely, threatening to mobilize the state militia and root out the Klan. If Brownlow tried, answered Forrest, "there will be war, and a bloodier one than we have ever witnessed. . . . If the militia attack us, we will resist to the last; and, if necessary, I think I could raise 40,000 men in five days, ready for the field."

For many months, Tennessee endured a high state of tension. In September 1868 a new law identified membership in the Klan as a felony, and the following February martial law was declared in nine Klan-ridden counties. But it was the Republicans, not the Klan, who cracked. In March 1869 Brownlow retreated to the U.S. Senate. The Democrats were on their way back to power, and the Klan, having served its purpose, was officially disbanded in Tennessee.

Like many other Confederate heroes, Forrest might now have anticipated a comfortable life in politics. But he had too much blood on his hands. He was among the very last to be pardoned by President Johnson. His appearance at the Democratic convention in 1868 brought forth bitter Republican denunciations against "the Fort Pillow Butcher." Physical violence, moreover, still dogged his life, including the killing (he claimed self-defense) of a sharecropper on his plantation. What sealed Forrest's political fate, however, was the Ku Klux Klan. Forrest had regarded the Klan's mission in strictly political terms, its violence calibrated to the task of driving the Republicans from power. In this Forrest only reflected what conservative Southerners generally favored.

KKK Flag
Striking fear in the hearts of its enemies was a favorite tactic of Forrest's Ku Klux Klan—hence this menacing ceremonial flag from Tennessee, with its fierce dragon and mysterious Latin motto, "Because it always is, because it is everywhere, because it is abominable." Chicago Historical Society.

But he could not curb the senseless brutality against blacks done in the Klan's name. Any ruffian, he complained, could put on a white sheet and go after his neighbors. But Forrest was the Grand Wizard, and even after he resigned, his name could not be dissociated from Klan savagery. Celebrated though he might have been, when it came to supporting him for political office, Democratic leaders kept their distance.

So Forrest had to cash in his chips elsewhere, which he did as president and chief promoter of the Memphis & Selma Railroad. Beginning in 1869 he hawked bonds to communities along the proposed right of way and lobbied for state and county subsidies, expending his considerable reputation on an ambitious project linking Memphis by rail to northern Alabama and eastern Mississippi: all in vain. The unfinished Memphis & Selma collapsed after the Panic of 1873, and Forrest was left with nothing. Resilient to the end, he contracted with Selby County for convicts to work 1,700 acres of land he had rented on President's Island, four miles from Memphis. Leasing convicts was a practice notorious for horrendous abuses, but none were reported on President's Island. The swamp-ridden island, however, proved hard on him; he contracted a debilitating intestinal illness that ultimately proved fatal. After so many setbacks, his luck turned at least in this regard: against all odds, Nathan Bedford Forrest died peacefully in his bed on October 29,1877. The legacy he left, however, gave the South no peace. Racial violence plagued the land, and in 1915 the Ku Klux Klan revived, its victims extending beyond the black community to include Jews, Catholics, and immigrants.

Harriet Hernandes

The Intimidation of Black Voters

The following testimony was given in 1871 by Harriet Hernandes, a black resident of Spartanburg, South Carolina, to the Joint Congressional Select Committee investigating conditions in the South. The terrorizing of black women through rape and other forms of physical violence was among the means of oppression used by the Ku Klux Klan.

Question: How old are you?
Answer: Going on thirty-four years....
Q: Are you married or single?
A: Married.
Q: Did the Ku-Klux come to your house at any time?
A: Yes, sir; twice....
Q: Go on to the second time....
A: They came in; I was lying in bed. Says he, "Come out here, sir; come out here, sir!" They took me out of bed; they would not let me get out, but they took me up in their arms and toted me out—me and my daughter Lucy. He struck me on the forehead with a pistol, and here is the scar above my eye now. Says he, "Damn you, fall." I fell. Says he, "Damn you, get up." I got up. Says he, "Damn you, get over this fence!" and he kicked me over when I went to get over; and then he went on to a brush pile, and they laid us right down there, both together. They laid us down twenty yards apart, I reckon. They had dragged and beat us along. They struck me right on

top of my head, and I thought they had killed me; and I said, "Lord o'mercy, don't, don't kill my child!" He gave me a lick on the head, and it liked to have killed me; I saw stars. He threw my arm over my head so I could not do anything with it for three weeks, and there are great knots on my wrist now.

Q: What did they say this was for?
A: They said, "You can tell your husband that when we see him we are going to kill him...."
Q: Did they say why they wanted to kill him?
A: They said, "He voted the radical ticket [slate of candidates], didn't he?" I said, "Yes," that very way....
Q: When did [your husband] get back home after this whipping? He was not at home, was he?
A: He was lying out; he couldn't stay at home, bless your soul! ...
Q: Has he been afraid for any length of time?
A: He has been afraid ever since last October. He has been lying out. He has not laid in the house ten nights since October.
Q: Is that the situation of the colored people down there to any extent?
A: That is the way they all have to do—men and women both.
Q: What are they afraid of?
A: Of being killed or whipped to death.
Q: What has made them afraid?
A: Because men that voted radical tickets they took the spite out on the women when they could get at them.
Q: How many colored people have been whipped in that neighborhood?
A: It is all of them, mighty near.

Source: Report of the Joint Congressional Select Committee to Inquire into the Condition of Affairs in the Late Insurrectionary States, House Report, 42nd Cong., 2nd sess. (Washington, DC: U.S. Government Printing Office, 1872), vol. 5, South Carolina, December 19, 1871.

their ex-Confederate enemies. Democrats overthrew Republican governments in Texas in 1873, in Alabama and Arkansas in 1874, and in Mississippi in 1875.

The Mississippi campaign showed all too clearly what the Republicans were up against. As elections neared in 1875, paramilitary groups such as the Rifle Clubs and Red Shirts operated openly. Often local Democrats paraded armed, as if they were militia companies. They identified black leaders in assassination lists called "dead books," broke up Republican meetings, provoked rioting that left hundreds of African Americans dead, and threat-

ened voters. Mississippi's Republican governor, Adelbert Ames, a Congressional Medal of Honor winner from Maine, appealed to President Grant for federal troops, but Grant refused. Ames then contemplated organizing a state militia but ultimately decided against it, believing that only blacks would join and that the state would be plunged into racial war. Brandishing their guns and stuffing the ballot boxes, the Redeemers swept the 1875 elections and took control of Mississippi. Facing impeachment by the new Democratic legislature, Governor Ames resigned his office and returned to the North.

By 1876 Republican governments, backed by token U.S. military units, remained in only three states— Louisiana, South Carolina, and Florida. Elsewhere, the former Confederates were back in the saddle.

The Acquiescent North

The faltering of Reconstruction stemmed from more than discouragement about prosecuting the Klan, however. Sympathy for the freedman began to wane. The North was flooded with one-sided, often racist reports, such as James M. Pike's *The Prostrate State* (1873), describing extravagant, corrupt Republican rule and a South in the grip of "a mass of black barbarism." The impact of this propaganda could be seen in the fate of the civil rights bill, which Charles Sumner introduced in 1870 at the height of radical Reconstruction. Sumner's bill was a remarkable application of federal power against discrimination in the country, guaranteeing citizens equal access to public accommodation, schools, and jury service. By the time the bill passed in 1875, it had been stripped of its key provisions and was of little account as a weapon against discriminatory treatment of African Americans. The Supreme Court finished the demolition job when it declared the remnant Civil Rights Act unconstitutional in 1883.

The political cynicism that overtook the Civil Rights Act signaled the Republican Party's reversion to the practical politics of earlier days. In many states a second generation took over the party—men like Roscoe Conkling of New York, who treated the Manhattan Customs House, with its regiment of political appointees, as an auxiliary of his machine. Conkling and similarly minded politicos had little enthusiasm for Reconstruction, except as it benefited the Republican Party. As the party lost headway in the South, they abandoned any interest in the battle for black rights. In Washington President Grant presided benignly over this transformation of his party, turning a blind eye on corruption even as it began to lap against the White House.

The Liberal Republicans and Election of 1872. As Grant's administration lapsed into cronyism, a revolt took shape inside the Republican Party, led by an influential collection of intellectuals, journalists, and reform-minded businessmen. The first order of business for them was civil service reform that would replace corrupt patronage with a merit-based system of appointments. The reformers also, however, disliked the government activism spawned by the Civil War crisis. They regarded themselves as liberals—believers in free trade, market competition, and limited government. And, with unabashed elitism, they spoke out against universal suffrage, which "can only mean in plain English the government of ignorance and vice." So it followed that liberal reformers would have little patience with the former slaves. Although mostly veterans of the antislavery movement, they now became strident critics of radical Reconstruction.

Unable to deny Grant renomination for a second term, the dissidents broke away and formed a new party under the name Liberal Republican. Their candidate was Horace Greeley, longtime editor and publisher of the *New York Tribune* and a warhorse of American reform in all its variety, including antislavery. The Democratic Party, still in disarray, also nominated Greeley, notwithstanding his editorial diatribes against Democrats as "murderers, adulterers, drunkards, liars, thieves." A poor campaigner, Greeley was assailed so bitterly during the campaign that, as he said, "I hardly knew whether I was running for the Presidency or the penitentiary."

Grant won overwhelmingly, capturing 56 percent of the popular vote and every electoral vote. Yet the Liberal Republicans had managed to shift the terms of political debate in the country. The new agenda they had established—civil service reform, limited government, reconciliation with the South—was adopted by the Democrats as they shed their disloyal reputation and reclaimed their place as a legitimate national party. In the 1874 elections the Democrats dealt the Republicans a heavy blow, gaining control of the House of Representatives for the first time since secession and capturing seven normally Republican states.

Scandal and Depression. Charges of Republican corruption, mounting ever since Grant's reelection, came to a head in 1875. The scandal involved the Whiskey Ring, a network of liquor distillers and treasury agents who defrauded the government of millions of dollars of excise taxes on whiskey. The ringleader was a Grant appointee, and Grant's own private secretary, Orville Babcock, had a hand in the thievery. The others went to prison, but Grant stood by Babcock, possibly perjuring himself to save his secretary from jail. The stench of scandal, however, had engulfed the White House.

On top of this the economy had fallen into a severe depression after 1873. The precipitating event was the bankruptcy of the Northern Pacific Railroad and its main investor, Jay Cooke. Both Cooke's privileged role as financier of the Civil War and the generous federal subsidies to the Northern Pacific suggested to many economically pressed Americans that Republican financial manipulations had caused the depression. Grant's administration responded ineffectually, rebuffing the pleas of debtors for relief by increasing the money supply (see Chapter 18). In 1874 Democrats gained enough Republican support to push through Congress a bill that would have increased the volume of currency in circulation and eased the money pinch. But President Grant vetoed it, fueling Democratic charges that the Republicans served only the business interests.

Among the casualties of the bad economy was the Freedman's Savings and Trust Company, which held the small deposits of thousands of ex-slaves. When the bank failed in 1874, Congress refused to compensate the depositors, and many lost their life savings. In denying their pathetic pleas, Congress was signaling also that Reconstruction had lost its moral claim on the country. National politics had moved on; other concerns absorbed the voter as another presidential election approached in 1876.

The Political Crisis of 1877

Abandoning Grant, the Republicans nominated Rutherford B. Hayes, governor of Ohio, a colorless figure, but untainted by corruption or by strong convictions—in a word, a safe man. His Democratic opponent was Samuel J. Tilden, governor of New York, a wealthy lawyer with ties to Wall Street and a reform reputation for helping to break the grip of the thieving Tweed Ring on New York City politics. The Democrat Tilden, of course, favored "**home rule**" for the South but so, more discreetly, did the Republican Hayes. Reconstruction actually did not figure prominently in the campaign and was mostly subsumed under broader Democratic charges of "corrupt centralism" and "incapacity, waste, and fraud." By now Republicans had essentially written off the South and scarcely campaigned there. Not a lot was said about the states still ruled by Reconstruction governments—Florida, South Carolina, and Louisiana.

Once the returns started coming in on election night, however, those three states began to loom very large indeed. Tilden led in the popular vote and, victorious in key northern states, he seemed headed for the White House. But sleepless politicians at Republican headquarters realized that if they kept Florida, South Carolina, and Louisiana, Hayes would win by a single electoral vote. The campaigns in those states had been bitterly fought, replicating the Democratic assaults on blacks that had overturned Republican regimes everywhere else in the South. But Republicans still controlled the election machinery in those states and, citing Democratic fraud and intimidation, they certified Republican victories. The audacious announcement came forth from Republican headquarters: Hayes had carried the three southern states and won the election. But, of course, newly elected Democratic officials in the three states also sent in electoral votes for Tilden, and, when Congress met in early 1877, it faced two sets of electoral votes from those states.

The Constitution does not provide for this contingency. All it says is that the President of the Senate (in 1877, a Republican) opens the electoral certificates before the House (Democratic) and the Senate (Republican) and that "the Votes shall then be counted" (Article 2, Section 1; see Documents, p. D-9). An air of crisis gripped the country. There was talk of inside deals, of a new election, even of a violent coup and civil war. Just in case, the commander of the army, General William T. Sherman,

deployed four artillery companies in Washington. Finally, Congress decided to appoint an electoral commission to settle the question. The commission included seven Republicans, seven Democrats, and, as the deciding member, David Davis, a Supreme Court justice not known to have fixed party loyalties. But Davis disqualified himself by accepting an Illinois seat in the Senate. He was replaced by Republican justice Joseph P. Bradley, and by 8 to 7 the commission awarded the disputed votes to Hayes.

Outraged Democrats had one more trick up their sleeves. They controlled the House, and they set about stalling a final count of the electoral votes so as to prevent Hayes's inauguration on March 4. But a week before, secret Washington talks had begun between southern Democrats and Ohio Republicans representing Hayes. Other issues may have been on the table, but the main thing was the situation in South Carolina and Louisiana, where rival governments were encamped at the state capitols, with federal soldiers holding the Democrats at bay. Exactly what deal was struck or how involved Hayes himself was will probably never be known, but on March 1 the House Democrats suddenly ended their filibuster, the ceremonial counting of votes went forward, and Hayes was inaugurated on schedule. He soon ordered the Union troops back to their barracks and the Republican regimes in South Carolina and Louisiana fell. Reconstruction had ended.

In 1877 political leaders on all sides seemed ready to say that what Lincoln had called "the work" was complete. But for the freedpeople, the work had only begun. Reconstruction turned out to have been a magnificent aberration, a leap beyond what most white Americans actually felt was due their black fellow citizens. Redemption represented a sad falling back to the norm. Still, something real had been achieved—three rights-defining amendments to the Constitution, some elbow room to advance economically, and, not least, a stubborn confidence among blacks that, by their own efforts, they could lift themselves up. Things would, in fact, get worse before they got better, but the work of Reconstruction was imperishable and could never be erased.

FOR FURTHER EXPLORATION

▶ For definitions of key terms boldface in this chapter, see the glossary at the end of the book.

▶ To assess your mastery of the material covered in this chapter, see the Online Study Guide at **bedfordstmartins.com/henretta**.

▶ For suggested references, including Web sites, see page SR-17 at the end of the book.

▶ For map resources and primary documents, see **bedfordstmartins.com/henretta**.

When the Civil War ended in 1865, no one could have foreseen the future course of Reconstruction. The slaves had been emancipated, but there was no consensus about their future status as citizens. The South had been defeated, but there was no consensus about its restoration to the Union. Had Abraham Lincoln lived, these great questions might have been settled peaceably, but with his assassination they were left to the mercy of unfolding events.

Without consulting Congress, Lincoln's successor, Andrew Johnson, offered the South easy terms for reentering the Union. This might have succeeded had the South responded with restraint, but instead a concerted effort was made to reenslave the freedmen through the Black Codes. In this opening round of freedom's struggle, the ex-slaves showed their determination to be agents of their own fate, resisting the Black Codes and demanding equal civil and political rights. Infuriated by southern intransigence, congressional Republicans closed ranks behind the Radicals, embraced the freedmen's demand for full equality, placed the South under military rule in 1867, and inaugurated radical Reconstruction.

The new Republican state governments that undertook to reconstruct the South through ambitious programs of economic and educational improvement. No amount of accomplishment, however, could have reconciled the ex-Confederates to Republican rule, and they staged a violent counterrevolution in the name of white supremacy and "redemption."

Despite an initially stern response, the Grant administration had no stomach for a protracted guerrilla war in the South. Northern politics moved on, increasingly absorbed by Republican scandals and, after depression hit in 1873, by the nation's economic problems. By allying with the Liberal Republicans in 1872, the discredited Democrats scrambled back into the political mainstream and began to compete on even terms with the Republicans. So close was the presidential election of 1876 that both parties claimed victory. The constitutional crisis was resolved only by Democratic agreement to accept the Republican Hayes as president in exchange for an end to Republican rule in South Carolina and Louisiana, signaling the conclusion of Reconstruction.

1863   Lincoln announces his Ten Percent Plan

1864   Wade-Davis Bill passed by Congress

Lincoln gives Wade-Davis Bill a "pocket" veto

1865   Freedmen's Bureau established

Lincoln assassinated; Andrew Johnson succeeds as president

Johnson implements his restoration plan

Joint Committee on Reconstruction formed

1866   Civil Rights Act passes over Johnson's veto

Memphis riots

Johnson makes disastrous "swing around the circle"; defeated in congressional elections

1867   Reconstruction Act

Tenure of Office Act

1868   Impeachment crisis

Fourteenth Amendment ratified

Ulysses S. Grant elected president

1870   Ku Klux Klan at peak of power

Fifteenth Amendment ratified

1872   Grant's reelection as president

1873   Panic of 1873 ushers in depression of 1873–1877

1874   Democrats win majority in House of Representatives

1875   Whiskey Ring scandal undermines Grant administration

1877   Compromise of 1877; Rutherford B. Hayes becomes president

Reconstruction ends

PART THREE

Religion in American Public Life

For Americans, reciting the Pledge of Allegiance is the most personal way they have for affirming their national identity. So students must think the words are in the same league with the Declaration of Independence and the Constitution. In fact, the pledge is of much later origin, composed in 1892 by Francis Bellamy, a Boston cleric-turned-social critic, who used its final words to promote his personal philosophy of "liberty and justice for all." Originally, it was an entirely secular document. Only in 1954 did "under God" become part of the pledge, inserted by Congress to further the cold war crusade against "godless Communism." Once in, however, that phrase, like the pledge itself, came to seem timeless and beyond questioning.

It therefore came as a shock in 2002 when a three-judge panel of the 9th U.S. Circuit Court of Appeals declared that a California law requiring students to recite the pledge was unconstitutional because of the words "under God." The political reaction to *Newdow v. U.S. Congress et al.* was quick and harsh. The Republican president George W. Bush denounced the decision, asserting, "America is a nation that values our relationship with an Almighty." Senator Joseph Lieberman, the Democratic vice presidential candidate in 2000 and an orthdox Jew, called for a constitutional amendment to make clear that "we are one nation because of our faith in God."

We have been down this road before. In 1863 the House of Representatives considered amending the Preamble of the Constitution to read: "Acknowledging the Lord Jesus Christ as the Governor among nations, His revealed will as the supreme law of the land, in order to constitute a Christian government, we the people of the United States. . . ." Like Senator Lieberman, living in the shadow of the terrorist attacks on America of September 11, 2001, the U.S. congressmen of 1863 were acting at a time of great national crisis, when Americans were pitted against their fellow citizens in a bloody civil war.

These professions of faith occupy one side of a great fault line in American public life. On the other side stands a secular constitutional tradition that goes back to the Revolutionary era and to the document that founded the national republic, the U.S. Constitution. The Constitution is a thoroughly secular document, containing no reference to God and mentioning religion in Article VI only to prohibit religious tests for federal office. Then came the Bill of Rights, the original ten amendments ratified in 1793. The First Amendment begins: "Congress shall make no law respecting an establishment of religion, or prohibiting the free exercise thereof. . . ." The first of these prohibitions, known as the Establishment Clause, mandates the separation of church and state and is the basis for the decision by the 9th Circuit Court in the *Newdow* case. The second, the "free exercise clause," also is germane, because freedom of conscience seems incompatible with state-mandated expressions of faith—like the phrase "under God" in the Pledge of Allegiance—that touch every citizen. These two provisions are, like freedom of speech and assembly, at the core of American civil liberties protected by the Bill of Rights.

This constitutional triumph was, however, by no means unqualified. The state constitutions of the 1770s and 1780s already in place were far from secular. Most New England states imposed taxes for the support of religion, and various states required elected officials to profess belief in "the Christian religion." Moreover, even at the federal level the secularist triumph was not quite what it seemed. As Akhil Reed Amar argues in *The Bill of Rights* (1998), many churchgoing Americans actually favored the Establishment Clause in hopes that it would shield state support of religion from federal interference. Separation of church and state, if a remarkable achievement, was tempered from the start by an abiding sense that the cohesion of the nation rested on Christian faith.

Ever since those nation-building years, religious belief and constitutional secularism have coexisted in this state of tension. And what determines which has the relative advantage? Primarily, scholars suggest, the varying intensity of religious belief. The Revolutionary era had been an age of rationalism. Thereafter, as the Second Great Awakening took hold, religious enthusiasm again swept the country. In *Southern Cross: The Beginnings of the Bible Belt* (1997), Christine Heyrman estimates that the number of white Southerners who attended evangelical churches jumped from 25 percent in 1776 to 65 percent in 1835. Alexis de Tocqueville remarked in

Democracy in America (1835) that the Great Awakening gave "the Christian religion . . . a greater influence over the souls of men" in the United States than in any other society. Modern scholars concur with Tocqueville. As we have shown in the preceding chapters, religious fervor prompted political activism on many fronts in the antebellum years—from abolitionism to temperance to the condemnation by 8,000 federal postmasters of mail delivery on Sunday, the Christian Sabbath, as "a disgrace to the nation, and an insult to the Supreme Lawgiver."

What this age of faith also revealed, however, was the staying power of constitutional secularism. Americans were coming to regard the Constitution itself as an inviolable document and a model for the states. Even in these fervent years, the bastions of public religion began to fall as churches were disestablished in the New England states and religious tests for officeholders were abandoned. New political realities set in. Irish Catholics arrived in great numbers and, ironically, the Second Great Awakening itself stimulated denominational diversity. Politicians took heed of President Andrew Jackson's warning that religiously inspired public policies would disturb "the security which religion now enjoys in this country in its complete separation from the political concerns of the General Government." Similar concerns sealed the fate of the Civil War amendment seeking to make Christianity the official federal creed.

As religious fervor waned after the Civil War, so did efforts to breach the wall of church/state separation. It is telling that the man who wrote the Pledge of Allegiance without invoking the Almighty was a Baptist minister. Moreover, the Establishment Clause proved not to be the shield for state support for religion that some of its original supporters had hoped for. In the twentieth century the courts began to move aggressively on this front. In *Everson v. Board of Education* (1947), a New Jersey case involving the use of public funds to transport students to Catholic schools, Justice Hugo Black declared that the Constitution erected "a wall of separation between church and state" that the courts would enforce. Then, in the landmark New York case of *Engel v. Vitale* (1962), the Court held that prayer in the public schools was "wholly inconsistent with the Establishment Clause," a decision that was a precedent for the *Newdow* decision and aroused even more controversy.

In each age, as the pendulum swings, a new balance has to be struck between the contradictory traditions of constitutional secularism and religious belief. That, at any rate, is what the history of church/state relations in America suggests. In our own time, a new age of faith, the courts have looked for legal accommodation. Thus laws limiting Sunday activities have been allowed on the secular grounds that they "provide a uniform day of rest for all citizens"; similarly, using a legal theory of "child benefit," judges have approved the use of public taxes to buy textbooks or defray tuition at religious schools. Such a strategy may be in the offing with respect to the pledge. Unlike President Bush and those who proclaim the centrality of faith in American public life, the Department of Justice has sought reconsideration of the *Newdow* case on the grounds that the words "under God" are essentially ritualistic, one of "many ceremonial references to our religious heritage and do not establish a religious faith." Such a legal tactic could well resolve the pledge controversy and satisfy the country. What do *you* think the outcome will be? And if, by the time you read this essay, the Supreme Court has decided this case, what did the judges actually do—and why?

Inculcating . . . What???

Three young children stare reverently at the American flag as they say (or listen to) the Pledge of Allegiance. Intended originally to promote national identity and social justice, during the twentieth century the pledge became a vehicle for inculcating patriotism and religious belief. Should children be required to recite the pledge? If so, what beliefs should it promote? Newsweek.

A Maturing Industrial Society

1877–1914

ECONOMY	SOCIETY	CULTURE	GOVERNMENT	DIPLOMACY
The Triumph of Industrialization	**Racial, Ethnic, and Gender Divisions**	**The Rise of the City**	**From Inaction to Progressive Reform**	**An Emerging World Power**
1877 ▸ Andrew Carnegie launches modern steel industry Knights of Labor becomes national movement (1878)	▸ Struggle for black equality defeated Nomadic Indian life ends	▸ National League founded (1876) Dwight L. Moody pioneers urban revivalism	▸ Election of Rutherford B. Hayes ends Reconstruction	▸ United States becomes net exporter
1880 ▸ Gustavus Swift pioneers vertically integrated firm American Federation of Labor (1886)	▸ Chinese Exclusion Act (1882) Dawes Act divides tribal lands (1887)	▸ Electrification transforms city life First Social Register defines high society (1888)	▸ Ethnocultural issues dominate state and local politics Civil service reform (1883)	▸ Diplomacy of inaction Naval buildup begins
1890 ▸ United States surpasses Britain in iron and steel output Economic depression (1893–1897) Era of farm prosperity begins	▸ Black disfranchisement and segregation in the South Immigration from southeastern Europe rises sharply	▸ Settlement houses spread progressive ideas to cities William Randolph Hearst's *New York Journal* pioneers yellow journalism	▸ Populist Party founded (1892) William McKinley wins presidency; defeats Bryan's free-silver crusade (1896)	▸ Social Darwinism and Anglo-Saxonism promote expansion Spanish-American War (1898–1899); conquest of the Philippines
1900 ▸ Great industrial merger movement Immigrants dominate factory work Industrial Workers of the World (1905)	▸ Women lead social reform Struggle for civil rights revived	▸ Muckraking journalism Movies begin to overtake vaudeville	▸ Progressivism in national politics Theodore Roosevelt attacks the trusts Hepburn Act regulates railroads (1906)	▸ Panama cedes Canal Zone to United States (1903) Roosevelt Corollary to Monroe Doctrine (1904)
1910 ▸ Henry Ford builds first automobile assembly line	▸ NAACP (1910) Women vote in western states World War I ends European migration	▸ Urban liberalism	▸ Woodrow Wilson elected (1912) New Freedom legislation creates Federal Reserve, FTC	▸ Taft's diplomacy promotes U.S. business Wilson proclaims U.S. neutrality in World War I

While the nation was absorbed by the political drama of Reconstruction, few people noticed an equally momentous watershed in American economic life. For the first time, as the decade of the 1870s passed, farmers no longer constituted a majority of working Americans. Henceforth America's future would be linked to its development as an industrial society.

ECONOMY The effects of accelerating industrialization were felt, first of all, in the manufacturing sector. Production became increasingly mechanized and increasingly directed at making the capital goods that undergirded economic growth. As the railroad system was completed, the vertically integrated model began to dominate American enterprise. The labor movement became firmly established, and as immigration surged the foreign-born and their children became America's workers. What had been partial and limited now became general and widespread; America turned into a land of factories, corporate enterprise, and industrial workers.

THE WEST The final surge of western settlement across the Great Plains was largely driven by the pressures of this industrializing economy. Cities demanded new sources of food; factories needed the Far West's mineral resources. Defending their way of life, western Indians were ultimately defeated not so much by army rifles as by the unceasing encroachment of railroads, mines, ranches, and proliferating farms. These same forces disrupted the old established Hispanic communities of the Southwest but spurred Asian, Mexican, and European migrations that made for a multiethnic western society.

THE CITY Industrialization also transformed the nation's urban life. By 1900 one in five Americans lived in cities. That was where the jobs were—as workers in the factories; as clerks and salespeople; as members of a new, salaried middle class of managers, engineers, and professionals; and at the apex as a wealthy elite of investors and entrepreneurs. The city was more than just a place to make a living, however. It provided a setting for an urban lifestyle unlike anything seen before in America.

GOVERNMENT The unfettered, booming economy of the Gilded Age tended at first to marginalize political life. The major parties remained robust not because they stood for much programmatically but because they exploited a culture of popular participation and embraced the ethnocultural interests of their constituencies. The depression of the 1890s triggered a major challenge to the political status quo by the agrarian Populist Party, with its demand for free silver. The election of 1896 turned back that challenge and established the Republicans as the dominant national party.

Still unresolved was the threat that corporate power posed to the marketplace and democratic politics. How to curb the trusts dominated national debate during the Progressive Era. In those years as well, the country took a critical look at its institutions and began to address its social ills. From different angles political reformers, women progressives, and urban liberals went about the business of cleaning up machine politics and making life better for America's urban masses. African Americans, victimized by disfranchisement and segregation, found allies among white Progressives and launched a new drive for racial equality.

DIPLOMACY Finally, the dynamism of America's economic development decisively altered the country's foreign relations. In the decades after the Civil War, America had been inward-looking, neglectful of its navy and inactive diplomatically. The business crisis of the 1890s, however, brought home the need for a more aggressive foreign policy that would advance the nation's overseas economic interests. In short order the United States went to war with Spain, acquired an overseas empire, and became actively engaged in Latin America and Asia. There was no mistaking America's standing as a Great Power and, as World War I approached, no evading the responsibilities and entanglements that came with that status.

CHAPTER 16

The American West

DURING THE LAST DECADES of the nineteenth century, America seemed like two nations. One was an advanced industrial society—the America of great factories and sprawling cities. But another America still remained frontier country, with pioneers streaming onto the Great Plains, repeating the old dramas of "settlement" they had been performing ever since Europeans had first set foot on the continent. Not until 1890 did the U.S. Census declare that a "frontier of settlement" no longer existed: the country's "unsettled area has been so broken into . . . that there can hardly be said to be a frontier line."

Eighteen-ninety also marked the year the country surpassed Great Britain in the production of iron and steel. Newspapers carried reports of Indian wars and industrial strikes in the same edition. The last tragic episode in the suppression of the Plains Indians, the massacre at Wounded Knee, South Dakota, occurred only eighteen months before the great Homestead steel strike of 1892. This alignment of events from the distant worlds of factory and frontier was not accidental. The final surge of settlement across the Great Plains and the Far West was powered primarily by the dynamism of American industrialism.

◀ **The Yo-Hamite Falls, 1855**
This is one of the earliest artistic renderings of Yosemite Valley, drawn, in fact, before the place came to be called Yosemite. The scale of the waterfall, which drops 2,300 feet to the valley below, is dramatized by artist Thomas A. Ayres's companions in the foreground. In this romantic lithograph one can already see the grandeur of the West that Yosemite came to represent for Americans.
University of California at Berkeley, Bancroft Library, Honeyman Collection.

The Great Plains

During the 1860s agricultural settlement reached the western margins of the tall-grass prairie. Beyond, roughly at the ninety-eighth meridian (Map 16.1), stretched vast, dry country, uninviting to farmers accustomed to woodlands and ample rainfall. They saw it much as did the New York publisher Horace Greeley on his way to California in 1859: "a land of starvation," "a treeless desert," baking in heat in the daytime and "chill and piercing" cold at night.

Greeley was describing the Great Plains. The geologic event creating the Great Plains occurred sixty million years ago when the Rocky Mountains arose out of the ocean covering western North America. With no outlet, the shallow inland sea to the east dried up, forming a hard pan on which sediment washing down from the mountains built up a loose, featureless surface layer. The mountain barrier also made for a dry climate because the moisture-laden winds from the Pacific spent themselves on the western slopes. Only vegetation capable of withstanding the bitter winters and periodic cycles of severe drought could take hold on the plains. The short grama grass, the linchpin of this fragile ecosystem, matted the easily blown soil into place and sustained a rich wildlife dominated by grazing antelope and buffalo. What the dry short-grass country had not sustained, until the past few centuries, was human settlement.

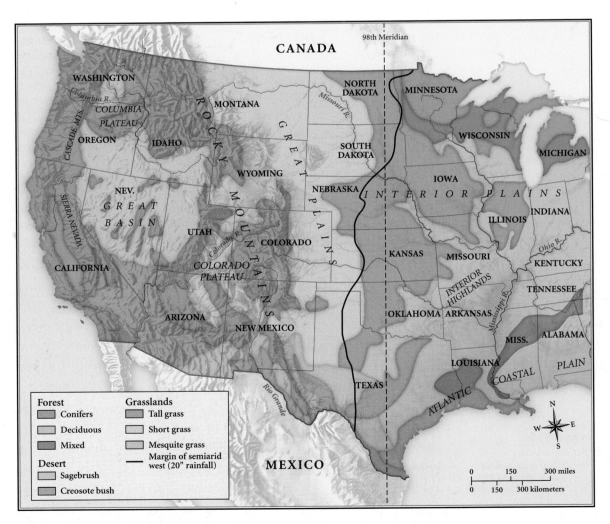

MAP 16.1 The Natural Environment of the West, 1860s

As settlers pushed into the Great Plains and beyond the line of semiaridity, they sensed the overwhelming power of the natural environment. In a landscape without trees for fences and barns, and without adequate rainfall, ranchers and farmers had to relearn their business. The Native Americans peopling the plains and mountains had in time learned to live in this environment, but this knowledge counted for little against the ruthless pressure of the settlers to domesticate the West.

Indians of the Great Plains

Probably 100,000 Native Americans lived on the Great Plains at mid-nineteenth century. They were a diverse people, divided into six linguistic families and at least thirty tribal groupings. On the eastern margins and along the Missouri River, the Mandans, Arikaras, and Pawnees planted corn and beans and lived in permanent villages. Smallpox and measles introduced by Europeans ravaged these settled tribes. Less vulnerable to epidemics because they were dispersed were the hunting tribes that had first arrived on the Great Plains in the seventeenth century: Kiowas and Comanches in the southwest; Arapahos and Cheyennes on the central plains; and, to the north, Blackfeet, Crows, Cheyennes, and the great Sioux nation.

The Teton Sioux.   Originally the Sioux had been eastern prairie people, occupying settlements in the lake country of northern Minnesota. With fish and game dwindling, some Sioux tribes drifted westward and around 1760 began to cross the Missouri River. These Sioux became nomadic, living in portable skin tepees and hunting the buffalo. From tribes to the southwest, they acquired horses. Once mounted, the Sioux became splendid hunters and formidable fighters, claiming the entire Great Plains north of the Arkansas River as their hunting grounds and driving out or subjugating longer-settled tribes.

A society that celebrates the heroic virtues of hunting and war is likely to define gender roles sharply. But before the Sioux had horses, chasing down the buffalo demanded the cooperation of the entire community, so that hunting could not be an exclusively male enterprise. It took the efforts of both men and women to construct the "pounds," into which, beating the brush side by side, they endeavored to stampede the herds. Once they had horses, however, the men rode off to the hunt while the women stayed behind to prepare the mounting piles of buffalo skins. This was laborious, painstaking work. Fanny Kelly, who had been a Sioux captive, considered the women's lives "a servitude"; but she noticed also that they were "very rebellious, often displaying ungovernable and violent temper." Subordination to the men was not how Sioux women understood their unrelenting labor; this was their allotted share in a partnership on which the proud, nomadic life of the Teton depended.

Teton Religion.   Living so close to wild nature, depending on its bounty for survival, the Sioux saw sacred meaning in every manifestation of the natural world. Unlike Europeans, they conceived of God not as a supreme being but, in the words of the pioneering ethnologist Clark Wissler, as a "series of powers pervading the universe"—Wi, the sun; Skan, the sky; Maka, the earth; Inyan, the rock. Below these came the moon, wind, and buffalo down through a hierarchy embodying the entire natural order.

By prayer and fasting Sioux prepared themselves to commune with these mysterious powers. Medicine men provided instruction, but the religious experience was personal and open to both sexes. The vision, when a supplicant achieved it, attached itself to some object—a feather, an animal skin, or a shell—that was tied into a sacred bundle and became the person's lifelong talisman. In the **Sun Dance** the entire tribe celebrated the rites of coming of

Tepee Liner
For the Plains Indians, tribal life revolved around the buffalo hunt and the battleground. These were the themes with which an unknown Indian artist decorated this dewcloth, which was hung inside a tepee to shield the occupants and provide some insulation from the cold. American Hurrah, New York City.

age, fertility, the hunt and combat, followed by four days of fasting and dancing in supplication to Wi, the sun.

The world of the Teton Sioux was not self-contained. All along they had exchanged pelts and buffalo robes for the produce of agriculturalist Pawnees and Mandans. When white traders appeared on the upper Missouri River during the eighteenth century, the Sioux began to trade with them. Although the buffalo remained their staff of life, the Sioux came to rely as well on the traders' pots, kettles, blankets, knives, and guns. The trade system they entered was linked to the Euro-American market economy, yet it was also integrated into the Sioux way of life. Everything depended on the survival of the Great Plains as the Sioux had found it—wild grassland on which the antelope and buffalo ranged free.

Wagon Trains, Railroads, and Ranchers

On first encountering the Great Plains, Euro-Americans thought these unforested lands best left to the Indians. After exploring a drought-stricken stretch in 1820, Major Stephen H. Long declared it "almost wholly unfit for cultivation, and of course uninhabitable by a people depending upon agriculture for their subsistence."

For years thereafter maps marked the plains as the **Great American Desert**. With that notion in mind Congress formally designated the Great Plains in 1834 as permanent Indian country. The army general in charge, Edmund Gaines, wanted the border forts, stretching from Lake Superior to Fort Worth, Texas, to be constructed of stone because they would be there forever. Trade with the Indians would continue, but now closely supervised and licensed by the federal government, with the Indian country otherwise off limits to whites.

Events swiftly overtook the nation's solemn commitment to the Native Americans. During the 1840s

Killing the Buffalo
This woodcut shows passengers shooting buffalo from a Kansas Pacific Railroad train—a small thrill added to the modern convenience of traveling west by rail. North Wind Picture Archives.

settlers began moving westward to Oregon and California. Instead of serving as a buffer against the Mexicans and British, Indian country became a bridge to the Pacific. The first wagon train headed west for Oregon from Missouri in 1842. Soon thousands of emigrants traveled the Oregon Trail to the Willamette Valley or cut south beyond Fort Hall down into California. Approaching Fort Hall in 1859, it seemed to Horace Greeley as if "the white coverings of the many emigrant and transport wagons dott[ing] the landscape" gave "the trail the appearance of a river running through great meadows, with many ships sailing on its bosom." Only these "ships" left behind, not a trailing wake of foam, but a rutted landscape devoid of grass and game and littered with abandoned wagons and rotting garbage.

The Railroads.   Talk about the need for a railroad to the Pacific soon began to be heard in Washington. How else could the distant territories formally acquired from Mexico and Britain in 1848 (see Chapter 13) be firmly linked to the Union or the ordeal of the overland journey by wagon train be alleviated? The project languished while North and South argued over the terminus for the route. Meanwhile, the Indian country was criss-crossed by overland freight lines and Pony Express riders delivered mail between Missouri and California. In 1861 telegraph lines brought San Francisco into instant communication with the East. The next year, with the South in rebellion, the federal government finally moved forward with the transcontinental rail project (Map 16.2).

No private company could be expected to foot the bill by itself. The construction costs were staggering, and in the short run not much traffic could be expected along the thinly populated route. So the federal government awarded generous land grants plus millions of dollars in loans to the two companies that undertook the transcontinental project.

The Union Pacific, building westward from Omaha, made little headway until the Civil War ended but then advanced rapidly across Indian country, reaching Cheyenne, Wyoming, in November 1867. It took the Central Pacific nearly that long moving eastward from Sacramento, California, to cross the crest of the Sierra Nevada. Both then worked furiously—since the government subsidy was based on miles of track laid—until, to great fanfare, the tracks met at **Promontory Point**, Utah, in 1869. None of the other railroads following other westward routes made it as far as the Rockies before the Panic of 1873 hit, throwing them into bankruptcy and bringing work to an abrupt halt.

By then, however, railroad tycoons had changed their minds about the Great Plains. No longer did they see it through the eyes of the Oregon-bound settlers— as a place to be gotten through en route to the Pacific. They realized rail transportation was laying the basis for the economic exploitation of the Great Plains. This

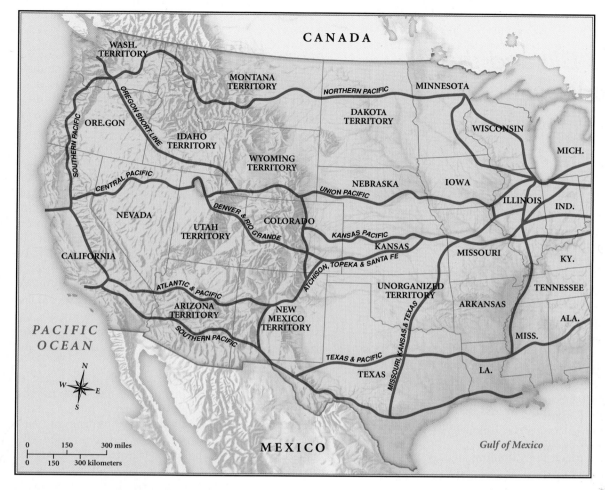

MAP 16.2 Western Trunk Lines, 1887

In the 1850s the talk in Washington had been about the need for a transcontinental railroad to bind the West to the Union. This map shows vividly how fully that talk had turned into reality in a matter of three decades. By 1887 no portion of the Pacific Coast lacked a rail connection to the East.

calculation spurred the railroad boom that followed economic recovery in 1878. Construction soared. During the 1880s, 40,000 miles of track were laid west of the Mississippi, including links from southern California via the Southern Pacific to New Orleans and via the Santa Fe to Kansas City, and from the Northwest via the Northern Pacific to St. Paul, Minnesota.

The Cattle Kingdom. Of all the opportunities beckoning, the most obvious was cattle raising. Grazing buffalo made it easy to imagine the plains as cow country. But first the buffalo had to go. A small market for buffalo robes had existed for years. And buffalo hunters like William F. Cody (see American Lives, "Buffalo Bill and the Mythic West," p. 462) made a good living provisioning army posts and leading hunting parties. Then in the early 1870s eastern tanneries discovered how to cure the hides, sparking a huge demand by shoe and harness manufacturers. Parties of professional hunters with high-powered

rifles swept across the plains and began a systematic slaughter of the buffalo. Already diminished by disease and shrinking pasturage, the great herds almost vanished within ten years. Many people spoke out against this mass killing, but no way existed to stop people bent on making a quick dollar. Besides, as General Philip H. Sheridan pointed out, exterminating the buffalo would starve the Indians into submission.

In south Texas about five million head of longhorn cattle grazed on Anglo ranches, hardly worth bothering about because they could not be profitably marketed. In 1865, however, the Missouri Pacific Railroad reached Sedalia, Missouri, far enough west to be accessible to Texas ranchers and their herds. At the Sedalia terminus, which connected to eastern markets, a longhorn worth $3 in Texas might command $40. With this incentive Texas ranchers inaugurated the famous **Long Drive**, hiring cowboys to herd the longhorn cattle hundreds of miles north to the railroads that were pushing west across Kansas.

Buffalo Bill and the Mythic West

Scott County, Iowa, was still frontier country when William F. Cody was born there on February 26, 1846. His family moved to Kansas in 1854, where it was even wilder, for it was not only frontier country but racked by bloody conflict between proslavery and free-soil settlers. Bill's father, Isaac Cody, was active on the free-soil side, serving in the Topeka legislature and frequently in harm's way from neighboring southern sympathizers and marauding Border Ruffians. One of Bill's first exploits was a wild gallop, with proslavery men in hot pursuit, to warn his father of a trap set for him near the family farm. Isaac Cody was less an idealist, however, than a typical enterprising westerner on the lookout for the main chance. He had been an Indian trader, a farm manager, a stagecoach operator, and, in Kansas, a land speculator around Grasshopper Falls. When he died suddenly in 1857, Cody left the family with a pile of land titles but little money.

Bill, never much for schooling anyway, had to find work. At age eleven he was taken on by Majors and Waddell, the firm that transported goods from Fort Leavenworth to army posts west of the Missouri River. Bill worked as a messenger boy, livestock herder, and teamster helper on the freight wagons. When his employers organized the short-lived Pony Express in 1860, Cody became a stock tender and an occasional rider in the Colorado–Nebraska division. Most of this was hard and tedious labor, but there were flashes of excitement—scrapes with Indians and with bandits (at fifteen, Bill killed one), buffalo stampedes, and brief encounters with Wild Bill Hickok and other tough western characters on whom Bill modeled himself. In the early part of the Civil War, Cody was at loose ends. Among other things, he engaged in horse thieving disguised as guerrilla activity in Missouri, and he became a heavy drinker. After a stint in the Seventh Kansas Cavalry and a halfhearted effort to settle down after the war (in what turned out to be an unhappy marriage), Cody got his lucky break in 1867.

The Kansas Pacific Railroad was building a line through Indian country to Sheridan, Kansas. To provision the work crews, the contractors hired Cody at $500 a month—excellent pay—to supply the cooks with buffalo meat. Cody was a crack shot and an excellent horseman, and he knew buffalo hunting. This assignment was duck soup for him, and the aplomb with which he carried it off soon gave him the name "Buffalo Bill."

Indian war broke out in Kansas in the summer of 1868, and Cody got his second claim to fame. He was hired as chief scout for the U.S. Fifth Cavalry. Cody knew the Kansas landscape intimately, he seemed to have a remarkable instinct for following a trail, and he was intrepid in the face of danger. At the height of the fighting in 1868 and 1869, Cody saw repeated action. In the climactic Battle of Summit Springs, his scouting played a decisive role, and he himself shot the Cheyenne chief Tall Bull. Although the legends later built up around Buffalo Bill have inclined scholars to be skeptical, he was in fact an authentic hero. Perhaps the best testimony was the extra $100 awarded him by the normally tight-fisted army "for extraordinarily good services as a trailer and fighter in the pursuit of hostile Indians."

Out of these promising materials there began to emerge a mythic figure. In July 1869 the dime novelist Ned Buntline (Edward Zane Carroll Judson) came through Kansas, met Cody, and, after returning to New York, wrote Buffalo Bill, the King of the Border Men—the first of some 1,700 potboilers to feature Cody's name and exploits. Then there were the buffalo-hunting parties of the rich and famous that Cody periodically led, including a royal hunt in 1872 with Grand Duke Alexis of Russia that had the entire country agog. With his white horse, buckskin suit, crimson shirt, and broad sombrero, Buffalo Bill began to play his part to the hilt. "He realized to perfection the bold hunter and gallant sportsman of the plains," wrote one appreciative participant. In 1872 Cody was persuaded to appear as himself in a play Ned Buntline proposed to put on in New York. Buntline was said to have dashed off The Scouts of the Prairie in four hours. Critics pronounced it "execrable." But Buffalo Bill, who mostly ad-libbed, was a great hit, and so was the production. Cody was launched on his career as a showman.

From then on the lines between reality and make-believe began to blur. Not only did Buffalo Bill draw on his past exploits when he went on stage, but he had the stage in mind when he returned to the real world. During the Sioux wars of 1875 and 1876 Cody was again out in the field as an army scout. (Fortunately, the fighting took place during the theatrical off-seasons in the East.) Shortly after

I AM COMING

Buffalo Bill's Wild West Show
Advertising the arrival of his troupe was a key function of Buffalo Bill's business enterprise. This brilliantly executed poster must have done duty all across the country, supplemented by flyers and newspaper ads announcing the date and place of the performance. The buffalo stampeding in the background were of course long gone by the time this poster appeared in the early twentieth century (judging by Buffalo Bill's gray beard). Library of Congress.

For more help analyzing this image, see the ONLINE STUDY GUIDE at bedfordstmartins.com/henretta.

the annihilation of Custer's troops at Little Big Horn, Cody gained a measure of vengeance in a famous skirmish in which he killed and scalped a Sioux chief named Yellow Hand. Cody rode into that engagement wearing his stage vaquero outfit—black velvet and scarlet with lace—so that when he reenacted the mayhem on stage, he could say he was wearing the very clothes in which he had seen action. Over time and with some help from Cody, the fight with Yellow Hand assumed legendary proportions, becoming a formal duel, with a challenge laid down by the Indian chief and troopers and Indian warriors lined up on opposing sides watching Buffalo Bill and Yellow Hand fight it out.

The mythic West that Cody was creating became full blown in his Wild West Show, first staged in 1883. Taking the circus and rodeo as his model, Cody put on an open-air extravaganza with displays of horsemanship, sharpshooting by Little Annie Oakley, real Indians (in one season Chief Sitting Bull toured with the company), and reenactments of stagecoach robberies and great events such as Custer's Last Stand. The Wild West Show toured the country every year and was a smashing success in Europe as well.

Buffalo Bill had been keen enough to see the hunger of city people for a legendary West. He traded on his talents as a showman, but he relied as well on his grasp of the authentic world behind the make-believe. When Cody died in 1917 that world was long gone, but his Wild West Show kept it alive in legend, where it still remains in the mythic figures of cowboys and Indians that populate our movies and television screens.

Cowboys on the Open Range

In open-range ranching, cattle from different ranches grazed together. At the roundup, cowboys separated the cattle by owner and branded the calves. Cowboys, celebrated in dime novels, were really farmhands on horseback, with the skills to work on the range. An ethnically diverse group, including blacks and Hispanics, they earned twenty-five dollars a month, plus meals and a bed in the bunkhouse, in return for long hours of grueling, lonesome work. Library of Congress.

At Abilene, Ellsworth, and Dodge City, ranchers sold their cattle, and trail-weary cowboys went on a binge. These cattle towns captured the nation's imagination as symbols of the Wild West. The reality was much more ordinary. The cowboys, many of them African Americans and Hispanics, were in fact farmhands on horseback who worked long hours under harsh conditions for small pay. Colorful though it seemed, the Long Drive was actually a makeshift method of bridging a gap in the developing transportation system. As soon as railroads reached the Texas range country during the 1870s, ranchers abandoned the Long Drive.

The Texas ranchers owned or leased the land they used, sometimes in huge tracts. North of Texas, where the land was in the public domain, cattlemen simply helped themselves. Hopeful ranchers would spot a likely area along a creek and claim as much land as they could qualify for as settlers under federal homesteading laws, plus what might be added by the fraudulent claims taken out by one or two ranch hands. By a common usage that quickly became established, ranchers had a "range right" to all the adjacent land rising up to the divide—the point where the land sloped down to the next creek.

News of easy money traveled fast. Calves cost $5; steers sold for maybe $60 on the Chicago market. Rail connections were in place or coming in. The grass was free. Profits of 40 percent per year seemed sure. The rush was on, drawing from as far away as Europe both hard-headed investors and romantics (like the recent Harvard graduate Teddy Roosevelt) eager for a taste of the Wild West. By the early 1880s the plains overflowed with cattle—as many as 7.5 million head decimating the grass and trampling the water holes.

A cycle of good weather only postponed the inevitable disaster. When it came—a hard winter in 1885, a severe drought the following summer, then record blizzards and bitter cold—cattle died by the hundreds of thousands. An awful scene of rotting carcasses greeted the cowhands riding out onto the range the following spring. Beef prices plunged when hard-pressed ranchers dumped the surviving cattle on the market. The boom collapsed and investors fled, leaving behind a more enduring ecological catastrophe: the destruction of native grasses from the relentless overgrazing in the drought cycle.

Open-range ranching came to an end. Ranchers fenced their land and planted hay. No longer would cattle be left to fend for themselves over the winters. Hispanic shepherds from New Mexico brought sheep in to feed on the mesquite and prickly pear that supplanted the native grasses. Sheep raising, previously scorned by ranchers as unmanly and resisted as a threat to cattle, became a major enterprise in the sparser high country. Some ranchers even sold out to the despised "nesters"—those who wanted to try farming the Great Plains.

Homesteaders

Potential settlers, of course, needed first to be persuaded that crops would grow in that dry country. Powerful interests worked hard to overcome the popular notion that the plains was a Great American Desert. Foremost were the railroads, eager to sell off the public land they had been granted—180 million acres of it—and develop traffic for their routes. They aggressively advertised, offered cut-rate tickets, and sold off their land holdings at bargain prices. Land speculators, transatlantic steamship lines, and the western states and territories did all they could to encourage settlers. And so did the federal government, which offered 160 acres of public land to all comers under the Homestead Act (1862).

"Why emigrate to Kansas?" asked a testimonial in *Western Trail*, the Rock Island Railroad's gazette. "Because it is the garden spot of the world. Because it will grow anything that any other country will grow, and with less work. Because it rains here more than any other place, and at just the right time."

As if to confirm the optimists, an exceptionally wet cycle occurred between 1878 and 1886. "As the plains are settled up we hear less and less of drouth, hot winds, alkali and other bugbears that used to hold back the adventurous," remarked one Nebraska man. Some settlers attributed the increased rainfall to soil cultivation and tree planting. Others credited God. As a settler on the southern plains remarked, "The Lord just knew we needed more land an' He's gone and changed the climate."

No amount of optimism, however, could dispel the pain of migration. "That last separating word of *Farewell!* sinks deeply into the heart," one pioneer woman recorded in her diary, thinking of family and friends left behind. But then came the treeless plains. "Such an air of desolation," wrote a Nebraska-bound woman; from another woman in Texas, "such a lonely country." One old hand likened these despairing feelings to an illness. "A stranger travelling on the prairie would get his hopes up, expecting to see something different on making the next rise." But all he found was "grass and then more grass—the monotonous, endless prairie! . . . To him the disappointment and monotony were terrible. 'He's got loneliness,' we would say of such a man." For a Swedish emigrant like Ida Lindgren (see American Voices, "Ida Lindgren: Swedish Emigrant in Frontier Kansas," p. 466) no place could have seemed so far from home and loved ones, and with so little hope of ever seeing family again.

Some women were liberated by this hard experience. Prescribed gender roles broke down as women shouldered men's work on new farms and became self-reliant in the face of danger and hardship. When husbands died or gave up, wives operated farms on their own. Under the Homestead Act, which accorded widows and single women the same rights as men, women filed 10 percent of the claims. "People afraid of coyotes and work and loneliness had better leave ranching alone," advised one woman homesteader. "At the same time, any woman who can stand her own company . . . and is willing to put in as much time at careful labor as she does at the washtub, will certainly succeed; will have independence, plenty to eat all the time, and a home of her own in the end."

Even with a man around, women contributed crucially to the farm enterprise. Farming might be thought of as a dual economy in which men's labor brought in the big wage at harvest time, while women provisioned the family day by day and produced a steady bit of money for groceries by selling eggs or butter. If the crop failed, it was women's labor that carried the family through. No wonder farming placed a high premium on marriage: a mere 2.4 percent of Nebraska women in 1900 had never married.

Male or female, the vision of new land beckoned people onto the plains. By the 1870s the older agricultural states had filled up, and farmers looked hungrily westward. "Hardly anything else was talked about," recalled the short-story writer Hamlin Garland about his Iowa neighbors. "Every man who could sell out had gone west or was going. . . . Farmer after farmer joined the march to Kansas, Nebraska, and Dakota. . . . The movement . . . had . . . become an exodus, a stampede."

The same excitement took hold in northern Europe, as Norwegians and Swedes for the first time joined the older German migration. At the peak of the "American fever" in 1882, over 105,000 Scandinavians emigrated to the United States. Swedish and Norwegian became the primary languages in parts of Minnesota and the Dakotas. Roughly a third of the farmers on the northern plains were foreign-born (Map 16.3).

The motivation for most settlers, American or European, was to better themselves economically. But for some southern blacks, Kansas briefly represented something more precious—the Promised Land of racial freedom. In the spring of 1879, with Reconstruction over and federal protection withdrawn, black communities fearful of white vengeance were swept by enthusiasm for Kansas. Within a month or so, some 6,000 blacks left Mississippi and Louisiana, most of them with nothing more than the clothes on their backs and faith in the Lord. They called themselves **Exodusters**, participants in the exodus to the dry prairie. How many of them remained is hard to say, but the 1880 census reported 40,000 blacks in Kansas—by far the largest African American concentration in the West aside from Texas—whose expanding cotton frontier attracted hundreds of thousands of black migrants during the 1870s and 1880s.

Farming the Plains. No matter where they came from, homesteaders found the plains an alien place. A cloud of grasshoppers might descend and destroy a crop in a day; a brushfire or hailstorm could do the job in an hour. What forested land had always provided—ample water, lumber for cabins and fencing, firewood—was absent. For shelter settlers often cut dugouts into hillsides and after a season or two erected houses made of turf cut from the ground.

The absence of trees, on the other hand, meant an easier time clearing the land. New technology overcame obstacles once thought insurmountable: steel plows enabled homesteaders to break the tightly matted ground, and barbed wire provided cheap, effective fencing against roaming cattle. Strains of hard-kernel wheat tolerant of the extreme temperatures of the plains came in from Europe. Homesteaders had good crops while the wet cycle held and began to anticipate the wood-frame house, deep well, and full coal bin that might make life tolerable on the plains.

In the later 1880s the dry years came and wrecked those hopeful calculations. "From day to day," reported the budding novelist Stephen Crane from Nebraska, "a wind hot as an oven's fury . . . raged like a pestilence,"

Ida Lindgren

Swedish Emigrant in Frontier Kansas

Like many emigrants, Ida Lindgren did not find it easy to adjust to the harsh new life on the frontier. Her diary entries and letters home show that the adjustment for the first generation was never complete.

May 15, 1870 [Lake Sibley, Nebraska]
What shall I say? Why has the lord brought us here? Oh, I feel so oppressed, so unhappy! Two whole days it took us to get here and they were not the least trying part of our travels. We sat on boards in the work-wagon packed in so tightly that we could not move a foot, and we drove across endless, endless prairies, on narrow roads; no, no, not roads, tracks like those in the fields at home when they harvested grain. No forest but only a few trees which grow along the rivers and creeks. And then here and there you see a homestead and pass a little settlement. The Indians are not so far away from here, I can understand, and all the men you see coming by, riding or driving wagons, are armed with revolvers and long carbines, and look like highway robbers.

No date [probably written July 1870]
Claus and his wife lost their youngest child at Lake Sibley and it was very sad in many ways. There was no real cemetery but out on the prairie stood a large, solitary tree, and around it they bury their dead, without tolling of bells, without a pastor, and sometimes without any coffin. A coffin was made here for their child, it was not painted black, but we lined it with flowers and one of the men read the funeral service, and then there was a hymn, and that was all.

August 25, 1874 [Manhattan, Kansas]
It has been a long time since I have written, hasn't it? . . . When one never has anything fun to write about, it is no fun to write. . . . We have not had rain since the beginning of June, and then with this heat and often strong winds as well, you can imagine how everything has dried out. There has also been a general lamentation and fear for the coming year. We are glad we have the oats (for many don't have any and must feed wheat to the stock) and had hoped to have the corn leaves to add to the fodder. But then one fine day there came millions, trillions of grasshoppers in great clouds, hiding the sun, and coming down into the fields, eating up everything that was still there, the leaves on the trees, peaches, grapes, cucumbers, onions, cabbage, everything, everything. Only the peach stones still hung on the trees, showing what had once been there.

July 1, 1877 [Manhattan, Kansas]
. . . It seems so strange to me when I think that more than seven years have passed since I have seen you all. . . . I can see so clearly that last glimpse I had of Mamma, standing alone amid all the tracks of Eslov station. Oliva I last saw sitting on her sofa in her red and black dress, holding little Brita, one month old, on her lap. And Wilhelm I last saw in Lund at the station, as he rolled away with the train, waving his last farewell to me. . . .

Source: H. Arnold Barton, ed., *Letters from the Promised Land* (Minneapolis: University of Minnesota Press, 1975), 143–45, 150–56.

---

destroying the crops and leaving farmers "helpless, with no weapon against this terrible and inscrutable wrath of nature." Land only recently settled emptied out as homesteaders fled in defeat. The Dakotas lost 50,000 settlers between 1885 and 1890, and comparable departures occurred up and down the drought-stricken plains.

Other settlers held on grimly. Stripped of the illusion that rain followed the plow, the survivors came to terms with the semiarid climate prevailing west of the ninety-eighth meridian. Mormons around the Great Salt Lake (see Chapter 12) had demonstrated how irrigation could turn a wasteland into a garden. But the Great Plains generally lacked the water reserves needed for irrigation. The answer lay in dry-farming methods, which involved deep planting to bring subsoil moisture to the roots and quick harrowing after rainfalls to turn over a dry mulch that slowed evaporation. Dry farming developed most fully on the corporate farms that covered up to 100,000 acres in the Red River Valley of North Dakota. But even family farms, which remained the norm elsewhere, could not survive with less than 300

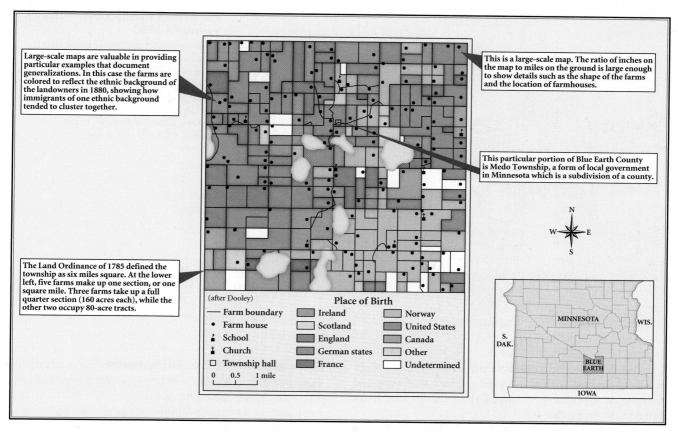

Large-scale maps are valuable in providing particular examples that document generalizations. In this case the farms are colored to reflect the ethnic background of the landowners in 1880, showing how immigrants of one ethnic background tended to cluster together.

This is a large-scale map. The ratio of inches on the map to miles on the ground is large enough to show details such as the shape of the farms and the location of farmhouses.

This particular portion of Blue Earth County is Medo Township, a form of local government in Minnesota which is a subdivision of a county.

The Land Ordinance of 1785 defined the township as six miles square. At the lower left, five farms make up one section, or one square mile. Three farms take up a full quarter section (160 acres each), while the other two occupy 80-acre tracts.

(after Dooley)

Place of Birth

— Farm boundary
• Farm house
School
Church
□ Township hall
0   0.5   1 mile

Ireland
Scotland
England
German states
France
Norway
United States
Canada
Other
Undetermined

S. DAK.   MINNESOTA   WIS.
BLUE EARTH
IOWA

MAP 16.3 The Rural Ethnic Mosaic: Blue Earth County, Minnesota, 1880
What could have been more natural for emigrants such as Ida Lindgren (see American Voices, p. 466) than to settle next to others sharing common ties to a homeland? This map of Medo township reveals that in rural America, no less than in the cities, ethnicity strongly influenced where people lived.

acres of grain crops and machinery for plowing, planting, and harvesting. Dry farming was not for the un-equipped homesteader.

By the turn of the century, the Great Plains had fully submitted to agricultural development. About half the nation's cattle and sheep, a third of its cereal crops, and nearly three-fifths of its wheat came from the newly settled lands. In this process there was little of the "pioneering" that Americans associated with the westward movement. The railroads came before the settlers, eastern capital financed the ranching bonanza, and agriculture depended on sophisticated dry-farming techniques and modern machinery.

Where was the economic capital of the Great Plains? Far off in Chicago. There, at the hub of the nation's rail system, the wheat pit traded western grain and consigned it to world markets; the great packing houses slaughtered western livestock and supplied the nation with sausage, bacon, and sides of beef. In return western ranchers and farmers received lumber, barbed wire, McCormick reapers, and Sears, Roebuck catalogues. Chicago was truly "nature's metropolis."

Farmers' Woes. American farmers embraced this commercial world. They relished the innovations of the industrial age, and supported whatever incentives it took, even public purchase of railway bonds, to attract rail lines to their towns. They had little of the passionate identification with the soil that tied European peasants to their inherited plots, regarding their acreage instead as a commodity. In frontier areas, where newly developed land appreciated rapidly, they anticipated as much profit, if not more, from the rising value of the land as from the crops it produced. American farmers were not averse to borrowing money. In boom times they rushed into debt to acquire more land and better farm equipment. All these enthusiasms—for cash crops, for land speculation, for borrowed money, for new technology—bore witness to the conviction that farming was, as one agricultural journal remarked, a business "like all other business."

Somehow, however, farmers went unrewarded for their faith in free enterprise. The basic problem was that they remained individual operators in an ever more complex and far-flung economic order. And they were, in certain ways, acutely aware of their predicament.

The Shores Family, Custer County, Nebraska, 1887

Whether the Shores family came west as Exodusters, we do not know. But in 1887, when this photograph was taken, they were well settled on their Nebraska farm, although still living in sod houses. The patriarch of the family, Jerry Shores, an ex-slave, is second from the right. Nebraska State Historical Society.

They understood, for example, the disadvantages they faced in dealing with the big businesses that supplied them with machinery, arranged their credit, and marketed their products.

One answer was cooperation. In 1867 Oliver H. Kelley, a government clerk, founded the National Grange of the Patrons of Husbandry mainly in hopes of improving the social life of farm families. Local granges spread by the thousands across rural America, providing meeting places and a rich array of dances, picnics, and lectures. The Grange soon added cooperative programs, purchasing in bulk from suppliers and setting up its own

banks, insurance companies, grain elevators, and processing plants. The Iowa Grange even attempted to manufacture farm implements. But private businesses fought back hard and generally got the better of the poorly managed and underfinanced Grange cooperatives. The cooperative idea was highly resilient, however, and would be embraced by every successive farmers' movement. Rural hostility to middlemen also left as a legacy the great mail-order house of Montgomery Ward, which had been founded in 1872 to serve Grange members.

The power of government might also be enlisted to counterbalance the organizational weakness of the

Buffalo Chips

With no trees around for firewood, settlers on the plains had to make do with dried cow and buffalo droppings. Gathering the "buffalo chips" must have been a regular chore for Ada McColl and her daughter on her homestead near Lakin, Kansas, in 1893. Kansas State Historical Society.

farmer in the marketplace. In the early 1870s the Grange encouraged independent political parties that ran on antimonopoly platforms. In a number of prairie states these agrarian parties enacted so-called Granger laws regulating grain elevators, fixing maximum railroad rates, and prohibiting discriminatory treatment of small and short-haul shippers.

Farmers turned to cooperatives and state regulation out of a deep sense of organizational disadvantage. But that disadvantage, tangible though it was, did not really account for the unprofitability of farming in this period. Manufacturers and banks lacked the degree of market control ascribed to them by angry farmers. The much-maligned mortgage companies actually could not rig credit markets in the western states; interest rates here matched those in the rest of the country. Nor for the period 1865 to 1890 could manufacturers establish a relative price advantage over agriculture. In fact, the wholesale prices of all commodities fell at a slightly faster pace than did farm prices during those years. As for the railroads, freight rates fell steadily as improved technology reduced operating costs and the volume of western traffic increased (Figure 16.1).

The general fall in prices, or deflation (see Chapter 17), did have dire consequences, however, for wheat farmers, who were subject to the wider, more unpredictable price swings of the international commodity markets. Also at risk in deflationary periods were farmers in debt, since falling prices forced them to pay back in real terms

more than they had borrowed. And who was most deeply in debt? The same group: wheat farmers.

In the 1870s the major wheat-growing states had been Illinois, Wisconsin, and Minnesota. These states had been at the center of the Granger agitation of that decade. By the 1880s wheat had moved onto the Great Plains. Among the indebted farmers of Kansas, Nebraska, and the Dakotas, the deflationary economy of the 1880s made for stubbornly hard times. All that was needed to bring on a real crisis was a sharp drop in world prices for wheat.

The Fate of the Indians

What of the Native Americans who had inhabited the Great Plains? Basically, their history has been told in the foregoing account of western settlement. "The white children have surrounded me and have left me nothing but an island," lamented the great Sioux chief Red Cloud in 1870, the year after the completion of the transcontinental railroad. "When we first had all this land we were strong; now we are all melting like snow on a hillside, while you are grown like spring grass."

Settlement occurred despite the provisions for a permanent Indian country that had been written into federal law and ratified by treaties with various tribes. As incursions into their lands increased from the late 1850s onward, the Indians resisted as best they could, striking back all along the frontier: the Apache in the Southwest, the Cheyenne and Arapaho in Colorado, and the Sioux in the Wyoming and Dakota territories. The Indians hoped that, if they resisted stubbornly enough, the whites would tire of the struggle and leave them in peace. This reasoning seemed not altogether fanciful given the country's exhaustion after the Civil War. But the federal government did not give up; instead it formulated a new policy for dealing with the western Indians.

The Reservation Solution. Few whites questioned the necessity of moving the Native Americans out of the path of settlement and into reservations. That, indeed, had been the fate of the eastern and southern tribes. Now, however, Indian removal included something new: a planned approach for weaning the Indians from their tribal way of life. The first step was a peace commission appointed in 1867 to negotiate an end to the fighting and sign treaties by which the western Indians would cede their lands and move to reservations. There, under the guidance of the Office of Indian Affairs, they would be wards of the government until they learned "to walk on the white man's road."

The government set aside two extensive areas. It allocated the southwestern quarter of the Dakota Territory—present-day South Dakota west of the Missouri River—to the Teton Sioux tribes. And it assigned what is now Oklahoma to the southern plains Indians, along with the major southern tribes—the Choctaw, Cherokee,

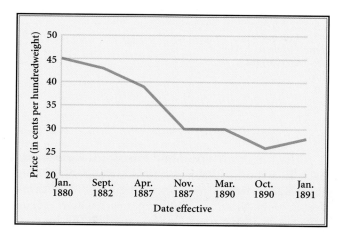

FIGURE 16.1 Freight Rates for Transporting Nebraska Crops

In railroading, a standard measure of operating efficiency is what it costs to move a given volume of goods a given distance. Thanks to improved technology and increasing traffic, costs so measured fell by 50 percent from 1870 to 1890 (see Chapter 17). Freight charges for shipping wheat from Grand Island, Nebraska, to Chicago fell at roughly the same rate (calculated for the years 1880 to 1891), an indication that savings from improved operations were being passed on to customers and that, at least in this respect, western farmers were benefiting from advances in the industrial economy.

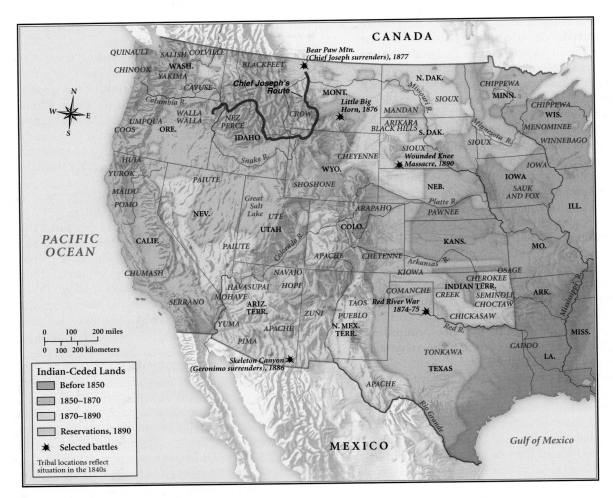

MAP 16.4 The Indian Frontier, to 1890

As settlement pushed onto the Great Plains after the Civil War, the Indians put up bitter resistance but ultimately to no avail. Over a period of decades, they ceded most of their lands to the federal government, and by 1890 they were confined to scattered reservations where the most they could expect was an impoverished and alien way of life.

For more help analyzing this map, see the ONLINE STUDY GUIDE at bedfordstmartins.com/henretta.

Chickasaw, Creek, and Seminole—and eastern Indians who had been removed there thirty years before. Scattered reservations went to the Apache, Navaho, and Ute in the Southwest and to the mountain Indians in the Rockies and beyond (Map 16.4).

That the Plains Indians would resist was inevitable. "You might as well expect the rivers to run backward as that any man who was born a free man should be contented when penned up and denied liberty to go where he pleases," said Chief Joseph of the Nez Percé, who led his people in 1877, including women and children, on an epic 1,500-mile march from eastern Oregon to escape confinement in a small reservation. In a series of heroic engagements, the Nez Percé fought off the pursuing U.S. Army until, after four months of extraordinary hardship, the remnants of the tribe were finally cornered and forced to surrender in Montana near the Canadian border.

The U.S. Army was thinly spread, having been cut back after the Civil War to a total force of 27,000. But these were veteran troops, including 2,000 black cavalrymen of the Ninth and Tenth regiments, whom Indians called, with grim respect, **buffalo soldiers.**" Technology also favored the army. Telegraph communications and railroads enabled the troops to be quickly concentrated; repeating rifles and Gatling machine guns increased their firepower. As fighting intensified in the mid-1870s, a reluctant Congress appropriated funds for more western troops. Because of tribal rivalries, the army could always find Indian allies. Worst of all, however, beyond the formidable U.S. Army or the Indians' disunity, was the overwhelming impact of white settlement.

Resisting the reservation solution, the Indians fought on for years—in Kansas in 1868 and 1869, in the Red River Valley of Texas in 1874, and sporadically among the fierce Apache, who made life miserable for white settlers in the Southwest until their wily chief Geronimo was finally captured in 1886. On the northern plains the crisis came in 1875, when the Indian Office—despite an 1868 treaty guaranteeing their Powder River rights—ordered the Sioux to vacate their Powder River hunting grounds and withdraw to the reservation.

Led by Sitting Bull, Sioux and Cheyenne warriors gathered on the Little Big Horn River to the west of the Powder River country. In a typical concentrating maneuver, army columns from widely separated forts converged on the Little Big Horn. The Seventh Cavalry, commanded by famous Civil War hero George A. Custer, came upon the Sioux encampment on June 25, 1876. Disregarding orders, the reckless Custer sought out battle on his own. He attacked from three sides, hoping to capitalize on the element of surprise. But his forces were spread too thin. The other two contingents fell back with heavy losses to defensive positions, but Custer's own force of 256 men was surrounded and annihilated by Crazy Horse's Sioux warriors. It was a great victory but not a decisive one. The day of reckoning was merely postponed.

Pursued by the military and physically exhausted, the Sioux bands one by one gave up and moved onto the reservation. Last to come in were Sitting Bull's followers. They had retreated to Canada, but in 1881 after five hard years they recrossed the border and surrendered at Fort Buford, Montana.

Not Indian resistance but white land hunger wrecked the reservation solution. In the mid-1870s prospectors began to dig for gold in the Black Hills, sacred land to the Sioux and entirely inside their Dakota reservation. Unable to hold back the prospectors or to buy out the Sioux, the government opened up the Black Hills to gold seekers at their own risk. In 1877, after Sioux resistance had crumbled, federal agents forced the tribes to cede the western third of their Dakota reservation (Map 16.5).

The Indian Territory of Oklahoma met the same fate. Two million acres in the heart of the territory had not been assigned to any tribe, and white homesteaders coveted that fertile land. The "Boomer" movement, stirred up initially by railroads operating in the Indian Territory, agitated tirelessly to open this so-called Oklahoma District to settlers. In 1889 the government gave in and placed the Oklahoma District under the Homestead Act. On April 22, 1889, a horde of claimants rushed in and staked out the entire district within a few hours. Two tent cities—Guthrie with 15,000 people and Oklahoma City with 10,000—were in full swing by nightfall.

Undermining Tribal Culture.
In the meantime the campaign to move the Indians on to "the white man's road" relentlessly went forward. During the 1870s the Office of Indian Affairs developed a program to train Indian children for farm work and prepare them for citizenship. Some

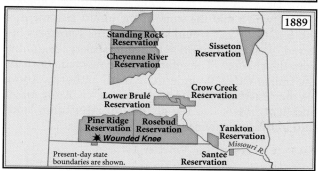

MAP 16.5 The Sioux Reservations in South Dakota, 1868–1889

In 1868, when they bent to the demand that they move onto the reservation, the Sioux thought they had gained secure rights to a substantial part of their ancestral hunting grounds. But as they learned to their sorrow, fixed boundary lines only increased their vulnerability to the land hunger of the whites and sped up the process of expropriation.

attended reservation schools, while the less lucky were sent to boarding schools far from home. Children as young as five were taken from their families and sent to Indian schools that taught them the rudiments of English while discouraging traditional tribal ways. The pupils were shorn of their braids and deprived of their moccasins and blankets. Mother Hubbard dresses and shirts and trousers visibly demonstrated that these bewildered children were being inducted into white society (see American Voices, "Zitkala-Ša [Gertrude Simmons Bonnin]: Becoming White," p. 473).

And not a moment too soon, believed many avowed friends of the Native Americans. The Indians had never lacked sympathizers—especially in the East, where

Indian School

In this photograph taken at the Riverside Indian School in Anadarko, Oklahoma Territory, the pupils have been shorn of their braids and dressed in laced shoes, Mother Hubbard dresses, and shirts and trousers—one step on the journey into the mainstream of white American society. Children as young as five were separated from their families and sent to Indian schools like this one that taught them new skills while encouraging them to abandon traditional Indian ways.
University of Oklahoma, Western History Collections.

reformers created the Indian Rights Association after the Civil War. The movement got a boost from Helen Hunt Jackson's influential book *A Century of Dishonor* (1881), which told the story of the unjust treatment of the Indians. What would save them, the reformers believed, was assimilation into white society, beginning with the children. The reformers also favored efforts by the Indian Office to undermine tribal authority. Above all, they esteemed private property as a "civilizing force" and hence advocated the division of reservation lands into individually owned parcels.

The result was the Dawes Act of 1887, authorizing the president to carve up tribal lands, with each family head receiving an allotment of 160 acres and individuals receiving smaller parcels. The land would be held in trust by the government for twenty-five years, and the Indians would become U.S. citizens. Remaining reservation lands would be sold off, with the proceeds placed in an Indian education fund.

The Last Battle: Wounded Knee.   The Sioux were among the first to bear the brunt of the Dawes Act. The

The Dead at Wounded Knee

In December 1890 U.S. soldiers massacred 146 Sioux men, women, and children in the Battle of Wounded Knee in South Dakota. It was the last big fight on the northern plains between the Indians and the whites. Black Elk, a Sioux holy man, related that "after the soldiers marched away from their dirty work, a heavy snow began to fall . . . and it grew very cold." The body of Yellow Bird lay frozen where it had fallen.
National Anthropological Archives, Smithsonian Institution, Washington, DC.

Zitkala-Ša (Gertrude Simmons Bonnin)

Becoming White

Zitkala-Ša, known later as the author Gertrude Simmons Bonnin, recalled in 1900 her painful transformation from Sioux child to pupil at a mission school.

The first day . . . a paleface woman, with white hair, came up after us. We were placed in a line of girls who were marching into the dining room. These were Indian girls, in stiff shoes and closely clinging dresses. The small girls wore sleeved aprons and shingled hair. As I walked noiselessly in my soft mocassins, I felt like sinking into the floor, for my blanket had been stripped from my shoulders. . . . Late in the morning, my friend Judewin gave me a terrible warning. Judewin knew a few words of English; and she had overheard the paleface woman talk about cutting our long, heavy hair. Our mothers had taught us that only unskilled warriors who were captured had their hair shingled by the enemy. Among our people, short hair was worn by mourners, and shingled hair by cowards! . . . In spite of myself, I was carried downstairs and tied fast in a chair. I cried aloud, shaking my head all the while until I felt the cold blades of the scissors against my neck, and heard them gnaw off one of my thick black braids. Then I lost my spirit. . . .

Now, as I look back upon the recent past, I see it from a distance, as a whole. I remember how, from morning till evening, many specimens of civilized peoples visited the Indian school. The city folks with canes and eyeglass, the countrymen with sunburned cheeks and clumsy feet . . . alike astounded at seeing the children of savage warriors so docile and industrious. . . .

In this fashion many have passed through the Indian schools during the last decade, afterward to boast of their charity to the North American Indian. But few there are who have paused to question whether real life or long lasting death lies beneath this semblance of civilization.

Source: Linda K. Kerber and Jane De-Hart Mathews, eds., *Women's America: Refocusing the Past*, 2nd ed. (New York: Oxford University Press, 1987), 254–57.

federal government, announcing it had gained tribal approval, opened their "surplus" land to white settlement on February 10, 1890. But no surveys had been made nor any provision for land allotments for the Indians living in the ceded areas. On top of these signs of bad faith by the whites, drought wiped out the Indians' crops that summer. It seemed beyond endurance. They had lost their ancestral lands. They faced a future as farmers, which was alien to their traditions. And immediately confronting them was a winter of starvation.

But news of salvation had also come. An Indian messiah, a holy man who called himself Wovoka, was preaching a new religion on a Paiute reservation in Nevada. In a vision Wovoka had gone to heaven and received God's word that the world would be regenerated. The whites would disappear, all the Indians of past generations would return to earth, and life on the Great Plains would be as it was before the white man appeared. All this would come to pass in the spring of 1891. Awaiting that great day the Indians should follow Wovoka's commandments and practice the **Ghost Dance**, a day-long ritual that sent the spirits of the dancers rising to heaven. As the frenzy of the Ghost Dance swept through some Sioux encampments in the fall of 1890, resident whites became alarmed and called for army intervention.

Wovoka had an especially fervent following among the Minneconjou, where the medicine man Yellow Bird held sway. But their chief, Big Foot, had fallen desperately ill with pneumonia, and the Minneconjou agreed to come in under military escort to an encampment at Wounded Knee Creek on December 28. The next morning, when the soldiers attempted to disarm the Indians, a battle exploded in the encampment. Among the U.S. troopers 25 died; among the Indians 146 men, women, and children perished, many of them shot down as they fled.

Wounded Knee was the final episode in the war against the Plains Indians but not the end of their story. The division of tribal lands now proceeded without hindrance. In the Dakota Territory the Teton Sioux fared relatively well, and many of the younger generation settled down as small farmers and stock grazers. Ironically, the more fortunate tribes were probably those occupying infertile land that did not attract white settlement and thus were spared the allotment process. The flood of whites into South Dakota and Oklahoma, on the other hand, left the Indians as small minorities in lands once wholly theirs—20,000 Sioux in a South Dakotan population of 400,000 in 1900; 70,000 of various tribes in a population of a million when Oklahoma became a state in 1907.

Even so, tribal life survived until, with the restoration of the reservation policy in 1934, it once again rested on a communal territorial basis. All along, Native American cultures had been adaptive, changing in the face of adversity and even absorbing features of white society including, in some cases, developing written languages. This cultural resilience persisted—in religion, in tribal structure, in crafts—but the fostering Native American world was gone, swept away, as an Oklahoma editor put it in the year of statehood, by "the onward march of empire."

The Far West

On the western edge of the Great Plains, the Rocky Mountains rise up to form a great barrier between the mostly flat eastern two-thirds of the country and the rugged Far West (see Map 16.1). Beyond the Rockies lie two vast plateaus: in the north the Columbia plateau, extending into eastern Oregon and Washington, and, flanking the southern Rockies, the Colorado plateau. Where they break off, the plateaus carve out the desert-like Great Basin that covers western Utah and all of Nevada. Separating this arid interior from the Pacific Ocean are two great mountain ranges—the Sierra Nevada and, to the north, the Cascades—beyond which lies a coastal region that is cool and rainy in the north but increasingly dry southward, until in southern California rainfall becomes almost as sparse as in the interior.

What most impressed white Americans about this far western country was its sheer inhospitability. The transmountain West could not be occupied in the standard American fashion—that is, by a multitude of settlers moving westward along a broad front, blanketing the land and, homestead by homestead, bringing it under cultivation. The wagon trains moving to Oregon's Willamette Valley adopted an entirely different strategy of occupation—the planting of scattered settlements in a vast, mostly barren landscape.

New Spain had pioneered this strategy when in 1598 it had sent the first wagon trains 700 miles northward from Mexico into the upper Rio Grande Valley. When the United States seized the Southwest 250 years later major Hispanic settlements existed in New Mexico and California, with lesser settlements scattered along the borderlands into south Texas. At that time, aside from Oregon, the only significant Anglo settlement was around the Great Salt Lake in Utah, where Mormons had moved to escape persecution and plant a New Zion. Fewer than 100,000 Euro-Americans—roughly 25,000 of them Anglo, the rest Hispanic—lived in the entire Far West when it became U.S. territory in 1848.

The Mining Frontier

More emigrants would be coming, certainly, but the Far West seemed unlikely to be much of a magnet. California

was "hilly and mountainous," noted a U.S. naval officer in 1849, too dry for farming and surely not "susceptible of supporting a very large population." He had not taken account of the recent discovery of gold in the Sierra foothills, however. California would indeed support a very large population, drawn not by arable land but by dreams of gold.

Extraction of mineral wealth became the basis for the Far West's development (Map 16.6). First of all, this meant explosive growth. By 1860, when the Great Plains was still Indian country, California was a booming state with 300,000 residents. There was also a burst of city building. Overnight San Francisco became a bustling metropolis—it had 57,000 residents by 1860—and was

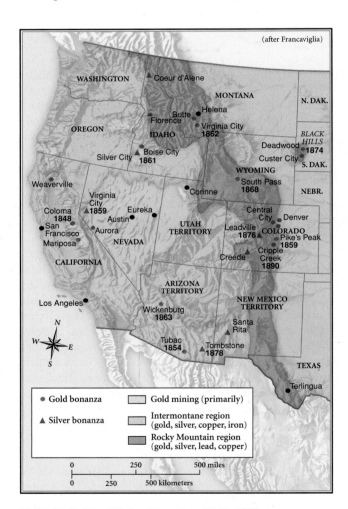

MAP 16.6 The Mining Frontier, 1848–1890

The Far West was America's gold country because of its geological history. Veins of gold and silver form when molten material from the earth's core is forced up into fissures caused by the tectonic movements that create mountain ranges, such as the ones that dominate the far western landscape. It was these veins, the product of mountain-forming activity many thousands of years earlier, that prospectors began to discover after 1848 and furiously exploit. Although widely dispersed across the Far West, the lodes that they found followed the mountain ranges bisecting the region and bypassing the great plateaus not shaped by the ancient tectonic activity.

the hub of a mining empire that stretched to the Rockies. Similarly, Denver mushroomed into the metropolis for the mining camps on the eastern slope.

In its swift urbanization the Far West resembled Australia, whose gold rush began in 1851, much more than it resembled the American Midwest. Like San Francisco, Melbourne was a city incongruously grand amid the empty spaces and rough mining camps of the Australian "outback." The distinctive pattern of isolated settlement persisted in the Far West, driven now, however, by a proliferation of mining sites and by people moving not east to west but west to east, coming mainly from California.

By the mid-1850s, as easy pickings in the California gold country diminished, prospectors began to pull out and spread across the West in hopes of striking it rich elsewhere. Gold was discovered on the Nevada side of the Sierra Nevada, in the Colorado Rockies, and along the Fraser River in British Columbia. New strikes occurred in Montana and Wyoming during the 1860s, a decade later in the Black Hills of South Dakota, and in the Coeur d'Alene region of Idaho during the 1880s.

As the news of each gold strike spread, a wild, remote area turned almost overnight into a mob scene of prospectors, traders, gamblers, prostitutes, and saloonkeepers. At least 100,000 fortune seekers flocked to the Pike's Peak area of Colorado in the spring of 1859. Trespassers on government or Indian land, the prospectors made their own law. The mining codes devised at community meetings limited the size of a mining claim to what a person could reasonably work. This kind of informal lawmaking also

Hydraulic Mining
When surface veins of gold were played out, miners turned to hydraulic mining, which was invented in California in 1853. The technology was simple, using high-pressure streams of water to wash away hillsides of gold-bearing soil. Although building the reservoirs, piping systems, and sluices cost money, the profits from hydraulic mining helped transform western mining into big business. But, as this daguerreotype suggests, hydraulic mining wreaked havoc on the environment. Collection of Matthew Isenburg.

Baron Joseph Alexander von Hübner

A Western Boom Town

During a leisurely trip around the world in 1871 Baron von Hübner, a distinguished Austrian diplomat, traveled across the United States, taking advantage of the newly completed transcontinental railroad to see the Wild West. After observing Mormon life in Salt Lake City, he went northward to Corinne, Utah, near the juncture where the Central and Union Pacific railroads met. He was struck not only by the crudeness of Corinne (see Map 16.6) but also by the tough "rowdies" inhabiting the place.

Corinne has only existed for four years. Sprung out of the earth as if by enchantment, this town now contains upwards of 2,000 inhabitants, and every day increases in importance. It is a victualing center for the advanced posts of the [miners] in Idaho and Montana. A coach runs twice a week to Virginia City and to Helena, 350 and 500 miles to the north. Despite the serious dangers and the terrible fatigue of the journeys, these diligences are always full of passengers. Various articles of consumption and dry goods of all sorts are sent in wagons. The "high road" is but a rough track in the soil left by the wheels of the previous vehicles.

The streets of Corinne are full of white men armed to the teeth, miserable looking Indians dressed in the ragged shirts and trousers furnished by the federal government, and yellow Chinese with a business-like air and hard, intelligent faces. No town in the Far West gave me so good an idea as this little place of what is meant by "border life," the struggle between civilization and savage men and things. . . .

All commercial business centers in Main Street. The houses on both sides are nothing but boarded huts. I have seen some with only canvas partitions. . . . The lanes alongside of the huts, which are generally the resort of Chinese women of bad character, lead into the desert, which begins at the doors of the last houses. . . .

To have on your conscience a number of manslaughters committed in full day, under the eyes of your fellow citizens; to have escaped the reach of justice by craft, audacity, or bribery; to have earned a reputation for being "sharp," that is, for knowing how to cheat all the world without being caught—those are the attributes of the true rowdy in the Far West. . . . Endowed as they often are with really fine qualities—courage, energy, and intellectual and physical strength—they might in another sphere and with the moral sense which they now lack, have become valuable members of society. But such as they are, these adventurers have a reason for being, a providential mission to fulfill. The qualities needed to struggle with and conquer savage nature have naturally their corresponding defects. Look back, and you will see the cradles of all civilization surrounded with giants of Herculean strength ready to run every risk and to shrink from neither danger nor crime to attain their ends. It is only by the peculiar temper of the time and place that we can distinguish them from the backwoodsman and rowdy of the United States.

Source: Oscar Handlin, ed., *This Was America* (Cambridge, MA: Harvard University Press, 1949), 313–15.

became an instrument for excluding or discriminating against Mexicans, Chinese, and African Americans in the gold fields. It turned into hangman's justice for the many outlaws who infested the mining camps. Supplying these camps were rough depots like Corinne, Utah (see Voices from Abroad, "Baron Joseph Alexander von Hübner: A Western Boom Town," above).

The heyday of the prospectors was always brief. They were equipped only to skim gold from the surface outcroppings and stream beds. Extracting the metal locked in underground lodes required mine shafts and crushing mills—hence capital, technology, and business organization. The original claim holders quickly sold out when a generous bidder came along. At every gold-rush site the prospector soon gave way to entrepreneurial development and large-scale mining. Rough mining camps turned into big towns.

Virginia City.   Nevada's Virginia City started out as a bawdy, ramshackle mining camp, but with the opening of the Comstock silver lode in 1859 it soon boasted a stock exchange, mansions for the mining kings, fancy hotels, and even Shakespearean theater. Virginia City remained a rough **boomtown** nonetheless. It was a magnet for job seekers of both sexes: the men laboring as miners below ground for $4 a day, many of the wage-earning women becoming dance-hall entertainers and prostitutes because that was the best they could do in Virginia City. In 1870 a hundred saloons operated day and night, brothels lined D Street, and men outnumbered women two to one.

When James Galloway arrived looking for work on February 4, 1875, however, he brought his family with him, as did many other miners. Galloway's diary describes a family life that was entirely ordinary—church-going, picnics, the purchase of a lot for a small house. But Galloway was infected by Virginia City's pervasive gambling fever: he speculated regularly in mining stock and always lost money. In the end, he fell victim to the extraordinary hazards of hard-rock mining. He was killed when his sleeve got caught in the gears of a mine machine. He might have survived had he permitted rescuers to hack off his arm, but he took a long chance on being cut loose and coming out whole, and lost.

In Galloway's time Virginia City became respectable and gave the appearance, with its churches and fine public buildings, of a place that would last forever. But in fact when the Comstock lode played out in the early 1880s, Virginia City declined and, in a fate all too familiar in bonanza mining, became a ghost town.

Industrialization of Western Mining. In its final stage the mining frontier passed into the industrial world. At some sites gold and silver proved less important than the commoner metals—copper, lead, and zinc—for which there was a huge demand in eastern manufacturing. Copper mining thrived in the Butte district of Montana. In the 1890s Idaho's Coeur d'Alene silver district became the nation's main source of lead and zinc.

Entrepreneurs raised capital, built rail connections, financed the technology for treating the lower-grade copper deposits, constructed smelting facilities, and recruited a labor force. As with other workers, western miners organized trade unions (see Chapter 17). As elsewhere in corporate America, the western mining industries went through a process of consolidation. The Anaconda Copper Mining Company and other Montana mining firms came under the control of the Amalgamated Copper Company in 1899. Also in that year the American Smelting and Refining Company brought together the bulk of the nation's lead-mining and copper-refining properties. Blackfeet and Crow country in the 1860s, the Butte copper district was a center of industrial capitalism thirty years later.

The Pacific Slope. But for its mineral wealth the Far West's history would certainly have been very different. Before the discovery of gold at Sutter's Mill in 1848, Oregon's Willamette Valley, not dry California, mostly attracted westward-bound settlers. And, but for the gold

rush, California would likely have remained like the Willamette Valley—an agricultural backwater with no markets for its products and a slow-growing population. In 1860, although already a state, Oregon had scarcely 25,000 inhabitants, and its principal city, Portland, was little more than a village. Booming California and its tributary mining country pulled Oregon from the doldrums by creating a market for the state's produce and timber. During the 1880s Oregon and Washington (which became a state in 1899) grew prodigiously. Where scarcely 100,000 settlers had lived twenty years earlier, there were nearly 750,000 by 1890 (Map 16.7). Portland and, even more dramatically, Seattle blossomed into important commercial centers, both prospering from a mixed economy of farming, ranching, logging, and fishing.

At a certain point, especially as railroads opened up eastern markets, this diversified growth became self-sustaining. But what had triggered it—what had provided the first markets and underwritten the economic infrastructure—was the bonanza mining economy, at the hub of which stood San Francisco, the metropolis for the entire Far West.

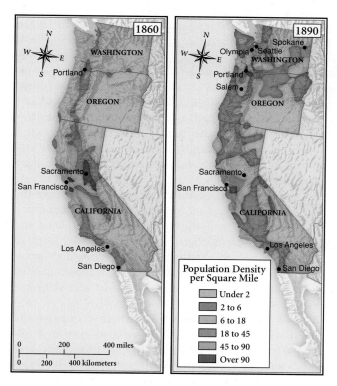

MAP 16.7 The Settlement of the Pacific Slope, 1860–1890

In 1860 the settlement of the Pacific slope was remarkably uneven—fully underway in northern California and scarcely begun anywhere else. By 1890 a new pattern had begun to emerge, with the swift growth of southern California foreshadowed and the settlement of the Pacific Northwest well launched.

Hispanics, Chinese, Anglos

California was the anchor of two distinct far western regions. First, it joined with Oregon and Washington to form the Pacific slope. Second, by climate and Hispanic heritage, California was linked to the Southwest, which today includes Arizona, New Mexico, and Texas.

The Hispanic Southwest. The first Europeans to enter the Far West—two centuries before the earliest Anglos—were Hispanics moving northward out of Mexico. There, along a 1,500-mile borderland, outposts had been planted over many years by the viceroys of New Spain. Most populous and best established were the settlements along New Mexico's upper Rio Grande Valley; the main town, Santa Fe, was over 200 years old and contained 4,635 residents in 1860. Farther down the Rio Grande was El Paso, nearly as old but much smaller, and, to the west in present-day Arizona, Tucson, an old presidio, or garrison, town. At the western end of this Hispanic crescent, in California, a Spanish-speaking population was spread thinly in the old presidio towns along the coast and on a patchwork of great ranches.

The economy of this Hispanic crescent was pastoral, consisting primarily of cattle and sheep ranching. In south Texas there were family-run ranches. Everywhere else the social order was highly stratified. At the top stood an elite—the beneficiaries of royal land grants, who were proudly Spanish and devoted to the traditional life of a landed aristocracy. Below them, with little in between, was a laboring class of servants, artisans, vaqueros (cowboys), and farmworkers. New Mexico also contained a large mestizo population—people of mixed Hispanic and Indian blood. They were a Spanish-speaking and Catholic peasantry but still faithful in their village life and farming methods to their Pueblo heritage.

Pueblo Indians, although their dominance over the Rio Grande Valley had long passed, still occupied much of the region, living in the old ways in adobe villages and making the New Mexico countryside a patchwork of Hispanic and Pueblo settlements. To the north a vibrant new people, the Navajo, had appeared, warriors like the Apache from which they descended but also skilled at crafts and sheep raising.

New Mexico was one place where European and Native American cultures managed a successful, if uneasy, coexistence and where the Indian inhabitants were equipped to hold their own against the Anglo challenge. In California, by contrast, the Hispanic occupation had been harder on the indigenous hunter-gatherer peoples, undermining their tribal structure, reducing them to forced labor, and making them easy prey for the aggressive Anglo miners and settlers, who, in short order, nearly wiped out California's once numerous Indian population.

Anglo-Hispanic Conflict. The fate of the Hispanic Southwest after its incorporation into the United States in 1848 depended on the rate of Anglo immigration. In New Mexico, which remained off the beaten track even after the arrival of railroads in the 1880s, the Santa Fe elite more than held its own, incorporating the Anglo newcomers into Hispanic society through intermarriage and business partnerships. In California, however, expropriation of the great ranches was relentless, even though the 1848 treaty with Mexico had recognized the property rights of the Californios and had made them U.S. citizens. Around San Francisco the great ranches disappeared almost in a puff of smoke. Farther south, where Anglos were slow to arrive, the dons held on longer, but by the 1880s just a handful of the original families still retained their Mexican land grants.

The New Mexico peasants found themselves equally embattled. Crucial to their livelihood were grazing rights on communal lands. But these were customary rights that could not withstand legal challenge when Anglo ranchers established title and began putting up fences. The peasants responded as best they could. Their subsistence economy relied on a division of labor that gave women a productive role in the village economy. Women tended the small gardens, engaged in village bartering, and maintained the households. With the loss of the communal lands, the men began migrating seasonally to railway work or the Colorado mines and sugar-beet fields, earning dollars while leaving the village economy in their wives' hands.

Elsewhere, hard-pressed Hispanics struck back for what they considered rightfully theirs. When Anglo ranchers began to fence in communal lands in San Miguel County, the New Mexicans long settled there, *los pobres* (the poor ones) organized themselves into masked night-riding raiders and in 1889 and 1890 mounted an effective campaign of harassment against the interlopers. After 1900, when Anglo farmers swarmed into south Texas bent on exploiting new irrigation methods, the displaced Tejanos responded with sporadic but persistent night-riding attacks. Much of the raiding by Mexican "bandits" from across the border in the years before World War I was really more in the nature of a civil war by embittered Tejanos who had lived north of the Rio Grande for generations.

But they, like the New Mexico villagers who became seasonal wage laborers, could not avoid being driven into the ranks of a Mexican American working class as the Anglo economy developed. This same development also began to attract increasing numbers of immigrants from Old Mexico.

Mexican Migrants. All along the Southwest borderlands, economic activity was picking up in the late nineteenth century. Railroads were being built, copper mines were opening in Arizona, cotton and

Mexican Miners

When large-scale mining began to develop in Arizona and New Mexico in the late nineteenth century, Mexicans crossed the border to earn Yankee dollars. In this unidentified photograph from the 1890s, the men are wearing traditional clothing, indicating perhaps that they are recent arrivals at the mine.

Division of Cultural Resource, Wyoming Department of Commerce.

vegetable agriculture was developing in south Texas, and orchards were planted in southern California. In Texas the Hispanic population increased from about 20,000 in 1850 to 165,000 in 1900. Some came as contract workers for railway gangs and harvest crews; virtually all were relegated to the lowest-paying and most back-breaking work; and everywhere they were discriminated against and reviled by Anglo workers.

What stimulated the Mexican migration was the enormous demand for workers by a region undergoing explosive development, which also accounted for the exceptionally high number of European immigrants in the West. In California, where they were most heavily concentrated, roughly one-third of the population was foreign-born, more than twice the level for the country as a whole. Most numerous were the Irish, followed by the Germans and British. But there was another group unique to the West—the Chinese.

The Chinese Migration. Attracted first by the California gold rush, 200,000 Chinese came to the United States between 1850 and 1880. In those years they constituted a considerable minority of California's population—around 9 percent—and because virtually all were actively employed, they represented a much larger proportion of the state's labor force—probably a quarter. Elsewhere in the West, at the crest of mining activity, their presence could surge remarkably, to over 25 percent of Idaho's population in 1870, for example.

The arrival of the Chinese in North America was part of a worldwide Asian migration that had begun in the mid-nineteenth century. Driven by poverty, the Chinese went to Australia, Hawaii, and Latin America; Indians to Fiji and South Africa; and Javanese to Dutch colonies in the Caribbean. Most of these Asians migrated as indentured servants, which in effect made them the property of others. In America, however, indentured servitude was no longer lawful—by the 1820s state courts were banning it as involuntary servitude—so the Chinese came as free workers, going into debt for their passage money but not surrendering their personal freedom or right to choose their employers.

Once in America, Chinese immigrants normally entered the orbit of the Six Companies, a powerful confederation of Chinese merchants in San Francisco's Chinatown. Most of the arrivals were young unmarried men eager to earn a stake and return to their native Cantonese villages. The Six Companies acted not only as an employment agency but provided new arrivals with the social and commercial services they needed to survive in an alien world. The few Chinese women—the male/female ratio was thirteen to one—worked mostly as servants and prostitutes, sad victims of the desperate poverty that drove the Chinese to America. Some were sold by impoverished parents; others were enticed or kidnapped by procurers and transported to America.

Until the early 1860s, when surface mining played out, Chinese men labored mainly in the California gold fields—as prospectors where white miners permitted it and as laborers and cooks where they did not. Then, when construction began on the transcontinental railroad, the Central Pacific hired Chinese workers. Eventually they constituted four-fifths of the railroad's labor force, doing most of the pick-and-shovel work laying the track across the Sierra Nevada. Many were recruited by labor agents and worked in labor gangs run

Building the Central Pacific
*Chinese laborers in 1867 at work on the great trestle spanning
the canyon at Secrettown in the Sierra Nevada.*
University of California at Berkeley, Bancroft Library.

by "China bosses," who not only supervised but fed, housed, paid, and often cheated them.

When the transcontinental railroad was completed in 1869, the Chinese scattered. Some stayed in railroad construction gangs, while others labored on swamp-drainage and irrigation projects in California's Central Valley or as agricultural workers and, if they were lucky, became small farmers and orchardists. The mining districts of Idaho, Montana, and Colorado also attracted large numbers of Chinese, but according to the 1880 census, nearly three-quarters remained in California. "Wherever we put them, we found them good," remarked Charles Crocker, one of the promoters of the Central Pacific. "Their orderly and industrious habits make them a very desirable class of immigrants."

Anti-Chinese Agitation.   White workers, however, did not share Crocker's enthusiasm for Chinese labor. In other parts of the country, racism was directed against African Americans; in California, where there were few blacks, it found a target in the Chinese. "They practice all the unnameable vices of the East," wrote the young journalist Henry George. "They are utter heathens, treacherous, sensual, cowardly and cruel." Sadly, this vicious racism was intertwined with labor's republican ideals. The Chinese, argued George, would "make nabobs and princes of our capitalists, and crush our working classes into the dust . . . substitut[ing] . . . a population of serfs and their masters for that population of intelligent freemen who are our glory and our strength."

The anti-Chinese frenzy climaxed in San Francisco in the late 1870s when mobs ruled the streets, at one point threatening to burn the docks of the Pacific Mail Steamship Company where the Chinese immigrants debarked. The fiercest agitator, an Irish teamster named Denis Kearney, quickly became a dominant figure in the California labor movement. Under the slogan "The Chinese Must Go!" Kearney led a Working Men's Party against the state's major parties. Democrats and Republicans, however, jumped on the bandwagon, joining together in 1879 to write a new state constitution replete with anti-Chinese provisions and pressuring Washington to take up the issue. In 1882 Congress passed the Chinese Exclusion Act, which barred further entry of Chinese laborers into the country.

The injustice of this law—no other nationality was similarly targeted—rankled the Chinese. Why us, protested one woman to a federal agent, and not the Irish, "who were always drunk and fighting?" Merchants and American-born Chinese, who were free to come and go, routinely registered a newly born son after each trip, enabling many an unrelated "paper son" to enter the country. Even so, resourceful as the Chinese were at evading the exclusion law, the flow of immigrants slowed to a trickle.

But the job opportunities that had attracted the Chinese to America did not subside. If anything, the West's agricultural development intensified the demand for cheap labor, especially in California, which was shifting from wheat, the state's first great cash crop, to fruits and vegetables. Such intensive agriculture required lots of workers: stoop labor, meagerly paid, and mostly seasonal. This was not, as one San Francisco journalist put it, "white men's work." That ugly phrase serves as a touchstone for California agricultural labor as it would thereafter develop—a kind of caste labor system, always drawing some downtrodden, footloose whites, yet basically defined along color lines.

But if not the Chinese, then who? First, Japanese immigrants, who came in increasing numbers and by the early twentieth century constituted half of the state's agricultural labor force. Then, when anti-Japanese agitation closed off that population flow in 1908, Mexico became the next, essentially permanent, source of migratory workers for California's booming commercial agriculture.

The irony of the state's social evolution is painful to behold. Here was California, a land of limitless opportunity, boastful of its democratic egalitarianism, and yet simultaneously, and from its very birth, a racially torn society, at once exploiting and despising the Hispanic and Asian minorities whose hard labor helped make California the enviable land it was.

Golden California

Life in California contained all that the modern world of 1890 had to offer—cosmopolitan San Francisco, comfortable travel, a high living standard, colleges and universities, even resident painters and writers. Yet California was still remote from the rest of America, still a long journey away and, of course, differently and spectacularly endowed by nature. Location, environment, and history all conspired to set California somewhat apart from the American nation. In certain ways so did the Californians.

Creating a California Culture.   What Californians yearned for was a cultural tradition of their own. Closest to hand was the bonanza era of the Forty-Niners, captured on paper by Samuel Clemens. Clemens did a bit of prospecting, worked as a reporter, and adopted the pen name Mark Twain. In 1864 he left for San Francisco, where he became a newspaper columnist writing about what he pronounced "the livest, heartiest community on our continent."

Listening to the old miners in Angel's Camp in 1865, Twain jotted down one tale in his notebook, as follows:

> *Coleman with his jumping frog—bet stranger $50—stranger had no frog, and C. got him one:—in the meantime stranger filled C's frog full of shot and he couldn't jump. The stranger's frog won.*

In Twain's hands, this fragment was transformed into a tall tale that caught the imagination of the country and made his reputation as a humorist. "The Celebrated Jumping Frog of Calaveras County" somehow encapsulated the entire world of make-or-break optimism in the mining camps.

In such short stories as "The Luck of Roaring Camp" and "The Outcasts of Poker Flat," Twain's fellow San Franciscan Bret Harte developed this theme in a more literary fashion and firmly implanted it in California's memory. But this past was too raw, too suggestive of the tattered beginnings of so many of the state's leading citizens—in short too disreputable—for an up-and-coming society.

Then in 1884 Helen Hunt Jackson published her novel *Ramona*. In this story of a half-Indian girl caught between two cultures, Jackson intended to advance the cause of the Native Americans, but she placed her tale in the evocative context of Old California and that rang a bell. By then the chain of missions planted by the Catholic Church had been long abandoned. The padres

were wholly forgotten, their Indian converts scattered and in dire poverty. Now that lost world of "sun, silence and adobe" became all the rage. Sentimental novels and histories appeared in abundance. There was a movement to restore the missions. Many communities began to stage Spanish fiestas, and the mission style of architecture enjoyed a great vogue among developers.

In its Spanish past California found the cultural traditions it needed. The same kind of discovery was taking place elsewhere in the Southwest, although in the case of Santa Fe and Taos there really were live Hispanic roots to celebrate.

Land of Sunshine.   All this enthusiasm was strongly tinged with commercialism. And so was a second distinctive feature of California's development—the exploitation of its climate. While northern California boomed, the southern part of the state was neglected and thinly populated, too dry for anything but grazing and some chancy wheat growing. What it did have, however, was an abundance of sunshine. At the beginning of the 1880s there burst upon the country amazing news of the charms of southern California. "There is not any malaria, hay fever, loss of appetite, or languor in the air; nor any thunder, lightning, mad dogs . . . or cold snaps." This publicity was mostly the work of the Southern Pacific Railroad, which had reached Los Angeles in 1876 and was eager for business.

A furious fare war broke out when the Santa Fe arrived in 1885, and it became possible to travel from Chicago or St. Louis to Los Angeles for $25 or less. Thousands of people, mostly Midwesterners, poured in. A dizzying real-estate boom developed, along with the frantic building of such resort hotels as San Diego's opulent Hotel del Coronado. Los Angeles County, which had less than 3 percent of the state's population in 1870, had 12 percent by 1900. By then southern California had firmly established itself as the land of sunshine and orange groves. It had found a way to translate climate into riches.

The Great Outdoors.   That California was specially favored by nature some Californians knew even as the great stands of redwoods and sugar pine were being hacked down, the soil depleted by the relentless cycle of wheat crops, the streams polluted, and the hills torn apart by reckless mining techniques. Back in 1864 influential Americans who had seen it prevailed on Congress to grant to the state of California "the Cleft, or Gorge in the granite peak of the Sierra Nevada Mountain, known as Yosemite Valley," which would be reserved "for public pleasuring, resort, and recreation." When the young naturalist John Muir arrived in California four years later, he headed straight for Yosemite. Its "grandeur . . . comes as an endless revelation," he wrote. Muir and others like him became

Kitty Tatch and Friend on Glacier Point, Yosemite
From the time the Yosemite Valley was set aside in 1864 as a place "for public pleasuring, resort, and recreation," it attracted a stream of tourists eager to experience the grandeur of the American West. As is suggested by this photograph taken sometime in the 1890s, the magic of Yosemite was enough to set even staid young ladies dancing. The Yosemite Museum.

devoted to studying the High Sierras and protecting them from "despoiling gain-seekers . . . eagerly trying to make everything immediately and selfishly commercial." One result was the creation of California's national parks in 1890—Yosemite, Sequoia, and General Grant (later part of King's Canyon). Another was the formation in 1892 of the Sierra Club, which became a powerful voice for the defenders of California's wilderness.

They won some and lost some. Advocates of water-resource development insisted that California's irrigated agriculture and thirsty cities could not grow without tapping the abundant snowpack of the Sierra Nevada. By the turn of the century, Los Angeles faced a water crisis that threatened its growth. The answer was a 238-mile aqueduct to the Owens River in the southern Sierra. A bitter controversy blew up over this immense project, driven by the resistance of local residents to the flooding of the beautiful Owens Valley. More painful for John Muir and his **preservationist** allies was their failure to save the Hetch Hetchy gorge north of Yosemite National Park. After years of controversy the federal government in 1913 approved the damming of Hetch Hetchy to serve the water needs of San Francisco.

When the stakes became high enough, nature lovers like John Muir generally came out on the short end. Even so, something original and distinctive had been added to California's heritage—the linking of a society's well-being with the preservation of its natural environment. This realization, in turn, said something important about the nation's relationship to the West. If the urge to conquer and exploit persisted, at least it was now tempered by a sense that nature's bounty was not limitless. And this, more than any announcement by the U.S. Census that a "frontier line" no longer existed, registered the country's acceptance that the age of heedless westward expansion had ended.

FOR FURTHER EXPLORATION

▶ For definitions of key terms boldfaced in this chapter, see the glossary at the end of the book.

▶ To assess your mastery of the material covered in this chapter, see the Online Study Guide at **bedfordstmartins.com/henretta**.

▶ For suggested references, including Web sites, see page SR-18 at the end of the book.

▶ For map resources and primary documents, see **bedfordstmartins.com/henretta**.

S U M M A R Y

In 1860 the Great Plains was still ancestral home to nomadic Indian tribes that had built a vibrant society based on the horse and the buffalo. By 1890 the Indians had been crowded onto reservations and forced to abandon their tribal way of life. With railroads leading the way, cattle ranchers and homesteaders in short order displaced the Indians and domesticated the Great Plains. Beyond the Rockies a different pattern of settlement occurred. Because so much of this region was arid and uninhabitable, occupation took the form of oases of settlement rather than progressive occupation along a broad frontier that had prevailed east of the Rockies. And while arable land had been the lure for settlers up to that point, what drove settlement beyond the Rockies was the discovery of mineral wealth. For the entire trans-Mississippi West, the pace of occupation was accelerated by the nation's economic development. Industry needed the West's mineral resources; the cities demanded agricultural products; and from railroads to barbed wire, the industrial economy provided the means for a swift and decisive conquest of the West. For Great Plains farmers suffering from weak markets, however, integration into this modern economy was no guarantee of prosperity.

By population, economy, and strategic position, California was the regional power dominating the Far West in the late nineteenth century. It was the anchor both of a crescent of Hispanic settlement to the Southwest and of the Pacific slope region stretching up to the Canadian border. The discovery of gold had set off a huge migration that overwhelmed the thinly spread Hispanic inhabitants and swiftly transformed California into a populous state with a large urban sector. California developed a distinctive culture that capitalized on its rediscovered Hispanic heritage and its climate and natural environment. The treatment of the Chinese, Japanese, and Mexicans who provided the state's cheap labor, however, infused a dark streak of racism into its society.

T I M E L I N E

1849   California gold rush

Chinese migration begins

1862   Homestead Act

1864   Yosemite Valley reserved as public park

1865   Long Drive of Texas longhorns begins

1867   Patrons of Husbandry (the Grange) founded

U.S. government adopts reservation policy for Plains Indians

1868   Indian treaty confirms Sioux rights to Powder River hunting grounds

1869   Union Pacific–Central Pacific transcontinental railroad completed

1875   Sioux ordered to vacate Powder River hunting grounds; war breaks out

1876   Battle of Little Big Horn

1877   San Francisco anti-Chinese riots

1879   Exoduster migration to Kansas

1882   Chinese Exclusion Act

1884   Helen Hunt Jackson's novel *Ramona*

1886   Dry cycle begins on the Great Plains

1887   Dawes Act

1889   Oklahoma opened to white settlement

1890   Indian massacre at Wounded Knee, South Dakota

U.S. Census declares end of the frontier

CHAPTER 17

Capital and Labor in the Age of Enterprise

1877–1900

THE YEAR THAT RECONSTRUCTION ENDED, 1877, also marked the end of the first great crisis of American industrial capitalism. In 1873, four years earlier, a severe depression had set in, bankrupting 47,000 firms and driving wholesale prices down by 30 percent. Railroad building ground to a halt. Orders for industrial goods disappeared. Hundreds of thousands of workers lost their jobs, and suffering was widespread. Across the country workers demanded "bread for the needy, clothing for the naked, and houses for the homeless." Before long the foundations of the social order began to shake.

On July 16, 1877, railroad workers went on strike to protest a wage cut at the Baltimore and Ohio Railroad. In towns along the B&O tracks, crowds cheered as the strikers attacked company property and prevented trains from running. The strike rippled across the country. In Pittsburgh the Pennsylvania Railroad's roundhouse went up in flames on July 21, and at many rail centers rioters and looters roamed freely. Only the arrival of federal troops restored order. On August 15 President Rutherford B. Hayes wrote in his diary: "The strikers have been put down *by force*." The Great Strike of 1877 had been crushed but only after raising the specter of social revolution.

And then recovery came. Within months the economy was booming again. In the next fifteen years, the output of manufactured goods increased by over 150 percent. Confidence in the nation's industrial future rebounded. "Upon [material progress] is founded all other progress," asserted a railroad president in 1888. "Can there be any doubt that cheapening the cost of necessaries and conveniences of life is the most powerful agent of civilization and progress?"

◀ **Homestead at Twilight**

In this evocative painting Aaron Henry Gorson (1872–1933) looks across the Monongahela River at Andrew Carnegie's great steel mill, a symbol of America's industrial prowess but also, as the clouds of smoke lighting the sky suggest, a major source of the Pittsburgh district's polluted air. Westmorland Museum of Art.

The rail magnate's boast represents the confident face of America's industrial revolution. President Hayes's anxious diary entries suggest a grimmer face, manifest for example in the armories built in cities across the country after 1877. They were fortresses designed to withstand assault by future strikers and rioters. It was a paradox of the nation's industrial history that an economy celebrated for its dynamism and inventiveness—a wealth-creating machine beyond anything the world had ever seen—was also brutally indifferent to the many who fell by the wayside, hence never secure and never free of social conflict.

Industrial Capitalism Triumphant

Economic historians speak of the late nineteenth century as the age of the Great Deflation. Prices fell steadily not only in the United States but worldwide (Figure 17.1). Falling prices normally signal economic stagnation: there is not enough demand for the available goods and services. For England, a mature industrial power, the Great Deflation did indeed signal economic decline. But not for the United States. Industrial expansion went into high gear during the Great Deflation. Because of increasing manufacturing efficiencies, American firms could cut prices and yet earn profits for financing still better equipment. This achievement meant higher real income for Americans, which increased by nearly 50 percent (from $388 in 1877 to $573 in 1900) in scarcely a quarter of a century.

Growth of the Industrial Base

By the 1870s factories were a familiar sight in America. But early manufacturing had really been an extension of the agricultural economy, producing consumer goods—textiles, shoes, paper, and furniture—that replaced articles made at home or by individual artisans. Gradually, however, a different kind of demand developed as the country's economy surged. Railroads needed locomotives; new factories needed machinery; cities needed trolley lines, sanitation systems, and commercial buildings. Railroad equipment, machinery, and construction materials were **capital goods**, that is, goods themselves adding to the nation's productive capacity. Although consumer goods remained very important, it was the manufacture of capital goods that now drove America's industrial economy.

Central to the capital-goods sector was technological revolution in steel making. The country already produced large quantities of wrought iron, a malleable metal easily worked by rural blacksmiths and farmers. But wrought iron was expensive—it was produced in small batches by skilled puddlers—and did not stand up under heavy use as railway track. In 1856 the British inventor Henry Bessemer designed a furnace—the Bessemer converter—that refined raw pig iron into an essentially new product, steel, a metal harder and more durable than wrought iron (see New Technology, "Iron and Steel," p. 488). Others adopted Bessemer's invention, but it was Andrew Carnegie who fully exploited its revolutionary potential.

Carnegie arrived from Scotland in 1848 at the age of twelve with his poverty-stricken family. He became a telegraph operator, then went to work for the Pennsylvania Railroad and rapidly climbed the managerial ladder. In 1865, having amassed a fortune in wartime speculation, Carnegie struck out on his own as an iron manufacturer. His main customers were his former associates in the railroad business.

In 1872 Carnegie erected a massive steel mill outside Pittsburgh, with the Bessemer converter as its centerpiece. The converter broke a bottleneck at the refining stage and enabled Carnegie's engineers to design a mill that functioned on the basis of integrated operation. Iron ore entered the blast furnaces at one end and emerged without interruption at the other end as finished steel rails.

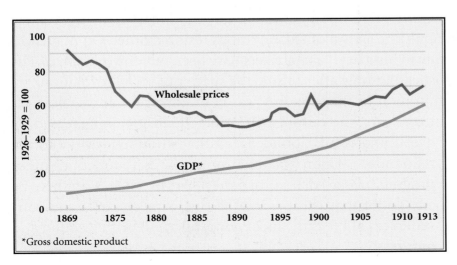

FIGURE 17.1 Business Activity and Wholesale Prices, 1869–1913
This graph shows the key feature of the performance of the late-nineteenth-century economy: while output was booming, the price of goods was falling.

Named after Carnegie's admired boss at the Pennsylvania Railroad, the Edgar Thompson Works became a model for the modern steel industry. Giant integrated steel plants swiftly replaced the puddling mills that had once dotted western Pennsylvania.

The technological breakthrough in steel spurred the intensive exploitation of the country's rich mineral resources. Once iron ore began to be shipped down the Great Lakes from the rich Mesabi Range in northern Minnesota, the industry was assured of an ample supply of its primary raw material. The other key ingredient, coal, came from the great Appalachian field that stretched from Pennsylvania to Alabama (Map 17.1). A minor enterprise before the Civil War, coal production doubled every decade after 1870, exceeding 400 million tons a year by 1910.

As steam engines became the nation's energy workhorse, prodigious amounts of coal began to be consumed by railroads and factories. Industries previously dependent on waterpower rapidly converted to steam. The turbine, utilizing continuous rotation rather than the steam engine's back-and-forth motion, marked another major advance during the 1880s. With the coupling of the steam turbine to the electric generator, the nation's energy revolution was completed, and after 1900 America's factories began a massive conversion to electric power.

▲ **The Corliss Engine**

The symbol of the Philadelphia Centennial in 1876 was the great Corliss engine, which towered over Machinery Hall and powered all the equipment on exhibit there. Yet the Corliss engine also signified the incomplete nature of American industrialism at that time; it soon became obsolete. Westinghouse turbines generating electricity would be the power source for the nation's next World's Fair in Chicago in 1893. Culver Pictures.

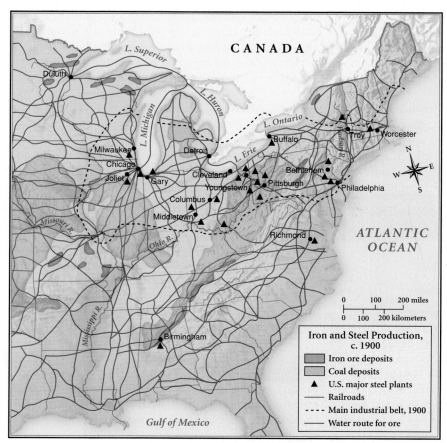

Iron and Steel Production, c. 1900

- ▇ Iron ore deposits
- ▨ Coal deposits
- ▲ U.S. major steel plants
- — Railroads
- --- Main industrial belt, 1900
- — Water route for ore

◀ **MAP 17.1 Iron and Steel Production, 1900**

Before the Civil War, the iron industry was concentrated in eastern Pennsylvania and northern New Jersey. With the shift to steel and the westward movement of population and industry, production moved first to western Pennsylvania and then to Ohio, Indiana, Illinois, and southward into Alabama. The specific locations—Pittsburgh, Youngstown, Chicago, and Birmingham—were dictated by the rail network, new sources of coal and iron ore, and markets for steel.

Iron and Steel

Iron was not a product new to the nineteenth century in the way that plastic was new to the twentieth century. Early Europeans had made iron tools and weapons at least a thousand years before Christ, and in the years since those remote times, the underlying processes did not change, for they are dictated by the nature of iron metallurgy. What did change were the techniques for carrying out those processes.

The first break from ancient methods came when blast furnaces appeared in Belgium around 1340. Ore was melted in a charcoal-burning furnace to which limestone had been added. A blast of air then set off a combustion process that combined carbon from the charcoal with the molten iron while the impurities combined with the limestone to form a slag. The slag was drawn off from the top while the molten iron was tapped from the bottom into sand forms resembling piglets feeding from a sow—hence the term *pig iron*.

By the late eighteenth century, Great Britain was running out of wood for charcoal. The substitution of coke, made by superheating coal, saved the industry and gave Britain the competitive edge it needed to launch the Industrial Revolution. Endowed with ample forests, the United States was slow to adopt coke-using furnaces, but by 1860 it had caught up with Britain technologically.

The search for a metal harder and more durable than wrought iron resulted in the invention in 1856 of an entirely different refining process by the Englishman Henry Bessemer. The Bessemer converter was a pear-shaped vessel that was open at the top and had a bottom perforated with many holes. Molten pig iron flowed into the top while the converter was tilted on its side. Air was blasted through the perforated bottom with great force, and the converter then swung back to its upright position. The resulting combustion set off a spectacular display of flame and smoke. Within fifteen minutes the impurities in the molten iron burned off, and the flames died down. The converter was again tilted on its side, and after manganese and other chemicals had been added, the purified iron was emptied into ingot molds. The refined metal, called *steel*, was ideally suited for use as railroad track.

Bessemer's device, though invented primarily with the aim of gaining a more durable metal, also proved vastly more efficient than the hand-operated puddling furnaces that produced wrought iron. The Bessemer converter turned out great quantities of steel with virtually no labor, and this forced changes up and down the line. To feed the converters' appetite for pig iron, blast furnaces were built larger and, with the introduction of the hot blast, became much faster. To handle the flow of steel from the converters, rolling mills became increasingly mechanized and automatic. Finally, blast furnaces, converters, and rolling mills were brought together and linked into a single processing operation. The integrated

Thus in the decades after the Civil War, the steel industry was established, the nation's mineral resources came under intensive development, and energy was harnessed to the manufacturing system. All these basic elements of modern industrialism—steel, coal, and energy—grew after 1870 at rates far exceeding manufacturing.

The Railroad Boom

Before the Civil War moving goods by water satisfied the country's transportation needs. But it was love at first sight when locomotives arrived from Britain in the early 1830s. Americans were impatient for the year-round, on-time service that canal barges and riverboats could not provide. By 1860, with a network of tracks already criss-crossing the country east of the Mississippi, the railroad clearly was on the way to being industrial America's mode of transportation (Map 17.2).

Constructing the Railroads. The question was, who would pay for it? Railroads could be state enterprises like the canals. Alternatively they could be financed by private investors. Unlike most European countries the United States chose free enterprise. Even so, government played a big role. Eager for the economic benefits, many states and localities lured railroads with offers of financial aid, mostly by buying railroad bonds. Land grants were the principle means by which the federal government encouraged interregional railroads; huge tracts went to the transcontinental railroads tying the Far West to the rest of the country.

The most important boost that government gave the railroads, however, was not money or land but a legal form of organization—the **corporation**—that enabled private capital to be raised in prodigious amounts. Investors who bought stock in the railroads enjoyed limited liability: they risked only the money they had invested and were not personally liable for the railroad's

steel plant of 1900—capable of producing 2,500 tons or more a day—became a voracious consumer of ore and coal.

The commanding lead the United States had built up by 1900 rested on the world's best reserves of coking coal in western Pennsylvania and the vast ore deposits in Minnesota's Mesabi Range, northern Michigan's older fields, and Alabama. The geographical face of American industrialism changed as the places best located in relation to raw materials, transportation, and markets—Pittsburgh, the steel towns along the Great Lakes, and Birmingham, Alabama—became the great centers of steel production. American cities relied on steel for the construction of skyscrapers, trolley lines, subways, and the vast underground complexes of pipe that supplied the urban millions with water and gas and carried away their sewage. Without steel the emerging automobile industry would not have grown, nor would a host of other industries.

It is no wonder that historians have called the last decades of the nineteenth century America's Age of Steel. What was overlooked at the time and for long afterward was the fact that the nation's natural resources were not inexhaustible. It is the exhaustion of the great Mesabi Range that has leveled the playing field among global competitors and helps explain the recent decline of the American steel industry.

Bessemer Converter, Bethlehem Works, Steelton, Pennsylvania, 1885

Workers for Bethlehem Steel in Steelton, Pennsylvania, pose for this 1885 photograph with a Bessemer converter. The late nineteenth century in America came to be known as "America's Age of Steel," thanks to the increased steel production that the Bessemer converter helped generate.
Hagley Museum and Library.

debts. A corporation could also borrow money by issuing interest-bearing bonds, which was how the railroads actually raised most of the money they needed.

Railroad building generally was handed over to construction companies, which, despite the name, were primarily another arm of the complex financing system. Hiring contractors and suppliers often involved persuading them to accept the railroad's bonds as payment and, when that failed, wheeling and dealing to raise cash by selling or borrowing on the bonds. Since the railroad promoters actually ran the construction companies, the opportunities for plunder were enormous. The most notorious, the Union Pacific's Credit Mobilier, siphoned probably half the money it paid out into the pockets of the promoters.

The railroad business was not for the faint of heart. Most successful were promoters with the best access to capital, such as John Murray Forbes, a great Boston merchant in the China trade who developed the Chicago, Burlington, and Quincy Railroad in the Midwest; or Cornelius Vanderbilt, who started with the fortune he had made in the steamboat business. Vanderbilt was primarily a consolidator, linking previously independent lines crossing New York State and ultimately developing the New York Central into a trunk line to Chicago. James J. Hill, who without federal subsidy made the Great Northern into the best of the transcontinental railroads, was certainly the nation's champion railroad builder. In contrast Jay Gould, at various times owner of the Erie, Wabash, Union Pacific, and Missouri Pacific systems, always remained a stock-market speculator at heart (see American Lives, "Jay Gould: Robber Baron?" p. 492).

Railroad development in the United States was often sordid, fiercely competitive, and subject to boom and bust. Yet vast sums of capital were raised and a network built exceeding that of the rest of the world combined. By 1900 virtually no corner of the country lacked rail service.

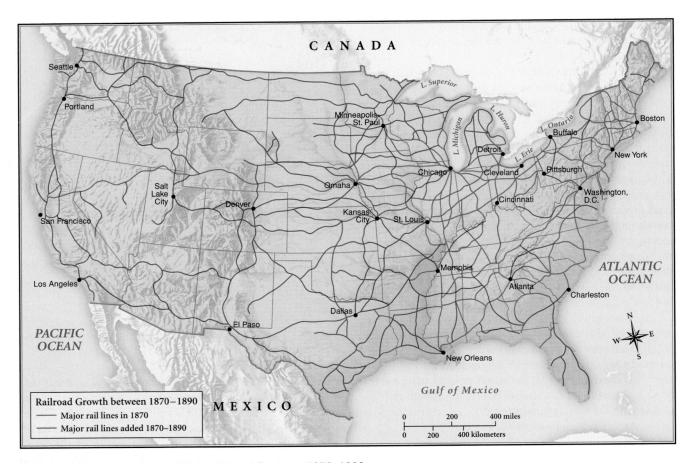

MAP 17.2 The Expansion of the Railroad System, 1870–1890
In 1870 the nation had 53,000 miles of rail track; in 1890 it had 167,000 miles. That burst of construction essentially completed the nation's rail network, although there would be additional expansion for the next two decades. The main areas of growth were in the South and west of the Mississippi. The Great Plains and the Far West accounted for over 40 percent of all railroad construction in this period.

The Railway System. Along with this prodigious growth came increasing efficiency. The early railroads, built by competing local companies, had been a jumble of discontinuous segments. Gauges of track—the width between the rails—varied widely and at terminal points railroads were not connected. As late as 1880 goods could not be shipped through from Massachusetts to South Carolina. Eight times along the way, freight cars had to be emptied and their contents transferred to other cars across a river or at a different terminal.

In 1883 the railroads rebelled against the jumble of local times that made scheduling a nightmare and, acting on their own, divided the country into the four standard time zones still in use. By the end of the 1880s, a standard track gauge (4 feet, 8½ inches) had been adopted everywhere. Fast-freight firms and standard accounting procedures enabled shippers to use the railroad network as if it were a single unit, moving their goods without breaks in transit, transfers between cars, or the other delays that had once bedeviled them.

At the same time railroad technology was advancing. Durable steel rails permitted heavier traffic. Locomotives became more powerful and capable of pulling more freight cars. To control the greater mass being hauled, the inventor George Westinghouse perfected the automatic coupler, the air brake, and the friction gear for starting and stopping a long line of cars. Costs per ton-mile fell by 50 percent between 1870 and 1890, resulting in a steady drop in freight rates for shippers.

The railroads more than met the transportation needs of the maturing industrial economy. For investors, however, the costs of freewheeling competition and unrestrained growth were painfully high. On the many routes served by too many railroads, competitors fought for the available traffic by cutting rates to the bone. Many were saddled with huge bonded debt from the extravagant construction years; about a fifth of these bonds failed to pay interest even in a pretty good year like 1889. When the economy turned bad, as it did in 1893, a third of the industry went into receivership.

Union Pacific's Engine No. 149
The railroads invoked a new notion of time. How fast could a person cross the continent? In 1876 a troupe of actors, scheduled to present Shakespeare's Henry V *in San Francisco, made the trip from New York City in eighty-four hours— a record. The Union Pacific's crack engine No. 149 carried them at open throttle on the last leg from Ogden, Utah.*
Union Pacific Museum Collection.

Out of the rubble came a major railroad reorganization. This was primarily the handiwork of Wall Street investment banks such as J. P. Morgan & Co. and Kuhn Loeb & Co., whose main role it had been to market railroad stocks and bonds. When railroads failed, the investment bankers stepped in to pick up the pieces. They persuaded investors to accept lower interest rates or put up more money. They eased competitive pressures by consolidating rivals. By the early twentieth century, half a dozen great regional systems had emerged, and the nerve center of American railroading had shifted to Wall Street.

Mass Markets and Large-Scale Enterprise

Until well into the industrial age, all but a few manufacturers operated on a small scale and mainly for nearby markets. They left distribution to wholesale merchants and commission agents. After the Civil War the scale of economic activity began to change. "Combinations of capital on a scale hitherto wholly unprecedented constitute one of the remarkable features of modern business methods," the economist David A. Wells wrote in 1889. He could see "no other way in which the work of production and distribution can be prosecuted." What was there about the nation's economy that led to Wells's sense that large-scale enterprise was inevitable?

Most of all the American market. Unlike Europe the United States was not carved up into many national markets; no political frontiers impeded the flow of goods across the continent. The population, swelled by immigration and a high birth rate, jumped from 40 million in 1870 to over 60 million in 1890. People flocked to the cities. The railroads brought these tightly packed markets within the reach of distant producers. The telegraph, fully operational by the Civil War, speeded communications.

Nowhere else did manufacturers have so vast and accessible a home market for their products.

Gustavus Swift and Vertical Integration. How that opportunity was seized is perhaps best revealed in the meat-packing industry. With the opening of the Union Stock Yards in 1865, Chicago became the cattle market for the country. Livestock came in by rail from the Great Plains, was auctioned off at the Chicago stockyards, and then shipped to eastern cities, where, as before, the cattle were slaughtered in local "butchertowns" (Map 17.3). Such an arrangement—a national livestock market but with its processing still local—adequately met the needs of an exploding urban population and could have done so indefinitely. In Europe no further development ever did occur.

Gustavus F. Swift, a shrewd Chicago cattle dealer from Massachusetts, saw the future differently. He recognized that livestock lost weight en route to the East and that local slaughterhouses lacked the scale to utilize waste by-products or cut labor costs. If it could be kept fresh in transit, however, dressed beef could be processed in bulk at the Chicago stockyards. Once his engineers developed an effective cooling system, Swift invested in a fleet of refrigerator cars and constructed a central beef-packing plant next to Chicago stockyards.

This was only the beginning of Swift's innovations. No refrigerated warehouses existed in the cities that received his chilled beef, so Swift built his own network of branch houses. Next he acquired a fleet of wagons to distribute his products to retail butcher shops. Swift constructed additional facilities to process the fertilizer, chemicals, and other usable by-products from his slaughtering operations. He also began to handle other perishable commodities to fully utilize his refrigerated cars and branch houses. As demand grew Swift built

Jay Gould: Robber Baron?

Jay Gould, c. 1882
Culver Pictures.

Jay Gould was an operator pure and simple. . . . It would be at least very difficult to show that the Nation as a whole is a dollar richer by the existence of JAY GOULD, while he himself has become the richer . . . from the expansion of the city and the Nation. He has simply absorbed what would have been made in spite of him.

Thus did the *New York Times* bid farewell to Jay Gould at his death on December 3, 1892. There was a name for the kind of businessman the *Times* thought Gould was: robber baron. In the Middle Ages the term described renegade knights who exacted tribute from all who passed by; by extension to Gould's time, robber baron referred to capitalists who extracted riches from the economic system while contributing nothing in return. By that definition was Gould a robber baron? Yes, said historians for many years, following the thesis first advanced by Matthew Josephson in his book *The Robber Barons* (1934). Today historians are no longer so sure.

Jay Gould was born on May 27, 1836, in Roxbury, New York, in the mountainous Catskill region. John Gould wanted Jay, his only son, to take over the family farm, but the boy was small and sickly, and he detested farmwork. By sheer tenacity Jay got more education than most farm boys, but even tenacity could not get him to Yale, which had been his dream. At sixteen he became a surveyor, at nineteen he wrote a flowery history of Delaware County for the money, and then at twenty he got a big break. An eccentric but wealthy tanner, Zadock Pratt, befriended Gould, taking him as a partner to set up a tannery in Pennsylvania, where Gould had located a rich new source of tanning bark. The venture succeeded thanks to Pratt's money and Gould's hard work, but after two years there was a falling-out and Pratt proposed terminating the partnership. He would buy Gould's share for $10,000 or sell out to the young man for $60,000. Gould found backers among the leather merchants who marketed the tannery's output and bought out the surprised Pratt. This was a typical Gould maneuver—bold, unexpected, and decisive. The new partnership quickly turned sour, primarily because of the collapse of the leather market. The damage to

well-reputed merchants left Gould discredited in the leather trade. He had made money amid the wreckage of other people's fortunes, another Gould trademark. In 1860 he settled in New York, bent on satisfying what had become his obsession: he wanted to be rich.

Enlisting in the Union army probably never occurred to him. The Civil War was too good a chance for turning quick profits; and besides, Gould had no taste for fighting. In 1863 he married the daughter of a wealthy New York merchant, sired six children in rapid succession, and became a devoted family man. These were, above all, schooling years for Gould. He learned about the railroads from a controlling interest he gained in a small Vermont railroad. And—no one knows exactly how—he developed a consummate mastery of Wall Street finance. Few could have been aware of this when Gould was elected in 1867 to the board of the Erie Railroad just as a titanic battle was taking shape for control of the Erie.

The aggressor was Cornelius Vanderbilt, who wanted to ally the Erie with his emerging New York

Central system. Vanderbilt began secretly buying up Erie stock, a maneuver by which he had captured other key railroad properties. This time, however, Erie stock mysteriously kept entering the market even though no more could legally be issued by the Erie. Gould was exploiting a dubious loophole: freshly minted convertible bonds that could immediately be converted to stock. Vanderbilt countered with court injunctions, forcing Gould and his confederates to decamp to New Jersey, while in Albany Vanderbilt lobbied to prevent legalization of the convertible-bond gambit. A bidding war began for legislators' votes, which, with the Erie dollars overflowing his satchel, Gould finally won. To settle things, Vanderbilt and his allies had to be compensated for their losses, which Gould ingeniously arranged by spending $9 million from the Erie treasury to buy back their stock at inflated prices. The Erie was effectively bankrupted, but it was now firmly in Gould's hands.

Gould was never able to shed the unsavory reputation he acquired during the Erie years. But even in that buccaneering period, there was another side to him as a railroad man. Indifferent to day-to-day operations, Gould had a brilliant strategic sense for how railroads should grow. The key, he knew, was integrated development, with trunk-line service between major centers. Right off Gould moved to take over the local western roads and make the Erie the dominant system linking the Atlantic seaboard and the Midwest. But he lacked the resources, and the Pennsylvania and the New York Central, spurred by his challenge, beat him out, capturing the key western lines and leaving the Erie a weak secondary system.

Yet the vision had been Gould's, and in 1879 he found greener fields for his strategic talents west of St. Louis and southward into Texas. The railroads in this region were a jumble of incomplete and disconnected lines. Gould began buying control, finishing the lines, and linking them into a regional system under his parent company, the Missouri Pacific. He also moved aggressively in other parts of the country, challenging established railroads and cutting rates ruthlessly to take traffic from them. By 1882 he controlled 15 percent of the nation's entire trackage, and Western Union and the New York Elevated besides.

The economic boom that fostered this empire building did not last, however, and after 1881 Gould found himself on the wrong side of the stock market, overextended in holdings that were falling in value. On the verge of ruin in early 1884, he managed to get a "corner" on the stock of the Missouri Pacific, forcing up its price and thus saving himself. But Gould was not the same man after that. He lost his iron nerve, and his health began to fail. He swore off speculation. His business dealings, while still far-flung, became more cautious and defensive. But to the end he remained a tough

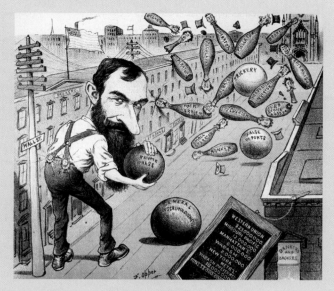

Wall Street: Gould's Private Bowling Alley
This 1882 cartoon testifies vividly to Gould's unsavory reputation as a financial manipulator, bowling over his adversaries with Trickery and False Reports and keeping score of his ill-gotten gains on the slate at lower right. Granger Collection.

customer, never justifying himself, never cloaking himself in religious piety, not even seeking to make amends by a show of philanthropy. In death he thumbed his nose at the world: his entire fortune—$75 million—went in trust to his family.

A century later historians can perhaps appreciate better than Gould's obituarists the positive side of Gould's amazing business career. The nation's railroad network bore in some considerable degree Gould's mark by virtue of his own system building and by virtue of the spur he gave to others. Moreover, his forays broke open monopoly markets and drove shipping prices down. Even Gould's purely speculative ventures may have contributed to the nation's economic growth. Economists say that money made in speculation is an especially efficient source of fresh capital, which is what Gould's winnings were to America's capital-hungry railroads.

Let us suppose that Gould never understood this. Let us grant further that he was motivated by greed, that his methods were unscrupulous, and that, had he lived at a later time, he probably would have ended up in prison. Are we justified in calling him a robber baron?

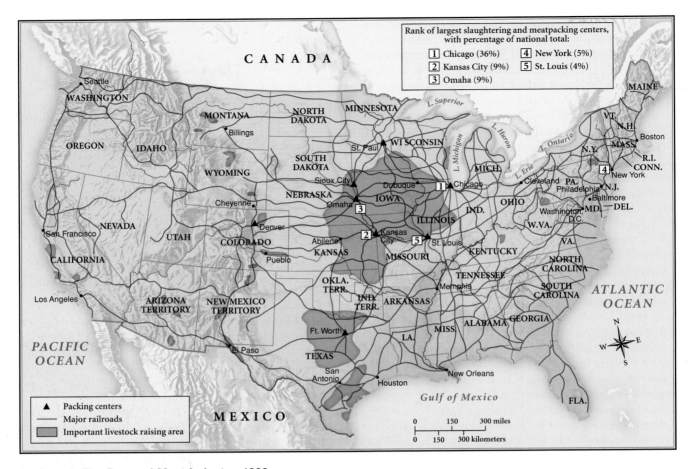

MAP 17.3 The Dressed Meat Industry, 1900

The meatpacking industry clearly shows how transportation, supply, and demand combined to foster the growth of the American industrial economy. The main centers of beef production in 1900—Chicago, Omaha, Kansas City, and St. Louis—were rail hubs with connections westward to the cattle regions and eastward to cities hungry for cheap supplies of meat. Vertically integrated enterprises sprang from these elements, linked together by an efficient and comprehensive railroad network.

For more help analyzing this map, see the ONLINE STUDY GUIDE at
bedfordstmartins.com/henretta.

more packing houses in other stockyard centers, including Kansas City, Fort Worth, and Omaha.

Step by step Swift created a new kind of enterprise—a national company capable of handling within its own structure all the functions of an industry. Swift & Co. pioneered **vertical integration**, by absorbing the activities of many small, specialized enterprises within a single national structure. Swift's lead was followed by several big Chicago packers already operating plants that preserved pork products. By 1900 five firms, all of them nationally organized and vertically integrated, produced nearly 90 percent of the meat shipped in interstate commerce.

The Birth of Mass Marketing. In most fields no single innovation was as decisive as Swift's refrigerator

car. But others did share Swift's insight that the essential step was to identify a mass market and then develop a national enterprise capable of serving it. In the petroleum industry John D. Rockefeller built the Standard Oil Company partly by taking over rival firms, but he also built a distribution system to reach the enormous market for kerosene for lighting and heating homes. The Singer Sewing Machine Company formed its own sales organization, using both retail stores and door-to-door salesmen. Through such distribution systems manufacturers were able also to provide technical information, credit, and repair facilities. Like the meat packers these companies became vertically integrated firms that served a national market.

Americans were ready consumers of standardized, mass-marketed goods. Because they were geographically mobile, they lost the local loyalties that were so strong in Europe. Social class in America, though by no means absent, was blurred at the edges and did not, for example, call for class-specific ways of dressing. Foreign visitors often noted that ready-made clothing made it difficult to tell salesgirls from debutantes on city streets.

To gain the benefits of mass distribution, retail business went through comparable changes. Montgomery Ward and Sears, Roebuck developed into national mail-order houses for rural consumers. From Vermont to California, farm families selected identical goods from catalogues and became part of the nationwide consumer market. Department stores, a form of retailing pioneered by John Wanamaker in Philadelphia in 1875, spread to every large city. An alternative route to urban distribution was through chain stores, which was the strategy of the Great Atlantic and Pacific Tea Company (A&P) and the F. W. Woolworth Company.

The American consumer's receptivity to standardized goods should not be exaggerated. Gustavus Swift, for example, encountered great resistance to his Chicago beef. How could it be wholesome weeks later in Boston or Philadelphia? Cheap prices helped, but advertising mattered more. Modern advertising was born in the late nineteenth century, bringing brand names and a billboard-cluttered urban landscape. By 1900 companies were spending over $90 million a year for space in newspapers and magazines. Advertisements urged readers to bathe with Pears' soap, eat Uneeda biscuits, sew on a Singer machine, and snap pictures with a Kodak camera. The active molding of demand for brand names became a major function of American business.

The New South

"Shall we dethrone our idols?" Southerners had to ask themselves that question as they observed the burst of economic activity in the North. For many, the answer was a resounding yes. Advocates of economic development argued that nostalgia for the Old South, with its leisurely plantation ways, had to be put aside. Led by Henry W. Grady, editor of the Atlanta *Constitution*, they made "the practical wisdom of businessmen" the credo of a New South.

Catching up with the North was no easy task. The slave economy had impeded industrial development. The Old South had few cities, a primitive distribution system, and not much manufacturing. This modest infrastructure, wrecked by the Civil War, was quickly restored. After Reconstruction a railroad boom developed. Track mileage doubled in the next decade, and at least by that measure, the South became nearly competitive with the rest of the country (Map 17.4).

But the South remained overwhelmingly agricultural. Farming and poverty are not necessarily linked, but in the South they were. The share-crop system re-

Kellogg's Toasted Corn Flakes
Like crackers, sugar, and other nonperishable products, cereal had been traditionally sold to consumers in bulk from barrels. In the 1880s the Quaker Oats Company hit on the idea of selling oatmeal in boxes of standard size and weight. A further wrinkle was to process the cereal so that it could be consumed right from the box (with milk) for breakfast. And lo and behold: Kellogg's Corn Flakes! This is one of Kellogg's earliest advertisements.
Picture Research Consultants & Archives.

For more help analyzing this image, see the ONLINE STUDY GUIDE at bedfordstmartins.com/henretta.

quired a cash crop (see Chapter 15), committing the South to cotton despite soil depletion, low productivity, and unprofitable prices. At a time of rapid advances in northern agriculture, cotton growing still relied on the mule, the plow, and the hoe. Wages for southern farm labor fell steadily, down to roughly 75 cents a day by the 1890s.

Southern Industry. From this low agricultural wage, surprisingly, sprang the South's hopes for industrialization. Consider, for example, how southern textile mills got started in the Piedmont country of North and

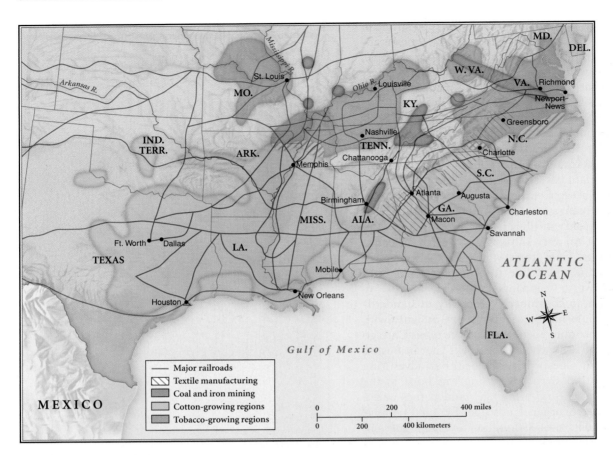

MAP 17.4 The New South, 1900

The economy of the Old South focused on raising staple crops, especially cotton and to-bacco. In the New South staple agriculture continued to dominate, but there was marked industrial development as well. Industrial regions developed, producing textiles, coal and iron, and wood products. By 1900 the South's industrial pattern was well defined.

South Carolina and Georgia in the mid-1870s. The mills recruited workers from the surrounding hill farms, where people struggled to make ends meet. To attract them mill wages had to exceed farm earnings but not by much. Paying rock-bottom wages the new mills had a competitive advantage over the long-established New England industry—as much as 40 percent in labor costs in 1897.

The labor system that evolved was based on hiring whole families. "Papa decided he would come because he didn't have nothing much but girls and they had to get out and work like men," recalled one woman. It was not Papa, in fact, but his girls whom the mills wanted, to work as spinners and loom tenders. Only they could not be recruited individually: no right-thinking parent would have permitted that. Hiring by families, on the other hand, was already familiar; after all everyone had been expected to work on the farm. So the family system of mill labor developed, with a labor force that was half female and very young. In the 1880s a quarter of all southern textile workers were under fifteen years of age.

The hours were long—twelve hours a day—but life in the mill villages was, in the words of one historian, "like a family." Employers tended to be paternalistic, providing company housing and a variety of services. The mill workers built close-knit, supportive communities, but for whites only. Although blacks sometimes worked as day laborers and janitors, they hardly ever got jobs as operatives in the cotton mills.

Cheap, abundant labor might have been termed the South's most valuable natural resource. But the region was blessed with other resources as well. From its rich soil came tobacco, the South's second cash crop. When cigarettes became fashionable in the 1880s, the young North Carolina entrepreneur James B. Duke seized the new market by taking advantage of a southern invention—James A. Bonsack's machine for producing cigarettes automatically. Blacks stemmed and stripped the leaf as they always had, but Duke followed the textile example and restricted machine tending to white women.

Lumbering, by contrast, was racially integrated, with a labor force evenly divided between black and

Houston's Cotton Depot

After the Civil War cotton-raising blossomed on the virgin lands of east Texas, and Houston simultaneously blossomed as the region's commercial center. This photograph from the 1890s reveals the tremendous volume of traffic that came through Houston as Texas cotton was unloaded and transshipped to be made into cloth in the mills of the Southeast and across the ocean in Britain.

Houston Public Library, Houston Metropolitan Research Center.

white men. Cutting down the South's pine forests was a growth business in these years. Alabama's coal and iron ore deposits also attracted investors; by 1890 the Birmingham district was producing nearly a million tons of iron and steel annually.

Economic Retardation. Despite the South's high hopes, this burst of industrial development did not lift the region out of poverty. In 1900 two-thirds of all southerners made their living from the soil, just as they had in 1870. Moreover the industries that did develop produced raw materials (forestry and mining) or engaged in the low-tech processing of coarse products. Industry by industry, the key statistic—the value added by manufacturing—showed the South lagging behind the North.

Southerners tended to blame the North: the South was a "colonial" economy controlled by New York and Chicago. There was some truth to this charge. Much of the capital—by no means all—did come from the North. And the integrating processes of the economy did subordinate regional to national interests. When the railway network moved to a uniform gauge in 1886, the southern railroads converted to the northern standard.

Northern firms did not hesitate to use their muscle to maintain the interregional status quo. Railroads, for example, manipulated freight rates so that it was cheap for southern cotton and timber to flow out and for northern manufactured goods to flow in.

Yet in the end the South's economic backwardness was mostly of its own making. The crowning irony was that the great advantage of the South—its cheap labor—also kept it from becoming a more technologically advanced economy. First, low wages discouraged employers from replacing workers with machinery. Second, low wages attracted labor-intensive industry, such as textiles. Third, a cheap labor market inhibited investment in education because of the likelihood that better-educated workers would flee to higher-wage markets.

What distinguished the southern labor market was that it was insulated from the rest of the country. Northern workers and European immigrants steered clear of the South because wages were too low and attractive jobs too scarce. Harder to explain is why so few southerners, black or white, left for the higher-wage North prior to World War I. At its core the explanation is that the South was a place apart, with social and racial mores that discouraged all but the most resourceful

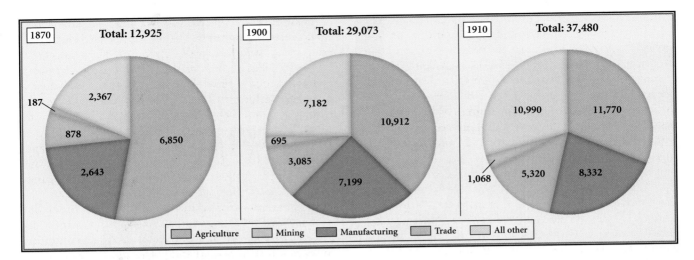

FIGURE 17.2 Changes in the Labor Force, 1870–1910

*The numbers represent thousands of people (for example, 12,925 = 12,925,000 workers).
They reveal both the enormous increase in the labor force between 1870 and 1910 and the
dramatic shift from agriculture to industry and other nonagricultural jobs.*

from seeking opportunity elsewhere. The result was that a normal flow of workers back and forth did not occur, and wage differentials did not narrow. So long as this isolation persisted, the South would remain a tributary economy, a supplier on unequal terms to the advanced industrial heartland of the North.

The World of Work

In a free-enterprise system, profit drives the entrepreneur. But the industrial order is not populated only by profit makers. It includes—in vastly larger numbers—wage earners. Economic change always affects working people but never so drastically as it did in the late nineteenth century.

Labor Recruits

Industrialism invariably set people in motion. Farm folk migrated to cities. Artisans entered factories. An industrial labor force emerged. This happened in the United States just as it did in Europe but with a difference: the United States did not rely primarily on its own population for a supply of workers.

The demand for labor was ravenous, tripling between 1870 and 1900 (Figure 17.2). Rural Americans were highly mobile in the late nineteenth century, and of those who moved, half ended up in cities. But the higher-paid jobs—puddlers, rollers, molders, machinists—required industrial skills not held by rural Americans. Except in the South, moreover, native-born whites

mostly rejected factory work. They had a basic education, they could read and calculate, and they understood American ways of doing things. City-bound white Americans found their opportunities in the multiplying white-collar jobs in offices and retail stores.

Modest numbers of blacks began to migrate out of the South—roughly 80,000 between 1870 and 1890 and another 200,000 between 1890 and 1910. Most of them settled in cities, but men were restricted to casual labor and janitorial work, while women were restricted to domestic service. Employers turned black applicants away from the factory gates—and away from their one best chance for a fair shake at American opportunity—because immigrant workers already supplied companies with as much cheap labor as they needed.

Immigrant Workers. The great migration from the Old World started in the 1840s, when over a million Irish fled the potato famine. In the following years, as European agriculture became increasingly commercialized, the peasant economies began to fail, first in Germany and Scandinavia and then, later in the nineteenth century, across Austria-Hungary, Russia, Italy, and the Balkans. This upheaval set off a great migration of Europeans, some of them going to Europe's own industrial centers, others heading for South America and Australia, but most coming to the United States.

Ethnic origin largely determined the work the immigrants took in America. Seeking the jobs in which they were already experienced, the Welsh labored as tinplate workers, the English as miners, the Germans as machinists and traditional artisans (for example, bakers and carpenters), the Belgians as glass workers, and

Scandinavians as seamen on Great Lakes boats. For common labor employers had long counted on the brawn of Irish rural immigrants, although all emigrating groups contributed to the pool of unskilled workers.

As technology advanced American employers needed fewer European craftsmen, while the demand for ordinary labor skyrocketed. The sources of immigration began to shift, and by the early twentieth century arrivals from southern and eastern Europe far outstripped immigration from western Europe (Figure 17.3). Italian and Slavic immigrants without industrial skills flooded into American factories. Heavy, low-paid labor became the domain of the recent immigrants (see Voices from Abroad, "Count Vay de Vaya und Luskod: Pittsburgh Inferno," p. 503). Blast-furnace jobs, a job-seeking investigator heard, were "Hunky work," not suitable for him or any other American. The derogatory term *Hunky* refers to Hungarian workers, but it was applied indiscriminately to Poles, Slovaks, and all other Slavic groups arriving in America's industrial districts.

Not only skill determined where immigrants ended up in American industry. The newcomers, although generally not traveling in groups, moved within well-defined networks, following relatives or fellow villagers already in America and relying on them to land a job. A high degree of ethnic clustering resulted, even within a single factory. At the Jones and Laughlin steel works in Pittsburgh, for example, the carpentry shop was German, the hammer shop Polish, and the blooming mill Serbian. Immigrants also had different job preferences. Men from Italy, for instance, liked outdoor work, often laboring in gangs under a *padrone* (boss), much as they had in Italy.

Immigrants entered a modern industrial order, but it was not a world they wanted. They were peasants, displaced by the breakdown of traditional rural economies. Many had lost their land and fallen into the class of dependent, propertyless servants. They could escape that bitter fate only if they had money to buy property. In Europe job-seeking peasants commonly tried seasonal agricultural labor or temporary work in nearby cities. America represented merely a larger leap, made possible by cheap and speedy steamships across the Atlantic. The peasant immigrants, most of them young and male, never intended to stay permanently. About half did return, departing in great numbers during depression years. No one knows how many left because they had saved enough and how many left for lack of work. For their American employers it scarcely mattered. What did matter was that the immigrants took the worst jobs and were always available when they were wanted. For the new industrial order, they made an ideal labor supply.

Working Women and the Family Economy.

Over four million women worked for wages in 1900. Representing a quarter of the nonfarm labor force, they played a vital part in the industrial economy. The opportunities they found were shaped by gender—by the fact that they were women. Contemporary beliefs about womanhood largely determined which women took jobs and how they were treated once they became wage earners.

Wives were not supposed to work outside the home, and in fact fewer than 5 percent did so in 1890. Only among African Americans did many married women—above 30 percent—work for wages. Among whites the typical working woman at that time was under twenty-four and unmarried. When older women worked, remarked one observer, it "was usually a sign that something had gone wrong"—their husbands had died, deserted them, or lost their jobs.

Since women were held to be inherently different from men, it followed that they not be permitted to do "men's work." Nor, regardless of their skills, could they be paid a man's wage. The dominant view was that a woman did not require a "living wage" because, as one investigator

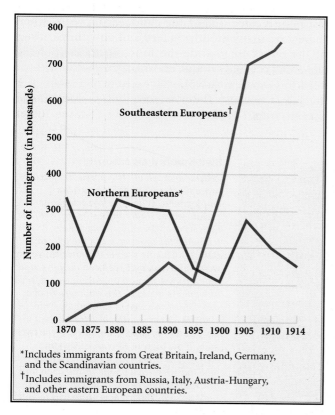

*Includes immigrants from Great Britain, Ireland, Germany, and the Scandinavian countries.

†Includes immigrants from Russia, Italy, Austria-Hungary, and other eastern European countries.

FIGURE 17.3 American Immigration, 1870–1914

This graph shows the surge of European immigration in the late nineteenth century. While northern Europe continued to send substantial numbers, it was overshadowed after 1895 by southern Europeans pouring into America to work in mines and factories. (See Map 19.3, Sources of European Immigration to the United States, 1871–1910, on p. 558.)

reported, "it is expected that she has men to support her." The occupation that served as the baseline for all women's jobs was domestic service, which was always very poorly paid or, in a woman's own home, not paid at all.

At the turn of the century, women's work fell into three categories. A third worked as domestic servants. Another third held "female" white-collar jobs in teaching, nursing, sales, and office work. The remaining third worked in industry, most heavily concentrated in the garment trades and textile mills, but present also in many other industries as inspectors, packers, assemblers and other "light" occupations. Few worked as supervisors, fewer in the crafts, and nearly none as day laborers.

Just how jobs came to be defined as male or female—in sociological lingo, the **sex typing** of occupations—is not easy to explain. Jobs as telephone operator and store clerk, originally male, had by the 1890s become female. Once women dominated an occupation, people came to think of it as having feminine attributes, even though very similar or even identical work elsewhere was done by men. Jobs identified as women's work became unsuitable for men. There were no male telephone operators by 1900.

Sex typing was justified by the sentimental view of women as the weaker sex, but powerful male interest also played a role. Craft workers protected their male domain, and employers profited from cut-rate work. Wherever they worked women earned less than the lowest paid males. At the turn of the century, the weekly wage of women factory workers came to roughly $7, $3 less than that of unskilled men and $5 below the average of all industrial workers.

As with male workers, ethnicity and race played a big part in the distribution of women's jobs. Exclusion from all but the most menial jobs applied as rigidly to black women as it did to black men. White-collar jobs were reserved for native-born women, which in the cities increasingly included the second-generation daughters of immigrants. And as with men, ethnicity created clustering patterns in women's jobs or, in the case of Italians, restricted them to sewing or other subcontracted tasks that could be done at home.

Disapproval of wives taking paying jobs, though expressed in sentimental and moral terms, was based on solid necessity. Cooking, cleaning, and tending the children were not income producing or reckoned in terms of money. But everyone knew that the family household could not function without the wife's contribution. Therefore, her place was in the home.

Working-class families, however, found the going hard on a single income. Only among highly skilled workers, wrote one investigator, "was it possible for the husband unaided to support his family." The rockiest period came during the childbearing years, when there were many mouths to feed and only the earnings of the father to provide the food. Thereafter, as the children grew old enough to work, the family income began to increase. Not only unmarried sons and daughters but also the younger children contributed their share. In 1900 one of every five children under

Switchboard Operators

Telephone work offers a prime historical example of sex typing in American employment. When the first telephone exchange was set up in Boston in 1878, the lines were operated by teenage boys, following the practice set in the telegraph industry. During the 1880s, however, young women increasingly replaced the boys, and by 1900 switchboard operation was defined as women's work. In this photograph of a telephone exchange in Columbus, Ohio, in 1907, the older woman at left has risen to the position of supervisor, but it is the two men in the picture who are clearly in charge. The other major occupations in this new industry—telephone installation and line maintenance—were just as strictly male as switchboard operation was female but of course on a higher pay scale.
Corbis-Bettmann.

Breaker Boys

In the anthracite districts of eastern Pennsylvania, giant machines called "breakers" processed the coal as it came out of the mines, crushing it and sorting it by size for sale as domestic fuel. The boys shown in this photograph had the job of picking out the slate and refuse as the processed coal came down the chutes, working long hours in a constant cloud of coal dust for less than a dollar a day. Breaker boy was the first job, often begun before the age of ten, in a lifetime in the mines. The photograph does not show any old men, but sick and disabled miners often ended their careers as breaker boys—hence the saying among coal diggers, "Twice a boy and once a man is the poor miner's life." Library of Congress.

sixteen worked. "When the people own houses," remarked a printer from Fall River, Massachusetts, "you will generally find that it is a large family all working together."

By the 1890s all the northern industrial states had passed laws prohibiting child labor and regulating work hours for teenagers. Most of these states also required children under fourteen to attend school for a certain number of weeks each year. Working-class families continued to need more than one income, but this money came increasingly from the wives. After 1890 the proportion of working married women crept steadily upward. About a fifth of the wives of unskilled and semiskilled men in Chicago held jobs in 1920. Wage-earning wives

and mothers were on their way to becoming a primary part of America's labor force.

Autonomous Labor

No one supervised the nineteenth-century coal miner (see American Voices, "John Brophy: A Miner's Son," p. 504). He was a tonnage worker who was paid for the amount of coal he produced. He provided his own tools, worked at his own pace, and knocked off early when he chose. Such autonomous craft workers—almost all of them men—flourished in many branches of nineteenth-century industry. They were mule spinners in cotton mills; puddlers and rollers in iron works; molders in stove making; and machinists, glass blowers, and skilled workers in many other industries.

In the shop they abided by the stint, a self-imposed limit on how much they would produce each day. This informal system of restricting output infuriated efficiency-minded engineers. But to the worker it signified personal dignity and "unselfish brotherhood" with fellow employees. The male craft worker took pride in a "manly" bearing, toward both his fellows and the boss. One day a shop in Lowell, Massachusetts, posted regulations requiring all employees to be at their posts in work clothes at the opening bell and to remain, with the shop door locked, until the dismissal bell. A machinist promptly packed his tools, declaring that he had not "been brought up under such a system of slavery."

Underlying this ethical code was a keen sense of the craft, each with its own history and customs. Hat finishers—masters of the art of applying fur felting to top hats and bowlers—had a language of their own. When a hatter was hired, he was "shopped"; if fired, he was "bagged"; when he quit work, he "cried off"; and when he took an apprentice, the boy was "under teach." The hatters, most of whom worked in Danbury, Connecticut, or Orange, New Jersey, formed a distinctive, self-contained community.

Women workers found much the same kind of social meaning in their jobs. Department store clerks, for example, developed a work culture and language just as robust as that of any male craft group. The most important fact about wage-earning women, however, was their youth. For many the first job was a chance to be independent, to form friendships with other young women, and to experience, however briefly, a fun-loving time of nice clothes, dancing, and other "cheap amusements." Young male workers, by contrast, underwent a process of job socialization presided over by seasoned, older coworkers. Being young mattered to male workers, certainly, but did not define work experience for them as it did for women.

Ironworkers—Noontime
The qualities of the nineteenth-century craft worker—dignity, "unselfish brotherhood," a "manly" bearing—shine through in this painting by Thomas P. Anschutz. Ironworkers—Noontime *became a popular painting when it was reproduced as an engraving in* Harper's Weekly *in 1884.* Fine Arts Museum of San Francisco.

To some degree their youthful preoccupations made it easier for working women to accept the miserable terms under which they labored. But this did not mean that they lacked a sense of solidarity or self-respect. A pretty dress might appear frivolous to the casual observer, but also conveyed the message that the working girl considered herself as good as anyone. Rebellious youth culture sometimes united with job grievances to produce astonishing strike movements, as demonstrated, for example, by the Jewish garment workers of New York and the Irish-American telephone operators of Boston.

Rarely, however, did women workers wield the kind of craft power that the skilled male worker commonly enjoyed. He hired his own helpers, supervised their work, and paid them from his earnings. In the late nineteenth century, when increasingly sophisticated production called for closer shop-floor supervision, many factory managers deliberately shifted this responsibility to craft workers. In metal-fabricating firms that did precise machining and complex assembling, a system of inside contracting developed in which skilled employees bid for a production run, taking full responsibility for the operation, paying their crew and pocketing the profits.

Dispersal of authority was characteristic of nineteenth-century industry. The aristocracy of the workers—the craftsmen, inside contractors, and foremen—enjoyed a high degree of autonomy. However, their subordinates often paid dearly for that independence. Any worker who paid his helpers from his own pocket might be tempted to exploit them. In the Pittsburgh area foremen were known as "pushers," notorious for driving their gangs mercilessly. On the other hand industrial labor in the nineteenth century remained on a human scale. People dealt with each other face to face, often developing cohesive ties within the shop. Striking craft workers commonly received the support of helpers and laborers, and labor gangs sometimes walked out on behalf of a popular foreman.

Systems of Control

As technology advanced, workers increasingly lost the proud independence characteristic of nineteenth-century craft work. One cause of this deskilling process was a new system of production—Henry Ford called it "**mass production**"—that lent itself to mechanization. Agricultural implements, typewriters, bicycles, and,

Count Vay de Vaya und Luskod

Pittsburgh Inferno

Count Vay de Vaya und Luskod, a Hungarian nobleman and high functionary in the Catholic Church, crossed the United States several times between 1903 and 1906 en route to his post as the Vatican's representative to Asia. In a book about his travels, he expresses his distress at the plight of his countrymen laboring in the mills of the Pittsburgh steel district.

The bells are tolling for a funeral. The modest train of mourners is just setting out for the little churchyard on the hill. Everything is shrouded in gloom, even the coffin lying upon the bier and the people who stand on each side in threadbare clothes and with heads bent. Such is my sad reception at the Hungarian working-men's colony at McKeesport. Everyone who has been in the United States has heard of this famous town, and of Pittsburgh, its close neighbor. . . .

Fourteen-thousand tall chimneys are silhouetted against the sky . . . discharg[ing] their burning sparks and smok[ing] incessantly. The realms of Vulcan could not be more somber or filthy than this valley of the Monongahela. On every hand are burning fires and spurting flames. Nothing is visible save the forging of iron and the smelting of metal. . . .

And this fearful place affects us very closely, for thousands of immigrants wander here from year to year. Here they fondly seek the realization of their cherished hopes, and here they suffer till they are swallowed up by the inferno. He whom we are now burying is the latest victim. Yesterday he was in full vigor and at work at the foundry, toiling, struggling, hoping—a chain broke, and he was killed. . . .

This is scarcely work for mankind. Americans will hardly take anything of the sort; only [the immigrant] rendered desperate by circumstances . . . and thus he is at the mercy of the tyrannous Trust, which gathers him into its clutches and transforms him into a regular slave.

This is one of the saddest features of the Hungarian emigration. In making a tour of these prisons, wherever the heat is most insupportable, the flames most scorching, the smoke and soot most choking, there we are certain to find compatriots bent and wasted with toil. Their thin, wrinkled, wan faces seem to show that in America the newcomers are of no use except to help fill the moneybags of the insatiable millionaires. . . . In this realm of Mammon and Moloch everything has a value—except human life. . . . Why? Because human life is a commodity the supply of which exceeds the demand. There are always fresh recruits to supply the place of those who have fallen in battle; and the steamships are constantly arriving at the neighboring ports, discharging their living human cargo still further to swell the phalanx of the instruments of cupidity.

Source: Oscar Handlin, ed., *This Was America* (Cambridge, MA: Harvard University Press, 1949), 407–10.

---

after 1900, automobiles were assembled from standardized parts. The machine tools that cut, drilled, and ground these metal parts were originally operated by skilled machinists. But because they produced long runs of a single item, these machine tools became more specialized; they became *dedicated* machines—machines set up to do the same job over and over—and the need for skilled operatives disappeared. In the manufacture of sewing machines, one machinist complained in 1883, "the trade is so subdivided that a man is not considered a machinist at all. One man may make just a particular part of a machine and may not know anything whatever about another part of the same machine." Such a worker, noted an observer, "cannot be master of a craft, but only master of a fragment."

Employers were attracted to automatic machinery because it increased output; the impact on workers was not uppermost in their minds. Employers recognized that mechanization made it easier to control workers, but that was only an incidental benefit. Gradually, however, the idea took hold that managing workers might itself be a way to reduce the cost of production.

The pioneer in this field was Frederick W. Taylor. An expert on metal-cutting methods, Taylor believed that the engineer's approach might be applied to managing workers, hence the name for his method: **scientific management**. To get the maximum work from the individual worker, Taylor suggested two basic reforms. The first would eliminate the brain work from manual labor. Managers would assume "the burden of

John Brophy

A Miner's Son

John Brophy (1883–1963), an important mine union official, recalls in an oral history what mining was like in his boyhood, a time when mining was strictly pick-and-shovel work and machinery had not yet eroded the prized skills of the miner.

I got a thrill at the thought of having an opportunity to go and work in the mine, to go and work along side my father. After . . . I got experience and some strength, and the ability to work with a little skill, I was conscious of the fact that my father was a good workman; that he had pride in his calling. . . . It was a great satisfaction to me that my father was a skilled, clean workman with everything kept in shape, and the timbering done well—all of these things: the rib side, the roadway, the timbering, the fact that you kept the loose coal clean rather than cluttered all over the workplace, the skill with which you undercut the vein, the judgment in drilling the coal after it had been undercut and placing the exact amount of explosive so that it would do an effective job of breaking the coal from the solid—indicated the quality of his work. . . .

It was skill in handling the pick and the shovel, the placing of timbers, and understanding the vagaries of the workplace—which is subject to certain pressures from the overhanging strata as you advance into the seam. It's an awareness of roof conditions. And it's something else too. Under the older conditions of mining under which I went to work with my father, the miner exercised considerable freedom in his working place in determining his pace of work and the selection of the order of time in the different work operations. Judgment was everywhere along the line, and there was also necessary skill. It was the feel of all this. You know that another workman in another place was a good miner, a passable miner, or an indifferent one. . . . I think that was one of the great satisfactions that

a miner had—that he was his own boss within his workplace. . . .

The miner is always aware of danger, that he lives under dangerous conditions in the workplace, because he's constantly uncovering new conditions as he advances in the workingplace, exposing new areas of roof, discovering some weakened condition or break which may bring some special danger. There is also the danger that comes from a piece of coal slipping off the fast and falling on the worker as he lays prone on the bottom doing his cutting. The worker has got to be aware of all these conditions that may be in the coal, that may be in the roof. . . .

Then there is the further fact that the miners by and large lived in purely mining communities which were often isolated. They developed a group loyalty under all these circumstances. They were both individualists and they were group conscious. . . . It made them an extraordinary body of workers, these miners, because of these very special conditions, because involved in it was not only earning a living, but a matter of health and safety, life and death were involved in every way. You find time and again miners, in an effort to rescue their fellow workers, taking chances which quite often meant death for themselves. . . .

Along with that is a sense of justice. There was the very fact the miner was a tonnage worker and that he could be short weighed and cheated in various ways, and that the only safeguard against it was [union] organization. In that case it was important to have a representative of the miners to see that the weight was properly done and properly credited to the individual miner. There was the whole complex of circumstances that had been in the mining industry for generations which had been their experience. The miner in my day in the United States was aware that all knowledge didn't start with his generation. . . . At least on one side of my family there are at least four generations of [British] miners, and I say this with a sense of pride; very much so. I'm very proud of the fact that there is this long tradition of miners who have struggled with the elements.

Source: Jerold S. Auerbach, ed., *American Labor: The Twentieth Century* (Indianapolis: Bobbs-Merrill, 1969), 44–48.

gathering together all of the traditional knowledge which in the past has been possessed by the workmen and then of classifying, tabulating, and reducing this knowledge to rules, laws, and formulae." The second reform, a logical consequence of the first, would deprive

workers of the authority they had exercised on the shop floor. Workers would "do what they are told promptly and without asking questions or making suggestions. . . . The duty of enforcing . . . rests with the management alone."

The Killing Floor
To the modern eye the labor process depicted in this 1882 engraving of a Chicago meatpacking plant seems primitive and inefficient, but it contains the seeds of America's mass-production revolution. At the far left the steer has already been stunned by one specialist, killed by a second, and attached to a chain that will lift it onto the overhead conveyor. The division of labor is already in place (each of the workers on the line does a single repetitive task), and the process is continuous. It would be only a small step from the killing floors of the Chicago packing plants to Henry Ford's assembly line. Library of Congress.

Once managers had the knowledge and the power, they would put labor on a "scientific" basis. This meant subjecting each task to **time-and-motion study** by an engineer who would analyze and time each job with a stopwatch. Workers would be paid at a differential rate—that is, a certain amount if they met the stopwatch standard and a higher rate for additional output. Taylor claimed that his techniques would guarantee optimum worker efficiency. His assumption was that only money mattered to workers and that they would automatically respond to the lure of higher earnings.

Scientific management was not, in practice, a roaring success. Implementing it proved to be very expensive, and workers stubbornly resisted the job-analysis method. "It looks to me like slavery to have a man stand over you with a stopwatch," complained one iron molder. A union leader insisted that "this system is wrong, because we want our heads left on us." Far from solving the labor problem, as Taylor claimed it would, scientific management embittered relations on the shop floor.

Yet Taylor achieved something of fundamental importance. He was a brilliant publicist, and his teachings spread throughout American industry. Taylor's disciples moved beyond his simplistic economic psychology, creating the new fields of personnel work and industrial psychology, whose practitioners purported to know how to extract more and better labor from workers. A threshold had been crossed into the modern era of labor management.

So the circle closed on American workers. With each advance the quest for efficiency eroded their cherished autonomy, diminishing them and cutting them down to fit the industrial system. The process occurred unevenly. For textile workers the loss had come early. Miners and ironworkers felt it much more slowly. Others, such as construction workers, escaped almost entirely. But increasing numbers of workers found themselves in an environment that crushed any sense of mastery or even understanding.

The Labor Movement

Wherever industrialization took hold, workers organized and formed labor unions. However, the movements they built varied from one industrial society to another. In the United States workers were especially uncertain about the path they wanted to take. Only in the 1880s did the American labor movement settle into a steady course.

Reformers and Unionists

Thomas B. McGuire, a New York wagon driver, was ambitious. He had saved $300 from his wages "so that I might become something of a capitalist eventually." But his venture as a cab driver in the early 1880s soon failed:

> Corporations usually take that business themselves. They can manage to get men, at starvation wages, and put them on a hack, and put a livery on them with a gold band and brass buttons, to show that they are slaves—I beg pardon; I did not intend to use the word slaves; there are no slaves in this country now—to show that they are merely servants.

Slave or liveried servant, the symbolic meaning was the same to McGuire. He was speaking of the crushed aspirations of the independent American worker.

**Terence V. Powderly,
Labor Peacemaker**

The Knights of Labor, unlike their trade union rivals, in principle opposed strikes. In this cartoon from Puck, *dated April 7, 1886, the little man depicted in the middle is Master Workman Powderly, leader of the Knights of Labor. The cartoon shows Powderly offering Capital and Labor the Knights' proposal for the peaceful settlement of labor disputes by means of "arbitration," which in those days meant mediation and negotiation rather than resolution by a third party. Powderly's judicious stance, however, could not keep the two sides from each other's throats, and in the national strikes soon to break out, Powderly's own members joined the picket lines.* Puck, *April 17, 1886.*

Labor Reform and the Knights of Labor. What would satisfy the Thomas McGuires of the nineteenth century? Only the establishment of an egalitarian society, one in which every citizen might hope to become economically independent. This republican goal did not mean returning to the agrarian past, but rather replacing the existing wage system with a more just order that did not distinguish between capitalists and workers. All would be "producers" laboring together in what was commonly called the "cooperative commonwealth." This was the ideal that inspired the Noble and Holy Order of the Knights of Labor.

Founded in 1869 as a secret society of garment workers in Philadelphia, the Knights of Labor spread to other cities and by 1878 emerged as a national movement. The Knights boasted an elaborate ritual calculated to appeal to the fraternal spirit of nineteenth-century workers. The local assemblies of the Knights engendered a spirit of comradeship very much like that offered by the Masons or Odd Fellows. For the Knights, however, fraternalism was harnessed to labor reform. The goal was to "give voice to that grand undercurrent of mighty thought, which is today [1880] crystallizing in the hearts of men, and urging them on to perfect organization through which to gain the power to make labor emancipation possible."

But how was "emancipation" to be achieved? Through cooperation, the Knights argued. They intended to set up factories and shops that would be owned and run by the employees. As these cooperatives flourished, American society would be transformed into a cooperative commonwealth. But little was actually done. Instead the Knights devoted themselves to "education." Their leader, Grand Master Workman Terence V. Powderly, regarded the organization as a vast labor

college open to all but lawyers and saloonkeepers. The cooperative commonwealth would arrive in some mysterious way as more and more "producers" became members and learned the group's message from lectures, discussions, and publications. Social evil would not end in a day but "must await the gradual development of educational enlightenment."

Trade Unionism. The labor reformers expressed the higher aspirations of American workers. Another kind of organization—the trade union—tended to their everyday needs. Unions had long been at the center of the lives of craft workers. Apprenticeship rules regulated entry into a trade, and the **closed shop**—by reserving all jobs for union members—kept out lower-wage and incompetent workers. Union rules specified the terms of work, sometimes in minute detail. Above all, trade unionism defended the craft worker's traditional skills and rights.

The trade union also expressed the social identity of the craft. Hatters took pride in their alcoholic consumption, an on-the-job privilege that was jealously guarded. More often craft unions had an uplifting character. A Birmingham iron puddler claimed that his union's "main object was to educate mechanics up to a standard of morality and temperance, and good workmanship." Some unions emphasized mutual aid. Because operating trains was a high-risk occupation, the railroad brotherhoods provided accident and death benefits and encouraged members to assist one another. On and off the job, the unions played a big part in the lives of craft workers.

The earliest unions were local organizations of workers in the same craft, that, especially among German workers, were sometimes limited to a single ethnic group. As expanding markets intruded, breaking down

A Railroad Brotherhood

Locomotive firemen, who fed the boilers on nineteenth-century steam engines, ranked below locomotive engineers but still considered theirs a privileged occupation. This union certificate conveys the respectable values to which locomotive firemen adhered and, as depicted in the scenes on the right-hand side, the need they felt to protect their families (through the affordable insurance provided by their union) in the event of accidents that were so much a part of the dangerous trade they followed. Library of Congress.

their ability to control local conditions, unions began to form national organizations. The first was the International Typographical Union in 1852. By the 1870s molders, ironworkers, bricklayers, and about thirty other trades had done likewise. The national union, uniting local unions of the same trade, was becoming the dominant organizational form for American trade unionism.

The practical job interests that trade unions espoused might have seemed a far cry from the idealism of the Knights of Labor. But both kinds of motives arose from a single workers' culture. Seeing no conflict many workers carried membership cards in both the Knights of Labor and a trade union. For many years little separated a trade assembly of the Knights from a local trade union; both engaged in fraternal and job-oriented activities. And because the Knights, once established in a town or city, tended to become politically active and

field independent slates of candidates, that too became a magnet attracting trade unionists.

Trade unions generally barred women, and so did the Knights until 1881, when women shoe workers in Philadelphia struck in support of their male coworkers and won the right to form their own local assembly. By 1886 probably 50,000 women belonged to the Knights of Labor. Their courage on the picket line prompted Powderly's rueful remark that women "are the best men in the Order." For a handful of women, such as the hosiery worker Leonora M. Barry, the Knights provided a rare chance to take up leadership roles as organizers and officials.

Similarly, the Knights of Labor grudgingly opened the door for black workers, out of the need for solidarity and, just as important, in deference to the Order's egalitarian principles. The Knights could rightly boast that

Samuel Gompers
This is a photograph of the labor leader in his forties taken when he was visiting striking miners in West Virginia, an area where mine operators resisted unions with special fierceness. The photograph was taken by a company detective.
George Meany Memorial Archives.

their "great work has been to organize labor which was previously unorganized."

The Triumph of "Pure and Simple" Unionism

In the early 1880s the Knights began to act more and more like trade unions. Boycott campaigns against the products of "unfair" employers achieved impressive results. With the economy booming and workers in short supply, the Knights began to win strikes, including a major victory against Jay Gould's Southwestern railway system in 1885. Workers flocked to the organization, and its membership jumped from 100,000 to perhaps 700,000. For a brief time the Knights stood poised as a potential industrial-union movement capable of bringing all workers into its fold.

The rapid growth of the Knights frightened the national trade unions. They began to insist on a clear separation of roles, with the Knights confined to labor reform. This was partly a battle over turf, but it reflected also a deepening divergence of labor philosophies.

Samuel Gompers, a cigar maker from New York City, led the ideological assault on the Knights. Gompers hammered out the philosophical position that would become known as "pure and simple" unionism. His starting point was that grand theories and schemes like those that excited the labor reformers should be strictly avoided. Unions, Gompers thought, should focus on concrete, achievable gains, and they should organize workers not as an undifferentiated mass of "producers" but by craft and occupation. The battleground should be at the workplace, where workers could best mobilize their power, not in the quicksands of politics.

Gompers developed these views as general propositions, but they were grounded in the hard experience of ordinary workers like Rose Schneiderman, striving to organize fellow workers and bring employers to the bargaining table (see American Voices, "Rose Schneiderman: Trade Unionist," p. 509). Schneiderman would have nodded in agreement with Gompers's assertion that "no matter how just . . . unless the cause is backed up with power to enforce it, it is going to be crushed and annihilated."

The struggle for the eight-hour day crystallized the conflict between the rival movements. Both, of course, favored a shorter workday but for different reasons. For the Knights more leisure was desirable because workers had duties "to perform as American citizens and members of society." Trade unionists took a more hard-boiled view: the eight-hour day would spread the available jobs among more workers, protect them against overwork, and give them an easier life. When the trade unions set May 1, 1886, as the deadline for achieving the eight-hour day, the leadership of Knights objected. But workers everywhere responded enthusiastically, and as the deadline approached, a wave of strikes and demonstrations broke out across the country.

At one such eight-hour strike, at the McCormick reaper works in Chicago, a battle erupted on May 3, leaving four strikers dead. Chicago was a hotbed of **anarchism**—the revolutionary advocacy of a stateless society—and local anarchists, most of them German immigrants, called a protest meeting the next evening at Haymarket Square. When police moved in to break it up, someone threw a bomb that killed and wounded several of the police, who responded with wild gunfire. Most of the casualties, including some police, came from police bullets. Despite no evidence of their involvement, the anarchists were tried and found guilty of murder and criminal conspiracy. Four were executed, one committed suicide, and the others received long prison sentences. They were victims of one of the great miscarriages of American justice.

Seizing on the antiunion hysteria set off by the Haymarket affair, employers took the offensive. They

Rose Schneiderman

Trade Unionist

Rose Schneiderman (1882–1972) typified the young Jewish garment workers who became the firebrands of their Manhattan industry. Schneiderman went on to an illustrious career as a labor organizer and social reformer (see photo on p. 579). At the time of her initiation, recorded below, she was twenty-one years old.

We had no idea that there was a union in our industry and that women could join it. Nor did we have a full realization of the hardships we were needlessly undergoing. There was the necessity of owning a sewing machine before you could work. Then you had to buy your own thread. But the worst of it was the incredibly inefficient way in which work was distributed. Because we were all pieceworkers, any time lost during the season was a real hardship. But because of poor management there never seemed to be any synchronizing between our available time and the supplying of materials we needed. . . .

[My friend] Bessie Braut pointed out all these things and more, insisting that it was possible to have all these hardships corrected if we complained as a group. An employer would think twice before telling a group what he would not hesitate to tell an individual employee: that if she didn't like it, she was free to take herself and her machine and go somewhere else where things would most likely be just as bad or perhaps worse. . . .

As her word began to sink in, we formed a committee composed of my friend Bessie Mannis, who worked with me, myself, and a third girl. Bravely we ventured into the office of the United Cloth Hat and Cap Makers Union and told the man in charge that we would like to be organized. . . .

We were told we would have to have least twenty-five women from a number of factories before we could acquire a charter. Novices that we were, we used the simplest methods. We waited at the doors of factories and, as the girls were leaving for the day, we would approach them and speak our piece. We had blank pledges of membership ready in case some could be persuaded to join us. Within days we had the necessary number. . . .

The only cloud in the picture was mother's attitude toward my being a trade unionist. She kept saying I'd never get married because I was so busy—a prophecy which came true. Of course, what she resented most of all was my being out of the house almost every evening. But for me it was the beginning of a period that molded all my subsequent life and opened wide many doors that might otherwise have remained closed to me. . . .

That June we decided to put our strength to the test. In the summer the men usually worked only a half-day on Saturdays, which was pay day. But even when there was no work we women had to hang around until three or four o'clock before getting our pay. I headed a committee which informed Mr. Fox that we wanted to be paid at the same time as the men. . . . He didn't say outright that he agreed, he wouldn't give us that much satisfaction. But on the first Sunday in July, when we went for our pay at twelve noon, there it was for us. . . .

Source: Rose Schneiderman, *All for One* (1967), reprinted in Irving Howe and Kenneth Lebo, eds., *How We Lived* (New York: New American Library, 1979), 139–41.

broke strikes violently, compiled blacklists of strikers, and forced workers to sign **yellow-dog contracts** guaranteeing that, as a condition of employment, they would not join a labor organization. If trade unionists needed any confirmation of the tough world in which they lived, they found it in Haymarket and its aftermath.

In December 1886, having failed to persuade the Knights of Labor to desist from union activity, the national trade unions formed the American Federation of Labor (AFL), with Samuel Gompers as president. The AFL in effect locked into place the trade union structure as it had evolved by the 1880s. Underlying this structure was the conviction that workers had to take the world as it was, not as they dreamed it might be. At this point the American movement definitely diverged from the European model, for fundamental to Gompers's AFL was opposition to a political party for workers.

The Knights of Labor never recovered from the Haymarket affair. Powderly retreated to the rhetoric of labor reform, but wage earners had lost interest, and he was unable to formulate a viable new strategy. By the mid-1890s the Knights of Labor had faded away. In the meantime the AFL took firm root, justifying Gompers's confidence that he had found the correct formula for the American labor movement.

Industrial War

American trade unions were conservative. They accepted the economic order. All they wanted was a larger share for working people. But it was precisely that claim against company earnings that made American employers so opposed to **collective bargaining**. In the 1890s they unleashed a fierce counterattack on the trade union movement.

The Homestead Strike. In Homestead, Pennsylvania, the site of one of Carnegie's steel mills, the skilled men thought themselves safe from that threat. They earned good wages, lived comfortably, and generally owned their own homes. They elected fellow workers to public office and considered the town very much their community. And they had faith in Andrew Carnegie—for had not Good Old Andy said in a famous magazine article that workers had as sacred a right to combine as did capitalists and that workers had a moral claim on their jobs that forbade the use of strikebreakers by employers?

Espousing high-toned principles made Carnegie feel good, but a healthy bottom line made him feel even better. He decided that collective bargaining had become too expensive, and he was confident that his skilled workers could be replaced by the advanced machinery he was installing. Lacking the stomach for the hard battle, Carnegie fled to a remote estate in Scotland, leaving behind a second-in-command well qualified to do the dirty work. This was Henry Clay Frick, a former coal baron and a veteran of labor wars in the coal fields.

After a brief pretense at bargaining, Frick announced that effective July 1, 1892, the company would no longer deal with the Amalgamated Association of Iron and Steel Workers. If the employees wanted to work, they would have to come back on an individual basis. The plant had already been fortified so that strikebreakers could be brought in to resume operations. At stake for Carnegie's employees now was not just wage cuts but the defense of a way of life. The town mayor, a union man, turned away the county sheriff when he tried to take possession of the plant. The entire community mobilized in defense of the union.

At dawn on July 6 barges were seen approaching Homestead up the Monongahela River. On board were armed guards hired by the Pinkerton Detective Agency to take control of the steel works. Behind hastily erected barricades the strikers opened fire, and a bloody battle ensued. When the Pinkertons surrendered they were mercilessly pummeled by the enraged women of Homestead as they retreated to the railway station.

Frick appealed to the governor of Pennsylvania, who called out the state militia and placed Homestead under martial law. The great steel works was taken over and opened to strikebreakers, while union leaders and town officials were arrested on charges of riot, murder, and treason.

The defeat at Homestead marked the beginning of the end for trade unions in the steel industry. Ended too were any lingering illusions about the sanctity of workers' communities like Homestead. "Men talk like anarchists or lunatics when they insist that the workmen of Homestead have done right," asserted one conservative journal. Nothing could be permitted to interfere with Carnegie's property rights or threaten law and order.

The Homestead strike ushered in a decade of strife that pitted working people against the formidable power of corporate industry and the even more formidable power of their own government. That hard reality was driven home to workers at a place that seemed an even less likely site for class warfare than Homestead.

The Great Pullman Boycott. Pullman, Illinois, was a model factory town, famous for the amenities it offered workers and the beauty of its landscaping and city plan. The town was named for its creator, George M. Pullman, inventor of the sleeping car that brought comfort and luxury to railway travel. When the Panic of 1893 struck, business fell off and Pullman cut wages but not the rents for company housing. When a workers' committee complained in May 1894, Pullman answered that there was no connection between his roles as employer and landlord. He then fired the workers' committee.

The strike that ensued would have warranted only a footnote in American labor history but for the fact that the Pullman workers belonged to the American Railway Union (ARU), a rapidly growing industrial union of railroad workers. Its leader, Eugene V. Debs, directed ARU members not to handle Pullman sleeping cars, which, although operated by the railroads, were owned and serviced by the Pullman Company. This was a **secondary labor boycott**: force was applied on a second party (the railroads) to bring pressure on the primary target (Pullman). Since the railroads insisted on running the Pullman cars, a far-flung strike soon spread across the country, threatening the entire economy.

Quite deliberately the railroads maneuvered to bring the federal government into the dispute. Their hook was the U.S. mail cars, which they attached to every train hauling Pullman cars. When strikers stopped these trains, the railroads appealed to President Cleveland to protect the U.S. mail and halt the growing violence. Richard Olney, Cleveland's attorney general, was a former railroad lawyer who unabashedly sided with his former employers. Disregarding the protests of the liberal Illinois governor, John P. Altgeld, Cleveland dispatched the U.S. Army. When federal troops failed to get the trains running again, Olney obtained court injunctions prohibiting the ARU leaders from conducting the strike. Debs and his associates refused to obey, were charged with contempt of court, and jailed. Now leaderless and uncoordinated, the strike quickly disintegrated.

No one could doubt why the great Pullman boycott had failed: it had been crushed by the naked use of government power on behalf of the railroad companies.

American Radicalism in the Making

Oppression does not radicalize every victim, but some it does radicalize. And when social injustice is most painfully felt, when the underlying power realities stand openly revealed, the process of radicalization speeds up. Such was the case during the depression of the 1890s. Out of the industrial strife of that decade emerged the main forces of twentieth-century American radicalism.

Eugene V. Debs and American Socialism. Very little in Eugene Debs's background would have suggested that he would one day become the nation's leading socialist. A native of Terre Haute, Indiana, a prosperous railroad town, Debs grew up believing in the essential goodness of American society. A popular young man-about-town, Debs considered a career in politics or business but instead became involved in the local labor movement. In 1880, at the age of twenty-five, he was elected national secretary-treasurer of the Brotherhood of Locomotive Firemen, one of the craft unions that represented the skilled operating trades on the railroads.

Troubled by his union's indifference to the low-paid track and yard laborers, Debs unexpectedly resigned from his comfortable post to devote himself to a new organization, the American Railway Union, that would organize all railroad workers irrespective of skill—that is, an **industrial union.**

The Pullman strike visibly changed Debs. Sentenced to six months in the federal penitentiary on what he considered to be trumped-up charges, Debs emerged an avowed radical, committed to a lifelong struggle against a system that enabled employers to enlist the powers of government to beat down working people. Initially, Debs identified himself as a Populist (see Chapter 18), but he quickly gravitated to the socialist camp.

German refugees had brought the ideas of Karl Marx, the radical German theorist, to America after the failed revolutions of 1848 in Europe. Marx postulated a class struggle between capitalists and workers, ending in a revolution that would abolish private ownership of the means of production and bring about a classless society.

Little noticed by most Americans, Marxist socialism struck deep roots in the German American communities of Chicago and New York. With the formation of the Socialist Labor Party in 1877, Marxist socialism established itself as a permanent, if narrowly based, presence in American politics.

When Eugene Debs appeared in their midst in 1897, the socialists were in disarray. American capitalism had just gone through its worst crisis, yet they had failed to make much headway. Many blamed the party head, Daniel De Leon, who considered ideological purity more important than winning elections. Debs joined in the revolt against the dogmatic De Leon and helped launch the rival Socialist Party of America in 1901.

A spellbinding campaigner, Debs talked socialism in an American idiom, making Marxism understandable and persuasive to many ordinary Americans. Under him the new party began to break out of its immigrant base and attract American-born voters. In Texas, Oklahoma, and Minnesota, socialism exerted a powerful appeal among distressed farmers radicalized by Populism. The party was also highly successful at attracting women activists. Inside of a decade, with a national network of branches and state organizations, the Socialist Party had become a force to be reckoned with in American politics.

Western Radicalism. In the meantime a different brand of American radicalism was taking shape in the West. After many years of mostly friendly relations, the atmosphere in the western mining camps turned ugly during the 1890s. Powerful new corporations were taking over, and they wanted to be rid of the miners' union, the Western Federation of Miners (WFM). Moreover, silver and copper prices began to drop, bringing pressure to cut miners' wages. When strikes resulted, they took an especially violent turn.

In 1892 at Coeur d'Alene, a silver-mining district in northern Idaho, striking miners engaged in gun battles with company guards, sent a car of explosive powder careering into the Frisco mine, and threatened to blow up the smelters. Martial law was declared, the strikers were imprisoned in stockades, and the strike was broken. Equally violent strikes took place at Cripple Creek, Colorado, in 1894; at Leadville, Colorado, in 1896; and again in Coeur d'Alene in 1899.

In these western strikes government intervention was naked and unrestrained. This was partly in response to labor's violence, but it stemmed also from the politics of the lightly settled western states: either the miners would dominate—as they did in coalition with the Populists during their successful strike at Cripple Creek—or, as was increasingly true, the mine owners would dominate, with disastrous consequences for the miners.

In 1897 WFM president Ed Boyce called on all union members to arm themselves with rifles, and his rhetoric—he called the wage system "slavery in its worst form"—had a hard edge. Any lingering faith in the political process died in the Colorado state elections of 1905, which the miners thought they had won, only to have the state supreme court overturn the results and reinstall their archenemy, Republican governor George H. Peabody.

In 1905 the Western Federation of Miners joined with left-wing socialists to create a new movement, the Industrial Workers of the World (IWW). The Wobblies, as IWW members were called, fervently supported the Marxist class struggle—but at the workplace rather than in politics. By resistance at the point of production and ultimately by means of a general strike, they believed that the workers would bring about a revolution. A new society would emerge, run directly by the workers through their industrial unions. The term **syndicalism** describes this brand of workers' radicalism.

In both its major forms—politically oriented Socialism and the syndicalist IWW—American radicalism flourished after the crisis of the 1890s but only on a limited basis and never with the possibility of seizing power. Nevertheless, Socialists and Wobblies served a larger purpose. American radicalism, by its sheer vitality, bore witness to what was exploitative and unjust in the new industrial order.

FOR FURTHER EXPLORATION

▶ For definitions of key terms boldfaced in this chapter, see the glossary at the end of the book.

▶ To assess your mastery of the material covered in this chapter, see the Online Study Guide at **bedfordstmartins.com/henretta**.

▶ For suggested references, including Web sites, see page SR-19 at the end of the book.

▶ For map resources and primary documents, see **bedfordstmartins.com/henretta**.

American industrialism took modern shape during the last decades of the nineteenth century. Central to this development were the shift from iron making to the manufacture of steel, the great expansion of coal mining, and the technology for generating steam and electrical power. These advances made possible the production of capital goods and energy required by an expanding manufacturing economy. An efficient railway system provided access to national markets. The scale of enterprise grew very large, and the vertically integrated firm became the predominant form of business organization. Only in the South did prevailing conditions—in particular the insulated low-wage labor market—retard the growth of an advanced industrial economy.

In the North the enormous demand for labor led to a great influx of immigrants, making ethnic diversity a distinctive feature of the American working class. Gender likewise defined occupational opportunity. Women joined the labor force in growing numbers but were almost universally subjected to a sex-typing process that relegated them to "women's work," always at the wage rates below those of men. Mass production—the volume output of standardized products—vastly improved the productivity of American manufacturing but also deskilled workers and mechanized their jobs. Scientific management, the brainchild of Frederick W. Taylor, cut further into the traditional autonomy of American workers by systematizing the labor process and shifting control into the hands of supervisors.

The late nineteenth century gave rise to the American labor movement in its modern form. In the Knights of Labor, labor reform enjoyed one final surge during the mid-1880s and then succumbed to the "pure and simple" unionism of the American Federation of Labor. The AFL was conservative in that it accepted the economic order, but its insistence on a larger share for workers guaranteed that employers would fiercely resist collective bargaining. The resulting industrial warfare of the 1890s stirred new radical impulses, leading both to the political socialism of Eugene Debs and to the industrial radicalism of the IWW.

1869	Knights of Labor founded in Philadelphia
1872	Andrew Carnegie starts construction of Edgar Thomson steelworks near Pittsburgh
1873	Panic of 1873 ushers in economic depression
1875	John Wanamaker establishes first department store in Philadelphia
1877	Baltimore and Ohio workers initiate nationwide railroad strike
1878	Gustavus Swift introduces refrigerator car
1879	Jay Gould begins to build Missouri Pacific railway system
1883	Railroads establish national time zones
1886	Haymarket Square bombing in Chicago
	American Federation of Labor (AFL) founded
1892	Homestead steel strike crushed
	Wave of western miners' strikes begins
1893	Panic of 1893 leads to national depression
	Surge of railroad bankruptcies; reorganization by investment bankers begins
1894	President Cleveland sends troops to break Pullman boycott
1895	Southeastern European immigration exceeds northern European immigration for first time
	F. W. Taylor formulates scientific management
1901	Eugene V. Debs helps found Socialist Party of America
1905	Industrial Workers of the World (IWW) launched

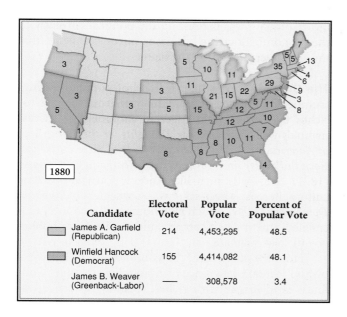

Candidate	Electoral Vote	Popular Vote	Percent of Popular Vote
James A. Garfield (Republican)	214	4,453,295	48.5
Winfield Hancock (Democrat)	155	4,414,082	48.1
James B. Weaver (Greenback-Labor)	—	308,578	3.4

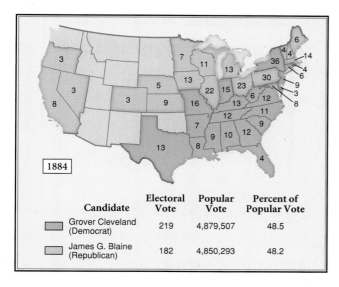

Candidate	Electoral Vote	Popular Vote	Percent of Popular Vote
Grover Cleveland (Democrat)	219	4,879,507	48.5
James G. Blaine (Republican)	182	4,850,293	48.2

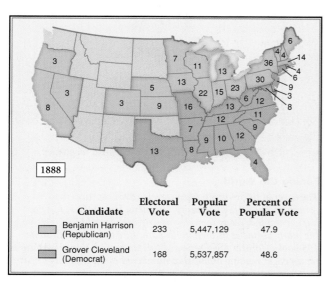

Candidate	Electoral Vote	Popular Vote	Percent of Popular Vote
Benjamin Harrison (Republican)	233	5,447,129	47.9
Grover Cleveland (Democrat)	168	5,537,857	48.6

sleepy places carrying on largely routine duties. Virtually all federal funding came from customs duties and excise taxes on liquor and tobacco. These sources produced more money than the government spent. How to reduce the federal surplus ranked as one of the most nettlesome issues of the 1880s.

As for setting a national agenda, this was—unlike in Lincoln's day—not to be looked for from the White House. "The office of President is essentially executive in nature," Cleveland insisted.

Party Politics. On matters of national policy, the presidents took a back seat to Congress. But Congress functioned badly. Procedural rules regularly impeded legislative business. The two parties were not especially eager to get things done. Historically, they represented somewhat different traditions. The Democrats favored states' rights, while the Republicans were heirs to the Whig enthusiasm for federally assisted economic development. After Reconstruction, however, the Republicans backed away from that interventionist position and, in truth, party differences became muddy. On most leading issues of the day—civil service reform, the currency, regulation of the railroads—the divisions occurred within the parties and not between them.

Only the **tariff** remained a fighting issue. From Lincoln's administration onward, high duties had protected American industry from imported goods. It was an article of Republican faith, as President Harrison said in 1892, that "the protective system . . . has been a mighty instrument for the development of the national wealth." The Democrats, free traders by tradition, regularly attacked Republican protectionism. Yet, in practice, even the tariff was a negotiable issue like any other. Congressmen voted their constituents' interests regardless of party rhetoric. As a result every tariff bill was a patchwork of bargains among special interests.

Campaign Politics. Issues were treated gingerly partly because the parties were so equally balanced. The Democrats, in retreat immediately after the Civil War, quickly regrouped and by the end of Reconstruction stood on virtually equal terms with the Republicans. Every presidential election from 1876 to 1892 was decided by a thin margin, and neither party gained permanent command of Congress (Map 18.1). Political

◄ **MAP 18.1 Presidential Elections of 1880, 1884, and 1888**

The anatomy of political stalemate is evident in this trio of electoral maps of the 1880s. First, note the equal division of the popular vote between Republicans and Democrats. Second, note the remarkable persistence in the pattern of electoral votes, in which overwhelmingly states went to the same party in all three elections. Finally, we can identify who determined the outcomes— the two "swing" states, New York and Indiana, whose vote shifted every four years and always in favor of the winning candidate.

caution seemed best; any false move on national issues might tip the scales to the other side. "Neither party has any principles, any distinctive tenets," grumbled James Bryce. "All has been lost, except office or the hope of it."

The weakening of principled politics was evident in the Republicans' retreat from their Civil War legacy. The major unfinished business after 1877 involved the plight of the former slaves. The Republican agenda called for federal funding to combat illiteracy and, even more contentious, federal protection for black voters in southern congressional elections. Neither measure managed to make it through Congress. With little mileage left in Reconstruction politics, the Republicans backpedaled on the race issue and abandoned the blacks to their fate.

That did not stop Republican orators from "waving the bloody shirt" against the Democrats. Service in the Union army gave candidates a strong claim to public office, and veterans' benefits always stood high on the Republican agenda. The Democrats played the same patriotic card in the South as defenders of the Lost Cause. Bryce rightly criticized American politicians for "clinging too long to outworn issues and neglecting the problems . . . which now perplex the country."

Alternatively, campaigns could descend into comedy. In the hard-fought election of 1884, for example, the Democrat Cleveland burst on the scene as a reformer, fresh from his victories over corrupt machine politics in New York State. But years earlier Cleveland, a bachelor, had fathered an illegitimate child, and throughout the campaign he was dogged by the ditty, "Maw, Maw, where's my Paw?" (After election day Cleveland's supporters gleefully responded, "He's in the White House, haw-haw-haw.") Cleveland's opponent, James G. Blaine, already on the defensive for taking favors from the railroads, was weakened by the unthinking charge of a too ardent Republican supporter that the Democrats were the party of "Rum, Romanism and Rebellion." In a twinkling he had insulted Catholic voters and possibly lost the election for Blaine. In the midst of all the mudslinging, the issues got lost.

The Ideology of Individualism

The characteristics of public life in the 1880s—the inactivity of the federal government, the evasiveness of the political parties, the absorption in politics for its own sake—derived ultimately from the conviction that little was at stake in public affairs. In 1887 Cleveland vetoed a small appropriation for drought-stricken Texas farmers with the remark that "though the people support the Government, the Government should not support the people." Governmental activity was itself considered a bad thing. All the state could do, said Republican senator Roscoe Conkling, was "to clear the way of impediments and dangers, and leave every class and every individual free and safe in the exertions and pursuits of life." Conkling was expressing the political corollary to the economic doctrine of **laissez-faire**—the belief that the less government did, the better.

The Gospel of Wealth.   A flood of popular writings trumpeted the creed of individualism, from the rags-to-riches tales of Horatio Alger to innumerable success manuals with such titles as *Thoughts for the Young Men of America, or a Few Practical Words of Advice to Those Born in Poverty and Destined to be Reared in Orphanages* (1871). Self-made men like Andrew Carnegie became cultural heroes. A best-seller was Carnegie's *Triumphant Democracy* (1886), which paid homage to a country that enabled a penniless Scottish child to rise from bobbin boy to steel magnate.

From the pulpit came the assurances of the Episcopal bishop William Lawrence of Massachusetts that "Godliness is in league with riches." Bishop Lawrence was

Facing the World

The cover of this Horatio Alger novel (1893) captures the American myth of opportunity. Our hero, Harry Vane, is a poor but earnest lad, ready to make his way in the world and, despite the many obstacles thrown in his path, sure to succeed. In some 135 books Horatio Alger repeated this story, with minor variations, for an eager reading public that numbered in the millions.

Frank and Marie-Therese Wood Print Collections, Alexandria, VA.

voicing a familiar theme of American Protestantism: success in one's earthly calling revealed the promise of eternal salvation. It was all too easy for a conservative ministry to make morally reassuring the furious acquisitiveness of industrial America. "To secure wealth is an honorable ambition," intoned the Baptist minister Russell H. Conwell in his lecture "Acres of Diamonds."

Social Darwinism. The celebration of American acquisitiveness drew strong intellectual support from science. In *On the Origin of Species* (1859), British naturalist Charles Darwin had developed a bold hypothesis to explain the evolution of plants and animals. In nature, Darwin wrote, all living things struggle to survive. Individual members of a species are born with genetic mutations that enable them to compete better in their particular environment—camouflage coloring for a bird, for example, or resistance to thirst in a camel. These survival characteristics, since they are genetically transmissible, become dominant in future generations, and the species evolves. This mechanism, which Darwin called *natural selection*, put evolution on a firm intellectual basis and revolutionized biological science.

Drawing on Darwin the British philosopher Herbert Spencer spun out an elaborate analysis of how human society had evolved through competition and "survival of the fittest." **Social Darwinism**, as Spencer's ideas became known, was championed in America by William Graham Sumner, a sociology professor at Yale. Competition, said Sumner, is a law of nature that "can no more be done away with than gravitation." And who are the fittest? "The millionaires. . . . They may fairly be regarded as the naturally selected agents of society. They get high wages and live in luxury, but the bargain is a good one for society."

Social Darwinists regarded with horror any interference with social processes. "The great stream of time and earthly things will sweep on just the same in spite of us," Sumner wrote in a famous essay, "The Absurd Attempt to Make the World Over" (1894). As for the government, it had "at bottom . . . two chief things . . . with which to deal. They are the property of men and the honor of women. These it has to defend against crime."

The Supremacy of the Courts

Suspicion of government not only paralyzed political initiative; it also shifted power away from the executive and legislative branches. "The task of constitutional government," declared Sumner, "is to devise institutions which shall come into play at critical periods to prevent the abusive control of the powers of a state by the controlling classes in it." Sumner meant the judiciary. From the 1870s onward the courts increasingly accepted the role that he assigned to them, becoming the guardians of the rights of private property against the grasping tentacles of government.

The main target of the courts was the states rather than the national government. This was because, under the federal system as it was understood in the late nineteenth century, the residual powers—those not delegated by the Constitution to the federal government—left to the states primary responsibility for social welfare and economic regulation. The states exercised their police powers to ensure the health, safety, and morals of their citizens. The leading question in American law was how to strike a balance between state responsibility for the general welfare and the liberty of individuals to pursue their private interests. Most states, caught up in the conservative ethos of the day, were cutting back on expenditures and public services. Even so, there were more than enough state initiatives to alarm vigilant judges. Thus in the landmark case *In Re Jacobs* (1885), the New York Supreme Court struck down a state law prohibiting cigar manufacturing in tenements on the grounds that such regulation exceeded the police powers of the state.

Increasingly, however, it was federal judges who took up the battle against state activism. The Supreme Court's crucial weapon in this campaign was the Fourteenth Amendment (1868), which prohibited the states from depriving "any person of life, liberty, or property, without due process of law." The due process clause had been adopted during Reconstruction to protect the civil rights of the former slaves. But due process protected the property rights and contractual liberty of any "person," and legally corporations counted as persons. So interpreted, the Fourteenth Amendment became by the turn of the century a powerful restraint on the states in the use of their police powers to regulate private business.

The Supreme Court similarly hamstrung the federal government. In 1895 the Court ruled that the federal power to regulate interstate commerce did not cover manufacturing and struck down a federal income tax law. And in areas where federal power was undeniable—such as the regulation of railroads—the Supreme Court scrutinized every measure for undue interference with the rights of property.

The preeminent conservative jurist of the day, Stephen J. Field, made no bones about the dangers he saw in the nation's headlong industrial development. "As the inequalities in the conditions of men become more and more marked and . . . angry menaces against order find vent in loud denunciations—it becomes more and more the imperative duty of the court to enforce with a firm hand every guarantee of the Constitution."

Power conferred status. The law, not politics, attracted the ablest people and held the public's esteem. A Wisconsin judge boasted: "The bench symbolizes on earth the throne of divine justice. . . . Law in its highest sense is the will of God." Judicial supremacy reflected how dominant the ideology of individualism had become in industrial America and also how low American politicians had fallen in the esteem of their countrymen.

Politics and the People

The country may have felt, as Kansas editor William Allen White wrote, "sick with politics" and "nauseated at all politicians," but somehow this did not reduce the people's appetite for politics. Proportionately more voters turned out in presidential elections from 1876 to 1892 than at any other time in American history. People voted Democratic or Republican loyally for a lifetime. National conventions attracted huge crowds. "The excitement, the mental and physical strains," remarked an Indiana Republican after the 1888 convention, "are surpassed only by prolonged battle in actual warfare, as I have been told by officers of the Civil War who latter engaged in convention struggles." The convention he described had nominated the colorless Benjamin Harrison on a routine platform. What was all the excitement about?

Cultural Politics: Party, Religion, and Ethnicity

In the late nineteenth century, politics was a vibrant part of the nation's culture. America "is a land of conventions and assemblies," a journalist noted, "where it is the most natural thing in the world for people to get together in meetings, where almost every event is the occasion for speechmaking." During the election season the party faithful marched in torchlight parades. Party paraphernalia flooded the country—handkerchiefs, mugs, posters, and buttons emblazoned with the Democratic donkey or the Republican elephant, symbols that had been adopted in the 1870s. In the 1888 campaign the candidates were featured on cards, like baseball players, packed into Honest Long Cut tobacco. In an age before movies and radio, politics ranked as one of the great American forms of entertainment.

Party loyalty was a deadly serious matter, however. Long after the killing ended, Civil War emotions ran high. Among family friends in Cleveland, recalled the urban reformer Brand Whitlock, the Republican Party was "a synonym for patriotism, another name for the nation. It was inconceivable that any self-respecting person should be a Democrat"—or, among ex-Confederates in the South, that any self-respecting person could be a Republican.

Beyond these sectional differences the most important determinants of party loyalty were religion and ethnicity (Figure 18.1). Statistically northern Democrats tended to be foreign-born and Catholic, while Republicans tended to be native-born and Protestant. Among Protestants, the more *pietistic* a person's faith—that is the more personal and direct the believer's relationship to God—the more likely he or she was to be a Republican and to favor using the powers of the state to uphold social values and regulate personal behavior.

During the 1880s, as ethnic tensions built up in many cities, education became an arena of bitter conflict. One issue was whether instruction would be in

The Presidential B.B. Club (1888)

On the left Grover Cleveland is the baseman; at center Benjamin Harrison is at bat; and on the right Cleveland tags Harrison out—not, alas, the right prediction, since Harrison won the 1888 election. Collection of Janice L. and David J. Frent.

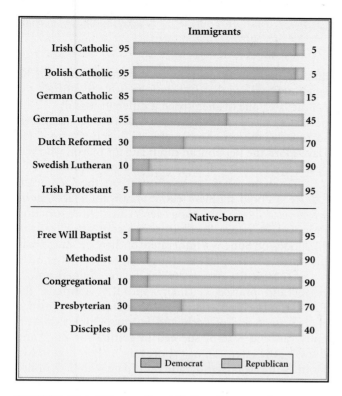

Immigrants

Irish Catholic   95 ——— 5

Polish Catholic   95 ——— 5

German Catholic   85 ——— 15

German Lutheran   55 ——— 45

Dutch Reformed   30 ——— 70

Swedish Lutheran   10 ——— 90

Irish Protestant   5 ——— 95

Native-born

Free Will Baptist   5 ——— 95

Methodist   10 ——— 90

Congregational   10 ——— 90

Presbyterian   30 ——— 70

Disciples   60 ——— 40

Democrat ▢   Republican ▢

FIGURE 18.1 Ethnocultural Voting Patterns in the Midwest, 1870–1892

These figures demonstrate how voting patterns among Midwesterners reflected ethnicity and religion in the late nineteenth century. Especially striking is the overwhelming preference by immigrant Catholics for the Democratic Party. Among Protestants there was an equally strong preference for the Republican Party by certain groups of immigrants (Swedish Lutherans and Irish Protestants) and native born (Free Will Baptists, Methodists, and Congregationalists), but other Protestant groups were more evenly divided in their party preferences.

English. Immigrant groups often wanted their children taught in their own languages. In St. Louis, a heavily German city, the long-standing policy of teaching German to all students was overturned after a heated campaign. Religion was an even more explosive educational issue. Catholics fought a losing battle over public aid for parochial schools, which by 1900 was prohibited by twenty-three states. In Boston a furious controversy broke out in 1888 over the use of an anti-Catholic history textbook. When the school board withdrew the offending book, angry Protestants elected a new board and returned the text to the curriculum.

Then there was the regulation of public morals. In many states so-called **blue laws** restricted activity on Sundays. When Nebraska banned Sunday baseball, the state supreme court approved the law as a blow struck in "the contest between Christianity and wrong." But German and Irish Catholics, who saw nothing evil in a bit of fun on Sunday, considered blue laws a violation of their personal freedom. Ethnocultural conflict also flared

over the liquor question (see Voices from Abroad, "Ernst Below: Beer and German American Politics," p. 522). Many states adopted strict licensing and local-option laws governing the sale of alcoholic beverages. Indiana permitted drinking but only joylessly in rooms containing "no devices for amusement or music . . . of any kind."

Because the hottest social issues of the day—education, the liquor question, and observance of the Sabbath— were also party issues, they lent deep significance to party affiliation. And because these issues were fought out mostly at the state and local levels, they hit very close to home. Crusading Methodists thought of Republicans as the party of morality. For embattled Irish and German Catholics, who favored "the largest individual liberty consistent with public order," the Democratic Party was the defender of their freedoms.

Organizational Politics

Politics was also important because of the organizational activity it generated. By the 1870s both major parties had evolved formal, well-organized structures. At the base lay the precinct or ward, where party meetings were open to all members. County, state, and national committees ran the ongoing business of the parties. Conventions determined party rules, adopted platforms, and selected the party's candidates.

At election time the party's main job was to get out the vote. Wherever elections were close and hard fought, the parties mounted intensive efforts organized down to the individual voter. In Indiana, for example, the Republicans appointed ten thousand "district men," each responsible for turning out a designated group of voters.

Machine Politics. Party governance seemed, on its face, highly democratic, since in theory all power derived from the party members in the precincts and wards. In practice, however, the parties were run by unofficial internal organizations—**political machines**—which consisted of insiders willing to do party work in exchange for public jobs or the sundry advantages of being connected. The machines tended toward one-man rule, although the "boss" ruled more by the consent of the secondary leaders than by his own absolute power.

Absorbed in the tasks of power brokerage, party bosses treated public issues as somewhat irrelevant. The high stakes of money, jobs, and influence made for intense factionalism. After Ulysses S. Grant left the White House in 1877, the Republican Party divided into two warring factions—the Stalwarts, led by Senator Roscoe Conkling of New York, and the Halfbreeds, led by James G. Blaine of Maine. The split was sparked by a personal feud between Conkling and Blaine, but it persisted because of a furious struggle over patronage. The Halfbreeds represented a newer Republican generation that was more favorably disposed than the Stalwarts to

Ernst Below

Beer and German American Politics

E rnst Below (1845–1910) toured the United States in the early 1890s, enjoying the hospitality of the prosperous German American communities he encountered along the way. Following is an excerpt from the book he published on his return to Germany, Bilder aus dem Westen (1894). Herr Below provides a vivid picture of America's ethnic politics, which he found highly distasteful. The reader will note that the action takes place at a turner festival. Turner is the German word for "gymnast." In the nineteenth century the gymnastic movement had an enormous vogue in Germany, helping to weld a spirit of German nationalism in that fragmented country before unification in 1871. In the United States the Turnverein took their place at the center of German American community life.

In Kansas City we sat on the veranda, taking coffee with Mr. Held, the attorney. The women turned the pages of a picture album; they were busy arranging an excursion to the pretty Missouri Valley. The men spoke of the chances of our host's election to Congress. Our friend, Karl, had the latest precise news from the battlefield and told of the stratagems used by one party or another in the attempt to make sure of victory. I showed my surprise that an educated, honest, thoughtful man, under such conditions, could bring himself to be concerned with politics. . . .

The next night the great *Turnverein* [Gymnastic Association] hall was brightly lighted. The stately redstone building with its impressive gabled facade at the corner of Oak and Twelfth Streets shone from the sparkle of electric lamps. . . . When I entered the hall the gymnastic exercises had already begun. . . . On the walls hung . . . pictures of Washington, Lincoln and Grant; side by side with William I, Bismarck and Moltke. . . . Below, the parents and members of the society intently watched the performances. Girls in becoming short-skirted gymnast uniforms rivaled the lively boys in agility and perseverance. . . .

At one end of the hall sat old Kumpf, the former mayor. Speaking to him from either side with great seriousness were two German Democrats, city officials. Kumpf was, like most of the old German turners, once a solid Republican. . . . Yet even he was displeased with the flirtation of his party with the temperance and prohibition forces in recent times. Nevertheless, he could not bring

himself publicly to go over to the Democrats, and he laughingly parried the attacks of the two city officials. . . . A little later one of them tried a different assault. . . . He pointed to the adjoining room, in which a great many men surrounded the refreshment table. In their midst stood Joe Davenport, the Republican candidate for mayor, who was ordering a round of drinks and cigars for everyone.

"Listen to what he says," went on the Democrat. ". . . He is a bold, faithless fellow. I know for a fact that he wrote yesterday to the Young Men's Christian Association promising in return for their votes a complete closing of all saloons on Sundays. Either here or there he must break his word. . . . Go up to the scamp and expose his game!"

. . . Now the mayoralty candidate climbed onto a barrel and praised Germany and the Germans, the Rhine and the "Fatherland." . . . After Davenport finished there was no end of *hochs* and *hurrays*. Only with difficulty did Old Kumpf succeed in getting the floor and drawing the attention of the crowd. . . . Pointing to Mr. Holmes the rival Democratic candidate who had, unnoticed, come into the hall during the concluding exercises [Kumpf said]: "Although I do not fight for exactly the same principles as this man, still I must acknowledge that he offers a true guarantee against the hypocritical attempts of the prohibitionists. . . . With this in mind, I say, 'long live our next mayor, Mister Holmes!'"

Loud applause arose from all sides; men, women, and children jostled about trying to shake the hand of the future mayor. The band struck up the "Star Spangled Banner" while the whole assemblage rose to its feet and loudly sang the words. . . .

Soon a loud uproar reigned in the refreshment room. One group yelled ridicule against another, as the satellites of Davenport sought to ridicule the sudden change in sentiment. After the beer had been poured out in streams on both sides for some time no one really knew what was going on; not a man could tell exactly who belonged to which party. . . .

As I left the hall I was greeted by Rothmann, the director of the German school. He was indignant at the scenes which had so unworthily closed a meeting that had begun so well. "This time at least," he said, "the Germans should have held together to show that they could unitedly support Held, our [Republican] candidate for Congress. But when it comes to the most vital interest of the Germans in America, they are only concerned with their little appetites, and let shortsighted politicians turn their festivals into carnivals, in which a glass of beer can purchase the allegiance of a man. This is indeed corruption of the worst kind."

Source: Oscar Handlin, ed., *This Was America* (Cambridge, MA: Harvard University Press, 1949), 383–89.

political reform and less committed to shopworn Civil War issues. But issues were secondary in the strife between Stalwarts and Halfbreeds. They were really fighting over the spoils of party politics.

Yet the record of machine politics was not wholly negative. In certain ways the standards of governance got better. Disciplined professionals, veterans of machine politics, proved effective as state legislators and congressmen because they were more experienced in the give-and-take of politics. More important, party machines filled a void in the nation's public life. They did informally much of what the governmental system left undone, especially in the cities.

The Mugwumps. But machine politics never managed to win the respect of the general public. Many of the nation's social elite—intellectuals, well-to-do businessmen, and old-line families—resented a politics that excluded people like themselves, the "best men." There was, too, a genuine clash of values. Political reformers called for "disinterestedness" and "independence"—the opposite of the self-serving careerism and party regularity fostered by the machine system. Many of these critics had earned their spurs as Liberal Republicans who had broken from the party and fought President Grant's reelection in 1872.

In 1884 Carl Schurz, Edwin L. Godkin, and Charles Francis Adams Jr. again left the Republican Party because they could not stomach its presidential candidate, James G. Blaine, whom they associated with corrupt politics. Mainly from New York and Massachusetts, these Republicans became known as Mugwumps—a derisive bit of contemporary slang, supposedly of Indian origin, referring to pompous or self-important persons. The Mugwumps threw their support to Democrat Grover Cleveland and may have ensured his election by giving him the winning margin in New York State.

After the 1884 election the enthusiasm for reform spilled over into local politics, spawning good-government campaigns across the country. Although they won some municipal victories, the Mugwumps were more adept at molding public opinion than at running government. Controlling the newspapers and journals read by the educated middle class, the Mugwumps defined the terms of political debate and denied the machine system public legitimacy.

The Mugwumps registered their biggest success in the battle for the secret ballot, which had been pioneered in Australia. Citizens in the privacy of a voting booth would mark an official ballot listing all the candidates instead of submitting a party-supplied ticket in public view at the polling place. Adopted in the early 1890s, the Australian ballot freed voters from party surveillance as they exercised the right to vote (Map 18.2).

The Mugwumps were reformers but not on behalf of social justice. The problems of working people meant little to them, nor did they favor using the state to help the poor. As far as the Mugwumps were concerned, the government that was best was the government that governed least. Theirs was the brand of "reform" perfectly in keeping with the conservative ethos of the time.

Women's Political Culture

The young Theodore Roosevelt, an up-and-coming Republican state politician in 1884, referred to the Mugwumps contemptuously as "man-milliners." The sexual slur was not accidental. In attacking organizational politics, the Mugwumps were challenging one of the bastions of male society. At party meetings and conventions, men carried on not only the business of politics but also the rituals of male sociability amid cigar smoke and whiskey. Politics was identified with manliness. It was competitive. It dealt in the commerce of power. It was frankly self-aggrandizing. Party politics, in short, was no place for a woman.

So, naturally, the woman suffrage movement met fierce opposition. Acknowledging the uphill battle that lay ahead, **suffragists** overcame the bitter divisions of the Reconstruction era (see Chapter 15) and in 1890 reunited in the National American Woman Suffrage Association. In that same spirit of realism, suffragists abandoned efforts to get a constitutional amendment and concentrated on state campaigns. Except out West—in Wyoming, Idaho, Colorado, and Utah—the most they could win was the right to vote for school boards or on tax issues. "Men are ordained to govern in all forceful and material things, because they are men," asserted an antisuffrage resolution, "while women, by the same decree of God and nature, are equally fitted to bear rule in a higher and more spiritual realm, where the strong frame and the weighty brain count for less"—that is to say, not in politics.

Yet this invocation of the doctrine of "separate spheres"—that men and women had different natures, and that women's nature fitted them for "a higher and more spiritual realm"—did open a channel for women to enter public life. "Women's place is Home," acknowledged the journalist Retha Childe Dorr. "But Home is not contained within the four walls of an individual house. Home is the community. The city full of people is the Family. . . . And badly do the Home and Family need their mother." Indeed, women had since the early nineteenth century engaged in charitable activities. Women's organizations fought prostitution, assisted the poor, agitated for prison reform, and tried to expand educational and job opportunities for women. Since many of these goals required state involvement, women's organizations of necessity became politically active. They stressed that partisan politics was not their game. Quite

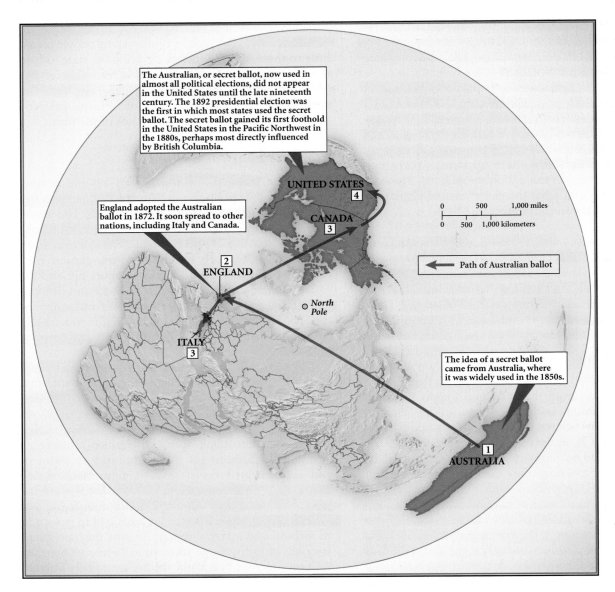

The Australian, or secret ballot, now used in almost all political elections, did not appear in the United States until the late nineteenth century. The 1892 presidential election was the first in which most states used the secret ballot. The secret ballot gained its first foothold in the United States in the Pacific Northwest in the 1880s, perhaps most directly influenced by British Columbia.

England adopted the Australian ballot in 1872. It soon spread to other nations, including Italy and Canada.

The idea of a secret ballot came from Australia, where it was widely used in the 1850s.

UNITED STATES 4
CANADA 3
ENGLAND 2
ITALY 3
AUSTRALIA 1

North Pole

| 0 | 500 | 1,000 miles |
| 0 | 500 | 1,000 kilometers |

← Path of Australian ballot

MAP 18.2 The Diffusion of the Australian Ballot

Although the foreign influences have not generally been acknowledged, many reforms that we think of as American are actually transnational phenomena, more often than not with the United States the beneficiary of advances elsewhere in the world. This was the case with the secret ballot, which originated in Australia in the 1850s and took four decades to reach the United States.

the contrary: women were bent on creating their own political sphere.

No issue joined home and politics more poignantly than did the liquor question. Just before Christmas in 1873 the women of Hillsboro, Ohio, began to hold vigils in front of the town's saloons, pleading with the owners to close and end the suffering of families of hard-drinking fathers. Thus began a spontaneous uprising of women that spread across the country. From this agitation came the Women's Christian Temperance Union (WCTU), which after its formation in 1874 rapidly blossomed into the largest women's organization in the country.

Because it excluded men, the WCTU was the spawning ground for a new generation of women leaders. Under the guidance of Frances Willard, who became president in 1879, the WCTU moved beyond temperance and adopted a "Do-Everything" policy. Women recognized that alcoholism was not simply a personal failing; it stemmed from larger social problems in American society. Willard also wanted to attract women who had no particular interest in the liquor question. Local affiliates were encouraged to undertake causes that were important in their own communities. By 1889 the WCTU had thirty-nine departments concerned with

The Levi P. Morton Association
The top-hatted gentlemen in this photograph constituted the local Republican Party organization of Newport, Rhode Island, named in honor of Levi P. Morton, Republican leader and vice president during the Benjamin Harrison administration (1889–1893). The maleness of party politics leaps from the photograph and asserts more clearly than a thousand words why the suffragist demand for the right to vote was met with ridicule and disbelief. Newport Historical Society.

labor, prostitution, health, international peace, and other issues.

Most important, the WCTU was drawn to woman suffrage. This was necessary, Willard argued, "because the liquor traffic is entrenched in law, and law grows out of the will of majorities, and majorities of women are against the liquor traffic." The WCTU began by stressing moral suasion and personal discipline—hence the word "temperance" in its name—but expanded its attack on liquor to include prohibition by law. Women needed the vote, said Willard, to fulfill their social responsibilities *as women* (see American Voices, "Helen Potter: The Case for Women's Political Rights," p. 527). This was very different from the claim made by the suffragists—that the ballot was an inherent right of all citizens *as individuals*—and was less threatening to masculine pride.

Not much changed in the short run. The WCTU was divided on the suffrage issue and did not become a major participant in later struggles for women's right to vote. But by linking women's social concerns to women's political participation, the WCTU helped lay the groundwork for a fresh attack on male electoral politics in the early twentieth century. And in the meantime, even without the vote, the WCTU demonstrated how potent a voice women could find in the public arena and how vibrant a political culture they could build.

Race and Politics in the New South

When Reconstruction ended in 1877, so did the hopes of African Americans that they would enjoy the equal rights of citizenship promised them by the Fourteenth and Fifteenth Amendments. Southern schools were strictly segregated. Access to jobs, the courts, and social services was racially determined and unequal. However, public accommodations were not yet legally segregated, and practices varied a good deal across the South. Only on the railroads, as rail travel became more common, did whites demand that blacks be excluded from first-class cars, with the result that southern railroads became after 1887 the first public accommodation subject to segregation laws.

In politics the situation was still more fluid. Blacks had not been driven from politics. On the contrary their turnout at elections was not far behind the turnout by whites. But blacks did not participate on equal terms with whites. In the Black Belt areas, where African Americans sometimes outnumbered whites, voting districts

Wanted, Sober Men

This drawing appeared in a magazine in 1899, twenty-five years after the women of Hillsboro, Ohio, rose in revolt against the town's saloonkeepers and launched the Woman's Christian Temperance Union (WCTU). But the emotion it expresses had not changed—that the saloon was the enemy of the family. Culver Pictures.

were designed to ensure that, while blacks got some offices, political control remained in white hands. Blacks, moreover, were routinely intimidated during political campaigns. Even so, an impressive majority remained staunchly Republican, refusing, as the last black congressman from Mississippi told his House colleagues in 1882, "to surrender their honest convictions, even upon the altar of their personal necessities."

Whatever hopes blacks entertained for better days, however, faded during the 1880s and then, in the next decade, expired in a terrible burst of racial terrorism.

Biracial Politics

No democratic society can survive if it does not enable competing economic and social interests to be heard. In the United States the two-party system performs that role. The Civil War crisis severely tested the two-party system because, in both North and South, political opposition came to be seen as treasonable. In the victorious North, despite the best efforts of the Republicans, the Democrats shed their disgrace after the war and

reclaimed their status as a major party. In the defeated South, however, the scars of war cut deep, and Reconstruction cut even deeper. The struggle for "home rule" empowered southern Democrats. They had "redeemed" the South from Republican domination—hence the name they adopted: Redeemers. Cloaked in the mantle of the Lost Cause, the Redeemers claimed a monopoly on political legitimacy.

The Republican Party in the South did not fold up, however. On the contrary, it soldiered on, sustained by tenacious black loyalty, by a hard core of white support, by patronage from Republican national administrations, and by a key Democratic vulnerability. This was the gap between the universality the Democrats claimed as the party of Redemption and its actual domination by a single interest—the South's economic elite.

Class antagonism, though masked by sectional patriotism, was never absent from southern society. The Civil War had brought out long-smoldering differences between planters and hill-country farmers, who were called on to shed blood for a slaveholding system in which they had no interest. Afterward, class tensions were exacerbated by the spread of farm tenancy and by an emergent class of low-wage industrial workers. Unable to make their grievances heard, economically distressed Southerners broke with the Democratic Party in the early 1880s and mounted insurgent movements across the region. Most notable were the Readjusters, who briefly gained power in Virginia over the issue of speculation in Reconstruction debt: they opposed repayment that would have rewarded bondholding speculators while leaving the state destitute. After subsiding briefly this agrarian discontent revived with a vengeance in the late 1880s, as tenant farmers now sought political power through farmers' alliances and the newly evolving Populist Party.

As this insurgency against the Democrats accelerated, the question of black participation became critical. Racism cut through southern society and, so some thought, most infected the lowest rungs. "The white laboring classes here," wrote an Alabamian in 1886, "are separated from the Negroes, working all day side by side with them, by an innate consciousness of race superiority," which "excites a sentiment of sympathy and equality with the classes above them." Yet when times got bad enough, hard-pressed whites could also see blacks as fellow victims. "They are in the ditch just like we are," asserted one white Texan. Southern Populists never fully reconciled these contradictory impulses. They did not question the conventions of social inequality. Nor were the interests of white farmers and black tenants and laborers always in concert. But once agrarian protest turned political, the logic of interracial solidarity became hard to deny.

Black farmers had developed a political structure of their own. The Colored Farmers' Alliance operated much

Helen Potter

The Case for Women's Political Rights

*I*n 1883 Helen Potter, a New York educator, testified before the Senate Committee on Education and Labor. She meant to speak about the sanitary conditions of the poor in New York City, but in the course of her testimony she delivered a powerful indictment of the unequal treatment of women that spoke volumes about the evolving women's political culture of the late nineteenth century.

The Witness. It is really an important question—this of the condition of women in our community. When I was a young girl I had some ambition, and when I heard a good speaker, or when I read something written by a good writer, I had an ambition to do something of that kind myself. I was exceedingly anxious to preach, but the churches would not have me; why, they said that a woman must not be heard. . . .

Question. I suppose you have an idea that women might abolish some of the tricks of the politician's trade?

Answer. Well, sir, it would take them a long time to learn to dare to do those things that men do in the way of politics—to sell and buy votes. . . .

Q. What would be the effect of conferring suffrage upon women? Would not the effect be injurious to the moral character and high influence of woman, if she should devote herself to the tricks of the politician's trade, which you very properly criticize so severely?

A. . . . I certainly think it would clean our streets, and I think it would purify politics, at least for the next two hundred years. It would take about that time to get

women to understand the tricks of politicians as at present practiced. I do not think that women would be injured by it. . . . This Government is based upon the will of the people—women are "people," yet we have not a word to say about the laws. You will hear women in the course of your acquaintance say they wish they were men; I never heard a man say he wished he was a woman. . . .

Q. Why do you think that the suffrage is not extended to women by men—what is the true reason, the radical reason, why men do not give up one half their political power to women?

A. Well, it may arise from a false notion of gallantry. I think most men feel like taking care of, and protecting the ladies. . . . It would be all very well, perhaps, if all women had representatives, and if all had a generous, straightforward honorable man to represent them. But take the case of a good woman who has a drunken husband; how can he represent her? He votes for liquor and for everything he may happen to want, even though it may ruin her and turn her out of doors, and even though it may ruin her children. If the husband is a bad man would it not be better for that woman to represent herself?

Q. What effect do you think the extension of the suffrage to women would have upon their material condition, their wage-earning power and the like?

A. They would get equal pay for equal work of equal value. I do not think a woman ought to be paid the price of an expert, when she is not herself an expert, but I believe there would be a stimulus for a woman to fit herself for the very best work. What stimulus is there for woman to fit herself properly, if she never can attain the highest pay, no matter what sort of work she does? If women had a vote I think larger avenues of livelihood would be opened for them and they would be more respected by the governmental powers.

Source: U.S. Senate, Committee on Education and Labor, *Report upon Relations between Labor and Capital,* II (1885), 627, 629–32.

---

less openly than its white counterparts—it could be worth a black man's life to make too open a show of his independence—but nevertheless made black voters a factor in the political calculations of southern Populists. The demands of partisan politics, once the break with the Democrats came, clinched the argument for interracial unity. Where the Populists fused with the Republican Party, as in North Carolina and Tennessee, they automatically became allies of black leaders. Where the Populists fielded separate third-party tickets, they needed to appeal directly to black voters. "The accident of color can make no difference in the interest of farmers, croppers, and laborers," argued the Georgian Tom Watson. "You are kept apart that you may be separately fleeced of your earnings" (see American Voices, "Tom Watson: The Case for Interracial Unity," p. 528). By making this interracial appeal, even if not

Tom Watson

The Case for Interracial Unity

In the post-Reconstruction South, racial animosities dividing poor whites from poor blacks enabled a conservative elite to maintain its grip on political power. Recognizing this, the fiery Georgia Populist Tom Watson appealed to whites and blacks to look to their class interests, most memorably in the following statement made in advance of the 1892 election. In the bitter aftermath Watson reversed course and rebuilt his career as a race-baiting politician exploiting the very hatreds that he had once so strenuously resisted.

The white tenant lives adjoining the colored tenant. Their houses are almost equally destitute of comforts. Their living is confined to bare necessities. . . . They pay the same enormous prices for farm supplies. Christmas finds them both without any satisfactory return for a year's toil. Dull and heavy and unhappy, they both start the plows again when "New Year's" passes.

Now the People's Party says to these two men, "You are kept apart that you may be separately fleeced of your earnings. You are made to hate each other because upon that hatred is rested the keystone of the arch of financial despotism which enslaves you both. You are deceived and blinded that you may not see how this race antagonism perpetuates a monetary system which beggars both."

This is so obviously true it is no wonder both these unhappy laborers stop to listen. No wonder they begin to realize that no change of law can benefit the white tenant which does not benefit the black one likewise;

that no system which now does injustice to one of them can fail to injure both. Their every material interest is identical. The moment this becomes a conviction, mere selfishness, the mere desire to better their conditions, escape onerous taxes, avoid usurious charges, lighten their rents, or change their precarious tenements into smiling, happy homes, will drive these two men together, just as their mutual inflamed prejudices now drive them apart.

. . . Why should the colored man always be taught that the white man of his neighborhood hates him, while a Northern man, who taxes every rag on his back, loves him? Why should not my tenant come to regard me as his friend rather than the manufacturer who plunders us both? Why should we perpetuate a policy which drives the black man into the arms of the Northern politician?

. . . To the emasculated individual who cries "Negro supremacy!" there is little to be said. . . . Not being prepared to make any such admission in favor of any race the sun ever shone on, I have no words which can portray my contempt for the white men, Anglo-Saxons, who can knock their knees together, and through their chattering teeth and pale lips admit they are afraid the Negroes will "dominate us." The question of social equality does not enter into the calculation at all. That is a thing each citizen decides for himself. No statute ever yet drew the latch of the humblest home—or ever will. Each citizen regulates his visiting list—and always will.

The conclusion, then, seems to me this: They will become political allies, and neither can injure the one without weakening both. It will be in the interest of both that each should have justice. And on these broad lines of mutual interest, mutual forbearance, and mutual support the present will be made the stepping-stone to future peace and prosperity.

Source: Paul F. Boller and Ronald Story, eds., *A More Perfect Union: Documents in U.S. History* (Boston, MA: Houghton Mifflin, 1984), 2: 83–85.

---

always wholeheartedly, the Populists put at risk the foundations of conservative southern politics.

One-Party Rule Triumphant

The conservative Democrats struck back with all their might. They played the race card to the hilt, parading as the "white man's party" while denouncing the Populists for promoting "Negro rule." Yet they shamelessly competed for the black vote. In this they had many advan-

tages: money, control of the local power structures, and a paternalistic relationship to the black community. When all else failed, mischief at the polls enabled the Democrats to beat back the Populists. Across the South in the 1892 elections, the Democrats snatched victory from defeat by a miraculous vote count of the blacks—including many long dead or gone. Thus the Mississippian Frank Burkitt's bitter attack on the conservatives: they were "a class of corrupt office-seekers" who had "hypocritically raised the howl of white supremacy while they debauched the ballot

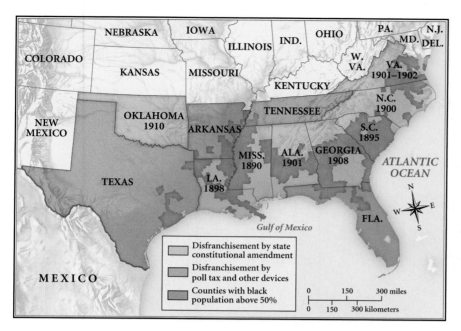

MAP 18.3 Disfranchisement in the New South

In the midst of the Populist challenge to Democratic one-party rule in the South, a movement to deprive blacks of the right to vote spread from Mississippi across the South. By 1910 every state in the region except Tennessee, Arkansas, Texas, and Florida had made constitutional changes designed to prevent blacks from voting, and these four states accomplished much the same result through poll taxes and other exclusionary methods. For the next half-century, the political process in the South would be for whites only.

For more help analyzing this map, see the ONLINE STUDY GUIDE at bedfordstmartins.com/henretta.

boxes . . . disregarded the rights of the blacks . . . and actually dominated the will of the white people through the instrumentality of the stolen negro vote."

Black Disfranchisement.   In the midst of these deadly struggles, the Democrats decided to settle matters once and for all. Disfranchising the blacks, hitherto pushed hesitantly, now became a potent section-wide movement (Map 18.3). In 1890 Mississippi adopted a literacy test that effectively drove the state's blacks out of politics. The motives behind it were cynical, but the literacy test could be dressed up as a reform for white Mississippians tired of electoral fraud and violence. Their children and grandchildren, argued one influential figure, should not be left "with shotguns in their hands, a lie in their mouths and perjury on their lips in order to defeat the negroes." Better, a Mississippi journalist wrote, to devise "some legal defensible substitute for the abhorrent and evil methods on which white supremacy lies." This logic even persuaded some weary Populists: Frank Burkitt, for example, was arguing *for* the Mississippi literacy test in the words quoted in the previous paragraph.

The race issue helped bring down the Populists; now it helped reconcile them to defeat. Embittered poor whites, deeply ambivalent all along about interracial cooperation, turned their fury on the blacks. Insofar as disfranchising measures asserted militant white supremacy, poor whites approved. Of course, it was important that their own vulnerability—their own lack of education—be partially offset by lenient enforcement of the literacy test. Thus to take a blatant instance, Louisiana's grandfather clause exempted from the test those entitled to vote on January 1, 1867 (before the Fifteenth Amendment gave freedmen that right), together

with their sons and grandsons. But poor whites were not protected from property and poll-tax requirements, and many stopped voting.

Poor whites might have objected more had their spokesmen not been conceded a voice within the Democratic Party. A new brand of demagogic politician came forward to speak for them, appealing not to their class interests but to their racial prejudices. Tom Watson, the Georgia Populist, rebuilt his political career as a brilliant practitioner of race baiting. Starting in the early 1900s, he and other race-baiting politicians thrived across the South.

The Ascendancy of Jim Crow.   With the collapse of Populism, a brand of white supremacy emerged that was more virulent than anything blacks had faced since Reconstruction. The color line, hitherto incomplete, became rigid and comprehensive. Segregated seating in trains, widely adopted in the late 1880s, provided a precedent for the legal separation of the races. The enforcing legislation, known as **Jim Crow** laws, soon applied to every type of public facility—restaurants, hotels, streetcars, and even cemeteries. In the 1890s the South became a region fully segregated by law for the first time.

The U.S. Supreme Court soon ratified the South's decision. In the case of *Plessy v. Ferguson* (1896), the Court ruled that segregation was not discriminatory—that is, it did not violate black civil rights under the Fourteenth Amendment—provided that blacks received accommodations equal to those of whites. The "separate but equal" doctrine ignored the realities of southern life: segregated facilities were rarely if ever "equal" in any material sense, and segregation was itself intended to underscore the

Disfranchisement

This political drawing that appeared in Judge *magazine on July 30, 1892, shows members of the Ku Klux Klan barring black voters from the polls. By 1892, in fact, this drawing was behind the times. Literacy tests and poll taxes were beginning to disfranchise blacks with less menace and more likelihood of evading the constitutional requirement (note the sign behind the Klansmen) under the Fifteenth Amendment that the right to vote not be denied "on account of race, color, or previous condition of servitude."*
Museum of American Political Life.

inferiority of blacks. With a similar disregard for reality, the Supreme Court in *Williams v. Mississippi* (1898) validated the disfranchising devices of the southern states: so long as race was not a specified criterion for disfranchisement, the Fifteenth Amendment was not being violated even though the practical effect was the virtual exclusion of blacks from politics in the South.

Race hatred manifested itself in a wave of lynchings and race riots. Public vilification of blacks became commonplace. Benjamin R. Tillman, governor of South Carolina and after 1895 a U.S. senator, called blacks "an ignorant and debased and debauched race." This ugly racism stemmed from several sources, including job competition between whites and blacks during the depressed 1890s and white anger at a less submissive black generation born after slavery. But what had triggered the antiblack impulse was the Populist challenge to one-party rule. From then on white supremacy propped up the one-party system that the Redeemers had been fighting for ever since Reconstruction. If power had to be shared with demagogic poor-white politicians, it would be on terms agreeable to the conservative elite—

the exclusion from politics of any serious challenge to the economic status quo.

The Case of Grimes County. In 1890 African Americans composed more than half of the population of Grimes County, a cotton-growing area in east Texas. They had kept the local Republican Party going after Reconstruction and regularly sent black representatives to the Texas legislature during the 1870s and 1880s. More remarkably, the local Populist Party that appeared among white farmers proved immune to Democrats' taunts of "black rule." A Populist-Republican coalition swept the county elections in 1896 and 1898, surviving well after the collapse of the Populist movement nationally.

In 1899 defeated Democratic candidates and prominent citizens organized the secret White Man's Union. Blacks were forcibly prevented from voting in town elections that year. The two most important black leaders were shot down in cold blood. Night riders terrorized both white Populists and black Republicans.

When the Populist sheriff proved incapable of enforcing the law, the game was up. The White Man's

Party, now out in the open, became the Democratic Party in a new guise. The Democrats carried Grimes County by an overwhelming vote in 1900. The day after the election, the Union laid siege to the sheriff's office. They killed his brother and a friend and drove him, badly wounded, out of the county forever.

The White Man's Party ruled Grimes County for the next fifty years. The whole episode was the handiwork of the county's "best citizens," suggesting how respectable the use of terror had become in the service of white supremacy. The Union intended, as one of its leaders said, to "force the African to keep his place." After Populism was crushed, blacks could survive in Grimes County only if they stayed out of politics and avoided trouble with whites.

Resisting White Supremacy

Like the blacks of Grimes County, southern blacks in many places resisted as best they could. When Georgia adopted the first Jim Crow law applying to streetcars in 1891, Atlanta blacks declared a boycott, and over the next fifteen years blacks boycotted segregated streetcars in at least twenty-five cities. "Do not trample on our pride by being 'jim crowed,'" the Savannah *Tribune* urged its readers: "Walk!" Ida Wells-Barnett emerged as the most outspoken black crusader against lynching, so enraging the Memphis white community by the editorials in her newspaper, *Free Speech,* that she was forced in 1892 to leave the city. Individual blacks who struck back, such as Robert Charles, often paid with their lives (see American Lives, "Robert Charles: Black Militant," p. 532).

Like Charles, some were drawn to the Back to Africa movement, abandoning all hope that they would ever find justice in America. But emigration was not a real choice, and African Americans everywhere had to bend to the raging forces of racism and find a way to survive.

The Atlanta Compromise. Booker T. Washington, the foremost black leader of his day, marked out the path in a famous speech in Atlanta in 1895. Washington retreated from the defiant stand of an older generation of black abolitionists exemplified by Frederick Douglass, who died the same year that the Atlanta speech launched Washington into national prominence. Conciliatory toward the South, Washington considered "the agitation of the question of social equality the extremest folly." He accepted segregation, provided that blacks had equal facilities. He accepted literacy tests and property qualifications for the vote, provided that they applied equally to blacks and whites. He was well aware, of course, that in practice neither proviso amounted to anything.

Washington's doctrine came to be known as the Atlanta Compromise. His approach was "accommodationist," in the sense that it avoided a direct assault on white supremacy. Despite the humble face he put on before white audiences, however, Washington did not concede

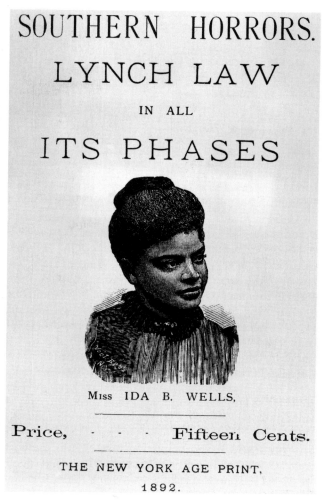

Miss Ida B. Wells

In 1887 Ida Wells (Wells-Barnett after she married in 1895) was thrown bodily from a train in Tennessee for refusing to vacate her seat in a section reserved for whites, launching her into a lifelong crusade for racial justice. Her mission was to expose the evil of lynching in the South. This portrait is from the title page of a pamphlet she published in 1892 entitled, "Southern Horrors. Lynch Law in All Its Phases."

Miriam and Ira D. Wallach Division of Art, Prints and Photographs, The New York Public Library. Astor, Lenox and Tilden Foundations.

the struggle. Behind the scenes he lobbied hard against Jim Crow laws and disfranchisement. More important, his Atlanta Compromise, while abandoning the field of political protest, opened up a second front of economic struggle.

Booker T. Washington sought to capitalize on a southern dilemma about the economic role of the black population. Racist dogma dictated that blacks be kept down and conform to their image as lazy, shiftless workers. But southern prosperity required an efficient labor force. Washington made this need the target of his efforts. As founder of the Tuskegee Institute in Alabama in 1881, Washington advocated *industrial education*— manual and agricultural training. He preached the virtues of thrift, hard work, and property ownership.

Robert Charles: Black Militant

The trouble began in an ordinary way. The two black men were sitting quietly on the steps of a house on Dryades Street in New Orleans, between Washington and Sixth Streets. It was Monday evening, July 24, 1900. One was nineteen-year-old Leonard Pierce; the other was an older man named Robert Charles. They were waiting for a friend of Charles's, Virginia Banks, and her roommate to return from a day in Baton Rouge. Around 11 P.M. three policemen approached Pierce and Charles and began to question them roughly. When Charles stood up, Officer Mora grabbed him. A scuffle followed, and Mora began to beat Charles about the head with his billy club. Charles, a big man, broke away. There was an exchange of gunfire, wounding both in the thigh, Officer Mora more seriously. In a hail of bullets, Charles ran off.

"In any law-abiding community Charles would have been justified in delivering himself up immediately to the properly constituted authorities and asking for a trial by a jury of his peers," wrote the antilynching crusader Ida Wells-Barnett in her pamphlet on what followed. "Charles knew that his arrest in New Orleans, even for defending his life, meant nothing short of a long term in the penitentiary, and still more probable death by lynching at the hands of a cowardly mob." Those must have been Charles's thoughts. He made his way back to the room he shared with Pierce on Fourth Street, took down his Winchester rifle, and got ready to fight.

In the meantime Pierce had been brought to the police station, where Charles's name and address were soon "sweated" out of him. Captain John T. Day, a local hero who had rescued fourteen people from a hotel fire, led a squad to bring in Charles. The entrance to Charles's room was along an alley. When the police arrived, Charles swung open the door, shot Day through the heart, then turned and fatally wounded a second officer. The other two policemen cowered along the wall and slipped into another house, where they hid in the dark. The officers on the street refused to enter the unlit alley. By the time reinforcements arrived at 5 A.M., Charles had slipped away, and the manhunt commenced.

The New Orleans newspapers labeled Charles a "fiend incarnate." No one who had known him would

Robert Charles
This is the only known picture of Charles, an engraving done for the cover of Ida Wells-Barnett's pamphlet on Charles's slaying.
Miriam and Ira D. Wallach Division of Art, Prints and Photographs, The New York Public Library. Astor, Lenox and Tilden Foundations.

have said so. Robert Charles was one of thousands of rural blacks who had sought to escape from grinding poverty by migrating to southern cities. Robert Charles was born just after the end of slavery, in 1865 or 1866, in Copiah County, Mississippi. His parents were sharecroppers, and he was one of ten children. He worked as a day laborer on the railroads and, after arriving in New

Orleans around 1894, at a variety of odd jobs. In July 1900 he was unemployed. Charles was unmarried and rather stylish in his dress, favoring a brown derby hat. Acquaintances remembered him as quiet and intelligent. He had received little education, but his room contained the well-thumbed books and papers of a studious man. One other thing about Charles: he ardently believed that blacks should return to Africa.

The Back to Africa movement, which enjoyed a revival in these hard years, reflected the despair that poor blacks like Robert Charles felt about life in America. Africa was their only salvation, preached Bishop Henry M. Turner, the combative leader of the movement. "I see no other shelter from the stormy blast, from the red tide of persecution, from the horrors of American prejudice." Charles was a reader of Bishop Turner's fiery paper *Voice of Missions*, and in 1899 he began to sell subscriptions. He also became a local agent for the International Migration Society, working on commission to sign up members who would secure transportation to Liberia by contributing a dollar a month for forty months.

Recent events had fortified Charles's conviction that blacks had no hope in America. He was said to have been infuriated by the most infamous lynching of the era, the burning and dismemberment of Sam Hose in Georgia in 1899. In Louisiana, moreover, blacks had been disfranchised in 1898, and a crisis was brewing in state politics. As the elections of 1900 approached, the Democrats vowed that on no account would they allow the Republicans and Populists to emerge as winners. In Charles's pocket was a newspaper clipping about an opposition leader who had called on his supporters to "oil up their Winchesters and prepare to fight" if Democrats tried to steal the election. In *Voice of Missions* there was a similarly desperate message: in one editorial Bishop Turner had urged that "Negroes Get Guns" in self-defense.

Charles, in fact, habitually carried a Colt .38 revolver; it was in his belt when Officer Mora accosted him. There is no knowing what went through his mind when he chose not to submit to the policeman's abuse. But by drawing his gun, Charles had stepped across the line. From then until his inevitable death, he was making a political statement.

That was how the whites of New Orleans saw Charles, too: he was challenging the white power structure. As a leader of the mob that gathered in the streets on Wednesday put it:

> The only way you can teach these niggers a lesson
> and put them in their place is to go out and lynch
> a few of them as an object lesson. String up a few
> of them, and the others will trouble you no more.
> . . . On to the Parish Prison and lynch Pierce!

The mob couldn't get at Pierce, but they took their fury out on any other unfortunate black they encountered as they surged through the city. In the next two days at least six people were killed, and dozens of others were brutally beaten. Only late on Thursday did the police and militia restore a semblance of law and order to New Orleans. But Charles remained at large. Then, on Friday afternoon, July 27, the police got a tip that he was hiding in a small house on Saratoga Street.

Springing from a back closet, Charles shot down the two police officers who came to investigate and then made his way up to the second story. A great crowd soon surrounded the house, peppering it with bullets. Dodging from window to window, Charles returned the fire for nearly two hours. In grudging admiration one reporter wrote of his "diabolical coolness" and "wonderful marksmanship [that] never failed him for a moment." More than twenty of his attackers were hit, three fatally. As dusk began to fall, the building was set ablaze, and Charles was forced out. Still defiant he almost made it across the courtyard when he was stopped by a bullet and went down. The crowd was at him in an instant, firing dozens of shots into him, and stomping on his head. His body was carried off in a police wagon, his battered head hanging grotesquely from the back. Later that night the mob broke loose again, burning buildings and murderously attacking six more blacks.

No New Orleans black would have dared say out loud that Robert Charles had done right. But Ida Wells-Barnett, writing from the safety of Chicago, insisted that he had. "The white people of this country may charge that he was a desperado, but to the people of his own race Robert Charles will always be regarded as the hero of New Orleans." Five weeks after Charles's burial, a neighbor of Fred Clark's on South Rampart Street came up behind Clark, put a gun to his head, and shot him dead. Fred Clark was the black man who had given away Charles's hiding place to the police.

Booker T. Washington

In an age of severe racial oppression, Washington emerged as the acknowledged leader of black people in the United States. He was remarkable both for his ability as spokesman to white Americans and for his deep understanding of the aspirations of black Americans. Born a slave, Washington suffered the indignities experienced by all blacks after emancipation. But having been befriended by several whites as he grew to manhood, he also understood what it took to gain white support—and maneuver around white hostility—in the black struggle for equality. Library of Congress.

For more help analyzing this image, see the ONLINE STUDY GUIDE at bedfordstmartins.com/henretta.

Washington's industrial education program won generous support from northern philanthropists and businessmen and, following his Atlanta speech, applause from local proponents of the New South.

Washington assumed that black economic progress would ultimately lead to political and civil rights. He regarded members of the white southern elite as crucial allies because only they had the power to change the South. More important, they could see "the close connection between labor, industry, education, and political institutions." When it was in their economic interest, when they had grown dependent on black labor and black enterprise, white men of business and property would recognize the justice of black rights. As Washington put it, "There is little race prejudice in the American dollar."

The Limits of Self-Help.   Do the facts suggest that Washington was right? Or, to put the question as an economist might, was it the impersonal market or race prejudice that most determined the economic treatment of blacks? For southern industry the answer seems mixed. Employers did not discriminate very much over wage rates—that is, they did not pay whites higher wages than they paid blacks for the same work. But racial barriers certainly prevented blacks from moving into better-paid jobs. This hard truth is made graphically clear in the comparative wage distribution of whites and blacks (Figure 18.2), which shows that at the low end whites were not paid more than blacks but that blacks were excluded from higher-paying jobs. In agriculture, too, the picture was mixed. The opportunity for black farmers to better themselves did exist. The proportion who became landowners inched slowly upward to roughly 25 percent by 1900. But the racial gap remained wide, with whites almost three times as likely to be landowners as blacks.

To what extent might black self-help—hard work, industrial education, the husbanding of small resources—counterbalance race prejudice? That was the nub of Booker T. Washington's problem. Where the almighty dollar reigned, there was some hope of progress. Elsewhere, as Washington saw it, there was none.

For twenty years after his Atlanta address, Washington dominated the organized African American community. In an age of severe racial oppression, no black dealt more skillfully with the elite of white America or wielded greater political influence. Black leaders knew Washington as a hard taskmaster. Intensely jealous of his authority, he did not regard opposition kindly. Black politicians, educators, and editors stood up to him at their peril.

Even so, opposition surfaced, especially among younger, educated blacks. They thought Washington was conceding too much. He instilled black pride, but of a narrowly middle-class and utilitarian kind. What about the special genius of blacks that W. E. B. Du Bois, a Harvard-trained African American sociologist, celebrated in his collection of essays, *The Souls of Black Folk* (1903)? And what of the "talented tenth" of the black population, whose promise could only be stifled by manual education? Blacks also became increasingly impatient with Washington's silence on segregation and lynching. By the time of his death in 1915, Washington's approach had been superseded by a more militant generation that relied on the courts and political protest, not on black self-help and accommodation.

The Crisis of American Politics: The 1890s

Populism was a catalyst for political crisis not only in the South but across the entire nation. But while in the South, the result was preservation of one-party rule; in national politics the result was a revitalized two-party system.

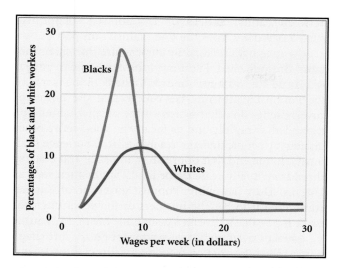

FIGURE 18.2 Distributions of Weekly Wages for Black and White Workers in Virginia, 1907

This graph reveals that wages for common labor in the South were nondiscriminatory (otherwise no or few whites would have been bunched at the low end of the wage scale) but that discrimination denied blacks entry into higher-paying jobs.
Source: Gavin Wright, *Old South, New South: Revolutions in the Southern Economy since the Civil War* (New York: Basic Books, 1986), 184.

Ever since Reconstruction, national politics had been stalemated by the even balance between the parties. In the late 1880s this equilibrium began to break down. Benjamin Harrison's election to the presidency in 1888 was the last of the cliff-hanger victories (Democrat Grover Cleveland actually got a larger popular vote). Thereafter, the tide turned against the Republicans. In 1890 Democrats took the House of Representatives decisively and won a number of governorships in normally Republican states. These losses can partly be explained by the lackluster performance of the Harrison administration and by the success of the Democrats at tarring the protectionist McKinley Tariff of 1890 as a giveaway for the vested interests. The Prohibition Party, which had first appeared in national elections in 1876, made inroads among pietistic Republicans, while the Democrats gained among moderates in local battles over education and public morality. In 1892 Cleveland regained the presidency by the largest margin in twenty years.

Had everything else remained equal, the events of 1890 and 1892 might have initiated an era of Democratic supremacy. But everything else did not remain equal. By the time of Cleveland's inauguration, farm foreclosures and railroad bankruptcies signaled economic trouble. On May 3, 1893, the stock market crashed. By year's end 16,000 firms and hundreds of banks had failed. In Chicago 100,000 jobless workers walked the streets; nationwide the unemployment rate soared to over 20 percent.

As depression set in, which party would prevail—and on what platform—became an open question. The first challenge to the status quo arrived from the West

and South, where falling grain and cotton prices were devastating farmers.

The Populist Revolt

Farmers were of necessity joiners. They needed organization to overcome their social isolation and provide economic services—hence the appeal of the Granger movement (see Chapter 16), which had spread across the Midwest after 1867, and, after the Grange's decline, the appeal of a new movement of farmers' alliances in many rural districts. From diffuse organizational beginnings, two dominant organizations emerged. One was the Farmers' Alliance of the Northwest, which was confined mainly to the midwestern states. More dynamic was the National (or Southern) Farmers' Alliance, which in the mid-1880s spread rapidly from Texas onto the Great Plains and eastward into the cotton South as "travelling lecturers" extolled the virtues of cooperative activity and reminded farmers of "their obligation to stand as a great conservative body against the encroachments of monopolies and . . . the growing corruption of wealth and power." While thus recapitulating Granger resentment against railroads and merchants that had fueled earlier third-party movements, the alliances conceived of themselves as agents of social and economic reform rather than as new political parties.

The Texas Alliance established a huge cooperative, the Texas Exchange, that marketed the crops of cotton farmers and provided them with cheap credit. When cotton prices fell sharply in 1891, the Texas Exchange failed. The Texas Alliance then proposed a new scheme—a **"subtreasury"** system, which would enable farmers to borrow against their unsold crops from a public fund until their cotton could be profitably marketed. The credit and marketing functions would be as in the defunct Texas Exchange but with a crucial difference: the federal government would play the key role. When the subtreasury plan was rejected by the Democratic Party as being too radical, the Texas Alliance decided to strike out in politics independently.

These events in Texas revealed, with special clarity, a process of politicization that rippled through the Alliance movement. Rebuffed by the established parties, alliancemen more or less reluctantly abandoned their Democratic and Republican allegiances. Across the South and West, as state alliances grew stronger and more impatient, they began to field independent slates. The confidence gained at the state level led to the formation of the national People's (Populist) Party in 1892. In the elections that year, with the veteran antimonopoly campaigner James B. Weaver as their presidential candidate, the Populists captured a million votes and carried four western states (Map 18.4). For the first time agrarian protest truly challenged the national two-party system.

Populism was distinguished by the many women in the movement. In established parties the grassroots political clubs were for men only. Populism, on the other hand, arose from a network of local alliances that had formed for largely social purposes and that welcomed women. Although they participated actively and served prominently as speakers and lecturers, few women became leaders of the alliance movement, and their role diminished with the shift into politics. In deference to the southern wing, the Populist platform was silent on woman suffrage. Still, neither Democrats nor Republicans would have countenanced a spokeswoman such as the fiery Mary Elizabeth Lease, who became famous for calling on farmers "to raise less corn and more hell." Mrs. Lease insisted just as strenuously on Populism's "grand and holy mission . . . to place the mothers of this nation on an equality with the fathers."

Populist Ideology. Populism was driven as much by ideology as by the quest for political power. Populists felt that the problems afflicting farmers could stem only from some basic evil. They identified this evil with the business interests controlling the levers of the economic system. "There are but two sides," proclaimed a Populist manifesto. "On the one side are the allied hosts of monopolies, the money power, great trusts and railroad corporations. . . . On the other are the farmers, laborers, merchants and all the people who produce wealth. . . . Between these two there is no middle ground."

By this reasoning farmers and workers formed a single producer class. The claim was not merely rhetorical. Texas railroad workers and Colorado miners cooperated with the farmers' alliances, got their support in strikes, and actively participated in forming state Populist parties. The national platform contained strong labor planks, and party leaders earnestly sought the support of the labor movement. In its explicit class appeal—in recognizing that "the irrepressible conflict between capital and labor is upon us"—Populism parted company from the two mainstream parties.

In an age dominated by laissez-faire doctrine, what most distinguished Populism from the major parties was its positive attitude toward the state. In the words of the Populist platform: "We believe that the power of government—in other words, of the people—should be expanded as rapidly and as far as the good sense of an intelligent people and the teachings of experience shall justify, to the end that oppression, injustice and poverty should eventually cease in the land." Spokesmen such as Lorenzo Dow Lewelling, Populist governor of Kansas, considered it to be "the business of the government to make it possible to live and sustain the life of my family."

At the founding Omaha convention in 1892 Populists called for nationalization of the railroads and communications; protection of the land, including natural resources, from monopoly and foreign ownership; a graduated income tax; the Texas Alliance's subtreasury plan; and the free and unlimited coinage of silver. From this array of issues, the last—free silver—emerged as the overriding demand of the Populist Party.

Free Silver. In the early 1890s, reeling from rock-bottom prices, embattled farmers gravitated to free silver because they hoped that an increase in the money supply would raise farm prices and give them some relief. In addition the party's slim resources would be fattened by hefty contributions from silver-mining interests who, scornful though they might be of Populist radicalism, yearned for the day when the government would buy at a premium all the silver they could produce.

Free silver triggered a debate for the soul of the Populist Party. Social democrats such as Henry Demarest Lloyd of Chicago and agrarian radicals such as Georgia's Tom Watson argued that free silver, if it became the

En Route to a Populist Rally, Dickinson County, Kansas

Farm people traveled miles to rallies and meetings for the chance to voice their grievances and socialize with like-minded folks. This tradition infused Populism with a special fervor. Gatherings such as the one these Kansans were heading to were a visible sign of what Populism meant—a movement of the "people."
Kansas State Historical Society.

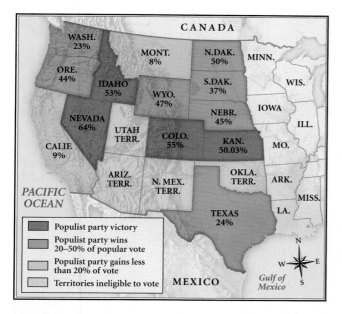

MAP 18.4 The Heyday of Western Populism, 1892

This map shows the percentage of the popular vote won by James B. Weaver, the People's Party candidate, in the presidential election of 1892. Except in California and Montana, the Populists won broad support across the West and genuinely threatened the established parties in that region.

Mary Elizabeth Lease

As a political movement the Populists were short on cash and organization but long on rank-and-file zeal and tub-thumping oratory. No one was more rousing on the stump than Mary Elizabeth Lease, who came from a Kansas homestead and pulled no punches. "What you farmers need to do," she proclaimed in her speeches, "is to raise less corn and more Hell!" Kansas State Historical Society.

defining party issue, would undercut the broader Populist program and alienate wage earners, who had no enthusiasm for inflationary measures. Any chance of a farmer-labor alliance that might transform Populism into an American version of the social-democratic parties of Europe would be doomed. The practical appeal of free silver, however, was simply too great.

But once Populists made that choice, they had fatally compromised their party's capacity to maintain an independent existence. Free silver was not an issue over which the Populists held a monopoly, but, on the contrary, a question at the very center of mainstream politics in the 1890s.

Money and Politics

In a rapidly developing economy, the money supply is bound to be a big political issue. Money has to increase rapidly enough to meet the economy's needs or growth will be stifled. How fast the money supply should grow, however, is a divisive question. Debtors and commodity producers want a larger money supply: more money in circulation inflates prices and reduces the real cost of borrowing. The "sound-money" people—creditors, individuals on fixed incomes, those in the slower-growing sectors of the economy—have an opposite interest.

Before the Civil War the main source of the nation's money supply had been state-chartered banks, several thousand of them, all issuing banknotes to borrowers that then circulated as money. The economy's need for money was amply met by the state banks, although the

soundness of the banknotes—the ability of the issuing banks to stand behind their notes and redeem them at face value—was always uncertain. This freewheeling activity was sharply curtailed by the U.S. Banking Act of 1863. However, because the Lincoln administration itself was printing paper money—**greenbacks**, so-called—to finance the Civil War, the economic impact of the Banking Act was not immediately felt.

After the war the sound money interests lobbied for a return to the traditional national policy, which was to base the federal currency on the amount of **specie**—gold and silver—held by the U.S. Treasury. The issue was hotly contested for a decade, but in 1875 the inflationists were defeated, and the circulation of greenbacks as legal tender—that is, backed by nothing more than the good faith of the federal government—came to an end. With state banknotes also in short supply, the country entered an era of chronic deflation and tight credit.

This was the context out of which the silver question emerged. The country had always operated on a bimetallic standard, but the supply of silver had gradually tightened and, as it became more valuable as metal than as money, silver coins disappeared from circulation. In 1873 silver was officially dropped as a medium of exchange. Soon afterward western mines began producing silver in abundance; silver prices plummeted. Inflationists began to agitate for a resumption of the bimetallic policy: if the government resumed buying at the fixed ratio prevailing before 1873—16 ounces of silver equaling 1 ounce of gold—silver would flow into the treasury and greatly expand the money in circulation.

With so much at stake for so many people, the currency question became one of the staples of post-Reconstruction politics. Twice the pro-silver coalition in Congress won modest victories. First, the Bland-Allison Act of 1878 required the U.S. Treasury to purchase and coin between $2 million and $4 million worth of silver each month. Then, in the more sweeping Sherman Silver Purchase Act of 1890, an additional 4.5 million ounces of silver bullion was to be purchased monthly, to serve as the basis for new issues of U.S. Treasury notes.

These legislative battles, although hard fought, cut across the parties in the familiar fashion of post-Reconstruction politics. But when the crash of 1893 hit, silver suddenly became a burning issue that divided politics along party lines.

The Cleveland Administration and the Silver Question.

As the party in power, the Democrats bore the brunt of responsibility for handling the economic crisis. Any Democratic president would have been hard pressed, but the man who actually had the job, Grover Cleveland, could hardly have made a bigger hash of it. When jobless marchers—the so-called Coxey's army— arrived in Washington in 1894 to demand federal relief, Cleveland's response was to disperse them forcibly and arrest their leader, Jacob S. Coxey, for trespassing on the Capitol grounds. Cleveland's brutal handling of the Pullman strike further alienated the labor vote. Nor did he live up to his reputation as a tariff reformer. Cleveland lost control of the battle when the protectionist McKinley Tariff of 1890 came up for revision in Congress. The resulting Wilson-Gorman Tariff of 1894, which Cleveland allowed to pass into law without his signature, caved in to special interests and left the most important rates unchanged.

Most disastrous, however, was Cleveland's rigidity on the silver question. Cleveland was a committed sound-money man. Nothing that happened after the depression set in—not collapsing prices, not the suffering of farmers, not the groundswell of support for free silver within his own party—budged Cleveland. Economic pressures, in fact, soon forced him to abandon a silver-based currency altogether. With the government's gold reserves dwindling, Cleveland persuaded Congress in 1893 to repeal the Sherman Silver Purchase Act, in effect sacrificing the country's painfully crafted program for maintaining a

Lawyers March for the Gold Standard
Presidential campaigns of the late nineteenth century were always hard fought, none more so than the 1896 election. Big issues were at stake: would the country stay on the gold standard or drastically expand the money supply through the free coinage of silver? Lawyers paraded in the streets of New York City to demonstrate their conviction that the nation's fate hung on sound money and the election of the Republican William McKinley. New-York Historical Society.

limited bimetallic standard. Then, as his administration's problems deepened, Cleveland turned in 1895 to a syndicate of private bankers led by J. P. Morgan to arrange the gold purchases needed to replenish the treasury's depleted reserves. The administration's secret negotiations with Wall Street, once discovered, enraged Democrats and completed Cleveland's isolation from his party.

The Election of 1896.

At their Chicago convention in 1896, the Democrats repudiated Cleveland and turned left. The leader of the triumphant silver Democrats was William Jennings Bryan of Nebraska. Bryan was a political phenomenon. Only thirty-six years old, he had already served two terms in Congress and become a passionate advocate of free silver. He was a consummate politician and, no less important, an inspiring public speaker. Bryan, remarked the journalist Frederic Howe, was "pre-eminently an evangelist," whose zeal sprang from "the Western self-righteous missionary mind." With biblical fervor Bryan swept up his audiences when he joined the debate on free silver at the Democratic convention. He locked up the presidential nomination with a stirring attack on the gold standard: "You shall not press down upon the brow of labor this crown of thorns, you shall not crucify mankind on a cross of gold."

Bryan's nomination meant that the Democrats had become the party of free silver; his "cross of gold" speech meant that he would turn the money question into a national crusade. No one could be neutral on this defining issue. Silver Republicans bolted their party; gold Democrats went for a splinter Democratic ticket or supported the Republican Party; even the Prohibitionist Party split into gold and silver wings. The Populists, meeting after the Democratic convention, accepted Bryan as their candidate. The free-silver issue had become so vital that they could not do otherwise. Although they nominated their own vice presidential candidate, Tom Watson of Georgia, the Populists found themselves for all practical purposes absorbed into the Democratic silver campaign.

The Republicans took up the challenge. Their party leader was the wealthy Cleveland iron maker Mark Hanna, a brilliant political manager and an exponent of the new industrial capitalism. Hanna orchestrated an unprecedented money-raising campaign among America's corporate interests. His candidate, William McKinley of Ohio, personified the virtues of Republicanism, standing solidly for high tariffs, sound money, and prosperity. While Bryan broke with tradition and crisscrossed the country in a furious whistle-stop campaign, the dignified McKinley received delegations at his home in Canton, Ohio. Bryan orated with moral fervor; McKinley talked of industrial progress and a full dinner pail.

Not since 1860 had the United States witnessed so hard fought an election over such high stakes. For the middle class, sound money stood symbolically for the soundness of the social order. With jobless workers tramping the streets and bankrupt farmers up in arms, Bryan's fervent assault on the gold standard struck fear in many hearts. Republicans denounced the Democratic platform as "revolutionary and anarchistic" and Bryan's supporters as "social misfits who have almost nothing in common but opposition to the existing order and institutions."

Though little noticed at the time, ethnocultural issues figured strongly in the campaign. The Republicans, the party of morality, beat a strategic retreat from temperance and Sunday laws. McKinley had represented an ethnically mixed district of northeastern Ohio in Congress. In appealing to his working-class constituents, he had learned the art of easy tolerance, expressed in his words, "live and let live." Of the two candidates the prairie orator Bryan, with his biblical language and moral righteousness, presented the more alien image to traditional Democratic voters in the big cities.

McKinley won handily, with 271 electoral votes to Bryan's 176. He kept the ground Republicans had regained in the 1894 midterm elections and pushed into Democratic strongholds, especially in the cities. Boston, New York, Chicago, and Minneapolis, all taken by Cleveland in 1892, went for McKinley in 1896. Bryan ran strongly only in the South, in silver-mining states, and in

The Candidates, 1896

The 1896 presidential campaign marked one small step in the technology of electioneering—the introduction of the celluloid campaign button, which a party supporter could pin on his lapel. It is doubtful, however, that this innovation made any difference in the outcome of the election. Collection of Janice L. and David J. Frent.

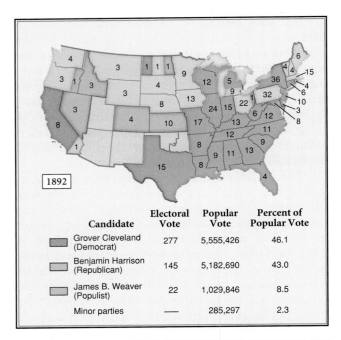

Candidate	Electoral Vote	Popular Vote	Percent of Popular Vote
Grover Cleveland (Democrat)	277	5,555,426	46.1
Benjamin Harrison (Republican)	145	5,182,690	43.0
James B. Weaver (Populist)	22	1,029,846	8.5
Minor parties	—	285,297	2.3

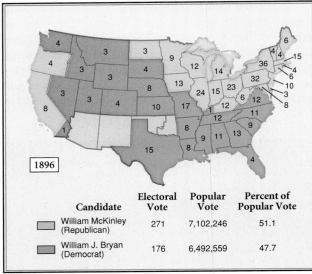

Candidate	Electoral Vote	Popular Vote	Percent of Popular Vote
William McKinley (Republican)	271	7,102,246	51.1
William J. Bryan (Democrat)	176	6,492,559	47.7

MAP 18.5 Presidential Elections of 1892 and 1896

In the 1890s the age of political stalemate came to an end. Students should compare the 1892 map with Map 18.1 on page 517 and note especially Cleveland's breakthrough in the normally Republican states of the upper Midwest. In 1896 the pendulum swung in the opposite direction, with McKinley's consolidation of Republican control over the Northeast and Midwest far overbalancing the Democratic advances in the thinly populated western states. The 1896 election marked the beginning of forty years of Republican dominance in national politics.

the Populist West (Map 18.5). But the gains his evangelical style brought him in some Republican rural areas did not compensate for his losses in traditionally Democratic urban districts.

The paralyzing equilibrium in American politics ended in 1896. The Republicans skillfully turned both economic and cultural challenges to their advantage. They persuaded the nation that they were the party of prosperity, and they persuaded many traditionally Democratic urban voters that they were sympathetic to ethnic diversity. In so doing the Republicans became the nation's majority party. In 1896, too, electoral politics regained its place as an arena for national debate.

The Decline of Agrarian Radicalism. As for Populism, it simply faded away. Fusion with the Democrats in 1896 deprived the People's Party of its identity and undermined its organizational structure. After the election the issue on which Populism had staked its fate—free silver—vanished. During the 1890s gold was discovered in South Africa, Colorado, and the Yukon, and the new cyanide refining process greatly increased ore yields. The newly abundant gold supply took the sting out of the lost battle for free silver. In 1897, moreover, the world market for agricultural commodities turned favorable. Wheat went from 72 cents a bushel in 1896 to 98 cents in 1909, corn from 27 cents a bushel to 57 cents, and cotton from 6 cents a pound to 14 cents. Farm prices rose faster than the prices of other products, and, as a result, so did the real income of farmers. A new spirit of optimism took hold in the "golden age" of American agriculture before World War I.

There would be times when distressed farmers would turn again to insurgent politics but never with the potency of the Populist Party. By 1900 scarcely a third of the labor force earned a living from the soil; the proportion would shrink in each succeeding census until, in our own time, less than 3 percent of the labor force is engaged in agriculture (see Appendix, p. A-14). It would be as an organized interest group, not as a protest movement, that farmers would ultimately find a way of advancing their interests in politics.

Agriculture had long been at the heart of American life. In the twentieth century agriculture became just one more economic interest—important but subordinate in the modern industrial order.

FOR FURTHER EXPLORATION

▶ For definitions of key terms boldfaced in this chapter, see the glossary at the end of the book.

▶ To assess your mastery of the material covered in this chapter, see the Online Study Guide at **bedfordstmartins.com/henretta**.

▶ For suggested references, including Web sites, see page SR-20 at the end of the book.

▶ For map resources and primary documents, see **bedfordstmartins.com/henretta**.

When Reconstruction ended in 1877, national politics became less issue oriented and, as a formal process, less important in American life. This situation resulted from weaknesses in governmental institutions, from the prevailing philosophy of laissez faire, and from the paralysis of evenly matched political parties. Yet post-Reconstruction politics displayed great vigor, as can be seen in the high levels of popular participation. For one thing, politics was the arena in which the nation's ethnic and religious conflicts were largely fought out. Equally important, the party machines were robust, engaging the energies of political activists and performing crucial functions that properly belonged to, but were still beyond the capacity of, governmental institutions. Finally, despite the slow headway made toward woman suffrage, women's organizations carved out for themselves a broader sphere of social reform activity.

In the South the political aftermath of Reconstruction was one-party rule by the "Redeemer" Democrats. Their appeal to sectional pride and white supremacy, potent though it was, could not quite contain the South's class tensions, which with the rise of Populism burst out in a full-fledged, biracial challenge to conservative Democratic rule. The defeat of southern Populism turned into a grim reaction that disfranchised African Americans, completed a rigid segregation system, and let loose a terrible cycle of racial violence. Blacks resisted but had to bend to overwhelming white power. The accommodationist strategy of Booker T. Washington seemed to offer the best hope for black survival in an age of extreme racism.

Elsewhere in the country the Populist challenge stirred new life into the two-party system. Seizing free silver from the Populists, the Democratic Party made the election of 1896 a contest of real programmatic significance. The Republicans won decisively, ending the paralyzing party stalemate of the previous twenty years. With electoral politics once more an arena of national debate, the stage was set for the reform politics of the Progressive Era.

1874 Woman's Christian Temperance Union founded

1877 Rutherford B. Hayes inaugurated as president, marking end of Reconstruction

1881 President James A. Garfield assassinated

1883 Pendleton Civil Service Act

Supreme Court strikes down Civil Rights Act of 1875

1884 Mugwump reformers leave Republican Party to support Grover Cleveland, first Democrat elected president since 1856

1887 Florida adopts first law segregating railroad travel

1888 James Bryce's *The American Commonwealth*

1890 McKinley Tariff

Democrats sweep congressional elections, inaugurating brief era of Democratic Party dominance

Mississippi becomes first state to adopt literacy test to disfranchise blacks

1892 People's (Populist) Party founded

1893 Panic of 1893 leads to national depression

Repeal of Sherman Silver Purchase Act (1890)

1894 "Coxey's army" of unemployed fails to win federal relief

1895 Booker T. Washington sets out Atlanta Compromise

1896 Election of Republican president William McKinley; free-silver campaign crushed

Plessy v. Ferguson upholds constitutionality of "separate but equal" facilities

Economic depression ends; era of agricultural prosperity begins

CHAPTER 19

The Rise of the City

VISITING HIS FIANCÉE'S MISSOURI HOMESTEAD IN 1894, Theodore Dreiser was struck by "the spirit of rural America, its idealism, its dreams." But this was an "American tradition in which I, alas!, could not share." Said Dreiser, "I had seen Pittsburgh. I had seen Lithuanians and Hungarians in their [alleys] and hovels. I had seen the girls of the city—walking the streets at night." Only twenty-three at the time, Dreiser would go on to write one of the great American urban novels, *Sister Carrie* (1900), about one young woman in the army of small-town Americans flocking to the Big City. But Dreiser, part of that army, already knew that between rural America and Pittsburgh an unbridgeable chasm had opened up.

◄ **Mulberry Street, New York City, c. 1900**

The influx of southern and Eastern Europeans created teeming ghettos in the heart of New York City and other major American cities. The view is of Mulberry Street, with its pushcarts, street peddlers, and bustling traffic. The inhabitants are mostly Italians, and some of them, noticing the photographer preparing his camera, have gathered to be in the picture.
Library of Congress.

For more help analyzing this image, see the ONLINE STUDY GUIDE at bedfordstmartins.com/henretta.

In 1820, after two hundred years of settlement, fewer than one in twenty Americans lived in a city of 10,000 people or more. After that, decade by decade, the urban population swelled until, by 1900, one of every five Americans was a city dweller. Nearly 6.5 million inhabited just three great cities: New York, Chicago, and Philadelphia (Table 19.1).

The city was the arena of the nation's vibrant economic life. Here the factories went up, and here the new immigrants settled, constituting in 1900 a third of the residents of the

TABLE 19.1 Ten Largest Cities by Population, 1870 and 1900

1870		1900	
City	Population	City	Population
1. New York	942,292	New York	3,437,202
2. Philadelphia	674,022	Chicago	1,698,575
3. Brooklyn*	419,921	Philadelphia	1,293,697
4. St. Louis	310,864	St. Louis	575,238
5. Chicago	298,977	Boston	560,892
6. Baltimore	267,354	Baltimore	508,957
7. Boston	250,526	Cleveland	381,768
8. Cincinnati	216,239	Buffalo, N.Y.	352,387
9. New Orleans	191,418	San Francisco	342,782
10. San Francisco	149,473	Cincinnati	325,902

*Brooklyn was consolidated with New York in 1898.
Source: U.S. Census data.

major American cities. Here, too, lived the millionaires and a growing white-collar middle class. For all these people the city was more than a place to make a living. It provided the setting for an urban culture unlike anything seen before in the United States. City people, although differing vastly among themselves, became distinctively and recognizably urban.

Urbanization

The march to the cities seemed irresistible to nineteenth-century Americans (Map 19.1). "The greater part of our population must live in cities—cities much greater than the world has yet known," declared the Congregational minister Josiah Strong. "There was no resisting the trend," said another writer. Urbanization became inevitable because of another inevitability of American life—industrialism.

Industrial Sources of City Growth

Until the Civil War cities were centers of commerce, not industry. They were the places where goods were bought and sold for distribution into the interior or shipment out to world markets. Early industry sprang up in the countryside because factories needed water power from streams, access to fuel and raw materials, and workers recruited from the countryside.

But once steam engines came along, mill operators no longer depended on water-driven power. In the iron industry coal replaced charcoal as the primary fuel, so it was not necessary to be near forests. Improved transportation, especially railroads, enabled entrepreneurs to locate in places most convenient to suppliers and markets. The result was a geographic concentration of industry. Iron makers gravitated to Pittsburgh because of its superior access to coal and ore fields and also to markets for iron products. Chicago, midway between western livestock suppliers and eastern markets, became a great meatpacking center (see Map 17.3 on p. 494).

The increasing size of factories contributed to urban growth. A plant that employed thousands of workers instantly created a small city in its vicinity, sometimes in the form of a company town like Aliquippa, Pennsylvania, which became body and soul the property of the Jones and Laughlin Steel Company. Many firms built plants near a large city so they could draw on its labor supply and transportation facilities, as George Pullman did in 1880 when he located his sleeping-car works and model town southwest of Chicago.

Sometimes the metropolis spread and absorbed nearby factory towns, which was the fate of Pullman. Elsewhere, as in northern New Jersey or along Lake

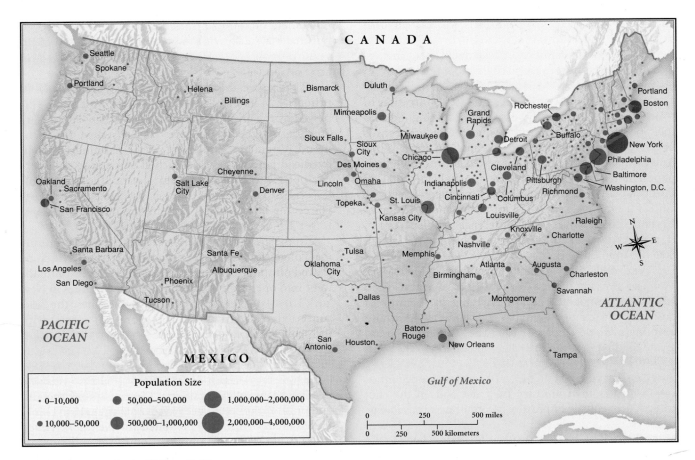

MAP 19.1 America's Cities, 1900

The number of Americans living in urban places more than doubled between 1880 and 1900, with the most dramatic increases in the largest metropolitan centers. New York grew from 1.2 million to 3.4 million, Chicago from 500,000 to 1.7 million.

For more help analyzing this map, see the ONLINE STUDY GUIDE at bedfordstmartins.com/henretta.

Michigan south of Chicago, the lines between industrial towns blurred and an extended urban-industrial area emerged. The same process occurred in Europe, where industrial regions were emerging in northeastern France around Lille and in Germany's Ruhr Valley.

Older commercial cities also became more industrial. Warehouse districts could readily be converted to small-scale manufacturing; a distribution network was right at hand. In addition, as gateways for immigrants, port cities offered abundant cheap labor. Boston, Philadelphia, Baltimore, and San Francisco became hives of small-scale, labor-intensive industrial activity. New York's enormous pool of immigrant workers made that city a magnet for the garment trades, cigarmaking, and diversified light industry. Preeminent as a city of trade and finance, New York also ranked as the nation's largest manufacturing center.

City Innovation

The commercial cities of the early nineteenth century had been compact places, densely settled around harbors or riverfronts. As late as 1850, when it had 565,000 people, Philadelphia covered only ten square miles. From the foot of Chestnut Street on the Delaware River, a person could walk almost anywhere in the city within forty-five minutes. Thereafter, as it developed, Philadelphia spilled out and, like American cities everywhere, engulfed the surrounding countryside.

A downtown area emerged, usually on the site of the original commercial city. Downtown in turn broke up into shopping, financial, warehousing, manufacturing, hotel and entertainment, and red-light districts. Moving out from the center, industrial development tended to follow the arteries of transportation—railroads, canals, and rivers—and, at the city's outskirts, to create concentrations of heavy industry.

Urban development was markedly different in continental Europe, where even cities growing rapidly in population remained physically compact, with built-up areas ending abruptly at the surrounding countryside. In America cities constantly expanded, spilling beyond their boundaries and forming what the federal census began to designate in 1910 as metropolitan areas. While American cities were highly congested at the center, their population density was actually much below that of European cities: 22 persons per acre for fifteen American cities, for example, versus 158 for a comparable group of German cities. Given this difference efficient urban transportation was a more urgent problem in the United States than in Europe.

"The only trouble about this town," wrote Mark Twain on arriving in New York in 1867, "is that it is too large. You cannot accomplish anything in the way of business, you cannot even pay a friendly call without devoting a whole day to it. . . . [The] distances are too great." Finding ways of moving nearly a million New Yorkers around was not as hopeless as Twain thought, but it did pose a challenge to city builders. The city demanded innovation no less than industry itself did and, in the end, compiled an equally impressive record of new technology.

Mass Transit. The first innovation, dating back to the 1820s, was the omnibus, an elongated version of the horse-drawn carriage. Much better was the horsecar, whose key advantage was that it ran on iron tracks so that the horses could pull more passengers and move them at a faster clip through congested city streets. All this happened because of a modest but crucial refinement on railroad track design in 1852—a grooved rail that was flush with the pavement. From the 1840s onward horsecars were the mainstay of urban transit across America.

Then came the electric trolley car, the brainchild primarily of Frank J. Sprague, an engineer once employed by the great inventor Thomas A. Edison. In 1887 Sprague designed an electric-driven system for Richmond, Virginia: a "trolley" carriage running along an overhead power line was attached by cable to streetcars equipped with an electric motor—hence the name "trolley car." After Sprague's success, the trolley swiftly displaced the horsecar and became the primary mode of transportation in most American cities.

In the great metropolitan centers, however, mounting congestion led to demands that transit lines be moved off the streets. In 1879 the first elevated railroads went into operation on Sixth and Ninth Avenues in New York City. Powered at first by steam engines, the "els" converted to electricity following Sprague's success with the trolley. Chicago developed elevated transit most fully (Map 19.2). New York, meanwhile, turned to the subway. Boston opened a short underground line in 1897, but it was the completion in 1904 of a subway running the length of Manhattan that demonstrated the full potential of the high-speed underground train. Thinly settled areas of the city, predicted the *New York Times,* would soon boast of "a population of ten millions . . . housed comfortably, healthfully and relatively cheaply." The subway would especially delight "all who travel with the sole purpose of 'getting there' in the least possible time." Mass transit had become *rapid* transit.

By 1890 the number of passengers carried on American street railways was more than 2 billion per

The Chicago Elevated, 1900
This is Wabash Avenue, looking north from Adams Street. For Americans from farms and small towns, this photograph by William Henry Jackson captured something of the peculiarity of the urban scene. What could be stranger than a railroad suspended above the streets in the midst of people's lives?
KEA Publishing Services Ltd.

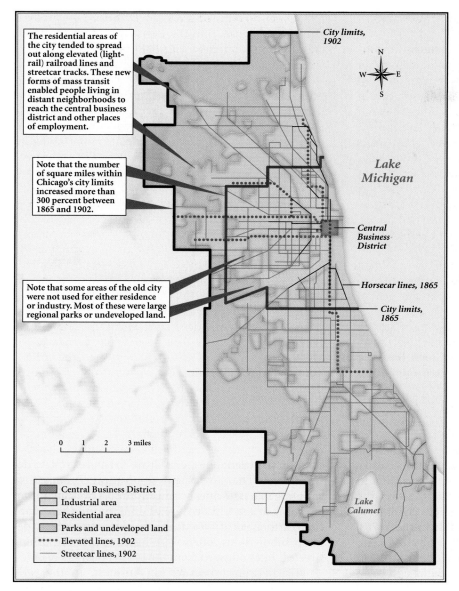

The residential areas of the city tended to spread out along elevated (light-rail) railroad lines and streetcar tracks. These new forms of mass transit enabled people living in distant neighborhoods to reach the central business district and other places of employment.

Note that the number of square miles within Chicago's city limits increased more than 300 percent between 1865 and 1902.

Note that some areas of the old city were not used for either residence or industry. Most of these were large regional parks or undeveloped land.

City limits, 1902

Lake Michigan

Central Business District

Horsecar lines, 1865

City limits, 1865

Lake Calumet

0   1   2   3 miles

Central Business District
Industrial area
Residential area
Parks and undeveloped land
••••• Elevated lines, 1902
— Streetcar lines, 1902

MAP 19.2 The Expansion of Chicago, 1865–1902

In 1865 Chicagoans depended on horsecar lines to get around town. By 1900 the city limits had expanded enormously, accompanied by an equally dramatic expansion of streetcar service, which was by then electrified. Elevated trains also helped to ease congestion in the urban core. New streetcar lines, some extending beyond the city limits, were important to suburban development in the coming years.

year, over twice that of the rest of the world combined. In Great Britain the horsecar remained dominant long after it had disappeared from American streets. In Tokyo, the largest Asian city, the horsecar was not even introduced until 1882, and electric streetcars first appeared there in 1903.

Skyscrapers. Equally remarkable was the architectural revolution sweeping metropolitan business districts. With steel girders, durable plate glass, and the passenger elevator available by the 1880s, a wholly new way of construction opened up. A steel skeleton supported the building, while the walls, previously weight bearing, served as curtains enclosing the structure. The sky, so to speak, became the limit.

The first "skyscraper" to be built on this principle was William Jenney's ten-story Home Insurance Building

(1885) in Chicago. Although this pioneering effort appeared unremarkable—it looked just like the other downtown buildings—the steel-girdered technology it contained liberated the aesthetic perceptions of American architects. A Chicago school sprang up, dedicated to the design of buildings whose form expressed, rather than masked, their structure and function. Chicago pioneered skyscraper construction, but New York, with its unrelenting need for prime downtown space, took the lead after the mid-1890s. The fifty-five story Woolworth Building, completed in 1913, marked the beginning of the modern Manhattan skyline.

The Electric City. For ordinary citizens the electric lights that dispelled the gloom of the city at night offered the most dramatic evidence that times had changed. Gaslight—illuminating gas produced from

Thomas Edison's Laboratories in Menlo Park, New Jersey, c. 1880
Thomas Edison's dream of illuminating the world is illustrated by this fanciful drawing of his laboratories in Menlo Park, New Jersey. For the time being, however, it was the American home that was the primary beneficiary of Edison's wonderful light bulb, since electricity was slow to arrive in many parts of the world.
U.S. Department of the Interior, National Park Service, Edison National Historic Site.

coal—had been in use since the early nineteenth century but, at 12 candlepower, the lamps were too dim to brighten the downtown streets and public spaces of the city. The first use of electricity, once generating technology made it commercially feasible in the 1870s, was for better city lighting. Charles F. Brush's electric arc lamps, installed in Wanamaker's department store in Philadelphia in 1878, threw a brilliant light and soon replaced gaslight on city streets and public buildings across the country. Electric lighting then entered the American home, thanks to Thomas Edison's invention of a serviceable incandescent bulb in 1879. Edison's motto—"Let there be light!"—truly described the experience of the modern city.

Before it had any significant effect on industry, electricity gave the city its modern tempo, lifting elevators, powering streetcars and subway trains, turning night into day. Meanwhile, Alexander Graham Bell's telephone (1876) sped communication beyond anything imagined previously. Twain's complaint of 1867 that it was impossible to carry on business in New York had been answered: all he needed to do was pick up the phone.

Private City, Public City

City building was very much an exercise in private enterprise. The lure of profit spurred the great innovations—the trolley car, electric lighting, the skyscraper, the elevator, the telephone—and drove urban real estate development. The investment opportunities looked so tempting that new cities sprang up almost overnight from the ruins of the Chicago fire of 1871 and the San Francisco earthquake of 1906. Real estate interests, eager to develop subdivisions, often were instrumental in pushing streetcar lines outward from the central districts of cities.

Urban transit became big business. In the early 1880s the streetcar lines of Philadelphia were merged into the Philadelphia Traction Company. The promoters, Peter A. B. Widener and William L. Elkins, then joined with financiers in Chicago and New York and built an immense syndicate that by 1900 controlled streetcar systems in over a hundred cities as well as utilities supplying gas and electricity to urban residents. The city, like industry, became an arena for enterprise and profit.

America gave birth to what one urban historian has called the "private city"—whose growth was shaped primarily by the actions of many individuals, all pursuing their own goals and bent on making money. The prevailing belief was that the sum of such private activity would far exceed what the community could accomplish through public effort.

Yet constitutionally it was up to the cities to draw the line between public and private. New York City was entirely within its rights to operate a municipally owned subway, the State Supreme Court ruled in 1897. Even the use of private land was subject to whatever regulations the city might impose. Thus the skylines of Chicago and Boston did not resemble Manhattan's because of the limits those cities imposed on the heights of buildings. Moreover, city governance improved impressively in the late nineteenth century. Though by no means free of the corruption of earlier days, municipal agencies became far better organized and staffed and, above all, more expansive in the functions they undertook. Nowhere in the world, indeed, were there more massive public projects—aqueducts, sewage systems, bridges, and spacious parks.

The Urban Environment. In the space between public and private, however, was an environmental no-man's land. City streets were often filthy and poorly maintained. "Three or four days of warm spring weather," remarked a New York journalist, would turn Manhattan's garbage-strewn, snow-clogged streets into "veritable mud rivers." Air quality likewise suffered. A visitor to Pittsburgh noted "the heavy pall of smoke which constantly overhangs her . . . until the very sun looks coppery through the sooty haze." As for the lovely hills rising from the rivers, "they have been leveled down, cut into, sliced off, and ruthlessly marred and mutilated." Pittsburgh presented "all that is unsightly and forbidding in appearance, the original beauties of nature having been ruthlessly sacrificed to utility."

Hardest hit by urban growth were the poor. In earlier times they had mainly lived in makeshift wooden structures in alleys and back streets and then, as more prosperous families moved away, in the subdivided homes left behind. As land values climbed after the Civil War, speculators tore down these houses and began to erect buildings specifically designed for the urban masses. In New York City the dreadful result was five- or six-story **tenements** housing twenty or more families in cramped, airless apartments (Figure 19.1). In New York's Eleventh Ward, an average of 986 persons occupied each acre, a density matched only in Bombay, India.

Reformers recognized the problem but seemed unable to solve it. Some favored model tenements financed by public-spirited citizens willing to accept a limited return on their investment. When private philanthropy failed to make much of a dent, cities turned to housing codes. The most advanced of these was New York's Tenement House Law of 1901, which required interior courts, indoor toilets, and fire safeguards for new structures but did little for existing housing stock. Commercial development had pushed up land values in downtown areas. Only high-density, cheaply built housing could earn a sufficient profit for the landlords of the poor. This economic fact defied nineteenth-century solutions.

It was not that America lacked an urban vision. On the contrary an abiding rural ideal had influenced American cities for many years. Frederick Law Olmsted, who designed New York's Central Park, wanted cities that exposed people to the beauties of nature. One of Olmsted's projects, the Chicago Columbian Exposition of 1893, gave rise to the influential "City Beautiful" movement. The results included larger park systems, broad boulevards and parkways, and after the turn of the century, zoning laws and planned suburbs.

But cities usually heeded urban planners too little and too late. "Fifteen or twenty years ago a plan might have been adopted that would have made this one of the most beautiful cities in the world," Kansas City's park commissioners reported in 1893. At that time "such a policy could not be fully appreciated." Nor, even if Kansas City had foreseen its future, would it have shouldered the "heavy burden" of trying to shape its development. The American city had placed its faith in the

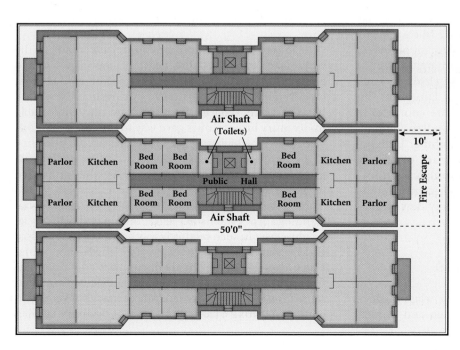

FIGURE 19.1 Floor Plan of a Dumbbell Tenement

In a contest for a design that met an 1879 requirement that every room have a window, the dumbbell tenement won. The interior indentation, which created an airshaft between adjoining buildings, gave the tenement its "dumbbell" shape. What was touted as a "model" tenement demonstrated instead the futility of trying to reconcile maximum land usage with decent housing. Each floor contained four apartments of three or four rooms, the largest only 10 by 11 feet. The two toilets in the hall became filthy or broke down under daily use by forty or more people. The narrow airshaft provided almost no light for the interior rooms and served mainly as a dumping ground for garbage. So deplorable were these tenements that they became the stimulus for the next wave of New York housing reform.

dynamics of the marketplace, not the restraints of a planned future. The pluses and minuses are perhaps best revealed by the following comparison.

A Balance Sheet: Chicago and Berlin. Chicago and Berlin had virtually equal populations in 1900. But they had very different histories. Seventy years earlier, when Chicago had been a muddy frontier outpost, Berlin was already a city of 250,000 and the royal seat of the Hohenzollerns of Prussia.

With German unification in 1871, the imperial authorities rebuilt Berlin on a grander scale. "A capital city is essential for the state, to act as a pivot for its culture," proclaimed the Prussian historian Heinrich von Treitschke. Berlin served that national purpose—"a center where Germany's political, intellectual, and material life is concentrated, and its people can feel united." Chicago had no such pretensions. It was strictly a place of business, made great by virtue of its strategic grip on the commerce of America's industrial heartland. Nothing in Chicago evoked the grandeur of Berlin's boulevards or its monumental palaces and public buildings, nor were Chicagoans witness to the pomp and ceremony of the imperial parades up broad, tree-lined Unter den Linden to the national cathedral.

Yet as a functioning city Chicago was in many ways superior to Berlin. Chicago's waterworks pumped 500 million gallons of water a day, or 139 gallons of water per person, while Berliners had to make do with 18 gallons. Flush toilets, a rarity in Berlin in 1900, could be found in 60 percent of Chicago's homes. Chicago's streets were lit by electricity, while Berlin still relied mostly on gaslight. Chicago had a much bigger streetcar system, twice as much acreage devoted to parks, and a public library containing many more volumes. And Chicago had just completed an amazing sanitation project, reversing the course of the Chicago River so that its waters—and the city's sewage—would flow away from Lake Michigan and southward down into the Illinois and Mississippi Rivers.

Giant sanitation projects were one thing; an inspiring urban environment was something else. For well-traveled Americans admiring of things European, the sense of inferiority was palpable. "We are enormously rich," admitted the journalist Edwin L. Godkin, "but . . . what have we got to show? Almost nothing. Ugliness from an artistic point of view is the mark of all our cities." Thus the urban balance sheet: a utilitarian infrastructure that was superb by nineteenth-century standards, but "no municipal splendors of any description, nothing but population and hotels."

Upper Class, Middle Class

In the compact city of the early republic, class distinctions had been expressed by the way men and women

dressed and by the deference they demanded from or granted to others. As the industrial city grew, these interpersonal marks of class began to lose their force. In the anonymity of a large city, recognition and deference no longer served as mechanisms for conferring status. Instead, people began to rely on external signs: conspicuous display of wealth, membership in exclusive clubs, and above all, choice of neighborhood.

For the poor, place of residence depended, as always, on being close to their jobs. But for higher-income urbanites, where to live became a matter of personal means and social preference.

The Urban Elite

As early as the 1840s, Boston merchants had taken advantage of the new railway service to escape the congested city. Fine rural estates appeared in Milton, Newton, and other outlying towns. By 1848 roughly 20 percent of Boston's businessmen were making the trip by train to their downtown offices. Ferries that plied the harbor between Manhattan and Brooklyn or New Jersey served the same purpose for New Yorkers.

Lifestyles of the Rich. As commercial development engulfed downtown residential areas, the exodus by the well-to-do spread across America. In Cincinnati wealthy families settled on the scenic hills rimming the crowded, humid tableland that ran down to the Ohio River. On those hillsides, a traveler noted in 1883, "the homes of Cincinnati's merchant princes and millionaires are found . . . elegant cottages, tasteful villas, and substantial mansions, surrounded by a paradise of grass, gardens, lawns, and tree-shaded roads." Residents of the area, called Hilltop, founded country clubs, five downtown gentlemen's clubs, and a host of other institutions that sustained an exclusive social life for Cincinnati's elite.

Despite the attractions of country life, many of the very richest preferred the heart of the city. Chicago boasted its Gold Coast; San Francisco, Nob Hill; Denver, Quality Hill; and Manhattan, Fifth Avenue. New York novelist Edith Wharton recalled how the comfortable midcentury brownstones gave way to the "'new' millionaire houses," which spread northward on Fifth Avenue along Central Park. Great mansions, emulating the aristocratic houses of Europe, lined Fifth Avenue at the turn of the century.

But great wealth did not automatically confer social standing. An established elite dominated the social heights, even in such relatively raw cities as San Francisco and Denver. It had taken only a generation—and sometimes less—for money made in commerce or real estate to shed its tarnish and become "old" and genteel. In long-settled Boston, wealth passed intact through several generations, creating a closely knit tribe of Brahmin families that kept moneyed newcomers at bay. Elsewhere urban elites tended to be more open, but only to the socially ambitious who were prepared to make visible and energetic use of their money.

New York's Metropolitan Opera was one product of this ongoing struggle among the wealthy. The Academy of Music, home to the city's opera since 1854, was controlled by the Livingstons, the Bayards, the Beekmans, and other old New York families. Denied boxes at the Academy, the Vanderbilts and their allies sponsored a rival opera house. In 1883, with its glittering opening to the strains of Gounod's *Faust,* the Metropolitan Opera proclaimed its ascendancy in the music world and in due course won the patronage even of the Beekmans and Bayards. During this war of the opera houses the Vanderbilt circle achieved social recognition.

"High Society." New York City became the home of a national elite as the most ambitious gravitated to this preeminent capital of American finance and culture. Manhattan's extraordinary vitality in turn kept the city's high society fluid and relatively open. In Theodore Dreiser's novel *The Titan* (1914), the tycoon Frank Cowperwood reassures his unhappy wife that if Chicago society will not accept them, "there are other cities. Money will arrange matters in New York—that I know. We can build a real place there, and go in on equal terms, if we have money enough." New York thus came to be a magnet for millionaires. The city attracted them not only because of its importance as a business center but for the opportunities it offered for display and social recognition.

This infusion of wealth shattered the older elite society of New York. Seeking to be assimilated into the upper class, the flood of moneyed newcomers simply overwhelmed it. There followed a curious process of reconstruction, a deliberate effort to define the rules of conduct and identify those who properly "belonged" in New York society.

The key figure was Ward McAllister, a southern-born lawyer who had made a quick fortune in gold-rush San Francisco and then devoted himself to a second career as the arbiter of New York society. In 1888 McAllister compiled the first *Social Register,* which announced that it would serve as a "record of society, comprising an accurate

Going to the Opera, 1873

In this painting by Seymour J. Guy, William H. Vanderbilt, eldest son and successor of the railroad tycoon Cornelius Vanderbilt, has gathered with his family and friends preparatory to attending the opera. It was the sponsorship of New York's Metropolitan Opera that helped the Vanderbilts achieve social recognition among the older, more established moneyed families of New York City. Courtesy, Biltmore Estate, Asheville, NC.

and careful list" of all those deemed eligible for New York society. McAllister instructed the socially ambitious on how to select guests, set a proper table, arrange a party, and launch a young lady into society. He presided over a round of assemblies, balls, and dinners that defined the boundaries of an elite society. At the apex stood "The Four Hundred"—the true cream of New York society. McAllister's list corresponded to those invited to Mrs. William Astor's gala ball of February 1, 1892.

Americans were adept at making money, remarked the journalist Edwin L. Godkin in 1896, but they lacked the aristocratic traditions of Europe for spending it. "Great wealth has not yet entered our manners," Godkin remarked. In their struggle to find the rules and establish the manners, the moneyed elite made an indelible mark on urban life. If there was magnificence in the American city, that was mainly their handiwork. And if there was conspicuous waste and display, that too was their doing.

The Suburban World

The middle class left a smaller imprint on the public face of urban society. Its members, unlike the rich, preferred privacy and retreated into the domesticity of suburban comfort and family life.

Since colonial times the American economy had spawned a robust middle class of mostly self-employed lawyers, doctors, merchants, and proprietors. This older middle class remained important, but it was joined by a new salaried middle class brought forth by industrialism. Corporate organizations required managers, accountants, and clerks. Technology advances called for engineers, chemists, and designers, while the distribution system needed salesmen, advertising executives, and accountants. These salaried ranks increased sevenfold between 1870 and 1910—much faster than any other occupational group. Nearly 9 million people held **white-collar** jobs in 1910, more than a fourth of all employed Americans.

Some members of this salaried class lived in the row houses of Baltimore and Boston or the comfortable apartment buildings of New York City. But more preferred to escape the clamor and congestion of the city. They were attracted by a persisting "rural ideal," agreeing with the landscape architect Andrew Jackson Downing that "nature and domestic life are better than the society and manners of town." As trolley service expanded out from the central city, middle-class Americans followed the wealthy into the countryside. All sought what one Chicago developer promised for his North Shore subdivision in 1875—"qualities of which the city is in a large degree bereft, namely, its pure air, peacefulness, quietude, and natural scenery."

No major American city escaped **suburbanization** during the late nineteenth century. City limits everywhere expanded rapidly, but even so, much of the suburban growth took place beyond city limits. By 1900 more than half of Boston's people lived in "streetcar suburbs" outside Boston proper; nationwide, according to the 1910 census, about 25 percent of the urban population lived in such autonomous suburbs.

On the European continent, by contrast, cities remained highly concentrated. When expansion did occur, it was the poor and not the well-to-do who inhabited the margins. Unlike its American counterpart, the European middle class was not attracted to the rural ideal and valued urban life for its own sake. The preconditions for suburbanization were likewise weaker in Europe: mass transit developed more slowly; traditional beam-and-post construction did not give way to the cheaper balloon frame techniques; and there was less of the freewheeling real estate development that spurred American suburbanization.

The geography of the suburbs was truly a map of class structure because where a family lived told where it ranked. The farther out from the city center, the finer the houses and the larger the lots. Affluent businessmen and professionals had the time and flexibility to travel a long distance into town. People closer in wanted transit lines that went straight into the city center and carried them quickly between home and office. Lower-income commuters were more likely to have more than one wage earner in the family, less secure employment, and jobs requiring movement around the city. It was better for them to be closer to the city center because they then had access to crosstown lines that afforded the mobility they needed for their work.

Suburban boundaries were ever shifting, as working-class city residents who wanted to better their lives moved to the cheapest suburbs, prompting an exodus of older residents who in turn pushed the next higher group farther out in search of space and greenery. Suburbanization was the sum of countless individual decisions. Each family's move represented an advance in living standards—not only more light, air, and quiet but better accommodation than the city afforded. Suburban houses were typically larger for the same money and came equipped with flush toilets, hot water, central heating, and, by the turn of the century, electricity.

The suburbs also restored an opportunity that rural Americans thought they had lost when they moved to the city. In the suburbs home ownership again became the norm. "A man is not really a true man until he owns his home," propounded the Reverend Russell H. Conwell in his famous sermon on the virtues of making money, "Acres of Diamonds."

The small towns of rural America had fostered community life. Not so the suburbs. The grid street pattern, while efficient for laying out lots, offered no natural focus for group life. Nor did the stores and services that lay scattered along the trolley-car streets. Suburban development conformed to the economics of real estate and transportation, and so did the thinking of middle-class home seekers entering the suburbs. They wanted a house that gave them good value and convenience to the trolley line.

The need for community had lost some of its force for middle-class Americans. Two other attachments assumed greater importance: one was work; the other, family.

Middle-Class Families

In the preindustrial economy there was little separation between work and family life. Farmers, merchants, and artisans generally worked at home, and everyone employed there, not only blood relatives, was considered part of the household. As industrialism progressed economic activity left the home. For the middle class in particular, the family became dissociated from employment. The father departed every morning for the office, and children spent more years in school. Clothing was bought ready made, and food came increasingly in cans and packages. Middle-class families became smaller, excluding all but nuclear members and consisting typically by 1900 of husband, wife, and three children.

Within this family circle relationships became intense and affectionate. "Home was the most expressive experience in life," recalled the literary critic Henry Seidel Canby of his growing up in the 1890s. "Though the family might quarrel and nag, the home held them all, protecting them against the outside world." The suburb provided a fit setting for such middle-class families. The quiet, tree-lined streets created a domestic space insulated from the hurly-burly of commerce and enterprise.

The Wife's Role.   The burdens of this domesticity fell heavily on the wife. It was nearly unheard of for her to seek an outside career—that was her husband's role. Her job was to manage the household. "The woman who could not make a home, like the man who could not support one, was condemned," Canby remembered. But with fewer children, the wife's workload declined. Moreover servants still played an important part in middle-class households. In 1910 there were about 2 million domestic servants, the largest job category for women.

As the physical burdens of household work eased, higher-quality homemaking became the new ideal. This was the message of Catharine Beecher's best-selling book *The American Woman's Home* (1869) and of such magazines as the *Ladies' Home Journal* and *Good Housekeeping*,

Middle-Class Domesticity

For middle-class Americans the home was a place of nurture, a refuge from the world of competitive commerce. Perhaps that explains why their residences were so heavily draped and cluttered with bric-a-brac. All of it emphasized privacy and pride of possession.

Culver Pictures.

which first appeared during the 1880s. This advice literature told wives that, in addition to their domestic duties, they were responsible for bringing sensibility, beauty, and love to the household. "We owe to women the charm and beauty of life," wrote one educator. "For the love that rests, strengthens and inspires, we look to women." In this idealized view the wife made the home a refuge for her husband and a place of nurture for their children.

Womanly virtue, even if much glorified, by no means put wives on equal terms with their husbands. Although the legal status of married women—their right to own property, control separate earnings, make contracts, and get a divorce—improved markedly during the nineteenth century, law and custom still dictated a wife's submission to her husband. She relied on his ability as the family breadwinner, and despite her superior virtues and graces she was thought below him in vigor and intellect. Her mind could be employed "but little and in trivial matters," wrote one prominent physician, and her proper place was as "the companion or ornamental appendage to man" (see American Voices, "M. Carey Thomas: 'We Did Not Know . . . Whether Women's Health Could Stand the Strain of College Education,'" p. 555).

Not surprisingly, many bright, independent-minded women rebelled against marriage. The marriage rate fell to its lowest point during the last forty years of the nineteenth century. More than 10 percent of women of marriageable age remained single, and the rate was much higher among college graduates and professionals. "I know that something perhaps, humanly speaking, supremely precious has passed me by," remarked the writer Vida Scudder. "But how much it would have excluded!" Married life "looks to me often as I watch it terribly impoverished, for women."

The Cult of Masculinity. If fewer women were marrying, of course, so were fewer men. We can, thanks to the census, trace the tardy progression into marriage of the male cohort born just after the Civil War: in 1890, when they were in their early thirties, two-fifths of this group remained unmarried; a decade later, in their early forties, a quarter still had not married; and ultimately, a hard-core, over 10 percent, never did. One historian has labeled the late nineteenth century the Age of the Bachelor, a time when being an unattached male lost its social stigma and, especially in large cities, became a happy alternative for many men of marriageable age.

A bachelor's counterpart to Vida Scudder's dim view of marriage was this ditty making the rounds in the early 1880s:

> No wife to scold me
> No children to squall
> God bless the happy man
> Who keeps bachelor's hall.

With its residential hotels, restaurants, and multifarious personal services, the urban scene afforded bachelors all the comforts of home and, doubtless more important, an ample array of men's clubs, saloons, and sporting events on which to erect a robust male subculture.

The appeal of the manly life was not, however, confined to confirmed bachelors. A larger crisis was overtaking American males, especially middle-class males. They inherited a pride in independence and autonomy, achieved above all by being one's own boss, but in the salaried jobs they increasingly held middle-class men were distinctly not their own bosses. Nor were they capable, once work and household had been severed, of exerting the patriarchal hold over family life that had empowered their fathers and grandfathers. A palpable anxiety arose that the American male was becoming, as one magazine editor warned, "weak, effeminate, decaying." There was a telling shift in language. While people had once spoken of *manhood*, which meant leaving *childhood* behind, they now spoke of *masculinity*, the opposite of *femininity*: being a man meant surmounting the feminizing influences of modern life.

And how was this to be accomplished? By engaging in competitive sports like football and boxing, which became hugely popular in this era. By working out and becoming fit because, as the psychologist G. Stanley Hall put it, "you can't have a firm will without firm muscles." By resorting to the great outdoors—preferably out West—and engaging in Theodore Roosevelt's "strenuous life." Or, vicariously, by reading Roosevelt's books or Owen Wister's best-selling cowboy novel, *The Virginian* (1902), or that paean to primitive man, Edgar Rice Burroughs's *Tarzan of the Apes* (1912). The surging popularity of westerns and adventure novels was surely a marker of the fears by urban dwellers that theirs was not a life for real men.

Changing Views of Sexuality. In earlier times sexuality and reproduction had been more or less in harmony. A large family was considered a good thing, and the heavy toll of repeated pregnancies on the wife was accepted as God's will. In middle-class families especially, this fatalism began to wane. Birth control, however, was not an easy matter. Beginning in the 1830s information about contraception became widely available, as did an array of commercial products. But the knowledge purveyed was imperfect or, like advice about the rhythm method, absolutely wrong (doctors thought women were fertile around the menstrual period). And contraceptive products were for the most part not very effective or, as in the case of the condom, stigmatized by association with the brothel.

Before these barriers could be surmounted, birth control was swept up by the social-purity campaign championed by Anthony Comstock. From the 1870s onward contraceptive devices and birth control information

M. Carey Thomas

"We Did Not Know . . . Whether Women's Health Could Stand the Strain of College Education"

President of Bryn Mawr College for many years, M. Carey Thomas (1857–1935) recalls in a retrospective essay her dreams of college as a girl growing up in Baltimore in the 1870s.

The passionate desire of women of my generation for higher education was accompanied thruout its course by the awful doubt, felt by women themselves as well as by men, as to whether women as a sex were physically and mentally fit for it. . . . I was always wondering whether it could be really true, as everyone always said, that boys were cleverer than girls. . . . I often remember praying about it, and begging God that if it were true that because I was a girl I could not successfully master Greek and go to college and understand things to kill me at once, as I could not bear to live in such an unjust world. When I was a little older I read the Bible entirely thru with passionate eagerness because I had heard it said that it proved that women were inferior to men. . . . To this day I can never read many parts of the Pauline epistles without feeling again the sinking of the heart with which I used to hurry over the verses referring to women's keeping silence in the churches and asking their husbands at home. . . .

It was not to be wondered at that we were uncertain in those old days as to the ultimate result of women's education. We did not know when we began whether women's health could stand the strain of college education. We were haunted in those early days by the clanging chains of that gloomy little specter, Dr. Edward H. Clarke's *Sex in Education*. With trepidation of spirit I made my mother read it, and was much cheered by her remark that, as neither she, nor any of the women she knew, had ever seen girls or women of the kind described in Dr. Clarke's book, we might as well act as if they did not exist. Still, we did not know whether college might not produce a crop of just such invalids. . . .

Before I myself went to college I had never seen but one college woman. I had heard that such a woman was staying at the house of an acquaintance. I went to see her with fear. Even if she had appeared in hoofs and horns I was determined to go to college all the same. But it was a relief to find this Vassar graduate tall and handsome and dressed like other women. When, five years later, I went to Leipzig to study after graduating from Cornell, my mother used to write me that my name was never mentioned to her by the women of her acquaintance. I was thought by them to be as much a disgrace to my family as if I had eloped with the coachman. . . .

We are now [1908] living in the midst of great and, I believe on the whole beneficent, social changes which are preparing the way for the coming economic independence of women. . . . The passionate desire of the women of my generation for a college education seems, as we study it now in the light of coming events, to have been part of this greater movement.

Source: Linda K. Kerber and Jane De Hart-Mathews, eds., *Women's America: Refocusing the Past*, 2nd ed. (New York: Oxford University Press, 1987), 263–65.

were legally classified as obscene, barred from the mails, and criminalized by many states. Abortion, long accepted by common law, became illegal except to save the mother's life. Although the practice of abortion remained widespread, it was expensive and dangerous—and considered shameful besides.

Around 1890 a change set in. Although the birthrate continued to decline, more young people married, and at an earlier age. These developments reflected the beginnings of a sexual revolution in the American middle-class family. Experts began to abandon the notion, put forth by one popular medical text, that "the majority of women (happily for society) are not very much troubled by sexual feeling of any kind." In succeeding editions of his book *Plain Home Talk on Love, Marriage, and Parentage*, physician Edward Bliss Foote began to favor a healthy sexuality that gave pleasure to women as well as men.

During the 1890s the artist Charles Dana Gibson created the image of the "new woman." In his drawings

The New Woman

John Singer Sargent's painting Mr. and Mrs. Isaac Newton
Phelps Stokes *(1897) captures on canvas the essence of the "new
woman" of the 1890s. Nothing about Mrs. Phelps Stokes, neither
how she is dressed nor how she presents herself, suggests physical
weakness or demure passivity. She confidently occupies center
stage, a fit partner for her husband, who is relegated to the
shadows of the picture.*

The Metropolitan Museum of Art. Bequest of Edith Minturn Phelps Stokes
(Mrs. I. N.), 1938 (38.104). Photo © 1992 The Metropolitan Museum of Art.

the **Gibson girl** was tall, spirited, athletic, and chastely
sexual. She rejected bustles, hoop skirts, and tightly laced
corsets, preferring shirtwaists and other natural styles
that did not disguise her female form. In the city women's
sphere began to take on a more public character. Among
the new urban institutions catering to women, the most
important was the department store, which became a
temple for their emerging role as consumers.

Attitudes toward Children. The offspring of the
middle class experienced their own revolution. In the past
children had been regarded as an economic asset—added
hands for the family farm, shop, or countinghouse.
Especially for the urban middle class, that no longer held
true. Parents stopped expecting their children to be
working members of the family. In the old days Ralph
Waldo Emerson remarked in 1880, "children had been
repressed and kept in the background; now they are
considered, cosseted, and pampered." There was such a
thing as "the juvenile mind," lectured Jacob Abbott in his
book *Gentle Measures in the Management and Training of
the Young* (1871). The family was responsible for
providing a nurturing environment in which the young
personality could grow and mature.

Preparation for adulthood became increasingly
linked to formal education. School enrollment went up
150 percent between 1870 and 1900. High school attendance, while still encompassing only a small percentage
of teenagers, increased at the fastest rate (Table 19.2). As
the years between childhood and adulthood began to
stretch out, a new stage of life—adolescence—emerged.
While rooted in longer years of family dependency, adolescence shifted much of the socializing role from parents to peer group. A youth culture—one of the
hallmarks of American life in the twentieth century—
was starting to take shape.

City Life

With its soaring skyscrapers, jostling traffic, and hum of
business, the city symbolized energy and enterprise.
When the budding writer Hamlin Garland and his
brother arrived in Chicago from Iowa in 1881, they
knew immediately that they had entered a new world:
"Everything interested us. . . . Nothing was commonplace, nothing was ugly to us." In one way or another
every city-bound migrant, whether from the American
countryside or from a foreign land, experienced something of this sense of wonder.

But with the boundless variety came disorder and uncertainty. The city was utterly unlike the rural world the
newcomers had left. In the countryside every person had
been known to his or her neighbors. Mark Twain found
New York "a splendid desert, where a stranger is lonely in

TABLE 19.2 High School Graduates, 1870–1910				
Year	Numbers	Percent 17-Year-Olds	Male	Female
1870	16,000	2.0	7,000	9,000
1890	44,000	3.0	19,000	25,000
1910	156,000	8.6	64,000	93,000

Source: Historical Statistics of the United States (1975), 1: 386.

the midst of a million of his race. . . . Every man rushes, rushes, rushes, and never has time to be companionable [or] to fool away on matters which do not involve dollars and duty and business." If rural roles and obligations had been well understood, in the city the only predictable relationships were those dictated by the marketplace.

Rural people could never re-create in the city the communities they had left behind. But they found ways to gain a sense of belonging, they built a multitude of new institutions, and they learned how to function in an impersonal, heterogeneous environment. An urban culture emerged, and through it there developed a new breed of American who was entirely at home in the modern city.

Newcomers

At the turn of the century, upwards of 30 percent of the residents of New York, Chicago, Boston, Cleveland, Minneapolis, and San Francisco were foreign-born. The biggest ethnic group in Boston was Irish; in Minneapolis, Swedish; in most other northern cities, German. But by 1910 the influx from southern and eastern Europe had changed the ethnic complexion of many of these cities (Map 19.3). In Chicago, Poles took the lead; in New York, eastern European Jews; in San Francisco, Italians.

For these later arrivals there was less intermingling with the resident populations than in the earlier "walking cities." By the 1880s observers were noticing that only immigrants lived in the dingier downtown areas. "One may find for the asking" ghettos of every kind, remarked Jacob Riis in his book about New York's poor, *How the Other Half Lives* (1890). "The one thing you shall vainly ask for in the chief city of America is a distinctly American community."

The arrivals from southern and eastern Europe had little choice about where they lived; they needed to find cheap housing near their jobs. Some gravitated to the outlying factory districts; others settled in the congested downtown **ghettos**. The immigrants tended to settle by ethnic group. In New York Italians crowded into the Irish neighborhoods west of Broadway, and Russian and Polish Jews pushed the Germans out of the Lower East Side (Map 19.4). A colony of Hungarians lived around Houston Street, and Bohemians occupied the poorer stretches of the Upper East Side between Fiftieth and Seventy-sixth Streets.

Within ethnic groups one could spot clusters from the same province or town. Among New York Italians, for example, Neapolitans and Calabrians populated the Mulberry Bend district, while Genoese lived on Baxter

Italian Bread Peddlers, New York City

Because of crowded conditions in East Side tenements, immigrant life spilled out onto the streets, which offered a bit of fresh air, a chance to socialize with neighbors, and a place to shop for food, including bread.
KEA Publishing Services Ltd.

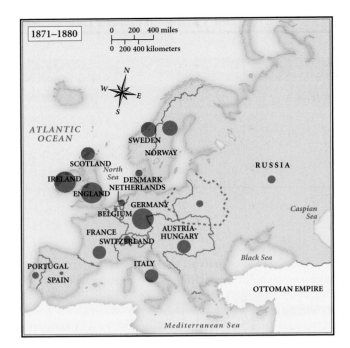

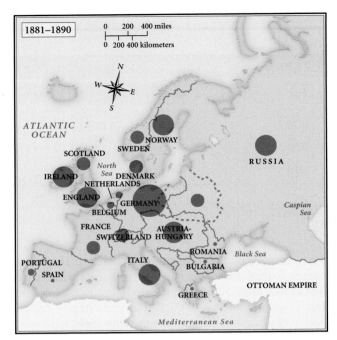

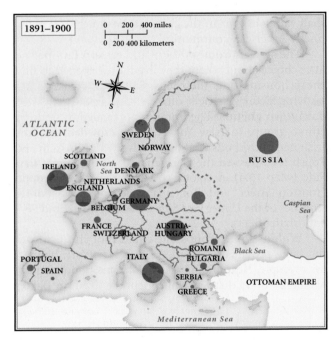

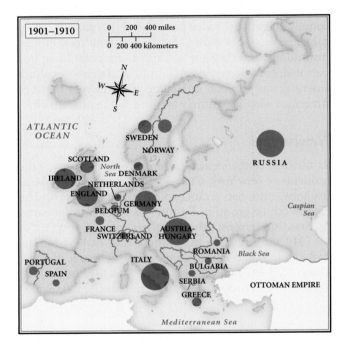

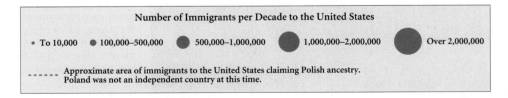

Number of Immigrants per Decade to the United States

• To 10,000   ● 100,000–500,000   ● 500,000–1,000,000   ● 1,000,000–2,000,000   ● Over 2,000,000

- - - - Approximate area of immigrants to the United States claiming Polish ancestry.
Poland was not an independent country at this time.

MAP 19.3 Sources of European Immigration to the United States, 1871–1910

Around 1900 Americans began to speak of the "new" immigration. They meant the large numbers of immigrants arriving from eastern and southern Europe—Poles, Slovaks and other Slavic groups, Yiddish-speaking Jews, Italians—and overwhelming the still substantial and more familiar immigrants from the British Isles and northern Europe (see Figure 17.3, American Immigration, 1870–1914, on p. 499).

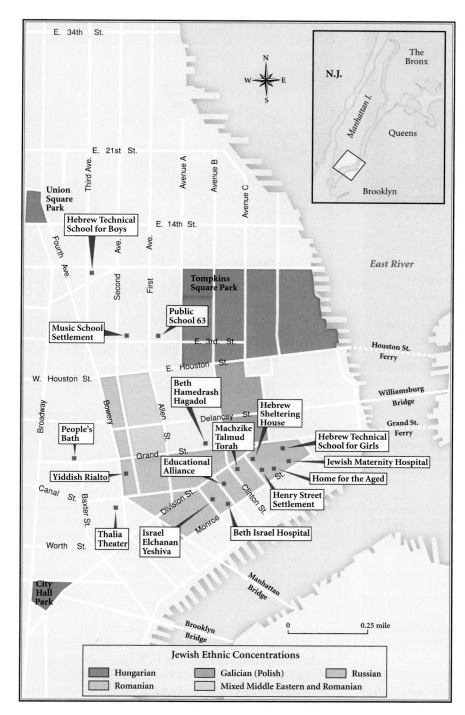

MAP 19.4 The Lower East Side, New York City, 1900

As this map shows, the Jewish immigrants dominating Manhattan's Lower East Side preferred living in neighborhoods populated by those from their home regions of eastern Europe. Their sense of a common identity made for a remarkable flowering of educational, cultural, and social institutions on the Jewish East Side.

Street. Along a short stretch of Elizabeth Street there lived several hundred families from a Sicilian fishing town, Sciacca, and Sciacca's patron saint was paraded on Elizabeth Street, as in Sicily.

Capitalizing on fellow feeling, institutions of many kinds sprang up to meet the immigrants' needs. Newspapers appeared wherever substantial numbers lived. In 1911 the 20,000 Poles in Buffalo, New York, supported two Polish-language daily papers. Immigrants throughout the country avidly read *Il Progresso Italo-Americano* and the Yiddish-language *Jewish Daily Forward*, both published in New York City (see American Voices, "Anonymous: Bintel Brief," p. 561). Companionship could always be found on street corners, in barbershops and club rooms, and in saloons. Italians marched in saint's day parades, Bohemians gathered in singing societies, and New York Jews patronized a lively Yiddish theater. To provide help in times of sickness and death, the immigrants organized mutual-aid societies. The Italians of Chicago had sixty-six of these organizations in 1903, mostly composed of people from

The Economy of the Ghetto
Downtown immigrant neighborhoods would not have struck the casual observer as industrial districts, but tucked away in the tenements were commercial lofts and small workshops. An entire ready-made clothing industry flourished within the ghettos of large cities, drawing especially on the young women of the neighborhood to perform the low-paid sewing tasks in often dangerous conditions. Brown Brothers.

particular provinces or towns. Immigrants built a rich and functional institutional life in urban America to an extent unimagined in their native places.

Urban Blacks. The great African American migration from the rural South to northern cities was just beginning at the turn of the century. The black population of New York increased by 30,000 between 1900 and 1910, making New York second only to Washington, D.C., as a black urban center, but the 91,000 African Americans in New York in 1910 represented fewer than 2 percent of the population, and that was true of Chicago and Cleveland as well.

Despite their relatively small numbers, urban blacks could not escape discrimination. They retreated from the scattered black neighborhoods of older times into concentrated ghettos—Chicago's Black Belt on the South Side, for example, or the early outlines of New York's Harlem. Race prejudice likewise cut down job opportunities. Twenty-six percent of Cleveland's blacks had been skilled workers in 1870, but only 12 percent were skilled by 1890; entire occupations such as barbering (except for a black clientele) became exclusively white. Two-thirds of Cleveland's blacks in 1910 worked as domestics and day laborers, with little hope of moving up the job ladder.

The Cherry Family, 1906
Wiley and Fannie Cherry migrated in 1893 from North Carolina to Chicago, settling in the small African American community on the West Side. The Cherrys apparently prospered, and by 1906, when this family portrait was taken, had entered the black middle class. When migration intensified after 1900, longer-settled urban blacks like the Cherrys became uncomfortable, and relations with the needy rural newcomers were often tense. Courtesy, Lorraine Heflin / Chicago Historical Society.

In the face of pervasive discrimination, urban blacks built their own communities. They created a flourishing press, fraternal orders, a vast array of women's organizations, and a middle class of doctors, lawyers, and small entrepreneurs. Above all, there were the black churches—twenty-five in Chicago in 1905, mainly Methodist and Baptist. More than any other institution, remarked one scholar in 1913, it was the church "which the Negro may call his own. . . . A new church may be built . . . and . . . all the machinery set in motion without ever consulting any white person. . . . [Religion] more than anything else represents the real life of the race." As in the southern countryside, the church was the central institution for city blacks, and the preacher was the most important local citizen. Manhattan's Union Baptist Church, housed like many others in a storefront, attracted the "very recent residents of this new, disturbing city" and, ringing with spirituals

Anonymous

Bintel Brief

In Yiddish bintel brief *means "bundle of letters." That was the name of the famous section of the* Jewish Daily Forward *devoted to letters from immigrant readers about their trials and tribulations in America.*

I am a girl sixteen years old. I live together with my parents and my two older sisters. Last year I met a young man. We love one another. He is a very respectable man, and makes a fine living. My sisters have no fiancés. I know that should I marry they will never talk to me. My parents are also strongly against it since I am the youngest child. I do not want to lose my parents' love, and neither do I want to lose my lover because that would break my heart. Give me some advice, dear Editor!

I was born in a small town in Russia, and until I was sixteen I studied in *Talmud Torahs* and *yeshivas*, but when I came to America I developed spiritually and became a freethinker. Yet every year when the time of *Rosh Hashana* and *Yom Kippur* comes around I become very gloomy. . . . So strong are my feelings that I enter the synagogue, not in order to pray to God but to heal and refresh my aching soul by sitting among *landsleit* [countrymen] and listening to the cantor's sweet melodies. The members of my Progressive Society don't understand. They say I am a hypocrite. . . . What do you think? *Answer.* No one can tell another what to do with himself on *Yom Kippur*.

I am a Russian revolutionist and a freethinker. Here in America I became acquainted with a girl who is also a freethinker. We decided to marry, but the problem is that she has Orthodox parents, and if we refuse a religious ceremony we will be cut off from them forever. I don't know what to do. Therefore, I ask you to advise me how to act. *Answer.* There are times when it is better to be kind in order not to grieve old parents.

To a man everything is permissible, to a woman nothing. A man is king over us and may do his will. When I argue that morality is more demanding on women, my husband gets angry and denies it with all his might. There is no such thing as a man with a bad name, but just let one spot fall upon a woman. . . . Why?!

I am in favor of giving women full rights, but most of my friends are against it. They argue that the woman would then no longer be the housewife, the mother to her children, the wife to her husband—in a word, everything would be destroyed. I do not agree because a woman is a human being just like a man, and if women are recognized as human beings, they must be granted all the rights of human beings. *Answer.* Justice can reign among people only when they all have equal rights.

Why do the police favor the clothing stores on Canal Street which remain open seven days a week? . . . Where else in the world do people sell their lives to make a living with no holidays and no rest? I am one of the corpses who works seven days a week in one of those electric-lit graves on Canal Street.

I am a young man of twenty-five, and I recently met a fine girl. She has a flaw, however—a dimple in her chin. It is said that people who have this lose their first husband or wife. I love her very much. But I'm afraid to marry her lest I die because of the dimple. *Answer.* The tragedy is not that the girl has a dimple in her chin but that some people have a screw loose in their heads.

Source: Irving Howe and Kenneth Libo, eds., *How We Lived* (New York: New American Library, 1979), 88–90.

and fervent prayer, made Christianity come "alive Sunday mornings."

Ward Politics

Race and ethnicity tended to divide newcomers and turn them in on themselves. Politics, by contrast, integrated them into the wider urban society. Every migrant to an American city automatically became a **ward** resident and acquired a spokesman at city hall in the form of his or her local alderman. Immigrants learned very quickly that if they needed anything from city hall, he was the man to see. He could arrange for streets to be paved, or water mains extended, or variances granted—so that, for example, in 1888 Vito Fortounescere could "place and keep a stand for the sale of fruit, inside the stoop-line, in front of the northeast corner of Twenty-eighth Street and Fourth Avenue" in Manhattan, or the parishioners of Saint Maria of Mount Carmel could set off fireworks at their Fourth of July picnic.

Machine control of political parties, although present at every level, flourished most luxuriantly in the big cities. Urban machines depended on a loyal grassroots constituency, so each ward was divided into a precinct of a few blocks. The precinct captain reported to the ward boss, who was likely also to be the alderman. The main job of these functionaries was to be accessible and, as best they could, serve the needs of the party faithful (see American Lives, "Big Tim Sullivan: Tammany Politican," p. 564).

The machine acted as a rough-and-ready social service agency, providing jobs for the jobless, a helping hand for a bereaved family, and intercession against an unfeeling city bureaucracy. The Tammany ward boss George Washington Plunkitt had a "regular system" when fires broke out in his district. He arranged for housing for burned-out families, "fix[ing] them up till they get things runnin' again. It's philanthropy, but it's politics, too—mighty good politics."

The business community was similarly served. Contractors sought city business; gas companies and streetcar lines wanted licenses and privileges; manufacturers needed services and not-too-nosy inspectors; and the liquor trade and numbers racket relied on a tolerant police force. All of them turned to the machine boss and his lieutenants.

Of course, the machine exacted a price for these services. The tenement dweller gave his vote. The businessman wrote a check. Naturally, some of the money that changed hands leaked into the pockets of machine politicians. This "boodle" could be blatantly corrupt—kickbacks by contractors; protection money from gamblers, saloonkeepers, and prostitutes; payoffs from gas and trolley companies. Tammany ward boss Plunkitt, however, insisted that he had no need for kickbacks and bribes. He favored what he called "**honest graft**," the easy profits that came to savvy insiders. Plunkitt made most of his money building wharves on Manhattan's waterfront. One way or another, legally or otherwise, machine politics rewarded its supporters.

For ambitious young people this was reason enough to favor the machine system. In the mid-1870s over half of Chicago's forty aldermen were foreign-born, sixteen of them Irish. The first Italian was elected in 1885, the first Pole in 1888. Blacks did not manage to get on Chicago's board of aldermen until after 1900, but Baltimore's Eleventh Ward elected an African American in 1890, and Philadelphia had three black aldermen by 1899. As a ladder for social mobility, machine politics (like professional sports, entertainment, and organized crime) was the most democratic of American institutions.

Ward boss Plunkitt was an Irishman, and so were most of the machine politicians controlling Tammany Hall. But by the 1890s Plunkitt's Fifteenth District was filling up with Italians and eastern European Jews. In general the New York Irish had no love for these newer immigrants, but Plunkitt played no favorites. On any given day (as recorded in a diary) he might attend an Italian funeral in the afternoon and a Jewish wedding in the evening, and at each he probably paid his respects with a few Italian words or a bit of Yiddish.

In an era when so many forces acted to isolate ghetto communities, politics served an *integrating* function, cutting across ethnic lines and giving immigrants and blacks a stake in the larger urban order.

Religion in the City

For African Americans, as we have seen, the church was a central institution of urban life. So it was for many other city dwellers. But the city was difficult ground for religious practice. All the great faiths present at the time—Judaism, Catholicism, and Protestantism—had to scramble to reconcile religious belief with the secular demands of the urban world.

Judaism: The Challenge to Orthodoxy. About 250,000 Jews, mostly of German origin, were living in America when the eastern European Jews began arriving in the 1880s. Well established and prosperous, the German Jews had embraced Reform Judaism, abandoning religious practices—from keeping a kosher kitchen to conducting services in Hebrew—"not adapted to the views and habits of modern civilization." This was not the way of the Yiddish-speaking Jews from eastern Europe. Anxious to preserve their traditional piety, they founded their own Orthodox synagogues, often in vacant stores and ramshackle buildings, and practiced Judaism as they had at home.

In the villages of eastern Europe, however, Judaism had involved not only worship and belief but an entire way of life. Insular though it might be, ghetto life in the American city could not re-create the communal environment on which strict religious observance depended. "The very clothes I wore and the very food I ate had a fatal effect on my religious habits," confessed the hero of Abraham Cahan's novel *The Rise of David Levinsky* (1917). "If you . . . attempt to bend your religion to the spirit of your surroundings, it breaks. It falls to pieces." Levinsky shaved off his beard and plunged into the Manhattan clothing business. Orthodox Judaism survived this shattering of faith but only by reducing its claims on the lives of the faithful.

"Americanism" and the Catholic Church. Catholics faced much the same problem. The issue, defined within the Roman Catholic Church as "Americanism," turned on the degree to which Catholicism should adapt to American society. Should Catholic children attend parochial or public schools? Should they intermarry with non-Catholics? Should the traditional education for the clergy be changed? Bishop John Ireland of St. Paul, Minnesota, felt that "the principles of the Church are in harmony with the interests of the Republic." But traditionalists, led by Archbishop Michael A. Corrigan of New York, denied the possibility of such harmony and argued in effect for insulating the Church from the pluralistic American environment, with its sharp separation of church and state.

Immigrant Catholics generally supported the Church's conservative wing because they wanted to preserve what they had known in Europe. But they also desired that church life express their ethnic identities. Settling in ethnically distinct neighborhoods, newly arrived Catholics wanted their own parishes where they could celebrate their customs, speak their languages, and establish their own parochial schools. When they became numerous enough, they also demanded their own bishops. The Catholic hierarchy, which was dominated by Irish Catholics, felt that the integrity of the Church itself was at stake. The demand for ethnic parishes implied local control of church property. And if there were bishops for specific ethnic groups, this would mean disrupting the diocesan structure that unified the Church.

The severity of the challenge depended partly on the religious convictions of each ethnic group. Italian men, for example, were known for religious apathy, and many Italians harbored strong anticlerical feelings because of the papacy's stand against the unification of Italy. But churchgoing played such an important part in the lives of Polish immigrants that they resented any interference by the Catholic hierarchy. Indeed fifty parishes in 1907 broke away and formed the Polish National Catholic Church of America, which adhered to Catholic ritual without recognizing the pope's authority.

On the whole, however, the Church managed to satisfy the immigrant faithful. It met the demand for representation in the hierarchy by appointing immigrant priests as auxiliary bishops within existing dioceses. Ethnic parishes also flourished. Before World War I American Catholics worshiped in more than two thousand foreign-language churches, and many others were bilingual. Not without strain the Catholic Church made itself a central institution for the expression of ethnic identity in urban America.

Protestantism: Regaining Lost Ground. For the Protestant churches the city posed different but not easier challenges. They had to find ways of attracting, or reaffiliating, the great numbers of native-born Americans flocking into the cities from the nation's farms and small towns. At the same time they had to keep up with congregations scattering into the suburbs as European immigrants occupied the older residential neighborhoods.

Every major city retained great downtown churches where wealthy Protestants worshiped. Some of these churches, richly endowed, took pride in nationally prominent pastors, such as Henry Ward Beecher of Plymouth Congregational Church in Brooklyn or Phillips Brooks of Trinity Episcopal Church in Boston. But the eminence of these churches, with their fashionable congregations and imposing edifices, could not disguise the growing remoteness of Protestantism from much of its urban constituency. "Where is the city in which the Sabbath day is not losing ground?" lamented a minister in 1887. The

Immaculate Heart of Mary Church, 1908

In crowded immigrant neighborhoods the church rose from undistinguished surroundings to assert the centrality of religious belief in the life of the community. This photograph is a view of Immaculate Heart of Mary Church, taken from Polish Hill in Pittsburgh in 1908.

Pittsburgh City Photographer Collection, Archives Service Center, University of Pittsburgh.

Big Tim Sullivan: Tammany Politician

Big Tim Sullivan Culver Pictures.

Timothy D. Sullivan was born on July 23, 1863, near the Hudson River docks in lower Manhattan. His parents were Irish immigrants, part of the mass migration of potato famine victims who flooded into New York in the 1840s. Four years later Tim's father died, leaving his young widow, Catherine Connelly Sullivan, with four small children. Soon after, Catherine married Lawrence Mulligan, an Irish laborer, and the family moved to the notorious Five Points district on the Lower East Side. There the 1870 census found them, a household of ten (including three boarders) living in an overcrowded tenement at 25 Baxter Street.

Tim had a harsh childhood. His stepfather drank heavily and beat his wife and children regularly. To make ends meet Catherine took in washing, and Tim went to work at age seven bundling papers for $1.50 a week on Newspaper Row across from City Hall. Tim got through grammar school, but his family needed his earnings too much for him to go on to high school. "Free as it was, he later remarked, "it was not free enough for me to go there." Instead—Horatio Alger style—he made his way up in the newspaper business and by age eighteen was well established as a wholesale newspaper dealer. He soon became the proprietor of two saloons and in his early twenties was ready for politics. A handsome fellow, over six feet tall, Sullivan was quick with his fists. He gained a local reputation by thrashing a tough he had encountered on the street beating up a woman. True or not, the story helped him win the Democratic nomination at age twenty-three for the New York State assembly from the Second District.

In 1889 Sullivan opposed a bill granting Manhattan's police virtually unlimited powers to detain people with jail records. The champion of the bill was Thomas F. Byrnes, chief inspector of the New York Police Department and the most celebrated detective in the country. Byrnes did not take kindly to opposition from small-time politicians. He raided Sullivan's saloons, arrested two barkeepers for excise tax violations, and denounced Sullivan as someone who consorted with criminals. Against the advice of friends, Sullivan took the assembly floor to answer the charge.

In tearful tones Sullivan cast himself as an "honest Bowery boy," describing his impoverished childhood, his saintly mother, and his struggle to rise in the world. "When, at the conclusion [so a reporter recorded], he asked if he had any time or money to spend with thieves, there was a 'No' on nearly every member's lips." The performance was the making of the obscure assemblyman. Although he gained notoriety with uptown New Yorkers that would dog him throughout his career, he won the hearts of his own constituents, who reveled in the success story of one of their own. They thought "Big Tim" a fine fellow, and so did the Tammany leaders.

When the Tammany machine swept into power in the 1892 elections, Boss Richard Croker tapped Sullivan to run the new Third Assembly District centering on the Bowery. Sullivan swiftly consolidated his power. His inner circle was all Irish, but for election district captains he appointed Jews, Italians, and Germans who were well connected in the immigrant communities that populated his fiefdom. Sullivan became famous for his summer "chowders," when he transported his constituents by riverboat to the country for a rowdy day of picnicking. At Christmas there was a fine dinner for all who were in

The Bowery at Night, 1895
This painting by W. Louis Sonntag Jr. shows Big Tim's stomping ground—the Bowery—crowded with shoppers and pleasure seekers. It was during this time that the Bowery gained its raffish reputation. Museum of the City of New York.

need. And in February Sullivan handed out wool socks and shoes—always with the sentimental tale of how a teacher had given him free shoes one cold winter.

Big Tim also attended assiduously to the nitty-gritty business of running a political machine. He got jobs for his supporters, visited the jails regularly to offer bail and other aid to the inmates, and on election day made sure his strong-arm crews patrolled the polling places. Sullivan's district became the best organized in the city, and Tammany hailed him as "the most popular man on the East Side."

In the meantime Sullivan was making his fortune. His particular form of "honest graft" was commercial entertainment. Big Tim knew instinctively how important a good time was to city people. Besides, the main street of his district, the Bowery, was the gaudy center of low-life entertainment for the entire city, lined with burlesque houses, concert saloons, restaurants, and cheap hotels. In the mid-1890s Sullivan formed a partnership with two theatrical producers and began to invest in vaudeville houses. He contributed not only money and a shrewd head but the political contacts that ensured lax enforcement of building codes and easy access to liquor licenses. Sullivan also became involved in professional boxing, horse racing, and, more illicitly, the gambling dens that dotted his district.

Sullivan was accused of trafficking in East Side prostitution, but this he indignantly denied: "Nobody who knows me well will believe I would take a penny from any woman, much less from the poor creatures who are more to be pitied than any other human beings

on earth. I'd be afraid to take a cent from a poor woman of the streets for fear my old mother would see me. I'd a good deal rather break into a bank and rob the safe. That would be a more manly and decent way of getting money."

When Boss Croker resigned in 1902, Sullivan might have succeeded him, but Big Tim preferred his own district and threw his support to Charles F. Murphy, who ruled Tammany for the next twenty-two years. Sullivan served briefly in Congress, made a lot more money investing in the early movie industry and in vaudeville syndicates across the country, and in the final phase of his career became a champion of progressive social legislation in the New York Senate. In 1912 Sullivan suffered a severe mental breakdown, possibly caused by tertiary syphilis. A year later he died under the wheels of a freight train after running off from his brother's house outside New York. His funeral procession down the Bowery was one of the largest in memory and brought out an immense crowd from every stratum of New York society, from statesmen to prizefighters to scrubwomen.

families of businessmen, lawyers, and doctors could be seen in any church on Sunday morning, he noted, "but the workingmen and their families are not there."

To counter this decline the Protestant churches responded by evangelizing among the unchurched and indifferent. Starting in the 1880s they also began providing reading rooms, day nurseries, clubhouses, vocational classes, and other services. The Salvation Army, which arrived from Great Britain in 1879, spread the gospel of repentance among the urban poor and built an assistance program that ranged from soup kitchens to shelters for former prostitutes. When all else failed the down-and-outers of American cities knew they could count on the Salvation Army.

For single people new to the city, there were the Young Men's and Women's Christian Associations, which had arrived from Britain before the Civil War. By the 1880s all large cities had YMCAs equipped with gymnasiums, meeting rooms, and dormitories. Housing for single women was an especially important mission of the YWCAs. The athletic facilities that made the YMCAs synonymous with "muscular Christianity" were equally important for young men. No other organizations so effectively combined activities for young people with an evangelizing appeal through Bible classes, nondenominational worship, and a religious atmosphere.

The social meaning that people sought in religion explained the enormous popularity of a book called *In His Steps* (1896). The author, a Congregational minister named Charles M. Sheldon, told the story of a congregation that resolved to live by Christ's precepts for one year. "If the church members were all doing as Jesus would do," Sheldon asked, "could it remain true that armies of men would walk the streets for jobs, and hundreds of them curse the church, and thousands of them find in the saloon their best friend?"

The most potent form of urban evangelism—revivalism—said little about social uplift. From their origins in the eighteenth century, revival movements had steadfastly focused on individual redemption. The resolution of earthly problems, revivalists believed, would follow the conversion of the people to Christ. Beginning in the mid-1870s, revival meetings swept through the cities.

The pioneering figure was Dwight L. Moody, a former Chicago shoe salesman and YMCA official. After preaching in Britain for two years, Moody returned to America in 1875 and began staging revival meetings that drew thousands. He preached an optimistic, uncomplicated, nondenominational message. Eternal life could be had for the asking, Moody shouted as he held up his Bible. His listeners needed only "to come forward and take, TAKE!"

Many other preachers followed in Moody's path. The most colorful was Billy Sunday, a hard-drinking former outfielder for the Chicago White Stockings who mended his ways and found religion. Like Moody and other city revivalists, Sunday was a farm boy. His rip-snorting attacks on fashionable ministers and the "booze traffic" carried the ring of rustic America. By realizing that many people remained villagers at heart, revivalists found a key for bringing city dwellers back into the church.

City Amusements

City people compartmentalized life's activities, setting workplace apart from home and working time apart from free time. "Going out" became a necessity, demanded not only as solace for a hard day's work but proof that life was better in the New World than in the Old. "He who can enjoy and does not enjoy commits a sin," a Yiddish-language paper told its readers. And enjoyment now meant buying a ticket and being entertained.

Amusement Park, Long Beach, California

The origins of the roller coaster go back to LaMarcus Thompson's Switchback Railway, installed at Coney Island in 1884 and featuring gentle dips and curves. By 1900, when Long Beach's Jack Rabbit Race was constructed, the goal was to create the biggest possible thrill. Angelenos journeyed out by trolley to Long Beach not only to take a dip in the ocean but to ride the new roller coaster. The airplane ride in the foreground is a further wrinkle on the peculiarly modern notion that the way to have fun is to be scared to death. Curt Teich Postcard Archives.

José Martí

Coney Island, 1881

José Martí, a Cuban patriot and revolutionary (see p. 609), was a journalist by profession. In exile from 1880 to 1895, he spent most of his time in New York City, reporting to his Latin American readers on the customs of the Yankees. Martí took special pleasure in observing Americans at play.

From all parts of the United States, legions of intrepid ladies and Sunday-best farmers arrive to admire the splendid sights, the unexampled wealth, the dizzying variety, the herculean surge, the striking appearance of Coney Island, the now famous island, four years ago an abandoned sand bank, that today is a spacious amusement area providing relaxation and recreation for hundreds of thousands of New Yorkers who throng to its pleasant beaches every day. . . .

Other nations—ourselves among them—live devoured by a sublime demon within that drives us to the tireless pursuit of an ideal of love or glory. . . . Not so with these tranquil souls, stimulated only by a desire for gain. One scans those shimmering beaches . . . one views the throngs seated in comfortable chairs along the seashore, filling their lungs with the fresh, invigorating air. But it is said that those from our lands who remain here long are overcome with melancholy . . . because this great nation is void of spirit.

But what coming and going! What torrents of money! What facilities for every pleasure! What absolute absence of any outward sadness or poverty! Everything in the open air: the animated groups, the immense dining rooms, the peculiar courtship of North Americans, which is virtually devoid of the elements that compose the shy, tender, elevated love in our lands, the theatre, the photographers' booth, the bathhouses! Some weigh themselves, for North Americans are greatly elated, or really concerned, if they find they have gained or lost a pound. . . .

This spending, this uproar, these crowds, the activity of this amazing ant hill never slackens from June to October, from morning 'til night. . . . Then, like a monster that vomits its contents into the hungry maw of another monster, that colossal crowd, that straining, crushing mass, forces its way onto the trains, which speed across wastes, groaning under their burden, until they surrender it to the tremendous steamers, enlivened by the sound of harps and violins, convey it to the piers, and debouch the weary merrymakers into the thousand trolleys that pursue the thousand tracks that spread through slumbering New York like veins of steel.

Source: Juan de Onís, trans., *The America of José Martí: Selected Writings* (New York: Noonday Press, 1954), 103–10.

Amusement parks went up on the outskirts of cities across the country. Most glittering was Luna Park at New York's Coney Island—"an enchanted, storybook land of trellises, columns, domes, minarets, lagoons, and lofty aerial flights. . . . It was a world removed—shut away from the sordid clatter and turmoil of the streets." In fact, escape from everyday urban life explains the appeal of amusement parks (see Voices from Abroad, "José Martí: Coney Island, 1881," above). The creators of Luna Park intended it to be "a different world—a dream world . . . where all is bizarre and fantastic . . . gayer and more different from the every-day world."

The theater likewise attracted huge audiences. Chicago had six **vaudeville** houses in 1896 and twenty-two in 1910. Evolving from tawdry variety and minstrel shows, vaudeville cleaned up its routines, making them suitable for the entire family, and turned into thoroughly professional entertainment handled by national booking agencies. With its standard program of nine singing, dancing, and comedy acts, vaudeville attained enormous popularity just as the movies arrived. The first primitive films, a minute or so of humor or glimpses of famous people, appeared in 1896 in penny arcades and as filler in vaudeville shows. Within a decade, millions of city people were watching films of increasing length and artistry at **nickelodeons** (named after the five-cent admission charge) across the country.

For young unmarried workers the cheap amusements of the city created a new social space. "I want a good time," a New York clothing operator told an investigator. "And there is no . . . way a girl can get it on $8 a week. I guess if anyone wants to take me to a dance he won't have to ask me twice." Hence the widespread ritual among the urban working class of "treating." The girls spent what money they had dressing up; their beaus were expected to pay for the fun. Parental control

The National Pastime

*In 1897, as today, the end-of-season games filled the bleachers. Here the Boston Beaneaters
are playing the Baltimore Orioles. Boston won. The Baltimore stadium would soon be
replaced by a bigger concrete and steel structure, but what is happening on the field needs
no updating. The scene is virtually identical to today's game.* Library of Congress.

over courtship broke down, and amid the bright lights
and lively music of the dance hall and amusement park
working-class youth forged a more easygoing culture of
sexual interaction and pleasure seeking.

The geography of the big city carved out ample
space for commercialized sex. Prostitution was not
new to urban life, but in the late nineteenth century it
became more open and more intermingled with other
forms of public entertainment. In New York the red-
light district was the Tenderloin, running northward
from Twenty-third Street between Fifth and Eighth
Avenues.

The Tenderloin and the Bowery farther downtown
were also the sites of a robust gay subculture. The long-
held notion that homosexual life was covert, in the
closet, in Victorian America appears not to be true, at
least not in the country's premier city. In certain corners
of the city, a gay world flourished, with a full array of saloons, meeting places, and drag balls, which were widely
known and patronized by uptown "slummers."

Baseball. Of all forms of (mostly) male diversion,
none was more specific to the city, or so spectacularly
successful, as professional baseball. The game's promoters
decreed that baseball had been created in 1839 by Abner
Doubleday in the village of Cooperstown, New York.
Actually, baseball was neither of American origin—it
developed from the British game of rounders—nor a
product of rural life. The game apparently first appeared
in the early 1840s in New York City, where a group of

gentlemen enthusiasts competed on an empty lot. Over
the next twenty years, the aristocratic tone of baseball
disappeared. Clubs sprang up across the country and
intercity competition developed on a scheduled basis. In
1868 baseball became openly professional, following the
lead of the Cincinnati Red Stockings in signing players to
contracts for the season.

Big-time commercial baseball came into its own
with the launching of the National League in 1876. The
team owners were profit-minded businessmen who
shaped the sport to please the fans. Wooden grand-
stands gave way to the concrete and steel stadiums of
the early twentieth century, such as Fenway Park in
Boston, Forbes Field in Pittsburgh, and Shibe Park in
Philadelphia.

For the urban multitudes baseball grew into something more than an afternoon at the ballpark. By root-
ing for the home team, fans found a way of identifying
with the city in which they lived. Amid the diversity and
anonymity of urban life, the common experience and
language of baseball acted as a bridge among strangers.

Newspapers. Most efficient at this task, however, was
the newspaper. James Gordon Bennett, founder of the
New York Herald in 1835, wanted "to record the facts . . .
for the great masses of the community." The news was
whatever interested city readers, starting with crime,
scandal, and sensational events. After the Civil War the
New York Sun added the human-interest story, which
made news of ordinary happenings. Newspapers also

TABLE 19.3 Newspaper Circulation

Year	Total Circulation
1870	2,602,000
1880	3,566,000
1890	8,387,000
1900	15,102,000
1909	24,212,000

Source: Historical Statistics of the United States (1975), 2: 810.

targeted specific audiences. A women's page offered recipes and fashion news, separate sections covered sports and high society, and the Sunday supplement helped fill the weekend hours.

The competition for readers became fierce when Joseph Pulitzer, the owner of the *St. Louis Post-Dispatch*, invaded New York in 1883 by buying the *New York World*. Pulitzer was in turn challenged by William Randolph Hearst, who arrived from San Francisco in 1895 prepared to beat the *New York World* at its own game (see Chapter 21, American Lives, "William Randolph Hearst: Jingo," p. 614). Hearst's sensationalist style of newspaper reporting became known as **yellow journalism**. The term, linked to the first comic strip to appear in color, *The Yellow Kid* (1895), meant a type of reporting in which accuracy came second to eliciting a "Gee Whiz!" feeling in the reader.

"He who is without a newspaper," said the great showman P. T. Barnum, "is cut off from his species." Barnum was speaking of city people and their hunger for information. By meeting this need, newspapers revealed their sensitivity to the public they served (Table 19.3).

The Higher Culture

In the midst of this popular ferment, new institutions of higher culture were taking shape in America's cities. A desire for the cultivated life was not, of course, specifically urban. Before the Civil War the lyceum movement had sent lecturers to the remotest towns, bearing messages of culture and learning. Chautauqua, founded in upstate New York in 1874, carried on this work of cultural dissemination. However, great institutions such as museums, public libraries, opera companies, and symphonic orchestras could flourish only in metropolitan centers.

Cultural Institutions. The nation's first major art museum, the Corcoran Gallery of Art, opened in Washington, D.C., in 1869. New York's Metropolitan Museum of Art started in rented quarters two years later, then moved in 1880 to its permanent site in Central Park and launched an ambitious program of art acquisition. When J. P. Morgan became chairman of the board in 1905, the Metropolitan's preeminence was assured. The Boston Museum of Fine Arts was founded in 1876 and Chicago's Art Institute in 1879.

Symphony orchestras also appeared, first in New York under the conductors Theodore Thomas and Leopold Damrosch in the 1870s and then in Boston and Chicago during the next decade. National tours by these leading orchestras planted the seeds for orchestral societies in many other cities. Public libraries grew from modest collections (in 1870 only seven had as many as fifty thousand books) into major urban institutions. The greatest library benefactor was Andrew Carnegie, who announced in 1881 that he would build a library in any town or city that was prepared to maintain it. By 1907 Carnegie had spent more than $32.7 million to establish about a thousand libraries throughout the country.

The late nineteenth century was the great age not only of moneymaking but of money *giving*. Generous with their surplus wealth, new millionaires patronized the arts partly as a civic duty and partly, as in the founding of the Metropolitan Opera, as a vehicle for establishing themselves in society. But museums and symphony orchestras also received support as an expression of national aspirations.

"In America there is no culture," pronounced the English critic G. Lowes Dickinson in 1909. Science and the practical arts, yes, "every possible application of life to purposes and ends," but "no life for life's sake." Such condescending remarks received a respectful American hearing out of a sense of cultural inferiority to the Old World. In 1873 Mark Twain and Charles Dudley Warner published a novel, *The Gilded Age*, satirizing America as a land of money grubbers and speculators. This enormously popular book touched a nerve in the American psyche. Its title has in fact been appropriated by historians to characterize the late nineteenth century—America's "Gilded Age"—as an era of materialism and cultural shallowness.

Some members of the upper class, like the novelist Henry James, despaired of the country and moved to Europe. But the more common response was to try to raise the nation's cultural level. The newly rich had a hard time of it. They did not have much opportunity to cultivate a taste for art, and a great deal of what they collected was mediocre and garish. On the other hand George W. Vanderbilt, grandson of the rough-hewn Cornelius Vanderbilt, was an early champion of French Impressionism, and the coal and steel baron Henry Clay Frick built a brilliant art collection that is still housed, as a public museum, in his mansion in New York City. The enthusiasm of moneyed Americans largely fueled the great cultural institutions that sprang up during the Gilded Age.

The Literary Scene.   A deeply conservative idea of culture sustained this generous patronage. The aim was to embellish life, not to probe or reveal its meaning. "Art," says the hero of the Reverend Henry Ward Beecher's sentimental novel *Norwood* (1867), "attempts to work out its end solely by the use of the beautiful, and the artist is to select out only such things as are beautiful." The idea of culture also took on an elitist cast: Shakespeare, once a staple of popular entertainment (in various bowdlerized versions), was appropriated into the domain of "serious" theater. And simultaneously the world of culture became feminized. "Husbands or sons rarely share those interests," noted one observer. In American life, remarked the clergyman Horace Bushnell, men represented the "force principle," women the "beauty principle."

The depiction of life, the eminent editor and novelist William Dean Howells wrote, "must be tinged with sufficient idealism to make it all of a truly uplifting character. We cannot admit stories which deal with false or immoral relations. . . . The finer side of things—the idealistic—is the answer for us." The "genteel tradition," as this literary school came to be known, dominated the nation's purveyors of elite culture—its universities and publishers—from the 1860s onward.

But the urban world could not finally be kept at bay. Howells himself resigned in 1881 as editor of the *Atlantic Monthly*, a stronghold of the genteel tradition, and called for a literature that seeks "to picture the daily life in the most exact terms possible." In a series of realistic novels—*A Modern Instance* (1882), *The Rise of Silas Lapham* (1885), and *A Hazard of New Fortunes* (1890)—Howells captured the urban middle class. Stephen Crane's *Maggie: Girl of the Streets* (1893), privately printed because no publisher would touch it, unflinchingly described the destruction of a slum girl. In another urban novel, *The Cliff-Dwellers* (1893), Henry Blake Fuller followed the fortunes of the occupants—"cliff-dwellers"—of a giant Chicago office building.

The city had entered the American imagination and become, by the early 1900s, a main theme of American art and literature. And because it challenged so many assumptions of an older, republican America, the city also became an overriding concern of reformers and a main theater in the drama of the Progressive Era.

FOR FURTHER EXPLORATION

▶ For definitions of key terms boldfaced in this chapter, see the glossary at the end of the book.

▶ To assess your mastery of the material covered in this chapter, see the Online Study Guide at **bedfordstmartins.com/henretta**.

▶ For suggested references, including Web sites, see page SR-21 at the end of the book.

▶ For map resources and primary documents, see **bedfordstmartins.com/henretta**.

SUMMARY

An agrarian society since birth, America became increasingly urbanized after the Civil War. By 1900 about 20 percent of the population was living in cities with 100,000 or more people. City growth stemmed mainly from industrialization—the concentration of industry at key locations, the increasing scale of production, and the need for financial and administrative services that were best located in urban centers. A burst of innovation, including mass transit systems, steel-framed buildings, the telephone, and electric lighting, solved the problems arising from the concentration of large populations in a confined area. Although the municipal sector became increasingly robust in these years, American cities left urban development as much as possible in the hands of private interests. The result was dramatic growth but little control over the impact of growth on the urban environment.

In the cities geography defined the social order. The poor were found in the city centers and factory districts. The middle class spread out into the suburbs, the rich lived insulated in favored sections of the city or beyond the suburbs. For the wealthy an elite society emerged, stressing an opulent lifestyle and exclusive social organizations. The middle class, by contrast, withdrew into the private world of the family. For middle-class wives the cult of domesticity reigned, but its more repressive features began to relax as a new attitude toward female sexuality took hold. Child nurture persisted, but as the years of dependency lengthened, a new phase—adolescence—began to emerge that would draw teenagers out of the family orbit.

A distinctive urban culture emerged, drawing heavily on ethnic social institutions and new leisure activities, enabling city dwellers to accommodate themselves to the urban world. Financed by the surplus wealth of American entrepreneurs, the great cities became sites of high culture, including art museums, opera companies, symphony orchestras, and libraries.

TIMELINE

1869 Corcoran Gallery of Art, nation's first major art museum, opens in Washington, D.C.

1871 Chicago fire

1873 Mark Twain and Charles Dudley Warner publish *The Gilded Age*

1875 Dwight L. Moody launches urban revivalist movement

1876 Alexander Graham Bell patents telephone

National Baseball League founded

1879 Thomas Edison creates practical incandescent light bulb

Salvation Army arrives from Britain

1881 Andrew Carnegie offers to build a library for every American city

1883 New York City's Metropolitan Opera founded

Joseph Pulitzer purchases *New York World*

1885 William Jenney builds first steel-framed structure, Chicago's Home Insurance Building

1887 First electric trolley line constructed in Richmond, Virginia

1893 Chicago World's Fair

"City Beautiful" movement

1895 William Randolph Hearst enters New York journalism

1897 Boston builds first American subway

1900 Theodore Dreiser publishes *Sister Carrie*

1901 New York Tenement House Law

1904 New York subway system opens

1906 San Francisco earthquake

1913 Fifty-five-story Woolworth Building opens in New York City

CHAPTER 20

The Progressive Era

O N THE FACE OF IT, the political ferment of the 1890s ended with the election of 1896. After the bitter struggle over free silver, the victorious Republicans had no stomach for political crusades. The McKinley administration devoted itself to maintaining business confidence: sound money and high tariffs were the order of the day. The main thing, as party chief Mark Hanna said, was to "stand pat and continue Republican prosperity."

Yet beneath the surface a deep unease had set in. The depression of the 1890s had unveiled truths not acknowledged in better days. The fury of the decade's industrial disputes, for example, revealed a frightening chasm between America's social classes. In Richard Olney's view, the great Pullman strike of 1894 had brought the country "to the ragged edge of anarchy." As Cleveland's attorney general, it had been Olney's job to crush the strike, which he had done with ruthless efficiency (see Chapter 17). But Olney took little joy in his success. He asked himself what might be done to avoid such repressive government actions in the future. His answer: by federal regulation of labor relations on the railroads so that crippling rail strikes would not happen. As a first step toward Olney's goal, Congress adopted the Erdman Mediation Act in 1898. In such ways did the crisis of the 1890s turn the nation's thinking to reform.

◀ **Reba Owen, Settlement-House Worker**

The settlement house was a hallmark of progressive America. Columbus, Ohio, had five, including Godman Guild House, where Reba Owen served as a visiting nurse, tending the pregnant mothers and children of the neighborhood.
LifeCare Alliance / Courtesy, Ohio Historical Society.

The problems themselves, however, were of much older origin. For many decades Americans had been absorbed in building the world's most advanced industrial economy. At the beginning of the twentieth century, they paused, looked around, and began to add up the costs—a frightening concentration of corporate power, a rebellious working class, misery in the cities, and the corruption of machine politics.

Now, with the crisis of the 1890s behind them, reform became an absorbing concern of many Americans. It was as if social awareness reached a critical mass around 1900 and set reform activity going as a major, self-sustaining phenomenon. For this reason the years from 1900 to World War I have come to be known as the Progressive Era.

The Course of Reform

Historians have sometimes spoken of a progressive "movement." But progressivism was not a movement in any meaningful sense. There was no single progressive constituency, no agreed-upon agenda, no unifying organization. At different times and places, different social groups became active. People who were reformers on one issue might be conservative on another. The term **progressivism** embraces a widespread, many-sided effort after 1900 to build a better society. Progressive reformers shared only this objective, plus an intellectual style that can be called "progressive."

The Progressive Mind

If the facts could be known, everything else was possible. That was the starting point for progressive thinking. Hence the burst of enthusiasm for scientific investigation—statistical studies by the federal government of immigration, child labor, and economic practices; social research by privately funded foundations into industrial conditions; vice commissions in many cities looking into prostitution, gambling, and other moral ills of an urban society. Progressives likewise placed great faith in academic expertise. In Wisconsin the state university became a key resource for Governor Robert La Follette's reform administration—the reason, one supporter boasted, for "the democracy, the thoroughness, and the accuracy of the state in its legislation."

Similarly, progressives were strongly attracted to scientific management, which had originally been intended to rationalize work in factories (see Chapter 17). But its founder, Frederick W. Taylor, argued that his basic approach—the "scientific" analysis of human activity—offered solutions to waste and inefficiency in municipal government, schools and hospitals, even at home. Scientific management, said Taylor, could solve all the social ills that arise from "such of our acts as are blundering, ill-directed, or inefficient."

The main thing, in the progressive view, was to resist ways of thinking that discouraged purposeful action. Social Darwinists who had so dominated Gilded Age thought (see Chapter 18) were wrong in their belief that society developed according to fixed and unchanging laws. "It is folly," pronounced the Harvard philosopher William James, "to speak of the 'laws of history,' as of something inevitable, which science only has to discover, and which anyone can then foretell and observe, but do nothing to alter or avert." Man could "shape environmental forces to his own advantage," argued the sociologist Lester F. Ward.

Nowhere were the battle lines more sharply drawn than in economics, where laissez-faire economists had long proceeded on the assumption that markets were perfectly competitive and perfectly responsive to supply and demand. Such an imagined world left no room for reform because any interference with the market could only disrupt what was already working perfectly. In response, reform-minded economists—founders of a new "institutional" school—turned to statistics and history to reveal how the economy really functioned and why, without trade unions and public regulation, the strong would devour the weak.

Progressives similarly opposed the reigning conception of the law that treated legal rights as if these arose from eternal principles not rooted in—or to be tested by—social reality. One such principle was liberty of contract, which the Supreme Court invoked in *Lochner v. New York* (1905) to strike down a state law limiting the working hours of bakers. Such a restriction, said the Court, violated the liberty of contract of the bakers (as well as their employers). Nonsense, responded the dissenting Justice Oliver Wendell Holmes. If the choice was between working and starving, could it really be said that bakers freely accepted jobs requiring them to labor fourteen hours a day? or that a law reducing their working hours violated their liberty of contract?

Legal realism, as Justice Holmes's reasoning came to be known, rested on his conviction that "the life of the law has not been logic; it has been experience." Dean Roscoe Pound of the Harvard Law School called for "the adjustment of principles and doctrines to the human conditions they are to govern rather than assumed first principles." The law, moreover, should not claim a false neutrality; on the contrary, as Pound's student Felix Frankfurter argued, law should be "a vital agency for human betterment."

The philosophical underpinnings for legal realism came from William James, who denied the existence of absolute truths and advocated instead a philosophy of **pragmatism**, which judged ideas by their consequences. Philosophy should be concerned with solving problems, James insisted, and not with contemplating ultimate ends.

Sources of Progressive Idealism. Progressives prided themselves on being tough minded, on being expert at making things happen. But they were not indifferent to the moral grounds for favoring reform.

Progressives were, in truth, unabashed idealists. The progressive cause, proclaimed Theodore Roosevelt, "is based on the eternal principles of righteousness."

Much of this idealism was rooted in American radical traditions. Many progressives traced their awakening to Henry George's *Progress and Poverty* (1879), which asked why, in the midst of fabulous wealth, so many Americans should be condemned to poverty. His answer was that private control of land siphoned the community's wealth into the hands of landlords. George's single-tax movement—advocating a confiscatory tax on the unearned value of land—served as a school for many budding progressives. Others credited Edward Bellamy's utopian novel, *Looking Backward* (1888), with its technocratic vision of an orderly, affluent American socialism, or Henry Demarest Lloyd's *Wealth against Commonwealth* (1894), with its searing indictment of the Standard Oil trust. In later years this radical tradition was transmitted mainly through the Socialist Party, which flourished after 1900 under the leadership of Eugene V. Debs. Many young reformers passed through socialism on the way to progressivism, although there were some, like Charlotte Perkins Gilman, who remained faithful to socialism.

The most important source of progressive idealism, however, was religion. Protestant churches, long troubled by the plight of the urban poor, now translated that concern into a major theological doctrine— the Social Gospel. Its leading exponent was the Baptist cleric Walter Rauschenbush, whose ideas had been forged by his ministry in the squalid Hell's Kitchen section of New York City. The churches could not wall themselves off from the misery and despair in their midst, he concluded. They had to embrace the "social aims of Jesus." The Kingdom of God on Earth would be achieved not by striving for personal salvation but in the cause of social justice.

Progressive leaders characteristically grew up in homes imbued with evangelical piety. Many went through a religious crisis, ultimately settling on a career in social work, education, or politics where religious striving might be translated into secular action. Jane Addams, for example, had taken up settlement-house work believing that by uplifting the poor, she would herself be uplifted: she would experience "the joy of finding Christ" by acting "in fellowship" with the needy.

The Muckrakers.   The progressive mode of thought— idealistic in intent, tough-minded in practice—nurtured a new kind of reform journalism. During the 1890s bright new magazines like *Collier's* and *McClure's* began to find an urban audience for lively, fact-filled reporting. At the turn of the century, almost by accident, editors discovered that what most interested readers was the exposure of mischief in American life. Investigative reporters fanned out on the trail of evildoers (see American Voices, "Charles Edward Russell: Muckraking," p. 576).

Ida Tarbell Takes on Rockefeller

A popular biographer of Napoleon and Lincoln in the 1890s, Ida Tarbell turned her journalistic talents to muckraking. Her first installment of "The History of the Standard Oil Company" appeared in McClure's *in November 1902. John D. Rockefeller, she wrote, "was willing to strain every nerve to obtain for himself special and illegal privileges from the railroads which were bound to ruin every man in the oil business not sharing them with him." As Tarbell built her case, criticism rained down on Rockefeller. A more sympathetic cartoon in* Judge *magazine pleads with Rockefeller's critics: "Boys, don't you think you have bothered the old man just about enough?"*

Charles Edward Russell

Muckraking

In this autobiographical account newspaperman Charles Russell describes how he got into muckraking journalism and what he thought it was all about. He never did, by the way, get back to writing music.

All America had been accustomed to laud and bepraise the makers of great fortunes. . . . Money had become the touchstone and perfect measure of worth. . . . Now, of a sudden, men began to discover that these great and adored fortunes had been gathered in ways that not only grazed the prison gate but imposed burdens and disadvantages upon the rest of the community; that vast hoards for one man meant much less for others. In the shock of this discovery, a literature of expos[ure] arose and daily the magazine editors looked for new dark, malodorous corners of money-grabbing upon which the spotlight could be turned.

Pure accident cast me, without the least desire, into the pursuit of this fashion. I had finally withdrawn from the newspaper business, and having enough money to live modestly I was bent upon carrying out a purpose long cherished in quite a different line. [I had concluded] that what we call the separate arts of music and poetry are really but one, and I now conceived that with

a piano, my Swinburne, and some sheets of music paper I could demonstrate this priceless fact to a palpitating world. Upon this task I was intent when the whole business was upset with a single telegram.

One day, Mr. J. W. Midgley, who was a famous expert on railroad rates and conditions . . . let loose a flood of startling facts about the impositions practised by the owners and operators of refrigerator cars. My friend, Mr. Erman J. Ridgway . . . of *Everybody's Magazine* wired asking me to see Mr. Midgley and get him to write for *Everybody's* an article along the lines of his testimony. I conferred accordingly and Mr. Midgley positively refused all offers to become an exposé writer. [So] Ridgway wire[d] asking me to furnish the article *Everybody's* wanted. I had not the least disposition to do so, except only that Ridgway was my friend. . . . The next thing I knew a muckrake was put into my hand and I was plunged into the midst of the game. . . .

I wrote two or three articles on the refrigerator car scandal and then went on to write a series on the methods of the Beef Trust and was not in the least astonished to find that I was become an unmitigated scoundrel, a hired assassin of character, a libeller of good men, an enemy of society and of the government, and probably an Anarchist in disguise. . . . We were all up and away, full of the pleasures of the chase . . . and all that business about poetry and music sheets forgotten. It was exhilarating sport, hunting the money octopus.

Source: Charles Edward Russell, *Bare Hands and Stone Walls* (New York: Charles Scribner's Sons, 1933), 135–39.

Lincoln Steffens's article "Tweed Days in St. Louis" in the October 1902 issue of *McClure's* is credited with starting the trend. In a powerful series Steffens wrote about "the shame of the cities"—the corrupt ties between business and political machines. Ida M. Tarbell attacked the Standard Oil monopoly and David Graham Phillips told how money controlled the Senate. William Hard exposed industrial accidents in "Making Steel and Killing Men" (1907) and child labor in "De Kid Wot Works at Night" (1908). Hardly a sordid corner of American life escaped the scrutiny of these tireless reporters. They were moralists as well, infusing their factual accounts with personal indignation. "The sights I saw," wrote the pioneering slum investigator Jacob Riis, "gripped my heart until I felt I must tell of them, or burst, or turn anarchist."

Theodore Roosevelt, among many others, thought these journalists went too far. In a 1906 speech he compared them to the man with a muckrake in *Pilgrim's Progress* (by the seventeenth-century English preacher John Bunyan) who was too absorbed with raking the filth on the floor to look up and accept a celestial crown. Thus the term **muckraker** became attached to journalists who exposed the underside of American life. Their efforts were in fact health giving. More than any other group, the muckrakers called the people to arms.

Women Progressives

Among the first to respond were middle-class women who, in their well-established role as "social housekeepers," had long shouldered the burden of humanitarian work in American cities. They were the foot soldiers for the charity organization societies that coordinated private relief, visiting needy families, assessing their problems, and referring them to relief agencies.

After many years of such dedicated labor, Josephine Shaw Lowell of New York City concluded that giving assistance to the poor was not enough. "If the working people had all they ought to have, we should not have the paupers and criminals," she declared. "It is better to save them before they go under, than to spend your life fishing them out afterward." Lowell founded the New York Consumers' League in 1890. Her goal was to improve the wages and working conditions of female clerks in the city's stores by issuing a "White List"—a very short list at first—of cooperating shops.

From these modest beginnings the league spread to other cities and blossomed into the National Consumers' League in 1899. By then the women at its head had lost faith in voluntary action; only the state had the resources to rescue poor families. Under the crusading leadership of Florence Kelley, formerly a chief factory inspector in Illinois, the Consumers' League became a powerful lobby for protective legislation for women and children.

Among its achievements, none was more important than the *Muller v. Oregon* decision (1908), which upheld an Oregon law limiting the workday for women to ten hours. The Consumers' League recruited the brilliant Boston lawyer Louis D. Brandeis to defend the Oregon law before the Supreme Court. In his brief Brandeis devoted a scant two pages to the narrow constitutional issue— whether, under its police powers, Oregon had the right to regulate women's working hours. Instead, Brandeis rested his case on data gathered by the Consumers' League describing the toll that long hours took on women's health and family roles. The *Muller* decision, by approving an expansive welfare role for the states, cleared the way for a wave of protective laws across the country (Table 20.1).

Women's organizations became a mighty lobby on behalf of women and children (see American Lives, "Frances Kellor: Woman Progressive," p. 580). Their victories included the first law providing public assistance for mothers with dependent children in Illinois in 1911; the first minimum wage law for women in Massachusetts in 1912; more effective child labor laws in many states; and at the federal level, the Children's and Women's bureaus in the Labor Department in 1912 and 1920, respectively. The welfare state, insofar as it arrived in America in these years, was what women progressives had made of it; they erected a "maternalist" welfare system.

Settlement Houses.   A parallel path for women's reform came via the settlement-house movement. The seed in America was Hull House, which Jane Addams and Ellen Gates Starr established in 1889 on Chicago's West Side after visiting Toynbee Hall in the London slums. During the progressive years scores of settlement houses sprang up in the poor neighborhoods of the nation's cities. The settlement houses served as community centers staffed by middle-class residents. Hull House had meeting rooms, an art gallery, clubs for children and adults, and a kindergarten. Addams herself led battles for garbage removal, playgrounds, better street lighting, and police protection.

In a famous essay Jane Addams spoke of the "subjective necessity" of the settlement house. She meant that it was as much for educated young men and women

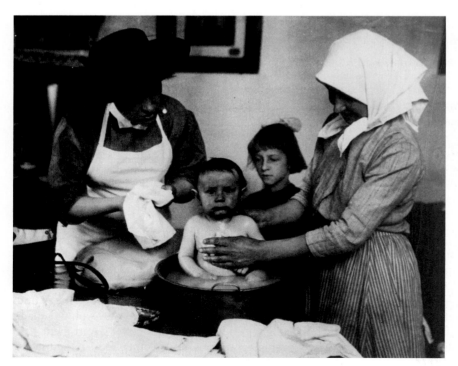

Saving the Children

In the early years at Hull House, Jane Addams recalled, toddlers sometimes arrived for kindergarten tipsy from a breakfast of bread soaked in wine. To settlement-house workers, the answer to such ignorance was in child-care education, and so began the program to send visiting nurses into immigrant homes. They taught mothers the proper methods of caring for children—including, as this photograph shows, the daily infant bath, given in a dishpan if necessary.

Chicago Historical Society.

TABLE 20.1 Progressive Legislation and Supreme Court Decisions

State Laws	
1903	Wisconsin primary law Oregon ten-hour law for women
1910	New York Bureau of Industries and Immigration Washington State adopts woman suffrage
1911	Illinois law providing aid for mothers with dependent children New York State Factory Commission
1912	Massachusetts minimum-wage law for women and children

Federal Laws	
1898	Erdman Railway Mediation Act
1902	Newlands Reclamation Act
1903	U.S. Bureau of Corporations Elkins Act
1906	Hepburn Railway Act Pure Food and Drug Act Meat Inspection Act
1909	Payne-Aldrich Tariff Act
1913	Underwood Tariff Act Federal Reserve Act
1914	Federal Trade Commission Act Clayton Antitrust Act
1916	Seamen's Act Federal Farm Loan Act

Supreme Court Decisions	
1895	*U.S. v. E. C. Knight* shelters manufacturing from antitrust law
1897	*U.S. v. Trans-Missouri* quashes "rule of reason" in antitrust suits
1904	*U.S. v. Northern Securities* orders dissolution of a company ruled a monopoly under Sherman Act
1905	*Lochner v. New York* invalidates a state law limiting hours of bakers
1908	*Muller v. Oregon* approves a state law limiting working hours of women *Loewe v. Lawlor* (*Danbury Hatters* case) finds a labor boycott to be a conspiracy in restraint of trade
1911	*U.S. v. Standard Oil* restores rule of reason as guiding principle in antitrust cases

eager to serve as a response to the needs of slum dwellers. Addams herself was a case in point. Born in 1860 in Cedarville, Illinois, she grew up in comfortable circumstances and graduated from Rockford College. Then Addams faced an empty future—an ornamental wife if she married, a sheltered spinster if she did not. Hull House became her salvation, enabling her to "begin with however small a group to accomplish and to live."

Revival of the Suffrage Movement. Almost imperceptibly, women activists like Jane Addams and Florence Kelley breathed new life into the suffrage movement. Why, they asked, should a woman who was capable of running a settlement house or lobbying a bill be denied the right to vote? If women had the right to vote, they would demand more enlightened legislation and better government. And by encouraging working-class women to help themselves,

Rose Schneiderman, 1913

In their battles for better conditions, women garment workers produced their own leaders, and none was more devoted to the cause or more fiery on the platform than Rose Schneiderman. The daughter of a widowed immigrant woman, Schneiderman went to work at thirteen, quickly got caught up in union activities, and fashioned for herself a lifelong career as a trade unionist, including becoming president of the National Women's Trade Union League. Brown Brothers.

women progressives got a whole new class interested in fighting for suffrage.

In 1903 social reformers founded the National Women's Trade Union League. Financed and led by wealthy supporters, the league organized women workers, played a considerable role in their strikes, and trained working-class leaders. One such was Rose Schneiderman (see Chapter 17, American Voices, p. 509), who became a union organizer among New York's garment workers; another was Agnes Nestor, who led Illinois glove workers. Although they often resented the patronizing ways of their well-to-do patrons, such trade union women identified their cause with the broader struggle for women's rights.

Around 1910, suffrage activity began to quicken, and tactics shifted. In Britain suffragists had begun to picket Parliament, assault politicians, and stage hunger strikes while in jail. Inspired by their example, Alice Paul, a young Quaker once resident in Britain, applied similar confrontational tactics to the American struggle. Although woman suffrage had been won in six western states since 1910, Paul rejected the state-by-state route as too slow (Map 20.1). She advocated a constitutional amendment that in one stroke would grant women everywhere the right to vote. In 1916 Paul organized the militant National Woman's Party.

The mainstream National American Woman Suffrage Association (NAWSA), from which Paul had split off, was also rejuvenated. Carrie Chapman Catt, a skilled organizer from the New York movement, took over as national leader in 1915. Under her guidance NAWSA brought a broad-based organization to the campaign for a federal amendment.

The Birth of Feminism. In the midst of this suffrage struggle, something new and more fundamental began

Suffragists on Parade, 1913

After 1910 the suffrage movement went into high gear. Suffragist leaders decided that a constitutional amendment was a more effective route than battling for the vote state by state. The impressive women's parade in Washington, D.C., at Woodrow Wilson's inauguration served notice on the incoming administration that the suffragists meant business. The new president was not pleased with his uninvited guests. Brown Brothers.

Frances Kellor:
Woman Progressive

From the day its doors opened in 1892, the University of Chicago was a major center of American learning. Financed by John D. Rockefeller, the university modeled itself on the great German research universities and, unlike Yale and Harvard, concentrated on graduate education. At Chicago and other American universities, modern social science was taking shape, breaking from its nineteenth-century moral foundations and seeking a scientific basis for the study of society. Economics, political science, and sociology demanded a rigorous course of study certified by the granting of the Ph.D. But if the social sciences were becoming professional, their guiding purpose was not yet disinterested research but the improvement of society. The University of Chicago saw the city surrounding it as a great laboratory for social betterment. Its students were being prepared, whether they knew it or not, to be in service to the American progressivism of the next decade. The University of Chicago, moreover, was receptive to the admission of women, and for them in particular, graduate education was a breeding ground for careers as social reformers.

Among the women entering in 1898 was Frances Alice Kellor, a recent graduate of Cornell University. Kellor was born in Columbus, Ohio, in 1873. Her father abandoned the family before she was two, and her mother made a hard living as a domestic and laundress. In 1875 her family moved to Coldwater, Michigan, a former abolitionist center (and station on the underground railroad) and a stronghold of Yankee culture. From the Coldwater community, with its high moral standards and strong educational institutions, Kellor received the reformist values that other budding progressives learned from their families. Her first patrons were the well-to-do librarians of Coldwater, Mary and Frances Eddy, who befriended her and took her into their home. Born Alice, Kellor began to call herself "Frances" as a sign that she considered herself adopted by the Eddy sisters. She graduated from high school, became a reporter for the *Coldwater Republican*, and then, with the backing of the Eddys, enrolled at Cornell in 1895. A natural athlete, Kellor made her first mark as a fighter for equal rights on a sports issue: she led the campaign for a women's crew. She got a

solid education in the social sciences at Cornell and decided to become a criminologist.

When Frances Kellor arrived in Chicago in 1898, sociology was an infant discipline, with an emphasis on high-minded investigations of social problems. Kellor's interest in crime was encouraged by the Chicago faculty. The prevailing theory of the time, advanced by the Italian Cesare Lombroso, was that criminality was an inherited trait—that criminals were born criminal and that this tendency was manifest in their physical features. Skeptical, Kellor conducted a study of the female inmates of five midwestern prisons. Comparing them with a control group of college women, she could find no physical differences. Kellor concluded that not heredity but social environment, economic disadvantage, and poverty produced criminality. Kellor also rejected "the prevailing opinion that when women are criminal they are more degraded and more abandoned than men." People thought so, she asserted, only because of "the difference in the standards which we set for the two sexes."

A project on criminality among southern blacks likewise rejected heredity and stressed environmental factors, but Kellor's conclusions were pessimistic and racially conservative: centuries of slavery and indolent southern life had left blacks so morally weakened that "the Negro at present has neither the perceptions nor the solidity of character that would enable him to lead his race." She considered the southern restrictions on blacks' legal and political rights unfortunate but necessary, and she believed that "the free intermingling of the two races is impossible, at least for many generations." In drawing these illiberal conclusions, Kellor was echoing the views of her teachers and indeed of most white progressives of her generation.

Despite her precocious record, Kellor left the university in 1902 without a degree. The reasons are not altogether clear but doubtless had something to do with the fact that the University of Chicago almost never placed its female graduate students in university teaching jobs. To be a professor, it seemed, was still a male prerogative. There was, however, a positive side to Kellor's decision. Like many of her fellow students, she had fallen under the spell of Jane Addams. Kellor lived periodically at Hull House and joined the circle of social reformers that congregated there. When she left Chicago, it was to do social research for New York's College Settlement Association.

Her first project was a study of unemployment. Kellor was among the first investigators to see that unemployment was an economic problem, not, as was generally believed, the result of individual shiftlessness or

Frances Kellor

This photograph of Kellor was taken in her early twenties when she was a student at Cornell University.

incompetence, but of the impersonal operations of the labor market. Her book *Out of Work* (1904) was a pioneering investigation, paving the way for the modern study of unemployment. Kellor was especially concerned with the plight of jobless women and their exploitation by commercial employment agencies. Representing the Women's Municipal League of New York, Kellor lobbied successfully for state regulation of these agencies. Kellor thus employed her research to bring about social change. The combination of professional investigation and robust political advocacy became the hallmark of Kellor's progressivism. Her next study, on the problems of immigrants in New York, led to the establishment of the New York State Bureau of Industries and Immigration in 1910. Kellor was chosen to be its head, the first woman to hold so high a post in New York State government.

The high point of Kellor's career came two years later, when Theodore Roosevelt launched the Progressive Party. Convinced that social reform required strong government, Kellor was drawn to the New Nationalism. She linked it with her own fervent advocacy of women's political rights. Always a fighter, she was entirely at ease in the

rough-and-tumble of partisan politics. After Roosevelt's defeat in 1912, the Progressive Party set up the National Progressive Service, a kind of think tank for studying social problems and formulating legislative proposals. The idea was mainly Kellor's, and she was tapped to chair the service. This was truly a pinnacle for a woman in American politics at a time when women in most states could not vote in national elections. Unfortunately, Kellor's emphasis on scientific investigation put her at odds with the practical politicians, and she was forced out in early 1914. Hers was a brief run in national politics, exhilarating while it lasted and unique for a woman of her generation.

Kellor never married. Like many other woman progressives, she found personal fulfillment in an enduring relationship with another woman. This was Mary Dreier, one of two wealthy sisters who played leading roles in New York progressivism. From the time Kellor moved into the Dreier home in Brooklyn Heights in 1904 until her death almost fifty years later, she and Mary were constant companions. Kellor's later professional life was devoted to a distinguished career with the American Arbitration Association.

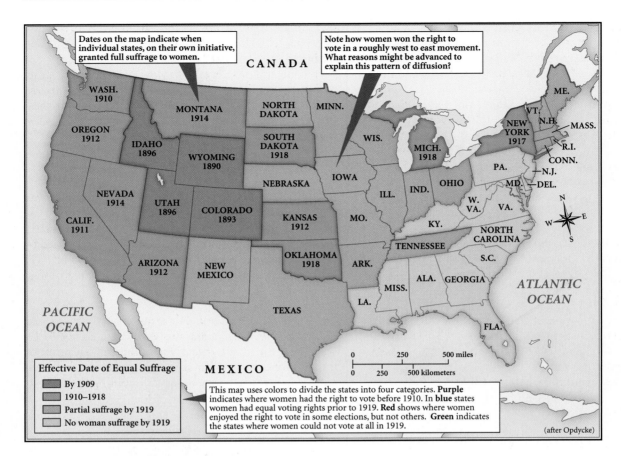

MAP 20.1 Woman Suffrage, 1890–1919

By 1909, after more than sixty years of agitation, only four lightly populated western states had granted women full voting rights. A number of other states offered partial suffrage, limited mostly to voting for school boards and such issues as taxes. Between 1910 and 1918, as the effort shifted to the struggle for a constitutional amendment, eleven states joined the list granting full suffrage. The most stubborn resistance was in the South.

For more help analyzing this map, see the ONLINE STUDY GUIDE at bedfordstmartins.com/henretta.

to happen. A younger generation of college-educated, self-supporting women refused to be hemmed in by the social constraints of women's "separate sphere." "Breaking into the Human Race" was the intention they proclaimed at a mass meeting in New York in 1914. "We intend simply to be ourselves," declared the chair Marie Jenny Howe, "not just our little female selves, but our whole big human selves."

The women at this meeting called themselves **feminists**, a term that was just coming into use. In this, its first incarnation, feminism meant freedom for full personal development. Thus did Charlotte Perkins Gilman, famous for her advocacy of communal kitchens as a means of liberating women from homemaking, imagine the new woman: "Here she comes, running, out of prison and off the pedestal; chains off, crown off, halo off, just a live woman."

Feminists were militantly prosuffrage, but unlike their more traditional suffragist sisters, they had no interest in arguing that women would have an uplifting effect on American politics. Rather, they demanded the right to vote because they considered themselves fully equal to men. At the point that the suffrage movement was about to triumph, it was overtaken by a larger revolution that redefined the struggle for women's rights as a battle against all the constraints that prevented women from achieving their potential as human beings.

Feminism brought forth a more radical type of woman social progressive—most notably, Margaret Sanger. As a public health nurse in New York City, Sanger had been repeatedly asked by immigrant women the "secret" about how to avoid having more babies. When one of her patients died of a botched abortion, Sanger decided to devote herself to the cause of birth control. This activity was illegal; nineteenth-century laws treated birth control literature and contraceptive devices as obscene materials. While the educated middle class readily evaded these laws, birth control could only reach the poor by an open campaign of education. Undeterred by police raids or public disapproval, Sanger gave speeches, published pamphlets, and in 1916 opened the first birth control clinic in the United States. If her ends were the same as Jane Addams's—both wanted to uplift the downtrodden—the means Sanger chose laid down a sharper challenge to the status quo.

Implicitly, however, feminism also challenged Addams's brand of social reform. Protection for working women, its premier legislative achievement, was premised on the argument that women were the weaker sex. It was just this argument, at the very heart of Brandeis's brief in the landmark *Muller* case, that rang true with the Supreme Court. "The two sexes differ in structure of body, in the functions to be performed by each, in the amount of physical strength," the Court agreed. "This difference justifies . . . legislation . . . designed to compensate for some of the burdens which rest upon her." But feminists wanted no such compensation. The progressive governor of Maryland, Charles J. Bonaparte,

was surprised to encounter opposition to his 1914 minimum wage bill for women's industries by suffragists objecting to the idea that "women need some special care, protection and privilege." This was the opening wedge of a dispute that would fracture the women's movement, dividing an older generation of progressives from their feminist successors who prized gender equality higher than any social benefit.

Reforming Politics

Like the Mugwumps of the Gilded Age, progressive reformers attacked the boss rule of the party system, but more adeptly and more aggressively. Indeed, because politics was about power, in this realm the motives of progressives were always mixed, with the ideals of civic betterment elbowing uneasily with the drive for self-aggrandizement.

La Follette: Political Reformer. Robert M. La Follette of Wisconsin led the way. Born in 1855, La Follette started as a conventional politician, rising from the Republican ranks to service in Congress for three terms. He was party regular, never doubting that he was

Robert M. La Follette
La Follette was transformed into a political reformer when a Wisconsin Republican boss attempted to bribe him in 1891 to influence a judge in a railway case. As he described it in his Autobiography, *"Out of this awful ordeal came understanding; and out of understanding came resolution. I determined that the power of this corrupt influence . . . should be broken." This photograph captures him at the top of his form, expounding his progressive vision to a rapt audience of Wisconsin citizens at an impromptu street gathering.* Library of Congress.

in honorable company until, by his own account, a Republican boss offered him a bribe to fix a judge in a railroad case. Awakened by this "awful ordeal," La Follette broke with the Wisconsin machine in 1891 and became a tireless advocate of political reform, which for him meant restoring America's democratic ideals. "Go back to the first principles of democracy; go back to the people," he told his audience when he launched his campaign against the state Republican machine. In 1900, after battling for a decade, La Follette won the Wisconsin governorship on a platform of higher taxes for corporations, stricter utility and railroad regulation, and political reform.

The key to party reform, La Follette felt, was to deny bosses the power to choose the party's candidates. This could be achieved by requiring that nominations be decided not in party conventions but by popular vote. Enacted in 1903, the direct primary expressed La Follette's democratic idealism, but it also suited his particular political talents. The party regulars opposing him were insiders, more comfortable in the caucus room than out on the stump. But that was where La Follette, a superb campaigner, excelled. The direct primary gave La Follette an iron grip on Republican politics in Wisconsin that lasted until his death twenty-five years later.

What was true of La Follette was more or less true of all successful progressive politicians. They typically described their work as political restoration, frequently confessing that they had converted to reform after discovering how far party politics had drifted from the ideals of representative government. Like La Follette, Albert B. Cummins of Iowa, Harold U'Ren of Oregon, and Hiram Johnson of California all espoused democratic ideals, and all skillfully used the direct primary as the stepping stone to political power. They practiced a new kind of popular politics, which in a reform age could be a more effective way to power than the backroom techniques of the old-fashioned machine politicians.

Even the most democratizing of reforms espoused by the progressives—the initiative and recall—were really exercises in power politics. The initiative enabled citizens to have issues placed on the ballot; recall empowered them to remove officeholders who had lost the public's confidence. It soon became clear, however, that direct democracy did not supplant organized politics. Initiative and recall campaigns required organization, money, and expertise, and these were attributes not of the people at large but of well-financed interests. Like the direct primary, the initiative and recall had as much to do with power relations as with political reform.

Municipal Reform.   And so, in many cities, did the demand for more efficient government. Taxes went up, local businessmen complained, but services always lagged. There had to be an end, as one manufacturer said, to "the inefficiency, the sloth, the carelessness, the injustice and the graft of city administrations." By making aldermanic elections citywide, municipal reformers attacked the ward politics that underlay the corrupting patronage system. A more radical strategy focused on the very structure of city governance that gave the masses a voice.

After a hurricane devastated Galveston, Texas, in 1901, business leaders impatient to rebuild the city persuaded voters to replace the mayor and board of aldermen with a nonpartisan five-member commission. This was the opening wedge in a nationwide drive to put municipal affairs, as John Patterson of the National Cash Register Company said, "on a strict business basis." In Dayton, Ohio, where Patterson was a leading citizen, the elected commission was combined with an appointed city manager, and this became the model for municipal reformers in medium-sized cities across the country. The commission-manager system aimed at running the city "in exactly the same way as a private business corporation." But of course there was nothing democratic about how private corporations operated. Some municipal reformers thought that was just as well. "Ignorance should be excluded from control," said former mayor Abram Hewitt of New York in 1901. "City business should be carried on by trained experts selected on some other principle than popular suffrage."

Urban Liberalism.   The antidemocratic strain in municipal reform was powerfully counterbalanced by the activation of the urban masses in progressive politics. When the Republican Hiram Johnson ran for California governor in 1910, he was the reform candidate of the state's middle class. Famous as prosecutor of the corrupt San Francisco boss Abe Ruef, Johnson pledged to purify California politics and curb the Southern Pacific Railroad—the dominating economic power in the state. By his second term, Johnson was championing social and labor legislation. His original base in the middle class had eroded, and he had become the champion of California's working class.

Johnson's career reflected a shift in the center of gravity of progressivism, which had begun as a movement of the middle class but then took on board America's working people. A new strain of progressive reform emerged that historians have labeled **urban liberalism**. To understand this phenomenon, we have to begin with city machine politics.

Thirty minutes before quitting time on Saturday afternoon, March 25, 1911, fire broke out at the Triangle Shirtwaist Company in downtown New York. The flames trapped the workers, who were mostly young immigrant women. Forty-seven leapt to their deaths; another ninety-nine never reached the windows.

In the wake of the tragedy, the New York State Factory Commission developed a remarkable program of labor reform over a four-year period: fifty-six laws dealing with

as an attack on back-room party rule, but it also served to deprive blacks of their political rights.

White Supremacy in the Progressive Vein.   How could democratic reform and white supremacy be thus wedded together? By the racism of the age. In a 1902 book on Reconstruction, Professor John W. Burgess of Columbia University denounced the Fifteenth Amendment: granting blacks the vote after the Civil War had been a "monstrous thing." Burgess was southern born, but he was confident that his northern audience saw the "vast differences in political capacity" between blacks and whites and approved of black disfranchisement. Even the Republican Party offered no rebuttal. Indeed, as president-elect in 1908, William Howard Taft applauded the southern laws as necessary to "prevent entirely the possibility of domination by . . . an ignorant electorate." Taft assured southerners that "the federal government has nothing to do with social equality."

Racial tensions were on the rise in the North. Over 200,000 blacks migrated from the South between 1900 and 1910. Their arrival in northern cities invariably sparked white resentment. Attacks on blacks became widespread, capped by a bloody race riot in Springfield, Illinois, in 1908. Equally reflective of racist sentiment was the huge success of D. W. Griffith's epic film *Birth of a Nation* (1915), which depicted Reconstruction as a moral struggle between rampaging blacks and a chivalrous Ku Klux Klan. Woodrow Wilson found the film's history "all so terribly true." His Democratic administration marked a low point for the federal government as the ultimate guarantor of equal rights: during Wilson's tenure, segregation of the U.S. civil service would have gone into effect but for an outcry among black leaders and influential white allies.

The Civil Rights Struggle Revived.   In these bleak years a core of young black professionals, mostly northern born, began to fight back. The key figure was William Monroe Trotter, the pugnacious editor of the *Boston Guardian* and an outspoken critic of Booker T. Washington. "The policy of compromise has failed," Trotter argued. "The policy of resistance and aggression deserves a trial." In this endeavor Trotter was joined by W. E. B. Du Bois, a Harvard-trained sociologist and author of *The Souls of Black Folk*. In 1906, after breaking with Washington, they called a meeting of twenty-nine supporters at Niagara Falls—but on the Canadian side because no hotel on the U.S. side would admit blacks.

The **Niagara Movement** resulting from that meeting had an impact far beyond the scattering of members and local bodies it organized. The principles it affirmed would define the struggle for the rights of African Americans: first, encouragement of black pride by all possible means; second, an uncompromising demand for full political and civil equality; and above all, the resolute denial "that the Negro-American assents to inferiority, is submissive under oppression and apologetic before insults."

W. E. B. Du Bois

No activity undertaken by the NAACP in the early years was more important than the publication of its journal, The Crisis, *which under the brilliant editorship of W. E. B. Du Bois became the strongest voice for equal rights and black pride in the country. In this photograph Du Bois is pictured at his desk at the magazine's editorial office.*

Schomburg Center for Research in Black Culture, New York Public Library.

Colored Women's League of Washington, D.C.

At a time when black men were being driven from politics in the South, their wives and sisters organized themselves and became an alternative voice of black conscience. Sara Iredell Fleetwood, superintendent of the Freedman's Hospital Training School for Nurses, founded the Colored Women's League of Washington, D.C., in 1892 for purposes of "racial uplift." This picture of the league was taken on the steps of Frederick Douglass's home in Anacostia, Washington. Mrs. Fleetwood is seated at the far right, third row from the bottom. The notations are by someone seeking to identify the other members, a modest effort to save for posterity these women, mostly teachers, who did their best for the good of the race. Library of Congress.

Going against the grain, a handful of white reformers rallied to the African American cause. Among the most devoted was Mary White Ovington, who grew up in an abolitionist family. Like Jane Addams, Ovington became a settlement-house worker, but among urban blacks in New York rather than in an immigrant Chicago neighborhood. News of the Springfield race riot of 1908 changed her life. Convinced that her duty was to fight racism, Ovington called a meeting of sympathetic white progressives, which led to the formation of the National Association for the Advancement of Colored People (NAACP) in 1909.

Torn by internal disagreements, the Niagara Movement was breaking up; most of the black activists joined the NAACP. The organization's national leadership was dominated by whites, with one crucial exception. Du Bois became the editor of the NAACP's journal, *The Crisis*. With a passion that only a black voice could provide, Du Bois used that platform to proclaim the demand for equal rights.

The National Urban League became the lead organization in social welfare, uniting in 1911 the many agencies serving black migrants arriving in northern cities. Like the NAACP, the Urban League was interracial, including both white reformers such as Ovington and black welfare activists such as William Lewis Bulkley, a New York school principal who was the league's main architect. In the South social welfare was very much the province of black women, whose civic activities to some extent filled the vacuum left by black disfranchisement. Mostly working in the churches and schools, they also utilized the southern branches of the National Association of Colored Women's Clubs, which had started in 1896. And because their activities seemed unthreatening to white supremacy, black women were able to reach across the color line and find allies and supporters among white women in the South.

Progressivism was a house of many chambers. Most were infected by the racism of the age, but not all. A saving remnant of white progressives rallied to the cause of racial justice. National institutions—the NAACP, Urban League, and such black organizations as the National Association of Colored Women's Clubs—took shape that would lead the black struggle for a better life over the next half-century.

Progressivism and National Politics

The gathering forces of progressivism reached the national scene slowly. Reformers had been spurred by immediate and visible problems, far from Washington. But in 1906 Robert La Follette left Wisconsin for the U.S. Senate. Other seasoned progressives, also ambitious for a wider stage, followed. By 1910 a vocal progressive bloc was making itself heard in both houses of Congress.

Progressivism came to national politics not via Congress, however, but by way of the presidency. This was partly because the White House provided a "bully pulpit"—to use Theodore Roosevelt's phrase. But just as important was the twist of fate that brought Roosevelt to the White House on September 14, 1901.

The Making of a Progressive President

Except for his upper-class background, Theodore Roosevelt was cut from much the same cloth as other progressive politicians. Born in 1858, he came from a wealthy, old-line New York family, attended Harvard, and might have led the life of a leisured man of letters. Instead, scarcely out of college, he plunged into Republican politics and entered the New York State legislature.

Like many other budding progressives, Roosevelt was motivated by a high-minded, Christian upbringing. He always identified himself—loudly—with the cause of righteousness. But Roosevelt did not scorn power and its uses. Contemptuous of the Mugwump reformers (see Chapter 18), he much preferred the company of party professionals. Roosevelt rose in the New York party because he skillfully developed broad popular support and thus forced himself on reluctant state Republican bosses.

Safely back from the Spanish-American War as the hero of San Juan Hill (see Chapter 21), Roosevelt won the New York governorship in 1898. During his single term he clearly signaled his progressivism by pushing through civil service reform and a tax on corporate franchises. He discharged the corrupt superintendent of insurance over the Republican Party's objections and asserted his confidence in the government's capacity to improve the life of the people.

Hoping to neutralize him, the party chieftains promoted Roosevelt in 1900 to what seemed a dead-end job, as William McKinley's vice president. Roosevelt accepted reluctantly. But on September 6, 1901, an anarchist named Leon F. Czolgosz shot the president. When McKinley died eight days later, Roosevelt became president. It was a sure bet, groaned Republican boss Mark Hanna, that "that damn cowboy" would make trouble in the White House.

Roosevelt in fact moved cautiously, attending first to politics. Well aware of the power of the conservative bloc in Congress, he adroitly used the patronage powers of the presidency to gain control of the Republican Party. But Roosevelt was also uncertain about what reform role the federal government should play. At first the new president might have been described as a progressive without a cause.

Even so, Roosevelt displayed his activist bent. An ardent outdoorsman, his first annual message to Congress emphasized **conservation**. Unlike John Muir (see Chapter 16), Roosevelt was not a preservationist wholly opposed to the exploitation of the nation's wilderness (Map 20.2). Rather, he wanted to conserve the country's resources and make certain that commercial development was mindful of the public interest. In 1902 he backed the Newlands Reclamation Act, which designated the proceeds from public land sales for irrigation in arid regions. His administration expanded the national forests, upgraded land management, and to the chagrin of some Republicans, energetically prosecuted violators of federal land laws. In the cause of conservation, Roosevelt showed his disdain for those who sought profit "by betraying the public."

That same energetic bent prompted Roosevelt's intervention in the miners' strike of 1902. Hard coal (anthracite) was the main fuel for home heating in those days. As cold weather approached it became urgent to settle the strike. The United Mine Workers, led by John Mitchell, was willing to submit to arbitration, but the coal operators would have nothing to do with the union. Although lacking any legal grounds for intervening, the president called both sides to a White House conference on October 1, 1902. When the operators balked Roosevelt threatened a government takeover of the mines. He also persuaded the financier J. P. Morgan to use his

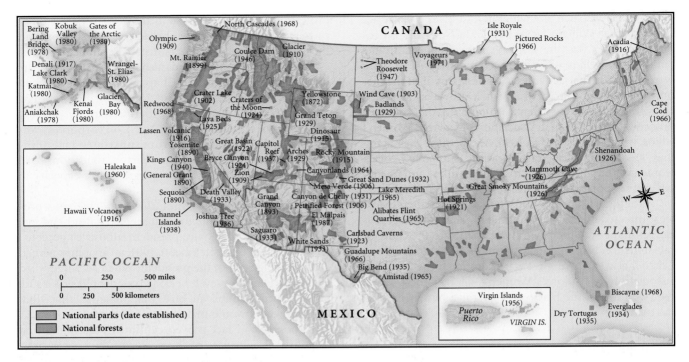

MAP 20.2 National Parks and Forests, 1872–1980

Close inspection of the above map illustrates that the national park system did not begin with the Progressive Era. Indeed, Yellowstone, the first park, dates from 1872. In 1893, the federal government began the protection of national forests. Without Roosevelt, however, the national forest program might have languished, and during his presidency he added 125 million acres to the forest system plus six national parks. More importantly, Roosevelt endowed these systems with a progressive, public-spirited stamp that has remained a principle resource of environmentalists striving to preserve the nation's natural heritage from over-development and destructive exploitation. In the list of progressive triumphs, a robust national park and forest system is one of the most enduring.

considerable influence. At that point the coal operators caved in. The strike ended with the appointment by Roosevelt of an arbitration commission—another unprecedented step. While not especially sympathetic to organized labor, Roosevelt blamed the crisis on the "arrogant stupidity" of the mine owners.

"Of all the forms of tyranny the least attractive and the most vulgar is the tyranny of mere wealth," Roosevelt wrote in his autobiography. He was prepared to deploy all his presidential authority against the "tyranny" of irresponsible business.

Regulating the Marketplace

The economic issue that most troubled Roosevelt was the threat posed by big business to competitive markets. The drift toward large-scale enterprise was itself not new; for many years efficiency-minded entrepreneurs had been building vertically integrated national firms (see Chapter 17). But bigger business, they knew, also meant power to control markets. And when, in the aftermath of the depression of the 1890s, promoters scrambled to merge

rival firms, the primary motive was not efficiency but the elimination of competition. These mergers—**trusts**, as they were called—greatly increased business concentration in the economy. By 1910, 1 percent of the nation's manufacturers accounted for 44 percent of the nation's industrial output (see Voices from Abroad, "James Bryce: America in 1905: 'Business Is King,'" p. 594).

As early as his first annual message, Roosevelt acknowledged the nation's uneasiness with the "real and grave evils" of economic concentration. But what weapons could the president use in response?

The legal principles upholding free competition were already firmly established under common law: anyone injured by monopoly or illegal restraint of trade could sue for damages. With the passage of the Sherman Antitrust Act of 1890, these common-law rights entered the U.S. statute books and could be enforced by the federal government where offenses involved interstate commerce. Neither Cleveland nor McKinley showed much interest, but the Sherman Act was there waiting to be used. Its potential consisted above all in the fact that it incorporated common-law principles of unimpeachable validity. In the

J. Pierpont Morgan

J. P. Morgan was a giant among American financiers. He had served an apprenticeship in investment banking under his father, a leading Anglo-American banker in London. A gruff man of few words, Morgan had a genius for instilling trust and the strength of will to persuade others to follow his lead and do his bidding—qualities the great photographer Edward Steichen captured in this portrait. Courtesy, George Eastman House, reprinted with permission of Joanna T. Steichen.

right hands the Sherman Act could be a mighty weapon against the abuse of economic power.

Trust-Busting.   Roosevelt made his opening move in 1903 by establishing a Bureau of Corporations empowered to investigate business practices and bolster the Justice Department's capacity to mount antitrust suits. The department had already filed such a suit in 1902 against the Northern Securities Company, a combination of the railroad systems of the Northwest. In a landmark decision the Supreme Court ordered Northern Securities dissolved in 1904.

In the presidential election that year, Roosevelt handily defeated a weak conservative Democratic candidate, Judge Alton B. Parker. Now president in his own right, Roosevelt stepped up the attack on the trusts. He took on forty-five of the nation's giant firms, including Standard Oil, American Tobacco, and DuPont. His rhetoric rising, Roosevelt became the nation's trust-buster, a crusader against "predatory wealth."

But Roosevelt was not antibusiness. He regarded large-scale enterprise as a natural tendency of modern industrialism. Only firms that abused their power deserved punishment. But how would those companies be identified? Under the Sherman Act, following common-law

Jack and the Wall Street Giants

In this vivid cartoon from the humor magazine Puck, *Jack (Theodore Roosevelt) has come to slay the giants of Wall Street. To the country, trust-busting took on the mythic qualities of the fairy tale—with about the same amount of awe for the fearsome Wall Street giants and hope in the prowess of the intrepid Roosevelt. J. P. Morgan is the giant leering at front right.* Library of Congress.

For more help analyzing this image, see the ONLINE STUDY GUIDE at **bedfordstmartins.com/henretta.**

practice, the courts decided whether an act in restraint of trade was "unreasonable"—that is, excessive and harmful of the public interest—on a case-by-case basis. In the *Trans-Missouri* decision of 1897, however, the Supreme Court abandoned this discretionary "rule of reason," holding now that actions that restrained or monopolized trade, regardless of the public impact, automatically violated the Sherman Act.

Little noticed at first, *Trans-Missouri* placed Roosevelt in a quandary. He had no desire to hamstring legitimate business activity, but he could not rely on the courts to distinguish between "good" and "bad" trusts. The only solution was for Roosevelt to do so himself, a power he had because as president it was up to him to

James Bryce

America in 1905: "Business Is King"

James Bryce, British author of The American Commonwealth *(1888), a great treatise on American politics, visited the United States regularly over many years. In an essay published in 1905, Lord Bryce took stock of the changes he had seen during the previous quarter century. What most impressed him, beyond the sheer growth of material wealth, was the loss of individualism and the intensifying concentration of corporate power. In this he was at one with his old friend Theodore Roosevelt, who at that very time was gearing up to do battle with the trusts.*

That which most strikes the visitor to America today is its prodigious material development. Industrial growth, swift thirty or forty years ago, advances more swiftly now. The rural districts are being studded with villages, the villages are growing into cities, the cities are stretching out long arms of suburbs, which follow the lines of road and railway in every direction. The increase of wealth, even more remarkable than the increase of population, impresses the European more than ever before because the contrast with Europe is greater. The huge fortunes, the fortunes of those whose income reaches or exceeds a million dollars a year, are of course far more numerous than in any other country. . . . With this extraordinary material development it is natural that in the United States, business, that is to say, industry, commerce, and finance, should have more and more come to overshadow and dwarf all other interests, all other occupations. . . . Business is king.

Commerce and industry themselves have developed new features. Twenty-two years ago there were no trusts. . . . Even then, however, corporations had covered a larger proportion of the whole field of industry and commerce in America than in Europe, and their structure was more flexible and efficient. Today this is still more the case; while as for trusts, they have become one of the most salient phenomena of the country. They fix the attention, they excite the alarm of economists and politicians as well as of traders in the Old World, while they exercise and baffle the ingenuity of American legislators. Workingmen follow, though hitherto with unequal steps, the efforts at combination which the lords of production and distribution have been making. The consumer stands, if not with folded hands, yet so far with no clear view of the steps he may make for his own protection. Perhaps his prosperity— for he is prosperous— helps him to be quiescent.

The example of the United States, the land in which individualism has been most conspicuously vigorous, may seem to suggest that the world is passing out of the stage of individualism and returning to that earlier stage in which groups of men formed the units of society. The bond of association was, in those early days, kinship, real or supposed, and a servile or quasi-servile dependence of the weak upon the strong. Now it is the power of wealth which enables the few to combine so as to gain command of the sources of wealth. . . . Is it a paradox to observe that it is because the Americans have been the most individualistic of peoples that they are now the people among whom the art of combination has reached its maximum? The amazing keenness and energy, which were stimulated by the commercial conditions of the country, have evoked and ripened a brilliant talent for organization. This talent has applied new methods to production and distribution and has enabled wealth, gathered into a small number of hands, to dominate even the enormous market of America.

Source: Allan Nevins, ed., *America through British Eyes* (Gloucester, MA: Peter Smith, 1968), 384–87.

decide whether to initiate antitrust prosecutions in the first place. It was his negative power that counted here: he could choose not to prosecute a trust.

In November 1904, with an antitrust suit looming, the United States Steel Corporation's chairman Elbert H. Gary approached Roosevelt with a deal: cooperation in exchange for preferential treatment. The company would open its books to the Bureau of Corporations; if it found evidence of wrongdoing, the company would be warned privately and given a chance to set matters right. Roosevelt accepted this "gentlemen's agreement" because it met his interest in accommodating the realities of the modern industrial order while maintaining his public image as slayer of the trusts.

Railroad Regulation. The railroads posed a different kind of problem. As quasi-public enterprises, they had always been subject to state regulation; in 1887 they came under federal regulation by the Interstate Commerce Commission (ICC). As with the Sherman Act, this assertion of federal authority was mostly symbolic at first. Convinced that the railroads needed firmer oversight, Roosevelt pushed through the Elkins Act of 1903, which prohibited discriminatory rates that gave an unfair advantage to preferred or powerful customers; and then, with the 1904 election behind him, he launched a drive for real railroad regulation.

In 1906, after nearly two years of wrangling, Congress passed the Hepburn Railway Act, which empowered the ICC to set maximum shipping rates and prescribe uniform methods of bookkeeping. As a concession to the conservative Republican bloc, however, the courts retained broad powers to review the ICC's rate decisions.

The Hepburn Act was a triumph of Roosevelt's skills as a political operator. He had maneuvered brilliantly against determined opposition and come away with the essentials of what he wanted. Despite grumbling by Senate progressives, Roosevelt was satisfied. He had achieved a landmark expansion of the government's regulatory powers over business.

Consumer Protection. The protection of consumers, another signature issue for progressives, was very much the handiwork of muckraking journalism. What sparked the issue was a riveting series of articles in *Collier's*. Samuel Hopkins Adams exposed the patent-medicine business as "undiluted fraud" dangerous to the nation's health and "exploited by the skillfullest of advertising bunco men." For a time industry lobbyists stymied legislative action.

Then, in 1906, Upton Sinclair's novel *The Jungle* appeared. Sinclair thought he was writing about the exploitation of workers in Chicago meatpacking plants, but what caught the nation's attention was his descriptions of rotten meat and filthy conditions. President Roosevelt, weighing into the legislative battle, authorized a federal investigation of the stockyards. Within months the Pure Food and Drug and the Meat Inspection Acts passed, and another administrative agency joined the expanding federal bureaucracy: the Food and Drug Administration.

The Square Deal. During the 1904 presidential campaign, Roosevelt had taken to calling his program the **Square Deal**. This kind of labeling was new to American politics, emblematic of a political style that dramatized issues, mobilized public opinion, and asserted leadership. But the label identified something of substance as well. After many years of passivity and weakness, the federal government was reclaiming the role it had abandoned after the Civil War. Now, however,

Campaigning for the Square Deal

When William McKinley ran for president in 1896, he sat on his front porch in Canton, Ohio, and received delegations of voters. That was not Theodore Roosevelt's way. He considered the presidency a "bully pulpit," and he used the office brilliantly to mobilize public opinion and to assert his leadership. The preeminence of the presidency in American public life begins with Roosevelt's administration. Here, at the height of his crusading power, Roosevelt stumps for the Square Deal in the 1904 election. Library of Congress.

the target was the new economic order. When companies abused their corporate power, the government would intercede to assure ordinary Americans a "square deal."

During his two terms as president, Roosevelt had struggled to bring a modern corporate economy under public control. He was well aware, however, that his Square Deal was built on nineteenth-century foundations. In particular, antitrust doctrine, which aimed at enforcing competition, seemed inadequate when the economy's tendency was toward industrial concentration. Better, Roosevelt felt, for the federal government to regulate big business than try to break it up. In his final presidential speeches, Roosevelt dwelled on the need for a reform agenda for the twentieth century. This was the task he bequeathed to his chosen successor, William Howard Taft.

The Fracturing of Republican Progressivism

William Howard Taft was an estimable man in many ways. An able jurist and superb administrator, he had served Roosevelt loyally as governor-general of the Philippines and as secretary of war. He was an avowed Square Dealer. But he was not by nature a progressive politician. He disliked the give-and-take of politics, he distrusted power, and he revered the processes of law. He could not, for example, have imagined intruding into the 1902 anthracite strike, as Roosevelt had done, or taken so flexible a view of the Sherman Act. He was, in fundamental ways, a conservative.

Taft's Democratic opponent in the 1908 campaign was William Jennings Bryan. This was Bryan's last hurrah, his third attempt at the presidency, and he made the most of it. Eloquent as ever, Bryan attacked the Republicans as the party of the "plutocrats" and outdid them in urging tougher antitrust legislation, lower tariffs, stricter railway regulation, and advanced labor legislation. Bryan's campaign moved the Democratic Party into the mainstream of national progressive politics, but it was not enough to offset Taft's advantages as Roosevelt's candidate.

Taft won comfortably, and he entered the White House with a mandate to pick up where Roosevelt left off. That, alas, was not to be.

Taft's Troubles.

By 1909 the ferment of reform had unsettled the Republican Party. On the right the conservatives were girding themselves against further losses. Led by the formidable Senator Nelson W. Aldrich of Rhode Island, they were still a force to be reckoned with. On the left progressive Republicans were rebellious. They had broad popular support—especially in the Midwest—and in Robert La Follette, a fiery leader. The progressives felt that Roosevelt had been too easy on business, and with him gone from the White House, they intended to make up for lost time. Reconciling these conflicting forces within the Republican Party would have been a daunting task for the most accomplished politician. For Taft it spelled disaster.

First there was the tariff. Progressives considered protective tariffs a major reason why competition had declined and the trusts had taken hold. Although Taft had campaigned for tariff reform, he was won over by the conservative Republican bloc and ended up approving the protectionist Payne-Aldrich Tariff Act of 1909, which critics charged sheltered eastern industry from foreign competition.

Next came the Pinchot-Ballinger affair. U.S. Chief Forester Gifford Pinchot, an ardent conservationist and a chum of Roosevelt's, accused Secretary of the Interior Richard A. Ballinger of conspiring to transfer Alaskan public land—rich in natural resources—to a private syndicate. When Pinchot aired these charges in January 1910, Taft fired him for insubordination. Despite Taft's strong conservationist credentials, in the eyes of the progressives the Pinchot-Ballinger affair marked him as a friend of the "interests" bent on plundering the nation's resources.

Taft found himself propelled into the conservative Republican camp, an ally of "Uncle Joe" Cannon, the dictatorial Speaker of the House of Representatives. When a House revolt finally broke Cannon's power in 1910, it was regarded as a defeat for the president as well. Galvanized by Taft's defection, the reformers in the Republican Party became a dissident faction, calling themselves "Progressives," or in more belligerent moments, "Insurgents." Taft answered by backing their conservative foes in the Republican primaries that year.

The Taft-Roosevelt Split.

The Progressives emerged from the 1910 elections stronger and angrier. In January 1911 they formed the National Progressive Republican League and began a drive to take over the Republican Party. Though La Follette was their leader, the Progressives knew that their best chance to topple Taft lay with Theodore Roosevelt.

Home from a year-long safari in Africa, Roosevelt yearned to reenter the political fray. Taft's dispute with the Progressives gave Roosevelt the cause he needed. But Roosevelt was a loyal party man and too astute a politician not to recognize that a party split would benefit the Democrats. He could be spurred into rebellion only by a true clash of principles. On the question of the trusts, just such a clash materialized.

By distinguishing between good and bad trusts, Roosevelt had managed to reconcile public policy (the Sherman Act) and economic reality (the tendency toward corporate concentration). But this was a makeshift solution that depended on a president who was willing to stretch his powers to the limit. Taft had no such inclination. His legalistic mind rebelled at the notion that as president he should decide which trusts should be prosecuted. The Sherman Act was on the books. "We are going to enforce that law or die in the attempt," Taft promised grimly.

In the *Standard Oil* decision (1911), the Supreme Court eased Taft's problem by reasserting the rule of reason, which meant that, once again, the courts themselves would distinguish between good and bad trusts. With that burden lifted from the executive branch, Attorney General George W. Wickersham stepped up the pace of antitrust actions.

The United States Steel Corporation became an immediate target. Among the charges against the steel trust was that it had violated the antimonopoly provision of the Sherman Act by acquiring the Tennessee Coal and Iron Company in 1907. Roosevelt had personally approved the acquisition, believing this was necessary—so U.S. Steel representatives had told him—to prevent a financial collapse on Wall Street. Taft's suit against U.S. Steel thus amounted to an attack on Roosevelt that he could not, without dishonor, ignore.

The New Nationalism.

Ever since leaving the White House, Roosevelt had been pondering the trust problem. There was, he concluded, a third way between breaking up big business and submitting to corporate rule. The federal government could be empowered to oversee the nation's industrial corporations to make sure they acted in the public interest. They would be regulated by a federal trade commission as if they were natural monopolies or public utilities.

In a speech in Osawatomie, Kansas, in August 1910, Roosevelt made the case for what he called the **New Nationalism**. The central issue, he argued, was human welfare versus property rights. In modern society, property had to be controlled "to whatever degree the public welfare may require it." The government would become "the steward of the public welfare."

This formulation unleashed Roosevelt's reformist bent. He took up the cause of social justice, adding to his program a federal child labor law, regulation of labor relations, and a national minimum wage for women. Most radical, perhaps, was Roosevelt's attack on the legal system. Insisting that the courts stood in the way of reform, Roosevelt proposed sharp curbs on their powers, even raising the possibility of popular recall of court decisions.

Early in 1912 Roosevelt announced his candidacy for the presidency and immediately swept the Progressive Republicans into his camp. A bitter party battle ensued. Roosevelt won the states that held primary elections, but Taft controlled the party machinery elsewhere. Dominated by the party regulars, the Republican convention chose Taft. Considering himself cheated out of the nomination, Roosevelt led his followers into a new Progressive Party, soon nicknamed the "Bull Moose" party. In a crusading campaign Roosevelt offered the New Nationalism to the people.

Woodrow Wilson and the New Freedom

While the Republicans battled among themselves, the Democrats were on the move. The scars caused by the free-silver campaign of 1896 had faded, and in the 1908 campaign William Jennings Bryan established the party's progressive credentials. The Democrats made

HARPER'S WEEKLY

EDITED BY GEORGE HARVEY

July 13 1912   THE NEW RIDER   Price 10 Cents

On to the White House

At the Democratic convention of 1912, Woodrow Wilson only narrowly defeated the front-runner, Champ Clark of Missouri. Harper's Weekly *triumphantly depicted Wilson immediately after his nomination—the scholar turned politician riding off on the Democratic donkey, with his running mate, Thomas R. Marshall, hanging on behind. The magazine's editor, George Harvey, had identified Wilson as presidential timber back in 1906, long before the Princeton president had thought of politics, and had worked on his behalf from then on.* Newberry Library.

dramatic gains in 1910, taking over the House of Representatives for the first time since 1892 and capturing a number of traditionally Republican governorships. After fourteen years as the party's standard-bearer, Bryan made way for a new generation of leaders.

The ablest was Woodrow Wilson of New Jersey, a noted political scientist who, as university president, had brought Princeton into the front rank of American universities. In 1910, with no political experience, he accepted the Democratic nomination for governor of New Jersey and won. Wilson compiled a sterling reform record, including the direct primary, workers' compensation, and stringent utility regulation. Wilson went on to win the Democratic presidential nomination in 1912 in a bruising battle.

Forging the New Freedom. Wilson possessed, to a fault, the moral certainty that characterized the progressive politician. A brilliant speaker, he instinctively assumed the mantle of righteousness. Only gradually, however, did Wilson hammer out, in reaction to Roosevelt's New Nationalism, a coherent reform program, which he called the **New Freedom**.

As he warmed to the debate, Wilson cast his differences with Roosevelt in fundamental terms of slavery and freedom. "This is a struggle for emancipation," he proclaimed in October 1912. "If America is not to have free enterprise, then she can have freedom of no sort whatever." Wilson also scorned Roosevelt's social program. Welfare might be benevolent, he declared, but it also would be paternalistic and contrary to the traditions of a free people. The New Nationalism represented a future of collectivism, Wilson warned, whereas the New Freedom would preserve political and economic liberty.

Wilson actually had much in common with Roosevelt. "The old time of individual competition is probably gone by," Wilson admitted. Like Roosevelt, he opposed not bigness but the abuse of economic power. Wilson agreed that the abuse of power could not be prevented without a strong federal government. He parted company from Roosevelt over *how* government should restrain private power.

Despite all the rhetoric, the 1912 election fell short of being a referendum on the New Nationalism versus the New Freedom. The outcome turned on a more humdrum reality: Wilson was elected because he kept the traditional Democratic vote, while the Republicans split between Roosevelt and Taft (Map 20.3). Despite a landslide in the electoral college, Wilson received only 42 percent of the popular vote. At best the 1912 election signified that the American public was in the mood for reform. Only 23 percent, after all, had voted for the one candidate who stood for the status quo, President Taft. Wilson's own program, however, had received no clear mandate from the people.

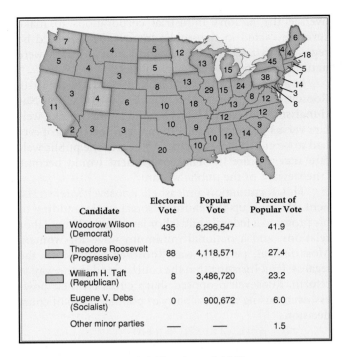

Candidate	Electoral Vote	Popular Vote	Percent of Popular Vote
Woodrow Wilson (Democrat)	435	6,296,547	41.9
Theodore Roosevelt (Progressive)	88	4,118,571	27.4
William H. Taft (Republican)	8	3,486,720	23.2
Eugene V. Debs (Socialist)	0	900,672	6.0
Other minor parties	—	—	1.5

MAP 20.3 Presidential Election of 1912
The 1912 election reveals why the two-party system is so strongly rooted in American politics. The Democrats, though a minority party, won an electoral landslide because the Republicans divided their vote between Roosevelt and Taft. This result indicates what is at stake when major parties splinter. The Socialists, despite a record vote of 900,000, received no electoral votes. To vote Socialist in 1912 meant in effect to throw away one's vote.

Yet the 1912 election proved decisive in the history of economic reform. The debate between Roosevelt and Wilson had brought forth, in the New Freedom, a program capable of finally resolving the crisis over corporate power that had gripped the nation for a decade. Just as important, the election created a rare legislative opportunity in Washington. With Congress in Democratic hands, the time was ripe to act on the New Freedom.

The First Phase: Tariff Reform and the Federal Reserve. Long out of power, the Democrats were hungry for tariff reform. From the prevailing average of 40 percent, the Underwood Tariff Act of 1913 pared rates down to 25 percent. Targeting especially the trust-dominated industries, Democrats confidently expected the Underwood Tariff to spur competition and reduce prices for consumers.

Wilson's administration then turned to the nation's banking system, whose key weakness was the absence of a central bank, or federal reserve. The main function of central banks at that time was to regulate commercial banks and back them up in case they could not meet their obligations to depositors. In the past this backup role had been assumed by the great New York banks that handled the accounts of outlying banks. If the New York banks weakened, the entire system could collapse. This nearly happened in 1907, when the Knickerbocker Trust Company failed and panic swept the nation's financial markets.

While the need for a central bank was clear, the form it should take was hotly disputed. Wall Street wanted a unified system run by the bankers. Rural Democrats and their spokesman, Senator Carter Glass of Virginia, preferred a decentralized network of reserve banks. Progressives in both parties agreed that the essential feature should be strong public control. The bankers, whose practices were already under scrutiny by Congress, were on the defensive.

President Wilson, initially no expert, learned quickly and reconciled the reformers and bankers. The monumental Federal Reserve Act of 1913 gave the nation a banking system that was resistant to financial panic. The act delegated financial functions to twelve district reserve banks that would be controlled by their member banks. The Federal Reserve Board imposed public regulation on this regional structure. In one stroke the act strengthened the banking system and placed a measure of restraint on Wall Street.

Settling the Trust Question. Having dealt with tariff and banking reform, Wilson turned to the big question of how to curb the trusts. In this effort Wilson relied heavily on a new advisor, Louis D. Brandeis, famous as the "people's lawyer" for his public service in many progressive causes (including the landmark *Muller* case). Brandeis denied that bigness meant efficiency. On the contrary, he argued, trusts were wasteful compared with firms that vigorously competed in a free market. The main thing was to prevent the trusts from unfairly using their power to curb free competition.

This could be done by strengthening the Sherman Act, but the obvious course—defining with precision what constituted anticompetitive practices—proved hard to implement. Was it feasible to say exactly when interlocking directorates, discriminatory pricing, or exclusive contracts became illegal? Brandeis decided that it was not, and Wilson assented. In the Clayton Antitrust Act of 1914, amending the Sherman Act, the definition of illegal practices was left flexible, subject to the test of whether an action "substantially lessen[ed] competition or tend[ed] to create a monopoly."

This retreat from a definitive antitrust prescription meant that a federal trade commission would be needed to back up the Sherman and Clayton Acts. Wilson was understandably hesitant, given his principled opposition to Roosevelt's powerful trade commission in the campaign. At first Wilson favored an advisory, information-gathering agency. But ultimately, under the 1914 law establishing it, the Federal Trade Commission (FTC) received broad powers to investigate companies and issue "cease and desist" orders against unfair trade practices that violated antitrust law.

Despite a good deal of commotion, this arduous legislative process was actually an exercise in consensus building. Wilson opened the debate in a conciliatory way. "The antagonism between business and government is over," he said, and the time ripe for a program representing the "best business judgment in America." Afterward, Wilson felt he had brought the long controversy over corporate power to a successful conclusion, and in fact he had. Steering a course between Taft's conservatism and Roosevelt's radicalism, Wilson had carved out a middle way that brought to bear the powers of government without threatening the constitutional order and curbed abuse of corporate power without threatening the capitalist system.

What few Americans recognized, in the midst of this protracted struggle, was how very odd it seemed from a European standpoint. Neither Britain nor Germany, America's industrial rivals, made such a fuss over competitive markets. It was true that the fundamental concept—restraint of trade—originated in English common law, but the British, free traders and export-oriented, lacked the opportunity to engage in market-controlling behavior and hence had no need for antitrust legislation. Germany, by contrast, was a veritable hotbed of conspiracies in restraint of trade, only they were called "cartels"—business groups that divided the market and set prices, operating with the approval of the imperial government.

Wilson's Social Program. On social policy, as with antitrust policy, Wilson charted a middle way. Having denounced Roosevelt's paternalism, he was at first unreceptive to what he saw as special-interest demands by labor and farm organizations. On the leading issue—that they be exempt from antitrust prosecution—the most Wilson was willing to accept was cosmetic language in the Clayton Act that did not grant them the immunity they sought.

The labor vote had grown increasingly important to the Democratic Party, however. Wilson's tenure in the White House, moreover, coincided with a burst of industrial conflict, including dramatic strikes by textile workers, mostly immigrant women, at Lawrence, Massachusetts, in 1912, and Paterson, New Jersey, in 1913, and a violent coal miners' strike in 1914 in Colorado, which climaxed with the torching of a tent city at Ludlow by state militia. The resulting asphyxiation of strikers' wives and children hiding in the tents horrified the nation and made Ludlow the focus of a wide-ranging investigation into the troubled industrial relations of the country. The "labor question" was suddenly prominent on the progressive agenda.

As his second presidential campaign drew near, Wilson lost some of his scruples about prolabor legislation.

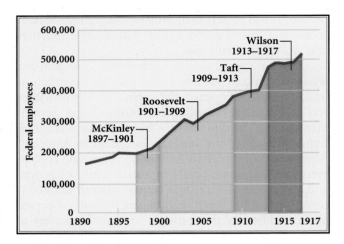

FIGURE 20.1 The Federal Bureaucracy, 1890–1917

The surge in federal employment after 1900 mirrored the surge in government authority under Theodore Roosevelt's progressive leadership. Not even Wilson, although he ran on a platform of limited government, could stem the tide. Numerically, in fact, the federal bureaucracy grew most rapidly during Wilson's first term.

In 1915 and 1916 he championed a host of bills beneficial to American workers: a federal child labor law, the Adamson eight-hour law for railroad workers, and the landmark Seamen's Act, which eliminated age-old abuses of sailors aboard ship. Likewise, after earlier resistance, Wilson approved in 1916 the Federal Farm Loan Act, which provided the low-interest rural credit system long demanded by farmers. Nor was it lost on observers that, his New Freedom rhetoric notwithstanding, Wilson presided over an ever more active federal government, and an ever-expanding federal bureaucracy (Figure 20.1).

Wilson encountered the same dilemma that confronted all successful progressives: the claims of moral principle versus the unyielding realities of political life. Progressives were high-minded but not radical. They saw evils in the system, but they did not consider the system itself to be evil. They also prided themselves on being realists as well as moralists. So it stood to reason that Wilson, like other progressives who achieved power, would find his place at the center.

But it would be wrong to underestimate their achievement. Progressives made presidential leadership important again, they brought government back into the nation's life, and they laid the foundation for twentieth-century social and economic policy.

FOR FURTHER EXPLORATION

▶ For definitions of key terms boldfaced in this chapter, see the glossary at the end of the book.

▶ To assess your mastery of the material covered in this chapter, see the Online Study Guide at **bedfordstmartins.com/henretta**.

▶ For suggested references, including Web sites, see page SR-22 at the end of the book.

▶ For map resources and primary documents, see **bedfordstmartins.com/henretta**.

A new chapter in American reform began at the start of the twentieth century. For decades the problems resulting from industrialization and urban growth had been mounting. Now, after 1900, reform began to dominate the nation's public life. The unifying element in progressivism was a common intellectual outlook, highly principled and idealistic as to goals and confident of the human capacity to find the means to achieve those goals.

Beyond this shared belief, progressives broke up into diverse and sometimes conflicting groups. Social welfare became the province of American women and that effort reinvigorated the struggle for women's voting rights. Suffragists divided over tactics, however, and the rise of feminism generated further strains in the women's movement. Political reformers included business groups concerned chiefly with improving the efficiency of city government. Other progressives, such as Robert La Follette, opposed privilege and wanted to democratize the political process. Both groups worked to enhance their power at the expense of entrenched party machines. In the cities working people and immigrants also became reform minded and set in motion a new political force—urban liberalism. While progressivism was infected by the endemic racism of American life, there was a reform wing that joined with black activists to forge the major institutions of black protest and uplift of the twentieth century: the NAACP and the Urban League.

At the national level, progressives focused primarily on controlling the economic power of corporate business. This overriding problem led to Theodore Roosevelt's Square Deal, then to his New Nationalism, and finally to Woodrow Wilson's New Freedom. The role of the federal government expanded dramatically but in service to a cautious and pragmatic approach to the country's problems.

1889 Jane Addams and Ellen Gates Starr found Hull House

1893 Panic of 1893 starts depression of the 1890s

1899 National Consumers' League founded

1900 Robert M. La Follette elected Wisconsin governor

Commission form of city government first appears, in Galveston, Texas

1901 President McKinley assassinated; Theodore Roosevelt succeeds him

1902 President Roosevelt settles national anthracite strike

1903 National Women's Trade Union League founded

1904 Supreme Court dissolves the Northern Securities Company

1905 *Lochner v. New York* overturns law restricting length of bakers' workday

1906 Upton Sinclair's *The Jungle*

Hepburn Railway Act

AFL adopts "Bill of Grievances"

1908 *Muller v. Oregon* upholds regulation of working hours for women

William Howard Taft elected president

1909 NAACP formed

1910 Roosevelt announces the New Nationalism

Woman suffrage movement revives

1911 *Standard Oil* decision restores "rule of reason"

Triangle Shirtwaist fire

1912 Progressive Party formed

Woodrow Wilson elected president

1913 Federal Reserve Act

Underwood Tariff Act

1914 Clayton Antitrust Act

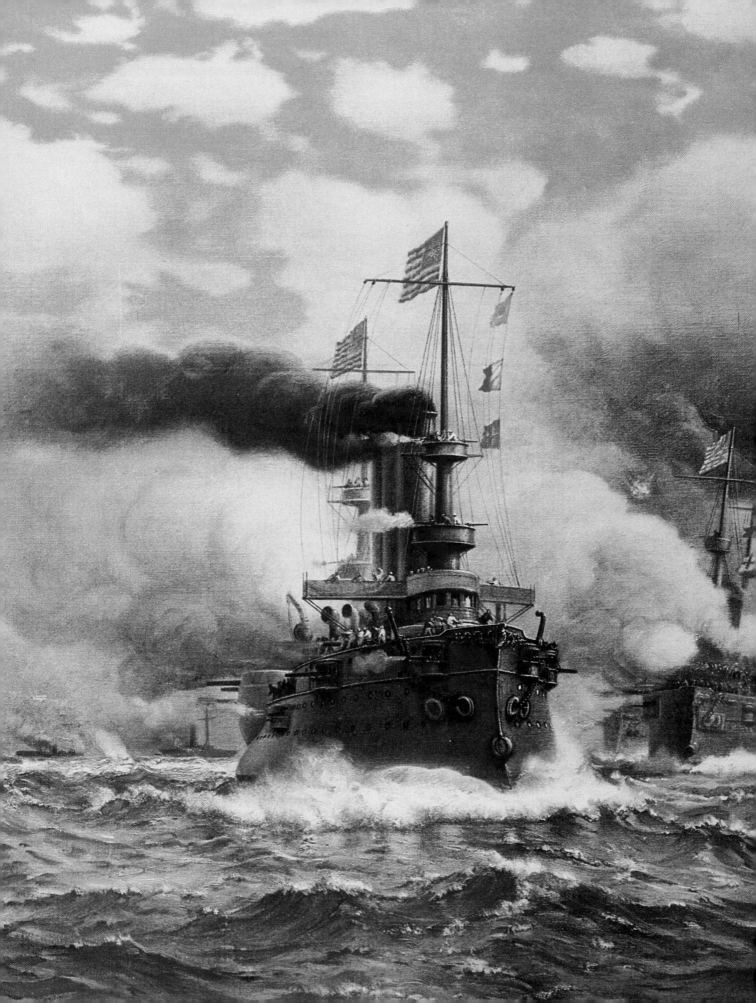

CHAPTER 21

An Emerging World Power

1877–1914

IN 1881 GREAT BRITAIN SENT A NEW ENVOY TO WASHINGTON. He was Sir Lionel Sackville-West, son of an earl and brother-in-law of the Tory leader Lord Denby, but otherwise distinguished only as the lover of a celebrated Spanish dancer. His well-connected friends wanted to park Sir Lionel somewhere comfortable, but out of harm's way. So they made him minister to the United States.

Twenty years later such an appointment would have been unthinkable. All the European powers had by then elevated their missions in Washington to embassies and staffed them with top-of-the-line ambassadors. And they treated the United States, without question, as a fellow Great Power.

In Sir Lionel's day the United States scarcely cast a shadow on world affairs. America's army was smaller than Bulgaria's; its navy ranked thirteenth in the world and was a threat mainly to the crews manning its unseaworthy ships. By 1900, however, the United States was flexing its muscles. It had just made short work of Spain in a brief but decisive war and acquired for itself an empire stretching from Puerto Rico to the Philippines. America's standing as a rising naval power was manifest, and so was its muscular assertion of national interest in the Caribbean and the Pacific.

◀ **Battle of Santiago de Cuba, 1898**
James G. Tyler's dramatic painting of the final sea battle of the Spanish-American War showcased America's newest weapon of war, the battleship.
Franklin D. Roosevelt Library.

In practice the United States still acted as a regional power, but Europeans were keenly aware of its capacity to cut a wider swath whenever it chose to do so. The notion of an "American peril" became a lively topic after 1900 among Europeans surveying America's industrial and military potential. No one could be sure what America's role would be, since the United States retained its traditional policy of nonalignment in European affairs. But by 1914, when a great war engulfed Europe, there was no question but that the United States would have a big role to play. How the United States emerged onto the world stage in the decades before World War I is the subject of this chapter.

The Roots of Expansion

In 1880 the United States had a population of 50 million, and by that measure ranked with the great European powers. In industrial production the nation stood second only to Britain and was rapidly closing the gap. Anyone who doubted the military prowess of Americans needed only to recall the ferocity with which they had fought one another in the Civil War. The great campaigns of Lee, Sherman, and Grant had entered the military textbooks and were closely studied by army strategists everywhere.

And when vital interests were at stake, the United States had not shown itself lacking in diplomatic vigor. The Civil War had put the United States at odds with both France and Britain. The dispute with France involved the establishment in Mexico of a French-sponsored regime under Archduke Maximilian, a move regarded by the United States as a threat to its security in the Southwest. When American troops under General Philip Sheridan began to mass on the Mexican border in 1867, the French military withdrew, abandoning Maximilian to a Mexican firing squad.

With Britain, the thorny issue involved damages to Union shipping by the *Alabama* and other Confederate sea raiders operating from English ports. American hopes of taking Canada as compensation were dashed by Britain's grant of dominion status to Canada in 1867. But four years later, after lengthy negotiations, Britain expressed regret for its unneutral acts and agreed to the arbitration of the *Alabama* claims, settling to America's satisfaction the last outstanding diplomatic issue of the Civil War.

Diplomacy in the Gilded Age

In the years that followed, the United States lapsed into diplomatic inactivity, not out of weakness but for lack of any clear national purpose in world affairs. The business of building the nation's industrial economy absorbed Americans and turned their attention inward. And while the new international telegraphic cables provided the country with swift overseas communication after the 1860s, wide oceans still kept the world at a distance and gave Americans a sense of isolation and security.

European power politics, which centered on Franco-German rivalry and on ethnic conflict in the Balkans, did not seem to matter very much. As far as President Cleveland's secretary of state, Thomas F. Bayard, was concerned, "we have not the slightest share or interest [in] the small politics and backstage intrigues of Europe."

As for the empires that the European powers were avidly building in Africa and Asia, this expression of national prowess did not tempt the United States. Even so ardent an American nationalist as the young Theodore Roosevelt saw the folly of overseas expansion. "We want no unwilling citizens to enter our Union," he wrote in 1886. "European nations war for possession of thickly settled districts. . . . We, wiser in our generation, have seized the waste solitudes that lay near us."

In these circumstances, with no external threat to be seen, why maintain a big navy? After the Civil War, the fleet gradually deteriorated. Of the 125 ships on the navy's active list, only about 25 were seaworthy at any one time. No effort was made to keep up with European advances in weaponry or battleship design; the American fleet consisted mainly of sailing ships and obsolete ironclads modeled on the *Monitor* of Civil War fame.

During the administration of Chester A. Arthur (1881–1885), the navy began a modest upgrading program, commissioning new ships, raising the standards for the officer corps, and founding the Naval War College. But the fleet remained small, without a unified naval command, and with little more to do than maintain coastal defenses.

The conduct of diplomacy was likewise of little account. Appointment to the foreign service was mostly through the spoils system. American envoys and consular officers were a mixed lot, with many idlers and drunkards among the hard working and competent. Domestic politics, moreover, made it difficult to develop a coherent foreign policy. Although diplomacy was a presidential responsibility, the U.S. Senate jealously guarded its constitutional right to give "advice and consent" on treaties and diplomatic appointments. For its part the State Department tended to be inactive, exerting little control over either policy or its missions abroad. In distant places the American presence was likely to be Christian missionaries proselytizing among the native populations of Asia, Africa, and the Pacific islands.

Latin American Diplomacy. In the Caribbean, the expansionist enthusiasms of the Civil War era subsided. William H. Seward, Lincoln and Andrew Johnson's secretary of state, had dreamed of an American empire extending from the Caribbean across Mexico to Hawaii.

Sugarcane Plantation, Hawaii

Over 300,000 Asians from China, Japan, Korea, and the Philippines came to work in the Hawaiian cane fields between 1850 and 1920. The hardships they endured are reflected in plantation work songs, such as this one by Japanese laborers:

Hawaii, Hawaii
But when I came what I saw was Hell
The boss was Satan
The lunas [overseers] his helpers.

George Bacon Collection, Hawaii State Archives.

Nothing came of his grandiose plans, nor of President Grant's efforts to purchase Santo Domingo (the future Dominican Republic) in 1870, and the Senate regularly blocked later moves to acquire bases in Haiti, Cuba, and Venezuela. The long-cherished interest in a canal across Central America also faded. Despite its claims of exclusive rights, the United States stood by when a French company headed by the builder of the Suez Canal, Ferdinand de Lesseps, started to dig across the Panama isthmus in 1880. That project failed after a decade, but the reason was bankruptcy and not American opposition.

Diplomatic activity quickened when the energetic James G. Blaine became secretary of state in 1881. He got involved in a border dispute between Mexico and Guatemala, tried to settle a war Chile was waging against Peru and Bolivia, and called the first Pan-American conference. Blaine's interventions in Latin American disputes went badly, however, and his successor canceled the Pan-American conference after Blaine left office in late 1881. This was a characteristic example of Gilded Age diplomacy, driven largely by partisan politics and carried out without any clear sense of national purpose.

Pan-Americanism—the notion of a community of western-hemispheric states—took root, however, and Blaine, returning in 1889 for a second stint at the State Department, took up the plans of the outgoing Cleveland administration for a new Pan-American conference. But little came of it, except for provisions for an agency in Washington that became the Pan-American Union. Any South American goodwill won by Blaine's efforts was soon blasted by the humiliation the United States visited upon Chile because of a riot against American sailors in the port of Valparaiso in 1891. Threatened with war, Chile was forced to apologize to the United States and pay an indemnity of $75,000.

Pacific Episodes.   In the Pacific, American interest centered on Hawaii, where prospects for raising sugarcane had attracted a horde of American planters and investors. Nominally an independent nation, Hawaii fell increasingly under American dominance. Under an 1875 treaty Hawaiian sugar gained duty-free entry in to the American market and the islands were declared off limits to other powers. A second treaty in 1887 granted the United States naval rights at Pearl Harbor.

When Hawaii's favored access to the American market was abruptly canceled by the McKinley Tariff of 1890, sugar planters began to plot an American takeover of Hawaii. They organized a revolt in January 1893 against Queen Liliuokalani and quickly negotiated a treaty of annexation with the Harrison administration. Before the Senate could approve, however, Grover Cleveland returned to the presidency and withdrew the treaty. To annex Hawaii, he declared, would violate America's "honor and morality" and an "unbroken tradition" against acquiring territory far from the nation's shores.

Meanwhile, the American presence elsewhere in the Pacific was growing. The purchase of Alaska from imperial

Russia in 1867 gave the United States not only a huge territory with vast natural resources but an unlooked-for presence stretching across the northern Pacific. And far to the south, in the Samoan islands, the United States secured rights in 1878 to a coaling station at Pago Pago harbor—a key link on the route to Australia—and established an informal protectorate there. In 1889, after some jostling with Germany and Britain, the rivalry over Samoa ended in a tripartite protectorate, with America retaining its rights in Pago Pago.

American diplomacy in these years has been characterized as a series of incidents, not the pursuit of a foreign policy. Many things happened, but intermittently and without any well-founded conception of national objectives. This was possible because, as the Englishman James Bryce remarked in 1888, America still sailed "upon a summer sea." In the stormier waters that lay ahead, a different kind of diplomacy would be required.

The Economy of Expansionism

"A policy of isolation did well enough when we were an embryo nation," remarked Senator Orville Platt of Connecticut in 1893. "But today things are different. . . . We are 65 million people, the most advanced and powerful on earth, and regard to our future welfare demands an abandonment of the doctrines of isolation." What especially demanded that Americans look outward was their enormously productive economy.

The Search for Foreign Markets.   America's gross domestic product—the total value of goods and services—quadrupled between 1870 and 1900. But were there markets big enough to absorb the output of America's farms and factories? Over 90 percent of

American goods in the late nineteenth century were consumed at home. Even so, foreign markets mattered. Roughly a fifth of the nation's agricultural output was exported, and as the industrial economy expanded, so did manufactured goods. Between 1880 and 1900, the industrial share of total exports jumped from 15 percent to over 30 percent.

American firms began to plant themselves overseas. As early as 1868 the Singer Sewing Machine Company established its first foreign factory in Glasgow, Scotland. The giant among American firms doing business abroad was Rockefeller's Standard Oil, with European branches operating tankers and marketing kerosene across the continent. In Asia Standard Oil cans, converted into utensils and roofing tin, became a visible sign of American market penetration. Brand names like Kodak (cameras), McCormick (agricultural equipment), and Ford (the Model T) became household words around the world.

Foreign trade was important partly for reasons of international finance. As a developing economy the United States attracted a lot of foreign capital. The result was a heavy outflow of dollars to pay interest and dividends to foreign investors. To balance this account, the United States needed to export more goods than it imported. In fact, a favorable import-export balance was achieved in 1876 (Figure 21.1). But because of its dependence on foreign capital, America had to be constantly vigilant about its export trade.

Even more important, however, was the relationship that many Americans perceived between foreign markets and the nation's social stability. Hard times always sparked agrarian unrest and labor strife. The problem, many thought, was that the nation's capacity to produce was outrunning its capacity to consume. When the economy

The Singer Sewing Machine

The sewing machine was an American invention that swiftly found markets abroad. The Singer Company, the dominant firm, not only exported large quantities but produced 200,000 machines annually at a Scottish plant that employed 6,000 workers. Singer's advertising rightly boasted of its prowess as an international company and of a product that was "The Universal Machine." New-York Historical Society.

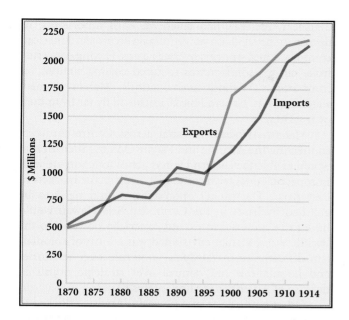

FIGURE 21.1 Balance of U.S. Imports, 1870–1914

By 1876 the United States had become a net exporting nation. The brief reversal after 1888 aroused fears that the United States was losing its foreign markets and helped fuel the expansionist drive of the 1890s.

economic interests. But in Asia, Latin America, and other regions that Americans considered "backward," a tougher brand of intervention seemed necessary because there the United States was competing with other industrial powers.

Asia and Latin America represented only a modest part of America's export trade—roughly an eighth of the total in the late nineteenth century. Still, this trade was growing—it was worth $200 million in 1900—and parts of it mattered a great deal to specific industries—for example, the Chinese market for American textiles. The real importance of these non-Western markets, however, was not so much their current value as their future promise. China especially exerted a powerful hold on the American mercantile imagination. Many felt that the China trade, although quite small at the time, would one day be the key to American prosperity. Therefore, China and other beckoning markets must not be closed to the United States.

In the mid-1880s the pace of European imperialism picked up. After the Berlin Conference of 1884, Africa was rapidly carved up by the European powers. In a burst of modernizing energy, Japan transformed itself into a major power and began to challenge China's claims to Korea. In the Sino-Japanese War of 1894–1895, Japan won an easy victory and started a scramble among the great powers, including Russia, to divide China up into spheres of influence. In Latin America, U.S. interests began to be challenged more aggressively by Britain, France, and Germany.

On top of all this came the Panic of 1893, setting in motion industrial strikes and agrarian protests that Cleveland's secretary of state, Walter Q. Gresham, like many other Americans, took to be "symptoms of revolution." With the nation's stability seemingly at risk, securing the markets of Latin America and Asia became an urgent necessity, inspiring the expansionist diplomacy of the 1890s.

slowed, cutbacks in domestic demand drove down farm prices and caused layoffs across the country. The answer was to make sure there would always be enough buyers for America's surplus products, and this meant, more than anything else, buyers in foreign markets.

Overseas Trade and Foreign Policy.   How did these concerns about overseas trade relate to America's foreign policy? The bulk of American exports in the late nineteenth century—over 80 percent—went to Europe and Canada (Table 21.1). In these countries the normal instruments of diplomacy sufficed to protect the nation's

TABLE 21.1 Exports to Canada and Europe Compared with Exports to Asia and Latin America, 1875–1900

Year	Exports to Canada and Europe ($)	Percentage of Total	Exports to Asia and Latin America ($)	Percentage of Total
1875	494,000,000	86.1	72,000,000	12.5
1885	637,000,000	85.8	87,000,000	11.7
1895	681,000,000	84.3	108,000,000	13.4
1900	1,135,000,000	81.4	200,000,000	14.3

Source: Compiled from information in *Historical Statistics of the United States* (1960); U.S. Department of Commerce, *Long Term Growth, 1860–1965* (1966); National Bureau of Economic Research, *Trends in the American Economy in the Nineteenth Century* (1960).

The Making of a "Large" Foreign Policy

"Whether they will or no, Americans must now begin to look outward. The growing production of the country requires it." So wrote Captain Alfred T. Mahan, America's leading naval strategist, in his book *The Influence of Seapower upon History* (1890). The key to imperial power was control of the seas, Mahan perceived, and from this insight he developed a naval analysis that became the cornerstone of American strategic thinking.

A Global Strategy. "When a question arises of control over distant regions . . . it must ultimately be decided by naval power," Mahan advised. The United States should regard the oceans not as barriers, but as "a great highway . . . over which men pass in all directions." Traversing that highway required a robust merchant

Alfred T. Mahan

Mahan's theory about the influence of sea power on history came to him while he was killing time on a tour of naval duty, reading Roman history in a library in Lima, Peru, in 1885. His insight was personal as well as intellectual: embarrassed by the decrepit ships on which he served, Mahan thought the United States should have a modern fleet in which officers like himself could serve with pride (and with some hope of professional advancement). U.S. Naval Historical Foundation.

marine (America's had fallen on hard times since its heyday in the 1850s), a powerful navy to protect American commerce, and strategic overseas bases. Having converted from sail to steam, navies required coaling stations far from home. Without such stations, Mahan warned, warships were "like land birds, unable to fly far from their own shores."

Mahan advocated a canal across Central America connecting the Atlantic and Pacific Oceans. Such a canal would enable the eastern United States to "compete with Europe, on equal terms as to distance, for the markets of East Asia." The canal's approaches would need to be guarded by bases in the Caribbean Sea. Hawaii would have to be annexed to extend American power into the Pacific. What Mahan envisioned was a form of colonialism different from Europe's—not rule over territories and populations but control over strategic points in defense of America's trading interests.

Other enthusiasts of a powerful America flocked to Mahan, including such up-and-coming politicians as Theodore Roosevelt and Henry Cabot Lodge. The influence of these men, few in number but well connected, increased during the 1890s. They pushed steadily for what Lodge called a "large policy." But mainstream politicians also accepted Mahan's arguments, and from the inauguration of Benjamin Harrison in 1889 onward, a surprising consistency emerged in the conduct of American foreign policy.

Rebuilding the Navy. Mahan wanted a battleship fleet capable of roaming the high seas and striking a decisive blow against an enemy. In 1890 Congress appropriated funds for three battleships as the first installment on a two-ocean navy. Battleships might be expensive, said Benjamin F. Tracy, Harrison's ambitious secretary of the navy, but they were "the premium paid by the United States for the insurance of its acquired wealth and its growing industries." The battleship took on a special aura for those—like the young Roosevelt—who had grand dreams for the United States. "Oh, Lord! if only the people who are ignorant about our Navy could see those great warships in all their majesty and beauty, and could realize how [well fitted they are] to uphold the honor of America!" (see New Technology, "The Battleship," p. 610).

The incoming Cleveland administration was less spread-eagled, and by canceling Harrison's scheme for annexing Hawaii, established its antiexpansionist credentials. But after hesitating briefly Cleveland picked up the naval program of his Republican predecessor, pressing Congress just as forcefully for more battleships (five were authorized) and making the same basic argument. The nation's commercial vitality—"free access to all markets," in the words of Cleveland's second secretary of state, Richard Olney—depended on its naval power.

While rejecting the territorial aspects of Mahan's thinking, Cleveland absorbed the underlying strategic arguments about where America's vital interests lay. This explains the remarkable crisis that suddenly blew up in 1895 over Venezuela.

The Venezuela Crisis. For years a border dispute had simmered between Venezuela and British Guiana. Now the United States demanded that it be resolved. The European powers were carving up Africa and Asia. How could the United States be sure that Europe did not have similar designs on Latin America? Secretary of State Olney made that point in a bristling note to London on July 25, 1895, insisting that Britain accept arbitration or face the consequences. Invoking the Monroe Doctrine, Olney warned that the United States would brook no challenge to its vital interests in the Caribbean. These vital interests were America's, not Venezuela's; Venezuela was not consulted during the entire dispute.

Despite its suddenness the pugnacious stand of the Cleveland administration was no aberration but a logical step in the new American foreign policy. Once the British realized that Cleveland meant business, they backed off and agreed to arbitration of the boundary dispute. Afterward, Olney remarked with satisfaction that, as a great industrial nation, the United States needed "to accept [a] commanding position" and take its place "among the Powers of the earth." Other countries would have to accommodate America's need for access to "more markets and larger markets for the consumption and products of the industry and inventive genius of the American people."

The Ideology of Expansionism

As policymakers hammered out a new foreign policy, a sustaining ideology took shape. One source of expansionist dogma was the Social Darwinist theory that dominated the political thought of this era (see Chapter 18). If, as Charles Darwin had shown, animals and plants evolved through the survival of the fittest, so did nations. "Nothing under the sun is stationary," warned the American social theorist Brooks Adams in *The Law of Civilization and Decay* (1895). "Not to advance is to recede." By this criterion the United States had no choice; if it wanted to survive, it had to expand.

Linked to Social Darwinism was a spreading belief in the inherent superiority of the Anglo-Saxon "race." In the late nineteenth century, Great Britain basked in the glory of its representative institutions, industrial prosperity, and far-flung empire—all ascribed to the supposed racial superiority of its people and, by extension, of their American cousins as well. On both sides of the Atlantic, **Anglo-Saxonism** was in vogue. Thus did John Fiske, an American philosopher and historian, lecture the nation on its future responsibilities: "The work

which the English race began when it colonized North America is destined to go on until every land on the earth's surface that is not already the seat of an old civilization shall become English in its language, in its religion, in its political habits, and to a predominant extent in the blood of its people."

Fiske titled his lecture "Manifest Destiny." A half century earlier this term had expressed the sense of national mission—America's "manifest destiny"—to sweep aside the Native American peoples and occupy the continent. In his widely read book *The Winning of the West* (1896), Theodore Roosevelt drew a parallel between the expansionism of his own time and the suppression of the Indians. To Roosevelt, what happened to "backward peoples" mattered little because their conquest was "for the benefit of civilization and in the interests of mankind." More than historical parallels, however, linked the Manifest Destiny of past and present.

In 1890 the U.S. Census reported the end of the westward movement on the North American continent: there was no longer a frontier beyond which land remained to be conquered. The psychological impact of that news on Americans was profound, spawning among other things a new historical interpretation that stressed the importance of the frontier in shaping the nation's character. In a landmark essay setting out this thesis—"The Significance of the Frontier in American History" (1893)—the young historian Frederick Jackson Turner suggested a link between the closing of the frontier and overseas expansion. "He would be a rash prophet who should assert that the expansive character of American life has now entirely ceased," Turner wrote. "Movement has been its dominant fact, and, unless this training has no effect upon a people, the American energy will continually demand a wider field for its exercise." As Turner predicted, Manifest Destiny did turn outward.

Thus a strong current of ideas, deeply rooted in American experience and traditions, justified the new diplomacy of expansionism. The United States was eager to step onto the world stage. All it needed was the right occasion.

An American Empire

Ever since Spain had lost its South American empire in the early nineteenth century, still-subjugated Cubans yearned to join their mainland brothers and sisters in freedom. In February 1895, inspired by the poet José Martí, Cuban patriots rebelled against Spain. Although Martí died in an early skirmish and no mass uprising occurred, the rebels built up substantial fighting forces and launched a guerrilla war. A standoff developed; the Spaniards controlled the towns, the insurgents much of the countryside. In early 1896 the newly appointed Spanish commander, Valeriano Weyler, adopted a harsh

The Battleship

In the annals of naval warfare, ancient gave way to modern when sea battles ceased to be combat between ship-borne soldiers. We can date that fault line quite precisely. It occurred at the defeat of the Spanish Armada in 1588, when the lumbering Spanish vessels of Philip II were pounded by the guns of the English ships without ever managing to board their troops on Elizabeth's nimble galleons. Ever since, the objective of naval combat has been to sink enemy ships. The tactical division of labor, as it evolved, called for sailing ships of many types—frigates, sloops-of-war, and smaller boats. But for a nation aspiring to command the seas, the essential weapon was the capital ship, carrying the biggest guns and heaviest armament. A superb example was the *Victory*, Lord Horatio Nelson's flagship at the battle against the Napoleonic fleet at Trafalgar in 1805. The *Victory* carried one hundred guns on three decks, and was among the most formidable fighting ships of her time. Because these capital ships entered battle in a line,

guns blazing against the enemy fleet, they were called ships of the line or line-of-battle ships—hence the name for the next generation of capital ships: battleships.

In this drama of capital ships, the United States figured not at all. Indeed, Trafalgar confirmed the nation's early policy against challenging Britain's command of the seas. In the War of 1812, the American fleet contained no ships of the line. At the time this strategy was recommended by the country's few naval resources, but even after the United States developed the means for challenging Britain, geography and aspirations argued against doing so. As long as the United States defined itself as a continental nation, the mission of the U.S. Navy could be limited to coastal defense and harassing enemy commerce. The ship of the line, glorious though it was, had no place in American naval doctrine.

Even so, given America's industrial prowess, the United States contributed to the battleship's emergence as the capital ship of the age of steam and iron. The first steam-powered vessel in any navy was the U.S.S. *Fulton* (1815), and another American warship, the *Princeton* (1844), first demonstrated the superiority of the screw propeller over paddle wheels. The Civil War taught the world that wooden warships were finished. In a celebrated battle on March 8, 1862, the Confederacy's

U.S.S. *Atlanta*
Pictured at its launching in 1884, the cruiser Atlanta *was the first step in the navy's modernization program. The ship's transitional nature is suggested by the sailors manning the yardarms, which were there to support the sails assisting the* Atlanta's *engines.* U.S. Naval Institute.

U.S.S. *Oregon*
Launched twelve years after the Atlanta, *the* Oregon *was in an altogether different league, not only because of heavier tonnage and weaponry but because this vessel had left the age of sail behind and was recognizably a modern battleship.*
U.S. Naval History Center.

ironclad *Merrimack* rammed a sloop-of-war, sank a frigate with its guns, and might have destroyed the entire Union fleet blockading the Chesapeake but for the arrival of the ironclad U.S.S. *Monitor*. Unlike its European predecessors or the *Merrimack*, the *Monitor* was not a converted man-of-war. Here was an entirely new design, a ship with a low, flat deck, a dominating turret mounting two cannons, and no auxiliary sails—a prototype of the modern battleship, in fact, but in miniature, since the *Monitor* was only a shallow-draft gunboat (soon fated to founder in high seas).

Though it had helped create these technological advances, the United States had little to do with incorporating them into the battleship. The first example, completed in late 1861, was Britain's 9,210-ton *Warrior*, with a speed of 14 knots, a crew of 707, and eight 7-inch guns. Over the next twenty-five years, all the essential features of battleship design fell into place: in weaponry, rifled guns mounted on revolving turrets (the H.M.S. *Monarch*, 1869); in motive power, steam engines exclusively (H.M.S. *Devastation*, 1873); in construction, all-steel hulls and superstructures (H.M.S. *Colossus*, 1886).

Only after the battleship was an accomplished fact did the United States, heeding Captain Alfred T. Mahan's advice, shed its small-navy doctrine and build capital ships. The *Indiana*, *Massachusetts*, and *Oregon*, authorized in 1890, were, at 11,700 tons, world-class battleships, but they had some flaws. They listed when the big guns pointed abeam; and the 8-inch turrets suffered blast effects from the 13-inch guns. Even so, these first American battleships proved more than adequate against the Spanish fleet in 1898, and the shipbuilding program then went into high gear, producing by 1914 the world's third most formidable battleship fleet, after Britain's and Germany's.

This achievement brought the United States into the front rank of twentieth-century sea powers; the battleship was Theodore Roosevelt's "big stick," and he took much pride in the Great White Fleet that circumnavigated the globe at the close of his administration. Yet after 1898 the American battleship's war record proved to be scant. By 1917, when the United States entered World War I, the German fleet had already been defeated, leaving for the U.S. Navy only convoy and blockading duties. By World War II battleships verged on obsolescence. Like the ships of the Spanish Armada, they were vessels of great power but incapable of closing with an elusive opponent—in this instance, the aircraft carrier, which launched its planes from one hundred miles off and hoped never to see the enemy's ships. Thus the Japanese attack on Pearl Harbor on December 7, 1941, meant little strategically because only the U.S. battleship fleet was at anchor on that Sunday morning; the U.S. aircraft carriers, safely at sea, were unscathed.

THE DUTY OF THE HOUR:—TO SAVE HER NOT ONLY FROM SPAIN BUT FROM A WORSE FATE.

Free Cuba?

Independence for Cuba was not an unalloyed good for many Americans, including this cartoonist. Here he depicts Cuba as a woman about to jump from the frying pan (Spanish misrule) into the fire (anarchy). Hence the revealing caption: "The Duty of the Hour:—To Save Her Not Only from Spain but from a Worse Fate." Granger Collection.

policy of *reconcentration,* forcing entire populations into guarded camps. Because no aggressive pursuit followed, reconcentration only inconvenienced the guerrilla fighters. The toll on civilians, however, was devastating. Out of a population of 1,600,000, as many as 200,000 died of starvation, exposure, or dysentery.

The Cuban Crisis

Rebel leaders shrewdly saw that their best hope was not military but political: they had to draw the United States into their struggle. A key group of exiles, the Junta, set up shop in New York to make the case for *Cuba Libre.* By itself, their cause might not have attracted much interest. The Spaniards were behaving no more dishonorably than any other colonial power in comparable circumstances; nor were atrocities in short supply elsewhere in the world. The Cuban exiles, however, came on the scene at a critical juncture in American sensationalist journalism. William Randolph Hearst had just purchased the *New York Journal,* and he was in a hurry to build readership. Cuba was ideal for Hearst's purposes. Locked in a furious circulation war with Joseph Pulitzer's *New York World,* Hearst elevated Cuba's agony into flaming front-page headlines (see American Lives, "William Randolph Hearst: Jingo," p. 614).

Across the country powerful sentiments stirred: humanitarian concern for the suffering Cubans, sympathy with their aspirations for freedom, and, as anger against Spain rose, a super-heated patriotism that became known as **jingoism.** Congress began calling for Cuban independence.

Presidential Politics.   Grover Cleveland, still in office when the rebellion broke out, took a cooler view of the situation. His concern was with America's vital interests, which, he told Congress, were "by no means of a wholly sentimental or philanthropic character." The Cuban civil war was disrupting the sizable trade between the two countries and destroying American property, especially in Cuban sugar plantations. Cleveland also was worried that Spain's troubles might draw in other European powers. A chronically unstable Cuba was incompatible with America's strategic interests, in particular, a planned interoceanic canal whose Caribbean approaches would have to be safeguarded. If Spain could put down the rebellion, that was fine with Cleveland. But there was a limit, he felt, to how long the United States could tolerate Spain's impotence.

The McKinley administration, on taking office in March 1897, adopted much the same pragmatic line.

Like Cleveland, McKinley was motivated by a conception of the United States as the dominant Caribbean power, with vital interests that had to be defended. McKinley, however, was inclined to be tougher on the Spaniards. He was upset by their "uncivilized and inhumane conduct" in Cuba. And he had to contend with rising jingoism in the Senate. But the notion, long held by historians, that McKinley was swept along against his better judgment by popular opinion and by a Republican war faction led by Henry Cabot Lodge, Alfred J. Beveridge, and other aggressive advocates of a "large policy" was not true. McKinley was very much his own man. He was a skilled politician and a canny, if undramatic, president. In particular, McKinley was sensitive to business fears of any rash action that might disrupt an economy just recovering from depression.

The Road to War. On September 18, 1897, the American minister in Madrid informed the Spanish government that it was time to "put a stop to this destructive war." If Spain could not ensure an "early and certain peace," the United States would take whatever steps it "should deem necessary to procure this result." At first America's hard line seemed to work. The conservative regime fell, and a liberal government, upon taking office in October 1897, moderated its Cuban policy. Spain recalled General Weyler, backed away from reconcentration, and offered Cuba a degree of self-rule but not independence. Madrid's incapacity soon became clear, however. In January 1898 Spanish loyalists in Havana rioted against the offer of autonomy. The Cuban rebels, encouraged by the prospect of American intervention, demanded full independence.

On February 9, 1898, Hearst's *New York Journal* published a private letter by Dupuy de Lôme, the Spanish minister to the United States. In it de Lôme called President McKinley "weak" and "a bidder for the admiration of the crowd." Worse, his letter suggested that the Spanish government was not taking the American demands seriously. De Lôme immediately resigned, but the damage had been done.

A week later the U.S. battlecruiser *Maine* blew up and sank in Havana harbor, with the loss of 260 seamen. "Whole Country Thrills with the War Fever," proclaimed the *New York Journal*. From that moment onward popular passions against Spain became a major factor in the march toward war.

McKinley kept his head. He assumed that the sinking had been accidental. A naval board of inquiry, however, issued a damaging report. Disagreeing with a

"Remember the *Maine*!"

In late January 1898 the Maine *entered Havana harbor on a courtesy call. On the evening of February 15, a mysterious blast sent the U.S. battleship to the bottom. This dramatic lithograph conveys something of the impact of that event on American public opinion. Although no evidence ever linked the Spanish authorities to the explosion, the sinking of the* Maine *fed the emotional fires that prepared the nation for war with Spain.*
Granger Collection.

William Randolph Hearst: Jingo

William Randolph Hearst, born in San Francisco on April 29, 1863, was no Horatio Alger hero. His father, George Hearst, had struck it rich in Nevada's Comstock Lode. Willie grew up in the lap of luxury—grand houses, trips to Europe, private tutors, Harvard. His mother, Phoebe, doted on him, at once indulging and smothering her only child. From these unpromising beginnings sprang a strappingly handsome young man of remarkable contradictions, beginning with his voice, which was incongruously thin and high pitched. Hearst was painfully shy but simultaneously hell bent on mischief; his pranks at Harvard (which finally got him expelled) were legendary. He was outwardly diffident but had to dominate everyone around him. When he wanted something, he really wanted it, and he was known late into his life to throw tantrums when he was denied. All this would be of no historical moment—doubtless there were others like him among the progeny of the new millionaires—except for one thing: Hearst did not end up a dissipated alcoholic or, as was known to happen, even a quietly exemplary citizen. Hearst became a great newspaperman and, driven by his inner demons, cut a swath through American history.

His father happened to own the *San Francisco Examiner*, a money loser that served as the elder Hearst's political organ. At Harvard the son took to reading the *Examiner* and decided that he wanted to run it. His inspiration was Joseph Pulitzer, who a few years earlier had taken over the moribund *New York World* and transformed it into a hugely successful daily. The elder Hearst was unimpressed. He was thinking about unloading the paper, not pouring more money into it. Supposing it became a great success, he asked the business manager, how much might it make? Maybe $100,000 a year, came the answer. "Hell!" snorted Hearst. "That ain't no money." But the son wasn't interested in the money; he was interested in the *circulation* and the delight he would take from orchestrating the emotions of thousands upon thousands of readers.

In early 1887 the young Hearst, not yet twenty-four, got his wish and, on taking command, immediately pronounced the sleepy *Examiner* "Monarch of the Dailies," bent on providing its readers with the best news and "THE LATEST AND MOST ORIGINAL SENSATIONS." Sensation was what Hearst was after—copy that would arouse, in his editor's words, "the gee-whiz emotion." For example, were any grizzly bears left in California? Hearst dispatched an intrepid newsman to the Tehachapi Mountains, where after three months of arduous trapping he caught a grizzly. The beast was chained in a beer wagon, paraded with great fanfare around San Francisco, and given a home in Golden Gate Park. Naturally it was named Monarch. All this the *Examiner* reported in exhaustive detail, building suspense as the search progressed and ending triumphantly with the carnival display of the unfortunate bear. There was much more of the same—rescues, murders, scandal, sob stories, anything that might give readers that "gee-whiz emotion." The other string in Hearst's bow was that he became a champion of "the people." The *Examiner* embarked on a series of noisy crusades—against the water trust, and got rates cut by 15 percent; against a city charter crafted by crooked politicos and their business cronies, and got it defeated; and, on many fronts, against the rapacious Southern Pacific Railroad.

By the early 1890s the *Examiner*'s circulation was soaring and Hearst was making money. Looking around for greener fields, his eye fixed on New York City. The *Journal* was for sale, and Hearst got it cheaply. It was an anemic paper, close to folding, but Hearst didn't care. He intended to transform it, applying everything he had learned in San Francisco. He was going to war against Pulitzer's *New York World*.

When Hearst took over the *Journal* in October 1895, the Cuban insurrection had already begun. Until then Hearst had shown no interest in foreign affairs, but he genuinely felt for the underdog Cubans and, more to the point, saw in their cause just what he needed to drive his circulation war against Pulitzer. Not much actual news could be extracted from Cuba, for the sporadic fighting took place in the remote interior, beyond the reach of Hearst's correspondents in Havana. It did not matter. Rebel claims were good enough for Hearst, and a drumbeat of superheated articles began to appear about mostly nonexistent battles and about Spanish atrocities.

The *Journal* was stridently for war. Hearst's jingoism sounded very much like his old crusade against the San Francisco water trust—it was the people versus the interests all over again, the freedom-loving masses against the peace-at-any-price plutocrats. President McKinley was Wall Street's puppet, with the nefarious Senator Hanna pulling the strings. When the *Maine* went down, the *Journal* was ablaze with fiery headlines charging

William Randolph Hearst

In this photograph, dated 1904, Hearst is forty-one and past his glory days as jingo-in-chief of American journalism. He had managed to get himself elected to Congress from New York City and at the time was maneuvering, unsuccessfully, for the Democratic nomination for president. Brown Brothers.

Spanish treachery. That week circulation passed a million. Impatient for action, Hearst found ammunition even in the suicide of poor Mrs. Mary Wayt:

GRIEVED OVER OUR DELAY

*"The Government May Live
in Dishonor," Said She,
"I Cannot."*

The next day, April 19, the Senate passed the war resolution, and hostilities commenced. The news from Manila Bay got this screaming headline: "VICTORY . . . Complete! . . . Glorious! . . . THE MAINE IS AVENGED." A few days later, the front page asked readers: "HOW DO YOU LIKE THE JOURNAL'S WAR?"

Was it true? Had Hearst caused the war? For many years historians thought so. Now, with a better understanding of McKinley's administration, they are more inclined to stress the country's endangered strategic interests. Yet there is no denying that Hearst's war hysteria helped force the president's hand. As for the war,

Hearst had a grand time of it. He hired a boat, took a crew of newsmen down to Cuba, came under fire, wrote some creditable dispatches when his star reporter was wounded, rounded up Spanish survivors of the Santiago naval battle, and returned to New York feeling that the world was his oyster.

At that time Hearst was thirty-five, with another fifty-three years to live. The news business, ultimately a huge empire, remained the core of his being. But he also entered New York politics in a quixotic quest for the presidency. He plunged into Hollywood moviemaking, built a castle at San Simeon, California, and extravagantly entertained the rich and famous. All the while he became more enigmatic, more dictatorial, more alone.

In the end Hearst gained immortality in an utterly modern way. He became the inspiration for Orson Welles's great film *Citizen Kane* (1941). Ordinarily we do not look to the movies for historical insight, but Welles captured something about Hearst. The plot turns on Kane's dying word, *Rosebud*, which proves to be only the name of a sled remembered from his childhood.

Spanish investigation, the American board concluded improbably that the sinking had been caused by a mine. (A 1976 naval inquiry faulted the ship's design, in particular, the fact that the explosive magazines were too close to coal bunkers that were prone to spontaneous fires.) No evidence linked the Spanish to the purported mine. But if a mine did sink the ship, then the Spanish were responsible for not protecting a peaceful American vessel within their jurisdiction.

President McKinley had no stomach for the martial spirit engulfing the country. He was not swept along by the calls for blood to avenge the *Maine*. But he could not ignore an aroused public opinion. Hesitant business leaders now also became impatient for the dispute with Spain to end. War was preferable to the unresolved Cuban crisis. On March 27 McKinley cabled to Madrid what was in effect an ultimatum: an immediate armistice for six months, abandonment of the practice of reconcentration, and, with the United States as mediator, peace negotiations with the rebels. A telegram the next day added that only Cuban independence would be regarded as a satisfactory outcome to the negotiations. Spain categorically rejected these humiliating demands.

On April 11 McKinley asked Congress for authority to intervene to end the fighting in Cuba. His motives were as he described them: "In the name of humanity, in the name of civilization, in behalf of endangered American interests which give us the right and the duty to speak and to act, the war in Cuba must stop." The War Hawks in Congress—a mixture of Republican and western Democrats—chafed under McKinley's cautious progress. But the president did not lose control, and he defeated the War Hawks' demand for recognition of the rebel republican government, which would have reduced the administration's freedom of action in dealing with Spain.

The resolutions authorizing intervention in Cuba contained an amendment by Senator Henry M. Teller of Colorado disclaiming any intention by the United States to take possession of Cuba. No European government should say that "when we go out to make battle for the liberty and freedom of Cuban patriots, that we are doing it for the purpose of aggrandizement." This had to be made clear with regard to Cuba, "whatever," Senator Teller added, "we may do as to some other islands."

Did McKinley have in mind "some other islands"? Was this really a war of aggression, secretly motivated by a desire to seize strategic territory from Spain? In a strict sense almost certainly no. It was not *because* of expansionist ambitions that McKinley forced Spain into a corner. But once war came McKinley saw it as an opportunity. As he wrote privately after hostilities began: "While we are conducting war and until its conclusion, we must keep all we get; when the war is over we must keep what we want." Precisely what

would be forthcoming, of course, depended on the fortunes of battle.

The Spoils of War

Hostilities formally began when Spain declared war on April 24, 1898. Across the country regiments began to form. Theodore Roosevelt immediately resigned as assistant secretary of the navy, ordered a fancy uniform, and accepted a commission as lieutenant colonel of a volunteer cavalry regiment that would become famous as the Rough Riders. Raw recruits poured into makeshift bases around Tampa, Florida. Confusion reigned. Tropical uniforms did not arrive; the food was bad, the sanitation worse; and rifles were in short supply. No provision had been made for getting the troops to Cuba; the government hastily began to collect a miscellaneous fleet of yachts, lake steamers, and commercial boats. Fortunately, the small regular army was a disciplined, highly professional force, and its 28,000 seasoned troops provided a nucleus for the 200,000 civilians who had to be turned into soldiers inside of a few weeks.

The navy was in better shape. Spain had nothing to match America's seven battleships and armored cruisers, and the ships it did have were undermanned and ill-prepared for battle. The Spanish admiral, Pascual Cervera, gloomily expected that his fleet would "like Don Quixote go out to fight windmills and come back with a broken head."

On April 23, acting on plans already drawn up, Commodore George Dewey's small Pacific fleet set sail from Hong Kong for the Philippines. Here, at this Spanish possession in the far Pacific, not in Cuba, the decisive engagement of the war took place. On May 1 American ships cornered the Spanish fleet in Manila Bay and destroyed it. The victory produced euphoria in the United States. Immediately, part of the army being trained for the Cuban campaign was diverted to the Philippines. Manila, the Philippine capital, fell on August 13, 1898.

With Dewey's naval victory, American strategic thinking clicked into place. "We hold the other side of the Pacific and the value to this country is almost beyond imagination," declared Senator Lodge. "We must on no account let the [Philippine] Islands go." President McKinley agreed, and so did his key advisors. Naval strategists had long coveted an anchor in the western Pacific. At this time, too, the Great Powers were carving up China into spheres of influence. If American merchants wanted a crack at that glittering market, the United States would have to project its power into Asia.

Once the decision for a Philippine base had been made, other decisions followed almost automatically. The question of Hawaii was quickly resolved. After stalling the previous year, Hawaiian annexation went through Congress by joint resolution in July 1898. Hawaii had suddenly acquired a crucial strategic value: it was a halfway station on the way to the Philippines. The navy pressed for a coaling base in the central Pacific; that meant Guam, a Spanish island in the Marianas. There was need also for a strategically located base in the Caribbean; that meant Puerto Rico. By July, before the assault on Cuba, the full scope of McKinley's war aims had crystallized. The American people were vociferously behind him. In the wake of Dewey's victory, enthusiasm for colonial annexations swept the country and, as one observer of the nation's press observed, was "getting so strong it will mean the political death of any man to oppose it pretty soon."

The campaign in Cuba was somewhat anticlimactic. Santiago, where the Spanish fleet was anchored, became the key to the military campaign (Map 21.1). Half-trained and ill-equipped, the American forces moving on the city might have been checked by a determined opponent. The Spaniards fought to maintain their honor, but they had no stomach for a real war against the Americans.

The main battle, on July 1, occurred near Santiago on the heights commanded by San Juan Hill. Roo-

sevelt's dismounted Rough Riders (there had been no room for horses on the transports) seized Kettle Hill. Then the frontal assault against the San Juan heights began. Four black regiments took the brunt of the fighting. White observers grudgingly credited much of the victory to the "superb gallantry" of the black soldiers (see American Voices, "George W. Prioleau: Black Soldiers in a White Man's War," p. 619). In fact it was not quite a victory. The Spaniards, driven from their forward positions, retreated to a well-fortified second line. The exhausted Americans had suffered heavy casualties; whether they could have mounted a second assault was questionable. They were spared this test, however, by the Spanish. On July 3 Cervera's fleet in Santiago harbor made a daylight attempt to run the American blockade and was destroyed. A few days later, convinced that Santiago could not be saved, the Spanish forces surrendered.

The two nations signed an armistice in which Spain agreed to liberate Cuba and cede Puerto Rico and Guam

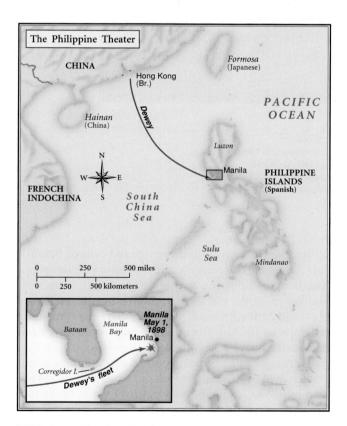

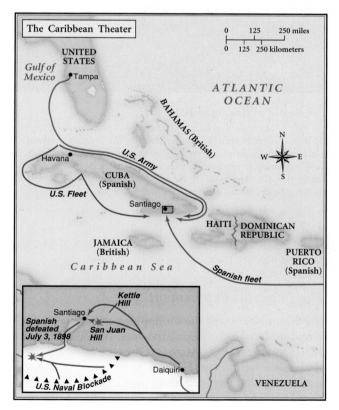

MAP 21.1 The Spanish-American War of 1898

The swift American victory in the Spanish-American War resulted from overwhelming naval superiority. Dewey's destruction of the Spanish fleet in Manila harbor doomed the Spaniards in the Philippines. In Cuba, American ground forces won a hard victory on San Juan Hill, for they were ill equipped and poorly supplied. With the United States in control of the seas, the Spaniards saw no choice but to give up the battle for Cuba.

For more help analyzing this map, see the ONLINE STUDY GUIDE at bedfordstmartins.com/henretta.

The Battle of San Juan Hill
On July 1, 1898, the key battle for Cuba took place on heights overlooking Santiago. African American troops bore the brunt of the fighting. Although generally overlooked, the black role in the San Juan battle is done justice in this contemporary lithograph, without the demeaning stereotypes by which blacks were normally depicted in an age of intensifying racism. Even so, the racial hierarchy is maintained. The blacks are the foot soldiers; their officers are white. Library of Congress.

to the United States. American forces occupied Manila pending a peace treaty.

The Imperial Experiment

The big question was the Philippines, an archipelago of over 7,000 islands populated—as William R. Day, McKinley's secretary of state, put it in the racist language of that era—by "eight or nine millions of absolutely ignorant and many degraded people." Not even avid American expansionists had advocated colonial rule over subject peoples—that was European-style imperialism, not the strategic bases that Mahan and his followers had in mind. Mahan and Lodge initially advocated keeping only Manila. It gradually became clear, however, that Manila was not defensible without the whole of Luzon, the large island on which the city was located.

Taking the Philippines. McKinley and his advisors surveyed the options. One possibility was to return most

of the islands to Spain, but the reputed evils of Spanish rule made that a "cowardly and dishonorable" solution. Another possibility was to partition the Philippines with one or more of the Great Powers. But as McKinley observed, to turn over valuable territory to "our commercial rivals in the Orient—that would have been bad business and discreditable."

Most plausible was the option of Philippine independence. As in Cuba, Spanish rule had already stirred up a rebellion, led by the fiery patriot Emilio Aguinaldo. An arrangement might have been possible like the one being negotiated with the Cubans over Guantanamo Bay: the lease of a naval base to the Americans as the price of freedom. But after some hesitation McKinley was persuaded that "we could not leave [the Filipinos] to themselves—they were unfit for self-rule—and they would soon have anarchy and misrule over there worse than Spain's was."

As for the Spaniards, they had little choice against what they considered "the immoderate demands of a

George W. Prioleau

Black Soldiers in a White Man's War

The chaplain of the Ninth Cavalry regiment expresses his bitterness toward the racism experienced by black troopers in the South on their way to battle in Cuba.

Hon. H. C. Smith
Editor, *Gazette*
Dear Sir:

The Ninth Cavalry left Chickamauga on the 30th of April for Tampa, Fla. We arrived here (nine miles from Tampa) on May 3. From this port the army will sail for Cuba. We have in this camp here and at Tampa between 7,000 and 8,000 soldiers, artillery, one regiment of cavalry (the famous fighting Ninth) and the Twenty-fourth and Twenty-fifth infantries. The Ninth Cavalry's bravery and their skillfulness with weapons of war . . . is well known by all who have read the history of the last Indian war. . . .

Yesterday, May 12, the Ninth was ordered to be ready to embark at a moment's notice for Cuba. . . .These men are anxious to go. The country will then hear and know of the bravery of these sable sons of Ham.

The American Negro is always ready and willing to take up arms, to fight and to lay down his life in defense of his country's flag and honor. All the way from northwest Nebraska this regiment was greeted with cheers and hurrahs. At places where we stopped the people assembled by the thousands. While the Ninth Cavalry band would play some national air the people would raise their hats, men, women and children would wave their handkerchiefs, and the heavens would resound with their hearty cheers. The white hand shaking the black hand. The hearty "goodbyes," "God bless you," and other expressions aroused the patriotism of our boys. . . . These

demonstrations, so enthusiastically given, greeted us all the way until we reached Nashville. At this point we arrived about 12:30 A.M. There were about 6,000 colored people there to greet us (very few white people) but not a man was allowed by the railroad officials to approach the cars. From there until we reached Chattanooga there was not a cheer given us, the people living in gross ignorance, rags and dirt. Both white and colored seemed amazed; they looked at us in wonder. Don't think they have intelligence enough to know that Andrew Jackson is dead. . . .

The prejudice against the Negro soldier and the Negro was great, but it was of heavenly origin to what it is in this part of Florida, and I suppose that what is true here is true in other parts of the state. Here, the Negro is not allowed to purchase over the same counter in some stores that the white man purchases over. The southerners have made their laws and the Negroes know and obey them. They never stop to ask a white man a question. He (Negro) never thinks of disobeying. You talk about freedom, liberty, etc. Why sir, the Negro of this country is a freeman and yet a slave. Talk about fighting and freeing poor Cuba and of Spain's brutality; of Cuba's murdered thousands, and starving reconcentradoes. Is America any better than Spain? Has she not subjects in her very midst who are murdered daily without a trial of judge or jury? Has she not subjects in her own borders whose children are half-fed and half-clothed, because their father's skin is black. . . . Yet the Negro is loyal to his country's flag. . . .

The four Negro regiments are going to help free Cuba, and they will return to their homes, some then mustered out and begin again to fight the battle of American prejudice. . . .

Yours truly,
Geo. W. Prioleau
Chaplain, Ninth Cavalry

Source: *Cleveland Gazette* (May 13, 1898), reprinted in Willard B. Gatewood, *"Smoked Yankees" and the Struggle for Empire, 1898–1902* (Urbana: University of Illinois Press, 1971), 27–29.

---

conquerer." In the Treaty of Paris they ceded the Philippines to the United States for a payment of $20 million. The treaty encountered harder going at home and was ratified by the Senate (requiring a two-thirds majority) on February 6, 1899, with only a single vote to spare.

The Anti-Imperialists. The administration's narrow margin signaled the revival of an antiexpansionist tradition that had been briefly silenced by the passions of a nation at war. In the Senate opponents of the treaty invoked the country's republican principles. Under the

Emilio Aguinaldo

At the start of the war with Spain, U.S. military leaders brought the Filipino patriot Emilio Aguinaldo back from Singapore because they thought he would stir up a popular uprising that would help defeat the Spaniards. Aguinaldo came because he thought the Americans favored an independent Philippines. These differing intentions—it has remained a matter of dispute what assurances Aguinaldo received—were the root cause of the Filipino insurrection that proved far costlier in American and Filipino lives than the war with Spain that preceded it.
Corbis-Bettmann.

Constitution, argued the conservative Republican George F. Hoar, "no power is given to the Federal Government to acquire territory to be held and governed permanently as colonies" or "to conquer alien people and hold them in subjugation." The alternative—making 8 million Filipinos American citizens—was equally unpalatable to the anti-imperialists, who were no more champions of "these savage people" than were the expansionists who denigrated the self-governing capacity of the Filipinos.

Leading citizens enlisted in the anti-imperialist cause, including the steel king Andrew Carnegie, who offered a check for $20 million to purchase the independence of the Philippines; the labor leader Samuel Gompers, who feared the competition of cheap Filipino labor; and Jane Addams, who believed that women

should stand for peace. The key group, however, was a social elite of old-line Mugwump reformers such as Carl Schurz, Charles Eliot Norton, and Charles Francis Adams. In November 1898 a Boston group formed the first of the Anti-Imperialist Leagues that began to spring up around the country.

Although skillful at publicizing their cause, the anti-imperialists never became a popular movement. They shared little but their anti-imperialism and, within the Mugwump core, lacked the common touch. Nor was anti-imperialism easily translated into a viable political cause because the Democrats, once the treaty had been adopted, waffled on the issue. Although an outspoken anti-imperialist, William Jennings Bryan, the Democratic standard-bearer, confounded his friends by favoring ratification of the treaty and afterward hesitated to stake his party's future on a crusade against a national policy he privately believed to be irreversible. Still, if it was an accomplished fact, Philippine annexation lost the moral high ground because of the grim events that began to unfold in the Philippines.

War in the Philippines. On February 4, 1899, two days before the Senate ratified the treaty, fighting broke out between American and Filipino patrols on the edge of Manila. Confronted by American annexation, Aguinaldo asserted his nation's independence and turned his guns on the occupying American forces.

The ensuing conflict far exceeded in ferocity the war just concluded with Spain. Fighting tenacious guerrillas, the U.S. Army resorted to the reconcentration tactic the Spaniards had employed in Cuba, moving people into towns, carrying out indiscriminate attacks beyond the perimeters, and burning crops and villages (see American Voices, "Daniel J. Evans and Seiward J. Norton: Fighting the Filipinos," p. 621). Atrocities became commonplace on both sides. In three years of warfare, 4,200 Americans and many thousands of Filipinos died. The fighting ended in 1902, and William Howard Taft, who had been appointed governor-general, set up a civilian administration. He intended to make the Philippines a model of American road-building and sanitary engineering.

Uneasy Aftermath. McKinley's convincing victory over William Jennings Bryan in the 1900 election, though by no means a referendum on American expansionism, suggested popular satisfaction with America's overseas adventure. Yet a strong undercurrent of misgivings was evident. Americans had not anticipated the brutal methods needed to subdue the Filipino guerrillas. "We are destroying these islanders by the thousands, their villages and cities," protested the philosopher William James. "No life shall you have, we say, except as a gift from our philanthropy after your unconditional surrender to our will. . . . Could there be any more damning

Daniel J. Evans and Seiward J. Norton

Fighting the Filipinos

*W*hen Arthur MacArthur, the commanding general of U.S. forces in the Philippines, appeared in 1902 before a Senate committee investigating the conduct of the war, he boasted of "planting the best traditions, the best characteristics of Americanism . . . deep down in that fertile soil." Two enlisted men offered the Senate committee a different picture of the implanting of American ideals in Filipino soil.

Daniel J. Evans, Twelfth Infantry

Q: The committee would like to hear . . . whether you were the witness to any cruelties inflicted upon the natives of the Philippine Islands; and if so, under what circumstances.—*A.* The case I had reference to was where they gave the water cure to a native in the Ilicano Province at Ilocos Norte . . . about the month of August 1900. There were two native scouts with the American forces. They went out and brought in a couple of insurgents. . . . They tried to get from this insurgent . . . where the rest of the insurgents were at that time. . . . The first thing one of the Americans—I mean one of the scouts for the Americans—grabbed one of the men by the head and jerked his head back, and then they took a tomato can and poured water down his throat until he could hold no more. . . . Then they forced a gag into his mouth; they stood him up . . . against a post and fastened him so that he could not move. Then one man, an American soldier, who was over six feet tall, and who was very strong, too, struck this native in the pit of the stomach as hard as he could. . . . They kept that operation up for quite a time, and finally I thought the fellow was about to die, but I don't believe he was as bad as that, because finally he told them he would tell, and from that on he was taken away, and I saw no more of him.

Seiward J. Norton, Eighteenth Infantry

Q: Did you witness the burning of any towns by the United States soldiers over there?—*A.* Oh, yes.

Q: Just state what towns you saw burned.—*A.* Well, we were out on an expedition this time; we started one morning at three o'clock and rode around the country to the north of Jaro to San Miguel, and came back down this road. It was not the town of San Miguel, but the houses built along the road side by side—barrios—and we burned that old string of houses there, it is my impression, to San Miguel. . . . Brown was acting corporal in the scouts and was ordered to go out with his squad and burn houses there, and he obeyed the order. . . .

Q: What other barrios and towns were burned besides those you mentioned, within your knowledge?—*A.* We burned a great many barrios which I did not know the names of. We burned a good deal of the country as were fired upon. It was the practice, in fact, if a column was marching along and was fired upon to burn the buildings in that neighborhood. That impressed the natives with the fact that they could not fire upon us with impunity, although they did not often do great damage. . . .

Q: Were the people in the houses warned to get out and then their houses were burned?—*A.* Oh, yes.

Q: You allowed the inmates to get out and then their houses were burned?—*A.* Yes, sir.

Q: You have stated that with the exception of isolated cases the treatment of Filipinos by the American soldiers was humane?—*A.* Yes, sir; very much so.

Q: And considerate?—*A.* So humane and considerate it was deemed a weakness on the part of the natives.

Source: Henry F. Graff, ed., *American Imperialism and the Philippine Insurrection* (Boston: Little, Brown, 1969), 80–81, 132–34.

indictment of that whole bloated ideal termed 'modern civilization'?"

There were, moreover, disturbing constitutional issues to be resolved. Did the Constitution extend to the acquired territories? Did their inhabitants automatically become U.S. citizens? In 1901 the Supreme Court ruled negatively on both questions; these were matters for Congress to decide. A special commission appointed by McKinley recommended independence for the islands after an indefinite period of U.S. rule, during which the Filipinos would be prepared for self-government. In 1916 the Jones Act formally committed the United States to granting Philippine independence but set no date.

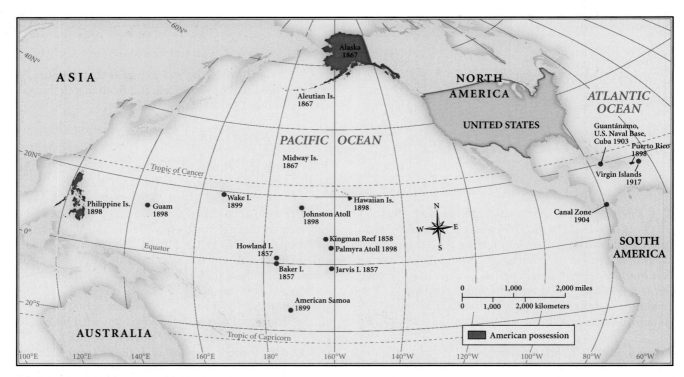

MAP 21.2 The American Empire, 1917

In 1890 Alfred T. Mahan wrote that the United States should regard the oceans as "a great highway" across which America would carry on world trade. That was precisely what resulted from the empire the United States acquired after the Spanish-American War. The Caribbean possessions, the strategically located Pacific islands, and, in 1903, the Panama Canal Zone gave the United States commercial and naval access to a wider world.

The brutal war in the Philippines rubbed off some of the moralizing gloss but left undeflected America's global aspirations. In a few years the United States had acquired the makings of an overseas empire: Hawaii, Puerto Rico, Guam, the Philippines, and finally, in 1900, several of the Samoan islands that had been jointly administered with Germany and Britain (Map 21.2). The United States, remarked the legal scholar John Bassett Moore in 1899, had moved "from a position of comparative freedom from entanglements into a position of what is commonly called a world power."

Onto the World Stage

In Europe the flexing of America's muscles against Spain caused a certain amount of consternation. At the instigation of Kaiser Wilhelm II of Germany, the major powers had tried before war broke out to intercede on Spain's behalf—but tentatively, because no one was looking for trouble with the Americans. President McKinley had listened politely to their envoys and had then proceeded with his war.

The decisive outcome confirmed what the Europeans already suspected. After Dewey's naval victory, the semiofficial French paper *Le Temps* observed that "what passes before our eyes is the appearance of a new power of the first order." And the *London Times* concluded: "This war must . . . effect a profound change in the whole attitude and policy of the United States. In the future America will play a part in the general affairs of the world such as she has never played before" (see Voices from Abroad, "Jean Hess, Émile Zola, and Ruben Dario: American Goliath," p. 624).

A Power among Powers

The politician most ardently agreeing with the *London Times*'s vision of America's future was the man who, with the assassination of William McKinley, became president on September 14, 1901. Unlike his predecessors in the White House, Theodore Roosevelt was an avid student of world affairs, widely traveled and acquainted with many European leaders. He had no doubt about America's role in the world.

It was important, first of all, to uphold the country's honor in the community of nations. "I am not

VOLUME XXXI.   NEW YORK, JUNE 16, 1898.   NUMBER 810.
Entered at the New York Post Office as Second-Class Mail Matter.
Copyright, 1898, by LIFE PUBLISHING COMPANY.

HURRAH FOR IMPERIALISM!

Hurrah for Imperialism!

Amid the patriotic frenzy over Dewey's naval victory, cooler heads wondered whether the United States knew what it was getting into with all the talk about creating an American empire. Here, Life *magazine, often a skeptical commentator on American public life, pictures a blindfolded Uncle Sam stepping off a cliff.*
Life, *1898, Newbury Library.*

For more help analyzing this image, see the ONLINE STUDY GUIDE at bedfordstmartins.com/henretta.

farsighted about the likelihood—in this he was truly exceptional among Americans—of a catastrophic world war. He believed in American responsibility for helping to maintain the balance of power.

Anglo-American Friendship. After the Spanish-American War, the European powers had been uncertain about how to deal with the victor. Germany toyed briefly with the notion of an American alliance, but only Great Britain had a clear view of what it wanted from the United States. In the late nineteenth century, Britain's position in Europe was steadily worsening in the face of a rising challenge from Germany and soured relations with France and Russia over clashing imperial ambitions in North Africa and across Asia.

In its growing isolation Britain turned to the United States. This explains why Britain bowed to American demands in the Venezuela dispute of 1895. From that time onward, after a century of cool relations (or worse) with its former colonies in North America, Britain strove for *rapprochement* (literally, a "coming together") with the United States. In the Hay-Pauncefote Agreement (1901), Britain gave up its treaty rights to participate in any Central American canal project, clearing the way for a canal under exclusive U.S. control. And two years later the last of the vexing U.S.–Canadian border disputes—this one involving British Columbia and Alaska—was settled, again to American satisfaction.

No formal alliance was forthcoming, but Anglo-American friendship had been placed on such a firm basis that after 1901 the British admiralty designed its war plans on the assumption that America was "a kindred state with whom we shall never have a parricidal war." Roosevelt heartily agreed: "England and the United States, beyond any other two powers, should be friendly." In his unflagging efforts to maintain a global balance of power, the cornerstone of Roosevelt's policy was the British relationship.

The Big Stick. Among nations, however, what counted was strength, not merely goodwill. Roosevelt wanted "to make all foreign powers understand that when we have adopted a line of policy we have adopted it definitely, and with the intention of backing it up with deeds as well as words." As Roosevelt famously said: "Speak softly and carry a big stick." By a "big stick" he meant above all naval power.

The battleship program went on apace under Roosevelt. By 1904 the U.S. Navy stood fifth in the world; by 1907 it was third. At the top of Roosevelt's agenda, however, was a canal across Central America. The Spanish-American War had graphically demonstrated the strategic need: the entire country had waited anxiously while the battleship *Oregon* steamed at full speed from the Pacific around the tip of South America to join the final action against the Spanish fleet in Cuba.

hostile to any European power in the abstract," Roosevelt once wrote. "I am simply American first and last, and therefore hostile to any power which wrongs us." Nor should the country shrink from righteous battle. "All the great masterful races have been fighting races," Roosevelt declared. But when he spoke of war, Roosevelt had in mind actions by the "civilized" nations against "backward peoples." Roosevelt felt "it incumbent on all the civilized and orderly powers to insist on the proper policing of the world." That was why Roosevelt sympathized with European imperialism and how he justified American dominance in the Caribbean.

As for the "civilized and orderly" policemen of the world, the worst thing that could happen was for them to fall to fighting among themselves. Roosevelt had an acute sense of the fragility of world peace, and he was

Jean Hess, Émile Zola, and Ruben Dario

American Goliath

America's emergence as an imperial power provoked much anxious comment abroad. Not surprisingly, this commentary tended to mirror the concerns of the commentators. What was unexpected, as the following excerpts suggest, was that they took seriously America's high estimate of itself. If its actions violated professed ideals, foreign critics were not averse to calling the United States to account.

Jean Hess, a Frenchman well traveled in East Asia, questioned American motives for intervening in the Philippines (1899).

Nowhere, in my opinion, better than in the Philippines, has it been shown that modern wars are simply "deals." The American intervention in the struggle engaged in by the revolutionary Tagals against the Spanish government has turned out to be nothing but a speculation of "business men," and not the generous effort of a people paying a debt in procuring for others the liberty that it concedes belongs to all. . . . Back of all these battles, this devastation and mourning, in spite of the newly-born Yankee imperialism, there was only, there is only, what the people of the Bourse [stock market] call a deal.

Émile Zola, the great French novelist, feared that America's military adventurism was dealing a blow to the cause of world peace (1900).

I know that, for belief in peace and future disarmament, the time is scarcely auspicious, as we are now beholding an alarming recrudescence of militarism. Nations which till now seem to have held aloof from the contagion, to have escaped this madness so prevalent in Europe, now appear to be attacked. Thus, since the Spanish war, the United States seems to have become a victim of the war fever. . . . I can see in that great nation a dangerous inclination toward war. I can detect the generation of vague ideas of future conquest. Until the present time that country wisely occupied itself with its domestic affairs and let Europe severely alone, but now it is donning plumes and epaulets, and will be dreaming of possible campaigns and be carried away with the idea of military glory—notions so perilous as to have been responsible for the downfall of nations.

In 1905, a year after the promulgation of the Roosevelt Corollary, the acclaimed Nicaraguan poet Ruben Dario issued an impassioned challenge from a small Central American country under the shadow of the Goliath. (Nicaragua was in fact occupied by U.S. Marines four years later.) Dario addressed his poem "To Roosevelt."

You are primitive and modern, simple and
    complex;
you are one part George Washington and one
    part Nimrod.
You are the United States,
future invader of our naive America
with its Indian blood, an America
that still prays to Christ and still speaks
    Spanish.
. . . .
The United States is grand and powerful.
. . . A wealthy country,
joining the cult of Mammon to the cult of
    Hercules;
while Liberty, lighting the path
to easy conflict, raises her torch in New York.

But our own America . . .
has lived, since the earliest moments of its life,
in light, in fire, in fragrance, and in love—
the America of Moctezuma and Atahuelpa. . . .
O men with Saxon eyes and barbarous souls,
our America lives. And dreams. And loves.
And it is the daughter of the Sun. Be Careful.
Long live Spanish America!

Sources: Philip S. Foner and Robert C. Winchester, eds., *The Anti-Imperialist Reader: A Documentary History of Anti-Imperialism in the United States*, 2 vols. (New York: Holmes and Meier Publishers, 1984), 1: 98–99, 417–18; Thomas G. Paterson and Dennis Merrill, eds., *Major Problems in American Foreign Relations*, 2 vols. (Lexington, MA: D. C. Heath Co., 1995), 1: 508–9; *Selected Poems of Ruben Dario*, tr. Lysander Kemp (Austin: University of Texas Press, 1965).

The Panama Canal. Having secured Britain's surrender of its joint canal rights in 1901, Roosevelt proceeded to the more troublesome task of leasing from Colombia the needed strip of land across Panama, a Colombian province. Furious when the Colombian legislature voted down the proposed treaty, Roosevelt contemplated outright seizure of Panama but settled on a more devious solution. With an independence movement brewing in Panama, the United States lent covert assistance that ensured the success of a bloodless revolution against Colombia. On November 7, 1901, the United States recognized Panama and received two weeks later a perpetually renewable lease on a canal zone. Roosevelt never regretted the victimization of Colombia, although the United States, as a kind of conscience money, paid Colombia $25 million in 1922.

Building the canal, one of the heroic engineering feats of the century, involved a swamp-clearing project to rid the area of malaria and yellow fever, the construction of a series of great locks, and the excavation of 240 million cubic yards of earth. It took the U.S. Army Corps of Engineers and the digging by thousands of hired laborers eight years to finish the huge project. When the Panama Canal opened in 1914, it gave the United States a commanding commercial and strategic position in the Western Hemisphere (Map 21.3).

Policeman of the Caribbean.   Next came the task of making the Caribbean basin secure. The countries there, said Secretary of State Elihu Root, had been placed "in the front yard of the United States" by the Panama Canal. Therefore, as Roosevelt put it, they had to "behave themselves."

In the case of Cuba, good behavior was readily managed by the settlement following the Spanish-American War. Before withdrawing in 1902 the United States reorganized Cuban public finances and concluded a swamp-clearing program that eliminated yellow fever, a disease that had ravaged Cuba for many years. As a condition for gaining independence, Cuba

The Panama Canal: Excavating the Culebra Cut

The Canal Zone was acquired through devious means from which Americans could take little pride (and which led in 1978 to the Senate's decision to restore the property to Panama). But the building of the Panama Canal itself was a triumph of American ingenuity and drive. Dr. William C. Gorgas cleaned out the malarial mosquitoes that had earlier stymied the French. Under Colonel George W. Goethals, the U.S. Army overcame formidable obstacles in a mighty feat of engineering. This photograph shows the massive effort under way in December 1904 to excavate the Culebra Cut so that oceangoing ships would be able to pass through. Corbis-Bettmann.

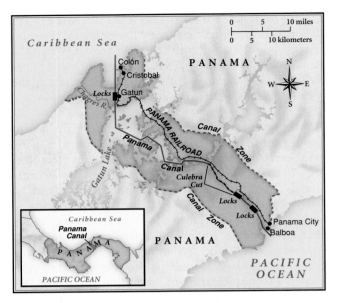

MAP 21.3 The Panama Canal: The Design

The forty-mile-long canal route zigzags to take maximum advantage of the regional topography, including an existing internal waterway via Gatun Lake. The lake is situated 85 feet above sea level, necessitating the use of locks to raise and lower ships as they approach the lake and the section known as the Culebra Cut, pictured on the previous page.

accepted a proviso in its constitution called the Platt Amendment, which gave the United States the right to intervene if Cuban independence was threatened or if internal order broke down. Cuba also granted the

United States a lease on Guantanamo Bay (which is still in effect), where the U.S. Navy built a large base.

Claiming that instability in the Caribbean invited the intervention of European powers, Roosevelt announced in 1904 that the United States would act as "policeman" of the region, stepping in, "however reluctantly, in flagrant cases . . . of wrong-doing or impotence" (Map 21.4). This policy, which became known as the Roosevelt Corollary to the Monroe Doctrine, transformed that doctrine's broad principle against European interference in Latin America into an unrestricted American right to regulate Caribbean affairs. The **Roosevelt Corollary** was not a treaty with other states; it was a unilateral declaration sanctioned only by American power and national interest.

Citing the Roosevelt Corollary, the United States intervened regularly in the internal affairs of Caribbean states. In 1905 American personnel took over the customs and debt management of the Dominican Republic, and, similarly, Nicaragua in 1911 and Haiti in 1916. When domestic order broke down, the U.S. Marines occupied Cuba in 1906, Nicaragua in 1909, and Haiti and the Dominican Republic in later years.

The Open Door in Asia

Commercial interest dominated American policy in East Asia, especially the prospect of the huge China market. By the late 1890s Japan, Russia, Germany, France, and Britain had all carved out spheres of influence in China (Map 21.5). Fearful of being frozen out, U.S. Secretary of

MAP 21.4 Policeman of the Caribbean

After the Spanish-American War, the United States vigorously asserted its interest in the affairs of its neighbors to the south. As the record of interventions shows, the United States truly became the "policeman" of the Caribbean.

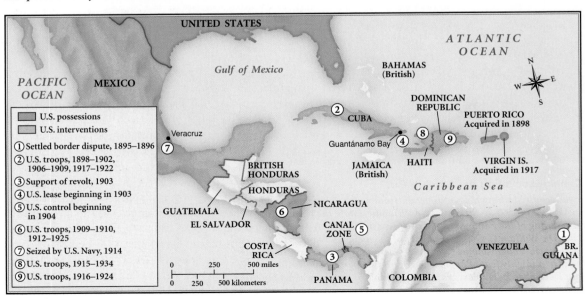

RUSSIA

L. Baikal

TRANS-SIBERIAN R.R.

Irkutsk

Chita

CHINESE EASTERN R.R.

Amur R.

Sakhalin

Boxer Rebellion (1900): Although the killing of missionaries and Chinese Christians was widespread across northeast China, the focus of the intervention by the Great Powers was Peking, the capital, where the embassy quarter was under siege by the anti-foreign Boxers.

OUTER MONGOLIA
(Russian influence)

INNER MONGOLIA

MANCHURIA   Harbin

Vladivostok

KURILE
IS.

SINKIANG

Hwang Ho

Peking
Tientsin

Sea of
Japan

JAPAN

An undeclared Japanese attack on the Russian fleet on February 9, 1904, opened the Russo-Japanese War. After eleven months of Japanese assaults, the 1905 surrender of Port Arthur—one in a train of defeats—concluded the war in Japan's favor and established its dominance over northeast China, Manchuria, and Korea.

Port
Arthur
Seoul

KOREA

Kobe

Tokyo
Yokohama

TIBET   Lhasa
NEPAL

CHINA

Chungking

Yangtze R.

Nanking
Hankow

Shanghai
Ningpo
Wenchow

RYUKYU IS.
(Japan)

N

W   E

S

INDIA   BHUTAN

Calcutta

BURMA

KWANGCHOWAN (Fr.)
Wuchow

Amoy

Foochow

Hanoi

Canton
Macao Hong Kong (Br.)
(Port.)

Formosa
(Taiwan)

PACIFIC
OCEAN

**Colonial
possessions**   **Spheres
of influence**

American

British

French

Japanese

Russian

German

SIAM

Bangkok

FRENCH
INDOCHINA

Saigon

South
China
Sea

Manila

PHILIPPINE
ISLANDS

▲ Chinese treaty ports
open for foreign trade

Place names in common use, 1910

0   500   1,000 miles

0   500   1,000 kilometers

**MAP 21.5 The Great Powers in
East Asia, 1898–1910**

The pattern of foreign dominance over China was via "treaty ports," where the powers based their naval forces, and "spheres of influence" extending from the ports into the hinterland. This map reveals why the United States had a weak hand; it lacked a presence on this colonized terrain. The Boxer Rebellion, by bringing an American expeditionary force to Peking, gave the United States a chance to insert itself onto the Chinese mainland, and American diplomats made the most of the opportunity to defend its commercial interest in China.

State John Hay in 1899 sent them an **Open Door note** claiming the right of equal trade access—an open door—for all nations that wanted to do business in China. Despite its Philippine bases, the United States lacked real leverage in East Asia and elicited only noncommittal responses from the occupying powers. But Hay chose to interpret them as accepting the American open-door position.

When a secret society of Chinese nationalists, the Boxers, rebelled against the foreigners in 1900, the United States sent 5,000 troops from the Philippines and joined the multinational campaign to break the Boxers' siege of the diplomatic missions in Peking (Beijing). America took this opportunity to assert a second principle of the Open Door: that China would be preserved as a "territorial and administrative entity." As long as the legal fiction of an independent China survived, so would American claims to equal access to the China market.

The European powers had acceded to American dominance in the Caribbean. But Britain, Germany, France, and Russia were strongly entrenched in East Asia and not inclined to defer to American interests. The United States also confronted a powerful Asian nation—Japan—that had its own vital interests. Although the open-door policy was important to him, Roosevelt sensed that there were higher stakes at risk in the Pacific.

Japan had unveiled its military strength in the Sino-Japanese War of 1894–1895, which began the dismemberment of China. A decade later, provoked by Russian rivalry in Manchuria and Korea, Japan suddenly attacked the tsar's fleet at Port Arthur, Russia's leased port in China. In a series of brilliant victories, the Japanese smashed the Russian forces in Asia. Anxious to restore a balance of power, Roosevelt mediated a settlement of the Russo-Japanese War at Portsmouth, New Hampshire, in 1905. Japan emerged as the dominant power in East Asia.

Contemptuous of other Asian nations, Roosevelt admired the Japanese—"a wonderful and civilized people . . . entitled to stand in absolute equality with all the other peoples of the civilized world." He conceded that Japan had "a paramount interest in what surrounds the Yellow Sea, just as the United States has a paramount interest in what surrounds the Caribbean." But American strategic and commercial interests in the Pacific had to be accommodated. The United States approved of Japan's protectorate over Korea in 1905, and then of its declaration of full sovereignty six years later. However, a surge of anti-Asian feeling in California complicated Roosevelt's efforts. In 1906 San Francisco's school board placed all Asian students in a segregated school, infuriating Japan. The "Gentlemen's Agreement" of 1907, in which Japan agreed to restrict immigration to the United States, smoothed matters over, but periodic racist slights by Americans made for continuing tensions with the Japanese.

Roosevelt meanwhile moved to balance Japan's military power by increasing American naval strength in the Pacific. American battleships visited Japan in 1908 on a global tour that impressively displayed U.S. sea power. Late that year, near the end of his administration, Roosevelt achieved a formal accommodation with Japan. The Root-Takahira Agreement confirmed the status quo in the Pacific, as well as the principles of free oceanic commerce and equal trade opportunity in China.

William Howard Taft, however, entered the White House in 1909 convinced that the United States had been short-changed. He pressed for a larger role for American investors, especially in the railroad construction going on in China. An exponent of **dollar diplomacy**—the aggressive coupling of American political and economic interests abroad—Taft hoped that American capital would counterbalance Japanese power and pave the way for increased commercial opportunities. When the Chinese Revolution of 1911 toppled the ruling Manchu dynasty, Taft supported the victorious Chinese Nationalists, who wanted to modernize their country and liberate it from Japanese domination. The United States thus entered a long-term rivalry with Japan that would end in war thirty years later.

The United States had become embroiled in a distant struggle heavy with future liabilities but little by way of the fabulous profits that had lured Americans to Asia.

Wilson and Mexico

When Woodrow Wilson became president in 1913, he was bent on reform in American foreign policy no less than in domestic politics. Wilson did not really differ with his predecessors on the importance of America's economic interests overseas. He applauded the "tides of commerce" that would arise from the Panama Canal. But he opposed dollar diplomacy, which he believed bullied weaker countries financially and gave undue advantage to American business. It seemed to Wilson "a very perilous thing to determine the foreign policy of a nation in terms of material interest."

The United States, Wilson insisted, should conduct its foreign policy in conformity with its democratic principles. He intended to foster the "development of constitutional liberty in the world," and above all in the nation's neighbors in Latin America. In a major foreign-policy speech in 1913, Wilson promised those nations that the United States would "never again seek one additional foot of territory by conquest." He was committed to advancing "human rights, national integrity, and opportunity" in

Latin America. To do otherwise would make "ourselves untrue to our own traditions."

Mexico became the primary object of Wilson's ministrations. A cycle of revolution had begun there in 1911. The dictator Porfirio Díaz was overthrown by Francisco Madero, who spoke much as Wilson did about liberty and constitutionalism. But before Madero got very far with his reforms, he was deposed and murdered in February 1913 by one of his generals, Victoriano Huerta. Other powers recognized Huerta's provisional government but not the United States, despite a long-standing tradition of granting quick recognition to new governments. Wilson abhorred Huerta, called him a murderer, and pledged "to force him out."

By intervening in this way, Wilson insisted, "we act in the interest of Mexico alone. . . . We are seeking to counsel Mexico for its own good." Wilson meant that he intended to put the Mexican Revolution back on the constitutional path started by Madero. Wilson was not deterred by the fact that American business interests, with big investments in Mexico, favored Huerta.

The emergence of armed opposition in northern Mexico under Venustiano Carranza strengthened Wilson's hand. But Carranza's Constitutionalist movement was ardently nationalist and had no desire for American intervention in Mexican affairs. Carranza angrily rebuffed Wilson's efforts to bring about elections by means of a compromise with the Huerta regime. He also vowed to fight any intrusion of U.S. troops in his country. All he wanted from Wilson, Carranza asserted, was recognition of the Constitutionalists' belligerent status, so that they could purchase arms in the United States. In exchange for vague promises to respect property rights and "fair" foreign concessions, Carranza finally got his way in 1914. American weapons began to flow to his troops.

When it became clear that Huerta was not about to fall, the United States threw its own forces into the conflict. On the pretext of a minor insult to the U.S. Navy at Tampico, Wilson ordered the occupation of the port of Veracruz on April 21, 1914, at the cost of 19 American and 126 Mexican lives. At that point the Huerta regime began to crumble. Carranza nevertheless condemned the United States, and his forces came close to engaging the Americans. When he entered Mexico City in triumph in August 1914, Carranza had some cause to thank the Yankees. But if any sense of gratitude existed, it was overshadowed by the anti-Americanism inspired by Wilson's insensitivity to Mexican pride and revolutionary zeal.

No sooner had the Constitutionalists triumphed than Carranza was challenged by his northern general, Pancho Villa, with some encouragement by American interests in Mexico. Defeated and driven northward, Villa began to stir up trouble along the border, killing sixteen American civilians taken from a train in January 1916 and two months later raiding the town of Columbus,

New Mexico. Wilson sent troops led by General John J. Pershing across the border after the elusive Villa. Soon Pershing's force resembled an army of occupation more than a punitive expedition. Mexican public opinion demanded that Pershing withdraw, and armed clashes with Mexican troops began. At the brink of war, the two governments backed off, and U.S. forces began to withdraw in early 1917. Soon after, with a new constitution ratified and elections completed, the Carranza government finally received official recognition from Washington.

The Gathering Storm in Europe

In the meantime Europe had begun to drift toward war. There were two main sources of tension. One was the rivalry between Germany, the new superpower of Europe, and the European states threatened by its might—above all France, which had been humiliated in the Franco-Prussian War of 1870. The second danger zone was the Balkans, where the Ottoman Empire was disintegrating and where, in the midst of explosive ethnic rivalries, Austria-Hungary and Russia were maneuvering for dominance. Out of these conflicts an alliance system had emerged, with Germany, Austria-Hungary, and Italy (the Triple Alliance) on one side and France and Russia (the Dual Alliance) on the other.

The tensions in Europe were partially released by European imperial adventures, especially by France in Africa and by Russia in Asia. These activities made France and Russia rivals of imperial Britain, effectively excluding Britain from the European alliance system. Fearful of Germany, however, Britain in 1904 resolved her differences with France, and the two countries reached a friendly understanding, or *entente*. When Britain came to a similar understanding with Russia in 1907, the basis was laid for the Triple Entente. A deadly confrontation between two great European power blocs became possible.

In these European quarrels Americans had no obvious stake nor any inclination, in the words of a cautionary Senate resolution, "to depart from the traditional American foreign policy which forbids participation . . . [in] political questions which are entirely European in scope." But on becoming president, Theodore Roosevelt took a lively interest in European affairs and was eager, as the head of a Great Power, to make a contribution to the cause of peace there. In 1905 he got his chance.

The Moroccan Crisis.　The Anglo-French entente of the previous year was based partly on an agreement over spheres of influence in North Africa: the Sudan went to Britain, Morocco to France. Then Germany suddenly challenged France over Morocco—a disastrous move, conflicting with Germany's self-interest in keeping France's attention diverted from Europe. The German ruler, Kaiser Wilhelm, turned to Roosevelt for help. Roosevelt arranged an international conference, which was held in January 1906 at Algeciras, Spain. With U.S. diplomats playing a key role, the crisis was defused. Germany got a few token concessions, but France's dominance over Morocco was sustained.

Algeciras marked an ominous turning point—the first time the power blocs that would become locked in battle in 1914 squared off against one another. But in 1906 the outcome of the conference seemed a diplomatic triumph. Roosevelt's secretary of state, Elihu Root, boasted of America's success in "preserv[ing] world peace because of the power of our detachment."

Root's words prefigured how the United States would define its role among the Great Powers: it would be the apostle of peace, distinguished by its "detachment," by its lack of selfish interest in European affairs. Opposing this internationalist impulse, however, was America's traditional isolationism.

The Peace Movement. Americans had applauded the international peace movement launched by the Hague Peace Conference of 1899. The Permanent Court of Arbitration that resulted offered new hope for the peaceful settlement of international disputes. Both the Roosevelt and the Taft administrations negotiated arbitration treaties with other countries, pledging to submit their disputes to the Hague Court, only to have the treaties emasculated by a Senate unwilling to permit any erosion of the nation's sovereignty. Nor was there any sequel to Roosevelt's initiative at Algeciras. It was coolly received in the Senate and by the nation's press.

When Wilson became president, he chose William Jennings Bryan to be secretary of state. An apostle of world peace, Bryan devoted himself to negotiating a series of "cooling off" treaties with other countries—so called because the parties agreed to wait for one year while disputed issues were submitted to a conciliation process. Although admirable, these bilateral agreements had no bearing on the explosive power politics of Europe. As tensions there reached the breaking point in 1914, the United States remained effectively on the sidelines.

Yet at Algeciras Roosevelt had correctly anticipated what the future would demand of America. So did the French journalist Andre Tardieu, who remarked in 1908:

> *The United States is . . . a world power. . . . Its power creates for it . . . a duty—to pronounce upon all those questions that hitherto have been arranged by agreement only among European powers. . . . The United States intervenes thus in the affairs of the universe. . . . It is seated at the table where the great game is played, and it cannot leave it.*

FOR FURTHER EXPLORATION

► For definitions of key terms boldfaced in this chapter, see the glossary at the end of the book.

► To assess your mastery of the material covered in this chapter, see the Online Study Guide at **bedfordstmartins.com/henretta.**

► For suggested references, including Web sites, see page SR-23 at the end of the book.

► For map resources and primary documents, see **bedfordstmartins.com/henretta.**

In 1877 the United States was, by any economic or demographic measure, already a great power. But America was inward looking. The lax conduct of its foreign policy and neglect of its naval power reflected the absence of significant overseas concerns. America's rapid economic development, however, began to force the country to look outward, in particular because of the felt need for outlets for its surplus products. By the early 1890s a new strategic outlook had taken hold, shaped mainly by the writings of Alfred T. Mahan. Mahan called for a battleship navy, an inter-oceanic canal, and overseas bases. Supporting this new expansionism were arguments drawn from Social Darwinism, Anglo-Saxon racism, and America's earlier tradition of Manifest Destiny.

The Spanish-American War created an opportunity for acting on these imperialist impulses. Swift victory enabled the United States to seize from Spain the key possessions it wanted, while wartime patriotism briefly silenced America's traditional anti-imperialism. In taking the Philippines, however, the United States overstepped the bounds of the colonialism palatable to the country. The result was a resurgence of anti-imperialist sentiment that was intensified by the sight of native patriots fighting Americans in the Philippines. Even so, the McKinley administration achieved the strategic goals it had set, and the United States entered the twentieth century poised to fulfill its destiny as a Great Power.

In Europe the immediate consequences were few. Only in its budding alliance with Britain and Roosevelt's involvement in the Moroccan crisis did the United States depart from its traditional policy of avoiding European entanglements. But in the Caribbean and Asia, where it had strong interests, the United States moved more decisively, building the Panama Canal, asserting its dominance over the nearby states, and pressing for an open door in China. In Japan the United States encountered a formidable opponent with interests not easily reconciled with America's. When Woodrow Wilson became president, he tried to conduct America's foreign policy more in conformity with the nation's political ideals, only to discover the limits of that approach when he intervened in the Mexican Revolution. As world war engulfed Europe in 1914, Wilson's idealism was about to receive a much harder test.

1875	Treaty brings Hawaii within U.S. orbit
1876	United States achieves favorable balance of trade
1881	Secretary of State James G. Blaine inaugurates Pan-Americanism
1889	Conflict with Germany in Samoa
1890	Alfred Thayer Mahan's *The Influence of Seapower upon History*
1893	Annexation of Hawaii fails
	Frederick Jackson Turner's "The Significance of the Frontier in American History"
1894	Sino-Japanese War begins breakup of China into spheres of influence
1895	Venezuela crisis
	Cuban civil war
1898	Spanish-American War
	Hawaii annexed
	Anti-imperialist movement launched
1899	Treaty of Paris
	Guerrilla war in the Philippines
	Open-door policy in China
1901	Theodore Roosevelt becomes president; diplomacy of the "big stick"
	Hay-Pauncefote Agreement
1902	United States withdraws from Cuba; Platt Amendment gives United States right of intervention
1903	United States recognizes Panama and receives grant of Canal Zone
1904	Roosevelt Corollary
1906	United States mediates Franco-German crisis over Morocco at Algeciras
1907	Gentlemen's Agreement with Japan
1908	Root-Takahira Agreement
1913	Wilson asserts new principles for American diplomacy
	Intervention in the Mexican Revolution
1914	Panama Canal opens
	World War I begins

PART FOUR

The Fate of the Great Plains

The founder of scientific management, Frederick W. Taylor, used to talk about "the one best way." There were many ways to organize work, said Taylor, but only one best, most efficient way (which of course only industrial engineers trained in his methods were capable of finding). More than one might think the writing of American history is infused with this kind of confident assumption: that there was "one best way" for history to unfold and that the historian's task is to explain why that way, and no other, was the one the nation had to take.

For in no period is this sense of inevitability more engrained than in the Age of Industrialism that you have just read about. Not in all its aspects, to be sure. On overseas expansion, which in some ways went contrary to the nation's self-conception, one can readily imagine paths other than to American empire. And, broadly speaking, this is true for politics generally. The abandonment of the southern blacks by the Republicans was not inevitable; nor was the failure of Populism; nor the progressive presidency of Theodore Roosevelt, who might have ended up just another obscure vice president but for McKinley's untimely death. But on the great social and economic developments—the onset of modern industrialism, the nation's urbanization, the settlement of the Great Plains—historians do indeed write as if it could not have been otherwise.

What might shake this sense of inevitability? Consider the settlement of the Great Plains. Every ten years the U.S. Census generates a new statistical portrait of American society. Always there are surprises, but none ever exceeded the discovery by the 2000 census that the Great Plains are emptying out. Sixty percent of the counties there lost population during the 1990s and huge stretches, equal in size to the original Louisiana Purchase, nearly 900,000 square miles, now count so few inhabitants as to meet the nineteenth-century census definition of frontier, with fewer than six people per square mile. There are, indeed, substantial areas even less populated than in the pre-settlement era, qualifying under the census definition as vacant, with fewer than two persons per square mile.

As the native grasses and wildlife return, the plains increasingly resemble the land it was before the settlers arrived, although their marks are still evident in abandoned farmhouses and ghost towns. The Native American popu-

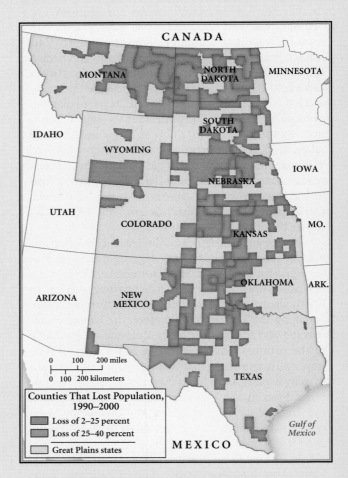

Population Losses: The American Plains, 1990–2000
The population losses shown on this map represent only the later stage in a long-term decline, especially among farmers, whose numbers in the northern plains states peaked in 1920. By mid-century, the farming population had already shrunk by a third.

lation meanwhile is returning—there are as many Indians on the Great Plains today as in the 1870s—although not of course as portrayed in the nomadic life they once led. Their ties to the buffalo, however, have revived. Roughly 300,000 head now graze on the northern plains, tended by more than 30 tribes, and buffalo management is being taught at many Indian colleges. We are realizing, as the Rutgers social scientists Frank and Deborah Popper who first identified this grand reversal in 1987 have said, that settlement of the Great Plains was "the largest, longest-run agricultural and environmental miscalculation in American history."

That conclusion, insofar as it is accepted, will surely prompt a rethinking of western history. For many years the dominant interpretation was Frederick Jackson Turner's frontier thesis, which celebrated the westward movement as an ever-renewable source of American democracy and individualism. Readers of Chapter 16's bibliographical essay will know that the Turnerian interpretation has come

Abandoned Farmhouse, North Dakota, 1996
Judging by the house depicted above, this had once been a large and prosperous farm. Now the cultivated acres have gone back to wild grass, and so, eventually, will the spacious house. For the long-departed family, the glorious sunsets will only be a memory. Annie Griffiths Belt / Corbis.

under fire in recent years from "new" western historians such as Patricia Nelson Limerick and Richard White, who have emphasized the rapacious and environmentally destructive underside of the westward movement. News that the Great Plains is emptying out will surely strengthen this critical assessment, but it will also expand what needs to be explained: not only why white settlement has not lasted but why it happened on the Great Plains in the first place.

Maps once called the Great Plains the "Great American Desert." This label has long been a source of mild amusement among historians, who regarded it as the error of easterners unaccustomed to the flat, unforested vistas of the Great Plains. Climatologists now tell us that there was something to the notion of a Great American Desert. A long-term drought cycle gripped the Great Plains in the early nineteenth century that in fact reduced much of it to shifting sands; eastern visitors did indeed see desert. Although that cycle ended before white settlement began, dry spells since then have produced incipient desert conditions, and another long-term drought cycle is only a matter of time, if indeed, under current conditions, it has not already arrived. So the question of a Great American Desert takes on new significance—why the truth it told was overridden and lands unsuitable for cultivation were put to the plow.

Or consider the question of why settlers undertook that ruinous task. The Turnerian view is that they acted as individuals, driven by pluck and courage to remake their lives on the frontier. To this day it remains an article of faith among westerners that they are the exemplars of American individualism and self-reliance. Nothing could be further from the truth, argue the new western historians. "More than any other region," says Richard White flatly, "the West has been historically a dependency of the federal government" (*It's Your Misfortune and None of My Own*, 1991), and this, indeed, in a nineteenth-century society otherwise remarkably free of any state presence.

Now that we know the Great Plains are emptying out—and that the ranching and farming remaining sur-

vive mostly on federal subsidies—the debunking argument opened by the new western historians is surely going to be pressed harder. The peopling of the Great Plains is increasingly going to be a history of how public subsidy, army protection, and federal land policy fostered a movement onto semiarid plains unlikely to have succeeded, or perhaps even attempted, by its individual members acting on their own.

In this textbook the westward movement, in its final phases, is linked to the industrial revolution and is likely to remain so linked in future editions. The industrial economy needed the mineral resources of the Far West, and once that region became economically important, railroads were certainly going to be built tying the Far West into the country. It does not follow, however, that railroads meant agricultural settlement of the Great Plains.

In the twenty-first century superhighways are still going to be crossing the Great Plains, but out the car windows travelers more and more will be seeing grasslands and buffalo. Some will be stopping on vacation to enjoy the sights as well as the casinos now undergirding many tribal economies. So it does not strain the mind to imagine a nineteenth-century counterpart—the Indian Country that was once American policy surviving in some fashion side by side with the railroads. And once we can imagine alternatives, we can no longer think of what actually happened as inevitable.

Historians know that the history they write is shaped by the times in which they live. That—as much as the uncovering of new facts—explains why history is constantly being revised. The question of inevitability we have been discussing is a central strand in this ongoing process of historical revision. Historians often speak of *contingency*. We call an event contingent if we find that prior events admit of more than one outcome. We can be sure that a sense of contingency will figure more strongly in future histories of the Age of Industrialism, including the treatment of that age in *America's History*.

The Modern State and Society

1914–1945

GOVERNMENT	DIPLOMACY	ECONOMY	SOCIETY	CULTURE
The Rise of the State	From Isolation to World Leadership	Prosperity, Depression, and War	Nativism, Migration, and Social Change	The Emergence of a Mass National Culture
1914 ▸ Wartime agencies expand power of federal government	▸ United States enters World War I (1917) Wilson's Fourteen Points (1918)	▸ Shift from debtor to creditor nation Agricultural glut	▸ Southern blacks begin migration to northern cities	▸ Silent screen; Hollywood becomes movie capital of the world
1920 ▸ Republican ascendancy Prohibition (1920–1933) Business-government partnership Nineteenth Amendment gives women the vote	▸ Treaty of Versailles rejected by U.S. Senate (1920) Washington Conference sets naval limits (1922)	▸ Economic recession (1920–1921) Booming prosperity (1922–1929) Rise of welfare capitalism	▸ Rise of nativism National Origins Act (1924) Mexican American immigration increases	▸ Consumer culture— advertising, radio, magazines, movies— flourishes Consumer culture promotes image of emancipated womanhood, the Flapper
1930 ▸ Franklin D. Roosevelt becomes president (1933) The New Deal: unprecedented government intervention in economy, social welfare, arts	▸ Roosevelt's Good Neighbor Policy toward Latin America (1933) Abraham Lincoln Brigade fights in Spanish Civil War U.S. neutrality proclaimed (1939)	▸ Great Depression (1929–1941) Rise of labor movement Married women increasingly participate in workforce	▸ Farming families migrate from Dust Bowl states to California and the West Indian New Deal	▸ Documentary impulse Federal patronage of the arts
1940 ▸ Government mobilizes industry for war production and rationing	▸ United States enters World War II (1941) Allies defeat Axis powers; bombing of Hiroshima (1945)	▸ War mobilization ends depression	▸ Rural whites and blacks migrate to war jobs in cities Civil rights movement revitalized	▸ Film industry enlisted to aid war effort

By 1914 industrialization, economic expansion abroad, massive immigration, and the growth of a vibrant urban culture had set the foundations for distinctly modern American society. In all facets of politics, the economy, and daily life, American society was becoming more organized, more bureaucratic, and more complex. By 1945, after having fought in two world wars and weathering a dozen years of economic depression, the edifice of the new society was largely complete.

GOVERNMENT First, an essential building block of modern American society was a strong national state. This state came late and haltingly to America compared with that of the industrialized countries of Western Europe. American participation in World War I called forth an unprecedented mobilization of the domestic economy, but policy makers quickly dismantled the centralized wartime bureaucracies in 1919. During the 1920s the Harding and Coolidge administrations embraced a philosophy of business-government partnership, believing that unrestricted corporate capitalism would provide for the welfare of the American people. Ultimately the Great Depression, with its countless business failures and unprecedented levels of unemployment, overthrew that long-cherished idea. Franklin D. Roosevelt's New Deal dramatically expanded federal responsibility for the economy and the welfare of ordinary citizens. An even greater expansion of the national state resulted from the massive mobilization necessitated by America's entry into World War II. Unlike the experience after World War I, the new state apparatus remained in place when the war ended.

DIPLOMACY Second, America was slowly and somewhat reluctantly drawn into a position of world leadership, which it continues to hold today. World War I provided the major impetus: before 1914 the world had been dominated by Europe, but from that point on the United States increasingly dominated the world. In 1918 American troops provided the margin of victory for the Allies, and President Wilson helped to shape the treaties that ended the war. The United States, however, refused to join the League of Nations. America's dominant economic position guaranteed an active role in world affairs in the 1920s and 1930s nonetheless. The globalization of America accelerated in 1941, when the nation threw all its energies into a second world war that had its roots in the imperfect settlement of the first one. Of all the powers that participated in this most devastating of global conflagrations, only America emerged physically unscathed from World War II. The country was also the only one to possess a dangerous new weapon—the atomic bomb. Within wartime decisions and strategies lay the roots of the Cold War that followed.

ECONOMY Third, modern America developed a strong domestic economy. In fact between 1914 and 1945 the nation's industrial economy was the most productive in the world. Even the Great Depression, which hit the United States harder than any other industrialized nation, did not permanently affect America's global economic standing. Indeed American businesses successfully competed in world markets, and American financial institutions played the leading role in international economic affairs. Large-scale corporate organizations replaced smaller family-run businesses. The automobile industry symbolized the ascendancy of mass-production techniques. Many workers shared in the general prosperity but also bore the brunt of economic downturns. These uncertainties fueled the dramatic growth of the labor movement in the 1930s.

SOCIETY Fourth, American society was transformed by the great wave of European immigration and the movement from farms to cities. The growth of metropolitan areas gave the nation an increasingly urban tone, and geographical mobility broke down regional differences. Many old-stock white Americans viewed these processes with alarm; in 1924 nativists succeeded in all but eliminating immigration except from within the Western Hemisphere, where migration across the border from Mexico continued to shape the West and Southwest. In other ways internal migration changed the face of America as African Americans moved north and west to take factory jobs, and Dust Bowl farmers in the 1930s moved to the Far West to find better livelihoods. World War II accelerated these migration patterns even more.

CULTURE Fifth, modern America saw the emergence of a mass national culture. By the 1920s Americans were increasingly drawn into a web of interlocking cultural experiences. Advertising and the new entertainment media—movies, radio, and magazines—disseminated the new values of consumerism; the movies exported this vision of the American experience worldwide. Not even the Great Depression could divert Americans from their desire for leisure, self-fulfillment, and consumer goods. The emphasis on consumption and a quest for a rising standard of living would define the American experience for the rest of the twentieth century.

SEPT 29th 1917

Price 10 Cents
In Canada, 15 Cents

Leslie's

Illustrated Weekly Newspaper

Notice to Reader

When you finish reading this magazine place a one cent stamp alongside of this notice, hand same to any postal employe and it will be placed in the hands of our soldiers or sailors at the front.

No wrapping—no address.

A. S. BURLESON,
Postmaster-General.

Paul Stahr

Be Patriotic

sign your country's pledge to save the food

CHAPTER 22

War and the American State

1914–1920

"I T,'s UP TO YOU—Protect the Nation's Honor—Enlist Now." "Turn Your Silver into Bullets at the Post Office." "Rivets Are Bayonets—Drive Them Home!" "Women! Help America's Sons Win the War: Buy U.S. Government Bonds." "Food Is Ammunition—Don't Waste It." At every turn during the eighteen months of U.S. participation in the Great War—at the movies, in schools and libraries, in shop windows and post offices, at train stations and factories— Americans encountered dramatic posters urging them to do their share. More than the colorful reminders of a bygone era they seem today, these propaganda tools were meant to unify the American people in voluntary, self-sacrificing service to the nation. They suggest not only that the federal government had increased its presence in the lives of Americans but also that in modern war victory demanded more than armies. On the home front, businessmen, workers, farmers, housewives, and even children had important roles to play.

Although the United States' participation in the conflict was of short duration, the war would have a lasting impact on the nation's domestic life as well as on its international position. The American decision to enter the conflict in 1917 confirmed one of the most important shifts of power in the twentieth century.

◀ **America and the War Effort**
Popular magazines like Leslie's Illustrated Weekly Newspaper *teamed up with the federal government to promote food conservation. This image features an idealized woman representing America and is directed at women. Eager to avoid food rationing and instead encourage voluntary sacrifice, the government mobilized 500,000 volunteers to go door to door to secure housewives' signatures on cards that pledged them to follow food conservation guidelines.*
Leslie's, September 29, 1917 / Picture Research Consultants & Archives.

Before the outbreak of the Great War in 1914, the world had been dominated by Europe; the postwar world was increasingly dominated by the United States as it spread its political, economic, and cultural influence across the globe. Related changes that shaped the country for the rest of the twentieth century also emerged at home. New federal bureaucracies had to be created to coordinate the efforts of business, labor, and agriculture—a process that hastened the emergence of a national administrative state. War meant new opportunities, albeit temporary, for white women and for members of ethnic minorities. It also meant new divisions among Americans and new hatreds, first of Germans and Austrians and then of "Bolshevik" Reds. When the war ended, the United States was forced to confront the deep class, racial, and ethnic divisions that had surfaced during wartime mobilization.

The Great War, 1914–1918

When war erupted in August 1914, most Americans saw no reason to involve themselves in the struggle among Europe's imperialistic powers. No vital U.S. interests were at stake. Indeed the United States had a good relationship with both sides, and its industries benefited from providing war material for the combatants. Many Americans placed their faith in what historians call *U.S. exceptionalism*—the belief that their superior democratic values and institutions made their country immune from the corruption and chaos of other nations. Horrified by the carnage and sympathetic to the suffering, Americans nevertheless expected that they would be able to follow their president's dictum "to be neutral in fact as well as in name."

War in Europe

Almost from the moment France, Russia, and Britain formed the Triple Entente in 1907 to counter the Triple Alliance of Germany, Austria-Hungary, and Italy (see Chapter 21), European leaders began to prepare for what they saw as an inevitable conflict. The spark that ignited the war came in Europe's perennial tinderbox, the Balkans, where Austria-Hungary and Russia competed for power and influence. Austria's seizure of the

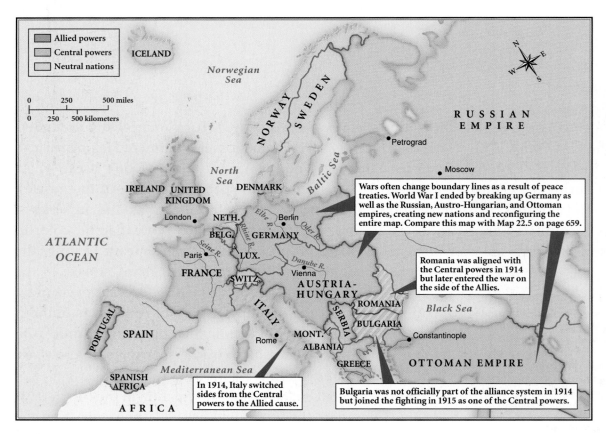

MAP 22.1 European Alliances in 1914
In early August 1914 a complex set of interlocking alliances drew the major European powers into war. At first the United States avoided the conflict. Not until April 1917 did America enter the war on the Allied side.

provinces of Bosnia and Herzegovina in 1908 had enraged Russia and its client, the independent state of Serbia. Serbian terrorists responded by recruiting Bosnians to agitate against Austrian rule. On June 28, 1914, a nineteen-year-old Bosnian student, Gavrilo Princip, assassinated Franz Ferdinand, the heir to the Austro-Hungarian throne, and his wife, the Duchess of Hohenberg, in the town of Sarajevo.

After the assassination the complex European alliance system, which had for years maintained a fragile peace, drew all the major powers into war. Austria-Hungary, blaming Serbia for the assassination, declared war on Serbia on July 28. Russia, which had a secret treaty with Serbia, mobilized its armies; Germany responded by declaring war on Russia and its ally, France, and by invading neutral Belgium. The brutality of the invasion, and Britain's commitment to Belgian neutrality, prompted Great Britain to declare war on Germany on August 4. Within a few days all the major European powers had formally entered the conflict.

The combatants were divided into two rival blocs. The Allied Powers—Great Britain, France, Japan, Russia, and, in 1915, Italy—were pitted against the Central Powers—Germany, Austria-Hungary, Turkey, and, in 1915, Bulgaria (Map 22.1). Because the alliance system encompassed competing imperial powers, the conflict spread to parts of the world far beyond Europe, including the Middle East, Africa, and China. Its worldwide scope gave it the name the Great War, or later, World War I.

The term *Great War* also suggested the terrible devastation the conflict produced. It was the first modern war in which extensive harm was done to civilian populations. New military technology, much of it from the United States, made armies more deadly than ever before. Soldiers carried long-range, high-velocity rifles that could hit a target at 1,000 yards—a vast technical improvement over the 300-yard range of the rifle-musket used in the American Civil War. Another innovation was the machine gun, whose American-born inventor, Hiram Maxim, moved to Great Britain in the

The Landscape of War
World War I devastated the countryside: this was the battleground at Ypres in western Belgium in 1915. The carnage of trench warfare also scarred the soldiers who served in these surreal settings, causing "gas neurosis," "burial-alive neurosis," and "soldiers' heart"—all symptoms of shell shock. Imperial War Museum, London.

1880s to follow a friend's advice: "If you want to make your fortune, invent something which will allow those fool Europeans to kill each other more quickly."

The concentrated firepower of rifles and machine guns gave troops in defensive positions a tremendous advantage. For four bloody years, between 1914 and 1918, the Allies and the Central Powers faced each other on the Western Front, a narrow swath of territory in Belgium and northern France crisscrossed by 25,000 miles of heavily fortified trenches, protected by deadly barbed wire (see American Voices, "Harry Curtin: Trench Warfare," p. 641). Trench warfare produced unprecedented numbers of casualties. If one side tried to break the stalemate by venturing into the "no man's land" between the trenches, its soldiers, caught in the sea of barbed wire, were mowed down by artillery fire or poison gas, first used by the Germans at Ypres in April 1915. Between February and December 1916, the French suffered 550,000 casualties and the Germans 450,000, as Germany tried to break through the French lines at Verdun. The front did not move.

The Perils of Neutrality

As the bloody stalemate continued, the United States grappled with its role in the international conflagration. Two weeks after the outbreak of war in Europe, President Woodrow Wilson had made the American position clear. In a message widely printed in the newspapers, the president called on Americans to be "neutral in fact as well as in name, impartial in thought as well as in action." Wilson wanted to keep the nation out of the war partly because he believed that if America kept aloof from the quarrel, he could arbitrate—and influence—its ultimate settlement.

The nation's divided loyalties also influenced Wilson's policy. Many Americans, including Wilson, felt deep cultural ties to the Allies, especially Britain and France. Yet most Irish Americans resented Britain's centuries-long occupation of their homeland and the cancellation of Home Rule in 1914. Pro-German sentiments drew strength from America's 10 million immigrants from Germany and Austria-Hungary. Indeed, German Americans made up one of the largest and best-established ethnic groups in the United States, and many aspects of German culture, including classical music and the German university system, were widely admired. Wilson could not easily have rallied the nation to the Allied side in 1914.

Many Americans had no strong sympathy for either side. Some progressive leaders—both Republicans and Democrats—vehemently opposed American participation in the European conflict. Virtually the entire political left, led principally by Eugene Debs and the Socialist Party, condemned the war as imperialistic. African American leaders such as A. Philip Randolph viewed it as a conflict of the white race only. Newly formed pacifist groups, among them the American Union against Militarism and the Women's Peace Party, both founded in 1915, also mobilized popular opposition. And some prominent industrialists bankrolled antiwar activities. In December 1915 Henry Ford spent almost half a million dollars to send more than a hundred men and women to Europe on a "peace ship" in an attempt to negotiate an end to the war.

Conflict on the High Seas.   These factors might have kept the nation neutral if the conflict had not spread to the high seas. Here the United States wished to assert its neutrality rights—freedom to trade with nations on both sides of a conflict. But the warring nations would not long let America trade in peace. By the end of August 1914, the British had imposed a naval blockade on the Central Powers, hoping to cut off military supplies and starve the German people into submission. But their actions also prevented neutral nations like the United States from trading with Germany and its allies. The United States chafed at the infringement of its neutral rights but chose to do little besides complain, largely because the war had produced a spectacular increase in trade with the Allies that more than made up for the lost commerce with the Central Powers. American trade with Britain and France grew from $824 million in 1914 to $3.2 billion in 1916. By 1917 U.S. banks had lent the Allies $2.5 billion. In contrast, American trade with and loans to Germany totaled only $29 million and $27 million, respectively, by 1917. This trade imbalance translated into closer U.S. ties with the Allies, despite the nation's official posture of neutrality.

To challenge British control of the seas, the German navy launched a devastating new weapon, the U-boat. In April 1915 the German embassy in the United States had issued a warning to civilians that all ships flying the flags of Britain or its allies were liable to destruction. A few weeks later, on May 7, a German U-boat off the coast of Ireland torpedoed the British luxury liner *Lusitania*, killing 1,198 people, 128 of them Americans. The attack on the unarmed passenger vessel (which was later revealed to have been carrying munitions) incensed Americans—newspapers branded it a "mass murder"—and prompted President Wilson to send a series of strongly worded protests to Germany. Mounting tension between the two nations temporarily subsided in September 1915, when Germany announced its submarines would no longer attack passenger ships without warning.

The *Lusitania* crisis was one factor that prompted Wilson to rethink his opposition to preparedness. He was further discouraged by the failure of his repeated attempts in 1915 and 1916 to mediate an end to the European conflict through his aide, Colonel Edward House. With neither side apparently interested in serious

Harry Curtin

Trench Warfare

Before the United States entered the Great War, many young American men, eager to get into the fight, enlisted in the British forces. In February 1918 Californian Harry Curtin wrote letters describing trench warfare in France that vividly captured the ravaged landscape and the pervasive tension as men waited fearfully for the next shell to hit.

Picture to yourself a scene of utter desolation and loneliness. A rolling plain of moist, black, sticky mud, so pitted by shell holes that they overlap shell holes all the way from three feet wide to twenty, and ranging from four to fifteen feet deep. These holes are filled with mud, riled up by continuous shell fire into the consistency of syrup, so that if one had the misfortune to slip into one, he is in a quagmire and dies a miserable death, unless his comrades drag him out.

Scattered in all directions are fragments of what were once trees, hedges, buildings, rusty barbed wire entanglements and dugouts; also corpses—horses, mules and humans. In all this scene man is as though he never was. Although his handiwork is everywhere evident, he is not visible.

There are no living things here—not even rats. I made a mistake. There are worms, any God's quantity of them.

Amidst this scene of ruin and death is a trench. It is one of many, but as it is the one I am in, it intimately concerns me and I will describe it.

This trench is about six feet deep, the excavated earth being thrown up in front to form a parapet which makes it apparently seven and a half feet. It ranges in width from eighteen inches at the bottom to three feet at the top and is about eighteen feet in length. About seven feet of this is roofed over with scantling and pieces of rubber sheeting, an outer covering of about eighteen inches of dirt being added. This portion is divided from the rest of the trench by walls made of rubber sheeting, and in it all cooking and sleeping is done. In this trench is a machine gun and its crew, of which I am one. There are others, but we are all segregated so as to minimize casualties.

It is pitch dark and the wind is moaning in a fashion to make one lose all belief in ghosts—for if there were such things as ghosts there should be troops of them here. . . .

Although the ground throbs with the concussion of heavy guns and shells, both our own and the enemy's, one experiences a sense of security and aloofness in these places which is peculiar. The talk ranges over a variety of subjects. Everything is discussed except the war, which is taboo.

Somebody looks at his watch and the next . . . guard listens to assure himself that there are no aeroplanes about, opens the flap and goes out, carefully tucking it down after him so that no gleam of light can escape. The man he relieves comes in a little later and casually remarks that "Fritz is throwing some ironmongery [shells] over." And he is!

Out of the black heavens outside is coming a rain of shells from 5.9 up to 9-inch, high explosives, which throw columns of dirt sixty feet high and make holes in the ground from eight feet in diameter to fifteen and ten feet deep. The gunners who fire these are miles away and don't know where their shells land. Their officers do, however, as they are "firing from the map." They are engaged in what is known as "searching"—firing shells here and there on our sector, sideways, backwards, and forwards with monotonous regularity. They are trying to blast us out of the ground.

I said that no one ever spoke about the war—with an exception, however. Whenever the concussion of a bursting shell puts the light out and a shower of dirt and stones patters into the trench, the discussion closes abruptly; someone says: "That was pretty close"—and we wait.

Source: Bulletin (Los Angeles Consistory, Scottish Rite) December 1918, p. 68.

---

peace negotiations, Wilson worried that the potential for the United States to be drawn into the conflict was deepening. In the fall of 1915, he endorsed a $1 billion buildup of the army and the navy, and in 1916 Congress passed the National Defense Act, which created the Council of National Defense, an agency charged with planning industrial mobilization in the event of war.

Toward War. Nevertheless, public opinion still ran against entering the war, a factor that profoundly shaped

The 1916 Campaign
This campaign van sponsored by the Women's Bureau of the Democratic National Committee linked Woodrow Wilson to the themes of progressivism, prosperity, and preparedness. Note the variation on the popular slogan, "He kept us out of war."
Corbis-Bettmann.

the election of 1916. The Republican Party passed over the belligerently prowar Theodore Roosevelt in favor of Supreme Court Justice Charles Evans Hughes, a former governor of New York. The Democrats renominated Wilson, whose campaign emphasized his progressive reform record (see Chapter 20) but whose telling campaign slogan was "He kept us out of war." Wilson won reelection by only 600,000 popular votes and by 23 votes in the electoral college, a slim margin that limited his options in mobilizing the nation for war.

The events of early 1917 diminished Wilson's lingering hopes of staying out of the conflict. On January 31 Germany announced the resumption of unrestricted submarine warfare, a decision dictated by the impasse in the land war. In response Wilson broke off diplomatic relations with Germany on February 3. A few weeks later, newspapers published an intercepted communication from Germany's foreign secretary, Arthur Zimmermann, to the German minister in Mexico City, in which Zimmermann urged Mexico to join the Central Powers

in the war. In return Germany promised to help Mexico recover "the lost territory of Texas, New Mexico, and Arizona." This threat to the territorial integrity of the United States jolted both congressional and public opinion, especially in the West, where opposition to entering the war was strong. Combined with the resumption of unrestricted submarine warfare, the Zimmermann telegram inflamed anti-German sentiment. Although the likelihood of Mexico's reconquering the border states was small, the continued instability there in the final phases of the Mexican Revolution (see Chapter 21) had led to border raids that killed sixteen U.S. citizens in January 1916 and made American policymakers take the German threat seriously.

Throughout March, U-boats attacked American ships without warning, sinking three on March 18 alone. On April 2, 1917, after consulting his cabinet, Wilson appeared before a special session of Congress to ask for a declaration of war. The rights of the nation had been trampled, and its trade and citizens' lives imperiled, he charged. But while U.S. self-interest shaped the decision to go to war, Americans' long-standing sense of their exceptionalism, coupled with Progressive Era zeal to right social injustices, also played a part. Believing that the United States, in sharp contrast to other nations, was uniquely high minded in the conduct of its international affairs, many Americans accepted Wilson's claim that America had no selfish aims: "We desire no conquest, no dominion. We seek no indemnities for ourselves, no material compensation for the sacrifices we shall freely make. We are but one of the champions of the rights of mankind." In a memorable phrase intended to ennoble the nation's role, Wilson proposed that U.S. participation in the war would make the world "safe for democracy."

Four days after Wilson's speech, on April 6, 1917, the United States declared war on Germany. Reflecting the divided feelings of the country as a whole, the vote was far from unanimous. Six senators and fifty members of the House voted against the action, including Representative Jeannette Rankin of Montana, the first woman elected to Congress. "I want to stand by my country," she declared, "but I cannot vote for war."

First Woman in Congress

In 1916 Jeannette Rankin, a former suffrage organizer, became the first woman elected to Congress. Her vote against U.S. entry into World War I cost her a chance for election to the Senate in 1918. In 1940 Rankin again won election to Congress from Montana. True to her lifelong pacifism, she cast the only vote against American entry into World War II. Corbis-Bettmann.

"Over There"

To native-born Americans, Europe seemed a great distance away—literally "over there," as the lyrics of George M. Cohan's popular song described it. After the declaration of war, many citizens were surprised to learn that the United States planned to send troops to Europe, optimistically having assumed that the nation's participation could be limited to military and economic aid. In May 1917 General John J. Pershing traveled to London and Paris to determine how the United States could best support the war effort. The answer, as Marshal Joseph Joffre of France put it, was clear: "Men, men, and more men."

Conscription. The problem was that the United States had never maintained a large standing army in peacetime. To field a fighting force strong enough to enter a global war, the government turned to conscription. The passage of the Selective Service Act in May 1917 demonstrated the increasing impact of the state on ordinary citizens. Though draft resistance had been common during the Civil War, no major riots occurred in 1917. The Selective Service system worked in part because it combined central direction from Washington with local administration and civilian control and thus did not tread on the nation's tradition of individual freedom and local autonomy. Draft registration also demonstrated the potential bureaucratic capacity of the American state. On a single day, June 5, 1917, more than 9.5 million men between the ages of twenty-one and thirty were processed for military service in their local voting precincts. By the end of the war almost 4 million men, popularly known as doughboys, plus a few thousand female navy clerks and army nurses, were in uniform. Another 300,000 men, called slackers, evaded the draft, and 4,000 were classified as conscientious objectors.

Wilson chose Pershing to head the American Expeditionary Force (AEF). But the newly raised army did not have an immediate impact on the fighting. The fresh recruits had to be trained and outfitted and then wait for transport across the submarine-infested Atlantic. The nation's first significant contribution was to secure the safety of the seas. Aiming for safety in numbers in the face of mounting German submarine activity, the government began sending armed convoys across the Atlantic. The plan worked: no American soldiers were killed on the way to Europe, and Allied shipping losses were cut dramatically.

The Western Front. Meanwhile, trench warfare on the Western Front continued its deadly grind. Allied commanders pleaded for American reinforcements, but Pershing was reluctant to put his soldiers under foreign commanders, preferring to delay introducing American troops until the AEF could be brought up to full strength and combat readiness. Thus, until May 1918, the brunt of the fighting continued to fall on the French and British.

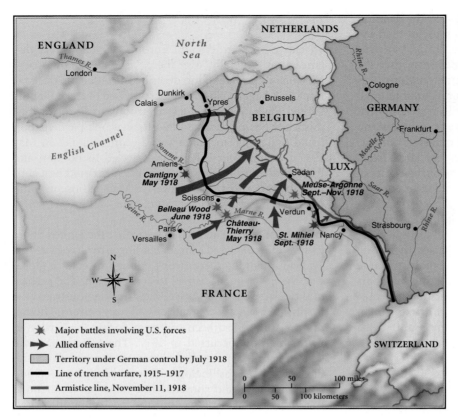

MAP 22.2 U.S. Participation on the Western Front, 1918

When American troops reached the European front in significant numbers in 1918, the Allied and Central Powers had been grinding each other down in a war of attrition for almost four years. The influx of American troops and supplies broke the stalemate. Successful offensive maneuvers by the American Expeditionary Force included those at Belleau Wood and Château-Thierry and the Meuse-Argonne campaign.

Their burden increased when the Eastern Front collapsed after the Russian Revolution in November 1917. Under the Treaty of Brest-Litovsk, the new **Bolshevik** regime under Vladimir Ilych Lenin surrendered about one-third of Russia's territories, including Russian Poland, Ukraine, and the Baltic provinces, in return for an end to hostilities.

When hostilities with Russia ended, the Germans launched a major offensive against the Allies on the Western Front on March 21, 1918. By May the German army had advanced to the Marne River, within 50 miles of Paris, and was attempting to subdue the city by bombardment. When Allied leaders intensified their calls for American troops, Pershing committed about 60,000 Americans to help the French repel the Germans in the battles of Château-Thierry and Belleau Wood (Map 22.2).

American reinforcements now began to arrive in large numbers. Slowly they worked their way to the front through the clogged French transportation system. Augmented by American troops, the Allied forces brought the German offensive to a halt in mid-July. The counteroffensive began with a successful campaign to drive the Germans back from the Marne. In mid-September 1918 American and French troops led by General Pershing forced the Germans to retreat at St. Mihiel. The last major assault of the war began on September 26, when Pershing pitted over a million American soldiers against vastly outnumbered and exhausted German troops. The Meuse-Argonne campaign pushed the enemy back across the Selle River near Ver-

dun and broke the German defenses, at a cost of over 26,000 American lives.

World War I ended on November 11, 1918, when German and Allied representatives signed an **armistice** in the railway car of Marshal Ferdinand Foch of France. The flood of American troops and supplies during the last six months of the war had helped secure the Allied victory. The nation's decisive contribution signaled a shift in international power as European diplomatic and economic dominance declined, and the United States emerged as a world leader.

The American Fighting Force

About 2 million American soldiers were in France at the war's end. Two-thirds of them had seen action at least briefly on the Western Front, but most Americans had escaped the horrors of sustained trench warfare that sapped the morale of Allied and German troops. During the eighteen months in which the United States fought, 48,000 American servicemen were killed in action or died from wounds. Another 27,000 died from other causes, mainly the influenza epidemic that swept the world in 1918 and 1919. But the nation's casualties were minimal compared with the 8 million soldiers lost by the Allies and Central Powers. The French lost far more soldiers in the siege of Verdun than the United States did in the entire war.

Although individual bravery was increasingly anachronistic in modern warfare, the war generated its

Fighting the Flu
The influenza epidemic of 1918 to 1919 strained the resources of a public health system already fully mobilized for the war effort. Here doctors, army officers, and reporters don surgical masks and gowns before touring hospitals that treat influenza patients. Note the patriotic poster entreating citizens to buy bonds on the wall behind them. Corbis-Bettmann.

share of American heroes. Sergeant Alvin York single-handedly killed 25 Germans and took 132 prisoners at the battle of Châtel-Chéhéry in the Meuse-Argonne campaign. Although air power played only a minor role in the conduct of the war, it captivated the popular imagination. One of America's best-known "aces" (the word coined for pilots who destroyed five or more enemy aircraft) was the former professional race-car driver Eddie Rickenbacker, known as the "American Ace of Aces" for shooting down more enemy aircraft than any other pilot. The aerial exploits of daredevil pilots, often fighting in single combat like medieval knights, provided a thrill that contrasted with the monotony of trench warfare. The popular fascination with York and Rickenbacker suggests a deep-seated need on the part of the American public to anoint heroes in what had become an increasingly depersonalized and mechanized pursuit of war.

Diversity and Racism in the Armed Forces. Most American soldiers were not aces or heroes, but rather ordinary men who reflected the heterogeneity of the nation's population. Approximately 12,000, or 25 percent, of the adult male Native American population served in the military. About one-fifth of the American soldiers had been born in another country, leading some people to call the AEF the American Foreign Legion. Army censors had to be able to read forty-nine languages to check letters written home by American servicemen. Although the diversity of the military worried some observers, most optimistically predicted that service in the armed forces would promote the Americanization of the nation's immigrants.

To sort its conscripts the army used the newly developed Stanford-Binet intelligence test, putting the progressive belief in social science at the service of wartime needs. Army psychologists, who administered the test to all recruits, expressed shock at the level of illiteracy among draftees—as high as 25 percent. Racial and ethnic variations in the test scores reinforced stereotypes about the supposed intellectual inferiority of blacks and immigrants, although in fact their lower scores stemmed from the cultural and environmental biases of the tests. The

Flying Aces
One of America's best-known aces was former professional race-car driver Eddie Ricken-backer (middle) of the Ninety- fourth Aero Pursuit Squadron. Note the insignia on the plane. The Ninety- fourth was known as the hat-in-the-ring squadron for the American custom of throwing a hat into the ring as an invitation to fight. Corbis-Bettmann.

army dropped the test in 1919, but revised versions of intelligence tests soon became a standard part of assessment measures in the American educational system.

The "Americanization" of the army remained imperfect at best, with African American soldiers receiving the worst treatment. Blacks were organized into rigidly segregated units, almost always under the control of white officers. In addition blacks were assigned to the most menial tasks, working as stevedores (workers who loaded and unloaded the ships) and messboys (workers who cleaned up kitchen and dining facilities). Although the policy of segregation minimized contact between black and white recruits, racial violence erupted at several camps. The worst incident occurred in Houston in August 1917, when black members of the Twenty-fourth Infantry's Third Battalion killed fifteen white soldiers and police officers in retaliation for a string of racial incidents, including the beating of a black woman by a white police officer. Sixty-four soldiers were tried in military courts, and nineteen were hanged. The army quickly disbanded the battalion, but the legacy of racial mistrust lingered throughout the rest of the war.

Racial equality had never been a central concern on the progressive agenda, and the black experience in World

War I reflected the persistent gap between democratic rhetoric and reality. Over 400,000 black men served in the military, accounting for 13 percent of the armed forces; 92 percent were draftees, a far higher rate than that of whites. Black soldiers often found the French more willing to socialize with them on an equal basis than white American soldiers. Despite documented cases of extreme heroism, no blacks received the Congressional Medal of Honor, the nation's highest military award, even though they had been so honored in the Civil War and the Spanish-American War. The French, however, had no qualms about awarding the Croix de Guerre (Legion of Honor) to several hundred African American soldiers (see Voices from Abroad, "A German Propaganda Appeal to Black Soldiers," p. 648).

Demobilization.   Just as it had taken months to get American troops to Europe to join the fighting, similar delays slowed demobilization at the war's end. June 1919 was the peak month for returns, with 368,000 men—plus the women who had served in France as telephone operators, canteen workers, and nurses—coming home to begin the process of readjusting to civilian life.

After the armistice the war lived on, however, in the minds of the men and women who had gone "over

World War I Veteran Fred Fast Horse

In contrast to the segregation African Americans experienced, Native Americans served in integrated combat units in the military. Ironically, racial stereotypes about their natural abilities as warriors, their adroit tactics, sense of strategy, and feats of camouflage both enhanced the reputation of Native Americans' military ability and meant that officers gave them hazardous duties as advance scouts, messengers, and snipers. Casualties were high. Roughly 5 percent died, compared to 1 percent for the military as a whole. Fred Fast Horse, a Rosebud Sioux, pictured here, was partially paralyzed in the Meuse-Argonne campaign.

William Hammond Mathers Museum, Indiana University.

there." Spared the trauma of sustained battle, many members of the AEF had experienced the war more as tourists than as soldiers. Before joining the army most recruits had barely traveled beyond their hometowns, and for them the journey across the ocean to Europe was a monumental, once-in-a-lifetime event. In 1919 a group of former AEF officers formed the American Legion "to preserve the memories and incidents of our association in the great war." The word *legion* perfectly captured the romantic, almost chivalric memories that many veterans held of their wartime service. Only later did disillusionment set in over the contested legacy of World War I.

War on the Home Front

Fighting World War I required extraordinary economic mobilization on the home front in which corporations, workers, and the general public cooperated. Although

the federal government did expand its power and presence during the emergency, the watchword was voluntarism. The government avoided compulsion as much as possible. Ambivalence about expanding state power, coupled with the pressures of wartime mobilization, severely damaged the impetus for progressive reforms that had characterized the prewar era. Yet even in the context of international crisis, some reformers expected that the war could serve the cause of improving American society.

Mobilizing Industry and the Economy

Even before the formal declaration of war, the United States had geared up as the arsenal for the Allied Powers. As hundreds of tons of American grain and military supplies crossed the Atlantic and the Allies paid for their purchases in gold, the United States reversed its historical position as a debtor and became a leading creditor. In addition, U.S. financial institutions increasingly provided capital for investment in the world market when British financial reserves started to be diverted to the war effort. This shift from debtor to creditor status, which would last until the 1980s, guaranteed the nation a major role in international financial affairs after the war and confirmed the new role of the United States as a world power.

Paying for the War. The continuing impact of the prewar progressive reform movement was evident in the financing of the war, the cost of which would eventually mount to $33 billion. The government paid for the war in part by using the Federal Reserve System established in 1913 (see Chapter 20) to expand the money supply, making it easier to borrow money. Two-thirds of the funds came from loans, especially the popular liberty bonds. Treasury Secretary William McAdoo encouraged the small, heavily advertised bond sales as a way of widening support for the war and demonstrating the voluntary self-sacrifice of the nation's citizenry. To augment the funds raised by bonds, McAdoo increased the federal income tax. Income taxes had been instituted by Congress after the passage of the Sixteenth Amendment to the Constitution in 1913. Now the War Revenue Bills of 1917 and 1918 transformed the tax into the foremost method of federal fund-raising. The Wilson administration took a progressive approach, rejecting a tax on all wages and salaries in favor of a tax on corporations and wealthy individuals. The **excess-profits tax** signaled a direct and unprecedented intrusion of the state into the workings of corporate capitalism. By 1918 U.S. corporations were paying over $2.5 billion in excess-profits taxes per year—more than half of all federal taxes.

Wartime Economic Regulation. The revenue bills should not mask the fact that the federal government for the most part took a collaborative rather than a coercive

A German Propaganda Appeal to Black Soldiers

In an effort to undermine enemy morale, each side distributed propaganda tracts behind the lines. This piece of German propaganda was directed toward black soldiers in France. According to Charles Williams—who, with the cooperation of the secretary of war, the Federal Council of Churches, and the Phelps-Stokes Fund, investigated conditions for black soldiers—the reaction of soldiers who read the propaganda was clear: "We know what they say is true, but don't worry; we're not going over."

To the Colored Soldiers of the U.S. Army, September, 1918, Vosges Mountains.

Hello, boys, what are you doing over there? Fighting the Germans? Why? Have they ever done you any harm? Of course, some white folks and the lying English-American papers told you that the Germans ought to be wiped out for the sake of humanity and democracy. What is democracy? Personal freedom, all citizens enjoying the same rights socially and before the law. Do you enjoy the same rights as the white people do in America, the land of freedom and democracy? Or aren't you rather rated over there as second class citizens? Can you go to a restaurant where white people dine, can you get a seat in a theatre where white people sit, can you get a pullman seat or berth in a railroad car, or can you ride in the South in the same street car with white people? And how about the law? Is lynching and the most horrible cruelties connected therewith a lawful proceeding in a democratic country?

Now all of this is entirely different in Germany, where they do like colored people, where they do treat them as gentlemen and not as second class citizens. They enjoy exactly the same social privileges as every white man, and quite a number of colored people have mighty fine positions in Berlin and other big German cities.

Why, then, fight the Germans only for the benefit of the Wall Street robbers to protect the millions they have lent to the English, French, and Italians? You have been made the tool of the egotistic and rapacious rich in England and America, and there is nothing in the whole game for you but broken bones, horrible wounds, broken health or—death. No satisfaction whatever will you get out of this unjust war. You have never seen Germany; so you are fools if you allow people to teach you to hate it. Come over and see for yourself. Let those do the fighting who make profit out of this war; don't allow them to use you as cannon food. To carry the gun in their defense is not an honor but a shame. Throw it away and come over to the German lines. You will find friends who will help you along.

Source: Charles H. Williams, *Sidelights on Negro Soldiers* (Boston: B. J. Brimmer Co., 1923), 70–71.

approach to big business during the war. To the dismay of many progressives who had hoped that the war emergency would increase federal regulation of business, the government suspended antitrust laws to encourage cooperation and promote efficiency. For economic expertise the administration turned to business executives who flocked to Washington, where they served with federal officials on a series of boards and agencies that sought a middle ground between total state control of the economy and total freedom for business.

The central agency for mobilizing wartime industry was the War Industries Board (WIB), established in July 1917. In March 1918, after a fumbling start that showed the limits of voluntarism in a national emergency, the Wilson administration reorganized the board under the direction of Bernard Baruch, a Wall Street financier. The WIB produced an unparalleled expansion of the federal government's economic powers: it allocated scarce resources, gathered economic data and statistics, controlled the flow of raw materials, ordered the conversion from peacetime to war production, set prices, imposed efficiency and standardization procedures, and coordinated purchasing. Though the board had the authority to compel compliance, Baruch preferred to win voluntary cooperation from industry, often through personal intervention. Business generally supported this governmental oversight because it coincided with its own interests in improving efficiency and productivity. Despite higher taxes corporate profits soared, aided by the suspension of antitrust laws and the institution of price guarantees for war work. War profits produced an economic boom that continued without interruption until 1920.

In some instances new federal agencies took dramatic, decisive action. In the face of the severe winter of

"Remember Your First Thrill of American Liberty"
American officials were adamant that all sectors of the population be reached by the propaganda campaigns that urged Americans to buy bonds, conserve food, enlist, and support the war effort in countless other ways. They targeted immigrants with posters such as this one for Liberty Bonds in the hopes not only that the foreign-born would buy bonds, but in doing so they would become more Americanized and more deeply committed to their adopted home. Library of Congress.

For more help analyzing this image, see the ONLINE STUDY GUIDE at bedfordstmartins.com/henretta.

1917 to 1918, which led to coal shortages in northeastern cities and industries, the Fuel Administration ordered all factories east of the Mississippi River to shut down for four days. An even more striking example of the temporary use of federal power came in December 1917. When a massive railroad traffic snarl interfered with the transport of troops, the Railroad War Board, which coordinated the nation's sprawling transportation system, took over the railroads. Guaranteeing railroad owners a "standard return" equal to their average earnings between 1915 and 1917, the board promised that the carriers would be returned to private control

no later than twenty-one months after the end of the war. Although reformers hoped to continue this experiment in government control on behalf of labor and consumers, the government fulfilled its pledge.

The Food Administration and Voluntarism.   Reliance on voluntary compliance in mobilizing for war was best exemplified in the Food Administration, created in August 1917 and led by Stanford-trained engineer Herbert Hoover, who proposed to "mobilize the spirit of self-denial and self-sacrifice in this country." Using the slogan "Food will win the war," Hoover encouraged farmers to expand production of wheat and other grains from 45 million acres in 1917 to 75 million in 1919. Although the Food Administration issued reams of rules and regulations for producers and retailers, at no time did the government contemplate domestic food rationing. Rather Hoover sent women volunteers from door to door to secure housewives' cooperation in observing "wheatless" Mondays, "meatless" Tuesdays, and "porkless" Thursdays and Saturdays—a campaign that resulted in substantial voluntary conservation of food resources. Hoover emerged from the war as one of the nation's most admired public figures.

The Legacy of Economic Mobilization.   With the signing of the armistice in November 1918, the United States scrambled to dismantle wartime controls. Wilson, determined to "take the harness off," disbanded the WIB on January 1, 1919, resisting suggestions that the board would help stabilize the economy during demobilization. Like most Americans, Wilson could tolerate government planning power during an emergency but not as a permanent feature of the economy.

Although the nation's participation in the war lasted just eighteen months, it left an enduring legacy, the modern bureaucratic state. Entire industries were organized as never before, linked to a maze of government agencies and executive departments. A modern system of income taxation was established, with the potential for vastly increasing federal reserves. Finally, the collaboration between business and government was mutually beneficial, teaching both partners a lesson they would put to use in state building in the 1920s and afterward.

Mobilizing American Workers

Modern wars are never won solely by armies and business and government leaders. Farmers, factory workers, and other civilians play crucial roles, ones that the federal government constantly promoted in its propaganda posters and other means of exhorting citizens "to do their bit for Uncle Sam." One result was that organized labor's position improved during the war, although it remained a junior partner to business and government.

Organized Labor. Besides mobilizing armies and businesses to wage war, the federal government also needed to ensure a reliable workforce, especially in war industries. Acute labor shortages, caused by the demands of the draft, the abrupt decline in European immigration, and the urgency of war production, had enhanced workers' bargaining power. The National War Labor Board (NWLB), formed in April 1918, also helped to improve labor's position. Composed of representatives of labor, management, and the public, the NWLB established an eight-hour day for war workers, with time and a half for overtime, and endorsed equal pay for women workers. Workers were not allowed to disrupt war production through strikes or other disturbances. In return the NWLB supported the workers' right to organize unions, required employers to deal with shop committees, and arbitrated labor disputes.

After years of federal hostility toward labor, the NWLB's actions brought a welcome change in labor's status and power. From 1916 to 1919 AFL membership grew by almost 1 million workers, reaching over 3 million at the end of the war. Few of the wartime gains lasted, however. Like other agencies, the NWLB was quickly disbanded. Wartime inflation ate up most of the wage hikes, and a virulent postwar antiunion movement caused a rapid decline in union membership that lasted into the 1930s.

Black and Mexican American Workers. While the war emergency benefited labor in general, it had a special effect on workers who were traditionally excluded from many industrial jobs. For the first time northern factories actively recruited African Americans, spawning the "Great Migration" (Map 22.3). Over 400,000 African Americans from the South moved northward to cities such as St. Louis, Chicago, New York, and Detroit during the war. The lure of decent jobs was potent. As one Mississippi man said in anticipation of working in northern meatpacking

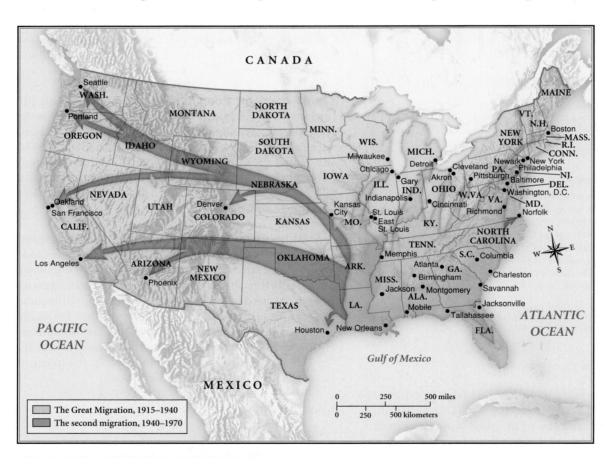

MAP 22.3 The Great Migration and Beyond

Employment opportunities that opened up during World War I and World War II served as catalysts for "great migrations" out of the rural South. In the first migration that began in 1915, African Americans headed primarily to industrial cities of the North and Midwest, such as Chicago, New York, and Pittsburgh. With the Second World War, their destinations expanded to include the West, especially Los Angeles, the San Francisco Bay area, and Seattle.

For more help analyzing this map, see the ONLINE STUDY GUIDE at bedfordstmartins.com/henretta.

houses: "You could not rest in your bed at night for thoughts of Chicago." African Americans encountered discrimination in the North—in jobs, housing, and education—but most were able to better their circumstances as they found new opportunities and an escape from the repressive southern agricultural system (see American Voices, "Southern Migrants," p. 652).

Mexican Americans in California, Texas, New Mexico, and Arizona also found new opportunities. Wartime labor shortages prompted many Mexican Americans to leave farm labor for industrial jobs in rapidly growing southwestern cities. Continuing political instability in Mexico following the revolution encouraged many Mexicans to relocate, temporarily or permanently, across the border, a process facilitated by newly opened railroad lines. At least 100,000 Mexicans entered the United States between 1917 and 1920, often settling in segregated neighborhoods (barrios) in urban areas, meeting discrimination similar to that faced by African Americans.

Women and the War Effort.   Women were the largest group to take advantage of new wartime opportunities. White women and, to a lesser degree, black and Mexican American women found that factory jobs usually reserved for men had been opened to them. About 1 million women joined the labor force for the first time, while many of the 8 million women who already held jobs switched from low-paying fields like domestic service to higher-paying industrial work. Americans soon got used to the sight of female streetcar conductors, train engineers, and defense workers. But everyone—including most working women—believed that those jobs would return to men after the war.

Wartime Reform: Woman Suffrage and Prohibition

Many progressive reformers had been active in the mobilization for war, hoping to keep alive the progressive spirit by pushing for a wide range of social reforms. They

Wartime Opportunities
Women took on new jobs during the war, working as mail carriers, police officers, drill-press operators, and farm laborers attached to the Women's Land Army. These women are riveters at the Puget Sound Navy Yard in Washington. Black women in particular, who customarily were limited to employment as domestic servants or agricultural laborers, found that the war opened up new opportunities and better wages in industry. When the war ended, black and white women alike usually lost jobs deemed to be men's work.
National Archives.

Southern Migrants

The Great Migration of southern African Americans to the cities of the North disrupted communities and families, but the migrants kept in touch with friends and kin through letters and visits. Cities like Chicago offered new opportunities and experiences, as these letters suggest, and migrants eagerly promoted their promise to the folks back home.

CHICAGO, ILLINOIS.

My dear Sister: I was agreeably surprised to hear from you and to hear from home. I am well and thankful to say I am doing well. The weather and everything else was a surprise to me when I came. I got here in time to attend one of the greatest revivals in the history of my life—over 500 people joined the church. We had a Holy Ghost shower. You know I like to have run wild. It was snowing some nights and if you didnt hurry you could not get standing room. Please remember me kindly to any who ask of me. The people are rushing here by the thousands and I know if you come and rent a big house you can get all the roomers you want. You write me exactly when you are coming. I am not keeping house yet I am living with my brother and his wife. My son is in California but will be home soon. He spends his winter in California. I can get a nice place for you to stop until you can look around and see what you want. I am quite busy. I work in Swifts packing Co. in the sausage department. My daughter and I work for the same company— We get $1.50 a day and we pack so many sausages we dont have much time to play but it is a matter of a dollar with me and I feel that God made the path and I am walking therein.

Tell your husband work is plentiful here and he wont have to loaf if he want to work. . . . Well goodbye from your sister in Christ.

CHICAGO, ILLINOIS, 11/13/17.

Mr. H———
Hattiesburg, Miss.
Dear M———: Yours received sometime ago and found all well and doing well. hope you and family are well.

I got my things alright the other day and they were in good condition. I am all fixed now and living well. I certainly appreciate what you done for us and I will remember you in the near future.

M, old boy, I was promoted on the first of the month I was made first assistant to the head carpenter when he is out of the place I take everything in charge and was raised to $95. a month. You know I know my stuff.

Whats the news generally around H'burg? I should have been here 20 years ago. I just begin to feel like a man. It's a great deal of pleasure in knowing that you have got some privilege My children are going to the same school with the whites and I dont have to umble to no one. I have registered—Will vote the next election and there isnt any "yes sir" and "no sir"—its all yes and no and Sam and Bill.

Florine says hello and would like very much to see you.

All joins me in sending love to you and family. How is times there now? Answer soon, from your friend and bro.

Source: *Journal of Negro History* 4, no. 4 (1919): 457, 458–59.

anticipated that the wartime expansion of federal power would lead to a more dramatic governmental activism in the postwar era. Their efforts met with limited success, but the war did help to get two amendments to the Constitution adopted that many reformers had long supported: woman suffrage and prohibition.

Suffrage Victory. Supporters of woman suffrage hoped that the war would reinvigorate their cause. The National American Woman Suffrage Association (NAWSA) continued to lobby for the proposed woman suffrage amendment to the Constitution. It also threw the support of its 2 million members behind the Wilson administration, encouraging women to do their part to win the war. Women in communities all over the country labored exhaustively to promote food conservation, to protect children and women workers, and to distribute emergency relief through organizations like the Red Cross. Many agreed with Carrie Chapman Catt, president of NAWSA, that women's patriotic service could advance the cause of woman's suffrage.

Alice Paul and the National Woman's Party (NWP) took a more militant tack. To the dismay of NAWSA leaders, NWP militants began picketing the White House in July 1917 to protest their lack of the vote. Arrested and sentenced to seven months in jail, Paul and other women prisoners went on a hunger strike, which prison authorities met with forced feeding. Public shock

Woman Suffrage Triumphant

This 1919 poster celebrating the passage of the Nineteenth Amendment by Congress promised that woman suffrage was coming, but it took still another year of intense lobbying to win the necessary ratification by the states. Then, finally, the woman's hour struck.

Poster Collection, US5084, Hoover Institution Archives, Stanford University, CA.

at the women's treatment made them martyrs, drawing attention to the issue of woman's suffrage.

The combination of the NWP's and NAWSA's policy of patient persuasion finally brought results. In January 1918 Woodrow Wilson withdrew his opposition to a federal woman suffrage amendment. The constitutional amendment quickly passed the House but took eighteen months to get through the Senate. Then came another year of hard work for ratification by the states. Finally, on August 26, 1920, Tennessee gave the Nineteenth Amendment the last vote it needed. The goal that had first been declared publicly at the Seneca Falls convention in 1848 was finally achieved seventy-two years later, in large part because of women's contributions to the war effort.

Moral Reform, Family Welfare, and Prohibition. Other activists also saw the war as an opportunity to further their long-standing goals. Moral reformers, concerned with vice and prostitution found that their

agenda meshed with the military's interest in army efficiency. With the slogan "Keeping fit to fight," the federal government launched an ambitious campaign against sexually transmitted diseases, forcing the shutdown of "red-light" districts in cities with military training camps. With the cooperation of the YMCA and the YWCA, the government undertook a far-reaching sex education program, designed to enlighten both men and women about the dangers of sexual activity and the value of "social purity."

While some reformers worried about soldiers' physical and moral welfare, others acted to protect the families they left behind. Responding to concerns about familial disruption and deprivation among working-class families, Congress enacted the War Risk Insurance Act in 1917, which required that enlisted men and noncommissioned officers allot $15 monthly from their military pay to their dependents, who also received allowances from the federal government, which disbursed almost $570 million for the program between 1917 and its end in 1921. The funds gave women some degree of financial security and even independence, but the program also reinforced expectations that women's proper role was in the home and men's was as the family breadwinner. This unprecedented expansion of the federal government into the private lives of families, although short lived, would shape the assumptions of the welfare programs established in the New Deal era (see Chapter 25).

A more dramatic enlargement of federal power resulted from the efforts of Prohibitionists who viewed alcoholic beverages as the nation's key social evil. In the early twentieth century, many Americans viewed the legal prohibition of alcohol as a progressive reform and not a denial of individual freedom. Urban reformers, concerned about good government, poverty, and public morality, supported a nationwide ban on drinking. The drive for Prohibition also had substantial backing in rural communities. Many people equated liquor with all the sins of the city: prostitution, crime, immigration, machine politics, and public disorder. The churches with the greatest strength in rural areas, including the Methodists, the Baptists, and the Mormons, also strongly condemned drinking. Protestants from rural areas dominated the membership of the Anti-Saloon League, which supplanted the Women's Christian Temperance Union as the leading proponent of Prohibition early in the century.

Temperance advocates were right in identifying cities as the sites of resistance to Prohibition. Alcoholic beverages, especially beer and whiskey, played an important role in the social life of certain ethnic cultures in the nation's heavily urbanized areas, especially those of German Americans and Irish Americans. Most saloons were in working-class neighborhoods and served as gathering places for workers. Machine politicians indeed conducted much of their business in bars. Thus many immigrants and working-class people opposed Prohibition, not only

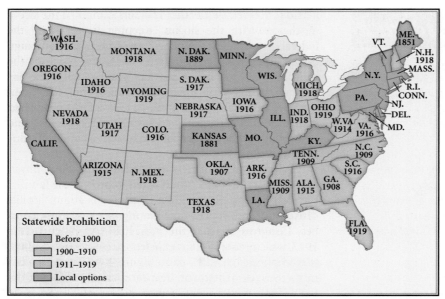

MAP 22.4 Prohibition on the Eve of the Eighteenth Amendment, 1919
Prohibition had already made headway in the states before the adoption of the Eighteenth Amendment in 1919. States such as Maine, North Dakota, and Kansas had been dry since the nineteenth century; by 1919 two-thirds of the states had passed laws banning liquor. Most states that resisted the trend were industrial centers or had large immigrant populations.

as an attack on drinking but as an attempt to impose middle-class cultural values on them.

Numerous states—mostly southern and midwestern states without a significant immigrant presence—already had Prohibition laws (Map 22.4), but World War I offered the impetus for national action. Because several major breweries had German names (Pabst and Busch, for example), beer drinking became unpatriotic in many people's minds. To conserve food Congress prohibited the use of foodstuffs such as hops and barley in breweries and distilleries. Finally, in December 1917, Congress passed the Eighteenth Amendment, which prohibited the "manufacture, sale, or transportation of intoxicating liquors." Ratified in 1919 and effective on January 16, 1920, the Eighteenth Amendment demonstrated the widening influence of the state in matters of personal behavior.

The Eighteenth Amendment was an example of how progressive reform efforts could benefit from the climate of war. But despite the stimulus the Great War gave to some types of reform, for the most part it blocked rather than furthered reforms. Though many Progressives had anticipated that the stronger federal presence in wartime would lead to stronger economic controls and corporate regulation, federal agencies were quickly disbanded once the war was over, reflecting the unease most Americans felt about a strong bureaucratic state. The wartime collaboration between government and business gave corporate leaders more influence in shaping the economy and government policy, not less.

Promoting National Unity

For the liberal reformers convinced that the war for democracy could promote a more just society at home, perhaps the most discouraging development was the

campaign to promote "One Hundred Percent Americanism," which meant an insistence on conformity and an intolerance of dissent. It was Woodrow Wilson who had predicted what came to pass: "Once lead this people into war, and they'll forget there ever was such a thing as tolerance." The president recognized the need to manufacture support for the war, but ironically his efforts encouraged a repressive spirit hostile to reform.

Wartime Propaganda.   In April 1917 Wilson formed the Committee on Public Information (CPI) to promote public support for the war. This government **propaganda** agency, headed by the journalist George Creel, quickly attracted progressive reformers and muckraking journalists (see American Lives, "George Creel: Holding Fast the Inner Lines," p. 656). Professing lofty-sounding goals such as educating citizens about democracy, promoting national unity, assimilating immigrants, and breaking down the isolation of rural life, the committee also acted as a nationalizing force by promoting the development of a common ideology.

During the war the CPI touched the lives of practically every American. It distributed 75 million pieces of patriotic literature and sponsored speeches at local movie theaters, reaching cumulative audiences estimated at more than 300 million—three times the population of the United States at the time. In its zeal the committee often ventured into hatemongering. In early 1918, for example, it encouraged speakers to use inflammatory stories of alleged German atrocities to build support for the war effort.

A Climate of Suspicion.   As a spirit of conformity pervaded the home front, many Americans found themselves targets of suspicion. Local businesses paid for newspaper and magazine ads that asked citizens to report to the Justice Department "the man who spreads pessimistic stories, cries for peace, or belittles our efforts to win the war." Posters encouraged Americans to be on the lookout for German spies. And quasi-vigilante groups such as the American Protective League mobilized about 250,000 self-appointed agents, furnished with badges issued by the Justice Department, to spy on neighbors and coworkers.

The CPI also urged ethnic groups to give up their Old World customs in the spirit of One Hundred Percent Americanism. German Americans bore the brunt of this campaign. In an orgy of hostility generated by propaganda about German militarism and outrages, everything associated with Germany became suspect. German music, especially opera, was banished from the concert halls. Publishers removed pro-German references from textbooks, and many communities banned the teaching of the German language. Sauerkraut was renamed "liberty cabbage," and hamburgers were transformed into "liberty sandwiches." Though anti-German hysteria dissipated when the war ended, hostility toward the "hyphenated" American survived into the 1920s.

Curbing Dissent. In law enforcement officials tolerated little criticism of established values and institutions. The main legal tools for curbing dissent were the Espionage Act of 1917 and the Sedition Act of 1918. The Espionage Act imposed stiff penalties for antiwar activities and allowed the federal government to ban treasonous materials from the mails. The postmaster general revoked the mailing privileges of groups considered to be radical, virtually shutting down their publications.

Individuals suffered as well. Because these acts defined treason and sedition loosely, they led to the conviction of more than a thousand people. The Justice Department focused particularly on socialists, who criticized the war and the draft, and on radicals like the Industrial Workers of the World (see Chapter 17), whose attacks on militarism threatened to disrupt war production in the western lumber and copper industries. Socialist party leader Eugene Debs was sentenced to ten years in jail for stating that the master classes declared war while the subject classes fought the battles. (Debs was pardoned by President Warren G. Harding in 1921.) Victor Berger, a Milwaukee socialist who had been jailed under the Espionage Act, was twice prevented from taking the seat to which he had been elected in the U.S. House of Representatives.

The courts rarely resisted these wartime excesses. In *Schenck v. United States* (1919), the Supreme Court upheld the conviction of the general secretary of the Socialist Party, Charles T. Schenck, who had been convicted of mailing pamphlets urging draftees to resist induction. In a unanimous decision Justice Oliver Wendell Holmes ruled that an act of speech uttered under circumstances that would "create a clear and present danger to the safety of the country" could be constitutionally restricted. Because of the national war emergency, then, the Court upheld limits on freedom of speech that would not have been acceptable in peacetime. In wartime, the drive for conformity reigned, dashing reformers' optimistic hopes that war could be what philosopher John Dewey had called a "plastic juncture," in which the country would be more open to progressive ideas.

An Unsettled Peace, 1919–1920

The war's end did not bring the tranquility Americans had hoped for. Demobilization proceeded with little planning, in part because Wilson was so preoccupied with the peacemaking process and his efforts to promote a league of nations. Spending only ten days in the United States between December 1918 and June 1919, for more than six months he was virtually an absentee president. Unfortunately, many urgent domestic issues demanded strong leadership that never emerged. In particular, racial, ethnic, and class tensions racked the nation as it attempted to adjust to a postwar order.

The Treaty of Versailles

In January 1917 Woodrow Wilson had proposed a "peace without victory," since only a "peace among equals" could last. His goal was "not a balance of power, but a community of power; not organized rivalries, but an organized common peace." The keystone of Wilson's postwar plans was a permanent league of nations. But he would first have to win over a Senate that was Republican controlled and openly hostile to the treaty he had brought home.

Negotiating the Treaty. President Wilson brought to the 1919 peace negotiations in France an almost missionary zeal. Confident in his own vision for a new world order, he believed that if necessary, "I can reach the peoples of Europe over the heads of their rulers." He scored an early victory when the Allies accepted his Fourteen Points as the basis for the peace negotiations that began in January 1919. In this blueprint for the postwar world, the president called for open diplomacy, "absolute freedom of navigation upon the seas," arms reduction, the removal of trade barriers, and an international commitment to national self-determination. Essential to Wilson's vision was the creation of a multinational organization "for the purpose of affording mutual guarantees of political independence and territorial integrity to great and small States alike." The League of Nations became Wilson's obsession.

The **Fourteen Points** were imbued with the spirit of progressivism. Widely distributed as propaganda during

George Creel: Holding Fast the Inner Lines

Woodrow Wilson called George Creel, his choice to lead the Committee on Public Information (CPI), a man with a "passion for adjectives." The forty-one-year-old Creel had already made a name for himself as a muckraking journalist and unabashed progressive, picking up a number of detractors along the way for his impetuous and flamboyant style. "A little shrimp of a man with burning dark eyes set in an ugly face under a shock of curly black hair" was how one critic described him; another called him "a fascinating talker who looked like a gargoyle." Whether it concerned his appearance or his politics, no one was neutral about George Creel.

George Creel was born on December 1, 1876, in Lafayette County, Missouri, the son of a Confederate officer who had moved west from Virginia after the Civil War. His mother, who ran a boardinghouse while his father brooded and drank, made sure that her son heard the Southern version of the War Between the States. "The battle of Antietam, indeed!" she exclaimed after he recounted one history lesson from school. "Why, honey, it was the battle of Sharpsburg, and we whipped them." The young boy concluded about his upbringing, "The open mind was no part of my inheritance. I took in prejudice with mother's milk, and was weaned on partisanship."

Quitting high school after one year, Creel worked briefly on a Kansas City newspaper before hopping on a cattle train to New York City to try his luck as a writer and freelance journalist. By 1900 he was back in the Midwest to found the *Kansas City Independent*, a weekly paper whose slogan was "A Clean, Clever Paper for Intelligent People." With zeal shared by early-twentieth-century urban progressives all around the country, he lead battles to clean up municipal government, pass laws to protect workers, and stop prostitution.

In 1909 Creel moved to Denver, which was a hotbed of progressive activity. When reformers won a majority in the 1912 city elections, he became police commissioner but was fired from the job a year later when his

George Creel
George Creel in 1917, at the time of his appointment as head of the Committee on Public Information. Corbis-Bettmann.

campaigns to dismiss political holdovers and rehabilitate criminals went too far even for his fellow progressives. Freed from the straitjacket of public office, he intensified his muckraking activities, exposing, for example, the glowing personal endorsements that often accompanied advertisements for quack medical remedies by printing the death dates of these supposedly cured patients. He was an ardent woman suffragist, and he coauthored a book on child labor with Edwin Markham and Denver's crusading judge, Ben Lindsey. Along the way he married Hollywood actress Blanche

Bates, star of *The Darling of the Gods* and other films, and starred in a cowboy movie himself. He also boxed professionally. Who says progressive reformers have to be dull?

Creel had been impressed by Woodrow Wilson's idealism as far back as 1905, and he became an enthusiastic backer of Wilson's presidential ambitions in 1912. In the 1916 campaign Creel wrote an influential pamphlet called *Wilson and the Issues*, which stressed Wilson's reform record and endorsed his stand of neutrality toward the European war. In return the reelected president offered him a position in Washington, but Creel declined. When America was on the verge of entering the war in the spring of 1917, Creel had a change of heart. If there was going to be someone in charge of public opinion, he told a Wilson aide, he wanted "to be it."

Reaction to Creel's appointment was decidedly mixed. Many newspapers, including the *New York Times*, saw him as "a radical writer" and questioned whether such an outspoken and thin-skinned figure would be able to work effectively with the press. Creel brushed these criticisms aside and promptly got down to work.

The jurisdiction of the Committee on Public Information was "everything related to public opinion, both at home and abroad," and Creel enlisted the cooperation of journalists, moviemakers, advertising executives, and others in the common battle of "holding fast the inner lines" of American public opinion during wartime. His goal was affirmative propaganda, not rank appeals to emotion—to "inspire, not inflame." So confident was he of "the absolute justice of America's cause, the absolute selflessness of America's aims," that he believed "no other argument was needed than the simple, straightforward presentation of the facts." "Words evaporate," he said repeatedly, but "facts remain."

Creel later called the CPI "the world's greatest adventure in advertising." In the days before radio, printed publicity played a crucial role in reaching, and then binding together, a diverse nation. By the end of 1917, the CPI was sending each newspaper in California an average of six pounds of publicity copy a day. One unintended by-product of this government-sponsored media campaign was the stimulation of the advertising industry, which became a major force in shaping patterns of consumption in the 1920s. The war also stimulated the nascent film industry, which cooperated wholeheartedly with CPI efforts.

George Creel quickly demonstrated that he aimed not just to shape the minds of American citizens but to "fight for the mind of mankind" worldwide. The foreign section of the CPI exported ideas about American life and values to three target audiences: neutral nations, America's allies, and the civilian populations of the Central Powers. German and Austrian citizens were bombarded with propaganda leaflets dropped from balloons and airplanes or smuggled behind enemy lines. And in the newly formed Soviet Union, the CPI distributed a million pamphlets, "sounding alarms against typhus as well as against Lenin and Trotsky." Propaganda became part of a global network.

At war's end the CPI was quickly dismantled and Creel returned to journalism. Always the publicist, he wrote a book about his CPI experiences entitled *How We Advertised America* (1920) in which he took great delight in settling old scores with his opponents, especially Republican members of Congress. He also ardently defended, to no avail, the Treaty of Versailles out of loyalty to his friend Woodrow Wilson. In 1926 he and his family moved to San Francisco, where he continued to write for national publications such as *Collier's* magazine, as well as publish books of popular history and biography.

The upheavals of the 1930s and 1940s drew Creel back into public life. He warmly supported Franklin Roosevelt's efforts to end the Great Depression and served on a variety of New Deal advisory boards. He was far more critical, however, of the administration's conduct of World War II, especially the "blundering" (in his words) propaganda efforts undertaken by the Office of War Information. With his usual inflated pride and self-justification, he commented, "A full twenty organizations now spend more than $130,000,000 a year to do the work that I did with $2,500,000 a year." By the 1940s he was moving away from his former progressive belief in reform, fearing that the federal government had gotten so big that it was stifling individual initiative. Creel died in 1951, having spent the last years of his life battling what he saw as a huge international conspiracy of Communists and their sympathizers.

George Creel always thought of himself as a "rebel at large," the title he chose for his 1947 autobiography. Reflecting on the changes that had occurred in America during his lifetime, he concluded, "At twenty, when I enlisted in the progressive movement, I was appalled at the magnitude of the task of reform. Today, at seventy, I am amazed at the swiftness of our approach to equal justice." Despite his ideological journey away from progressivism toward the end of his life, Creel never deviated from his wartime creed: "Democracy is a religion with me, and throughout my adult life I have preached America as the hope of the world."

The Peace at Versailles
This painting by Sir William Orpen of the signing of the peace treaty in the Hall of Mirrors at Versailles in June 1919 captures the solemnity of the occasion and the grandeur of the surroundings. Wilson was justifiably proud of his role in the peace negotiations, but he faced strong opposition in the Senate. Imperial War Museum, London.

the final months of the war, Wilson's plan proposed to extend the ideals of America—democracy, freedom, and peaceful economic expansion—to the rest of the world. The League of Nations, acting as a kind of international Federal Trade Commission, would supervise disarmament and—according to the crucial Article X of its covenant—curb aggressor nations through collective military action. More grandiosely, Wilson anticipated that the league would mediate disputes between nations, preventing future wars, and thus ensuring that the Great War would be "the war to end all wars." By emphasizing these lofty goals, Wilson set the stage for disappointment: his ideals for world reformation proved too far-reaching to be practical or attainable.

Twenty-seven countries sent representatives to the peace conference in Versailles, near Paris. Distrustful of the new Bolshevik regime in Russia and its call for proletarian revolution against capitalism and imperialism, the Allies deliberately excluded its representatives. Nor was Germany invited. The Big Four—Wilson, Prime Minister David Lloyd George of Great Britain, Premier Georges Clemenceau of France, and Prime Minister Vittorio Orlando of Italy—did most of the negotiating. The three European leaders sought a peace that differed radically from Wilson's plan. They wanted to punish Ger-

many and treat themselves to the spoils of war by demanding heavy **reparations**. In fact, before the war ended, Britain, France, and Italy had already made secret agreements to divide up the German colonies.

It is a tribute to Wilson that he managed to influence the peace settlement as much as he did. He was able to soften some of the harshest demands for reprisal against Germany. National self-determination, a fundamental principle of Wilson's Fourteen Points, bore fruit in the creation of the independent states of Austria, Hungary, Poland, Yugoslavia, and Czechoslovakia from the defeated empires of the Central Powers (Map 22.5). The establishment of the new nations of Finland, Estonia, Lithuania, and Latvia not only upheld the principle of self-determination but also served Wilson's (and the Allies') desire to isolate Soviet Russia from the rest of Europe.

The Battle for Ratification and the League. Wilson had less success in achieving other goals. He won only limited concessions regarding the colonial empires of the defeated powers. The old central and eastern European colonial empires in Africa, Asia, and the Middle East were dismantled, but instead of becoming independent countries the colonies were assigned to victorious Allied

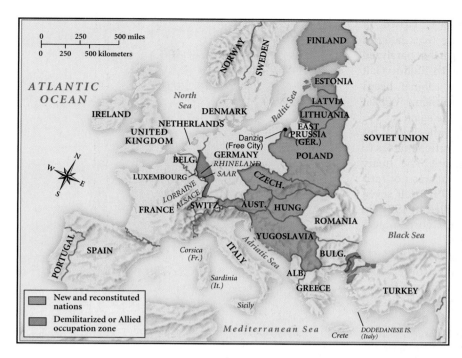

MAP 22.5 Europe after World War I
World War I and its aftermath dramatically altered the landscape of Europe, most notably with the reunification of countries such as Poland, Yugoslavia, and Czechoslovakia from territory of the defeated powers of Germany and Russia. Twenty years later, these new countries were the battlegrounds of the next world war.

nations to administer as trustees, a far cry from Wilson's ideal of national self-determination. Certain topics, such as freedom of the seas and free trade, never even appeared on the agenda because of Allied resistance. Finally Wilson had only partial success in scaling back French and British demands for reparations from Germany, which eventually were set at $33 billion.

In the face of these disappointments, Wilson consoled himself with the negotiators' commitment to his proposed League of Nations. He acknowledged that the peace treaty had defects but expressed confidence that they could be resolved by a permanent international organization dedicated to the peaceful resolution of disputes.

On June 28, 1919, representatives gathered in the Hall of Mirrors at the Palace of Versailles to sign the peace treaty. Wilson sailed home to a public enthusiastic about a league of nations in principle. Major newspapers and the Federal Council of Churches of Christ of America supported the treaty, and even an enemy of the proposed league, Senator Henry Cabot Lodge of Massachusetts, acknowledged that "[T]he people of the country are very naturally fascinated by the idea of eternal preservation of the world's peace."

But by the time Wilson presented the treaty to the Senate on July 10, it was clear that the treaty was in trouble, with support in the Senate being far short of the two-thirds vote necessary for ratification. Wilson had not paid much attention to the political realities of building support for the League of Nations and the treaty in the Senate. He had failed to include a prominent Republican in the American commission that represented the United States at Versailles. Stubbornly convinced of his own rectitude and ability, he had kept

the negotiations firmly in his own hands. When the Senate balked at the treaty, Wilson adamantly refused to compromise. "I shall consent to nothing," he told the French ambassador. "The Senate must take its medicine."

The Senate, however, did not oblige. And despite the president's attempt to make the 1918 congressional elections a referendum for his peace plans, Americans returned a Republican majority to Congress. Wilson and the league faced stiff opposition in the Senate. Some progressive senators, who endorsed the idea of American internationalism, felt that the peace agreement was too conservative, that it served to "validate existing empires" of the victorious Allies. The "irreconcilables," including progressive senators William E. Borah of Idaho, Hiram W. Johnson of California, and Robert M. La Follette of Wisconsin, disagreed fundamentally with the premise of permanent U.S. participation in European affairs. More influential was a group of Republicans led by Lodge. They proposed a list of amendments that focused on Article X, the section of the league covenant that called for collective security measures when a member nation was attacked. This provision, they argued, would restrict Congress's constitutional authority to declare war and would limit the freedom of the United States to pursue a unilateral foreign policy.

Defeat. Wilson refused to budge, especially not to placate Lodge, his hated political rival. Hoping to mobilize support for the treaty, in September 1919 the president launched an extensive speaking tour during which he brought large audiences to tears with his impassioned defense of the treaty. But the strain proved too much, and the ailing sixty-two-year-old president collapsed in Pueblo, Colorado, late in September. One week later, in Washington, Wilson suffered a severe stroke that paralyzed one side of his body. While his wife, Edith Bolling Galt Wilson, his physician, and the various cabinet heads oversaw the routine business of government, Wilson slowly recovered, but he was never the same again.

From his sickbed Wilson remained inflexible in his refusal to compromise, ordering Democratic senators to vote against all Republican amendments. The treaty came up for a vote in November 1919 but was not ratified. When another attempt in March 1920 fell seven votes short, the issue was dead. Wilson died in 1924 "as much a victim of the war," David Lloyd George noted, "as any soldier who died in the trenches."

The United States never ratified the Versailles treaty or joined the League of Nations. Many wartime issues were only partially resolved, notably Germany's future, the fate of the colonial empires, and rising nationalist demands for self-determination. These unsolved problems played a major role in the coming of World War II; some, like the competing ethnic nationalisms in the Balkans, remain unresolved today.

Racial Strife, Labor Unrest, and the Red Scare

Shortly after the end of the war, an author in the popular periodical *World's Work* observed that "the World War has accentuated all our differences. It has not created those differences, but it has revealed and emphasized them." These differences virtually exploded in the aftermath of war. Race riots exposed white resistance to the rising expectations of African Americans. Thousands of strikes signified class tensions, and a witch hunt for foreign radicals reflected anxieties about social order and the nation's ethnic pluralism.

Riots in Chicago.   Many African Americans emerged from the war determined to stand up for their rights, and they contributed to a spirit of black militancy that characterized the early 1920s. The volatile mix of black migration and raised expectations of blacks as a result of service in World War I combined to exacerbate white racism. In the South the number of lynchings rose from forty-eight in 1917 to seventy-eight in 1919. Several African American men were lynched while wearing military uniforms. In the North race riots broke out in more than twenty-five cities, with one of the first and most deadly occurring in 1917 in East St. Louis, Illinois, where nine whites and more than forty blacks died in a conflict sparked by competition over jobs at a defense plant.

By the summer of 1919, the death toll from racial violence had reached 120. One of the worst race riots in American history took place in Chicago in July, where five days of rioting left twenty-three blacks and fifteen whites

Chicago Race Riot
Racial violence exploded in Chicago during the summer of 1919, and photographer Jun Fujita was on the scene to capture it. As one of the few Japanese immigrants in Chicago at the time, Fujita was probably no stranger to racism, but it took personal courage to put himself in the midst of the escalating violence. When the riot finally ended, thirty-eight people were dead and more than five hundred were injured.
Chicago Historical Society / Photo by Jun Fujita.

dead. A variety of tensions were at work in cities where violence erupted. Black voters often determined the winners of close elections, thereby enraging white racists who resented black political influence. Blacks also competed with whites for jobs and scarce housing. Even before the July riot, blacks in Chicago had suffered the bombing of their homes and other forms of harassment. They did not sit meekly by as whites destroyed their neighborhoods: they fought back in self-defense and for their rights as citizens. Wilson's rhetoric about democracy and self-determination had raised their expectations, too.

1919—A Year of Strikes.   Workers of all races harbored similar hopes for a better life after the war. The war years had brought them higher pay, shorter hours, and better working conditions. Yet many native-born Americans continued to identify unions with radicalism and foreigners, and soon after the armistice many employers resumed their attacks on union activity. In addition rapidly rising inflation—in 1919 the cost of living was 77 percent higher than its prewar level—threatened to wipe out workers' wage increases. Nevertheless, workers hoped to hold onto and perhaps even expand their wartime gains.

The result of workers' determination—and employers' resistance—was a dramatic wave of strikes. More than four million workers—one in every five—went on strike in 1919, a proportion never since equaled. The year began with a walkout by shipyard workers in Seattle, a strong union town. Their action spread into a general strike that crippled the city. Another hard-fought strike disrupted the steel industry when 350,000 steel workers demanded union recognition and an end to twelve-hour shifts and the seven-day workweek. And in the fall the Boston police force shocked many Americans by going on strike. Governor Calvin Coolidge of Massachusetts propelled himself into the political spotlight by declaring, "There is no right to strike against the public safety by anybody, anywhere, any time." Coolidge fired the entire police force, and the strike failed. The public supported this harsh reprisal, and Coolidge was rewarded with the Republican vice presidential nomination in 1920.

The Red Scare and the Palmer Raids.   A crucial factor in organized labor's failure to win many of its strikes in the postwar period was the pervasive fear of radicalism. This concern coincided with mainstream Americans' long-standing anxiety about unassimilated immigrants—an anxiety the war had made worse. The Russian Revolution of 1917 so alarmed the Allies that Wilson sent several thousand troops to Russia in the summer of 1918 in hopes of weakening the Bolshevik regime. When the Bolsheviks founded the Third International (or Comintern) in 1919 to export Communist doctrine throughout the world, American fears deepened. As domestic labor unrest increased, Americans began to see

radicals everywhere. Hatred of the German Hun was quickly replaced by hostility toward the Bolshevik Reds.

Ironically, as public concern about domestic Bolshevism increased, radicals were rapidly losing members and political power. No more than 70,000 Americans belonged to either the fledgling U.S. Communist Party or the Communist Labor Party in 1919. Both the IWW and the Socialist Party had been weakened by wartime repression and internal dissent. Yet the public and the press continued to blame almost every disturbance, especially labor conflicts, on alien radicals. "REDS DIRECTING SEATTLE STRIKE—TO TEST CHANCE FOR REVOLUTION," warned a typical newspaper headline.

Tensions mounted with a series of bombings in the early spring. "The word 'radical' in 1919," as one historian observed, "automatically carried with it the implication of dynamite." In June a bomb detonated outside the Washington townhouse of the recently appointed attorney general, A. Mitchell Palmer. His family escaped unharmed, but the bomber was blown to bits. Angling for the presidential nomination, Palmer capitalized on the event, fanning fears of domestic radicalism.

In November 1919, on the second anniversary of the Russian Revolution, the attorney general staged the first of what became known as "Palmer raids." Federal agents stormed the headquarters of radical organizations, capturing supposedly revolutionary booty such as a set of blueprints for a phonograph (at first thought to be sketches for a bomb). The dragnet pulled in thousands of aliens who had committed no crime but were suspect because of their anarchist or revolutionary beliefs or their immigrant backgrounds. Lacking the protection of U.S.

citizenship, they faced deportation without formal trial or indictment. In December 1919 the U.S.S. *Buford*, nicknamed the "Soviet Ark," embarked for Finland and the Soviet state with a cargo of 294 deported radicals.

The peak of Palmer's power came with his New Year's raids in January 1920. In one night, with the greatest possible publicity, federal agents rounded up 6,000 radicals, invading private homes, union headquarters, and meeting halls, arresting citizens and aliens alike. Palmer was riding high in his ambitions for the presidency, but then he overstepped himself. He predicted that on May Day 1920 an unnamed conspiracy would attempt to overthrow the U.S. government. State militia units and police went on twenty-four-hour alert to guard the nation against the threat of revolutionary violence, but not a single incident occurred. As the summer of 1920 passed without major labor strikes or renewed bombings, the hysteria of the Red Scare began to abate.

The Sacco-Vanzetti Case.   The wartime legacy of antiradicalism and anti-immigrant sentiment, however, persisted well into the next decade. In May 1920, at the height of the Red Scare, Nicola Sacco, a shoemaker, and Bartolomeo Vanzetti, a fish peddler, were arrested for the robbery and murder of a shoe company's paymaster in South Braintree, Massachusetts. The two men, self-proclaimed anarchists and alien draft evaders, were both armed at the time of their arrest.

Convicted in 1921, Sacco and Vanzetti sat on death row for six years while supporters appealed their verdicts. Although new evidence suggesting their innocence surfaced, Judge Webster Thayer denied a motion for a new trial. Scholars still debate the question of their guilt, but most agree that the two anarchists did not receive a fair trial and that the evidence and procedures were tainted. The verdict stemmed as much from their status as radicals and immigrants as it did from evidence. As future Supreme Court jurist Felix Frankfurter said at the time, "The District Attorney invoked against them a riot of political passion and patriotic sentiment." Nevertheless, shortly before his execution in the electric chair on August 23, 1927, Vanzetti claimed triumph:

If it had not been for these thing, I might have live out my life among scorning men. I might have die, unmarked, unknown, a failure. . . . Never in our full life can we hope to do such work for tolerance, for justice, for man's understanding of man, as now we do by an accident.

This oft-quoted elegy captures the eloquence and tolerance of a man caught in the last spasm of antiradicalism and fear that capped America's participation in the Great War.

The war—with its nationalistic emphasis on conformity—left racial, ethnic, and class tensions in its wake. But there were other legacies as well. World War I did not have the catastrophic effect on the United States that it did on European countries. With relatively few casualties and no physical destruction at home, America emerged from the conflict stronger than ever before. Consolidating developments that had begun with the Spanish-American War, the United States became a major international power, both economically and politically. Increased efficiency and technological advancements fostered exceptional industrial productivity, making the United States the envy of the rest of the world in the postwar decade.

FOR FURTHER EXPLORATION

▶ For definitions of key terms boldfaced in this chapter, see the glossary at the end of the book.

▶ To assess your mastery of the material covered in this chapter, see the Online Study Guide at **bedfordstmartins.com/henretta**.

▶ For suggested references, including Web sites, see page SR-24 at the end of the book.

▶ For map resources and primary documents, see **bedfordstmartins.com/henretta**.

American participation in World War I set in motion one of the most important shifts in international power in the twentieth century, as the United States emerged from the war as a dominant world power. The outbreak of the Great War in 1914 initially posed a great challenge to American diplomacy. For more than two years, President Wilson attempted to use American power and prestige to mediate between the two sides. The United States finally entered the war in 1917 because of violations of its neutral rights at sea but, more broadly, because the country's foreign policy reflected the same sentiments that animated the domestic reform movement, Americans anticipated spreading their political and social ideals to the rest of the world. On April 6, 1917, Congress declared war on Germany.

American participation in the war was brief but decisive. Two million freshly recruited doughboys helped to turn the tide for the Allies on the Western Front in 1918. Flush with victory Wilson sought to bring about a peace that would reflect his vision of a new world order. Yet the Versailles treaty only partially reflected the president's hopes for freedom of the seas, peaceful economic expansion, and national self-determination. His postwar plans suffered a worse blow when the U.S. Senate refused to ratify the treaty, which included American participation in the League of Nations.

As the Wilson administration put the nation on a war footing, progressive reform energies were largely diverted to the war effort. An army had to be created almost from scratch, American agriculture and manufacturing had to be federally coordinated to produce for the Allies as well as for the home market, and American workers had to be recruited for war work and kept on the job. All this absorbed the energies of a new group of professional-experts-turned-government-bureaucrats. World War I thus helped create the tools of the modern bureaucratic state, which (though laid aside temporarily at the war's end) would be taken up again during the nation's worst peacetime crisis, the Great Depression.

The government tried to mobilize the minds of the American people as well but succeeded mainly in inflaming passions. Certain groups, such as woman suffragists, found success during the war. But others became targets of repression, including blacks who migrated to northern cities, labor activists, and socialists and other radicals who criticized the government. Domestic tensions erupted in race riots in many northern cities, widespread labor strikes in 1919, and the Red Scare of 1919–1920. The story of U.S. involvement in World War I, then, is a story of battles and diplomacy abroad, and mobilization and strife at home—all of which profoundly affected the nation's future.

1914   Outbreak of war in Europe

United States declares neutrality

1915   German submarine sinks *Lusitania*

1916   Woodrow Wilson reelected president

Revenue Act of 1916

National Defense Act

1916–1919   Height of "Great Migration" of blacks

1917   United States enters World War I

Selective Service Act

War Risk Insurance Act

War Industries Board established

Suffrage militancy

East St. Louis race riot

Espionage Act

Bolshevik Revolution

Committee on Public Information established

1918   Wilson proposes Fourteen Points peace plan

Meuse-Argonne campaign

Eugene Debs imprisoned under Sedition Act

Armistice ends war

U.S. troops intervene in Russia

1919   Treaty of Versailles

Chicago race riot

Steel strike

Red Scare and Palmer raids

Schenck v. United States

American Legion founded

League of Nations defeated in Senate

Eighteenth Amendment (Prohibition) ratified

War Industries Board disbanded

1920   Nineteenth Amendment (woman suffrage)

Sacco and Vanzetti arrested

1924   Woodrow Wilson dies

Through her dealings as business manager of the home, the modern woman brings sound commercial sense to bear on her judgment of a Ford closed car.

She knows that its low first cost, its small upkeep and operation costs, and its long-sustained usefulness make it a genuine economy. She is aware that the ease

with which she can get expert attention for it anywhere and at any time is an asset of great dollar-and-cents value to her.

And she is delighted to find this value in a car that she drives so easily, and whose outward style and inward comfort she so whole-heartedly approves.

TUDOR SEDAN, $590   FORDOR SEDAN, $685   COUPE, $525   (All prices f. o. b. Detroit)

Ford
CLOSED CARS

CHAPTER 23

Modern Times
The 1920s

IN 1924 SOCIOLOGISTS ROBERT LYND AND HELEN MERRELL LYND arrived in Muncie, Indiana, to study the life of a small American city. They observed how the citizens of Middletown (the fictional name they gave the city) made a living, maintained a home, educated their young, practiced their religion, organized community activities, and spent their leisure time. As the Lynds' fieldwork proceeded, they were struck by how much had changed over the past thirty-five years—the lifetime of a middle-aged Middletown resident—and decided to contrast the Muncie of the 1890s with the Muncie of the 1920s. When *Middletown* was published in 1929, this "study in modern American culture" became an unexpected best-seller. Its success spoke to Americans' desire to understand the forces that were transforming their society.

This transformation began with World War I. The United States emerged from the war as a powerful modern state and a major player in the world economy. The 1920s, however, rather than World War I were the watershed in the development of a mass national culture. Only then did the Protestant work ethic and the old values of self-denial and frugality begin to give way to the fascination with consumption, leisure, and self-realization that is the essence of modern American culture.

◄ **Selling Mrs. Consumer**
No other image captures the spirit of the consumer culture of the 1920s more emphatically than the Ford Model T. With the Ford Company in the lead, automobiles revolutionized Americans' patterns of spending money and spending leisure— with the help of the rapidly expanding advertising industry. This 1924 ad in the Ladies' Home Journal, *reflects advertisers' sense of the growing importance of the role of the "modern" housewife as the family's purchasing agent.*
Ladies' Home Journal, August 1924.

In economic organization, political outlook, and cultural values, the 1920s had more in common with the United States today than with the industrializing America of the late nineteenth century.

Business-Government Partnership of the 1920s

The business-government partnership fostered by World War I continued on an informal basis throughout the 1920s. As the *Wall Street Journal* enthusiastically proclaimed, "Never before, here or anywhere else, has a government been so completely fused with business." While the *Journal* exaggerated the fusion, it did convey the way in which business interests exerted powerful influence on public policy. From 1922 to 1929 the nation's prosperity seemed to confirm the economy's ability to regulate itself with minimal government regulation. Gone or at least submerged was the reform impulse of the Progressive Era. Business leaders were no longer villains but respected public figures. President Warren G. Harding captured the prevailing political mood when he offered the American public "not heroics but healing, not nostrums but normalcy."

Politics in the Republican "New Era"

Except for Woodrow Wilson's two terms, the Republican Party had controlled the presidency since 1896. When Wilson's progressive coalition floundered in 1918, the Republicans had a chance to regain the White House. With the ailing Wilson out of the picture, in the 1920 election the Democrats nominated Governor James M. Cox of Ohio for president and Assistant Secretary of the Navy Franklin D. Roosevelt as vice president. The Democratic platform called for U.S. participation in the League of Nations and a continuation of Wilson's progressivism. The Republicans, led by Warren G. Harding and Calvin Coolidge, promised a return to "normalcy," which meant a strong probusiness stance and conservative cultural values. Reflecting many Americans' desire to put the war and the stresses of 1919 behind them, voters rejected the party in power. Harding and Coolidge won in a landslide, marking the beginning of a Republican dominance that would last until 1932.

Government-Business Cooperation. Central to what Republicans termed the "New Era" was business-government cooperation. Although Republican administrations generally opposed expanding state power to promote progressive reforms, they had no qualms about using federal policy and power to assist corporations. In other words, some extensions of government activity seemed acceptable, while others did not. Thus Harding's

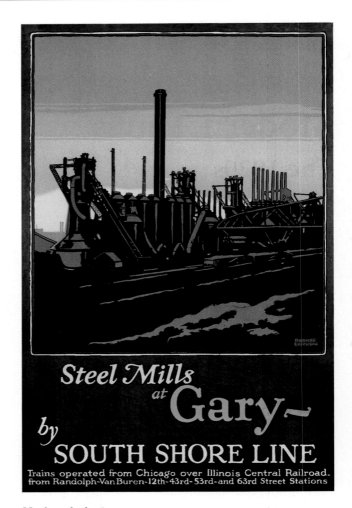

Modern Industry
This highly stylized 1928 poster promotes the steel mills of Gary, Indiana, as a tourist attraction on par with Yellowstone or Yosemite. The Gary that steelworkers experienced was more likely to be full of soot, grime, and hard work than recreation or beauty. The sky in Gary was often similar in color to that eerie shade of orange shown in the poster due to the high levels of pollution generated by the steel mills. Chicago Historical Society.

secretary of the treasury, financier Andrew W. Mellon, engineered a tax cut that undercut the wartime Revenue Acts, benefiting wealthy individuals and corporations. The Republican-dominated Federal Trade Commission (FTC) for the most part ignored the antitrust laws rather than using federal power to police industry. In this the commission followed the lead of the Supreme Court, which in 1920 had dismissed the long-pending antitrust case against U.S. Steel, ruling that largeness in business was not against the law as long as some competition remained.

Perhaps the best example of government-business cooperation emerged in the Department of Commerce, headed by Herbert Hoover. Hoover thought that with the offer of government assistance, businessmen would voluntarily run their enterprises in ways that would benefit the public interest, thereby benefiting the entire country. Under Hoover the Commerce Department expanded dramatically, offering new services like the compilation and distribution of trade and production statistics to American business. It also assisted private trade associations in their efforts to rationalize and make more efficient major sectors of industry and commerce by using such tools as product standardization and wage and price controls.

Unfortunately, not all government-business cooperation was as high minded as Hoover had anticipated. President Harding was basically an honest man, but some of his political associates were not. When Harding died suddenly of a heart attack in San Francisco in August 1923, evidence of widespread fraud and corruption in his administration had just come to light. In 1924 a particularly damaging scandal concerned the secret leasing of government oil reserves in Teapot Dome, Wyoming, and in Elk Hills, California, without competitive bidding. Secretary of the Interior Albert Fall was eventually convicted of taking $300,000 in bribes; he became the first cabinet officer in American history to serve a prison sentence.

After Harding's death, the taciturn vice president, Calvin Coolidge, moved into the White House. In contrast to his predecessor's political cronyism and outgoing style, Coolidge personified an austere rectitude. As vice president "Silent Cal" often sat through official functions without uttering a word. A dinner partner once challenged him by saying, "Mr. Coolidge, I've made a rather sizable bet with my friends that I can get you to speak three words this evening." Responded Coolidge icily, "You lose." Although Coolidge was quiet and unimaginative, his image of unimpeachable integrity reassured voters, and he soon announced his candidacy for the presidency in 1924.

The 1924 Election. When the Democrats gathered that July in the sweltering heat of New York City, they faced a divided party that drew its support mainly from the South and from northern urban political machines like Tammany Hall in New York. These two constituencies often collided. They disagreed mightily over Prohibition, immigration restriction, and most seriously, the mounting power of the racist and anti-immigrant Ku Klux Klan. The resolutions committee remained deadlocked for days over whether the party should condemn the Klan, eventually reaching a weak compromise that affirmed its general opposition to "any effort to arouse religious or racial dissension."

With this contentious background, the convention took 103 ballots to nominate John W. Davis, a Wall Street lawyer, for the presidency. To attract rural voters the Democrats chose as their vice presidential candidate Governor Charles W. Bryan of Nebraska, William Jennings Bryan's brother. But the Democrats could not mount an effective challenge to their more popular and

On the Campaign Trail
Although Calvin Coolidge was a man of few words, with little charisma, he recognized the importance of modern campaigning. In 1924 he hired advertising man Bruce Barton as a consultant to his presidential campaign. Here, Coolidge is pictured with an automobile decked out with radio equipment for broadcasting to potential voters in the streets. Library of Congress.

better-financed Republican rivals, whose strength came chiefly from the native-born Protestant middle class, augmented by small-business people, skilled workers, farmers, northern blacks, and wealthy industrialists. Until the Democrats could overcome their sectional and cultural divisions and build an effective national organization to rival that of the Republicans, they would remain a minority party.

The 1924 campaign also featured a third-party challenge by Senator Robert M. La Follette of Wisconsin, who ran on the Progressive Party ticket. La Follette's candidacy mobilized reformers and labor leaders as well as disgruntled farmers in an effort to reinvigorate the reform movement both major parties had abandoned. Their platform called for nationalization of railroads, public ownership of utilities, and the right of Congress to overrule Supreme Court decisions. It also favored the direct election of the president by the voters rather than by indirect election through the electoral college.

In an impressive Republican victory, Coolidge received 15.7 million popular votes to Davis's 8.4 million and won a decisive margin in the electoral college. La Follette chalked up almost 5 million popular votes, but he carried only Wisconsin in the electoral college.

Perhaps the most significant aspect of the election was the low voter turnout. Only 52 percent of the electorate cast their ballots in 1924, compared to more than 70 percent in presidential elections of the late nineteenth century. Newly enfranchised women voters were not to blame, however; a long-term drop in voting by men, rather than apathy among women, caused the decline.

Women in Politics. Instead of resting after their suffrage victory, women increased their political activism in the 1920s. African American women struggled for voting rights in the Jim Crow South and pushed unsuccessfully for a federal antilynching law. Many women tried to break into party politics, but Democrats and Republicans granted them only token positions on party committees. Women were more influential as lobbyists. The Women's Joint Congressional Committee, a Washington-based coalition of ten major white women's organizations, including the newly formed League of Women Voters, lobbied actively for reform legislation (see American Voices, "Women Write the Children's Bureau," p. 669). Its major accomplishment was the passage in 1921 of the Sheppard-Towner Federal Maternity and Infancy Act, which appropriated $1.25 million for well-baby clinics, educational programs, and visiting nurse projects. Such major reform legislation was rare in the 1920s, however, and its success was short lived. The Sheppard-Towner Act had passed in part because politicians feared that if it did not pass, women would vote them out of office. Once politicians realized that women did not vote as a bloc, they stopped listening to the women's lobby, and in 1929 Congress cut off the act's funding.

The roadblocks women activists faced were part of a broader public antipathy to ambitious reforms. Although some states—such as New York, where an urban liberalism was coalescing under leaders like Al Smith—did enact a flurry of legislation that promoted workmen's compensation, public health programs, and conservation measures, on the national level reforms that would strengthen federal power made little headway. After years of progressive reforms and an expanded federal presence in World War I, Americans were unenthusiastic about increased taxation or more governmental bureaucracy. The Red Scare had given ammunition to opponents of reform by making it easy to claim that legislation calling for governmental activism was the first step toward Bolshevism. The general prosperity of the 1920s further hampered the reform spirit. With a strong economy, the Republican policy of an informal partnership between business and government seemed to work and made reforms regulating corporations and the economy seem unnecessary and even harmful.

The Economy

Although prosperity and the 1920s seem almost synonymous, the decade got off to a bumpy start in the transition from a wartime to a peacetime economy. In the immediate postwar years, the nation suffered rampant inflation: prices jumped by a third in 1919, accompanied by feverish business activity. Federal efforts to halt inflation—through spending cuts and a contraction of the supply of credit—produced the recession of 1920 and 1921, the sharpest short-term downturn the United States had ever faced. Unemployment reached 10 percent. Foreign trade dropped by almost half as European nations resumed production after the disruptions of war. Prices fell dramatically—more than 20 percent—and reversed much of the wartime inflation.

The recession was short. In 1922, stimulated by an abundance of consumer products, particularly automobiles, the economy began a recovery that continued with only brief interruptions through 1929. Between 1922 and 1929 the gross domestic product (GDP) grew from $74.1 billion to $103.1 billion, approximately 40 percent. Per capita income rose from $641 in 1921 to $847 in 1929. Soon the federal government was recording a budget surplus. This economic expansion provided the backdrop for the partnership between business and government.

As industries churned out an abundance of new consumer products—cars, appliances, chemicals, electricity, radios, aircraft, and movies—manufacturing output expanded 64 percent. Behind the growth lay new techniques of management and mass production, which brought a 40 percent increase in workers' productivity. The demand for goods and services kept unemployment low in most industries throughout the decade. High employment rates combined with low inflation enhanced the spending power of many Americans, especially skilled workers and the middle class.

The economy had some weaknesses, however. Income distribution reflected significant disparity: 5 percent of the nation's families received one-third of all income. In addition a number of industries were unhealthy. Agriculture never fully recovered from the 1920 and 1921 recession. During the inflationary period of 1914 to 1920, farmers had borrowed heavily to finance mortgages and equipment in response to government incentives, increased demand, and rising prices. When the war ended, European countries resumed agricultural production, glutting the world market. The price of wheat dropped 40 percent as the government withdrew wartime price supports. Corn prices fell 32 percent, and hog prices declined 50 percent. Farmers were not the only ones whose incomes plunged. Certain "sick industries," such as coal and textiles, had also expanded in response to wartime demand, which dropped sharply at war's end. Their troubles foreshadowed the Great Depression of the 1930s.

Women Write the Children's Bureau

The Children's Bureau in the Department of Labor was in charge of administering the Sheppard-Towner Act from 1921 to 1929. In addition to setting up clinics and offering correspondence courses, the staff answered letters from anxious mothers, such as the two excerpted here—yet another example of how the state was becoming part of everyday life.

Dear Doctor Sherbon:

You can not imagine how much I have enjoyed the Course. As soon as I received it I lay down and never stopped until I read it through. It is splendid, and if every woman could follow each lesson to the letter there would be less suffering. But how are we going to convince our families that such care is necessary? Of course the children can be taught these things, but the husbands and our mothers think it is foolishness to take such care of ourselves.

Do you think it proper to explain to children where they come from and the science of life? I have told my stepson, age 18, all of these things and how he should take care of himself, and also how he should treat girls and how much suffering there was to childbirth, and I was very much criticized by some of the family.

I must close. I am taking up your valuable time and am losing much time of my own. Thank you for all the help and the good you are doing, not only for myself but others.

Dear Madam:

I took your correspondence course last winter and enjoyed it very much although I have been a mother three times and expect to be again as [I] am pregnant three months now. Maybe you have something for me or that might help me in some way, so [I] thot that I would drop you a line.

We are a poor family and live in western Kansas and [are] heavily in debt, so this ordeal is hard for me at present. But what I would like to ask you is if a poor mother can get any county or state aid. My teeth are badly in need of dental work, and [I have] no money to pay the bill and the doctor bill worries me too. The doctor we have gone to is so high I don't see how we can afford it. We owe $125 in doctor bills in another county . . . and I dread any more until back ones are paid.

Isn't there a law in Kansas that unless a confinement case is obstetrical the limit charge is $15 and if obstetrical the limit is $25? He says he charges $25 for a confinement case and $1.00 mileage which would make a total of $37 for us for doctor bill, besides a nurse or lady to nurse and do the work too. But if you know anything about such things you know that mother and babe are sadly neglected if the nurse has all the house work to do too. . . .

Does the county doctor tend to such cases and look to the community for his money? It looks like we ought to be able to do and care for such things without asking for help, but you know there are just lots and lots of mothers in my fix that just drag along and worry because they have no way of buying the most needy things at such a time and are too proud to find out if there is any way to get help. My husband thinks it's awful to get help in any way besides paying for it, but when I know he is not financially able to help, I don't see why I should suffer if there is any way to help me, as any mother or doctor knows at that time a mother needs the best of care in every way. And it's because I have always had to work too soon after childbirth that I am broken down now.

I will see what I hear from you before going into details any more. Hoping you will not think it too trifling a matter to interest you and will answer me as soon as possible. Yours truly.

Source: Molly Ladd-Taylor, *Raising a Baby the Government Way: Mothers' Letters to the Children's Bureau, 1915–1932* (New Brunswick, NJ: Rutgers University Press, 1986), 131–32, 136–38.

The Heyday of Big Business

But for the most part, despite these ominous signs, the nation was in a confident mood about the economy and the corporations that shaped it. Throughout the decade business leaders enjoyed enormous popularity and respect; their reputations often surpassed those of the era's lackluster politicians. The most revered businessman of the decade was Henry Ford, whose rise from poor farm boy to corporate giant embodied both the traditional value of individualism and the triumph of mass production. Success stories like Ford's prompted

President Calvin Coolidge to declare solemnly, "The man who builds a factory builds a temple. The man who works there worships there."

Corporate Consolidation and the Managerial Revolution. This apotheosis of big business was accompanied by a vigorous trend toward consolidation. There were more mergers in the 1920s than at any time since the flourishing of business combinations in the 1880s and 1890s, with the largest number occurring in rapidly growing industries like chemicals, electrical appliances, and automobiles. By 1930 the 200 largest corporations controlled almost half the nonbanking corporate wealth in the United States. Rarely did any single corporation monopolize an entire industry; instead, **oligopolies**, in which a few large producers controlled an industry, became the norm, as in auto manufacturing, oil, and steel. The nation's financial institutions expanded and consolidated along with its corporations. Total bank assets rose dramatically as mergers between Wall Street banks enhanced New York's role as the financial center of the world. In 1929 almost half the nation's banking resources were controlled by 1 percent of American banks (250 banks).

The 1920s also saw the triumph of the managerial revolution that had been reshaping American business since the late nineteenth century (see Chapter 17), as large-scale corporate organizations with bureaucratic structures of authority replaced family-run enterprises. By 1920 many American industries, especially in manufacturing, had modern organizational structures. The multiunit enterprise coordinated production and distribution through divisions organized by functions, such as sales, operations, and investment. Alfred P. Sloan Jr., an engineer and midlevel manager at General Motors in the 1920s, refined this structure by relieving top management of the day-to-day control of production, freeing it to concentrate on long-range planning while autonomous, integrated divisions met short-range production goals.

Most Americans benefited from corporate success in the 1920s. Although unskilled African Americans and immigrants participated far less fully in the prosperity of the decade, many members of the working class enjoyed higher wages and a better standard of living. A shorter workweek (five full days and a half day on Saturday) and paid vacations gave many more leisure time. But in the workplace itself, labor had less power (see Voices from Abroad, "The Ford Miracle: 'Slaves' to the Assembly Line," p. 671). Scientific management techniques, first introduced in 1895 by Frederick W. Taylor but widely implemented only in the 1920s, reduced workers' control over their labor.

Welfare Capitalism. The 1920s were also the heyday of welfare capitalism, a system of labor relations that stressed management's responsibility for employees' well-being. At a time when unemployment compensation and government-sponsored pensions did not exist, large corporations offered workers stock plans, health insurance, and old-age pension plans. Employee security was not, however, the primary aim of the programs that were established mainly to deter the formation of unions. The approach reflected the conservative values of the 1920s, which placed the responsibility for economic welfare in the private sector to avoid government interference on the side of labor. Coupled with an aggressive drive for what corporate leaders called the American Plan (or an open, nonunion shop) and with Supreme Court decisions that limited workers' ability to strike, welfare capitalism helped to erode the unions' strength. Membership dropped from 5.1 million in 1920 to 3.6 million in 1929—about 10 percent of the nonagricultural workforce—and the number of strikes also fell dramatically from the level in 1919. Technology and management had combined to undermine workers' power.

Economic Expansion Abroad

The power of American corporations emerged also in the international arena. During the 1920s the United States was the most productive country in the world, with an enormous capacity to compete in foreign markets that eagerly desired American consumer products. Manufacturers led the way in foreign investment. Electric companies, including General Electric, built new plants in Latin America, China, Japan, and Australia. Ford had major facilities throughout the British empire, and General Motors took over established automakers such as Vauxhall in England and Opel in Germany. The International Telephone and Telegraph Corporation, founded in 1920, employed 95,000 workers outside the country, more than did any other U.S. company.

Other American companies invested internationally during the 1920s to take advantage of lower production costs or to procure raw materials and supplies, concentrating mainly on Latin America. The three major American meat packers—Swift, Armour, and Wilson—built plants in Argentina to capitalize on low livestock prices there. Fruit growers such as the United Fruit Company established plantations in Costa Rica, Honduras, and Guatemala. American capital ran sugar plantations in Cuba and rubber plantations in the Philippines, Sumatra, and Malaya. The Anaconda Copper Corporation owned Chile's largest copper mine, and Standard Oil of New Jersey led American oil companies in acquiring oil reserves in Mexico and Venezuela. (American involvement in the oil-rich Persian Gulf became significant only after World War II.)

The demand for U.S. capital was just as great. American investment abroad more than doubled between 1919 and 1930: by the end of the 1920s, American

The Ford Miracle: "Slaves" to the Assembly Line

During the 1920s many foreign observers came to the United States to witness firsthand the drama of mass production industries, particularly the Ford plant at Rouge River and what was often termed "the Ford miracle." While most observers commented approvingly on the impressive advances Americans had made in manufacturing, some were critical. Australian journalist Hugh Grant Adams, traveling with a delegation of trade unionists from his own country, offered a scathing attack on American mass production industries for the way in which they undermined the skill and power of workers. In this passage from An Australian Looks at America, *he paints a depressing picture of work on the assembly line.*

Here are the facts. In industries that have adopted the methods of mass production, the worker needs no trade and no skill. Whether he is making telephones, bathroom taps, sausages, reapers, or motor-cars, the only difference is in the design of the machinery he tends. Four times in four different places I saw the famous chain at one end of which motor-cars begin as a nut and at the other end are driven off under their own power without a craftsman having touched them. The man in the workshop does nothing but fetch and carry for machines while the metal is being transformed into a motor-car.

The inventor, the designer of the machine, is the maker of industrial America. When he has put the machine in place it becomes the god of the factory, tireless, inexorable, whom all men must serve. Out of every hundred men employed in a mass-production factory only ten men require technical skill. These ten are the men who keep the machines in running order—the mechanics and the tool-makers, whose skill is not used in making the product of the factory but only in making the machines that make the product. The others are employed fetching and carrying for the machines, taking the product off one machine and fitting it to the product of another, doing their narrow job with the mechanical efficiency that comes from endless repetition.

Take a motor-car plant for example. At 8 A.M. the worker takes his place at the side of a narrow platform down the centre of which runs a great chain moving at the rate of a foot a minute. His tool is an electrically-driven riveter. As he stands, riveter poised, the half-built framework of the car passes slowly in front of him. On the opposite side of the chain, one foot farther up the line, a workman with a long pair of tongs has slipped two red-hot bolts through two holes that seem to be just always there. Once, twice, he plunges the riveter down upon the hot metal . . . once, twice . . . once, twice. . . . And so on for six, eight or ten hours, whatever the rule of the factory may be, day after day, year after year—if he can keep the job.

There is not a job on the mass-production chain more complicated technically than that. The chain never stops. The pace never varies. The man is part of the chain, the feeder and the slave of it. He must keep going—always the same action and always at the same speed—or the chain would jam, and he would be execrated all along the line; for each man is paid not according to what he himself does, but according to the progress of the chain. If one man holds up the chain every man in the line loses wages.

The man flattening these two red-hot rivets, doing that and nothing else throughout his working hours, can learn his work from A to Z in five minutes. This is true of every other job in the actual building of motor-cars as they are being built in these mass-production factories of America.

You can see why it follows that ninety out of every hundred workmen employed in these great manufacturing industries need neither training nor skill. These secondary industries have the whole field of labour—skilled and unskilled, intelligent and unintelligent, American and foreign, black and white—to draw upon. For its purposes, all are on the same level, and must be kept on the same level.

What a happy circumstance for industry! Here we find the manufacture of the most ingenious products of human skill demanding no skill in the making, able to continue, and able to develop indefinitely without asking or paying for more than the mere ability to lift a hammer or turn a screw or drive a nail. Out of every hundred workers in these industries, ninety are denied the opportunity to give more than that—and this in a country that, having practically closed its doors against fresh supplies of raw labour, is preaching and teaching individualism, the ambition to push ahead, and the shame of staying the rut.

America cannot have it both ways. . . .

Source: Hugh Grant Adams, *An Australian Looks at America: Are Wages Really Higher?* (Sydney, Australia: Cornstalk Publishing Co, 1927), 21–23.

corporations had invested $15.2 billion in foreign countries. Soon the United States became the world's largest creditor nation, reversing its pre–World War I status as a debtor and causing a dramatic shift of power in the world's capital markets. European countries, particularly Germany, needed American capital to finance their economic recovery following World War I. Germany had to rebuild its economy and pay reparations to the Allies; Britain and France had to repay wartime loans. As late as 1930 the Allies still owed the United States $4.3 billion. American political leaders, responding to voters' disenchantment with the cost of the war, rigidly demanded payment. "They hired the money, didn't they?" President Coolidge scoffed.

European countries had difficulty repaying their debts because the United States was maintaining high protective tariffs against foreign-made goods. The Fordney-McCumber Tariff of 1922 and the Hawley-Smoot Tariff of 1930 advanced the long-standing Republican policy of protectionism and economic nationalism. Most American manufacturers favored high tariffs because they feared foreign competition would reduce their profits. But the difficulty of selling goods in the United States hindered European nations' efforts to pay off their debts in dollars.

In 1924, at the prodding of the United States, the nations of France, Great Britain, and Germany joined with the United States in a plan to promote European financial stability. The Dawes Plan (named for Charles G. Dawes, the Chicago banker who negotiated the agreement) offered Germany substantial loans from American banks and a reduction in the amount of reparations owed to the Allies. But the Dawes Plan did not provide a permanent solution because the international economic system was inherently unstable. It depended on the flow of American capital to Germany, reparations payments from Germany to the Allies, and the repayment of the Allies' debts to the United States. If the outflow of capital from the United States were to slow or stop, the international financial structure could collapse.

Foreign Policy in the 1920s

American efforts to shore up the international economy belie the common view of U.S. foreign affairs as **isolationist** in the interwar period—as representing a time when the United States, disillusioned after World War I, willfully retreated from involvement in the rest of the world. In fact the United States played an active role in world affairs during this period. Expansion into new markets was fundamental to the prosperity of the 1920s. U.S. officials ardently sought a stable international order to facilitate American investments in Latin American, European, and Asian markets.

The United States continued the quest for peaceful ways to dominate the Western Hemisphere both economically and diplomatically but retreated slightly from military intervention in Latin America. U.S. troops withdrew from the Dominican Republic in 1924 but remained in Nicaragua almost continuously from 1912 to 1933 and in Haiti from 1915 to 1934. Relations with Mexico remained tense, a legacy of U.S. intervention during the Mexican Revolution (see Chapter 21) and of U.S. resentment over the Mexican government's efforts to wrest control of its oil and mineral deposits away from foreign owners, a policy that particularly alarmed American oil companies.

There was little popular or political support, however, for entangling diplomatic commitments to allies, European or otherwise. The United States never joined the League of Nations or the Court of International Justice (the World Court). International cooperation came through other forums, such as the 1921 Washington Naval Arms Conference. At that meeting the leading naval powers—Britain, the United States, Japan, Italy, and France—agreed to halt construction of large battleships for ten years and to limit their future shipbuilding to a set ratio between the five nations of 5 to 5 to 3 to 1.75 to 1.75, respectively. By placing limits on naval expansion, policymakers hoped to encourage stability in areas like the Far East and to protect the fragile postwar economy from an expensive arms race. A thinly veiled agenda was to contain Japan, whose expansionist tendencies in Asia were alarming other nations.

Seven years later, in a similar spirit of international cooperation, the United States joined other nations in condemning militarism through the Kellogg-Briand Peace Pact. Fifteen nations signed the pact in Paris in 1928; forty-eight more approved it later. The signatories agreed to "condemn recourse to war for the solution of international controversies, and renounce it as an instrument of national policy." U.S. peace groups such as the Women's International League for Peace and Freedom enthusiastically supported the pact, and the U.S. Senate ratified it eighty-five to one. Yet critics complained that it lacked mechanisms for enforcement, calling it nothing more than an "international kiss."

In the end, fervent hopes and pious declarations were no cure for the massive economic, political, and territorial problems created by World War I. U.S. policymakers vacillated, as they would in the 1930s, between wanting to play a larger role in world events and fearing that treaties and responsibilities would limit their ability to act unilaterally. Their diplomatic efforts ultimately proved inadequate to the mounting crises that followed in the wake of the war.

A New National Culture

The 1920s represented an important watershed in the development of a mass national culture. A new emphasis on leisure, consumption, and amusement characterized the era, although their benefits were more accessible to the middle class than to disadvantaged groups. Automobiles, paved roads, the parcel post service, movies, radios, telephones, mass-circulation magazines, brand names, chain stores—all linked mill towns in the southern Piedmont, rural outposts on the Oklahoma plains, and ethnic enclaves on the coasts in an expanding web of national experience. In fact with the exportation of automobiles, radios, and movies to consumers throughout the world, American culture became a global model.

A Consumer Culture

In homes across the country, Americans sat down to a breakfast of Kellogg's corn flakes and toast from a General Electric toaster. Then they got into a Ford Model T to go about their business, perhaps shopping at one of the chain stores that had sprung up across the country, such as Safeway or A&P. In the evening the family gathered to listen to radio programs like *Great Moments in History* or to read the latest issue of the *Saturday Evening Post*; on weekends they might go to see the newest Charlie Chaplin film at the local theater. Millions of Americans, in other words, now shared similar daily experiences.

Yet participation in commercial mass culture was not universal, nor did it necessarily mean total conversion to mainstream values, as is often assumed. The historian Lizabeth Cohen concluded that "Chicago's ethnic workers were not transformed into more Americanized, middle-class people by the objects they consumed. Buying an electric vacuum cleaner did not turn Josef Dobrowolski into *True Story*'s Jim Smith." What is more, the unequal distribution of income limited many consumers' ability to buy the enticing new products. At the height of the nation's prosperity in the 1920s, about 65 percent of families had incomes of less than $2,000 a year, which barely supported a decent standard of living. Poor minority families in particular were isolated from the new consumerism.

Many Americans stretched their incomes by buying on the newly devised installment plan. In those days, "buy now, pay later" for consumer goods was a revolutionary concept. Before World War I most urban families paid cash for everything except a house, but in the 1920s the automobile became such an object of desire that consumers put aside their fears of buying "on time." In 1927 two-thirds of the cars in the United States

were being paid for on the installment plan. Once people saw how easy it was to finance a car, they bought radios, refrigerators, and sewing machines on credit. "A dollar down and a dollar forever," a cynic remarked. By 1929 banks, finance companies, credit unions, and other institutions were lending consumers over $7 billion a year, and consumer lending had become the tenth largest business in the United States.

Many of the new products were household appliances, made feasible by the rapid electrification that had reached 85 percent of American nonfarm households by 1930. Irons and vacuum cleaners were the most popular appliances, followed by phonographs, sewing machines, and washing machines. Radios, whose production increased twenty-five-fold in the 1920s, sold for around $75. One of the most expensive items was a refrigerator, which cost $900 at the beginning of the decade. Technological improvements soon brought the price down to

$180, but many families still had to make do with an old-fashioned icebox, which supplied cooling through blocks of ice delivered to the house.

Because much of the new technology was concentrated in the home, it had a dramatic impact on women's lives, especially prosperous white women. Despite enfranchisement and participation in the work force, the primary role for most women remained that of housewife. Electric appliances made housewives' chores less arduous: plugging in an electric iron was far easier than heating an iron on the stove; using a vacuum cleaner was quicker and easier than wielding a broom and a rug beater. Paradoxically, however, the time women spent on housework did not decline. More middle-class women began to do their own housework and laundry as electric servants replaced human ones. Technology also raised standards of cleanliness so that a man could wear a clean shirt every day instead of just on

Sunday, and a house could be vacuumed daily rather than swept weekly.

Few of the new consumer products could be considered necessities, so the advertising industry spent billions of dollars (in 1929 an average of $15 annually on every man, woman, and child in the United States) to entice consumers to buy their products. Advertisements appealed to people's social aspirations by projecting images of successful and elegant sophisticates who smoked a certain brand of cigarettes or drove a recognizable make of car. Ad writers also sold products by preying on people's insecurities, coming up with a variety of socially unacceptable "diseases," including "office hips," "ashtray breath," and the dreaded "BO" (body odor). After the term *halitosis* was discovered in a British medical journal, many consumers rushed out to buy Listerine mouthwash. Advertising became a big business in the 1920s, accounting for 3 percent of the gross national product, comparable to its share after World War II.

Yet consumers were not merely passive victims. Advertisers recognized that the buying public made choices and struggled to offer messages that appealed to their targeted audiences. In the process they made consumption a cultural ideal for most of the middle class. Character, religion, and social standing, once the main criteria for judging self-worth, became less important than the gratification of personal desires through the acquisition of more and better possessions.

The Automobile Culture

No possession typified the new consumer culture better than the automobile. "Why on earth do you need to study what's changing this country?" a Muncie, Indiana, resident asked sociologists Robert and Helen Lynd. "I can tell you what's happening in just four letters: A-U-T-O!" The showpiece of modern capitalism, the automobile revolutionized the way Americans spent their money and leisure time. In the wake of the automobile, the isolation of rural life broke down. Cars touched so many aspects of American life that the word *automobility* was coined to describe their impact on production methods, the landscape, and American values.

Mass production of cars stimulated the prosperity of the 1920s. Before the introduction of the moving assembly line in 1913, Ford workers took twelve and a half hours to put together an auto; on an assembly line they took only ninety-three minutes. By 1927 Ford was producing a car every twenty-four seconds. Auto sales climbed from 1.5 million in 1921 to 5 million in 1929, a year in which Americans spent $2.58 billion on cars. By the end of the decade, Americans owned about 80 percent of the world's automobiles—an average of one car for every five people.

The success of the auto industry had a ripple effect on the American economy. In 1929, 3.7 million workers owed their jobs to the automobile, either directly or indirectly. Auto production stimulated the steel, petroleum, chemical, rubber, and glass industries. Highway construction became a billion-dollar-a-year enterprise, financed by federal subsidies and state gasoline taxes. Car ownership also spurred the growth of suburbs, contributed to real-estate speculation, and in 1924 spawned the first shopping center, Country Club Plaza in Kansas City. Not even the death of 25,000 people a year in traffic accidents—70 percent of them pedestrians—could dampen America's passion for the automobile.

The auto also changed the way Americans spent their leisure time. They took to the roads, becoming a nation of tourists. The American Automobile Association, founded in 1902, reported that in 1929 about 45 million people—almost a third of the population—took vacations by automobile, patronizing the "autocamps" and tourist cabins that were the forerunners of motels. And like movies and other products of the new mass culture, cars changed the dating patterns of young Americans. Contrary to many parents' views, premarital sex was not invented in the backseat of a Ford, but a Model T offered more privacy and comfort than did the family living room or the front porch and contributed to increased sexual experimentation among the young.

Mass Media and New Patterns of Leisure

Equal in importance to the automobile in transforming American culture were the increasingly significant mass media. Innovations in the movies, radio, and the print media helped to spread common values and attitudes throughout the United States and offered Americans new ways to "spend" their leisure time.

Moving Pictures.   The movie industry probably did more than anything else to disseminate common values and attitudes. In contrast to Europe where cinema developed as an avant-garde, highbrow art form, in America movies were part of popular culture almost from the start. They began around the turn of the century in nickelodeons, where for a nickel the mostly working-class audience could see a one-reel silent film like the spectacularly successful *The Great Train Robbery* (1903). Because the films, mostly comedies and melodramas, were silent, they could be understood by immigrants who did not speak English. Both democratic and highly lucrative, the new medium quickly became popular.

By 1910 the moviemaking industry had concentrated in southern California, which had cheap land, plenty of sunshine, and varied scenery—mountains, deserts, cities, and the Pacific Ocean—within easy reach. Another attraction was Los Angeles's reputation as an antiunion town. By war's end the United States was producing 90 percent of the world's films. Foreign distribution of

The Tramp

Charlie Chaplin did not invent the tragicomic figure of the tramp, but it soon became his screen persona. Chaplin grew up poor in the London slums, but the movies brought him wealth and fame. In 1919 he joined Douglas Fairbanks, Mary Pickford, and D. W. Griffith to form United Artists. Archive Photos.

The Flapper

The flapper phenomenon was not limited to Anglos. This 1921 photograph of a young Mexican American woman named Luisa Ronstadt Espinel shows how American fads and fashions reached into Latino communities across the country.
Arizona Historical Society.

Hollywood films stimulated the market for the material culture so lavishly displayed on the screen.

As directors turned to feature films and began exhibiting them in large, ornate theaters, movies quickly outgrew their working-class audiences and began to appeal to the middle class. Early movie stars—the comedians Buster Keaton, Charlie Chaplin, and Harold Lloyd; Mary Pickford ("America's Sweetheart," though born in Canada); and dashing leading men Douglas Fairbanks, Wallace Reid, and John Gilbert—became national idols who helped to set national trends in clothing and hairstyles. Then a new cultural icon, the **flapper**, burst on the scene to represent emancipated womanhood. Clara Bow was Hollywood's favorite flapper, a bobbed-hair "jazz baby" who rose to stardom almost overnight (see American Lives, "Clara Bow: The

'It' Girl," p. 678). Decked out in short skirt and rolled-down silk stockings, the flapper wore makeup (once assumed to be a sign of sexual availability in lower-class women), smoked, and danced to jazz, flaunting her liberated lifestyle. Like so many cultural icons, the flapper represented only a tiny minority of women. Yet the movies, along with advertising, mass-marketed this symbol of women's emancipation, suggesting it was the norm.

Movies became even more powerful cultural influences with the advent of the "talkies." Warner Brothers' *The Jazz Singer* (1927), starring Al Jolson, was the first feature-length film to offer sound. Two years later all the major studios had made the transition to talkies. By the end of the 1920s, the nation had almost 23,000

CRAZY BLUES

By PERRY BRADFORD

MAMIE SMITH AND HER JAZZ HOUNDS

Get this number for your phonograph on Okeh Record No. 4169

PUBLISHED BY
PERRY BRADFORD
MUSIC PUB. CO.
1547 BROADWAY, N. Y. C.

movie theaters, including elaborate picture palaces built by the studios in major cities. Movie attendance rose from 60 million in 1927 to 90 million in 1930. In two short decades movies had become thoroughly entrenched as the most popular—and probably the most influential—form of urban-based mass media.

Jazz. That the first talkie was *The Jazz Singer* was perhaps no coincidence. Jazz was such an important part of the new mass culture that the 1920s are often referred to as the Jazz Age. An improvisational style whose notes were (and are) rarely written down, jazz originated in the dance halls and bordellos of New Orleans around the turn of the century. A synthesis of African American music forms, such as ragtime and the blues, it also drew on African and European styles. Most of the early jazz musicians were blacks who

brought music that originated in the South to Chicago, New York, and other northern cities. Some of the best-known performers were composer-pianist Ferdinand "Jelly Roll" Morton, trumpeter Louis Armstrong, composer-bandleader Edward "Duke" Ellington, and singer Bessie Smith.

Although Smith was known as the "Empress of the Blues," numerous other women—Ida Cox, Ma Rainey, Mamie Smith, and Ethel Waters among them—also made a name for themselves singing the blues and bringing a modern form of this rural music to a broader audience. While many of their songs described a woman lamenting the man "who done her wrong," others, like "Young Woman's Blues," exuberantly expressed women's enjoyment of sexuality as well as their resilience and desire for personal autonomy in the face of harsh circumstances. As they performed in urban clubs or

Clara Bow: The "It" Girl

When Clara Bow, the "It" Girl of the 1920s, was asked to define what "it" meant, she replied, "I ain't real sure." To most fans "it" was synonymous with sex appeal, but Elinor Glyn, the British writer who coined the phrase, had a more nuanced definition: "To have 'It' the fortunate possessor must have that strange magnetism which attracts both sexes. 'It' is a purely virile quality belonging to a strong character. . . . There must be physical attraction, but beauty is unnecessary. Conceit or self-consciousness destroys 'It' immediately." Whatever "it" was, when Paramount released a movie in 1927 based on the Elinor Glyn novella of the same name and starring Clara Bow, the film grossed $1 million. Soon Bow was receiving almost 35,000 fan letters a month, many addressed simply to "The 'It' Girl, Hollywood U.S.A." In 1927 she was all of twenty-two years old.

The thin plot of the film hardly seems capable of launching a national obsession. Bow played a department store clerk named Betty Lou Spense who is out to catch her rich, handsome boss. He too is smitten, and when he calls on her in her modest home, he finds her minding a friend's baby. However, he jumps to the mistaken conclusion that she is an unmarried mother and propositions her. She is indignant at the insult, but after several plot twists they resolve their differences. In the final scene they kiss on the store owner's yacht, *Itola*, with the embrace obscuring all but the first two letters of the yacht's name. That's right—IT!

"It" was typical of Hollywood's fascination with flapper themes in the 1920s. On screen and off the flapper was emancipated, urban, and young, befitting the worship of youth that was characteristic of the 1920s. The flapper was a working girl with money to spend, time on her hands, and a wardrobe of mass-produced fashions, especially short skirts suitable for dancing and dating. On screen she was sensual but not promiscuous, often marrying the male lead at the film's end. The Hollywood stars Colleen Moore and Louise Brooks also played flapper roles.

Before Bow became indelibly known as the "It" Girl, her studio had tried to promote her as the "Brooklyn Bonfire." The name never stuck, but it revealed her background. Clara Bow was born on July 29, 1905, into an extremely poor family in Brooklyn, New York; her mother was mentally unstable, and her father was often unemployed. She dropped out of school during the eighth grade. The only place she found refuge from her grim family life was at the movies. Like many other young girls, Bow decided that she wanted to be an actress.

Her break came when she won a 1921 "Fame and Fortune" beauty contest sponsored by three movie magazines, which helped her land a bit part in *Beyond the Rainbow* (1922). Her scenes ended up on the cutting-room floor, but they were restored after she became a star. In 1923 Bow won a Hollywood contract, and by 1924 she had made thirteen films, none of which were memorable. Her roles improved when she signed with Paramount in 1925; her performances in *Dancing Mothers* (1926) and *Mantrap* (1926), two movies with Jazz Age themes, led Elinor Glyn to pronounce that Bow had "it" on the screen.

Clara Bow had an amazing presence in her films. On screen she never seemed to stay still. Studio executive B. P. Schulberg called her "the hottest jazz baby in films." A young man who first saw her at age seventeen observed, "I've never taken dope, but it was like a shot of dope when you looked at this girl." The *New York Times* wrote of her performance in *Mantrap*: "She could flirt with a grizzly bear." She had a boyish figure and what one reviewer called "flirt's eyes." She was especially known for her shock of red hair. In the 1920s redheads were thought to be highly sexed. Just as the vamp of the 1910s had dark hair and the typical star of the 1930s was a platinum blonde, the 1920s was the decade of the redhead.

Yet Bow's career lasted less than five years after the success of *It*. Somewhat unstable emotionally, she had several nervous breakdowns. As she once said, "A sex symbol is a heavy load to carry when one is tired, hurt, and bewildered." She was also hurt by scandals in her personal life, including widely publicized affairs with actor Gary Cooper and director Victor Fleming and a legal dispute with a former secretary. Furthermore, like many silent stars, she found the transition to talkies difficult. It was not just her Brooklyn accent—voice lessons could have smoothed that out. Her whole style of acting, which was very emotional and involved constant movement around the set, was not suited to the early days of sound recording, when an actor had to stay close to a stationary microphone to speak dialogue.

In 1931 Bow announced that she was leaving Hollywood to live with Rex Bell, a Nevada rancher whom

Twenties Sex Symbol
Clara Bow was not the girl next door, as this seductive film still from Her Wedding Night
(1930) confirms. Culver Pictures.

she married later that year. She returned briefly to make two films before declaring "I've had enough" in 1933. She devoted her time to marriage and the two sons she and Bell had in 1934 and 1938, but her emotional instability made it hard for her to find happiness, and she and Bell eventually separated. She died in Los Angeles in 1965, long before her films had become cult classics. On seeing *It* for the first time in 1987, sixty years after its release, her son said, "If I ever saw Mother, I saw her in that movie. The tremendous facial expression. . . . It brought back so vividly what she was like." But it also reinforced the deep

gulf between the on-screen charisma of the "It" Girl and Bow's fragile off-screen persona.

Toward the end of her life, Bow reflected on the differences between Hollywood in the 1920s and the 1960s in a way that makes clear where her sympathies lay: "We had individuality. We did as we pleased. We stayed up late. We dressed the way we wanted. Today stars are sensible and end up with better health. But we had more fun."

makeshift rural honky-tonks, showing off elaborate gowns as well as their musical talent, blues women offered a glamorous image of successful black womanhood that belied the difficult lives that many of them experienced. Novelist Ralph Ellison expressed their importance to the black community in his description of Bessie Smith, noting that she "might have been a 'blues Queen' to the society at large, but within the tighter Negro community where the blues were a total way of life, and major expression of an attitude toward life, she was a priestess, a celebrant who affirmed the values of the group and man's ability to deal with chaos."

Phonograph records increased the appeal of jazz and the blues by capturing its spontaneity and distributing it to a wide audience; jazz, in turn, boosted the infant recording industry. Soon this uniquely American art form had caught on in Europe, especially in France. That jazz, which often expressed black dissent in the face of mainstream white values, also appealed to white audiences signifies the role that African Americans played in shaping the contours of American popular culture.

Journalism and the Radio.   Other forms of mass media also helped to establish national standards of taste and behavior. In 1922 ten magazines claimed a circulation of at least 2.5 million, including the *Saturday Evening Post*, the *Ladies' Home Journal*, *Collier's Weekly*, and *Good Housekeeping*. *Reader's Digest*, *Time*, and the *New Yorker*, still found today in homes throughout the country, all started publication in the 1920s. Tabloid newspapers, which were half the size of standard papers and highlighted crime, sports, comics, and scandals, also became part of the national scene. Thanks to syndicated newspaper columns and features, people across the United States could read the same articles. They could also read the same books, preselected by a board of expert judges for the Book-of-the-Month Club, founded in 1926.

The newest instrument of mass culture, professional radio broadcasting, took off on November 2, 1920, when station KDKA in Pittsburgh carried the presidential election returns. By 1929 about 40 percent of the nation's households owned a radio. More than 800 stations, most affiliated with the Columbia Broadcasting Service (CBS) or the National Broadcasting Company (NBC), were on the air. Unlike European networks, which were government monopolies, American radio stations operated for profit. Though the federal government licensed the stations, their revenue came primarily from advertisers and corporate sponsors.

Americans loved radio. They listened avidly to the World Series and other sports events and to variety shows sponsored by advertisers. One of the most popular radio shows of all time, *Amos 'n' Andy* premiered on NBC in 1928, featuring two white actors playing stereotypical black characters. Soon fractured phrases from *Amos 'n' Andy*, such as "check and double check," became part of everyday speech. So many people "tuned in" (another new phrase of the 1920s) that the country seemed to come to a halt during popular programs—a striking example of the pervasiveness of mass media.

Leisure and Sports.   The automobile and new forms of entertainment like movies and radio pointed to a new emphasis on leisure. As the workweek shrank and some workers won the right to paid vacations, Americans had more time and energy to spend on recreation. Like so much else in the 1920s, leisure became increasingly tied to consumption and mass culture. Public recreation flourished as cities and suburbs built baseball diamonds, tennis courts, swimming pools, and golf courses. Americans not only played sports but had the time and money to watch professional athletes perform in increasingly commercialized enterprises. They could see a game in a comfortable stadium, listen to it on the radio, or catch highlights in the newsreel at the local movie theater.

Americans reveled vicariously in the accomplishments of the superb athletes of the 1920s. Baseball continued to be the national pastime, drawing as many as 10 million fans a year. Tarnished in 1919 by the "Black Sox" scandal, in which some Chicago White Sox players took bribes to throw the World Series, baseball bounced back with the rise of stars like Babe Ruth of the New York Yankees. African Americans, however, had different heroes from whites. Excluded from the white teams, black athletes like Satchel Paige played in Negro leagues formed in the 1920s.

Thanks to the media's attention, the popularity of sports figures rivaled that of movie stars. In football Red Grange of the University of Illinois was a major star, while Jack Dempsey and Gene Tunney attracted a loyal following in boxing and Bobby Jones helped to popularize golf. Bill Tilden dominated men's tennis, while Helen Wills and Suzanne Lenglen reigned in the women's game. The decade's best-known swimmer was Gertrude Ederle, who crossed the English Channel in 1926 in just over fourteen hours.

The decade's most popular hero, however, was neither an athlete nor a movie star. On May 20, 1927, aviator Charles Lindbergh, flying the small plane *The Spirit of St. Louis*, made the first successful nonstop solo flight between New York and Paris, a distance of 3,610 miles, in $33\frac{1}{2}$ hours (see New Technology, "Aviation," p. 682). Returning home to tickertape parades and effusive celebrations, he became *Time* magazine's first Man of the Year in 1928. Lindbergh captivated the nation by combining his mastery of the new technology (the airplane) with the pioneer virtues of individualism, self-reliance, and hard work. He symbolized Americans' desire to

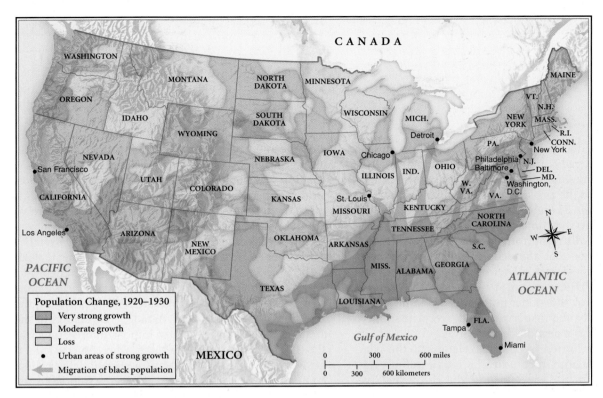

MAP 23.1 The Shift from Rural to Urban Population, 1920–1930

Despite the increasingly urban tone of modern America after 1920, regional patterns of population growth and decline were far from uniform. Cities in the South and West grew most dramatically as southern farmers moved to more promising areas with familiar climates. An important factor in the growth of northern cities, such as New York and Chicago, was the migration of southern blacks set in motion by World War I (see Map 22.3).

For more help analyzing this map, see the Online Study Guide at bedfordstmartins.com/henretta.

enjoy the benefits of modern industrialism without renouncing their traditional values.

Dissenting Values and Cultural Conflict

As movies, radio, advertising, and mass-production industries helped to transform the country into a modern, cosmopolitan nation, many Americans welcomed them as exciting evidence of progress. But others were uneasy. Flappers dancing to jazz, youthful sexual experimentation in the back of Ford Model Ts, hints of a decline in religious values: these harbingers of a new era worried more tradition-minded folk. In the nation's cities the powerful presence of immigrants and African Americans suggested the waning of white Protestant cultural dominance. Beneath the clichés of the Roaring Twenties were deeply felt tensions that surfaced in conflicts over immigration, religion, Prohibition, and race relations.

The Rise of Nativism

Tensions between the fast-paced city and the traditional, small-town values of the country partially explain the decade's conflicts. As farmers struggled with severe economic problems, rural communities lost residents to the cities at an alarming rate. The 1920 census revealed that for the first time in the nation's history city people outnumbered rural people: 52 percent of the population lived in urban areas, compared with just 28 percent in 1870. Though the census exaggerated the extent of urbanization—its guidelines classified towns with only 2,500 people as cities—there was no mistaking the trend (Map 23.1). By 1929 ninety-three cities had populations over 100,000. The mass media generally reflected the cosmopolitan values of these urban centers, and many old-stock Americans worried that the cities and the immigrants who clustered there would soon dominate the culture.

Yet the polarities between city and country should not be overstated. Rural and small-town people were affected

Aviation

Charles Lindbergh captivated an American public that was already captivated by aviation. In the 1910s and 1920s, many Americans embraced this new technology, investing in the airplane almost utopian hopes for a new world order. There was something about seeing an airplane for the first time that called forth these feelings—it was so different from anything that anyone had ever seen before that they could only describe it in miraculous, almost mystical, terms. As a Chicago minister said of his first experience at an airshow, "Never have I seen such a look of wonder in the faces of a multitude. From the gray-haired man to the child, everyone seemed to feel that it was a new day in their lives."

World War I acted as a great accelerator to the aviation industry in both its commercial and its military applications. When the war ended, a glut of inexpensive training planes became available, and these craft became the vehicles of choice for the barnstorming pilots of the 1920s. With their open cockpits, canvas wings, and rudimentary controls, these planes were tricky and often dangerous to fly, but that did not stop the pilots from spreading the "winged gospel" through stunts, shows, and air races. These "birdmen"—and a fair number of "birdwomen"—brought aviation to towns and hamlets all across America. Said Amelia Earhart, who learned to fly in 1921, "Not to have had a ride in an airplane today is like not having heard the radio."

Hollywood discovered aviation in the 1920s, cranking out dozens of aviation-related films whose plots, often on World War I themes, featured production thrillers like dogfights and fiery crashes. Flying became a popular hobby for Hollywood celebrities like Cecil B. DeMille and Colleen Moore, which further added to its allure. In newspapers and tabloids across the country, aviation was front-page news precisely because aviation stories, especially crashes (of which there were many, given the technologically unsophisticated equipment of the time), sold papers. So did coverage of long-distance record-setting flights. When Admiral Richard Byrd became the first person to fly over the North Pole in 1926, he became a national hero.

It took railroads half a century to complete a cycle of pioneering, merger, regulation, and stabilization; the airlines did it in just over a decade, culminating in the 1938 Civil Aeronautics Act. An important milestone was the 1925 Contract Air Mail Act, whereby the federal government awarded contracts for airmail delivery on a competitive basis. These contracts were essential to the emergence of modern airlines because they offered a guaranteed profit at a time when neither the technology nor the demand existed for commercial transport of passengers. Charles Lindbergh had been both a stunt pilot and an airmail pilot in Minnesota before his record-breaking flight.

Lindbergh's transatlantic solo set off a boom—often called the Lindbergh boom—that saw the number of airlines expand from sixteen in 1927 to forty-seven in 1930. But commercial air travel was still very much in its infancy. In 1929 Lindbergh joined other investors to

by the same forces that influenced urban residents. Much of the new technology—especially automobiles—enhanced rural life. Country people, like their urban counterparts, were tempted by the materialistic new values proclaimed on the radio, in magazines, and in movies. Moreover, many urban residents—immigrant Catholics, for example—were just as alarmed about declining moral standards as rural Protestants were. A simplified urban-rural dichotomy misrepresents the complexity of the decade's cultural and ethnic conflicts.

Immigration Restriction. These conflicts often centered on the question of growing racial and ethnic pluralism. When native-born white Protestants—both rural and city dwellers—looked at their communities in 1920, they saw a nation that had changed dramatically in only forty years. During that time more than 23 million immigrants had come to America, many of them Jews or Catholics, most of peasant stock. Senator William Bruce of Maryland branded them "indigestible lumps" in the "national stomach," implying that mainstream society could not absorb their large numbers and foreign customs. This sentiment, termed **nativism**, was widely shared.

Nativist animosity fueled a new drive against immigration. The Chinese had been excluded in 1882, and Theodore Roosevelt had negotiated a "gentleman's agreement" to limit Japanese immigration in 1908. Yet efforts to restrict European immigration did not meet with much success until after World War I, which had heightened

customers.) TAT was not that much more efficient than the fastest train, however, and was much more expensive, so it never turned much of a profit despite its nickname of "the Lindbergh line." The airline was soon absorbed into Trans World Airlines (TWA). In fact by the early 1930s, the outlines of the other major airline dynasties, including United, Eastern, and Northwest, were firmly in place. These companies would dominate the domestic and, in the case of Pan American, the international markets until airline deregulation in the 1970s.

Aviation technology took a quantum leap forward with the introduction in 1936 of the DC-3. With its seating capacity of twenty-one passengers, the DC-3 offered airlines the possibility of generating profits through passenger travel rather than being dependent on airmail contracts. The DC-3, manufactured by the Douglas Aircraft Company, proved to be the most influential piece of aircraft in history as well as one of the most dependable. Hundreds of its models are still flying today.

found Transcontinental Air Transport (TAT), which promised passengers coast-to-coast passage in forty-eight hours by flying during the day and taking the train at night. (Night flying, especially over mountainous regions, was considered too dangerous a risk to paying

suspicion of "hyphenated" Americans. During the Red Scare, nativists had played up the supposed association of the immigrants with radicalism and labor unrest, charging that southern and eastern European Catholics and Jews were incapable of becoming true Americans.

In response Congress passed an emergency bill in 1921, limiting the number of immigrants to 3 percent of the foreign born from each national group as represented in the 1910 census. President Woodrow Wilson refused to sign it, but the bill was reintroduced and passed under Warren Harding. In 1924 a more restrictive measure, the National Origins Act, reduced immigration until 1927 to 2 percent of each nationality's representation in the 1890 census—which had included relatively small numbers of people from southeastern Europe and Russia. After 1927

(later postponed to 1929) the law set a cap of 150,000 immigrants per year and continued to tie admission into the United States to the quota system. Japanese immigrants were excluded entirely. While limiting all immigration, the act clearly privileged older immigrant groups whose "national origins" were northern and western European at the expense of more recent southern and eastern Europeans. By placing Japanese immigrants outside the quota system, the act also drew sharp racial lines as to who was welcome to American shores (see American Voices, "Kazuo Kawai: A Foreigner in America," p. 686).

Puerto Rico provided a different source of immigration. After the Jones Act of 1917 conferred U.S. citizenship on Puerto Ricans, they could go to and from the mainland without restriction. Most of the movement

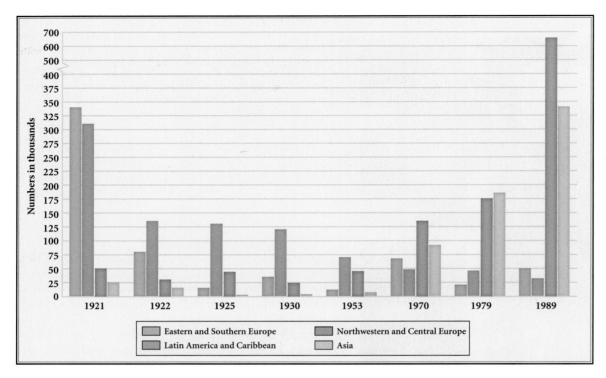

FIGURE 23.1 American Immigration after World War I
Legislation reflecting nativism slowed the influx of immigrants after 1920, as did the dislocations brought on by depression and war in the 1930s and 1940s. Note the higher rate of non-European immigration since the 1970s.

was to New York, which was only a four-day sea voyage away. Thriving Puerto Rican communities, or *colonias*, sprang up in East Harlem and the Greenpoint section of Brooklyn. As it was for other migrants, the lure of New York City was primarily economic, and Puerto Ricans took jobs that had previously gone to European immigrants. But when hard times hit in the 1930s, the flow of Puerto Ricans stopped temporarily.

One remaining loophole in immigration law permitted unrestricted immigration from countries in the Western Hemisphere. This source became increasingly significant over the years (Figure 23.1), as Mexicans and Central and South Americans crossed the border to fill jobs made available by the cutoff of immigration from Europe and Asia. Over 1 million Mexicans entered the United States between 1900 and 1930, including a wave who crossed the border after the Mexican Revolution of 1910 and another who entered during the labor shortages of World War I. Nativists and representatives of organized labor, who viewed Mexican immigrants as unwanted competition, lobbied Congress to close the loophole but were unsuccessful until the 1930s when the economic devastation of the Great Depression minimized the need for immigrant labor.

The New Klan.   Another expression of nativism in the 1920s was the revival of the Ku Klux Klan. Shortly after

the premiere of *Birth of a Nation* in 1915, a popular film glorifying the Reconstruction-era Ku Klux Klan, a group of southerners had gathered on Stone Mountain outside Atlanta to revive the racist organization. Taking as its motto "Native, white, Protestant supremacy," the modern Klan appealed to both urban and rural folk, though its largest "klaverns" were in urban areas. Spreading out from its southern base, the group found significant support in the Far West, the Southwest, and the Midwest, especially Oregon, Indiana, and Oklahoma. Unlike the Klan that was founded after the Civil War, the Klan of the 1920s did not limit its harassment to blacks; Catholics and Jews were just as likely to be its targets. Many of its tactics, however, were the same: arson, physical intimidation, and economic boycotts (Map 23.2). The new Klan also turned to politics, succeeding in electing hundreds of Klansmen to public office. At the height of its power in 1925, the Klan had over 3 million members— including a strong contingent of women who pursued a political agenda that combined racism, nativism, and equal rights for white Protestant women.

After 1925 the Klan declined rapidly. Internal rivalries and the disclosure of rampant corruption hurt the group's image. Especially damaging was the revelation that Grand Dragon David Stephenson, the Klan's national leader, had kidnapped and sexually assaulted his former secretary, driving her to suicide. And the passage

Patrolling the Texas Border

These Border Patrol officers in Laredo, Texas, in 1926 were deputized to stop illegal immigration from Mexico. Their guns, military uniforms, and stern expressions did not present a warm welcome to immigrants arriving from south of the border.
University of Texas at Austin.

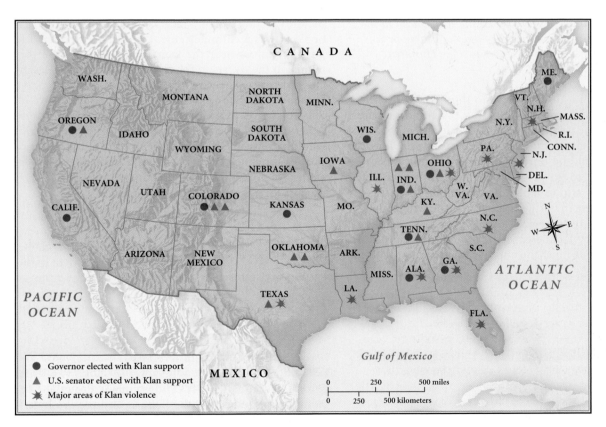

MAP 23.2 Ku Klux Klan Politics and Violence in the 1920s

Unlike the Reconstruction-era Klan, the Klan of the 1920s was geographically dispersed, achieving substantial strength in the West and Midwest. Although the Klan is often thought of as a rural movement, some of its strongest "klaverns" were in such cities as Chicago, Los Angeles, Atlanta, and Detroit. The organization's violence included vigilante acts, but small Klan riots also erupted in many communities where ethnic tensions led to confrontations between Klansmen and their opponents.

Kazuo Kawai

A Foreigner in America

Before the 1920s the laws regulating immigration from Asia contained more loopholes for the Japanese than the Chinese. As a result there were approximately 110,000 Japanese living in the United States in 1920. Asian immigrants' experience of prejudice was much sharper than that of Europeans; in California, for example, the Alien Land Law of 1913 barred foreign-born Japanese from purchasing land or leasing it for more than three years. At the same time the experiences of Japanese immigrants such as Kazuo Kawai echoed the problems that many young ethnic Americans faced in the 1920s as they recognized that they did not belong in the old country but were not accepted as "One Hundred Percent Americans."

Then, for the first time, I began to think about my trip to Japan. I found myself wondering if I could prepare myself for some work there. . . . I began to feel that no matter for what position I prepared myself for in America, I would be unrecognized and handicapped. I would be able to go just so high and no higher. But thinking of my trip to Japan, I realized that there was a nation, complete in itself, great, wonderful, with a glorious future, where every position from the bottom to the top was filled by Japanese. There, I would meet no cool unrecognition. If I had the ability, I could go to the top,

and set the limit myself. . . . For the first time, I felt myself becoming identified with Japan, and began to realize that I was a Japanese. But there was another side. Was I a Japanese? What could I be able to do in Japan? I couldn't read or write Japanese. I didn't know any of the customs or traditions of Japan. How could I do anything there? I realized with a shock that I was not a Japanese. Thus, at the same time that I came to realize that I was a Japanese, I came to realize also that I was not a Japanese. Where did I belong? I realized with a pang that I was a "man without a country." . . . [I]t hurt because I couldn't say: "This is my own, my native land." What was my native land? Japan? True, I was born there. But it had seemed a queer, foreign land to me when I visited it. America? I had, until now, thought so. I had even told my father once that even in case of war between Japan and America, I would consider America as my country. In language, in thought, in ideals, in custom, in everything, I was American. But America wouldn't have me. She wouldn't recognize me in high school. She put the pictures of those of my race at the tail end of the year book. (I was a commencement speaker, so they had to put my picture near the front.) She won't let me play tennis on the courts in the city parks of Los Angeles, by city ordinance. She won't give me service when I go to a barber's shop. She won't let me own a house to live in. She won't give me a job, unless it is a menial one that no American wants. I thought I was American, but America wouldn't have me. Once I was American, but America made a foreigner out of me—not a Japanese, but a foreigner—a foreigner to any country, for I am just as much a foreigner to Japan as to America.

Source: Stanford Survey of Race Relations (Stanford, CA: Stanford University, 1924), Hoover Institute Archives.

---

of the National Origins Act in 1924 reduced the nativist fervor, robbing the Klan of its most potent issue.

Legislating Values: The Scopes Trial and Prohibition

Other cultural tensions erupted over religion. The debate between modernist and fundamentalist Protestants, which had been simmering since the 1890s (see Chapter 19), came to a boil in the 1920s. Modernists, or liberal Protestants, tried to reconcile religion with Charles Dar-

win's theory of evolution and recent technological and scientific discoveries. **Fundamentalists** clung to a literal interpretation of the Bible. Most major Protestant denominations, especially the Baptists and the Presbyterians, experienced heated internal conflicts over these issues. However, the most conspicuous evangelical figures came from outside mainstream denominations. Popular preachers like Billy Sunday and Aimee Semple McPherson used revivals, storefront churches, and open-air preaching to popularize their own blends of charismatic fundamentalism and traditional values.

Ku Klux Klan Women Parade in Washington, D.C.

The Ku Klux Klan was so well integrated into the daily life of some white Protestants that one woman from rural Indiana remembered her time in the KKK in the 1920s as "just a celebration . . . a way of growing up." Perhaps as many as 500,000 women joined the Women of the Ku Klux Klan (WKKK) in the 1920s, including these women who paraded down Pennsylvania Avenue in Washington, D.C., in 1928. National Archives at College Park, MD.

For more help analyzing this image, see the ONLINE STUDY GUIDE at **bedfordstmartins.com/henretta.**

The Scopes Trial. Religious controversy soon entered the political arena when fundamentalists, worried about increasing secularism and declining morality, turned to the law to shore up their vision of a righteous Protestant nation. Some states enacted legislation to block the teaching of evolution in the schools. In 1925, for instance, Tennessee passed a law declaring that "it shall be unlawful . . . to teach any theory that denies the story of the Divine creation of man as taught in the Bible, and to teach instead that man has descended from a lower order of animals." In a test case involving John T. Scopes, a high school biology teacher in Dayton, Tennessee, the fledgling American Civil Liberties Union (ACLU) challenged the constitutionality of that law. Clarence

Darrow, the famous criminal lawyer, defended Scopes; the spellbinding orator William Jennings Bryan, three-time presidential candidate and ardent fundamentalist, was the most prominent member of the prosecution's team.

The Scopes trial was quickly dubbed the "monkey trial," referring both to Darwin's theory that human beings and primates share a common ancestor and to the circus atmosphere in the courtroom. In July 1925 more than 100 journalists crowded the sweltering courthouse in Dayton, Tennessee, giving massive publicity to the knotty questions of faith and scientific theory that the trial addressed. The jury took only eight minutes to deliver its verdict: guilty. Though the Tennessee Supreme Court later overturned the conviction on a technicality,

Scopes Trial

As this picture of a stall selling antievolution material in Dayton, Tennessee, suggests, the Scopes trial in 1925 became a focus of the antievolution movement. Pitting the old-time religion of rural America against modern values, the trial symbolized much of the cultural conflict of the 1920s and demonstrated the continued importance of religion to many Americans. Corbis-Bettmann.

the reversal prevented further appeals of the case, and the controversial law remained on the books for more than thirty years. Historically, the trial symbolizes the conflict between the two competing value systems, cosmopolitan and traditional, that clashed in the 1920s. It suggests that despite the period's image as a frivolous and decadent time, traditional religious values of spirituality and morality continued to matter deeply to many Americans.

Prohibition. Like the dispute over evolution, Prohibition involved the power of the state to enforce social values. Americans did drink less overall after passage of the Eighteenth Amendment, which took effect in January of 1920 (see Chapter 22). Yet more than any other issue, Prohibition gave the decade its reputation as the Roaring Twenties. In major cities, whose ethnic populations had always opposed Prohibition, noncompliance was widespread. People imitated rural moonshiners by distilling "bathtub gin." Illegal saloons called **speakeasies** sprang up everywhere—more than 30,000 of them in New York City alone. Liquor smugglers operated with ease along borders and coastlines. Organized crime, already a presence in major cities, supplied a ready-made distribution network for the bootleg liquor, using the "noble experiment," as Prohibition was called, to entrench itself more deeply in city politics. Said the decade's most notorious gangster, Al Capone, "Everybody calls me a racketeer. I call myself a businessman. When I sell liquor, it's bootlegging. When my patrons serve it on a silver tray on Lake Shore Drive, it's hospitality."

By the middle of the decade, Prohibition was clearly failing. Government appropriations for its enforcement were woefully inadequate; the few highly publicized raids hardly made a dent in the liquor trade. Forces for repeal—the "wets," as opposed to the "drys," who continued to support the Eighteenth Amendment—began the long process to obtain the necessary votes in Congress and state legislatures to amend the Constitution once more. The wets argued that Prohibition had undermined respect for the law and had seriously impinged on individuals' liberty. The onset of the Great Depression hastened the repeal process, as politicians began to see alcohol production as a way to create jobs and prop up the faltering economy. On December 5, 1933, the Eighteenth Amendment was repealed. Ironically, drinking became more socially acceptable, though not necessarily more widespread, than it had been before the experiment began.

Intellectual Crosscurrents

The most articulate and embittered dissenters of the 1920s were writers and intellectuals disillusioned by the horrors of World War I and the crass materialism of the new consumer culture. Some artists were so repelled by what they saw as the complacent, moralistic, and anti-intellectual tone of American life that they settled in Europe—some temporarily, like the novelists Ernest Hemingway and F. Scott Fitzgerald, others permanently, like writer Gertrude Stein. Prominent African American artists, such as dancer Josephine Baker and writer

Ignoring Prohibition

Despite their popularity, speakeasies were rarely drawn or photographed; after all, they were supposed to be private clubs tucked away beyond the reach of the law. Fancy hotels were unable to compete with speakeasies once their bars were shut down, and many went out of business in the 1920s. But John Sloan's 1928 painting shows the rich enjoying themselves at New York's posh Lafayette Hotel. It is likely that these gentlemen and ladies had flasks concealed somewhere in their evening finery.

John Sloan, *The Lafayette*, 1928, Metropolitan Museum of Art, New York. Gift of Friends of John Sloan, 1929 (28.18).

Langston Hughes, sought temporary escape from racism in France. The poet T. S. Eliot, who left the United States before the war, ultimately became a British citizen. His despairing poem *The Waste Land* (1922), with its images of a fragmented civilization in ruins after the war, influenced a generation of writers.

Other writers also made powerful statements against war and contemporary culture, including John Dos Passos, whose first novel, *The Three Soldiers* (1921), was inspired by the war, and whose *1919* (1932), the second volume in his *USA* trilogy, railed against the obscenity of "Mr. Wilson's war." Ernest Hemingway's novels *In Our Time* (1924), *The Sun Also Rises* (1926), and *A Farewell to Arms* (1929) also powerfully described the dehumanizing consequences and the futility of war. In 1925 F. Scott Fitzgerald published *The Great Gatsby*, which showed the corrosive consequences of the mindless pursuit of wealth.

But the artists and writers who migrated to Europe, particularly Paris, were not simply a "lost generation" fleeing America. They were also drawn to Paris as the cultural and artistic capital of the world and a beacon of modernism. Paris, as Gertrude Stein put it, was "where the twentieth century was happening." Indeed, the **modernist movement**, which was marked by skepticism and technical experimentation in literature, art, and music, invigorated American writing both abroad and at home. Many American writers, whether they settled in Paris or remained in their home country, joined the movement, which had begun before the war as intellectuals reacted with excitement to the cultural and social changes that science, industrialization, and urbanization had brought.

In the 1920s the business culture and political corruption of the Harding years caused intellectuals to cast a more critical eye on American society. One of the sharpest critics, the Baltimore journalist H. L. Mencken, directed his mordant wit against mass culture, small-town America with its guardians of public morals, and the *booboisie,* his contemptuous term for the middle class. In the *American Mercury,* the journal he founded in 1922, Mencken championed writers like Sherwood Anderson, Sinclair Lewis, and Theodore Dreiser, who satirized the provincialism of American society.

The literature of the 1920s was rich and varied. Poetry enjoyed a renaissance in the works of Robert Frost, Wallace Stevens, Marianne Moore, and William Carlos Williams. Edith Wharton won a Pulitzer Prize—the first woman so honored—for *The Age of Innocence* (1920). Influenced by Freudian psychology, William Faulkner achieved his first critical success with *The Sound and the Fury* (1929), set in the fictional Mississippi county of Yoknapatawpha, where inhabitants clung to the values of the old agrarian South as they struggled to adjust to modern industrial capitalism. Playwright Eugene O'Neill showed the influence of Freudian psychology in his experimental plays, including *The Hairy Ape* (1922) and *Desire Under the Elms* (1924). Although both Faulkner and O'Neill went on to produce additional major works in the 1930s, on the whole the creative energy of the literary renaissance of the 1920s did not survive into the 1930s. The Great Depression, social and ideological unrest, and the rise of totalitarianism would reshape the intellectual landscape.

Harlem Renaissance. A different kind of cultural affirmation took place in the African American community of Harlem in the 1920s. In the words of the Reverend Adam Clayton Powell Sr., pastor of the influential Abyssinian Baptist Church, Harlem loomed as "the symbol of liberty and the Promised Land to Negroes everywhere." The migration of African Americans out of the South and into the cities during the war years had continued into the 1920s, helping to make Harlem in particular a vital place that attracted talented artists and writers. Here they created the Harlem Renaissance, which broke with older genteel traditions of black literature to reclaim a cultural identity with African roots. Alain Locke, editor of the anthology *The New Negro* (1926), summed up the movement when he stated that, through art, "Negro life is seizing its first chances for group expression and self-determination."

The Harlem Renaissance championed racial pride and cultural identity in the midst of white society. The poet Langston Hughes, who became a leading exponent of the Harlem Renaissance, captured its affirmative spirit when he asserted, "I am a Negro—and beautiful." Authors such as Claude McKay, Jean Toomer, Jessie

The Harlem Renaissance
The Crisis, *edited by W. E. B. Du Bois, was the magazine of the National Association for the Advancement of Colored People (NAACP). This 1929 cover suggests the cultural and political awakenings associated with the Harlem Renaissance.*
Henry Lee Moon Library and Civil Rights Archive, NAACP, Washington, DC.

Fauset, and Zora Neale Hurston explored the black experience and represented the "**New Negro**" in fiction. Countee Cullen and Langston Hughes turned to poetry, and Augusta Savage used sculpture to draw attention to black accomplishments. Their production of creative work showed the ongoing African American struggle to find a way, as W. E. B. Du Bois put it, "to be both a Negro and an American."

The artistic outpouring encouraged a wide range of creative expression. Jean Toomer, a writer passionately committed to black self-expression, wrote the influential novel *Cane* in 1923. With its poems, sketches, and stories about a northern black's discovery of the rural black South, it inspired other African American artists and writers. Langston Hughes drew on the black artistic forms of blues and jazz in *The Weary Blues* (1926), a groundbreaking collection of poems. Considered the most original black poet and the most representative African American writer of the time, Hughes also wrote novels, plays, and essays. Zora Neale Hurston, born in

Florida to a family of poor tenant farmers, attended Howard University in Washington, D.C., and won a scholarship to study anthropology at Barnard College in New York City. She spent a decade collecting folklore in the South and the Caribbean and incorporated that material into her short stories and novels. Her genius for storytelling won her acclaim.

The vitality of the Harlem Renaissance was short-lived. Although the NAACP's magazine *The Crisis* was a forum for the Harlem writers, the black middle class and the intellectual elite in Harlem were relatively small and could not support the group's efforts. Its main audience consisted of white intellectuals and philanthropists, and many writers were ambivalent about depending on white patronage as they struggled to attain an authentic voice in their fiction. Langston Hughes became disillusioned with his white patron when she withdrew support as he began to write about common black people in Kansas and New York rather than keeping with African themes.

During the Jazz Age, when Harlem was in vogue, the publishing industry courted its writers, but the stock market crash of 1929 brought that interest to a sudden end. The movement waned in the 1930s as the depression deepened. Nonetheless, the writers of the Harlem Renaissance would influence a future generation of black writers when their works were rediscovered by black intellectuals during the civil rights movement of the 1960s.

Marcus Garvey and the UNIA.   Although the Harlem Renaissance had little impact on the masses of African Americans, other movements built racial pride and challenged white political and cultural hegemony. The most successful was the Universal Negro Improvement Association (UNIA), which championed black separatism under the leadership of the Jamaican-born Marcus Garvey. Based in Harlem, the UNIA was the black working class's first mass movement. At its height it claimed 4 million followers, many of whom were recent migrants to northern cities. Like several nineteenth-century reformers, Marcus Garvey urged blacks to return to Africa because, he reasoned, blacks would never be treated justly in countries ruled by whites. Although he did not anticipate a massive migration, he did envision a strong black Africa that could use its power to protect blacks everywhere. Garvey's wife, Amy Jacques Garvey, appealed to black women by combining black nationalism with an emphasis on women's contributions to culture and politics.

The UNIA grew rapidly in the early 1920s. It published a newspaper called *Negro World* and undertook extensive business ventures to support black enterprise. The most ambitious project, the Black Star Line steamship company, was supposed to ferry cargo between the West Indies and the United States and take African Americans back to Africa. Irregularities in fund-raising for the project, however, led to Garvey's conviction for mail fraud in

1925, and he was sentenced to five years in prison. President Coolidge commuted his sentence in 1927, but Garvey was deported to Jamaica. Without his charismatic leadership, the movement collapsed.

Cultural Clash in the Election of 1928

The works of the lost generation and the Harlem Renaissance touched only a small minority of Americans in the 1920s, but emotionally charged issues like Prohibition, fundamentalism, and nativism eventually spilled over into national politics. The Democratic Party, which attracted both rural Protestants in the South and the West and ethnic minorities in northern cities, was especially vulnerable to the cultural conflicts of the time. The 1924 Democratic National Convention had revealed an intensely polarized party, split between the urban machines and the rural wing.

In 1928 the urban wing held sway and succeeded in nominating New York's Governor Alfred E. Smith, a descendant of Irish immigrants and a product of Tammany Hall. Proud of his background, Smith adopted "The Sidewalks of New York" as his campaign song. His candidacy troubled many voters, however. His heavy New York accent, his brown derby, and his colorful style highlighted his urban, ethnic, working-class origins, and his early career in Tammany Hall suggested incorrectly that he was little more than a cog in the machine. Smith's stand on Prohibition—although he promised to enforce it, he wanted it repealed—alienated even more voters.

An equally serious handicap, however, was his religion. In 1928 most Protestants were not ready for a Catholic president. Although Smith insisted that his religion would not interfere with his duties as president, his perceived allegiance to Rome cost him the support of Democrats and Republicans alike. Protestant clergymen, who already opposed Smith because he supported the repeal of Prohibition, led the drive against him. "No Governor can kiss the papal ring and get within gunshot of the White House," declared one Methodist bishop.

Smith's candidacy met with much opposition, but for his supporters he embodied a new America. Throughout the decade, attacks on immigrants, Catholics, and Jews had repeatedly labeled them as unwelcome outsiders. Ethnic and religious leaders and communities had vehemently countered these criticisms by offering a more inclusive vision of citizenship. One Catholic bishop summed it up neatly in 1921, stating that "National aspirations constitute Americanism. We are the blend of all the peoples of the world, and I think we are much the better for that. Americanism is not a matter of birth, Americanism is a matter of faith, of consecration to the ideals of America." That Al Smith, a man of Catholic immigrant stock, could be the Democratic Party's nominee for president suggested to many in 1928 that the country might yet embrace a more pluralistic conception of American identity.

Just as Smith was a new kind of presidential candidate for the Democrats, so was Herbert Hoover for the Republicans. As a professional administrator and engineer who had never before been elected to political office, Hoover embodied the new managerial and technological elite that was restructuring the nation's economic order. During his campaign, in which he gave only seven speeches, Hoover asserted that his vision of individualism and cooperative endeavor would banish poverty from the United States. That rhetoric, as well as his reputation for organizing a drive for humanitarian relief during the war, caused many voters to see him as more progressive than Smith. Hoover won a stunning victory, receiving 58 percent of the popular vote to Smith's 41 percent and 444 electoral votes to Smith's 87 (Map 23.3). The election suggested important underlying political changes. Despite the

overwhelming loss, the Democrats' turnout increased substantially in urban areas with significant concentrations of ethnic voters. Smith also won the industrialized states of Massachusetts and Rhode Island. The Democrats were on their way to fashioning a new identity as the party of the urban masses, a reorientation the New Deal would complete in the 1930s.

It is unlikely that any Democratic candidate, let alone a Catholic, could have won the presidency in 1928. With a seemingly prosperous economy, national consensus on foreign policy, and strong support from the business community, the Republicans were unbeatable. Ironically, Herbert Hoover's victory would put him in the unenviable position of leading the United States when the Great Depression struck in 1929. Having claimed credit for the prosperity of the 1920s, the Republicans could not escape blame for the depression; twenty-four years would pass before a Republican won the presidency again.

But as Hoover began his presidency in early 1929, most Americans expected progress and prosperity to continue. The New Era the Republicans had touted meant more than Republican ascendancy in politics, more than business-government cooperation, and more than a decline in the progressive reform movement. To most Americans the New Era embodied the industrial productivity and technological advances that made consumer goods widely available and the movies and the radio an exciting part of American life. At home and abroad the nation seemed unprecedentedly vigorous and powerful. Despite disruptive cultural conflicts and a changing workplace that undermined workers' power, despite inequities in the racial order and in the distribution of income, the general tone was one of optimism, of faith in the modern society the country had become.

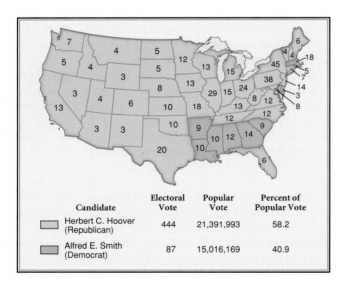

Candidate	Electoral Vote	Popular Vote	Percent of Popular Vote
Herbert C. Hoover (Republican)	444	21,391,993	58.2
Alfred E. Smith (Democrat)	87	15,016,169	40.9

MAP 23.3 Presidential Election of 1928

Historians still debate the extent to which 1928 was a critical election—an election that produced a significant realignment in voting behavior. Although the Republican Herbert Hoover swept the electoral college, Democrats were heartened by the fact that Alfred E. Smith won the heavily industrialized states of Rhode Island and Massachusetts. Not evident in this map is that Democratic turnout increased substantially in urban areas with a significant concentration of ethnic voters, a trend that would eventually lead to a new identity for the Democrats as the party of the urban masses.

FOR FURTHER EXPLORATION

► For definitions of key terms boldfaced in this chapter, see the glossary at the end of the book.

► To assess your mastery of the material covered in this chapter, see the Online Study Guide at **bedfordstmartins.com/henretta**.

► For suggested references, including Web sites, see page SR-25 at the end of the book.

► For map resources and primary documents, see **bedfordstmartins.com/henretta**.

By the 1920s modern America had arrived, a transformation that had begun with World War I. The Republican Party controlled the national government and cemented the partnership between business and government that had been accelerated by the war and that characterized the pattern of state building during the era. In foreign policy the United States promoted disarmament and the reduction of German war reparations but otherwise generally steered clear of European political affairs. The chief U.S. interest was to ensure a stable environment for economic expansion abroad, especially in the Western Hemisphere. With the exception of the 1920–1921 recession, the economy performed well, although agriculture never recovered from the postwar slump, and some industries remained overextended after their wartime expansion. The automobile industry typified the new mass-production techniques that dominated economic life in the United States and revolutionized American society.

During the 1920s a national culture began to develop. It was characterized by new ways of spending leisure time, a heightened emphasis on consumption and advertising, and the wide diffusion of new, more secular ideas and values through movies, radio, and other mass media. The new lifestyles of the decade, often called the Roaring Twenties or the Jazz Age, captured the popular imagination but were limited to a minority of the population. Families needed a middle-class income to buy cars, radios, vacuum cleaners, and toasters. Those left outside the circle of prosperity included farmers, blacks, and Mexican Americans.

Not everyone welcomed the new secular values of the 1920s. Conflicts arose over Prohibition, religion, race, and immigration. Those cultural disputes spilled over into politics, disrupting the already fractured Democratic Party. The 1928 election showed that the nation could not yet accept a Catholic as president. The Republican ascendancy continued under Herbert Hoover, who looked forward to a term filled with even greater prosperity and progress. The advances of the New Era, and the expectation that the nation would continue to be vigorous and powerful at home and abroad, made the harsh realities of the Great Depression that would follow all the more shocking.

1920 Eighteenth Amendment outlawing alcohol takes effect

First commercial radio broadcast

Warren G. Harding elected president

Census reveals shift in population from farms to cities

Edith Wharton, *The Age of Innocence*

1920–1921 National economic recession

1921 Sheppard-Towner Act

Immigration Act limits immigration

Washington Conference supports naval disarmament

1922 T. S. Eliot, *The Waste Land*

1922–1929 Record economic expansion

1923 Harding dies in office: succeeded by Calvin Coolidge as president

Time magazine founded

Jean Toomer, *Cane*

1924 Dawes Plan reduces German reparation payments

Teapot Dome scandal

U.S. troops withdraw from Dominican Republic

National Origins Act further limits immigration

1925 F. Scott Fitzgerald, *The Great Gatsby*

Height of Ku Klux Klan's power

Scopes ("monkey") trial

1926 Alain Locke, *The New Negro*

The Book-of-the-Month Club is founded

1927 First "talkies"

Charles Lindbergh's solo flight

Ford's Model A car

1928 Herbert Hoover elected president

Kellogg-Briand Pact condemning militarism signed

1929 *Middletown* published

Ernest Hemingway, *A Farewell to Arms*

William Faulkner, *The Sound and the Fury*

CHAPTER 24

The Great Depression

Our images of the 1920s and the decade that followed are polar opposites. Flappers and movie stars, admen and stockbrokers, caught up in what F. Scott Fitzgerald called the "world's most expensive orgy"—these are our conceptions of the Jazz Age. The 1930s we remember in terms of breadlines and hobos, dust bowl devastation and hapless migrants piled into dilapidated jalopies. Almost all our impressions of that decade are black and white, in part because widely distributed photographs taken by Farm Security Administration photographers etched this dark visual image of depression America on the popular consciousness.

But this contrast between the flush times of the 1920s and the hard times of the 1930s is too stark. The vaunted prosperity of the 1920s was never as widespread or as deeply rooted as many believed. Though America's mass-consumption economy was the envy of the world, many people lived on its margins. However, not all Americans were devastated by the depression. Those with secure jobs or fixed incomes survived the economic downturn in relatively good shape. Yet few could escape the depression's wide-ranging social, political, and cultural effects. Whatever their personal situation was, Americans understood that the nation was deeply scarred by the pervasive struggle to survive and overcome "hard times."

◀ **Looking for Work**
This detail of Moses Soyer's painting Employment Agency *(1940) captures the despair and bleak resignation of a victim of the Great Depression—a white male, down on his luck but still trying to keep up appearances and hope.*
Collection of Philip J. and Suzanne Schiller.

Wall Street, October 1929

Crowds gather in front of the New York Stock Exchange on October 25, 1929, the day after "Black Thursday." The mood would be even darker after "Black Tuesday," October 29, the day the bubble burst. Corbis-Bettmann.

The Coming of the Great Depression

Booms and busts are a permanent feature of the business cycle in capitalist economies. Since the beginning of the Industrial Revolution early in the nineteenth century, the United States had experienced recessions or panics at least once every twenty years. But none was as severe as the Great Depression of the 1930s. The country would not recover from the depression until World War II put American factories and people back to work.

Causes of the Depression

The downturn began slowly and almost imperceptibly. After 1927 consumer spending declined, and housing construction slowed. Soon inventories piled up; in 1928 manufacturers began to cut back production and lay off workers, reducing incomes and buying power and reinforcing the slowdown. By the summer of 1929, the economy was clearly in recession.

Stock Market Speculation and the Great Crash. Yet stock market activity continued unabated. By 1929 the stock market had become the symbol of the nation's prosperity, an icon of American business culture. In a *Ladies' Home Journal* article titled "Everyone Ought to Be Rich," financier John J. Raskob advised that $15 a month invested in sound common stocks would grow to $80,000 in twenty years. Not everyone was playing the market, however. Only about 4 million Americans, or roughly 10 percent of the nation's households, owned stock in 1929.

Stock prices had been rising steadily since 1921, but in 1928 and 1929 they surged forward, rising on average over 40 percent. At the time market activity was essentially unregulated. **Margin buying** in particular proceeded at a feverish pace, as customers were encouraged to buy stocks with a small down payment and finance the rest with a broker loan. But then on "Black Thursday," October 24, 1929, and again on "Black Tuesday," October 29, the bubble burst. On those two bleak days, more than 28 million shares changed hands in frantic trading. Overextended investors, suddenly finding themselves heavily in debt, began to sell their portfolios. Waves of panic selling ensued. Practically overnight stock values fell from a peak of $87 billion (at least on paper) to $55 billion.

The impact of what became known as the Great Crash was felt far beyond the trading floors of Wall Street. Commercial banks had invested heavily in corporate stock. Speculators who had borrowed from banks to buy their stocks could not repay their loans because they could not sell their shares. Throughout the nation bank failures multiplied. Since bank deposits were uninsured, a bank collapse meant that depositors lost all their money. The sudden loss of their life savings was a tremendous shock to members of the middle class, many of whom had no other resources to cope with the crisis. More symbolically, the crash destroyed the faith of those who viewed the stock market as the crowning symbol of American prosperity, precipitating a crisis of confidence that prolonged the depression.

Structural Weaknesses. Although the stock market crash triggered the Great Depression, long-standing weaknesses in the economy accounted for its length and severity. Agriculture, in particular, had never recovered from the recession of 1920 and 1921. Farmers faced high fixed costs for equipment and mortgages, which they had incurred during the inflationary war years. When prices fell because of overproduction, many farmers defaulted on their mortgage payments, risking foreclosure. Because farmers accounted for about a fourth of the nation's gainfully employed workers in 1929, their difficulties weakened the general economic structure.

Certain basic industries also had economic setbacks during the prosperous 1920s. Textiles, facing a steady decline after the war, abandoned New England for cheaper labor in the South but suffered still from decreased demand and overproduction. Mining and lumbering, which had expanded in response to wartime demand, confronted the same problems. The railroad industry, damaged by stiff competition from trucks, faced shrinking passenger revenues and stagnant freight levels, worsened by inefficient management. While these older sectors of the economy faltered, newer and more successful consumer-based industries, such as chemicals, appliances and food processing, proved not yet strong enough to lead the way to recovery.

Unequal Distribution of Wealth. The unequal distribution of the nation's wealth was another underlying weakness of the economy. During the 1920s the share of national income going to families in the upper- and middle-income brackets increased. The tax policies of Secretary of the Treasury Andrew Mellon contributed to a concentration of wealth by lowering personal income tax rates, eliminating the wartime excess-profits tax, and increasing deductions that favored corporations and the affluent. In 1929 the lowest 40 percent of the population received only 12.5 percent of aggregate family income, while the top 5 percent of the population received 30 percent. Once the depression began, this skewed income distribution left the majority of people unable to spend the amount of money that was needed to revive the economy.

The Deepening Economic Crisis

The Great Depression became self-perpetuating. The more the economy contracted, the longer people expected the depression to last. The longer they expected it to last, the more afraid they became to spend or invest their money, if they had any—and spending and investment was exactly what was needed to stimulate economic recovery. The economy showed some improvement in the summer of 1931, when low prices encouraged consumption but plunged again late that fall.

The nation's banks, already weakened by the stock market crash, continued to collapse. When agricultural prices and income fell more steeply than usual in 1930, many farmers went bankrupt, causing rural banks to fail. By December 1930 so many rural banks had defaulted on their obligations that urban banks too began to collapse. The wave of bank failures frightened depositors, who withdrew their savings, deepening the crisis.

In 1931 a change in the nation's monetary policy compounded the banks' problems. In the first phase of the depression, the Federal Reserve System had reacted cautiously. But in October 1931 the Federal Reserve Bank of New York significantly increased the **discount rate**—the interest rate charged on loans to member banks—and reduced the amount of money placed in circulation through the purchase of government securities. This miscalculation squeezed the money supply, forcing prices down and depriving businesses of funds for investment. In the face of the money shortage, the American people could have pulled the country out of the depression only by spending faster. But because of falling prices, rising unemployment, and a troubled banking system, Americans preferred to keep their dollars, stashing them under the mattress rather than depositing them in the bank, further limiting the amount of money in circulation. Economic stagnation solidified.

The Worldwide Depression

President Hoover later blamed the severity of the depression on the international economic situation. Although domestic factors far outweighed international causes of America's protracted decline, Hoover was correct in surmising that economic problems in the rest of the world affected the United States and vice versa. Indeed, the international economic system had been out of kilter since World War I. It functioned only as long as American banks exported enough capital to allow European countries to repay their debts and to buy U.S. manufactured goods and foodstuffs. By the late 1920s European economies were staggering under the weight of huge debts and trade imbalances with the United States, which effectively undercut their recovery from the war. By 1931 most European economies had collapsed.

In an interdependent world the economic downturn in America had enormous repercussions. When U.S. companies cut back production, they also cut their purchases of raw materials and supplies abroad, devastating many foreign economies. When American financiers sharply reduced their foreign investment and consumers bought fewer European goods, debt repayment became even more difficult, straining the gold standard, the foundation of international commerce in the interwar period. As European economic conditions worsened, demand for American exports fell drastically. Finally, when the Hawley-Smoot Tariff of 1930 went into effect, raising rates to all-time highs, foreign governments retaliated by imposing their own trade restrictions, further limiting the market for American goods and intensifying the worldwide depression.

No other nation was as hard hit as the United States (Figure 24.1). From the height of its prosperity before the stock market crash in 1929 to the depths of the

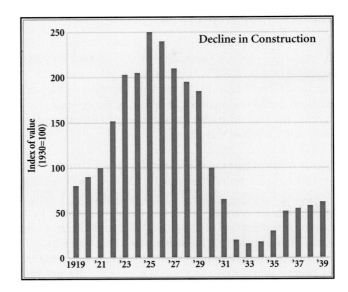

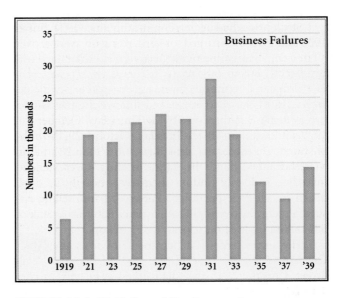

FIGURE 24.1 Statistics of the Depression
The top graph shows the decline in construction, as reflected in the value of new building permits; the bottom graph shows the number of business failures.
Source: Historical Statistics of the United States, Colonial Times to 1970 (Washington, DC: U.S. Government Printing Office, 1975), 626, 912.

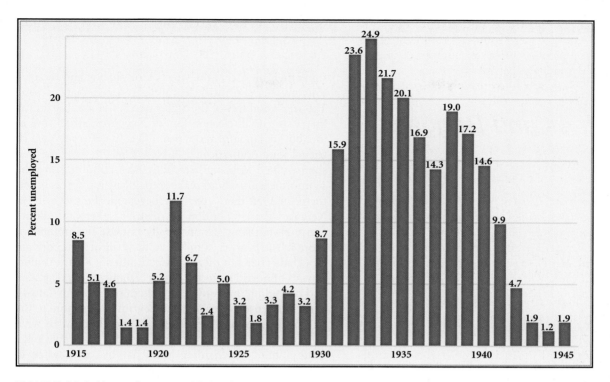

FIGURE 24.2 Unemployment, 1915–1945
This graph shows how the historically low unemployment levels of the 1920s began to rise in 1930. By 1933 one in four American workers was out of a job.

depression in 1932 and 1933, the U.S. gross domestic product (GDP) was cut almost in half, declining from $103.1 billion to $58 billion in 1932. Consumption expenditures dropped by 18 percent, construction by 78 percent; private investment plummeted 88 percent, and farm income, already low, was more than halved. In this period 9,000 banks went bankrupt or closed their doors and 100,000 businesses failed. The consumer price index (CPI) declined by 25 percent, and corporate profits fell from $10 billion to $1 billion.

Most tellingly, unemployment rose from 3.2 percent to 24.9 percent, affecting approximately 12 million workers (Figure 24.2). Statistical measures at the time were fairly crude, so the figures were probably understated. At least one in four workers was out of a job, and even those who had jobs faced wage cuts, work for which they were overqualified, or layoffs. Their stories put a human face on the almost incomprehensible dimensions of the economic downturn.

Hard Times

"We didn't go hungry, but we lived lean." That statement sums up the experiences of many families during the Great Depression. The majority of Americans were neither very rich nor very poor. For most the depression did not mean losing thousands of dollars in the stock market or pulling children out of boarding school; nor did it mean going on relief or living in a shantytown. In a typical family in the 1930s, the husband still had a job, and the wife was still a homemaker. Families usually managed to "make do." But life was far from easy, and most Americans worried about an uncertain future that might bring even harder times into their lives.

The Invisible Scar

"You could feel the depression deepen," recalled the writer Caroline Bird, "but you could not look out the window and see it." Many people never saw a breadline or a man selling apples on the corner. The depression caused a private kind of despair that often simmered behind closed doors. "I've lived in cities for many months broke, without help, too timid to get in breadlines," the writer Meridel LeSueur remembered. "A woman will shut herself up in a room until it is taken away from her, and eat a cracker a day and be as quiet as a mouse" (see Voices from Abroad, "Mary Agnes Hamilton: Breadlines and Beggars," p. 700).

Many variables—race, ethnicity, age, class, and gender—influenced how Americans experienced the depression. Blacks, Mexican Americans, and others already on the economic margins saw their opportunities shrink

Mary Agnes Hamilton

Breadlines and Beggars

British writer and Labor Party activist Mary Agnes Hamilton arrived in the United States on a gloomy morning in December 1931 for a lecture tour that eventually took her as far west as Nebraska and as far south as Virginia. Her observations of conditions in New York during that grim winter confirm the devastation and despair gripping urban America.

One does not need to be long in New York (or for that matter in Chicago, in Cleveland, in Detroit, in Kansas, or in Buffalo) to see that there are plenty of real tragedies, as well as plenty of not-so-real ones. If those who have turned in the second or third car talk the most, the others talk—when they get the chance. In New York, one has only to pass outside the central island bounded by Lexington and Sixth Avenues to see hardship, misery, and degradation, accentuated by the shoddy grimness of the shabby houses and broken pavements. Look down from the Elevated, and there are long queues of dreary-looking men and women standing in "breadlines" outside the relief offices and the various church and other charitable institutions. Times Square, at any hour of the day and late into the evening, offers an exhibit for the edification of the theater-goer, for it is packed with shabby, utterly dumb and apathetic-looking men, who stand there, waiting for the advent of the coffee wagon run by Mr. W. R. Hearst of the New York American. Nowhere, in New York or any other city, can one escape from the visible presence of those who with perhaps unconscious cruelty are called "the idle." At every street corner, and wherever taxi or car has to pause, men try to sell one apples, oranges, or picture papers. Not matches—matches, in book form, are given away with every fifteen-cent package of cigarettes, lie on every restaurant table, litter the street, half used, and exemplify how little, as yet, the depression has done to overcome the national habit of easy-going wastefulness. On a fine day, men will press on one gardenias at fifteen cents apiece; on any day, rows of them line every relatively open space, eager to shine one's shoes. It is perhaps because so many people are doing without this "shine," or attempting with unfamiliar hands and a sense of deep indignity to shine their own, that the streets look shabby and the persons on them so much less well-groomed than of yore. The well-shod feet of the States struck me forcibly on my first visit; the ill-cleaned feet of New York struck me as forcibly in January and April 1932. In 1930 an English friend, long domesticated in New England, told me that she hesitated to bring her children to London, since the sight of beggars would make so painful an impression on them; in 1932 there are more beggars to be met with in New York than in London. Yes, distress is there; the idle are there. How many, no one really knows. Ten million or more in the country; a million and a half in New York are reported. They are there; as is, admittedly a dark undergrowth of horrid suffering that is certainly more degraded and degrading than anything Britain or Germany knows. Their immense presence makes a grim background to the talk of depression: there is an obscure alarm as to what they may do "if this goes on," and the charitable relief funds (about which more later) dry up, as they are in many centers already doing; their existence, in numbers that grow instead of diminishing, constitutes the fact that largely justifies the feeling of gloom. . . .

The American people, unfamiliar with suffering, with none of that long history of catastrophe and calamity behind it which makes the experience of European nations, is outraged and baffled by misfortune. Depression blocks its view: it cannot see round it. Misled in the onset by leaders who assured it, in every soothing term and tone, that reverse was to last but for a little while; that it was the preliminary to recovery; that American institutions were immune to the ills that had laid the countries of the rest of the world upon their backs; that prosperity was native to the soil of the Union, and all that was needed was to wait till the clouds, blown up by the wickedness of other lands, rolled by, as they were bound to do, and that speedily; the nation now suffers from a despair of any and every kind of leadership. Every institution is assailed; even the sacred foundations of democracy are being undermined. The defeatism that has been so lamentably evidenced in Congress is not peculiar to Congressmen, any more than is the crude individualism of their reactions. It lies like a pall over the spirit of the nation. It is felt by most people to be, in fact, the greatest obstacle to recovery, to that restoration of confidence for which everybody pleads, which everybody sees as necessary. But how to break it nobody knows.

Source: Mary Agnes Hamilton, *In America Today* (1932), in Allan Nevins, ed., *America through British Eyes* (Gloucester, MA: Peter Smith, 1968), 443–44.

The Breadline

Some of the most vivid images from the depression were breadlines and men selling apples on street corners. Note that all the people in this breadline are men. Women rarely appeared in breadlines, often preferring to endure private deprivation rather than violate standards of respectable behavior by appearing in public to ask for help.

Franklin D. Roosevelt Library, Hyde Park, NY.

further. Often the last hired they were the first fired. Hard times weighed heavily on the nation's senior citizens of all races, many of whom faced destitution. Many white middle-class Americans experienced downward mobility for the first time. An unemployed man in Pittsburgh told the journalist Lorena Hickok, "Lady, you just can't know what it's like to have to move your family out of the nice house you had in the suburbs, part paid for, down into an apartment, down into another apartment, smaller and in a worse neighborhood, down, down, down, until finally you end up in the slums." People like this, who strongly believed in the Horatio Alger ethic of upward mobility through hard work, suddenly found themselves floundering in a society that did not reward them for that work as they had expected. Thus the depression challenged basic American tenets of individualism and success. Yet even in the midst of pervasive unemployment, many people blamed themselves for their misfortune. This sense of damaged pride pervaded letters written to President Franklin D. Roosevelt and his wife Eleanor, summed up succinctly in one woman's plea for assistance: "Please don't think me unworthy."

After exhausting their savings and credit, many families found the traditional path of turning to relatives, neighbors, church, and mutual-aid societies in time of need blocked. Private charities and benefit societies were overwhelmed by the needy, and individuals often had too few resources to share. For many the only alternative was the humiliation of going on relief—seeking aid from state or local governments (Map 24.1). Even if families endured the demeaning process of certification for state or local relief, the amount they received was a pittance. In New York State, where benefits were among the highest in the nation, a family on relief received only $2.39 a week. Such hardships left a deep wound: one historian described it as the "invisible scar." And the scar branded more than those who were forced onto the relief rolls. For the majority of Americans, the fear of losing control over their lives was the crux of the Great Depression.

Families Face the Depression

Sociologists who studied family life during the 1930s found that the depression usually intensified existing behavior. If a family had been stable and cohesive before the depression, then members pulled together to overcome the new obstacles. But if a family had shown signs of disintegration, the depression made the situation worse. On the whole far more families hung together than broke apart.

Gender Roles. Men and women experienced the Great Depression differently, partly because of the gender roles that governed male and female behavior in the 1930s. From childhood men had been trained to be

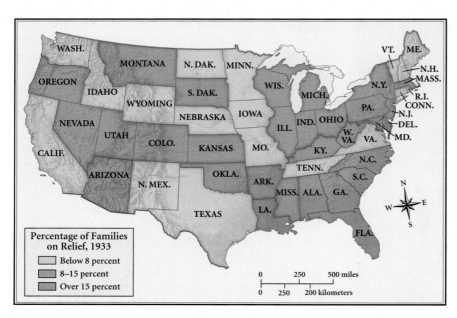

MAP 24.1 The Great Depression: Families on Relief, to 1933

Although the Great Depression was a nationwide crisis, some regions were hit harder than others, with the worst of the economic decline concentrating in the South and Appalachia. In the worst years of the depression (1929–1933), local and state governments, as well as charitable organizations, were overwhelmed by the demand for relief and could offer only minimal assistance. It was not until after Franklin D. Roosevelt assumed the presidency in 1933 and implemented his "New Deal" that the national government began a massive program of federal aid to the unemployed through the Federal Emergency Relief Administration (FERA).

breadwinners; they considered themselves failures if they could no longer support their families (see American Voices, "A Working-Class Family Encounters the Great Depression," p. 703). But while millions of men lost their jobs, few of the nation's 28 million homemakers lost their positions in the home. In contrast to men, women's sense of self-importance increased as they struggled to keep their families afloat. Sociologists Robert and Helen Lynd noticed this phenomenon in their follow-up study of *Middletown* (Muncie, Indiana), published in 1937: "The men, cut adrift from their usual routine, lost much of their sense of time and dawdled helplessly and dully about the streets; while in the homes the women's world remained largely intact and the round of cooking, housecleaning, and mending became if anything more absorbing."

Even if a wife took a job when her husband lost his, she retained almost total responsibility for housework and child care. To economize women sewed their own clothes and canned fruits and vegetables. They bought day-old bread and heated several dishes in the oven at once to save fuel. Women who had once employed servants did their own housework. Eleanor Roosevelt described the stressful effects of the depression on these women's lives: "It means endless little economies and constant anxiety for fear of some catastrophe such as accident or illness which may completely swamp the family budget." Housewives' ability to watch every penny often made the difference in a family's survival.

Consumption Trends.   Despite hard times Americans as a whole maintained a fairly high level of consumption. As in the 1920s households in the middle-income range—in 1935 the 50.2 percent of American families

with an annual income of $500 to $1,500—did much of the buying. Several trends allowed those families to maintain their former standard of living despite pay cuts and unemployment. Between 1929 and 1935 deflation lowered the cost of living almost 20 percent. And buying on the installment plan increased in the 1930s, permitting many families to stretch their reduced incomes.

Americans spent their money differently in the depression, though. Telephone use and clothing sales dropped sharply, but cigarettes, movies, radios, and newspapers, once considered luxuries, became necessities. The automobile proved one of the most depression-proof items in the family budget. Though sales of new cars dropped, gasoline sales held stable, suggesting that families bought used cars or kept their old models running longer.

Demographics of the Great Depression.   Another measure of the impact of the depression on family life was the change in demographic trends. The marriage rate fell from 10.14 per thousand persons in 1929 to 7.87 per thousand in 1932. The divorce rate decreased as well because couples could not afford the legal expense of dissolving failed unions. And between 1930 and 1933, the birthrate, which had fallen steadily since 1800, dropped from 21.3 live births per thousand to 18.4, a dramatic 14 percent decrease. The new level would have produced a decline in population if maintained. Though it rose slightly after 1934, by the end of the decade it was still only 18.8. (In contrast, at the height of the baby boom following World War II, the birthrate was 25 per thousand.)

The drop in the birthrate during the Great Depression could not have happened without increased access to effective contraception. In 1936, in *United States v.*

Larry Van Dusen

A Working-Class Family Encounters the Great Depression

Although many families endured the privations of the Great Depression with equanimity, others, like Larry Van Dusen's family, experienced tremendous strains. In this passage from his oral history account to journalist Studs Terkel, he describes the pressures on male wage earners and their children.

One of the most common things—and it certainly happened to me—was this feeling of your father's failure. That somehow he hadn't beaten the rap. Sure things were tough, but why should I be the kid who had to put a piece of cardboard into the sole of my shoe to go to school? It was not a thing coupled with resentment against my father. It was simply this feeling of regret, that somehow he hadn't done better, that he hadn't gotten the breaks. Also a feeling of uneasiness about my father's rage against the way things are.

My father was very much of an individualist, as craftsmen usually are. He would get jobs he considered beneath his status during this period. Something would happen: he'd quarrel with the foreman, he'd have a fight with the boss. He was a carpenter. He couldn't be happy fixing a roadbed or driving a cab or something like that. He was a skilled tradesman and this whole thing had him beat. I think it bugged the family a lot.

Remember, too, the shock, the confusion, the hurt that many kids felt about their fathers not being able to provide for them. This reflected itself very often in bitter quarrels between father and son. I recall I had one. I was the oldest of six children. I think there was a special feeling between the father and the oldest son. . . .

My father led a rough life: he drank. During the Depression, he drank more. There was more conflict in the home. A lot of fathers—mine, among them—had a habit of taking off. They'd go to Chicago to look for work. To Topeka. This left the family at home, waiting and hoping that the old man would find something. And there was always the Saturday night ordeal as to whether or not the old man would get home with his paycheck. Everything was sharpened and hurt more by the Depression.

Heaven would break out once in a while, and the old man would get a week's work. I remember he'd come home at night, and he'd come down the path through the trees. He always rode a bicycle. He'd stop and sometimes say hello, or give me a hug. And that smell of fresh sawdust on those carpenter overalls, and the fact that Dad was home, and there was a week's wages—well, this is something you remember, too. That's the good you remember.

And then there was always the bad part. That's when you'd see your father coming home with the toolbox on his shoulder. Or carrying it. That meant the job was over. The tools were home now, and we were back on the treadmill again.

I remember coming back home, many years afterwards. Things were better. It was after the Depression, after the war. To me, it was hardly the same house. My father turned into an angel. They weren't wealthy, but they were making it. They didn't have the acid and the recriminations and the bitterness that I had felt as a child.

Source: Studs Terkel, *Hard Times* (New York: Pantheon Books, 1986), 107–18.

One Package of Japanese Pessaries, a federal court struck down all federal restrictions on the dissemination of contraceptive information. The decision gave doctors wide discretion in prescribing birth control for married couples, making it legal everywhere except the heavily Catholic states of Massachusetts and Connecticut. While abortion remained illegal the number of women who underwent the procedure increased. Because many abortionists operated under unsafe or unsanitary conditions, between 8,000 and 10,000 women died each year from the illegal operations.

Margaret Sanger played a major role in encouraging the availability and popular acceptance of birth control (see Chapter 20). Sanger began her career as a public-health nurse in the 1910s in the slums of New York City. At first she joined forces with socialists trying to help working-class families to control their fertility. In the 1920s and 1930s, however, she appealed to the middle

It's Up to the Women

Ironically, as women struggled to cope with their own unemployment or to help their families weather the hard times, advertisers relentlessly urged middle-class women to maintain their consumption patterns as a means of stimulating the economy and bringing about recovery. This 1932 cover for **Ladies' Home Journal** *not only emphasizes the perception of women's pivotal role as consumers but also evokes the patriotism of World War I through use of the icon of Uncle Sam, so familiar in World War I posters. The analogy between fighting a war and fighting the depression was a common theme throughout the decade.* Ladies' Home Journal, *February 1932.*

class for support, identifying those families as the key to the movement's success. Sanger also courted the medical profession, pioneering the establishment of professionally staffed birth control clinics and winning the American Medical Association's endorsement of contraception in 1937. As a result of Sanger's efforts, birth control became less a feminist issue and more a medical question. And in the context of the depression it became an economic issue as well, as financially pressed couples sought to delay or limit their childbearing while they weathered hard times.

Women and Work.   One way for families to make ends meet was to send an additional member of the household to work. Whereas in African American families that role already often fell to a married woman by the turn of the century, it was not until the 1930s that married white women expanded their presence in the labor

market, too, and the total number of married women employed outside the home rose 50 percent. Working women, especially white married women, encountered sharp resentment and outright discrimination in the workplace. When asked in a 1936 Gallup poll whether wives should work when their husbands had jobs, 82 percent of those interviewed said no. Such public disapproval encouraged restrictions on women's right to work. From 1932 to 1937 the federal government would not allow a husband and a wife to hold government jobs at the same time. Many states adopted laws that prohibited married women from working.

Married or not, most women worked because they had to. A sizable minority were the sole support of their families because their husbands had left home or lost their jobs. Single, divorced, deserted, or widowed women had no husbands to support them. This was especially true of poor black women. A survey of Chicago revealed that two-fifths of adult black women in the city were single. These working women rarely took jobs away from men. "Few of the people who oppose married women's employment," observed one feminist in 1940, "seem to realize that a coal miner or steel worker cannot very well fill the jobs of nursemaids, cleaning women, or the factory and clerical jobs now filled by women." Custom made gender crossovers from one field to another rare.

The division of the workforce by gender gave white women a small edge during the depression. Many fields where they had concentrated—including clerical, sales, and service and trade occupations—reinforced the traditional stereotypes of female work but suffered less from economic contraction than heavy industry, which employed men almost exclusively. As a result unemployment rates for white women, although extremely high, were somewhat lower than those for their male counterparts. This small bonus came at a high price, however. When the depression ended, women were even more concentrated in low-paying, dead-end jobs than when it began. White women also benefited at the expense of minority women. To make ends meet white women willingly sought jobs usually held by blacks or other minority workers—domestic service jobs, for example—and employers were quick to act on their preference for white workers.

White men also took jobs once held by minority males. Contemporary observers' concerns about the crisis of the male breadwinner or married women in the workforce rarely extended to blacks. Most commentators paid scant attention to the impact of the depression on the black family, focusing instead on the perceived threats to the stability of white households. As historian Jacqueline Jones explains it, few leaders worried "over the baneful effects of economic independence on the male ego when the ego in question was that of a black husband."

During the Great Depression there were few feminist demands for equal rights, at home or on the job. On an individual basis, women's self-esteem probably rose because of the importance of their work to family survival. Most men and women, however, continued to believe that the two sexes should have fundamentally different roles and responsibilities and that a woman's life cycle should be shaped by marriage and her husband's career.

Hard Times for Youth.   The depression hit another segment of the family—the nation's 21 million young people—especially hard. Though small children often escaped the sense of bitterness and failure that gripped their elders, hard times made children grow up fast. About 250,000 young people became so demoralized that they took to the road as hobos and "sisters of the road," as female tramps were called. Others chose to stay in school longer: public schools were free, and they were warm in the winter. In 1930 less than half the nation's youth attended high school, compared with three-fourths in 1940, at the end of the depression. College, however, remained the privilege of a distinct minority. About 1.2 million young people, or 7.5 percent of the population between eighteen and twenty-four, attended college in the 1930s. Forty percent of them were women. After 1935 college became slightly more affordable when the National Youth Administration (NYA) gave part-time employment to more than 2 million college and high school students. The government agency also provided work for 2.6 million out-of-school youths.

College students worked hard in the 1930s; financial sacrifice encouraged seriousness of purpose. Interest in fraternities and sororities declined as many students became involved in political movements. Fueled by disillusionment with World War I, thousands of youth took the "Oxford Pledge" never to support United States involvement in a war. In 1936 the Student Strike against War drew support from several hundred thousand students across the country.

Although many youths enjoyed more education in the 1930s, the depression damaged their future prospects. Studies of social mobility confirm that young men who entered their twenties during the depression era had less successful careers than those who came before or after. After extensive interviews with these youths all over the nation, the writer Maxine Davis described them as "runners, delayed at the gun," adding, "The depression years have left us with a generation robbed of time and opportunity just as the Great War left the world its heritage of a lost generation."

Popular Culture Views the Depression

Americans turned to popular culture to alleviate some of the trauma of the Great Depression. In June 1935 a Chicago radio listener wrote station WLS, "I feel your music and songs are what pulled me through this

winter." She explained that "Half the time we were blue and broke. One year during the depression and no work. Kept from going on relief but lost everything we possessed doing so. So thanks for the songs, for they make life seem more like living." Mass culture flourished in the 1930s, offering not just entertainment but commentary on the problems that beset the nation. Movies and radio served as a forum for criticizing the system—especially politicians and bankers—as well as vehicles for reaffirming traditional ideals.

Movies.   Despite the closing of one-third of the country's theaters by 1933, the movie industry and its studio system flourished. Sixty percent of Americans—some 60 to 75 million people—flocked to the cinema each week, seeking solace from the pain of the depression. In the early thirties moviegoers might be

Dancing Cheek to Cheek
During the Great Depression Americans turned to inexpensive recreational activities such as listening to the radio and going to the movies. One of the most popular attractions in Hollywood movies was the dance team of Fred Astaire and Ginger Rogers, who starred together in ten movies. Steve Schapiro.

titillated or scandalized by Mae West, who was noted for her sexual innuendoes: "I used to be Snow White, but I drifted." But in response to public outcry against immorality in the movies, especially from the Protestant and Catholic churches, the industry established a means of self-censorship, the Production Code Administration. After 1934 somewhat racy films were supplanted by sophisticated, fast-paced, screwball comedies like *It Happened One Night*, which swept the Oscars in 1934. The musical comedies of Fred Astaire and Ginger Rogers, including *Top Hat* (1935) and *The Gay Divorcee* (1934), in which the two dancers seemed to glide effortlessly through opulent sets, provided a stark contrast with most moviegoers' own lives.

But Hollywood, which produced 5,000 films during the decade, offered much more than what on the surface might seem to be escapist entertainment. Many of its movies contained complex messages that reflected a real sense of the societal crisis that engulfed the nation. Depression-era films repeatedly portrayed politicians as cynical and corrupt. In *Washington Merry-Go-Round* (1932), lobbyists manipulated weak congressmen to undermine democratic rule. The Marx Brothers' irreverent comedies more humorously criticized authority—and most everything else. In *Duck Soup* (1933) Groucho Marx played Rufus T. Firefly, president of the mythical Freedonia, who sings gleefully:

> *The last man nearly ruined this place,*
> *He didn't know what to do with it.*
> *If you think this country's bad off now,*
> *Just wait till I get through with it.*

Even if they did not deal specifically with the economic or political crisis, many films reaffirmed traditional values like democracy, individualism, and egalitarianism. They also contained criticisms—suggestions that the system was not working or that law and order had broken down. Thus popular gangster movies, such as *Public Enemy* (1931), with James Cagney, or *Little Caesar* (1930), starring Edward G. Robinson, could be seen as perverse Horatio Alger tales, in which the main character struggled to succeed in a harsh environment. Often these movies suggested that incompetent or corrupt politicians, police, and businessmen were as much to blame for organized crime as the gangsters themselves.

Few filmmakers left more of a mark on the decade than Frank Capra. An Italian immigrant who personified the possibilities for success that the United States offered, Capra made films that spoke to Americans' idealism. In movies like *Mr. Deeds Goes to Town* (1936) and *Mr. Smith Goes to Washington* (1939), he pitted the virtuous small-town hero against corrupt urban shysters—businessmen, politicians, lobbyists, and newspaper publishers—whose machinations subverted the nation's ideals. Though the hero usually prevailed, Capra was realistic enough to suggest that the victory

Mr. Smith Goes to Washington
In this classic 1939 film, directed by Frank Capra, actor Jimmy Stewart plays an idealistic young senator who exposes the unscrupulous political machine that dominates his home state. In response, the machine frames Senator Smith for corruption, and he must struggle to vindicate himself. Although the movie has a romantic subplot as Stewart's character wins over the cynical woman played by costar Jean Arthur, this light-hearted advertising poster belies the more serious tone of the movie.
Collection of Hershenson-Allen Archives.

was not necessarily permanent and that the problems the nation faced were serious.

Radio.   Radio occupied an increasingly important place in popular culture during the 1930s (Map 24.2). At the beginning of the decade, about 13 million households had radios; by the end 27.5 million owned them. Listeners tuned in to daytime serials like *Ma Perkins*, picked up useful household hints on *The Betty Crocker Hour*, or enjoyed the Big Band "swing" of Benny Goodman, Duke Ellington, and Tommy Dorsey. Weekly variety shows featured Jack Benny; George Burns and Gracie Allen; and the ventriloquist Edgar Bergen and his impudent dummy, Charlie McCarthy. And millions of listeners followed the adventures of the Lone Ranger, Superman, and Dick Tracy.

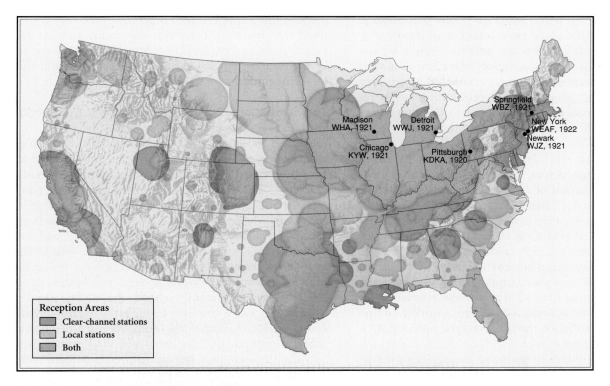

MAP 24.2 The Spread of Radio, to 1939
In 1938 more than 26 million American households, or about three-quarters of the population, had a radio. Four national networks dominated the field, broadcasting news and entertainment across the country. Powerful clear-channel stations reached listeners hundreds of miles away. By 1939, only sparsely populated areas were beyond radio's reach.

Like movies, radio offered Americans more than escape. A running gag in comedian Jack Benny's show was his stinginess; audiences could identify with an unwillingness—or inability—to spend money. Even more relevant was Benny's distrust of banks. He kept his money in an underground vault guarded by a pet polar bear named Carmichael—presumably a more reliable place than the nation's financial institutions. *Amos 'n' Andy* (see Chapter 23) is remembered primarily for its racial stereotyping. But the exceptionally popular show also dealt with hard times, often referring explicitly to the depression. A central theme was the contrast between Amos's hard work and Andy's more carefree approach to life. Amos, tending to believe that the nation's economic crisis had been brought about by the extravagant spending of the 1920s, criticized his friend's fiscal irresponsibility. Though *Amos 'n' Andy* reinforced racial stereotypes, it also reaffirmed the traditional values of "diligence, saving, and generosity."

Americans did not spend all their leisure time in commercial entertainment. In a resurgence of traditionalism, attendance at religious services rose, and the home again became a center for pleasurable pastimes. Amateur photography and stamp collecting enjoyed tremendous vogues, as did the new board game Monopoly, invented in 1934 by an unemployed Germantown, Pennsylvania,

man. Reading aloud from books borrowed from the public library was another affordable diversion. But Americans bought books, too. Taking advantage of new manufacturing processes that made books cheaper, they made best-sellers of Margaret Mitchell's *Gone with the Wind* (1936), James Hilton's *Lost Horizon* (1933), and Pearl Buck's *The Good Earth* (1932).

Harder Times

Much writing about the 1930s has focused on white working-class or middle-class families caught suddenly in a downward spiral. For African Americans, farmers, Mexican Americans, and Asian Americans, times had always been hard; during the 1930s they got much harder. As the poet Langston Hughes noted, "The depression brought everybody down a peg or two. And the Negroes had but few pegs to fall."

African Americans in the Depression

The African American worker had always known discrimination and limited opportunities and thus viewed the depression differently from most whites. "It didn't mean too much to him, the Great American Depression, as you call it," one man remarked. "There was no such thing. The best he could be is a janitor or a porter or shoeshine boy. It only became official when it hit the white man." The novelist and poet Maya Angelou, who grew up in Stamps, Arkansas, recalled, "The country had been in the throes of the Depression for two years before the Negroes in Stamps knew it. I think that everyone thought the Depression, like everything else, was for the white folks."

Despite the black migration to northern cities, which had begun before World War I, as late as 1940 more than 75 percent of African Americans still lived in the South. Nearly all black farmers lived in the South, their condition scarcely better than it had been at the end of Reconstruction. Only 20 percent of black farmers owned their land; the rest toiled at the bottom of the South's exploitative agricultural system as tenant farmers, farm hands, and sharecroppers. African Americans rarely earned more than $200 a year, less than a quarter of the annual average wages of a factory worker. In one Louisiana parish black women averaged only $41.67 a year picking cotton.

Throughout the 1920s southern agriculture had suffered from falling prices and overproduction. The depression made an already desperate situation worse. Some black farmers tried to protect themselves by joining the Southern Tenant Farmers Union (STFU), which was founded in 1934. The STFU was one of the few southern groups that welcomed both blacks and whites. "The same chain that holds you hold my people, too," an elderly black farmer reminded whites on the organizing committee. Landowners, however, had a stake in keeping sharecroppers from organizing, and they countered the union's efforts with repression and harassment. In the end the STFU could do little to reform an agricultural system based on such deep economic and racial inequities.

The Scottsboro Case. All blacks faced harsh social and political discrimination throughout the South. In a celebrated 1931 case in Scottsboro, Alabama, two white women who had been riding a freight train claimed to have been raped by nine black youths, all under twenty years old. The two women's stories contained many inconsistencies, and one woman later recanted. But in the South when a white woman claimed to have been raped by a black, she was taken at her word and the accused man's guilt was taken for granted. Two weeks later juries composed entirely of white men found all nine defendants guilty of rape; eight were sentenced to death. (One defendant escaped the death penalty because he was a minor.) Though the U.S. Supreme Court overturned the sentences in 1932 and ordered new trials on grounds that the defendants had been denied adequate legal counsel, five of the men eventually were again convicted and sentenced to long prison terms.

The hasty trials and the harsh sentences, especially given the defendants' young age, stirred public protest, prompting the International Labor Defense (ILD), a labor organization tied closely to the Communist Party, to take over the defense. Though the Communist Party had targeted the struggle against racism as a priority in the early 1930s, it was making little headway recruiting African Americans. "It's bad enough being black, why be red?" was

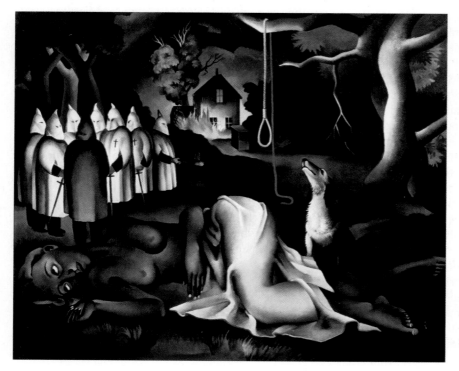

Lynching

The threat of lynching remained a terrifying part of life for African Americans in the 1930s and not just in the South. Artist Joe Jones set this canvas in 1933, perhaps influenced by the fact that twenty-four blacks were lynched that year. He gave it the ironic title of American Justice, 1933 (White Justice).

Collection of Philip J. and Suzanne Schiller.

Drought Refugees
Like the Joad family in John Steinbeck's powerful novel The Grapes of Wrath *(1939), many thousands of poor people hit hard by the drought, dust, and debt of farm life in the Great Plains loaded all their possessions in a pick-up truck and set out for a new start in the West. In this 1937 photograph of Missouri drought refugees on Highway 99 near Tracy, California, photographer Dorothea Lange vividly captured the migrants' bleak circumstances.* Library of Congress.

For more help analyzing this image, see the ONLINE STUDY GUIDE at bedfordstmartins.com/henretta.

a common reaction. White southerners resented radical groups' interference, noting that almost all those involved in the Scottsboro defense were northerners and Jews. Declared a local solicitor, "Alabama justice cannot be bought and sold with Jew money from New York." The Scottsboro case received wide coverage in black communities across the country. Along with an increase in lynching in the early 1930s (twenty blacks were lynched in 1930, twenty-four in 1933), it gave black Americans a strong incentive to head for the North and the Midwest.

Harlem in the 1930s. Harlem, one of their main destinations, was already strained by the enormous influx of African Americans in the 1920s. The depression only aggravated the housing shortage. Residential segregation kept blacks from moving elsewhere, so they paid excessive rents to live in deteriorating buildings where crowded living conditions fostered disease and premature death. As whites clamored for jobs traditionally held by blacks—as waiters, domestic servants, elevator operators, and garbage collectors—unemployment in Harlem rose to 50 percent, twice the national rate. At the height of the depression, shelters and soup kitchens staffed by the Divine Peace Mission, under the leadership of the charismatic black religious leader Father Divine, provided 3,000 meals a day for Harlem's destitute.

In March 1935 Harlem exploded in the only major race riot of the decade. Anger about the lack of jobs, a slowdown in relief services, and economic exploitation of the black community had been building for years. Although white-owned stores were entirely dependent on black trade, store owners would not employ blacks. The arrest of a black shoplifter, followed by rumors that he had been severely beaten by white police, triggered the riot. Four blacks were killed, and $2 million worth of property was damaged.

There were some signs of hope for African Americans in the 1930s. Partly in response to the 1935 riot but mainly in return for growing black allegiance to the Democratic Party (see Chapter 25), the New Deal would channel significant amounts of relief money toward blacks outside the South. And the National Association for the Advancement of Colored People (NAACP) continued to challenge the status quo of race relations. Though calls for racial justice went largely unheeded during the depression, World War II and its aftermath would further the struggle for black equality.

Dust Bowl Migrations

A distressed agricultural sector had been one of the causes of the Great Depression. In the 1930s conditions

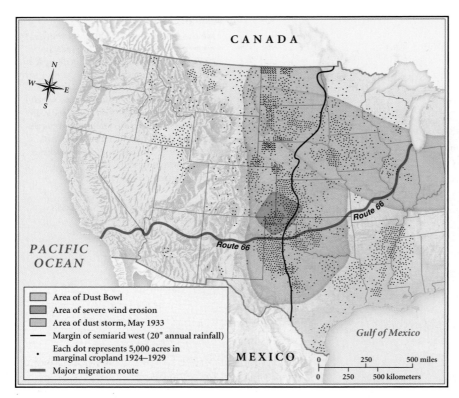

MAP 24.3 The Dust Bowl, 1930–1941

A U.S. Weather Bureau scientist called the drought of the 1930s "the worst in the climatological history of the country." Conditions were especially severe in the southern plains, where the dramatic increases in farming on marginal land had strained production even before the drought struck. Many farm families saw no choice but to follow Route 66, the highway that went west through Missouri, Oklahoma, and north Texas to California, the promised land.

For more help analyzing this map, see the ONLINE STUDY GUIDE at bedfordstmartins.com/henretta.

only got worse, especially for farmers on the Great Plains. In the semiarid states of Oklahoma, Texas, New Mexico, Colorado, Arkansas, and Kansas, farmers had always risked the ravages of drought (see Chapter 16), but the years 1930 to 1941 witnessed the worst drought in the country's history. Low rainfall alone did not create the Dust Bowl, however. National and international market forces, like the rising demand for wheat during World War I, had caused farmers to push the farming frontier beyond its natural limits. To capture a profit they had stripped the land of its natural vegetation, destroying the delicate ecological balance of the plains (Map 24.3). When the rains dried up and the winds came, nothing remained to hold the soil. Huge clouds of dust rolled over the plains, causing streetlights to blink on as if night had fallen. Dust seeped into houses and "blackened the pillow around one's head, the dinner plates on the table, the bread dough on the back of the stove."

The ecological disaster prompted a mass exodus from the plains. Their crops ruined, their lands barren and dry, their homes foreclosed for debts they could not pay, at least 350,000 "Okies" (so-called whether or not they were from Oklahoma) loaded their belongings into beat-up Fords and headed west, encouraged by handbills distributed by growers that promised good jobs in California. Some went to metropolitan areas, but about half settled in rural areas where they worked for low wages as migratory farm laborers. John Steinbeck's novel *The Grapes of Wrath* (1939) immortalized them and their journey. In the novel the Joads abandon their land not only because of drought

but also as a result of the economic transformation of American agriculture that had begun during World War I. By the 1930s large-scale commercialized farming had spread to the plains, where family farmers still used draft animals. In Steinbeck's novel, after the bank forecloses on the Joads' farm, a gasoline-engine tractor, the symbol of mechanized farming, plows under their crops and demolishes their home. Though it was a powerful novel, *The Grapes of Wrath* did not convey the diversity of the westward migration. Not all Okies were destitute dirt farmers; perhaps one in six was a professional, a business proprietor, or a white-collar worker. For most the drive west was fairly easy. Route 66 was a paved two-lane road; in a decent car the journey from Oklahoma or Texas to California took only three to four days.

Before the 1930s, Californians had developed a different type of agriculture from that practiced in the Southwest and Midwest. Basically industrial in nature, California agriculture was large-scale, intensive, and diversified, ironically requiring a massive irrigation system that would lay the groundwork for serious future environmental problems. The key crops were specialty foods—citruses, grapes, potatoes—whose staggered harvests required a great deal of transient labor during short picking seasons. A steady supply of cheap migrant labor provided by Chinese, Mexicans, Okies, Filipinos, and, briefly, East Indians made this type of farming economically feasible.

The migrants had a lasting impact on California culture. At first they met outright hostility from old-time

A Bitter Harvest

In the early 1930s California was rocked by strikes, and one of the largest was the cotton-pickers' strike of 1933. Demanding higher wages and better working conditions, the predominantly Mexican American work force set up camps for the duration of the strike. As usual, it was the women who bore most of the responsibility for cooking, cleaning, and child care.

Bancroft Library, University of California, Berkeley.

Californians—a demoralizing experience for white native-born Protestants, who were ashamed of the Okie stereotype. But they stayed, filling important roles in California's expanding economy. Soon some communities in the San Joaquin Valley—Bakersfield, Fresno, Merced, Modesto, and Stockton—took on a distinctly Okie cast, identifiable by southern-influenced evangelical religion and the growing popularity of country music.

Mexican American Communities

As Okies arrived in California, many Mexican Americans were leaving. In the depths of the depression, with fear of competition from foreign workers at a peak, perhaps a third of the Mexican American population, most of them immigrants, returned to Mexico. A federal deportation policy—fostered by racism and made feasible by the proximity of Mexico—was partly responsible for the exodus, but many more Mexicans left voluntarily when work ran out and local relief agencies refused to assist them. Los Angeles lost approximately one-third of its Mexican community of 150,000—the largest concentration of Mexicans outside Mexico—during the deportations, which separated families, disrupted children's education, and caused extreme financial hardship during the worst years of the depression. They also created a leadership vacuum in Mexican American community and labor organizations, as leaders of these groups returned—sometimes involuntarily—to Mexico. Although forced repatriation slowed after 1932, for those who remained in America deportation was still a constant threat, an unmistakable reminder of their fragile status in the United States.

Discrimination and exploitation were omnipresent in the Mexican community. The harsh experiences of

migrant workers influenced a young Mexican American named César Chávez, who would become one of the twentieth century's most influential labor organizers. In the mid-1930s Chávez's father became involved in several bitter labor struggles in California's Imperial Valley. Thirty-seven major agricultural strikes occurred in California in 1933 alone, including one in the San Joaquin Valley that mobilized 18,000 cotton pickers—the largest agricultural strike to date. All these strikes failed, but they gave the young Chávez a background in labor organizing, which he would use to found a national farm workers' union in 1962.

Not all Mexican Americans were migrant farm workers. A significant number lived in urban areas and held industrial jobs, especially in steel mills, meat-packing plants, and refineries, where they established a strong tradition of labor activism. Mexican American smelter and refinery workers joined the International Union of Mine, Mill and Smelter Workers (known colloquially as "Mine-Mill") in large numbers and became key leaders. Bert Corona launched his career as a labor organizer with the International Longshoremen's and Warehousemen's Union in Los Angeles (see American Lives, "Bert Corona and the Mexican American Generation," p. 712). In California, Mexican Americans also found employment in fruit- and vegetable-processing plants. Young single women especially preferred the higher-paying cannery work to domestic service, needlework, and farm labor. In plants owned by corporate giants like Del Monte, McNeill, and Libby, Mexican American women earned around $2.50 a day, while their male counterparts received $3.50 to $4.50. Labor unions came to the canneries in 1939 with the formation of the United Cannery, Agricultural, Packing, and Allied Workers of America, an

Bert Corona and the Mexican American Generation

Bert Corona

Bert Corona addresses a press conference at the National Chicano Political Caucus in 1972. Bert Corona.

Bert Corona always considered himself a child of the revolution—the Mexican Revolution. His father, Noe Corona, had crossed the border from Mexico to the United States around 1915 or 1916, seeking safety after being wounded while fighting in Pancho Villa's army. Settling temporarily in El Paso, he married Margarita Escápite Salayandia, and they had four children, including Humberto (his Anglo teachers later Americanized his name to Bert), who was born in 1918.

The border is an apt metaphor for Mexican American life, capturing the fluidity of crossing back and forth between two countries and two cultures. Bert's family returned to Mexico in 1922, where two years later Noe Corona was assassinated by unknown assailants, presumably political enemies. This loss had a profound effect on Noe's six-year-old son: "The Revolution, my father's role in it, and his martyrdom symbolized the struggle for social justice. This would be the same struggle I would later pursue."

Strong female role models influenced Bert as well. The Corona family resettled in El Paso, where Bert's mother secured a job at the Mexican customs house on the El Paso–Ciudad Juarez border, and his grandmother, a doctor, pursued her practice of medicine and midwifery. The El Paso school system provided a searing introduction to the discrimination and unequal treatment that Mexican immigrants in the Southwest faced. Corona's segregated "Mexican" school in the barrio, geared primarily toward vocational education, was far inferior to white schools. Although he attended an integrated high school with a good academic reputation, racism and discrimination remained very much a part of his education, both in daily encounters with his Anglo teachers and classmates and in the general lack of respect for Mexican history and culture in the curriculum. His grandmother said tartly, "Well, you have to understand that the United States writes its history to its own convenience. It always has, and these people always will."

When Bert graduated from high school in 1934 at age sixteen, it was the height of the Great Depression, and El Paso was hard hit. Fortunately, his mother kept her job at the Juarez customs house, but hard times forced many Mexicans to leave. El Paso was a major border crossing for *los repatriados* (those returning to their old country), as they fled the depression and the threat of deportation, but Mexicans were not the only group on the move. The Corona backyard faced the train tracks, and Bert vividly remembered the thousands of Dust Bowl migrants traveling through El Paso on their way west. A hundred-car freight train could carry a thousand Dust Bowlers, and there were three trains in the morning and three in the evening. "It was like the population of a small town coming in every day," he later recalled.

After working for two years in El Paso, Bert headed to the University of Southern California, where he hoped to play basketball and continue his education on an athletic scholarship. But an injury cut short his sports career, and he soon found new interests that took him away from his studies, although he later regretted not getting a college degree. What took precedence over his family's strong belief in education? Participating in the revitalized labor movement and fostering Mexican American political consciousness—the two causes that shaped the rest of Corona's life.

The Congress of Industrial Organizations, or CIO (see Chapter 25), became his vehicle for labor activism: "I had a sense of the historical importance of the CIO, and I viewed the CIO as a movement whose time had come. Nothing could stop it, and—for a time—nothing did." In the 1930s many labor activists focused on organizing Mexican American migrant workers in the fields, but Corona concentrated on recruiting Los Angeles industrial workers into the newly constituted International Longshoremen's and Warehousemen's Union (ILWU). His organizing was not restricted to Mexican workers, however. Like the CIO, he wanted the entire working class to join unions to work for social change in the workplace and in society as a whole. While organizing at an aviation plant in 1941, he met his future wife, Blanche Taff. The daughter of Polish Jewish immigrants, she shared his commitment to progressive social change. Their marriage fit right in with the interracial and interethnic culture of the CIO. So great was their commitment to organized labor that they gave up their honeymoon to participate in a major CIO organizing drive.

In addition to labor organizing, Bert Corona felt a deep commitment to the political mobilization of Spanish-speaking peoples throughout the United States. In 1939 he joined El Congreso Nacional del Pueblo de Habla Español (the National Congress of Spanish-Speaking Peoples), a militant organization founded to fight for the rights of Mexican Americans and other Latinos as part of the larger struggle against racial and class oppression. There he worked with noted activists such as Luisa Moreno, a Guatemalan-born CIO organizer who had been active in the cannery industry, and Josefina Fierro, a radical young Mexican American married to the screenwriter John Bright, who was part of Hollywood's leftist community. Their activist agenda was far to the left of that of organizations such as the League of United Latin American Citizens (LULAC), founded in 1929, which focused on assimilation and citizenship from a distinctly middle-class perspective.

After serving in the armed forces during World War II, Corona continued to be a labor and community activist. In the 1960s he became involved in the Mexican American Political Association, or MAPA, which mobilized Latino political power to force the Kennedy and Johnson administrations to do more for those constituencies. Since then he has been involved in community organizing, especially of undocumented Mexican workers, arguing that they have just as legitimate claims to live, work, and be protected by the basic guarantees of American law as any other workers.

Bert Corona exemplifies what the historian Mario Garcia has called the "Mexican-American Generation." These men and women, who were born and raised in the United States, came of political age between the 1930s and the 1950s. They filled the leadership vacuum created when *los repatriados,* mainly older and Mexican-born, returned permanently to that country in the 1930s. Even before terms such as *Mexican American, Hispanic,* and *Latino* were widely used, this generation had the "double consciousness" that W. E. B. Du Bois described in African Americans: a sense of being both *Mexicanos* and American citizens. Many members of the Mexican American Generation shared Corona's commitment to organizing for social change—in their communities, on the job, and in the wider political arena. Tracing their political activism over the years provides a window on the changing character of Mexican American communities in the United States.

Since the 1930s Bert Corona has seen a dramatic expansion of Latino empowerment, but he remains modest about his role in this story. "It's hard for me to think how I would like to be remembered by history," he told Mario Garcia as they collaborated on a book about his life. "I never planned my life. It just happened the way it did. . . . If my life has meant anything, I would say that it shows that you can organize workers and poor people if you work hard, are persistent, remain optimistic, and reach out to involve as many people as possible. . . . But my life is not over yet, and I continue *la lucha,* the struggle." For Bert Corona, that commitment to *la lucha* had its roots in his Mexican heritage, but it first began to flower during the turbulent 1930s.

unusually democratic union in which women, the majority of the rank-and-file workers, played a leading role.

Activism in the fields and factories demonstrated how a second generation of Mexican Americans, born in the United States, had turned increasingly to the struggle for political and economic justice in the United States rather than retaining primary allegiance to Mexico. Joining American labor unions and becoming more involved in American politics (see Chapter 25) were important steps in the creation of a distinct Mexican American ethnic identity.

Asian Americans Face the Depression

Men and women of Asian descent—mostly from China, Japan, and the Philippines—constituted a tiny minority that concentrated primarily in the western states. Their experiences during the depression were as diverse as the people themselves, although all were subject to a pervasive anti-Asian racism. Second-generation Japanese Americans, for example, had eagerly pursued higher education, finishing an average of two years of college during the period of 1925 to 1935, but relatively few professional jobs were open to them as white firms refused to hire them. They and their families concentrated in farming and small ethnic enterprises, often linked to agriculture, such as fruit and vegetable vendors. They had carved out a modest success by the time of the depression, despite a 1913 California law, strengthened in 1920, that prohibited Japanese immigrants from owning land. Having circumvented the laws by various devices—including putting land titles in the names of their citizen children—during the depression, most Japanese farmers managed to hold on to their land, and the amount of acreage owned actually increased. But times were hard, and many farm families barely eked out a decent subsistence. Twenty-two percent of the immigrant population—presumably the poorest—returned to Japan during the depression. And toward the end of the decade, economic anxieties were compounded by renewed anti-Japanese sentiment, stemming from mounting tensions between the United States and Japan over the latter's aggression in Asia (see Chapter 26).

Chinese Americans as a rule had not prospered as much as the Japanese. For example statistics show that as late as 1940, only around 3 percent of Chinese Americans were engaged in professional and technical occupations. But ironically the discrimination that had kept them isolated from the mainstream economy may have proved somewhat beneficial as they weathered the 1930s. In San Francisco, where Chinese were excluded from most industrial jobs, they clustered in ethnic enterprises in the city's Chinatown. Like the rest of the nation's small enterprises, Chinatown's businesses and their employees suffered during the depression, but they bounced back much more quickly. And similar to the experience of white working women, Chinese women found that the labor market that had limited them to a handful of low-paid job categories in light industry and service work in good times worked to their advantage in hard times. They were far less likely to be unemployed than Chinese men. Despite these factors that may have meliorated the hardships of the depression, most Chinese immigrants and their families were on the margins economically. In hard times they turned inward to the community, getting assistance from traditional Chinese social organizations such as *huiguan* (district associations) and kin networks until San Francisco finally extended relief assistance to them—approximately one-sixth of the city's Chinese population was on public assistance in 1931. The New Deal aided them as well, although many programs were limited to citizens and thus barred Chinese immigrants who were "aliens ineligible for citizenship" until the repeal of the Chinese Exclusion Act in 1943.

Filipinos differed from the Japanese and Chinese in that they alone were not affected by the ban on Asian immigration passed in 1924 (see Chapter 23) because the Philippines were a U.S. territory. Consequently their numbers swelled during the 1920s, and by 1930 over 45,000 had emigrated, concentrating mostly along the Pacific Coast. Relegated primarily to menial labor, 60 percent found jobs in agriculture, where they were preferred for the arduous stoop labor for which growers believed they were exceptionally well suited. When the depression struck, Filipinos were among the most militant of the agricultural workers who organized to try to extract decent pay from their employers. Although their first major strike in 1933 was broken, in part by the use of Mexican, Japanese, and Asian Indian strikebreakers, they later enjoyed some success in extracting wage concessions. In 1936 Filipinos and Mexican workers came together in a Field Workers Union chartered by the American Federation of Labor.

Just as the depression focused attention on Mexican immigration, hard times also led to demands that Filipino immigration be restricted. Racial hostility, as well as a concern about Filipinos as competitors for jobs and public relief, fueled the drive to bring about immigration exclusion by making the Philippines an independent nation. In 1934 Congress passed the Tydings-McDuffie Act, which granted independence, classified all Filipinos in the United States as aliens, and restricted immigration to fifty persons per year. By the time the act passed, immigration had slowed to a trickle, but their new status as aliens ineligible for citizenship—or most New Deal assistance programs—had a powerful impact on the Filipinos who remained as unwelcome interlopers.

Herbert Hoover and the Great Depression

Had Herbert Hoover been elected in 1920 instead of 1928, he probably would have been a popular president. As the director of successful food conservation programs at home and charitable food relief abroad during World War I, he was respected as an intelligent and able administrator. Although Hoover's name frequently emerged as a possible candidate in 1920, he did not run for president until the end of the decade. Timing was against him. Although his optimistic predictions in the 1928 campaign—that "the poorhouse is vanishing from among us" and that America was "nearer to the final triumph over poverty than ever before in the history of any land"—reflected beliefs that many Americans shared, that prosperity and Hoover's reputation were soon to be dramatically undermined. When the stock market crashed in 1929, Hoover stubbornly insisted that the downturn was only temporary. In June 1930 he greeted a business delegation with the words "Gentlemen, you have come sixty days too late. The Depression is over." As the country hit rock bottom in 1931 and 1932, the president finally acted, but by then it was too little, too late.

Hoover Responds

Hoover's approach to the Great Depression was shaped by his priorities as secretary of commerce. Hoping to avoid coercive measures on the part of the federal government, he turned to the business community for leadership in overcoming the economic downturn. Hoover asked business executives to maintain wages and production levels voluntarily and to work with the government to build people's confidence in the economic system.

Fiscal Policy. Hoover did not rely solely on public pronouncements, however; he also used public funds and federal action to encourage recovery. Soon after the stock market crash, he cut federal taxes and called on state and local governments to increase their expenditures on public construction projects. He signed the 1929 Agricultural Marketing Act, which gave the federal government an unprecedented role in stabilizing agriculture. In 1930 and the first half of 1931, Hoover raised the federal budget for public works to $423 million, a dramatic increase in expenditures not traditionally considered to be the federal government's responsibility. Hoover also eased the international crisis by declaring a moratorium on the payment of Allied debts and reparations early in the summer of 1931. The depression continued, however. When the president, alarmed about the federal deficit, asked Congress for a 33-percent tax increase to balance the budget, the ill-advised move choked investment and, to a lesser extent, consumption, contributing significantly to the continuation of the depression.

Not all the steps taken by the Hoover administration were so ill conceived. The president pushed Congress to create a system of government home-loan banks in 1932 and supported the Glass-Steagall Banking Act of 1932, which made government securities available to guarantee Federal Reserve notes and thus temporarily propped up the ailing banking system. The federal government under Hoover also spent $700 million—an unprecedented sum for the time—on public works.

The Reconstruction Finance Corporation. Hoover's most innovative program to aid the economy—one the New Deal would later draw on—was the Reconstruction Finance Corporation (RFC), approved by Congress in January 1932. Modeled on the War Finance Corporation of World War I and developed in collaboration with the business and banking communities, the RFC was the first federal institution created to intervene directly in the economy during peacetime. To alleviate the credit crunch for business, the RFC would provide federal loans to railroads, financial institutions, banks, and insurance companies in a strategy that has been called **pump priming**. In theory, money lent at the top of the economic structure would stimulate production, creating new jobs and increasing consumer spending. These benefits would eventually "trickle down" to the rest of the economy.

Unfortunately, the RFC lent its funds too cautiously to make a significant difference. Nonetheless, it represents a watershed in American political history and the growth of the federal government: when voluntary cooperation failed, the president turned to federal action to stimulate the economy. Yet Hoover's break with the past had clear limits. In many ways his support of the RFC was just another attempt to encourage business confidence. Compared with previous chief executives—and in contrast to his popular image as a "do-nothing" president—Hoover responded to the national emergency on an unprecedented scale. But the nation's needs were also unprecedented, and Hoover's programs failed to meet them (see American Voices, "Public Assistance Fails a Southern Farm Family," p. 716).

In particular, federal programs fell short of helping the growing ranks of the unemployed. Hoover remained adamant in his refusal to consider any plan for direct federal relief to those out of work. Throughout his career he had believed that privately organized charities were sufficient to meet the nation's social welfare needs. During World War I he had headed the Commission for Relief of Belgium, a private group that distributed 5 million tons of food to Europe's suffering civilian population. And in 1927 he had coordinated a rescue and cleanup operation after a devastating flood of the Mississippi River left 16.5 million acres of land under water in seven states. The success of these and other predominantly voluntary responses to public emergencies had confirmed Hoover's belief that private charity, not federal aid, was the "American way" of solving social problems. He would not undermine the country's hallowed faith in individualism, even in the face of evidence that charities and state and local relief agencies could not meet the needs of a growing unemployed population.

Public Assistance Fails a Southern Farm Family

When times were bad, even public assistance could be bad for a family in dire straits. Here a young mother living in the farming community of Commerce, Georgia, relates how relief efforts ironically proved to be a burden to her family of eight. She also indicates the strains that "making do" put on poor women.

I've just met with a problem I cannot solve alone. I am a Mother of six children the oldest is only 11 years old the youngest 18 months and I'm expecting another in March. We couldn't get any crop for 1936 because we could neither furnish ourselves or had any stock. So here we are having made out on a little work once in a while all summer. And then in Aug I had to have a serious operation and now I'm not able to feed & clothe our six children as my husband couldnt find anything at all to do was compelled to get on relief job at $1.28 a day 16 days a month. Well you take 8 meals 3 times a day out of $1.28 and what will you have left is 24 meals and what kind of meals do you have? We have to buy everything we eat. We have nothing except what we buy. Our bed-clothes are threadbare our clothes the same. No shoes and no money to buy yet the relief say that cant help us as he is working. Can he work naked. Can he sleep cold. I don't know of any one at all that can help me and I know we cant go on like this.

We have four children in school and they cant go on unless thay [sic] have some warm clothes when cold weather sets in. . . . Do you know of any people in Atlanta that have any used clothes they would give in exchange for piecing quilts or quilting. Id be glad to do anything I can in exchange for clothes to keep our children in school.

I hate to be like this but can a person that is willing to work for a living and that honest and disable to help themselves sit idle and see their small children suffer day after day without enough food or clothes to keep their bodies warm when there are thousands of people with plenty to give if they knew your need.

How it hurts to know that you are almost starving in the land of plenty.

Source: Julia Kirk Blackwelder, "Letters from the Great Depression," in *Southern Exposure* 6, no. 3 (Fall 1978): 77.

Rising Discontent

As the depression deepened many citizens came to hate Herbert Hoover. Once the symbol of business prosperity, he became the scapegoat for the depression. "In Hoover we trusted, now we are busted," declared the hand-lettered signs carried by the down and out. New terms entered the vocabulary: *Hoovervilles* (shantytowns where people lived in packing crates and other makeshift shelters), *Hoover flags* (empty pockets turned inside out), and *Hoover blankets* (newspapers). Hoover's declarations that nobody was starving, that hobos were better fed than ever before, seemed cruel and insensitive. His apparent willingness to bail out businesses and banks while leaving individuals to fend for themselves added to his reputation for coldheartedness.

As the country entered the fourth year of depression, signs of rising discontent and rebellion emerged. Farmers were among the most vocal protestors, banding together to harass the bank agents and government officers who enforced evictions and foreclosures and to protest the low prices they received for their crops. Midwestern farmers had watched the price of wheat fall from $3 a bushel in 1920 to barely 30 cents in 1932. Now they formed the Farm Holiday Association, barricaded local roads, and dumped milk, vegetables, and other farm produce in the dirt rather than accept prices that would not cover their costs. Nothing better captured the cruel irony of maldistribution than farmers destroying food at a time when thousands were going hungry.

Protest was not confined to rural America, however. Bitter labor strikes occurred in the depths of the depression, despite the threat that strikers would lose their jobs. In Harlan County, Kentucky, in 1931 miners struck over a 10 percent wage cut. Their union was crushed by mine owners and the National Guard. In 1932 at Ford's River Rouge factory outside Detroit, a demonstration provoked violence from police and Ford security forces; three demonstrators were killed, and fifty more were seriously injured. Later some 40,000 people viewed the coffins under a banner charging that "Ford Gave Bullets for Bread."

Hoovervilles
By 1930 shantytowns had sprung up in most of the nation's cities. In New York City squatters camped out along the Hudson River railroad tracks, built makeshift homes in Central Park, or lived in the city dump. This scene from the old reservoir in Central Park looks east toward the fancy apartment buildings of Fifth Avenue and the Metropolitan Museum of Art, at left. Grant Smith / Corbis.

In 1931 and 1932 violence broke out in the nation's cities. Groups of the unemployed battled local authorities over inadequate relief, staging rent riots and hunger marches. Some of these actions were organized by the Communist Party—still a tiny organization with only 12,000 members—as a challenge to the capitalist system, such as "unemployment councils" that agitated for jobs and food and a hunger march on Washington, D.C., in 1931. Though the marches were well attended and often got results from local and federal authorities, they did not necessarily win converts to communism.

Not radicals but veterans staged the most publicized—and most tragic—protest. In the summer of 1932, the "Bonus Army," a ragtag group of about 15,000 unemployed World War I veterans, hitchhiked to Washington to demand immediate payment of their bonuses, originally scheduled for distribution in 1945. While their leaders lobbied Congress, the Bonus Army camped out in the capital. "We were heroes in 1917, but we're bums now," one veteran complained bitterly. When the marchers refused to leave their Anacostia Flats camp, Hoover called out riot troops to clear the area. Led by General Douglas MacArthur, and assisted by Major Dwight D. Eisenhower and Major George S. Patton, the troops burned the encampment to the ground. In the fight that followed, more than a hundred marchers were injured. Newsreel footage captured the deeply disturbing spectacle of the U.S. Army moving against its own veterans, and Hoover's popularity plunged even lower.

The 1932 Election: A New Order

Despite the evidence of discontent, the nation overall was not in a revolutionary mood as it approached the 1932 election. Having internalized Horatio Alger's ideal of the self-made man, many Americans initially blamed themselves rather than the system for their hardship. Despair and apathy, not anger, was their mood. The Republicans, who could find no credible way to dump an incumbent president, unenthusiastically again nominated Hoover. The Democrats turned to Governor Franklin Delano Roosevelt of New York, who won the nomination by capitalizing on that state's reputation for innovative relief and unemployment programs.

Roosevelt, born into a wealthy New York family in 1882, had attended Harvard College and Columbia Law School. He had served in the New York State legislature and as assistant secretary of the navy in the Wilson administration, a post that had earned him the vice presidential nomination on the Democratic ticket in 1920. Roosevelt's rise to the presidency was interrupted in 1921 by an attack of polio that left both his legs paralyzed for life. But he fought back from illness, emerging from the ordeal a stronger, more resilient man. "If you had spent two years in bed trying to wiggle your toe, after that anything would seem easy," he explained. His wife, Eleanor, strongly supported his return to public life and helped to mastermind his successful campaign for the governorship of New York in 1928.

The 1932 campaign for the presidency foreshadowed little of the New Deal. Roosevelt hinted only vaguely at new approaches to alleviating the depression: "The country needs and, unless I mistake its temper, the country demands bold, persistent experimentation." He won easily, receiving 22.8 million votes to Hoover's 15.7 million. Despite the nation's economic collapse, Americans remained firmly committed to the two-party system. The Socialist Party candidate, Norman Thomas, got fewer than a million votes, and the Communist Party candidate, party leader William Z. Foster, drew only 100,000 votes (Map 24.4).

The 1932 election marked a turning point in American politics—the emergence of a Democratic coalition that would help to shape national politics for the next four decades. Roosevelt won the support of the Solid South, which returned to the Democratic fold after defecting in 1928 because of Al Smith's Catholicism and his views on Prohibition. Roosevelt drew substantial support in the West and in the cities, continuing a trend first noticed in 1928, when the Democrats appealed successfully to recent immigrants and urban ethnic groups. However, Roosevelt's election was hardly a mandate to reshape American political and economic institutions. Many people voted as much against Hoover as for Roosevelt.

Having spoken, the voters had to wait until Roosevelt's inauguration in March 1933 to see him put his ideas into action. (The four-month interval between the election and the inauguration was shortened by the Twentieth Amendment in 1933.) In the worst winter of the depression, Americans could do little but hope that things would get better. According to the most conservative estimates, unemployment stood at 20 to 25 percent nationwide. The rate was 50 percent in Cleveland, 60 percent in Akron, and 80 percent in Toledo—cities dependent on manufacturing jobs in industries that had essentially shut down. The nation's banking system was so close to collapse that many state governors closed banks temporarily to avoid further panic.

By the winter of 1932–33, the depression had totally overwhelmed public welfare institutions. Private charity and public relief, both of whose expenditures had risen dramatically, still reached only a fraction of the needy. Hunger haunted cities and rural areas alike. When a teacher tried to send a coal miner's daughter home from school because she was weak from hunger, the girl replied, "It won't do any good . . . because this is sister's day to eat." In New York City hospitals reported ninety-five deaths from starvation. This was the America that Roosevelt inherited when he took the oath of office on March 4, 1933.

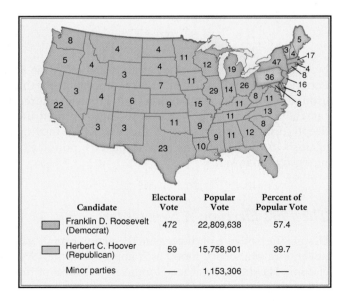

Candidate	Electoral Vote	Popular Vote	Percent of Popular Vote
Franklin D. Roosevelt (Democrat)	472	22,809,638	57.4
Herbert C. Hoover (Republican)	59	15,758,901	39.7
Minor parties	—	1,153,306	—

MAP 24.4 Presidential Election of 1932

Franklin Roosevelt's convincing electoral victory over Herbert Hoover in 1932 resulted from a political realignment and dissatisfaction with the incumbent president. Even in the midst of the gravest crisis capitalism ever faced, candidates of the Communist and Socialist Parties received fewer than 1 million votes out of almost 40 million cast.

FOR FURTHER EXPLORATION

► For definitions of key terms boldfaced in this chapter, see the glossary at the end of the book.

► To assess your mastery of the material covered in this chapter, see the Online Study Guide at **bedfordstmartins.com/henretta**.

► For suggested references, including Web sites, see page SR-26 at the end of the book.

► For map resources and primary documents, see **bedfordstmartins.com/henretta**.

The Great Depression of the 1930s was the longest and most severe economic downturn the United States had ever faced, and it had wide-ranging social, political, and cultural effects. The economic prosperity of the 1920s had rested on shaky ground. After the stock market crash of 1929, the economy entered a downward spiral that did not bottom out until 1932 to 1933. In addition to the collapse of the stock market, the main causes of the depression were underconsumption, an unequal distribution of wealth, an unstable international financial situation, a legacy of "sick industries" and agricultural distress from the 1920s, and the flawed monetary policies of the Federal Reserve System. At first President Hoover did not want to intervene in the economy because of his reliance on private charities and his adamant stance on maintaining a balanced budget. Then in 1932 the Hoover administration authorized the first direct federal intervention in the economy during peacetime, the Reconstruction Finance Corporation, to win business and public confidence. Though unprecedented, such measures did not end the Great Depression. In 1932 the nation turned to Franklin D. Roosevelt and the Democrats.

The Great Depression left an invisible scar on many people who lived through the 1930s, especially white middle-class Americans. Those who wanted to work blamed themselves if they could not find a job. The impact of the depression was especially catastrophic for African Americans and Mexican Americans, for whom times had always been hard, and left a scar with many Asian Americans as well. And for farmers in the Midwest, things got even worse than they had been in the 1920s. Misguided agricultural practices and drought created the Dust Bowl, forcing many farmers off their land.

Despite the devastating impact of the depression, many aspects of American life and culture continued to conform to traditional patterns. Families pulled together, with women taking on expanded roles—and often new jobs—to help support their households. Young people stayed in school longer. Families sought relief in popular culture, especially movies and radio programs, which played an especially important role in reaffirming—and obliquely criticizing—traditional American ideals and institutions.

1929 Stock market crash

Agricultural Marketing Act to stabilize agriculture

1930 Midwestern drought begins

Hawley-Smoot Tariff

1931 *Scottsboro* case

Hoover declares moratorium on Allied war sdebts

Miners strike in Harlan County, Kentucky

1932 Reconstruction Finance Corporation created

Bonus Army rebuffed in Washington

Height of deportation of Mexican migrant workers

Farm Holiday Association dumps produce

Strike at Ford's River Rouge plant in Michigan

Communist-led hunger marches

1933 Unemployment rises to highest level

Franklin Delano Roosevelt becomes president

Birthrate drops to lowest level due to depression

The Marx Brothers in *Duck Soup*

1934 Southern Tenant Farmers Union founded

It Happened One Night sweeps Oscars

Tydings-McDuffie Act grants Philippine independence and curtails immigration

1935 National Youth Administration created

Harlem race riot

1936 Student Strike against War

Margaret Mitchell, *Gone with the Wind*

Birth control legalized

1939 John Steinbeck, *The Grapes of Wrath*

Frank Capra, *Mr. Smith Goes to Washington*

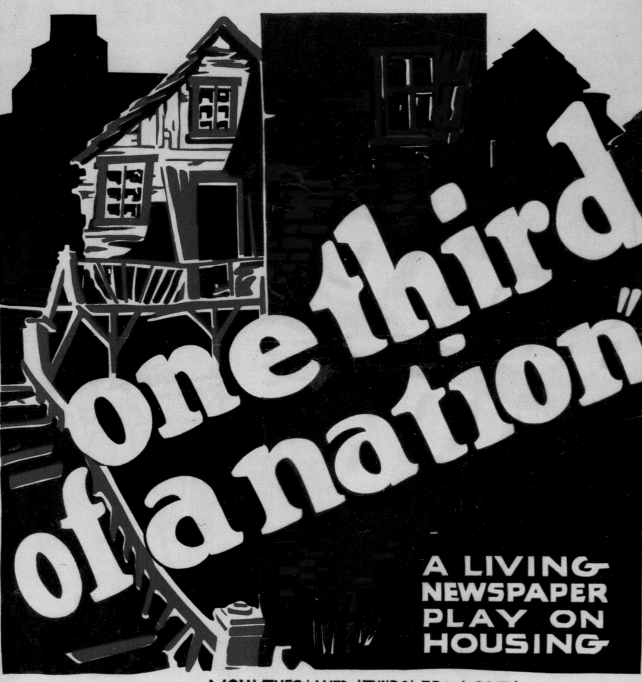

CHAPTER 25

The New Deal

1933–1939

I N HIS BOLD INAUGURAL ADDRESS on March 4, 1933, President Franklin Delano Roosevelt told a despondent, impoverished nation, "The only thing we have to fear is fear itself." That memorable phrase rallied a nation that had already endured almost four years of the worst economic contraction in its history, with no end in sight. His demeanor grim and purposeful, Roosevelt preached his first inaugural address like a sermon. Issuing ringing declarations of his vision of governmental activism—"This Nation asks for action, and action now"—he repeatedly compared combating the Great Depression to fighting a war. The new president was willing to ask Congress for "broad Executive power to wage a war against the emergency, as great as the power that would be given to me if we were in fact invaded by a foreign foe." He promised to "assume unhesitatingly the leadership of this great army of our people dedicated to a disciplined attack upon our common problems."

◄ **"One Third of a Nation"**
One of the more innovative New Deal programs was the Federal Theatre Project. Its director, Hallie Flanagan, envisioned a nationwide network of community theaters that would produce plays of social relevance. "Living Newspaper" productions, such as the one advertised in this 1938 poster for a performance in Oregon, were documentary plays designed to expose Americans to contemporary social problems. One Third of a Nation by Arthur Arent tackled the history of New York City's housing problems, while at the same time it promoted New Deal housing legislation. National Archives.

To wage this war Roosevelt proposed the *New Deal*, a term that he first used in his acceptance speech at the Democratic National Convention in 1932 and that eventually came to stand for his administration's complex set of responses to the nation's economic collapse. The New Deal was never a definitive plan of action but rather evolved and expanded over the course of Roosevelt's presidency.

In a time of major crisis, it was meant to relieve suffering yet conserve the nation's political and economic institutions through unprecedented activity on the part of the national government. Its legacy would be an expanded federal presence in the economy and in the lives of ordinary citizens.

The New Deal Takes Over, 1933–1935

The Great Depression destroyed Herbert Hoover's political reputation and helped to make Roosevelt's. Although some Americans—especially wealthy conservatives—hated Roosevelt, he was immensely popular and beloved by many. Ironically, the ideological differences between Hoover and Roosevelt were not that vast. Both were committed to maintaining the nation's basic institutional structure. Both believed in the basic morality of a balanced budget and extolled the values of hard work, cooperation, and sacrifice. But Roosevelt's personal charisma, his political savvy, and his willingness to experiment made all the difference. Above all, his New Deal programs put people to work, instilling hope and restoring the nation's confidence.

The Roosevelt Style of Leadership

While the New Deal involved hundreds of programs and thousands of people, the leadership of Franklin Roosevelt tied it all together. A superb and pragmatic politician, Roosevelt crafted his administration's program in response to shifting political and economic conditions rather than according to a set ideology or plan. He experimented with an idea; if it did not work, he tried another. "I have no expectation of making a hit every time I come to bat," Roosevelt told his critics. "What I seek is the highest possible batting average."

Roosevelt established an unusually close rapport with the American people. "Mr. Roosevelt is the only man we ever had in the White House who would understand that my boss is a son of a bitch," remarked one worker. Many ordinary citizens credited Roosevelt with the positive changes in their lives, saying "He gave me a job" or "He saved my home." Roosevelt's masterful use of the new medium of radio, typified by the "**fireside chats**" he broadcast during his first two terms, fostered this personal identification. In the week after the inauguration, more than 450,000 letters, many of which addressed Roosevelt as a friend or a member of the family, poured into the White House. An average of 5,000 to 8,000 arrived weekly for the rest of the decade. Whereas one person had handled public correspondence during the Hoover administration, a staff of fifty was required under Roosevelt.

Roosevelt's charisma allowed him to continue the expansion of presidential power begun in the administrations of Theodore Roosevelt and Woodrow Wilson. From the beginning he dramatically enlarged the role of the executive branch in initiating policy, thereby helping to create the modern presidency. For policy formulation he turned to his talented cabinet, which included Secretary of the Interior Harold Ickes, Frances Perkins at Labor, Henry A. Wallace at Agriculture, and an old friend, Henry Morgenthau Jr. at Treasury. During the interregnum (the period between election and inauguration), Roosevelt relied so heavily on the advice of the Columbia University

FDR

President Franklin Delano Roosevelt was a consummate politician who loved the adulation of a crowd, such as this one greeting him in Warm Springs, Georgia, in 1933. He consciously adopted a cheerful mien to keep people from feeling sorry for him because of his infirmity, knowing that he could not be a successful politician if the public pitied him. He so zealously avoided having photographs taken that might show his leg braces or limited mobility that many Americans thought FDR had recovered from the polio that had stricken him in 1921. Corbis-Bettmann.

Joe Marcus

A New Deal Activist

As an economist working for Harry Hopkins, Joe Marcus was one of thousands who formed the growing New Deal bureaucracy. Marcus's account, as told to Studs Terkel, captures some of the excitement that the New Deal generated. Marcus also suggests the way in which Roosevelt's administration expanded opportunities for Jews and other "outsiders."

I graduated college in '35. I went down to Washington and started to work in the spring of '36. The New Deal was a young man's world. Young people, if they showed any ability, got an opportunity. I was a kid, twenty-two or twenty-three. In a few months I was made head of the department. We had a meeting with hot shots: What's to be done? I pointed out some problems: let's define what we're looking for. They immediately had me take over. I had to set up the organization and hire seventy-five people. Given a chance as a youngster to try out ideas, I learned a fantastic amount. The challenge itself was great.

It was the idea of being asked big questions. The technical problems were small. These you had to solve by yourself. But the context was broad: Where was society going? Your statistical questions became questions of full employment. You were not prepared for it in school. If you wanted new answers, you needed a new kind of people. This is what was exciting.

Ordinarily, I might have had a job at the university, marking papers or helping a professor. All of a sudden, I'm doing original research and asking basic questions about how our society works. What makes a Depression?

What makes for pulling out of it? Once you start thinking in these terms, you're in a different ball game.

The climate was exciting. You were part of a society that was on the move. You were involved in something that could make a difference. Laws could be changed. So could the conditions of people.

The idea of being involved close to the center of political life was unthinkable, just two or three years before all this happened. Unthinkable for someone like me, of lower middle-class, close to ghetto, Jewish life. Suddenly you were a significant member of society. It was not the kind of closed society you had lived in before.

. . . You were really part of something, changes could be made. Bringing immediate results to people who were starving. You could do something about it: that was the most important thing. This you felt.

A feeling that if you had something to say, it would get to the top. As I look back now, memoranda I had written reached the White House, one way or another. The biggest thrill of my life was hearing a speech of Roosevelt's, using a selection from a memorandum I had written.

Everybody was searching for ideas. A lot of guys were opportunists, some were crackpots. But there was a search, a sense of values . . . that would make a difference in the lives of people.

We weren't thinking of remaking society. That wasn't it. I didn't buy this dream stuff. What was happening was a complete change in social attitudes at the central government level. The question was: How can you do it within this system? People working in all the New Deal agencies were dominated by this spirit. . . .

It was an exciting community, where we lived in Washington. The basic feeling—and I don't think this is just nostalgia—was one of excitement, of achievement, of happiness. Life was important, life was significant.

Source: Studs Terkel, *Hard Times* (New York: Pantheon Books, 1986), 265–66.

professors Raymond Moley, Rexford Tugwell, and Adolph A. Berle Jr. that the press dubbed them the "Brain Trust."

When searching for new ideas and fresh faces, Roosevelt was just as likely to turn to advisors and administrators scattered throughout the New Deal bureaucracy. Eager young people flocked to Washington to join the New Deal—"men with long hair and women with short hair," wags quipped (see American Voices, "Joe Marcus: A New Deal Activist," above). Lawyers in their mid-

twenties and fresh out of Harvard found themselves drafting legislation or being called to the White House for strategy sessions with the president. Paul Freund, a Harvard Law School professor who worked in the Department of Justice, remembered, "It was a glorious time for obscure people." Many young New Dealers who went on to distinguished careers in government or public service later recalled that nothing could match the excitement of the early New Deal.

The Hundred Days

The first problem the new president confronted was the banking crisis, which, far more than the stock market crash, had brought the depression home to the middle class. Since the onset of the depression, about 9 million people had lost their savings. On the eve of the inauguration, thirty-eight states had closed their banks, and the remaining ten had restricted their hours of operation. On March 5, the day after the inauguration, the president declared a national "**bank holiday**"—a euphemism for closing all the banks—and called Congress into special session. Four days later Congress, which responded enthusiastically to most early New Deal legislative proposals, passed Roosevelt's proposed emergency banking bill, which permitted banks to reopen beginning on March 13 but only if a Treasury Department inspection showed they had sufficient cash reserves. The House approved the plan after only thirty-eight minutes of debate.

The Emergency Banking Act. The Emergency Banking Act, which Roosevelt developed in consultation with banking leaders, was a conservative document that mirrored Herbert Hoover's proposals. The difference was the public's reaction. On the Sunday evening before the banks reopened, Roosevelt broadcast his first fireside chat to a radio audience estimated at 60 million. In simple terms he reassured citizens that the banks were safe, and Americans believed him. When the banks reopened on Monday morning, deposits exceeded withdrawals. "Capitalism was saved in eight days," observed Raymond Moley, who had served as Roosevelt's speech writer in the 1932 campaign. By using the federal government to investigate the nation's banks and restore confidence in the system, the banking act did its job. Though more than 4,000 banks failed in 1933—the majority in the months before the law was passed—only 61 closed their doors in 1934 (Table 25.1).

The banking act was the first of fifteen pieces of major legislation enacted by Congress in the opening months of the Roosevelt administration. This legislative session, known as the "Hundred Days," remains one of the most productive ever. Congress created the Home Owners Loan Corporation to refinance home mortgages threatened by foreclosure. A second banking law, the Glass-Steagall Act, curbed speculation by separating investment banking from commercial banking and created the Federal Deposit Insurance Corporation (FDIC), which insured deposits up to $2,500. Another act established the Civilian Conservation Corps (CCC), which sent 250,000 young men to do reforestation and conservation work. The Tennessee Valley Authority (TVA) received legislative approval for its innovative plan of government-sponsored regional development and public energy. And in a move that lifted public spirits immeasurably, Roosevelt legalized beer in April. Full repeal of Prohibition came eight months later in December 1933.

TABLE 25.1 American Banks and Bank Failures, 1920–1940

Year	Total Number of Banks	Total Assets ($ billion)	Bank Failures
1920	30,909	53.1	168
1929	25,568	72.3	659
1931	22,242	70.1	2,294
1933	14,771	51.4	4,004
1934	15,913	55.9	61
1940	15,076	79.7	48

Source: Historical Statistics of the United States: Colonial Times to 1970 (Washington, DC: U.S. Government Printing Office, 1975), 1019, 1038–39.

The Agricultural Adjustment Act. To speed economic recovery the Roosevelt administration targeted three pressing problems: agricultural overproduction, business failures, and unemployment relief. Roosevelt considered a healthy farming sector crucial to the nation's economic well-being. As he put it in 1929, "If farmers starve today, we will all starve tomorrow." Thus he viewed the Agricultural Adjustment Act (AAA) as a key step toward the nation's recovery. The AAA established a system for seven major commodities (wheat, cotton, corn, hogs, rice, tobacco, and dairy products) that provided cash subsidies to farmers who cut production—a policy that continues to the present day. These benefits were financed by a tax on processing (such as the milling of wheat), which was passed on to consumers. New Deal planners hoped prices would rise in response to the federally subsidized scarcity, spurring a general recovery.

Though the AAA stabilized the agricultural sector, its benefits were distributed unevenly. Subsidies for reducing production went primarily to the owners of large and medium-size farms, who often cut production by reducing their renters' and sharecroppers' acreage rather than their own. In the South, where many sharecroppers were black and the landowners and government administrators were white, that strategy had racial overtones. As many as 200,000 black tenant farmers were displaced from their land by the AAA. Thus New Deal agricultural policies fostered the migration of marginal farmers in the South and Midwest to northern cities and California, while they consolidated the economic and political clout of larger landholders.

The National Recovery Administration. The New Deal's major response to the problem of economic recovery, the National Industrial Recovery Act, launched the National Recovery Administration (NRA). The NRA, which drew on the World War I experience of Bernard Baruch's War Industries Board, established a system of industrial self-government to handle the problems of overproduction, cutthroat competition, and price instability that had caused business failures. Each industry—ranging from large industries such as coal, cotton, and steel to small ones such as dog food, costume jewelry, and even burlesque theaters—hammered out a code of prices and production quotas, similar to those for farm products. In effect, these legally enforceable agreements suspended the antitrust laws. The codes also established minimum wages and maximum hours and outlawed child labor. One of the most far-reaching provisions, Section 7(a), guaranteed workers the right to organize and bargain collectively, "through representatives of their own choosing." These union rights dramatically spurred the growth of the labor movement in the 1930s.

Yet trade associations, controlled by large companies, tended to dominate the code-drafting process, thus solidifying the power of large businesses at the expense of smaller enterprises. Labor had little input, and consumer interests almost none. To sell the program to skeptical consumers and businesspeople, the NRA launched an extensive public relations campaign, complete with plugs in Hollywood films and stickers with the NRA slogan, "We Do Our Part."

Unemployment Legislation.

The early New Deal also addressed the critical problem of unemployment. In the fourth year of the depression, the total exhaustion of private and local sources of charity made some form of federal relief essential. Reluctantly, Roosevelt moved toward federal assumption of responsibility for the unemployed. The Federal Emergency Relief Administration (FERA), set up in May 1933 under the direction of Harry Hopkins, a social worker from New York, offered federal money to the states for relief programs. FERA was designed to keep people from starving until other recovery measures took hold. In his first two hours in office, Hopkins distributed $5 million. When told that some of the projects he had authorized might not be sound in the long run, Hopkins replied, "People don't eat in the long run—they eat every day." Over the program's two-year existence, FERA spent $1 billion.

Roosevelt and his advisors maintained a strong distaste for the **dole**. As Hopkins worried, "I don't think anybody can go year after year, month after month, accepting relief without affecting his character in some ways unfavorably. It is probably going to undermine the independence of hundreds of thousands of families." Whenever possible New Deal administrators promoted work relief over cash subsidies, and they consistently favored jobs that would not compete directly with the private sector. When the Public Works Administration (PWA), under Secretary of the Interior Harold L. Ickes, received a $3.3 billion appropriation in 1933, Ickes's cautiousness in initiating public works projects limited the agency's effectiveness. But in November 1933 Roosevelt established the Civil Works Administration (CWA) and named Harry Hopkins its head. Within thirty days the CWA had put 2.6 million men and women to work; at its peak in January 1934, it employed 4 million in jobs such as repairing bridges, building highways, constructing public buildings, and setting up community projects. The CWA, regarded as a stopgap measure

"Gulliver's Travels"

So many new agencies flooded out of Washington in the 1930s that one almost needed a scorecard to keep them straight. Here a July 1935 Vanity Fair *cartoon by William Gropper substitutes Uncle Sam for Captain Lemuel Gulliver, tied to the ground by Lilliputians, in a parody of Jonathan Swift's* Gulliver's Travels.

Courtesy, *Vanity Fair*. © 1935 (renewed 1963) by The Conde Nast Publications, Inc.

to get the country through the winter of 1933–1934, lapsed the next spring after spending all its funds.

Many of these early emergency measures were deliberately inflationary. They were designed to trigger price increases, which were thought necessary to stimulate recovery and halt the steep deflation. Another element of this strategy was Roosevelt's executive order of April 18, 1933, to abandon the international gold standard and allow gold to rise in value like any other commodity. As the price of gold rose, administrators hoped, so too would the prices of manufactured and agricultural goods. Though removing the country from the gold standard did not accomplish much toward economic recovery, it did provide the Federal Reserve System freedom to attempt to promote stable prices and full employment without being tied to the value of gold on the international market. Now it could manipulate the value of the dollar in response to fluctuating economic conditions.

When an exhausted Congress recessed in June 1933, much had been accomplished. Rarely had a president so dominated a legislative session. A mass of "**alphabet soup agencies**," as the New Deal programs came to be known, had been created. But though they gave the impression of action and initiated a slight economic upturn, they did not turn the economy around.

After the Hundred Days, with no end to the depression in sight, Roosevelt and Congress continued to pass legislation to promote recovery and restore confidence. Much of it focused on reforming business practices to prevent future depressions. In 1934 Congress established the Securities and Exchange Commission (SEC) to regulate the stock market. The commission had the power to regulate the purchase of stocks on credit, or **margin buying**, and to restrict speculation by those with inside information on corporate plans. The Banking Act of 1935 authorized the president to appoint a new Board of Governors of the Federal Reserve System, placing control of interest rates and other money-market policies at the federal level rather than with regional banks. By requiring all large state banks to join the Federal Reserve System by 1942 to take advantage of the federal deposit insurance system, the law further encouraged centralization of the nation's banking system.

The New Deal under Attack

As Congress and the president consolidated the New Deal, their work came under attack from several quarters. Although Roosevelt billed himself as the savior of capitalism, noting that "to preserve we had to reform," his actions provoked strong hostility from many Americans who charged that he was undermining capitalism. To the wealthy Roosevelt became simply "that man," a traitor to his class. Business leaders and conservative Democrats formed the Liberty League in

1934 to lobby against the New Deal and its "reckless spending" and "socialist" reforms.

The conservative majority on the Supreme Court also disagreed with the direction of the New Deal. On "Black Monday," May 27, 1935, the Supreme Court struck down the NRA in *Schechter v. United States*, ruling unanimously that the National Industrial Recovery Act represented an unconstitutional delegation of legislative power to the executive. The so-called sick-chicken case concerned a Brooklyn, New York, firm convicted of violating NRA codes by selling diseased poultry. The Court found in favor of the poultry firm, stating in its decision that the NRA illegally regulated commerce within states, while the Constitution limited federal regulation to interstate commerce. Roosevelt protested that the Court's narrow interpretation would return the Constitution "to the horse-and-buggy definition of interstate commerce" and worried privately that the Court might invalidate the entire New Deal.

Other citizens thought the New Deal had not gone far enough. Francis Townsend, a Long Beach, California, doctor, spoke for the nation's elderly. Many Americans feared poverty in old age because few had pension plans, and many had lost their life savings in bank failures. In 1933 Townsend proposed the Old Age Revolving Pension Plan, which would give $200 a month—a considerable sum at the time—to citizens over the age of sixty. To receive payments the elderly would have to retire from their jobs, thus opening their positions to others, and would also have to agree to spend the money within a month. Townsend Clubs soon sprang up across the country, particularly in the Far West and mobilized mass support for old-age pensions that would eventually help secure the passage of the far less ambitious plan created by the Social Security Act of 1935.

Father Charles Coughlin also challenged Roosevelt's leadership, attracting a large following, especially in the Midwest. A parish priest in the Detroit suburb of Royal Oak, Coughlin had turned to the radio in the mid-1920s to enlarge his pastorate. In 1933 about 40 million Americans listened regularly to the Radio Priest's broadcasts. At first Coughlin supported the New Deal, but he soon broke with Roosevelt over the president's refusal to support the nationalization of the banking system and expansion of the money supply. Although Coughlin offered varying solutions to the economic crisis, he tended to rely heavily on inflationary schemes that harked back to the Populist era (see Chapter 18). In 1935 he organized the National Union for Social Justice to promote his views, billing them as an alternative to those of "Franklin Double-Crossing Roosevelt." Because he was Canadian born and a priest, Coughlin was not likely to make a run for president, but his rapidly growing constituency threatened to complicate the 1936 election.

The most direct threat to Roosevelt came from Senator Huey Long. In a single term as governor of

Louisiana, the flamboyant Long had achieved stunning popularity. He had increased the share of state taxes paid by corporations and had embarked on a program of public works that included construction of new highways, bridges, hospitals, and schools. But Long's accomplishments came at a price: to push through his reforms he had seized almost dictatorial control of the state government. He maintained control over Louisiana's political machine even after his election to the U.S. Senate in 1930. Though he supported Roosevelt in 1932, he made no secret of his own presidential ambitions.

In 1934 Senator Long broke with the New Deal, arguing that its programs did not go far enough. Like Coughlin he established his own national movement, the Share Our Wealth Society, which boasted over 4 million followers by 1935. Arguing that the unequal distribution of wealth in the United States was the fundamental cause of the depression, Long advocated taxing 100 percent of all incomes over $1 million and all inheritances over $5 million, distributing the money to the rest of the population.

He knew his plan was unworkable but confided privately, "When they figure that out, I'll have something new for them."

Like Coughlin, Long offered quick-fix solutions to the nation's economic ills that only addressed part of the complex problems that fueled the continuing depression. Their extreme proposals alarmed liberals, as both men showed little regard for the niceties of representative government. Coughlin had actually promised to dictate if necessary to preserve democracy. And the demagogic Long had dismissed complaints about his unconstitutional interference with the Louisiana legislative process by announcing, "I'm the Constitution around here." Coughlin's rhetoric, furthermore, often had disturbingly anti-Semitic overtones. Long and Coughlin's ideas and their rapid rise in popularity suggested strong currents of public dissatisfaction with the Roosevelt administration. The president's strategists feared that Long might join forces with Coughlin and Townsend to form a third party, enabling the Republicans to win the 1936 election.

The Kingfish
Huey Long, the Louisiana governor and senator, called himself "the Kingfish" because "I'm a small fish here in Washington. But I'm the Kingfish to the folks down in Louisiana." An exceptionally charismatic man and a brilliant campaigner, he attracted a significant following with his "Share Our Wealth Plan," which aimed to redistribute the nation's wealth. Democrats worried that he might run for president in 1936 on a third-party ticket, thus threatening Franklin Roosevelt's reelection, but his assassination in 1935 at the hands of a Louisiana doctor put an end to his political ambitions. Long is seen here on the right, hat in hand.
Louisiana State Museum.

The Second New Deal, 1935–1938

As the depression continued and attacks on the New Deal mounted, Roosevelt and his advisors embarked on a new course, which historians have labeled the Second New Deal. By 1935, frustrated by his inability to win the support of big business, Roosevelt began to openly criticize the "money classes," proudly stating of his administration that "We have earned the hatred of entrenched greed." Pushed to the left by the popularity of movements like Long's as well as by signs of militancy among workers, Roosevelt, his eye fixed firmly on the 1936 election, began to construct a new coalition and broaden the scope of his response to the depression.

Legislative Accomplishments

Unlike the First New Deal, which focused on recovery, the Second New Deal emphasized reform and promoted legislation to increase the role of the federal government in providing for the welfare of citizens. While one of the most dramatic programs, the Works Progress Administration, did not last beyond the crisis of the depression, the Wagner Act and the Social Security Act would become permanent features of American life.

The Wagner Act and Social Security. The first beneficiary of Roosevelt's change in direction was the labor movement. The rising number of strikes in 1934—about 1,800 involving a total of 1.5 million workers—reflected the dramatic growth of rank-and-file militancy. After the Supreme Court declared the NRA unconstitutional in 1935, invalidating Section 7(a), labor representatives demanded effective legislation that would protect the right to organize and bargain collectively. Named for its sponsor, Senator Robert F. Wagner of New York, the Wagner Act (1935) offered a degree of protection to labor. It upheld the right of industrial workers to join a union (farm workers were not covered) and outlawed many unfair labor practices used to squelch unions, such as firing workers for union activities. The act also established the nonpartisan National Labor Relations Board (NLRB) to protect workers from employer coercion, supervise elections for union representation, and guarantee the process of collective bargaining.

The Social Security Act signed by Roosevelt on August 14, 1935, was partly a response to the political mobilization of the nation's elderly through the Townsend and Long movements. But it also reflected prodding from social reformers like Grace Abbott, head of the Children's Bureau, and Secretary of Labor Frances Perkins. The Social Security Act provided pensions for most workers in the private sector, although originally agricultural workers and domestics were not covered, a limitation that disproportionately disadvantaged poor blacks, especially women. Pensions were to be financed

General Strike, San Francisco, 1934
A general strike in San Francisco began with the longshoremen and soon spread to almost every union member (and some middle-class supporters as well) in the city. This striker has been shot in the head during an altercation with police. On July 19, union leaders voted to accept government arbitration, and the strike ended. Corbis-Bettmann.

by a federal tax that both employers and employees would pay. The act also established a joint federal-state system of unemployment compensation, funded by an unemployment tax on employers.

The Social Security Act was a milestone in the creation of the modern **welfare state**. Now the United States joined industrialized countries like Great Britain and Germany in providing old-age pensions and unemployment compensation to citizens. (The Roosevelt administration chose not to push for national health insurance, even though most other industrialized nations offered such protection.) The act also mandated categorical assistance to the blind, deaf, and disabled and to dependent children—the so-called deserving poor, who clearly could not support themselves. Categorical assistance programs, only a small part of the New Deal, gradually expanded over the years until they became an integral part of the American welfare system.

The Works Progress Administration.   Roosevelt was never enthusiastic about large expenditures for social welfare programs. But in the sixth year of the depression, 10 million Americans were still out of work, creating a pressing moral and political issue for FDR and the Democrats. Under Harry Hopkins the Works Progress Administration (WPA) became the main federal relief agency for the rest of the depression. While FERA had supplied grants to state relief programs, the WPA put relief workers directly onto the federal payroll. Between 1935 and 1943 the WPA employed 8.5 million Americans, spending $10.5 billion. The agency's employees constructed 651,087 miles of roads, 125,110 public buildings, 8,192 parks, and 853 airports and built or repaired 124,087 bridges (Map 25.1).

Though the WPA was an extravagant operation by the standards of the 1930s (it inspired nicknames such as "We Putter Around" and "We Poke Along"), it never reached more than a third of the nation's unemployed. The average

See America

During the New Deal, the United States Travel Bureau encouraged Americans to explore the nation's wide variety of vacation destinations and commissioned travel posters from the WPA's Federal Art Project. This example highlighting Montana was typical of the emphasis on regional distinctiveness as well as natural beauty. The imagery also often invoked a sense of power and encouraged Americans not just to "see America" but to see its strength and potential, a message designed to offset the pessimism created by the economic crisis. Library of Congress.

wage of $55 a month—well below the government-defined subsistence level of $100 a month—barely enabled workers to eke out a living. In 1941 the government cut the program severely. It ended in 1943 when the economy returned to full employment during World War II.

The Revenue Act of 1935.   The Revenue Act of 1935, a tax reform bill that increased estate and corporate taxes and instituted higher personal income tax rates in the top brackets, showed Roosevelt's willingness to push for reforms that were considered too controversial earlier in his presidency. Much of the business community had already turned violently against Roosevelt in reaction to the NRA, the Social Security Act, and the Wagner Act. Now wealthy conservatives quickly labeled the Revenue Act an attempt to "soak the rich." Roosevelt, seeking to defuse the popularity of Huey Long's Share Our Wealth plan, was just as interested in the political mileage of the tax bill as in its actual results, which increased federal revenue by only $250 million a year.

The 1936 Election

As the 1936 election approached, the broad range of New Deal programs (Table 25.2) brought new voters into the Democratic coalition. Many had been personally helped by federal programs. Others benefited because their interests had found new support in the federal expansion: Roosevelt could count on a potent coalition of urban-based workers, organized labor, northern blacks, farmers, white ethnic groups, Catholics, Jews, liberals, intellectuals, progressive Republicans, and middle-class families concerned about unemployment and old-age dependence. The Democrats also held on, though with some difficulty, to their traditional constituency of white southerners.

The Republicans realized that they could not directly oppose Roosevelt and the New Deal. To run against the president, they chose the progressive governor of Kansas, Alfred M. Landon, who accepted the general precepts of the New Deal. Landon and the Republicans concentrated on criticizing the inefficiency and expense of many New Deal programs, stridently accusing FDR of harboring dictatorial ambitions.

Roosevelt's victory in 1936 was one of the biggest landslides in American history. The assassination of Huey Long in September 1935 had deflated the threat of a serious third-party challenge; the candidate of the combined Long-Townsend-Coughlin camp, Congressman William Lemke of North Dakota, garnered fewer than 900,000 votes (1.9 percent) for the Union Party ticket. Roosevelt received 60.8 percent of the popular vote and carried every state except Maine and Vermont. Landon fought such an uphill battle that the columnist Dorothy Thompson quipped, "If Landon had given one more speech, Roosevelt would have carried Canada." The New Deal was at high tide.

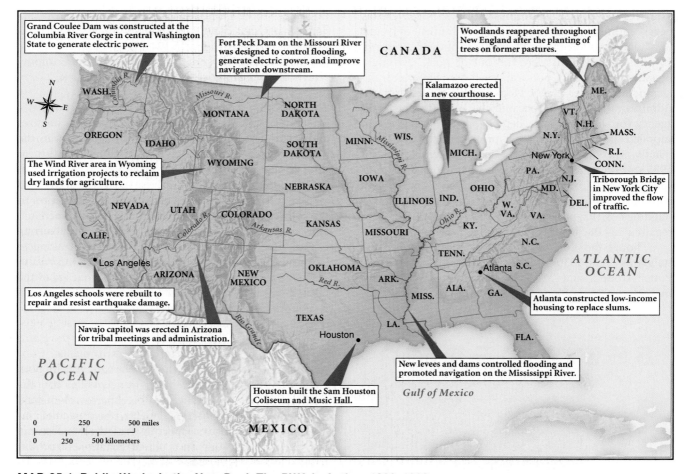

MAP 25.1 **Public Works in the New Deal: The PWA in Action, 1933–1939**

Between 1933 and 1939, the New Deal agencies of the Civilian Conservation Corps (CCC), the Works Progress Administration (WPA), and the Public Works Administration (PWA) created public works projects designed to put unemployed Americans to work and prime the economy with federal dollars, while simultaneously making lasting contributions to the nation's communities. The PWA, established in 1933 and directed by Harold Ickes, was the first federal agency to undertake extensive public projects that ranged from courthouses to swimming pools, airports to aircraft carriers, the Triborough Bridge to the Grand Coulee Dam.

Stalemate

"I see one-third of a nation ill-housed, ill-clad, ill-nourished," the president declared in his second inaugural address in January 1937. Roosevelt's appraisal suggested that he was considering further expansion of the welfare state that had begun to form late in this first term. However, retrenchment, controversy, and stalemate—not further reform—marked the second term.

The Supreme Court Fight. Only two weeks after his inauguration, Roosevelt stunned Congress and the nation by asking for fundamental changes in the structure of the Supreme Court. Shortly after finding the NRA unconstitutional in *Schechter v. United States,* the Court had struck down the Agricultural Adjustment

Act, a coal conservation act, and New York State's minimum wage law. With the Wagner Act, the TVA, and Social Security coming up on appeal, the future of New Deal reform measures seemed in doubt.

Roosevelt responded by proposing the addition of one new justice for each sitting justice over the age of seventy—a scheme that would have increased the number of justices from nine to fifteen. Roosevelt's opponents quickly protested that he was trying to "pack" the Court with justices who favored the New Deal. The president's proposal was also regarded as an assault on the principle of the separation of powers. Congress blocked the proposal, but Roosevelt ultimately achieved some part of what he wanted, as the Supreme Court upheld several key pieces of New Deal legislation, and a series of resignations created vacancies on the Court. Within four

TABLE 25.2 Major New Deal Legislation

Agriculture

1933	Agricultural Adjustment Act (AAA)
1935	Resettlement Administration (RA) Rural Electrification Administration
1937	Farm Security Administration (FSA)
1938	Agricultural Adjustment Act of 1938

Business and Industry

1933	Emergency Banking Act Glass-Steagall Act (FDIC) National Industrial Recovery Act (NIRA)
1934	Securities and Exchange Commission (SEC)
1935	Banking Act of 1935 Revenue Act (wealth tax)

Conservation and the Environment

1933	Tennessee Valley Authority (TVA) Civilian Conservation Corps (CCC)
1936	Soil Conservation and Domestic Allotment Act

Labor and Social Welfare

1933	Section 7(a) of NIRA
1935	National Labor Relations Act (Wagner Act) National Labor Relations Board (NLRB) Social Security Act
1937	National Housing Act
1938	Fair Labor Standards Act (FLSA)

Relief

1933	Federal Emergency Relief Administration (FERA) Civil Works Administration (CWA) Public Works Administration (PWA)
1935	Works Progress Administration (WPA) National Youth Administration (NYA)

years, retirements allowed Roosevelt to reshape the Supreme Court to suit his liberal philosophy through seven new appointments, including Hugo Black, Felix Frankfurter, and William O. Douglas. Yet his court scheme was a costly blunder at a time when his second-term administration was vulnerable to the lame-duck syndrome, in which Congress traditionally is less responsive to the proposals of a second-term president, knowing

he will soon be out of office. No one yet suspected that FDR would break with tradition by seeking a third term.

Congressional Opposition. Congressional conservatives had long opposed the direction of the New Deal, but the court-packing episode galvanized them by demonstrating that Roosevelt was no longer politically invincible. Throughout Roosevelt's second term a conservative coalition composed mainly of southern Democrats and Republicans from rural areas blocked or impeded social legislation. Two pieces of reform legislation that did win passage were the National Housing Act of 1937, which mandated the construction of low-cost public housing, and the Fair Labor Standards Act of 1938, which made permanent the minimum wage, maximum hours, and anti–child labor provisions in the NRA codes.

Roosevelt's attempts to reorganize the executive branch met a different fate. When Roosevelt inherited the presidency, the executive branch was still relatively weak. The enormity of the economic crisis gave the president far more influence in proposing and passing legislation, and the administration of New Deal programs significantly expanded the executive's influence. Congress resisted this accrual of power, however. In both 1937 and 1938, it refused to consider a plan to consolidate all independent agencies into cabinet-rank departments, extend the civil service system, and create the new position of auditor general. Conservatives effectively played on lawmakers' fears that centralized executive management would dramatically reduce congressional power and linked the plan to popular fears of fascism and dictatorship abroad, fears fanned by Hitler's rise to power in Germany. Roosevelt settled for a less ambitious bill in 1939 that allowed him to create the Executive Office of the President and name six administrative assistants to the White House staff. The White House also took control of the all-important budget process by moving the Bureau of the Budget to the Executive Office from its old home in the Treasury department.

The Roosevelt Recession. The "Roosevelt recession" of 1937 to 1938 dealt the most devastating blow to the president's political standing in the second term. Until that point the economy had made steady progress. From 1933 to 1937 the gross domestic product had grown at a yearly rate of about 10 percent, and by 1937 industrial output and real income had finally returned to 1929 levels. Unemployment had declined from 25 percent to 14 percent. Many Americans agreed with Senator James F. Byrnes of South Carolina that "the emergency has passed."

The steady improvement of the economy cheered Roosevelt, who had never been comfortable with large federal expenditures. Accordingly, Roosevelt slashed the federal budget in 1937. Between January and August Congress cut the WPA's funding in half, causing layoffs of about 1.5 million workers. Fearing inflation, the Federal Reserve tightened credit, creating a sharp drop in the stock market. Unemployment soared to 19 percent, which translated into more than 10 million workers without jobs. Roosevelt soon found himself in the same situation that had confounded Hoover. Having taken credit for the recovery between 1933 and 1937, he had to take the blame for the recession.

Shifting gears, Roosevelt spent his way out of the downturn. Large WPA appropriations and a resumption of public works projects poured enough money into the economy to lift it out of the recession by early 1938. Roosevelt and his economic advisors were groping their way toward the general theory advanced by John Maynard Keynes, a British economist who proposed that governments use **deficit spending** (the spending of public funds obtained by borrowing rather than through taxation) to stimulate the economy when private spending proves insufficient. But Keynes's theory would not be widely accepted until a dramatic increase in defense spending for World War II finally ended the Great Depression.

Still struggling with attacks on the New Deal, Roosevelt decided to "purge" the Democratic Party of some of his most conservative opponents as the 1938 election approached. In the spring primaries he campaigned against members of his own party who had been hostile or unsympathetic to New Deal initiatives. The purge failed abysmally and widened the liberal-conservative rift in the party. In the general election of 1938, Republicans capitalized on the "Roosevelt recession" and the backlash against the court-packing attempt: they picked up eight seats in the Senate and eighty-one in the House. The Republicans also gained thirteen governorships.

Even without these political reversals, the reform impetus of the New Deal probably would not have continued. Roosevelt had always set clear limits on how far he was willing to go. His instincts were basically conservative, not revolutionary; he had wanted only to save the capitalist economic system by reforming it. The new activism of the Second New Deal was a major step beyond the informal, one-sided business-government partnership of the preceding decade, but it was a step Roosevelt took only because the emergency of the depression had pushed him in that direction.

The New Deal's Impact on Society

Despite the limits of the New Deal, it had a tremendous impact on the nation and fundamentally altered Americans' relationship to their government. With an optimistic faith in using government for social purposes, New Dealers sponsored programs in the arts. They created vast projects to conserve the country's natural beauty and

resources and to make them more accessible to its citizens. The broker state that emerged in the New Deal also brought the voices of more citizens—women, blacks, labor, Mexican Americans—into the public arena, helping to promote the view that Roosevelt and his party represented and mediated for the common people.

New Deal Constituencies and the Broker State

The New Deal accelerated the expansion of the federal bureaucracy that had been under way since the turn of the century. In a decade the number of civilian government employees increased 80 percent, exceeding a million by 1940. The number of federal employees who worked in Washington grew at an even faster rate, doubling between 1929 and 1940. Power was increasingly centered in the nation's capital and not in the states. In 1939 a British observer summed up the new orientation: "Just as in 1929 the whole country was 'Wall Street conscious', now it is 'Washington conscious'."

The growth of the federal government increased the potential impact of its decisions (and spending) on various constituencies. During the 1930s the federal government operated as a broker state, mediating between contending pressure groups seeking power and benefits. Democrats recognized the importance of satisfying certain blocs of voters to cement their allegiance to the party. Even before the depression they had begun to build a coalition based on urban political machines and white ethnic voters. In the 1930s organized labor, women, African Americans, and other groups joined that coalition, receiving increased attention from the Democrats and the federal government they controlled.

Organized Labor. During the 1930s, after decades of federal hostility or inattention to the rights of workers, labor relations became a legitimate arena for federal action and intervention, and organized labor claimed a place in national political life. Labor's dramatic growth in the 1930s represented one of the most important social and economic changes of the decade, an enormous contrast to its demoralized state at the end of the 1920s. Several factors encouraged the growth of the labor movement: the inadequacy of welfare capitalism in the face of the depression, New Deal legislation like the Wagner Act, the rise of the Congress of Industrial Organizations (CIO), and the growing militancy of rank-and-file workers. By the end of the decade, the number of unionized workers had tripled to almost 9 million, or 23 percent of the nonfarm workforce. Organized labor won the battle not only for union recognition but for higher wages, seniority systems, and grievance procedures.

The CIO served as the cutting edge of the union movement by promoting "industrial unionism"—that is, organizing all the workers in an industry, both skilled and unskilled, into one union. John L. Lewis, leader of the United Mine Workers (UMW) and the foremost exponent of industrial unionism, broke with the American Federation of Labor, which favored organizing workers on a craft-by-craft basis, and in 1935 helped to found the CIO. The CIO achieved some of its momentum through the presence in its ranks of members of the Communist Party. The rise of fascism in Europe had prompted the Soviet Union to mobilize support in democratic countries. In Europe and the United States, Communist parties called for a "popular front," welcoming the cooperation of any group concerned about the threat of fascism to civil rights, organized labor, and world peace. Under the popular front Communists softened their revolutionary rhetoric and concentrated on becoming active leaders in many CIO unions. While few workers actually joined the Communist Party, its influence in labor organizing in the

Organize

The Steel Workers Organizing Committee was one of the most vital labor organizations contributing to the rise of the CIO. Note that artist Ben Shahn chose a male figure to represent the American labor movement in this poster from the late 1930s. Such iconography reinforced the notion that the typical worker was male, despite the large number of women who joined the CIO. Library of Congress.

For more help analyzing this image, see the ONLINE STUDY GUIDE at bedfordstmartins.com/henretta.

thirties was far greater than its numbers, which in 1936 reached 40,000.

The CIO's success also stemmed from the recognition that unions must be more inclusive in order to succeed. The CIO worked deliberately to attract new groups to the labor movement. Mexican Americans and African Americans found the CIO's commitment to racial justice a strong contrast to the AFL's long-established patterns of exclusion and segregation. And about 800,000 women workers also found a limited welcome in the CIO. Few blacks, Mexican Americans, or women held leadership positions, however.

The CIO scored its first major victory in the automobile industry. On December 31, 1936, General Motors workers in Flint, Michigan, staged a sit-down strike, vowing to stay at their machines until management agreed to collective bargaining. The workers lived in the factories and machine shops for forty-four days before General Motors recognized their union, the United Automobile Workers (UAW). Shortly thereafter the CIO won another major victory, at the U.S. Steel Corporation. Despite a long history of bitter opposition to unionization, as demonstrated in the 1919 steel strike (see Chapter 22), Big Steel executives capitulated without a fight and recognized the Steel Workers Organizing Committee (SWOC) on March 2, 1937.

The victory in the steel industry was not complete, however. A group of companies known as "Little Steel" chose not to follow the lead of U.S. Steel in making peace with the CIO, causing steelworkers to strike the Republic Steel Corporation plant in South Chicago. On Memorial Day, May 31, 1937, strikers and their families gathered for a holiday picnic and rallied outside the plant's gates. Tension mounted, rocks were thrown, and the police fired on the crowd, killing ten protesters. All were shot in the back. A newsreel photographer recorded the scene, but Paramount Pictures considered the film of the "Memorial Day Massacre" too inflammatory for distribution. Workers in Little Steel did not win union recognition until 1941. The road to recognition for labor, even with New Deal protections, was still long and violent.

The 1930s constituted one of the most active periods of labor solidarity in American history (Map 25.2). The sit-down tactic spread rapidly. In March 1937 a total of 167,210 workers staged 170 sit-down strikes. Labor unions called for nearly 5,000 strikes that year and won favorable terms in 80 percent of them. Yet large numbers of middle-class Americans felt alienated by sit-down strikes, which they considered attacks on private property. The Supreme Court agreed and in 1939 upheld a law that banned the practice.

Labor's new vitality spilled over into political action. The AFL generally had stood aloof from partisan politics, but the CIO quickly allied itself with the Democratic Party, hoping to use its influence to elect candidates sympathetic to labor and social justice. Establishing a

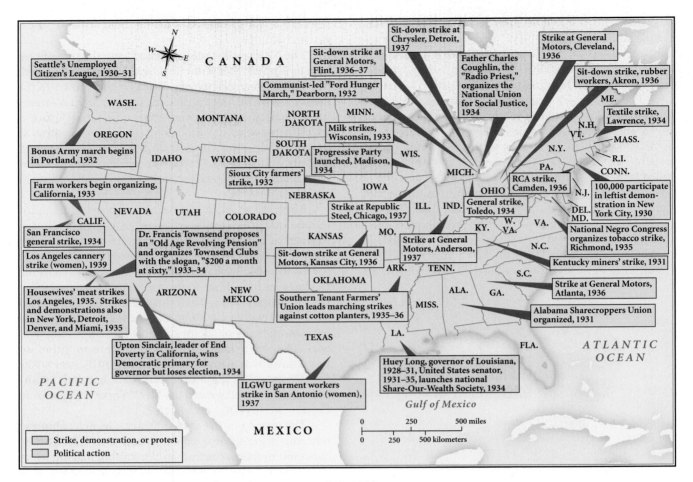

MAP 25.2 Popular Protest in the Great Depression, 1933–1939

Throughout the Depression, Americans protested the harsh conditions brought about by economic collapse. Some expressed their discontent through large social movements like Upton Sinclair's EPIC (End Poverty in California) or Huey Long's Share Our Wealth movement. Others turned to Communist-led demonstrations such as the 1932 "Ford Hunger March" in Dearborn, Michigan. Independent farmers in Iowa's Farm Holiday Association organized to bring about higher prices in 1932, while in 1935, the socialist-led Southern Tenant Farmers' Union challenged cotton planters over their restriction of tenants' rights. Also in 1935, militant housewives staged meat strikes in cities countrywide to protest high meat prices. Everywhere, it seemed, American workers were striking against their employers. Despite this wellspring of popular protest, discontent in the 1930s did not lead to a radical restructuring of politics or the economy, in large measure because Franklin Roosevelt's New Deal shored up confidence and deflected dissent.

group it rather misleadingly called Labor's Nonpartisan League, the CIO gave $770,000 to Democratic campaigns in 1936. Labor also provided solid support for Roosevelt's plan to reorganize the Supreme Court.

Despite the breakthroughs of the New Deal, the labor movement never developed into a dominant force in American life. Roosevelt never made the growth of the labor movement a high priority, and many workers remained indifferent or even hostile to unionization. And although the Wagner Act guaranteed unions a permanent place in American industrial relations, it did not revolutionize working conditions. The right to collective bargaining, rather than redistributing power in Ameri-

can industry, merely granted labor a measure of legitimacy. Management even found that unions could be used as a buffer against rank-and-file militancy. New Deal social welfare programs also tended to diffuse some of the pre-1937 radical spirit by channeling economic benefits to workers whether or not they belonged to unions. The road to union power, even with New Deal protection, continued to be a rocky and uncertain one.

Women and the New Deal. Like organized workers white women achieved new influence in the experimental climate of the New Deal, as unprecedented numbers of them were offered positions in the Roosevelt

A First Lady without Precedent

Reflecting Eleanor Roosevelt's tendency to turn up in odd places, a famous 1933 New Yorker *cartoon has one coal miner saying to another, "For gosh sakes, here comes Mrs. Roosevelt."* Life *soon imitated art. Here, the first lady emerges from a coal mine in Dellaire, Ohio, still carrying her miner's cap in her left hand, while speaking with Joseph Bainbridge on May 22, 1935.*
Wide World Photos, Inc.

administration. Frances Perkins, the first woman named to a cabinet post, served as secretary of labor throughout Roosevelt's presidency. Molly Dewson, a social reformer turned politician, headed the Women's Division of the Democratic National Committee, where she pushed an issue-oriented program that supported New Deal reforms. Roosevelt's woman appointees also included the first female director of the mint, the head of a major WPA division, and a judge on a circuit court of appeals. Many of those women were close friends as well as professional colleagues and cooperated in an informal network to advance feminist and reform causes.

Eleanor Roosevelt exemplified the growing prominence of women in public life. In the 1920s she had worked closely with other reformers to increase women's power in political parties, labor unions, and education. The experience proved an invaluable apprenticeship for her White House years, when her marriage to FDR developed into one of the most successful political partnerships of all time. He was the pragmatic politician, always aware of what could be done; she was the idealist, the gadfly, always pushing him—and the New Deal—to

do more. Eleanor Roosevelt served as the conscience of the New Deal.

Despite the advocacy by a female political network for equal opportunity for women, grave flaws still marred New Deal programs. A fourth of the NRA codes set a lower minimum wage for women than for men performing the same jobs. New Deal agencies like the Civil Works Administration and the Public Works Administration gave jobs almost exclusively to men: only 7 percent of CWA workers were female. And the CCC excluded women entirely, prompting critics to ask, "Where is the 'she-she-she'?"

When they did hire women, New Deal programs tended to reinforce the broader society's gender and racial attitudes. Thus program administrators resisted placing women in nontraditional jobs. Under the WPA, sewing rooms became a sort of dumping ground for unemployed women. African American and Mexican American women, if they had access to work relief at all, often found themselves shunted into training as domestics, whose work was not covered by the Social Security and Fair Labor Standards Acts. For the most part, progress for women did not come from specific attempts to recognize them as a group but occurred as part of a broader effort to improve the economic security of all Americans.

Blacks and the New Deal.   Just as the New Deal did not seriously challenge gender inequities, it did little to battle racial discrimination. In the 1930s the majority of the American people did not regard civil rights as a legitimate area for federal intervention. Indeed many New Deal programs reflected prevailing racist attitudes. CCC camps segregated blacks and whites, and many NRA codes did not protect black workers. Most tellingly, Franklin Roosevelt repeatedly refused to support legislation to make lynching a federal crime, claiming it would antagonize southern members of Congress whose support he needed to pass New Deal measures.

Nevertheless, blacks did receive significant benefits from those New Deal relief programs that were directed toward the poor regardless of their race or ethnic background. Blacks made up about 18 percent of the WPA's recipients, although they constituted only 10 percent of the population. The Resettlement Administration, established in 1935 to help small farmers buy land and to resettle sharecroppers and tenant farmers on more productive land, fought for the rights of black tenant farmers in the South, until angry southerners in Congress drastically cut its appropriations. Still, many blacks reasoned that the tangible aid from Washington outweighed the discrimination that marred many federal programs.

African Americans were also pleased to see blacks appointed to federal office. Mary McLeod Bethune, an educator who ran the Office of Minority Affairs of the National Youth Administration, headed the "black cabinet" (see American Lives, "Mary McLeod Bethune: Black Braintruster," p. 736). This informal network worked for

Mary McLeod Bethune: Black Braintruster

The New Deal brought many remarkable people to Washington, but few had traveled as far as Mary McLeod Bethune. As the Reverend Adam Clayton Powell Sr. wrote to her in 1935 when she received the prestigious Spingarn Medal from the National Association for the Advancement of Colored People, "It is a long way from the rice and cotton fields of South Carolina to this distinguished recognition, but you have made it in such a short span of years that I am afraid you are going to be arrested for breaking the speed limit." In terms of her contributions to black history, Mary McLeod Bethune deserves to be remembered alongside such luminaries as Frederick Douglass, W. E. B. Du Bois, and Martin Luther King Jr.

Born on July 10, 1875, near Mayesville, South Carolina, Mary was the fifteenth of seventeen children born to Sam and Patsy McLeod, former slaves liberated after the Civil War. She was educated at the Scotia Seminary in Concord, North Carolina, and the Bible Institute for Home and Foreign Missions in Chicago (later the Moody Bible Institute) in preparation for her chosen career as a missionary. Turning from her original plan to go to Africa, she redirected her missionary zeal to the United States and the field of education and racial uplift. In 1898 she married Albertus Bethune, and their only child, Albert McLeod Bethune, was born in 1899. The family moved to Florida, but the marriage foundered and the couple separated in 1907. She never remarried, and Albertus Bethune died in 1918.

In 1904, "with $1.50 and a prayer," Mary McLeod Bethune opened the school in Daytona Beach, Florida, that eventually became the prestigious Bethune-Cookman College, the only historically black college founded by a black woman that continues to thrive today. The initial student body consisted of five girls and her son; by 1923 the school had more than 300 students and a faculty and staff of twenty-five. Bethune was intimately involved with this institution—and by extension with the issue of providing expanded educational opportunities for African Americans—for the rest of her life. Through her extensive civic involvement in Daytona

Mary McLeod Bethune

This 1943 painting by Betsy Graves Reyneau captures the strength and dignity of one of the twentieth century's most important African Americans. Behind Bethune is a picture of the first building at the Daytona Literary and Industrial School for Training of Negro Girls, which later became Bethune-Cookman College.

National Portrait Gallery, Smithsonian Institution / Art Resource, NY.

Beach and the constant fundraising needed to keep her school afloat, she was quickly drawn into wider national networks, especially through the National Association of Colored Women (NACW)—the leading black women's organization in the first quarter of the twentieth century. Bethune served as president of that organization from 1924 to 1928. In 1935 she organized the National Council of Negro Women (NCNW), a coalition of the major national black women's associations, serving as its president until 1949.

Mary McLeod Bethune was a forceful personality and a born leader. The New Deal offered her a national platform through which to promote her agendas on race, education, women, and youth when she was named—at Eleanor Roosevelt's suggestion—to the advisory committee of the National Youth Administration in 1935. In the next year she was named director of the division of Negro Affairs in the NYA, where she served until 1944. One of her greatest contributions was the leadership she provided to the other black administrators who found opportunities in the New Deal. The Federal Council of Negro Affairs, known informally as the Black Cabinet, met on Sunday nights at her home in Washington. As the Washington correspondent for the Associated Negro Press noted, "Mrs. Bethune has gathered everything and everybody under her very ample wing since her arrival last June." Along with NAACP general secretary Walter White, she was the only ranking black administrator who had access to the White House.

Bethune recognized the limits of the New Deal's commitment to civil rights, but she remained a loyal supporter of Franklin Roosevelt, with whom she enjoyed an easy friendship. But it was Eleanor Roosevelt who became her staunchest political ally. When funding for a black housing project in Daytona Beach was stalled by bureaucratic red tape, local activists contacted Bethune, who in turn reached Eleanor Roosevelt, who with one call to the head of the Federal Housing Authority had the project back on track. On several occasions the first lady opened the White House to Bethune for conferences, thereby ensuring that they would receive national attention. Along the way the two women became personal friends as well as allies, although Roosevelt admitted that it took her a while to feel comfortable giving Bethune the customary peck on the cheek she bestowed when greeting white friends. Not until she kissed Mrs. Bethune without thinking about it, she told her daughter, did she feel that she had overcome the racial prejudice that was so much a part of Roosevelt's—and many white Americans'—background.

Bethune's basic strategy was to win policymaking positions for African Americans and then use those bases to work for more equitable treatment for blacks throughout the New Deal. Sometimes her small gestures were just as telling as her larger public stances. She always insisted on being called "Mrs. Bethune" as a term of respect, refusing to go down in history as "Mary from Florida." When a White House guard addressed her as "Auntie," a name whites often used indiscriminately for older black women, she looked at him sweetly and asked, "Which one of my brother's children are you?" Her entire adult life was devoted to improving conditions and access for her race. "The drums of Africa beat in my heart," she often said. "I cannot rest while there is a single Negro boy or girl lacking a chance to prove his worth."

There must have been many times when Bethune, a deeply religious woman, had to suppress personal feelings of disappointment or outright anger at the pace of change, but she always favored conciliation and compromise over confrontation. "I am diplomatic about certain things. I let people infer a great many things, but I am careful about what I say because I want to do certain things." But she also knew when to apply pressure, twist arms, appeal to publicity, and move a group toward concensus. As she once said forthrightly, "The White man has been thinking for us too long. We want him to think with us instead of for us."

When the National Youth Administration ceased operation in 1944, Bethune left government service but continued to be active in educational and charitable work. In 1952 she fulfilled a lifelong dream when she visited Liberia as an official U.S. representative at the inauguration of William Tubman as that country's president. She died of a heart attack in 1955 and was buried on the Bethune-Cookman campus. In 1974, on the ninety-ninth anniversary of her birth, the National Council of Negro Women dedicated the Mary McLeod Bethune Memorial Statue at Lincoln Park in Washington, D.C., just a short distance from the Capitol.

"Most people think I am a dreamer," Mary McLeod Bethune once said. "Through dreams many things come true." A dream come true was the 1938 gathering organized in conjunction with the National Council of Negro Women that brought sixty-seven black women leaders to the White House. Bethune recalled its significance soon thereafter:

> It certainly was history-making. . . . The pressure we have been making, the intercessions . . . they are finding their way. . . . The position I hold now—I give you that as an example. The first time in history that a Negro woman filled a national, federal position with the leeway, the opportunity . . . the contacts. Because one got in there, sixty-seven got in one day and many others are getting in here and there and there and there.

"A door has been sealed up for two hundred years," she concluded. "You can't open it overnight but little crevices are coming." Mary McLeod Bethune cracked open that door, and generations of African American activists, male and female, have been opening it wider and wider ever since.

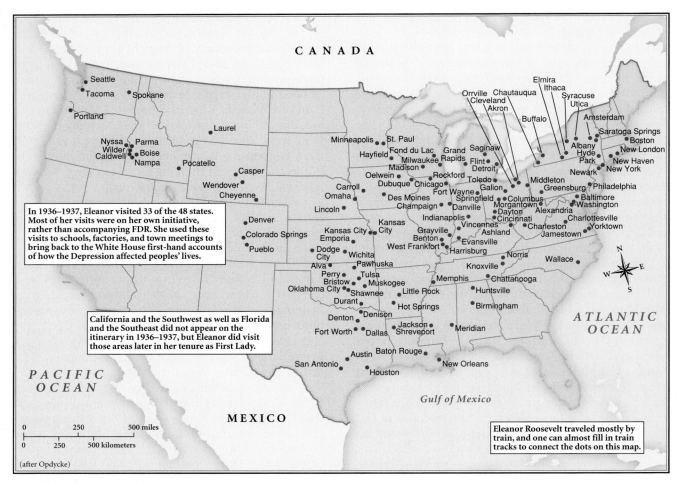

In 1936–1937, Eleanor visited 33 of the 48 states. Most of her visits were on her own initiative, rather than accompanying FDR. She used these visits to schools, factories, and town meetings to bring back to the White House first-hand accounts of how the Depression affected peoples' lives.

California and the Southwest as well as Florida and the Southeast did not appear on the itinerary in 1936–1937, but Eleanor did visit those areas later in her tenure as First Lady.

Eleanor Roosevelt traveled mostly by train, and one can almost fill in train tracks to connect the dots on this map.

(after Opdycke)

MAP 25.3 Eleanor Roosevelt's Travels, 1936–1937

First Lady Eleanor Roosevelt quickly achieved a reputation as a seemingly inexhaustible traveler, who often served as "the eyes and ears of the New Deal." The high public profile produced by her heavily publicized appearances throughout the nation helped to create an image of both Eleanor and Franklin as caring, humane people. Throughout FDR's twelve years as president, it is not surprising that many of the millions of letters that poured into the White House addressed Eleanor as though she was a friend or family member.

fairer treatment of blacks by New Deal agencies in the same way the white women's network advocated feminist causes. Both groups benefited greatly from the support of Eleanor Roosevelt. The first lady's promotion of equal treatment for blacks ranks as one of her greatest legacies.

Help from the WPA and other New Deal programs and a belief that the White House—or at least Eleanor Roosevelt—cared about their plight, caused a dramatic change in African Americans' voting behavior (Map 25.3). Since the Civil War, blacks had voted Republican, a loyalty based on Abraham Lincoln's freeing of the slaves. As late as 1932 black voters in northern cities overwhelmingly supported Republican candidates. But in 1936 black Americans outside the South (where blacks were still

largely prevented from voting) gave Roosevelt 71 percent of their votes. In Harlem, where relief dollars increased dramatically in the wake of the 1935 riot (see Chapter 24), their support for Roosevelt was an extraordinary 81.3 percent. Black voters have remained overwhelmingly Democratic ever since.

The Politicization of Mexican Americans. The election of Franklin Roosevelt also had an immediate effect on Mexican American communities, demoralized by the depression and the deportations of the Hoover years. In cities like Los Angeles and El Paso, Mexican Americans qualified for relief more easily under New Deal guidelines, and there was more relief to go around (see American Voices, "Susana Archuleta: A Chicana

Susana Archuleta

A Chicana Youth Gets New Deal Work

Although African Americans and Chicanos often experienced discrimination in New Deal programs, many did find opportunities in agencies like the Civilian Conservation Corps, the National Youth Administration, or the Works Progress Administration. They attributed the help they received directly to Franklin Delano Roosevelt's election, as Susana Archuleta's reminiscence of life in Wyoming suggests.

I was born in New Mexico, on a farm up North in Mora County. I was the fifth of eight children. When I was very little, my dad moved us all to Wyoming. You see, he heard that they had free textbooks in Wyoming, while here in New Mexico the parents had to pay for the books. Daddy didn't have much money, and he felt that we all needed an opportunity for education. We left the farm—the animals, the machinery, everything—and he went to work in the mines up in Rock Springs, Wyoming. . . .

During the Depression, things got bad. My dad passed away when I was about twelve, leaving my mother with eight children and no means of support. There wasn't any welfare. My mother took in washings to make a living, and our job was to pick up the washings on the way home from school. We'd pick up clothes from the school-teachers, the attorney, and what-have-you. Then, at night, we'd help iron them and fold them. On Saturdays we'd help with the wash, too. We'd put a big old fire out in the patio and a big old tub of water on top of it. Then we'd bring the tub in and wash the clothes.

Summer months would come along and everybody had their chores. My oldest brother always went out and worked, delivering papers, things like that. Two of my sisters did the housework. My next oldest brother and I used to fill up the coal bin for the winter months. We'd go down to the pits where the coal cars would come out. They'd come out loaded full, and some of the coals would fall off. So during the hours when the cars weren't working, we'd go with the other kids from town and fill up our sacks with the coal from the tracks. It took a long time, because that coal bin would hold about three tons of coal. I used to carry a good fifty-pound sack on my back.

When I was a teenager, the Depression began to take a turn. Franklin Roosevelt was elected, and the works projects started. The boys and young men who'd been laid off at the mines went to the CCC camps, and the girls joined the NYA. When school was over, we'd go and work right there in the school building. We'd help out in the office, do filing and other things. Actually, we didn't do much work—it was our first job. But we learned a lot. It was good experience.

They paid us about twenty-one dollars a month. Out of that we got five and the other sixteen was directly issued to our parents. The same was true of the boys working in the camps. They got about thirty dollars a month. They were allowed to keep five of it. The rest was sent to their families. All of us were hired according to our family income. If a man with a lot of children was unemployed, he was given preference over someone who had less children. They also had projects for women who were widows. They made quilts and mattresses. Those programs were great. Everybody got a chance to work. I think there should be more training programs like that, instead of giveaway programs like welfare. . . .

Source: Nan Elsasser, "Susana Archuleta," in Nan Elsasser et al., *Las Mujeres: Conversations from a Hispanic Community* (New York: Feminist Press, 1980), 36–37.

Youth Gets New Deal Work," above). Even though New Deal regulations prohibited discrimination based on an immigrant's legal status, the new climate encouraged a marked rise in requests for naturalization papers. Mexican Americans also benefited from New Deal labor policies; joining the CIO was an important stage for many in becoming Americans. Inspired by New Deal rhetoric about economic recovery and social progress through

cooperation, Mexican Americans increasingly identified with the United States rather than with Mexico. This shift was especially evident among American-born children of Mexican immigrants.

Participating in the political system increasingly became part of Mexican American life. Los Angeles activist Beatrice Griffith noted, "Franklin D. Roosevelt's name was the spark that started thousands of Spanish-speaking

A New Deal for Indians

John Collier, the New Deal's Commissioner for Indian Affairs, was a former social worker who had become interested in Native American tribal cultures in the 1920s. Here, Collier speaks with Chief Richard of the Blackfoot Nation, one of the Indian chiefs attending the Four Nation celebration at historic Old Fort Niagara, New York, in 1934. Corbis-Bettmann.

persons to the polls." In 1939 El Congreso Nacional del Pueblo de Habla Español, the first national civil rights conference for Spanish-speaking peoples, called on its members to become American citizens and vote. The Democrats made it clear that they welcomed Mexican American voters and considered them an important part of the New Deal coalition. This politicization provided additional spurs to political activism after World War II.

The Indian Reorganization Act. But what about groups that did not mobilize politically or were not recognized as key participants in the New Deal coalition? Native Americans were one of the nation's most disadvantaged and powerless minorities. The average annual income of a Native American in 1934 was only $48; the unemployment rate among Native Americans was three times the national average. Concerned New Deal administrators like Secretary of the Interior Harold Ickes and Commissioner of the Bureau of Indian Affairs John Collier tried to correct some of those inequities. The Indian Section of the Civilian Conservation Corps brought needed money and projects to reservations throughout the West. Indians also received benefits from FERA and CWA work relief projects.

More ambitious was the Indian Reorganization Act of 1934, sometimes called the "Indian New Deal." That law reversed the Dawes Act of 1887 by promoting more extensive self-government through tribal councils and constitutions. The government also abandoned the attempt to force Native Americans to assimilate into mainstream society in favor of promoting cultural pluralism. The New Deal pledged to help preserve Indian languages, arts, and traditions and to restore some lands lost in the allotment program (see Chapter 16).

Despite the intention to redress some of the ills produced by earlier government policies, the Indian New Deal was profoundly flawed. Reflecting Collier's paternalistic approach, it tended to treat all tribes as identical, with the same needs and structures. Ironically, its imposition of United States–style democracy did not always mesh with Native Americans' consensus style of decision making. The Seneca, for example, argued that the Indian Reorganization Act violated their treaty rights and the system of self-government they had adopted in 1848. Only 174 nations accepted the reorganization policy, while 78 refused to participate. While some native groups may have benefited from the Indian New Deal, the problems of Native Americans were so severe that these changes in federal policy did little to improve their lives or reinvigorate tribal communities.

The New Deal and the Land

Concern for the land was one of the dominant motifs of the New Deal, and the shaping of the public landscape was among its most visible legacies. During the 1920s conservation supporters allied themselves with business interests and focused primarily on the commercial benefits of responsible use of natural resources. The expansion of federal responsibilities in the 1930s created a climate conducive to a broader vision of conservation efforts, as did public concern heightened by the dramatic images of drought and devastation in the Dust Bowl. Roosevelt's own strong commitment to what he called "the gospel of conservation" helped to bring a more public-oriented, while still practical, approach to the fore. Although the long-term success of New Deal resources policy was mixed, it innovatively stressed scientific management of the land, conservation instead of commercial development, and the aggressive use of public authority to safeguard both private and public holdings.

The most extensive New Deal environmental undertaking was the Tennessee Valley Authority. Since World War I, experts had recognized the need for dams to control flooding and erosion in the Tennessee River Basin, a seven-state area with some of the country's heaviest rainfall, and in the 1920s a small group of progressive reformers had hoped to create a model of publicly owned power in the region. It took the crisis of the depression and the rise of the New Deal to create in 1933 the Tennessee Valley Authority, charged with developing the region's resources under public control (Map 25.4). Roosevelt had high hopes for the project, claiming that "What we are doing there is taking a watershed with about three and half million people in it, almost all of them rural, and we are

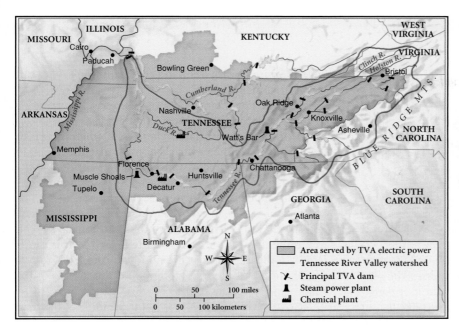

MAP 25.4 The Tennessee Valley Authority, 1933–1952

The Tennessee Valley Authority was one of the New Deal's most far-reaching environmental projects. Between 1933 and 1952, the TVA built twenty dams and improved five others. The cheap hydroelectric power generated by the dams brought electricity to hundreds of thousands of area residents.

For more help analyzing this map, see the ONLINE STUDY GUIDE at bedfordstmartins.com/henretta.

trying to make a different type of citizen out of them. . . . TVA is primarily intended to change and improve the standards of living of the people of that Valley." The TVA was the ultimate watershed demonstration area, integrating flood control, reforestation, and agricultural and industrial development, including the production of chemical fertilizers. A hydroelectric grid provided cheap electric power for the valley's residents (see Voices from Abroad, "Odette Keun: A Foreigner Looks at the Tennessee Valley Authority," p. 742).

The Dust Bowl helped to focus attention on land management and ecological balance. Agents from the Soil Conservation Service in the Department of Agriculture taught farmers the proper technique for tilling hillsides. Government agronomists also tried to remove marginal land from cultivation and to prevent soil erosion through better agricultural practices. One of their most widely publicized programs was the creation of the Shelterbelts, which involved the planting of 220 million trees running along roughly the ninety-ninth meridian from Abilene, Texas, to the Canadian border. Planted as a windbreak, the trees also prevented soil erosion. Another priority of the Roosevelt administration was helping rural Americans to stay on the land. The Rural Electrification Administration, established in 1935, brought power to farms in an attempt to improve the quality of rural life (see New Technology, "Rural Electrification," p. 744).

Today New Deal projects affecting the environment can be seen throughout the country. CCC and WPA workers built the Blue Ridge Parkway, which connects the Shenandoah National Park in Virginia with the Great Smoky Mountain National Park in North Carolina. In the West government workers built the San Francisco Zoo, Berkeley's Tilden Park, and the canals of San Antonio. The CCC helped to complete the East Coast's Appalachian Trail and the West Coast's Pacific Crest Trail through the Sierra Nevada. In state parks across the country, cabins, shelters, picnic areas, lodges, and observation towers, built in a style that has been called "government rustic," are witness to the New Deal ethos of recreation coexisting with conservation.

Although the New Deal was ahead of its time in its attention to conservation, its legacy to later environmental movements is mixed. Many of the tactics used in New Deal projects—damming rivers, blasting fire roads, altering the natural landscape through the construction of buildings and shelters—are now considered intrusive. In the 1970s the TVA came under attack for its longstanding practice of strip mining and the pollution caused by its power plants and chemical factories. Because of environmental concerns, a project as massive as the TVA probably could not be built today—an ironic comment on what was once hailed as an enlightened use of government power.

The New Deal and the Arts

In the arts the depression dried up traditional sources of patronage. Like most Americans, creative artists had nowhere to turn but Washington. A WPA project known as "Federal One" put unemployed artists, actors, and writers to work, but its spirit and purpose extended far beyond relief. New Deal administrators wanted to redefine the relationship between artists and the community so that art would no longer be the exclusive province of the elite. "Art for the millions" became a popular New Deal slogan.

The Federal Art Project (FAP) gave work to many of the twentieth century's leading painters, muralists, and

Odette Keun

A Foreigner Looks at the Tennessee Valley Authority

French writer Odette Keun visited the United States in 1936 and was so impressed by the Tennessee Valley Authority (TVA) that she wrote a book about it. Among other observations, Keun felt that experiments like the TVA might help inhibit the development of an American variety of fascism.

The vital question before democracy is, therefore, not how to bring back an economic freedom which is irretrievably lost, but how to prevent the intellectual freedom, which is still our heritage, from being submerged. It is already threatened. It will be threatened more and more strongly in the years ahead—and the menace, of course, is dictatorship. But to fight dictatorship it is necessary first to understand in what circumstances it arises, and then to think out the counterattack which democracy can launch against its approaching force.

Dictatorship springs from two very clear causes. One is the total incapacity of parliamentary government: total, as in Germany in 1933 and in Spain in 1935. To such a breakdown neither the democratic nations of Europe nor America have yet been reduced, although everywhere there are very ominous creaks and cracks, and the authority and prestige of parliamentary institutions have greatly and perilously diminished. The other cause, infinitely closer to us and more dynamic, is the failure of the economic machine to function properly, and by functioning properly I mean ensuring a livelihood for the entire population. No system can survive if it cannot procure food and wages for the people who live under it. Man has to get subsistence from his rulers, for the most immediate and the most imperious law of our nature is that the belly must be filled. It is perfectly futile to orate on fine, high, and abstract principles to human beings who are permanently hungry, permanently harassed, permanently uncertain, who hear their wives begging for the rent and their children crying out for nourishment. . . .

One of the main tenets of liberalism—I reiterate this like a gramophone, but I must get it to sink in—is that all necessary overhauling and adjustment ought to be done in a manner which will minimize the shock to the greatest number, and soften as much as possible the unavoidable human suffering which these changes entail. This opposition to extremes, this practice of a graduated change, we can call "the middle of the road in time and space." But it is not nearly enough to conceive it and to bestow upon it a name. We must reach it. It is unutterably foolish to look at the middle of the road, to talk of the middle of the road, to hope for the middle of the road—and never get there.

Now I have tried to show that the middle of the road is already being laid down in America. The Tennessee Valley Authority is laying it down. Handicapped and restricted though it is in all sorts of ways, it is the noblest, the most intelligent, and the best attempt made in this country or in any other democratic country to economize, marshal, and integrate the actual assets of a region, plan its development and future, ameliorate its standards of living, establish it in a more enduring security, and render available to the people the benefits of the wealth of their district, and the results of science, discovery, invention, and disinterested forethought. In its inspiration and its goal there is goodness, for goodness is that which makes for unity of purpose with love, compassion, and respect for every life and every pattern of living. The economic machine, bad though it is, has not been smashed in the Tennessee Watershed; it is being very gradually, very carefully, very equitably reviewed and amended, and the citizens are being taught and directed, but not bullied, not coerced, not regimented, not frightened, within the constitutional frame the nation itself elected to build. It is not while the Tennessee Valley Authority has the valley in its keeping that despair or disintegration can prepare the ground for a dictatorship and the loss of freedom. The immortal contribution of the TVA to liberalism, not only in America but all over the world, is the blueprint it has drawn, and that it is now transforming into a living reality, of the road which liberals believe is the only road mankind should travel.

Source: Odette Keun, A *Foreigner Looks at the TVA* (1937), in Oscar Handlin, ed., *This Was America* (Cambridge, MA: Harvard University Press, 1949), 547–49.

"The Promise of the New Deal"

This 1936 mural by noted artist Ben Shahn depicts the beginnings of Roosevelt, New Jersey, originally called "Jersey Homesteads." The product of a New Deal planning initiative, the town included a cooperative consisting of retail stores, a factory, and a farm, and was designed for poor immigrants from New York City. While the mural includes the intended beneficiaries of the new community in the background and acknowledges the powerful presence of Franklin D. Roosevelt with the image on the wall, it focuses on the New Deal planners themselves, capturing some of the faith in experts and social planning of the New Deal era. Roosevelt Arts Project.

sculptors at a point in their careers when the lack of private patronage might have prevented them from continuing their artistic production. Under the direction of Holger Cahill, an expert on American folk art, the FAP commissioned murals for public buildings and post offices across the country. Jackson Pollock, Alice Neel, Willem de Kooning, and Louise Nevelson all received support from the FAP.

The Federal Music Project employed 15,000 musicians under the direction of Nicholas Sokoloff, the conductor of the Cleveland Symphony Orchestra. Government-sponsored orchestras toured the country, presenting free concerts of both classical and popular music. Like many New Deal programs, the Music Project emphasized American themes. The composer Aaron Copland wrote his ballets *Billy the Kid* (1938) and *Rodeo* (1942) for the WPA, basing the compositions on western folk motifs. The distinctive "American" sound and athletic dance style of these works made them immensely appealing to audiences. The federal government also employed the musicologist Charles Seeger and his wife, the composer Ruth Crawford Seeger, to catalog hundreds of American folk songs.

The former journalist Henry Alsberg headed the Federal Writers' Project (FWP), which at its height employed about 5,000 writers. Young FWP employees who later achieved fame included Saul Bellow, Ralph Ellison, Tillie Olsen, and John Cheever. The black folklorist and novelist Zora Neale Hurston finished three novels while on the Florida FWP, among them *Their Eyes Were Watching God* (1937). And Richard Wright won the 1938 *Story* magazine prize for the best tale by a WPA writer. Wright used his spare time to complete his novel *Native Son* (1940).

Of all the New Deal arts programs, the Federal Theatre Project (FTP) was the most ambitious. American drama thrived in the 1930s, the only time at which the United States had a federally supported national theater. Under the gifted direction of Hallie Flanagan, former head of Vassar College's Experimental Theater, the FTP reached an audience of 25 to 30 million people in the four years of its existence. Talented directors, actors, and playwrights, including Orson Welles, John Houseman, and Arthur Miller, offered their services. The tendency to take a hard and critical look at social problems, however, made the program vulnerable to **red-baiting**. After a series of

Rural Electrification

In 1935 fewer than one-tenth of the nation's 6.8 million farms had electricity. For millions of farm families, that stark fact meant a life of unremitting toil made even harsher by the lack of simple conveniences. Farm families used an average of 200 gallons of water a day. Any chore requiring water—and most did—meant pumping the water from a distant well and carrying it to the house or barn in a pair of buckets that weighed as much as 30 pounds each. Water had to be heated on a woodstove that required constant tending. Meeting a family's yearly water needs took 63 eight-hour days and involved carrying water a distance of 1,750 miles.

Rural women suffered especially from the lack of electricity. Canning, a necessity before refrigeration, kept women standing over steaming vats of fruit or vegetables, often in the worst summer heat, before the freshly harvested produce spoiled. Wash day, traditionally Monday, called for three large zinc washtubs for washing, rinsing, and bleaching. A week's wash consisted of four to eight loads, each requiring three washtubs of clean water hauled from the well. Few rural households could afford commercial soap, so women used lye, which barely removed ground-in dirt from soiled clothes and was very harsh on hands. But if farm women dreaded Monday, they hated Tuesday even more. Tuesday meant ironing, another all-day job. The iron, a 6- or 7-pound wedge of metal, had to be heated on the stove, and, because it did not retain heat for more than a few minutes, it took several irons to do a shirt. The women in Texas's hill country called them "sad irons."

A day that began in darkness and was given over to twelve hours of backbreaking toil brought few comforts in the evening. Reading by kerosene lamps strained the eyes. Children's eyes might be strong enough to read in the semidarkness, but few older people could read without squinting. The absence of electricity also meant no radios, which meant no contact with the outside world.

Studies showed that farmers would find many uses for electricity and would make good customers, but power companies balked at the prospect of bringing electricity to the countryside, claiming that it was not economically feasible to run lines to individual farms. In 1935 the federal government made a commitment to bring power to rural America. The Rural Electrification Administration, an independent agency, promoted the formation of nonprofit farm cooperatives to bring electricity to their regions. For a $5 down payment, local farmers could join an association and become eligible for low-interest federal loans covering the cost of installing power lines. Each household was committed to a monthly minimum usage, usually about $3, but as usage increased, the rates came down. By 1940, 40 percent of the nation's farms had electricity; in 1950 the rate reached 90 percent.

Electricity brought relief from the drudgery and isolation of farm life. An electric milking machine saved hours of manual labor, most of it previously done before dawn by the faint glow of a kerosene lamp so farmers could devote the daylight hours to outdoor chores. An electric water pump lightened many chores, especially the hauling of water. Electric irons, vacuum cleaners, and washing machines eased women's burdens.

People's responses to rural electrification were poignant. A small child told his mother, "I didn't realize how dark our house was until we got electric lights." One farm woman remembered, "I just turned on the light and kept looking at Paw. It was the first time I'd ever really seen him after dark." Another family, caught unaware by the timing of the hookup, saw their house from a distance and thought it was on fire. Schoolteachers noticed that children did better at school when they had light to do homework by at night. Along with the automobile, electricity probably did more than any other technological innovation to break down the barriers between urban and rural life in twentieth-century America.

"Blue Monday"

Laundry was one of women's hardest household chores. Although this woman did not have to haul water from an outdoor well, she still had to pump it by hand in order to do the wash because her home lacked electricity. She also had to wring out the wet clothes manually—another arduous task. Corbis-Bettmann.

investigations as to alleged Communist influence, Congress terminated the FTP in 1939. Director Flanagan wryly remarked, "I could see why certain powers would not want even 10% of the Federal Theatre plays to be the sort to make people in our democracy think. Such forces might well be afraid of thinking people."

The WPA arts projects were influenced by a broad artistic trend called the "**documentary impulse**." Combining social relevance with distinctively American themes, this approach, which presented actual facts and events in a way that aroused the interest and emotions of the audience, characterized the artistic expression of the 1930s. The documentary, probably the decade's most distinctive genre, influenced practically every aspect of American culture—literature, photography, art, music, film, dance, theater, and radio. It is evident in John Steinbeck's fiction (see Chapter 24) and in John Dos Passos's *USA* trilogy, which used actual newspaper clippings, dispatches, and headlines in its fictional story. *The March of Time* newsreels, which movie audiences saw before feature films, presented the news of the world for the pretelevision age. The filmmaker Pare Lorentz commissioned the composer Virgil Thompson to create music that set the mood for documentary movies such as *The Plow That Broke the Plains* (1936) and *The River* (1936). The new photojournalism magazines, including *Life* and *Look*, also reflected this documentary approach. And the New Deal institutionalized the trend by sending investigators like the journalist Lorena Hickok and the writer Martha Gellhorn into the field to report on the conditions of people on relief.

Finally, the federal government played a leading role in compiling the photographic record of the 1930s. The Historical Section of the Resettlement Administration had a mandate to document and photograph the American scene for the government. Through their haunting images of sharecroppers, Dust Bowl migrants, and the urban homeless, photographers Dorothea Lange, Walker Evans, Ben Shahn, and Margaret Bourke-White permanently shaped the image of the Great Depression. The government hired photographers solely for their professional skills, not to provide them relief, as in Federal One projects. Their photographs, collected by the Historical Section, which in 1937 became part of the newly created Farm Security Administration (FSA), rank as the best visual representation of life in the United States during the depression years.

The Human Face of the Great Depression
Migrant Mother by Dorothea Lange is perhaps the most famous documentary photograph of the 1930s. Lange spent only ten minutes in the pea-picker's camp in California where she captured this image and did not even get the name of the woman whose despair and resignation she so powerfully recorded. She was later identified as Florence Thompson, a full-blooded Cherokee from Oklahoma. Library of Congress.

The Legacies of the New Deal

The New Deal set in motion far-reaching changes, notably the growth of a modern state of significant size. For the first time people experienced the federal government as a concrete part of everyday life. During the 1930s more than a third of the population received direct government assistance from new federal programs, including Social Security payments, farm loans, relief work, and mortgage guarantees. Furthermore, the government had made a commitment to intervene in the economy when the private sector could not guarantee economic stability. New legislation regulated the stock market, reformed the Federal Reserve System by placing more power in the hands of Washington policymakers, and brought many practices of modern corporate life under federal regulation. Thus the New Deal accelerated the pattern begun during the Progressive Era of using federal regulation to bring order and regularity to economic life, a pattern that would persist for the rest of the twentieth century, despite recurring criticism about the increased presence of the state in American life.

One particularly important arena of expansion was the development of America's welfare state—that is, the federal government's acceptance of primary responsibility for the individual and collective welfare of the people. Although the New Deal offered more benefits to American citizens than they had ever received before, its safety net had many holes, especially in comparison with the far more extensive welfare systems of Western Europe.

The Social Security Act did not include national health care. Another serious defect of the emerging welfare system was its failure to reach a significant minority of American workers, including domestics and farm workers, for many years. Since state governments administered the programs, benefits varied widely, with southern states consistently providing the lowest amounts.

Another shortcoming of the welfare system stemmed from male and female New Dealers' gendered conceptions of the "family wage," an ideal that assumed men were workers and women were homemakers. The old-age pensions and unemployment compensation provisions in the Social Security Act, which were designed primarily with men in mind and with the hope of maintaining the dignity of the male breadwinner, tended to be more generous and applied universally, regardless of need. Moreover, Social Security policies discriminated against married women until the 1970s. The programs for dependent children of poor women, usually referred to as simply "welfare," by contrast, applied means and morals tests and provided funds to keep women out of the workforce and in their proper place in the home. Denying the growing presence of women in the workforce, welfare made no provisions for helping poor working women sustain their families. A highly stigmatized program, welfare rarely offered enough for a decent standard of living or a means for poor women to get out of poverty (see Thinking about History, "Women, Gender, and the Welfare System," p. 778).

To its credit the New Deal recognized that poverty was an economic problem and not a matter of personal failure. However, it did not come up with the perfect economic solution. Reformers assumed that once the depression was over, full employment and an active economy would take care of the nation's welfare needs, and poverty would wither away. It did not. When later administrations confronted the persistence of inequality and unemployment, they grafted welfare programs onto the jerry-built system left over from the New Deal. Thus the American welfare system would always be marked by its birth during the crisis atmosphere of the Great Depression.

Even if the depression-era welfare system had some serious flaws, it was brilliant politics. The Democratic Party courted the allegiance of citizens who benefited from New Deal programs. Organized labor aligned itself with the administration that had made it a legitimate force in modern industrial life. Blacks voted Democratic in direct relation to the economic benefits that poured into their communities. At the grassroots level the Women's Division of the Democratic National Committee mobilized 80,000 women who recognized what the New Deal had done for their communities. The unemployed also looked kindly on the Roosevelt administration. According to one of the earliest Gallup polls, 84 percent of those on relief voted the Democratic ticket in 1936.

But the Democratic Party did not attract only the down-and-out. Roosevelt's magnetic personality and the dispersal of New Deal benefits to families throughout the social structure brought middle-class voters, many of them first- or second-generation immigrants, into the Democratic fold. Thus the New Deal completed the transformation of the Democratic Party that had begun in the 1920s toward a coalition of ethnic groups, city dwellers, organized labor, blacks, and a broad cross section of the middle class. Those voters would form the backbone of the Democratic coalition for decades to come and would provide support for liberal reforms that extended the promise of the New Deal.

The New Deal coalition contained potentially fatal contradictions involving mainly the issue of race. Because Roosevelt depended on the support of southern white Democrats to pass New Deal legislation, he was unwilling to challenge the economic and political marginalization of blacks in the South. At the same time New Deal programs were changing the face of southern agriculture by undermining the sharecropping system and encouraging the migration of southern blacks to northern and western cities. Outside the South blacks were not prevented from voting, guaranteeing that civil rights would enter the national agenda. The resulting fissures would eventually weaken the coalition that seemed so invincible at the height of Roosevelt's power.

With all its shortcomings the New Deal nonetheless had a profound impact on the nation, all the more remarkable in light of its short duration—most of its legislation passed between 1933 and 1936. While the Supreme Court–packing scheme, the "Roosevelt recession," and the political successes of Republicans in 1938 helped to bring an end to the New Deal, the darkening international scene also played a part. As Europe moved toward war, and Japan flexed its muscles in the Far East, Roosevelt became increasingly preoccupied with international relations and pushed domestic reform further and further into the background.

FOR FURTHER EXPLORATION

▶ For definitions of key terms boldfaced in this chapter, see the glossary at the end of the book.

▶ To assess your mastery of the material covered in this chapter, see the Online Study Guide at **bedfordstmartins.com/henretta**.

▶ For suggested references, including Web sites, see page SR-27 at the end of the book.

▶ For map resources and primary documents, see **bedfordstmartins.com/henretta**.

The New Deal was the response of Franklin Roosevelt and the Democratic Party to the crisis of the Great Depression. It offered a broad-based program of political and economic reform, but its programs were hardly revolutionary. President Hoover had taken the first steps toward involving the federal government more actively in economic life, a trend that Roosevelt continued and expanded, pushed in part by growing protest on the part of the workers, the elderly, and supporters of programs like Huey Long's Share Our Wealth movement. The New Deal never cured the depression, but it restored confidence that Americans could overcome hard times. It provided a measure of economic security against the worst depression in American history by relieving many of its tragic effects. Legislation such as the Social Security Act of 1935 laid the foundation of the modern welfare state, bringing the United States more in line with other industrialized countries in its acceptance of responsibility for the collective welfare of its citizens.

The New Deal dramatically expanded the size and power of the federal government, continuing a trend that had begun in the late nineteenth and early twentieth centuries. Decisions made in Washington touched millions of individual lives. The New Deal provided new opportunities and a larger role in public life for blacks, women, Mexican Americans, and the labor movement. The collapse of the economy encouraged a reassertion of American values in literature and the arts. This artistic flowering was partly supported by a unique experiment in government patronage of the arts through the WPA. In politics the Democratic coalition of white southerners and the urban working class that had begun to emerge in the 1920s reached a climax in the landslide presidential victory of 1936. The coalition provided the Democrats with electoral success but also contained the seeds of future conflict, especially over the issue of race.

Although the hard times were far from over, by 1938 the New Deal had run out of steam. It was not until the United States entered the war in 1941 that Roosevelt made the end of his depression program official when he announced in 1943 that it was time for "Dr. Win the War" to take the place of "Dr. New Deal." But in reality the New Deal had long ceased to propel the nation toward social reform.

1933	FDR's inaugural address and first fireside chat
	Emergency Banking Act begins the Hundred Days
	Glass-Steagall Act establishes Federal Deposit Insurance Corporation (FDIC)
	Civilian Conservation Corps (CCC)
	Agricultural Adjustment Act (AAA)
	National Industrial Recovery Act (NIRA)
	Tennessee Valley Authority (TVA)
	United States abandons gold standard
	Townsend Clubs promote Old Age Revolving Pension Plan
	Twenty-First Amendment repeals Prohibition
1934	Securities and Exchange Commission (SEC)
	Indian Reorganization Act
	Share Our Wealth Society established by Senator Huey Long
1935	Supreme Court finds the NRA unconstitutional in *Schechter v. United States*
	National Union for Social Justice (Father Charles Coughlin)
	National Labor Relations (Wagner) Act
	Social Security Act
	Works Progress Administration (WPA)
	Huey Long assassinated
	Rural Electrification Administration (REA)
	Supreme Court finds Agricultural Adjustment Act unconstitutional
	Congress of Industrial Organizations (CIO) formed
1935–1939	Communist Party at height of influence
1936	General Motors sit-down strike
	Landslide reelection of FDR marks peak of New Deal power
	The Plow That Broke the Plains and *The River*, documentary movies by Pare Lorentz
1937	FDR's attempted Supreme Court reorganization fails
1937–1938	"Roosevelt recession"
1938	Aaron Copland's *Billy the Kid*
	Fair Labor Standards Act (FLSA)
1939	Federal Theatre Project terminated

CHAPTER 26

The World at War

1939–1945

Times Square in New York City on August 15, 1945, was awash with people celebrating V-J (Victory over Japan) Day. World War II was over. Civilians and soldiers "jived in the streets and the crowd was so large that traffic was halted and sprinkler trucks were used to disperse pedestrians." The spontaneous street party seemed a fitting end to what had been the country's most popular war. For many Americans World War II had been what one man described to journalist Studs Terkel as "an unreal period for us here at home. Those who lost nobody at the front had a pretty good time."

Americans had many reasons to view World War II as the "good war." Shocked by the Japanese attack on Pearl Harbor on December 7, 1941, they united in their determination to fight German and Japanese totalitarianism in defense of their way of life. When evidence of the grim reality of the Jewish Holocaust came to light, U.S. participation in the war seemed even more just. And despite their sacrifices, many people found the war a positive experience because it ended the devastating Great Depression, bringing full employment and prosperity. The unambiguous nature of the victory and the subsequent emergence of the United States as an unprecedentedly powerful nation further contributed to the sense of the war as one worth fighting.

◀ **A B-17 Crew "Somewhere in England"**
The cheerful camaraderie evident in this photograph of crew members as they rode to their B-17G "Flying Fortress" bomber on an airfield in England is the type of image that fuels Americans' memories of World War II as "The Good War." With over 100 bombing missions over Germany, their plane, named I'll Get By, *chalked up one of the highest records of the war. Boeing manufactured 12,713 B-17s during World War II, of which 4,753 were lost in combat.*
National Archives.

But the good war had other sides. The period brought significant social disruption, accompanied by widespread anxiety about women's presence in the workforce and a rise in juvenile delinquency. In a massive violation of civil liberties, over 100,000 people of Japanese ancestry were incarcerated in internment camps, victims of racially based hysteria. African Americans served in a segregated military and, with Chicanos, faced discrimination and violence at home. World War II also fostered the rise of a **military-industrial complex** and unleashed the terrible potential of the atomic bomb. Finally, another enduring legacy developed out of the unresolved issues of the wartime alliance: the debilitating cold war, which would dominate American foreign policy for decades.

The Road to War

While Americans focused on getting through the Great Depression, trouble was massing overseas. The right wing antidemocratic totalitarian movement known as **fascism** had begun to emerge in Europe in the 1920s, and by the 1930s fascist states had emerged, characterized by strong dictators backed by the military, such as Adolph Hitler in Nazi Germany, Benito Mussolini in Italy, and Francisco Franco in Spain. Their aggression in Europe, as well as Japan's increasingly militaristic and expansionist trajectory in Asia, threatened the fragile peace that had prevailed since the end of World War I. When the League of Nations proved too weak to deal with the emerging crises, President Roosevelt foresaw the possibility of America's participation in another war. An internationalist at heart, he wanted the United States to play a prominent role in world affairs to foster the long-term prosperity necessary for a lasting peace. Hampered at first by the pervasive isolationist sentiment in the country, by 1939 he was leading the nation toward war.

The Rise of Fascism

As early as 1936, President Roosevelt had foreseen the possibility of U.S. participation in another European war, but he was determined to stay in line with public opinion. Gallup polls showed that two-thirds of the American people believed the United States had made a mistake in entering World War I. During the 1936 campaign Roosevelt made a stirring antiwar statement that drew on his experience as assistant secretary of the navy during World War I: "I have seen blood running from the wounded. I have seen men coughing out their gassed lungs. . . . I have seen children starving. I have seen the agony of mothers and wives. I hate war." However, the aggressive actions of Germany, Italy, and Japan, all determined to expand their borders and their influence, challenged American neutrality repeatedly.

The first crisis was precipitated by Japan, a country whose militaristic regime was intent on dominating the Pacific basin. In 1931 Japan occupied Manchuria, the northernmost province of China; then in 1937 it launched a full-scale invasion of China. In both instances the League of Nations condemned Japan's action but was helpless to stop the aggression. Japan simply served the required one-year notice of withdrawal from the league.

Japan's defiance of the league encouraged a fascist dictator half a world away. Italy's Benito Mussolini had long been unhappy with the Versailles treaty, which had not awarded Italy any formerly German or Turkish colonies. In 1935 Italy invaded Ethiopia, one of the few independent countries left in Africa. The Ethiopian emperor, Haile Selassie, appealed to the League of Nations, which condemned the invasion and imposed sanctions but to little effect. By 1936 the Italian subjugation of Ethiopia was complete.

The Rise of Hitler.   Not Italy but Germany presented the gravest threat to the world order in the 1930s. There, huge reparations payments, economic depression, fear of Communism, labor unrest, and rising unemployment fueled the rise of Adolf Hitler and his National Socialist (Nazi) Party. In 1933 Hitler became chancellor of Germany and assumed dictatorial powers. Aiming at nothing short of world domination, as he made clear in his book *Mein Kampf* (My Struggle), Hitler sought to overturn the territorial settlements of the Versailles treaty, to "restore" all the Germans of central and Eastern Europe to a single greater German fatherland, and to annex large areas of Eastern Europe. In his warped vision, "inferior races" such as Jews, Gypsies, and Slavs, as well as "undesirables" such as homosexuals and the mentally impaired, would have to make way for the "master race." In 1933 Hitler established the first concentration camp at Dachau and opened a campaign of persecution against Jews, which expanded to a campaign of extermination when the war began.

Appeasement.   Hitler's strategy for gaining territory through the use of troops and intimidation provoked a series of crises that gave Britain and France no alternative but to let him have his way or risk war. Prime Minister Neville Chamberlain of Britain was a particularly insistent proponent of what became known as **appeasement.** Germany withdrew from the League of Nations in 1933; two years later Hitler announced that he planned to rearm the nation in violation of the Versailles treaty. Not willing to risk war, no one stopped him. In 1936 Germany reoccupied the Rhineland, a region that had been declared a demilitarized zone under the treaty. Once again, France and Britain took no action. Later that year, Hitler and Mussolini joined forces in the Rome-Berlin Axis, a political and military alliance. When the Spanish civil war broke out, Germany and Italy armed the Spanish Fascists. The same year, Germany and Japan signed the Anti-Comintern Pact, a precursor to the military alliance between Japan and the Axis that was formalized in 1940.

Depression-Era Isolationism

During the early years of the New Deal, America's involvement in international affairs, especially those in Europe, remained limited. One of Roosevelt's few diplomatic initiatives had been the formal recognition of the Soviet Union in November 1933. A second significant development was the Good Neighbor Policy, under which the United States voluntarily renounced the use of military force and armed intervention in the Western Hemisphere. This policy recognized that the friendship of Latin American countries was essential to the security of the United States. One practical outcome came in 1934 when Congress repealed the Platt Amendment, a relic of the Spanish-American War, which asserted the United States' right to intervene in Cuba's affairs. Indicating the limits to the Good Neighbor Policy, the U.S. Navy kept (and still maintains) a major base at Cuba's Guantanamo Bay and continued to meddle in Cuban politics. And in numerous Latin American countries, U.S. diplomats frequently resorted to economic pressure to solidify the influence of the United States and benefit its international corporations.

Roosevelt and his secretary of state, Cordell Hull, might have hoped to pursue more far-reaching diplomatic initiatives. But **isolationism** had been building in both Congress and the nation throughout the 1920s, a product in part of disillusionment with American participation in World War I. In 1934 Gerald P. Nye, a Republican senator from North Dakota, began a congressional investigation into the profits of munitions makers during World War I and then widened the investigation to determine the influence of economic interests on America's decision to declare war. Nye's committee concluded that war profiteers, whom it called "merchants of death," had maneuvered the nation into World War I for financial gain.

Though most of the committee's charges were dubious or simplistic, they gave momentum to the isolationist movement, contributing to the passage of the Neutrality Act of 1935. Designed explicitly to prevent a recurrence of the events that had pulled the United States into World War I, the act imposed an embargo on arms trading with countries at war and declared that American citizens traveled on the ships of belligerent nations at their own risk. In 1936 Congress expanded the Neutrality Act to ban loans to belligerents, and in 1937 it adopted a "cash-and-carry" provision: if a country at war wanted to purchase nonmilitary goods from the United States, it had to pay for them in cash and pick them up in its own ships.

The same year, Congress explicitly reinforced earlier bans on sales of arms to Spain, when the bloody civil war erupted in 1936. There, Francisco Franco, strongly supported by the Fascist regimes in Germany and Italy, was leading a rebellion against the democratically elected Republican government. Backed officially only by the Soviet Union and Mexico, the Republicans, or Loyalists, relied heavily on individual volunteers from other countries, including the American Lincoln Brigade, which fought courageously and sustained heavy losses throughout the war. The governments of the United States, Great Britain, and France, despite their Loyalist sympathies, remained neutral—a policy that dismayed many American intellectuals and activists and virtually ensured a Fascist victory.

In the meantime Roosevelt seemed to take a small step away from isolationism. In October 1937 he denounced "the present reign of terror and international lawlessness" and called on peace-loving nations to oppose such aggression through a "quarantine." Roosevelt's statement reflected general antimilitarism rhetoric rather than a specific call for collective security, for he knew there was no broad-based support in the nation for changing the isolationist course.

The Failure of Appeasement.   In 1938 Hitler's ambitions expanded: he sent troops to annex Austria, while simultaneously scheming to seize part of Czechoslovakia. Because Czechoslovakia had an alliance with France, war seemed imminent. But at the Munich Conference in September 1938, Britain and France capitulated, agreeing to let Germany annex the Sudetenland—the German-speaking border areas of Czechoslovakia—in return for Hitler's pledge to seek no more territory.

Within six months, however, Hitler's forces had overrun the rest of Czechoslovakia and were threatening to march into Poland. Britain and France realized that their policy of appeasement had been disastrous and prepared to take a stand. Then in August 1939 Hitler shocked the world by signing the Nonaggression Pact with the Soviet Union, which assured Germany it would not have to wage war on two fronts at once. On September 1, 1939, German troops attacked Poland; two days later Britain and France declared war on Germany. World War II had begun (Map 26.1).

Retreat from Isolationism

Because the United States had become a major world power, its response would affect the course of the European conflict. Two days after the war started, the United States officially declared its neutrality. Roosevelt made no secret of his sympathies, however. He pointedly rephrased Woodrow Wilson's declaration of 1914: "This nation will remain a neutral nation, but I cannot ask that every American remain neutral in thought as well." The

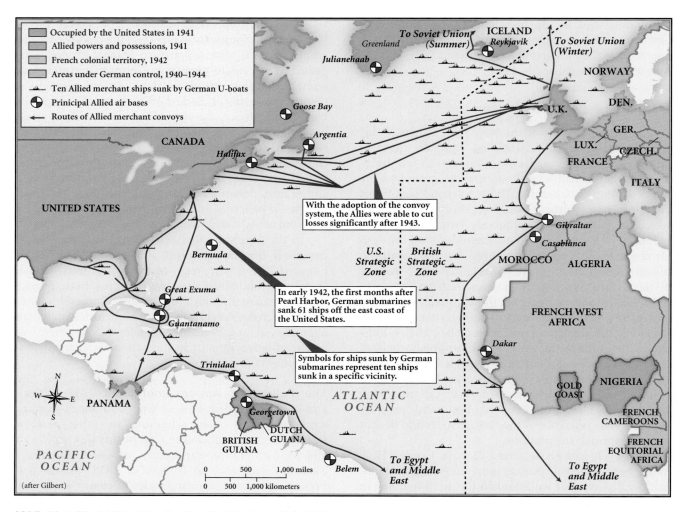

MAP 26.1 World War II in the North Atlantic, 1939–1943

After the start of the war in Europe in September 1939, Germany escalated its attacks on Allied and American merchant shipping in the Atlantic, spurring Congress to pass the Lend-Lease Act in March 1941 and President Roosevelt and Prime Minister Churchill to issue the Atlantic Charter in August. A pivotal factor in the Allied victory in Europe would be countering the German submarine threat in the Atlantic so that U.S. troops and materiel could be transported safely overseas. With the establishment of the convoy system—the protection of merchant shipping with destroyers—the Atlantic shipping lanes became safer, and the numbers of ships sunk after 1943 declined.

overwhelming majority of Americans supported the Allies (Britain and France) over the Nazis, but most Americans did not want to be drawn into another world war.

At first the need for American intervention seemed remote. After the German conquest of Poland in September 1939, a false calm settled over Europe. But then on April 9, 1940, Nazi tanks overran Denmark. Norway fell to the Nazi *blitzkrieg* ("lightning war") next, then the Netherlands, Belgium, and Luxembourg. Finally, on June 22, 1940, France fell. Britain stood alone against Hitler's plans for world domination.

Support for Intervention Grows. In America the developments in Europe stirred debate over neutrality.

The journalist William Allen White and his Committee to Defend America by Aiding the Allies led the interventionists. Isolationists, including the aviator Charles Lindbergh, formed the **America First Committee** to keep the nation out of the war; they attracted the support of the *Chicago Tribune*, the Hearst newspapers, and other conservative publications.

Despite the isolationist pressure, in 1940 the United States moved closer to involvement in the war. In May Roosevelt began putting the economy and the government on a defense footing by creating the National Defense Advisory Commission and the Council of National Defense. During the summer he traded fifty World War I destroyers to Great Britain in exchange for the right to build military bases on British possessions in the Atlantic, thus circumventing the nation's neutrality law by executive order. In October Congress approved a large increase in defense spending and instituted the first peacetime draft registration and conscription in American history.

While the war expanded in Europe, Asia, North Africa, and the Middle East, the United States was preparing for the 1940 presidential election. The conflict had convinced Roosevelt that he should seek an unprecedented third term. Despite some conservative opposition, Roosevelt chose the liberal secretary of agriculture Henry A. Wallace as his running mate. The Republicans nominated Wendell Willkie of Indiana, a former Democrat who supported many New Deal policies. The two parties' platforms differed only slightly. Both pledged aid to the Allies but stopped short of calling for American participation in the war. Though Willkie's spirited campaign resulted in a closer election than those of 1932 or 1936, Roosevelt and the Democrats won 55 percent of the popular vote and a lopsided total in the electoral college.

The Lend-Lease Act.   With the election behind him, Roosevelt concentrated on persuading the American people to increase aid to Britain, whose survival he viewed as the key to American security. In November 1939 FDR had won a bitter battle in Congress to amend the Neutrality Act of 1937 to allow the Allies to buy weapons from the United States—but only on the cash-and-carry basis the act had established for nonmilitary goods. In March 1941, with German submarines sinking British ships faster than they could be replaced and Britain no longer able to afford to pay cash for arms, Roosevelt convinced Congress to pass the Lend-Lease Act. The legislation authorized the president to "lease, lend, or otherwise dispose of" arms and other equipment to any country whose defense was considered vital to the security of the United States. After Germany invaded the Soviet Union in June 1941 (abandoning the Nazi-Soviet Nonaggression Pact of two years earlier), the United States extended lend-lease to the Soviet Union, which became part of the Allied coalition.

In his State of the Union address to Congress in January 1941, Roosevelt connected lend-lease to the defense of democracy at home as well as in Europe. He spoke about what he called "four essential human freedoms everywhere in the world"—freedom of speech and expression, freedom of worship, freedom from want, and freedom from fear. Although Roosevelt avoided stating explicitly that America had to enter the war to protect those freedoms, he intended to justify exactly that, for he regarded the United States' entry in the war as inevitable. And indeed the implementation of lend-lease marked the unofficial entrance of the United States into the European war.

The Atlantic Charter.   The United States became even more involved in August 1941, when Roosevelt and

Winston Churchill, who had become British prime minister in 1940, conferred secretly to discuss goals and military strategy. Their joint press release, which became known as the Atlantic Charter, provided the ideological foundation of the Western cause and of the peace to follow. Like Wilson's Fourteen Points, the charter called for economic collaboration and guarantees of political stability after the war ended to ensure that "all men in all the lands may live out their lives in freedom from fear and want." The charter also supported free trade, national self-determination, and the principle of collective security.

As in World War I, when Americans started supplying the Allies, Germany attacked American and Allied ships. By September 1941 Nazi submarines and American vessels were fighting an undeclared naval war in the Atlantic, unknown to the American public. Without a dramatic enemy attack, however, and with the public reluctant to enter the war, Roosevelt hesitated to ask Congress for a declaration of war.

The Attack on Pearl Harbor

The final provocation came not from Germany but from Japan. Throughout the 1930s, Japanese military advances in China had upset the balance of political and economic power in the Pacific, where the United States had long enjoyed the benefits of the open-door policy (see Chapter 21), even though the fabled "China Market" had never met American exporters' expectations. After the Japanese invasion of China in 1937, Roosevelt denounced "the present reign of terror and international lawlessness," suggesting that aggressors such as Japan be "quarantined" by peace-loving nations. Despite such rhetoric, however, the United States avoided taking a stand. During the brutal sack of Nanking in 1937, the Japanese sunk an American gunboat, the *Panay*, in the Yangtze River. The crisis was smoothed over, however, when the United States accepted Japan's apology and more than $2 million in damages.

Japan soon became more expansionist in its intentions, signing the Tri-Partite Pact with Germany and Italy in 1940. In the fall of 1940, Japanese troops occupied the northern part of French Indochina. The United States retaliated by restricting trade with Japan and placing an embargo on aviation-grade gasoline and scrap metal. Despite mounting tensions, Roosevelt hoped to avoid war with Japan. But in July 1941 Japanese troops occupied the rest of Indochina. Roosevelt responded by freezing Japanese assets in the United States and instituting an embargo on all trade with Japan, including vital oil shipments that accounted for almost 80 percent of Japanese consumption.

In September 1941 the government of Prime Minister Hideki Tojo began secret preparations for war against the United States. By November American military

Pearl Harbor
The U.S. destroyer West Virginia *exploded into flames after receiving a direct hit during the surprise Japanese attack on Pearl Harbor on December 7, 1941. It was early Sunday morning, and many of the servicemen were still asleep. More than 2,400 Americans were killed; the Japanese suffered only light losses.* U.S. Navy.

intelligence knew that Japan was planning an attack but did not know where it would come. Early on Sunday morning, December 7, 1941, Japanese bombers attacked Pearl Harbor in Hawaii, killing more than 2,400 Americans. Eight battleships, three cruisers, three destroyers, and almost two hundred airplanes were destroyed or heavily damaged.

Although the attack was devastating, it infused the American people with a determination to fight. Pearl Harbor Day is still etched in the memories of millions of Americans who remember precisely what they were doing when they heard about the attack. The next day Roosevelt went before Congress. Calling December 7 "a date which will live in infamy," he asked for a declaration of war against Japan. The Senate voted unanimously for war, and the House concurred by a vote of 388 to 1. The lone dissenter was Jeannette Rankin of Montana, who had also opposed American entry into World War I.

Three days later Germany and Italy declared war on the United States, and the United States in turn declared war on those nations.

Organizing for Victory

The task of fighting a global war accelerated the growing influence of the state on all aspects of American life. A dramatic expansion of power occurred at the presidential level when Congress passed the War Powers Act of December 18, 1941, giving Roosevelt unprecedented authority over all aspects of the conduct of the war. Coordinating the changeover from civilian to war production, raising an army, and assembling the necessary workforce taxed government agencies to the limit. Mobilization on such a scale demanded cooperation between business executives and political leaders in

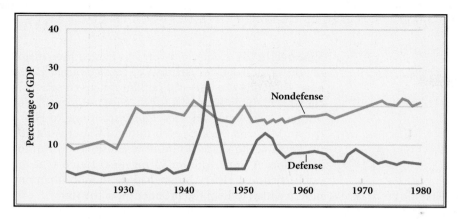

FIGURE 26.1 Government Spending as a Percentage of GDP

Government defense spending was a minuscule percentage of the gross domestic product in the 1930s, but it ballooned during World War II and rose again during the Korean War and, to a lesser degree, during the Vietnam War. Nondefense government spending did not display such wild fluctuations—just a steady, upward trend.

Washington, solidifying a partnership that had been growing since World War I.

Financing the War

Defense mobilization had a powerful impact on the federal government's role in the economy (Figure 26.1). The federal budget of $95.2 billion in 1945 was ten times that of 1939, and the national debt grew sixfold, topping out at $258.6 billion in 1945. Along with huge federal budgets came greater acceptance of Keynesian economics, that is, the use of government fiscal policy to stimulate economic growth. At the same time, the national government became more closely tied to its citizens' pocketbooks. The Revenue Act of 1942 continued the income tax reform that had begun during World War I by taxing not just wealthy individuals and corporations but average citizens as well. Tax collections rose from $2.2 billion to $35.1 billion, facilitated by payroll deductions and tax withholding instituted in 1943. This system of mass taxation, a revolutionary change in the financing of the modern state, was sold to the taxpayers as a way to express their patriotism.

The war also brought significant changes in the federal bureaucracy. The number of civilians employed by the government increased almost fourfold, to 3.8 million—a far more dramatic growth than the New Deal period had witnessed. Leadership of federal agencies also changed as the Roosevelt administration turned to business executives to replace the reformers who had staffed New Deal relief agencies in the 1930s. The executives became known as "**dollar-a-year men**" because they volunteered for government service while remaining on the corporate payroll. Many wartime agencies extended the power of the federal government. The Office of Price Administration (OPA) supervised the domestic economy, allocating resources and trying to keep inflation down. By February 1942 retail prices were rising by 2 percent a month, as consumers had more income to spend than there were available goods and services. In April the OPA froze most prices and rents at their March 1942 levels. When loopholes, especially regarding food prices, undermined that effort, Congress passed the Anti-Inflation Act, which stabilized prices, wages, and salaries. The consumer price index rose by 28.3 percent between 1940 and 1945, but most of the inflation occurred before 1943.

One of the most important wartime agencies was the War Production Board (WPB), which awarded defense contracts, evaluated military and civilian requests for scarce resources, and oversaw the conversion of industry to military production. The WPB used the carrot more often than the stick. To encourage businesses to convert to war production, the board granted generous tax write-offs for plant construction and approved contracts with **cost-plus provisions** that guaranteed a profit and promised that businesses could keep the new factories after the war. As Secretary of War Henry Stimson put it, in capitalist countries at war "you had better let business make money out of the process or business won't work."

In the interest of efficiency and maximum production, the WPB preferred to deal with major corporations rather than with small businesses. The fifty-six largest corporations received three-fourths of the war contracts; the top ten received a third. This system of allocating contracts, along with the suspension of antitrust prosecution during the war, hastened the trend toward large corporate structures. In 1940 the hundred largest companies manufactured 30 percent of the nation's industrial output; by 1945 their share was 70 percent. These very large businesses would form the core of the military-industrial complex of the postwar years, which linked the federal government, corporations, and the military in an interdependent partnership (see Chapter 27).

Together business and government produced an astonishing number of military goods. By 1945 the United States had turned out 86,000 tanks, 296,000 airplanes, 15 million rifles and machine guns, 64,000 landing craft, and 6,500 ships. Henry J. Kaiser, a West coast shipbuilder, performed shipyard production miracles. Using the mass-production techniques of the automobile industry, Kaiser cut the time needed to build a transport ship from 300 days to 17 (see American Lives, "Henry J. Kaiser: World War II's 'Miracle Man,'" p. 756). Mobilization on this gigantic scale gave a tremendous boost to the economy, causing it to more than double, rising from a gross

Henry J. Kaiser: World War II's "Miracle Man"

Henry Kaiser was a workaholic. His motto was "Find a Need and Fill It." He hated being alone and hated taking vacations. He worked twenty-hour days and expected his top managers to do the same. If ordinary mortals were trying to sleep in California, he made long-distance calls to associates in other time zones. "Whenever he had a new idea—and he commonly had a score or so daily—he reached for the telephone," noted his biographer, Mark Foster. As early as 1942 his company was running up then-extravagant phone bills of $250,000 a year.

Kaiser was one of the most widely known figures of the 1940s, a genuine folk hero to many for his ability to get things done. After shipyard triumphs such as the construction of an entire Liberty ship in four days, fifteen hours, and twenty-six minutes in November 1942, the press dubbed him the "Miracle Man." He was a special darling of media mogul Henry Luce: 40 percent of the popular articles on Kaiser between 1941 and 1943 appeared in *Time*, *Life*, and *Fortune*, Luce's three major publications. Even the staid *Wall Street Journal* called him "Fabulous Mr. Kaiser." Franklin Roosevelt seriously considered the industrialist for the vice presidential slot on the 1944 Democratic ticket and, according to FDR's cousin Margaret Suckley, even thought Kaiser would be the best man to succeed him if he chose not to run for reelection. A Roper poll in spring 1945 found that the public believed Henry Kaiser had done more than any other civilian to help the president win the war.

Kaiser's career and the rise of the modern American West went hand in hand. Born in upstate New York in 1882 to German immigrant parents, he left school at age thirteen to make his way in the world. In 1906 he headed west to Spokane, Washington, to establish himself in business so that he could marry his fiancée; in 1921 he and his family settled permanently in Oakland, California. From 1914 to 1931 Kaiser's contracting business built roads, trying to keep up with the West's insatiable demand for highways for the new cars rolling off the assembly lines in Detroit. In the 1930s Kaiser was part of a six-company partnership that successfully bid for massive engineering projects such as building the Hoover and Grand Coulee Dams, federally funded public works projects that permanently changed the western landscape. In the 1930s he also lobbied extensively in Washington, developing contacts with New Deal bureaucrats that would prove invaluable during the war years.

The Miracle Man

In November 1942 Henry Kaiser used an 81-piece, 14-foot-long model of the 10,400-ton Liberty freighter to show shipowners and navy representatives how it was built in the amazing time of 4 days, 15 hours, and 26 minutes. Corbis-Bettmann.

Moved largely by wartime opportunities, Kaiser left construction to launch a career as an industrialist. He made his first big splash—literally—building Liberty ships faster and better than anyone else. Shipbuilding was an ideal choice for an inveterate self-promoter like Henry Kaiser. The World War II era boasted few photo opportunities better than a ship launching, and Kaiser invited Hollywood stars, members of the president's family, and a host of other celebrities to christen the ships, always with the newsreel cameras rolling and the photographers' flash bulbs popping. Thanks to his public relations machine, Kaiser's name was all over the news.

But before Kaiser could build ships, he had to build shipyards. Drawing on the availability of vacant tracts of West Coast waterfront (something the older shipyards in the East did not have), he constructed work spaces large enough to accommodate the assembly of prefabricated ship components. Kaiser's shipyards in Richmond, California, were designed like a city grid, complete with numbered and lettered streets. "It was a city without houses," remembered one worker, "but the traffic was heavy. Cranes, trucks, trains noised by." Recalled a recent migrant from a small Iowa town, "It was such a huge place, something I had never been in. People from all walks of life, all coming and going and working, and the noise. The whole atmosphere was overwhelming to me."

Although Kaiser did not invent the subassembly technique, he was the most successful at applying mass production to shipbuilding. Previously, most jobs in shipbuilding had been skilled or semiskilled, requiring apprenticeship and training far too lengthy for the wartime emergency. To train new workers more quickly, the work process was broken down into small, specialized tasks, in effect removing the skill from what had previously been a craft. As Kaiser put it, "production is not labor anymore, but a process."

The Kaiser shipyards were known as much for their corporate welfare programs as for their bureaucratized work climate. Kaiser offered his workers day care, financial and job counseling, subsidized housing, and especially health care, his most significant long-term contribution. The Kaiser Permanente Medical Care Program was founded in 1942, an outgrowth of prepaid health-care plans first tried on remote federal construction projects in the 1930s. This health-care system, the forerunner of today's health maintenance organizations (HMOs), was available to Kaiser workers for a nominal paycheck deduction of 50 cents a week. Almost 90 percent of his workers chose that option. Kaiser provided health care for both philanthropic and business reasons. The initial investment was quickly repaid in the form of healthier workers, lower absenteeism, and greater productivity. As a Permanente executive explained, "To the private physician, a sick person is an asset. To Permanente, a sick person is a liability. We'd go bankrupt if we didn't keep most of our members and their families well most of the time."

At the core of Kaiser's popularity was a dichotomy. The public saw him as a man who broke the rules for them, a self-made outsider who made things happen in wartime Washington despite the bureaucrats. Yet Kaiser could never have achieved his business miracles without a close working relationship with the federal government, which, for example, allowed him to borrow $300 million from the Reconstruction Finance Corporation during World War II to construct new plants. Noting the symbiotic relationship between business and government that increasingly characterized the twentieth century, historian Stephen B. Adams called Henry Kaiser a government entrepreneur. But the public persisted in seeing him as an individualist, a symbol of a "can-do" age.

While many business executives faced the postwar period with caution, Kaiser looked forward to peacetime reconversion with the boundless optimism of a far-sighted entrepreneur. He was especially excited about opportunities for industrial expansion in the West. Between 1944 and 1946 he identified opportunities in areas such as steel, magnesium, and aluminum as well as foresaw a demand for mass-produced suburban tract housing. In the 1950s he headed a multinational corporate empire that included many companies with assets close to $1 billion. In 1965 he became the first industrialist to win the AFL-CIO's highest honor, the Philip Murray–William Green Award.

To many Americans Henry Kaiser was a twentieth-century incarnation of Horatio Alger, even though he was a portly sixty years old in 1942 when he launched the Richmond shipyards. In terms of managerial style, he was more an old-style "seat-of-the-pants" entrepreneur than a modern corporate bureaucrat. He was a maverick, challenging traditional ways of doing business at every stage of his career at the same time that he seized the opportunities presented by the growth of the administrative state. He was a visionary in the role that he saw for an industrial West, a dream that was amply fulfilled during the postwar era. But he was also lucky, his success being the product of a highly favorable set of economic conditions both regionally in the West and globally during World War II and its aftermath. After his death in 1967, his industrial empire largely disappeared, but Kaiser Permanente lives on, one of the country's largest and most successful health maintenance organizations.

domestic product in 1940 of $99.7 billion to $211 billion by the end of the war. After years of depression, Americans' faith in the capitalist system was restored. But it was a transformed system that relied heavily on the federal government's participation in the economy.

Mobilizing the American Fighting Force

An expanded state presence was also evident in the government's mobilization of a fighting force. By the end of World War II, the armed forces of the United States numbered more than 15 million men and women. Draft boards had registered about 31 million men between the ages of eighteen and forty-four. More than half the men failed to meet the physical standards: many were rejected because of defective teeth or poor vision. The military

Why We Fight

This 1942 award-winning lithograph by Karl Koehler and Victor Ancona painted a sinister, menacing portrait of a Nazi officer, leaving little room for doubt as to why it was necessary to end Nazism.

National Museum of American Art, Smithsonian Institution, Washington, DC.

also tried to screen out homosexuals, but its attempts were ineffectual. Once in service homosexuals found opportunities to participate in a gay subculture more extensive than that in civilian life, where they were often channeled into marriage and heterosexual societal roles.

Racial discrimination prevailed in the armed forces, directed mainly against the approximately 700,000 blacks who fought in all branches of the armed forces in segregated units. Though the National Association for the Advancement of Colored People (NAACP) and other civil rights groups chided the government with reminders such as "A Jim Crow army cannot fight for a free world," the military continued to segregate African Americans and to assign them the most menial duties. In contrast Mexican Americans were never officially segregated. Unlike blacks they were welcomed into combat units, and seventeen Mexican Americans won the Congressional Medal of Honor. Native Americans also served in nonsegregated combat, and some, like the Navajo Code Talkers, played a unique role in circumventing Japanese codebreaking efforts by using their native language to send military messages.

Women found both opportunities and discrimination in the armed services. Approximately 350,000 American women enlisted in the armed services and achieved a permanent status in the military. There were about 140,000 WAC (Women's Army Corps) members; 100,000 naval WAVES (Women Accepted for Volunteer Emergency Service); 23,000 members of the Marine Corps Women's Reserve; and 13,000 SPARs (for *Semper Paratus*, or Always Ready, the coast guard's motto) in the coast guard. One-third of the nation's registered nurses, almost 75,000 overall, volunteered for military duty. In addition about 1,000 WASPs (Women's Airforce Service Pilots) ferried planes and supplies in noncombat areas. The government refused to incorporate the WASPs as part of the military, primarily because male pilots resented women's encroachment on their high-status preserve. Not until 1977 did a congressional act accord them veterans' benefits, a belated recognition of their wartime service.

The armed forces limited the types of duty assigned to women, as it did with blacks. Women were barred from combat, although nurses and medical personnel sometimes served close to the front lines, risking capture or death. The social lives of women soldiers, most of whom were single, were more strictly regulated than those of their male counterparts, mainly to prevent sexual impropriety. Most military jobs reflected stereotypes of women's roles in civilian life—clerical work, communications, and health care. The widely distributed pinups of Betty Grable in a bathing suit, Rita Hayworth in a flimsy nightgown, and, for the black soldiers, the singer Lena Horne were probably closer to the average GI's view of women than was a WAC or a WAVE.

The WACs Overseas
Not all military women were relegated to stateside duty. These eager WACs, members of the first Women's Army Corps unit to go overseas, have just arrived in North Africa in 1943 to begin their assignments, most likely as nurses, clerks, drivers, or telephone operators. Archive Photos.

Workers and the War Effort

When millions of citizens entered military service, a huge hole opened in the American workforce. The backlog of depression-era unemployment quickly disappeared, and the United States faced a critical labor shortage. The nation's defense industries provided jobs for about 7 million new workers, including great numbers of women, who were given employment opportunities for the first time.

Rosie the Riveter. Government planners "discovered" women while looking for workers to fill the jobs vacated by departing servicemen. Well-organized government propaganda stressed patriotism as it urged women into the workforce. "Longing won't bring him back sooner . . . GET A WAR JOB!" one poster beckoned, while the artist Norman Rockwell's famous "Rosie the Riveter" appealed to women from the cover of the *Saturday Evening Post.*

Although the government directed its propaganda at housewives, women who were already employed gladly abandoned low-paying "women's" jobs as domestic servants or file clerks for higher-paying jobs in the defense industry. Suddenly the nation's factories were full of women working as riveters, welders, and drill-press operators. Women made up 36 percent of the labor force in 1945, compared with 24 percent at the beginning of the war.

Government planners and employers regarded women as just "filling in" while the men were away. Employers rarely offered day care or flexible hours, and government child-care programs established by the 1940 Lanham Act reached only 10 percent of those who needed them. Because women were responsible for home care as well as their jobs, they had a higher absentee rate than did men. Often, the only way to get shopping done or take a child to the doctor was to skip work. Women war workers also faced discrimination on the job. In shipyards women with the most seniority and responsibility earned $6.95 a day, whereas the top men made as much as $22.

When the men came home from war, and the nation's plants returned to peacetime operations, Rosie the Riveter was out of a job. But many women refused to put on aprons and stay home. Though women's participation in the labor force dropped temporarily when the war ended, it rebounded steadily for the rest of the 1940s, especially among married women (see Chapter 27).

Organized Labor. Wartime mobilization also opened up opportunities to advance the labor movement. Organized labor responded to the war with an initial burst of patriotic unity. On December 23, 1941, representatives of the major unions made a "no-strike" pledge—though it was nonbinding—for the duration of the war. In January 1942 Roosevelt set up the National War Labor Board (NWLB), composed of representatives of labor, management, and the public. The NWLB established wages, hours, and working conditions and had the authority to order government seizure of plants that did not comply. Forty plants were seized during the war.

During its tenure the NWLB handled 17,650 disputes affecting 12 million workers. It resolved the controversial issue of union membership through a compromise. New hires did not have to join a union, but those who already belonged had to maintain their membership over the life of a contract. Agitation for wage increases caused a more serious disagreement. Because managers wanted to keep production running smoothly and profitably, they were willing to pay higher wages. However, pay raises would conflict with the government's efforts to combat inflation, which drove up prices dramatically in the early war years. Incomes rose as much as 70 percent during the war because workers earned overtime pay, which was not covered by wage ceilings.

Although incomes were higher than anyone could have dreamed during the depression, many union members felt cheated as they watched corporate profits soar in relation to wages. Dissatisfaction peaked in 1943. That year a nationwide railroad strike was narrowly averted. Then John L. Lewis led more than half a million United Mine Workers out on strike, demanding an increase in wages over that recommended by the NWLB.

Though Lewis won concessions, he alienated Congress, and because he had defied the government, he became one of the most disliked public figures of the 1940s.

Congress countered Lewis's action by overriding Roosevelt's veto of the Smith-Connally Labor Act of 1943, which required a thirty-day cooling-off period before a strike and prohibited entirely strikes in defense industries. Nevertheless, about 15,000 walkouts occurred during the war. Though less than one-tenth of 1 percent of working hours were lost to labor disputes, the public perceived the disruptions to be far more extensive. Thus although union membership increased dramatically during the war, from 9 million to almost 15 million workers—a third of the nonagricultural workforce—the labor movement also evoked significant public and congressional hostility that would hamper it in the postwar years.

Civil Rights during Wartime

Just as labor sought to benefit from the war, African Americans manifested a new mood of militancy. "A wind is rising throughout the world of free men everywhere," Eleanor Roosevelt wrote during the war, "and they will not be kept in bondage." Black leaders pointed out parallels between anti-Semitism in Germany and racial discrimination in America and pledged themselves to a "Double V" campaign: victory over Nazism abroad and victory over racism and inequality at home.

Even before Pearl Harbor, black activism was on the rise. In 1940 only 240 of the nation's 100,000 aircraft workers were black, and most of them were janitors. Black leaders demanded that the government require defense contractors to integrate their workforces. When the government took no action, A. Philip Randolph, head of the Brotherhood of Sleeping Car Porters, a black union, announced plans for a "March on Washington" in the summer of 1941. Though Roosevelt was not a strong supporter of civil rights, he feared the embarrassment of a massive public protest. Even more, he worried about a disruption of the nation's war preparations.

In June 1941, in exchange for Randolph's cancellation of the march, Roosevelt issued Executive Order 8802, declaring "that there shall be no discrimination in the employment of workers in defense industries or government because of race, creed, color, or national origin," and established the Fair Employment Practices Commission (FEPC). Though this federal commitment to minority employment rights was unprecedented, it was limited in scope; for instance, it did not affect segregation in the armed forces. Moreover, the FEPC could not require compliance with its orders and often found that the needs of defense production took precedence over fair employment practices. The committee resolved only about a third of the more than 8,000 complaints it received.

Fighting for Freedom at Home and Abroad
This protester from the Negro Labor Relations League pointedly drew the parallel between blacks serving in the armed forces and a 1941 labor discrimination dispute at a Chicago dairy.
Library of Congress.

Encouraged by the ideological climate of the war years, civil rights organizations increased their pressure for reform. The League of United Latin American Citizens (LULAC) built on their community's patriotic contributions to national defense and the armed services to challenge long-standing patterns of discrimination and exclusion. In Texas, where it was still common to see signs reading, "No Dogs or Mexicans Allowed," the organization protested segregation in schools and public facilities. African American groups also flourished. The NAACP grew ninefold to 450,000 by 1945. Although the NAACP generally favored lobbying and legal strategies, a student chapter of the NAACP at Howard University

German POWs

American Race Relations

During World War II Nazi prisoners of war were assigned to various army camps throughout the United States, where their labor was often contracted out to help with the acute shortage of workers caused by war mobilization. German prisoners thus had a unique opportunity to observe American life. Here are some of their observations, mainly centered on the issue of race.

We picked cotton the length of the Mississippi. I'm an agriculturalist, and I know how to handle hard work, but there it was truly very, very hard. It was terribly hot, and we had to bend over all day. We had nothing to drink. . . . There were a great number of Blacks on the plantation. They required us to gather 100 lbs. of cotton a day; but of the Blacks, they demanded two or three times more. . . . For them it was worse than for us. And

you have to see how they lived. Their farms: very ugly, very primitive. These people were so exploited. . . .

Me, I was in peas; picking and the canning factory. The farmers liked me, and wanted me to stay after the war, but I wasn't sure. . . . I met some old people of German origin one day, and these poor old people told me: "We feel alone here. It's sad. It's too big. If we could, we would walk back to Germany on foot. . . ." And the Blacks! They were always saying: "We are just like you: Prisoners; Oppressed; Second-class men. . . ."

There was a plumber who came to work in the camp. His name was Gutierrez, and he was Mexican. . . . He was a very nice guy. When he went to the barbershop, he stood in the corner, he did not move, and, as he was "colored," he had to wait until all the Whites were done. You know, things like that upset us very much. . . .

I was in a camp near Miami in Florida. I was one of the scavenger commandos; every morning we went to gather the garbage in the city. . . . People of German origin were the least nice to us. . . . Those who helped us the most, on the contrary, were the Jews. . . . Ah, the Jews and the Blacks.

Source: Arnold Krammer, *Nazi Prisoners of War in America* (New York: Stein and Day, 1979), 92–93.

used direct tactics. In 1944 it forced several restaurants in Washington, D.C., to serve blacks after picketing them with signs that read "Are You for Hitler's Way or the American Way? Make Up Your Mind." In Chicago James Farmer helped to found the Congress of Racial Equality (CORE), a group that became known nationwide for its use of direct action like demonstrations and sit-ins. These wartime developments—both federal intervention and resurgent African American militancy—laid the groundwork for the civil rights revolution of the 1950s and 1960s (see Voices from Abroad, "German POWs: American Race Relations," above).

Politics in Wartime

Although the federal government expanded dramatically during the war years, there was little attempt to use the state to promote social reform on the home front, as in World War I. An enlarged federal presence was justified only insofar as it assisted war aims. During the early years

of the war, Roosevelt rarely pressed for social and economic change, in part because he was preoccupied with the war but also because he wanted to counteract Republican political gains. Republicans had picked up ten seats in the Senate and forty-seven seats in the House in the 1942 elections, thus bolstering conservatives in Congress who sought to roll back New Deal measures. With little protest Roosevelt agreed to drop several popular New Deal programs, including the Civilian Conservation Corps and the National Youth Administration, which were less necessary once war mobilization brought full employment.

Later in the war Roosevelt began to promise new social welfare measures. In his State of the Union address in 1944, he called for a second bill of rights, which would serve as "a new basis of security and prosperity." This extension of the New Deal identified jobs, adequate food and clothing, decent homes, medical care, and education as basic rights. But the president's commitment to them remained largely rhetorical; congressional support for this vast extension of the welfare state did not exist in 1944. Some of those rights did become realities for veterans, however. The Servicemen's Readjustment Act (1944), known as the GI Bill of Rights, provided education, job training, medical care, pensions, and mortgage loans for men and women who had served in the armed forces during the war. An extraordinarily influential program, particularly in making higher education more widely available, it distributed almost four billion dollars worth of benefits to 9 million veterans between 1944 and 1949 and in the 1950s would be extended to veterans of the Korean War era.

Roosevelt's renewed call for social legislation was part of a plan to woo Democratic voters after the congressional setbacks of the 1942 elections. The Democrats realized they would have to work hard to maintain their strong coalition in 1944. Once again Roosevelt headed the ticket, reasoning that the continuation of the war made a fourth term necessary. Democrats, concerned about Roosevelt's health and the need for a successor, dropped Vice President Henry Wallace, whose outspoken support for labor, civil rights, and domestic reform was too extreme for many party leaders. In his place they chose Senator Harry S Truman of Missouri, known for heading a Senate investigation of government efficiency in awarding wartime defense contracts.

The Republicans nominated Governor Thomas E. Dewey of New York. Only forty-two years old, Dewey had won fame fighting organized crime as a U.S. attorney. He accepted the broad outlines of the welfare state and was among those Republicans who rejected isolationism in favor of an internationalist stance. The 1944 election was the closest since 1916: Roosevelt received only 53.5 percent of the popular vote. The party's margin of victory came from the cities: in urban areas of more than 100,000 people the president drew 60 percent of the vote, reflecting in part ethnic minorities' loyalty to the Democratic Party. A significant segment of this urban support came from organized labor. The CIO's Political Action Committee made substantial contributions to the party, canvassed door to door, and conducted voter registration campaigns—a role organized labor would continue to play after the war.

Life on the Home Front

Although the United States did not suffer the physical devastation that ravaged much of Europe and the Pacific, the war affected the lives of those who stayed behind. Every time relatives of a loved one overseas saw the Western Union boy on his bicycle, they feared a telegram from the War Department saying that their son, husband, or father would not be coming home. All Americans tolerated small deprivations daily. "Don't you know there's a war on?" became the standard reply to any request that could not be fulfilled. People accepted the fact that their lives would be different "for the duration." They also accepted, however grudgingly, the increased role of the federal government in shaping their daily lives.

"For the Duration"

Just like the soldiers in uniform, people on the home front had a job to do. They worked on civilian defense committees, collected old newspapers and scrap material, and served on local rationing and draft boards. About 20 million home "Victory gardens" produced 40 percent of the nation's vegetables. All these endeavors were encouraged by various federal agencies, especially the Office of War Information (OWI), which strove to disseminate information and promote patriotism. Working closely with advertising agencies, the OWI urged them to link their clients' products to the "four freedoms," explaining that patriotic ads would not only sell goods but would "invigorate, instruct and inspire [the citizen] as a functioning unit in his country's greatest effort."

Popular Culture. Popular culture, especially the movies, reinforced the connections between the home front and troops serving overseas. Average weekly movie attendance soared to over 100 million during the war. Demand was so high that many theaters operated around the clock to accommodate defense workers on the swing and night shifts. Many movies, encouraged in part by the OWI, had patriotic themes; stars such as John Wayne, Anthony Quinn, and Spencer Tracy portrayed the heroism of American fighting men in films like *Back to Bataan* (1945), *Guadalcanal Diary* (1943), and *Thirty Seconds over Tokyo* (1945). Other movies, such as *Watch on the Rhine* (1943), warned of the danger of fascism at home and abroad, while the Academy Award–winning *Casablanca* (1943) demonstrated the heroism and patriotism of ordinary citizens. *Since You Went Away* (1943), starring Claudette Colbert as a wife who took a war job after her husband left for war, was one of many films that portrayed struggles on the home front. Newsreels accompanying the feature films kept the public up-to-date on the war, as did on-the-spot radio broadcasts by commentators such as Edward R. Murrow. Thus popular culture reflected America's new international involvement at the same time that it built morale on the home front.

Consumption Patterns and Rationing. Perhaps the major source of Americans' high morale was wartime prosperity. Federal defense spending had solved the depression; unemployment had disappeared, and per capita income had risen from $691 in 1939 to $1,515 in 1945. Despite geographical dislocations and shortages of many items, about 70 percent of Americans admitted midway through the war that they had personally experienced "no real sacrifices." A Red Cross worker put it bluntly: "The war was fun for America. I'm not talking

Entertaining the Troops

The original Stage Door Canteen opened in the basement of a Broadway theater in 1942. It provided servicemen with coffee, doughnuts, and big-time entertainment volunteered by Broadway and Hollywood stars. The canteen's popular weekly radio show was the inspiration for the 1943 movie Stage Door Canteen. Lee Boltin Picture Library.

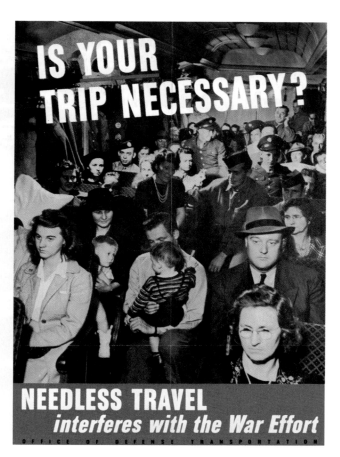

Please Stay Home

With the economy booming and most citizens reporting no great hardships or dislocations, Americans sometimes had to be reminded that there was a war on. A poster from the Office of Defense Transportation pointing out that needless travel interfered with the war effort jogged their memory. Picture Research Consultants & Archives.

about the poor souls who lost sons and daughters. But for the rest of us, the war was a hell of a good time."

For many Americans the major inconveniences of the war were the limitations placed on their consumption. In contrast to the largely voluntaristic approach used during World War I, federal agencies such as the Office of Price Administration subjected almost everything Americans ate, wore, or used during World War II to rationing or regulation. In response to depleted domestic gasoline supplies and a shortage of rubber—the Japanese had conquered Malaysia and Netherlands' East Indies, the source of 97 percent of American rubber—the government restricted the sale of tires, rationed gas, and imposed a nationwide speed limit of 35 miles per hour, which cut highway deaths dramatically. By 1943 the amount of meat, butter, sugar, and other foods Americans could buy was also regulated. Most people cooperated with the complicated system of restrictions, but almost a fourth occasionally bought items on the black market, especially meat, gasoline, and cigarettes. People found it especially hard to

cut back on sugar. When sugar disappeared from grocery shelves, the government rationed it at a rate of 1 to $1\frac{1}{2}$ cups per person a week. However, the manufacturers of products such as Coca-Cola and Wrigley's chewing gum received unlimited quantities of sugar by convincing the government that the products helped the morale of the men and women in the armed forces.

Migration and Family Life. The war and the government affected not only what people ate, drank, and wore, but also where they lived. When men entered the armed services, their families often followed them to training bases or points of debarkation. The lure of high-paying defense jobs encouraged others—Native Americans on reservations, white southerners in the hills of Appalachia, African Americans in the rural South—to move. About 15 million Americans changed residence during the war years, half of them moving to another state.

Anton Bilek

The War in the Pacific

Anton Bilek grew up in southern Illinois and enlisted in the army in 1939 at nineteen because jobs were hard to get. Sent to the Philippines in 1940, he was taken prisoner when the Japanese overran the Bataan peninsula in April 1942. He describes the infamous "Bataan Death March" and its aftermath.

The next morning, we got orders to get rid of all our arms and wait for the Japanese to come. General King had surrendered Bataan. They came in. First thing they did, they lined us up and started searchin' us. Anybody that had a ring or a wristwatch or a pair of gold-rimmed spectacles, they took 'em. Glasses they'd throw on the floor and break 'em and put the gold rims in their pockets. If you had a ring, you handed it over. If you couldn't get it off, the guy'd put the bayonet right up against your neck. Fortunately I never wore a ring. I couldn't afford one.

They moved us about on the road. Here was a big stream of Americans and Filipinos marchin' by. They told us to get in the back of this column. This was the start of the Death March. (A long, deep sigh.) That was a sixty-mile walk. Here we were, three, four months on half-rations, less. The men were already thin, in shock. Undernourished, full of malaria. Dysentery is beginning to spread. This is even before the surrender. We had two hospitals chuck-full of men. Bataan peninsula was the worst malaria-infected province of the Philippines.

The Japanese emptied out the hospitals. Anybody that could walk, they forced 'em into line. You found all kinda bodies along the road. Some of 'em bloated, some had just been killed. If you fell out to the side, you were either shot by the guards or you were bayoneted and left there. We lost somewhere between six hundred and seven hundred Americans in the four days of the march. The Filipinos lost close to ten thousand. At San Fernando, we were stuffed into boxcars and taken about thirty-five miles further north. The cars were closed, you couldn't get air. In the hot sun, the temperature got up there. You couldn't fall down because you were held up by the guys stacked around you. You had a lot of guys blow their top, start screamin'. From there, they marched us another seven, eight miles to Camp O'Donnell, which was built hurriedly for the Philippine army. It was built like the huts were built, of native bamboo and nipa and grass. There must've been about nine thousand of us and about fifty thousand Filipinos. Americans in one camp, Filipinos in the other. We had to leave after a month and a half. The monsoon season was starting. A hurricane blew down two of the barracks. Eighty men were killed. Just crushed.

I went blind, momentarily. It scared the hell out of me. I was at the hospital for about two weeks, and the doctor, an American, said, "There's nothing I can do with you. Rest is the only thing. Eat all the rice you can get. That's your only medicine." That's the one thing that pulled me through. He said, "You won't have to go on details." The Japanese were comin' in and they'd take two, three hundred and start 'em repairing a bridge that was blown up. We were losin' a lot of men there. They couldn't work any more. They were dyin'. . . .

I'm back home. It's all over with. I'd like to forget it. I had nothin' against the Japanese. But I don't drive a Toyota or own a Sony. . . . A lotta friends I lost. We had 185 men in our squadron when the war started. Three and a half years later, when we were liberated from a prison camp in Japan, we were 39 left. It's them I think about. Men I played ball with, men I worked with, men I associated with. I miss 'em.

Source: Studs Terkel, "The Good War": An Oral History of World War Two (New York: Pantheon Books, 1984), 85, 90–91, 95–96.

return pledged to hold "free and unfettered elections" at an unspecified time. (Those elections never took place.) The compromise reached by the three leaders at Yalta was open to multiple interpretations. Admiral William D. Leahy, Roosevelt's chief military aide, described the agreement as "so elastic that the Russians can stretch it all the way from Yalta to Washington without ever technically breaking it."

The three leaders proceeded with plans to divide Germany into four zones to be controlled by the United States, Great Britain, France, and the Soviet Union. The capital city, Berlin, which lay in the middle of the Soviet zone, would also be partitioned among the four powers. The issue of German reparations remained unsettled.

The Big Three made further progress toward the establishment of an international organization in the form of the United Nations. They agreed that the Security Council of the United Nations would include the five

The Big Three at Yalta
With victory in Europe at hand, Roosevelt journeyed in 1945 to Yalta, on the Black Sea, to meet one last time with Churchill and Stalin. It was here that they discussed the problems of peace settlements. The Yalta agreement mirrored a new balance of power and set the stage for the cold war. Franklin D. Roosevelt Library.

major Allied powers—the United States, Britain, France, China, and the Soviet Union—plus six other nations elected on a rotating basis. They also decided that the permanent members of the Security Council should have veto power over decisions of the General Assembly, in which all nations would be represented. Roosevelt, Churchill, and Stalin announced that the United Nations would convene in San Francisco on April 25, 1945.

Roosevelt returned to the United States in February, visibly exhausted by his 14,000-mile trip. He neglected to inform the American public of the concessions he had made to maintain the increasingly fragile wartime alliance. When he reported to Congress on the Yalta agreements, he made an unusual acknowledgment of his physical infirmity. Referring to the heavy steel braces he wore on his legs, he asked Congress to excuse him for giving his speech while sitting down. The sixty-three-year-old president was a sick man, suffering from heart failure and high blood pressure. On April 12, 1945, during a short visit to his vacation home in Warm Springs, Georgia, Roosevelt suffered a cerebral hemorrhage and died.

The Onset of the Atomic Age and the War's End

When Harry S Truman assumed the presidency, he learned about the top-secret Manhattan Project, charged with developing an atomic bomb. The project, which cost $2 billion and employed 120,000 people, culminated in Los Alamos, New Mexico, where the country's top physicists assembled the first bomb. Not until the first test—at Alamogordo, New Mexico, on July 16, 1945—did scientists know that the bomb would work. A month later Truman ordered the dropping of atomic bombs on two Japanese cities, Hiroshima on August 6 and Nagasaki on August 9.

Many later questioned why the United States did not warn Japan about the attack or choose a noncivilian target; the rationale for dropping the second bomb was even less clear. Some historians have argued that American

Hiroshima

This aerial view of Hiroshima after the dropping of an atomic bomb on August 6, 1945, shows the terrible devastation of the city. A U.S. Army report prepared in 1946 describes the bomb exploding "with a blinding flash in the sky, and a great rush of air and a loud rumble of noise extended for many miles around the city; the first blast was soon followed by the sounds of falling buildings and of growing fires, and a great cloud of dust and smoke began to cast a pall of darkness over the city." With the exception of around 50 concrete-reinforced buildings designed to withstand earthquakes, every structure within one mile of the center of the bomb blast was reduced to rubble. The physical destruction was second to the human cost: with a population estimated at between 300,000 and 400,000 people, Hiroshima lost 100,000 in the initial explosion and many thousands more died slowly of radiation poisoning. U.S. Air Force.

policymakers, already worried about potential conflicts with the Soviets over the postwar order, used the bomb to intimidate the Soviets. Others have suggested the fact that the Japanese were a nonwhite race facilitated the momentous decision to use the new, alarming weapon. At the time, however, the belief that Japan's military leaders would never surrender unless their country was utterly devastated convinced policymakers that they had to deploy the atom bomb. One hundred thousand people died at Hiroshima and sixty thousand at Nagasaki; tens of thousands more died slowly of radiation poisoning. Japan offered to surrender on August 10 and signed a formal treaty of surrender on September 2, 1945.

FOR FURTHER EXPLORATION

▶ For definitions of the key terms boldfaced in this chapter, see the glossary at the end of the book.

▶ To assess your mastery of the material covered in this chapter, see the Online Study Guide at **bedfordstmartins.com/henretta**.

▶ For suggested references, including Web sites, see page SR-28 at the end of the book.

▶ For map resources and primary documents, see **bedfordstmartins.com/henretta**.

SUMMARY

World War II was a global war, consisting of massive military campaigns in both Europe and the Pacific. With the rise of fascism and imperialism in Germany, Italy, and Japan, the world was at war by 1939. Although most Americans clung to strong isolationist sentiment, as evidenced by the series of Neutrality Acts during the 1930s, by the end of the decade President Roosevelt had begun mobilizing public opinion for intervention and converting the economy to war production. The Japanese attack on Pearl Harbor on December 7, 1941, brought the nation into World War II.

Defense mobilization ended the Great Depression and caused the economy to rebound. As with World War I, mobilization led to a dramatic expansion of the state. On the home front the war resulted in rationing and shortages of many items but no serious hardships. Geographical mobility increased as labor shortages opened job opportunities for women, blacks, and Mexican Americans. The labor movement surged, and the ideological climate of fighting Nazism aided the cause of civil rights. However, Japanese Americans on the West Coast suffered a devastating denial of civil liberties when the government moved them into internment camps.

The war news was bleak at first, but by 1943 the Allies had started to move toward victory, first in Europe and then in the Pacific. Soviet forces bore the brunt of the fighting in the European theater, while American forces primarily orchestrated the war effort in the Pacific. More than 15 million American men and women served in the armed forces, and at least 405,000 lost their lives.

While the Allied forces mobilized to defeat Germany and Japan, Roosevelt attempted to maintain harmony among the United States, Great Britain, and the Soviet Union. Many of the disagreements over wartime diplomacy would become serious problems in the postwar world, especially the fate of Eastern Europe and the intentions of the Soviet Union. Of all the major powers that fought in World War II, only the United States emerged physically unharmed. And at the end of the war, only the United States had a powerful new weapon—the atomic bomb. But the most enduring legacy of World War II was the onset of the cold war, which would dominate American foreign policy for the next four decades.

TIMELINE

1933	Adolf Hitler becomes chancellor of Germany
1935	Italy invades Ethiopia
1935–1937	U.S. Neutrality Acts
1936	Germany reoccupies Rhineland demilitarized zone
	Rome-Berlin Axis established
	Japan and Germany sign Anti-Comintern Pact
1937	Japan invades China
1938	Munich agreement between Germany, Britain, and France
1939	Nazi-Soviet Nonaggression Pact
	Germany invades Poland
	Britain and France declare war on Germany
1940	American conscription reinstated
	Germany, Italy, and Japan sign Tri-Partite Pact
1941	Roosevelt promulgates Four Freedoms
	Germany invades Soviet Union
	Lend-Lease Act passed
	Fair Employment Practices Commission
	Atlantic Charter
	Japanese attack Pearl Harbor
1942	Allies suffer severe defeats in Europe and Asia
	Executive Order 9066 leads to Japanese internment camps
	Battles of Coral Sea and Midway halt Japanese advance
	Women recruited for war industries
1942–1945	Rationing
1943	Race riots in Detroit and Los Angeles
	Fascism falls in Italy
1944	D-Day
	GI Bill of Rights
1945	Yalta Conference
	Battles of Iwo Jima and Okinawa
	Germany surrenders
	Harry S Truman becomes president after Roosevelt's death
	United Nations convenes
	Atomic bombs dropped on Hiroshima and Nagasaki
	Japan surrenders

PART FIVE

Women, Gender, and the Welfare System

Would it surprise you to learn that as recently as twenty-five years ago the experiences of women were virtually absent from U.S. history books? Now, thanks in large part to the feminist movement that began in the 1960s, women's history is flourishing. Initially, the aim was simply to include women in the central narrative of the nation's history—to make them visible. This effort continues, but as scholars have discovered that women's experience often cannot be extricated from men's experience, they have increasingly made *gender*, encompassing both women's and men's roles, a preferred strategy of analysis. Gendered analysis has, in turn, proved to have life of its own, spilling from its original confines in women's history and illuminating subjects seemingly far removed from the intimate realm of sexual identity. The welfare system that originated in the New Deal era is a key case in point.

The cornerstone for welfare was the Social Security Act of 1935, which provided old-age pensions for most workers, a joint federal-state system of unemployment compensation, and direct federal assistance for the blind, deaf, and disabled and for single mothers with dependent children. The first generation of scholars after the New Deal, such as the eminent historian Arthur Schlesinger Jr., not surprisingly identified the Social Security Act with the progressive thrust of the federal government under Franklin D. Roosevelt. As witnesses to the Great Depression, these historians celebrated the Social Security Act for providing Americans with a much needed safety net.

Subsequent interpretation has been more critical, however. Some scholars have stressed how business interests managed to reshape the proposed legislation so that its pension and unemployment provisions were much more limited than Social Security advocates had intended. Other scholars noted the denial of coverage to farm workers because of the power of the farm lobby, dominated by agribusiness leaders who wanted no federal interference with their control over the farm labor force. That decision, along with the exclusion of domestic household workers from coverage, meant that two-thirds of African American workers were left out of the Social Security system in 1935. A rich body of literature has emerged, contrasting the conservative tone of the Roosevelt administration's approach with the more generous and comprehensive systems of Western European

nations and stressing the powerful impact of American racial inequality in shaping social welfare legislation.

Now gendered analysis has come into play, focusing through works of such feminist scholars as Alice Kessler-Harris (*In Pursuit of Equity: Women, Men, and the Quest for Economic Citizenship in Twentieth-Century America*, 2001), Gwendolyn Mink (*The Wages of Motherhood: Inequality in the Welfare State, 1917–1942*, 1995), and Linda Gordon (*Pitied But Not Entitled: Single Mothers and the History of Welfare*, 1994) on the way policymakers' assumptions about men's and women's proper roles framed the initial Social Security legislation and its implementation. The starting point for this critique is the distinction embedded in the Social Security Act of 1935 between *social security*, which applies to old-age pensions, and *welfare*, which usually describes aid to families with dependent children. In *Pitied But Not Entitled*, Gordon traces welfare's beginnings to the white women's social reform network established in the late nineteenth and early twentieth centuries, which supported a wide range of government programs to assist the urban poor (see Chapter 20). Between 1910 and 1920, pressure from these reformers led most states to enact mothers' pension programs that provided cash subsidies to poor women and their children in the absence of a male breadwinner.

With the coming of the Great Depression, welfare issues, traditionally the sphere of women, moved to the center of public policy. Men dominated the planning of Social Security and relegated the women within the

Creating the Welfare System

When FDR signed the Social Security bill on August 14, 1935, he set in motion a system that shaped social benefits, including social security and welfare, for decades. Behind him is Frances Perkins, the first woman to hold a cabinet position. The Children's Bureau, so crucial to the framing of the provisions for Aid to Dependent Children, was housed in Perkins's Department of Labor. Associated Press.

Job Training for Welfare Recipients

One of the most widely touted aspects of President Clinton's 1996 Personal Responsibility and Work Opportunity Act was the requirement that welfare recipients find work within two years. This act gave states more discretion in running welfare programs, and many implemented job-training programs, such as this one in California. It is still too soon to evaluate the long-term impact of the welfare reforms put in place in the 1990s. Lava Jo Regan / Saba.

Children's Bureau—Grace Abbott, Katherine Lenroot, Martha Eliot, and others—to planning one small piece of the omnibus legislation, a federal program for dependent mothers and children.

Although the planning process suggests marginalization of the women's network and the poor mothers who were the objects of their concern, both male and female New Dealers believed in the concept of the "family wage"—in which the husband earned enough money to support his family, preventing the need for the wife to enter the work force. Concerned about the crippling impact of joblessness and aging on the masculine role of breadwinner, New Dealers hoped to ensure that men—and, through them, their families—could weather unemployment and have a cushion for old age. They created social insurance programs tied to a payroll tax system, still in use today, that enabled supporters to describe old-age pensions and unemployment compensation as "rights" based on payroll taxation and therefore "earned."

In contrast to these programs designed primarily for male breadwinners, Gordon argues that the system established for poor women and children was not portrayed as a "right" linked to participation in the workforce but rather as aid founded on "need." Drawing upon the family wage concept, which had also shaped the mothers' pension programs enacted earlier by states, women New Dealers designed the policy of Aid to Dependent Children (ADC, later called AFDC) to keep poor women out of the workforce and in the home with their children—a policy that ignored the growing numbers of working mothers and reinforced notions of women's dependence. Rather than develop a program that would make it feasible for single mothers to work to support their families (for example, through subsidies to supplement their low wages or child

care), New Dealers opted for one that would keep women in the home at a bare subsistence. It stigmatized these mothers as "needy" and failed to protect poor children.

Other factors contributed to the stigma attached to AFDC, Gordon points out. Initially, relatively few black women received welfare benefits, primarily because southern congressmen had balked at national welfare standards, insisting instead on local control of welfare payments. This demand led to a shared federal-state program that in the short term gave localities the power to refuse aid to poor black women, making them more easily exploitable as farm labor. By the 1960s, however, in part because of black migration to the cities of the north, African American women began to swell the ranks of welfare mothers. Never a majority, their numbers were nonetheless proportionately higher than other groups, and racist attitudes, intersecting with the association of black women with welfare, led to further stigmatization of AFDC.

By the 1980s welfare was widely condemned, both by feminist and welfare-rights activists for its failure to provide for the needs of the poor and by conservatives who criticized it for supporting "irresponsible" mothers at taxpayers' expense and undermining the work ethic. Bowing to demands for reform, in 1996 President Bill Clinton signed the Personal Responsibility and Work Opportunity Act, which he promised "would end welfare as we know it." The new program eliminated the federal guarantee of cash assistance to poor children by abolishing AFDC, required most adult recipients to find work within two years, set a five-year limit on payments to any one family, and gave states wide discretion in running their welfare programs.

Gordon wrote her book in 1994, when the older order was still in effect. What might she say today about gender and the reform of welfare? To some extent, the 1996 act continued to rely on traditional gender assumptions, especially in urging states to "encourage the formation and maintenance of two-parent families." However, in their emphasis on putting welfare mothers to work, contemporary policymakers have clearly broken with early reformers who idealized women in the home, supported by a family wage. Gordon would likely argue that the long-term success of welfare reform, measured not just in reducing the welfare rolls but in reducing poverty itself, will rest on its ability to address what the original Social Security Act of 1935, with its assumptions about men's and women's proper roles, neglected: the problem of providing poor working mothers access to jobs that offer adequate wages and benefits as well as to affordable child and medical care, a proposal that for many Americans would seem almost as contentious as welfare itself. Feminist scholars like Gordon may have limited success in influencing contemporary public policy, but they have made important contributions to the history of the American welfare state. Introducing gender into our analysis of Social Security legislation is, moreover, just one example of how women's history has broadened our understanding of the factors shaping politics and policy.

CHAPTER 27

Cold War America

1945–1960

WHEN HARRY TRUMAN ARRIVED at the White House on April 12, 1945, after Franklin Roosevelt died, he asked the president's widow, "Is there anything I can do for you?" Eleanor Roosevelt responded, "Is there anything we can do for you? For you are the one in trouble now." Truman inherited the presidency at one of the most perilous times in modern history. Unscathed by bombs and battles on the home front, U.S. industry and agriculture had grown rapidly during World War II. The nation wielded enormous military power as the sole possessor of the atomic bomb. The most powerful country in the world, the United States had become a preeminent force in the international arena. Only the Soviet Union represented an obstacle to American **hegemony**, or dominance, in global affairs. Soon the two superpowers were locked in a cold war of economic, political, and military rivalry but no direct engagement on the battlefield.

Soviet-American confrontations during the postwar years had important domestic repercussions. The cold war boosted military expenditures, fueling a growing arms race. It fostered a climate of fear and suspicion of "subversives" in government, education, and the media who might undermine American

◀ **Protect Them**

*The cold war and nuclear arms race
pervaded American culture in the
post–World War II years. The government's
Civil Defense Agency, founded in 1950,
mounted an extensive campaign to alert
the nation to the need for civil defense
plans, including the construction of public
shelters and the development of emergency
evacuation strategies. This Teaneck, New
Jersey, poster not only reminded Americans
of the potential for attack, but also, by
picturing a mother and child in need of
protection, reinforced the era's emphasis on
family and traditional gender roles.*
Collection of Janice L. and David J. Frent.

democratic institutions. It both constrained and assisted the emerging civil rights movement. The economic benefits of internationalism also gave rise to a period of unprecedented affluence and prosperity during which the United States enjoyed the highest standard of living in the world (see Chapter 28). That prosperity helped to continue and in some cases to expand federal power, perpetuating the New Deal state in the postwar era.

The Cold War Abroad

The defeat of Germany and Japan did not bring stability to the world. Six years of devastating warfare had destroyed prewar governments and geographical boundaries, creating new power relationships that helped to dissolve colonial empires. Even before the war ended, the United States and the Soviet Union were struggling for advantage in those unstable areas; after the war they engaged in a protracted global conflict. Hailed as a battle between communism and capitalism, the cold war was in reality a more complex power struggle covering a range of economic, strategic, and ideological issues. As each side tried to protect its own national security and way of life, its actions aroused fear in the other, contributing to a cycle of distrust and animosity that would shape U.S.-Soviet relations for decades to come.

Descent into Cold War, 1945–1946

During the war Franklin Roosevelt worked effectively with Soviet leader Joseph Stalin and determined to continue

Postwar Devastation

Berlin, Germany, was one of many European cities reduced to rubble during World War II. Both Allied bombing and brutal fighting in April 1945, when Soviet troops entered Berlin, devastated the once impressive capital city. Here, in a telling statement about the collapse of Hitler's Third Reich, German refugees walk in front of what was once Goebbels's Propaganda Ministry. U.S. policymakers feared that this type of destruction and the economic disorder that accompanied it would make many areas of postwar Europe vulnerable to Communist influence. National Archives.

For more help analyzing this image, see the ONLINE STUDY GUIDE at **bedfordstmartins.com/henretta.**

good relations with the Soviet Union in peacetime. In particular he hoped that the United Nations would provide a forum for resolving postwar conflicts. Avoiding the disagreements that had doomed American membership in the League of Nations after World War I, the Senate approved America's participation in the United Nations in December 1945. Coming eight months after Roosevelt's death, the vote was in part a memorial to the late president's hopes for peace.

Shortly before his death, however, Roosevelt had been disturbed by Soviet actions in Eastern Europe. As the Soviet army drove the Germans out of Russia and back through Eastern Europe, the Soviet Union sponsored provisional governments in the occupied countries. Since the Soviet Union had been a victim of German aggression in both world wars, Stalin was determined to prevent the rebuilding and rearming of its traditional foe, and he insisted on a security zone of friendly governments in Eastern Europe for further protection. At the Yalta Conference in February, both America and Britain had agreed to recognize this Soviet **"sphere of influence,"** with the proviso that "free and unfettered elections" would be held as soon as possible. But in succeeding months the Soviets made no move to hold elections and rebuffed Western attempts to reorganize the Soviet-installed governments.

When Truman assumed the presidency after Roosevelt's death, he took a belligerent stance toward the Soviet Union. Recalling Britain's disastrous appeasement of Hitler in 1938, he had decided that the United States had to take a hard line against Soviet expansion. "There isn't any difference in totalitarian states," he said, "Nazi, Communist, or Fascist." At a meeting held shortly after he took office, the new president berated the Soviet foreign minister, V. M. Molotov, over the Soviets' failure to honor their Yalta agreement to support free elections in Poland. Truman used what he called "tough methods" that July at the Potsdam Conference, which brought together the United States, Britain, and the Soviet Union. After learning of the successful test of America's atomic bomb, Truman "told the Russians just where they got off and generally bossed the whole meeting," recalled British prime minister Winston Churchill. Negotiations on critical postwar issues deadlocked, revealing serious cracks in the Grand Alliance.

One issue tentatively resolved at Potsdam was the fate of occupied Germany. At Yalta the defeated German state had been divided into four zones of occupation, controlled by the United States, France, Britain, and the Soviet Union. At Potsdam the Allies agreed to disarm the country, dismantle its military production facilities, and permit the occupying powers to extract reparations from the zones they controlled. Plans for future reunification stalled, however, as the United States and the Soviet Union each worried that a united Germany would fall into the other's sphere. The foundation was thus laid for what would become the political division into East and West Germany four years later (Map 27.1).

As tensions over Europe divided the former Allies, hopes of international cooperation in the control of atomic weapons faded as well. In the Baruch Plan, submitted to the United Nations in 1946, the United States proposed a system of international control that relied on mandatory inspection and supervision but preserved American nuclear monopoly. The Soviets, profoundly uneasy about this monopoly, rejected the plan and worked assiduously to complete their own bomb. Meanwhile, the Truman administration pursued plans to develop nuclear energy and weapons further. Thus the failure of the Baruch Plan signaled the hardening of tensions and the beginning of a frenzied nuclear arms race between the two superpowers.

The Truman Doctrine and Containment

As tensions mounted between the superpowers, the United States increasingly perceived Soviet expansionism as a threat to its own interests, and a new American policy, **containment**, began to take shape. The most influential expression of the policy came in February 1946 from George F. Kennan in an 8,000-word cable, dubbed the "Long Telegram," from his post at the U.S. embassy in Moscow to his superiors in Washington. Kennan, who was identified only as "X," warned that the Soviet Union was moving "inexorably along the prescribed path, like a persistent toy automobile wound up and headed in a given direction, stopping only when it meets unanswerable force" (see American Lives, "George F. Kennan: Architect of Containment," p. 786). To stop Soviet expansionism, Kennan argued, the United States should pursue a policy of "firm containment . . . at every point where [the Russians] show signs of encroaching upon the interests of a peaceful and stable world."

The Truman Doctrine and the National Security Act. The emerging policy of containment crystallized in 1947 over a crisis in Greece. In the spring of 1946, several thousand local Communist guerrillas, whom American advisors mistakenly believed were taking orders from Moscow, launched a full-scale civil war against the government and the British occupation authorities. In February 1947 the British informed Truman that they could no longer afford to assist anti-Communists in Greece. American policymakers worried that Soviet influence in Greece threatened American and European interests in the eastern Mediterranean and the Middle East, especially in strategically located Turkey and the oil-rich state of Iran.

In response the president announced what would be known as the Truman Doctrine. In a speech to the Republican-controlled Congress on March 12, he

George F. Kennan: Architect of Containment

On February 22, 1946, a diplomatic advisor named George Kennan dictated an 8,000-word telegram from the U.S. embassy in Moscow. Responding to a Department of State request for an assessment of Soviet foreign policy, Kennan described the Soviet Union as an insecure state intent on expansion, subversion, and the export of Communist revolution. It was, he argued, "a political force committed fanatically to the belief that with the U.S. there can be no permanent modus vivendi." A preliminary blueprint of the containment theory, this "Long Telegram" was a confidential communiqué to President Harry Truman and Secretary of State James Byrnes. Within weeks, however, it became required reading for hundreds of U.S. military and diplomatic personnel around the world.

Kennan's Long Telegram found an enthusiastic audience among Washington policymakers who were eager to redefine U.S.-Soviet relations in the early postwar period. Its alarmist language helped convince the Truman administration to take a harder line against the Soviet Union and provided the ideological foundations for the emerging cold war. Summoned back to Washington a few months later, Kennan became one of the most influential advisors in the Truman administration. Writing and lecturing continuously for the next forty years, he would also become one of the foremost foreign policy theorists of the twentieth century.

Kennan's containment theory was shaped by his many years of experience in the diplomatic corps. Born in Milwaukee in 1904, Kennan graduated from Princeton University in 1925 and entered the foreign service the following year. After holding minor positions in Switzerland and Germany, he was offered training as a Soviet specialist in 1929. Under the tutelage of anti-Communist Russian émigrés in Berlin, Kennan studied Russian history, language, and literature and later served as a Soviet expert at the U.S. embassy in Latvia. In 1933, when Franklin Roosevelt initiated diplomatic relations with the Soviet Union, Kennan helped open the new U.S. embassy in Moscow and joined the embassy staff. During his four years in the Soviet Union, he witnessed the horrors of the Stalinist purges, an experience that fueled his animosity toward the Russian leader Joseph Stalin and

the Soviet Communist regime. Between 1937 and 1944 Kennan occupied a variety of diplomatic posts in the United States and Europe, none of which truly satisfied him. When the new ambassador to the Soviet Union, Averell Harriman, requested him as an advisor in 1944, he jumped at the opportunity to return to Moscow.

Still deeply antagonistic toward the Soviet Union, Kennan disagreed with Roosevelt's wartime alliance with Stalin and issued a steady stream of anti-Soviet memoranda. During the war most of these pronouncements fell on deaf ears. With the end of the war and the rise of Soviet-American conflict over Poland, however, Harriman and other members of the Truman administration became more receptive to Kennan's views. Widespread praise for his Long Telegram won Kennan an offer to lecture at the National War College in Washington in April 1946. A year later, Secretary of State George Marshall appointed him director of the department's new Policy Planning Staff (PPS), which helped devise the Marshall Plan and other long-range foreign-policy initiatives.

While serving as PPS director from 1947 to 1950, Kennan refined his ideas about containment. His best-known articulation of the theory appeared in a July 1947 article in *Foreign Affairs*, which he wrote anonymously as "Mr. X." Kennan's identity, however, was soon revealed, and his views of an antagonistic and deceitful Soviet state won wide currency. Conceding Soviet influence in Eastern Europe, he urged the United States and its Allies to contain the Soviet threat through "the adroit and vigilant application of counter-force at a series of constantly shifting geographical and political points." By pursuing such a policy, Kennan speculated, Soviet power could be diminished since it "bears within it the seeds of its own decay."

As Kennan himself would later admit, his formulation of containment was ambiguous and imprecise. His use of the term *force* was vague; he failed to specify whether the United States should use political, economic, or military force to contain the Soviets. And he placed no geographical limits on American intervention. Although Kennan later claimed that containment was primarily a political/economic strategy intended to protect the world's key industrial areas, the ambiguity of the 1947 article invited American policymakers to interpret containment in the broadest possible fashion.

By 1950 Truman's increasingly hard-line approach toward the Soviet Union had alienated Kennan. He criticized the open-ended commitment of the Truman Doctrine, the militarization of containment under NSC-68, and the division of Europe under the NATO treaty. Increasingly marginalized by the new secretary of state, Dean Acheson, Kennan took a leave of absence to attend the Institute for Advanced Study at Princeton University.

George F. Kennan

As a diplomat, foreign policy theorist, and historian, George F. Kennan has enjoyed a long and distinguished career spanning more than seventy years. This portrait by Guy Rowe dates from 1955.

National Portrait Gallery, Smithsonian Institution / Art Resource, NY.

In 1952 he returned to the administration to serve as ambassador to the Soviet Union; within months, however, he was forced to resign after making disparaging remarks comparing Stalin's regime to Nazism.

With the election of Republican Dwight D. Eisenhower in 1952, Kennan's influence in Washington was further diminished. Eisenhower's secretary of state, the staunchly conservative John Foster Dulles, condemned containment as immoral and denounced Kennan for his "appeasement" of the Soviets in Eastern Europe. Kennan briefly returned to the diplomatic corps in 1961 as ambassador to Yugoslavia under President John F. Kennedy. Two years later, however, Congress revoked that country's most-favored-nation trading status, undermining Kennan's work and prompting his permanent retirement from government service.

As Kennan's diplomatic career waned, he became a renowned historian and theorist of American foreign relations. Working from his office at the Institute for Advanced Studies, he produced dozens of books and articles, including two Pulitzer Prize–winning works, *Russia Leaves the War* (1950) and his often-quoted *Memoirs* (1967). His popular historical text *American Diplomacy, 1900–1950* (1951) introduced millions of Americans to the "realist" critique of foreign policy—an approach that stresses national interests and power politics over the idealistic motives of both conservatives and liberals.

On numerous occasions Kennan aired his realist views of controversial cold war developments. During the 1950s he condemned McCarthyism and advocated Soviet and U.S. disengagement from Europe. Later he became an outspoken opponent of the Vietnam War, testifying before the Senate Foreign Relations Committee in 1966 that the containment doctrine was poorly suited to Indochina. Opposing moralistic foreign policy, he criticized Jimmy Carter's preoccupation with human rights in the 1970s and Ronald Reagan's dramatic arms buildup and anti-Soviet pronouncements in the 1980s. As an outspoken critic of the nuclear arms race, he called for "no first use" of nuclear weapons in 1984 and pressed for comprehensive arms control agreements.

The demise of the Soviet Union in 1991 seemed to fulfill Kennan's prophecy in the 1947 article and brought him renewed public attention. But historians continue to debate the usefulness of containment in ending the cold war. During his long career, Kennan served as both chief architect and key critic of containment. His evolving views highlight the complexities and perils of cold war policymaking in the late twentieth century.

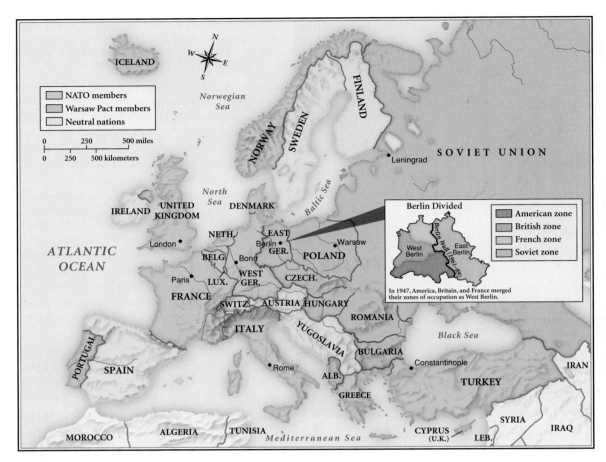

MAP 27.1 Cold War in Europe, 1955

In 1949 the United States sponsored the creation of the North Atlantic Treaty Organization (NATO)—an alliance of ten European nations, the United States, and Canada. West Germany was formally admitted to NATO in May 1955. A few days later the Soviet Union and seven other Communist nations established a rival alliance, the Warsaw Pact. The divided city of Berlin, with West Berlin located deep in Communist East Germany, was a major flash point in cold war controversies.

requested large-scale military and economic assistance for Greece and Turkey. If Greece fell to communism, Truman warned, the effects would be serious not only for Turkey but for the entire Middle East. This notion of an escalating Communist contagion was an early version of what Dwight Eisenhower would later call the "domino theory." Not just Greece but freedom itself was at issue, Truman declared: "If we falter in our leadership, we may endanger the peace of the world," and "we shall surely endanger the welfare of our own nation." Despite the open-endedness of this military commitment, Congress quickly approved Truman's request for $300 million in aid to Greece and $100 million for Turkey. The appropriation reversed the postwar trend toward sharp cuts in foreign spending and marked a new level of commitment to the emerging cold war.

The Marshall Plan. During this period Secretary of State George Marshall proposed a plan to provide

economic as well as military aid to Europe. In June 1947 Marshall urged the nations of Europe to construct a comprehensive recovery program and then ask the United States for aid. By bolstering European economies devastated by war, Marshall and Truman believed, the United States could forestall severe economic dislocation, which might give rise to communism. American economic self-interest was also a contributing factor; the legislation required that foreign-aid dollars be spent on U.S. goods and services. A revitalized Europe centered on a strong West German economy would provide a better market for U.S. goods.

Truman's pledge of economic aid to European economies, however, met with significant opposition in Congress. Republicans castigated the Marshall Plan as a huge "international W.P.A." But in the midst of the congressional stalemate, on February 25, 1948, came a Communist coup in Czechoslovakia. A stark reminder of the menace of Soviet expansion in Europe, the coup

Charting a New Course for Europe with the Marshall Plan

Between 1948 and 1951 the European Recovery Program—popularly known as the Marshall Plan, after Secretary of State George C. Marshall—contributed over $12 billion toward its objective of "restoring the confidence of the European people in the economic future of their own countries and of Europe as a whole." This poster, targeted at Great Britain, stresses European cooperation in the rebuilding effort. Courtesy, Marshall Foundation.

rallied congressional support for the Marshall Plan. In March 1948 Congress voted overwhelmingly to approve funds for the program. Like most other foreign-policy initiatives of the 1940s and 1950s, the Marshall Plan won bipartisan support despite the opposition of an isolationist wing of the Republican Party.

Over the next four years, the United States contributed nearly $13 billion to a highly successful recovery effort. Western European economies revived, and industrial production increased 64 percent, opening new opportunities for international trade (see Voices from Abroad, "Jean Monnet: Truman's Generous Proposal," p. 790). The Marshall Plan did not specifically exclude Eastern Europe or the Soviet Union, but it required that all participating nations exchange economic information and work toward the elimination of tariffs and other trade barriers. Denouncing those conditions as attempts to draw Eastern Europe into the American orbit, Soviet leaders forbade the satellite states of Czechoslovakia, Poland, and Hungary to participate.

The Berlin Airlift and the Creation of NATO. The Marshall Plan accelerated American and European efforts to rebuild and unify the West German economy. In June 1948, after agreeing to fuse their zones of occupation, the United States, France, and Britain initiated a program of currency reform in West Berlin. The economic revitalization of Berlin, located deep within the Soviet zone of occupation, alarmed the Soviets, who feared a resurgent Germany aligned with the West. As a response, they imposed a blockade on all highway, rail, and river traffic to West Berlin. Truman countered with an airlift: for nearly a year American and British pilots, who had been dropping bombs on Berlin only four years earlier, flew in 2.5 million tons of food and fuel—nearly a ton

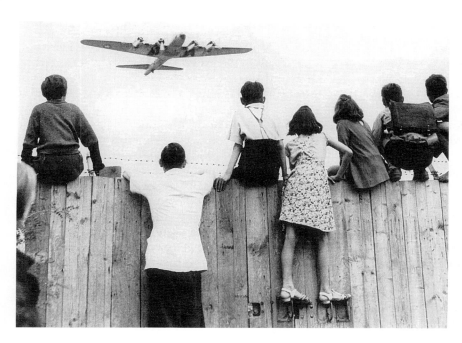

The Berlin Airlift

For 321 days American planes like this one flew 272,000 missions to bring food and other supplies to Berlin after the Soviet Union had blocked all surface routes into the former German capital. The blockade was finally lifted on May 12, 1949, after the Soviets conceded that it had been a failure. Wide World Photos, Inc.

Jean Monnet

Truman's Generous Proposal

Jean Monnet was an eminent French statesman and a tireless promoter of postwar European union. As head of a French postwar planning commission, he helped oversee the dispersal of Marshall Plan funds, the importance of which he described in his memoirs.

So we had at last concerted our efforts to halt France's economic decline; but now, once more, everything seemed to be at risk. Two years earlier [1947], we thought that we had plumbed the depths of material poverty. Now we were threatened with the loss of even basic essentials. . . . Our dollar resources were melting away at an alarming rate, because we were having to buy American wheat to replace the crops we had lost during the winter. This alone cost us $200m. instead of the $30m. we had expected to pay. In addition, we had to increase our coal imports at a time when prices had risen in the United States. In June, we met the cost with gold bullion from the Bank of France; in August, we cut off inessential imports. A further American loan was soon exhausted.

Nor was this grim situation confined to France. Britain too had come to the end of her resources. In February 1947 she had abruptly cancelled her aid to Greece and Turkey, whose burdens she had seemed able to assume in 1945. Overnight, this abrupt abdication gave the United States direct responsibility for part of Europe. Truman did not hesitate for a moment: with the decisiveness that was to mark his actions as President, he at once asked for credits and arms for both Turkey and Greece. . . . [Soon after], he announced the Truman Doctrine of March 12, 1947. Its significance was general: it meant that the United States would prevent Europe from becoming a depressed area at the mercy of Communist advance. On the very same day, the Four-Power Conference began in Moscow. There, for a whole month, George Marshall, Ernest Bevin, and Georges Bidault argued with Vyacheslav Molotov about all the problems of the peace, and above all about Germany.

When Marshall returned to Washington, he knew that for a long time there would be no further genuine dialogue with Stalin's Russia. The "cold war," as it was soon to be known, had begun. . . . Information from a number of sources convinced Marshall and his Under-Secretary Dean Acheson that once again, as in 1941, the United States had a great historic duty. And once again there took place what I had witnessed in Washington a few years earlier: a small group of men brought to rapid maturity an idea which, when the Executive gave the word, turned into vigorous action. This time, it was done by five or six people, in total secrecy and at lightning speed. Marshall, Acheson, Clayton, Averell Harriman, and George Kennan worked out a proposal of unprecedented scope and generosity. It took us all by surprise when we read the speech that George Marshall made at Harvard on June 5, 1947. Chance had led him to choose the University's Commencement Day to launch something new in international relations: helping others to help themselves.

Source: Jean Monnet, *Memoirs*, trans. Richard Mayne (New York: Doubleday, 1978), 264–66.

for each resident. On May 12, 1949, Stalin lifted the blockade, which had made West Berlin a symbol of resistance to communism.

The coup in Czechoslovakia and the crisis in Berlin convinced U.S. policymakers of the need for a collective security pact. In April 1949, for the first time since the end of the American Revolution, the United States entered into a peacetime military alliance, the North Atlantic Treaty Organization (NATO). Truman asked Congress for $1.3 billion in military assistance to NATO and authorized the basing of four U.S. Army divisions in Western Europe. Under the NATO pact, twelve nations—the United States, Canada, Britain, France, Italy, Belgium, the Netherlands, Luxembourg, Denmark, Norway, Portugal, and Iceland—agreed that "an armed attack against one or more of them in Europe or North America shall be considered an attack against them all." In May 1949 those nations also agreed to the creation of the Federal Republic of Germany (West Germany), which joined NATO in 1955.

In October 1949, in response to the creation of NATO, the Soviet Union tightened its grip on Eastern Europe by creating a separate government for East Germany, which became the German Democratic

Republic. The Soviets also organized an economic association, the Council for Mutual Economic Assistance (COMECON) in 1949, and a military alliance for Eastern Europe, the Warsaw Pact, in 1955. The postwar division of Europe was nearly complete.

Containment Militarized: NSC-68. New impetus for the policy of containment came in September 1949, when American military intelligence detected a rise in radioactivity in the atmosphere—proof that the Soviet Union had detonated an atomic bomb. The American atomic monopoly, which some military and political advisors had argued would last for decades, had ended in just four years, forcing a major reassessment of the nation's foreign policy.

To devise a new diplomatic and military blueprint, Truman turned to the National Security Council (NSC), an advisory body established in 1947 to set defense and military priorities. In April 1950 the NSC delivered its report, known as "NSC-68," to the president. Filled with alarmist rhetoric and exaggerated assessments of Soviet capabilities, the document made several specific recommendations, including the development of a hydrogen bomb, an advanced weapon a thousand times more destructive than the atomic bombs that had destroyed Hiroshima and Nagasaki. (The United States would explode its first hydrogen bomb in November 1952 and the Soviet Union its first in 1953.) NSC-68 also supported increases in U.S. conventional forces and the establishment of a strong system of alliances. Most important, it called for increased taxes to finance "a bold and massive program of rebuilding the West's defensive potential to surpass that of the Soviet world."

Though Truman was an aggressive anti-Communist, he was reluctant to commit to a major defense buildup, fearing that it would overburden the budget. But the Korean War, which began just two months after NSC-68 was completed, helped to transform the report's recommendations into reality, as the cold war spawned a hot war.

Containment in Asia and the Korean War

As mutual suspicion deepened between the United States and the Soviet Union, cold war doctrines began to influence the American position in Asia as well. American policy there was based on Asia's importance to the world economy as much as on the desire to contain communism. At first American plans for the region centered on a revitalized China, but political instability there prompted the Truman administration to focus on developing the Japanese economy instead. After dismantling Japan's military forces and weaponry, American occupation forces under General Douglas MacArthur began the job of transforming the country into a bulwark of Asian capitalism. MacArthur drafted a democratic constitution and oversaw the rebuilding of the economy, paving the way for the restoration of Japanese sovereignty in 1951.

The "Fall" of China. In China the situation was more precarious. Since the 1930s a civil war had been raging, as Communist forces led by Mao Zedong (Mao Tsetung) and Zhou Enlai (Chou En-lai) contended for power with conservative Nationalist forces under Jiang Jieshi (Chiang Kai-shek). Although dissatisfied with the corrupt and inefficient Jiang regime, officials for the Truman administration did not see Mao as a good alternative, and they resigned themselves to working with the Nationalists. Between 1945 and 1949 the United States provided more than $2 billion to Jiang's forces but to no avail. In 1947 General Albert Wedemeyer, who had tried to work with Jiang, reported to President Truman that, until the "corrupt, reactionary, and inefficient Chinese National government" undertook "drastic political and economic reforms," the United States could not accomplish its purpose. In August 1949, when those reforms did not occur, the Truman administration cut off aid to the Nationalists, sealing their fate. The People's Republic of China was formally established under Mao on October 1, 1949, and what was left of Jiang's government fled to Taiwan.

Although nothing less than a massive U.S. military commitment could have stopped the Chinese Communists, many Americans viewed Mao's success as a defeat for the United States. A pro-Nationalist "China lobby," supported by the powerful publisher Henry R. Luce and by Republican senators Karl Mundt of South Dakota and William S. Knowland of California, protested that under Truman's newly appointed secretary of state, Dean Acheson, the State Department was responsible for the "loss of China." The China lobby's influence led to the United States' refusal to recognize what it called "Red China"; instead, the nation recognized the exiled Nationalist government in Taiwan. The United States also used its influence to block China's admission to the United Nations. For almost twenty years U.S. administrations treated mainland China, the world's most populous country, as a diplomatic nonentity.

The Korean War Begins. In Korea as in China, cold-war confrontation grew out of World War II roots. Both the United States and the Soviet Union had troops in Korea at the end of the war and had agreed to occupy the nation jointly. They divided Korea into competing spheres of influence at the thirty-eighth parallel. The Soviets supported a Communist government, led by Kim Il Sung, in North Korea; the United States backed a long-time Korean nationalist, Syngman Rhee, in South Korea. Soon sporadic fighting broke out along the thirty-eighth parallel, and a civil war began.

The Korean War

These men of the Second Infantry Battalion, shown here in Korea in 1950, helped pave the way for the formal integration of all U.S. Army units by 1954. The Korean War marked the first time in the nation's history that all troops served in racially integrated combat units.
National Archives.

On June 25, 1950, the North Koreans launched a surprise attack across the thirty-eighth parallel (Map 27.2). The attack was part of an initiative for Korean reunification that came from Kim Il Sung, with Stalin's support (although the extent of Soviet involvement was unknown at the time). Soviet and North Korean leaders may have expected Truman to ignore this armed challenge, but the president felt that the United States must take a firm stance against the spread of communism. "There's no telling what they'll do if we don't put up a fight now," he said. Truman immediately asked the U.N. Security Council to authorize a "**police action**" against the invaders. Because the Soviet Union was temporarily boycotting the Security Council to protest the exclusion of the People's Republic of China from the United Nations, it could not veto Truman's request. Three days after the Security Council voted to send what was called a "peacekeeping force," Truman ordered U.S. troops to Korea.

Fighting the War. Though fourteen other non-Communist nations sent troops, the rapidly assembled United Nations army in Korea was overwhelmingly American. At the request of the Security Council, President Truman named General Douglas MacArthur to head the U.N. forces. At first the North Koreans held an overwhelming advantage, controlling practically the entire peninsula except for the area around Pusan. But on September 15, 1950, MacArthur launched a surprise amphibious attack at Inchon, far behind the North Korean front line, while U.N. forces staged a breakout from Pusan. Within two weeks the U.N. forces controlled Seoul, the South Korean capital, and almost all the territory up to the thirty-eighth parallel.

Encouraged by this success MacArthur sought the authority to lead his forces across the thirty-eighth parallel and into North Korea. Truman's initial plan had been to restore the 1945 border, but he managed to win U.N. support for the broader goal of creating "a unified, independent and democratic Korea." Though the Chinese government in Beijing warned repeatedly that such a move would provoke retaliation, American officials ignored the warnings. MacArthur's troops crossed the thirty-eighth parallel on October 9, reaching the Chinese border at the Yalu River by the end of the month. Just after Thanksgiving a massive Chinese counterattack of almost 300,000 troops forced MacArthur to retreat south of the thirty-eighth parallel. Then on January 4, 1951, Communist troops reoccupied Seoul.

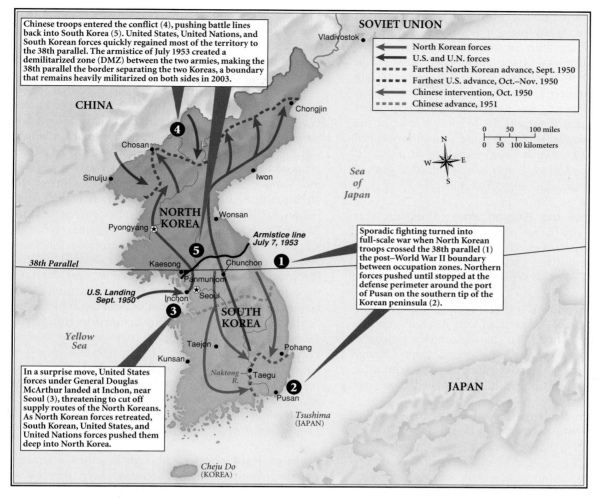

MAP 27.2 The Korean War, 1950–1953

The Korean War, which the United Nations officially deemed a "police action," lasted three years and cost the lives of over 36,000 U.S. troops. South and North Korean deaths were estimated at over 900,000. Although hostilities ceased in 1953, the U.S. military and the North Korean army faced each other across the Demilitarized Zone for the next fifty years.

Two months later American forces and their Allies counterattacked, regained Seoul, and pushed back to the thirty-eighth parallel. Then stalemate set in. Public support in the United States had dropped after Chinese intervention increased the likelihood of a long war. A poll revealed in early January 1951 that 66 percent of Americans thought the United States should withdraw; 49 percent felt intervening in the war had been a mistake. Given domestic opinions and the stalemate in Korea, Truman and his advisors decided to work for a negotiated peace. They did not want to tie down large numbers of U.S. troops in Asia, far from what were considered more strategically important trouble spots in Europe and the Middle East.

The Fate of Douglas MacArthur. MacArthur disagreed. Headstrong, arrogant, and brilliant, the general

fervently believed that the nation's future lay in Asia, not Europe. Disregarding Truman's instructions MacArthur traveled to Taiwan and urged the Nationalists to join in an attack on mainland China. He pleaded for permission to use the atomic bomb against China. In an inflammatory letter to the House minority leader, Republican Joseph J. Martin of Massachusetts, he denounced the Korean stalemate. "We must win," MacArthur declared. "There is no substitute for victory."

Martin released MacArthur's letter on April 6, 1951, as part of a concerted Republican campaign to challenge Truman's conduct of the war. The strategy backfired. On April 11 Truman relieved MacArthur of his command in Korea and Japan, accusing him of insubordination—a decision the Joint Chiefs of Staff supported. Truman's decision was nonetheless highly unpopular. But when the shouting subsided, Truman had the last word. After failing to win the Republican presidential nomination in 1952, MacArthur faded from public view.

The war dragged on for more than two years after MacArthur's dismissal. Truce talks began in Korea in July 1951, but a final armistice was not signed until July 1953. Approximately 45 percent of American casualties were sustained during this period. The final settlement left Korea divided very near the original border at the thirty-eighth parallel, with a demilitarized zone between the two countries. North Korea remained firmly allied with the Soviet Union; South Korea signed a mutual defense treaty with the United States in 1954.

The Impact of the Korean War.   The three-year conflict was costly for the United States: 36,516 American soldiers died, 103,000 were wounded, and military expenditures totaled $54 billion. Defense mobilization helped stimulate the American economy but did not foster the patriotic fervor that had characterized World War II. Struggling against heavy snow and subzero cold, American troops in Korea grew to hate the endless fighting that characterized the stalemate. "I'll fight for my country," a corporal from Chicago complained, "but I'm damned if I see why I'm fighting for this hell-hole." When the armistice was signed, there were few public celebrations.

The Korean War had a lasting impact on the conduct of American foreign policy. Truman's decision to commit troops to Korea without congressional approval set a precedent for future undeclared wars. The war also expanded American involvement in Asia, transforming containment into a truly global policy. During and after the war, the United States stationed large numbers of troops in South Korea and increased military aid to French forces fighting Communist insurgents in Indochina (see Chapter 29). Such commitments were costly. Overall defense expenditures grew from $13 billion in 1950, roughly one-third of the federal budget, to $50 billion in 1953, nearly two-thirds of the budget. Although military expenditures dropped briefly after the Korean War, defense spending remained at over $35 billion annually throughout the 1950s. American foreign policy had become more global, more militarized, and more expensive. Even in times of peace, the United States now functioned in a state of permanent mobilization.

Eisenhower and the "New Look" of Foreign Policy

The election of 1952 brought Republican Dwight D. Eisenhower to the White House. Despite his lack of political experience, Eisenhower's military reputation— he had been Supreme Commander of Allied forces in Europe—engendered confidence in his leadership. Although Eisenhower shared many of Truman's and the Democrats' assumptions about the cold war, his administration's policies were distinctive. Eisenhower's "New Look" in foreign policy continued the nation's commitment to containment but sought less expensive ways of implementing the nation's predominance in the cold war struggle against international communism.

One of Eisenhower's first acts as president was to use his negotiating skills to bring an end to the Korean War. As he had pledged in the campaign, Eisenhower visited Korea in December 1952. The final settlement was signed in July 1953, after the parties reached a compromise on the tricky issue of prisoner exchange. With the Korean War concluded, Eisenhower turned his attention to Europe and the Soviet Union. Stalin's death in March 1953 precipitated an intraparty struggle in the Soviet Union, which lasted until 1956, when Nikita S. Khrushchev emerged as Stalin's successor. Although Khrushchev surprised westerners by calling for **"peaceful coexistence"** between Communist and capitalist societies, he made certain that the Soviet Union's Eastern European satellites did not deviate too far from the Soviet path. When nationalists revolted in Hungary in 1956 and moved to take the country out of the Warsaw Pact, Soviet tanks moved rapidly into Budapest—an action the United States could condemn but could not realistically resist. Soviet repression of the Hungarian revolt showed that American policymakers had few, if any, options for rolling back Soviet power in Eastern Europe, short of going to war with the Soviet Union.

Massive Retaliation.   Although Eisenhower strongly opposed communism, he hoped to keep the cost of containment at a manageable level. Under his "New Look" defense policy, Eisenhower and Secretary of State John Foster Dulles decided to economize by developing a massive nuclear arsenal as an alternative to more expensive conventional forces. Nuclear weapons delivered "more bang for the buck," explained Defense Secretary Charles E. Wilson. To that end the Eisenhower administration expanded its commitment to the hydrogen bomb, approving extensive atmospheric testing in the South Pacific and in western states such as Nevada, Colorado, and Utah. To improve the nation's defenses against an air attack from the Soviet Union, the administration made a commitment to develop the long-range bombing capabilities of the Strategic Air Command and installed the Distant Early Warning line of radar stations in Alaska and Canada in 1958.

Those measures did little to improve the nation's security, however, as the Soviets matched the United States weapon for weapon in an escalating arms race. The Soviet Union carried out its own atmospheric tests of hydrogen bombs between 1953 and 1958 and developed a fleet of long-range bombers. By 1958 both nations had intercontinental ballistic missiles (ICBMs). When an American nuclear submarine launched an atomic-tipped Polaris missile in 1960, Soviet engineers raced to produce

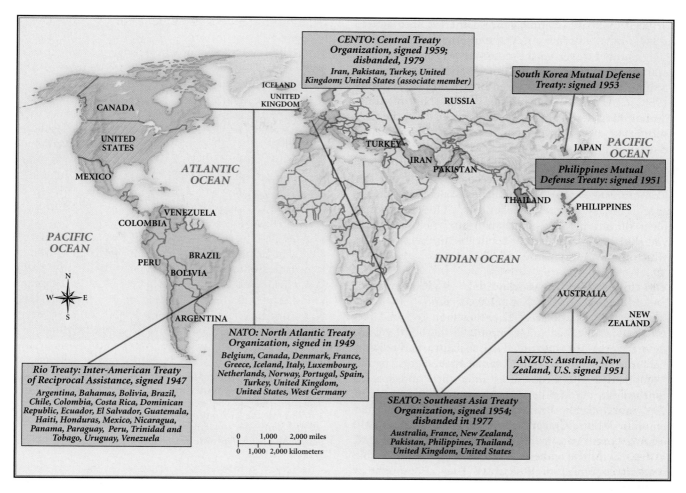

MAP 27.3 American Global Defense Treaties in the Cold War Era

The experience of World War II and the advent of the cold war led to a major shift in American foreign policy—the signing of mutual defense treaties. Dating back to George Washington's call "to steer clear of permanent alliances with any portion of the foreign world," the United States had remained officially neutral in conflicts between other nations. As late as 1919, the U.S. Senate had rejected the principle of "collective security," the centerpiece of the League of Nations established by the Treaty of Versailles that ended World War I. In response to fears of Soviet expansion globally, in the late 1940s and 1950s, the United States pledged to defend much of the non-Communist world. As illustrated by the map, major treaty organizations to which the United States belonged included NATO, SEATO, CENTO, ANZUS, and the Rio Treaty.

an equivalent weapon. While the arms race boosted the military-industrial sectors of both nations, it debilitated their social welfare programs by funneling immense resources into soon-to-be-obsolete weapons systems.

Collective Security. The New Look policy also extended collective security agreements between the United States and its Allies. To complement the NATO alliance in Europe, for example, Secretary of State Dulles orchestrated the creation of the Southeast Asia Treaty Organization (SEATO), which in 1954 linked America and its major European allies with Australia, Pakistan, Thailand, New Zealand, and the Philippines. This

extensive system of defense tied the United States to more than forty other countries (Map 27.3).

U.S. policymakers tended to support stable governments, no matter how repressive, as long as they were overtly anti-Communist. Some of America's staunchest Allies—the Philippines, Iran, Cuba, South Vietnam, and Nicaragua—were governed by dictatorships or repressive right-wing regimes that lacked broad-based popular support. In fact, Dulles often resorted to **covert interventions** against governments that were, in his opinion, too closely aligned with communism.

For such tasks he used the newly formed Central Intelligence Agency (CIA), which had moved beyond its original mandate of intelligence gathering into active, albeit covert, involvement in the internal affairs of foreign countries, even to the extent of overthrowing several governments. When Iran's nationalist premier, Muhammad Mossadegh, seized British oil properties in 1953, CIA agents helped the young shah of Iran, Muhammad Reza Pahlavi, depose him. In 1954 the CIA supported a coup in Guatemala against the popularly elected Jacobo Arbenz Guzman, who had expropriated 250,000 uncultivated acres held by the American-owned United Fruit Company and accepted arms from the Communist government of Czechoslovakia. Eisenhower specifically approved those efforts. "Our traditional ideas of international sportsmanship," he wrote privately in 1955, "are scarcely applicable in the morass in which the world now flounders."

The Cold War in the Middle East.

American leaders had devised the containment policy in response to Soviet expansion in Eastern Europe, but they soon extended it to the new nations that were emerging in the Third World. Before World War II, nationalism, socialism, and religion had inspired powerful anticolonial movements; in the 1940s and 1950s those forces intensified and spread, especially in the Middle East, Africa, and Asia. Between 1947 and 1962 the British, French, Dutch, and Belgian empires all but disintegrated. Seeking to draw the newly created countries into an American-led world system, U.S. policymakers encouraged the development of stable market economies in those areas. They also sought to further the ideal of national self-determination. But under the growing East-West tensions of the cold war, both the Truman and the Eisenhower administrations often failed to recognize that indigenous nationalist or socialist movements in emerging nations had their own goals and were not necessarily under the control of either local Communists or the Soviet Union.

The Middle East, an oil-rich area that was playing an increasingly central role in the strategic planning of the United States and the Soviet Union, presented one of the most complicated challenges. Zionism, the Jewish nationalist movement, had long encouraged Jews to return to their ancient homeland of Israel (Palestine). After World War II, many Jewish survivors of the Nazi extermination camps had resettled in Palestine, which was still controlled by Britain under a World War I mandate. On November 29, 1947, the U.N. General Assembly voted to partition Palestine into two states, Jewish and Arab—a decision that Egypt, Jordan, and other Arab League states resisted. On May 14, 1948, the British mandate ended, and Zionist leaders proclaimed the state of Israel. President Truman quickly recognized the new state, alienating the Arabs but winning crucial support from Jewish voters in the 1948 election.

Egypt was another site of conflict with the Arab nations, one that reflected the way in which Third World

Future Israelis

In 1945 these survivors of the Buchenwald concentration camp, like many other Jewish survivors of the Holocaust, resettled in Palestine. International outrage over Hitler's effort to exterminate the Jewish people was one of the factors that led the United Nations in 1947 to partition Palestine into two states, Jewish and Arab. The state of Israel was established in 1948.
National Archives.

countries became embroiled in the cold war. When Gamal Abdel Nasser came to power in Egypt in 1954, two years after independence from Britain, he pledged to lead not just his country but the entire Middle East out of its dependent, colonial relationship through a form of pan-Arab socialism. Nasser obtained arms and promises of economic assistance from the Soviet Union, including help in building the Aswan Dam on the Nile, a major water and energy development project. Secretary of State Dulles countered with an offer of American assistance, but Nasser refused to distance himself from the Soviets, declaring Egypt's neutrality in the cold war. Unwilling to accept this stance of nonalignment, Dulles abruptly withdrew his offer in July 1956.

A week later Nasser retaliated against the withdrawal of Western financial aid by seizing and nationalizing the Suez Canal, over which Britain had retained administrative authority and through which three-quarters of Western Europe's oil was transported. Nasser said he would use the tolls from the canal to build the dam himself. After several months of fruitless negotiation, Britain and France, in alliance with Israel, attacked Egypt and retook the canal. Their attack occurred at the same time as the Soviet repression of the Hungarian revolt, placing the United States in the potentially awkward position of denouncing Soviet aggression while tolerating a similar action by its own Allies. Eisenhower and the United Nations forced France and Britain to pull back. Egypt retook the Suez Canal and built the Aswan Dam with Soviet support. In the end the Suez crisis increased Soviet influence in the Third World, intensified anti-Western sentiment in Arab countries, and produced dissension among leading members of the NATO alliance.

The Eisenhower Doctrine. In early 1957, in the aftermath of the Suez crisis, the president persuaded Congress to approve the Eisenhower Doctrine. Addressing concerns over declining British influence in the Middle East, the policy stated that American forces would assist any nation in the region "requiring such aid, against overt armed aggression from any nation controlled by International Communism." Later that year Eisenhower invoked the doctrine when he sent the U.S. Sixth Fleet to the Mediterranean Sea to aid King Hussein of Jordan against a Nasser-backed revolt. A year later he landed 14,000 troops to back up a pro-U.S. government in Lebanon.

The attention that the Eisenhower administration paid to developments in the Middle East in the 1950s demonstrated how the desire for access to steady supplies of oil increasingly affected foreign policy. More broadly, attention to the Middle East confirmed the global scope of American interests. Just as the Korean War had stretched the application of containment from Europe to Asia, the Eisenhower Doctrine revealed U.S. intentions to influence events in the Middle East as well.

The Cold War at Home

As the cold war took shape, Americans had to grapple with a new and often alarming world order. Fears about the menace of Soviet communism pervaded the culture, as did anxieties about the destructive capabilities of nuclear weaponry. These factors would have a powerful impact on domestic politics, especially in the hunt for internal Communist subversives, but other issues, including the conversion to a peacetime economy, the call for black civil rights, and the legacy of the New Deal, also influenced politics on the "home front" of the cold war.

Postwar Domestic Challenges

The public's main fear in 1945—that the depression would return once war production had ended—proved unfounded. Despite a drop in government spending after the war, consumer spending increased; workers had amassed substantial wartime savings and were eager to spend them. The Servicemen's Readjustment Act of 1944, popularly known as the GI Bill, also put money into the economy by providing educational and economic assistance to returning veterans. Despite some temporary dislocations as war production shifted back to civilian production and veterans entered the workforce, unemployment did not soar.

Economic Policy. But the transition was hardly trouble free. The main domestic problem was inflation. Consumers wanted to end wartime restrictions and price rationing, but Truman feared economic chaos if he lifted all controls immediately. In the summer of 1945, he eased industrial controls but retained the wartime Office of Price Administration (OPA). When he disbanded the OPA and lifted almost all the remaining controls in the following year, prices soared, producing an annual inflation rate of 18.2 percent. Rising prices and persistent shortages of food and household goods irritated consumers.

With the Employment Act of 1946, the federal government began developing mechanisms to pursue a more coherent economic policy. The legislation introduced federal fiscal planning on a permanent basis—not just in times of economic crisis—to achieve full employment. Besides supporting the Keynesian notion of government spending to spur economic growth, the act promoted the use of tax policy as a tool for managing the economy, using tax cuts to spur economic growth and tax increases to slow inflation. Yet the legislation was weak. It merely advocated rather than mandated such planning measures and gave the new three-member Council of Economic Advisors only an advisory role. It also failed to establish clear economic priorities, such as the proper relationship between the commitment to full employment and the need for a balanced budget. Nevertheless, the Employment Act of 1946 was an important milestone in establishing federal responsibility for the performance of the economy.

Postwar Strikes. The rapidly rising cost of living prompted workers' demands for higher wages. Under government-sanctioned agreements the labor movement held the line on salary increases during the war. But after the war ended, union leaders expressed frustration. Corporate profits had doubled while real wages had declined as a result of inflation and the loss of overtime pay. Determined to make up for their war-induced sacrifices, workers mounted crippling strikes in the automobile, steel, and coal industries. General strikes effectively closed down business in more than a half dozen cities in 1946. By the end of that year, 5 million workers had idled factories and mines for a total of 107,476,000 workdays.

Truman responded dramatically. In the face of a devastating railway strike, he used his executive authority to place the nation's railroad system under federal control and asked Congress for the power to draft striking workers into the army—a move that infuriated labor leaders but pressured strikers to go back to work. Three days later he seized control of the nation's coal mines to end a strike by the United Mine Workers. Such actions won Truman support from many Americans but outraged organized labor, an important partner in the Democratic coalition.

The Taft-Hartley Act. These domestic upheavals did not bode well for the Democrats at the polls. In 1946 the Republicans gained control of both houses of Congress and set about undoing New Deal social welfare measures, especially targeting labor legislation. In 1947 Congress passed the Taft-Hartley Act, a rollback of several provisions of the 1935 National Labor Relations Act. Unions especially disliked Section 14b of Taft-Hartley, which outlawed the closed shop and allowed states to pass "right-to-work" laws that further limited unions' operations. The act also restricted unions' political power by prohibiting use of their dues for political activity and allowed the president to declare an eighty-day cooling-off period in strikes that had a national impact. Truman issued a ringing veto of the Taft-Hartley bill in June 1947, calling it "bad for labor, bad for management, and bad for the country." Congress easily overrode the veto, but Truman's actions countered some of workers' hostility to his earlier antistrike activity and kept labor in the Democratic fold.

The 1948 Election. Most observers believed that Truman faced an impossible task in the presidential campaign of 1948. The Republicans were united, and with Thomas E. Dewey, the politically moderate governor of New York, as their candidate once again, they had a good chance of attracting traditional Democratic voters. To increase their appeal in the West, the Republicans nominated Earl Warren, governor of California, for vice president. In their platform they promised to continue most New Deal reforms and to support a bipartisan foreign policy.

Truman, in contrast, led a party in disarray. Both the left and the right wings of the Democratic Party split off and nominated their own candidates. Henry A. Wallace, a former New Deal liberal whom Truman had fired as secretary of commerce in 1946 because he was perceived as too "soft" on communism, ran as the candidate of the new Progressive Party. Wallace advocated increased government intervention in the economy, more power for labor unions, and cooperation with the Soviet Union. The right-wing challenge came from the South. At the Democratic national convention, northern liberals such as Mayor Hubert H. Humphrey of Minneapolis had pushed through a platform calling for the repeal of the Taft-Hartley Act and increased federal commitment to civil rights. Southern Democrats, unwilling to tolerate federal interference in race

relations, bolted the convention and created the States' Rights Party, popularly known as the "Dixiecrats." They nominated Governor J. Strom Thurmond of South Carolina for president.

Truman responded to these challenges with one of the most effective presidential campaigns ever waged. He launched a strenuous cross-country speaking tour in which he hammered away at the Republicans' support for the antilabor Taft-Hartley Act. He also criticized Republicans for opposing legislation for housing, medical insurance, and civil rights. By combining these issues with attacks on the Soviet menace abroad, Truman began to salvage his troubled campaign. At his rallies enthusiastic listeners shouted, "Give 'em hell, Harry!"

Truman won a remarkable victory, receiving 49.6 percent of the vote to Dewey's 45.1 percent (Map 27.4). The Democrats also regained control of both houses of Congress. Strom Thurmond carried only four southern states, and Henry Wallace failed to win any electoral votes. Truman retained the support of organized labor. Jewish and Catholic voters in the big cities and black voters in the North offset his losses to the Dixiecrats. Most importantly, Truman appealed effectively to people like himself from the farms, towns, and small cities in the nation's heartland.

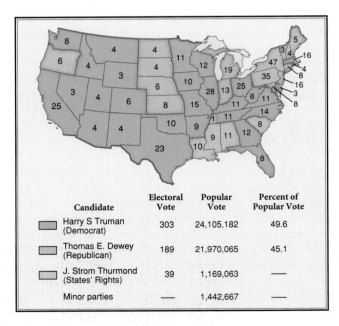

Candidate	Electoral Vote	Popular Vote	Percent of Popular Vote
Harry S Truman (Democrat)	303	24,105,182	49.6
Thomas E. Dewey (Republican)	189	21,970,065	45.1
J. Strom Thurmond (States' Rights)	39	1,169,063	—
Minor parties	—	1,442,667	—

MAP 27.4 Presidential Election of 1948

Political advisor Clark Clifford planned Truman's electoral strategy in 1948, arguing that the president should concentrate his campaign in urban areas where the Democrats had their greatest strength. In an election with a low turnout, Truman held onto enough support from the Roosevelt coalition of blacks, union members, and farmers to defeat Dewey by more than 2 million votes. In December 2002, Mississippi senator Trent Lott's comments suggesting approval of Strom Thurmond's support for segregation sparked a political uproar and cost Lott the position of majority leader in the 108th Congress.

Fair Deal Liberalism

Shortly after becoming president Truman proposed to Congress a twenty-one-point plan for expanded federal programs based on individual "rights," including the right to a "useful and remunerative" job, controls over monopolies, good housing, "adequate medical care," "protection from the economic fears of old age," and a "good education." Later Truman added support for civil rights and in his 1949 State of the Union address christened his program the Fair Deal. Although to some extent the Fair Deal represented an extension of the New Deal's liberalism—with faith in the positive influence of government and the use of federal power to ensure public welfare—it also took some new directions. Its attention to civil rights reflected the growing importance of African Americans to the Democratic Party's coalition of urban voters. And the desire to extend a high standard of living and other benefits of capitalism to an ever-greater number of citizens reflected a new liberal vision of the role of the state. Economically, the liberals of Truman's era were more moderate than the Progressive Era and New Deal reformers who had proposed extensive federal regulation of corporations and intrusive planning of the economy. They believed that the essential role of the federal government was to manage the economy indirectly through fiscal policy. Drawing on the Keynesian notion of using government spending to spur economic growth, they expected that welfare programs not only would provide a safety net for disadvantaged citizens but also would maintain consumer purchasing power, keeping the economy healthy.

Truman's agenda met with a generally hostile Congress, despite the Democratic majority. The same conservative coalition that had blocked Roosevelt's initiatives in his second term and dismantled or cut popular New Deal programs during wartime continued to fight against Truman's proposals. Only parts of the Fair Deal won adoption: the minimum wage was raised; the Social Security program was extended to cover 10 million new workers; and Social Security benefits were increased by 75 percent. The National Housing Act of 1949 called for the construction of 810,000 units of low-income housing, but only half that number were actually built.

Interest groups successfully opposed other key items in the Fair Deal. The American Medical Association (AMA) quashed a labor-backed movement for national health insurance by denouncing it as the first step toward "**socialized medicine**." Catholics successfully opposed aid to education because it did not include subsidies for parochial schools. Trade associations, the National Association of Manufacturers, and other business groups also actively opposed what they called "creeping socialism." Though most corporate leaders recognized that some state involvement in the economy was necessary and even beneficial to business interests, they felt the Fair Deal went too far. As a lobbyist for the National Association of Real Estate Boards explained, "In our country we prefer that government activity shall take the form of assisting and aiding private business rather than undertake great public projects of a governmental character." Through extensive lobbying and public relations campaigns, business groups agitated not only to defeat specific pieces of Fair Deal legislation but also to forestall increased taxes, antitrust activity, and other unwanted federal interference in corporate affairs. Their activities helped to block support for enlarged federal responsibilities for economic and social welfare. The outbreak of the Korean War in 1950 also limited the chances of the Fair Deal being passed by diverting national attention and federal funds from domestic affairs. So did the nation's growing paranoia concerning internal subversion, the most dramatic manifestation of the cold war's effect on American life.

Truman Triumphant

In one of the most famous photographs in American political history, Harry S Truman gloats over an inaccurate headline in the Chicago Daily Tribune. *Pollsters had predicted an overwhelming victory for Thomas E. Dewey. Their primitive techniques, however, did not reflect the dramatic surge in support for Truman during the last days of the campaign.*
Corbis-Bettmann.

The Great Fear

As American relations with the Soviet Union deteriorated, fear of communism at home fueled a widespread campaign of domestic repression. Americans often call this phenomenon "McCarthyism," after Senator Joseph R. McCarthy of Wisconsin, the decade's most vocal anti-Communist, but more was involved than the work of just one man. The Great Fear built on the long-standing distrust of radicals and foreigners that had exploded in the Red Scare after World War I. Worsening cold war tensions intersected with both those deep-seated anxieties and partisan politics to spawn an obsessive concern with internal subversion. Ultimately, few Communists were found in positions of power; far more Americans became innocent victims of false accusations and innuendos.

HUAC. The roots of postwar anticommunism dated back to 1938, when Congressman Martin Dies of Texas and other conservatives launched the House Committee on Un-American Activities (HUAC) to investigate alleged fascist and Communist influence in labor unions and New Deal agencies. HUAC gained heightened visibility after the war, especially after revelations in 1946 of a Soviet spy ring operating in Canada and the United States' accentuated fears of Soviet subversion.

In 1947 HUAC helped spark the "Great Fear" by holding widely publicized hearings on alleged Communist infiltration in the film industry. A group of writers and directors, soon dubbed the Hollywood Ten, went to jail for contempt of Congress when they cited the First Amendment while refusing to testify about their past associations. Hundreds of other actors, directors, and writers whose names had been mentioned in the HUAC investigation or whose associates and friends the committee had labeled as "reds" were unable to get work, victims of an unacknowledged but very real **blacklist** honored by industry executives. HUAC also investigated playwrights, authors, university professors, labor activists, organizations, and government officials thought to be "left wing."

Truman's Loyalty Program. Although HUAC bore much of the responsibility for spawning the witch hunt, its effects spread far beyond the congressional committee. In March 1947 President Truman issued an executive order initiating a comprehensive investigation into the loyalty of federal employees. Following Washington's lead many state and local governments, universities, political organizations, churches, and businesses undertook their own antisubversion campaigns, including the requirement that employees take loyalty oaths. In the labor movement, which Communists had been active in organizing in the 1930s, charges that Soviet-led Communists were taking over American unions led to a purge of Communist members. Civil rights organizations such as the NAACP and the National Urban League also expelled Communists or "fellow travelers"—words used to describe people viewed as left-wing—or as Communist sympathizers who were not members of the Communist Party. Thus the Great Fear was particularly devastating to the political left; accusations of guilt by association affected progressives of all stripes.

The anti-Communist crusade intensified in 1948 when HUAC began an investigation of Alger Hiss, a former New Dealer and a State Department official who had accompanied Franklin Roosevelt to Yalta. A former Communist, Whittaker Chambers, claimed that Hiss was a member of a secret Communist cell operating within the government and had passed him classified documents in the 1930s. Hiss categorically denied the allegations and denied even knowing Chambers. HUAC's investigation was orchestrated by Republican congressman Richard M. Nixon of California. Because the statute of limitations on the crime of which Hiss was accused had expired, he was charged instead with perjury for lying about his Communist affiliations and acquaintance with Chambers. In early 1950 Hiss was found guilty and sentenced to five years in federal prison. Although recently released evidence from Soviet archives has helped to harden the case against Hiss, the question of his guilt continues to be a contentious one among historians and journalists.

The Rise and Fall of McCarthy. Hiss's conviction fueled the paranoia about a Communist conspiracy in the federal government, contributing to the meteoric rise of Senator Joseph McCarthy of Wisconsin. In February 1950 McCarthy delivered a bombshell during a speech in Wheeling, West Virginia: "I have here in my hand a list of the names of 205 men that were known to the Secretary of State as being members of the Communist Party and who nevertheless are still working and shaping the policy of the State Department." McCarthy later reduced his numbers, first to fifty-seven, then to one "policy risk," and he never released any names or proof, but he had gained the attention he sought. For the next four years, he was the central figure in a virulent campaign of anticommunism. Like other Republicans in the late 1940s, McCarthy leveled accusations of Communist subversion in the government to embarrass President Truman and the Democratic Party. Critics who disagreed with him exposed themselves to charges of being "soft" on communism. Because McCarthy charged that his critics were themselves part of "this conspiracy so immense," few political leaders challenged him. Truman called McCarthy's charges "slander, lies, character assassination" but could do nothing to curb them. When Republican Dwight D. Eisenhower was elected president in 1952, he refrained from publicly challenging his party's most outspoken senator.

Despite McCarthy's failure to identify a single Communist in government, a series of national and international events allowed him to retain credibility. Besides the Hiss case, the sensational 1951 espionage trial of Julius and Ethel Rosenberg fueled McCarthy's allegations. Convicted of passing atomic secrets to the Soviet Union in a highly controversial trial, the Rosenbergs were executed in 1953. (As in the case of Hiss, their convictions continue to be debated; the recent release of declassified documents from a top-secret intelligence

McCarthy's Assault on Civil Liberties

Senator Joseph McCarthy's reckless attacks on alleged Communists in the U.S. government stirred widespread public fears of Soviet subversion in the 1950s. His critics, such as cartoonist Al Hirschfeld, expressed alarm at what they saw as McCarthy's assault on American liberty.

© Al Hirschfeld. Drawing reproduced by special arrangement with The Margo Feiden Galleries, NY.

mission has provided some new evidence of Julius Rosenberg's guilt.) The Korean War, which embroiled the United States in a frustrating fight against communism in a faraway land, also made Americans susceptible to McCarthy's claims. Blaming disloyal individuals rather than complex international factors for the problems of the cold war undoubtedly helped many Americans make sense of a disordered world of nuclear bombs, "police actions," and other world crises that seemed to come with alarming regularity.

In early 1954 McCarthy overreached himself by launching an investigation into possible subversion in the U.S. Army. When the lengthy televised hearings brought McCarthy's smear tactics and leering innuendoes into the nation's living rooms, support for him declined. The end of the Korean War and the death of Stalin in 1953 also undercut public interest in McCarthy's red-baiting campaign. In December 1954 the Senate voted sixty-seven to twenty-two to censure McCarthy for unbecoming conduct. He died from an alcohol-related illness three years later at the age of forty-eight, his name forever attached to a period of political repression of which he was only the most flagrant manifestation (see American Voices, "Mark

Goodson: Red Hunting on the Quiz Shows; or, What's My Party Line?," p. 802).

"Modern Republicanism"

At the height of the Great Fear, Dwight D. Eisenhower became president. Having secured the 1952 Republican nomination, he asked Senator Richard M. Nixon of California to be his running mate. Nixon, young, tirelessly partisan, and with a strong anti-Communist record from his crusade against Alger Hiss, brought an aggressive campaign style as well as regional balance to the Republican ticket. The new administration set the tone for what historians have called "modern Republicanism," an updated party philosophy that emphasized a slowdown, rather than a dismantling, of federal responsibilities. Compared with their predecessors in the 1920s and their successors in the 1980s and 1990s, modern Republicans were more tolerant of government intervention in social and economic affairs, though they did seek to limit the scope of federal action.

The 1952 Election. The Democrats never seriously considered renominating Harry Truman, who by 1952

Mark Goodson

Red Hunting on the Quiz Shows; or, What's My Party Line?

Active in the television industry from its earliest days, Mark Goodson was a highly successful producer whose game shows included What's My Line?, To Tell the Truth, Password, *and* Family Feud. *In this interview Goodson recalls his experience in the industry in the early 1950s when rampant anticommunism plagued the entertainment business.*

I'm not sure when it began, but I believe it was early 1950. At that point I had no connection with the blacklisting that was going on, although I heard about it in the motion picture business and heard rumors about things that had happened on other shows, like *The Aldrich Family. . . .*

Soon afterwards, CBS installed a clearance division. There wasn't any discussion. We would just get the word—"drop that person"—and that was supposed to be it. Whenever I booked a guest or a panelist on *What's My Line?* or *I've Got a Secret*, one of our assistants would phone up and say, "We're going to use so-and-so." We'd either get the okay, or they'd call back and say, "Not clear," or "Sorry, we can't use them." Even advertising agencies—big ones, like Young & Rubicam and BBD&O—had their own clearance departments. They would never come out and say it. They would just write off somebody by saying, "He's a bad actor." You were never supposed to tell the person what it was about;

you'd just unbook them. They never admitted there was a blacklist. It just wasn't done. . . .

Anna Lee was an English actress on a later show of ours called *It's News to Me*. The sponsor was Sanka Coffee, a product of General Foods. The advertising agency was Young & Rubicam. One day, I received a call telling me we had to drop one of our panelists, Anna Lee, immediately. They said she was a radical, that she wrote a column for the *Daily Worker*. They couldn't allow that kind of stuff on the air. They claimed they were getting all kinds of mail. It seemed incongruous to me that this little English girl, someone who seemed very conservative, would be writing for a Communist newspaper. It just didn't sound right.

I took her out to lunch. After a little social conversation, I asked her about her politics. She told me that she wasn't political, except she voted Conservative in England. Her husband was a Republican from Texas.

I went to the agency and said, "You guys are really off your rocker. Anna Lee is nothing close to a liberal." They told me, "Oh, you're right. We checked on that. It's a different Anna Lee who writes for the *Daily Worker*." I remember being relieved and saying, "Well, that's good. You just made a mistake. Now we can forget this." But that wasn't the case. They told me, "We've still got to get rid of her, because the illusion is just as good as the reality. If our client continues to get the mail, no one is going to believe him when he says there's a second Anna Lee." At that point I lost it. I told them their demand was outrageous. They could cancel the show if they wanted to, but I would not drop somebody whose only crime was sharing a name. When I got back to my office, there was a phone call waiting for me. It was from a friend of mine at the agency. He said, "If I were you, I would not lose my temper like that. If you want to argue, do it quietly. After you left, somebody said, 'Is Goodson a pinko?'"

Source: Griffin Fariello, *Red Scare* (New York: Norton, 1995), 320–24.

was a thoroughly discredited leader. Lack of popular enthusiasm for the Korean War had dealt the most severe blow to Truman's support, but a series of scandals involving federal officials in bribery, kickback, and influence-peddling schemes also had caused a public outcry about the "mess in Washington." With a certain relief the Democrats turned to Governor Adlai E. Stevenson of Illinois, who enjoyed the support of respected liberals such as Eleanor Roosevelt and of organized labor. To appease southern voters who feared Stevenson's liberal agenda, the Democrats nominated Senator John A. Sparkman of Alabama for vice president.

Throughout the 1952 campaign Stevenson advocated New Deal and Fair Deal policies with an almost literary eloquence. But Eisenhower's artfully unpretentious speeches and "I Like Ike" slogan were more

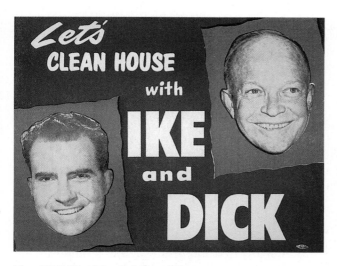

The 1952 Presidential Campaign

The 1952 Republican ticket of Dwight D. Eisenhower and Richard M. Nixon launched an effective attack on the Democratic leadership by stressing the Truman administration's involvement in bribery and influence-peddling scandals and by capitalizing on Truman's failure to end the war in Korea. Collection of Janice L. and David J. Frent.

The *Sputnik* Crisis

The Soviet launching of the Sputnik *space satellite in 1957 precipitated a crisis of confidence in American science and education. That sense of crisis was reflected in a 1950s "Space Race" card game, in which those dealt the* Sputnik *card would lose two turns.* The Michael Barson Collection / Past Perfect.

effective with voters. Eager to win the support of the broadest electorate possible, Eisenhower played down specific questions of policy. Instead, he attacked the Democrats with the "K_1C_2" formula—"Korea, Communism, and Corruption."

That November Eisenhower won 55 percent of the popular vote, carrying all the northern and western states and four southern states. Republican candidates for Congress did not fare quite as well. They regained the Senate from the Democrats but took the House of Representatives by a slender margin of only four seats. In 1954 they would lose control of both houses to the Democrats. Even though the enormously popular Eisenhower would easily win reelection over Adlai Stevenson in 1956, the Republicans would remain in the minority in Congress.

The Hidden-Hand Presidency. The political scientist Fred Greenstein has characterized Eisenhower's style of leadership as the "hidden-hand presidency," pointing out that the president maneuvered deftly behind the scenes while seeming not to concern himself in public with partisan questions. Seeking a middle ground between liberalism and conservatism, Eisenhower did his best to set a quieter national mood, hoping to decrease the need for federal intervention in social and economic issues, while avoiding conservative demands for a complete rollback of the New Deal.

Eisenhower nonetheless presided over new increases in federal activity. When the Soviet Union launched the first satellite, *Sputnik,* in 1957, Eisenhower

supported a U.S. space program to catch up in this new cold war competition. The National Aeronautics and Space Administration (NASA) was founded the following year. Alarmed that the United States was falling behind the Soviets in technological expertise, the president also persuaded Congress to appropriate additional money for college scholarships and for research and development at universities and in industry. After 1954, when the Democrats took over control over Congress, the Eisenhower administration also acceded to legislation promoting social welfare. Federal outlays for veterans' benefits, unemployment compensation, housing, and Social Security were increased, and the minimum wage was raised from 75 cents an hour to $1. The creation of the new Department of Health, Education, and Welfare (HEW) in 1953 consolidated government control of social welfare programs, confirming federal commitments in that area. Congress also passed the Interstate Highway Act of 1956, which authorized $26 billion over a ten-year period for the construction of a nationally integrated highway system. This enormous public works program surpassed anything undertaken during the New Deal.

Thus Republicans, though they resisted the unchecked expansion of the state, did not generally cut back federal power. In social welfare programs and defense expenditures, modern Republicanism signaled an abandonment of the traditional Republican commitment to limited government. When Eisenhower retired from public life in 1961, the federal government had become an even greater presence in everyday life than it had been when he took office. Some of the most controversial federal initiatives occurred in the area of civil rights.

The Emergence of Civil Rights as a National Issue

The civil rights movement was arguably the most important force for change in postwar America, and its accelerating momentum had profound implications for the federal government. The movement built upon a long tradition of African American protest but was also shaped by the climate of the cold war that so pervaded American politics and society.

Civil Rights under Truman

Beginning with World War II, the National Association for the Advancement of Colored People (NAACP) had redoubled its efforts to combat segregation in housing, transportation, and other areas. Black demands for justice continued into the postwar years, spurred by symbolic victories such as Jackie Robinson's breaking through the color line in major league baseball by joining the Brooklyn Dodgers in 1947. African American leaders were cautiously optimistic about extracting support from President Truman. Although capable of using racist language in private, Truman was moderately sympathetic to civil rights on moral grounds, a sympathy that was reinforced not just by cold war considerations but also by the realization that black voters were playing an increasingly large role in the Democratic Party as they migrated from the South, where they were effectively disenfranchised, to northern and western cities.

Lacking a popular mandate on civil rights, Truman turned to executive action. In 1946 he appointed a National Civil Rights Commission. Basing its arguments on moral, economic, and international grounds, its 1947 report called for an expanded federal role in civil rights that foreshadowed much of the civil rights legislation of the 1960s. Truman also ordered the Justice Department to prepare an amicus curiae ("friend of the court") brief in the Supreme Court case of *Shelley v. Kraemer* (1948),

which ruled that states that enforced restrictive covenants maintaining residential segregation by barring home buyers of a certain race or religion violated the Fourteenth Amendment. In this and other briefs, the Justice Department explicitly referred to the way in which "the United States has been embarrassed in the conduct of foreign relations by acts of discrimination taking place in this country." Also in 1948, under pressure from the Committee Against Jim Crow in Military Service organized by World War II's March on Washington's founder, A. Philip Randolph, Truman signed an executive order desegregating the armed forces. His administration also proposed a federal antilynching law, federal protection of voting rights (such as an end to poll taxes), and a permanent federal agency to guarantee equal employment opportunity, but a filibuster by southern conservatives blocked the legislation.

Challenging Segregation

In addition to exerting pressure on white politicians like Truman, civil rights leaders in the early 1950s continued their long-standing battle to challenge segregation in the courts and adopted a new strategy of nonviolent protest. They were determined to overturn the legal segregation of the races that still governed southern society in the early 1950s. In most southern states whites and blacks could not eat in the same rooms at restaurants and luncheonettes or use the same waiting rooms and toilets at bus and train stations. All forms of public transportation were rigidly segregated by custom or by law. Even drinking fountains were labeled "White" and "Colored."

Brown v. Board of Education of Topeka. The first significant victory came in 1954, when the Supreme Court handed down its most far-reaching decision in *Brown v. Board of Education of Topeka*. The NAACP's chief legal counsel, Thurgood Marshall, had argued that the segregated schools mandated by the Board of Education in Topeka, Kansas, were inherently unconstitutional because they stigmatized an entire race, denying black children the "equal protection of the laws" guaranteed by the Fourteenth Amendment. In a unanimous decision announced on May 17, 1954, the Supreme Court, following the lead of Chief Justice Earl Warren (see Chapter 30), agreed with Marshall and overturned the long-standing "separate but equal" doctrine of *Plessy v. Ferguson* (see Chapter 19).

Over the next several years, in response to NAACP suits, the Supreme Court used the *Brown* precedent to overturn segregation at city parks, public beaches, and golf courses; in interstate and intrastate transportation; and in public housing. In the face of these Court decisions, white resistance to integration solidified. In 1956,

Integration at Little Rock, Arkansas
With chants such as "Two-four-six-eight, we ain't gonna integrate," angry crowds taunted Elizabeth Eckford (shown here walking past white students and National Guardsmen) and eight other black students who tried to register at the previously all-white Central High School in Little Rock, Arkansas, on September 4, 1957. The court-ordered integration proceeded only after President Eisenhower reluctantly nationalized the Arkansas National Guard to protect the students. Francis Miller, LIFE Magazine, © Time, Inc.

101 members of Congress signed the Southern Manifesto, denouncing the *Brown* decision as "a clear abuse of judicial power" and encouraging their constituents to defy it. That same year, 500,000 southerners joined White Citizens' Councils dedicated to blocking school integration and other civil rights measures. Some whites revived old tactics of violence and intimidation, swelling the ranks of the Ku Klux Klan to levels not seen since the 1920s.

Eisenhower and Civil Rights. Unlike Harry Truman, Eisenhower showed little interest in civil rights. Though he proved extremely reluctant to intervene in what was widely seen as a state issue, entrenched southern resistance to federal authority eventually forced his hand. In 1957 in response to the *Brown* decision, racial moderates on the Little Rock, Arkansas, school board had designed a desegregation plan. But pressure from Citizens' Councils and others groups led the governor of Arkansas, Orval Faubus, to defy a federal court order to desegregate Little Rock's Central High School. Faubus called out the National Guard to bar nine black students who were attempting to enroll in the all-white school. When scenes of vicious mobs harassing the determined students aired on television,

the crisis rocked the nation and provoked a storm of criticism abroad. President Eisenhower—concerned about the nation's international image and Faubus's defiance of federal authority—reluctantly intervened, sending 1,000 federal troops and 10,000 nationalized members of the Arkansas National Guard to protect the students. Eisenhower thus became the first president since Reconstruction to use federal troops to enforce the rights of blacks.

The Montgomery Bus Boycott. White resistance to the *Brown* decision, as well as Eisenhower's hesitancy to act in Little Rock, showed that court victories were not enough to overturn segregation. In 1955 a single act of defiance gave black leaders an opportunity to implement a new strategy—nonviolent protest. On December 1 Rosa Parks, a seamstress and a member of the NAACP in Montgomery, Alabama, refused to give up her seat on a city bus to a white man. "I felt it was just something I had to do," Parks stated. She was promptly arrested and charged with violating a local segregation ordinance. When the black community in Montgomery met to discuss the proper response, they turned to the Reverend Martin Luther King Jr., who had become the

Martin Luther King in Montgomery

After the arrest of Rosa Parks in December 1955, the black community of Montgomery, Alabama, organized a citywide bus boycott with the help of Dr. Martin Luther King Jr., a local Baptist pastor. Many black women served as grassroots organizers of the boycott, but it was King who rose to prominence as an eloquent and highly respected spokesperson for the emerging civil rights movement in the region.

Dan Weiner / Courtesy, Sandra Weiner.

pastor at a local church the year before. King endorsed a plan by a Montgomery black women's organization to boycott the city's bus system until it was integrated. For the next 381 days, members of a united black community formed carpools or walked to work. The bus company neared bankruptcy, and downtown stores saw their business decline. But not until the Supreme Court ruled in November 1956 that bus segregation was unconstitutional did the city of Montgomery finally relent, prompting one woman boycotter to proclaim, "My feets is tired, but my soul is rested."

The Montgomery bus boycott catapulted King to national prominence. In 1957, with the Reverend Ralph Abernathy and other southern black clergy, King founded the Southern Christian Leadership Conference

(SCLC), based in Atlanta. The black church had long been the center of African American social and cultural life. Through the SCLC the church lent its moral and organizational strength, as well as the voices of its most inspirational preachers, to the civil rights movement. Black churchwomen flocked to the movement, transferring the skills they had honed through years of church work to the fight for racial change. Soon the SCLC joined the NAACP as one of the major advocates for racial justice. While the two groups achieved only limited victories in the 1950s, they laid the organizational groundwork for the dynamic civil rights movement that would become one of the defining issues of the 1960s and would open the door to wide-ranging dissent from America's cold war culture of consensus and conformity.

The Civil Rights Movement and the Cold War

One effect of the cold war on civil rights was the way in which the hunt for internal subversives stifled dissent in American culture in the late 1940s and 1950s. Black activists were often "red-baited," branded as "Communist agitators," and harassed in a variety of ways. Paul Robeson, a charismatic actor and singer who had long sympathized with the political left and had made positive statements about the Soviet Union, had his passport revoked in 1950. State Department officials explained that allowing him to "travel abroad . . . would be contrary to the best interests of the United States," because of "his frequent criticism of the treatment of blacks in the United States." When Communists and fellow travelers were ousted from the NAACP and labor unions, other militant voices were silenced. This suppression helped to shape the direction of the civil rights movement in the postwar era, minimizing the attention given to class and economic issues and focusing attention on the legal discrimination and violence African Americans faced in the South.

But if the cold war constrained the postwar civil rights movement, it also engendered support for reforms. The fight against the spread of international communism was in many ways a war of words, and American leaders were well aware that the world press reported on incidents of lynching and other violence as well as on the disenfranchisement and segregation of blacks in the South. Chester Bowles, U.S. ambassador to India, noted in 1952 that "the colored peoples of Asia and Africa, who total two-thirds of the world's population, seldom think about the United States without considering the limitations under which our 13 million Negroes are living." The Soviets capitalized on the issue, repeatedly hammering on the fact that the United States fell far short of realizing its ideals of democracy and equality. Black activists invoked the cold war as a justification for pursuing racial reform, increasingly forcing U.S. presidents and their administrations to view black civil rights at home in the context of international politics.

The Impact of the Cold War

The cold war extended to the most distant areas of the globe, but it also had powerful effects on the domestic economy, politics, and cultural values of the United States. It permeated domestic politics, helped to shape the response to the civil rights movement, and created an atmosphere that stifled dissent. Moreover, the implications of the nation's extensive military mobilization, even in times of peace, were far ranging. For the first time in the nation's history, there was a peacetime draft. In the past the armed forces had shrunk to a skeleton volunteer force at the end of each war or foreign engagement. But when World War II ended, the draft was kept in place to meet the military commitments associated with the cold war: occupation forces in defeated Axis countries, missile deployment operations in Europe, and counterinsurgency forces in the Third World.

The postwar expansion of the military produced a dramatic shift in the country's economic priorities, as military spending took up a greater percentage of national income. Between 1900 and 1930, except for the two years that the United States fought in World War I, the country spent less than 1 percent of its GDP for military purposes. When Eisenhower left office in January 1961, the figure was closer to 10 percent, fully half of the federal budget (Figure 27.1). Even though the country was at peace during most of his administration, the

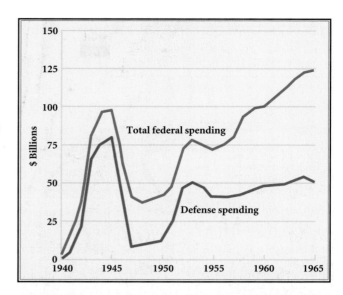

FIGURE 27.1 National Defense Spending, 1940–1965
In 1950 the defense budget was $13 billion, less than a third of total federal outlays. In 1961 defense spending reached $47 billion, fully half of the federal budget and almost 10 percent of the gross domestic product.

economy and the government operated practically on a war footing.

Nuclear Proliferation

One of the most alarming aspects of the nation's militarization was the dangerous cycle of nuclear proliferation

Duck and Cover
The nation's Civil Defense Agency's efforts to alert Americans to the threat of a nuclear attack extended to children in schools, where repeated drills taught them to "duck and cover" as protection against the impact of an atomic blast. Variations of this 1954 scene at Franklin Township School in Quakertown, New Jersey, were repeated all over the nation.
Paul F. Kutta / Courtesy, *Reminiscences* Magazine.

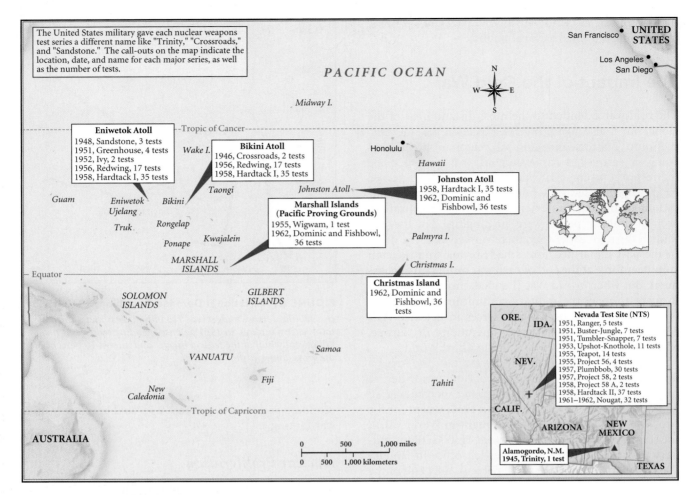

The United States military gave each nuclear weapons test series a different name like "Trinity," "Crossroads," and "Sandstone." The call-outs on the map indicate the location, date, and name for each major series, as well as the number of tests.

Eniwetok Atoll
1948, Sandstone, 3 tests
1951, Greenhouse, 4 tests
1952, Ivy, 2 tests
1956, Redwing, 17 tests
1958, Hardtack I, 35 tests

Bikini Atoll
1946, Crossroads, 2 tests
1956, Redwing, 17 tests
1958, Hardtack I, 35 tests

Johnston Atoll
1958, Hardtack I, 35 tests
1962, Dominic and Fishbowl, 36 tests

Marshall Islands (Pacific Proving Grounds)
1955, Wigwam, 1 test
1962, Dominic and Fishbowl, 36 tests

Christmas Island
1962, Dominic and Fishbowl, 36 tests

Nevada Test Site (NTS)
1951, Ranger, 5 tests
1951, Buster-Jungle, 7 tests
1951, Tumbler-Snapper, 7 tests
1953, Upshot-Knothole, 11 tests
1955, Teapot, 14 tests
1955, Project 56, 4 tests
1957, Plumbbob, 30 tests
1957, Project 58, 2 tests
1958, Project 58 A, 2 tests
1958, Hardtack II, 37 tests
1961–1962, Nougat, 32 tests

Alamogordo, N.M.
1945, Trinity, 1 test

MAP 27.5 Atmospheric Nuclear Weapons Testing in the Pacific and at Home, 1945–1962

On July 16, 1945, with the detonation of the world's first atomic bomb at the Trinity test site in Alamogordo, New Mexico, the United States began, as a critical part of its growing cold war conflict with the Soviet Union, what would become nearly two decades of nuclear weapons testing in the atmosphere (as opposed to underground explosions). While the U.S. military conducted numerous aboveground tests at the Nevada Test Site, the majority of atmospheric tests were conducted in the Pacific in the area of Bikini, Eniwetok, and Christmas Islands. In response to mounting scientific evidence and a growing worldwide fear of radioactive nuclear "fallout," the United States and the Soviet Union signed a test-ban treaty in 1963 pledging a halt to atmospheric weapons testing, although nations like France and China continued to test above ground. Underground testing by all nations possessing nuclear weapons continued into the 1990s.

For more help analyzing this map, see the ONLINE STUDY GUIDE at **bedfordstmartins.com/henretta**.

that would outlive the Soviet-American conflict that spawned it. The nuclear arms race affected all Americans by fostering a climate of fear and uncertainty. Bomb shelters and civil defense drills provided a daily reminder of the threat of nuclear war, and atomic research and testing had a devastating impact on human health. In the late 1950s a small but growing number of citizens

became concerned about the effects of radioactive fallout from above-ground bomb tests (Map 27.5). In later years federal investigators documented a host of illnesses, deaths, and birth defects among families of veterans who had worked on weapons tests and among "down-winders"—people who lived near nuclear test sites and weapons facilities (see American Voices, "Isaac Nelson:

Isaac Nelson

Atomic Witness

Isaac Nelson, a naval veteran of World War II, returned to his hometown of Cedar City, Utah, in 1945 and went to work for a nearby hardware company. Like many other residents of southern Utah, he and his wife Oleta lived downwind from the Nevada Test Site, where the U.S. government detonated 126 atomic bombs into the atmosphere between 1951 and 1963.

After 1951 they were going to start the testing in Nevada, and everybody was really excited, and thought maybe we'd get a part to play in it and show our patriotism. We wanted to help out what little we could. My wife and I and a hundred or so residents of Cedar drove out to see the first one. We huddled up, our blankets around us because it was cold, so early in the morning before daylight, and we were chattering like chipmunks, so excited! Pretty soon, why, the whole sky just flared up in an orange-red flash, and it was so brilliant that you could easily see the trees ten miles across the valley, and if you had a newspaper you could have easily read it, it was so bright. . . .

Later on in the day, you'd see these fallout clouds drifting down in Kanarraville, and up through Cedar, and if you'd ever seen one you'd never mistake it because it was definitely different from any rain cloud, kind of a pinkish-tan color strung out all down through the valley there for several miles. They'd float over the city and everyone would go out and ooh and aah just like a bunch of hicks. We was never warned that there was any danger involved in going out and being under these fallout clouds all the time I lived here. . . .

Along about 1955 a cloud came over Cedar, and my wife and I, the kids and the neighbors stood outside looking at it and talking about it. Later on towards evening, my wife, her skin, her hands, arms, neck, face, legs, anything that was exposed just turned a beet red. . . . She got a severe headache, and nausea, diarrhea, really miserable. We drove out to the hospital, and the doctor said, "Well it looks like sunburn, but then it doesn't." Her headache persisted for several months, and the diarrhea and nausea for a few weeks.

Four weeks after that I was sittin' in the front room reading the paper and she'd gone into the bathroom to wash her hair. All at once she let out the most ungodly scream, and I run in there and there's about half her hair layin' in the washbasin! You can imagine a woman with beautiful, raven-black hair, so black it would glint green in the sunlight just like a raven's wing. . . . She was in a state of panic. . . . After that she kept getting weaker, and listless, and she didn't even have any desire to go out in the garden to work with her flowers. . . . Finally [the doctors] said it looked like a large tumor in her brain, and they operated and removed a tumor about the size of a large orange or softball, but they couldn't get it all out, it was too embedded in the brain tissue. Oleta lived two years or so after that operation. She started going downhill from 1955 and died in 1965 at 41.

Source: Carole Gallagher, *American Ground Zero* (Cambridge, MA: MIT Press, 1993), 133–35.

Atomic Witness," above). The most shocking revelations, however, came to light in 1993, when the Department of Energy released millions of previously classified documents on human radiation experiments conducted in the late 1940s and 1950s under the auspices of the Atomic Energy Commission (AEC) and other federal agencies. Many of the subjects were irradiated without their consent or understanding.

By the late 1950s, public concern over nuclear testing and fallout had become a high-profile issue, and new antinuclear groups such as SANE (the National Committee for a Sane Nuclear Policy) and Physicians for Social Responsibility called for an international test ban.

Eisenhower himself had second thoughts about a nuclear policy based on the premise of annihilating the enemy even if one's own country was destroyed—the aptly named **MAD (Mutually Assured Destruction)** policy. He also found spiraling arms expenditures a serious hindrance to balancing the federal budget, one of his chief fiscal goals. Consequently, Eisenhower tried to negotiate an arms-limitation agreement with the Soviet Union. Progress along those lines was cut short, however, when on May 5, 1960, the Soviets shot down an American U-2 spy plane over their territory and captured and imprisoned its pilot, Francis Gary Powers. Eisenhower at first denied that the plane was engaged in

The Computer Revolution

The first modern computers—information-processing machines capable of storing and manipulating data according to specified programs—appeared in the 1940s. During World War II engineers and mathematicians at the University of Pennsylvania developed a general-purpose, programmable electronic calculator called ENIAC (Electronic Numerical Integrator and Computer), which could add 5,000 ten-digit decimal numbers in one second. It stood 8 feet tall, measured 80 feet long, and weighed 30 tons; it used 18,000 vacuum tubes for computations. When it performed complex mathematical computations, one scientist noted, ENIAC sounded "like a roomful of ladies knitting." Although ENIAC lacked a central memory and could not store a program, it was the bridge to the modern computer revolution.

Six computers were under construction by 1947, including UNIVAC (Universal Automatic Computer), the first commercial computer system. To the general public in the 1950s, the word UNIVAC was synonymous with computer. UNIVAC was basically a data-processing system that could be tailored to a customer's needs. In 1951 the U.S. Census Bureau bought the first UNIVAC. Soon CBS-TV signed on, using a UNIVAC to predict the outcome of the 1952 presidential election. At 9 P.M., after only the East Coast polls had closed and with only 7 percent of the votes counted, UNIVAC predicted that Dwight D. Eisenhower would sweep the election with 438 electoral votes. CBS programmers and network executives, who had expected a closer election, got jittery and altered the program to give Eisenhower a far narrower margin. When the final tally gave him 442 electoral votes, only 4 votes off the original projection, commentator Edward R. Murrow observed, "The trouble with machines is people."

Computers are essentially collections of switches; the programs tell the machine which switches to turn on and off. The puzzle early computer scientists had to solve was how to increase the speed of this basic operation while lowering the cost. The first generation of computers needed vacuum tubes for computation power and used punched cards for writing programs and analyzing data. Computers such as ENIAC were room-size machines, and programming them could take several days because the programmers had to manually set thousands of switches in the on or off position. The vacuum tubes were the weakest part of early computers; the burnout of just a few of them could shut down the entire system. Furthermore, the tubes gave off enormous amounts of heat, necessitating noisy and cumbersome air-conditioning units wherever computers operated. After a critical signal relay stopped one early program, scientists finally located the problem—a dead moth trapped in the apparatus, the origin of the term *debugging*.

The 1948 invention of the transistor revolutionized computers and the whole field of electronics, making the second generation of computers possible. Like vacuum tubes, transistors served as on-off switches, but they did not generate heat, burn out, or consume a lot of energy. They also were inexpensive to manufacture. The invention of integrated circuits in 1959 ushered in the third computer generation, characterized by greater sophistication in miniaturization: the number of transistors that could be installed on a silicon chip increased dramatically, with a corresponding increase in computational power. The fourth computer generation arrived

espionage but later admitted that he had authorized the mission and other secret flights over the Soviet Union. In the midst of the dispute, a proposed summit meeting was canceled, and Eisenhower's last chance to negotiate an arms agreement evaporated.

The Military-Industrial Complex

With its headquarters at the sprawling Pentagon in Arlington, Virginia, the Department of Defense evolved into a massive bureaucracy that profoundly influenced the postwar economy. Federal money underwrote 90 percent of the cost of research on aviation and space and also subsidized the scientific instruments, automobile, and electronics industries. With the government paying part of the bill, corporations developed products with unprecedented speed. After the Pentagon backed IBM's investment in integrated circuits in the 1960s, these new devices—crucial to the computer revolution (see New Technology, "The

in 1971 with the development of the microprocessor, which placed the entire central processing unit (CPU) of a computer on a single silicon chip (about the size of the letter "O" on this page).

Miniaturization progressed so rapidly that by the mid-1970s a $1 chip provided as much processing power as had the ENIAC of thirty years earlier. Since then, transistor size has continued to shrink, resulting in chips with twice as many transistors roughly every eighteen months. The increased speed and memory of these chips, together with the immense data storage capabili-

ties of the Internet (an online network first established by the Department of Defense in 1969), have made today's compact personal computers incredibly powerful tools. At the same time, scientists have been developing large-scale "supercomputers"—an integrated series of smaller computers that can be used to simulate complex natural and human phenomena such as weather, transportation systems, and genetics. Computers and computer technology have become so much a part of modern life that it is hard to remember how recent are the origins of this technological revolution.

The First Electronic Computer
Betty Holberton, one of many women technical experts involved in ENIAC (Electronic Numerical Integrator and Computer), programs the first electronic computer. Frances Miller / Timepix.

Computer Revolution," above)—were in commercial production within three years. More directly, Pentagon spending created a powerful defense industry. Aircraft companies such as Boeing and Lockheed did so much of their business with the government that they became dependent on Defense Department orders. By the 1960s perhaps as many as one American in seven owed his or her job to the military-industrial complex. In the South and West, where much of the new military

activity was concentrated, dependence on federal defense spending was even greater (Map 27.6). That increased spending put money in the pockets of the millions of people working in defense-related industries, but it also limited the resources available for domestic needs.

In his final address to the nation, Eisenhower warned against the power of what he called the "military-industrial complex," which by then was employing

CHAPTER 28

The Affluent Society and the Liberal Consensus

1945–1965

IN 1959 VICE PRESIDENT RICHARD NIXON TRAVELED to Moscow to open the American National Exhibit, one of several efforts to reduce cold war tensions in the period. While touring the kitchen of a model American home, Nixon and Soviet Premier Nikita Khrushchev got into a heated debate about the relative merits of Soviet and American societies. Instead of discussing rockets, submarines, and missiles, however, they talked dishwashers, toasters, and televisions. In what was quickly dubbed the "kitchen debate," Nixon used the exhibit and its representation of American affluence and mass consumption to assert the superiority of capitalism over communism and inevitable American victory in the cold war.

During the postwar era millions of Americans, enjoying the highest standard of living in the nation's history, pursued the promise of consumer society in the burgeoning suburbs. But affluence was never as widespread as the Moscow exhibit implied. The middle-class suburban lifestyle was beyond the reach of many poor and nonwhite Americans, particularly those in the decaying central cities. Hoping to spread the abundance of a flourishing economy to greater numbers of Americans, the Democratic administrations of the early 1960s pressed for the expansion of New Deal social welfare programs.

◄ **The Growing Middle Class**
Postwar affluence resulted in an unprecedented standard of living for the rapidly expanding middle class of the 1950s and 1960s. This 1951 photograph shows DuPont worker Steve Czekalinski and his family amid a year's supply of food. Prior to the 1950s, most families relied on a diet of starches and smoked meats. The newfound prosperity of the growing middle class enabled families like the Czekalinskis to enrich their diets with fresh meats and vegetables and frozen food. The cost to the Czekalinskis in 1951 for a year's supply of food: $1,300.
Alexander Henderson / Hagley Museum and Library.

815

The administrations of John F. Kennedy and—to a much greater extent—Lyndon B. Johnson tried to use federal power to ensure the public welfare in areas such as health care, education, and civil rights. In the Great Society program—a burst of social legislation in 1964 and 1965 that marked the high tide of postwar liberalism—the Johnson administration attempted to use the fiscal powers of the state to redress the imbalances of the economy without directly challenging capitalism.

Liberal politicians also pursued an activist stance abroad. Continuing and in some cases expanding the cold war policies of Truman and Eisenhower, the Kennedy and Johnson administrations took aggressive action against Communist influence in Europe, the Caribbean, Vietnam (see Chapter 29), and other areas. The growing financial and political costs of that ambitious agenda, however, hampered further progress on the domestic front and revealed ominous cracks in the postwar liberal coalition.

The Affluent Society

By the end of 1945, war-induced prosperity had made the United States the richest country in the world, a preeminence that would continue unchallenged for twenty years. U.S. corporations and banking institutions so dominated the world economy that the period has been called the *Pax Americana* (American peace). U.S. military policy and foreign aid, as well as the absence of major economic competitors, were vital factors in extending the global reach of American corporate capitalism, which enjoyed remarkable growth in productivity and profits. American economic leadership abroad translated into affluence at home. As many Americans, especially whites, moved to home ownership in new suburban communities, it was clear that domestic prosperity was benefiting a wider segment of society than anyone would have dreamed possible in the dark days of the Great Depression.

The Economic Record

The predominant thrust of modern corporate life in this period was the consolidation of economic and financial resources by **oligopolies**—a few large producers that controlled the national and, increasingly, the world market. In 1970, for example, the top four American firms produced 91 percent of the motor vehicles sold in the domestic market. Large firms maintained their dominance by diversifying. Combining companies in unrelated industries, these **conglomerates** ensured for themselves protection from instability in any single market, making them more effective international competitors. International Telephone and Telegraph became a diversified conglomerate by acquiring companies in

unrelated industries, including Continental Baking, Sheraton Hotels, Avis Rent-a-Car, Levitt and Sons home builders, and Hartford Fire Insurance. This pattern of corporate acquisition developed into a great wave of mergers that peaked in the 1960s.

The development of giant corporations also depended on the penetration of foreign markets. Unlike the Soviet Union, Western Europe, and Japan, America emerged physically unscathed from the war, with its defense industries eager to convert to consumer production. The weakness of the competition enabled American business to enter foreign regions when domestic markets became saturated or when American recessions cut into sales. Soon American companies provided products and services for war-torn European and Asian markets, giving the nation a trade surplus close to $5 billion in 1960.

The Bretton Woods System. American global supremacy rested in part on decisions made at a United Nations economic conference held in Bretton Woods, New Hampshire, in July 1944, which established the U.S. dollar as the capitalist world's principal reserve currency. Two global institutions—the International Bank for Reconstruction and Development (commonly known as the World Bank) and the International Monetary Fund (IMF)—resulted from this meeting. The World Bank provided private loans for the reconstruction of war-torn Europe as well as for the development of Third World countries. The IMF was set up to stabilize the value of currencies, providing a secure and predictable monetary environment for trade. It did this by encouraging fixed exchange rates, which facilitated the free convertibility of currencies to gold or to the currencies of other trading nations; the strong U.S. dollar served as the benchmark. In 1947 multinational trade negotiations resulted in the first General Agreement on Tariffs and Trade (GATT), which led to the establishment of an international body to oversee trade rules and practices.

The World Bank, the IMF, and GATT were the cornerstones of the so-called Bretton Woods system, which guided the world economy after the war. The United States dominated the World Bank and the IMF because it contributed the most capital to them and because the U.S. dollar had a pivotal role in international currency exchange. Thus these independent international organizations worked along lines that favored American-style internationalism over the economic nationalism that was traditional in most other countries. The World Bank, the IMF, and GATT encouraged stable prices, the liberalization of trade barriers and the reduction of tariffs, flexible domestic markets, and free trade based on fixed exchange rates. As long as the U.S. dollar remained the strongest currency, the Bretton Woods system would effectively serve America's global economic interests.

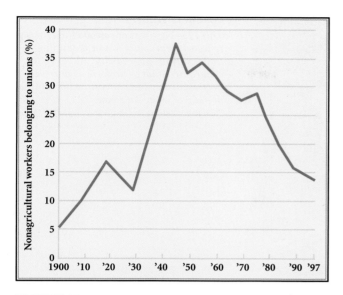

FIGURE 28.1 Labor Union Strength, 1900–1997

Labor unions reached their peak strength immediately after World War II. For the next thirty years, they consistently represented more than a quarter of the nonfarm workforce. After 1975 the influence of labor unions declined dramatically.
Source: AFL-CIO Information Bureau, Washington, DC.

Postwar Prosperity. U.S. economic supremacy abroad helped boost the domestic economy, creating millions of new jobs. One of the fastest-growing groups was salaried office workers, whose numbers increased by 61 percent between 1947 and 1957. Growing corporate bureaucracies and increased access to a college education through the GI Bill helped expand the male white-collar ranks. These "organization men," as sociologist William Whyte called them, were joined by millions of women who moved into clerical work and other lower-paying service-sector occupations. Although the percentage of blue-collar manufacturing jobs declined slightly during this period, the power of organized labor reached an all-time high (Figure 28.1). In 1955 the Congress of Industrial Organizations made a formal alliance with its old adversary, the American Federation of Labor. That merger created a single organization—the AFL-CIO—which represented more than 90 percent of the nation's 17.5 million union members. In exchange for labor peace and stability—that is, fewer strikes—corporate managers often cooperated with unions, agreeing to contracts that gave many workers secure, predictable, and steadily rising incomes, guaranteeing them a share in the new prosperity.

As the income of many American workers grew, consumer spending soared. That spending, combined with federal outlays for defense and domestic programs, seemed to promise a continuously rising standard of living. The gross domestic product (GDP) grew from $213 billion in 1945 to more than $500 billion in 1960 (Figure 28.2). With the inflation rate under 3 percent in

the 1950s, this steady economic growth meant a 25 percent rise in real income between 1946 and 1959. American homeownership rates reflected the rising standard of living: in 1940, 43 percent of American families owned their homes; by 1960, 62 percent owned them. The postwar boom was marred, however, by periodic bouts of recession and unemployment that particularly hurt low-income and nonwhite workers. Moreover, the rising standard of living was not accompanied by a redistribution of income: the top 10 percent of Americans still earned more than the bottom 50 percent. Nevertheless, most Americans had more money to spend than ever before.

The Suburban Explosion

Although Americans had been gravitating toward urban areas throughout the twentieth century, the postwar period was characterized by two new patterns: one was a shift away from older cities in the Northeast and Midwest and toward newer urban centers in the South and West; the other, a mass defection from the cities to the suburbs. Both processes were stimulated by the dramatic growth of a car culture and the federal government's support of housing and highway initiatives.

The Housing Boom. At the end of World War II, many cities were surrounded by pastures and working farms, but just five to ten years later those cities were surrounded by tract housing, factories, and shopping centers. By 1960 more Americans—particularly whites—lived in suburbs than in cities. People flocked to the suburbs in part because they followed the available housing. Few new dwellings had been built during the depression or war years, and the returning veterans and their families faced a critical housing shortage. The difficulty was partly resolved by an innovative Long Island building contractor. Arthur Levitt revolutionized the suburban housing market by applying mass-production techniques to home construction. Levitt's company could build 150 homes per week. In Levittown a basic four-room house, complete with kitchen appliances and an attic that

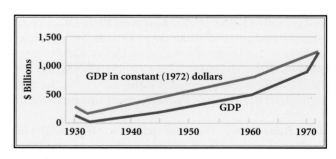

FIGURE 28.2 Gross Domestic Product, 1930–1972

After a sharp dip during the Great Depression, the gross domestic product (GDP) rose steadily in both real and constant dollars in the postwar period.

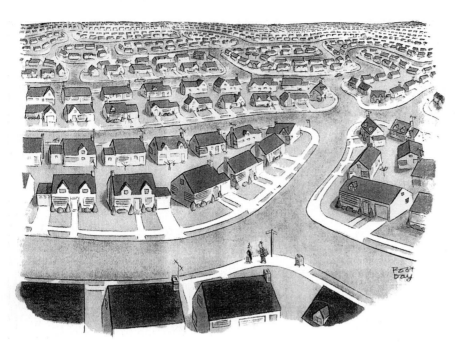

"I'm Mrs. Edward M. Barnes. Where do I live?"

Lost in Levittown

This 1954 New Yorker *cartoon humorously reflected what critics saw as the stifling uniformity of suburban life. Although the suburbs were not as uniform as they were portrayed, they were almost exclusively the domain of white Americans.*

a handy homeowner could convert into two additional bedrooms, was priced at less than $10,000 in 1947. Other developers soon followed suit in subdivisions all over the country, hastening the exodus from the farm and central city.

Many families financed their homes with mortgages from the Federal Housing Administration (FHA) and the Veterans Administration at rates dramatically lower than those offered by private lenders. In 1955 those two agencies wrote 41 percent of all nonfarm mortgages. Such lending demonstrated the quiet yet revolutionary way in which the federal government was entering and influencing daily life.

The new suburban homes—and much of the FHA and Veterans Administration loan funds—were reserved almost exclusively for whites. Levittown homeowners had to sign a covenant prohibiting occupation "by members of other than the Caucasian Race"; Levitt did not sell houses directly to blacks until 1960. Other communities adopted similar covenants to exclude Jews or Asians. Although the Supreme Court had ruled in *Shelley v. Kraemer* (1948) that **restrictive covenants** were illegal, the custom continued informally until the civil rights laws of the 1960s banned private discrimination.

The Sun Belt. The new patterns of growth and development were most striking in the South and West, where open space allowed for sprawling suburban-style expansion. Fueled by World War II defense spending, the postwar development of the southern and western cities accelerated as industry took advantage of

inexpensive land, unorganized labor, low taxes, and warm climates (now made livable through the new technology of air conditioning). Some of the most explosive growth occurred in Florida, Texas, and California—states that would become the industrial leaders of the emerging **Sun Belt** economy (Map 28.1). Between 1940 and 1970 Miami's metropolitan population increased by 79 percent with the addition of more than a million new residents, many of them older or retired. Texas cities, especially Houston and Dallas, grew as the petrochemical industry expanded rapidly after 1945. Spurred by massive defense spending, California grew the most rapidly, adding 2.6 million people in the 1940s and 3.1 million more in the 1950s. In 1970 California had about a tenth of the U.S. population, and in 1972 it replaced New York as the state with the largest number of electoral votes.

Business boosters in California and other Sun Belt states worked tirelessly to promote regional development. Local leaders lobbied for new defense installations and contracts, wooed scientific and artistic talent from the Northeast, and even purchased professional sports teams. In 1958 investors moved the Brooklyn Dodgers to Los Angeles and the New York Giants to San Francisco, allowing boosters to promote their towns as "big-league" cities. In subsequent decades, however, the success of Sun Belt cities raised new problems and challenges. Booming urban populations brought higher crime and poverty rates, making southern and western cities more like those in the Northeast. In the arid Southwest, increasing demands for water and energy

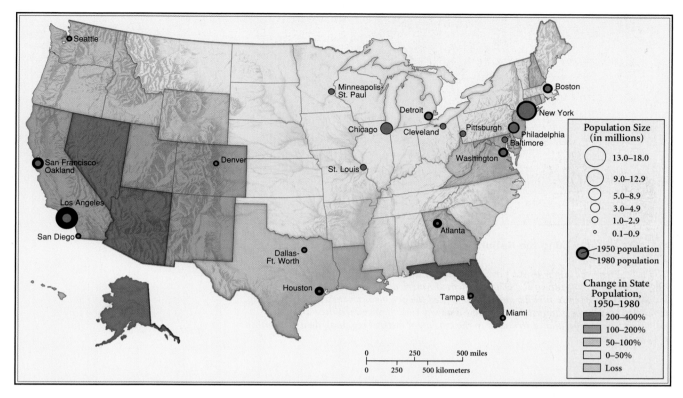

MAP 28.1 Metropolitan Growth, 1950–1980

A metropolitan area is generally defined as a central city that in combination with its surrounding territory forms an integrated economic and social unit. The U.S. Census Bureau introduced the Standard Metropolitan Statistical Area (SMSA) in 1950, but later changes in the definition of SMSA have made it difficult to generalize from the 1950 figures. This map compares the population of central cities in 1950 with population figures for the more broadly defined metropolitan areas in 1980 to illustrate the extent and geographical distribution of metropolitan growth in the postwar period.

resulted in environmental and health problems. As cities competed for scarce water resources, they depleted underground aquifers and dammed scenic rivers. The proliferation of coal-burning power plants increased air pollution and scarred rural landscapes through strip mining. The nuclear industry, which brought jobs and income to the West, also brought radiation contamination to residents near atomic test sites, nuclear waste facilities, and uranium mines. In the West, as elsewhere, postwar economic development often carried a significant social cost.

Cars and Highways. Automobiles were essential both to suburban growth and to the development of the Sun Belt states of the South and the West. Suburbanites throughout the country needed cars to get to work and to take their children to school and piano lessons (see Voices from Abroad, "Hanoch Bartov: Everyone Has a Car," p. 821). In 1945 Americans owned 25 million cars; by 1965 the number had tripled to 75 million. As the car

culture that first emerged in the 1920s expanded dramatically in the 1950s, cars—extravagant gas guzzlers with elaborate tail fins and ostentatious chrome detail—became symbols of status and success.

More cars required more highways, which were funded largely by the federal government. In 1947 Congress authorized the construction of 37,000 miles of highways; the National Interstate and Defense Highway Act of 1956 increased this commitment by another 42,500 miles (Map 28.2). One of the largest civil engineering projects in world history, the new interstate system would link the entire country with roads at least four lanes wide. The interstate system changed both the cities and the countryside. It rerouted traffic away from small towns and through rural areas, creating isolated pockets of gas stations, fast-food outlets, and motels along highway exits. In urban areas new highways cut wide swaths through old neighborhoods and caused air pollution and traffic jams; critics complained about "autosclerosis," a hardening of the urban arteries.

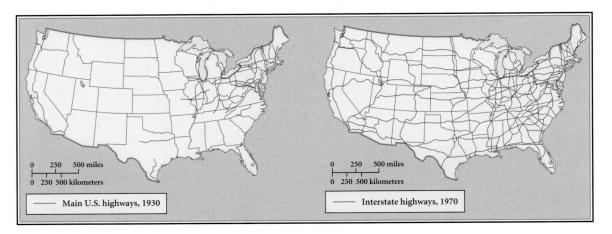

MAP 28.2 Connecting the Nation: The Interstate Highway System, 1930 and 1970

The 1956 Interstate Highway Act paved the way for an extensive network of federal highways throughout the nation. The act pleased American drivers and enhanced their love affair with the automobile, and also benefited the petroleum, construction, trucking, real estate, and tourist industries. The new highway system promoted the nation's economic integration and contributed to the erosion of distinct regional identities within the United States.

Highway construction had far-reaching effects on patterns of consumption and shopping. Instead of taking a train into the city or walking to a corner grocery store, people drove to suburban shopping malls and supermarkets. The first mall appeared in Kansas City in the 1920s, and there were still only eight in 1945; by 1960 the number mushroomed to almost 4,000. When a 110-store complex at Roosevelt Field on suburban Long Island opened in 1956, it was conveniently situated at an expressway exit and had parking for 11,000 cars. Downtown department stores and other retail outlets soon declined, helping to precipitate the decay of American central cities.

At the time few Americans understood that trade-offs were involved in the postwar economic boom. With a strong economic position internationally and government spending to help fuel expansion at home, Americans expected an unending trajectory of progress. Their faith led to complacency—an unwillingness to look beneath the surface for the hidden implications of the forces that were transforming America.

American Life during the Baby Boom

Hula Hoops and poodle skirts, sock hops and rock 'n' roll, and shiny cars and gleaming appliances—all signify the "fifties," a period that really stretched from 1945 through the early 1960s. The postwar years are remembered as a time of affluence and stability, a time when Americans enjoyed an optimistic faith in progress and technology and a serene family-centered culture, reflected in a booming birthrate known as the baby

boom and enshrined in television sitcoms such as *Father Knows Best*. This powerful myth, like many myths, has some truth to it, but there were other sides to the story. Focusing solely on affluence, popular culture, and consumption does not do justice to this complex period of economic and social transformation, which included challenges to the status quo as well as conformity.

Consumer Culture. The new prosperity of the 1950s was aided by a dramatic increase in consumer credit, which enabled families to stretch their incomes. Between 1946 and 1958 short-term consumer credit rose from $8.4 billion to almost $45 billion. The Diners Club introduced the first credit card in 1950, followed by the American Express card and Bank Americard in 1959. By the 1970s the omnipresent plastic credit card had revolutionized personal and family finances.

Aggressive advertising contributed to the massive increase in consumer spending. In 1951 businesses spent more on advertising ($6.5 billion) than taxpayers did on primary and secondary education ($5 billion). The 1950s gave Americans the Marlboro man; M&Ms that "melt in your mouth, not in your hand"; Wonder Bread to "build strong bodies in twelve ways"; and the "Does she or doesn't she?" Clairol woman.

Consumers had more free time in which to spend their money than ever before. In 1960 the average worker put in a five-day week, with eight paid holidays a year (double the 1946 standard) plus a two-week paid vacation. Americans took to the interstate highway system by the millions, encouraging dramatic growth in motel chains, roadside restaurants, and fast-food eateries.

Hanoch Bartov

Everyone Has a Car

O*ne of Israel's foremost writers and journalists, Hanoch Bartov spent two years in the United States working as a correspondent for the newspaper Lamerchav. As a newcomer to Los Angeles in the early 1960s, he was both fascinated and appalled by Americans' love affair with the automobile.*

Our immediate decision to buy a car sprang from healthy instincts. Only later did I learn from bitter experience that in California, death was preferable to living without one. Neither the views from the plane nor the weird excursion that first evening hinted at what I would go through that first week.

Very simple—the nearest supermarket was about half a kilometer south of our apartment, the regional primary school two kilometers east, and my son's kindergarten even farther away. A trip to the post office—an undertaking, to the bank—an ordeal, to work—an impossibility.

Truth be told: the Los Angeles municipality . . . does have public transportation.

Buses go once an hour along the city's boulevards and avenues, gathering all the wretched of the earth, the poor and the needy, the old ladies forbidden by their grandchildren to drive, and other eccentric types. But few people can depend on buses, even should they swear never to deviate from the fixed routes. . . . There are no tramways. No one thought of a subway. Railroads—not now and not in the future.

Why? Because everyone has a car. A man invited me to his house, saying, "We are neighbors, within ten minutes of each other." After walking for an hour and a half

I realized what he meant—"ten minute drive within the speed limit." Simply put, he never thought I might interpret his remark to refer to the walking distance. The moment a baby sees the light of day in Los Angeles, a car is registered in his name in Detroit. . . .

At first perhaps people relished the freedom and independence a car provided. You get in, sit down, and grab the steering wheel, your mobility exceeding that of any other generation. No wonder people refuse to live downtown, where they can hear their neighbors, smell their cooking, and suffer frayed nerves as trains pass by bedroom windows. Instead, they get a piece of the desert, far from town, at half price, drag a water hose, grow grass, flowers, and trees, and build their dream house. . . .

The result? A widely scattered city, its houses far apart, its streets stretched in all directions. Olympic Boulevard from west to east, forty kilometers. Sepulveda Boulevard, from Long Beach in the south to the edge of the desert, forty kilometers. Altogether covering 1,200 square kilometers. As of now.

Why "as of now"? Because greater distances mean more commuting, and more commuting leads to more cars. More cars means problems that push people even farther away from the city, which chases after them.

The urban sprawl is only one side effect. Two, some say three, million cars require an array of services. . . .

. . . Why bother parking, getting out, getting in, getting up and sitting down, when you can simply "drive in"? Mailboxes have their slots facing the road, at the level of the driver's hand. That is how dirty laundry is deposited, electricity and water bills paid. That is how love is made, how children are taken to school. That is how the anniversary wreath is laid on the graves of loved ones. There are drive-in movies. And, yes, we saw it with our own eyes: drive-in churches. Only in death is a man separated from his car and buried alone. . . .

Source: Oscar and Lilian Handlin, eds., *From the Outer World* (Cambridge, MA: Harvard University Press, 1997), 293–96.

(The first McDonald's restaurant opened in 1954 in San Bernardino, California; the Holiday Inn motel chain started in Memphis in 1952.) Among the most popular destinations were state and national parks and Disneyland, which opened in Anaheim, California, in 1955.

Television. Perhaps the most significant hallmark of postwar consumer culture was television. Television's leap

to cultural prominence was swift and overpowering. There were only ten broadcasting stations in the country and a meager 7,000 sets in American homes in 1947. By 1960, 87 percent of American families had at least one television set. Soon television supplanted radio as the chief diffuser of popular culture, its national programming promoting shared interests and tastes and reducing regional and ethnic differences.

Advertising in the TV Age

Aggressive advertising and the development of new products, such as the color television, helped fuel the surge in consumer spending during the 1950s. Both marketing experts and social commentators emphasized the role of television in promoting family togetherness, while interior designers offered decorating tips that placed the television at the focal point of living rooms and the increasingly popular "family rooms." Here, the family watches a variety program starring singer Dinah Shore, who was the television spokeswoman for Chevrolet cars, yet another example of the burgeoning consumer market of the period.
Gaslight Advertising Archives.

What Americans saw on television, besides the omnipresent commercials, was an overwhelmingly white, middle-class world of nuclear families living in suburban homes. *Leave It to Beaver, Ozzie and Harriet,* and similar sitcoms featured characters who adhered to clear-cut gender roles and plots based on minor family crises that were always happily resolved by the end of the show. Programs such as *The Honeymooners,* starring Jackie Gleason as a Brooklyn bus driver, and *Life of Reilly,* a situation comedy featuring a California aircraft worker, were rare in their treatment of working-class lives. Nonwhite characters appeared mainly as servants, such as comedian Jack Benny's black "houseboy" Rochester or the Latino gardener with the anglicized name "Frank Smith" on *Father Knows Best.* Although

the new medium did offer some serious programming, notably live theater and documentaries, Federal Communications Commissioner Newton Minow concluded in 1963 that television was "a vast wasteland." Its reassuring images of family life and postwar society, however, dovetailed with the social expectations of many Americans.

Religion and the Search for Security. The dislocations of the depression and war years made Americans yearn for security and a reaffirmation of traditional values. Some of this sentiment was expressed in a renewed emphasis on religion. Church membership rose from 49 percent of the population in 1940 to 69 percent in 1960. All the major denominations shared in the growth, which was accompanied by an ecumenical movement to bring Catholics, Protestants, and Jews together. The stress on religion meshed with cold war Americans' view of themselves as a righteous people opposed to "godless communism." In 1954 the phrase "under God" was inserted into the Pledge of Allegiance, and in 1956 Congress added "In God We Trust" to all U.S. coins.

Beyond patriotism, religion also served more deeply felt needs. In his popular television program, Bishop Fulton Sheen asked, "Is life worth living?" He and countless others optimistically answered in the affirmative. None was more positive than Norman Vincent Peale, whose best-selling book *The Power of Positive Thinking* (1952) embodied the trend toward the therapeutic use of religion to assist men and women in coping with the stresses of modern life. Evangelical religion also experienced a resurgence, most evident in the dramatic rise to popularity of the Reverend Billy Graham, who used television, radio, advertising, and print media to spread the gospel. Although critics suggested that middle-class interest in religion stemmed not so much from a renewed spirituality as from a surging impulse toward conformity, the revival nonetheless spoke to Americans' search for spiritual meaning in uncertain times.

The Baby Boom. Even more dramatic testimony to the desire for stability in the postwar era was the emphasis Americans placed on the family and children. As one popular advice book put it, "The family is the center of your living. If it isn't, you've gone far astray." Family demographics between 1940 and 1960 moved notably away from depression and war trends. Marriages were remarkably stable; not until the mid-1960s did the divorce rate begin to rise sharply. But the average age at marriage fell during the period, to twenty-two for men and twenty for women. In 1951 a third of all women were married by age nineteen. More important, the drop in the average age at marriage resulted in a surge of young married couples who produced a bumper crop of

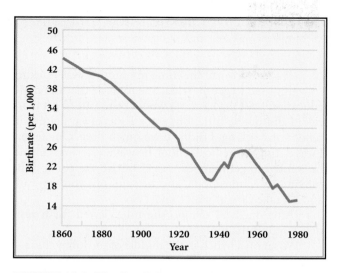

FIGURE 28.3 The Declining American Birthrate, 1860–1980

When birthrates are viewed over more than a century, the postwar baby boom is clearly an aberration.

children. After a century and a half of declining family size, the birthrate shot up and peaked in 1957: more babies were born between 1948 and 1953 than had been born in the previous thirty years (Figure 28.3). As a result of this trend and a lengthened life expectancy because of improvements in diet, public health, and medicine, the American population rose dramatically from 140 million in 1945 to 179 million in 1960, and to 203 million in 1970.

The baby boom had a broad and immediate impact on American society. It prompted a major expansion of the nation's educational system: by 1970 school expenditures were double those of the 1950 level. In addition, babies' consumer needs fueled the economy as families bought food, diapers, toys, and clothing for their expanding broods. Together with federal expenditures on national security, family spending on consumer goods fueled the unparalleled prosperity and economic growth of the 1950s and 1960s.

Contradictions in Women's Lives. The parents of baby boomers experienced multiple economic and social pressures. In addition to providing for their children materially and emotionally, they were expected to adhere to rigid gender roles as a way of maintaining the family and undergirding the social order. The mass media, educators, and experts urged men to conform to a masculine ideal that emphasized their role as responsible breadwinners. Women's proper place, they advised, was in the home. Endorsing what Betty Friedan has called the "**feminine mystique**" of the 1950s—the ideal that "the highest value and the only commitment for women is the fulfillment of their own femininity"— many psychologists pronounced motherhood the only "normal" female gender role and berated mothers who worked outside the home, charging that they damaged their children's development.

Though the power of these ideas stunted the lives of many women, not all housewives were unhappy or neurotic, as Friedan would later charge in her 1963 best-seller, *The Feminine Mystique*. Many working-class women embraced their new roles as housewives; unlike their mothers and unmarried sisters, they were not compelled to take low-paid employment outside the home. But not all Americans could or did live by the

A Woman's Dilemma in Postwar America

This 1959 cover of the Saturday Evening Post *depicts some of the difficult choices facing women in the postwar era. Women's consignment to low-paid, dead-end jobs in the service sector encouraged many to become full-time homemakers. Once back in their suburban homes, however, many middle-class women felt isolated and trapped amid endless rounds of cooking, cleaning, and diaper changing.*

A Woman Encounters the Feminine Mystique

The power of the feminine mystique in the 1950s made it difficult for middle-class women who challenged the view that women's proper place was in the home. In this oral history account, "Sylvia" describes her struggle to pursue a career as an ophthalmologist. She began her medical training in nursing, even though she knew when she entered college at Adelphi University that she wanted to become a doctor.

My mother's notion was, "You don't know anything about being a doctor. Become a nurse first and then if you like it, become a doctor." This dean [at Adelphi] said to me, "Well, what do you want to be, a doctor or a nurse?" What came out of my mouth was, "I want to be a nurse." To this day I'm not sure why. In a way I was trying to be practical. We didn't have that much money and I thought I could pay for medical school with a profession. You know, what women earned in those days was pathetic. One of my classmates worked in a bank and made two hundred to three hundred dollars a month. I had no artistic talent and I didn't like teaching, that was the other women's profession. What else was there? And then, I thought, what if I didn't get accepted into medical school?

[She worked for four years as a nurse. Here she describes her first, unsuccessful interview for medical school.] I'd traveled all day to get there, and I was anxious and it was a rigorous interview. At the end of the interview, that man said to me, "You know, I don't know if I could ever recommend accepting a woman here. She'd have to be better than the best man . . . and even then, I'm not sure." This was in 1957. You don't forget things like that.

. . . Of course, all this time my mother was hocking [nagging] me to get married. She told me that the more education I got the harder it would be for me to get married. I did date a little, but since I was always either in school or working, I didn't have much time. One fellow I was dating in medical school, he was a veterinarian and he wanted to get married. I said, but you're going to be moving to Minneapolis, and he said, oh, you can quit and I'll take care of you. I said, "Go."

[After medical school, she interviewed for a residency in ophthalmology.]

We sat on a bench in the middle of the lobby there— I remember it looked like a train station—and he [her professor] said, "Do you plan to get pregnant or married?" I promised him I wouldn't do either. I felt like I was about ten years old. They gave me a year's trial in the research department and after that I could get a residency. Most people there, the men, had a three-year residency. I was only the second woman they'd ever accepted, and I was the only woman out of twenty men.

I had a fellowship, so when I finished with my work I'd have to go over to see how my research projects were coming along. I never, never, goofed off. These guys were watching me all the time and complaining that I wasn't doing my work. It was hard enough to be a first-year resident, where you're the bottom person who gets kicked by everybody. I had no friends. My fellow physicians were constantly telling me I should switch to obstetrics or pediatrics, I should be home having babies, that a man could earn a wonderful living for his family in my place. Finally I was at my wits' end and I called my old ophthalmology professor and told him I didn't know if I could psychologically take this for another two and a half years. He said, "You know, if you give up now I'll never be able to get another woman in there." So I went on.

Source: Brett Harvey, *The Fifties: A Women's Oral History* (New York: Harper, 1993), 154–55.

norms of suburban domesticity, ideals that were out of reach of or irrelevant to many racial minorities, inner-city residents, recent immigrants, rural Americans, and homosexuals. At the height of the postwar period, more than one-third of American women held jobs outside the home (see American Voices, "A Woman Encounters the Feminine Mystique," above). The increase in the number of working women coincided with another change of equal significance—a dramatic rise in the number of older, married middle-class women who took jobs.

How could the society of the 1950s cling so steadfastly to the domestic ideal while an increasing number of wives and mothers worked? Often women justified their jobs as an extension of their family responsibilities, enabling their families to enjoy more of the fruits of the consumer culture. Working women also still bore full responsibility for child care and household management, allowing families and society to avoid facing the implications of their new roles. Thus the reality of women's lives departed significantly from the cultural stereotypes glorified in advertising, sitcoms, and women's magazines.

Youth Culture. Beneath the surface of family togetherness lay other tensions—those between parents and children. Dating back to the 1920s, the emergence of a mass youth culture had its roots in the democratization of education and the increasing purchasing power of teenagers in an age of affluence. Youth, eager to escape the climate of suburban conformity of their parents, had become a distinct new market that advertisers eagerly exploited. In 1956 advertisers projected an adolescent market of $9 billion for items such as transistor radios (introduced in 1952), clothing, and fads such as Hula Hoops (1958).

What really defined this generation's youth culture, however, was its music. Rejecting the rigid boundaries of traditional popular music, teenagers in the 1950s discovered **rock 'n' roll**, an amalgam of white country and western music and the black urban music known as rhythm and blues. The Cleveland disc jockey Alan Freed played a major role in introducing white America to the new African American sound by playing rhythm and blues records on white radio stations beginning in 1954. Young white performers such as Bill Haley, Buddy Holly, and especially Elvis Presley incorporated the new mixture into their own music and capitalized on the new youth market. Between 1953 and 1959 record sales increased from $213 million to $603 million, with 45-rpm rock 'n' roll records as the driving force (see American Lives, "Elvis Presley: Teen Idol of the 1950s," p. 826). The new teen music shocked many white adults, who saw rock 'n' roll as an invitation to race-mixing, sexual promiscuity, and juvenile delinquency.

Cultural Dissenters. The youth rebellion was only one aspect of a broader undercurrent of discontent with the conformist culture of the 1950s. In major cities across the nation, gay men and women, many of whom had served in the military during World War II, fought back against homophobic laws and personal attacks. In Los Angeles homosexual men founded the Mattachine Society, a gay rights organization, in 1951, and in 1954 lesbians established the Daughters of Bilitis. While for the most part the gay subculture remained closeted, this did not stop gay baiting or local police raids on gay bars. And because homosexuals were viewed as emotionally unstable or vulnerable to blackmail, they were assumed to be security risks. As a result of publicity attached to raids, as well as government investigations, many gays lost their jobs, a testament to the perceived threat they represented to mainstream sexual and cultural norms.

Postwar artists, musicians, and writers expressed their alienation from mainstream society through intensely personal, introspective art forms. In New York Jackson Pollock and other painters rejected the social realism of the 1930s for an unconventional style that became known as abstract expressionism. Swirling and splattering paint onto giant canvases, Pollock emphasized self-expression in the act of painting, capturing the chaotic atmosphere of the nuclear age.

A similar trend developed in jazz, as black musicians originated a hard-driving improvisational style known as "bebop." Black jazz musicians found eager fans not only in the African American community but among young white Beats in New York and San Francisco. Disdaining middle-class conformity, corporate capitalism, and suburban materialism, the Beats were a group of writers and poets who were both literary innovators and outspoken social critics. In his poem "Howl" (1956), which became a manifesto of the Beat generation, Allen Ginsberg lamented: "I saw the best minds of my generation destroyed by madness, starving hysterical naked, dragging themselves through the angry negro streets at dawn looking for an angry fix." In works such as Jack Kerouac's novel *On the Road* (1957) the Beats glorified spontaneity, sexual adventurism, drug use, and spirituality. Although they were most often apolitical—their rebellion was strictly cultural—in the 1960s they inspired a new generation of rebels who would champion both political and cultural change.

The Other America

As middle-class whites flocked to the suburbs, a diverse group of poor and working-class migrants, many of them nonwhite, moved into the central cities. With jobs and financial resources flowing to the suburbs, urban newcomers inherited a declining economy and a decaying environment. To those enjoying new prosperity, "the Other America"—as the social critic Michael Harrington called it in 1962—remained largely invisible.

Migration to Cities

Newly arrived immigrants were one of several groups moving into the nation's cities in the postwar era. Although until 1965 U.S. immigration policy followed the restrictive national origins quota system set up in 1924 (see Chapter 23), Congress modified the law during and after World War II. The War Brides Act of 1945, permitting the entry and naturalization of the wives and children of Americans living abroad (mainly servicemen), brought thousands of new immigrants between 1950 and 1965, including some 17,000 Koreans. Three years later the Displaced Persons Act admitted approximately 415,000 European refugees. The repeal of the Chinese Exclusion Act in 1943, in deference to America's wartime alliance with China, and the passage of the

Elvis Presley: Teen Idol of the 1950s

When Elvis Presley performed on *The Ed Sullivan Show* in 1956, the television cameras zoomed in on his head and shoulders. The closeups were inspired not by the young singer's good looks but by a desire to conceal his lower body. After several scandalous TV appearances earlier that season, CBS decided that Presley's sexually suggestive bumping and grinding were unsuitable for family viewing. Despite the censorship, Presley's performance was an unprecedented success, claiming over 80 percent of the television audience. His records sold 10 million copies that year alone and would account for a quarter of RCA's record sales over the next decade. More than any other recording artist of the 1950s, Presley popularized the new hybrid music known as "rock 'n' roll."

Born in East Tupelo, Mississippi, in 1935, Elvis Aron Presley grew up in a white working-class family that keenly felt the hardships of the Great Depression. Like many poor southerners, the Presleys moved frequently in search of work as laborers and mill hands. When Elvis was thirteen, his father found a job at a paint factory in Memphis, and the Presleys settled in one of that city's new public-housing projects.

Elvis's earliest exposure to music came through gospel singing at the Pentecostal First Assembly of God Church, where his uncle was pastor. Later, when his family lived in or adjacent to the black districts of Tupelo and Memphis (as the South's poorest whites often did), Elvis gravitated toward local churches, bars, and clubs, where he gained a lifelong love of blues, gospel, and other black music.

Local radio was an equally powerful force in his musical education. In the late 1940s commercial radio offered a diverse selection of musical programming, catering to the growing audience of rural migrants who had been moving to southern cities since World War II. Although there had always been significant cross-fertilization between white and black musical styles, industry promoters maintained an artificial distinction between "hillbilly" and "race" music. After World War II, those derogatory labels gave way to the more respectable labels "country and western" and "rhythm and blues," but the programming remained rigidly segregated.

Young white southerners like Presley listened to both types of programs. They admired the traditional vocal styles and guitar picking they heard on *The Grand Ole Opry* and other country shows, and they developed a keen appreciation for the blues progressions and driving rhythms of black music. White youngsters' growing fascination with rhythm and blues was not generally acknowledged and was considered somewhat scandalous. But a small group of disc jockeys and record promoters spotted the potential of the new market. As Memphis record producer Sam Phillips once said, "If I could find a white man who had the Negro sound and the Negro feel, I could make a billion dollars."

Phillips found that man in Elvis Presley. In 1953 nineteen-year-old Presley was working as a truck driver and occasionally stopped by Phillips's Sun Studios to make sample recordings for his friends and family. Phillips remembered his unusual vocal style and later asked him to cut a record with a local band. The result was an eclectic mix of musical styles: on one side a white version of a black blues song, "That's All Right," on the other side a black-influenced interpretation of a bluegrass number, "Blue Moon of Kentucky." The record was an overnight local sensation and launched Presley into a national recording career the following year. Over the next decade he produced dozens of hits for RCA, including "Hound Dog," "Heartbreak Hotel," "Jailhouse Rock," and "Blue Suede Shoes."

Presley's success was based not only on his music but also on his stage presence and his relationship with the audience. With his slicked-back hair, long sideburns, and tight pants, Presley cultivated a lower-class "greaser" look that proved immensely popular with teenage fans. His quivering legs, gyrating pelvis, and playful sneer drove young female fans wild; they frequently mobbed the stage, grabbing at his clothes for souvenirs. Many adults, however, condemned such antics, associating them with juvenile delinquency, sexual immorality, and race-mixing. After his first television appearance, one critic described Presley's performance as "suggestive and vulgar, tinged with the kind of animalism that should be

Elvis Presley
The young Elvis Presley, shown here on the cover of his first album in 1956, embodied cultural rebellion against the conservatism and triviality of adult life in the 1950s.
© 1956 BGM Music.

confined to dives and bordellos," and another critic called it "a strip-tease with clothes on." To many adults rock 'n' roll seemed an invitation to rebellion by the younger generation.

African Americans found Presley's success and notoriety somewhat ironic. Chuck Berry and other black musicians had been performing such music for years—but with little commercial success among white audiences. Many of them viewed the appropriation of black rhythm and blues by white artists as out-and-out theft. In the long run, however, the popularity of rock 'n' roll introduced black performers such as Little Richard, Fats Domino, and James Brown to white as well as black audiences.

Presley's musical popularity declined with his induction into the army in 1958 (the long arm of the state reached even the most popular stars). Afterward he headed for Hollywood, acting and singing in dozens of mostly mediocre teen-oriented movies. He enjoyed a comeback starting in 1968, but his career was hampered by personal problems. In 1977 he died of an accidental drug overdose. Since then he has become a cult figure, spawning hundreds of books and articles and a spate of Elvis impersonators. Graceland, his ornate home in Memphis, attracts more visitors per year than does George Washington's estate at Mount Vernon.

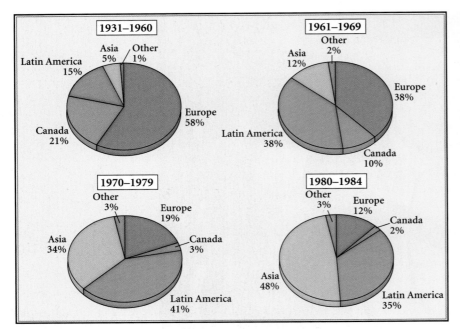

FIGURE 28.4 Legal Immigration to the United States by Region, 1931–1984

As immigration law shifted in the postwar era, the sources of immigration to the United States shifted from Europe to Latin America and Asia.

Source: Robert W. Gardner, Bryant Robie, and Peter C. Smith, "Asian Americans: Growth, Change, and Diversity," *Population Bulletin*, vol. 40, no. 4 (Washington, DC: Population Reference Bureau, 1985), 2.

McCarran-Walter Act in 1952 ended the exclusion of Chinese, Japanese, Korean, and Southeast Asian immigrants. Finally, in recognition of the freeing of the Philippines from American control in 1946, Filipinos received their own quota (Figure 28.4).

Latino Immigration. One of the largest groups of postwar migrants came from Mexico. Nearly 275,000 Mexicans came in the 1950s and almost 444,000 in the 1960s. They moved primarily to western and southwestern cities such as Los Angeles, El Paso, and Phoenix, where they found jobs as migrant workers or in the expanding service sector. Before World War II most Mexican Americans had lived in rural areas and engaged in agricultural work; by 1960 a majority were living in urban areas where they joined more settled communities of service and manufacturing workers.

Part of the stimulus for Mexican immigration was the reinstitution of the bracero program from 1951 to 1964. Originally devised as a means of importing temporary labor during World War II, the program brought 450,000 Mexican workers to the United States at its peak in 1959. But even as the federal government welcomed braceros, it deported those who stayed on illegally. In response to the recession of 1953 to 1954 and the resulting high rate of unemployment throughout the nation, federal authorities deported nearly 4 million Mexicans in a program called "Operation Wetback." The deportations discouraged illegal immigration for a few years, but the level increased again after the bracero program ended.

Another group of Spanish-speaking migrants came from the American-controlled territory of Puerto Rico. Residents of that island had been American citizens since 1917, so their migration was not subject to immigration laws. The inflow from the territory increased dramatically after World War II, when mechanization of the island's sugarcane industry pushed many rural Puerto Ricans off the land. When airlines began to offer cheap direct flights between San Juan and New York City (in the 1940s the fare was about $50, or two weeks' wages), Puerto Ricans—most of whom settled in New York—became this country's first group to immigrate by air.

Cuban refugees constituted the third large group of Spanish-speaking immigrants. In the six years after Communist Fidel Castro's overthrow of the Batista dictatorship in 1959, an estimated 180,000 people fled Cuba for the United States. The Cuban refugee community grew so quickly that it turned Miami into a cosmopolitan, bilingual city almost overnight. Unlike most new immigrants, Miami's Cubans prospered, in large part because they had arrived with more resources.

Internal Migration. Internal migration from rural areas also brought large numbers of people to the cities, especially African Americans, continuing a trend that had begun during World War I (see Chapter 22). Although both whites and blacks left the land, the starkest decline was among black farmers. Their migration was hastened by the transformation of southern agriculture, especially by the introduction of innovations like the mechanical cotton picker, which significantly reduced the demand for farm labor.

Some of the migrants settled in southern cities, where they found industrial jobs. White southerners from Appalachia moved north to "hillbilly" ghettos such as Cincinnati's Over the Rhine neighborhood and Chicago's

Uptown. As many as 3 million blacks headed to Chicago, New York, Washington, Detroit, Los Angeles, and other cities between 1940 and 1960. So pervasive were the migrants that certain sections of Chicago seemed like the Mississippi Delta transplanted. By 1960 about half of the nation's black population was living outside the South, compared with only 23 percent before World War II.

In western cities an influx of Native Americans also contributed to the rise in the nonwhite urban population. Seeking to end federal responsibility for Indian affairs, Congress in 1953 authorized a "termination" program aimed at liquidating the reservation system and integrating Native Americans into mainstream society. The program, which reflected a cold war preoccupation with conformity and assimilation, enjoyed strong support from mining, timber, and agricultural interests that wanted to open reservation lands for private development. The Bureau of Indian Affairs encouraged voluntary relocation to urban areas with a program subsidizing moving costs and establishing relocation centers in San Francisco, Denver, Chicago, and other cities. The relocation program proved problematic, however, as many Native Americans found it difficult to adjust to an urban environment and culture. Although forced termination was halted in 1958, by 1960 some 60,000 Native Americans had moved to the cities. Despite the program's stated goal of assimilation, most Native American migrants settled together in poor urban neighborhoods alongside other nonwhite groups.

The Urban Crisis

American cities thus saw their nonwhite populations swell at the same time that whites were flocking to the suburbs. From 1950 to 1960 the nation's twelve largest cities lost 3.6 million whites and gained 4.5 million nonwhites. As affluent whites left the cities, urban tax revenues shrank, leading to the decay of services and infrastructure, which, coupled with growing racial fears, accelerated white suburban flight in the 1960s.

By the time that blacks, Latinos, and Native Americans moved into the inner cities, urban America was in poor shape. Housing continued to be a crucial problem. City planners, politicians, and real estate developers responded with urban renewal programs, razing blighted city neighborhoods to make way for modern construction projects. Local residents were rarely consulted about whether they wanted their neighborhoods "renewed," and redevelopment programs often produced grim high-rise housing projects that destroyed community bonds and created anonymous open areas that were vulnerable to crime. Between 1949 and 1967 **urban renewal** demolished almost 400,000 buildings and displaced 1.4 million people.

Postwar urban areas were increasingly becoming places of last resort for the nation's poor. Lured to the

Harlem in the Fifties

During and after World War II, thousands of African Americans left the rural South for northern and western cities, expanding the population of Harlem and other black neighborhoods. Ironically, the migrants arrived just as declining employment, deteriorating housing, and shrinking tax revenues were making life more difficult for inner-city residents. Henry Hammond.

cities by the promise of plentiful jobs, migrants found that many of those opportunities had relocated to the suburban fringe, putting steady employment out of reach for those who needed it most. Migrants to the city, especially blacks, also faced racial hostility and institutional barriers to mobility—biased school funding, hiring and promotion decisions, and credit practices. Two separate Americas were emerging: a largely white society in suburbs and peripheral areas and an inner city populated by blacks, Latinos, and other disadvantaged groups.

The stereotypes of boundless affluence and contentment in the 1950s—of "Happy Days"—are thus misleading, for they hide those persons who did not share equally in the American dream—displaced factory workers, destitute old people, female heads of households, blacks and other racial minority groups. In the turbulent decade to come, the contrast between suburban affluence and the "other America," between the lure of the city for the poor and minorities and its grim, segregated reality, and between a heightened emphasis on domesticity and the widening opportunities for women

The Other America
While many celebrated the "affluent society" of the postwar era, critics like Michael Harrington noted that thousands of Americans remained in poverty. Among them were many elderly people who struggled to survive on fixed incomes and without medical insurance. Cincinnati Historical Society.

second Amendment prevented them from doing so. Passed in 1951 by a Republican-controlled Congress to prevent a repetition of Franklin Roosevelt's four-term presidency, the amendment limited future presidents to two full terms. So in 1960 the Republicans turned to Vice President Richard M. Nixon, who campaigned for an updated version of Eisenhower's policies but was hampered by lukewarm support from the popular president.

The Democrats chose Senator John F. Kennedy of Massachusetts, with the Senate majority leader, Lyndon B. Johnson of Texas, as the vice presidential nominee. First elected to Congress in 1946, John Kennedy moved to the Senate in 1952. Ambitious and hard driven, Kennedy launched his campaign in 1960 with a platform calling for civil rights legislation, health care for the elderly, aid to education, urban renewal, expanded military and space programs, and containment of communism abroad.

At forty-three Kennedy was poised to become the youngest man ever elected to the presidency and the nation's first Catholic chief executive. Turning his age into a powerful campaign asset, Kennedy practiced what came to be called the "**new politics**," an approach that emphasized youthful charisma, style, and personality more than issues and platforms. Using the power of the media—particularly television—to reach voters directly, practitioners of the new politics relied on professional media consultants, political pollsters, and mass fund-raising.

A series of four televised debates between the two principal candidates, a major innovation of the 1960 campaign, showed how important television was becoming to political life. Nixon, far less photogenic than

would spawn growing demands for social change that the nation's leaders in the 1960s could not ignore.

John F. Kennedy and the Politics of Expectation

In his 1961 inaugural address President John Fitzgerald Kennedy challenged a "new generation of Americans" to take responsibility for the future: "Ask not what your country can do for you, ask what you can do for your country." Few presidents came to Washington more primed for action than John F. Kennedy. His **New Frontier** program promised to "get America moving again" through vigorous governmental activism at home and abroad. But the legislative achievements of Kennedy's New Frontier, particularly in domestic affairs, were modest.

The New Politics

The Republicans would have been happy to renominate Dwight D. Eisenhower for president, but the Twenty-

The Kennedy Magnetism
John Kennedy, the Democratic candidate for president in 1960, used his youth and personality to attract voters. Here, the Massachusetts senator draws an enthusiastic crowd on a campaign stop in Elgin, Illinois. Wide World Photos, Inc.

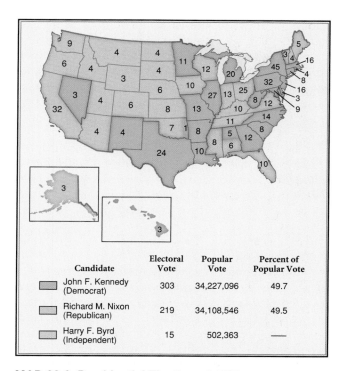

Candidate	Electoral Vote	Popular Vote	Percent of Popular Vote
John F. Kennedy (Democrat)	303	34,227,096	49.7
Richard M. Nixon (Republican)	219	34,108,546	49.5
Harry F. Byrd (Independent)	15	502,363	—

MAP 28.3 Presidential Election of 1960

The Kennedy-Nixon contest was the closest since 1884. Kennedy won twelve states, including Illinois, by less than 2 percent of the two-party vote tally; he lost six others, including California, by a similarly small margin. Fifteen electors cast their votes for the Independent Democrat, Harry F. Byrd. Despite his razor-thin margin of victory, Kennedy won 303 electoral votes, the same number Truman had won in 1948, showing that the electoral college vote can be a misleading indicator of popular support.

Kennedy, looked sallow and unshaven under the intense studio lights. Kennedy, in contrast, looked vigorous, cool, and self-confident on screen. Polls showed that television did sway political perceptions: voters who listened to the first debate on the radio concluded that Nixon had won, but those who viewed it on television judged in Kennedy's favor.

Despite the edge Kennedy enjoyed in the debates, he won only the narrowest of electoral victories, receiving 49.7 percent of the popular vote to Nixon's 49.5 percent (Map 28.3). Kennedy successfully appealed to the diverse elements of the Democratic coalition, attracting large numbers of Catholic and black voters and a significant sector of the middle class; the vice presidential nominee, Lyndon Johnson, brought in southern white Democrats. Yet only 120,000 votes separated the two candidates, and the shift of a few thousand votes in key states such as Illinois (where there were confirmed cases of voting fraud) would have reversed the outcome.

Activism Abroad

Kennedy's greatest priority as president was foreign affairs. A resolute cold warrior, Kennedy took a hard line against Communist expansionism. In contrast to Eisenhower, whose cost-saving New Look program had built up the American nuclear arsenal at the expense of conventional weapons, Kennedy proposed a new policy of "**flexible response**," stating that the nation must be prepared "to deter all wars, general or limited, nuclear or conventional, large or small." Congress quickly granted Kennedy's military requests, and by 1963 the defense budget reached its highest level as a percentage of total federal expenditures in the cold war era, greatly expanding the military-industrial complex.

Flexible response measures were designed to deter direct attacks by the Soviet Union. To prepare for a new kind of warfare, evident in the **wars of national liberation** that had broken out in many developing countries, Kennedy adopted a new military doctrine of **counterinsurgency**. Soon U.S. Army Special Forces, called "Green Berets" for their distinctive headgear, were receiving intensive training in repelling the random, small-scale

The Peace Corps

The Peace Corps, a New Frontier program initiated in 1961, attracted thousands of idealistic young Americans, including these volunteers who worked in a vaccination program in Bolivia. David S. Boyer / National Geographic Society Image Collection.

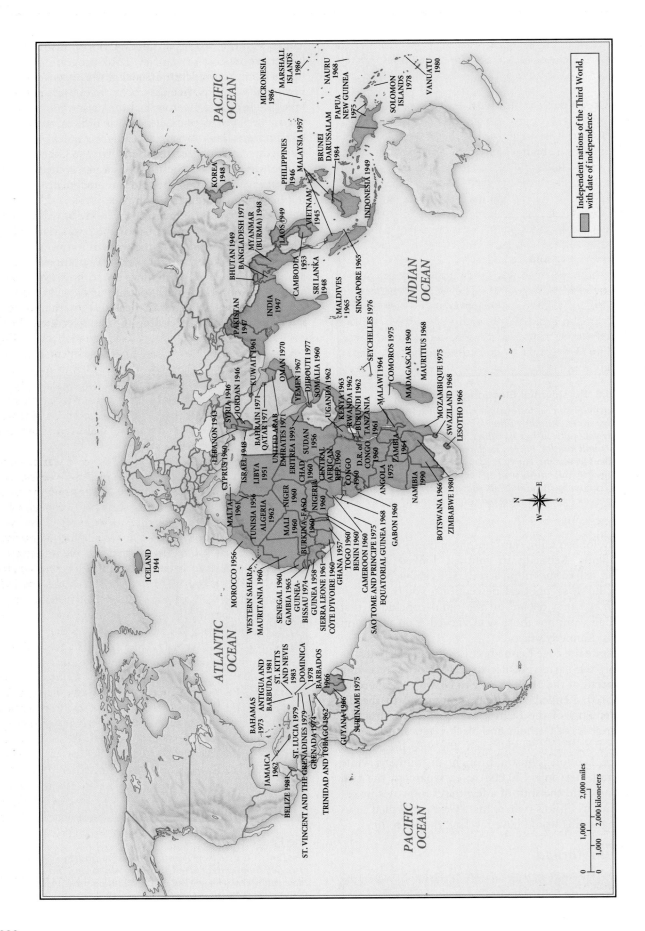

Independent nations of the Third World, with date of independence

PACIFIC OCEAN

ATLANTIC OCEAN

INDIAN OCEAN

PACIFIC OCEAN

ICELAND 1944

MOROCCO 1956
WESTERN SAHARA
MAURITANIA 1960
SENEGAL 1960
GAMBIA 1965
GUINEA-BISSAU 1974
GUINEA 1958
SIERRA LEONE 1961
COTE D'IVOIRE 1960
GHANA 1957
TOGO 1960
BENIN 1960
CAMEROON 1960
SAO TOME AND PRINCIPE 1975
EQUATORIAL GUINEA 1968
GABON 1960

MALTA 1961
TUNISIA 1956
ALGERIA 1962
MALI 1960
NIGER 1960
BURKINA-FASO 1960
NIGERIA 1960
LIBYA 1951

LEBANON 1943
SYRIA 1946
CYPRUS 1960
ISRAEL 1948
JORDAN 1946
KUWAIT 1961
BAHRAIN 1971
QATAR 1971
UNITED ARAB EMIRATES 1971
OMAN 1970
YEMEN 1967

CHAD 1960
SUDAN 1956
ERITREA 1993
CENTRAL AFRICAN REP. 1960
CONGO 1960
D.R. of CONGO 1960
ANGOLA 1975
NAMIBIA 1990
BOTSWANA 1966
ZIMBABWE 1980

UGANDA 1962
KENYA 1963
RWANDA 1962
BURUNDI 1962
TANZANIA 1961
ZAMBIA 1964
MALAWI 1964
SOMALIA 1960
DJIBOUTI 1977
SEYCHELLES 1976
COMOROS 1975
MADAGASCAR 1960
MAURITIUS 1968
MOZAMBIQUE 1975
SWAZILAND 1968
LESOTHO 1966

PAKISTAN 1947
INDIA 1947
BHUTAN 1949
BANGLADESH 1971
MYANMAR (BURMA) 1948
LAOS 1949
CAMBODIA 1953
VIETNAM 1945
SRI LANKA 1948
MALDIVES 1965
SINGAPORE 1965
KOREA 1948

PHILIPPINES 1946
MALAYSIA 1957
BRUNEI DARUSSALAM 1984
INDONESIA 1949

MICRONESIA 1986
MARSHALL ISLANDS 1986
NAURU 1968
PAPUA NEW GUINEA 1975
SOLOMON ISLANDS 1978
VANUATU 1980

BAHAMAS 1973
JAMAICA 1962
BELIZE 1981
ST. VINCENT AND THE GRENADINES 1979
ST. LUCIA 1979
GRENADA 1974
TRINIDAD AND TOBAGO 1962
ANTIGUA AND BARBUDA 1981
ST. KITTS AND NEVIS 1983
DOMINICA 1978
BARBADOS 1966
GUYANA 1966
SURINAME 1975

N
E
S
W

0   1,000   2,000 miles
0   1,000   2,000 kilometers

attacks typical of guerrilla warfare. Vietnam would soon provide a testing ground for counterinsurgency techniques (see Chapter 29).

Peace Corps and Foreign Aid.   Another of Kennedy's projects, the Peace Corps, established in 1961, embodied the commitment to public service that the president had called for in his inaugural address. Thousands of men and women agreed to devote two or more years to programs that had them teaching English to Filipino schoolchildren or helping African villagers obtain adequate supplies of water. Embodying the idealism of the early 1960s, the Peace Corps was also a cold war weapon intended to bring developing countries into the American orbit and away from Communist influence.

For the same reason Kennedy pushed for economic aid to developing countries. The State Department's Agency for International Development coordinated foreign aid for the Third World, including surplus agricultural products distributed to developing nations through its Food for Peace program. In Latin America the Alliance for Progress provided funds for food, education, medicine, and other services, although it did little to enhance economic growth or improve social conditions there (Map 28.4).

Crises in Cuba.   Latin America was the site of Kennedy's first major foreign-policy initiative and one of his biggest failures—an effort to overthrow the new Soviet-supported regime in Cuba. The United States had long exercised nearly total economic and political dominance of the island. But on New Year's Day in 1959, the revolutionary Fidel Castro overthrew the corrupt and unpopular dictator Fulgencio Batista. When Castro began agrarian reforms and nationalized American-owned banks and industries, relations with Washington deteriorated. By early 1961 the United States had declared an embargo on all exports to Cuba, cut back on imports of Cuban sugar, and broken off diplomatic relations with Castro's regime.

Isolated by the United States, Cuba turned increasingly toward the Soviet Union for economic and military support. Concerned about Castro's growing friendliness with the Soviets, in early 1961 Kennedy used plans originally drawn up by the Eisenhower administration to dispatch Cuban exiles living in Nicaragua to foment an anti-Castro uprising. Although the invaders had been trained by the Central Intelligence Agency (CIA), they were ill prepared for their task and had little popular support. After landing at Cuba's Bay of Pigs on April 17, the tiny force of 1,400 men was crushed by Castro's troops (Map 28.5).

Already weakened by the Bay of Pigs invasion, U.S.-Soviet relations deteriorated further in June 1961 when Soviet Premier Khrushchev deployed soldiers to isolate Communist-controlled East Berlin from the western sector of the city controlled by West Germany. With congressional approval Kennedy responded by adding 300,000 troops to the armed forces and promptly dispatching 40,000 of them to Europe. In mid-August, to stop the exodus of East Germans to the West, the Soviets ordered construction of the Berlin Wall, and East German guards began policing the border. Until it was dismantled in 1989, the Berlin Wall remained the supreme symbol of the cold war.

The climactic confrontation of the cold war came in October 1962. After the failed Bay of Pigs invasion, the Kennedy administration increased economic pressure against Cuba and resumed covert efforts to overthrow the Castro regime. In response the Soviets stepped up military aid to Cuba, including the installation of nuclear missiles. In early October American reconnaissance planes photographed Soviet-built bases for intermediate-range ballistic missiles (IRBMs), which could reach U.S. targets as far as 2,200 miles away. Some of those weapons had already been installed, and more were on the way.

In a somber televised address on Monday, October 22, Kennedy confronted the Soviet Union and announced that the United States would impose a "quarantine on all offensive military equipment" intended for Cuba. As the two superpowers went on full military alert, people around the world feared that the confrontation would end in nuclear war. Americans living within range of the missiles restocked their bomb shelters or calculated the fastest route out of town. When Khrushchev denounced the quarantine, tension mounted. But as the world held its breath, ships carrying the Soviet-made missiles turned back. After a week of tense negotiations, both Kennedy and Khrushchev made concessions: Kennedy pledged not to invade Cuba, and Khrushchev promised to dismantle the missile bases.

Although the risk of nuclear war was greater during the Cuban missile crisis than it was at any other time in the postwar period, it led to a slight thaw in U.S.-Soviet

◀ **MAP 28.4 Decolonization and the Third World, 1943–1990**

Instigated by the upheaval of World War II and continuing for several decades, peoples throughout the globe challenged the long-standing colonial order and demanded independence. After 1945, movements for national self-determination swept across Africa, India, Southeast Asia, and other parts of the "third world," a cold war term designating countries not formally aligned with the United States ("first world") or the Soviet Union ("second world"). Courted with weapons and promises of aid by both the United States and the Soviet Union, many Third World nations like Vietnam and Angola became key battlegrounds of the cold war, often with disastrous results for the local populations.

For more help analyzing this map, see the ONLINE STUDY GUIDE at bedfordstmartins.com/henretta.

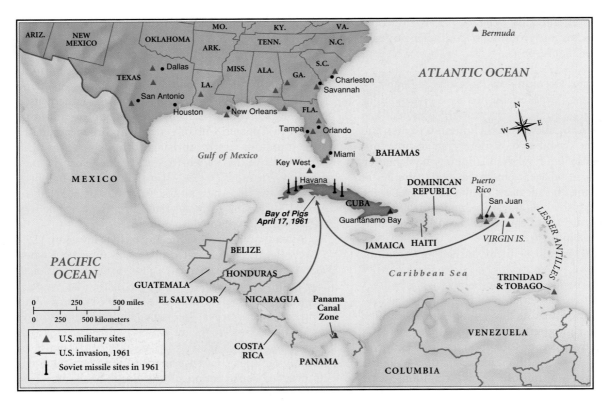

MAP 28.5 The United States and Cuba, 1961–1962
Fidel Castro's takeover in Cuba in 1959 brought cold war tensions to the Caribbean. In 1961 the United States tried unsuccessfully to overthrow Castro's regime by supporting the Bay of Pigs invasion of Cuban exiles launched from Nicaragua and other points in the Caribbean. In 1962 a major confrontation with the Soviet Union occurred over Soviet construction of nuclear missile sites in Cuba. The Soviets removed the missiles after President Kennedy ordered a naval blockade of the island, which lies just 90 miles south of Florida. Despite the fall of the Soviet Union in 1991 and the official end of the cold war, the United States continues to view Cuba, still governed in 2003 by Fidel Castro, as an enemy nation.

relations. In the words of national security advisor McGeorge Bundy, "having come so close to the edge, the leaders of the two governments have since taken care to keep away from the cliff." Kennedy softened his cold war rhetoric and began to strive for peaceful coexistence. Soviet leaders, similarly chastened, were willing to talk. In August 1963 the three nuclear powers—the United States, the Soviet Union, and Great Britain—agreed to ban the testing of nuclear weapons in the atmosphere, in space, and under water. Underground testing, however, was allowed to continue. The new emphasis on peaceful coexistence also led to the establishment of a Washington-Moscow telecommunications "hot line" in 1963 so that leaders could contact each other quickly during potential crises.

But no matter how often American leaders talked about opening channels of communication with the Soviets, the preoccupation with the Soviet military threat to American security remained a cornerstone of U.S. policy. And Soviet leaders did not moderate their concern over the threat that they believed the United States posed to the survival of the Soviet Union. The cold war, and the escalating arms race that accompanied it, would continue for another twenty-five years.

The New Frontier at Home

The expansive vision of presidential leadership that Kennedy and his advisors brought to the White House worked less well at home than it did abroad. Hampered by the lack of a popular mandate in the 1960 election, Kennedy could not mobilize public support for the domestic agenda of the New Frontier. A conservative coalition of southern Democrats and western and midwestern Republicans effectively stalled most liberal initiatives. More important, Kennedy was not nearly as impassioned about domestic reform as he was about foreign policy.

One program that did win both popular and congressional support was increased funding for the National Aeronautics and Space Administration (NASA),

Following the Cuban Missile Crisis

In the tense days of the Cuban missile crisis in October 1962, Americans, fearful that the Soviet Union and the United States were on the verge of war, followed the news intently. In this photograph Cuban refugees in a New York hotel room watched as President Kennedy outlined his plans to impose a quarantine of Cuba and warned of U.S. instant retaliation if the Soviet Union launched an attack from Cuba on any Western Hemisphere nation.
Corbis-Bettmann.

whose Mercury space program had begun in 1958. On May 5, 1961, just three months after Kennedy took office, Alan Shepard became the first American in space. (The Soviet cosmonaut Yuri Gagarin became the first person in space when he made a 108-hour flight in April 1961.) The following year, American astronaut John Glenn manned the first space mission to orbit the earth. At the height of American fascination with space flight, Kennedy proposed that the nation commit itself to landing a man on the moon within the decade. To support this mission (accomplished in 1969), Kennedy persuaded Congress to greatly increase NASA's budget.

Kennedy's most striking domestic achievement was his use of modern economic theory to shape government fiscal policy. New Dealers had gradually moved away from the ideal of a balanced budget, turning instead to deliberate deficit spending to stimulate economic growth. In addition to relying on federal spending to create the desired deficit, Kennedy and his advisors proposed a reduction in income taxes. A tax cut, they argued, would put more money in the hands of taxpayers, who would

spend it, thereby creating more jobs. For a time federal expenditures would exceed federal income, but after a year or two the expanding economy would raise American incomes and generate higher tax revenues.

Congress balked at this unorthodox proposal, and the measure failed to pass. But Lyndon Johnson pressed for it after Kennedy's assassination, signing it into law in February 1964. The Kennedy-Johnson tax cut—the Tax Reduction Act (1964)—marked a milestone in the use of fiscal policy to encourage economic growth, an approach that Republicans and other fiscal conservatives would later embrace.

Kennedy's interest in stimulating economic growth did not include a commitment to spending for domestic social needs, although he did not entirely ignore the liberal legislative agenda of Franklin Roosevelt and Harry Truman. Kennedy managed to push through legislation raising the minimum wage and expanding Social Security benefits. But on other issues—federal aid to education, wilderness preservation, federal investment in mass transportation, and medical insurance for the elderly—he ran into determined congressional

Civil Rights Protesters in Selma
Protesting the killing of a black voting-rights advocate, thousands of civil rights activists staged a 54-mile march from Selma to Montgomery, Alabama, on March 7, 1965. The men and women in this photograph, shown here singing songs of freedom, were part of the historic march. The peaceful protest turned violent when state troopers clubbed and tear-gassed demonstrators on the Pettus Bridge outside Selma. Public outrage over the violence on "Bloody Sunday," as the incident became known, helped Johnson push the Voting Rights Act through Congress that summer. Bob Adelman / Magnum Photos, Inc.

Alabama, to the state capital in Montgomery to protest the murder of a voting-rights activist. As soon as the marchers left Selma, mounted state troopers attacked them with tear gas and clubs. The scene was shown on national television that night.

Calling the episode "an American tragedy," President Johnson redoubled his efforts to persuade Congress to pass the pending voting-rights legislation. In a televised speech to a joint session of Congress on March 15, quoting the best-known slogan of the civil rights movement, "We shall overcome," he proclaimed voting rights a moral imperative.

On August 6 Congress passed the Voting Rights Act of 1965, which suspended the literacy tests and other measures most southern states used to prevent blacks from registering to vote. The act authorized the attorney general to send federal examiners to register voters in any county where less than 50 percent of the voting-age population was registered. Together with the adoption in 1964 of the Twenty-fourth Amendment to the Constitution, which outlawed the poll tax in federal elections, and successful legal challenges to state and local poll taxes, the Voting Rights Act allowed millions of blacks to register and vote for the first time. Congress reauthorized the Voting Rights Act in 1970, 1975, and 1982.

In the South the results were stunning. In 1960 only 20 percent of blacks of voting age had been registered to vote; by 1964 the figure had risen to 39 percent, and by 1971 it was 62 percent (Map 28.7). As Hartman Turnbow, a Mississippi farmer who risked his life to register in 1964, later declared, "It won't never go back where it was."

Enacting the Liberal Agenda

Johnson's success in pushing through the 1965 Voting Rights Act stemmed in part from the 1964 election, in which he won the presidency in his own right by defeating the conservative Republican senator Barry Goldwater of Arizona. With his running mate, Senator Hubert H. Humphrey of Minnesota, Johnson achieved one of the largest margins in history, 61.1 percent of the popular vote (Map 28.8). And Johnson's coattails were long—his sweeping victory brought democratic gains in both Congress and the state legislatures. Thus strengthened politically, he used this mandate not only to promote a civil rights agenda but also to bring to fruition what he called the "Great Society."

Like most New Deal liberals, Johnson took an expansive view of presidential leadership and the role of the federal government. Johnson's first major success came in education. The Elementary and Secondary Education Act, passed in 1965, authorized $1 billion in federal funds to benefit impoverished children. The same year the Higher Education Act provided the first federal scholarships for college students. The Eighty-ninth Congress also gave Johnson enough votes to enact the federal health insurance legislation first proposed by Truman. The result was two new programs: Medicare, a health plan for the elderly funded by a surcharge on Social Security payroll taxes, and Medicaid, a health plan for the poor paid for by general tax revenues.

Although the Great Society is usually associated with programs for the disadvantaged, many Johnson administration initiatives actually benefited a wide spectrum of Americans. Federal urban renewal and home mortgage assistance helped those who could afford to live in single-family homes or modern apartments. Medicare covered every elderly person eligible for Social Security, regardless of need. Much of the federal aid to

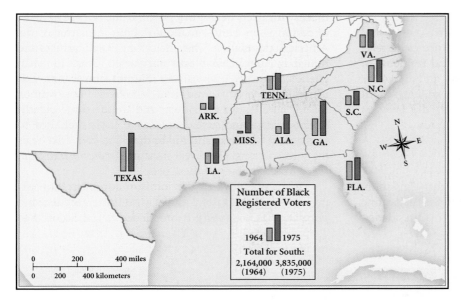

MAP 28.7 Black Voter Registration in the South, 1964 and 1975

After passage of the Voting Rights Act of 1965, black registration in the South increased dramatically. The bars on the map show the number of blacks registered in 1964, before the act was passed, and in 1975, after it had been in effect for ten years. States in the Deep South, such as Mississippi, Alabama, and Georgia, had the biggest rises.

education benefited the children of the middle class. Finally, the creation of the National Endowment for the Arts and the National Endowment for the Humanities in 1965 supported artists and historians in their efforts to understand and interpret the nation's cultural and historical heritage.

Another aspect of public welfare addressed by the Great Society was the environment. President Johnson pressed for expansion of the national park system, improvement of the nation's air and water, and increased land-use planning. At the insistence of his wife, Lady Bird Johnson, he promoted the Highway Beautification Act of 1965. His approach marked a significant break

with past conservation efforts, that had tended to concentrate on maintaining natural resources and national wealth. Under Secretary of the Interior Stewart Udall, Great Society programs emphasized quality of life, battling the problem "of vanishing beauty, of increasing ugliness, of shrinking open space, and of an overall environment that is diminished daily by pollution and noise and blight."

Taking advantage of the Great Society's reform climate, liberal Democrats also brought about significant changes in immigration policy. The Immigration Act of 1965 abandoned the quota system of the 1920s that had discriminated against Asians and southern and Eastern

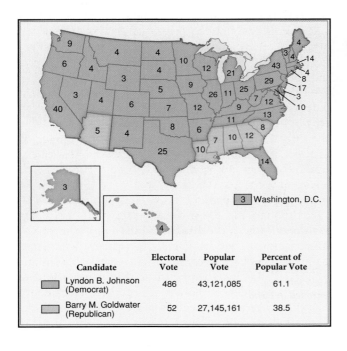

◄ MAP 28.8 Presidential Election of 1964

A landslide victory in 1964, along with significant Democratic gains in Congress and the states, helped President Lyndon B. Johnson to claim that he had a mandate for social reform. Johnson's ambitious "Great Society" led to extensive federal programs in the areas of education, housing, health, transportation, welfare, civil rights, and the environment. Although the conservative Republican senator Barry Goldwater of Arizona was soundly defeated in 1964, a Republican resurgence in the 1980s would be based on Goldwater's critique of the "big government" unleashed by the Great Society.

Europeans, replacing it with more equitable numerical limits on immigration from Europe, Africa, Asia, and countries in the Western Hemisphere. Since close relatives of individuals who were already legal residents of the United States could be admitted over and above the numerical limits, the legislation led to an immigrant influx far greater than anticipated, with the heaviest volume coming from Asia and Latin America.

War on Poverty

In the midst of his campaign for civil rights legislation, Johnson was also pursuing his ambitious goal of putting "an end to poverty in our time." During his presidency,

those who lived below the poverty line—three-fourths of whom were white—made up about a quarter of the American population. They included isolated farmers and miners in Appalachia, blacks and Puerto Ricans in urban ghettos, Mexican Americans in migrant labor camps and urban *barrios*, Native Americans on reservations, women raising families on their own, and the destitute elderly. Because programs such as Old Age Assistance, Aid to Dependent Children, and Aid to the Blind had strict eligibility restrictions, New Deal social welfare programs had failed to reach many of these people.

To reduce poverty, the Johnson administration expanded long-established social insurance, welfare, and public works programs. It broadened Social Security to

Project Head Start
Project Head Start, which offered free early education programs for poor children, was one of the most acclaimed programs of Lyndon Johnson's War on Poverty. In 1965 folk singer Tom Glazer staged a series of concerts for the more than 25,000 children enrolled in Head Start throughout New York City. Wide World Photos, Inc.

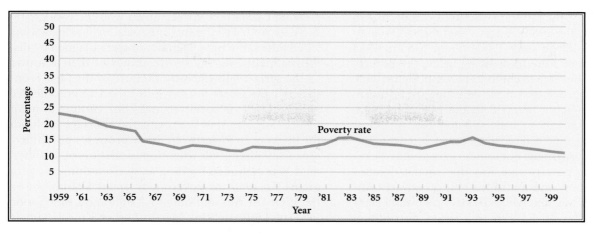

FIGURE 28.5 Americans in Poverty, 1959–2000
During the 1960s the poverty rate among American families dropped from 20 percent to 11 percent, suggesting that the War on Poverty was bringing more Americans into the economic mainstream. Critics charged, however, that economic growth spurred by the Vietnam War accounted for the decrease.

include waiters and waitresses, domestic servants, farmworkers, and hospital employees. Social welfare expenditures increased rapidly, especially for Aid to Families with Dependent Children (AFDC), as did public housing and rent subsidy programs. Food Stamps, begun in 1964 largely to stabilize farm prices, grew into a major program of assistance to low-income families. The Appalachian Regional Development Act of 1965 provided federal funding for local roads, health clinics, and other public works projects in that poverty-stricken region. As during the New Deal, these social welfare programs developed in piecemeal fashion, without overall coordination.

The Office of Economic Opportunity (OEO), established by the Economic Opportunity Act of 1964, was the Great Society's showcase in the War on Poverty. Built around the twin strategies of equal opportunity and community action, OEO programs were so numerous and diverse that they recalled the alphabet agencies of the New Deal. Sargent Shriver, who moved from the Peace Corps to head the new agency, admitted, "It's like we went down to Cape Kennedy [the NASA space center in Florida] and launched a half dozen rockets at once."

OEO programs produced some of the most innovative measures of the Johnson administration. Head Start provided free nursery schools to prepare disadvantaged preschoolers for kindergarten. The Job Corps and the Neighborhood Youth Corps provided jobs and vocational training for young people. Upward Bound gave low-income teenagers the skills and motivation to go to college. Volunteers in Service to America (VISTA), modeled on the Peace Corps, promoted community service among youths in impoverished rural and urban areas. The Community Action Program encouraged the poor

to demand "maximum feasible participation" in decisions that affected them. Community Action organizers worked closely with 2,000 lawyers employed by the Legal Services Program to provide the poor with free legal aid.

By the end of 1965, the Johnson administration had compiled the most impressive legislative record of liberal reforms since the New Deal. It had put issues of poverty, justice, and access at the center of national political life, and it had expanded the federal government's role in protecting citizens' welfare. Yet the Great Society never quite measured up to the extravagant promises made for it, and by the end of the decade, many of its programs were under attack.

In part the political necessity of bowing to pressure from various interest groups hampered Great Society programs. For example, the American Medical Association (AMA) used its influence to shape the Medicare and Medicaid programs to ensure that Congress did not impose a cap on medical expenses. Its intervention produced escalating federal expenditures and contributed to skyrocketing medical costs. And Democratic-controlled urban political machines criticized VISTA and Community Action Program agents who encouraged poor people to demand the public services long withheld by unresponsive local governments. In response to such political pressure, the Johnson administration gradually phased out the Community Action Program and instead channeled spending for housing, social services, and other urban poverty programs through local municipal governments.

Another inherent problem was the limited funding of Great Society programs. The annual budget for the War on Poverty was less than $2 billion. Despite the limited nature of the program, the statistical decline in poverty during the 1960s suggests that the Great Society was successful on some levels. From 1963 to 1968 the proportion of Americans living below the poverty line dropped from 20 percent to 13 percent (Figure 28.5, p. 845). Among African Americans economic advancement was even more marked. In the 1960s the black poverty rate was cut in half, and millions of blacks moved into the middle class, some through federal jobs in antipoverty programs. But critics charged that the reduction in the poverty rate was due to the decade's booming economy and not to the War on Poverty. Another criticism was that while the nation's overall standard of living increased during this period, distribution of wealth was still uneven. The poor were better off in an absolute sense, but they remained far behind the middle class in a relative sense.

Other factors also hampered the success of the Great Society. Following in the steps of Roosevelt's New Deal coalition, Kennedy and Johnson had gathered an extraordinarily diverse set of groups—middle-class and poor; white and nonwhite; Protestant, Jewish, and Catholic; urban and rural—in support of an unprecedented level of federal activism. For a brief period between 1964 and 1966, the coalition held together. But inevitably the demands of certain groups—such as blacks' demands for civil rights and the urban poor's demands for increased political power—conflicted with the interests of other Democrats, such as white southerners and northern political bosses. In the end the Democratic coalition could not sustain a consensus on the purposes of governmental activism powerful enough to resist a growing backlash of conservatives who increasingly resisted expanded civil rights and social welfare legislation.

At the same time, Democrats were plagued by disillusionment over the shortcomings of their reforms. In the early 1960s the lofty rhetoric of the New Frontier and the Great Society had raised unprecedented expectations for social change. But competition for federal largesse was keen, and the shortage of funds for the War on Poverty left many promises unfulfilled, especially after 1965 when the escalation of the Vietnam War siphoned funding away from domestic programs. In 1966 the government spent $22 billion on the Vietnam War and only $1.2 billion on the War on Poverty. Ultimately, as Martin Luther King Jr. put it, the Great Society was "shot down on the battlefields of Vietnam."

FOR FURTHER EXPLORATION

▶ For definitions of key terms boldfaced in this chapter, see the glossary at the end of the book.

▶ To assess your mastery of the material covered in this chapter, see the Online Study Guide at **bedfordstmartins.com/henretta**.

▶ For suggested references, including Web sites, see page SR-30 at the end of the book.

▶ For map resources and primary documents, see **bedfordstmartins.com/henretta**.

SUMMARY

In the postwar era, American dominance of the global economy ensured an unprecedented level of domestic prosperity. Increased levels of spending on defense and consumer goods led to new economic development concentrated in the southern and western states and in the suburbs. Federal intervention in the economy, especially cold war defense spending, boosted the economies and populations of California, Texas, Florida, and other emerging Sun Belt states. Federal home loan programs and highway construction spurred rapid suburban development, siphoning jobs and middle-class residents out of the central cities. At the same time, many blacks, Latinos, Native Americans, and other low-income groups were migrating into these declining urban areas, where they encountered growing unemployment, rising crime, and deteriorating housing and education.

After years of depression and war-induced insecurity, Americans turned inward toward religion, home, and family. Postwar couples married young, had several children, and—if they were white and middle class—raised their children in a climate of suburban affluence and consumerism. The profamily orientation of the 1950s celebrated social conformity and traditional gender roles, even though millions of women entered the workforce in those years. Many of the smoldering contradictions of the postwar period—unequally shared affluence, institutionalized racism, tensions in women's lives—helped spur the civil rights movement and other social reform efforts of the 1960s.

As Americans looked to Washington for solutions to the nation's social and economic ills, the Democrats offered a diverse array of federal programs designed to appeal to a broad range of constituencies. John F. Kennedy first set the agenda for this politics of expectation in his 1960 presidential bid, but the domestic accomplishments of his New Frontier were limited. Kennedy's activism was more evident in foreign policy, where he proved a resolute Cold Warrior. Following Kennedy's assassination in 1963, Lyndon Johnson played a critical role in pushing civil rights legislation through Congress. Moreover, Johnson used his formidable political skills to usher in the most ambitious legislative reform program since the New Deal. Congress funded an array of Great Society programs in education, medical care, social welfare, housing, transportation, and environmental protection. But although the Great Society raised hopes, it could not always deliver on its promises. Increasing military expenditures for the Vietnam conflict limited federal funds for domestic programs. And as federal functions and responsibilities grew, accommodating the diverse and often competing constituencies in the Democratic coalition became increasingly difficult. By the mid-1960s the liberal consensus was breaking apart.

TIMELINE

1944 Bretton Woods economic conference

World Bank and International Monetary Fund (IMF) founded

1947 Levittown, New York, built

1953– 1958 Operation Wetback and Indian termination programs

1954 *Brown v. Board of Education of Topeka*

1955 AFL and CIO merge

Montgomery bus boycott

1956 National Interstate and Defense Highway Act

1957 Peak of postwar baby boom

School desegregation battle in Little Rock, Arkansas

Southern Christian Leadership Conference (SCLC) founded

1960 Sit-ins in Greensboro, North Carolina

John F. Kennedy elected president

1961 Peace Corps established

Freedom rides

Bay of Pigs invasion

Berlin Wall erected

1962 Michael Harrington's *The Other America*

Cuban missile crisis

1963 Betty Friedan's *The Feminine Mystique*

Civil rights protest in Birmingham, Alabama

March on Washington

Nuclear test-ban treaty

John F. Kennedy assassinated; Lyndon B. Johnson assumes presidency

1964 Freedom Summer

Civil Rights Act

Economic Opportunity Act inaugurates War on Poverty

Johnson elected president

1965 Immigration Act abolishes national quota system

Civil rights march from Selma to Montgomery

Voting Rights Act

Medicare and Medicaid programs established

Elementary and Secondary Education Act

CHAPTER 29

War Abroad and at Home: The Vietnam Era

1961–1975

IN FEBRUARY 1969, while conducting his first mass as a Catholic priest, James Carroll seized the opportunity to criticize the U.S. war in Vietnam. Carroll's public pronouncement against the war, delivered in a U.S. Air Force base chapel before an audience of high-ranking officers, among them his father, opened a rift in his family that never healed. Carroll's stand was not unique; he joined countless other ministers and priests who used their pulpits to condemn the war. His experience provides a dramatic example of the ruptures the Vietnam War brought to families, institutions, and the American social fabric.

Vietnam spawned a vibrant antiwar protest movement, which intersected with a broader youth movement that questioned traditional American political and cultural values. The challenges posed by youth, together with the revival of feminism, the rise of the black and Chicano power movements, and explosive riots in the cities, produced a profound sense of social disorder at home. Vietnam split the Democratic Party and shattered the liberal consensus. The high monetary cost of the war diverted resources from domestic uses, spelling an end to the Great Society. Beyond its domestic impact the war wreaked extraordinary damage on the country of Vietnam and undermined U.S. credibility abroad. For the first time average Americans began to question their assumptions about the nation's cold war objectives and the beneficence of American foreign policy.

◀ **The Longest War**
American combat troops fought in Vietnam from 1965 to 1973, making it the longest war in the nation's history. Ambushed during a search-and-destroy mission, these soldiers await the arrival of a medical evacuation helicopter. The red smoke, produced by a grenade, designated the clearing in the jungle where the helicopter could land. More than 58,000 Americans lost their lives in the conflict, while another 300,000 were injured.
© Tim Page.

Into the Quagmire, 1945–1968

Like many new nations that emerged from the dissolution of European empires after World War II, Vietnam was characterized by a volatile mix of nationalist sentiment, religious and cultural conflict, economic need, and political turmoil. The rise of communism there was just one phase of the nation's larger struggle, which would eventually climax in a bloody civil war. But American policymakers viewed these events through the lens of the cold war, interpreting them as part of an international Communist movement toward global domination. Their failure to understand the complexity of Vietnam's internal conflicts led to a long and ultimately disastrous attempt to influence the course of the war.

America in Vietnam: From Truman to Kennedy

Vietnam had been part of the French colony of Indochina since the late nineteenth century but had been occupied by Japan during World War II. When the Japanese surrendered in 1945, Ho Chi Minh and the Vietminh, the Communist nationalist group that had led Vietnamese resistance to the Japanese, took advantage of the resulting power vacuum. With words drawn from the American Declaration of Independence, Ho proclaimed the establishment of the independent republic of Vietnam that September. The next year, when France rejected his claim and reasserted control over the country, an eight-year struggle ensued that the Vietminh called the Anti-French War of Resistance. Appealing to American anticolonial sentiment Ho called on President Truman to support the struggle for Vietnamese independence. But Truman ignored his pleas and instead offered covert financial support to the French, in hopes of stabilizing the politically chaotic region and rebuilding the French economy.

By the end of the decade cold war developments had prompted the United States to step up its assistance to the French. After the Chinese Revolution of 1949, the United States became concerned that China—along with the Soviet Union—might actively support anticolonial struggles in Asia and that newly independent countries might align themselves with the Communists. At the same time Republican charges that the Democrats had "lost" China influenced Truman to take a firmer stand against perceived Communist aggression in Korea and Vietnam. Truman also wanted to maintain good relations with France, whose support was crucial to the success of the new NATO alliance. Finally, Indochina played a strategic role in Secretary of State Dean Acheson's plans for an integrated Pacific Rim economy centered on a reindustrialized Japan.

For all these reasons, when the Soviet Union and the new Chinese leaders recognized Ho's republic early in 1950, the United States—along with Great Britain—recognized the French-installed puppet government of Bao Dai. Subsequently, both the Truman and the Eisenhower administrations provided substantial military support to the French in Vietnam. President Eisenhower argued that such aid was essential to prevent the collapse of all non-Communist governments in the area, in a chain reaction he called the **domino effect**: "You have a row of dominoes set up, you knock over the first one, and what will happen to the last one is the certainty that it will go over very quickly."

Despite joint French-American efforts, the Vietminh forces gained strength in northern Vietnam. In the spring of 1954, they seized the isolated administrative fortress of Dienbienphu after a fifty-six-day siege. The spectacular victory gave the Vietminh negotiating leverage in the 1954 Geneva accords, which partitioned Vietnam temporarily at the seventeenth parallel (Map 29.1) and committed France to withdraw its forces from the area north of that line. The accords also provided that within two years, in free elections, the voters in the two sectors would choose a unified government for the entire nation. The United States considered the agreements a "disaster," especially provisions for elections that it feared would be won by the Communists. It refused to sign the accords and instead issued a separate protocol acknowledging them and promising to "refrain from the threat or use of force to disturb them."

Eisenhower had no intention of allowing a Communist victory in Vietnam's upcoming election. With the help of the CIA, he made sure that a pro-American government took power in South Vietnam in June 1954, just before the accords were signed. Ngo Dinh Diem, an anti-Communist Catholic who had spent eight years in the United States, returned to Vietnam as the premier of the French-backed South Vietnamese government. The next year, in a rigged election, Diem became president of an independent South Vietnam. Realizing that the popular Ho Chi Minh would easily win in both the north and south, Diem called off the reunification elections that were scheduled for 1956—a move the United States supported.

In March 1956 the last French soldiers left Saigon, the capital of South Vietnam, and the United States replaced France as the dominant foreign power in the region. American policymakers quickly asserted that a non-Communist South Vietnam was vital to U.S. security interests. In reality, Vietnam was too small a country to upset the international balance of power, and its Communist movement was regional and intensely nationalistic rather than expansionist. Nevertheless, Eisenhower and subsequent U.S. presidents persisted in viewing Vietnam as part of the cold war struggle to contain the Communist threat to the free world. Between 1955 and 1961 the Eisenhower administration sent

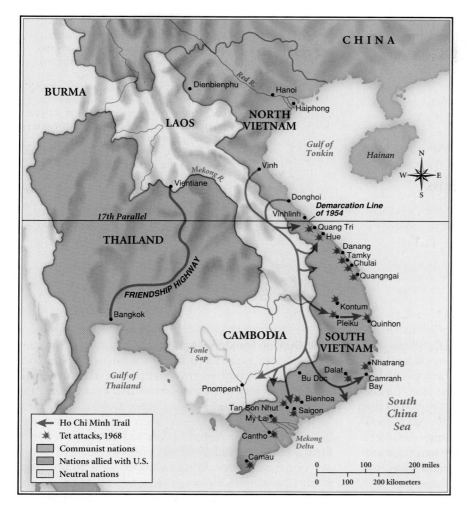

MAP 29.1 The Vietnam War, 1954–1975

The Vietnam War was a guerrilla war, fought in skirmishes and inconclusive encounters rather than decisive battles. Supporters of the National Liberation Front filtered into South Vietnam along the Ho Chi Minh Trail, which wound through Laos and Cambodia. In January 1968 Vietcong forces launched the Tet offensive, a surprise attack on several South Vietnamese cities and provincial centers. American vulnerability to these attacks served to undermine U.S. credibility and fueled opposition to the war. After a 1973 cease-fire was signed, the United States withdrew its troops, and in 1975 South Vietnam fell to the northern forces. The country was reunited under Communist rule in April of that year.

Diem an average of $200 million a year in aid and stationed approximately 675 American military advisors in Saigon. Having stepped up U.S. involvement there considerably, Eisenhower left office, passing the Vietnam situation to his successor, John F. Kennedy.

President Kennedy saw Vietnam as an ideal testing ground for the counterinsurgency techniques that formed the centerpiece of his military policy (see Chapter 28). But he first had to prop up Diem's unpopular regime, which faced a growing military threat. In December 1960 the Communist Party in North Vietnam organized most of Diem's opponents in South Vietnam into a revolutionary movement known as the National Liberation Front (NLF). In response, Kennedy increased the number of American military "advisors" (an elastic term that included helicopter units and special forces), raising it to more than 16,000 by November 1963. To win the "hearts and minds" of Vietnamese peasants away from the insurgents and to increase agricultural production, he also sent economic development specialists. But Kennedy refused to send combat troops to assist the South Vietnamese in what had become a guerrilla-style civil war with the north.

American aid did little good in South Vietnam. Diem's political inexperience and corruption, combined with his Catholicism in a predominantly Buddhist country, prevented him from creating a stable popular government. The NLF's guerrilla forces—called the Vietcong by their opponents—made considerable headway against Diem's regime, using the revolutionary tactics of the Chinese leader Mao Zedong to blend into South Vietnam's civilian population "like fish in the water." They found a receptive audience among peasants who had been alienated by Diem's "strategic hamlet" program, which uprooted families and whole villages and moved them into barbed-wire compounds in a vain attempt to separate them from Ho Chi Minh's sympathizers.

Anti-Diem sentiment also flourished among Buddhists, who charged the government with religious persecution. Starting in May 1963 militant Buddhists staged a dramatic series of demonstrations against Diem, including several self-immolations that were recorded by American television crews. Diem's regime retaliated with raids on temples and mass arrests of Buddhist priests in August, prompting more antigovernment demonstrations.

Buddhist Protesters, 1966
Beginning in 1963, militant Buddhist monks staged a series of protests against the war that helped bring down the American-backed regime of Ngo Dinh Diem. Here, robed monks, part of a group of 250 Buddhist protesters, stage an antigovernment demonstration in Saigon. They are surrounded by barbed wire put there by government troops. Strongly nationalistic, the monks appealed for peace talks with the Vietcong and for free elections that would allow the Vietnamese to decide their fate. The South Vietnamese military government arrested Buddhist leaders in 1966 and effectively crushed their movement. Wide World Photos, Inc.

As opposition to Diem deepened, Kennedy decided that he would have to be removed. Ambassador Henry Cabot Lodge Jr. let it be known in Saigon that the United States would support a military coup that had "a good chance of succeeding." On November 1, 1963, Diem was driven from office and assassinated by officers in the South Vietnamese army. America's role in the coup reinforced the links between the United States and the new regime in South Vietnam, making the prospect of withdrawal from the region less acceptable to U.S. policymakers.

Less than a month later, Kennedy was assassinated. Although historians continue to debate whether Kennedy would have withdrawn American forces from Vietnam had he lived, his administration's actions clearly accelerated U.S. involvement. When Lyndon Johnson became president, he retained many of Kennedy's foreign-policy advisors. Asserting that "I am not going to be the President who saw Southeast Asia go the way China went," he quickly declared he would maintain U.S. support for South Vietnam.

Escalation: The Johnson Years

The removal of Diem did not improve the efficiency or popularity of the Saigon government. Secretary of Defense Robert McNamara and other top advisors argued that only a rapid, full-scale deployment of U.S. forces could prevent the imminent defeat of the South Vietnamese. But Johnson would need at least tacit congressional support, perhaps even a declaration of war, to commit U.S. forces to an offensive strategy. Originally, Johnson wanted to wait until after the 1964 election to place this controversial request before Congress, but events gave him an opportunity to win authorization sooner.

The Gulf of Tonkin Resolution. During the summer of 1964, American naval forces conducted surveillance missions off the North Vietnamese coast to aid amphibious attacks by the South Vietnamese. When the North Vietnamese resisted the attacks, President Johnson told the nation that on two separate occasions North Vietnamese torpedo boats had fired on American destroyers in international waters in the Gulf of Tonkin. At Johnson's request, Congress authorized him to "take all necessary measures to repel any armed attack against the forces of the United States and to prevent further aggression." On August 7 the Gulf of Tonkin Resolution passed by 88 to 2 votes in the Senate and 416 to 0 in the House. Only Senators Wayne Morse of Oregon and Ernest Gruening of Alaska opposed it as a "predated declaration of war" that further increased the president's ability to carry out foreign policy without consulting Congress.

Many questions were later raised about the resolution. A draft version had been ready for several months, awaiting just such an incident. The evidence of a North Vietnamese attack was sketchy at best. As the president admitted to his advisors soon afterward, "For all I know, our navy was shooting at whales out there." But this unverified attack got Johnson what he wanted—a sweeping mandate to conduct Vietnam operations as he saw fit. It was the only formal approval of American intervention in Vietnam that Congress ever granted.

During the 1964 presidential campaign, Johnson declared, "We are not going to send American boys nine or ten thousand miles away from home to do what Asian boys ought to be doing for themselves." Yet plans were already being drawn up for a possible escalation of American efforts. With congressional support assured and the 1964 election safely over, the Johnson administration began the fateful move toward the total Americanization of the war. The escalation, which was accomplished during the first several months of 1965, took two forms: the initiation of direct bombing campaigns against North Vietnam and the deployment of ground troops.

Operation Rolling Thunder.   The first phase of escalation began on March 2, 1965, with Operation Rolling Thunder, a protracted campaign of bombing attacks against North Vietnam designed to cripple the economy and force the Communists to the bargaining table. A special target was the Ho Chi Minh Trail, an elaborate network of paths, bridges, and shelters that stretched from North Vietnam through Cambodia and Laos into South Vietnam (see Map 29.1). By 1967 some 20,000 Vietnamese soldiers were moving southward along that route each month, along with the military equipment and other resources necessary to supply them.

Between 1965 and 1968 Operation Rolling Thunder (named for a Protestant hymn) dropped a million tons of bombs on North Vietnam, 800 tons a day for three and a half years. Each B-52 bombing sortie cost $30,000, and by early 1966 the direct costs of the air war had exceeded $1.7 billion. From 1965 to 1973 the United States dropped three times as many bombs on North Vietnam, a country roughly the size of Texas, as had fallen on Europe, Asia, and Africa during World War II. The several hundred captured American pilots downed in the raids then became pawns in negotiations with the North Vietnamese over the fate of prisoners of war.

To the amazement of American advisors, the bombing had little effect on the ability of the Vietnamese to wage war. Despite continuous sorties and the use of chemical defoliants to deny the Vietcong cover, the flow of troops and supplies to the south continued. The North Vietnamese quickly rebuilt roads and bridges, moved munitions plants underground, and constructed a network of tunnels and shelters. Instead of destroying enemy morale and bringing the North Vietnamese to the bargaining table, Operation Rolling Thunder intensified their will to fight. The bombing continued nevertheless.

The Arrival of U.S. Ground Troops.   A week after the launch of Operation Rolling Thunder, the United States sent its first official ground troops into combat duty. Soon U.S. Marines were skirmishing with the enemy. Over the next three years, the number of American troops in Vietnam grew dramatically. Although U.S. troops were accompanied by military forces from Australia, New Zealand, and South Korea, the war increasingly became an American war, fought for American aims. By 1966 more than 380,000 American soldiers were stationed in Vietnam; by 1967, 485,000; by 1968, 536,000 (Figure 29.1).

The massive commitment of troops and air power threatened to destroy Vietnam's countryside. The defoliation campaign had seriously damaged agricultural production, undercutting the economic and cultural base of Vietnamese society. After one devastating but not unusual engagement, a commanding officer reported, using the logic of the time, "It became necessary to destroy the town in order to save it." Graffiti on a plane that dropped defoliants read "Only you can prevent forests." (In later years defoliants such as Agent Orange were found to have highly toxic effects on both humans and the environment.) The destruction was not limited to North Vietnam; South Vietnam, America's ally, absorbed more than twice the bomb tonnage dropped on the North, as U.S. forces tried to flush out

Aerial Bombing in Vietnam
The bombs dropped by U.S. forces in an attempt to root out Vietcong sympathizers inflicted heavy damage on the countryside and caused many civilian deaths. B-52 jets dropped most of the bombs.
Larry Burrows / LIFE Magazine © Time, Inc.

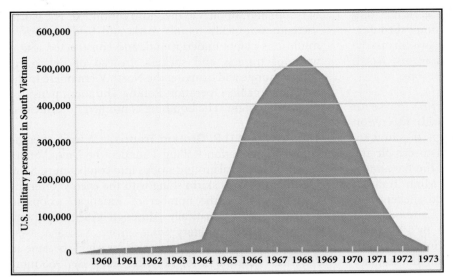

FIGURE 29.1 U.S. Troops in Vietnam, 1960–1973

When Lyndon Johnson escalated the Vietnam War, troop levels rose from 23,300 in December 1964 to 184,300 a year later. Troop levels eventually peaked at more than 543,000 personnel. Under Richard Nixon's Vietnamization program, beginning in the summer of 1969, levels drastically declined; the last U.S. military forces left South Vietnam on March 29, 1973.

Vietcong sympathizers. In Saigon and other South Vietnamese cities, the influx of American soldiers and dollars distorted local economies, spread corruption and prostitution, and triggered uncontrollable inflation and black-market activity.

Why did the dramatically increased American presence in Vietnam fail to turn the tide of the war? Some advisors argued that military intervention could accomplish little without simultaneous reform in Saigon and increased popular support in the countryside. Other critics claimed that the United States never fully committed itself to a "total victory"—although what that term meant was never settled. Military strategy was inextricably tied to political considerations. For domestic reasons policymakers often searched for an elusive "middle ground" between all-out invasion of North Vietnam (and the possibility of sparking a nuclear exchange between the two superpowers) and the politically unacceptable alternative of disengagement. Hoping to win a war of attrition, the Johnson administration assumed that American superiority in personnel and weaponry would ultimately triumph. But that limited commitment was never enough to ensure victory—however it was defined.

American Soldiers' Perspectives on the War

Approximately 2.8 million Americans served in Vietnam. At an average age of only nineteen, most of those servicemen and women were too young to vote or drink (the voting age was twenty-one until passage of the Twenty-sixth Amendment in 1971), but they were old enough to fight and die. Some were volunteers, including 7,000 women enlistees. Many others served because they were drafted. Until the nation shifted to an all-volunteer force in 1973, the draft stood as a concrete

reminder of the government's impact on the lives of ordinary Americans. Even more than in other recent wars, sons of the poor and the working class shouldered a disproportionate amount of the fighting, forming an estimated 80 percent of the enlisted ranks. Young men from more affluent backgrounds were more likely to avoid combat through student deferments, medical exemptions, and appointments to National Guard and reserve units—alternatives that made Johnson's Vietnam policy more acceptable to the middle class. Although over the course of the war blacks were drafted and died roughly in the same proportion as their share of the draft-age population (about 12 to 13 percent), black casualty rates were significantly higher than average in the early 1960s.

At first many draftees and enlistees shared common cold war assumptions about the need to fight communism and the superiority of the American military. However, their experience in Vietnam quickly challenged simple notions of patriotism and the inevitability of victory (see American Voices, "Dave Cline: A Vietnam Vet Remembers," p. 855). In "Nam" long days of boring menial work were punctuated by brief flashes of intense fighting. "Most of the time, nothing happened," a soldier recalled, "but when something did, it happened instantaneously and without warning." Rarely were there large-scale battles, only skirmishes; rather than front lines and conquered territory, there were only daytime operations in areas the Vietcong controlled at night.

Racism was a fact of everyday life. Because differentiating between friendly South Vietnamese and Vietcong sympathizers was difficult, many soldiers lumped them together as "gooks." As a draftee noted of his indoctrination, "The only thing they told us about the Vietcong was they were gooks. They were to be killed.

Dave Cline

A Vietnam Vet Remembers

Born in 1947, Dave Cline grew up in a working-class family outside Buffalo, New York. Drafted by the army in 1967, the twenty-year-old Cline was eager to help fight Communist aggression in Vietnam. But after his arrival in Danang seven months later, his attitude toward the war quickly changed. Cline described this transformation in an interview conducted in 1992.

I went to basic training at Fort Dix. . . .

Down there, they used to give you basically two raps on why you were going to Vietnam. One was that rap about we're going to help the heroic South Vietnamese people. We're going to go fight for freedom [and repel] communist aggression. They'd show you the maps and stuff, the domino theory, the Red Chinese are trying to engulf all of southeast Asia. The other rap was: killing communists was your duty. . . .

The boat came into Danang, and then they flew us from Danang to Cu Chi. I remember it was humid and hot and smelled. First thing you do when you get in-country is, they give you these indoctrination classes and they say, "Forget all that shit they told; you can't trust any of these people. They're not really people anyway; they're gooks." . . . In other words: You see anyone with slant eyes, that's your potential enemy—don't trust them. That sort of blows away any "help the people" thing. . . .

I got wounded the last time out near the Cambodian border. This happened on December 20, 1967. Again, we were doing these sweeps and we were overrun about two in the morning. The North Vietnamese launched a massive human wave attack. We could hear them yelling orders maybe 25, 30 feet away, and these guys were charging. . . .

A guy came running up to my foxhole. We saw him coming from the next hole over and we didn't know if it was an American retreating over to us or a Vietnamese, because it was two in the morning. So we didn't shoot him.

I was sitting there with my rifle waiting to see, and all of a sudden he stuck his rifle in. I saw the front side of an AK-47 and a muzzle flash, and then I pulled my trigger. I shot him through his chest. I blacked out initially, but then I came to and found a round went right through my knee. They threw me in a foxhole and gave me a bottle of Darvons. I lay there until the battle ended. In the morning they medivaced me out.

They carried me over to this guy I had shot. He was sitting up against this tree stump. He was just sitting there with his rifle across his lap. He was dead. The sergeant started giving me this pep talk, "Here's the gook you killed!" In my unit they had a big thing about confirmed kills. If you had a confirmed kill and the person had an automatic weapon, then you were supposed to get a three-day in-country pass. . . .

This kid looked about the same age as me. The first thing I started thinking was, Why is he dead and I'm alive? . . .

Then after going into the hospital, I started thinking about that guy. I wonder if his mother knows he's dead? I wonder if he had a girlfriend? Looking back, I think I was retaining the sense that he was a human being.

Source: Richard Stacewicz, *Winter Soldiers: An Oral History of the Vietnam Veterans against the War* (New York: Twayne Publishers, 1997), 135–36, 140–41.

Nobody sits around and gives you their historical and cultural background. They're the enemy. Kill, kill, kill."

Fighting and surviving under such conditions took its toll. One veteran explained that "the hardest thing to come to grips with was the fact that making it through Vietnam—surviving—is probably the only worthwhile part of the experience. It wasn't going over there and saving the world from communism or defending the country." Cynicism and bitterness were common. The pressure of waging war under such conditions drove many soldiers to seek escape in alcohol or drugs, which were cheap and readily available.

The women who served in Vietnam shared many of these experiences. As WACs, nurses, and civilians serving with organizations such as the USO, women volunteers witnessed death and mutilation on a massive scale. Though they tried to maintain a professional distance, as a navy nurse recalled, "It's pretty damn hard not getting involved when you see a nineteen- or twenty-year-old blond kid from the Midwest or California or the East Coast screaming and dying. A piece of my heart would go with each."

The Cold War Consensus Unravels

In the twenty years following World War II, despite widespread affluence and confidence in the nation's cold war leadership, there had emerged a variety of challenges to the status quo. From the nonconforming Beats came a critical assault on corporate capitalism. Teenagers' embrace of rock 'n' roll defied the cultural norms of their elders. African Americans' boycotts, sit-ins, and freedom rides signaled a rising wind of protest against racial injustice. By 1965 such angry expressions of disaffection from mainstream America had multiplied dramatically. Criticism of the war in Vietnam mounted, as youthful protesters rebelled against traditional respect for the "system." The civil rights movement took on a more militant thrust and expanded beyond African Americans to other minority groups, while the feminist movement revived to challenge social values and the family structure itself. Together the various movements forced Americans to reassess basic assumptions about the nature of their society.

A Televised War

This harrowing scene from Saigon during the Tet offensive in 1968 was broadcast on U.S. network news. The NBC bureau chief described the film in a terse telex message: "A VC officer was captured. The troops beat him. They bring him to [Brigadier General Nguyen Ngoc] Loan who is head of South Vietnamese national police. Loan pulls out his pistol, fires at the head of the VC, the VC falls, zoom on his head, blood spraying out. If he has it all it's startling stuff." Wide World Photos, Inc.

Public Opinion on Vietnam

President Kennedy and at first President Johnson enjoyed broad support for their conduct of foreign affairs. Both Democrats and Republicans approved Johnson's escalation of the war, and public opinion polls in 1965 and 1966 showed strong popular support for his policies. But in the late 1960s, public opinion began to turn against the war. In July 1967 a Gallup poll revealed that for the first time a majority of Americans disapproved of Johnson's Vietnam policy and believed the war had reached a stalemate. Television had much to do with these attitudes. Vietnam was the first war in which television brought film of the fighting directly into the nation's living rooms.

The Credibility Gap. Despite the glowing reports filed by the media and the administration on the progress of the war, by 1967 many administration officials had privately reached a more pessimistic conclusion. In November Secretary of Defense Robert McNamara sent a memo to the president arguing that continued escalation "would be dangerous, costly in lives, and unsatisfactory to the American people," but President Johnson continued to insist that victory in Vietnam was vital to U.S. national security and prestige. Journalists, especially those who had spent time in Vietnam, soon began to warn that the Johnson administration suffered from a "**credibility gap.**" The administration, they charged, was concealing important and discouraging information about the war's progress. In February 1966 television coverage of hearings by the Senate Foreign Relations Committee (chaired by J. William Fulbright, an outspoken critic of the war) raised further questions about the administration's policy.

Economic developments put Johnson and his advisors even more on the defensive. In 1966 the federal deficit was $9.8 billion; in 1967 the Vietnam War cost the taxpayers $27 billion, and the deficit jumped to $23 billion. Although the war consumed just 3 percent of the gross national product, its costs became more evident as the growing federal deficit nudged the inflation rate upward. Only in the summer of 1967 did Johnson ask for a 10 percent surcharge on individual and corporate income taxes, an increase that Congress did not approve until 1968. By then the inflationary spiral that would plague the U.S. economy throughout the 1970s was well under way.

The Rise of the Antiwar Movement. As a result of these troubling political and economic developments, more Americans than during previous American wars began to question the war effort in Vietnam. As in every American military conflict, a small group of dissenters opposed the war from the beginning, including pacifist organizations such as the War Resisters League and the

Women's International League for Peace and Freedom and religious groups such as the Quakers and the Fellowship for Reconciliation. Those groups were joined by a new generation of activists who had emerged in the 1950s in groups such as SANE (the National Committee for a Sane Nuclear Policy), Physicians for Social Responsibility, and Women Strike for Peace. These activists opposed the accelerating arms race in general and atmospheric testing in particular and lobbied successfully for the 1963 nuclear test-ban treaty between the United States and the Soviet Union (see Chapter 28).

Between 1963 and 1965, peace activists in both older and newer organizations staged protests, vigils, and letter-writing campaigns against U.S. involvement in the war. After the escalation in the spring of 1965, various antiwar coalitions, swelled by growing numbers of students, clergy, housewives, politicians, artists, and others opposed to the war, organized several mass demonstrations in Washington, bringing out 20,000 to 30,000 people at a time. A diverse lot, participants in these rallies shared a common skepticism about the means and aims of U.S. policy. The war was morally wrong, they argued, and antithetical to American ideals; the goal of an independent, anti-Communist South Vietnam was unattainable; and American military involvement would not help the Vietnamese people.

Student Activism

Youth were among the key protestors of the era. Not all youth challenged authority in the 1960s, but those who did had a powerful impact. It was primarily college students—many of whom had been raised in a privileged environment, showered with consumer goods, and inculcated with faith in American institutions and leaders—who began to question U.S. foreign policy, racial injustice, and middle-class morals and conformity.

In June 1962 forty students from Big Ten and Ivy League universities, disturbed by the gap they perceived between the ideals they had been taught to revere and the realities in American life, met in Port Huron, Michigan, to found Students for a Democratic Society (SDS). Tom Hayden wrote their manifesto, the Port Huron Statement, which expressed their disillusionment with the consumer culture and the gulf between the prosperous and the poor. These students rejected cold war ideology and foreign policy, including but not limited to the Vietnam conflict. The founders of SDS referred to their movement as the "**New Left**" to distinguish themselves from the "Old Left"—Communists and socialists of the 1930s and 1940s. Consciously adopting the activist tactics pioneered by members of the civil rights movement, they turned to grassroots organizing in cities and on college campuses.

The Free Speech Movement. The first major student protests erupted in the fall of 1964 at the University of California at Berkeley, after administrators banned political activity near the Telegraph Avenue entrance, where student groups had traditionally distributed leaflets and recruited volunteers. In protest the major student organizations formed a coalition called the Free Speech Movement (FSM) and organized a sit-in at the administration building. The FSM owed a strong debt to the civil rights movement. Some students had just returned from Freedom Summer in Mississippi, radicalized by their experience. Mario Savio spoke for many of them:

> Last summer I went to Mississippi to join the struggle there for civil rights. This fall I am engaged in another phase of the same struggle, this time in Berkeley. The two battlefields may seem quite different to some observers, but this is not the case. The same rights are at stake in both places—the right to participate as citizens in a democratic society and to struggle against the same enemy. In Mississippi an autocratic and powerful minority rules, through organized violence, to suppress the vast, virtually powerless majority. In California, the privileged minority manipulates the university bureaucracy to suppress the students' political expression.

Free Speech at Berkeley, 1964
Students at the University of California's Berkeley campus protested the administration's decision to ban political activity in the school plaza. Free speech demonstrators, many of them active in the civil rights movement, relied on tactics and arguments that they learned during that struggle.
University of California at Berkeley, Bancroft Library.

Columbia University Protests, 1968
At the height of the Vietnam War in 1968, Columbia University students launched a series of protests against military research contracts, university governance, and the construction of a gymnasium in a nearby Harlem neighborhood. Steve Schapiro / Black Star.

On a deeper level Berkeley students were challenging a university that in their view had grown too big and was too far removed from the major social issues of the day. Emboldened by the Berkeley movement, students across the nation were soon protesting their universities' academic policies and then, more passionately, the Vietnam War.

The Antiwar Movement. The highly politicized activists of the New Left, who had developed a wide-ranging critique of American society, increasingly focused on the war, and they were joined by thousands of other students in protesting American participation in the Vietnam conflict. When President Johnson escalated the war in March 1965, faculty and students at the University of Michigan organized a **teach-in** against the war. Abandoning their classes, they debated the political, diplomatic, and moral aspects of the nation's involvement in Vietnam. Teach-ins quickly spread to other universities as students turned from their studies to protest the war.

Many protests centered on the draft, especially after the Selective Service system abolished automatic student deferments in January 1966. To avoid the draft some young men enlisted in the National Guard or the reserves; others declared themselves conscientious objectors. Several thousand young men ignored their induction notices, risking prosecution for draft evasion.

Others left the country, most often for Canada or Sweden. In public demonstrations of civil disobedience, opponents of the war burned their draft cards, closed down induction centers, and on a few occasions broke into Selective Service offices.

As antiwar and draft protests multiplied, students realized that their universities were deeply implicated in the war effort. In some cases as much as 60 percent of a university's research budget came from government contracts, especially those of the Defense Department. Protesters blocked recruiters from the Dow Chemical Company, the producer of napalm and Agent Orange. Arguing that universities should not train students for war, they demanded that the Reserve Officer Training Corps (ROTC) be removed from college campuses.

After 1967 nationwide student strikes, mass demonstrations, and other organized protests became commonplace. In October 1967 more than 100,000 antiwar demonstrators marched on Washington, D.C., as part of "Stop the Draft Week." The event culminated in a "siege of the Pentagon," in which protesters clashed with police and federal marshals. Hundreds of people were arrested and several demonstrators beaten. Lyndon Johnson, who had once dismissed antiwar protesters as "nervous Nellies," rebellious children, or Communist dupes, now had to face the reality of large-scale public opposition to his policies. Criticism of American policy also came

Che Guevara

Vietnam and the World Freedom Struggle

Che Guevara, a leader of the Cuban Revolution, later worked with revolutionary nationalist movements in Africa and Latin America. Between his departure from Cuba in 1965 and his death in Bolivia in 1967, he made only one public statement. His message, "Vietnam and the World Freedom Struggle," helped convince some young American radicals of the necessity of armed struggle at home and abroad.

This is the painful reality: Vietnam, a nation representing the aspirations and the hopes for victory of the entire world of the disinherited, is tragically alone. . . .

And—what grandeur has been shown by this people! What stoicism and valor in this people! And what a lesson for the world their struggle holds!

It will be a long time before we know if President Johnson ever seriously thought of initiating some of the popular reforms necessary to soften the sharpness of the class contradictions that are appearing with explosive force and more and more frequently.

What is certain is that the improvements announced under the pompous label of the Great Society have gone down the drain in Vietnam.

The greatest of the imperialist powers feels in its own heart the drain caused by a poor, backward country; and its fabulous economy feels the effect of the war. . . .

And for us, the exploited of the world, what should our role be in this? . . .

Our part, the responsibility of the exploited and backward areas of the world, is to eliminate the bases sustaining imperialism—our oppressed peoples, from whom capital, raw materials, technicians and cheap labor are extracted, and to whom new capital, means of domination, arms and all kinds of goods are exported, submerging us in absolute dependence.

The fundamental element of this strategic goal will be, then, the real liberation of the peoples, a liberation that will be obtained through armed struggle in the majority of cases, and which, in the Americas, will have almost unfailingly the property of becoming converted into a socialist revolution.

In focusing on the destruction of imperialism, it is necessary to identify its head, which is none other than the United States of North America. . . .

The adversary must not be underestimated; the North American soldier has technical ability and is backed by means of such magnitude as to make him formidable. He lacks the essential ideological motivation which his most hated rivals of today have to the highest degree—the Vietnamese soldiers. . . .

Over there, the imperialist troops encounter the discomforts of those accustomed to the standard of living which the North American nation boasts. They have to confront a hostile land, the insecurity of those who cannot move without feeling that they are walking on enemy territory; death for those who go outside of fortified redoubts; the permanent hostility of the entire population.

All this continues to provoke repercussions inside the United States; it is going to arouse a factor that was attenuated in the days of the full vigor of imperialism—the class struggle inside its own territory.

Source: Ernesto C. Guevara, *Che Guevara Speaks* (New York: Pathfinder Press, 1967), 144–59.

---

from abroad. Cuban revolutionary leader Che Guevara denounced the war as an imperialist struggle, a view embraced by a growing number of young American radicals (see Voices from Abroad, "Che Guevara: Vietnam and the World Freedom Struggle," above).

The Rise of the Counterculture

While the New Left took to the streets in protest, a growing number of young Americans embarked on a general revolution against authority and middle-class respectability. The "**hippie**"—attired in ragged blue jeans, tie-dyed T-shirt, beads, and army fatigues, with long, unkempt hair—symbolized the new counterculture, a youthful movement that glorified liberation from traditional social strictures.

Not surprisingly, given the importance of rock 'n' roll to 1950s youth culture, popular music formed an important part of the counterculture. The folk singer Pete Seeger set the tone for the era's political idealism with songs such as the antiwar ballad "Where Have All the Flowers Gone?" Another folk singer, Joan Baez, gained national prominence for her rendition of the African American protest song "We Shall Overcome" and other folk and political anthems she performed at protest rallies in the mid-1960s. In 1963, the year of the Birmingham demonstrations and President Kennedy's assassination, Bob Dylan's "Blowin' in the Wind" reflected the impatience of people whose faith in "the system" was wearing thin.

Other winds of change in popular music came from the Beatles, four English working-class youths who burst onto the American scene early in 1964. The Beatles' music, by turns lyrical and driving, was phenomenally successful, spawning a commercial and cultural phenomenon called "Beatlemania." American youth's eager embrace of the Beatles deepened the generational divide between teenagers and their elders already set in motion by the popularity of rock 'n' roll in the 1950s. The Beatles also helped to pave the way for the more rebellious, angrier music of other British groups, notably the Rolling Stones, whose raunchy 1965 "(I Can't Get No) Satisfaction" not only signaled a new openness about sexuality but also made fun of the consumer culture ("He can't be a man 'cause he doesn't smoke the same cigarettes as me").

Drugs intertwined with music as a crucial element of the youth culture. The recreational use of drugs—especially marijuana and lysergic acid diethylamide, the hallucinogen popularly known as LSD, or "acid"—was celebrated in popular music. San Francisco bands such as the Grateful Dead and Jefferson Airplane and musicians like the Seattle-born guitarist Jimi Hendrix developed a musical style known as "acid rock," which was characterized by long, heavily amplified guitar solos

accompanied by psychedelic lighting effects. In August 1969, 400,000 young people journeyed to Bethel, New York, to "get high" on music, drugs, and sex at the three-day Woodstock Music and Art Fair. Despite torrential rain and numerous drug overdoses, most enjoyed the festival, which was heralded as the birth of the "Woodstock nation."

For a brief time adherents of the counterculture believed a new age was dawning. They experimented in communal living and glorified uninhibited sexuality. In 1967 the "world's first Human Be-In" drew 20,000 people to Golden Gate Park in San Francisco. The Beat poet Allen Ginsberg "purified" the site with a Buddhist ritual, and the LSD advocate Timothy Leary, a former Harvard psychology instructor, urged the gathering to "turn on to the scene, tune in to what is happening, and drop out." That summer—dubbed the "Summer of Love"—San Francisco's Haight-Ashbury, New York's East Village, and Chicago's Uptown neighborhoods swelled with young dropouts, drifters, and teenage runaways dubbed "flower children" by observers. Their faith in instant love and peace quickly turned sour, however, as they suffered bad drug trips, sexually transmitted diseases, loneliness, and violence. Although many young people kept their distance from both the counterculture and the antiwar movement, to many adult observers it seemed that all of American youth were rejecting political, social, and cultural norms.

The Widening Struggle for Civil Rights

The counterculture and the antiwar movement were not the only social movements to challenge the status quo in the 1960s. The frustration and anger of blacks boiled

Jimi Hendrix at Woodstock
The three-day outdoor "Woodstock" concert in August 1969 was a defining moment in the counterculture as 400,000 young people journeyed to Bethel, New York, for music, drugs, and sex. Jimi Hendrix closed the show with an electrifying version of "The Star Spangled Banner." More overtly political than most counterculture music, Hendrix's rendition featured sound effects that seemed to evoke the violence of the Vietnam War. Michael Wadleigh, who directed the documentary Woodstock, *called Hendrix's performance "his challenge to American foreign policy."*
Allan Koss / Image Bank.

over in a new racial militance as the civil rights struggle moved outside the South and took on the more stubborn problems of entrenched poverty and racism. The rhetoric and tactics of the emerging black-power movement shattered the existing civil rights coalition and galvanized white opposition.

Rising Militance. Once the system of legal, or de jure, segregation had fallen, the civil rights movement turned to the more difficult task of eliminating the de facto segregation, enforced by custom, that made blacks second-class citizens throughout the nation. Outside the South racial discrimination was less flagrant, but it was pervasive, especially in education, housing, and employment. Although the *Brown* decision outlawed separate schools, it did nothing to change the educational system in areas where schools were all-black or all-white because of residential segregation. Not until 1973 did federal judges begin to extend the desegregation of schools, which had begun in the South two decades earlier, to the rest of the country.

As civil rights leaders took on northern racism, the movement fractured along generational lines. Some younger activists, eager for confrontation and rapid social change, questioned the very goal of integration into white society. Black separatism, espoused by earlier black leaders such as Marcus Garvey in the 1920s (see Chapter 23), was revived in the 1960s by the Nation of Islam, a religious group with more than 10,000 members and many more sympathizers. Popularly known as the Black Muslims, the organization was hostile to whites and stressed black pride, unity, and self-help.

The Black Muslims' most charismatic figure was Malcolm X. A brilliant debater and spellbinding speaker, Malcolm X preached a philosophy quite different from Martin Luther King's. He advocated militant protest and separatism, though he condoned the use of violence only for self-defense. Hostile to the traditional civil rights organizations, he caustically referred to the 1963 March on Washington as the "Farce on Washington." In 1964, after a power struggle with the founder of the Black Muslims, Elijah Muhammad, Malcolm X broke with the Nation of Islam. Following a pilgrimage to Mecca and a tour of Africa, he embraced the liberation struggles of all colonized peoples. But before he could fully pursue his new agenda, he was assassinated while delivering a speech at the Audubon Ballroom in Harlem on February 21, 1965. Three Black Muslims were later convicted of his murder.

Black Power. A more secular black nationalist movement emerged in 1966 when young black SNCC and CORE activists, following the lead of Stokely Carmichael, began to call for black self-reliance and racial pride under the banner of "Black Power." Amid growing distrust of white domination, SNCC effectively ejected its white members. In the same year Huey Newton and Bobby Seale, two college students in Oakland, California, founded the Black Panthers, a militant self-defense organization dedicated to protecting local blacks from police violence. The Panthers' organization quickly spread to other cities, where members undertook a wide range of community organizing projects, including interracial efforts, but their affinity for Third World revolutionary movements and armed struggle became their most publicized attribute.

Among the most significant legacies of black power was the assertion of racial pride. Many young blacks insisted on using the term *Afro-American* rather than *Negro*, a term they found demeaning because of its historical association with slavery and racism. Rejecting white tastes and standards, blacks wore African clothing and hairstyles and helped to awaken interest in black history, art, and literature. By the 1970s many colleges and universities were offering programs in black studies.

The new black assertiveness alarmed many white Americans. They had been willing to go along with the moderate reforms of the 1950s and early 1960s but became wary when blacks began demanding immediate access to higher-paying jobs, housing in white neighborhoods, proactive integration of public schools, and increased political power. Another major reason for the erosion of white support was a wave of riots that struck the nation's cities. Lacking education and skills, successive generations of blacks had moved out of the rural South in search of work that paid an adequate wage. In the North many remained unemployed. Resentful of white landlords, who owned the substandard housing they were forced to live in, and white shopkeepers, who denied them jobs in their neighborhoods, many blacks also hated police, whose violent presence in black neighborhoods seemed that of "an occupying army." Stimulated by the successes of southern blacks who had challenged whites and gotten results, young urban blacks expressed their grievances through their own brand of direct action.

Summer in the City. The first "long hot summer" began in July 1964 in New York City, when police shot a young black criminal suspect in Harlem. Angry youths looted and rioted there for a week. Over the next four years, the volatile issue of police brutality set off riots in dozens of cities. In August 1965 the arrest of a young black motorist in the Watts section of Los Angeles sparked six days of rioting that left thirty-four blacks dead. The riots of 1967 were the most serious, engulfing twenty-two cities in July and August (Map 29.2). The most devastating outbreaks occurred in Newark and Detroit. Forty-three people were killed in Detroit alone, nearly all of them

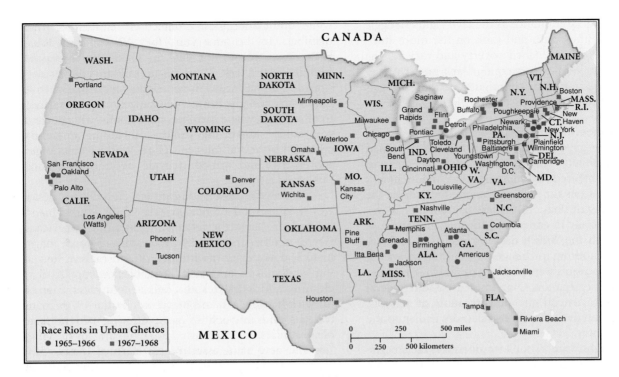

MAP 29.2 Racial Unrest in America's Cities, 1965–1968

American cities suffered through four "long hot summers" of rioting in the mid-1960s. In 1967, the worst year, riots broke out across the United States, including numerous locations in the South and West. The 1968 report of the National Advisory Commission on Civil Disorders targeted racism as the source of black rage: "What white Americans have never fully understood—but what the Negro can never forget—is that white society is deeply implicated in the ghetto. . . . White institutions created it, white institutions maintain it, and white society condones it." The riots' major impact on white America was to create a climate of fear that helped drain support from the larger civil rights movement.

For more help analyzing this map, see the ONLINE STUDY GUIDE at
bedfordstmartins.com/henretta.

black, and $50 million worth of property was destroyed. As in most of the riots, the arson and looting in Detroit targeted white-owned stores and property, but there was little physical violence against white people.

On July 29, 1967, President Johnson appointed a special commission to investigate the riots. The final report of the National Advisory Commission on Civil Disorders (also known as the Kerner Commission), released in March 1968, detailed the continuing inequality and racism of urban life. It also issued a warning: "Our nation is moving toward two societies, one black, one white—separate and unequal. . . . What white Americans have never fully understood—but what the Negro can never forget—is that white society is deeply implicated in the ghetto. White institutions created it, white institutions maintain it, and white society condones it."

The Assassination of Martin Luther King Jr. On April 4, 1968, barely a month after the Kerner

Commission released its report, Martin Luther King Jr. was assassinated in Memphis, Tennessee, where he had gone to support a strike by predominantly black sanitation workers. King's death set off an explosion of urban rioting, with major violence breaking out in more than a hundred cities.

With King's assassination, the civil rights movement lost the black leader best able to stir the conscience of white America. At the time of his death, King was only thirty-nine years old. During the last years of his life, he had moved toward a broader view of the structural problems of poverty and racism faced by blacks in contemporary America. He spoke out eloquently against the Vietnam War, and in 1968 he was planning a poor people's campaign to raise issues of economic injustice and inequality. How successful King would have been in those endeavors will never be known, but his death marked the passing of an important national leader and symbolized the troubled course of the civil rights movement.

The Legacy of the Civil Rights Movement

The 1960s brought permanent, indeed revolutionary, changes in American race relations. Jim Crow segregation was overturned and federal legislation passed to ensure protection of black Americans' most basic civil rights. The enfranchisement of blacks in the southern states ended political control by all-white state Democratic parties and allowed black candidates to enter the political arena. White candidates who had once been ardent segregationists began to court the black vote. In time Martin Luther King Jr.'s greatness was recognized even among whites in the South; in 1986 his birthday became a national holiday.

Yet much remained undone. The more entrenched forms of segregation and discrimination persisted. African Americans, particularly those in the central cities, continued to make up a disproportionate number of the poor, the unemployed, and the undereducated. As the civil rights movement gradually splintered, its agenda remained unfinished. Yet, even as African Americans experienced frustration with the slow rate of change, their movement provided a fresh and innovative model for other groups seeking to expand their rights.

The Chicano Movement. Although Mexican Americans had been working actively for civil rights since the 1930s (see Chapter 24), poverty, an uncertain legal status, and language barriers made their political mobilization difficult. That situation began to change when the Mexican American Political Association (MAPA) mobilized support for John F. Kennedy; in return Kennedy appointed several Mexican American leaders to posts in Washington. Over the next four years, MAPA and other political organizations worked successfully to elect Mexican American candidates to Congress: Edward Roybal of California and Henry González and Elizo de la Garza of Texas in the House, and Joseph Montoya of New Mexico in the Senate.

Younger Mexican Americans quickly grew impatient with MAPA, however. The barrios of Los Angeles and other western cities produced the militant Brown Berets, modeled on the Black Panthers (who wore black berets). Rejecting the assimilationist approach of their elders, 1,500 Mexican American students met in Denver in 1969 to hammer out a new nationalist political and cultural agenda. They proclaimed a new term, *Chicano*, to replace *Mexican American*, and later organized a new political party, La Raza Unida (The United Race), to promote Chicano interests and candidates. In California and other southwestern states, students staged demonstrations and boycotts to press for bilingual education, the hiring of more Chicano teachers, and the creation of Chicano studies programs. By the 1970s dozens of such programs were offered at universities throughout the region.

Chicano strategists also pursued economic objectives. Working in the fields around Delano, California, labor leader César Chávez organized the United Farm Workers (UFW), the first union to represent migrant workers successfully. A 1965 grape pickers' strike and a nationwide boycott of table grapes brought Chávez and his union national publicity and won support from the AFL-CIO and from Senator Robert F. Kennedy of New York. Victory came in 1970 when California grape growers signed contracts recognizing the UFW.

The Native American Movement. North American Indians also found a model in the civil rights movement. Numbering nearly 800,000 in the 1960s, Native Americans were an exceedingly diverse group, divided by language, tribal history, region, and degree of integration into the mainstream of American life. The termination policy that had begun in the 1950s had accelerated the breakdown of tribal life and the dispersal of Native American populations—although it could also be said to have fostered a sense of "American Indian" identity by bringing diverse Native Americans together. As a group, they shared an unemployment rate ten times the national average as well as the worst poverty, the most inadequate housing, the highest disease rates, and the least access to education of any group in the United States.

As early as World War II, the National Council of American Indians had lobbied for improvement of those conditions. In the 1960s some Indian groups became more assertive. Like the young militants in the black civil rights movement, they challenged the accommodationist approach of their elders. Proposing a new name for themselves—*Native Americans*—they organized protests and demonstrations to build support for their cause. In 1968 several Chippewas from Minnesota organized the militant American Indian Movement (AIM), which drew its strength from the third of the Native American population who lived in "red ghettos" in cities throughout the West.

In November 1969 a group calling themselves "Indians of All Tribes" seized the deserted federal penitentiary on Alcatraz Island in San Francisco Bay, offering the government $24 worth of trinkets to pay for it, supposedly the sum the Dutch had paid the native inhabitants for Manhattan Island in 1626. The occupation of Alcatraz lasted until the summer of 1971. A year later a thousand protesters occupied the headquarters of the Federal Bureau of Indian Affairs in Washington, D.C., which was to many Native Americans a hated symbol of the inconsistent federal policy on tribal welfare (see American Voices, "Mary Crow Dog: The Trail of Broken Treaties," p. 864).

In February 1973, 200 Sioux organized by AIM leaders began an occupation of the tiny village of Wounded Knee, South Dakota, the site of an army massacre of the Sioux in 1890 (see Chapter 16). They were protesting the light sentences given to a group of white men convicted

Mary Crow Dog

The Trail of Broken Treaties

In November 1972, nineteen-year-old Mary Crow Dog traveled to Washington, D.C., with several hundred other Sioux from the Rosebud and Pine Ridge reservations in South Dakota. As she explains in her autobiography, their group was one of several caravans participating in a protest known as the "Trail of Broken Treaties," which ended in a six-day occupation of the Bureau of Indian Affairs headquarters.

When we arrived in Washington we got lost. We had been promised food and accommodation, but due to government pressure many church groups which had offered to put us up and feed us got scared and backed off. . . .

Somebody suggested, "Let's all go to the BIA." It seemed the natural thing to do, to go to the Bureau of Indian Affairs building on Constitution Avenue. They would have to put us up. It was "our" building after all. Besides, that was what we had come for, to complain about the treatment the bureau was dishing out to us. . . . Next thing I knew we were in it. We spilled into the building like a great avalanche. Some people put up a tipi on the front lawn. . . . The building finally belonged to us and we lost no time turning it into a tribal village. . . .

We pushed the police and guards out of the building. Some did not wait to be pushed but jumped out of the ground-floor windows like so many frogs. We had formulated twenty Indian demands. These were all rejected by the few bureaucrats sent to negotiate with us. . . . Soon we listened to other voices as the occupation turned into a siege. I heard somebody yelling, "The pigs are here." I could see from the window that it was true. The whole building was surrounded by helmeted police armed with all kinds of guns. A fight broke out between the police and our security. Some of our young men got hit over the head with police clubs and we saw the blood streaming down their faces. . . .

We barricaded all doors and the lowest windows with document boxes, Xerox machines, tables, file cabinets, anything we could lay our hands on. . . .

From then on, every morning we were given a court order to get out by six P.M. Come six o'clock and we would be standing there ready to join battle. I think many brothers and sisters were prepared to die right on the steps of the BIA building. . . .

In the end a compromise was reached. The government said . . . they would appoint two high administration officials to seriously consider our twenty demands. Our expenses to get home would be paid. Nobody would be prosecuted. Of course, our twenty points were never gone into afterward. From the practical point of view, nothing had been achieved. . . . But morally it had been a great victory. We had faced White America collectively, not as individual tribes. We had stood up to the government and gone through our baptism of fire. We had not run.

Source: Mary Crow Dog, *Lakota Woman* (New York: Grove Weidenfeld, 1990), 84–85, 88–91.

---

of killing a Sioux in 1972. To dramatize their cause the protesters took eleven hostages and occupied several buildings. But when a gun battle with the FBI left one protester dead and another wounded, the seventy-one-day siege collapsed. Although the new Native American activism helped to alienate many white onlookers, it did spur government action on tribal issues (see Chapter 31).

Identity Politics. Civil rights, once seen as a movement exclusively for the rights of black people, also sparked a new awareness among some predominantly white groups. Americans of Polish, Italian, Greek, and Slavic descent, most of them working class and Catholic, proudly embraced their ethnic identities. Through groups like the Grey Panthers, elderly Americans organized to demand better health, Social Security, and other benefits.

Homosexual men and women also banded together to protest legal and social oppression based on their sexual orientation. In 1969 the gay liberation movement gained momentum in the "Stonewall riot" in New York City, when patrons of a gay bar fought back against police harassment. The assertion of gay pride that followed the incident drew heavily on the language and tactics of the civil rights movement. Activists took the new name of *gay* rather than *homosexual*; founded advocacy groups, newspapers, and political organizations to challenge

Wounded Knee Revisited

In 1973 members of the American Indian Movement staged a seventy-one-day protest at Wounded Knee, South Dakota, the site of the 1890 massacre of 200 Sioux by U.S. soldiers. (See Map 16.4, The Indian Frontier, to 1890, p. 470.) The takeover was sparked by the murder of a local Sioux by a group of whites but quickly expanded to include demands for basic reforms in federal Indian policy and tribal governance. Corbis-Bettmann.

discrimination and prejudice; and offered emotional support to those who "came out" and publicly affirmed their homosexuality. For gays as well as members of various ethnic and cultural groups, political activism based on heightened group identity represented one of the most significant legacies of the African American struggle.

The Revival of Feminism

The black civil rights movement also helped to reactivate **feminism**, a movement that had been languishing since the 1920s. Just as the abolition movement had been the training ground for women's rights advocates in the nineteenth century, the black struggle became an inspiration for young feminists in the 1960s. But the revival of feminism also sprang from social and demographic changes that affected women young and old.

Changing Social Conditions.   By 1970, 42.6 percent of women were working, and four out of ten working women were married. Especially significant was the growth in the number of working women with preschool children—up from 12 percent in 1950 to 30 percent in 1970.

Another significant change was increased access to education for women. Immediately after World War II, the percentage of college students who were women declined, as the GI Bill gave men a temporary advantage in access to higher education. At the height of the baby boom, many college women dropped out of school to marry and raise families. By 1960, however, the percentage of college students who were women had risen to 35 percent; in 1970 it reached 41 percent.

The meaning of marriage was changing, too. The baby boom turned out to be only a temporary interruption of a century-long decline in the birthrate. The introduction of the birth control pill, first marketed in 1960, and the intrauterine device (IUD) helped women control their fertility. Women had fewer children, and because of an increased life expectancy (seventy-five years in 1970, up from fifty-four years in 1920), they devoted proportionally fewer years to raising children. At the same time the divorce rate, which had risen slowly throughout the twentieth century, rose markedly as the states liberalized divorce laws. As a result of these changes, traditional gender expectations were dramatically undermined. American women's lives now usually included work and marriage, often childrearing and a career, and possibly bringing up children alone after a divorce. Those changing social realities created a major constituency for the emerging women's movement of the 1960s.

Older, politically active professional women sought change by working through the political system. This group was galvanized in part by a report by the Presidential Commission on the Status of Women (1963), which documented the employment and educational discrimination women faced. More important than the report's rather conservative recommendations was the rudimentary nationwide network of women in public life that formed in the course of the commission's work.

Another spark that ignited the revival of feminism was Betty Friedan's pointed indictment of suburban domesticity, *The Feminine Mystique*, published in 1963 (see Chapter 28). Women responded enthusiastically to Friedan's book—especially white, college-educated, middle-class women. The book sold 3 million copies and was excerpted in many women's magazines. *The Feminine Mystique* gave women a vocabulary with which to express their dissatisfaction and promoted women's self-realization through employment, continuing education, and other activities outside the home.

Like so many other constituencies in postwar America, women's rights activists looked to the federal government for help. Especially important was the Civil Rights Act of 1964, which had as great an impact on women as it did on blacks and other minorities. Title VII, which barred discrimination in employment on the basis of race, religion, national origin, or sex, eventually became a powerful tool in the fight against sex discrimination. At first, however, the Equal Employment Opportunity Commission (EEOC) avoided implementing it.

The National Organization for Women.

Dissatisfied with the Commission's reluctance to defend women's rights, Friedan and others founded the National Organization for Women (NOW) in 1966. Modeling itself on groups such as the NAACP, NOW aimed to be a civil rights organization for women. "The purpose of NOW," an early statement declared, "is to take action to bring women into full participation in the mainstream of American society now, exercising all the privileges and responsibilities thereof in truly equal partnership with men." Under Friedan, who served as NOW's first president, membership grew from 1,000 in 1967 to 15,000 in 1971. Men made up a fourth of NOW's early membership. The group is still the largest feminist organization in the United States.

Women's Liberation.

Another group of new feminists, the women's liberationists, came to the women's movement through their civil rights work. White college women had made up about half the students who went south with SNCC in the Freedom Summer project of 1964. Young women like Casey Hayden and Mary King found role models in older southern women like Ella Baker, Anne Braden, and Virginia Foster Durr, who were prominent in the civil rights movement. They also appreciated the work of local black women who were in the forefront of community organizing and who put their lives on the line by housing SNCC workers. As Dorothy Burlage noted, these women "inspired me to think that women could do anything." As the white college women developed self-confidence and organizational skills working in the South, some of them began to question what would later be called the sexism of the male-dominated leadership.

After 1965 black militants made whites unwelcome in the civil rights movement. But when white women transferred their energies to the antiwar groups that were emerging in that period, they found the New Left even more male dominated. When the antiwar movement adopted draft resistance as a central strategy, women found themselves marginalized. Those women who tried to raise feminist issues at conventions were shouted off the platform with jeers such as "Move on, little girl, we have more important issues to talk about here than women's liberation."

Around 1967 the contradiction between the New Left's lip service to egalitarianism and women's treatment by male leaders caused women radicals to realize

Women's Liberation
Arguing that beauty contests were degrading to women, members of the National Women's Liberation Party staged a protest against the Miss America pageant held in Atlantic City, New Jersey, in September 1968. Wide World Photos, Inc.

that they needed their own movement. In contrast to groups such as NOW, which had traditional organizational structures and dues-paying members, these women formed loose collectives whose shifting membership often lacked any formal structure. They organized independently in five or six different cities, including Chicago, San Francisco, and New York.

Members of the women's liberation movement (or "women's lib," as it was dubbed by the somewhat hostile media) went public in 1968 in a protest at the Miss America pageant. Their demonstration featured a "freedom trash can" into which they encouraged women to throw false eyelashes, hair curlers, brassieres, and girdles—all of which they branded as symbols of female oppression. An activity with a more lasting impact was "consciousness raising"—group sessions in which women shared their experiences of being female. Swapping stories about being passed over for a promotion, needing a husband's signature on a credit card application, or enduring the whistles and leers of men while walking down the street helped participants to realize that their individual problems were part of a wider pattern of oppression. The slogan "The personal is political" became a rallying cry of the movement.

By 1970 a growing convergence of interests began to blur the distinction between women's rights and women's liberation. Radical women realized that key feminist goals—child care, equal pay, and abortion rights—could best be achieved in the political arena. At the same time more traditional activists developed a broader view of the women's movement, tentatively including divisive issues such as abortion and lesbian rights. Although the movement remained largely white and middle class, feminists were beginning to think of themselves as part of a broad, growing, and increasingly influential social crusade that would continue to grow.

The Long Road Home, 1968–1975

The United States in 1968 was deeply polarized. Riots in the cities, black and Chicano power, campus unrest, and a host of protests and challenges were, in the eyes of many citizens, tearing the country in two. But Vietnam remained the central domestic and foreign-policy issue. Although the Johnson administration insisted that there was "light at the end of the tunnel," the reality was otherwise. The war would continue, at home and in Vietnam, for another five years.

1968: A Year of Shocks

In 1968, as Lyndon Johnson planned his reelection campaign, antiwar protests and rising battlefield casualties had begun to erode public support for a war that seemed to have no end. Since Diem's assassination in 1963, South Vietnam had undergone a confusing series of military coups and countercoups. In the spring of 1966, the Johnson administration pressured the unpopular South Vietnamese government to adopt democratic reforms, including a new constitution and popular elections. In September 1967 U.S. officials helped to elect General Nguyen Van Thieu president of South Vietnam. Thieu's regime, the administration hoped, would stabilize politics in South Vietnam, advance the military struggle against the Communists, and legitimize the South Vietnamese government in the eyes of the American public.

The Tet Offensive. The administration's hopes evaporated on January 30, 1968, when the Viet Cong unleashed a massive, well-coordinated assault on major urban areas in South Vietnam. Known as the "Tet" offensive, the assault was timed to coincide with the lunar new year, a festive Vietnamese holiday. Viet Cong forces struck thirty-six of the forty-four provincial capitals and five of the six major cities, including Saigon, where they raided the supposedly impregnable U.S. embassy (see Map 29.1). In strict military terms the Tet offensive was a failure for the Viet Cong since it did not provoke the intended collapse of the South Vietnamese government. But its long-term effect was quite different. The daring attack made a mockery of official pronouncements that the United States was winning the war and swung American public opinion more strongly against the war. Just before the offensive a Gallup poll found that 56 percent of Americans considered themselves "hawks" (supporters of the war), while only 28 percent identified with the "doves" (opponents). Three months after Tet the doves outnumbered the hawks 42 to 41 percent. This turnaround in public opinion did not mean that a majority of Americans supported the peace movement, however. Many who called themselves doves had simply concluded that the war was unwinnable and were therefore opposed to it on pragmatic rather than moral grounds. As a housewife told a pollster, "I want to get out, but I don't want to give up."

Political Turmoil. The growing opposition to the war spilled over into the 1968 presidential campaign. Even before Tet, Senator Eugene J. McCarthy of Minnesota had entered the Democratic primaries as an antiwar candidate. President Johnson won the early New Hampshire primary, but McCarthy received a stunning 42.2 percent of the vote. His strong showing against the president reflected profound public dissatisfaction with the course of the war, even among those who were hawks.

Johnson realized that his political support was evaporating. On March 31 and at the end of an otherwise mundane televised address, he stunned the nation by announcing that he would not seek reelection. Johnson had already reversed his policy of incremental escalation of the war. Now he called a partial bombing halt and vowed to devote his remaining months in office to the search for peace. On May 10, 1968, preliminary peace talks between the United States and North Vietnam opened in Paris.

Just four days after Johnson's withdrawal from the presidential race, Martin Luther King Jr. was assassinated in Memphis. The ensuing riots in cities across the country left forty-three people dead. Soon afterward, students protesting Columbia University's plans for expanding into a neighboring ghetto and displacing its residents occupied several campus buildings. The brutal response of the New York City police helped to radicalize even more students. The next month a massive strike by students and labor unions toppled the French government. Student unrest seemed likely to become a worldwide phenomenon.

Then came the final tragedy of the year. Senator Robert Kennedy, who had entered the Democratic presidential primaries in March, had quickly become a frontrunner. On June 5, 1968, as he celebrated his victory in the California primary, he was shot dead by a young Palestinian who was thought to oppose Kennedy's pro-Israeli stance. Robert Kennedy's assassination shattered the dreams of many who had hoped that social change could be achieved by working through the political system. His death also weakened the Democratic Party. In his brief but dramatic campaign, Kennedy had excited and energized the traditional members of the New Deal coalition, including blue-collar workers and black voters, in a way that the more cerebral Eugene McCarthy, who appealed mostly to the antiwar movement, never did.

The Democratic Party never fully recovered from Johnson's withdrawal and Kennedy's assassination. McCarthy's campaign limped along, while Senator George S. McGovern of South Dakota entered the Democratic race in an effort to keep the Kennedy forces together. Meanwhile, Vice President Hubert H. Humphrey lined up pledges from traditional Democratic constituencies—unions, urban machines, and state political organizations. Democrats found themselves on the verge of nominating not an antiwar candidate but a public figure closely associated with Johnson's war policies.

The Siege of Chicago. At the August Democratic nominating convention, the political divisions generated by the war consumed the party. Most of the drama occurred not in the convention hall but outside on the streets of Chicago. Led by activists Jerry Rubin and Abbie Hoffman, around 10,000 protesters descended on the city, calling for an end to the war, the legalization of marijuana, and the abolition of money. To mock those inside the convention hall, these "Yippies," as the group called themselves, nominated a pig for president. Their

RFK

Bobby Kennedy inspired strong passions during his 1968 campaign. Followers often tore off his cuff links as they tried to touch him or shake his hand. Steve Schapiro / Black Star.

stunts, geared toward maximizing their media exposure, diverted attention from the more serious and far more numerous antiwar activists who had come to Chicago as convention delegates or volunteers.

Richard J. Daley, the Democratic mayor of Chicago who had grown increasingly angry as protesters disrupted his convention, called out the police to break up the demonstrations. Several nights of skirmishes between protesters and police culminated on the evening of the nominations. In what an official report later described as a "police riot," patrolmen attacked protesters with mace, tear gas, and clubs as demonstrators chanted, "The whole world is watching!" Television networks broadcast a film of the riot as the nominating speeches were being made, cementing a popular impression of the Democrats as the party of disorder. Inside the hall the Democrats dispiritedly nominated Hubert H. Humphrey, who chose Senator Edmund S. Muskie of

Maine as his running mate. The delegates approved a middle-of-the-road platform that endorsed continued fighting in Vietnam while the administration explored diplomatic means of ending the conflict.

Backlash. The disruptive Democratic convention unleashed a backlash against antiwar protesters. The general public did not differentiate between the disruptive antics of the Yippies and the more responsible behavior of those activists who were trying to work within the system. Polls showed overwhelming support for Mayor Daley and the police.

The turmoil surrounding the New Left and the antiwar movement strengthened support for proponents of "law and order," which became a conservative catch phrase for the next several years. Indeed, many Americans, though opposed to the war, were fed up with protest and dissent. Governor George C. Wallace of Alabama, a third-party candidate, skillfully exploited their growing disapproval of the antiwar movement by making student protests and urban riots his chief campaign issues. But Wallace, who in 1963 had promised to enforce "segregation now . . . segregation tomorrow . . . and segregation forever," also exploited the mounting backlash against the civil rights movement. Articulating the resentments of many working-class whites, he combined attacks on liberal intellectuals and government elites with strident denunciations of school desegregation and forced busing.

Even more than George Wallace, Richard Nixon tapped the increasingly conservative mood of the electorate. After his unsuccessful presidential campaign in 1960 and his loss in the California gubernatorial race in 1962, Nixon engineered an amazing political comeback and in 1968 won the Republican presidential nomination. As part of what his advisors called the "southern strategy," he chose Spiro Agnew, the conservative governor of Maryland, as his running mate to help him make inroads into the once solidly Democratic South. Nixon hoped to attract southern voters, especially Wallace supporters, who opposed Democratic civil rights legislation. He also used traditional populist appeals, pledging, to represent the "quiet voice" of the "great majority of Americans, the forgotten Americans, the nonshouters, the nondemonstrators."

Despite the Democratic debacle in Chicago, the election was a close one. In the last weeks of the campaign, Humphrey rallied by gingerly disassociating himself from Johnson's war policies. Then in a televised address on October 31, President Johnson announced a complete halt to the bombing of North Vietnam. Nixon countered by intimating that he had his own plan to end the war— although in reality no such plan existed. On election day Nixon received 43.4 percent of the vote to Humphrey's 42.7 percent, defeating him by a scant 510,000 votes out

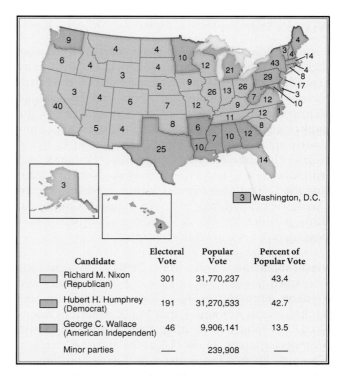

MAP 29.3 Presidential Election of 1968

Candidate	Electoral Vote	Popular Vote	Percent of Popular Vote
Richard M. Nixon (Republican)	301	31,770,237	43.4
Hubert H. Humphrey (Democrat)	191	31,270,533	42.7
George C. Wallace (American Independent)	46	9,906,141	13.5
Minor parties	—	239,908	

With Lyndon B. Johnson's surprise decision not to run for another term and, less than three month's later, the assassination of the party's most charismatic contender for the presidential nomination, Robert Kennedy, the Democrats faced the election of 1968 in disarray. Controversy over the Vietnam War fractured the party, as did the appeal of Governor George Wallace of Alabama, who left the Democrats to run as a third-party candidate and campaigned on the backlash against the civil rights movement. As late as mid-September Wallace held the support of 21 percent of the voters. But in November he received only 13.5 percent of the vote, winning five states and showing that the South was no longer solidly Democratic. Republican Richard M. Nixon, who like Wallace emphasized "law and order" in his campaign, defeated Hubert H. Humphrey with only 43.4 percent of the popular vote.

of the 73 million that were cast (Map 29.3). Wallace finished with 13.5 percent of the popular vote. Though Nixon owed his election largely to the split in the Democratic coalition, the success of his southern strategy presaged the emergence of a new Republican majority. In the meantime, however, the Democrats retained a majority in both houses of Congress.

The closeness of the 1968 election suggested how polarized American society had become. Nixon appealed to a segment of society that came to be known as the **silent majority**—hard-working, nonprotesting, generally white Americans. Although his victory suggested a growing consensus among voters who were "unblack, unpoor, and unyoung," heated protest and controversy would persist until the war ended.

Nixon's War

Vietnam, long Lyndon Johnson's war, now became Richard Nixon's. At first Nixon sought to end the war by expanding its scope, as a means of pressuring the North Vietnamese to negotiate. But Nixon and his national security advisor, Henry Kissinger, soon realized that the public would not support such an approach. Thus shortly after Nixon took office, he sent a letter to the North Vietnamese leaders proposing mutual troop withdrawals. In March 1969, to convince North Vietnam that the United States meant business, Nixon ordered clandestine bombing raids on neutral Cambodia, through which the North Vietnamese had been transporting supplies and reinforcements.

Vietnamization and Its Critics. When the intensified bombing failed to end the war, Nixon and Kissinger adopted a policy of Vietnamization. On June 8, 1969, Nixon announced that 25,000 American troops would be withdrawn by August and replaced by South Vietnamese forces. As the U.S. ambassador to Vietnam, Ellsworth Bunker, noted cynically, Vietnamization was just a matter of changing "the color of the bodies." Antiwar demonstrators denounced the new policy, which protected American lives at the expense of the Vietnamese but would not end the war. On October 15, 1969, in cities across the country, millions of Americans joined a one-day "moratorium" against the war. A month later more than a quarter of a million people mobilized in Washington in the largest antiwar demonstration to date.

To discredit his critics Nixon denounced student demonstrators as "bums" and stated that "North Vietnam cannot defeat or humiliate the United States. Only Americans can do that." Vice President Spiro Agnew attacked dissenters as "ideological eunuchs" and "nattering nabobs of negativism." Nixon staunchly insisted that he would not be swayed by the mounting protests against the war. During the November 1969 March on Washington, the president barricaded himself in the White House and watched football on television.

Invasion in Cambodia. On April 30, 1970, the bombing of Cambodia, which Nixon had kept secret from both the public and from Congress, culminated in an "incursion" into Cambodia by American ground forces to destroy enemy havens there. The invasion proved only a short-term setback for the North Vietnamese. More critically, the American action in Cambodia—along with the ongoing North Vietnamese intervention there—destabilized the country, exposing it to a takeover by the ruthless Khmer Rouge later in the 1970s.

When the *New York Times* uncovered the secret invasion of Cambodia, outrage led antiwar leaders to organize a national student strike. On May 4 at Kent State University outside Cleveland, panicky National Guardsmen fired into a crowd of students at an antiwar rally. Four people were killed and eleven more wounded. Only two of those who were killed had been attending the demonstration; the other two were just passing by on their way to class. Soon afterward, National Guardsmen stormed a dormitory at Jackson State College in Mississippi, killing two black students. More than 450 colleges closed in protest, and 80 percent of all campuses experienced some kind of disturbance. In June 1970, immediately after the Kent State slayings, a Gallup poll identified campus unrest as the issue that most troubled Americans.

At the same time, however, dissatisfaction with the war continued to spread. Congressional opposition to the war, which had been growing since the Fulbright hearings in 1966, intensified with the invasion of Cambodia. In June 1970 the Senate expressed its disapproval by voting to repeal the Gulf of Tonkin resolution and by cutting off funding for operations in Cambodia. Even the soldiers in Vietnam were showing mounting opposition to their mission. The number of troops who refused to follow combat orders increased steadily, and thousands of U.S. soldiers deserted. Among the majority who fought on, many sewed peace symbols on their uniforms. In the heat of battle, a number of overbearing junior officers were sometimes "fragged"—killed or wounded in grenade attacks by their own soldiers. At home, members of a group called Vietnam Veterans Against the War turned in their combat medals at demonstrations outside the U.S. Capitol.

The My Lai Massacre. In 1971 Americans were appalled by revelations of the sheer brutality of the war when Lieutenant William L. Calley was court-martialed for atrocities committed in the village of My Lai. In March 1968 Calley and the platoon under his command had apparently murdered 350 Vietnamese villagers in retaliation for casualties sustained in an earlier engagement. The incident came to light because one member of the platoon refused to go along with a military cover-up; investigative reporter Seymour Hersh of the *New York Times* broke the story in November 1969. The military court sentenced Calley to life in prison for his part in the massacre. Yet George Wallace and some congressional conservatives called him a hero. President Nixon had Calley's sentence reduced; he was paroled in 1974.

The Decline of Antiwar Protest. After a final outbreak of protest and violence following the incident at Kent State, antiwar activism began to ebb. The antiwar movement was weakened in part by internal divisions within the New Left. In the late 1960s SDS and other antiwar groups fell victim to police harassment, and Federal Bureau of Investigation (FBI) and Central Intelligence Agency (CIA) agents infiltrated and disrupted

WHO LOST VIET NAM?

"NOT I," SAID IKE. "I JUST SENT MONEY."

"NOT I," SAID JACK. "I JUST SENT ADVISORS."

"NOT I," SAID LYNDON. "I JUST FOLLOWED JACK."

"NOT I," SAID DICK. "I JUST HONORED JACK AND LYNDON'S COMMITMENTS."

"NOT I," SAID JERRY. "WHAT WAS THE QUESTION?"

"**YOU** LOST VIETNAM," SAID HENRY, "BECAUSE YOU DIDN'T TRUST YOUR LEADERS."

Passing the Buck

Highlighting the long and tortured history of the war, Jules Feiffer's 1975 cartoon offered a biting commentary on the lack of presidential accountability for U.S. policies in Vietnam.

radical organizations. After 1968 the New Left splintered into factions, its energy spent. One radical faction broke off from SDS and formed the Weathermen, a tiny band of self-styled revolutionaries who embraced terrorist tactics that alienated more moderate activists.

Nixon's Vietnamization policy also played a role in the decline of antiwar protest by dramatically reducing the number of soldiers in combat. When Nixon took office, more than 543,000 American soldiers were serving in Vietnam; by the end of 1970, there were 334,000, and two years later there were 24,200. Nixon's promise to continue troop withdrawals, end the draft, and institute an all-volunteer army by 1973 further deprived the antiwar movement of important organizing issues, particularly on college campuses. Student commitment to social causes, however, did not disappear altogether. In the early 1970s many student activists refocused their energies on issues such as feminism and environmentalism.

Withdrawal from Vietnam and Détente

At the same time Nixon had been prosecuting the war in Vietnam, ostensibly to halt the spread of communism, he had been formulating a new policy toward the Soviet Union and China. Known as **détente** (the French word for a relaxation of tensions), Nixon's policy was to seek peaceful coexistence with the two Communist powers and to link his overtures of friendship with a plan to end the Vietnam War. In his talks with Chinese and Soviet leaders, Nixon urged them to reduce their military aid to the North Vietnamese as a means of pressuring the North Vietnamese to the negotiating table.

A lifelong anti-Communist crusader, Nixon was better able to reach out to the two Communist superpowers without arousing American mistrust than a Democratic president would have been. Since the Chinese revolution of 1949, the United States had refused to recognize the government of the People's Republic of China. Instead, the State Department had recognized the Nationalist Chinese government in Taiwan. Nixon moved away from that policy, reasoning that the United States could exploit the growing rift between the People's Republic of China and the Soviet Union. In February 1972 Nixon journeyed to China in a symbolic visit that set the stage for the establishment of formal diplomatic relations in 1979.

In a similar spirit Nixon journeyed to Moscow in May 1972 to sign the first Strategic Arms Limitations Treaty (SALT I) between the United States and the Soviet Union. Although SALT I fell far short of ending the arms race, it did limit the production and deployment of intercontinental ballistic missiles (ICBMs) and antiballistic missile systems (ABMs). The treaty also signified that the United States could no longer afford the massive military spending that would have been necessary to regain the

The Fall of Saigon

After the 1973 U.S. withdrawal from Vietnam, the South Vietnamese government lasted another two years. In March 1975 the North Vietnamese forces launched a final offensive against the south and by April had surrounded the capital of Saigon. Here, panicked Vietnamese seek sanctuary at the U.S. embassy compound. Vietnam was united on April 29, 1975. Nik Wheeler / Sipa.

nuclear and military superiority it had enjoyed immediately following World War II. By the early 1970s inflation, domestic dissent, and the decline in American hegemony had limited and reshaped American aims and options in international relations. Most of all Nixon hoped that a rapprochement with the Soviets would help to resolve the prolonged crisis in Vietnam.

The Paris peace talks had been in stalemate since 1968. Though the war had been "Vietnamized," and American casualties had decreased, the South Vietnamese military proved unable to hold its own. In late 1971, as American troops withdrew from the region, Communist forces stepped up their attacks on Laos, Cambodia, and South Vietnam. The next spring North Vietnamese forces launched a major new offensive against South Vietnam. In April, as the fighting intensified, Nixon ordered B-52 bombing raids against North Vietnam, and a month later he approved the mining of North Vietnamese ports (see American Lives, "John Paul Vann: Dissident Patriot," p. 874).

That spring the increased combat activity and growing political pressure at home helped revive the Paris peace negotiations. Nixon hoped to undercut antiwar critics by making concessions to the North Vietnamese in the peace talks. In October Henry Kissinger and the North Vietnamese negotiator Le Duc Tho reached a cease-fire agreement calling for the withdrawal of the remaining U.S. troops, the return of all American prisoners of war, and the continued presence of North Vietnamese troops in South Vietnam. Nixon and Kissinger also promised the North Vietnamese substantial aid for postwar reconstruction. On the eve of the 1972 presidential election, Kissinger announced "peace is at hand," and Nixon returned to the White House with a resounding electoral victory (see Chapter 30).

The peace initiative, however, soon stalled when the South Vietnamese rejected the provision concerning North Vietnamese troop positions, and the North declined to compromise further. With negotiations deadlocked, Nixon stepped up military action once more. From December 17 to December 30, 1972, American planes subjected civilian and military targets in Hanoi and Haiphong to the most devastating bombing of the war, referred to in the press as the "Christmas bombings."

Finally, on January 27, 1973, representatives of the United States, North and South Vietnam, and the Viet Cong signed a cease-fire in Paris. But the Paris Peace accords, which differed little from the proposal that had been rejected in October, did not fulfill Nixon's promise of "peace with honor." Basically, they mandated the unilateral withdrawal of American troops in exchange for the return of American prisoners of war from North Vietnam. For most Americans that was enough.

Without massive U.S. military and economic aid and with North Vietnamese guerrillas operating freely throughout the countryside, the South Vietnamese government of General Nguyen Van Thieu soon fell to the more disciplined and popular Communist forces. In March 1975 North Vietnamese forces launched a final offensive. Horrified American television viewers watched as South Vietnamese officials and soldiers struggled with American embassy personnel to board the last helicopters that would fly out of Saigon before

North Vietnamese troops entered the city. On April 29, 1975, Vietnam was reunited, and Saigon was renamed Ho Chi Minh City in honor of the Communist leader who had died in 1969.

The Legacy of Vietnam

Spanning nearly thirty years, the American involvement in Vietnam occupied administrations from Truman to Nixon's successor Gerald Ford. U.S. troops fought in Vietnam for more than eleven years, from 1961 to 1973. In human terms the nation's longest war exacted an enormous cost. Some 58,000 U.S. troops died, and another 300,000 were wounded. Even those who returned unharmed encountered a sometimes hostile or indifferent reception. Arriving home alone without the fanfare that had greeted soldiers of America's victorious wars, most Vietnam veterans found the transition to civilian life abrupt and disorienting. The psychological tensions

The Vietnam Veterans' Memorial
Conceived and funded by a small group of veterans, the Vietnam Veterans' Memorial was dedicated in Washington, D.C., in November 1982. The memorial, designed by Maya Ling Lin, a Yale architecture student, consists of two walls of black granite inscribed with the names of 58,183 men and women who died in the war. The wall of names has tremendous emotional impact on viewers and has become one of the most popular tourist destinations in the nation's capital. Peter Marlow / Magnum Photos, Inc.

John Paul Vann: Dissident Patriot

The divisions caused by the Vietnam War haunted Arlington National Cemetery on June 16, 1972, when three hundred mourners assembled for the funeral of John Paul Vann. "The soldier of the war in Vietnam," Vann had been killed in a helicopter crash in the Central Highlands the week before. Politicians and military leaders closely associated with the war effort were very much in evidence—General William Westmoreland, CIA Director William Colby, the conservative journalist Joseph Alsop, and Secretary of State William Rogers. But so were Daniel Ellsberg, a former Pentagon official who had publicly turned against the war, and Senator Edward Kennedy, another war opponent who had shared Vann's concern about the plight of Vietnamese refugees. In a time of intense polarization over a war that was still going on, this assemblage of hawks and doves was an exceptional sight.

Vann's family also showed the rifts over Vietnam that day. His wife of twenty-six years, Mary Jane, had requested two pieces of music: the upbeat "Colonel Bogie March" from the film *The Bridge on the River Kwai*, one of her husband's favorites, and the haunting antiwar ballad "Where Have All the Flowers Gone?" to express her opposition to the war. One of Vann's sons, twenty-one-year-old Jesse, hated the war so profoundly that he tore his draft card in two at the funeral, placing half of it on his father's casket. He planned to give the other half to President Richard Nixon at the White House ceremony after the funeral, where his father would be presented posthumously with the Presidential Medal of Freedom. Only at the last moment was Jesse talked out of his act of defiance, agreeing that this was, after all, his father's day.

Also at the funeral was *New York Times* reporter Neil Sheehan, who decided at that moment to write a biography of Vann, which he published sixteen years later, *A Bright and Shining Lie*. Sheehan, along with David Halberstam and other reporters, had fallen under Vann's spell during his first tour of duty in Vietnam in 1963, when Vann seemed to be the only American official who was willing to admit that the war was not going well. Sheehan had continued to rely on Vann's outspoken assessments for the rest of the war. "In this war without heroes, this man had been the one compelling figure," Sheehan concluded. "By an obsession, by an unyielding dedication to the war, he had come to personify the American endeavor in Vietnam."

John Paul Vann was an enormously complicated person—a born leader, a visionary, a man who knew no physical fear, but most of all a true believer in America's mission to share democracy with countries "less fortunate" than the United States. His early years were shaped by poverty and lack of opportunity. Born in 1924 to a working-class family in Norfolk, Virginia, he grew up poor during the Great Depression. A colleague later remembered him as a "cocky little red-necked guy with a rural Virginia twang." World War II offered a ticket out; when Vann turned eighteen in 1943, he enlisted and made the army his career. He served with distinction in the Korean War and then took assignments in West Germany and the United States. But in 1959 his service record was stained by accusations of the statutory rape of a fifteen-year-old girl. Even though the army eventually dropped the charges, the scandal effectively prevented him from moving up in the military bureaucracy. Neil Sheehan later concluded that Vann's "moral heroism" in speaking out against the conduct of the war to the seeming detriment of his career was rooted in his awareness that he had nothing to lose, although reporters did not know the full story at the time.

In 1963 thirty-nine-year-old Lieutenant Colonel Vann was sent to Vietnam, where he served as a senior advisor to a South Vietnamese infantry division in the Mekong Delta. At the battle of Ap Bac, he watched his South Vietnamese counterpart purposely refuse to fight the battle the way it had been planned and let the enemy escape. In a moment of epiphany, Vann realized that the rosy reports being fed to Saigon and Washington were false and that Saigon suffered from "an institutionalized unwillingness to fight." After unsuccessful attempts to enlighten his superiors, he leaked his meticulously documented assessments to reporters such as Halberstam and Sheehan. His candor won him few friends in the military, and at the end of his tour of duty, he was reassigned to the Pentagon. He tried to alert the Joint Chiefs of Staff that the war was not being won, but at the last moment the scheduled briefing was canceled, in large

Planning Strategy
Lieutenant Colonel John P. Vann (left) shown during his tour of duty in Vietnam in 1963, discussing a tactical decision. U.S. Army Photo / U.S. Department of Defense, Still Media Records Center, Washington, DC.

For more help analyzing this image, see the ONLINE STUDY GUIDE at bedfordstmartins.com/henretta.

part because the Joint Chiefs did not want to hear his version of the problem. Frustrated and disillusioned, Vann resigned from the army soon afterward and went to work for a civilian defense contractor.

Before long, however, Vann grew restless with stateside life and tried to rejoin the military. Wary of Vann's public criticism of the war, the army refused to accept him. In 1965 Vann found civilian employment with the Agency for International Development in a pacification program to win over the peasants to the South Vietnamese side rather than the National Liberation Front. Arriving just as the major escalation of the war was getting underway, Vann would stay in Vietnam (except for brief trips home) until his death. His honesty and unmatched familiarity with conditions in the countryside led him to conclude that the Communists were doing a far better job at appealing to the local population than was the corrupt Saigon government. As he wrote to a friend in 1965, "If I were a lad of eighteen faced with the same choice—whether to support the GVN [Government of Vietnam] or the NLF—and a member of a rural community, I would surely choose the NLF." His concern for winning over the local peasantry made him an outspoken opponent of the heavy bombing inflicted on the Vietnamese countryside to roust Vietcong sympathizers. He also strongly criticized General Westmoreland's strategy of sending in more American troops to wear down the Vietcong in a war of attrition, arguing that this would be useless without major reforms in the Saigon government.

Despite his role as a gadfly and even though he was now a civilian, Vann assumed more and more responsibility in the day-to-day conduct of the war. In 1971 he was given authority over all the U.S. military forces in the Central Highlands, the equivalent of the position of major general. But by then, according to Sheehan, Vann had "lost his compass." He was no longer able to assess realistically the ability or will of the South Vietnamese to fight without American aid. He continued to insist that the war could be won through pacification and reform in Saigon despite evidence of growing Vietcong strength. When his helicopter went down at Kontum in 1972, he had almost single-handedly saved the Central Highlands from a North Vietnamese offensive. Within six months the United States formally ended its involvement. Two years later Vietnam was reunited under Communist rule.

John Paul Vann never wavered in his belief that in Vietnam America's cause was just and its intentions good. He had no quarrel with the war itself, just with the way it was fought. Vann thought he knew the answers, but Saigon and Washington chose not to listen. His life and death serve as a reminder of the complexities of the Vietnam experience: could it ever really have been "won," and what would "winning" have meant? Neil Sheehan is convinced that Vann "died believing he had won his war."

of serving in Vietnam and the difficulty of reentry sowed the seeds of what is now recognized as posttraumatic stress disorder—recurring physical and psychological problems that often lead to divorce, unemployment, and suicide. Only in the 1980s did America begin to make its peace with those who had served in the nation's most unpopular war.

In Southeast Asia the damage was far greater. The war claimed an estimated 1.5 million Vietnamese lives and devastated the country's physical and economic infrastructure. Neighboring Laos and Cambodia also suffered, particularly Cambodia, where between 1975 and 1979 the Khmer Rouge killed an estimated 2 million Cambodians—a quarter of the population—in a brutal relocation campaign. All told, the war produced nearly 10 million refugees, many of whom immigrated to the United States. Among them were thousands of Amerasians, the offspring of American soldiers and Vietnamese women. Spurned by their fathers and by most Vietnamese, more than 30,000 Amerasians arrived in the 1990s.

The defeat in Vietnam prompted Americans to think differently about foreign affairs and to acknowledge the limits of U.S. power abroad. The United States became less willing to plunge into overseas military commitments, a controversial change that conservatives dubbed the "Vietnam syndrome." In 1973 Congress declared its hostility to undeclared wars like those in Vietnam and Korea by passing the War Powers Act, which required the president to report any use of military force within forty-eight hours and directed that without a declaration of war by Congress hostilities must cease within sixty days. On those occasions when Congress did agree to foreign intervention, as in the Persian Gulf War of 1990 to 1991, American leaders would insist on obtainable military objectives and

carefully channeled information to the news media. In the future any foreign entanglement would be evaluated in terms of its potential to become "another Vietnam."

The Vietnam War also distorted American economic and social affairs. At a total price of over $150 billion, the war siphoned resources from domestic needs, added to the deficit, and fueled inflation. Lyndon Johnson's Great Society programs had been pared down, and domestic reform efforts slowed thereafter. Moreover, the war shattered the liberal consensus that had supported the Democratic coalition. Even more seriously, the conduct of the war—the questionable representation of events in the Gulf of Tonkin, the lies about American successes on the battlefield, the secret war in Cambodia—spawned a deep distrust of government among American citizens. The discrediting of liberalism, the increased cynicism toward government, and the growing social turmoil that accompanied the war would continue into the next decade, paving the way for a resurgence of the Republican Party and a new mood of conservatism.

FOR FURTHER EXPLORATION

▶ For definitions of key terms boldfaced in this chapter, see the glossary at the end of the book.

▶ To assess your mastery of the material covered in this chapter, see the Online Study Guide at **bedfordstmartins.com/henretta**.

▶ For suggested references, including Web sites, see page SR-32 at the end of the book.

▶ For map resources and primary documents, see **bedfordstmartins.com/henretta**.

S U M M A R Y

America's involvement in Vietnam lasted nearly thirty years. Under Truman, Eisenhower, and Kennedy, the United States threw its support behind the French and later the South Vietnamese government in an effort to contain the Communist threat in Asia. Lyndon Johnson transformed the war in 1965 to an offensive combat mission. Between 1965 and 1968 sustained bombing attacks on North Vietnam were accompanied by ever larger infusions of U.S. ground troops. But the Tet offensive of January 1968 highlighted the discrepancy between the administration's glowing accounts of the war and its tortuous reality and marked the beginning of U.S. efforts to disengage from the conflict. Richard Nixon spent another five years trying to end the war, promising Americans "peace with honor." Under his program of Vietnamization, Nixon gradually withdrew U.S. troops while secretly bombing and later invading Cambodia in a futile attempt to destroy enemy havens. The final withdrawal of American troops took place in 1973 under the terms of the Paris Peace accords. The war marked a turning point in U.S. foreign relations, revealing the limitations of American military power in a complex postwar world.

The war also had serious consequences at home, as different viewpoints bitterly divided Americans. Galvanized by opposition to military escalation and the draft, the antiwar movement spread rapidly among young people who staged a series of mass protests between 1967 and 1971. The spirit of rebellion was not limited to the antiwar movement. The New Left challenged university policies and corporate dominance of society, while the more apolitical counterculture preached personal liberation through sex, drugs, music, and spirituality. As the civil rights struggle moved beyond the South, rising militancy and racial strife divided the movement and fueled white opposition to change. At the same time, however, the new black-power movement encouraged racial pride and assertiveness, serving as a model for Mexican Americans, Native Americans, and other ethnic groups. The civil rights movement also helped to inspire a resurgence of feminism and the birth of the gay liberation movement.

The domestic struggle over the war and other issues divided the Democratic Party, resulting in a Democratic National Convention riven with protest and violence in the summer of 1968. The assassinations of Martin Luther King Jr. and Robert Kennedy and a series of urban riots that year further shocked the nation, fueling a growing public desire for law and order. Although antiwar protests continued into the early 1970s, a new mood of conservatism took hold in the country, contributing to the resurgence of the Republican Party under Richard Nixon.

T I M E L I N E

1946 War begins between French and Vietminh over control of Vietnam

1950 United States recognizes French-backed government of Bao Dai and sends military aid

1954 French defeat at Dienbienphu

Geneva accords partition Vietnam at 17th parallel

1962 Students for a Democratic Society (SDS) founded

1963 Coup ousts Ngo Dinh Diem in South Vietnam

Presidential Commission on the Status of Women

1964 Free Speech Movement at Berkeley

Gulf of Tonkin Resolution authorizes military action in Vietnam

1965 Malcolm X assassinated

Operation Rolling Thunder escalates war through mass bombing campaigns

First U.S. combat troops arrive in Vietnam

Race riot in Watts district of Los Angeles

1966 National Organization for Women (NOW) founded

Stokely Carmichael proclaims black power

1967 Hippie counterculture's "Summer of Love"

Race riots in Detroit and Newark

100,000 march in antiwar protest in Washington, D.C.

1968 Tet offensive dashes American hopes of victory

Martin Luther King Jr. and Robert F. Kennedy assassinated

Riot at Democratic National Convention in Chicago

Women's liberation movement emerges

American Indian Movement (AIM) organized

1969 Stonewall riot leads to gay liberation movement

Woodstock Music and Art Fair

Vietnam moratorium called in protest of war

1970 Nixon orders invasion of Cambodia; renewed antiwar protests

Killings at Kent State and Jackson State

1972 Nixon visits People's Republic of China

SALT I Treaty with Soviet Union

1973 Paris Peace accords

War Powers Act

1975 Fall of Saigon

CHAPTER 30

The Lean Years

1969–1980

"THE UNITED STATES STEEL CORPORATION ANNOUNCED yesterday that it was closing 14 plants and mills in 8 states. About 13,000 production and white-collar workers will lose their jobs." "Weyerhaeuser Co. may trim about 1,000 salaried employees from its 11,000 member workforce over the next year." "Philadelphia: Food Fair Inc. plans to close 89 supermarkets in New York and Connecticut." Newspaper articles in the 1970s told the story of the widespread downsizing that cost millions of workers their jobs when rising oil prices, runaway inflation, declining productivity, and stagnating incomes caused the biggest economic downturn in three decades. Beyond the individual hard-luck stories of demeaning low-paid jobs, lost homes, forced relocations, broken marriages, and alcoholism, the economic uncertainties facing working-

and middle-class Americans in this period created a sense of disillusionment about the nation's future. Already reeling from the nation's withdrawal from Vietnam and its implications for the United States' international power, many people also grew disenchanted with their political leadership in the 1970s, as one public official after another, including President Richard Nixon, resigned for misconduct. In the wake of Nixon's resignation, the lackluster administrations of Presidents Gerald Ford and Jimmy Carter failed to provide

◀ **No Gas**
During the energy crisis of 1973 to 1974, American motorists faced widespread gasoline shortages for the first time since World War II. Although gas was not rationed, gas stations were closed on Sundays, and some communities instituted further restrictions such as creating systems by which motorists with license plates ending in even numbers could purchase gas on certain days, with alternate days being reserved for odd numbers. Ken Regan.

the leadership necessary to cope with the nation's economic and international insecurities—failure that fed Americans' growing skepticism about government and its capacity to improve people's lives.

Paradoxically, in the midst of this growing disaffection and skepticism, a commitment to social change persisted. Some of the social movements born in the 1960s, such as feminism and environmentalism, had their greatest impact in the 1970s. As former student radicals moved into the political mainstream, they took their struggles with them, from streets and campuses into courts, schools, workplaces, and community organizations. But like the civil rights and antiwar movements of the 1960s, the social activism of the 1970s stirred fears and uncertainties among many Americans. Furthermore, the darkening economic climate of the new decade undercut the sense of social generosity that had characterized the 1960s, fueling a new conservatism that would become a potent political force by the decade's end.

The Nixon Years

Richard Nixon set the stage for the conservative political resurgence. His election gave impetus to a long-standing Republican effort to trim back the Great Society and shift some federal responsibilities back to the states. At the same time facing a Democratic Congress, Nixon embraced the use of federal power—within limits—to uphold governmental responsibility for social welfare, environmental protection, and economic stability. The president's domestic accomplishments, however, as well as his international initiatives, were ultimately overshadowed by the Watergate scandal, which swept him from office in disgrace and undermined Americans' confidence in their political leaders.

The Republican Domestic Agenda

In a 1968 campaign pledge to "the average American," Nixon vowed to "reverse the flow of power and resources from the states and communities to Washington and start power and resources flowing back . . . to the people." One hallmark of this approach was the 1972 revenue-sharing program, which distributed a portion of federal tax revenues to the states as block grants to be spent as state officials saw fit. In later years revenue sharing would become a key Republican strategy for reducing federal social programs and federal bureaucracy.

Nixon also worked to scale down certain government programs that had grown dramatically during the Johnson administration. Viewing many Democratic social programs as bloated and inefficient, he reduced funding for most of the War on Poverty and dismantled the Office of Economic Opportunity altogether in 1971. Nixon also **impounded** (refused to spend) billions of dollars appropriated by Congress for urban renewal, pollution control, and other environmental initiatives. Although his administration claimed to support civil rights, Nixon adopted a cautious approach toward racial issues so as not to alienate southern white voters. In a leaked 1970 memo, presidential advisor Daniel Patrick Moynihan, a Democrat who had joined the Nixon White House, suggested that "the issue of race could benefit from a period of benign neglect"—a revelation that scandalized liberals and embarrassed the administration. Nixon also vetoed a 1971 bill to establish a comprehensive national child-care system, fearing that such "communal approaches to child rearing" would "Sovietize" American children.

As an alternative to Democratic social legislation, the administration put forward its own antipoverty program in an ambitious attempt to overhaul the jerrybuilt welfare system. In 1969, following the advice of Moynihan, Nixon proposed a Family Assistance Plan that would provide a family of four a small but guaranteed annual income. The appeal of this proposal lay in its simplicity: it would eliminate the multiple layers of bureaucrats (caseworkers, local and state officials, and federal employees) who administered Aid to Families with Dependent Children (AFDC), the nation's largest welfare program. But the bill floundered in the Senate: conservatives attacked it for putting the federal government too deeply into the welfare business, and liberals and social welfare activists opposed it for not going far enough. Welfare reform would remain a contentious political issue for the next thirty years.

Although Nixon sought to streamline or scale back certain antipoverty programs, he actively expanded federal entitlement programs and the regulatory apparatus. Facing Democratic majorities in both houses of Congress, Nixon agreed to the growth of major entitlement programs such as Medicare, Medicaid, and Social Security. In 1970 he signed a bill establishing the Environmental Protection Agency (EPA) to coordinate the growing federal responsibilities for environmental action. In 1972, to monitor the health and safety of workers and consumers, Nixon approved legislation creating the Occupational Safety and Health Administration (OSHA) and the Consumer Products Safety Commission. As inflation spiraled upward in 1971, he also made use of the federal powers granted under the Economic Stabilization Act of 1970 to institute wage and price controls, the first such measures since World War II. Although Nixon offered only lukewarm support for much of this legislation, his administration generally continued the expansion of federal power that had been under way since the New Deal.

Nixon demonstrated his conservative social values most clearly in his appointments to the Supreme Court. The liberal thrust of the Court under the direction of Chief Justice Earl Warren (1953–1969) had disturbed many conservatives. Its *Brown v. Board of Education* decision in 1954 requiring the desegregation of public schools (see Chapter 27) was followed by other landmark decisions in the 1960s. The *Miranda v. Arizona* (1966) decision reinforced defendants' rights by requiring arresting officers to notify suspects of their legal rights. In *Baker v. Carr* (1962) and *Reynolds v. Sims* (1964), the Court put forth the doctrine of "one person, one vote," meaning that all citizens' votes should have equal weight, no matter where they lived, a challenge to disproportionately rural weighted voting districts. The ruling substantially increased the representation in state legislatures and Congress of both suburban and urban areas (with their concentrations of African American and Spanish-speaking residents) at the expense of rural regions. One of the most controversial decisions was *Engel v. Vitale* (1962), which banned organized prayer in public schools as a violation of the First Amendment. When Justice Warren retired in 1969, President Nixon took the opportunity to begin reshaping the Court and nominated conservative Warren Burger to become chief justice. After some difficulties in getting nominees confirmed by the Senate, Nixon eventually named three other justices: Harry Blackmun (who proved more liberal than expected), Lewis F. Powell Jr., and William Rehnquist.

Nixon's appointees did not always hand down decisions the president approved, however. Despite attempts by the Justice Department to halt further desegregation in the face of determined white opposition, the Court ordered busing of public school students to nonneighborhood schools in order to achieve racial balance in the classroom. In 1972 it issued restrictions on the implementation of capital punishment, though it did not rule the death penalty unconstitutional. And in the controversial 1973 case *Roe v. Wade*, Justice Blackmun wrote the decision that struck down laws prohibiting abortion in Texas and Georgia.

The 1972 Election

Nixon's reelection in 1972 was never much in doubt. In May the threat of a conservative third-party challenge from Alabama governor George Wallace ended abruptly when an assailant shot Wallace, paralyzing him from the waist down. With Wallace out of the picture, Nixon's strategy of wooing southern white voters away from the Democrats got a boost. Nixon also benefited from the disarray of the Democratic Party. Divided over Vietnam and civil rights, the Democrats were plagued by tensions between their newer, more liberal constituencies— women, minorities, and young adults—and the old-line officeholders and labor union leaders who had always dominated the party. Recent changes in the party's system of selecting delegates and candidates benefited the newer groups, and they helped to nominate Senator

Nixon Triumphant

One of the most resilient political figures in American history, Richard Nixon won the presidential elections of 1968 and 1972 after losing campaigns for president in 1960 and for governor of California in 1962. Even after his resignation in 1974, Nixon reemerged as an elder statesman and was frequently consulted for his views on foreign affairs. Here, he exults in an enthusiastic welcome from supporters in Savannah, Georgia, in 1970.
Charles Moore / Black Star.

George McGovern of South Dakota, a noted liberal and an outspoken opponent of the Vietnam War.

McGovern's campaign quickly ran into trouble. On learning that his running mate, Senator Thomas F. Eagleton of Missouri, had undergone electroshock therapy for depression some years earlier, McGovern first supported him and then abruptly insisted that he quit the ticket. But McGovern's waffling on the matter made him appear weak and indecisive. Moreover, he was far too liberal for many traditional Democrats, who rejected his ill-defined proposals for welfare reform and his call for unilateral withdrawal from Vietnam.

Nixon's campaign took full advantage of McGovern's weaknesses. Although the president had failed to end the war, his Vietnamization policy had virtually eliminated American combat deaths by 1972. Henry Kissinger's premature declaration that "peace is at hand" raised voters' hopes for a negotiated settlement (see Chapter 29). Not only did those initiatives rob the Democrats of their greatest appeal—their antiwar stance—but a short-term upturn in the economy further favored the Republicans. Nixon won handily, receiving nearly 61 percent of the popular vote and carrying every state except Massachusetts and the District of Columbia. Yet the president failed to kindle strong loyalty in the electorate. Only 55.7 percent of eligible voters bothered to go to the polls, and the Democrats maintained control of both houses of Congress. A far graver threat to Nixon's leadership would emerge shortly after the election, when the news broke that the White House was implicated in the 1972 break-in at the Democratic National Committee's headquarters at the Watergate apartment complex in Washington, D.C.

Watergate

Watergate, one of the great constitutional crises of the twentieth century, was a direct result of Nixon's ruthless political tactics, his secretive style of governing, and his obsession with the antiwar movement. But though many Americans saw Watergate as consisting of only the evil deeds of one person (Richard Nixon) and one unlawful act (obstruction of justice), Watergate was not an isolated incident. It was part of a broad pattern of illegality and misuse of power that flourished in the crisis atmosphere of the Vietnam War.

Before the Break-In.   Though the Watergate scandal began in 1972, its roots lay in the early years of Nixon's first administration. Obsessed with the antiwar movement, the White House had repeatedly authorized illegal surveillance—opening mail, tapping phones, arranging break-ins—of citizens such as Daniel Ellsberg, a former Defense Department analyst who had become disillusioned with the war. In 1971 Ellsberg had leaked the so-called Pentagon Papers to the *New York Times*. This secret study, commissioned by Secretary of Defense McNamara in 1967, detailed so many American blunders in Vietnam that, after reading it, McNamara had commented, "You know, they could hang people for what is in there." To discredit Ellsberg, White House underlings broke into his psychiatrist's office in an unsuccessful search for damaging personal information. When their break-in was revealed, the court dismissed the government's case against Ellsberg.

In another abuse of presidential power, the White House had established a clandestine intelligence group known as the "plumbers" that was supposed to plug leaks of government information. The plumbers relied on tactics such as using the Internal Revenue Service to harass the administration's opponents, who were named on an "enemies list" drawn up by presidential counsel John Dean. One of the plumbers' major targets was the Democratic Party, whose front-running primary candidate in 1972, Senator Edmund Muskie of Maine,

became the object of several of their "dirty tricks," including the distribution of phony campaign posters reading "Help Muskie in Busing More Children Now."

These secret and highly questionable activities were financed by massive illegal fund-raising efforts by Nixon's Committee to Re-Elect the President (known as CREEP). To obtain contributions from major corporations, Nixon's fund-raisers had used high-pressure tactics that included implied threats of federal tax audits if companies failed to cooperate. CREEP raised over $20 million, a portion of which was used to finance the plumbers' dirty tricks, including the Watergate break-in.

The Break-In.   Early in the morning of June 17, 1972, police arrested five men carrying cameras, wiretapping equipment, and a large amount of cash and charged them with breaking into the Democratic National Committee's headquarters at the Watergate apartment complex in Washington, D.C. Two accomplices were apprehended soon afterward. Three of the men had worked in the White House or for CREEP, and four had CIA connections. Nixon later claimed that White House counsel John Dean had conducted a full investigation of the incident (no such investigation ever took place) and that "no one on the White House staff, no one in this administration, presently employed, was involved in this very bizarre incident."

Subsequent investigations revealed that shortly after the break-in the president had ordered his chief of staff, H. R. Haldeman, to instruct the CIA to tell the FBI not to probe too deeply into connections between the White House and the burglars. When the burglars were convicted in January 1973, John Dean, with Nixon's approval, tried to buy their continued silence with $400,000 in hush money and hints of presidential pardons.

The cover-up of the White House's involvement began to unravel when one of the convicted burglars began to talk. Two tenacious investigative reporters at the *Washington Post*, Carl Bernstein and Bob Woodward, exposed the attempt to hide the truth and traced it back to the White House. Reports of CREEP's "dirty tricks" and illegal fund-raising soon compounded the public's suspicions about the president. In February the Senate voted 77 to 0 to establish an investigative committee. Two months later Nixon accepted the resignations of Haldeman, Assistant Secretary of Commerce Jeb Stuart Magruder, and Chief Domestic Advisor John Ehrlichman, all of whom had been implicated in the cover-up. He fired Dean, who had agreed to testify in the case in exchange for immunity from prosecution. In May the Senate Watergate committee began holding nationally televised hearings. In June Magruder testified before the committee, confessing his guilt and implicating former Attorney General John Mitchell, Dean, and others. Dean, in turn, implicated Nixon in the plot. Even more startling testimony from a Nixon aide revealed that Nixon had installed a secret taping system in the Oval Office.

The president steadfastly "stonewalled" the committee's demand that he surrender the tapes, citing executive privilege and national security. But Archibald Cox, a special prosecutor whom Nixon had appointed to investigate the case, successfully petitioned a federal court to order the president to hand the tapes over. Still Nixon refused to comply. After receiving additional federal subpoenas the following spring, Nixon finally released a heavily edited transcript of the tapes, peppered with the words "expletive deleted." Senate Republican leader Hugh Scott called the transcripts "deplorable, disgusting, shabby, immoral." Most suspicious was an eighteen-minute gap in the tape covering a crucial meeting between Nixon, Haldeman, and Ehrlichman on June 20, 1972—three days after the break-in.

The Final Days.   The Watergate affair moved into its final phase when on June 30 the House of Representatives' Judiciary Committee voted three articles of impeachment against Richard Nixon: obstruction of justice, abuse of power, and acting to subvert the Constitution. Two days later the Supreme Court ruled unanimously that Nixon could not claim executive privilege as a justification for refusing to turn over additional tapes. Under duress, on August 5 Nixon released the unexpurgated tapes, which contained evidence that he had ordered the cover-up as early as six days after the break-in. Facing certain conviction if impeached, on August 9, 1974, Nixon became the first U.S. president to resign.

The next day Vice President Gerald Ford was sworn in as president. Ford, a former Michigan congressman and house minority leader, had replaced Vice President Spiro Agnew in 1973 after Agnew resigned under indictment for accepting kickbacks on construction contracts. The transfer of power proceeded smoothly. A month later, however, Ford stunned the nation by granting Nixon a "full, free, and absolute" pardon "for all offenses he had committed or might have committed during his presidency." Ford took that action, he said, to spare the country the agony of rehashing Watergate in a criminal prosecution. Twenty-five members of Nixon's administration went to prison, but he refused to admit guilt for what had happened, conceding only that he had made an error in judgment.

The Aftermath.   In response to the abuses of the Nixon administration and to contain the power of what the historian Arthur M. Schlesinger Jr. called "the imperial presidency," Congress adopted several reforms. In 1974 a strengthened Freedom of Information Act gave citizens greater access to files federal agencies had amassed on them. The Fair Campaign Practices Act of 1974 limited campaign contributions and provided for stricter accountability and public financing of presidential

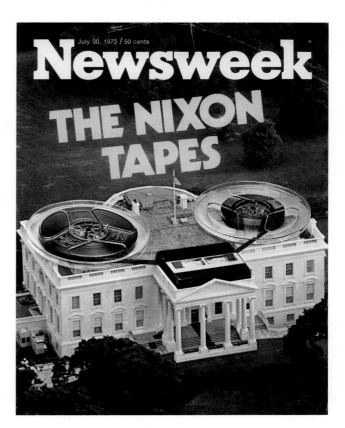

Watergate

In July 1973 White House aide Alexander Butterfield testified before the Senate Watergate Committee that all Oval Office telephone communications had been recorded on a secret taping system. Although Nixon tried in vain to suppress the tapes by claiming executive privilege, their eventual release—including statements directly implicating the president in the Watergate cover-up—led to Nixon's resignation in August of 1974.

campaigns. Ironically, because the act allowed an unlimited number of political action committees (PACs) to donate up to $5,000 per candidate, corporations and lobbying groups found they could actually increase their influence by making multiple donations. By the end of the decade, close to 3,000 PACs were playing an increasingly pivotal—and some would argue unethical—role in national elections.

Perhaps the most significant legacy of Watergate, however, was the wave of cynicism that swept the country in its wake. Beginning with Lyndon Johnson's "credibility gap" during the Vietnam War, public distrust of government had risen steadily with the disclosure of the secret bombing of Cambodia and the illegal surveillance and harassment of antiwar protesters and other political opponents. The saga of Watergate confirmed what many Americans had long suspected: that politicians were hopelessly corrupt and that the federal government was out of control.

An Economy of Diminished Expectations

Economic difficulties compounded Americans' political disillusionment. Growing international demand for natural resources, particularly oil, coupled with unstable access to foreign oil supplies wreaked havoc with the American economy. At the same time foreign competitors in varied industries successfully expanded their share of the world market, edging out American-made products. The resulting sharp downturn in the domestic economy marked the end of America's twenty-five-year dominance of the world economy.

Energy Crisis

Until the mid-twentieth century the United States was the world's leading producer and consumer of oil. During World War II the nation had produced two-thirds of the world's oil, but by 1972 its share had fallen to only 22 percent, even though domestic production had continued to rise. By the late 1960s the United States was buying more and more of its oil on the world market to keep up with shrinking domestic reserves and growing demand.

The imported oil came primarily from the Middle East, where production had increased a stupendous 1,500 percent in the twenty-five years following World War II. The rise of nationalism and the corresponding decline of colonialism in the postwar era had encouraged the Persian Gulf nations to wrest control from the European and American oil companies that once dominated petroleum exploration and production in that region. In 1960, joining with other oil-producing developing countries, they had formed the Organization of Petroleum Exporting Countries (OPEC). Just five of the founding countries—the Middle Eastern states of Saudi Arabia, Kuwait, Iran, and Iraq, plus Venezuela—were the source of more than 80 percent of the world's crude oil exports. During the early 1970s, when world demand climbed and oil reserves fell, they took advantage of market forces to maximize their profits. Between 1973 and 1975 OPEC raised the price of a barrel of oil from $3 to $12. By the end of the decade, the price had peaked at $34 a barrel, setting off a round of furious inflation in the oil-dependent United States.

OPEC members also found that oil could be used as a weapon in global politics. In 1973 OPEC instituted an oil embargo against the United States, Western Europe, and Japan in retaliation for their aid to Israel during the Yom Kippur War, which had begun when Egypt and Syria invaded Israel. The embargo, which lasted six months, forced Americans to curtail their driving or spend long hours in line at the pumps; in a matter of months, gas prices climbed 40 percent. Since the U.S. automobile industry had little to offer except "gas-guzzlers" built to run on cheap fuel, Americans turned to cheaper, more fuel-efficient foreign cars manufactured in Japan and West Germany. Soon the auto industry was in a slump, weakening the American economy.

The energy crisis was an enormous shock to the American psyche. Suddenly, Americans felt like hostages to economic forces that were beyond their control. As OPEC's leaders pushed prices higher and higher, they seemed to be able to determine whether Western economies would grow or stagnate. Despite an extensive public conservation campaign and a second gas shortage in 1979 caused by the Iranian revolution, Americans could not wean themselves from foreign oil. In fact, they used even more foreign oil after the energy crisis than they had before—a testimony to the enormous thirst of modern industrial and consumer societies for petroleum (Figure 30.1).

Economic Woes

While the energy crisis dealt a swift blow to the U.S. economy, other developments had equally damaging results. The high cost of the Vietnam War and the Great Society had contributed to a steadily growing federal deficit and spiraling inflation. A business downturn in 1970 had led to rising unemployment and declining productivity. In the industrial sector the reviving economies of West Germany and Japan over time had reduced demand for American goods worldwide. As a result, in 1971 the dollar fell to its lowest level on the world market since 1949, and the United States posted its first **trade deficit**, importing more than it exported, in almost a century.

Nixon's Remedies. That year Nixon took several bold steps to turn the economy around. To stem the decline in currency and trade, he suspended the Bretton Woods system that had been established at the United Nations monetary conference in 1944 (see Chapter 28). Once again the dollar would fluctuate in relation to the price of an ounce of gold. The change, which effectively devalued the dollar in hopes of encouraging foreign trade, represented a frank acknowledgment that America's currency was no longer the world's strongest. Nixon also instituted wage and price controls to curb inflation, and to boost the sluggish economy he offered a "full employment" budget for 1972, including $11 billion in deficit spending.

Though these measures brought a temporary improvement in the economy, the general decline persisted. Overall economic growth, as measured by the gross domestic product (GDP), had averaged 4.1 percent per year in the 1960s; in the 1970s it dropped to only 2.9 percent, contributing to a noticeable decline in most Americans' standard of living. At the same time galloping inflation forced consumer prices upward (Figure 30.2). Housing prices, in particular, rose rapidly: the average

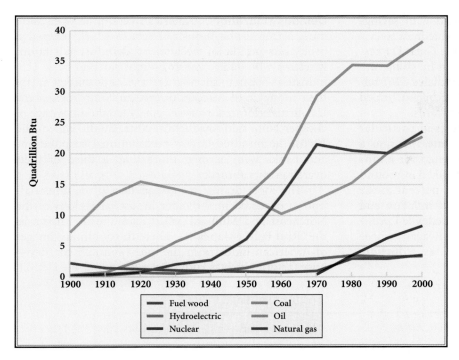

FIGURE 30.1 U.S. Energy Consumption, 1900–2000

Coal was the nation's primary source of energy until the 1950s, when oil and natural gas became the dominant fuels. The use of nuclear and hydroelectric power also rose substantially in the postwar era. During the 1980s fuel-efficient automobiles and conservation measures reduced total energy use, but in the 1990s energy consumption rose significantly.
Source: World Almanac 2002.

cost of a single-family home more than doubled in the 1970s, making homeownership inaccessible to a growing segment of the working and middle classes.

The inflationary crisis helped to forge new attitudes about saving and spending. With bank savings accounts' interests rates unable to keep up with inflation, many Americans turned to the stock market, taking advantage of the appearance of new discount brokerage firms like Charles Schwab, whose low commission fees made it easier for small investors to take the plunge. The money market mutual fund also emerged in this decade, offering investors uninsured but relatively safe investment opportunities overseen by a fund manager. The inflation-afflicted middle class responded enthusiastically, and by 1982 more than $200 billion dollars were in mutual funds. While these investors sought new ways to increase their

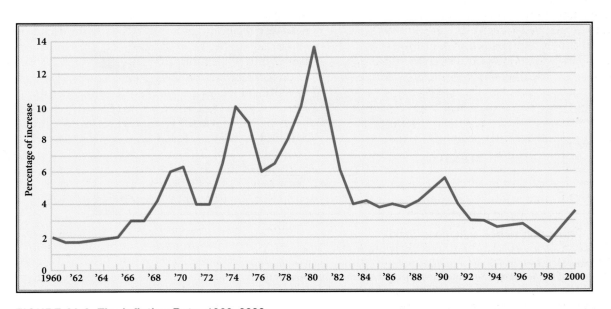

FIGURE 30.2 The Inflation Rate, 1960–2000

One common measure of inflation is the percent change per year in the consumer price index as calculated by the Bureau of Labor Statistics. The annual inflation rate peaked in 1980, the last year of Carter's presidency. Source: Statistical Abstract of the United States, 2000.

savings, millions of Americans dispensed with savings altogether. Putting behind the fear of indebtedness so evident in people who had lived through the Great Depression, now Americans coped with inflation by going into debt. By mid-1975 consumer borrowing totaled $167 billion, but by 1979 it had skyrocketed to $315 billion, helped by a dramatic increase in the use of credit cards.

In addition to inflation young adults in particular faced a constricted job market in the late 1970s, as a record number of baby boomers competed for a limited number of jobs. Unemployment peaked at around 9 percent in 1975 and hovered at 6 to 7 percent in the late 1970s. A devastating combination of inflation and unemployment—dubbed **stagflation**—bedeviled presidential administrations from Nixon to Reagan, whose remedies, such as deficit spending and tax reduction, failed to eradicate the double scourge.

Deindustrialization.   American economic woes were most acute in the industrial sector, which entered a prolonged period of decline, or **deindustrialization.** Investors who had formerly bought stock in basic U.S. industries began to speculate on the stock market or put their money into mergers or foreign companies. Many U.S. firms relocated overseas, partly to take advantage of cheaper labor and production costs. By the end of the 1970s, the hundred largest multinational corporations and banks were earning more than a third of their overall profits abroad.

The most dramatic consequences of deindustrialization occurred in the older industrial regions of the Northeast and Midwest, which came to be known as the "Rust Belt" (Map 30.1). There the dominant images of American industry in the mid-twentieth century—huge factories such as Ford's River Rouge outside Detroit;

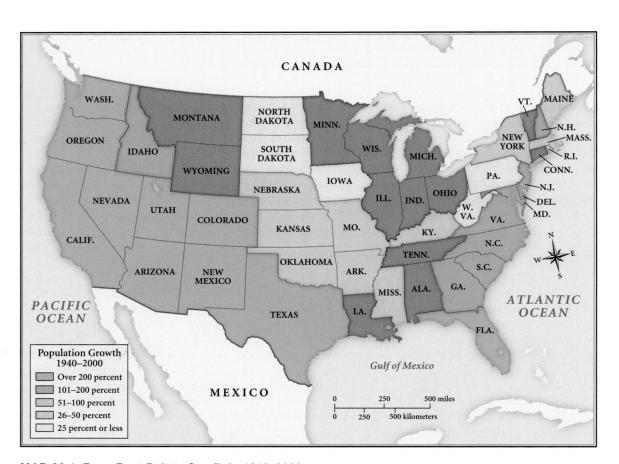

MAP 30.1 From Rust Belt to Sun Belt, 1940–2000

One of the most significant developments of the post–World War II era was the growth of the Sun Belt. Sparked by federal spending for military bases, the defense industry, and the space program, states of the South and Southwest experienced an economic boom in the 1950s. This growth was further enhanced in the 1970s, as the heavily industrialized regions of the Northeast and Midwest declined, and migrants from what was quickly dubbed the "Rust Belt" headed to the South and West in search of jobs. Rising political influence accompanied the economic and demographic growth of the Sun Belt: since Lyndon B. Johnson, all presidents but Gerald Ford have hailed from a Sun Belt state, and the region has provided an important base for the conservative wing of the Republican Party.

Deindustrialization

Scores of industrial plants closed in the 1970s, putting many Americans out of work. At the same time more Americans were buying cheaper imported cars, fueling anger toward foreign competitors. David Helfferich of Greenburg, Pennsylvania, bashed this Japanese-made Honda Civic and urged others to "buy American" as a means of protecting U.S. jobs. Wide World Photos, Inc.

the United States Steel Corporation compound in Gary, Indiana; and the General Electric plant in Lynn, Massachusetts—were fast becoming relics.

When a community's major employer closed up shop and left town, the effect was devastating. In 1977 the Lykes Corporation shut the Campbell Works of the Youngstown Sheet and Tube Company, laying off 4,100 Ohio steelworkers. Two years later Youngstown was still reeling. A third of the displaced workers, considered too old to retrain for new positions, had been forced to take early retirement at half of their previous salaries. Ten percent had moved. Another 15 percent were still looking for work, their unemployment compensation long since exhausted. Among the 40 percent who were the "success stories" (those who had found other jobs), many had taken huge wage cuts. A former rigger, for instance, was selling women's shoes for $2.37 an hour. The impact of such plant closings rippled through communities across America's heartland.

Many of the displaced workers relocated to the Sun Belt, which continued its postwar expansion with the spectacular growth of cities like Houston, Los Angeles, San Diego, and Atlanta (see Chapter 28). Even the least booming of the southern rim states—Alabama—saw its job rolls expanding at four times the rate of New York and Pennsylvania. As the *New York Times* described the out-migration from the North, "All day and through the lonely night, the moving vans push southward, the 14-wheeled boxcars of the highway, changing the demographic face of America." The growth of the Sun Belt owed much to federal spending for defense contracts, military bases, and the space program in the region. The oil industry and agribusiness also benefited from federal

subsidies and tax breaks. Equally important, however, in the creation of new jobs were low labor costs. "Right-to-work" laws that made it difficult to build strong labor unions made these states, unlike those of the Rust Belt, inhospitable to organized labor.

Deindustrialization, the population shift to the Sun Belt, and the changing economic conditions of the 1970s posed a critical problem for the labor movement. In the heyday of labor during the 1940s and 1950s, American managers had often cooperated with unions; with profits high there was room for accommodation. But as foreign competition cut into corporate profits in the 1970s, industry became less willing to bargain, and the labor movement's power declined. In the 1970s union membership dropped from 28 to 23 percent of the American workforce. In the South membership was 14 percent. By the end of the 1980s, only 16 percent of American workers were organized. Operations moving abroad also hurt labor, as the new overseas workforce was beyond American labor's organizing influence. In a competitive global environment, labor's prospects seemed dim.

Reform and Reaction in the 1970s

The nation's economic problems and growing cynicism about government led to deep public anxiety and resentment. Many Americans turned inward to private satisfactions, prompting the journalist Tom Wolfe to label the 1970s the "Me Decade." Yet such a label hardly does justice to a decade in which environmentalism, feminism, lesbian and gay rights, and other social movements blossomed. Furthermore, such characterizations neglect the growing social conservatism that was in part a response to such movements. In fact, the confluence of these trends produced a pattern of shifting crosscurrents that made the 1970s a complex transitional decade.

The New Activism: Environmental and Consumer Movements

After 1970 many baby boomers left the counterculture behind and settled down to pursue careers and material goods. But these young adults sought personal fulfillment as well. In a quest for physical well-being, millions of Americans began jogging, riding bicycles, and working out at the gym. The fitness craze coincided with a heightened environmental awareness that spurred the demand for pesticide-free foods and vegetarian cookbooks. For spiritual support some young people embraced the self-help techniques of the human-potential, or New Age, movement; others turned to alternative religious groups such as the Hare Krishna, the Church of Scientology, and the Unification Church of Reverend Sun Myung Moon.

A few baby boomers continued to pursue the unfinished social and political agendas of the 1960s. Moving into law, education, social work, medicine, and other fields, these former radicals continued their activism on a grassroots level. Some joined the left wing of the Democratic Party; others helped to establish community-based organizations, including health clinics, food co-ops, and day-care centers. On the local level, at least, the progressive spirit of the 1960s lived on.

Environmental Awareness. Many of these 1960s-style activists helped to invigorate the environmental movement, which had been energized by the publication in 1962 of Rachel Carson's *Silent Spring*, a powerful analysis of the impact of pesticides on the food chain. Activists brought their radical political sensibilities to the environmental movement, using sit-ins and other protest tactics developed in the civil rights and antiwar movements to mobilize mass support and infuse the movement with new life. For example, they construed the search for alternative technologies (especially solar power) as a political statement against a corporate structure that was increasingly inhospitable to human-scale technology—and to humans as well.

Other issues that galvanized public opinion included the environmental impact of industrial projects such as an Alaskan oil pipeline and the harmful effects of chlorofluorocarbons and increased carbon dioxide levels on the earth's atmosphere. In January 1969 a huge oil spill off the coast of Santa Barbara, California, provoked an outcry, as did the discovery in 1978 that a housing development outside Niagara Falls,

Rachel Carson

A pioneer of the modern environmental movement, biologist Rachel Carson documented the adverse effects of DDT and other pesticides in her 1962 best-seller, Silent Spring. *This photograph, taken in 1961, shows Carson conducting fieldwork.*
Alfred Eisenstadt / LIFE Magazine © Time, Inc.

New York, had been built on a toxic waste site. Lois Gibbs and other residents became aware of abnormally high rates of illness, miscarriage, and birth defects among Love Canal families, and the New York State government paid homeowners to relocate (see American Lives, "Lois Marie Gibbs: Environmental Activist," p. 890).

Nuclear Power. Nuclear energy became the subject of citizen action in the 1970s, when rising prices and oil shortages led to the expansion of nuclear power, pitting environmental concerns against the need for alternative energy sources. By January 1974 forty-two nuclear power plants were in operation, and over a hundred more were planned. Suddenly the proliferation of nuclear power plants and reactors, which had gone largely unchallenged in the 1950s and 1960s, raised public concerns about safety. Community activists protested plans for new reactors, citing inadequate evacuation plans and the unresolved problem of the disposal of radioactive waste.

Their fears seemed to be confirmed in March 1979 when a nuclear plant at Three Mile Island near Harrisburg, Pennsylvania, came critically close to a meltdown of its central core reactor. A prompt shutdown of the plant brought the problem under control before radioactive material seeped into the environment, but as a member of the panel who investigated the accident admitted, "We were damn lucky." Ultimately, Three Mile Island caused Americans to rethink the question of whether nuclear power could be a viable solution to the nation's energy needs. Grassroots activism, combined with public fear of the potential dangers of nuclear energy, convinced many utility companies to abandon nuclear power, despite its short-term economic advantages.

Environmental Legislation. Americans' concerns about nuclear power, chemical contamination, pesticides, and other environmental issues helped to turn environmentalism into a mass movement. On the first Earth Day, April 22, 1970, 20 million citizens gathered in communities across the country to show their support for the endangered planet. Their efforts helped to create bipartisan support for a spate of new federal legislation. In 1969 Congress passed the National Environmental Policy Act, which required the developers of public projects to file an environmental impact statement. The next year Nixon established the Environmental Protection Agency (EPA) and signed the Clean Air Act, which toughened standards for auto emissions in order to reduce smog and air pollution. Two years later Congress banned the use of the pesticide DDT. And in 1973 the Endangered Species Act expanded the protection provided by the Endangered Animals Act of 1964, granting species such as snail darters and spotted owls protected status. Thus environmental protection joined social welfare, defense, and national security as areas of federal intervention.

The environmental movement did not go uncontested. The EPA-mandated fuel-economy standards for cars provoked criticism for threatening the health of the auto industry as it struggled to keep up with foreign competitors. Corporations resented environmental regulations, but so did many of their workers, who believed that tightened standards threatened their jobs and privileged nature over human beings. "IF YOU'RE HUNGRY AND OUT OF WORK, EAT AN ENVIRONMENTALIST" read one labor union's bumper sticker. In a time of rising unemployment and deindustrialization, activists clashed head-on with proponents of economic development, full employment, and global competitiveness.

The Consumer Movement. Paralleling the rise of environmentalism was a growing consumer protection movement to eliminate harmful consumer products and curb dangerous practices by American corporations. The consumer movement had originated in the Progressive Era with the founding of government agencies such as the Food and Drug Administration (see Chapter 20). After decades of inertia, the consumer movement reemerged in the 1960s under the leadership of Ralph Nader, a young Harvard-educated lawyer whose book *Unsafe at Any Speed* (1965) attacked General Motors for putting flashy style ahead of safe

handling and fuel economy in its engineering of the Chevrolet Corvair.

In 1969 Nader launched a Washington-based consumer protection organization that gave rise to the Public Interest Research Group, a national network of consumer groups that focused on issues ranging from product safety to consumer fraud and environmental pollution. Staffed by a handful of lawyers and hundreds of student volunteers known as "Nader's Raiders," the organization pioneered legal tactics such as the class-action suit, which allowed people with common grievances to sue as a group. Nader's organization became a model for dozens of other groups that emerged in the 1970s and afterward to combat the health hazards of smoking, unethical insurance and credit practices, and other consumer problems. The establishment of the federal Consumer Products Safety Commission in 1972 reflected the growing importance of consumer protection in American life.

Challenges to Tradition: The Women's Movement and Gay Rights

Feminism proved the most enduring movement to emerge from the 1960s. In the next decade the women's movement grew more sophisticated, generating an array of services and organizations, from rape crisis centers and battered women's shelters to feminist health collectives and women's bookstores. In 1972 Gloria Steinem and other journalists founded *Ms.* magazine, the first consumer magazine aimed at a feminist audience. Formerly all-male bastions, such as Yale, Princeton, and the U.S. Military Academy, admitted women undergraduates for the first time, while the proportion of women attending graduate and professional schools rose markedly. Several new national women's organizations emerged, and established groups such as the National Organization for Women (NOW) continued to grow. In 1977, 20,000 women went to Houston for the first National Women's Conference. Their "National Plan of Action" represented a hard-won consensus on topics ranging from violence against women to homemakers' rights, the needs of older women, and, most controversially, abortion and other reproductive issues.

Women were also increasingly visible in politics and public life. The National Women's Political Caucus, founded in 1971, actively promoted the election of women to public office. Their success stories included Shirley Chisholm, Patricia Schroeder, and Geraldine Ferraro, all of whom served in Congress, and Ella T. Grasso, who won election as Connecticut's governor in 1974.

Women's political mobilization produced significant legislative and administrative gains. With the passage of Title IX of the Educational Amendments Act of 1972, which broadened the 1964 Civil Rights Act to include educational institutions, Congress prohibited colleges and

Lois Marie Gibbs: Environmental Activist

In 1978 Lois Gibbs was a twenty-seven-year-old housewife living in Niagara Falls, New York. A chemical worker's wife and the mother of two children, Gibbs spent her days cooking, shopping, and cleaning the family's modest three-bedroom home. Two years later Gibbs was a nationally known figure. As leader of the fight against toxic waste at Love Canal, she organized hundreds of local families, squared off with the governor of New York State, testified before Congress, appeared on national television, and was recognized by President Jimmy Carter for her efforts. She was, as she liked to put it, "the housewife who went to Washington."

Born in Grand Island, New York, in 1951, Lois Conn was one of six children in a blue-collar family in the industrial region surrounding Buffalo. After graduating from high school in 1969, she worked as a nurse's aide at a convalescent home and married Harry Gibbs, a worker at a local chemical plant. After the birth of their first child, Michael, they purchased a home in a quiet, tree-lined neighborhood. Lois quit her job to stay at home and in 1975 gave birth to a daughter. With no inkling of what lay beneath them, the Gibbses finished their basement, tended their garden, and enjoyed a peaceful suburban existence.

The first sign of trouble came in 1977, when their son Michael entered kindergarten at the neighborhood school. Within three months he developed epilepsy and soon contracted asthma and chronic urinary and ear infections. The following spring Gibbs read newspaper reports about toxic chemicals buried beneath the school and tried to have her son transferred. When school officials rejected her request, insisting that the school was safe, Gibbs launched a petition drive to have the school closed.

At first Gibbs was reticent about approaching her neighbors, afraid of having doors slammed in her face. But what she found surprised her. Not only were people interested in and concerned about the dangers of chemicals, but many of them had health problems of their own, including respiratory ailments, cancer, miscarriages, and birth defects. "The more I heard, the more frightened I became," said Gibbs. "The entire community seemed to be sick."

Gibbs set out to educate herself about the area's history. Consulting local newspaper files, she learned about Love Canal, a six-mile-long canal project developed by William T. Love in the 1890s to connect the upper and lower branches of the Niagara River. Construction had been under way when the depression of 1893 doomed the project, leaving a partially dug trench. The land later became a dump site used mainly by the Hooker Chemical Corporation, which disposed of 22,000 tons of chemical wastes there between 1942 and 1953. (Health officials eventually identified over 200 different compounds at the site, including highly toxic substances such as dioxin—used in the herbicide Agent Orange—toluene, and benzene.) After filling and covering over the site in 1953, Hooker sold the land to the Board of Education for one dollar, stipulating that the company not be held responsible for any future injury or death. Housing subdivisions soon sprang up around the site, and a new elementary school near the corner of the canal opened in 1955.

By the time Gibbs began meeting with her neighbors in 1978, rusted metal drums were surfacing in backyards, chemical sludge was seeping into basements, and residents were complaining about dead trees, burned feet, and a recurring stench. In June of that year, the New York State Health Department began collecting air, soil, and blood samples from households closest to the canal. After finding abnormally high rates of birth defects and miscarriages, the health department issued an order on August 2 for reconstruction of the canal site and recommended the evacuation of all pregnant women and children under age two. Soon afterward, concerned residents established the Love Canal Homeowners Association (LCHA) to fight for permanent relocation of Love Canal families and elected Lois Gibbs as LCHA president. Under pressure from Gibbs and the LCHA, New York's governor, Hugh Carey, agreed a few days later to relocate the 239 families closest to the canal, purchasing their homes at the replacement value.

While Gibbs and the LCHA applauded Carey's action, they worried about the other 810 families remaining in the neighborhood, many of whose homes also showed dangerous levels of chemicals. Gibbs appealed to federal and local officials for further action but encountered repeated delays, denials, and rebuffs. The mayor of Niagara Falls denounced Gibbs's efforts, claiming that the adverse publicity would destroy the

Lois Marie Gibbs

A twenty-seven-year-old housewife in Niagara Falls, New York, Lois Gibbs became the leader of a campaign against toxic waste in her neighborhood in 1978. As president of the Love Canal Homeowners Association, Gibbs fought successfully for the permanent relocation of more than a thousand Love Canal families. Corbis-Bettmann.

city's tourist industry. Meanwhile, the state health department refused to relocate more families until it could complete further studies. At one point in 1979, the department claimed to have lost the residents' health records and instructed them to start the lengthy documentation process all over again.

Faced with bureaucratic inertia, Gibbs sought out sympathetic scientists to help the residents conduct their own studies. Their most important finding came from a neighborhood survey showing health problems clustered around swales—underground drainage ditches that led away from the canal—and suggesting more widespread contamination. The LCHA promptly released the findings to the media. Gibbs got publicity in other ways as well: she appeared on talk shows, organized picketing at the canal construction site, and was arrested for blocking truck traffic. When state officials still failed to take action, Gibbs led a group of citizens to the state capitol in Albany, bearing cardboard coffins symbolizing

Love Canal victims. Throughout the Love Canal crisis Gibbs made frequent trips to Albany and Washington to negotiate with state officials, the governor's office, Senator Daniel Patrick Moynihan, and other federal representatives.

Like other housewives involved in the crisis, Gibbs gained a new independence through her activities outside the home. Those activities, however, also caused tension in her marriage. "My husband was getting upset with me," she recalled. "I was never home . . . dinner was never on time." She and her husband divorced in 1980.

In May of that year, events at Love Canal came to a head when the U.S. Environmental Protection Agency released a study showing abnormally high levels of chromosome breakage in Love Canal residents (suggesting increased risks of cancer, miscarriage, and birth defects). In an act of desperation, Gibbs and two other housewives took two EPA officials hostage in the LCHA office while hundreds of angry residents surrounded the building, demanding federal relocation of Love Canal families. Coming in the middle of the Iranian hostage crisis, the women's ploy brought national media coverage but also a threat of reprisal from the FBI. To avoid violence Gibbs released the officials, but she also demanded a response from President Jimmy Carter within forty-eight hours. Two days later, on May 21, Carter declared a health emergency at Love Canal, authorizing the temporary relocation of the remaining 810 families. Later that year he signed a bill permitting the permanent relocation of those families and the purchase of their homes; he also signed a bill establishing a "Superfund" to clean up Love Canal and thousands of other toxic waste sites identified by the EPA.

Using part of the $30,000 the state paid for her home, Gibbs and her children moved to Washington, D.C., in 1981. There she founded the Citizens Clearinghouse for Hazardous Waste, a consulting group for grassroots organizations working on problems related to pesticides, solid waste, asbestos, and other toxic substances. She married a toxicologist, gave birth to two more children, and continues to work as director of the Citizens Clearinghouse.

One of the communities the Citizens Clearinghouse has been watching is Love Canal. In 1990 the EPA declared Love Canal habitable again after a twelve-year, $250 million cleanup. The elementary school and the 239 houses closest to the canal had been demolished, but 236 other homes were rehabilitated and sold at discount prices to eager buyers. Public officials insist the new containment system has safely and permanently sealed off the dump. Lois Gibbs is not so sure.

universities that received federal funds from discriminating on the basis of sex, a change that particularly benefited women athletes. Another federal initiative was **affirmative action**. Originally instituted in 1966 under Lyndon Johnson's administration to redress a history of discrimination against nonwhites in employment and education, affirmative action procedures—hiring and enrollment goals and recruitment training programs—were extended to women the following year and gave many women, especially educated white ones, more opportunities for educational and career advancement. In 1972 Congress authorized child-care deductions for working parents; in 1974 it passed the Equal Credit Opportunity Act, which significantly improved women's access to credit.

Abortion Rights.

The Supreme Court also significantly advanced women's rights. In several rulings the Court gave women more control over their reproductive lives by reading a right of privacy into the Ninth and Fourteenth Amendments' concept of personal liberty. In 1965 *Griswold v. Connecticut* had overturned state laws against the sale of contraceptive devices to married adults, an option that was later extended to single persons. In 1973, in *Roe v. Wade*, the Court struck down Texas and Georgia statutes that allowed an abortion only if the mother's life was in danger. According to this seven-to-two decision, states could no longer outlaw abortions performed during the first trimester of pregnancy.

Roe v. Wade nationalized the liberalization of state abortion laws, which had begun in New York in 1970, but also fueled the development of a powerful antiabortion movement. Charging that the rights of a fetus took precedence over a woman's right to decide whether or not to terminate a pregnancy, abortion opponents worked to circumvent or overturn *Roe v. Wade*. In 1976 they convinced Congress to deny Medicaid funds for abortions for poor women, one of the opening rounds in a protracted legislative and judicial campaign to chip away at the *Roe* decision.

The Equal Rights Amendment.

Another battlefront for the women's movement was the proposed Equal Rights Amendment (ERA) to the Constitution. The ERA, first introduced in Congress in 1923 by the National Woman's Party, stated in its entirety, "Equality of rights under the law shall not be denied or abridged by the United States or any State on the basis of sex." In 1970 feminists revived the amendment, which passed the House but died in the Senate. In the next session it passed both houses and was submitted to the states for ratification.

Thirty-four states quickly passed the ERA between 1972 and the end of 1974, but then the momentum stopped (Map 30.2). Only Indiana ratified after that point, leaving the amendment three states short of the necessary three-fourths' majority. Most of the nonratifying states were in the South and the West; Illinois also held out

despite spirited campaigns there by ERA supporters. Congress extended the deadline for ratification until June 30, 1982, but the Equal Rights Amendment still fell short.

Challenges to Feminism.

The fate of the ERA and the battle over abortion rights showed that by the mid-1970s the women's movement was beginning to weaken. Increasingly its members were divided by issues of race, class, age, and sexual orientation. For many nonwhite and working-class women, the feminist movement seemed to stand for the interests of self-seeking white career women. At the same time, the women's movement faced growing social conservatism among Americans in general. Although 63 percent of women polled in 1975 said they favored "efforts to strengthen and change women's status in society," a growing minority of both sexes expressed concern over what seemed to be revolutionary changes in women's traditional roles.

Lawyer Phyllis Schlafly, long active in conservative causes, led the antifeminist backlash. Despite the active career she had pursued while raising five children, Schlafly advocated traditional roles for women. Schlafly's STOP ERA organization claimed that the amendment

The Expanding Women's Movement
By the late 1970s the feminist movement had broadened its base, attracting women of all ages and backgrounds, such as this delegate to the 1977 National Women's Conference in Houston, Texas. As the slogan on her hat implies, though, the movement was already on the defensive against right-wing claims that it undermined traditional values. Bettye Lane.

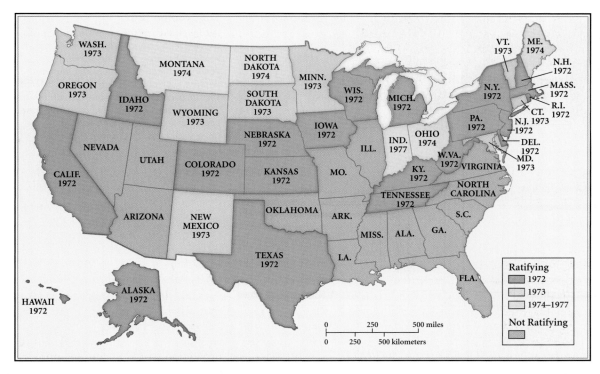

MAP 30.2 States Ratifying the Equal Rights Amendment, 1972–1977

The Equal Rights Amendment (ERA) quickly won support in 1972 and 1973 but then stalled. ERAmerica, a coalition of women's groups formed in 1976, lobbied extensively, particularly in Florida, North Carolina, and Illinois, but failed to sway the conservative legislatures in those states. After Indiana ratified in 1977, the amendment still lacked three votes toward the three-fourths majority needed to pass. Efforts to revive the ERA in the 1980s were unsuccessful, and it remains a dead issue.

would create a "unisex society" in which women could be drafted, homosexuals could be married, and separate toilets for men and women would be prohibited. Alarmed, conservative women in grassroots networks mobilized, showing up at statehouses with home-baked bread and apple pies, symbols of their traditional domestic role. As labels on baked goods at one anti-ERA rally expressed it, "My heart and hand went into this dough / For the sake of the family please vote no." Their message, that women would lose more than they would gain if the ERA passed, resonated with many men and women, especially those who were troubled by the rapid pace of social change.

Women's Changing Roles. Although the feminist movement was on the defensive by the mid-1970s, women's lives showed no signs of returning to the patterns of the 1950s. Because of increasing economic pressures, the proportion of women in the paid workforce continued to rise, from 44 percent in 1970 to 51 percent in 1980. In their private lives easier access to birth control permitted married and unmarried women to enjoy greater sexual freedom (although they also became more vulnerable to male sexual pressure). With a growing number of career options available to them,

many women, particularly educated white women, stayed single or delayed marriage and childrearing. The birthrate continued its postwar decline, reaching an all-time low in the mid-1970s. At the same time the divorce rate rose 82 percent in the 1970s, as more men and women elected to leave unhappy marriages.

Although such changes brought increased autonomy for many women, they also caused new hardships, particularly in poor and working-class families. Divorce left many women with low-paying jobs and inadequate child care. Meanwhile, more tolerant attitudes toward premarital sex, along with other social and economic factors, had contributed to rising teenage pregnancy rates. The rise in divorce and adolescent pregnancy produced a sharp increase in the number of female-headed families, contributing to the "feminization" of poverty. By 1980 women accounted for 66 percent of adults who lived below the poverty line, a development that fueled a growing wave of social reaction.

Gays and Lesbians. Another major focus of social activism, the gay liberation movement, achieved heightened visibility in the 1970s. Thousands of gay men and lesbians "came out," publicly proclaiming their sexual

The Income Gap

Although the feminist movement helped create greater opportunities for women, it could not redress the long-standing economic inequalities between men and women. Cartoonist Doug Marlette offered this satirical look at the income gap in 1982, when women earned only fifty-nine cents for every dollar men earned.
Doug Marlette. © The *Charlotte Observer*.

orientation (see American Voices, "David Kopay: The Real Score: A Gay Athlete Comes Out," p. 895). In New York's Greenwich Village, San Francisco's Castro neighborhood, and other urban enclaves, growing gay communities gave rise to hundreds of new gay and lesbian clubs, churches, businesses, and political organizations. In 1973 the National Gay Task Force launched a campaign to include gay men and lesbians as a protected group under laws covering employment and housing rights. Such efforts were most successful on the local level; during the 1970s Detroit, Boston, Los Angeles, Miami, San Francisco, and other cities passed laws barring discrimination on the basis of sexual preference.

Like abortion and the ERA, gay rights came under attack from conservatives, who believed that granting gay lifestyles legal protection would encourage immoral behavior. When the Miami city council passed a measure banning discrimination against gay men and lesbians in 1977, the singer Anita Bryant led a campaign to repeal the law by popular referendum. Later that year voters overturned the measure by a two-to-one majority, prompting similar antigay campaigns around the country.

Racial Minorities

Although the civil rights movement was in disarray by the late 1960s, continued minority-group protests brought social and economic gains in the next decade. Native Americans realized some of the most significant changes. In 1971 the Alaska Native Land Claims Act

An Antibusing Confrontation in Boston

Tensions over court-ordered busing ran high in Boston in 1976. When a black lawyer tried to cross the city hall plaza during an antibusing demonstration, he became a victim of Boston's climate of racial hatred and violence. This Pulitzer Prize–winning photograph by Stanley Forman for the Boston Herald American *shows a protester trying to impale the man with a flagstaff.* Stanley Forman.

David Kopay

The Real Score: A Gay Athlete Comes Out

For ten years David Kopay played professional football for the San Francisco Forty-Niners, the Detroit Lions, the Washington Redskins, the New Orleans Saints, and the Green Bay Packers. In 1975, at the end of his playing career, Kopay publicly acknowledged his homosexuality, creating a national furor in the sports world.

I always knew I was a bit different, but I kept it kind of quiet. I didn't think of myself as queer. In fact I couldn't even say that word for years and years. . . .

When I thought about the future, I assumed I'd be able to get a job in coaching because I was a player-coach my last few years playing. I was always working behind the scenes with the young ballplayers, coaching them. But I wasn't getting any interviews. There were all kinds of rumors about me being gay. . . .

By the time I spoke out, I really had nothing left to lose. It felt like I didn't have a choice—I just had to do it. Then one morning in 1975 I saw an article in the *Washington Star* about homosexual athletes and why they had everything to lose. There was an interview in the article with Jerry Smith [Washington Redskins tight end who died of AIDS in 1986]. . . .

. . . I was at a time and place in my own coming out where I felt that if I was going to survive, I had to speak out. It was do that or maybe go crazy.

So I called Lynn Rosellini, who was the reporter for the article that quoted Jerry Smith. Lynn was doing an entire series on gay athletes. . . .

Everybody said there was going to be a terrible backlash against me when Lynn's article was published. But there wasn't a backlash against me personally: There was a backlash against all the television shows and radio stations that I went on. And the newspapers. The *Washington Star* said they had never received more negative mail for anything they'd ever done—hundreds of horrible hate letters. Only two or three were addressed to me directly; the rest were addressed to the *Washington Star* editor and Lynn Rosellini for doing the series on gay athletes. The letters said things like, "It doesn't belong on the sports page as a model for our young boys and girls." "How could the *Washington Star* run an article like this?" I got letters that said, "I hope you never get a coaching job. Yours in Christ. Love. . . ." Just horrible things.

I never did get a coaching job. I was really quite frightened because I didn't know what I was going to do. No one would hire me to be a coach, I think, because of the image problem. They didn't think I could fill the role of the coach as guardian of the morals of the young students—the father figure. I also knew that I probably wouldn't get that really good sales-rep job that a lot of the other guys got. I had to make a spot for myself somehow, so I wound up working with Perry Young for a year on my book, *The Dave Kopay Story*.

I think we knew we were doing something good. . . .

A lot of kids still write. They say that the book meant so much to them. They remember that it changed them a lot or made a difference.

Source: Eric Marcus, *Making History* (New York: Harper Collins, 1992), 275–77.

restored 40 million acres to Eskimos, Aleuts, and other native peoples, along with $960 million in compensation. Most important, the federal government abandoned the tribal termination program of the 1950s (see Chapter 28). Under the Indian Self-Determination Act of 1974, Congress restored the tribes' right to govern themselves and gave them authority over federal programs on their reservations (Map 30.3).

Busing. The busing of children to achieve school desegregation proved the most disruptive social issue of the 1970s. Progress in achieving the desegregation

mandated by *Brown v. Board of Education of Topeka* had been slow. In the 1970s both the courts and the Justice Department pushed for more action, not just in the South but in other parts of the country. In *Milliken v. Bradley* (1974), the Supreme Court ordered cities with deeply ingrained patterns of residential segregation to use busing of black and white students from segregated neighborhoods to nonneighborhood schools to integrate their classrooms.

The decision sparked intense and sometimes violent opposition. In Boston in 1974 and 1975, the strongly Irish-Catholic working-class neighborhood of

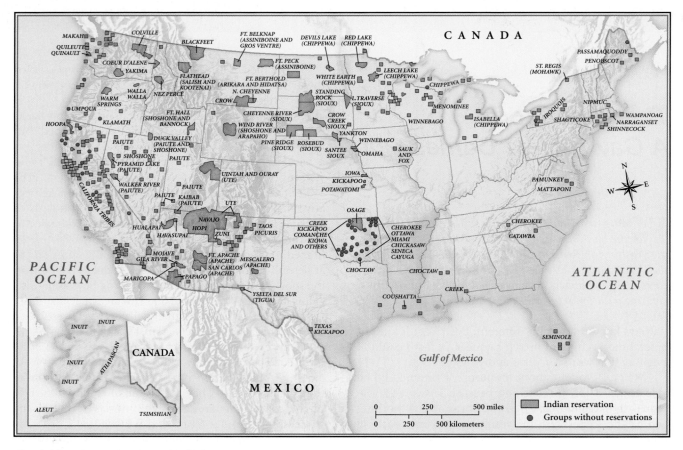

MAP 30.3 American Indian Reservations

Although Native Americans have been able to preserve small enclaves in the northeastern states, most Indian reservations are in the West. Beginning in the 1970s various nations filed land claims against federal and state governments.

For more help analyzing this map, see the ONLINE STUDY GUIDE at bedfordstmartins.com/henretta.

South Boston responded to the arrival of African American students from Roxbury with mob action reminiscent of that in Little Rock in 1957 (see American Voices, "Phyllis Ellison: Busing in Boston," p. 897). Threatened by court-ordered busing, many white parents transferred their children to private schools or moved to the suburbs. The resulting "white flight" exacerbated the racial imbalance busing was supposed to redress. Some black parents also opposed busing, calling instead for better schools in predominantly black neighborhoods. By the late 1970s federal courts had begun to back away from their insistence on busing to achieve racial balance.

Affirmative Action.   Almost as divisive as busing was the issue of affirmative action procedures, which had expanded opportunities for blacks and Latinos. The number of African American students enrolled in colleges and universities doubled between 1970 and 1977 to 1.1

million, or 9.3 percent of the total student enrollment. A small but growing number of African Americans moved into white-collar professions in corporations and universities. Others found new opportunities in civil service occupations such as law enforcement or entered apprenticeships in the skilled construction trades. Latinos experienced similar gains in education and employment. On the whole, however, both groups enjoyed only marginal economic improvement, since poor and working-class nonwhites bore the brunt of job loss and unemployment in the 1970s.

Nevertheless, many whites, who were also feeling the economic pinch, came to resent affirmative action programs as an infringement of their rights. White men especially complained of "reverse discrimination" against them. In 1978 Allan Bakke, a white man, sued the University of California Medical School at Davis for rejecting him in favor of less qualified minority candidates.

Phyllis Ellison

Busing in Boston

Nowhere in the North was busing more divisive than in Boston from 1974 to 1975. Phyllis Ellison was one of fifty-six black students from the predominantly black neighborhoods of Columbia Point and Roxbury who were assigned to South Boston High School. In this interview she describes incidents from her sophomore year, including the day a white student was stabbed by a black student during a melee at the school. The student's wound was not fatal, but the incident led to heightened resistance and recriminations.

I remember my first day going on the bus to South Boston High School. I wasn't afraid because I felt important. I didn't know what to expect, what was waiting for me up the hill. We had police escorts. I think there was three motorcycle cops and then two police cruisers in front of the bus, and so I felt really important at that time, not knowing what was on the other side of the hill.

Well, when we started up the hill you could hear people saying, "Niggers go home." There were signs, they had made a sign saying, "Black people stay out. We don't want any niggers in our school." And there were people on the corners holding bananas like we were apes, monkeys. "Monkeys get out, get them out of our neighborhood. We don't want you in our schools." . . .

You can't imagine how tense it was inside the classroom. A teacher was almost afraid to say the wrong thing, because they knew that that would excite the whole class, a disturbance in the classroom. The black students sat on one side of the classes. The white students sat on the other side of the classes. . . . In the lunchrooms . . . [it] was the same thing. . . . So really, it was separate, I mean, we attended the same school, but we really never did anything together. . . .

I remember the day Michael Faith got stabbed vividly, because I was in the principal's office and all of a sudden you heard a lot of commotion and you heard kids screaming and yelling and saying, "He's dead, he's dead. That black nigger killed him. He's dead, he's dead." And then the principal running out of the office. There was a lot of commotion and screaming, yelling, hollering, "Get the niggers at Southie." I was really afraid. And the principal came back into the office and said, Call the ambulance and tell all the black students that were in the office to stay there. A police officer was in there and they were trying to get the white students out of the building, because they had just gone on a rampage and they were just going to hurt the first black student that they saw. . . . The black students were locked in their rooms and all the white students were let go out of their classrooms. I remember us going into a room, and outside you just saw a crowd of people, I mean, just so many people, I can't even count. . . . I remember the police cars coming up the street, attempting to, and people turning over the police cars, and I was just amazed that they could do something like that. The police tried to get horses up. They wouldn't let the horses get up. They stoned the horses. They stoned the cars. And I thought that day that we would never get out of South Boston High School. . . .

Source: Henry Hampton and Steve Fayer, *Voices of Freedom: An Oral History of the Civil Rights Movement from the 1950s through the 1980s* (New York: Bantam, 1990), 600, 610, 612–13.

The Supreme Court ruling in *Bakke v. University of California* was inconclusive. Though it branded the medical school's strict quota system illegal and ordered Bakke admitted, it stated that racial factors could be considered in hiring and admission decisions, thus upholding the principle of affirmative action. But the *Bakke* decision was a setback for proponents of affirmative action, and it prepared the way for subsequent efforts to eliminate those programs.

Though activists who supported racial minorities, women, gays, consumers, and the environment had distinct agendas, they also had much in common. They were part of "a rights revolution"—a wide-ranging movement in the 1960s and 1970s to bring issues of social justice and welfare to the forefront of public policy. Influenced by the Great Society's liberalism, they invariably turned to the federal government for protection of individual rights and—in the case of environmentalists—the world's natural resources. The activists of this period made substantial progress in widening the notion of the federal government's responsibilities, but by the end of the 1970s their movements faced growing opposition.

The Politics of Resentment

Together with the rapidly growing antiabortion movement, the often vociferous public opposition to busing, affirmative action, gay rights ordinances, and the Equal Rights Amendment constituted a broad backlash against the social changes of the previous decade. Many Americans believed that their interests had been slighted by the rights revolution and resented a federal government that protected women who sought abortions or minorities who benefited from affirmative action. The economic changes of the 1970s, which left many working- and middle-class Americans with lower disposable incomes, rising prices, and higher taxes, further fueled what the conservative writer Alan Crawford has termed the *politics of resentment*—a grassroots revolt against "special-interest groups" (women, minorities, gays, and so on) and growing expenditures on social welfare. Special groups and programs, conservatives believed, robbed other Americans of educational and employment opportunities and saddled the working and middle classes with an extra financial burden.

One manifestation of the politics of resentment was a wave of local taxpayers' revolts. In 1978 California voters passed Proposition 13, a measure that reduced property taxes and eventually undercut local governments' ability to maintain schools and other essential services. Promising tax relief to middle-class homeowners and reduced funding for busing and other programs to benefit the poor—who were invariably assumed to be nonwhite—Proposition 13 became the model for similar tax measures around the country in the late 1970s and 1980s.

Evangelical Religion.   The rising popularity of evangelical religion also fueled the conservative resurgence of the 1970s. Fundamentalist groups that fostered a "born-again" experience had been growing steadily since World War II, under the leadership of charismatic preachers such as Billy Graham. According to a Gallup poll conducted in 1976, some 50 million Americans—about a quarter of the population—were affiliated with evangelical movements. These groups set up their own school systems and newspapers. Through broadcasting networks like the Christian Broadcasting Network, founded by the Virginia preacher Pat Robertson, a new breed of televangelists such as Jerry Falwell built vast and influential electronic ministries.

Many of these evangelicals spoke out on a broad range of issues, denouncing abortion, busing, sex education, pornography, feminism, and gay rights and bringing their religious values to a wider public. In 1979 Jerry Falwell founded the Moral Majority, a political pressure group that promoted Christian "family values"—traditional gender roles, heterosexuality, family cohesion—and staunch anticommunism. The extensive

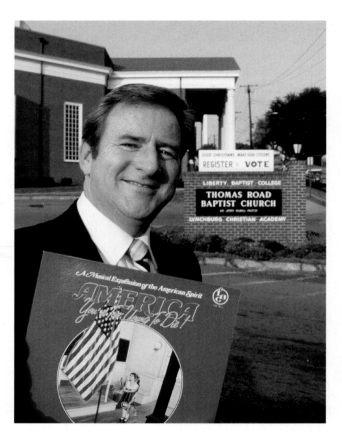

Jerry Falwell

The resurgence of evangelical religion in the 1970s was accompanied by a conservative movement in politics known as the "New Right." Founded in 1979 by televangelist Jerry Falwell, the Moral Majority was one of the earliest New Right groups, committed to promoting "family values" in American society and politics.   Dennis Brack / Black Star.

media and fund-raising networks of the Christian right contributed to the organizational base for a larger conservative movement known as the **New Right.**

The New Right.   The New Right's constituency was complex. Conservatives of the early cold war era had focused on resisting creeping socialism at home and abroad and were often identified with corporate business interests. In the 1970s they were joined not only by evangelical Christian groups but by "neoconservatives," intellectuals such as sociologist Nathan Glazier and Norman Podhoretz, editor of *Commentary* magazine, who had been associated with radical or liberal agendas in the past and now vehemently recanted their former political views. Articulate in their criticisms of affirmative action, the welfare state, and changing gender and sexual values, they helped to give conservative values a heightened respectability and reinforced much of the "politics of resentment." The New Right's diverse constituents shared a hostility toward a powerful federal government and a fear of declining social morality. Backed by wealthy corporate interests and using sophisticated computerized mass-mailing campaigns, a variety of New Right political groups mobilized thousands of followers and millions of dollars to support conservative candidates and causes.

Politics in the Wake of Watergate

It is not surprising that in the wake of Watergate many citizens had become cynical about the federal government and about politicians in general. "Don't vote. It only encourages them" read one bumper sticker during the 1976 campaign. Nixon's successors, Gerald Ford and Jimmy Carter, plagued by foreign-policy crises and continued economic woes, did little to restore public confidence. In the 1980 elections voter apathy persisted, but Ronald Reagan's lopsided presidential victory signified a hope that the charismatic former actor could restore America's traditional values and its economic and international power.

Ford's Caretaker Presidency

During the two years Gerald Ford held the nation's highest office, he failed to establish his legitimacy as president. Ford's pardon of Nixon hurt his credibility as a political leader, but an even bigger problem was his handling of the economy, which was reeling from the inflation set in motion by the Vietnam War, rising oil prices, and the growing trade deficit. In 1974 the inflation rate soared to almost 12 percent, and in the following year the economy entered its deepest downturn since the Great Depression. Though many of the nation's economic problems were beyond the president's control, Ford's failure to take more vigorous action made him appear timid and powerless.

In foreign policy Ford was equally lacking in leadership. He maintained Nixon's détente initiatives by asking Henry Kissinger to stay on as secretary of state. Though Ford met with Soviet leaders hoping to hammer out the details of a SALT II (Strategic Arms Limitation Treaty) agreement, he made little progress. Ford and Kissinger also continued Nixon's policy of increasing support for the shah of Iran, ignoring the bitter opposition and anti-Western sentiment that the shah's policy of rapid modernization was provoking among the growing Muslim fundamentalist population in Iran.

Jimmy Carter: The Outsider as President

The 1976 presidential campaign was one of the blandest in years. President Ford chose as his running mate the conservative Senator Robert J. Dole of Kansas. The Democratic choice, James E. (Jimmy) Carter, governor of Georgia, shared the ticket with Senator Walter F. Mondale of Minnesota, who had ties to the traditional Democratic constituencies of labor, liberals, blacks, and big-city machines. Avoiding issues and controversy, Carter played up his role as a Washington outsider, pledging to restore morality to government. "I will never lie to you," he earnestly told voters. Carter won the election with 50 percent of the popular vote to Ford's 48 percent.

Despite his efforts to overcome the post-Watergate climate of skepticism and apathy, Carter never became an effective leader. His outsider strategy distanced him from traditional sources of power, and he did little to heal the breach. Shying away from established Democratic leaders, Carter turned to advisors and friends who had worked with him in Georgia, none of whom had national experience. When his budget director, Bert Lance, was questioned about financial irregularities at the Atlanta bank he had headed, Carter's campaign pledge to restore integrity and morality to the government rang hollow.

Coping with Hard Economic Times. Inflation was Carter's major domestic challenge. When he took office, the nation was still recovering from the severe recession of 1975 and 1976. Carter embarked on a fiscal policy that eroded both business and consumer confidence. To counter inflation the Federal Reserve Board raised interest rates repeatedly; in 1980 they topped 20 percent, a historic high. A deep recession finally broke the inflationary spiral in 1982, a year after Carter left office.

The Carter administration expanded the federal bureaucracy in some cases and limited its reach in others. Carter enlarged the cabinet by creating the Departments of Energy and Education and approved new environmental protection measures, such as the $1.6 billion "Superfund" to clean up chemical pollution sites as well as new park and forest lands in Alaska. But he continued President Nixon's efforts to reduce the scope of federal activities by reforming the civil service and deregulating the airline, trucking, and railroad industries. With deregulation, prices often dropped, but the resulting cutthroat competition drove many firms out of business and encouraged corporate consolidation. Carter also failed in his effort to decontrol oil and natural gas prices as a spur to domestic production and conservation.

Carter's attempt to provide leadership during the energy crisis also faltered. He called energy conservation efforts "the moral equivalent of war," but the media reduced the phrase to "MEOW" (see Voices from Abroad, "Fei Xiaotong: America's Crisis of Faith," p. 900). In early 1979 a revolution in Iran again raised oil prices, and gas lines again reminded Americans of their dependence on foreign oil. That summer, Carter's approval rating dropped to 26 percent—lower than Richard Nixon's during the worst part of the Watergate scandal.

Fei Xiaotong

America's Crisis of Faith

Fei Xiaotong, a Chinese anthropologist and sociologist, wrote influential books on the United States during World War II and the 1950s. Despite his criticism of U.S. foreign policy, his often sympathetic treatment of America contributed to twenty years of political ostracism in China. Returning to prominence in the late 1970s, he joined an official delegation to the United States in 1979. In this passage written shortly after his return to China, Fei responds to President Jimmy Carter's assessment of the problems Americans faced as a spiritual crisis. Despite Fei's Marxist critique of American capitalism, his concluding remarks indicate a broadly positive attitude about the United States.

I read in the newspaper that the energy crisis in the United States is getting worse and worse. I hear that after spending several days of quiet thought in his mountain retreat, President Carter decided that America's real problem is not the energy crisis but a "crisis of faith." The way it is told is that vast numbers of people have lost their faith in the present government and in the political system, and do not believe that the people in the government working with current government methods can solve the present series of crises. Even more serious, he believes that the masses have come to have doubts about traditional American values, and if this continues, in his opinion, the future of America is terrible to imagine. He made a sad and worried speech. I have not had an opportunity to read the text of his speech, but if he has truly realized that the present American social system has lost popular support, that should be considered a good thing because at least it shows that the old method of just treating the symptoms will no longer work.

In fact, loss of faith in the present social system on the part of the broad masses of the American people did not begin with the energy crisis. The spectacular advances in science and technology in America in the last decade or two and the unceasing rise in the forces of production are good. But the social system remains unchanged, and the relations of production are basically the same old capitalism. This contradiction between the forces of production and the relations of production has not lessened but become deeper. The ruling class, to be sure, still has the power to keep on finding ways of dealing with the endless series of crises, but the masses of people are coming increasingly to feel that they have fallen unwittingly into a situation where their fate is controlled by others, like a moth in a spiderweb, unable to struggle free. Not only the blacks of Harlem—who are clearly able to earn their own living but still have to rely on welfare to support themselves without dignity—but even well-off families in garden-like suburban residences worry all day that some accident may suddenly rob them of everything. As the dependence of individuals on others grows heavier and heavier, each person feels in his heart that this society is no longer to be relied on. . . . No wonder people complain that civilization was created by humans, but humans have been enslaved by it. Such a feeling is natural in a society like America's. Carter is right to call this feeling of helplessness a "crisis of faith," for it is a doubting of the present culture. Only he should realize that the present crisis has been long in the making and is already deep. . . .

These "Glimpses of America" essays may be brought to a close here, but to end with the crisis of faith does violence to my original intention. History is a stream that flows on and cannot be stopped. Words must be cut off, but history goes bubbling on. It is inconceivable that America will come to a standstill at any crisis point. I have full faith in the great American people and hope that they will continue to make even greater contributions to the progress of mankind. . . .

Source: R. David Arkush and Leo O. Lee, trans. and eds., *Land Without Ghosts: Chinese Impressions of America From the Mid-Nineteenth Century to the Present* (Berkeley: University of California Press, 1989).

Foreign Policy and Diplomacy. In foreign affairs President Carter made human rights the centerpiece of his policy. He criticized the suppression of dissent in the Soviet Union—especially as it affected the right of Jewish citizens to emigrate—and withdrew economic and military aid from Argentina, Uruguay, Ethiopia, and other countries that violated human rights. Carter also established the Office of Human Rights in the State Department. Unable to change the internal policies of longtime U.S. allies who were serious violators of human rights, such as the Philippines, South Korea, and South Africa, he did manage to raise public awareness of the human rights issue, making it one future administrations would have to address.

In Latin America Carter's most important contribution was the resolution of the lingering dispute over control of the Panama Canal. In a treaty signed on September 7, 1977, the United States agreed to turn over control of the canal to Panama on December 31, 1999. In return the United States retained the right to send its ships through the canal in case of war, even though the canal itself would be declared neutral territory. Despite a conservative outcry that the United States was giving away more than it got, the Senate narrowly approved the treaty.

Though Carter had campaigned to free the United States from its "inordinate fear of Communism," relations with the Soviet Union soon became tense, largely because of problems surrounding arms-limitation talks. Eventually the Soviet leader Leonid Brezhnev signed SALT II (1979), but hopes for Senate ratification of the treaty collapsed when the Soviet Union invaded Afghanistan that December. In retaliation for this aggression, which Carter viewed as a threat to Middle Eastern oil supplies, the United States curtailed grain sales to the Soviet Union and boycotted the 1980 summer Olympics in Moscow. (The Soviets returned the gesture by boycotting the 1984 summer games in Los Angeles.) In a move with more long-term impact, Carter and his successor Ronald Reagan also provided covert assistance to an Afghan group who called themselves *mujahideen*, or holy warriors. With funding provided by Saudia Arabia and Pakistan, the CIA supported these radical Islamic fundamentalists, whose numbers would eventually include Osama bin Laden, in their efforts to drive the Russians from Afghanistan in the 1980s, thereby helping to establish the now infamous Taliban.

President Carter achieved both his most stunning success and his greatest failure in the Middle East. Relations between Egypt and Israel had remained tense since the 1973 Yom Kippur War. In 1978 Carter helped

A Framework for Peace

President Jimmy Carter's greatest foreign-policy achievement was the personal diplomacy he exerted to persuade President Anwar al-Sadat of Egypt (left) and Prime Minister Menachem Begin of Israel (right) to sign a peace treaty in 1978. The signing of the Camp David accords marked an important first step in constructing a framework for peace in the Middle East. In 2002 Carter received the Nobel Peace Prize in recognition of his "untiring effort to find peaceful solutions to international conflicts, to advance democracy and human rights, and to promote economic and social development."

Jimmy Carter Presidential Library.

to break the diplomatic stalemate by inviting Israel's prime minister Menachem Begin and Egyptian president Anwar al-Sadat to Camp David, the presidential retreat in Maryland. Two weeks of discussions and Carter's promise of additional foreign aid to Egypt persuaded Sadat and Begin to adopt a "framework for peace." The framework included Egypt's recognition of Israel's right to exist and Israel's return of the Sinai Peninsula, which it had occupied since 1967. Transfer of the territory to Egypt took place from 1979 to 1982.

The Iranian Hostage Crisis. Dramatically less successful was U.S. foreign policy toward Iran. Ever since the CIA had helped to install Muhammad Reza Pahlavi on the throne in 1953, the United States had counted Iran as a faithful ally in the troubled Middle East. Overlooking the repressive tactics of Iran's CIA-trained secret police, SAVAK, Carter followed in the footsteps of previous cold war policymakers for whom access to Iranian oil reserves and the shah's consistently anti-Communist stance outweighed all other considerations.

Early in 1979, however, the shah's government was overthrown and driven into exile by a revolution led by fundamentalist Muslim leader Ayatollah Ruhollah Khomeini. In late October 1979 the Carter administration admitted the deposed shah, who was suffering from incurable cancer, to the United States for medical treatment. Though Iran's new leaders had warned that such an action would provoke retaliation, Henry Kissinger and other foreign-policy leaders had argued

that the United States should assist the shah, both for humanitarian reasons and in return for his years of support for American policy. In response, on November 4, 1979, fundamentalist Muslim students under Khomeini's direction seized the U.S. embassy in Tehran, taking Americans there hostage in a flagrant violation of the principle of diplomatic immunity. The hostage takers demanded that the shah be returned to Iran for trial and punishment, but the United States refused. Instead, President Carter suspended arms sales to Iran, froze Iranian assets in American banks, and threatened to deport Iranian students in the United States.

For the next fourteen months, the Iranian hostage crisis paralyzed Jimmy Carter's presidency. Night after night, humiliating pictures of blindfolded hostages appeared on television newscasts. The extensive media coverage and Carter's insistence that the safe return of the fifty-two hostages was his top priority enhanced the value of the hostages to their captors. An attempt to mount a military rescue of the hostages failed miserably in April 1980, six months into the crisis, because of helicopter equipment failures in the desert. The abortive rescue mission reinforced the public's view of Carter as a bumbling and ineffective executive.

The Reagan Revolution

With Carter embroiled in the hostage crisis, the Republicans gained momentum by nominating former California governor Ronald Reagan. A movie actor from the late 1930s to the early 1950s, Reagan had served as president of

American Hostages in Iran

Images of blindfolded, handcuffed American hostages seized by Iranian militants at the American embassy in Tehran in November 1979 shocked the nation and created a foreign-policy crisis that eventually cost President Carter his chance for reelection.

Mingam / Liaison.

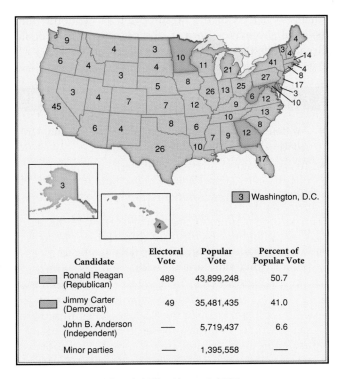

MAP 30.4 Presidential Election of 1980

Ronald Reagan defeated Democratic incumbent Jimmy Carter, winning all but six states and the District of Columbia. Winning 51 percent of the popular vote, Reagan cut deeply into the traditional Democratic coalition by wooing many southern whites, urban ethnics, and blue-collar workers and setting the stage for the "Reagan Revolution" and the conservative swing in American politics that characterized the 1980s and 1990s. Republicans also won control of the Senate for the first time since 1954.

the Screen Actors Guild and had been active in the post-war anti-Communist crusade in Hollywood. He had endorsed conservative presidential candidate Barry Goldwater in 1964 and had begun his own political career shortly thereafter, serving as governor of California from 1967 to 1975. After losing a bid for the Republican nomination in 1976, Reagan secured it easily in 1980 and chose former CIA director George Bush as his running mate.

In the final months of the campaign, Carter took on an embattled and defensive tone, while Reagan remained upbeat and decisive. The Republicans benefited from superior financial resources, which allowed them to make sophisticated use of television and direct-mail appeals. Reagan also had a powerful issue to exploit: the hostage stalemate. Calling the Iranians "barbarians" and "common criminals," he hinted that he would take strong action to win the hostages' return. More important, Reagan effectively appealed to the politics of resentment that flourished during the lean years of the 1970s. In a televised debate between the candidates, Reagan emphasized the economic plight of working- and middle-class Americans when he posed the rhetorical question, "Are you better off today than you were four years ago?"

In November Reagan won easily, with 51 percent of the popular vote to Carter's 41 percent (Map 30.4). The landslide also gave the Republicans control of the Senate for the first time since 1954, though the Democrats maintained their hold on the House. Voter turnout, however, was at its lowest since the 1920s: only 53 percent of those eligible to vote went to the polls. Many poor and working-class voters stayed home. Nevertheless, the election confirmed the growth in the power of the Republican Party since Richard Nixon's victory in 1968.

Superior financial resources and a realignment of the electorate contributed to the Republican resurgence of the 1970s. The political action committees that had proliferated under the Fair Campaign Practices Act of 1974 collected large sums for both parties, but particularly for the Republicans. While the Democratic Party saw its key constituency—organized labor—dwindle, the GOP's financial superiority enabled it to make sophisticated and effective use of television and direct mail to reach voters. This aggressive outreach helped bring about a realignment of the electorate. The core of the Republican Party that elected Ronald Reagan remained the upper-middle-class white Protestant voters who supported balanced budgets, disliked government activism, feared crime and communism, and believed in a strong national defense. But new groups had gravitated toward the Republican vision: southern whites disaffected by big government and black civil rights gains; blue-collar workers, especially culturally conservative Catholics; young voters who identified themselves as conservatives; and residents in the West, especially those in the rapidly growing suburbs. By wooing these "Reagan Democrats," the Republican Party made deep inroads into Democratic territory, eroding that party's traditional coalition of southerners, blacks, laborers, and urban ethnics.

The New Right was another significant contributor to the Republican victory, especially the religious right, associated with groups like the Moral Majority, whose emphasis on traditional values and Christian morality dovetailed well with conservative Republican ideology. In 1980 these concerns formed the basis for the party's platform, which called for a constitutional ban on abortion, voluntary prayer in public schools, and a mandatory death penalty for certain crimes. The Republicans also demanded an end to court-mandated busing and for the first time in forty years opposed the Equal Rights Amendment. A key factor in the 1980 election, the New Right contributed to the rebirth of the Republican Party under Ronald Reagan.

On January 20, 1981, at the moment Carter turned over the presidency to Ronald Reagan, the Iranian government released the American hostages. After 444 days of captivity, the hostages returned home to an ecstatic welcome, a reflection of the public's frustration over their long ordeal. While most Americans continued to maintain "We're Number One," the hostage crisis in Iran came to symbolize the loss of America's power to control world affairs. Its psychological impact was enhanced by its occurrence at the end of a decade that had witnessed Watergate, the American defeat in Vietnam, and the OPEC embargo.

To a great extent, the decline in American influence had been magnified by the unusual predominance the United States had enjoyed after World War II—an advantage that should not have been expected to last forever. The return of Japan and Western Europe to economic and political power, the control of vital oil resources by Middle Eastern countries, and the industrialization of some developing nations had widened the cast of characters on the international stage. Still, many Americans were unable to let go of the presumption of economic and political supremacy born in the postwar years. Ronald Reagan rode their frustrations to victory in 1980.

FOR FURTHER EXPLORATION

▶ For definitions of key terms boldfaced in this chapter, see the glossary at the end of the book.

▶ To assess your mastery of the material covered in this chapter, see the Online Study Guide at **bedfordstmartins.com/henretta**.

▶ For suggested references, including Web sites, see page SR-33 at the end of the book.

▶ For map resources and primary documents, see **bedfordstmartins.com/henretta**.

With his election to the presidency in 1968, Richard Nixon became a harbinger of more conservative times in American social and political life. During his five years in the White House, Nixon sought to trim back the welfare state through federal revenue sharing, cutbacks in Great Society antipoverty programs, and a reduced commitment to civil rights. But when he deemed it necessary, Nixon did not shrink from the use of executive power; he implemented wage and price controls to fight inflation, periodically impounded federal funds, and expanded the role of the government in environmental and consumer affairs. Nixon's plans, however, were cut short after his administration took part in a series of illegal acts during his campaign for reelection in 1972. The resulting Watergate scandal forced him to resign in 1974.

For much of the decade, the United States struggled with economic problems, including high inflation, skyrocketing energy costs, stagnation of income, and a diminished position in world trade. A series of gas shortages during the Arab oil embargo of 1973 to 1974 and the Iranian revolution in 1979 had a devastating impact on American society and caused many people to question the country's voracious pattern of energy consumption.

Although many Americans became cynical about politics after Watergate and Vietnam, some continued to pursue the unfinished social agendas of the 1960s. Most notably, the environmental and women's movements showed dynamic growth and activism at the grassroots level. Movements for consumer protection, gay and lesbian rights, and racial equality also continued to make modest gains. By the late 1970s, however, a new, more conservative social mood—based in part on the resurgence of evangelical Christianity—limited activists' advances on issues such as abortion rights, the Equal Rights Amendment, gay and lesbian rights, busing, and affirmative action.

On the national level ineffective political leadership by Gerald Ford led to his defeat in 1976 by Jimmy Carter of Georgia, who campaigned as a Washington outsider. Taking a high moral tone, Carter made human rights a priority of his administration and helped to negotiate the Camp David Peace accords between Egypt and Israel in 1978. But his own inexperience, mounting economic problems, and growing troubles abroad plagued his administration. The end of the decade was dominated by the Iranian hostage crisis, as Islamic fundamentalists held fifty-two hostages at the U.S. embassy in Tehran for 444 days. The hostage crisis virtually paralyzed Carter's presidency, helping Ronald Reagan to win election in 1980.

1968 Richard Nixon elected president

1970 Earth Day first observed

Environmental Protection Agency established

1971 Pentagon Papers published

Nixon suspends Bretton Woods system

Swann v. Charlotte-Mecklenburg institutes busing

1972–1974 Watergate investigation

1972 Revenue sharing begins

Watergate break-in; Nixon reelected

Congress passes Equal Rights Amendment

Ms. magazine founded

1973 Spiro Agnew resigns; Gerald Ford appointed vice president

Roe v. Wade legalizes abortion

Endangered Species Act

1973–1974 Arab oil embargo; gas shortages

Nixon resigns; Ford becomes president and pardons Nixon

Freedom of Information Act strengthened

Fair Campaign Practices Act passed

1974–1975 Busing controversy in Boston

1975–1976 Recession

Jimmy Carter elected president

First National Women's Conference in Houston

Voters overturn a Miami city council's gay rights measure

Carter brokers Camp David accords between Egypt and Israel

Proposition 13 reduces California taxes

Bakke v. University of California limits affirmative action

Love Canal crisis begins

1979 Three Mile Island nuclear accident

Moral Majority founded

Second oil crisis triggered by revolution in Iran

Hostages seized at American embassy in Teheran, Iran

Soviet Union invades Afghanistan

1980 "Superfund" created to clean up chemical pollution

Ronald Reagan elected president

CHAPTER 31

A New Domestic and World Order

1981–2001

O N NOVEMBER 9, 1989, MILLIONS of television viewers worldwide watched jubilant Germans swarm through the Berlin Wall after the East German government lifted all restrictions on passage between the eastern and western sectors of the city. The Berlin Wall, which had divided the city since 1961, was the foremost symbol of Communist repression and the cold war division of Europe. Over the years, more than 400 East Germans had lost their lives trying to escape to the freedom of the other side. Now East and West Berliners, young and old, danced and mingled on what remained of the structure.

When the Berlin Wall came down, it brought communism's grip over Eastern Europe down with it. The Soviet Union would dissolve in 1991, ending the cold war. But new sources of conflict soon threatened world peace. International terrorism, instability in developing nations, and ethnic conflict loomed as potentially serious threats. In the new world order, the United States was increasingly linked to a global economy that directly affected American interest rates, consumption patterns, and job opportunities. At home, Americans grappled with racial, ethnic, and cultural conflict; crime and economic inequities; the shrinking role of the federal government; and disenchantment with political leaders' failure to solve many of the nation's pressing social problems.

◄ **The Wall Comes Tumbling Down**
The destruction of the Berlin Wall in
November 1989 symbolized the end of the
cold war.
Alexandra Avakian / Woodfin Camp & Associates.

The Reagan-Bush Years, 1981–1993

First elected at age sixty-nine, Ronald Reagan was the oldest man ever to serve as president, yet he conveyed a sense of physical vigor. By capitalizing on his skills as an actor and public speaker and by winning the support of the emerging New Right within the Republican Party, Reagan became one of the most popular presidents of the twentieth century. George Bush paled in comparison. His one term as president often seems indistinguishable from the two terms of his predecessor, in part because Bush was overshadowed by Reagan's extraordinary charisma but also because he followed the basic policies of the previous administration. Distrustful of the federal government, both Bush and Reagan turned away from the state as a source of solutions to America's social problems, calling into question almost a half cen-

Festive Times at the Reagan White House

Since Ronald and Nancy Reagan were both former actors, perhaps they thought of Fred Astaire and Ginger Rogers (see p. 705) when they struck this pose at a White House state dinner in May 1985. Some former White House staffers now suspect that Reagan was showing signs of early Alzheimer's disease by that point.

Photo by Harry Benson. Cover courtesy VANITY FAIR. © 1985 by Condé-Nast Publications, Inc.

tury of governmental activism. "Government is not the solution to our problem," Reagan declared. "Government is the problem."

Reaganomics

The economic and tax policies that emerged under Reagan, quickly dubbed **Reaganomics**, were based on supply-side economics theory. According to the theory, high taxes siphoned off capital that would otherwise be invested, stimulating growth. Tax cuts would therefore promote investment, causing an economic expansion that would increase tax revenues. Together with reductions in government spending, tax cuts would also shrink the federal budget deficit. Critics charged that conservative Republicans deliberately cut taxes to force reductions in federal funding for the social programs they disliked.

The Economic Recovery Tax Act passed in 1981 reduced income tax rates by 25 percent over three years. The reductions were supposed to be linked to drastic cutbacks in federal expenditures. But while cuts were made in food stamps, unemployment compensation, and welfare programs such as Aid to Families with Dependent Children (AFDC), congressional resistance kept the Social Security and Medicare programs intact. The net impact of Reaganomics was to further the redistribution of income from the poor to the wealthy.

Another tenet of Reaganomics was that many federal regulations impeded economic growth and productivity. The administration moved to abolish or reduce federal regulation of the workplace, health care, consumer protection, and the environment. The responsibility for and cost of such regulations were transferred to the states. One of the results of this policy was the deinstitutionalization of many of the mentally ill, forcing them onto the streets.

The money saved by these means—and more—was plowed into a five-year, $1.2 trillion defense buildup. This huge increase fulfilled Reagan's campaign pledge to "make America number one again," a slogan that tapped anxieties about the nation's foreign-policy failures, most recently symbolized by the Iranian hostage fiasco. The B-1 bomber, which President Carter had canceled, was resurrected, and development of a new missile system, the MX, was begun. Reagan's most ambitious and controversial weapons plan, proposed in 1983, was the Strategic Defense Initiative (SDI), popularly known as "Star Wars." A computerized satellite and laser shield for detecting and intercepting incoming missiles, SDI would supposedly render nuclear war obsolete.

Reagan's programs benefited from the Federal Reserve Board's tight money policies as well as a serendipitous drop in world oil prices, which reduced the disastrous inflation rates that had bedeviled the nation in the 1970s. Between 1980 and 1982 the inflation rate dropped from 12.4 percent to just 4 percent. Unfortunately, the Fed's tightening of the money supply also brought on the "Reagan recession" of 1981 to 1982, which threw some 10 million Americans out of work. But as the recession bottomed out in early 1983 the economy began to grow, and for the rest of the decade, inflation remained low. Despite rather unexceptional growth in the gross domestic product, the Reagan administration presided over the longest peacetime economic expansion in American history.

Reagan's Second Term

Economic growth played a role in the 1984 elections. Reagan campaigned on the theme "It's Morning in America," suggesting that a new day of prosperity and pride was dawning. The Democrats nominated former vice president Walter Mondale of Minnesota to run against Reagan. With strong ties to labor unions, minority groups, and party leaders, Mondale epitomized the New Deal coalition that had dominated the Democratic Party since Roosevelt. To appeal to women voters, Mondale selected Representative Geraldine Ferraro of New York as his running mate—the first woman to run on a major party ticket. Nevertheless, Reagan won a landslide victory, carrying the entire nation except for Minnesota and the District of Columbia. Democrats, however, held onto the House and in 1986 would regain control of the Senate.

The Iran-Contra Affair. A major scandal marred Reagan's second term when in 1986 news leaked out that the administration had negotiated an arms-for-hostages deal with the revolutionary government of Iran—the same government Reagan had denounced during the 1980 hostage crisis. In an attempt to gain Iran's help in freeing some American hostages held by pro-Iranian forces in Lebanon, the United States had covertly sold arms to Iran. Some of the profits generated by the arms sales were diverted to the **Contras**, counterrevolutionaries in Nicaragua, whom the administration supported over the leftist regime of the Sandinistas. The covert diversion of funds, which was both illegal and unconstitutional, seemed to have been the brainstorm of Marine Lieutenant Colonel Oliver North, a National Security Council aide at the time. One key memo linked the White House to his plan. But when Congress investigated the mounting scandal in 1986 and 1987, White House officials testified that the president knew nothing about the diversion. Ronald Reagan's defense remained simple and consistent: "I don't remember."

The scandal bore many similarities to Watergate, including the possibility that the president had acted illegally. Yet early in Reagan's administration, one of his critics had coined the phrase "Teflon presidency" to describe Reagan's resiliency: bad news did not stick; it

just rolled off. The public seemed untroubled that the president was often confused or ill informed. Even the news that Nancy Reagan was in the habit of consulting an astrologer before planning major White House events failed to shake public confidence in the president. Reagan weathered "Iran-Contragate," but the scandal weakened his presidency.

The Reagan Legacy. The president proposed no bold domestic policy initiatives in his last two years in office. He had promised to place drastic limits on the federal government and to give free-market forces freer reign. Despite reordering the federal government's priorities, he failed to reduce its size or scope. Social Security and other entitlement programs remained untouched, and the military buildup counteracted cuts in other programs. Nevertheless, those spending cuts and Reagan's antigovernment rhetoric shaped the terms of political debate for the rest of the century.

One of Reagan's most significant legacies was his conservative judicial appointments. In 1981 he appointed Sandra Day O'Connor, the first woman ever to serve on the Supreme Court. In his second term he appointed two more justices, Antonin Scalia (1986) and Anthony Kennedy (1988), both far more conservative than the moderate O'Connor. Justice William Rehnquist, a noted conservative, was elevated to Chief Justice of the

Another Barrier Falls

In 1981 Sandra Day O'Connor (shown here with Chief Justice Warren Burger) became the first woman appointed to the Supreme Court. In 1993 she was joined by Ruth Bader Ginsburg.
Fred Ward / Black Star.

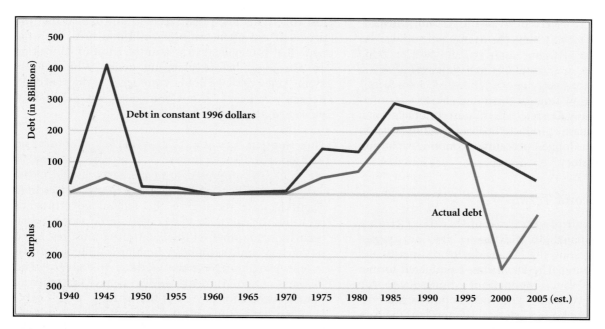

FIGURE 31.1 The Escalating Federal Debt, 1939–2000

The federal debt, which soared during World War II, remained fairly stable until the huge annual deficits of the 1980s. Deficits remained high in the 1990s, but political pressure to balance the budget promised reductions in the national debt.

Source: *Statistical Abstract of the United States, 2000* and Historical Tables, Budget for Fiscal Year 2003.

United States in 1986. Under his leadership the Court, often by a five-to-four margin, chipped away at the Warren Court's legacy in decisions on individual liberties, affirmative action, and the rights of criminal defendants.

Ironically, though Reagan had promised to balance the budget by 1984, his most enduring legacy was the national debt, which tripled during his two terms. The huge deficit reflected the combined effects of increased military spending, tax reductions for high-income taxpayers, and Congress's refusal to approve deep cuts in domestic programs (Figure 31.1). By 1989 the national debt had climbed to $2.8 trillion—more than $11,000 for every American citizen.

The nation was also running an annual deficit in its trade with other nations. Exports had been falling since the 1970s, when American products began to encounter increasing competition in world markets. In the early 1980s a high exchange rate for dollars made U.S. goods more expensive for foreign buyers and imports more affordable for Americans. The budget and trade deficits contributed to a major shift in 1985: for the first time since 1915, the United States became a debtor rather than a creditor nation.

The Bush Presidency

George Bush won the Republican nomination in 1988 and chose for his vice president a young conservative Indiana senator, Dan Quayle. In the Democratic primaries the

Patriotism and Politics

At a confetti parade for the 1988 Summer Olympic team held at Disneyland, California, in September 1988, Republican presidential candidate George Bush and his wife Barbara bask in the glow of America's success. Cynthia Johnson. © TIME Magazine.

most important contest was between Governor Michael Dukakis of Massachusetts and the charismatic civil rights leader Jesse Jackson, whose populist Rainbow Coalition had embraced the diversity of Democratic constituencies. Dukakis received the party's nomination and chose Senator Lloyd Bentsen of Texas as his running mate.

The 1988 campaign had a harsh tone: brief televised attack ads replaced meaningful discussion of the issues. The sound bite "Read My Lips: No New Taxes," drawn from George Bush's acceptance speech at the Republican convention, became the party's campaign mantra. In a racially charged television ad featuring Willie Horton, a black man convicted of murder who had killed again while on furlough from a Massachusetts prison, Republicans charged Dukakis with being soft on crime. Dukakis, forced on the defensive, failed to mount an effective counterattack. Bush carried thirty-eight states, winning the popular vote by 53.4 percent to 45.6 percent.

Supreme Court Conservatism. The judiciary rather than the executive branch determined some of the more significant domestic trends of the Bush era. Under Reagan's appointees the Supreme Court continued to move away from liberal activism toward a more conservative stance, especially on the issue of abortion. The 1989 *Webster v. Reproductive Health Services* decision upheld the right of states to limit the use of public funds and institutions for abortions. The next year the Court upheld a federal regulation barring personnel at federally funded health clinics from discussing abortion with their clients. In 1992 the Court upheld a Pennsylvania law mandating informed consent and a twenty-four-hour waiting period before an abortion could be performed. But the justices also reaffirmed the "essential holding" in *Roe v. Wade:* women had a constitutional right to abortion.

In 1990 David Souter, a little-known federal judge from New Hampshire, easily won confirmation to the Supreme Court. But the next year a major controversy erupted over President Bush's nomination of Clarence Thomas, an African American conservative with little judicial experience. Just as Thomas's confirmation hearings were drawing to a close, a former colleague, Anita Hill, testified publicly that Thomas had sexually harassed her in the early 1980s. After widely watched and widely debated televised testimony by both Thomas and Hill before the all-male Senate Judiciary Committee, the Senate confirmed Thomas by a narrow margin. In the wake of the hearings, national polls confirmed the pervasiveness of sexual harassment on the job: four out of ten women said that they had been the object of unwanted sexual advances from men at work.

Domestic and Economic Policy. Bush's record on the economy was crippled by his predecessor's failed economic policies, especially the budget deficit. The

A Woman of Conscience
Accusations by University of Oklahoma law professor Anita Hill that Supreme Court nominee Clarence Thomas had sexually harassed her sparked fierce debate. Many felt that had there been more women in the Senate, Hill's charges would have been treated more seriously. After the 1992 election women's representation did in fact increase to six women in the Senate and forty-seven in the House of Representatives. Markel / Gamma Liaison.

Gramm-Rudman Act, passed in 1985, had mandated automatic cuts if budget targets were not met in 1991. Facing the prospect of a halt in nonessential government services and the layoff of thousands of government employees, Congress resorted to new spending cuts and one of the largest tax increases in history. Bush's failure to keep his "No New Taxes" promise earned him the enmity of Republican conservatives, which dramatically hurt his chances for reelection in 1992.

Reagan's decision to shift the cost of many federal programs—including housing, education, public works, and social services—to state and local governments caused problems for Bush. In 1990 a recession began to erode state and local tax revenues. As incomes declined and industrial and white-collar layoffs increased, poverty and homelessness increased sharply. In 1991 unemployment approached 7 percent nationwide. To save money, state and local governments laid off workers even as demand for social services climbed.

The Savings and Loan Crisis.   Another drag on the economy was the collapse of the savings and loan industry. Savings and loan associations (S & Ls), also called "thrifts," invested depositors' savings in home mortgages. Since 1934 deposits in S & Ls had been insured by the Federal Savings and Loan Insurance Corporation (FSLIC). After S & Ls complained in 1982 that high inflation and soaring interest rates were reducing their profits, Reagan's deregulation program permitted them to invest in commercial real estate and businesses. The real estate market boomed for most of the 1980s, so the loans and investments were profitable. But when construction and the oil boom in the Southwest slowed and the stock market tumbled sharply in 1987, savings and loan associations' losses mounted, and the value of their assets plummeted. Some S & Ls were taken over by commercial banks, but many simply went bankrupt, forcing the federal government to make good its guarantee to depositors. To recoup some of the massive losses, the Bush administration set up a temporary agency in 1989 to sell the remaining assets—primarily defaulted real estate. It took the Resolution Trust Corporation six years to clean up the mess, at a total cost to American taxpayers of $150 billion.

Foreign Relations under Reagan and Bush

The collapse of détente during the Carter administration, after the Soviet invasion of Afghanistan, prompted Reagan's confrontational approach to what he called the "evil empire." Backed by Republican hard-liners and determined to reduce Communist influence in developing nations, Reagan articulated some of the harshest anti-Soviet rhetoric since the 1950s. The collapse of the Soviet Union in 1991 removed that nation as a credible threat, but new post–cold war challenges quickly appeared.

Interventions in Developing Countries

Despite Reagan's rhetoric, not all his international problems involved U.S.-Soviet confrontations. In 1983, after Israel invaded Lebanon, the U.S. Embassy in Beirut was bombed by anti-Israeli Muslim fundamentalists. A second bombing killed 241 marine peacekeepers barracked in the city. Around the world, terrorist assassins struck down Indira Gandhi in India and Anwar al-Sadat in Egypt. But it was the airplane hijackings and numerous terrorist incidents in the Middle East that led Reagan to order air strikes against one highly visible source of terrorism, Muammar al-Qaddafi of Libya.

The administration reserved its most concerted attention for Central America. Halting what was seen as the spread of communism in that region became an obsession. In 1983 Reagan ordered the marines to invade the tiny Caribbean island of Grenada, claiming that its Cuban-supported Communist regime posed a threat to other states in the region. Reagan's top priority, however, was to topple the leftist Sandinista government in Nicaragua (Map 31.1). In 1981 the United States suspended aid to Nicaragua, charging that the Sandinistas were supplying arms to rebels against a repressive but non-Communist right-wing regime in El Salvador. At the same time the CIA began to provide extensive covert support to the Nicaraguan opposition, the Contras, who Reagan called "freedom fighters." Congress, wary of the assumption of unconstitutional powers by the executive branch, responded in 1984 by passing the Boland Amendment, which banned the CIA and other intelligence agencies from providing military support to the Contras—a provision violated in the Iran-Contra affair.

The End of the Cold War

Surprisingly, given Reagan's rhetoric, his second term brought a reduction in tensions with the Soviet Union. In 1985 Reagan met with the new Soviet premier, Mikhail Gorbachev, at the first superpower summit meeting since 1979. Two years later the two leaders agreed to eliminate all intermediate-range missiles based in Europe. During the Bush administration even more dramatic changes abroad brought an end to the cold war. In 1989 the grip of communism on Eastern Europe eroded in a series of mostly nonviolent revolutions that climaxed in the destruction of the Berlin Wall in November. Soon the Soviet Union itself began to succumb to the forces of change.

The background for these dramatic upheavals was established by Soviet president Mikhail Gorbachev. His policies of *glasnost* (openness) and *perestroika* (economic restructuring) after 1985 signaled a willingness to tolerate significant changes in Soviet society.

Alarmed by Gorbachev's shift, on August 19, 1991, Soviet military leaders seized Gorbachev and attempted unsuccessfully to oust him. The failure of the coup broke the Communist Party's dominance over the Soviet Union. In December the Union of Soviet Socialist Republics formally dissolved itself to make way for an eleven-member Commonwealth of Independent States (CIS) (Map 31.2). Gorbachev resigned, and Boris Yeltsin, president of the new state of Russia, the largest and most populous republic, became the preeminent leader in the region.

The unexpected collapse of the Soviet Union and the end of the cold war stunned America and the world. In the absence of bipolar superpower confrontations, future international conflicts would arise from varied regional, religious, and ethnic differences. Suddenly, the United States faced unfamiliar military and diplomatic challenges.

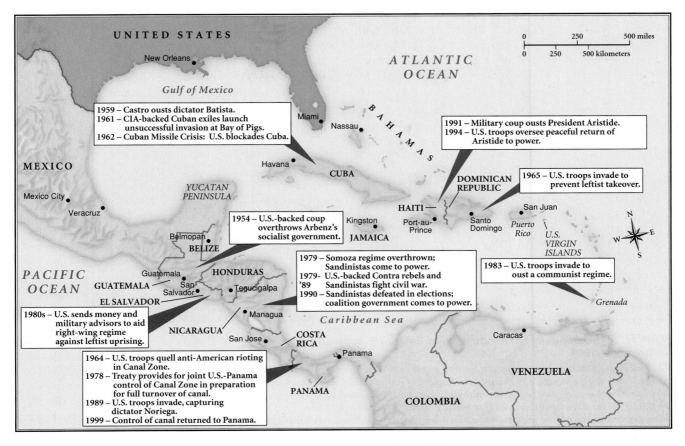

MAP 31.1 U.S. Involvement in Latin America and the Caribbean, 1954–2000

Ever since the Monroe Doctrine (1823), the United States has claimed a special interest in Latin America. During the cold war, U.S. foreign policy throughout Latin America focused on containing instability and the appeal of communism in a region plagued by poverty and military dictatorships. Providing foreign aid was one approach to addressing social and economic needs, but, more typically, U.S. policy concentrated on supporting U.S. business interests. The desire for stability and governments friendly to the United States also led to repeated military interventions, both overt and covert, throughout the cold war decades.

War in the Persian Gulf, 1990–1991

The first challenge had already surfaced in the Middle East. On August 2, 1990, Iraq, led by Saddam Hussein, invaded Kuwait, its small but oil-rich neighbor, and threatened Saudi Arabia, the site of one-fifth of the world's known oil reserves (see Voices from Abroad, "Saddam Hussein: Calling for a Holy War against the United States," p. 915). Concerned about this threat to Middle East stability as well as to U.S. access to oil, President Bush sponsored a series of resolutions in the United Nations Security Council condemning Iraq, calling for its withdrawal, and imposing an embargo and trade sanctions. When Hussein showed no signs of yielding, Bush prodded the international organization to create a legal framework for a military offensive against the man he called "the butcher of Baghdad." In November the Security Council voted to use force if Iraq

did not withdraw by January 15. In a close vote of 52 to 48 on January 12, the U.S. Senate authorized military action. Four days later President Bush announced to the nation that "the liberation of Kuwait has begun."

The forty-two-day war was a resounding success for the United Nations' coalition forces, which were predominantly American. Under the leadership of General Colin Powell, chairman of the Joint Chiefs of Staff, and the commanding general, H. Norman Schwarzkopf, Operation Desert Storm opened with a month of air strikes to crush communications, destroy armaments, and pummel Iraqi ground troops. A land offensive followed. Within days, thousands of Iraqi troops had fled or surrendered, and the fighting quickly ended, although Hussein remained in power (Map 31.3).

Operation Desert Storm's success and the few U.S. casualties (145 Americans were killed in action) produced a euphoric reaction at home. For many the American

MAP 31.2 The Collapse of Communism in Eastern Europe and the Soviet Union, 1989–1991

The end of the Soviet empire in Eastern Europe and the collapse of communism in the Soviet Union itself dramatically changed the borders of Europe and Central Asia. West and East Germany reunited, while the nations of Czechoslovakia and Yugoslavia, created by the 1919 Versailles treaty, divided into smaller states. The old Soviet Union produced fifteen new countries, of which eleven remained loosely bound in the Commonwealth of Independent States (CIS).

Women at War

Women played key and visible roles in the Persian Gulf War, comprising approximately 10 percent of the American troops. Increasing numbers of women are choosing military careers, despite widespread reports of sexual harassment and other forms of discrimination. Luc Delahaye / SIPA Press.

victory over a vastly inferior fighting force seemed to banish the ghost of Vietnam. "By God, we've kicked the Vietnam syndrome once and for all," Bush gloated. The president's approval rating shot up precipitously but declined almost as quickly when a new recession showed that the easy victory had masked the country's serious economic problems.

Uncertain Times: Economic and Social Trends, 1980–2000

Opinion polls taken in the early 1990s showed that Americans were deeply concerned about the future. They worried about crime in the streets, increases in poverty and homelessness, the decline of the inner cities, illegal immigration, the environment, the failure of public schools, the unresolved abortion issue, and AIDS. But above all they worried about their own economic security—whether they would be able to keep their jobs in an era of global competition. By the end of the decade, a vastly improved economic picture would lessen—but not erase—Americans' concerns for the future.

Saddam Hussein

Calling for a Holy War against the United States

After Iraq invaded Kuwait in August 1990, President Saddam Hussein of Iraq justified the action in the language of jihad, *the Muslim holy war. Coming from a secular ruler committed to the suppression of religion in public life, Hussein's call for a holy war against the United States suggested the ways in which Islamic fundamentalism had become part of the larger political discourse of the Arab world, particularly in political relations with Western nations.*

This great crisis started on the 2nd of August, between the faithful rulers and presidents of these nations—the unjust rulers who have abused everything that is noble and holy until they are now standing in a position which enables the devil to manipulate them. This is the great crisis of this age in this great part of the world where the material side of life has surpassed the spiritual one and the moral one. . . . This is the war of right against wrong and is a crisis between Allah's teachings and the devil.

Allah the Almighty has made his choice—the choice for the fighters and the strugglers who are in favor of principles, God has chosen the arena for this crisis to be the Arab World, and has put the Arabs in a progressive position in which the Iraqis are among the foremost. And to confirm once more the meaning that God taught us ever since the first light of faith and belief, which is that the arena of the Arab world is the arena of the first belief and Arabs have always been an example and a model for belief and faith in God Almighty and are the ones who are worthy of true happiness.

It is now your turn, Arabs, to save all humanity and not just save yourselves, and to show the principles and meanings of the message of Islam, of which you are all believers and of which you are all leaders.

It is now your turn to save humanity from the unjust powers who are corrupt and exploit us and are so proud of their positions, and these are led by the United States of America. . . .

For, as we know out of a story from the Holy Koran, the rulers, the corrupt rulers, have always been ousted by their people for it is a right on all of us to carry out the holy jihad, the holy war of Islam, to liberate the holy shrines of Islam. While the ruler of Saudi Arabia called himself the custodian of the two holy shrines, while in fact he is an agent, for he has given away his land to the foreigners.

We call upon all Arabs, each according to his potentials and capabilities within the teachings of Allah and according to the Muslim holy war of jihad, to fight this U.S. presence of nonbelievers and to fight the stance taken by the Arab agents who have followed these foreigners. And we hail the people of Saudi Arabia who are being fooled by their rulers, as well as the people of dear Egypt, as well as all the people of the Arab nations who are not of the same position as their leaders, and they believe in their pride and their sovereignty over their land. We call on them to revolt against their traitors, their rulers, and to fight foreign presence in the holy lands. And we support them, and more important, that God is with them.

Source: New York Times, September 6, 1990, A19.

The Economy

Between 1980 and 2000, the nation's economic mood swung from despairing to optimistic. At the beginning of this two-decade period, Americans struggled with such problems as growing trade deficits, declining productivity, and a widening gap between rich and poor. By 2000, productivity had improved, the federal deficit had disappeared, and the stock market boomed. Despite Americans' optimism, however, many observers warned of danger signs that threatened to reverse the country's future economic outlook.

Economic Pressures. In the 1980s and early 1990s, Americans viewed with alarm the economic success of Germany and Japan, the growing U.S. trade deficit, and the infusion of foreign workers and investment money into the United States. While other nations improved their competitive edge, Americans grappled with a worrisome decline in productivity. In contrast to the period of 1945 to 1973, when productivity had grown 2.8 percent annually, in the next quarter century that figure had dropped to less than 1 percent annually.

As productivity declined, economic inequality increased: the rich got richer, the poor got poorer, and

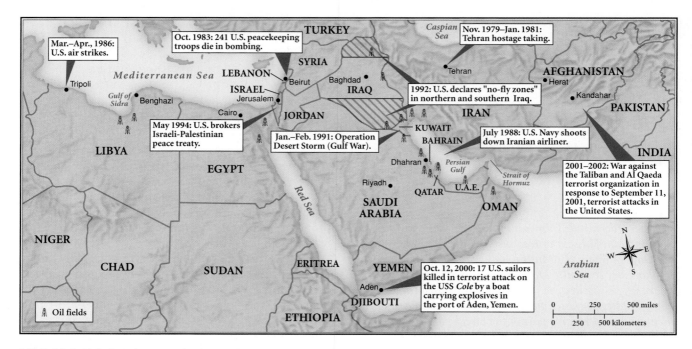

MAP 31.3 U.S. Involvement in the Middle East, 1980–2002
The United States has long played an active role in the Middle East, pursuing the twin goals of protecting Israel's security and ensuring a reliable supply of low-cost oil from the Persian Gulf states. The Middle East has also been the site of terrorist activities targeting U.S. interests, most notably the suicide attack, presumably by Al Qaeda operatives, on the USS Cole *refueling in Yemen. Al Qaeda terrorism against sites in the United States on September 11, 2001, provoked a U.S.-led United Nations attack on Afghanistan that drove the Islamic fundamentalist Taliban government from power.*

the middle class shrank (Figure 31.2). By 1996 the United States was the most economically stratified industrial nation in the world. Statistics from the Congressional Budget Office showed that the richest 1 percent of American families reaped most of the gains of Reaganomics.

Even relatively well-advantaged Americans felt a sense of diminished expectations, in part from changes in the job market. Following an established pattern, the number of minimum-wage service jobs continued to grow, while the number of union-protected manufacturing jobs was shrinking. One-fifth of the labor force in 1994 held only part-time or temporary work. Moreover, in the 1980s and 1990s the downsizing trend, in which companies deliberately shed permanent workers to cut wage costs, spread to middle management. From 1980 to 1995 IBM shrank its mostly white-collar workforce from 400,000 to 220,000. Although most laid-off middle managers eventually found new jobs, many took a large pay cut.

These economic trends put even more pressure on women to seek paid employment. In 1994, 58.8 percent of women were in the labor force, up from 38 percent in 1962, compared with 75.1 percent of men. The stereotypical nuclear family of employed father, homemaker wife, and children characterized less than 15 percent of U.S.

households. Although women continued to make inroads in traditionally male-dominated fields—medicine, law, law enforcement, the military, and skilled trades—one out of five held a clerical or secretarial job, the same proportion as in 1950. Women's pay lagged behind men's; for black and Latino women, the gender gap in pay was especially wide.

At the same time, the labor movement—hurt by downsizing, foreign competition, fear of layoffs, government hostility during the Reagan-Bush years, and its own failure to organize unskilled workers—continued to decline. The number of union members dropped from 20 million in 1978 to 16.2 million in 1998, representing only 13.9 percent of the labor force. Although union membership was more than one-third female and one-fifth black, union leadership remained overwhelmingly white and male.

Economic Turnaround. The discouraging economic picture began to improve by the mid-1980s. To compete with the economic success of Germany and Japan, American corporations had adopted new technologies, including microelectronics, biotechnology, computers, and robots, and by the late 1990s saw their competi-

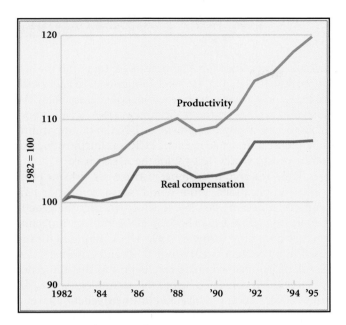

FIGURE 31.2 Productivity and Wages, 1982–1995
Usually as productivity increases, so does labor's share of national income. In the 1990s, however, workers failed to reap the rewards of the increased productivity shown here. Labor's relative loss in real compensation in turn contributed to a rise in corporate profits.
Source: *New York Times,* January 2, 1996, C20. Copyright © 1996 by The New York Times Co. Reprinted by permission.

tiveness return (see New Technology, "The Biotech Revolution," p. 918). Bethlehem Steel, which invested $6 billion to modernize its operations, doubled its productivity between 1989 and 1997. By 1997, U.S. economic growth, measured at 4 percent, was among the healthiest in the world, while one of the country's most serious competitors in the 1980s, Japan, limped along with only a 1.1 percent growth rate.

Working Americans benefited from these developments: new jobs were added to the economy at the rate of 213,000 per month in 1997, and unemployment dropped from 7.5 percent in 1992 to barely over 4 percent in the first half of 2000. A booming stock market, energized by a flow of funds into the high-tech sector and the highly touted emergence of e-commerce (firms doing business over the Internet), seemed to reach new highs daily and fueled the wealth and retirement savings of middle- and upper-income Americans. By 2000, as a result of the economy's strong performance and the spending cuts in the federal budget, the nagging deficit was wiped out: the Congressional Budget Office projected an astonishing surplus of $4.6 trillion in the next ten years.

But there were downsides to the picture as well. Many stock market analysts worried that a steep drop in the

stock market might create a recession, although the country weathered a stunning market plunge of 554 points in 1997. Other experts warned that the consumer spending fueling economic growth was tied to growing debts. The median family indebtedness was $33,300 in 1998, up from $23,400 in 1995. An economic downturn could have serious repercussions for overextended families' ability to repay their debts. Moreover, prosperity was not equally distributed. A federal survey released in January 2000 reported that the earnings of the top one-fifth of Americans grew 15 percent in the preceding decade, while the bottom one-fifth grew less than 1 percent. By the end of 2000, the collapse of many e-commerce enterprises and the declining value of many blue-chip technology stocks signaled that the boom was over. In the final quarter of that year, economic growth slowed to 2.2 percent, a pattern that would intensify in 2001.

Popular Culture and Popular Technology

Image was everything in the 1980s and 1990s—or so commentators said, pointing to rock stars Michael Jackson and Madonna and even to President Reagan. One strong influence on popular culture was MTV, a television channel that premiered in 1981 and featured short visual pieces accompanying popular songs. The MTV style—with its creative choreography, flashy colors, and rapid cuts—soon showed up in mainstream media and even political campaigns, which adapted the 30-second sound bites common on television news shows to campaigning purposes. The national newspaper *USA Today,* which debuted in 1982, also adopted the style, featuring eye-catching graphics, color photographs, and short, easy-to-read articles. Soon more staid newspapers followed suit.

At the same time, new technology, especially satellite transmission and live "minicam" broadcasting, reshaped the television industry. Cable and satellite dishes were increasingly available. By the mid-1990s viewers could choose from well over 100 channels, including upstarts such as Ted Turner's Cable News Network (CNN) and the Entertainment Sports Network (ESPN), an all-sports channel. Media, communications, and entertainment were big business, increasingly drawn into global financial networks, markets, and mergers.

Technology also reshaped the home in the late twentieth century. The 1980s saw the introduction of videocassette recorders (VCRs), compact disc (CD) players, cellular telephones, and inexpensive fax machines. By 1993 more than three-quarters of American households had VCRs. Video was everywhere—stores, airplanes, tennis courts, operating rooms. With the introduction of camcorders, the family photo album could be supplemented by a video of a high school graduation, a marriage, or a birth.

The Biotech Revolution

Was Zachary Taylor poisoned? Did Abraham Lincoln have a rare disease called Marfan's syndrome? Were Tsar Nicholas II and his family executed during the Bolshevik Revolution in 1918? Was the Vietnam serviceman buried in Arlington National Cemetery's Tomb of the Unknowns really Air Force Lieutenant Michael Blassie? Recent advances in DNA testing, part of the dramatic growth in biotechnology in the 1980s and 1990s, mean that these historical questions, plus a host of contemporary ones, can be answered. With promises of breakthroughs in medicine (gene therapy and cancer research), the environment (genetically altered microorganisms for pollution cleanup), and agriculture (genetically engineered foods), biotechnology offers the possibility not just to understand but also to manipulate the processes of life.

The essence of biotechnology is exploiting genes, a process revolutionized by the 1953 discovery of DNA by scientists James Watson and Francis Crick. DNA (deoxyribonucleic acid) is the molecule that carries the genetic blueprint of all living things; genes are DNA chains made up of hundreds or sometimes thousands of simple molecules. Like fingerprints, no two people (other than identical twins) have the same genetic characteristics. Once DNA's structure was understood, it became theoretically possible to isolate the genetic codes that control everything from hair color to height to inherited diseases and certain cancers. But DNA samples were often too meager to work with. Then in the 1980s laboratory advances such as PCR (polymerase chain reaction, polymerase being the enzyme that triggers the replication of DNA) made it possible to take a single fragment of DNA and copy it infinitely. One immediate result of PCR was the introduction of the most sensitive test yet for the AIDS virus.

DNA research in criminal justice cases was one of its earliest applications. From blood, saliva, semen, or hair samples, it became possible to show whether the genetic profile of a suspect matched the DNA information gathered at the crime scene. By 1995 DNA testing had been used in more than twenty-four thousand criminal cases. Some of its most dramatic results proved the innocence of individuals convicted before this technology was available; DNA testing established that their genetic makeup was so markedly different from the surviving evidence that they could not possibly have committed the crimes for which they were imprisoned. Even so, as the 1995 murder trial and acquittal of former football star O. J. Simpson showed, DNA testing remained controversial. Simpson's defense team was able to raise doubts about possible contamination of Simpson's blood samples by faulty laboratory procedures and to counter seemingly overwhelming DNA-based medical evidence that linked bloodstains on Simpson's socks, gloves, and car to the victims.

DNA testing was just one of many promising medical and scientific discoveries to emerge in the 1980s and 1990s. Biotech companies such as Genentech, Amgen, and Biogen pioneered in finding practical—and potentially profitable—applications for the new technology, making biotech companies hot tickets for investors.

But it was the personal computer that revolutionized the home and office. The big breakthrough came in 1977 when the Apple Computer Company offered the Apple II personal computer for $1,195—a price middle-class Americans could afford. When the Apple II became a runaway success, other companies scrambled to get into the market. IBM offered its first personal computer in the summer of 1981. Software companies such as Microsoft, whose founder Bill Gates is now the richest person in America (see American Lives, "Bill Gates: Microsoft's Leader in the Computer Revolution," p. 922) grew rapidly by providing operating systems and other software for the expanding personal-computer market. By 2000, 77 percent of American households had at least one personal computer.

More than any other technological advance, the computer created the modern electronic office. Even the smallest business could afford to keep its records and do all its correspondence, billing, and other business on a single desktop machine. The very concept of the office was changing as a new class of telecommuters worked at home via computer, fax machine, and electronic mail. Today, new technologies utilizing fiberoptics, microwave relays, and satellites can transmit massive quantities of information to and from almost any place on earth, even in outer space.

By 2000, almost 300 million people—approximately 43 percent of them in the United States—used the Internet. At first scientists and other professionals, who communicated with their peers through electronic mail (e-mail), were the primary users of the Internet. But the

Cracking the Genetic Code

A researcher enters DNA sequences into a computer as part of the effort to map the human genome.

© J. Griffin / The Image Works.

Nowhere was the promise of this research more evident than in medical technology, where biotechnology became the driving force in the creation of genetically engineered drugs and vaccines, the identification of specific genes that cause cystic fibrosis and sickle-cell anemia, and the transplantation of either healthy or genetically altered cells to treat cancer. But initial excitement palled as companies found it difficult to translate this new understanding into products that could actually be shown in clinical trials to benefit humans. So volatile has the biotech business been that one analyst called it "free fall" rather than free enterprise—bungee jumping without the bungee.

One of the most ambitious projects undertaken to date is the Human Genome Project, launched in 1988 with the goal of deciphering the entire human genetic code (the entirety of the DNA in an organism is called its genome). In June 2000 scientists on the project announced that they had produced a "Book of Life," a genetic blueprint that would serve a purpose not unlike the periodic table of elements, the basis for twentieth-century research in chemistry. Given that there are approximately three billion nucleic acid–base pairs in a set of human chromosomes, the success of this project was intricately linked to the expanding capacities of modern computers. Biochemistry, medical research, and computer science are increasingly intertwined as earlier technological revolutions spawn new ones.

debut of the World Wide Web in 1991 enhanced the commercial possibilities of the Internet. The Web allowed companies, organizations, political campaigns, and even the White House to create their own "home pages," incorporating both visual and textual information. Businesses and entrepreneurs began to use the Internet to sell their products and services.

The glories of cyberspace are still limited mostly to those who can afford them: in 1997, 65 percent of Americans who used the Internet had incomes of $50,000 or more. But the trend continues to change. In 1998 only 25 percent of all households had access to cyberspace, but by 2000 the figure had grown to 50 percent. Additionally, programs to wire public schools and libraries have significantly increased access to the new technology. In 2000, 63 percent of public classrooms were connected to the Internet.

An Increasingly Pluralistic Society

As technological change reshaped the nation, significant demographic developments emerged as well. Ethnic and racial diversity, always a source of conflict in American culture, became a defining theme of the 1990s. Between 1981 and 1996 almost 13.5 million immigrants entered the country.

Latino and Asian Immigration. The greatest number of newcomers were Latinos. Although Mexico continued to provide the largest group of Spanish-speaking

Honey, Where's the Remote?

How many channels can you watch? How many Web sites can you visit? In the 1990s Americans began to complain of information overload. This image of a person viewing 500 cable TV stations simultaneously was created by photographer Louis Psihoyos for an article on technology that appeared in National Geographic.
© 1995 Louis Psihoyos / Matrix.

immigrants, many also arrived from El Salvador and the Dominican Republic. The Latino population grew at a rate of 18 percent in the 1990s to reach 31 million in 1999, making Latinos the second-largest minority group in the United States after African Americans and the second fastest-growing after Asians. Once concentrated in California, Texas, and New Mexico, Latinos now lived in urban areas throughout the country and made up about 16 percent of the population of Florida and New York (Map 31.4). Their growing numbers have increased their significance as consumers and voters and have led advertisers and politicians alike to vie for their loyalty.

Asia was the other major source of new immigrants. Asian migration, which increased almost 108 percent from 1980 to 1990, consisted mainly of people from China, the Philippines, Vietnam, Laos, Cambodia, Korea, India, and Pakistan. More than 700,000 Indochinese refugees came to escape upheavals in Southeast Asia in the decade following the Vietnam War. The first arrivals, many of them well educated, adapted successfully to their new homeland. Later refugees lacked professional or vocational skills and took low-paying jobs where they could find them.

The Face of Ethnic Pluralism.   The new immigrants' impact on the country's social, economic, and cultural landscape has been tremendous. In many places they have created thriving ethnic communities, such as Koreatown in Los Angeles. In the 1980s tens of thousands of Jews

New Immigrants

In the 1980s many Korean immigrants got their start by opening small grocery stores in urban neighborhoods. Their success sometimes led to conflicts with other racial groups, such as blacks and Hispanics, who were often their customers as well as competitors. Kay Chernush / The Image Bank.

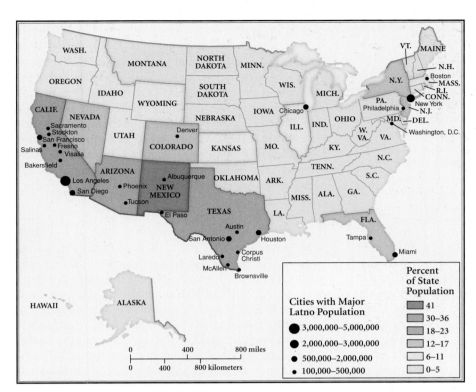

MAP 31.4 Latino Population and Asian Population, 2000

In 2000 Latinos made up over 11 percent of the U.S. population and Asian Americans 4 percent. Demographers predict that Latinos will overtake African Americans as the largest minority group early in the twenty-first century and that by the year 2050 only about half the U.S. population will be composed of non-Latino whites.

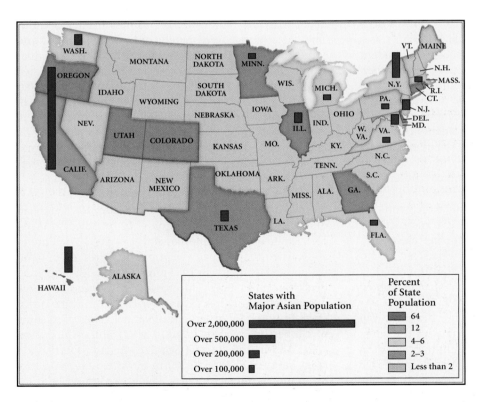

fleeing religious and political persecution in the Soviet Union created Little Odessa in Brooklyn, New York. Ethnic restaurants and shops have sprung up across the country, while some 300 specialized periodicals serve immigrant readers.

The U.S. Census Bureau predicts that in the year 2050, whites will make up 52.7 percent of the American population (down from 75.7 percent in 1990), with Latinos accounting for 21.1 percent, blacks 15 percent, and Asians 10.1 percent. If projected intermarriage is

Bill Gates: Microsoft's Leader in the Computer Revolution

In the eleventh grade Bill Gates told a friend that he would be a millionaire by the time he was thirty. When Gates went to Harvard two years later, he revised his prediction downward to twenty-five. He was being far too modest. At the age of thirty-one, Bill Gates became the youngest self-made billionaire ever. In 1992 *Forbes* magazine named him the richest person in America. What was the source of all this wealth? Microsoft Corporation, whose software runs on nine of every ten personal computers sold in the United States. Microsoft is the most successful start-up company in the history of American business.

This is no Horatio Alger, rags-to-riches story. William Henry Gates III was born into a wealthy Seattle family on October 28, 1955. His father, William Gates Jr., is a successful corporate lawyer and former president of the Washington State Bar Association; his mother, Mary, was a prominent United Way volunteer who also served as a regent of the University of Washington. Gates attended the exclusive Lakeside School, one of the first schools in the country to offer students computer access, thanks to a time-sharing arrangement paid for by the school's mothers' club. The eighth-grader was hooked. Another Lakeside classmate and computer whiz was tenth-grader Paul Allen, who joined Gates in 1972 to found a company called Traf-O-Data, which counted vehicles at busy intersections by using a rudimentary computer device. In 1975 these two former classmates founded Microsoft. Allen was twenty-one; Gates, who would soon drop out of Harvard, was all of nineteen.

Gates looked even younger. When Miriam Lubow became Microsoft's office manager in 1977, she was appalled when some "kid" whipped by her desk into the office of "Mr. Gates" and began playing with the computer terminal. That kid was Bill Gates. In the early days of Microsoft, Gates was too young to rent a car or have a drink with prospective clients on a business trip. His smudged glasses and unkempt hair became trademarks. But looks can be deceiving, as competitors have found out ever since.

In certain ways Gates and Allen were classic hackers—nerdy, mathematically inclined, and fascinated by the possibilities for computation (and mischief) that early computers provided. But most hackers saw computers as a hobby or a game. Back then, the thought of owning a computer seemed as far-fetched as owning a nuclear submarine. But right from the start, Gates and Allen saw commercial possibilities in the new field, long before the personal computer revolution of the 1980s. They anticipated that there would be money to be made writing, and especially marketing, software for the new machines. Microsoft's domination has resulted less from developing innovative products than from anticipating trends in the industry, getting products quickly into the marketplace, and then using its market share to bludgeon the competition. The phenomenal success of products such as MS-DOS and Windows was due as much to Microsoft's relentless marketing barrage as to any inherent technological superiority of its products. One Microsoft veteran described the corporate strategy in this way: "See where everybody's headed then catch up and go past them."

In the early days Microsoft was more like a college dorm than the billion-dollar business it later became. The "Microkids" were barely out of their teens, and some were still in high school. Nobody kept regular hours (in fact, the walls lacked clocks), and they existed on junk food, rock music, and free Coke, a tradition that Microsoft still maintains. A married employee was an oddity, and almost all the programmers were men. Parking slots were unnumbered as a way to reward early arrivals. Gates's competitive and confrontational managerial style set the tone: "That's the stupidest thing I ever heard" was a frequently heard comment.

Gates literally could not sit still, and Seattle-based Microsoft continued to grow at a fantastic rate. Gates had once thought it might employ 20 people; by 1982 Microsoft had 200 employees and sales of $32 million. In 1985, when the company went public, Gates, Allen (who had left the company in 1983 after a bout with Hodgkin's disease), and many Microsoft employees became overnight millionaires. Allen later cashed in some of his stock to buy the Portland Trailblazers. Gates used some of his personal wealth to build a $53 million house on Lake Washington outside Seattle, whose property taxes alone (estimated at $620,000 in 1998) would buy a luxury home in most U.S. cities. The house is a series of interconnected pavilions set deep into a hillside, with its own salmon estuary, a twenty-car subterranean garage, a trampoline room, and video "walls" in every room to

Microsoft Employees, 1978

This group portrait shows eleven of Microsoft's thirteen employees as the company was about to relocate from Albuquerque, New Mexico, to Seattle, Washington. Bill Gates is in the front row, far left; Paul Allen is in the front row, far right. They may look geeky or weird, but they built Microsoft into a multibillion-dollar corporation.
Courtesy, Bob Wallace.

display changing electronic images of art (for which Gates has bought the rights from major museums). "Working for Bill, you design for change," said the architect. That sums up Gates's approach to business as well.

The next step for Gates and Microsoft was onto the information superhighway. Internet commerce was projected to generate $180 billion of business a year by the beginning of the twenty-first century, and Gates wanted Microsoft to be part of that connection. But if Microsoft was able to use its market share to force consumers to use its applications and links to the World Wide Web rather than competitors' browsers, thereby controlling access to the information, entertainment, shopping, real estate, and travel services that the Web provides, its dominance would increase even more. When the Justice Department took Microsoft to court in 1998 for violating antitrust laws, Gates brashly replied that he was simply giving consumers what they wanted. The fact that Attorney General Janet Reno did not even use a personal computer seemed to confirm Microsoft's view that the Department of Justice was out

of touch with the importance of computers to modern life.

Friends note Bill Gates's "extraordinary bandwidth"—that is, the amount of information he can absorb—but it is his insights into business rather than technology that set Gates apart. His entrepreneurial streak would have made Henry Ford or John D. Rockefeller proud. The future, however, comes quickly in the computer field, and Gates keenly worries about being left behind in the next stage of the revolution: "It's a little scary that as computer technology has moved ahead there's never been a leader from one era who was also a leader in the next." He takes this as a warning and a challenge: "I want to defy historical tradition."

"Software is cool," Gates told CNN's Larry King to explain the hoopla surrounding the release of Microsoft's Windows 95. To the computer crowd, cool is the opposite of random, which means out of it, wrong, or inane. No one, especially not his competitors, has ever accused Bill Gates of being random.

factored in (Latinos and Asians marry outside their racial groups much more frequently than blacks), the estimated white "majority" will probably slip to a white "minority." At the close of the twentieth century, already one out of twenty-five married couples were interracial, and at least 3 million children were of mixed-race parentage in the country.

Anti-Immigrant Sentiment.

While many Americans celebrated the nation's ethnic pluralism as a source of strength, others viewed the new immigrants as scapegoats for all that was wrong with the United States. Though a 1997 study by the National Academy of Science reported that immigration has benefited the nation, adding some $10 billion a year to the economy, many American-born workers felt threatened by immigrants. The unfounded assumption that immigrants were lured to the United States by generous public services influenced provisions of a 1996 welfare reform act (see p. 930), which severely curtailed legal immigrants' access to welfare benefits, especially food stamps. Also in 1996, Congress enacted legislation that increased the financial requirements for sponsors of new immigrants.

The most dramatic challenges to immigrants have emerged on the state level. In the 1980s California absorbed far more immigrants than any other state: more than a third of its population growth in that decade came from foreign immigration. In 1994 California voters overwhelmingly approved Proposition 187, a ballot initiative provocatively named "Save Our State," which barred undocumented aliens from public schools, non-emergency care at public health clinics, and all other state social services. The initiative also required law enforcement officers, school administrators, and social workers to report suspected illegal immigrants to the Immigration and Naturalization Service. Though opponents challenged the constitutionality of Proposition 187, anti-immigrant feeling soon spread to other parts of the country, becoming a hotly debated issue in the 1996 election.

The Plight of Urban America.

Though the National Academy of Sciences report did find that "some black workers have lost their jobs to immigrants," for the most part African Americans were not adversely affected by the new immigration. But in the cities, African Americans and new immigrants were forced by economic necessity and entrenched segregation patterns to fight for space in decaying, crime-ridden ghettos, where unemployment rates sometimes hit 60 percent. Overcrowded and underfunded, inner-city schools had fallen into disrepair and were unable to provide a proper education.

In April 1992 the frustration and anger of impoverished urban Americans erupted in five days of race riots in Los Angeles. The worst civil disorder since the 1960s, the violence took sixty lives and caused $850 million in damage. The riot was set off by the acquittal (on all but one

To Live and Die in L.A.
The images from South-Central Los Angeles in the wake of the 1992 riots looked eerily similar to those from Watts in 1965. The underlying causes of both riots were similar as well—police brutality, racism, and frustration about lack of jobs and opportunity. Sylvie Kreiss / Liaison.

charge) of four white Los Angeles police officers accused of using excessive force in arresting a black motorist, Rodney King. A graphic amateur video showing the policemen kicking, clubbing, and beating King had not swayed the predominantly white jury. Three of the officers were later convicted on federal civil rights charges.

The Los Angeles riot exposed the rifts in urban neighborhoods. Trapped in the nation's inner cities, many blacks resented recent immigrants who were struggling to get ahead and often succeeding. As a result some blacks had targeted Korean-owned stores during the arson and looting. Latinos were also frustrated by high unemployment and crowded housing conditions. According to the Los Angeles Police Department, Latinos accounted for more than half of those arrested and a third of those killed during the rioting. Thus the riots were not simply a case of black rage at white injustice; they contained a strong element of class-based protest against the failure of the American system to address the needs of all poor people.

One of the ways federal and state governments tried to help poor blacks and Latinos was through the establishment of affirmative action programs in government hiring, contracts, and university admissions. In 1995, however, under pressure from the Republican governor, Pete Wilson, the Regents of the University of California voted to scrap the university's twenty-year-old policy of affirmative action, despite protests from the faculty and from university presidents. In the November 1996 elections, the struggle over affirmative action was intensified by California's passage of Proposition 209. It banned all preference based on race or gender in state government hiring and contracting and in public education. As appeals worked their way through the federal courts and black and Latino enrollments declined, the University of California sought new admissions criteria that would circumvent the restrictions imposed by Proposition 209.

One reason affirmative action became a political issue in the 1990s was that many people, including prominent conservatives like George F. Will, William Bennett, and Patrick Buchanan, saw it as a threat to core American values. Lumping affirmative action together with multiculturalism—the attempt to represent the diversity of American society and its peoples—critics feared that all this counting by race, gender, sexual preference, and age would lead to a "balkanization," or fragmentation, of American society. Attempts to revise American history textbooks along multicultural lines aroused much anger, as did efforts by universities such as Stanford to revise college curricula to include the study of non-European cultures. Conservatives also took aim at the antiracist and antisexist regulations and speech codes that had been adopted by many colleges. Arguing for the need to protect First Amendment rights, conservatives derided the attempt to regulate hate speech as "politically correct" (PC).

Backlash against Women's and Gay Rights

Conservative critics also targeted the women's movement. In the widely read *Backlash: The Undeclared War on American Women* (1991), the journalist Susan Faludi described a powerful reaction against the gains American women had won in the 1960s and 1970s. Spearheaded by New Right leaders and aided by the media, conservatives held the women's movement responsible for every ill afflicting modern women, from infertility to rising divorce rates. Yet polls showed strong support for many feminist demands, including equal pay, reproductive rights, and a more equitable distribution of household and child-care responsibilities.

Feminism was also weakened by racial and generational fault lines. Despite the attempts of prominent feminist organizations such as the National Organization for Women (NOW) to focus on racial and ethnic differences among women, African Americans and other women of color often felt themselves to be tokens in a predominantly white movement. Many young women felt that the movement had become too obsessed with women as passive victims (of date rape, discrimination, sexual harassment, the media's beauty myth, and so forth) rather than offering women models of empowerment. Other young women, influenced by women's studies programs and the explosion of feminist scholarship, forged a third wave of feminism in the 1990s (see

American Voices, "Laurie Ouellette: A Third-Wave Feminist," p. 926).

The deep national divide over abortion, one of the main issues associated with feminism, continued to polarize the country. In the 1980s and 1990s, harassment and violence toward those who sought or provided abortions became common. In 1994 two workers were gunned down at Massachusetts abortion clinics, and five people were wounded in the attacks. Although only a fraction of antiabortion activists supported such extreme acts, disruptive confrontational tactics made receiving what was still a woman's legal right more dangerous.

Gay rights was another field of battle. As gays and lesbians gained legal protection against housing and job discrimination across the country, Pat Robertson, North Carolina senator Jesse Helms, and others denounced these civil rights gains as undeserved "special rights." To conservatives, gay rights threatened America's traditional family values. In 1992 Coloradans passed a referendum (overturned by the Supreme Court in 1996) that barred local jurisdictions from passing ordinances protecting gays and lesbians. Across the nation, "gay bashing" and other forms of violence against homosexuals continued.

The AIDS Epidemic

A grim backdrop to gay men's struggle against discrimination was the AIDS epidemic. Acquired immune deficiency syndrome (AIDS) was first recognized by physicians in 1981 in the gay male population and its cause identified as the human immunodeficiency virus (HIV). At first, little government funding was directed toward AIDS research or treatment; critics charged that the lack of attention to the syndrome reflected society's antipathy toward gay men. Only when heterosexuals, such as hemophiliacs who had received the virus through blood transfusions, began to be affected did AIDS gain significant public attention. The death of the film star Rock Hudson from AIDS in 1985 finally broke the barrier of public apathy. Another galvanizing moment came in 1991, when the basketball great Earvin "Magic" Johnson announced that he was HIV-positive.

To date more Americans have died of AIDS than were killed in the Korean and Vietnam wars combined. Between 1995 and 1999, however, deaths from AIDS in the United States dropped 30 percent. This decline—in part the result of new treatment strategies using a combination of drugs, or a "cocktail"—has led to cautious optimism about controlling the disease. Yet the drugs' high costs limit their availability and make distribution particularly limited in poor nations. As AIDS deaths decline in developed countries like the United States, the epidemic has reached crisis proportions in sub-Saharan Africa, which accounts for 30 million of the 40 million infections worldwide. Approximately 95 percent of people infected with HIV live in the developing world.

Laurie Ouellette

A Third-Wave Feminist

Born in 1966 and educated at the University of Minnesota, Laurie Ouellette represents the generation of women who benefited from the changes set in motion by the revival of feminism but who are confused about what feminism means. She calls on the movement to broaden its vision.

As a member of the first generation of women to benefit from the gains of the '70s women's movement without participating in its struggles, I grew up on the sidelines of feminism—too young to take part in those moments, debates, and events that would define the women's movement but old enough to experience firsthand the societal changes it had wrought.

Ironically, it is due to the modest success of feminism that many young women like myself were raised with an illusion of equality. Like most women my age, I never really thought much about feminism while I was growing up. Looking back, though, I believe it has always influenced me. Growing up with divorced parents, especially a father who was ambivalent about parental responsibilities, probably has much to do with this fact. I was only five when my parents separated in 1971, and I couldn't possibly have imagined or understood the ERA marches or the triumphal result of *Roe v. Wade* that would make history in just a few short years. Certainly I couldn't have defined the word *feminism*. Still, watching my mother struggle emotionally and financially as a single parent made the concept of gender injustice painfully clear. . . .

It was at the University of Minnesota that I first took an interest in feminist classics like *The Feminine Mystique, Sisterhood Is Powerful*, and *Sexual Politics*. They expressed the anger of an earlier generation that simultaneously captivated me and excluded me. Reading them so long after the excitement of their publication made my own consciousness-raising seem anticlimactic. Like many of my white middle-class friends, I believed that we wouldn't have to worry about issues like discrimination, oppression, and getting stuck in the housewife role. We wondered why we should join forces with a battle for women's equality that the media repeatedly declared was already "won."

My experiences after college made me think again about feminism. A public television internship where I was expected to perform menial secretarial tasks while my male (and, I might add, less experienced) co-interns worked on interesting and challenging projects shocked me into realizing the difficulties facing women in the workplace. Likewise, living in an inner-city neighborhood and being involved in community issues there showed me the dire need for feminism in the lives of the poor women, elderly women, and women of color who were my neighbors. Watching these women, many of them single mothers, struggle daily to find shelter, child care, and food made me realize that they had not been touched at all by the women's movement gains of the '70s. . . .

My 24-year-old sister stands out as an example of other routes that feminism must move toward. Whereas I have focused my energies on attending graduate school and working toward a professional career, she has chosen to forfeit similar plans, for now, in favor of marrying young, moving to the country, and raising a family. Does she signify a regression into the homemaker role of the 1950s? On the contrary. For her, issues such as getting midwifery legalized and insured, providing information about breast-feeding to rural mothers, countering the male-dominated medical establishment by using and recommending natural and alternative healing methods, and raising her own daughter with positive gender esteem are central to a feminist agenda.

Only by recognizing and helping to provide choices—both lifestyle and reproductive—for women of all races, economic levels, and ages, as well as supporting all women in their struggles to make those choices, will the women of my generation, the first to be raised in the shadow of feminism and witness its successes and failures, be able to build a successful third wave of the feminist movement.

Source: Laurie Ouellette, "Our Turn Now: Reflections of a 26-Year-Old Feminist," *Utne Reader* (July–August 1992), 118–20.

The Environmental Movement at Twenty-five

Another pressing issue that the United States shared with other countries was the environment. On April 26, 1995, when Americans came together for the twenty-fifth anniversary of Earth Day, they had much to celebrate. The nation's rivers and waterways were cleaner; air pollution had been reduced by a third; and lead emissions from fuel, a cause of retardation in children, had been cut by an astounding 98 percent. The bald eagle and the California condor had come back from the brink of extinction. More than six thousand communities across the country had recycling programs.

Be Kind to Your Mother (Earth)

This poster, created by Jennifer Morla to commemorate the twenty-fifth anniversary of Earth Day in 1995, urges people to celebrate the event by "making everyday [sic] Earth Day." Simple things that ordinary citizens can do to save the earth include stopping junk mail, recycling cans and bottles, carpooling, taking shorter showers, and recharging batteries rather than throwing them away. © 1995 Morla Design, San Francisco.

In addition to addressing problems in their own communities, Americans were increasingly aware that the environment required action not just from the United States but from the entire global community. An important precedent for international action was set by the 1987 Montreal protocol, in which thirty-four nations agreed to phase out ozone-damaging chlorofluorocarbons (CFCs) by 1999. In June 1992 delegates from 170 countries to the United Nations Earth Summit in Rio de Janeiro adopted a treaty on global warming, and in 1994 the United States joined sixty-three other countries in signing the Basel Convention, which banned the export of hazardous wastes from industrialized to developing countries. In 1997, reflecting continuing concern about global warming, the international community drafted the Kyoto accord, which would require industrialized countries to reduce greenhouse-gas emissions over the next fifteen years, while leaving the problem of developing nation's emissions unresolved. In late 1998, President Bill Clinton signed the Kyoto Treaty, but it was never ratified by the United States Senate, primarily because of fears that the United States, which was responsible for 36.1 percent of the industrialized nations' emissions, would be hurt economically.

Other signs of U.S. failure to address environmental issues emerged at home. By the late 1990s Americans were using almost as much energy per capita as they had in 1973, wiping out practically all the savings achieved through conservation and efficiency in between. Despite efforts to reduce urban smog, two of five Americans lived in areas with unhealthy air. Many rivers and lakes were still unsafe for fishing and swimming. One of four Americans lived within four miles of a toxic waste dump, a trend that activists termed *environmental racism* because it disproportionally affected lower-income communities. Even though energy experts warned that a tightening of oil supplies and higher prices were inevitable—a prediction that came true in 2000—few consumers changed their lifestyles by reducing energy consumption.

Restructuring the Domestic Order: Public Life, 1992–2001

If Americans hoped to make progress on the economy, environment, and the deep social cleavages surrounding race, gender, and sexual orientation, they would need strong leadership. Yet low voter turnout and the strong showing of independent candidates in the 1992 presidential election signaled deep dissatisfaction with the American political system. In the ensuing years Americans' disaffection helped to continue the rollback of federal power begun by Reagan and Bush.

Clinton's First Term

As the 1992 election campaign got under way, the economy was the overriding issue, for the recession that had begun in 1990 showed no sign of abating. George Bush easily won renomination as the Republican candidate. To solidify the support of the New Right, his running mate, J. Danforth (Dan) Quayle, spoke out strongly for "family values" and other conservative social agendas. William Jefferson (Bill) Clinton, the longtime governor of Arkansas, survived charges of marital infidelity and draft dodging as well as questions about a dubious Arkansas real estate deal called "Whitewater," to win the Democratic nomination. For his running mate he chose Albert (Al) Gore Jr., a second-term senator from Tennessee. At age forty-four Gore was a year and a half younger than Clinton, making the two men the first of the baby-boom generation to occupy the national ticket.

In the middle of the primary season, Texas billionaire H. Ross Perot, capitalizing on voters' desire for a change from politics as usual, announced he would run as an independent candidate. Although Perot dropped out of the race on the last day of the Democratic convention, he reentered it less than five weeks before the election, adding a well-financed wild card to an unusual election year.

The Democrats mounted an effective, aggressive campaign that highlighted Clinton's plans to solve domestic problems, especially in education, health care, and the economy. Gore added expertise on defense and environmental issues. Bush was hurt by the weak economy and especially by reneging on his "No New Taxes" pledge. On election day Clinton received 43 percent of the popular vote to Bush's 38 percent and Perot's 19 percent (Map 31.5). Although Perot did not win a single state, his popular vote was the highest for an independent candidate since Theodore Roosevelt's in 1912. The Democrats retained control of both houses of Congress, ending twelve years of divided government. But the narrowness of Clinton's victory and the public's perception that he did not really stand for anything did not augur well for his ability to lead the country.

Clinton's Early Record.   The liberals who supported Clinton hoped that a Democratic presidency could erase the Reagan-Bush legacy and oversee the creation of a new Democratic social agenda. Initially, Clinton seemed to fulfill that promise. He nominated the liberal Ruth Bader Ginsberg for a seat on the Supreme Court; she was confirmed. The president also appointed Janet Reno as attorney general—the first woman to head the Department of Justice. Other trailblazing cabinet appointments included Secretary of Health and Human Services Donna E. Shalala and, in Clinton's second term, Secretary of State Madeline Albright. Clinton chose an African American,

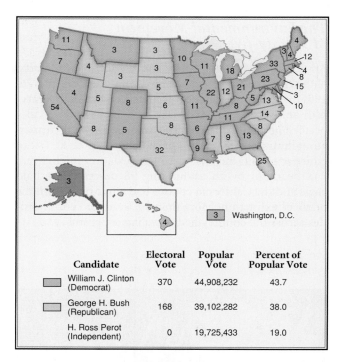

MAP 31.5 Presidential Election of 1992

The first national election after the end of the cold war was dominated by concern over the economy. The first-ever all-southerner Democratic ticket of Bill Clinton and Al Gore won broad support across the country, cutting into Republican strongholds in the South and West. The independent candidate, H. Ross Perot, won no electoral votes but polled an impressive 19 percent of the popular vote. In 1996 Clinton and Gore won reelection against Republican challengers Senate majority leader Bob Dole and Jack Kemp.

Ron Brown, as secretary of commerce, and two Latinos, Henry Cisneros and Frederico Peña, to head the Department of Housing and Urban Development (HUD) and the Department of Transportation, respectively.

Clinton's early legislative and administrative record was mixed. In early 1993 he signed into law the Family and Medical Leave Act, twice vetoed by Bush, which provided workers with up to twelve weeks of unpaid leave to tend to a newborn or an adopted child or to respond to a family medical emergency. But when Clinton tried to implement a campaign promise to lift the ban on gays serving in the armed forces, he ran into such ferocious opposition that he backed off, offering instead a weak compromise policy—"Don't ask, don't tell, don't pursue." The solution was an ineffective palliative at best, one that called into question Clinton's willingness to stand firm on issues of principle.

By the time Clinton took office, the economy had pulled out of the 1990 recession, enabling him to focus on other economic issues, especially the opening of foreign markets to U.S. goods. In 1992 President Bush signed the North American Free Trade Agreement (NAFTA), in which the United States, Canada, and Mexico agreed to make all of North America a free-trade zone. Strongly supported by the business community, NAFTA was bitterly opposed by labor unions worried about the loss of jobs to lower-paid Mexican workers and by environmentalists concerned about the weak enforcement of antipollution laws south of the border. Nonetheless, Congress narrowly passed NAFTA in November 1993.

Health-Care Reform Failure.

Clinton staked his political fortunes on his campaign promise of universal health care. Though the United States spent more on health care than any other country in the world, it remained the only major industrialized country not to provide national health insurance to all. Spiraling medical costs and rising insurance premiums had brought the health-care system to a crisis.

The president chose his wife, attorney Hillary Rodham Clinton, to head the task force that would draft the legislation—a controversial move since no first lady had ever played a formal role in policymaking. The resulting proposal was based on the idea of managed competition: market forces, not the government, would control health-care costs and expand citizen's access to health care. But even this mild form of social engineering ran into intense opposition from the well-financed pharmaceutical and insurance industries. By September 1994 congressional leaders were admitting that health reform was dead. In 1995 an estimated 40.3 million Americans had no health insurance, and experts predicted that the number would climb.

Post–Cold War Foreign Policy.

Clinton seemed to never have the time to devote his full attention to pushing health reform through Congress. Three days before assuming office, he had to commit his support to a missile attack President Bush had ordered on Iraq. In February foreign terrorists bombed the World Trade Center in New York City, and in April FBI agents made a misguided assault on the Branch Davidian compound in Waco, Texas. At the White House in September, Israeli prime minister Yitzhak Rabin and Yasir Arafat, chairman of the Palestine Liberation Organization, signed an agreement allowing limited Palestinian self-rule in the Gaza Strip and Jericho. In October 1993, just after Clinton announced his health plan, twelve American soldiers were killed on a United Nations peacekeeping mission in Somalia. Constantly shifting from crisis to crisis, Clinton appeared to the American public to be vacillating, indecisive, and lacking in vision, especially in his handling of foreign affairs.

Nothing seemed more intractable than the problems that engulfed the former state of Yugoslavia, which had split into five independent states in 1991. The province of Bosnia and Herzegovina, made up largely of Muslims and committed to a multiethnic state—Serb, Croat, and Muslim—had declared its independence in 1992. But Bosnian Serbs, supported financially and militarily by what remained of Yugoslavia, formed their own breakaway state and began a siege of the Bosnian capital, Sarajevo. In the countryside the Serbs launched a ruthless campaign of "ethnic cleansing," driving Bosnian Muslims and Croats from their homes and into concentration camps or shooting them in mass executions. More than 250,000 people were killed or reported missing after the outbreak of war in April 1992. After three years of unsuccessful efforts by the European powers to stop the carnage, President Clinton and Secretary of State Warren Christopher facilitated a peace accord in November 1995. A NATO-led peacekeeping force, backed by U.S. troops, would end the fighting, at least temporarily.

At the same time the end of cold war superpower rivalry presented unexpected opportunities to resolve other long-standing conflicts. In Haiti the threat of a U.S. invasion in October 1993 led to the restoration of the exiled president, Jean-Bertrand Aristide, who had been ousted by a military coup in 1991. In South Africa the end of a fifty-year policy of racial separation was capped in May 1994 by the election of the rebel leader Nelson

A Forceful and Controversial First Lady

Drawing inspiration from Eleanor Roosevelt, Hillary Rodham Clinton hoped the country would be ready for a first lady who could play a role in shaping health-care policy. It wasn't.

Robert Trippet / SIPA Press.

Mandela, who had spent twenty-seven years in prison for challenging apartheid, as the country's first black president. And in a move that was seen as the symbolic end to the American experience in Vietnam, the United States established diplomatic relations with Hanoi in July 1995, two decades after the fall of Saigon.

"The Era of Big Government Is Over"

In the 1994 midterm elections, Republicans gained fifty-two seats in the House of Representatives, which gave them a majority in the House as well as the Senate. In the House the centerpiece of the new Republican majority was the "Contract with America," a list of proposals that Newt Gingrich of Georgia, the new Speaker of the House, vowed would be voted on in the first 100 days of the new session. The contract included constitutional amendments to balance the budget and set term limits for congressional office, significant tax cuts, reductions in welfare and other entitlement programs, anticrime initiatives, and cutbacks in federal regulations. President Clinton, bowing to political reality, acknowledged in his State of the Union message in January 1996 that "the era of big government is over."

Balancing the Budget. But the Republicans were frustrated in their commitment to cut taxes and balance the budget by the year 2002 because both practical and political considerations made many items in the budget immune to serious reductions. Interest on the national debt had to be paid. Defense spending had declined only slightly in the post–cold war world. Since Social Security was considered as being untouchable, Congress looked to health care and discretionary spending as places to save.

In the fall of 1995, Congress passed a budget that cut $270 billion from projected spending on Medicare and $170 billion from spending on Medicaid over the next seven years. Other savings came from cuts in discretionary programs, including education and the environment. Clinton accepted Congress's resolve to balance the budget in seven years but, vowing to protect the nation from an "extremist" Congress, vetoed the budget itself. In the standoff that followed, nonessential departments of the government were forced to shut down twice for lack of funding, but polls showed that a majority of Americans held Congress, not the president, responsible. The budget that Clinton finally signed in April 1996 left Medicare and Social Security intact, though it did meet the Republicans' goal of cutting $23 billion from discretionary spending.

As part of the Contract with America, House Republicans were especially determined to cut welfare, a joint federal-state program that represented a fairly small part of the budget. The benefits of the main welfare program, Aid for Dependent Children (AFDC), were far from generous: the average annual welfare payment to families (including food stamps) was $7,740, well below the established poverty line. Still, in the 1990s both Democratic and Republican statehouses sought ways to change the behavior of welfare recipients by imposing work requirements or denying benefits for additional children born to women on AFDC. In August 1996, after vetoing two Republican-authored bills, President Clinton signed into law the Personal Responsibility and Work Opportunity Act, a historic overhaul of federal entitlements. The 1996 law ended the federal guarantee of cash assistance to poor children by abolishing AFDC, required most adult recipients to find work within two years, set a five-year limit on payments to any one family, and gave states wide discretion in running their welfare programs.

The 1996 Election. The Republican takeover of Congress had one unintended consequence: it united the usually fractious Democrats behind the president. Unopposed in the 1996 primaries, Clinton was able to burnish his image as a moderate "New Democrat." His political fortunes were aided by the unpopularity of the Republican Congress following the government shutdowns. He also benefited from the continuing strength of the economy. Economic indicators released shortly before election day showed that the "misery index"—a combination of the unemployment rate and inflation—was the lowest it had been in twenty-seven years.

The Republicans settled on Senate Majority Leader Bob Dole of Kansas as their presidential candidate. Acceptable to both the conservative and the moderate wings of the party, Dole selected former representative Jack Kemp, a leading proponent of supply-side economics, as his running mate. Dole made a 15 percent across-the-board tax cut the centerpiece of his campaign, while Clinton emphasized an improved economy. Americans seemed to have made up their minds early about the candidates. With the lowest voter turnout since Calvin Coolidge won the presidency in 1924, Clinton became the first Democratic president since Franklin Roosevelt to win reelection. Republicans retained control of a majority of the nation's statehouses and the House of Representatives and increased their majority in the Senate. Thus a key factor in Bill Clinton's second term was the necessity, as a Democratic president working with a Republican-dominated Congress, of pursuing bipartisan policies or facing stalemate.

Second-Term Stalemates

In his 1998 State of the Union address, Bill Clinton outlined an impressive program of federal spending for schools, tax credits for child care, a hike in the minimum wage, and protection for the beleaguered Social Security system. His ability to pursue this domestic agenda was seriously compromised, however, by a scandal

A Bipartisan Balanced Budget
*On August 5, 1997, a smiling President Clinton signed the balanced budget bill,
surrounded by congressional leaders including House Speaker Newt Gingrich of Georgia
(second from right) and House Budget Committee Chairman John Kasich of Ohio (far
right). Also looking on with satisfaction was Vice President Al Gore, who already had
hopes for the presidency in 2000.* Ron Edmonds / Wide World Photos, Inc.

that eventually led to his impeachment and by international crises.

Crises Abroad. The first of these foreign crises emerged in Iraq, where Saddam Hussein was still in power despite his 1991 defeat in Operation Desert Storm and the United Nations' imposition of economic sanctions. In late 1997 Hussein ejected American members of a UN inspection team that was searching Iraqi sites for hidden "weapons of mass destruction," which included nuclear, biological, and chemical warfare materials. In response, the United States, with limited international support, began a military buildup in the Gulf. The threatened air strike against Iraq was averted when United Nations Secretary-General Kofi Annan brokered an agreement that temporarily put an end to the crisis. But in December 1998 the same issues led to an intense four-day joint U.S.-British bombing campaign, "Desert Fox." Neither that effort, periodic missile strikes against Iraq, nor economic sanctions seem to have compromised the Iraqis' ability to build "weapons of mass destruction" or to have undercut Hussein's regime.

The second major international crisis began in March 1999 in Kosovo, a province of the Serbian-dominated Federal Republic of Yugoslavia (FRY). There, NATO, strongly influenced by the United States, intervened to protect ethnic Albanians from the Serbians who were determined to drive them out of the region. Three months of bombing eventually forced the Serbians to agree to remove their troops from Kosovo and to agree to a multinational peacekeeping force. Yet, as in the Middle East, no long-term solutions were found to the problems generated by ethnic conflict. The region was devastated and its people impoverished, and a year later most observers considered the war a "hollow triumph" for NATO and the United States. Only in 2000 was the brutal Serbian president Slobodan Milosevic pushed from office (Map 31.6).

In the post–cold war era, terrorism constituted yet another challenge to world peace. In October 2000 a suicide attack on the USS *Cole*, a navy guided-missile destroyer that was refueling in the Yemeni port of Aden, blew a huge hole in the ship's hull, killing seventeen sailors. The United States immediately lay the blame on Saudi exile and Muslim extremist Osama bin Laden. In Yemen six suspects were arrested on suspicion of complicity in the attack, but bin Laden remained at large. The Iraqi and Kosovo crises and the *Cole* incident served as potent reminders that despite its position as the most powerful nation in the world, the United States was limited in its ability to achieve its foreign-policy aims.

Clinton's Impeachment.

Although international events deflected President Clinton from his domestic agenda, far more damaging was the crisis that stemmed from a problem that had plagued him since 1992: allegations of sexual misconduct. In January 1998 attorneys representing Paula Jones, who claimed that the then-governor Clinton had propositioned her when she was an Arkansas state employee, revealed that they planned to depose a former White House intern, Monica Lewinsky, about an alleged affair with President Clinton. Kenneth Starr, the independent counsel initially charged with investigating the Whitewater scandal, widened his investigation to explore whether Clinton or his aides had encouraged Lewinsky to lie in her statement. Clinton consistently denied having a sexual relationship with Lewinsky—both on national television and in deposition before a federal grand jury.

In September 1998, after Starr issued a report that concluded that the president had committed impeachable offenses, the House of Representatives began its inquiry. On December 20 the House narrowly approved two articles of impeachment against Clinton, one for perjury before a grand jury concerning his liaison with Lewinsky and a second for obstruction of justice, in which he was accused of encouraging others to lie on his behalf. Yet on the evening of the House vote, a CBS news poll reported that 58 percent of its respondents opposed impeachment, while only 38 percent supported it.

Throughout the ensuing trial conducted by the Senate, Clinton's approval rating remained exceptionally high, perhaps because most Americans doubted the political motives of his attackers and almost certainly because a strong economy kept most citizens content with the

MAP 31.6 Ethnic Conflict in the Balkans: The Breakup of Yugoslavia, 1991–1992

The collapse of the Soviet Union and the end of the cold war released a wave of ethnic conflicts in the Balkans among rival groups forced to live together under Communist rule. Fanned by ethnic hatreds, in the early 1990s Yugoslavia splintered into warring states, with Serbs, Croats, and Muslims fighting for control of their own territories. Serbian president Slobodan Milosevic's brutal aggression against Muslims in Bosnia and later in Kosovo, a province of Serbia, prompted NATO to launch its first offensive war to end the conflict.

For more help analyzing this map, see the ONLINE STUDY GUIDE at bedfordstmartins.com/henretta.

president's performance, even if they disapproved of his personal morality. Finally, after a five-week trial and hours of televised debate, with Democrats voting solidly against impeachment and enough Republicans breaking with their party, the Senate acquitted Clinton on both charges. Like Andrew Johnson, the only other president to be impeached (see Chapter 15), Bill Clinton survived the process, but the scandal, the trial, and the profoundly partisan sentiments that surrounded it limited his ability to be an effective president and deepened public cynicism about politics and its practitioners.

For if Clinton had been hampered by the controversy, so too had Republicans. The November 1998 elections took place while the House was considering impeachment. Despite polls that indicated that Americans did not place much emphasis on the Lewinsky scandal, in many localities and on the national level Republican leaders made Clinton's moral character the focus of the campaign. The Democrats, in contrast, focused on issues like Social Security and education. They also employed vigorous get-out-the-vote drives, particularly among traditional Democratic constituencies—labor unions and African Americans. When the ballots were counted, for the first time since 1934 the party of the incumbent president gained seats—five—in a midterm election, shrinking the Republican majority in Congress to twelve. Although a variety of factors influenced voting patterns, including the improving economy, many observers pointed to a backlash against the drive for impeachment.

Because of the controversies surrounding Clinton and the weakened state of the Republicans, neither party was able to secure significant legislation. For the rest of Clinton's term, shoring up Social Security, addressing the high cost of medical care, and passing an effective gun-control law eluded the president and his supporters, while Republicans were stymied in their efforts to cut taxes and further roll back the federal government. The stalemate was exacerbated by politicians' focus on positioning themselves for the election of 2000. As Senator Joseph I. Lieberman, a Democrat from Connecticut, described the 106th Congress in November 1999, "This was not a session of great initiatives. . . . This was a session that was post-impeachment and preelection."

An Unprecedented Election

Lieberman was to become much better known when the Democratic Party nominated him as Vice President Al Gore's running mate for the 2000 presidential election. The Republicans chose Governor George W. Bush of Texas to head their ticket and Richard Cheney for their vice presidential nominee. Although both Bush and Gore were considered moderate centrists, they had ideological differences over the role of the federal government and how best to use the large projected budget surpluses. Bush proposed a major tax cut that critics claimed would benefit primarily the wealthiest 10 percent of Americans, a partial privatization of Social Security, and the use of government-issued vouchers to pay for private education. Gore argued for using the surplus to shore up the Social Security funds, for a tax-break incentive for college tuition, and for expansion of Medicare. The two candidates disagreed on the abortion issue, with Bush opposing abortion and Gore supporting a woman's right to choose. While Pat Buchanan of the Reform Party fared poorly and was not able to make significant inroads among conservative Republicans, Ralph Nader, the Green Party representative, did appeal to many in the left wing of the Democratic Party who were disenchanted with Gore's centrist position. Nader received over two and a half million votes and detracted enough ballots from Gore in New Hampshire, New Mexico, and Florida to give those states to Bush. Nader's 97,419 votes in Florida (2 percent) contributed to making that state's presidential election a virtual tie between Bush and Gore.

As Florida hung in the balance, returns from the rest of the country showed that Gore had a lead of 337,000 in the popular vote and had won the District of Columbia and twenty states, mostly in the Northeast and Far West, with 267 electoral votes, while Bush had triumphed in twenty-nine states, mostly in the South and Midwest, with 246 electoral votes. In four states, however, fewer than 7,500 votes separated the two major candidates. In such a tight election, the results in Florida became crucial because the electoral college victory would come down to which candidate could claim that state's twenty-five electoral votes (Map 31.7).

At stake were protested "butterfly ballots," which had apparently misled some Gore voters into voting for Buchanan, and "under votes," (ballots not clearly marked)

Recount Nightmare

In the aftermath of the 2000 presidential election, the eyes of the nation, and indeed the world, were riveted on Florida's challenged election result. When the Democrats demanded a hand recount, a crucial issue became how to evaluate dimpled, pregnant, and hanging "chads"— the tiny cardboard pieces punched from the ballot. Here, Judge Robert Rosenberg of the electoral canvassing board of Broward County scrutinizes a Fort Lauderdale ballot. When the Supreme Court put an end to the hand-count process, Vice President Gore conceded the election and George W. Bush announced his victory— 37 days after the election.
AFP Photo / Pool / Allen Eyestone / Corbis.

which resulted from antiquated voting machines and inattentive voters (see American Voices, "John Lewis: We Marched to Be Counted," p. 935). To make certain all votes were tabulated, Gore forces demanded hand recounts in several counties. How to evaluate dimpled, pregnant, and hanging "chads"—the tiny cardboard pieces punched from the ballot—became a hotly contested issue. On November 27, Florida's Secretary of State Katherine Harris halted the recount process and declared Governor Bush the winner by a mere 537 votes. The struggle, however, continued. Gore appealed twice to the Florida Supreme Court in an attempt to get a hand recount. When that court ordered the hand count to continue, Bush went to the United States Supreme Court, which then ordered it stopped.

Finally, on December 12, a deeply divided Supreme Court, in a 5-to-4 decision marked by acrimonious dissenting opinions, declared that the equal protection clause of the Fourteenth Amendment required that all ballots had to be counted in the same way and that time did not permit a statewide hand count. Justice Stephen G. Breyer in dissent angrily pointed out that the majority's opinion was clearly a political one that "runs the risk of undermining the public's confidence in the Court itself." On the following day Vice President Gore gave his concession speech, and George W. Bush announced his victory to become the forty-third president. It took thirty-seven dramatic days and the intervention of the Supreme Court to resolve the controversies surrounding the Florida vote and determine the new president, making the election one of the most remarkable in American history.

George W. Bush's Early Presidency

As President Bush took office, the nation witnessed one more Clinton scandal. In the last hours of his administration, Clinton granted a series of dubious pardons, including most notoriously one for fugitive financier Mark Rich, the ex-husband of Denise Rich, who had contributed heavily to Clinton's political campaign. The incident not only further tarnished Clinton's reputation but also deepened Americans' cynicism about politicians that had been fueled by the 2000 election.

In his first seven months in office, Bush compiled a mixed record of success. He pleased the right wing of his party on his first day in office when he banned the use of foreign-aid funds for family-planning programs abroad that included abortion counseling among their services. Then, despite vigorous opposition, he secured Senate approval for his appointment of John Ashcroft, noted for his conservative social values concerning homosexuality, abortion, and religion, as Attorney General. Other major Bush appointees were Donald Rumsfeld as Secretary of Defense, a position he had also filled under President Gerald Ford, and the widely regarded Gulf War hero Colin Powell as the first black Secretary of State.

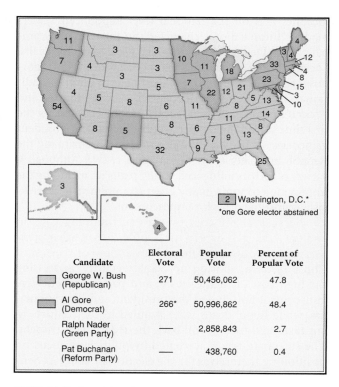

Candidate	Electoral Vote	Popular Vote	Percent of Popular Vote
George W. Bush (Republican)	271	50,456,062	47.8
Al Gore (Democrat)	266*	50,996,862	48.4
Ralph Nader (Green Party)	—	2,858,843	2.7
Pat Buchanan (Reform Party)	—	438,760	0.4

MAP 31.7 Presidential Election of 2000

This map illustrates clearly the closeness of the 2000 presidential contest. Democrat Al Gore tallied 337,576 more popular votes than his opponent, Republican George W. Bush, but lost the election. Bush, drawing upon solid support in the South and Midwest, and assisted by Green Party candidate Ralph Nader's drawing votes away from the Democrats, won in the electoral college by only four votes, thus securing the presidency. What the map does not reveal is the extraordinary controversy over Florida's 25 electoral votes that eventually was resolved—37 days after the election—by the United States Supreme Court.

Bush also made good on his campaign pledge to cut taxes, which he claimed would stimulate the slowing economy. The tax act refunded money retroactively to taxpayers ($300–$600 per person). However, it not only failed to stimulate the economy but contributed to the rapid decline of the federal budget surplus, which opened Bush to significant criticism. His economic headaches intensified in March, when the stock market took a dive, marking the greatest loss in eleven years. In September another market dive—the Dow Jones Industrial Average dropped 234 points—coupled with a jump in unemployment figures and slowing economic growth (0.7 percent in the third quarter) led to serious fears that a recession lurked just around the corner.

Other economic woes emerged in the summer, when sharply escalating gasoline prices alarmed consumers, and severe power shortages on the West Coast led to rolling blackouts and increased energy costs there. President Bush resisted calls for federal price controls and emphasized instead the need for the creation of more

John Lewis

We Marched to Be Counted

Emerging from the furor over apparent voting irregularities in Florida in the 2000 presidential election is a concern that uncounted and disqualified voters were more likely to be poor people, especially African Americans. John Lewis, a civil rights activist who had marched from Selma to Montgomery in 1965 to demonstrate for African American voting rights in Alabama, reflects on the relationship between the 1960s civil rights movement and the Florida voting controversy. Lewis is now a congressman from Atlanta.

What's happening in Florida and in Washington is more than a game for pundits. The whole mess reminds African Americans of an era when we had to pass literacy tests, pay poll taxes, and cross every *t* and dot every *i* to get to be able to vote. . . . For all the political maneuvering and legal wrangling, many people have missed an important point: the story of the 2000 election is about more than George W. Bush and Al Gore. It's about the right to vote. And you cannot understand the true implications of this campaign and the subsequent litigation without grasping how deeply many minorities feel about the seemingly simple matter of the sanctity of the ballot box.

There is a lot of troubling new talk of "political profiling"—allegations that officials tried to suppress the black vote on Election Day and may be maneuvering now to make sure it isn't counted. There are reports that officials put new voting machines in white areas but not black ones and that African Americans were asked to present two, not just one, forms of identification to be allowed to vote. These charges should be looked into. But I like to believe that no one met in some smoke-filled room and said, "We're going to keep black voters out, we're going to keep Jewish voters out." . . .

My greatest fear today is that the perception our votes were not counted may usher in a period of great cynicism. On the other hand—and I bet this is more likely—it may give people a greater sense of the importance of voting and of vigilance. The vote, after all, is the real heart of the movement. Younger people shouldn't think civil rights was just about water fountains or stirring speeches on TV. Late in the summer of 1961, after the Freedom Rides, we realized it was not enough to integrate lunch counters and buses. We had to get the vote.

Source: John Lewis, "We Marched to Be Counted," *Newsweek* (December 11, 2000), 38.

power plants and for oil drilling in Alaska and the Arctic, a move that infuriated environmentalists. The political falling-out was compounded by complaints that President Bush's and Vice President Cheney's close personal ties to the energy industry were guiding administration policies. Many observers claimed that energy companies were manipulating the market, pointing for example to Enron Corporation, a Houston-based firm that had been a major contributor to Bush's campaign.

A major political challenge to the administration erupted in late May when Vermont Republican senator Jim Jeffords announced that he was leaving the party to become an independent. The moderate Jeffords had grown disenchanted with the rising influence of the right wing in his party and announced he feared that in the future "I can see more and more instances where I'll disagree with the president on very fundamental issues—the issues of choice, the direction of the judiciary, tax and spending decisions, missile defense, energy and the environment, and a host of other issues, large and small." Jeffords's decision was not only an embarrassment to the president but also had dramatic consequences, as it meant that the Republicans lost their majority status in the Senate. Democrat Tom Daschle then stepped into the position of Senate majority leader, ensuring that Bush's ability to implement his policies would be severely hampered.

Abroad, Bush took steps to heighten his credibility as a world leader, a task made difficult both by the controversial nature of his election and his total inexperience in foreign affairs. Indeed, before he took office, he had barely been outside the United States. His major initiatives were to call for maintaining UN sanctions against Iraq and for increased efforts to destabilize Saddam Hussein's regime. In contrast to his predecessor, Bush decided that the United States would withdraw from active

"We Are under Attack"

On September 11, 2001, President Bush learned that a plane had crashed into one of New York's World Trade Center towers shortly before he entered Emma T. Booker Elementary School in Sarasota, Florida, where he listened to second graders read from the story "Pet Goat." As he listened an aide informed him of a second plane's crash into the other tower and that "America was under attack." Bush waited until the lesson was finished before complimenting the students on their reading and leaving the room. He later recounted his thoughts at this dramatic moment: "I'm being briefed about a reading program that works and I was looking at these little children and, all of the sudden, we were at war. So, I had to maintain my composure. I can remember noticing the press pool and the press corps beginning to get the calls and seeing the look on their face, and it became evident that we were, you know, that the world had changed." Doug Mills.

participation in negotiations in the Palestinian-Israeli conflict. He also announced that the United States would return to creating a missile defense shield, an updated version of Ronald Reagan's discredited "Star Wars." Implementing the plan would violate the 1972 Antiballistic Missile Treaty signed between the United States and Russia, a move that disturbed many U.S. allies.

The domestic and foreign issues that shaped the Bush administration in its first days would soon take a backseat to a sobering challenge when terrorists, later identified as members of Osama bin Laden's Al Qaeda, hijacked four commercial airliners on September 11, 2001. Two plowed into New York's World Trade Center, destroying its twin towers and killing over 2,700 persons. A third plane seriously damaged the Pentagon, but the fourth, headed for the White House, crashed in Pennsylvania when passengers thwarted the hijackers' efforts. As discussed in the Epilogue, the events of September 11 not only

profoundly altered the problems the nation and the world faced in maintaining a stable world order but also affected the domestic economic, political, and social landscape.

FOR FURTHER EXPLORATION

► For definitions of key terms boldfaced in this chapter, see the glossary at the end of the book.

► To assess your mastery of the material covered in this chapter, see the Online Study Guide at **bedfordstmartins.com/henretta**.

► For suggested references, including Web sites, see page SR-35 at the end of the book.

► For map resources and primary documents, see **bedfordstmartins.com/henretta**.

The last two decades of the twentieth century brought enormous changes. In the international arena, the collapse of the Soviet Union and the end of the cold war produced repercussions that are still evolving. The United States became the world's only superpower, but as the conflict in Iraq suggested, the nation's dominance in the new world order was limited, and the problem of global terrorism loomed menacingly, its implications not yet fully understood.

In politics, Republican Presidents Ronald Reagan and George Bush advocated a smaller role for the federal government in domestic programs. Though the Democrats regained the White House with the election of Bill Clinton in 1992, the Republican congressional landslide of 1994 helped continue the drive toward a balanced budget, tax cuts, deregulation, and federal government retrenchment. In other political developments, low voter turnout, the popularity of third-party candidates like Ralph Nader, and the controversies surrounding the impeachment of Bill Clinton and the 2000 election of George W. Bush pointed to widespread cynicism about politics.

In social and economic developments, increased immigration, notably from Latin America and Asia, changed the demographic balance of many areas, especially the cities, and the strains of an increasingly diverse society were reflected in debates over affirmative action and multiculturalism. Slow productivity growth, wage stagnation, and growing income inequality were the major domestic economic trends in the 1980s and early 1990s. By the late 1990s the United States had dramatically improved its position in the world economy, but decisions made beyond its borders continued to affect the daily lives of American workers, managers, and consumers.

Despite the problems the nation faced, Americans were relatively confident as the twentieth century ended. Economic prosperity deflected serious discontent. Following the September 11, 2001, terrorist attacks, fears about terrorism and concern about instability around the globe have made Americans and the rest of the world worried and uncertain. Moreover, economic problems—the slowing of the economy and the repercussions from immense corporate scandals—have undercut the confidence the nation felt at the end of the 1990s. How Americans come to interpret the last two decades of the twentieth century in the future will certainly be shaped by their experiences in the twenty-first century.

1981	Sandra Day O'Connor nominated to Supreme Court MTV premieres Beginning of AIDS epidemic IBM markets its first personal computer
1981–1983	Recession
1981–1989	National debt triples
1983	Star Wars proposed
1985	Gramm-Rudman Balanced Budget Act United States becomes a debtor nation Mikhail Gorbachev takes power in Soviet Union
1986	Iran-Contra affair Simpson-Mazzoli Immigration Act
1987	Montreal environmental protocol Stock market collapse
1988	George Bush elected president
1989	Savings and loan crisis *Webster v. Reproductive Health Services*
1990–1991	Persian Gulf War
1990–1992	Recession
1991	Dissolution of Soviet Union ends cold war Clarence Thomas–Anita Hill hearings Susan Faludi, *Backlash: The Undeclared War on American Women*
1992	Los Angeles riots Earth Summit in Rio de Janeiro Bill Clinton elected president
1993	Family and Medical Leave Act North American Free Trade Agreement (NAFTA)
1994	Health-care reform fails Republicans gain control of Congress
1995	U.S. troops enforce peace in Bosnia
1996	Personal Responsibility and Work Opportunity Act Clinton reelected
1998–1999	Bill Clinton impeached and acquitted
2000	Terrorists attack USS *Cole* in Yemen George W. Bush elected president in contested election
2001	Tax-cut refunds $300–$600 to taxpayers Worst stock market loss in eleven years Terrorists destroy New York's World Trade Center and attack Pentagon

Thinking about Contemporary History

Wᴴᴇɴ ʏᴏᴜ ɢᴏ ᴛᴏ ѕᴇᴇ ᴀ ᴍᴏᴠɪᴇ ᴀɴᴅ ᴛʜᴇ ꜰɪʟᴍ ᴇɴᴅѕ, the credits roll, the lights come on, and you go home. The movie is over. But for the writers of a history textbook, there is no "end" because history does not stop. The process of creating the next edition is already under way when the last sentence is written and the product of their work is sent to the printer. But which events should be included in the next edition? Just as a movie editor has to determine which sequences to follow and which scenes to cut or include, the authors of the next edition of *America's History* must determine which events will be thought important enough to warrant inclusion in a broad synthesis of American history and culture and which events will be judged as merely interesting occurrences of passing significance. Today's headlines do not always become tomorrow's history.

In a 1992 interview, former president Richard M. Nixon stated bluntly, "In my view, history is never worth reading until it's fifty years old. It takes fifty years before you're able to come back and evaluate a man or a period of time." Yet if textbook writers took Nixon's advice literally, they would end their books just after World War II and the onset of the cold war. Of course, this isn't desirable, and the enormous outpouring of

◄ **A Poignant Symbol**
This striking photograph captures one of the nation's most revered symbols, the Statue of Liberty, against a backdrop of smoke from the collapse of New York's World Trade Center following the terrorist attacks of September 11, 2001.
Daniel Hulshizer / AP / Wide World.

September 11, 2001

Photographers capturing the aftermath of a plane crash into the north tower of New York's World Trade Center found themselves recording an extraordinary moment in the nation's history. When a second plane approached and then slammed into the building's south tower at 9:03 A.M., which erupted into flames, the nation knew it was under attack. Of the estimated 2,843 people who died in the September 11 terrorist attacks, 2,617 were at the World Trade Center. Robert Clark / AURORA.

excellent scholarship that informs Part Six of this textbook demonstrates that it is indeed possible to assess and interpret historically events of the fairly recent past such as the cold war, the civil rights movement, the growth of suburbia, and the changing contours of the global economy.

The closer the past gets to the present, however, the harder the task becomes. Consider the terrorist attacks of September 11, 2001. No reader of this text could possibly have missed the television images of the two Boeing 767s hurtling into New York City's World Trade Center, or the Twin Towers collapsing into rubble, or the crowds fleeing the cascading clouds of dust, and then, as the cameras

switched to Washington, D.C., the flames engulfing a wing of the Pentagon. Few will forget the accounts of survivors who, clambering down the staircases, encountered firefighters laboring upward overloaded with equipment, some to their death, or of the passengers of United Airlines Flight 93 who, learning on their cell phones about what had happened, took on the terrorists and brought down the plane in rural Pennsylvania before it could reach its probable target, the White House. Given the emotional impact of those searing images and the poignant stories of courage and mourning that continue to unfold, historians have a daunting task in trying to

Americans, Think!

For extremist Islamic groups in Pakistan, neighbor to Taliban-controlled Afghanistan, the terrorist attacks on the United States on September 11, 2001, brought to the fore long-standing resentment toward the United States. Their resentment is based in part on U.S. support for Israel, but also stems from the way in which America—with its great power and wealth—exemplifies the corrosive effects of Western capitalism and modernism. Here, Pakistani activists demonstrate at an anti-America rally in Islamabad held on September 15, 2001.
B. K. Bangash / AP / Wide World.

step back from their experience as witnesses of contemporary events to place the trauma of September 11 into a broad historical perspective.

What follows in this epilogue is a preview, to follow our movie analogy, of how we anticipate incorporating the terrorist attacks and their aftermath into the final chapter of the next edition of *America's History*. We offer an overview of the key areas in modern American life that have been traced throughout this book—politics, society and culture, the economy, and diplomacy—in light of September 11, a day that has led many contemporary observers to conclude that "the world will never be the same again." Just as in earlier chapters, we will examine the larger themes, shifting perspectives, and emerging syntheses in these areas but with a more tentative and open-ended perspective. Think of this part of *America's History* as a historical document: how a group of American historians viewed the nation during a heightened time of crisis. Look at the choice of issues and mode of analysis they used to gather and evaluate evidence, how they linked complex events surrounding the terrorist attacks to larger patterns and themes.

We are writing this epilogue in April 2003, nearly eighteen months after the events of September 11. By the time you read this you will know how some of the themes we touch upon have turned out. To reiterate Nixon's remark, "It takes fifty years before you're able to come back and evaluate a man or a period of time." Perhaps, many years from now, you will look back over your copy of *America's History* and judge how well we did.

September 11 and International Affairs

Almost three thousand men and women from over eighty countries perished in the terrorist attacks on the United States on September 11, 2001. For the first time since the War of 1812, foreign agents attacked the continental United States, targeting symbols of American capitalism and government. Within minutes of the first plane's collision into one of the Twin Towers, television crews were on the scene; by the time the second plane hit the other tower, seventeen minutes later, the event was covered live. America was under attack in living color for the entire world to see.

The Search for Al Qaeda
After the terrorist attacks on New York's World Trade Center and the Pentagon, the United States succeeded in marshalling a multinational force to attack Afghanistan, where the repressive anti-American Taliban regime harbored a significant component of the Al Qaeda network. Here, Canadian infantry soldiers board a U.S. Army Ch-47 Chinook helicopter in the Shahi Kot mountains of Afghanistan in March 2002. Later they teamed up with U.S. Army soldiers to search remote mountain regions for Taliban and Al Qaeda personnel. © Jim Hollander / AFP / Corbis.

Within hours, the United States had traced the origins of the attack to a militant Muslim sect, Al Qaeda, under the leadership of Osama bin Laden, a Saudi exile living among and supported by Taliban leaders in Afghanistan. The Taliban was itself a fundamentalist Muslim organization that had seized control of Afghanistan in 1996, following the overthrow of a Soviet-backed regime by forces supplied and assisted by the United States in the heat of the cold war.

In response to the attacks, President George W. Bush and his advisors proclaimed a "war on terrorism," working to forge a broad international coalition that included Great Britain, Canada, Russia, most of Europe, and many Muslim countries, notably Pakistan and Saudi Arabia. In seeking international assistance against terror as a common enemy to all, the Bush administration shifted away from its preference for unilateral action, which had earlier prompted its withdrawal from the Kyoto environmental agreements, the Comprehensive Test Ban Treaty, and participation in the International Criminal Court. These international treaties, which

sought worldwide participation to end global warming, an end to atomic testing and proliferation, and the establishment of a world court, all ran counter to Bush's policies. As the world's only superpower following the collapse of the Soviet Union in 1991, the failure of the United States to participate deeply undermined these international goals and provoked much criticism of its go-it-alone stance.

In response to the September 11 attacks, the United States successfully called upon its allies to support military strikes against Osama bin Laden and the Taliban. Within weeks, the United States and its allies, relying on massive air power and deployment of special forces, routed the Taliban and rolled up the Al Qaeda network's center of operations. Afghanistan was liberated from its Taliban dictators, who had squelched all civil liberties in the name of their fundamentalist beliefs. As television news reported on the change in regime, it particularly celebrated how Afghani women were freed from an exceptionally repressive way of life. In the wake of this victory, the United States and its allies attacked terrorist

Surrender

After a week of being surrounded by 50,000 rival Afghani troops and being subjected to intense American bombing, Taliban forces in Kunduz surrendered on November 25, 2001, marking a significant gain in America's fight against the Taliban. Here a Taliban fighter gives up a rocket launcher to a soldier of the Northern Alliance, a rebel Islamic faction that had resisted the Taliban since its takeover in 1996. The Northern Alliance became a major component of the American strategy to destroy the Taliban.

© Jean-Philippe Ksiazak / AFP / Corbis.

networks throughout the world, destroying many of their secret cells and capturing and killing large numbers of anti-American militants. Despite these successes in the war on terrorism, however, U.S. officials as of this writing believe Osama bin Laden to be alive and the Al Qaeda network active once again in "holy war" against the United States and its allies.

In his State of the Union address on January 29, 2002, President Bush stressed that the world still faced the threat of an international web of radical Muslim terrorists, ranging from Somalia to Bosnia to the Philippines and beyond. He signaled an intention to carry the fight to other nations that harbor terrorists or develop weapons of mass destruction—hence his characterization of Iran, Iraq, and North Korea as "an axis of evil." By the first anniversary of September 11, President Bush was threatening to attack Iraq, a controversial plan that divided his advisors and provoked heated public debate.

To quiet some of the opposition, and more importantly to garner international support for the war on Iraq, President Bush presented his case to the United Nations. On November 8, the Security Council approved Resolution 1441, which included the return of UN weapons inspectors to Iraq and a requirement that

Saddam Hussein's government submit to the Security Council a full account of its weapons, stockpiles, facilities, and delivery capabilities. To achieve passage of the resolution, the United States stepped back from its demand for regime change in Iraq, but it has still reserved the right of unilateral action. As weapons inspections proceeded in December 2002, the Bush administration continued its war preparations, and when it failed to obtain international, UN-sanctioned support for a preemptive strike, the United States and Britain launched an armed attack against Iraq without it. Whatever the results, how the United States chooses to exercise its immense power will undoubtedly be a major theme in future editions of *America's History*.

We will also have to assess the impact of the events of September 11 on other simmering hot spots in the world, where U.S. leadership will play an important role. The long-brewing crisis in the Middle East over Israeli resistance to demands for a Palestinian homeland has deepened since the attacks on the United States, with both sides adopting a harder position, particularly regarding Israeli settlements in the West Bank and the Palestinian use of terrorism, including suicide bombings against Israeli citizens. The Palestinian-Israeli conflict

Antiwar Voices
As President Bush accelerated his calls for war on Iraq in fall 2002, a peace movement emerged in communities throughout the country. These Maine residents were part of a crowd of 2,500 who turned out for an antiwar protest in Augusta, Maine, on October 26, 2002. Jill Brady / Maine Sunday Telegram.

Preparing for War

En route to the Middle East as part of the build-up for what the United States called a possible "pre-emptive strike" against Iraq, the aircraft carrier USS Constellation made a routine stop in Hong Kong where a crew member worked on one of the fighter jets in November 2002. By mid-January 2003, more than 65,000 U.S. military personnel were in the Persian Gulf region in preparation for war with Iraq.

Anat Givon / AP / Wide World.

Another area of major concern is the continuing threat of war between India, a predominately Hindu nation, and Pakistan, a mostly Muslim state. Both countries possess atomic weapons that they have expressed willingness to use. For many years armed conflicts have erupted along the borders between the two nations, particularly over the issue of Kashmir, a region that lies between them and has both Hindu and Muslim populations. Following India's achievement of independence in 1947, Kashmir declared itself a sovereign nation. Since then, in three Indian-Pakistani wars over Kashmir, some 70,000 Kashmiris have been killed, another 40,000 have been placed in Indian jails, and over 150,000 have become homeless. Tensions in Kashmir have greatly accelerated since September 11, with relations between Pakistan and India strained as well over the issue of Muslim terrorists based in Pakistan.

That so much international anxiety about the future is tied to Muslim extremists also raises the alarming specter of a world divided in two, of the followers of Islam pitted against the rest of the world. Such a division is certainly the goal of the terrorists, who hope to galvanize Muslims into a holy war against the capitalist West. With few exceptions, leaders in Muslim nations have roundly condemned extremism and terrorism in the name of Islam, while the United States and its allies have insisted that their targets are terrorists, not Muslims. President Bush emphasized this point in a highly publicized speech given on September 17, 2001, just days after the attacks. Standing in a mosque in Washington, D.C., the president commented, "These acts of violence against innocents violate the fundamental tenets of the Islamic faith, and it's important for my fellow Americans to understand that."

How can the growth of such religious extremism be understood? As historians grapple with this question, they will need to take into consideration U.S. foreign policy, including its efforts to secure and protect American access to Middle Eastern oil, an objective made clear by its role in unseating Muhammad Mossadegh in Iran in 1954 as well as by its support for Kuwait against Iraq in the Gulf War of 1991. And, despite U.S. efforts to broker peace between Israel and the Palestinians, long-standing American support of Israelis constitutes yet another major source of resentment throughout the Muslim world that historians will have to consider. So, too, they will have to assess the circumstances that led the United States during Jimmy Carter's and Ronald Reagan's presidential administrations to support radical Islamic fundamentalists, including Osama bin Laden, in their efforts to drive the Russians out of Afghanistan in the 1980s. As part of the long-standing cold war tactic of resisting Communist encroachment in developing countries, the CIA trained and partially funded many leaders who eventually formed the Taliban. This is certainly one of the tragic ironies of recent history.

affects the entire Middle East; thus its escalation adds to the enormous problems that face the United States in formulating an effective policy in the region.

Observers also question the stability of other Middle Eastern countries. Saudi Arabia has been an invaluable ally to the United States, but its ruling elite has engaged in a delicate balancing act of maintaining good relations with America while placating militant fundamentalist clerics within the country. Some observers worry that Saudi Arabia could be ripe for a fundamentalist revolution on the order of the Iranian revolution of the 1970s. Moreover, they fear that anger over the U.S. bombing of Muslims in Afghanistan could deepen anti-American sentiment throughout the Muslim world.

Mideast Crisis
With extremist Palestinian suicide bombers wreaking havoc and killing hundreds in Israel and Israeli officials mounting an aggressive offensive against Palestinians, a solution to the long-standing crisis seems remote. Here, Palestinians survey the rubble in Jenin on the West Bank after an intense Israeli attack in April 2002. In eight days of close-range bloody fighting, twenty-three Israeli soldiers and over fifty Palestinians died. VII Photo Agency.

September 11 and Domestic Issues

The implications of September 11 for international stability are far reaching. Perhaps of less long-term importance but nonetheless significant is the impact on the nation's domestic politics and policies. Put simply, the crisis has been a boon to George W. Bush's administration. Prior to the attacks, Bush was being lampooned in the media for the "dyselection of 2000." Jokes that Vice President Dick Cheney, a far more experienced and sophisticated policymaker, was the real president abounded. Opinion polls in Europe indicated that Bush was not taken seriously as a world leader, while the president's approval rating at home sagged steadily during the summer of 2001, registering only 52 percent in early July. By January 2002, however, Bush's approval rating had soared to an exceptional 83 percent. Some critics flinched at Bush's Wild West rhetoric—"bring them back dead or alive"—and promotion of strident nationalism, but the majority of the public approved the president's handling of the crisis.

As during any war, the power and influence of the executive have increased, and many observers agree that Bush's demeanor has become more "presidential."

Beyond the direction of foreign policy, however, Bush's new strength may have significant effects on domestic policy as well. Most indices suggested that Americans have more confidence in Bush than in his Democratic opposition in Congress. And although the Republicans have not yet been able to use the president's popularity to make substantial progress on their conservative domestic agenda concerning the economy, abortion, and education, this may change as a result of the November 2002 elections. With Republicans gaining two seats, the Senate reverted to Republican control, and in the House they picked up five seats, increasing their majority to 228 out of the total of 435 representatives.

The election results were striking, as this was the first time since 1934 that the party of the president scored gains in both houses of Congress in his administration's first midterm election. In 1934 Democratic candidates rode Franklin D. Roosevelt's coattails into office; in 2002 Republican candidates clearly benefited from President Bush's personal popularity and the voting public's belief that he handled the terrorist crisis well. Moreover, the administration's aggressive posture in challenging Saddam Hussein and success in pushing a resolution through

Minority Whip

San Francisco representative Nancy Pelosi made history when she became the Democrat's House of Representatives leader, the "Minority Whip," and the first woman of either party to hold that position. The selection of the liberal Pelosi came on the heels of significant Republican victories in the 2002 elections and may indicate a shift away from the centrist politics of Democrats in the Clinton era.
Joe Marquette / AP / Wide World.

Congress authorizing military action against Iraq reinforced Bush's status as a forceful leader in uncertain times.

For their part, the Democrats suffered from unimaginative leadership and an inability to offer little that seemed distinctive from the Republicans. Moreover, Republicans mounted an unprecedented get-out-the-vote effort, while Democrats proved unable to energize their constituents to get to the polls. Already looking to the 2004 elections, and perhaps a sign that they are rejecting their move toward the more centrist leanings of the Clinton years, the Democrats have revamped their leadership, selecting Nancy Pelosi, a liberal San Francisco congressional representative, as the House Democratic leader—the first time a woman of either party has held this position.

International issues will undoubtedly remain a crucial factor in partisan politics in the near future. The Democrats will be particularly challenged to find a way of presenting themselves as supporting a forceful U.S. presence in the world—something the American public seems to want—while simultaneously challenging the Republican leadership in charge of that policy. Two other issues—the economy and corporate corruption—were expected, incorrectly, to be important factors in the 2002 midterm elections, but they may yet surface as vital issues in future political confrontations.

Figures released in August 2002 by the Commerce Department reveal that the economy was in recession months before the terrorist attacks and had begun to recover by the end of 2001. By the summer of 2002, however, that recovery had stalled, with most economic indicators looking bleak, leading *The Economist* to describe the outlook as "decidedly wobbly." Certainly, September 11 contributed to the economic woes, most noticeably in damage to the airline industry. Faced with reluctant air travelers, airlines cut schedules between 15 and 20 percent after September 11; within a year, in August 2002, U.S. Airways announced that it had filed for bankruptcy protection. In the same week, United Airlines indicated it was considering the same option, and American Airlines reported that it was overhauling its operation and eliminating 7,000 jobs, or 6 percent of its workforce.

But the fragility of the airline industry paled in comparison to broader economic problems that were unconnected to the terrorist attacks. Just weeks after the destruction of the Twin Towers, the energy giant Enron, a company that brokered electricity and natural gas, collapsed on Wall Street after its announcement of a $618 million third-quarter loss. The Securities and Exchange Commission discovered that the auditing firm Arthur Andersen, which handled Enron's accounts, had been shredding and destroying documents related to the company's collapse. A scandal of huge proportions, it reached into centers of government, including the White House. Kenneth Lay, the CEO of Enron, with a long history of involvement in Republican Party affairs, had been a strong financial backer and personal friend of President Bush, donating over $290,000 to his presidential campaign.

During the summer of 2002, other corporate giants, including WorldCom and Adelphia Communications, fell with regularity, costing thousands of jobs and threatening the nation's economy. By midsummer the unemployment rate stood at 5.9 percent as compared to 4.6 percent the previous year. The accompanying decline in the stock market wiped out $7.7 trillion of paper wealth—an outcome devastating for many Americans, roughly half of whom owned stock. As falling stock prices depleted 401(k) accounts and retirement funds, the elderly found their real incomes reduced and for many their hopes of retirement put on hold.

Hard Times for the Airlines

The most obvious economic impact of the terrorist attacks of September 11 has been on the airline industry since many Americans are now reluctant to fly. The industry has witnessed significant cutbacks in schedules, layoffs of employees, and declarations of bankruptcy. Symbolic of the industry's woes is this photograph of a virtually empty United Airlines terminal at Boston's Logan Airport on the first anniversary of the attacks. Indicative of the increased security precautions for airports, State Police Trooper Maureen Lewis patrols with Bara, a dog trained to detect explosives. Charles Krupa / AP / Wide World.

The corporate scandals and their economic fallout have helped to erode the nation's trust in corporate America. Polls also suggest that they have deflected some attention away from the issues connected to the events of September 11, as economic anxieties are supplanting Americans' fears about terrorism as their number one concern. Recognizing the importance of turning the economy around, the Bush administration instituted a dramatic shakeup of economic appointees in December 2002, replacing the secretary of the treasury, the head of the Securities and Exchange Commission, and the chief economic advisor to the president. Although the faltering economy, corporate scandals, and the terrorist attacks of September 11 are unrelated issues, together they have fostered a widespread uneasiness and have undermined Americans' confidence about the future.

In addition to assessing the impact of September 11 on politics and the economy, future editions of *America's History* will need to analyze another important domestic ramification of the terrorist attacks: the efforts to ensure "homeland security." To improve the nation's domestic defenses, the Bush administration increased security at

The Fall of Enron

Two weeks after the terrorist attacks of September 11, Americans faced more unsettling news as they learned that the energy firm Enron, one of the nation's ten largest corporations, had collapsed on Wall Street, taking the investments and retirement funds of many thousands of people with it. Subsequent investigation revealed the firm had lied about its losses and that its auditing firm had shredded and destroyed documents related to the company's collapse. The full impact of the scandal has yet to be evaluated, but in Texas, one quick result was the change of the name for the Houston Astros' baseball park—from Enron Field to Minute Maid Park. Brett Coomer / AP / Wide World.

Homeland Security

One of the most far-reaching domestic results of the terrorist attacks on the World Trade Center and the Pentagon was the call for heightened defense at home. At a July 2002 speech in Washington, D.C., President Bush outlined his plan for an Office of Homeland Security designed to thwart the terrorist threat and control the nation's borders. The following November, Congress approved the president's proposal, which combined approximately twenty-two different government departments under a single cabinet-level agency, making it the largest federal government reorganization since 1947. President Bush nominated former Pennsylvania governor Thomas Ridge to head up the new office.
Paul J. Richards / AFP / Corbis.

airports, government buildings, and popular tourist attractions, while proposing legislation that would enhance federal investigative capabilities. The USA PATRIOT (Uniting and Strengthening America by Providing Appropriate Tools Required to Intercept and Obstruct Terrorism) Act of 2002, which passed with only one dissenting vote, gave unparalleled powers to the federal government to investigate and detain immigrants suspected of terrorist activity, all surrounded by a high degree of secrecy in the name of national security. One result of these powers was that the hunt for suspected terrorists threatened to bring about a new type of racial profiling, whereby young Muslim men could become subject to investigations not bound by traditional protections of civil liberties. Other threats to civil liberties included President Bush's executive order of November 2001 that suspected terrorists be tried in military tribunals rather than in the civil courts where they would have the full protections provided in the Constitution.

Similarly, programs such as TIPS (Terrorism Information and Prevention System) put forth by Attorney General John D. Ashcroft have drawn fire for proposing a citizen-spy network that would use mail carriers, utility workers, truckers, dock workers, and others to report on suspicious activities. Responding to criticism, the Justice Department has scaled back its program, but it remains worrisome to many civil liberty advocates. The Justice Department also suffered setbacks in August 2002, when a Federal Appeals Court ruled that the Justice Department's "blanket" policy of secret deportation hearings was unconstitutional and the United States Foreign Intelligence Surveillance Court (created in 1978) placed limits on the USA PATRIOT Act's authorization of electronic surveillance of people accused of spying.

Another important domestic initiative called for the creation of the Office of Homeland Security, which Congress approved in November 2002. The initiative combines approximately twenty-two different government departments into a single cabinet-level agency operating with a budget of $40 billion, with about 170,000 employees. The largest governmental reorganization since the creation of the Department of Defense in 1947, this centralized agency will be responsible for the protection

Stars and Stripes

After September 11, 2001, American flags abounded—from car windows to T-shirts. Less conventional ways to display the stars and stripes also emerged, such as this painted lawn in South Mitford, Indiana. While many Americans praised the pervasive appearance of the flag as a sign of much-needed unity and patriotism, some criticized it as excessive nationalism that did little to address the serious problems the nation faced.
Samuel Hoffman / The Fort Wayne Journal Gazette / AP / Wide World.

of American life and property from terrorist activities and for controlling the nation's borders. It will bring together the U.S. Customs Service, the Coast Guard, the Immigration and Naturalization Service, and the Transportation Security Administration but not the CIA and FBI, even though in the aftermath of September 11 the two agencies were chastened for their mishandling of information relevant to the attacks.

Supporters hope that this monumental reorganization will bring efficiency and coordination to the myriad government agencies engaged in national security. Critics worry that it will create a bureaucracy too unwieldy to operate effectively and that it will center too much power in the president and the executive branch. Historians in the future not only will need to analyze the effectiveness of the USA PATRIOT Act and the new cabinet position in the efforts to weed out terrorism, but they also will need to evaluate the costs entailed in enhanced governmental authority and the reduction of Americans' civil liberties and privacy rights.

September 11 and the American People

Both in the passage of the USA PATRIOT Act and in approval of U.S. bombing in Afghanistan, President Bush enjoyed bipartisan support. This bipartisan spirit formed part of what commentators described as a new sense of unity in the nation. Observers praised the renewed spirit of patriotism—most obviously in the display of the American flag everywhere from taxi cabs to football fields.

It is not surprising that Americans would crave expressions of unity and higher purpose in the aftermath of September 11. During any war, such spirit helps individuals to cope with the vulnerability and uncertainty they face. In the case of America's war on terrorism, moreover, rallying around the flag gave the nation a respite from the disruptions that characterized its recent domestic history. In focusing on coming together for a victory against

terrorism, the American people could ignore, at least for a while, underlying sources of disunity—racial and ethnic conflict and disparate views on issues ranging from taxes and welfare reform to affirmative action and abortion to health care and immigration. They also could hope to have moved beyond such disheartening political controversies as the impeachment of Bill Clinton, the divisive nature of the 2000 elections, and the three-ring circus of media coverage of political sex scandals. But as uplifting as the spirit of a new America might be, historians know that this sort of war-inspired sentiment rarely lasts when the war is over. But the war on terrorism is a different kind of war. How long will it last? How long will the American people—and the rest of the world—support its current trajectories?

Many observers have compared the September 11 attacks to the December 7, 1941, attack on Pearl Harbor. Indeed, within days of September 11 the authors of this textbook were exchanging e-mails and debating the usefulness of the World War II analogy. Certainly, like December 7, 1941, and November 22, 1963, the day John F. Kennedy was shot, September 11, 2001, will be one of those defining dates that contemporaries are sure to remember in precise detail. And, like the bombing of Pearl Harbor, the terrorist attacks touched off an exceptional sense of American unity and determination to defeat the enemy. But important differences stand out. This war is against an elusive enemy—not nation-states with explicit territory and armed forces to be attacked but scattered cells of determined people who can wreak destruction cheaply and quickly and then virtually disappear.

Thus the aftermath of September 11 resembles not so much World War II as the cold war between the United States and the Soviet Union. Certainly, the rhetoric of the current war against terrorists evokes the cold war—a rhetoric of simple dichotomies, of good versus evil, and a tendency to dismiss criticism of U.S. policy as "un-American." And, like containing the Communists, containing the terrorists requires attention to wide-ranging

and no fact tried by a jury, shall be otherwise reexamined in any Court of the United States, than according to the Rules of the common law.

. . .

This amendment guarantees people the same right to a trial by jury as was guaranteed by English common law in 1791. Under common law, in civil trials (those involving money damages) the role of the judge was to settle questions of law and that of the jury was to settle questions of fact. The amendment does not specify the size of the jury or its role in a trial, however. The Supreme Court has generally held that those issues be determined by English common law of 1791, which stated that a jury consists of twelve people, that a trial must be conducted before a judge who instructs the jury on the law and advises it on facts, and that a verdict must be unanimous.

Amendment VIII [1791]

Excessive bail shall not be required, nor excessive fines imposed, nor cruel and unusual punishments inflicted.

. . .

The language used to guarantee the three rights in this amendment was inspired by the English Bill of Rights of 1689. The Supreme Court has not had a lot to say about "excessive fines." In recent years it has agreed that despite the provision against "excessive bail," persons who are believed to be dangerous to others can be held without bail even before they have been convicted.

Although opponents of the death penalty have not succeeded in using the Eighth Amendment to achieve the end of capital punishment, the clause regarding "cruel and unusual punishments" has been used to prohibit capital punishment in certain cases.

Amendment IX [1791]

The enumeration in the Constitution, of certain rights, shall not be construed to deny or disparage others retained by the people.

. . .

Some Federalists feared that inclusion of the Bill of Rights in the Constitution would allow later generations of interpreters to claim that the people had surrendered all rights not specifically enumerated there. To guard against this, James Madison added language that became the Ninth Amendment. Interest in this heretofore largely ignored amendment revived in 1965 when it was used in a concurring opinion in Griswold v. Connecticut (1965). While Justice William O. Douglas called on the Third Amendment to support the right to privacy in deciding that case, Justice Arthur Goldberg, in the concurring opinion, argued that the right to privacy regarding contraception was an unenumerated right that was protected by the Ninth Amendment.

In 1980 the Court ruled that the right of the press to attend a public trial was protected by the Ninth Amendment. Although some scholars argue that modern judges cannot identify the unenumerated rights that the framers were trying to protect, others argue that the Ninth Amendment should be read as providing a constitutional "presumption of liberty" that allows people to act in any way that does not violate the rights of others.

Amendment X [1791]

The powers not delegated to the United States by the Constitution, nor prohibited by it to the States, are reserved to the States respectively, or to the people.

. . .

The Antifederalists were especially eager to see a "reserved powers clause" explicitly guaranteeing the states control over their internal affairs. Not surprisingly, the Tenth Amendment has been a frequent battleground in the struggle over states' rights and federal supremacy. Prior to the Civil War, the Jeffersonian Republican Party and Jacksonian Democrats invoked the Tenth Amendment to prohibit the federal government from making decisions about whether people in individual states could own slaves. The Tenth Amendment was virtually suspended during Reconstruction following the Civil War. In 1883, however, the Supreme Court declared the Civil Rights Act of 1875 unconstitutional on the grounds that it violated the Tenth Amendment. Business interests also called on the amendment to block efforts at federal regulation.

The Court was inconsistent over the next several decades as it attempted to resolve the tension between the restrictions of the Tenth Amendment and the powers the Constitution granted to Congress to regulate interstate commerce and levy taxes. The Court upheld the Pure Food and Drug Act (1906), the Meat Inspection Acts (1906 and 1907), and the White Slave Traffic Act (1910), all of which affected the states, but it struck down an act prohibiting interstate shipment of goods produced through child labor. Between 1934 and 1935 a number of New Deal programs created by Franklin D. Roosevelt were declared unconstitutional on the grounds that they violated the Tenth Amendment. As Roosevelt appointees changed the composition of the Court, the Tenth Amendment was declared to have no substantive meaning. Generally, the amendment is held to protect the rights of states to regulate internal matters such as local government, education, commerce, labor, and business as well as matters involving families such as marriage, divorce, and inheritance within the state.

Unratified Amendment

Reapportionment Amendment (proposed by Congress September 25, 1789, along with the Bill of Rights)

After the first enumeration required by the first article of the Constitution, there shall be one Representative for every thirty thousand, until the number shall amount to one hundred, after which the proportion shall be so regulated by Congress, that there shall be not less than one hundred Representatives, nor less than one Representative for every forty thousand persons, until the number of Representatives shall amount to two hundred; after which the proportion shall be so regulated by Congress, that there shall not be less than two hundred Representatives, nor more than one Representative for every fifty thousand persons.

. . .

If the Reapportionment Amendment had passed and remained in effect, the House of Representatives today would have more than 5,000 members rather than 435 to reflect the current U.S. population.

Amendment XI [1798]

The Judicial power of the United States shall not be construed to extend to any suit in law or equity, commenced or prosecuted against one of the United States by Citizens of another State, or by Citizens or subjects of any foreign state.

• • •

In 1793 the Supreme Court ruled in favor of Alexander Chisholm, executor of the estate of a deceased South Carolina merchant. Chisholm was suing the state of Georgia because the merchant had never been paid for provisions he had supplied during the Revolution. Many regarded this Court decision as an error that violated the intent of the Constitution.

Antifederalists and many other Americans feared a powerful federal court system because they worried that it would become like the British courts of this period, which were accountable only to the monarch. Furthermore, Chisholm v. Georgia *prompted a series of suits against state governments by creditors and suppliers who had made loans during the war.*

In addition, state legislators and Congress feared that the shaky economies of the new states, as well as the country as a whole, would be destroyed, especially if Loyalists who had fled to other countries sought reimbursement for land and property that had been seized. The day after the Supreme Court announced its decision, a resolution proposing the Eleventh Amendment, which overturned the decision in Chisholm v. Georgia, *was introduced in the U.S. Senate.*

Amendment XII [1804]

The Electors shall meet in their respective States and vote by ballot for President and Vice-President, one of whom, at least, shall not be an inhabitant of the same State with themselves; they shall name in their ballots the person voted for as President, and in distinct ballots the person voted for as Vice-President, and they shall make distinct lists of all persons voted for as President, and of all persons voted for as Vice-President, and of the number of votes for each, which lists they shall sign and certify, and transmit sealed to the seat of government of the United States, directed to the President of the Senate;—the President of the Senate shall, in the presence of the Senate and House of Representatives, open all the certificates and the votes shall then be counted;—The person having the greatest number of votes for President, shall be the President, if such number be a majority of the whole number of Electors appointed; and if no person have such majority, then from the persons having the highest numbers not exceeding three on the list of those voted for as President, the House of Representatives shall choose immediately, by ballot, the President. But in choosing the President, the votes shall be taken by States, the representation from each State having one vote; a quorum for this purpose shall consist of a member or members from two-thirds of the States, and a majority of all the States shall be necessary to a choice. And if the House of Representatives shall not choose a President whenever the right of choice shall devolve upon them, before *the fourth day of March* next following, then the Vice-President shall act as President, as in the case of the death or other constitutional disability of the President.[*]—The person having the greatest number of votes as Vice-President, shall be the Vice-

President, if such number be a majority of the whole number of Electors appointed; and if no person have a majority, then from the two highest numbers on the list, the Senate shall choose the Vice-President; a quorum for the purpose shall consist of two-thirds of the whole number of Senators, and a majority of the whole number shall be necessary to a choice. But no person constitutionally ineligible to the office of President shall be eligible to that of Vice-President of the United States.

• • •

The framers of the Constitution disliked political parties and assumed that none would ever form. Under the original system, electors chosen by the states would each vote for two candidates. The candidate who won the most votes would become president, and the person who won the second-highest number of votes would become vice president. Rivalries between Federalists and Republicans led to the formation of political parties, however, even before George Washington had left office. In 1796 Federalist John Adams was chosen as president, and his great rival, Thomas Jefferson (whose party was called the Republican Party), became his vice president. In 1800 all the electors cast their two votes as one of two party blocs. Jefferson and his fellow Republican nominee, Aaron Burr, were tied with seventy-three votes each. The contest went to the House of Representatives, which finally elected Jefferson after thirty-six ballots. The Twelfth Amendment prevents these problems by requiring electors to vote separately for the president and vice president.

Unratified Amendment

Titles of Nobility Amendment (proposed by Congress May 1, 1810)

If any citizen of the United States shall accept, claim, receive or retain any title of nobility or honor or shall, without the consent of Congress, accept and retain any present, pension, office or emolument of any kind whatever, from any emperor, king, prince or foreign power, such person shall cease to be a citizen of the United States, and shall be incapable of holding any office of trust or profit under them, or either of them.

• • •

This amendment would have extended Article I, Section 9, Clause 8 of the Constitution, which prevents the awarding of titles by the United States and the acceptance of such awards from foreign powers without congressional consent. Historians speculate that general nervousness about the power of the Emperor Napoleon, who was at that time extending France's empire throughout Europe, may have prompted the proposal. Though it fell one vote short of ratification, Congress and the American people thought the proposal had been ratified, and it was included in many nineteenth-century editions of the Constitution.

The Civil War and Reconstruction Amendments (Thirteenth, Fourteenth, and Fifteenth Amendments)

In the four months between the election of Abraham Lincoln and his inauguration, more than two hundred proposed constitutional amendments were presented to Congress as part of a desperate attempt to hold the rapidly dissolving Union together. Most of these were efforts to appease the southern states by protecting

---

[*]Superseded by Section 3 of the Twentieth Amendment.

the right to own slaves or by disfranchising African Americans through constitutional amendment. None were able to win the votes required from Congress to send them to the states. Ultimately, the Corwin Amendment seemed to be the only hope for preserving the Union by amending the Constitution.

The northern victors in the Civil War tried to restructure the Constitution just as the war had restructured the nation. Yet they were often divided in their goals. Some wanted to end slavery; others hoped for social and economic equality regardless of race; others hoped that extending the power of the ballot box to former slaves would help create a new political order. The debates over the Thirteenth, Fourteenth, and Fifteenth Amendments were bitter. Few of those who fought for these changes were satisfied with the amendments themselves; fewer still were satisfied with their interpretation. Although the amendments put an end to the legal status of slavery, it was nearly a hundred years after the amendments' passage before most of the descendants of former slaves could begin to experience the economic, social, and political equality the amendments were intended to provide.

Unratified Amendment

Corwin Amendment
(proposed by Congress March 2, 1861)

No amendment shall be made to the Constitution which will authorize or give to Congress the power to abolish or interfere, within any State, with the domestic institutions thereof, including that of persons held to labor or service by the laws of said State.

• • •

Following the election of Abraham Lincoln, Congress scrambled to try to prevent the secession of the slaveholding states. House member Thomas Corwin of Ohio proposed the "unamendable" amendment in the hope that by protecting slavery where it existed, Congress would keep the southern states in the Union. Lincoln indicated his support for the proposed amendment in his first inaugural address. Only Ohio and Maryland ratified the Corwin Amendment before the war caused it to be forgotten.

Amendment XIII [1865]

Section 1.   Neither slavery nor involuntary servitude, except as a punishment for crime whereof the party shall have been duly convicted, shall exist within the United States, or any place subject to their jurisdiction.

Section 2.   Congress shall have power to enforce this article by appropriate legislation.

• • •

Because the Emancipation Proclamation of 1863 abolished slavery only in the parts of the Confederacy still in rebellion, Republicans proposed a Thirteenth Amendment that would extend abolition to the entire South. In February 1865, when the proposal was approved by the House, the gallery of the House was newly opened to black Americans who had a chance at last to see their government at work. Passage of the proposal was greeted by wild cheers from the gallery as well as tears on the House floor, where congressional representatives openly embraced one another.

The problem of ratification remained, however. The Union position was that the Confederate states were part of the country of thirty-six states. Therefore, twenty-seven states were needed to ratify the amendment. When Kentucky and Delaware rejected it, backers realized that without approval from at least four former Confederate states, the amendment would fail. Lincoln's successor, President Andrew Johnson, made ratification of the Thirteenth Amendment a condition for southern states to rejoin the Union. Under those terms, all the former Confederate states except Mississippi accepted the Thirteenth Amendment, and by the end of 1865 the amendment had become part of the Constitution and slavery had been prohibited in the United States.

Amendment XIV [1868]

Section 1.   All persons born or naturalized in the United States, and subject to the jurisdiction thereof, are citizens of the United States and of the State wherein they reside. No State shall make or enforce any law which shall abridge the privileges or immunities of citizens of the United States; nor shall any State deprive any person of life, liberty, or property, without due process of law; nor deny to any person within its jurisdiction the equal protection of the laws.

Section 2.   Representatives shall be apportioned among the several States according to their respective numbers, counting the whole number of persons in each State, excluding Indians not taxed. But when the right to vote at any election for the choice of electors for President and Vice-President of the United States, Representatives in Congress, the Executive and Judicial officers of a State, or the members of the Legislature thereof, is denied to any of the male inhabitants of such State, being twenty-one years of age and citizens of the United States, or in any way abridged, except for participation in rebellion, or other crime, the basis of representation therein shall be reduced in the proportion which the number of such male citizens shall bear to the whole number of male citizens twenty-one years of age in such State.

Section 3.   No person shall be a Senator or Representative in Congress, or Elector of President and Vice-President, or hold any office, civil or military, under the United States, or under any State, who, having previously taken an oath, as a member of Congress, or as an officer of the United States, or as a member of any State legislature, or as an executive or judicial officer of any State, to support the Constitution of the United States, shall have engaged in insurrection or rebellion against the same, or given aid or comfort to the enemies thereof. Congress may, by a vote of two-thirds of each house, remove such disability.

Section 4.   The validity of the public debt of the United States, authorized by law, including debts incurred for payment of pensions and bounties for services in suppressing insurrection or rebellion, shall not be questioned. But neither the United States nor any State shall assume or pay any debt or obligation incurred in aid of insurrection or rebellion against the United States, or any claim for the loss or emancipation of any slave; but all such debts, obligations, and claims shall be held illegal and void.

Section 5. The Congress shall have power to enforce, by appropriate legislation, the provisions of this article.

• • •

Without Lincoln's leadership in the reconstruction of the nation following the Civil War, it soon became clear that the Thirteenth Amendment needed additional constitutional support. Less than a year after Lincoln's assassination, Andrew Johnson was ready to bring the former Confederate states back into the Union with few changes in their governments or politics. Anxious Republicans drafted the Fourteenth Amendment to prevent that from happening. The most important provisions of this complex amendment made all native-born or naturalized persons American citizens and prohibited states from abridging the "privileges or immunities" of citizens; depriving them of "life, liberty, or property, without due process of law"; and denying them "equal protection of the laws." In essence, it made all former slaves citizens and protected the rights of all citizens against violation by their own state governments.

As occurred in the case of the Thirteenth Amendment, former Confederate states were forced to ratify the amendment as a condition of representation in the House and the Senate. The intentions of the Fourteenth Amendment, and how those intentions should be enforced, have been the most debated point of constitutional history. The terms due process *and* equal protection *have been especially troublesome. Was the amendment designed to outlaw racial segregation? Or was the goal simply to prevent the leaders of the rebellious South from gaining political power?*

The framers of the Fourteenth Amendment hoped Section 2 would produce black voters who would increase the power of the Republican Party. The federal government, however, never used its power to punish states for denying blacks their right to vote. Although the Fourteenth Amendment had an immediate impact in giving black Americans citizenship, it did nothing to protect blacks from the vengeance of whites once Reconstruction ended. In the late nineteenth and early twentieth centuries, Section 1 of the Fourteenth Amendment was often used to protect business interests and strike down laws protecting workers on the grounds that the rights of "persons," that is, corporations, were protected by "due process." More recently, the Fourteenth Amendment has been used to justify school desegregation and affirmative action programs, as well as to dismantle such programs.

Amendment XV [1870]

Section 1. The right of citizens of the United States to vote shall not be denied or abridged by the United States or by any State on account of race, color, or previous condition of servitude—

Section 2. The Congress shall have power to enforce this article by appropriate legislation.

• • •

The Fifteenth Amendment was the last major piece of Reconstruction legislation. Although earlier Reconstruction acts had already required black suffrage in the South, the Fifteenth Amendment extended black voting rights to the entire nation. Some Republicans felt morally obligated to do away with the double standard between the North and South because many northern states had stubbornly refused to enfranchise blacks. Others believed that the freedman's ballot required the extra protection of a constitutional amendment to shield it from white counterattack. But partisan advantage also played an important role in the amendment's passage because Republicans hoped that by giving the ballot to northern blacks, they could lessen their party's political vulnerability.

Many women's rights advocates had fought for the amendment. They had felt betrayed by the inclusion of the word male *in Section 2 of the Fourteenth Amendment and were further angered when the proposed Fifteenth Amendment failed to prohibit denial of the right to vote on the grounds of sex as well as "race, color, or previous condition of servitude." In this amendment, for the first time, the federal government claimed the power to regulate the franchise, or vote. It was also the first time the Constitution placed limits on the power of the states to regulate access to the franchise. Although ratified in 1870, however, the amendment was not enforced until the twentieth century.*

The Progressive Amendments
(Sixteenth–Nineteenth Amendments)

No amendments were added to the Constitution between the Civil War and the Progressive Era. America was changing, however, in fundamental ways. The rapid industrialization of the United States after the Civil War led to many social and economic problems. Hundreds of amendments were proposed, but none received enough support in Congress to be sent to the states. Some scholars believe that regional differences and rivalries were so strong during this period that it was almost impossible to gain a consensus on a constitutional amendment. During the Progressive Era, however, the Constitution was amended four times in seven years.

Amendment XVI [1913]

The Congress shall have power to lay and collect taxes on incomes, from whatever source derived, without apportionment among the several States, and without regard to any census or enumeration.

• • •

Until passage of the Sixteenth Amendment, most of the money used to run the federal government came from customs duties and taxes on specific items, such as liquor. During the Civil War the federal government taxed incomes as an emergency measure. Pressure to enact an income tax came from those who were concerned about the growing gap between rich and poor in the United States. The Populist Party began campaigning for a graduated income tax in 1892, and support continued to grow. By 1909 thirty-three proposed income tax amendments had been presented in Congress, but lobbying by corporate and other special interests had defeated them all. In June 1909 the growing pressure for an income tax, which had been endorsed by Presidents Roosevelt and Taft, finally pushed an amendment through the Senate. The required thirty-six states had ratified the amendment by February 1913.

Amendment XVII [1913]

Section 1. The Senate of the United States shall be composed of two Senators from each State, elected by the people thereof, for six years; and each Senator shall have one vote. The electors in each State shall have the qualifications requisite for electors of [voters for] the most numerous branch of the State legislatures.

Section 2. When vacancies happen in the representation of any State in the Senate, the executive authority of such State shall issue writs of election to fill such vacancies: Provided, that the Legislature of any State may empower the executive thereof to make temporary appointments until the people fill the vacancies by election as the Legislature may direct.

Section 3. This amendment shall not be so construed as to affect the election or term of any Senator chosen before it becomes valid as part of the Constitution.

• • •

The framers of the Constitution saw the members of the House as the representatives of the people and the members of the Senate as the representatives of the states. Originally, senators were to be chosen by the state legislators. According to reform advocates, however, the growth of private industry and transportation conglomerates during the late nineteenth century had created a network of corruption in which wealth and power were exchanged for influence and votes in the Senate. Senator Nelson Aldrich, who represented Rhode Island in this period, for example, was known as "the senator from Standard Oil" because of his open support of special business interests.

Efforts to amend the Constitution to allow direct election of senators had begun in 1826, but because any proposal had to be approved by the Senate, reform seemed impossible. Progressives tried to gain influence in the Senate by instituting party caucuses and primary elections, which gave citizens the chance to express their choice of a senator who could then be officially elected by the state legislature. By 1910 fourteen of the country's thirty senators received popular votes through a state primary before the state legislature made its selection. Despairing of getting a proposal through the Senate, supporters of a direct-election amendment had begun in 1893 to seek a convention of representatives from two-thirds of the states to propose an amendment that could then be ratified. By 1905 thirty-one of forty-five states had endorsed such an amendment. Finally, in 1911, despite extraordinary opposition, a proposed amendment passed the Senate; by 1913 it had been ratified.

Amendment XVIII [1919; repealed 1933 by Amendment XXI]

Section 1. After one year from the ratification of this article the manufacture, sale, or transportation of intoxicating liquors within, the importation thereof into, or the exportation thereof from the United States and all territory subject to the jurisdiction thereof, for beverage purposes, is hereby prohibited.

Section 2. The Congress and the several States shall have concurrent power to enforce this article by appropriate legislation.

Section 3. This article shall be inoperative unless it shall have been ratified as an amendment to the Constitution by the legislatures of the several States, as provided by the Constitution, within seven years from the date of the submission thereof to the States by the Congress.

• • •

The Prohibition Party, formed in 1869, began calling for a constitutional amendment to outlaw alcoholic beverages in 1872. A prohibition amendment was first proposed in the Senate in 1876 and was revived eighteen times before 1913. Between 1913 and 1919 another thirty-nine attempts were made to prohibit liquor in the United States through a constitutional amendment. Prohibition became a key element of the Progressive agenda as reformers linked alcohol and drunkenness to numerous social problems, including the corruption of immigrant voters. Whereas opponents of such an amendment argued that it was undemocratic, supporters claimed that their efforts had widespread public support. The admission of twelve "dry" western states to the Union in the early twentieth century and the spirit of sacrifice during World War I laid the groundwork for passage and ratification of the Eighteenth Amendment in 1919. Opponents added a time limit to the amendment in the hope that they could thereby block ratification, but this effort failed. (See also Amendment XXI.)

Amendment XIX [1920]

Section 1. The right of citizens of the United States to vote shall not be denied or abridged by the United States or by any State on account of sex.

Section 2. Congress shall have the power to enforce this article by appropriate legislation.

• • •

Advocates of women's rights tried and failed to link woman suffrage to the Fourteenth and Fifteenth Amendments. Nonetheless, the effort for woman suffrage continued. Between 1878 and 1912 at least one and sometimes as many as four proposed amendments were introduced in Congress each year to grant women the right to vote. Although over time women won very limited voting rights in some states, at both the state and federal levels opposition to an amendment for woman suffrage remained very strong. President Woodrow Wilson and other officials felt that the federal government should not interfere with the power of the states in this matter. And many people were concerned that giving women the vote would result in their abandoning traditional gender roles. In 1919, following a protracted and often bitter campaign of protest in which women went on hunger strikes and chained themselves to fences, an amendment was introduced with the backing of President Wilson. It narrowly passed the Senate (after efforts to limit the suffrage to white women failed) and was adopted in 1920 after Tennessee became the thirty-sixth state to ratify it.

Unratified Amendment

Child Labor Amendment
(proposed by Congress June 2, 1924)

Section 1.   The Congress shall have power to limit, regulate, and prohibit the labor of persons under eighteen years of age.

Section 2.   The power of the several States is unimpaired by this article except that the operation of State laws shall be suspended to the extent necessary to give effect to legislation enacted by Congress.

• • •

Throughout the late nineteenth and early twentieth centuries, alarm over the condition of child workers grew. Opponents of child labor argued that children worked in dangerous and unhealthy conditions, that they took jobs from adult workers, that they depressed wages in certain industries, and that states that allowed child labor had an economic advantage over those that did not. Defenders of child labor claimed that children provided needed income in many families, that working at a young age helped to develop character, and that the effort to prohibit the practice constituted an invasion of family privacy.

In 1916 Congress passed a law that made it illegal to sell through interstate commerce goods made by children. The Supreme Court, however, ruled that the law violated the limits on the power of Congress to regulate interstate commerce. Congress then tried to penalize industries that used child labor by taxing such goods. This measure was also thrown out by the courts. In response, reformers set out to amend the Constitution. The proposed amendment was ratified by twenty-eight states, but by 1925 thirteen states had rejected it. Passage of the Fair Labor Standards Act in 1938, which was upheld by the Supreme Court in 1941, made the amendment irrelevant.

Amendment XX [1933]

Section 1.   The terms of the President and Vice-President shall end at noon on the 20th day of January, and the terms of Senators and Representatives at noon on the 3rd day of January, of the years in which such terms would have ended if this article had not been ratified; and the terms of their successors shall then begin.

Section 2.   The Congress shall assemble at least once in every year, and such meeting shall begin at noon on the 3rd day of January, unless they shall by law appoint a different day.

Section 3.   If, at the time fixed for the beginning of the term of the President, the President-elect shall have died, the Vice-President-elect shall become President. If a President shall not have been chosen before the time fixed for the beginning of his term, or if the President-elect shall have failed to qualify, then the Vice-President-elect shall act as President until a President shall have qualified; and the Congress may by law provide for the case wherein neither a President-elect nor a Vice-President-elect shall have qualified, declaring who shall then act as President, or the manner in which one who is to act shall be selected, and such person shall act accordingly until a President or Vice-President shall have qualified.

Section 4.   The Congress may by law provide for the case of the death of any of the persons from whom the House of Representatives may choose a President whenever the right of choice shall have devolved upon them, and for the case of the death of any of the persons from whom the Senate may choose a Vice-President whenever the right of choice shall have devolved upon them.

Section 5.   Sections 1 and 2 shall take effect on the 15th day of October following the ratification of this article.

Section 6.   This article shall be inoperative unless it shall have been ratified as an amendment to the Constitution by the Legislatures of three-fourths of the several States within seven years from the date of its submission.

• • •

Until 1933, presidents took office on March 4. Because elections are held in early November and electoral votes are counted in mid-December, this meant that more than three months passed between the time a new president was elected and when he took office. Moving the inauguration to January shortened the transition period and allowed Congress to begin its term closer to the time of the president's inauguration. Although this seems like a minor change, an amendment was required because the Constitution specifies terms of office. This amendment also deals with questions of succession in the event that a president- or vice-president-elect dies before assuming office. Section 3 also clarifies a method for resolving a deadlock in the electoral college.

Amendment XXI [1933]

Section 1.   The eighteenth article of amendment to the Constitution of the United States is hereby repealed.

Section 2.   The transportation or importation into any State, Territory, or Possession of the United States for delivery or use therein of intoxicating liquors, in violation of the laws thereof, is hereby prohibited.

Section 3.   This article shall be inoperative unless it shall have been ratified as an amendment to the Constitution by conventions in the several States, as provided in the Constitution, within seven years from the date of the submission thereof to the States by the Congress.

• • •

Widespread violation of the Volstead Act, the law enacted to enforce prohibition, made the United States a nation of lawbreakers. Prohibition caused more problems than it solved by encouraging crime, bribery, and corruption. Further, a coalition of liquor and beer manufacturers, personal liberty advocates, and constitutional scholars joined forces to challenge the amendment. By 1929 thirty proposed repeal amendments had been introduced in Congress, and the Democratic Party made repeal part of its platform in the 1932 presidential campaign. The Twenty-first Amendment was proposed in February 1933 and ratified less than a year later. The failure of the effort to enforce prohibition through a constitutional amendment has often been cited by opponents of subsequent efforts to shape public virtue and private morality.

Amendment XXII [1951]

Section 1. No person shall be elected to the office of the President more than twice, and no person who has held the office of President, or acted as President, for more than two years of a term to which some other person was elected President shall be elected to the office of President more than once. But this article shall not apply to any person holding the office of President when this Article was proposed by the Congress, and shall not prevent any person who may be holding the office of President, or acting as President, during the term within which this Article becomes operative from holding the office of President or acting as President during the remainder of such term.

Section 2. This article shall be inoperative unless it shall have been ratified as an amendment to the Constitution by the legislatures of three-fourths of the several States within seven years from the date of its submission to the States by the Congress.

• • •

George Washington's refusal to seek a third term of office set a precedent that stood until 1912, when former president Theodore Roosevelt sought, without success, another term as an independent candidate. Democrat Franklin Roosevelt was the only president to seek and win a fourth term, though he did so amid great controversy. Roosevelt died in April 1945, a few months after the beginning of his fourth term. In 1946 Republicans won control of the House and the Senate, and early in 1947 a proposal for an amendment to limit future presidents to two four-year terms was offered to the states for ratification. Democratic critics of the Twenty-second Amendment charged that it was a partisan posthumous jab at Roosevelt.

Since the Twenty-second Amendment was adopted, two of the three presidents who might have been able to seek a third term, had it not existed, were Republicans Dwight Eisenhower and Ronald Reagan. Since 1826, Congress has entertained 160 proposed amendments to limit the president to one six-year term. Such amendments have been backed by fifteen presidents, including Gerald Ford and Jimmy Carter.

Amendment XXIII [1961]

Section 1. The District constituting the seat of Government of the United States shall appoint in such manner as the Congress may direct: A number of electors of President and Vice-President equal to the whole number of Senators and Representatives in Congress to which the District would be entitled if it were a State, but in no event more than the least populous State; they shall be in addition to those appointed by the States, but they shall be considered for the purposes of the election of President and Vice-President, to be electors appointed by a State; and they shall meet in the District and perform such duties as provided by the twelfth article of amendment.

Section 2. The Congress shall have the power to enforce this article by appropriate legislation.

• • •

When Washington, D.C., was established as a federal district, no one expected that a significant number of people would make it their permanent and primary residence. A proposal to allow citizens of the district to vote in presidential elections was approved by Congress in June 1960 and was ratified on March 29, 1961.

Amendment XXIV [1964]

Section 1. The right of citizens of the United States to vote in any primary or other election for President or Vice-President, for electors for President or Vice-President, or for Senator or Representative in Congress, shall not be denied or abridged by the United States or any State by reason of failure to pay any poll tax or other tax.

Section 2. The Congress shall have the power to enforce this article by appropriate legislation.

• • •

In the colonial and Revolutionary eras, financial independence was seen as necessary to political independence, and the poll tax was used as a requirement for voting. By the twentieth century, however, the poll tax was used mostly to bar poor people, especially southern blacks, from voting. Although conservatives complained that the amendment interfered with states' rights, liberals thought that the amendment did not go far enough because it barred the poll tax only in national elections and not in state or local elections. The amendment was ratified in 1964, however, and two years later the Supreme Court ruled that poll taxes in state and local elections also violated the equal protection clause of the Fourteenth Amendment.

Amendment XXV [1967]

Section 1. In case of the removal of the President from office or of his death or resignation, the Vice-President shall become President.

Section 2. Whenever there is a vacancy in the office of the Vice-President, the President shall nominate a Vice-President who shall take office upon confirmation by a majority vote of both Houses of Congress.

Section 3. Whenever the President transmits to the President pro tempore of the Senate and the Speaker of the House of Representatives his written declaration that he is unable to discharge the powers and duties of his office, and until he transmits to them a written declaration to the contrary, such powers and duties shall be discharged by the Vice-President as Acting President.

Section 4. Whenever the Vice-President and a majority of either the principal officers of the executive departments or of such other body as Congress may by law provide, transmit to the President pro tempore of the Senate and the Speaker of the House of Representatives their written declaration that the President is unable to discharge the powers and duties of his office, the Vice-President shall immediately assume the powers and duties of the office as Acting President.

Thereafter, when the President transmits to the President pro tempore of the Senate and the Speaker of the House of Representatives his written declaration that no inability exists, he shall resume the powers and duties of his office unless the Vice-President and a majority of either the principal officers of the executive department[s] or of such other body as Congress may by law provide, transmit within four days to the President pro tempore of the Senate and the Speaker of the House of Representatives their written declaration that the President is unable to discharge the powers and duties of his office. Thereupon Congress shall decide the issue, assembling within forty-eight hours for that purpose if not in session. If the Congress, within twenty-one days after receipt of the latter written declaration, or, if Congress is not in session, within twenty-one days after Congress is required to assemble, determines by two-thirds vote of both Houses that the President is unable to discharge the powers and duties of his office, the Vice-President shall continue to discharge the same as Acting President; otherwise, the President shall resume the powers and duties of his office.

• • •

The framers of the Constitution established the office of vice president because someone was needed to preside over the Senate. The first president to die in office was William Henry Harrison, in 1841. Vice President John Tyler had himself sworn in as president, setting a precedent that was followed when seven later presidents died in office. The assassination of President James A. Garfield in 1881 posed a new problem, however. After he was shot, the president was incapacitated for two months before he died; he was unable to lead the country, and his vice president, Chester A. Arthur, was unable to assume leadership. Efforts to resolve questions of succession in the event of a presidential disability thus began with the death of Garfield.

In 1963 the assassination of President John F. Kennedy galvanized Congress to action. Vice President Lyndon Johnson was a chain-smoker with a history of heart trouble. According to the 1947 Presidential Succession Act, the two men who stood in line to succeed him were the seventy-two-year-old Speaker of the House and the eighty-six-year-old president of the Senate. There were serious concerns that any of these men might become incapacitated while serving as chief executive. The first time the Twenty-fifth Amendment was used, however, was not in the case of presidential death or illness, but during the Watergate crisis. When Vice President Spiro T. Agnew was forced to resign following allegations of bribery and tax violations, President Richard M. Nixon appointed House Minority Leader Gerald R. Ford vice president. Ford became president following Nixon's resignation eight months later and named Nelson A. Rockefeller as his vice president. Thus, for more than two years, the two highest offices in the country were held by people who had not been elected to them.

Amendment XXVI [1971]

Section 1.   The right of citizens of the United States, who are eighteen years of age or older, to vote shall not be denied or abridged by the United States or by any State on account of age.

Section 2.   The Congress shall have power to enforce this article by appropriate legislation.

• • •

Efforts to lower the voting age from twenty-one to eighteen began during World War II. Recognizing that those who were old enough to fight a war should have some say in the government policies that involved them in the war, Presidents Eisenhower, Johnson, and Nixon endorsed the idea. In 1970 the combined pressure of the antiwar movement and the demographic pressure of the baby-boom generation led to a Voting Rights Act lowering the voting age in federal, state, and local elections.

In Oregon v. Mitchell (1970), the state of Oregon challenged the right of Congress to determine the age at which people could vote in state or local elections. The Supreme Court agreed with Oregon. Because the Voting Rights Act was ruled unconstitutional, the Constitution had to be amended to allow passage of a law that would lower the voting age. The amendment was ratified in a little more than three months, making it the most rapidly ratified amendment in U.S. history.

Unratified Amendment

Equal Rights Amendment (proposed by Congress March 22, 1972; seven-year deadline for ratification extended, June 30, 1982)

Section 1.   Equality of rights under the law shall not be denied or abridged by the United States or by any State on account of sex.

Section 2.   The Congress shall have the power to enforce, by appropriate legislation, the provisions of this article.

Section 3.   This amendment shall take effect two years after the date of ratification.

• • •

In 1923, soon after women had won the right to vote, Alice Paul, a leading activist in the woman suffrage movement, proposed an amendment requiring equal treatment of men and women. Opponents of the proposal argued that such an amendment would invalidate laws that protected women and would make women subject to the military draft. After the 1964 Civil Rights Act was adopted, protective workplace legislation was removed anyway.

The renewal of the women's movement, as a by-product of the civil rights and antiwar movements, led to a revival of the Equal Rights Amendment (ERA) in Congress. Disagreements over language held up congressional passage of the proposed amendment, but on March 22, 1972, the Senate approved the ERA by a vote of 84 to 8, and it was sent to the states. Six states ratified the amendment within two days, and by the middle of 1973 the amendment seemed well on its way to adoption, with thirty of the needed thirty-eight states having ratified it. In the mid-1970s, however, a powerful "Stop ERA" campaign developed. The campaign portrayed the ERA as a threat to "family values" and traditional relationships between men and women. Although thirty-five states ratified the ERA, five of those state legislatures voted to rescind ratification, and the amendment was never adopted.

Unratified Amendment

D.C. Statehood Amendment
(proposed by Congress August 22, 1978)

Section 1.   For purposes of representation in the Congress, election of the President and Vice President, and article V of this Constitution, the District constituting the seat of government of the United States shall be treated as though it were a State.

Section 2.   The exercise of the rights and powers conferred under this article shall be by the people of the District constituting the seat of government, and as shall be provided by Congress.

Section 3.   The twenty-third article of amendment to the Constitution of the United States is hereby repealed.

Section 4.   This article shall be inoperative, unless it shall have been ratified as an amendment to the Constitution by the legislatures of three-fourths of the several states within seven years from the date of its submission.

• • •

The 1961 ratification of the Twenty-third Amendment, giving residents of the District of Columbia the right to vote for a president and vice president, inspired an effort to give residents of the district full voting rights. In 1966 President Lyndon Johnson appointed a mayor and city council; in 1971 D.C. residents were allowed to name a nonvoting delegate to the House; and in 1981 residents were allowed to elect the mayor and city council. Congress retained the right to overrule laws that might affect commuters, the height of federal buildings, and selection of judges and prosecutors. The district's nonvoting delegate to Congress, Walter Fauntroy, lobbied fiercely for a congressional amendment granting statehood to the district. In 1978 a proposed amendment was approved and sent to the states. A number of states quickly ratified the amendment, but, like the ERA, the D.C. Statehood Amendment ran into trouble. Opponents argued that Section 2 created a separate category of "nominal" statehood. They argued that the federal district should be eliminated and that the territory should be reabsorbed into the state of Maryland. Most scholars believe that the fears of Republicans that the predominantly black population of the city would consistently elect Democratic senators constituted a major factor leading to the defeat of the amendment.

Amendment XXVII [1992]

No law varying the compensation for the services of the Senators and Representatives, shall take effect, until an election of Representatives shall have intervened.

• • •

Whereas the Twenty-sixth Amendment was the most rapidly ratified amendment in U.S. history, the Twenty-seventh Amendment had the longest journey to ratification. First proposed by James Madison in 1789 as part of the package that included the Bill of Rights, this amendment had been ratified by only six states by 1791. In 1873, however, it was ratified by Ohio to protest a massive retroactive salary increase by the federal government. Unlike later proposed amendments, this one came with no time limit on ratification. In the early 1980s Gregory D. Watson, a University of Texas economics major, discovered the "lost" amendment and began a single-handed campaign to get state legislators to introduce it for ratification. In 1983 it was accepted by Maine. In 1984 it passed the Colorado legislature. Ratifications trickled in slowly until May 1992, when Michigan and New Jersey became the thirty-eighth and thirty-ninth states, respectively, to ratify. This amendment prevents members of Congress from raising their own salaries without giving voters a chance to vote them out of office before they can benefit from the raises.

The American Nation

Admission of States into the Union

State	Date of Admission	State	Date of Admission	State	Date of Admission
1. Delaware	December 7, 1787	18. Louisiana	April 30, 1812	35. West Virginia	June 20, 1863
2. Pennsylvania	December 12, 1787	19. Indiana	December 11, 1816	36. Nevada	October 31, 1864
3. New Jersey	December 18, 1787	20. Mississippi	December 10, 1817	37. Nebraska	March 1, 1867
4. Georgia	January 2, 1788	21. Illinois	December 3, 1818	38. Colorado	August 1, 1876
5. Connecticut	January 9, 1788	22. Alabama	December 14, 1819	39. North Dakota	November 2, 1889
6. Massachusetts	February 6, 1788	23. Maine	March 15, 1820	40. South Dakota	November 2, 1889
7. Maryland	April 28, 1788	24. Missouri	August 10, 1821	41. Montana	November 8, 1889
8. South Carolina	May 23, 1788	25. Arkansas	June 15, 1836	42. Washington	November 11, 1889
9. New Hampshire	June 21, 1788	26. Michigan	January 26, 1837	43. Idaho	July 3, 1890
10. Virginia	June 25, 1788	27. Florida	March 3, 1845	44. Wyoming	July 10, 1890
11. New York	July 26, 1788	28. Texas	December 29, 1845	45. Utah	January 4, 1896
12. North Carolina	November 21, 1789	29. Iowa	December 28, 1846	46. Oklahoma	November 16, 1907
13. Rhode Island	May 29, 1790	30. Wisconsin	May 29, 1848	47. New Mexico	January 6, 1912
14. Vermont	March 4, 1791	31. California	September 9, 1850	48. Arizona	February 14, 1912
15. Kentucky	June 1, 1792	32. Minnesota	May 11, 1858	49. Alaska	January 3, 1959
16. Tennessee	June 1, 1796	33. Oregon	February 14, 1859	50. Hawaii	August 21, 1959
17. Ohio	March 1, 1803	34. Kansas	January 29, 1861		

Territorial Expansion

Territory	Date Acquired	Square Miles	How Acquired
Original states and territories	1783	888,685	Treaty of Paris
Louisiana Purchase	1803	827,192	Purchased from France
Florida	1819	72,003	Adams-Onís Treaty
Texas	1845	390,143	Annexation of independent country
Oregon	1846	285,580	Oregon Boundary Treaty
Mexican cession	1848	529,017	Treaty of Guadalupe Hidalgo
Gadsden Purchase	1853	29,640	Purchased from Mexico
Midway Islands	1867	2	Annexation of uninhabited islands
Alaska	1867	589,757	Purchased from Russia
Hawaii	1898	6,450	Annexation of independent country
Wake Island	1898	3	Annexation of uninhabited island
Puerto Rico	1899	3,435	Treaty of Paris
Guam	1899	212	Treaty of Paris
The Philippines	1899–1946	115,600	Treaty of Paris; granted independence
American Samoa	1900	76	Treaty with Germany and Great Britain
Panama Canal Zone	1904–1978	553	Hay–Bunau-Varilla Treaty
U.S. Virgin Islands	1917	133	Purchased from Denmark
Trust Territory of the Pacific Islands*	1947	717	United Nations Trusteeship

*A number of these islands have recently been granted independence: Federated States of Micronesia, 1990; Marshall Islands, 1991; Palau, 1994.

Presidential Elections

Year	Candidates	Parties	Percentage of Popular Vote	Electoral Vote	Percentage of Voter Participation
1789	**George Washington**	No party designations	*	69	
	John Adams†			34	
	Other candidates			35	
1792	**George Washington**	No party designations		132	
	John Adams			77	
	George Clinton			50	
	Other candidates			5	
1796	**John Adams**	Federalist		71	
	Thomas Jefferson	Democratic-Republican		68	
	Thomas Pinckney	Federalist		59	
	Aaron Burr	Democratic-Republican		30	
	Other candidates			48	
1800	**Thomas Jefferson**	Democratic-Republican		73	
	Aaron Burr	Democratic-Republican		73	
	John Adams	Federalist		65	
	Charles C. Pinckney	Federalist		64	
	John Jay	Federalist		1	
1804	**Thomas Jefferson**	Democratic-Republican		162	
	Charles C. Pinckney	Federalist		14	
1808	**James Madison**	Democratic-Republican		122	
	Charles C. Pinckney	Federalist		47	
	George Clinton	Democratic-Republican		6	
1812	**James Madison**	Democratic-Republican		128	
	De Witt Clinton	Federalist		89	
1816	**James Monroe**	Democratic-Republican		183	
	Rufus King	Federalist		34	
1820	**James Monroe**	Democratic-Republican		231	
	John Quincy Adams	Independent Republican		1	
1824	**John Quincy Adams**	Democratic-Republican	30.5	84	26.9
	Andrew Jackson	Democratic-Republican	43.1	99	
	Henry Clay	Democratic-Republican	13.2	37	
	William H. Crawford	Democratic-Republican	13.1	41	
1828	**Andrew Jackson**	Democratic	56.0	178	57.6
	John Quincy Adams	National Republican	44.0	83	
1832	**Andrew Jackson**	Democratic	54.5	219	55.4
	Henry Clay	National Republican	37.5	49	
	William Wirt	Anti-Masonic	8.0	7	
	John Floyd	Democratic	‡	11	
1836	**Martin Van Buren**	Democratic	50.9	170	57.8
	William H. Harrison	Whig		73	
	Hugh L. White	Whig		26	
	Daniel Webster	Whig	49.1	14	
	W. P. Mangum	Whig		11	
1840	**William H. Harrison**	Whig	53.1	234	80.2
	Martin Van Buren	Democratic	46.9	60	
1844	**James K. Polk**	Democratic	49.6	170	78.9
	Henry Clay	Whig	48.1	105	
	James G. Birney	Liberty	2.3		

(*continued on next page*)

*Prior to 1824, most presidential electors were chosen by state legislators rather than by popular vote.

†Before the Twelfth Amendment was passed in 1804, the electoral college voted for two presidential candidates; the runner-up became vice-president.

‡Percentages below 2.5 have been omitted. Hence the percentage of popular vote might not total 100 percent.

Year	Candidates	Parties	Percentage of Popular Vote	Electoral Vote	Percentage of Voter Participation
1848	**Zachary Taylor**	Whig	47.4	163	72.7
	Lewis Cass	Democratic	42.5	127	
	Martin Van Buren	Free Soil	10.1		
1852	**Franklin Pierce**	Democratic	50.9	254	69.6
	Winfield Scott	Whig	44.1	42	
	John P. Hale	Free Soil	5.0		
1856	**James Buchanan**	Democratic	45.3	174	78.9
	John C. Frémont	Republican	33.1	114	
	Millard Fillmore	American	21.6	8	
1860	**Abraham Lincoln**	Republican	39.8	180	81.2
	Stephen A. Douglas	Democratic	29.5	12	
	John C. Breckinridge	Democratic	18.1	72	
	John Bell	Constitutional Union	12.6	39	
1864	**Abraham Lincoln**	Republican	55.0	212	73.8
	George B. McClellan	Democratic	45.0	21	
1868	**Ulysses S. Grant**	Republican	52.7	214	78.1
	Horatio Seymour	Democratic	47.3	80	
1872	**Ulysses S. Grant**	Republican	55.6	286	71.3
	Horace Greeley	Democratic	43.9		
1876	**Rutherford B. Hayes**	Republican	48.0	185	81.8
	Samuel J. Tilden	Democratic	51.0	184	
1880	**James A. Garfield**	Republican	48.5	214	79.4
	Winfield S. Hancock	Democratic	48.1	155	
	James B. Weaver	Greenback-Labor	3.4		
1884	**Grover Cleveland**	Democratic	48.5	219	77.5
	James G. Blaine	Republican	48.2	182	
1888	**Benjamin Harrison**	Republican	47.9	233	79.3
	Grover Cleveland	Democratic	48.6	168	
1892	**Grover Cleveland**	Democratic	46.1	277	74.7
	Benjamin Harrison	Republican	43.0	145	
	James B. Weaver	People's	8.5	22	
1896	**William McKinley**	Republican	51.1	271	79.3
	William J. Bryan	Democratic	47.7	176	
1900	**William McKinley**	Republican	51.7	292	73.2
	William J. Bryan	Democratic; Populist	45.5	155	
1904	**Theodore Roosevelt**	Republican	57.4	336	65.2
	Alton B. Parker	Democratic	37.6	140	
	Eugene V. Debs	Socialist	3.0		
1908	**William H. Taft**	Republican	51.6	321	65.4
	William J. Bryan	Democratic	43.1	162	
	Eugene V. Debs	Socialist	2.8		
1912	**Woodrow Wilson**	Democratic	41.9	435	58.8
	Theodore Roosevelt	Progressive	27.4	88	
	William H. Taft	Republican	23.2	8	
	Eugene V. Debs	Socialist	6.0		
1916	**Woodrow Wilson**	Democratic	49.4	277	61.6
	Charles E. Hughes	Republican	46.2	254	
	A. L. Benson	Socialist	3.2		

(*continued on next page*)

Year	Candidates	Parties	Percentage of Popular Vote	Electoral Vote	Percentage of Voter Participation
1920	**Warren G. Harding**	Republican	60.4	404	49.2
	James M. Cox	Democratic	34.2	127	
	Eugene V. Debs	Socialist	3.4		
1924	**Calvin Coolidge**	Republican	54.0	382	48.9
	John W. Davis	Democratic	28.8	136	
	Robert M. La Follette	Progressive	16.6	13	
1928	**Herbert C. Hoover**	Republican	58.2	444	56.9
	Alfred E. Smith	Democratic	40.9	87	
1932	**Franklin D. Roosevelt**	Democratic	57.4	472	56.9
	Herbert C. Hoover	Republican	39.7	59	
1936	**Franklin D. Roosevelt**	Democratic	60.8	523	61.0
	Alfred M. Landon	Republican	36.5	8	
1940	**Franklin D. Roosevelt**	Democratic	54.8	449	62.5
	Wendell L. Willkie	Republican	44.8	82	
1944	**Franklin D. Roosevelt**	Democratic	53.5	432	55.9
	Thomas E. Dewey	Republican	46.0	99	
1948	**Harry S Truman**	Democratic	49.6	303	53.0
	Thomas E. Dewey	Republican	45.1	189	
1952	**Dwight D. Eisenhower**	Republican	55.1	442	63.3
	Adlai E. Stevenson	Democratic	44.4	89	
1956	**Dwight D. Eisenhower**	Republican	57.6	457	60.6
	Adlai E. Stevenson	Democratic	42.1	73	
1960	**John F. Kennedy**	Democratic	49.7	303	64.0
	Richard M. Nixon	Republican	49.5	219	
1964	**Lyndon B. Johnson**	Democratic	61.1	486	61.7
	Barry M. Goldwater	Republican	38.5	52	
1968	**Richard M. Nixon**	Republican	43.4	301	60.6
	Hubert H. Humphrey	Democratic	42.7	191	
	George C. Wallace	American Independent	13.5	46	
1972	**Richard M. Nixon**	Republican	60.7	520	55.5
	George S. McGovern	Democratic	37.5	17	
1976	**Jimmy Carter**	Democratic	50.1	297	54.3
	Gerald R. Ford	Republican	48.0	240	
1980	**Ronald W. Reagan**	Republican	50.7	489	53.0
	Jimmy Carter	Democratic	41.0	49	
	John B. Anderson	Independent	6.6	0	
1984	**Ronald W. Reagan**	Republican	58.4	525	52.9
	Walter F. Mondale	Democratic	41.6	13	
1988	**George H. W. Bush**	Republican	53.4	426	50.3
	Michael Dukakis	Democratic	45.6	111*	
1992	**Bill Clinton**	Democratic	43.7	370	55.1
	George H. W. Bush	Republican	38.0	168	
	H. Ross Perot	Independent	19.0	0	
1996	**Bill Clinton**	Democratic	49	379	49.0
	Robert J. Dole	Republican	41	159	
	H. Ross Perot	Reform	8	0	
2000	**George W. Bush**	Republican	47.8	271	51.3
	Albert Gore	Democratic	48.4	267	
	Ralph Nader	Green	0.4	0	

*One Dukakis elector cast a vote for Lloyd Bentsen.

Supreme Court Justices

Name	Terms of Service	Appointed by	Name	Terms of Service	Appointed by
John Jay*, N.Y.	1789–1795	Washington	Joseph McKenna, Cal.	1898–1925	McKinley
James Wilson, Pa.	1789–1798	Washington	Oliver W. Holmes, Mass.	1902–1932	T. Roosevelt
John Rutledge, S.C.	1790–1791	Washington	William R. Day, Ohio	1903–1922	T. Roosevelt
William Cushing, Mass.	1790–1810	Washington	William H. Moody, Mass.	1906–1910	T. Roosevelt
John Blair, Va.	1790–1796	Washington	Horace H. Lurton, Tenn.	1910–1914	Taft
James Iredell, N.C.	1790–1799	Washington	Charles E. Hughes, N.Y.	1910–1916	Taft
Thomas Johnson, Md.	1792–1793	Washington	**Edward D. White**, La.	1910–1921	Taft
William Paterson, N.J.	1793–1806	Washington	Willis Van Devanter, Wy.	1911–1937	Taft
John Rutledge, S.C.	1795	Washington	Joseph R. Lamar, Ga.	1911–1916	Taft
Samuel Chase, Md.	1796–1811	Washington	Mahlon Pitney, N.J.	1912–1922	Taft
Oliver Ellsworth, Conn.	1796–1800	Washington	James C. McReynolds, Tenn.	1914–1941	Wilson
Bushrod Washington, Va.	1799–1829	J. Adams	Louis D. Brandeis, Mass.	1916–1939	Wilson
Alfred Moore, N.C.	1800–1804	J. Adams	John H. Clarke, Ohio	1916–1922	Wilson
John Marshall, Va.	1801–1835	J. Adams	**William H. Taft**, Conn.	1921–1930	Harding
William Johnson, S.C.	1804–1834	Jefferson	George Sutherland, Utah	1922–1938	Harding
Brockholst Livingston, N.Y.	1807–1823	Jefferson	Pierce Butler, Minn.	1923–1939	Harding
Thomas Todd, Ky.	1807–1826	Jefferson	Edward T. Sanford, Tenn.	1923–1930	Harding
Gabriel Duvall, Md.	1811–1835	Madison	Harlan F. Stone, N.Y.	1925–1941	Coolidge
Joseph Story, Mass.	1812–1845	Madison	**Charles E. Hughes**, N.Y.	1930–1941	Hoover
Smith Thompson, N.Y.	1823–1843	Monroe	Owen J. Roberts, Pa.	1930–1945	Hoover
Robert Trimble, Ky.	1826–1828	J. Q. Adams	Benjamin N. Cardozo, N.Y.	1932–1938	Hoover
John McLean, Ohio	1830–1861	Jackson	Hugo L. Black, Ala.	1937–1971	F. Roosevelt
Henry Baldwin, Pa.	1830–1844	Jackson	Stanley F. Reed, Ky.	1938–1957	F. Roosevelt
James M. Wayne, Ga.	1835–1867	Jackson	Felix Frankfurter, Mass.	1939–1962	F. Roosevelt
Roger B. Taney, Md.	1836–1864	Jackson	William O. Douglas, Conn.	1939–1975	F. Roosevelt
Philip P. Barbour, Va.	1836–1841	Jackson	Frank Murphy, Mich.	1940–1949	F. Roosevelt
John Cartron, Tenn.	1837–1865	Van Buren	**Harlan F. Stone**, N.Y.	1941–1946	F. Roosevelt
John McKinley, Ala.	1838–1852	Van Buren	James R. Byrnes, S.C.	1941–1942	F. Roosevelt
Peter V. Daniel, Va.	1842–1860	Van Buren	Robert H. Jackson, N.Y.	1941–1954	F. Roosevelt
Samuel Nelson, N.Y.	1845–1872	Tyler	Wiley B. Rutledge, Iowa	1943–1949	F. Roosevelt
Levi Woodbury, N.H.	1845–1851	Polk	Harold H. Burton, Ohio	1945–1958	Truman
Robert C. Grier, Pa.	1846–1870	Polk	**Frederick M. Vinson**, Ky.	1946–1953	Truman
Benjamin R. Curtis, Mass.	1851–1857	Fillmore	Tom C. Clark, Texas	1949–1967	Truman
John A. Campbell, Ala.	1853–1861	Pierce	Sherman Minton, Ind.	1949–1956	Truman
Nathan Clifford, Me.	1858–1881	Buchanan	**Earl Warren**, Cal.	1953–1969	Eisenhower
Noah H. Swayne, Ohio	1862–1881	Lincoln	John Marshall Harlan, N.Y.	1955–1971	Eisenhower
Samuel F. Miller, Iowa	1862–1890	Lincoln	William J. Brennan Jr., N.J.	1956–1990	Eisenhower
David Davis, Ill.	1862–1877	Lincoln	Charles E. Whittaker, Mo.	1957–1962	Eisenhower
Stephen J. Field, Cal.	1863–1897	Lincoln	Potter Stewart, Ohio	1958–1981	Eisenhower
Salmon P. Chase, Ohio	1864–1873	Lincoln	Bryon R. White, Colo.	1962–1993	Kennedy
William Strong, Pa.	1870–1880	Grant	Arthur J. Goldberg, Ill.	1962–1965	Kennedy
Joseph P. Bradley, N.J.	1870–1892	Grant	Abe Fortas, Tenn.	1965–1969	Johnson
Ward Hunt, N.Y.	1873–1882	Grant	Thurgood Marshall, Md.	1967–1991	Johnson
Morrison R. Waite, Ohio	1874–1888	Grant	**Warren E. Burger**, Minn.	1969–1986	Nixon
John M. Harlan, Ky.	1877–1911	Hayes	Harry A. Blackmun, Minn.	1970–1994	Nixon
William B. Woods, Ga.	1881–1887	Hayes	Lewis F. Powell Jr., Va.	1971–1987	Nixon
Stanley Matthews, Ohio	1881–1889	Garfield	William H. Rehnquist, Ariz.	1971–1986	Nixon
Horace Gray, Mass.	1882–1902	Arthur	John Paul Stevens, Ill.	1975–	Ford
Samuel Blatchford, N.Y.	1882–1893	Arthur	Sandra Day O'Connor, Ariz.	1981–	Reagan
Lucius Q. C. Lamar, Miss.	1888–1893	Cleveland	**William H. Rehnquist**, Ariz.	1986–	Reagan
Melville W. Fuller, Ill.	1888–1910	Cleveland	Antonin Scalia, Va.	1986–	Reagan
David J. Brewer, Kan.	1890–1910	B. Harrison	Anthony M. Kennedy, Cal.	1988–	Reagan
Henry B. Brown, Mich.	1891–1906	B. Harrison	David H. Souter, N.H.	1990–	Bush
George Shiras Jr., Pa.	1892–1903	B. Harrison	Clarence Thomas, Ga.	1991–	Bush
Howell E. Jackson, Tenn.	1893–1895	B. Harrison	Ruth Bader Ginsburg, N.Y.	1993–	Clinton
Edward D. White, La.	1894–1910	Cleveland	Stephen G. Breyer, Mass.	1994–	Clinton
Rufus W. Peckham, N.Y.	1896–1909	Cleveland			

*Chief Justices are printed in bold type.

The American People: A Demographic Survey

A Demographic Profile of the American People							
	Life Expectancy from Birth		Average Age at First Marriage		Number of Children Under 5 (per 1,000 Women Aged 20–44)	Percentage of Women in Paid Employment	Percentage of Paid Workers Who Are Women
Year	White	Black	Men	Women			
1820					1,295	6.2	7.3
1830					1,145	6.4	7.4
1840					1,085	8.4	9.6
1850					923	10.1	10.8
1860					929	9.7	10.2
1870					839	13.7	14.8
1880					822	14.7	15.2
1890			26.1	22.0	716	18.2	17.0
1900	47.6	33.0	25.9	21.9	688	21.2	18.1
1910	50.3	35.6	25.1	21.6	643	24.8	20.0
1920	54.9	45.3	24.6	21.2	604	23.9	20.4
1930	61.4	48.1	24.3	21.3	511	24.4	21.9
1940	64.2	53.1	24.3	21.5	429	25.4	24.6
1950	69.1	60.8	22.8	20.3	589	29.1	27.8
1960	70.6	63.6	22.8	20.3	737	34.8	32.3
1970	71.7	65.3	22.5	20.6	530	43.3	38.0
1980	74.4	68.1	24.7	22.0	440	51.5	42.6
1990	76.2	71.4	26.1	23.9	377	57.4	45.2
1999	77.5	72.2	27.0	25.0	375	60.0	46.6

Source: Historical Statistics of the United States, Colonial Times to 1970 (1975); Statistical Abstract of the United States, 2001.

American Population

Year	Population	Percentage Increase	Year	Population	Percentage Increase
1610	350	—	1810	7,239,881	36.4
1620	2,300	557.1	1820	9,638,453	33.1
1630	4,600	100.0	1830	12,866,020	33.5
1640	26,600	478.3	1840	17,069,453	32.7
1650	50,400	90.8	1850	23,191,876	35.9
1660	75,100	49.0	1860	31,443,321	35.6
1670	111,900	49.0	1870	39,818,449	26.6
1680	151,500	35.4	1880	50,155,783	26.0
1690	210,400	38.9	1890	62,947,714	25.5
1700	250,900	19.2	1900	75,994,575	20.7
1710	331,700	32.2	1910	91,972,266	21.0
1720	466,200	40.5	1920	105,710,620	14.9
1730	629,400	35.0	1930	122,775,046	16.1
1740	905,600	43.9	1940	131,669,275	7.2
1750	1,170,800	29.3	1950	150,697,361	14.5
1760	1,593,600	36.1	1960	179,323,175	19.0
1770	2,148,100	34.8	1970	203,235,298	13.3
1780	2,780,400	29.4	1980	226,545,805	11.5
1790	3,929,214	41.3	1990	248,709,873	9.8
1800	5,308,483	35.1	2000	281,421,906	13.2

Note: These figures largely ignore the Native American population. Census takers never made any effort to count the Native American population that lived outside their political jurisdictions and compiled only casual and incomplete enumerations of those living within their jurisdictions until 1890. In that year the federal government attempted a full count of the Indian population: the Census found 125,719 Indians in 1890, compared with only 12,543 in 1870 and 33,985 in 1880.

Source: Historical Statistics of the United States, Colonial Times to 1970 (1975); Statistical Abstract of the United States, 2001.

White/Nonwhite Population

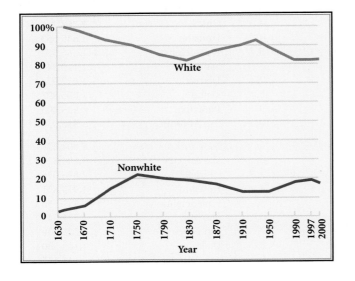

Urban/Rural Population

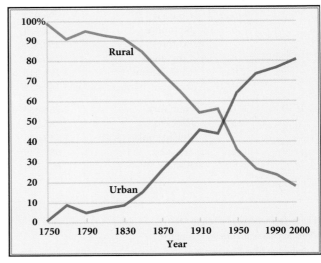

The Ten Largest Cities by Population, 1700–2000

		City	Population			City	Population
1700	1.	Boston	6,700		6.	Cleveland	560,663
	2.	New York	4,937*		7.	Baltimore	558,485
	3.	Philadelphia	4,400†		8.	Pittsburgh	533,905
1790	1.	Philadelphia	42,520		9.	Detroit	465,766
	2.	New York	33,131		10.	Buffalo	423,715
	3.	Boston	18,038	**1930**	1.	New York	6,930,446
	4.	Charleston, S.C.	16,359		2.	Chicago	3,376,438
	5.	Baltimore	13,503		3.	Philadelphia	1,950,961
	6.	Salem, Mass.	7,921		4.	Detroit	1,568,662
	7.	Newport, R.I.	6,716		5.	Los Angeles	1,238,048
	8.	Providence, R.I.	6,380		6.	Cleveland	900,429
	9.	Marblehead, Mass.	5,661		7.	St. Louis	821,960
	10.	Portsmouth, N.H.	4,720		8.	Baltimore	804,874
1830	1.	New York	197,112		9.	Boston	781,188
	2.	Philadelphia	161,410		10.	Pittsburgh	669,817
	3.	Baltimore	80,620	**1950**	1.	New York	7,891,957
	4.	Boston	61,392		2.	Chicago	3,620,962
	5.	Charleston, S.C.	30,289		3.	Philadelphia	2,071,605
	6.	New Orleans	29,737		4.	Los Angeles	1,970,358
	7.	Cincinnati	24,831		5.	Detroit	1,849,568
	8.	Albany, N.Y.	24,209		6.	Baltimore	949,708
	9.	Brooklyn, N.Y.	20,535		7.	Cleveland	914,808
	10.	Washington, D.C.	18,826		8.	St. Louis	856,796
1850	1.	New York	515,547		9.	Washington, D.C.	802,178
	2.	Philadelphia	340,045		10.	Boston	801,444
	3.	Baltimore	169,054	**1970**	1.	New York	7,895,563
	4.	Boston	136,881		2.	Chicago	3,369,357
	5.	New Orleans	116,375		3.	Los Angeles	2,811,801
	6.	Cincinnati	115,435		4.	Philadelphia	1,949,996
	7.	Brooklyn, N.Y.	96,838		5.	Detroit	1,514,063
	8.	St. Louis	77,860		6.	Houston	1,233,535
	9.	Albany, N.Y.	50,763		7.	Baltimore	905,787
	10.	Pittsburgh	46,601		8.	Dallas	844,401
1870	1.	New York	942,292		9.	Washington, D.C.	756,668
	2.	Philadelphia	674,022		10.	Cleveland	750,879
	3.	Brooklyn, N.Y.	419,921‡	**1990**	1.	New York	7,322,564
	4.	St. Louis	310,864		2.	Los Angeles	3,485,398
	5.	Chicago	298,977		3.	Chicago	2,783,726
	6.	Baltimore	267,354		4.	Houston	1,630,553
	7.	Boston	250,526		5.	Philadelphia	1,585,577
	8.	Cincinnati	216,239		6.	San Diego	1,110,549
	9.	New Orleans	191,418		7.	Detroit	1,027,974
	10.	San Francisco	149,473		8.	Dallas	1,006,877
1910	1.	New York	4,766,883		9.	Phoenix	983,403
	2.	Chicago	2,185,283		10.	San Antonio	935,933
	3.	Philadelphia	1,549,008	**2000**	1.	New York	8,008,278
	4.	St. Louis	687,029		2.	Los Angeles	3,694,820
	5.	Boston	670,585		3.	Chicago	2,896,016
					4.	Houston	1,953,631
					5.	Philadelphia	1,517,550
					6.	Phoenix	1,321,045
					7.	San Diego	1,223,400
					8.	Dallas	1,188,580
					9.	San Antonio	1,144,646
					10.	Detroit	951,270

*Figure from a census taken in 1698.

†Philadelphia figures include suburbs.

‡Annexed to New York in 1898.

Source: U.S. Census data.

Immigration by Decade

Year	Number	Percentage of Total Population	Year	Number	Percentage of Total Population
1821–1830	151,824	1.6	1921–1930	4,107,209	3.9
1831–1840	599,125	4.6	1931–1940	528,431	0.4
1841–1850	1,713,251	10.0	1941–1950	1,035,039	0.7
1851–1860	2,598,214	11.2	1951–1960	2,515,479	1.6
1861–1870	2,314,824	7.4	1961–1970	3,321,677	1.8
1871–1880	2,812,191	7.1	1971–1980	4,493,000	2.2
1881–1890	5,246,613	10.5	1981–1990	7,338,000	3.0
1891–1900	3,687,546	5.8	1991–2000	9,095,083	3.66
1901–1910	8,795,386	11.6	**Total**	**32,433,918**	
1911–1920	5,735,811	6.2			
Total	**33,654,785**		1821–2000 **GRAND TOTAL**	**66,088,703**	

Sources: U.S. Bureau of the Census, *Historical Statistics of the United States, Colonial Times to 1970* (1975), part 1,105–106; *Statistical Abstract of the United States, 2001.*

Regional Origins

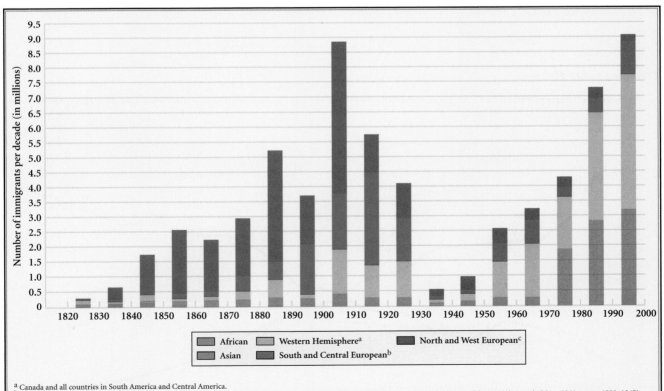

[a] Canada and all countries in South America and Central America.
[b] Italy, Spain, Portugal, Greece, Germany (Austria included, 1938–1945), Poland, Czechoslovakia (since 1920), Yugoslavia (since1920), Hungary (since 1861), Austria (since 1861, except 1938–1945), former USSR (excludes Asian USSR between 1931 and 1963), Latvia, Estonia, Lithuania, Finland, Romania, Bulgaria, Turkey (in Europe), and other European countries not classified elsewhere.
[c] Great Britain, Ireland, Norway, Sweden, Denmark, Iceland, Netherlands, Belgium, Luxembourg, Switzerland, France.
Source: Stephan Thernstrom, ed., *Harvard Encyclopedia of American Ethnic Groups* (1980), 480; U.S. Bureau of the Census, *Statistical Abstract of the United States, 1991;* U.S. Immigration and Naturalization Service, *Statistical Yearbook, 2000.*

The Labor Force (Thousands of Workers)

Year	Agriculture	Mining	Manufacturing	Construction	Trade	Other	Total
1810	1,950	11	75	—	—	294	2,330
1840	3,570	32	500	290	350	918	5,660
1850	4,520	102	1,200	410	530	1,488	8,250
1860	5,880	176	1,530	520	890	2,114	11,110
1870	6,790	180	2,470	780	1,310	1,400	12,930
1880	8,920	280	3,290	900	1,930	2,070	17,390
1890	9,960	440	4,390	1,510	2,960	4,060	23,320
1900	11,680	637	5,895	1,665	3,970	5,223	29,070
1910	11,770	1,068	8,332	1,949	5,320	9,041	37,480
1920	10,790	1,180	11,190	1,233	5,845	11,372	41,610
1930	10,560	1,009	9,884	1,988	8,122	17,267	48,830
1940	9,575	925	11,309	1,876	9,328	23,277	56,290
1950	7,870	901	15,648	3,029	12,152	25,870	65,470
1960	5,970	709	17,145	3,640	14,051	32,545	74,060
1970	3,463	516	20,746	4,818	15,008	34,127	78,678
1980	3,364	979	21,942	6,215	20,191	46,612	99,303
1990	3,223	724	21,346	7,764	24,622	60,849	118,793
1999	3,281	565	20,070	8,987	27,572	74,733	135,208

Source: *Historical Statistics of the United States, Colonial Times to 1970* (1975), 139; *Statistical Abstract of the United States, 1998*, table 675.

Changing Labor Patterns

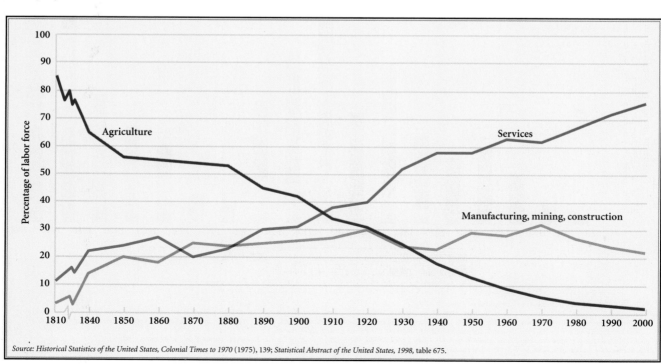

Source: *Historical Statistics of the United States, Colonial Times to 1970* (1975), 139; *Statistical Abstract of the United States, 1998*, table 675.

Birth Rate, 1820–2000

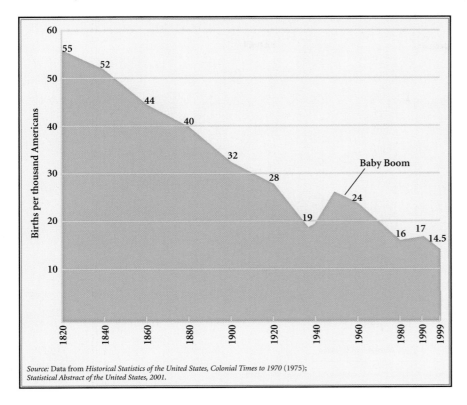

Source: Data from *Historical Statistics of the United States, Colonial Times to 1970* (1975);
Statistical Abstract of the United States, 2001.

Death Rate, 1900–2000

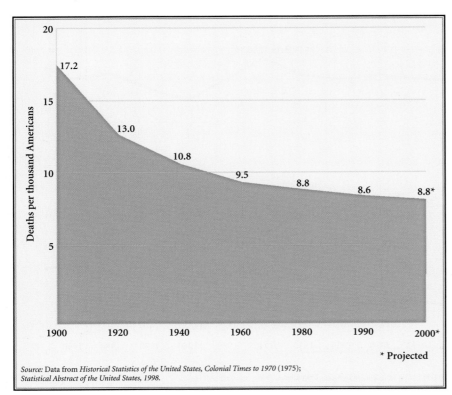

Source: Data from *Historical Statistics of the United States, Colonial Times to 1970* (1975);
Statistical Abstract of the United States, 1998.

Life Expectancy (at birth), 1900–2000

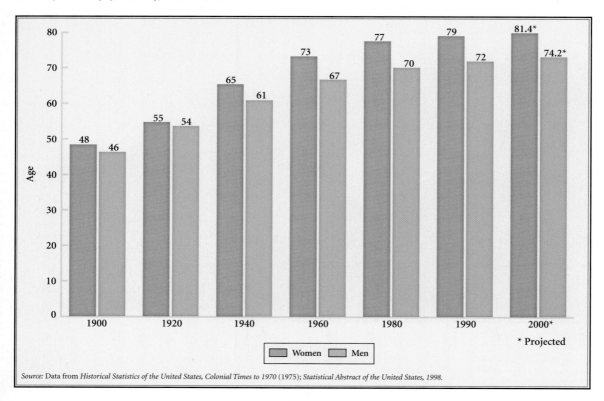

Source: Data from *Historical Statistics of the United States, Colonial Times to 1970* (1975); *Statistical Abstract of the United States, 1998.*

The Aging of the U.S. Population, 1850–1999

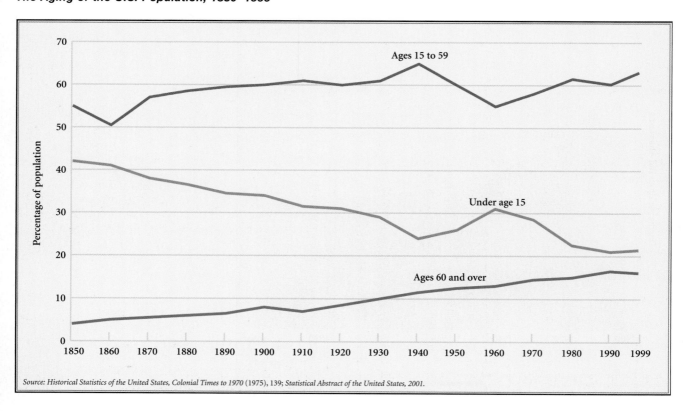

Source: *Historical Statistics of the United States, Colonial Times to 1970* (1975), 139; *Statistical Abstract of the United States, 2001.*

The American Government and Economy

The Growth of the Federal Government

| Year | Employees (millions) | | Receipts and Outlays ($ millions) | |
	Civilian	Military	Receipts	Outlays
1900	0.23	0.12	567	521
1910	0.38	0.13	676	694
1920	0.65	0.34	6,649	6,358
1930	0.61	0.25	4,058	3,320
1940	1.04	0.45	6,900	9,600
1950	1.96	1.46	40,900	43,100
1960	2.38	2.47	92,500	92,200
1970	3.00	3.06	193,700	196,600
1980	2.99	2.05	517,112	590,920
1990	3.13	2.07	1,031,321	1,252,705
2000	2.88	1.38	2,025,200	1,788,800

Source: Statistical Profile of the United States, 1900-1980; Statistical Abstract of the United States, 2001.

Gross Domestic Product, 1840–2000

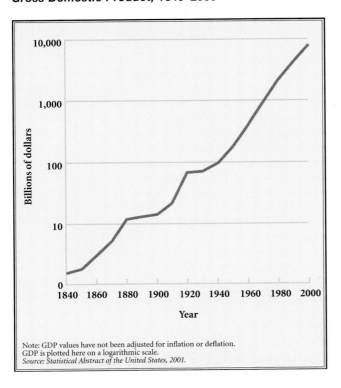

Note: GDP values have not been adjusted for inflation or deflation. GDP is plotted here on a logarithmic scale.
Source: Statistical Abstract of the United States, 2001.

GDP per Capita, 1840–2000

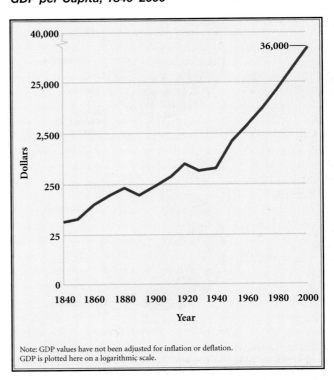

Note: GDP values have not been adjusted for inflation or deflation. GDP is plotted here on a logarithmic scale.

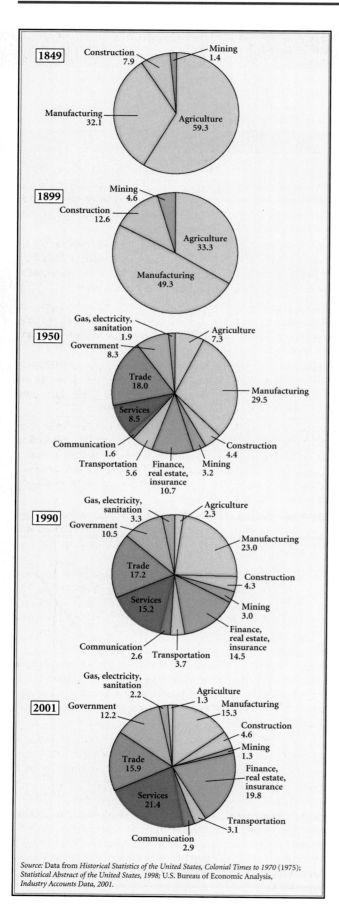

Source: Data from *Historical Statistics of the United States, Colonial Times to 1970* (1975); *Statistical Abstract of the United States, 1998*; U.S. Bureau of Economic Analysis, *Industry Accounts Data, 2001*.

Consumer Price Index

$100 in the year	1790	is equivalent to	$1,920	in 2001
	1800		1,400	
	1810		1,430	
	1820		1,500	
	1830		1,900	
	1840		2,030	
	1850		2,250	
	1860		2,110	
	1870		1,340	
	1880		1,720	
	1890		1,940	
	1900		2,090	
	1910		1,850	
	1920		882	
	1930		1,050	
	1940		1,260	
	1950		735	
	1960		598	
	1970		456	
	1980		215	
	1990		135	

This index provides a very rough guide to the purchasing power of $100 in various periods of American history. For example, in the early 1830s, day laborers earned about $1 a day or about $300 a year. This sum is the equivalent of about $5,700 a year in 2001 (3 × $1,900 = $5,700), or about one-half the gross income of a worker earning the federal government-designated minimum wage of $5.15 per hour.

Source: Samuel H. Williamson, "What Is the Relative Value?" Economic History Services, April 2002, <http://www.eh.net/ hmit/compare/>

◀ **Main Sectors of the U.S. Economy: 1849, 1899, 1950, 1990, and 2001**

affirmative action   Government mandates beginning in the 1970s that unions, businesses, and educational institutions make a deliberate effort to achieve a better measure of racial and gender equality in their recruitment and hiring. While the civil rights movement had achieved significant legal and political victories, historic patterns of racial and gender discrimination proved difficult to overcome without the assistance of government.

alphabet soup agencies   Nickname for the vast number of new federal agencies created by the New Deal that were usually referred to by their initial letters, for example, the AAA, CCC, NRA, and TVA.

America First Committee   A committee organized by isolationists in 1940 to oppose American entrance into the war. The membership of the committee included senators, journalists, and publishers. Perhaps the most well-known member was Charles Lindbergh, the famous aviator.

anarchism   Advocates the revolutionary creation of a stateless society. Anarchists' revolutionary views made them scapegoats for the 1886 Haymarket Square bombing.

Anglo-Saxonism   A theory that the English, and by extension their American cousins, were successful because of racial superiority. Combined with Social Darwinism, this notion fueled American expansionism in the late nineteenth century.

appeasement   Pacifying an enemy by making concessions. In the context of the coming of World War II, it refers specifically to the agreement reached at Munich in 1938 when England and France agreed to allow Hitler to annex the Sudetenland in exchange for his promise not to take more territory.

armistice   The equivalent of a cease-fire during which peace negotiations take place. Signed on November 11, 1918, an armistice marked the effective end to World War I.

bank holiday   State or federal government closure of lending institutions to prevent their going broke; President Franklin Roosevelt's use of this euphemism during the Great Depression was an attempt to put a positive face on an unpleasant reality.

Black Codes   After the Civil War, southern states passed these laws to keep African Americans in conditions close to slavery, forcing them back to the plantations and denying them civil rights.

blacklist   Procedure used by employers to label and identify undesirable workers.

blitzkrieg   Literally "lightning war," this expression describes the tactics followed by the Germans in 1939–1940 when they used massed armored and air forces to overrun Poland and the countries of Western Europe.

blue laws   Term used to refer to the legal restriction of activity on Sundays. In the late nineteenth century, Sunday closings were encouraged by Protestants as part of their crusade to uphold social values, but considered by immigrant Catholics as a violation of their personal freedom.

Bolsheviks   Russia's communist revolutionary party in the early twentieth century. Led by Lenin, they took Russia out of the war in early 1917, giving up huge territories to the Germans in the Treaty of Brest-Litovsk.

boomtowns   Mid-to-late nineteenth-century frontier settlements created virtually overnight following the news of a gold strike. A high ratio of men to women and a transient population added to their rough-and-tumble atmosphere.

buffalo soldiers   The name Native Americans gave to African American U.S. cavalrymen, most of them Civil War veterans stationed in the West to fight the Indian wars of the 1870s and 1880s.

capital goods   Products used by manufacturers to add to the productive capacity of the economy, such as machinery. In the late nineteenth century, the dramatic increase in products used by businesses drove industrial expansion.

carpetbaggers   A derisive name given by Southerners to Northerners who moved to the South during Reconstruction to help develop the region's economic potential. Former Confederates despised these Northerners as transient exploiters. Carpetbaggers included former Union army officers and also educated professionals.

closed shop   Workplace in which one had to be a union member to gain employment. In the late nineteenth century, craft unions began using them to keep out incompetent and lower-wage workers.

collective bargaining   A process of negotiation between labor unions and employers, particularly followed by the American Federation of Labor (AFL) in the late nineteenth century. Led by Samuel Gompers, the AFL accepted the new industrial order, but fought for a bigger share of the profits for the workers.

conglomerate   The business structure created when firms in different industries are purchased and combined into a single large firm. One purpose of this process is to assure an overall profit even if one part of the firm operates at a loss.

conservation   The process of protecting the natural environment for sustained use. As applied by Theodore Roosevelt at the start of the twentieth century, conservation protected public lands from development that was not in the public interest, in contrast to preservationists and later environmentalists, who sought to prevent almost all exploitation of wilderness land.

containment   American cold war policy designed to prevent Soviet expansionism, articulated most forcefully in 1946 by American diplomatic advisor George Kennan. For over forty years, American defense policy was guided by Kennan's argument that the Soviets would stop only when met with "unanswerable force."

convoy   In the face of threatening submarine warfare during World War I, U.S. and British merchant and troop ships traveled in large numbers bunched together and escorted by armed naval vessels. Organization in convoys greatly reduced the number of ships lost to the U-boats.

corporation   A business organization in which stockholders own the company and that has the ability to issue interest-bearing bonds to raise money. In the late nineteenth century, corporate charters allowed businesses of all sorts—especially the railroads—to raise large amounts of capital to finance expansion.

cost-plus provisions   Agreement between business and government in which industries were guaranteed a profit no matter what the cost of war production turned out to be; designed to enlist American industry in the World War II effort.

counterinsurgency   A military operation using specially trained forces to defend against guerrilla warfare. The U.S. military created the Green Berets in the early 1960s to fight this type of nontraditional warfare, characteristic of the fighting in Vietnam.

covert interventions   Secret undertakings by a country in pursuit of foreign policy goals, as evidenced by the Central Intelligence Agency, started in the 1950s, when operating in the interests of the United States. Knowledge of these acts, like U.S. participation in the overthrow of the government of Guatemala in 1954 and support for the Contras in Nicaragua in the 1980s, was kept from the American people and most members of Congress.

credibility gap   Term referring to the wide discrepancy between what was actually happening in Vietnam and what the public was being told. With the war dragging on in the late 1960s, the credibility of the U.S. position was increasingly undermined as more factual details were made public.

cyberspace   The information superhighway exists in this virtual world, the vast universe behind a computer screen. By 2000, 50 percent of all American households and 63 percent of public classrooms were connected to the Internet.

deficit spending   High government spending based on the ideas of economist John Maynard Keynes, who proposed in the 1930s that governments should be prepared to go into debt to stimulate a stagnant economy.

deindustrialization   A long period of decline in the industrial sector. In the 1970s American business reduced its investment in domestic production: capital was diverted to speculation, mergers and acquisitions, and foreign investment, resulting in massive unemployment and a decline in the labor movement.

détente   From a French word for a relaxation of tension, this term was used to signify the new foreign policy of President Nixon, which sought a reduction of tension and hostility between the United States and the Soviet Union and China in the early 1970s.

discount rate   The interest level charged by the Federal Reserve for money it loans to member banks. Since its establishment in 1913, the Federal Reserve's ability to manipulate the discount rate has given the "Fed" a powerful influence in the U.S. economy.

documentary impulse   Desire to present real-life situations in such a way as to evoke an emotional response; creating a document such as a film or photograph intended to elicit an empathetic reaction from its audience. During the New Deal, the WPA arts projects were influenced by documentary impulse.

dole   Expression referring to direct payment of relief to recipients during the Great Depression, suggesting recipients got relief money without having to perform work.

dollar-a-year men   Leading businessmen called to Washington to help organize war mobilization at the beginning of World War II. Many of them stayed on the payrolls of their corporations and volunteered their services to the administration.

dollar diplomacy   Term coined to describe the U.S. government's diplomatic initiatives to protect and enhance America's expanding business interests abroad in the early twentieth century.

domino effect   President Eisenhower used this metaphor to illustrate what would happen if the United States allowed Vietnam to be united, most assuredly under Communist rule, in free elections in 1956 as called for in the Geneva Accords. Once one country in a region became Communist, others would topple under the Soviet Union's influence almost automatically. The metaphor was used to support an aggressive American foreign policy.

downsizing   The deliberate laying off of permanent employees to cut company costs and raise profits. In the 1980s and 1990s the downsizing trend spread to middle management.

electronic mail (e-mail)   This electronic message system operating on the Internet gives individuals the ability to communicate directly with each other through cyberspace.

ethnic cleansing   The practice of entering a populated area during a time of civil strife and killing or driving away a significant portion of the population based on their ethnicity. The term was first used by Serbs seeking to seize territory from Muslims and Croats in the former Yugoslav provinces of Croatia and Bosnia.

excess-profits tax   This levy on corporate profits and the wealthiest individuals during World War I accounted for more than half of all federal taxes, and was a new source of federal government revenue.

Exodusters   Term used to describe the thousands of African Americans who migrated to Kansas in the spring of 1879 to escape from the post-Reconstruction violence of the South. By 1880, 40,000 blacks lived in Kansas.

fascism   Right-wing antidemocratic movements that began in Europe after World War I, characterized by strong dictators backed by the military. The dictatorships of Benito Mussolini in Italy, Adolph Hitler in Germany, and Francisco Franco in Spain represent three fascist states.

feminine mystique   The title of Betty Friedan's influential 1963 book, this expression refers to the ideal whereby women were encouraged to confine themselves to roles within the domestic sphere. The feminist movements of recent years emerged in reaction to this ideology.

feminism (feminists)   This theory developed in the early twentieth century among female activists who believed that women should be equal to men in all areas of life. Many women activists had accepted the notion of separate spheres for men and women, but feminists sought to overcome all barriers to equality.

fireside chat   President Franklin Roosevelt's regularly scheduled talks with the public in the 1930s and 1940s; the name suggested an intimate conversation and demonstrated the president's effective use of the new electronic political medium of radio.

flapper   A young woman of the 1920s who defied conventional standards of conduct. She wore short skirts and makeup, danced to jazz, and flaunted her liberated lifestyle. The flapper was a cultural icon of the era, but actually represented only a small minority of women.

flexible response   Strategy adopted by the Kennedy administration in the early 1960s that called for a military establishment that had to be prepared to fight any foe, large or small, conventional- or nuclear-armed, which was seen as a threat to American interests.

Fourteen Points   President Wilson proposed these as a basis for peace negotiations at Versailles in 1919. Among them were open diplomacy, freedom of the seas, free trade, territorial integrity, arms reduction, national self-determination, and the League of Nations.

freedom rides   A form of civil rights protest for which the Congress of Racial Equality (CORE) organized racially mixed groups to travel by bus through the South in 1961 to test compliance with federal laws banning racial segregation on interstate transportation. These activists were subjected to violence in several southern cities and drew the Kennedy administration further into the struggle for equal rights.

Fundamentalists (Fundamentalism)   Conservative Protestants who believe in a literal interpretation of the Bible. In the 1920s, Fundamentalists opposed modernist Protestants, who tried to reconcile Christianity with Darwin's theory of evolution and recent technological and scientific discoveries, and instigated the famous Scopes trial of 1925.

ghetto   Term describing an urban neighborhood composed of the poor, and occasionally used to describe any tight-knit community containing a single ethnic or class group. Ghettos came into being in the nineteenth century, in tandem with the enormous influx of immigrants to American cities.

Ghost Dance   A religious movement that swept the Plains Indians in 1890. It stemmed from the preaching of the Paiute prophet Wovoka who claimed that the whites would disappear from the Great Plains and that Indians would reclaim their lands.

Gibson girl   Image of the "new woman" created during the 1890s, which represented a stronger, more independent vision of women, as well as a more sexual one.

glasnost and **perestroika**   Policies introduced by Soviet president Mikhail Gorbachev during the 1980s that referred to openness and economic restructuring, respectively. Gorbachev's policies contributed to the freeing of Eastern Europe from Soviet domination and led, unintentionally, to the breakup of the Soviet Union.

Great American Desert   The name given to the drought-stricken Great Plains by Euro-Americans in the early nineteenth century. Believing the region was unfit for cultivation or agriculture, Congress designated the Great Plains as permanent Indian country in 1834.

greenbacks   First issued by the Union during the Civil War to finance the war effort, greenbacks became a general term to describe any paper currency issued by the federal government as legal tender. The value of greenbacks is supported by the good faith of the government rather than specie: gold or silver.

hegemony   Dominance in global affairs by a nation. The United States and Soviet Union emerged from World War II as the world's leading powers, each exercising a tremendous influence within their respective spheres of influence.

hippie   Young person who participated in the 1960s counterculture, a lifestyle in which drug use, rock music, uninhibited sexuality, and vivid self-expression were celebrated.

home rule   White southern Democrats referred to their desire to overthrow legitimately elected Reconstruction governments and replace them with white supremacy with this euphemism. By 1876, both national parties favored home rule.

honest graft   This notion, described by George Washington Plunkitt of Tammany Hall in the 1890s, indicates one aspect of machine politics. It refers to the financial advantages of insider information in the awarding of city contracts.

impeachment   First step in the constitutional process for removing the president from office in which charges of wrongdoing (articles of impeachment) are passed by the House of Representatives and then judged in a trial conducted by the Senate.

imperial presidency   Historian Arthur M. Schlesinger Jr. used this phrase to describe the growth of executive power, which up to that time reached its highest point in President Nixon's attempts in 1972 to subvert the constitutional restraints on his authority.

impoundment   President Nixon hoped to slow the growth of the federal government and reduce funding for programs he opposed by refusing to spend money appropriated by the Democratic-controlled Congress for urban renewal and pollution control in the early 1970s.

industrial union   A group of workers in a single industry (for example, automobile, railroad, or mining) organized into a single association, regardless of skill, rather than into separate craft-based organizations. The American Railway Union, formed in the 1880s, was one of the first industrial unions in the nation.

Internet   A vast network of communication technology made possible by the computer revolution and supporting tools like e-mail and the World Wide Web that became increasingly popular in the 1990s.

isolationism   Supporting the withdrawal of the United States from involvement with nations beyond its borders, especially avoidance of entangling diplomatic relations. The common view of post–World War I U.S. foreign policy is one of isolationism, when in fact the United States played an active role in world affairs, especially in trade and finance.

Jim Crow   The system of racial segregation in the South that was created in the late nineteenth century following the end of slavery. Jim Crow laws written in the 1880s and 1890s mandated segregation in public facilities.

jingoism   This term came to refer to superpatriotism in the late nineteenth and early twentieth centuries that favored a military solution to all international disputes.

kamikaze   Aerial Japanese suicide attacks during World War II in which pilots crashed their planes into U.S. ships in a last-ditch effort to destroy the American naval forces. This tactic became more common as the war in the Pacific turned more desperate for Japan.

laissez-faire Doctrine characterized by the belief that the less government does, the better. This was the philosophy of American government in the late nineteenth century and the guiding light of "conservative" politics in the twentieth. In 1980, Republican Party candidate Ronald Reagan ran for the presidency under the slogan, "The government is the problem, not the solution."

lien (crop lien) Southern redemption governments passed laws in the late nineteenth century allowing furnishing merchants to assume ownership, or lien, of a borrower's (usually sharecroppers) crops as collateral for loans of seed, tools, and fertilizer. This system trapped farmers in a cycle of debt and prevented economic diversification away from the increasingly unprofitable cotton-based agriculture.

Long Drive The moving of wild longhorn cattle hundreds of miles from Texas to the railheads of Kansas, where they could be shipped to eastern markets. This seemingly colorful event was actually a makeshift means of bridging a gap in the developing transportation system, and was abandoned when the railroads reached the Texas range country during the 1870s.

los pobres Literally, "the poor ones"; Hispanic residents of New Mexico who were displaced when Anglo ranchers fenced communal lands. They organized themselves as masked raiders and in 1889 and 1890 mounted an effective campaign of harassment against the interloping ranchers.

MAD (Mutually Assured Destruction) policy This U.S. nuclear policy, purportedly a theory of nuclear deterrence, called for a massive and unstoppable nuclear response if the Soviet Union were to launch an attack on the United States in the 1950s. This program of nuclear reciprocation would result in the total annihilation of both countries.

managed competition This idea was the heart of the failed Clinton health-care-reform initiative in the early 1990s. This policy would have depended on market forces rather than government controls to reduce the cost of health insurance and medical care.

margin buying The purchase of stocks or securities with a small down payment while financing the rest with a broker loan. When stock prices started to fall in 1929, brokers requested repayment of the loans and the funds were often not forthcoming, leading to the crash of the stock market in October of that year.

mass production In contrast to custom or handwork, this industrial process was designed to produce a great number of identical items to be sold to the public on a large scale. In the late nineteenth century most factories came to use the assembly line to maintain high volume.

military-industrial complex Term used to describe the close relationship of military spending and defense contractors that emerged during World War II and grew with the cold war. In the 1950s and 1960s, federal defense spending came to have a tremendous influence on the national economy, particularly in the South and West where many defense contractors were located. In his farewell address in 1961, President Eisenhower raised troubling questions about the influence of this new power in a democracy and warned the nation to be vigilant.

misery index Derived by adding the national unemployment rate and the average annual rate of inflation, the misery index first appeared in the 1970s to measure economic suffering. It reappeared during the 1996 election to underscore a healthy economy. The rate at that time was the lowest it had been in twenty-seven years.

modernist movement (modernism) A literary and artistic style and movement in the 1920s that broke sharply with past traditions and was marked by skepticism and stylistic experimentation. Modernist writers included Gertrude Stein, T. S. Eliot, and F. Scott Fitzgerald.

muckrakers These journalists in the early twentieth century were crusaders who exposed the corruption of big business and government. Theodore Roosevelt gave them the name as a term of reproach. The term comes from a character in *Pilgrim's Progress*, a religious allegory by John Bunyan.

multiculturalism The policy of promoting diversity—gender, race, ethnicity, and sexual preference.

nativism Antiforeign sentiment in the United States that fueled a drive against immigration. In the 1920s, many native-born white Protestants reacted with bitter animosity to the more than 23 million immigrants who had come to America during the previous forty years.

New Freedom President Woodrow Wilson's domestic agenda that called for a limitation of the abuses of economic power by large corporations. Wilson's program differed from Teddy Roosevelt's "New Nationalism" in that it sought to revive competition rather than regulate large corporations.

New Frontier President John F. Kennedy's activist program "to get America moving again" after the Eisenhower administration of the 1950s. In his inaugural speech, Kennedy called for vigorous activism at home and abroad. Although his legislative achievements were limited, Kennedy's example proved inspirational, particularly to the young.

New Left Radical students of the 1960s and 1970s adopted this term to refer to their activist movement, distinguishing themselves from the "Old Left"—the communists and socialists of the 1930s and 1940s. They turned to grassroots organizing in cities and college campuses in their protest against the status quo and what they saw as the accommodationist stance of older generations.

New Nationalism Theodore Roosevelt's program for reform and the cause of social justice, first articulated in 1910 after he left the presidency. Roosevelt called for a strong central government concerned with the interests of the common person.

New Negro Term taken from the title of an anthology of writings from the Harlem Renaissance, edited by Alain Locke; the expression was used to describe the artists and intellectuals of Black America who came to prominence in the 1920s.

new politics The shift in political campaigning from issues-based to image-based strategies. Mass media played a major role in this transformation during the election of 1960.

New Right Conservative political movement that achieved considerable success beginning in the 1970s, helping to elect Ronald Reagan president in 1980 and enabling the Republican Party to retake both houses of Congress in the 1994 elections. Riding the support of evangelical Christians and organizations like Jerry Falwell's Moral Majority, New Right activists mobilized thousands of followers and millions of dollars to combat federal activism and declining social morality.

Niagara Movement   Brought together in 1906 by the black activists William Monroe Trotter and W. E. B. Du Bois, this organization defined the agenda for the racial struggle in the early twentieth century.

nickelodeon   In the early days of the film industry, the late 1890s, this was the most common movie spot: a working-class theater with a five-cent admission charge.

oligopolies   Situations in which a few large corporations control an industry. This became the norm in the 1920s.

Open-Door Notes   Sent by U.S. Secretary of State John Hay to Japan, Russia, Germany, and France in 1899, this policy claimed the right of equal trade for all nations that wanted to do business in China. Because it lacked colonial possessions in China, free trade was crucial to the United States to gain access to China's large markets.

Pan-Americanism   In the abstract, this phrase suggests a belief in a community of all Western Hemisphere nations, north and south. In practical terms, it encompassed early twentieth-century theories that ranged from a political confederation to international arbitration.

peaceful coexistence   Premier Khrushchev of the Soviet Union used this term in 1956 to call for diminished tensions between capitalist and communist nations in the cold war. As a sign of the reduced hostility, Khrushchev and Vice President Nixon exchanged official visits.

peonage (debt peonage)   As cotton prices declined during the 1870s, many sharecroppers fell into permanent debt. Merchants often conspired with landowners to make the debt a pretext for forced labor, or peonage.

pocket veto   Presidential way to kill a piece of legislation without issuing a formal veto. When congressional Republicans passed the Wade-Davis Bill in 1864, a harsher alternative to President Lincoln's restoration plan, Lincoln used this method to kill it by simply not signing the bill and letting it expire after Congress adjourned.

police action   A military action, undertaken without a formal declaration of war, by regular armed forces against perceived violators of international peace. This term was applied to the participation of U.N. authorized troops in the Korean War against communist North Korea.

political machine   Nineteenth-century term for a highly organized political party, which was often compared to new technological innovations because of its efficiency and complexity.

politics of resentment   The various social reform movements of the 1960s and 1970s aroused animosity on the part of those who felt change had gone too far, spurring a grassroots conservative backlash against social reform, special-interest groups, and governmental activism.

poll tax   Legal device used throughout the South beginning during Reconstruction to prevent freedmen from voting. Nationally, the northern states used poll taxes to keep immigrants and others deemed unworthy from the polls.

pragmatism   Philosophy popular with Progressives, developed by Harvard psychologist William James in the early

twentieth century. It judged ideas by their consequences and was concerned with solving problems rather than seeking ultimate truths.

Preservationists   Early-twentieth-century activists like John Muir who fought to protect the natural environment from commercial exploitation, particularly in the American West. Notable achievements include the establishment of many national parks like Yosemite, Sequoia, and King's Canyon in California.

progressivism   This term embraces a widespread, many-sided effort in the years after 1900 to build a better society. The movement rejected the fatalism of earlier social thought in analyzing social problems and replaced it with empirical social science and a belief in administrative efficiency.

Promontory Point   Site in Utah where the railway lines built by the Union Pacific and Central Pacific met in 1869, completing the first transcontinental railroad line and contributing to the integration of the western territories into the rest of the Union and the development of the Great Plains.

propaganda   The spreading of ideas that support a particular cause. Although this process does not require a distortion of the facts, it usually involves a misrepresentation of the views or policies of one's opponents. During World War I, the U.S. Committee on Public Information, led by George Creel, published literature and sponsored speeches to increase public hostility toward Germany.

pump priming   Term first used during the Great Depression of the 1930s to describe the practice of pouring money into the financial system and the industrial structure in the hope that it will generate economic activity throughout the system; the beginning of the process that is supposed to lead to significant economic recovery.

Reaganomics   The policy enacted by the Reagan administration in the 1980s calling for tax cuts and reductions in domestic spending in order to reduce the size of the federal government.

Reconstruction   Post–Civil War policies whereby the freedmen, abolitionists, and radical Republican politicians hoped to make changes in the South that would ensure political equality for the freedmen and grant them greater economic rights.

red-baiting   Tactics used to identify, accuse, or raise suspicion of communist sympathies. In the 1930s, critics of the New Deal charged the Federal Theatre Project with being under the influence of communists, leading to its termination in 1939.

Redeemers   Ex-Confederates who sought to return the political and economic control of the South to white southerners in the decades after the Civil War. They believed that Union support of the freedmen had deprived the South of democratic self-government and organized secret societies and campaigns of terror to regain it, leading to the undoing of Reconstruction.

reparations   Payments by a defeated enemy to the victors following a war. After World War I, the European Allies required Germany to pay vast sums for expenses incurred during the war and as a long-term punishment.

restrictive covenant   Limiting clauses in real estate transactions intended to prevent the sale or rental of properties to classes of the population considered "undesirable," such as African Americans, Jews, or Asians. Such clauses were declared unenforceable by the Supreme Court decision in *Shelley v. Kraemer* (1948), but continued to be instituted informally in spite of the ruling.

revenue sharing   The return of federal tax money to the states for use as they saw fit. President Nixon sought to reverse the concentration of power in Washington by initiating a decentralization of governmental functions in 1972.

rock 'n' roll   Style of popular music, an amalgam of white country-and-western music and urban black rhythm and blues. White performers, like Elvis Presley, dramatically increased its popularity with white audiences in the 1950s.

Roosevelt corollary   This 1904 assertion by President Theodore Roosevelt expanded the Monroe Doctrine. It stated that the United States would act as a "policeman" in the Caribbean region and intervene in the affairs of nations that were guilty of "wrongdoing or impotence," in order to protect U.S. interests in Latin America.

scalawags   Southern whites who joined the Republicans during Reconstruction and were ridiculed by ex-Confederates as worthless traitors. They included wealthy ex-Whigs and yeomen farmers who had not supported the Confederacy and who believed that an alliance with the Republicans was the best way to attract northern capital to the South.

scientific management   A system of organizing work, developed by Frederick W. Taylor in the late nineteenth century, designed to get the maximum output from the individual worker and reduce the cost of production, using methods such as the time-and-motion study to determine how factory work should be organized. The rigid structure of the system was never applied in its totality in any industry, but it contributed to the rise of the "efficiency expert" and the field of industrial psychology.

secondary labor boycott   Technique used by unions during a strike in which force is applied on a second party to bring pressure on the primary target and force it to accept demands. A secondary labor boycott was used in the Great Pullman Boycott of 1894 and failed when the government intervened.

sex typing   Process by which occupations become categorized as either "male" or "female" jobs. In the late nineteenth century, jobs characterized as "female" came to be seen as having feminine attributes, even if the same work had been done by men before.

sharecropping   Labor system developed during Reconstruction by which freedmen agreed to work the land and pay a portion of their harvested crops to the landowner in exchange for land, a house, and tools. A compromise between freedmen and white landowners, this system developed in the cash-strapped South because the freedmen wanted to work their own land but lacked the money to buy it, while the white landowners needed agricultural laborers, but did not have money to pay wages.

silent majority   This term, derived from Ben J. Wattenberg and Richard Scammon's book, applies to the segment of American society to whom Nixon appealed—generally the "un-black, unpoor, and unyoung."

sit-in   Nonviolent protest tactic first popularized by African American students for civil rights in Greensboro, North Carolina, in 1960. As protest in the 1960s spread beyond civil rights, many groups adopted the sit-in as their method of activism.

social Darwinism   A social application of Charles Darwin's biological theory of evolution by natural selection, this late-nineteenth-century theory encouraged the notion of human competition and opposed intervention in the natural human order. Social Darwinists justified the increasing inequality of late-nineteenth-century industrial American society as natural.

socialized medicine   Label applied by the American Medical Association in the early 1950s in a campaign against Truman's recommendation that a federally underwritten national health-care system be enacted. The attempt to link Truman's program with leftist politics was successful in arousing congressional and public opinion against the plan.

speakeasies   Illegal saloons that sold alcohol to the public during Prohibition (starting in 1920).

sphere of influence   A geographical area beyond a nation's borders over which it claims control. The Soviet Union's domination of Eastern European countries after World War II, which created a communist buffer zone between the USSR and Western Europe, extended the Soviet sphere of influence dangerously close to the U.S. sphere of influence.

Square Deal   President Theodore Roosevelt's domestic reform program, begun in 1904, calling for government control of corporate abuses.

stagflation   An economic condition that results when inflation and unemployment rise at the same time. This condition does not respond to traditional governmental remedies, such as deficit spending and tax reduction.

"subtreasury" system   A scheme under which the federal government would provide localized banking functions for farmers, allowing them credit and marketing opportunities not controlled by private firms. This banking reform was promoted by the Populist Party in the late nineteenth century.

suburbanization   The movement of the upper and middle classes beyond city limits to less crowded areas with larger homes and that are connected to city centers by streetcar or subway lines. By 1910, 25 percent of the population lived in these new communities. The 1990 census revealed that the majority of Americans lived in the suburbs.

suffragists   Those (mostly female) who were active in seeking voting rights for women as an inherent right for all individuals in the nineteenth and early twentieth centuries.

Sun Belt   The southern and western United States in the 1950s and 1960s, where many firms moved their operations during the industrial development of the postwar era. Population followed this industrial migration and led to an enormous growth in economic activity and political influence of the Sun Belt states.

Sun Dance   Sioux Indian ceremony in which an entire tribe celebrated the rites of coming of age, fertility, the hunt, and combat. The ritual involved four days of fasting and dancing in supplication to Wi, the sun.

supply-side economics   This theory, the basis for Reaganomics, argued that a large tax cut would empower individuals and businesses to invest more money. Otherwise known as "trickle-down economics," the subsequent increase in economic activity, the reasoning went, would create jobs, generate more taxable income, and increase government revenues.

syndicalism A revolutionary movement that, like socialism, believed in the Marxist principle of class struggle and advocated the organization of society on the basis of industrial unionism. This approach was advocated by the Industrial Workers of the World (IWW) at the start of the twentieth century.

tariff A tax on imports, which has two purposes: raising revenue for the government and protecting domestic products from foreign competition. A hot political issue throughout much of American history, in the late nineteenth century the tariff became particularly controversial as Republicans, who viewed it as a protective system, and Democrats, who were free traders by tradition, made the tariff the centerpiece of their political campaigns.

teach-in University gatherings in the 1960s where the political, diplomatic, and moral aspects of the nation's involvement in Vietnam were debated. College students and faculty abandoned structured class time to explore these issues.

telecommuters People who perform their jobs at home with the use of electronic communication devices (computers, modems, faxes). Telecommuting became common in the 1990s as the growth and development of the Internet and World Wide Web revolutionized communications.

tenements High-density, cheap, five- or six-story housing units designed for large urban populations built in the late nineteenth century. New York's tenements were known for their horrible crowding and lack of ventilation or plumbing.

time-and-motion study An engineer's study of a particular industrial task to determine the most efficient method for producing the greatest amount in the least amount of time. The factory would then set this time as the standard to which workers would be expected to conform.

trade deficit The importation by a nation of more than it exports. Contributing to the economic problems of the 1970s, the United States posted its first trade deficit in more than a century as the emerging industrial economies of Germany and Japan began to provide stiff international competition.

trusts Large business mergers in the late nineteenth and early twentieth centuries. These combinations became a problem because their size gave them the ability to inhibit competition and control the market for their products.

urban liberalism An early twentieth-century reform movement organized by unions and politicians who sought state measures to improve the life of the working class of the cities.

urban renewal Process by which city planners, politicians, and real estate developers leveled urban tenements and replaced them with modern construction projects in the 1950s and 1960s. High-rise housing projects, however, destroyed community bonds and led to an increase in crime.

vaudeville A professional stage show composed of singing, dancing, and comedy routines that changed live entertainment from its seedier predecessors like minstrel shows to family entertainment for the urban masses. Vaudeville became popular in the 1880s and 1890s, the years just before the introduction of movies.

vertical integration A national company's capability of handling, within its own structure, all the functions of an industry. Pioneered in the late nineteenth century by Gustavus F. Swift in the meatpacking industry, his Swift & Co. was organized so that it could manage all of the aspects of its operations, from obtaining raw materials to marketing the final product.

ward The basic unit of municipal government in the late nineteenth century. City councils were made up of representatives from these districts, and it was through the ward system that the urban political machine operated.

wars of national liberation Leftist movements rebelling against colonial or oligarchic governments in the Third World. In the 1960s the United States saw many of these struggles as attempts to extend the reach of Soviet communism, while the Soviet Union saw them, as legitimate struggles for freedom and national self-determination.

welfare state A nation that provides for the basic needs of its citizens, including such provisions as old-age pensions, unemployment compensation, child-care facilities, education, and other social policies. Unlike the major European countries, such provisions appeared in the United States only with the coming of the New Deal in the 1930s.

white-collar Middle-class professionals, who are salaried workers as opposed to business owners or wage laborers; they first appeared in large numbers during the industrial expansion in the late nineteenth century. Their ranks were composed of lawyers, engineers, and chemists, as well as salesmen, accountants, and advertising managers.

white primary Southern states accepted the progressive idea of a direct selection of party candidates in the early twentieth century but used this device as a way of reducing the effect of black voting in the general election.

yellow-dog contract When a worker, as a condition of employment, promises not to join a union. Employers in the late nineteenth century used this along with the blacklist and violent strikebreaking to fight unionization of their workforce.

yellow journalism Term that refers to newspapers that specialize in sensationalistic reporting. The name came from the ink used in Hearst's *New York Journal* to print the first comic strip to appear in color in 1895 and is generally associated with the inflammatory reporting leading up to the Spanish-American War of 1898.

Chapter 15: Reconstruction, 1865–1877

The starting point for the study of Reconstruction is Eric Foner's major synthesis, *Reconstruction: America's Unfinished Revolution, 1863–1877* (1988), which is also available in a shorter version. Two older surveys that provide useful introductions are John Hope Franklin, *Reconstruction: After the Civil War* (1961), and Kenneth M. Stampp, *The Era of Reconstruction* (1965). *Black Reconstruction in America* (1935), by the black activist and scholar W. E. B. Du Bois, deserves attention as the first book to challenge traditional racist interpretations of Reconstruction as carpetbagger rule unjustly imposed on the defeated South by radical Republicans. The Web site <http://lcweb2.loc.gov/ammem/aaohtml/exhibit/aopart5.html> provides Library of Congress documents and illustrations on African Americans during Reconstruction.

Presidential Reconstruction

For important studies of presidential efforts to rebuild the Union, see the books on Abraham Lincoln listed in Chapter 14 and the following works on Andrew Johnson: Albert Castel, *The Presidency of Andrew Johnson* (1979); Eric L. McKitrick, *Andrew Johnson and Reconstruction* (1960); and James Sefton, *Andrew Johnson and the Uses of Constitutional Power* (1979). On the radical resistance to presidential Reconstruction, see James M. McPherson, *The Struggle for Equality: Abolitionists and the Negro in the Civil War and Reconstruction* (1965). Books that focus on Congress include LaWanda Cox and John H. Cox, *Politics, Principle, and Prejudice, 1865–1867* (1963); David Donald, *The Politics of Reconstruction, 1863–1867* (1965); and William B. Brock, *An American Crisis: Congress and Reconstruction, 1865–1867* (1963). For insight into developments in the South, see Dan T. Carter, *When the War Was Over: The Failure of Self-Reconstruction in the South, 1865–1867* (1985). Michael Perman, *Reunion without Compromise: The South and Reconstruction, 1865–1868* (1973), stresses the South's relations with Johnson. On the freedmen, see Willie Lee Rose, *Rehearsal for Reconstruction: The Port Royal Experiment* (1964); Peter Kolchin, *First Freedom: The Responses of Alabama's Blacks to Emancipation and Reconstruction* (1972); and Leon F. Litwack, *Been in the Storm So Long: The Aftermath of Slavery* (1979). More recent emancipation studies emphasize slavery as a labor system: Barbara Fields, *Slavery and Freedom on the Middle Ground: Maryland during the Nineteenth Century* (1985); Julie Saville, *The Work of Reconstruction: From Slave to Wage Laborer in South Carolina, 1860–1870* (1994); Ira Berlin et al., *Slaves No More: Three Essays on Emancipation and the Civil War* (1992); and Amy Dru Stanley, *From Bondage to Contract: Wage Labor, Marriage, and the Market in the Age of Slave Emancipation* (1999), which expands the discussion to show what the onset of wage labor meant for freedwomen. Other books that deal with the impact of emancipation on black women are Jacqueline Jones, *Labor of Love, Labor of Sorrow: Black Women, Work, and the Family from Slavery to the Present* (1985), a pioneering work, and an important case study, Leslie A. Schwalm, *A Hard Fight for We: Women's Transition from Slavery to Freedom in South Carolina* (1997). For a Web site that explores how white northern women attempted to assist freed people during Reconstruction, see <http://womhist.binghamton.edu/aid/intro.htm>. Eric Foner, *Nothing But Freedom: Emancipation and Its Legacy* (1983), helpfully places emancipation in a comparative context.

Radical Reconstruction

For Congress's role in radical Reconstruction, see Michael Les Benedict, *A Compromise of Principle: Congressional Republicans and Reconstruction* (1974), and Hans L. Trefousse, *Impeachment of a President: Andrew Johnson, the Blacks, and Reconstruction* (1975). William S. McFeely, *Grant: A Biography* (1981), deftly explains the politics of Reconstruction. Also helpful is Brooks D. Simpson, *Let Us Have Peace: Ulysses S. Grant and the Politics of War and Reconstruction, 1861–1868* (1991). State studies of Reconstruction include Richard Lowe, *Republicans and Reconstruction in Virginia, 1856–1870* (1991), and Otto Olsen, ed., *Reconstruction and Redemption in the South* (1980). The best account of carpetbaggers is Richard N. Current, *Those Terrible Carpetbaggers: A Reinterpretation* (1988). On blacks during radical Reconstruction, see Joel Williamson, *After Slavery: The Negro in South Carolina during Reconstruction, 1861–1877* (1965); Robert Cruden, *The Negro in Reconstruction* (1969); John Blassingame, *Black New Orleans, 1860–1880* (1973); Thomas Holt, *Black over White: Negro Political Leadership in South Carolina during Reconstruction* (1977); and Barry A. Crouch, *The Freedmen's Bureau and Black Texans* (1992). The emergence of the sharecropping system is explored in Roger L. Ransom and Richard Sutch, *One Kind of Freedom: The Economic Consequences of Emancipation* (1977); Jay Mandle, *The Roots of Black Poverty: The Southern Plantation Economy after the Civil War* (1978); Gavin Wright, *Old South, New South: Revolutions in the Southern Economy since the Civil War* (1986); Edward Royce, *The Origins of Southern Sharecropping* (1993); Harold Woodman, *New South, New Law: The Legal Foundations of Credit and Labor Relations in the Postbellum Agricultural South* (1995).

The Undoing of Reconstruction

The most thorough study of the Ku Klux Klan is Allen W. Trelease, *White Terror: The Ku Klux Klan Conspiracy and Southern Reconstruction* (1972), and on its founder, Brian S. Wills, *A Battle from the Start: The Life of Nathan Bedford Forrest* (1992). To survey Reconstruction politics in the South, consult Michael Perman, *The Road to Redemption: Southern Politics, 1869–1879* (1984). On politics in the North, see James Mohr, ed., *The Radical Republicans in the North: State Politics during Reconstruction* (1976), and William Gillette, *Retreat from Reconstruction, 1863–1879* (1979). Laura F. Edwards, *Gendered Strife and Confusion: The Political Culture of Reconstruction*

(1997) is an innovative study that explores the gendered dimension of Reconstruction politics in a North Carolina county. Equally illuminating as a more traditional political narrative is Jonathan M. Bryant, *How Curious a Land: Conflict and Change in Greene County, Georgia, 1850–1885* (1996). For the impact of Reconstruction on the national state, see Morton Keller, *Affairs of State: Public Life in Late Nineteenth-Century America* (1977), and Richard F. Bensel, *Yankee Leviathan: The Origins of Central State Authority in America, 1859–1877* (1990). On political corruption, see Mark W. Summers, *The Era of Good Stealings* (1993). On the Compromise of 1877, see C. Vann Woodward's classic *Reunion and Reaction* (1956), and K. I. Polakoff, *The Politics of Inertia: The Election of 1876 and the End of Reconstruction* (1973).

Chapter 16: The American West

Western history has become a bitterly contested ground in recent years. The fountainhead of the voluminous traditional scholarship is Frederick Jackson Turner's famous essay "The Significance of the Frontier in American History" (1893), reprinted in Ray A. Billington, ed., *Frontier and Section: Selected Essays of Frederick Jackson Turner* (1961). The "new" western history is critical of Turnerian scholarship for being "Eurocentric"—for seeing western history only through the eyes of frontiersmen and settlers—and for masking the rapacious and environmentally destructive underside of western settlement. Patricia N. Limerick's skillfully argued *The Legacy of Conquest: The Unbroken Past of the American West* (1987) opened the debate. Richard White, *"It's Your Misfortune and None of My Own": A New History of the American West* (1991), provides the fullest synthesis of the new scholarship. For an authoritative, balanced treatment of the main themes of western history, see the essays in Clyde A. Milner II et al., *The Oxford History of the American West* (1994); and, for some of the most debated issues, Clyde A. Milner II, ed., *A New Significance: Re-Envisioning the History of the American West* (1996). On women's experience—another primary concern of the new western history—the starting point is Susan Armitage and Elizabeth Jameson, eds., *The Women's West* (1987). There are incisive environmental essays in Donald Worster, *Under Western Skies: Nature and History in the American West* (1992). D. W. Meinig, *Transcontinental America, 1850–1915* (1998), the third volume of his monumental *The Shaping of America: A Geographical Perspective on 500 Years of History*, is illuminating on the geography of western development. A comprehensive Web site with many links is <http://americanwest.com>.

The Great Plains

The classic book, stressing the settlers' adaptation to climate and environment, is Walter P. Webb, *The Great Plains* (1931). There is an excellent chapter on the ecological history of the southern plains in Donald Worster, *The Great Plains* (1979). Robert M. Utley, *The Indian Frontier of the American West, 1846–1890* (1984), is a good introduction; Robert H. Lowie, *Indians of the Great Plains* (1954), is a classic anthropological study. On the religious life of the Plains Indians, see Howard L. Harrod, *Renewing the World: Plains Indian Religion and Morality* (1987). The assault on Indian culture is recounted in Frederick E. Hoxie, *A Final Promise: The Campaign to Assimilate the Indians, 1880–1920* (1984). On phases of plains settlement see Oscar Winther, *The Transportation Frontier: The Trans-Mississippi West, 1865–1890* (1964); Lewis Atherton, *The Cattle Kings* (1964); Gilbert Fite, *The Farmer's Frontier, 1865–1900* (1966); and Mary W. M. Hargreaves, *Dry-Farming in the Northern Great Plains* (1954). The ecological impact is subtly probed in Frieda Knobloch, *The Culture of Wilderness: Agriculture as Colonization in the American West* (1996). One facet of this subject is reconsidered in Andrew C. Isenberg, *The Destruction of the Bison: An Environmental History* (2000). Richard Slotkin, *The Fatal Environment: The Myth of the Frontier in the Age of Industrialization, 1800–1890* (1985), deals with the process by which Americans translated the hard realities of conquering the West into a national mythology. A case in point is Joy Kasson, *Buffalo Bill's Wild West: Celebrity, Memory, and Popular History* (2000).

The peopling of the plains can be explored in Craig Miner, *West of Wichita: Settling the High Plains of Kansas, 1865–1890* (1986); Frederick C. Luebke, ed., *Ethnicity and the Great Plains* (1980); Jon Gjerde, *The Minds of the West: Ethnocultural Evolution in the Rural Middle West, 1830–1917* (1997); Nell Irvin Painter, *Exodusters: Black Migration to Kansas after Reconstruction* (1976); Julie Roy Jeffrey, *Frontier Women: The Trans-Mississippi West, 1840–1880* (1979); Deborah Fink, *Agrarian Women: Wives and Mothers in Rural Nebraska, 1880–1940* (1992); and Elaine Lindgren, *Land in Her Own Name: Women as Homesteaders in North Dakota* (1991). On the integration of the plains economy with the wider world, an especially rich book is William Cronon, *Nature's Metropolis: Chicago and the Great West* (1991).

The Far West

Two valuable regional histories are David Alan Johnson, *Founding the Far West: California, Oregon, and Nevada* (1992), and Carlos A. Schwantes, *The Pacific Northwest: An Interpretive History* (1989). The best book on western mining is Rodman Paul, *Mining Frontiers of the Far West: 1848–1880* (1963). Two case studies of life in mining towns are Paula Petrik, *Women and Family on the Rocky Mountain Frontier: Helena, Montana, 1865–1900* (1987), and Elizabeth Jameson, *All That Glitters: Class, Conflict, and Community in Cripple Creek* (1998). An imaginative treatment of the New Mexico peasantry is Sarah Deutsch, *No Separate Refuge* (1987). On Hispanic Texas an important book is David Montejano, *Anglos and Mexicans in the Making of Texas* (1987). Local studies of laboring Hispanics and their communities are Mario T. Garcia, *Desert Immigrants: The Mexicans of El Paso, 1880–1920* (1981), and Richard Griswold del Castillo, *The Los Angeles Barrio, 1850–1890* (1979). On the Asian migration to America, the best introduction is Ronald Takaki, *Strangers from a Different Shore: A History of Asian Americans* (1989), which can be supplemented with Sucheng Chan, *This Bittersweet Soil: The Chinese in California Agriculture, 1860–1910* (1986); Yong Chen, *Chinese San Francisco, 1850–1943: A Trans-Pacific Community* (2000); and, on the impact of the exclusion laws, Lucy E. Salyer, *Laws Harsh as Tigers: Chinese Immigrants and the Shaping of Modern Immigration Law* (1995). Labor's opposition to the Chinese is skillfully treated in Alexander Saxton, *The Indispensable Enemy: Labor and the Anti-Chinese Movement in California* (1971). Kevin Starr, *California and the American Dream, 1850–1915* (1973), provides a comprehensive account of the emergence of a distinctive California culture. On John Muir and the California wilderness, see Michael L. Smith, *Pacific Visions: California Scientists and the Environment, 1850–1915* (1987), and on water, with special emphasis on California, Donald J. Pisani, *Water, Land, and Law in the West: The Limits of Public Policy, 1850–1920* (1996).

Chapter 17: Capital and Labor in the Age of Enterprise, 1877–1900

The most useful introduction to the economic history of this period is Edward C. Kirkland, *Industry Comes of Age, 1860–1897* (1961). A more sophisticated analysis can be found in W. Elliot Brownlee, *Dynamics of Ascent* (rev. ed., 1979). For essays on many of the topics covered in this chapter, consult Glenn Porter, ed., *Encyclopedia of American Economic History* (3 vols., 1980).

Industrial Capitalism Triumphant

On railroads a convenient introduction is John F. Stover, *American Railroads* (1970). The growth of the railroads as an integrated system has been treated in George R. Taylor and Irene D. Neu, *The American Railway Network, 1861–1890* (1956). On the key link to the Pacific, see David Haward Bain, *Empire Express: Building the First Transcontinental Railroad* (1999). Julius Grodinsky, *Jay Gould: His Business Career, 1867–1892* (1957), is a complex study demonstrating the contributions this railroad buccaneer made to the transportation system. Books such as Cochran's and Grodinsky's have gone a long way to resurrect Gilded Age businessmen from the debunking tradition first set forth with great power in Matthew Josephson, *Robber Barons: Great American Fortunes* (1934). Important business biographies include Joseph F. Wall, *Andrew Carnegie* (1970); Ron Chernow, *Titan: The Life of John D. Rockefeller* (1998); and Jean Strouse, *Morgan: American Financier* (1999). There is an excellent Web site on Andrew Carnegie <http://pbs.org/wgbh/amex/carnegie/>. Peter Temin, *Iron and Steel in the Nineteenth Century* (1964), is the best treatment of that industry. On the development of mass production the key book is David A. Hounshell, *From the American System to Mass Production, 1800–1932* (1984). Alfred D. Chandler, *The Visible Hand: The Managerial Revolution in American Business* (1977), is not an easy book but will amply repay the labors of interested students.

On the New South, the standard work has long been C. Vann Woodward, *Origins of the New South, 1877–1913* (1951). Equally essential as a modern reconsideration is Edward L. Ayers, *The Promise of the New South: Life after Reconstruction* (1992). A brilliant reinterpretation of the causes of the South's economic retardation is Gavin Wright, *Old South, New South* (1986). Jacqueline Jones, *The Dispossessed: America's Underclasses from the Civil War to the Present* (1992), contains an excellent treatment of southern labor.

The World of Work

To understand the impact of industrialism on American workers, three collections of essays make the best starting points: Herbert G. Gutman, *Work, Culture and Society in In-* *dustrializing America* (1976); Michael S. Frisch and Daniel J. Walkowitz, eds., *Working-Class America: Essays on Labor, Community and American Society* (1983); and Leon Fink, *In Search of the Working Class* (1994). On the introduction of Taylorism, the most useful books are Daniel Nelson, *Managers and Workers: Origins of the New Factory System* (2nd ed., 1995); and Robert Kanigel, *The One Best Way: Frederick W. Taylor and the Enigma of Efficiency* (1997). The impact of Taylorism on American workers is treated with insight in David Montgomery, *The Fall of the House of Labor: The Workplace, the State, and American Labor Activism, 1865–1925* (1987).

Two valuable collections of essays on immigrant workers are Richard Ehrlich, ed., *Immigrants in Industrial America* (1977), and Dirk Hoerder, ed., *American Labor and Immigration History, 1877–1920: Recent European Research* (1983). John Bodnar, *Immigration and Industrialization: Ethnicity in an American Mill Town* (1977), and David M. Emmons, *The Butte Irish: Class and Ethnicity in an American Mining Town* (1989), are important case studies of single communities. On women workers, the best introduction is Alice Kessler-Harris, *Out to Work* (1982). Ava Baron, ed., *Work Engendered: Toward a New History of American Labor* (1991), is a rich collection of essays that apply gender analysis to the history of working people. Two excellent case studies in this vein are Mary Blewett, *Men, Women, and Work: Class, Gender, and Protest in the New England Shoe Industry, 1780–1910* (1988), and Stephen H. Norwood, *Labor's Flaming Youth: Telephone Operators and Worker Militancy, 1878–1923* (1990). On black workers useful introductions are William H. Harris, *The Harder We Run: Black Workers Since the Civil War* (1982), and Philip S. Foner, *Organized Labor and the Black Worker* (1974). Walter Licht, *Getting Work: Philadelphia, 1840–1950* (1992), is a pioneering history of a labor market in operation.

The Labor Movement

The standard book on the struggle between labor reform and trade unionism is Gerald N. Grob, *Workers and Utopia, 1865–1900* (1961). For the Knights of Labor, it should be supplemented by Leon Fink, *Workingmen's Democracy: The Knights of Labor and American Politics* (1983), which captures the cultural dimensions of labor reform not seen by earlier historians. Labor's place in the political environment is the subject of David Montgomery, *Citizen Worker* (1993), and, in an innovative comparative study of a single occupation, John H. M. Laslett, *Colliers Across the Seas: A Comparative Study of Class Formation in Scotland and the American Midwest, 1880–1924* (2000). On the emergence of a political strategy, see Julie Greene, *Pure and Simple Politics: The American Federation of Labor, 1881–1915* (1997). Paul Krause, *The Battle for Homestead, 1880–1892* (1992), puts the great strike in a larger social context. Another landmark conflict is considered from many angles in Richard Schneirov et al., ed., *The Pullman Strike and the Crisis of the 1890s* (1999).

The founder of the AFL is the subject of a lively brief biography by Harold Livesay, *Samuel Gompers and Organized Labor in America* (1978). Among the many books on individual unions, Robert Christie, *Empire in Wood* (1956), best reveals the way pure-and-simple unionism worked out in practice. On the western labor movement, important new interpretations are David Brundage, *The Making of Western Working-Class Radicalism: Denver's Organized Workers,*

1878–1905 (1994) and Elizabeth Jameson, *All That Glitters: Class, Conflict, and Community in Cripple Creek* (1998). The best book on the IWW is Melvyn Dubofsky, *We Shall Be All* (1969). On socialism, David Shannon, *The Socialist Party of America* (1955), remains the standard account. There is, however, a fine biography of that party's leader that supersedes previous studies: Nick Salvatore, *Eugene V. Debs: Citizen and Socialist* (1982). A dimension of American radicalism long neglected has received sensitive attention in Mari Jo Buhle, *Women and American Socialism, 1870–1920* (1982).

Chapter 18: The Politics of Late-Nineteenth-Century America

The best introductions to American politics in the late nineteenth century are John A. Garraty, *The New Commonwealth, 1877–1890* (1968), and R. Hal Williams, *Years of Decision: American Politics in the 1890s* (1978). More detailed and comprehensive is Morton Keller, *Affairs of State: Public Life in Late-Nineteenth-Century America* (1977). Joel L. Silbey, *The American Political Nation, 1838–1893* (1991), focuses on the party system and political behavior.

The Politics of the Status Quo, 1877–1893

Various aspects of national politics are discussed in Robert D. Marcus, *Grand Old Party: Political Structure in the Gilded Age* (1971); H. Wayne Morgan, *From Hayes to McKinley: National Party Politics, 1877–1896* (1969); and David J. Rothman, *Politics and Power: The Senate, 1869–1901* (1966). Heather Cox Richardson, *The Death of Reconstruction: Race, Labor, and Politics in the Post–Civil War North, 1865–1901* (2001), extends the politics of Reconstruction beyond 1877 to the turn of the century. The process of sectional reconciliation is imaginatively studied in David W. Blight, *Race and Reunion: The Civil War in American Memory* (2001). On the development of public administration, see Stephen Skowronek, *Building a New American State: The Expansion of National Administrative Capacities* (1982). The ideological basis for conservative national politics is fully treated in Sidney Fine, *Laissez Faire and the General Welfare State, 1865–1901* (1956), and Robert G. McCloskey, *American Conservatism in the Age of Enterprise* (1951). Much information on the Gilded Age presidents can be found at the Web site <http://americanpresident.org/presidentialresources.htm>. A useful introduction to the legal history of this era is Morton J. Horwitz, *The Transformation of American Law, 1870–1960* (1992).

Politics and the People

On popular participation in politics see especially Michael E. McGerr, *The Decline of Popular Politics: The American North, 1865–1928* (1986), and Paul Kleppner, *The Third Electoral Party System, 1853–1892: Parties, Voters, and Political Cultures* (1979). On the Mugwump reformers see John G. Sproat, *The "Best Men": Liberal Reformers in the Gilded Age* (1965); and Ari Arthur Hoogenboom, *Outlawing the Spoils: The Civil Service Reform Movement, 1865–1883* (1961). Alexander Keyssar, *The Right to Vote: The Contested History of Democracy in the United States* (2000) is illuminating on the assault on voting rights in the late nineteenth century. Kathryn Kish Sklar, *Florence Kelley and the Nation's Work* (1995) traces the emergence of women's political culture through the life of a leading reformer. A valuable book setting the stage is Ellen Carol DuBois, *Feminism and Suffrage: The Emergence of an Independent Women's Movement in America, 1848–1869* (1978). The political role of the WCTU is one of the themes of Suzanne M. Marilley, *Woman Suffrage and the Origins of Liberal Feminism in the United States* (1997).

Race and Politics in the New South

On southern politics the seminal book for the post-Reconstruction period is C. Vann Woodward, *Origins of the New South, 1877–1913* (1951), which still defines the terms of discussion among historians. The most far-reaching revision is Edward L. Ayers, *The Promise of the New South* (1992). Complementary books on the social basis of southern politics are Paul Escott, *Many Excellent People: Power and Privilege in North Carolina, 1850–1900* (1985), and Michael R. Hyman, *The Anti-Redeemers: Hill Country Political Dissenters in the Lower South* (1990).

The classic book on segregation is C. Vann Woodward, *The Strange Career of Jim Crow* (2nd ed., 1968). A powerful analysis of southern racism, stressing its psychosocial roots, is Joel Williamson, *A Rage for Order: Black/White Relations in the American South since Emancipation* (1986). Disfranchisement is treated with great analytic sophistication in J. Morgan Kousser, *The Shaping of Southern Politics: Suffrage Restriction and the Establishment of the One-Party South, 1880–1910* (1974), and Michael Perman, *Struggle for Mastery: Disfranchisement in the South, 1888–1908* (2001). The experience of being black in the South in this era is brilliantly evoked in Leon F. Litwack, *Trouble in Mind: Black Southerners in the Age of Jim Crow* (1998). The preeminent exponent of black accommodation is the subject of a superb two-volume biography by Louis B. Harlan, *Booker T. Washington: The Making of a Black Leader* (1973) and *Wizard of Tuskegee* (1983); and equally fine on Washington's main critic is David Levering Lewis, *W. E. B. Du Bois: Biography of a Race, 1868–1919* (1993).

The Crisis of American Politics: The 1890s

The most recent synthesis on Populism is Robert C. McMath, *American Populism* (1993). Richard D. Hofstadter, *The Age of Reform* (1955), stresses the darker side of Populism, in which intolerance and paranoia figure heavily. Hofstadter's thesis, which once dominated debate among historians, has given way to a more positive assessment. The key book here is Lawrence Goodwyn, *Democratic Promise: The Populist Moment in America* (1976), which argues that Populism was a broadly based radical response to industrial capitalism. Peter H. Argesinger, *The Limits of Agrarian Radicalism: Western Politics and American Politics* (1995), stresses the capacity of the political status quo to frustrate western Populism. Two stimulating books that follow the history of Populism into the twentieth century are Grant McConnell, *The Decline of Agrarian Democracy* (1953), which focuses on farm organizations, and Michael Kazin, *The Populist Persuasion* (1995), which describes how the language of Populism entered the discourse of mainstream American politics.

The money question is elucidated in Allan Weinstein, *Prelude to Populism: Origins of the Silver Issue* (1970), and, in the most recent and sophisticated account, Gretchen Ritter, *Goldbugs and Greenbacks: The Antimonopoly Tradition and the Politics of Finance in America, 1865–1896* (1997). On the politics of the 1890s, see especially Robert F. Durden, *Climax of Populism: The Election of 1896* (1965), and Paul W. Glad, *McKinley, Bryan, and the People* (1964).

Chapter 19: The Rise of the City

Useful introductions to urban history are Charles N. Glaab and A. Theodore Brown, *A History of Urban America* (1967), and Raymond A. Mohl, ed., *The Making of Urban America* (1997). Arthur M. Schlesinger, *The Rise of the City* (1936), is a pioneering study. A sampling of the innovative scholarship that opened new historical paths can be found in Stephan Thernstrom and Richard Sennett, eds., *Nineteenth-Century Cities: Essays in the New Urban History* (1969). Allan Pred, *Spatial Dynamics of U.S. Urban Growth, 1800–1914* (1971), traces the patterns in which cities grew. On the revolution in urban transit see the pioneering book by Sam B. Warner, *Streetcar Suburbs: The Process of Growth in Boston, 1870–1900* (1962). In a subsequent work, *The Private City: Philadelphia in Three Periods* (1968), Warner broadened his analysis to show how private decision making shaped the character of the American city.

Urbanization

Innovations in urban construction are treated in two works by Carl Condit, *American Building Art: Nineteenth Century* (1969) and *Rise of the New York Skyscraper, 1865–1913* (1996); Robert C. Twombly, *Louis Sullivan* (1986); Alan Trachtenberg, *The Brooklyn Bridge* (1965); Harold L. Platt, *The Electric City: Energy and the Growth of the Chicago Area, 1880–1930* (1991); and Mark H. Rose, *Cities of Light and Heat: Domesticating Gas and Electricity in Urban America* (1995). The problems of meeting basic human needs are treated in Jon C. Teaford, *The Unheralded Triumph: City Government in America, 1870–1900* (1984); Eric H. Monkkonen, *Police in Urban America, 1860–1920* (1981); and David B. Tyack, *The One Best System: A History of American Urban Education* (1974). The struggle to reshape the chaotic nineteenth-century city can be explored in John D. Fairchild, *The Mysteries of the Great City: The Politics of Urban Design, 1877–1937* (1993); James Machor, *Pastoral Cities: Urban Ideals and the Symbolic Landscape of America* (1987); and David Schuyler, *The New Urban Landscape: The Redefinition of City Form in Nineteenth-Century America* (1986). On the Columbian Exposition of 1893, an excellent Web site is "The World's Columbian Exposition: Idea, Experience, Aftermath" at <http://xroads.virginia.edu/~MA96/WCE/title.html>, including detailed guides to every site at the fair and analysis of its lasting impact.

Upper Class, Middle Class

Urban social mobility is the focus of Stephan Thernstrom, *The Other Bostonians: Poverty and Progress in an American City, 1880–1970* (1973), which also contains a useful summary of mobility research on other cities. On the social elite, see Frederic C. Jaher, *The Urban Establishment: Upper Strata in Boston, New York, Charleston, Chicago, and Los Angeles* (1982). Sven Beckert, *The Moneyed Metropolis: New York City and the Con-*

solidation of the American Bourgeoisie, 1850–1896 (2001), delves more deeply into the New York story. Two incisive books greatly advance our understanding of the urban middle class: Stuart S. Blumin, *The Emergence of the Middle Class: Social Experience in the American City, 1760–1900* (1989), and Olivier Zunz, *Making Corporate America, 1870–1920* (1990). Aspects of middle-class life are revealed in Margaret Marsh, *Suburban Lives* (1990); Michael A. Ebner, *Creating Chicago's North Shore: A Suburban History* (1988); Gwendolyn Wright, *Moralism and the Model Home: Domestic Architecture and Cultural Conflict in Chicago, 1873–1913* (1980); John F. Kasson, *Rudeness and Civility: Manners in Nineteenth-Century America* (1990); and, on the entry of immigrants into the middle class, Andrew R. Heinze, *Adapting to Abundance: Jewish Immigrants, Mass Consumption, and the Search for American Identity* (1990).

John D'Amelio and Estelle Freedman, *Intimate Matters: A History of Sexuality in America* is a good introduction. Contemporary notions of sexuality are skillfully captured in John S. Haller and Robin M. Haller, *The Physician and Sexuality in Victorian America* (1980). Whether those views actually applied to the private world of the middle class is strongly questioned in Karen Lystra, *The Searching Heart: Women, Men, and Romantic Love in Nineteenth-Century America* (1989). Control over reproduction is fully explored in Janet Farrell Brodie, *Contraception and Abortion in Nineteenth-Century America* (1994); and the moral counterattack, in Nicola Beisel, *Imperiled Innocents: Anthony Comstock and Family Reproduction in Victorian America* (1997). A good introduction to family development, including childhood, is Steven Mintz and Susan Kellog, *Domestic Revolutions: A Social History of the American Family* (1988). The weakening of those bonds is the subject of Howard P. Chudacoff, *The Age of the Bachelor: Creating an American Subculture* (1999). One aspect of that subculture is treated in Clifford Putney, *Muscular Christianity: Manhood and Sports in Protestant America, 1880–1920* (2001).

City Life

A useful introduction to American immigration history is John Bodnar, *The Transplanted* (1986). Among the leading monographs are Moses Rischin, *The Promised City: New York's Jews, 1870–1914* (1962); Joseph Barton, *Peasants and Strangers: Italians, Rumanians, and Slovaks in an American City, 1890–1950* (1975); and Robert A. Orsi, *The Madonna of 115th Street: Faith and Community in Italian Harlem, 1880–1950* (1985). On blacks in the city, see Gilbert Osofsky, *Harlem: The Making of a Ghetto, 1890–1930* (1966); Allan H. Spear, *Black Chicago, 1860–1920* (1966); and Kenneth L. Kusmer, *A Ghetto Takes Shape: Black Cleveland, 1870–1930* (1976). David C. Hammack, *Power and Society: Greater New York at the Turn of the Century* (1982), is a sophisticated treatment that places the party machine in the larger context of municipal power politics. The Web site <http://acad.smumn.edu/history/contents.html> offers a collection of first-rate articles and documents written at the turn of the century about life on New York's Lower East Side, from housing and child labor to ethnic communities and pushcarts. The encounter of Protestantism with the city is treated in William G. McLoughlin, *Modern Revivalism* (1959), and Paul Boyer, *Urban Masses and Moral Order in America, 1820–1920* (1978). On the Catholic Church, see Robert D. Cross, *Liberal Catholicism in America* (1958). Aspects of an emerging city culture are studied in Gunther Barth, *City People: The Rise of Modern City Culture in Nineteenth-Century America* (1982); Susan Porter Benson, *Counter Cultures: Saleswomen, Managers, and Customers in American Department Stores, 1890–1940* (1986); John F. Kasson, *Amusing the Million: Coney Island at the Turn of the Century* (1978); Timothy J. Gilfoyle, *City of Eros: New York City, Prostitution and the Commercialization of Sex, 1790–1920* (1991); Kathy Peiss, *Cheap Amusements: Working Women and Leisure in Turn-of-the-Century New York* (1986); Robert W. Snyder, *The Voice of the City: Vaudeville and Popular Culture in New York City, 1880–1930* (1998); and David Nasaw, *Going Out: The Rise and Fall of Public Amusements* (1993). George Chauncey, *Gay New York: Gender, Urban Culture, and the Making of the Gay New York World, 1890–1940* (1994), reveals a terrain hitherto invisible to the historian. On the fostering of high culture in the American city, see Daniel M. Fox, *Engines of Culture: Philanthropy and Art Museums* (1963). The best introduction to intellectual currents in the emerging urban society is Alan Trachtenberg, *The Incorporation of America: Culture and Society, 1865–1893* (1983).

Chapter 20: The Progressive Era

A good survey of the Progressive Era is John Milton Cooper, *Pivotal Decades: The United States, 1900–1920* (1990). Two older but still serviceable narrative accounts are George E. Mowry, *The Era of Theodore Roosevelt, 1900–1912* (1958), and Arthur S. Link, *Woodrow Wilson and the Progressive Era, 1910–1917* (1954). A highly influential interpretation of progressive reform that is worth reading despite its disputed central arguments is Richard Hofstadter, *Age of Reform* (1955). Robert H. Wiebe, *The Search for Order, 1877–1920* (1967), places progressive reform in a broader context of organizational development.

The Course of Reform

Nancy Cohen, *The Reconstruction of American Liberalism: 1865–1914* (2002), is a good introduction to the intellectual origins of progressivism. The religious underpinnings are stressed in Robert M. Crunden, *Ministers of Reform: The Progressives' Achievement in American Civilization, 1889–1920* (1982). In *The New Radicalism in America, 1889–1963* (1965), Christopher Lasch sees progressivism as a form of cultural revolt. Most useful on political thinkers are Charles Forcey, *The Crossroads of Liberalism: Croly, Weyl, Lippmann, and the Progressive Era* (1961), and Leon Fink, *Progressive Intellectuals and the Dilemmas of Democratic Commitment* (1997). Albert W. Alschuler, *Law Without Values: The Life, Work, and Legacy of Justice Holmes* (2000), is the most recent study of the towering figure in legal realism. Two provocative studies set in an international context are James T. Kloppenberg, *Uncertain Victory: Social Democracy and Progressivism in European and American Thought, 1870–1920* (1986), and Daniel T. Rodgers, *Atlantic Crossings: Social Politics in a Progressive Age* (1998). On the journalists, see David M. Chalmers, *The Social and Political Ideas of the Muckrakers* (1964), and Harold S. Wilson, *McClure's Magazine and the Muckrakers* (1970).

Political reform has been the subject of a voluminous literature. Wisconsin progressivism can be studied in David P. Thelen, *The New Citizenship: Origins of Progressivism in Wisconsin, 1885–1900* (1972). Important progressives are discussed in Spencer C. Olin, *California's Prodigal Son: Hiram Johnson and the Progressive Movement* (1968), and Richard Lowitt, *George W. Norris: The Making of a Progressive* (1963). On city reform see Bradley R. Rice, *Progressive Cities: The Commission Government Movement* (1972); Jack Tager, *The Intellectual as Urban Reformer: Brand Whitlock and the Progressive Movement* (1968); and Melvin G. Holli, *Reform in Detroit: Hazen S. Pingree and Urban Politics* (1969). The best treatment of the settlement-house movement is Allen F. Davis, *Spearheads of Reform* (1967). Allen F. Davis, *American Heroine: Jane Addams* (1973); George Martin, *Madame Secretary: Frances Perkins* (1976); and Kathryn Kish Sklar, *Florence Kelley and the Nation's Work: The Rise of Women's Political Culture* (1995), deal with leading women progressives. The connection to working women is effectively treated in Nancy S. Dye, *As Equals and Sisters: Feminism, the Labor Movement, and the Women's Trade Union League of New York* (1980). Women garment workers, the key labor constituency for women progressives, are studied with great skill and insight in Susan A. Glenn, *Daughters of the Shtetl: Life and Labor in the Immigrant Generation* (1990). Two path-breaking books on the origins of American feminism are Rosalind Rosenberg, *Beyond Separate Spheres: The Intellectual Origins of Modern Feminism* (1982), and Nancy F. Cott, *The Grounding of Modern Feminism* (1987). Sara Hunter Graham, *Woman Suffrage and the New Democracy* (1996), treats the battle for the suffrage as a precocious exercise of single-issue pressure politics. "Votes for Women: Selections from the National American Woman Suffrage Association Collection, 1848–1921" at <http://memory.loc.gov/ammem/naw/nawshome.html> is a searchable archive of over 160 documents pertaining to the campaign for suffrage. Ellen Carol DuBois, *Harriot Stanton Blatch and the Winning of Woman Suffrage* (1997), studies one of the key suffragist leaders. The most prominent social reformer to spring from feminism is treated in Ellen Chesler, *Woman of Valor: Margaret Sanger and the Birth Control Movement* (1992).

On urban liberalism, the standard book is John D. Buenker, *Urban Liberalism and Progressive Reform* (1973). Richard Schneirov, *Labor and Urban Politics: Class Conflict and the Origins of Modern Liberalism in Chicago, 1864–97* (1998), traces the origins of urban liberalism back into the nineteenth century. The relationship to organized labor can be followed in Irwin Yellowitz, *Labor and the Progressive Movement in New York State* (1965). An incisive study of labor's legal problems is William E. Forbath, *Law and the Shaping of the American Labor Movement* (1991). Two important books by historical sociologists treat the halting progress toward the welfare state: Theda Skocpol, *Protecting Soldiers and Mothers* (1992), and, in a comparison of the United States with Canada and Britain, Ann Shola Orloff, *The Politics of Pensions* (1993). Linda Gordon, *Pitied but Not Entitled: Single Mothers and the History of Welfare, 1890–1935* (1994), brilliantly uses the contemporary crisis over welfare reform as a lens for probing the tangled history of this central concern of social progressives. The most comprehensive survey is Morton Keller, *Regulating a New Society: Public Policy and Social Change in America, 1900–1933* (1994). On the South, see Jack Temple Kirby, *Darkness at the Dawning: Race and Reform in the Progressive South* (1972), and Dewey Grantham, *Southern Progressivism* (1983); on southern black women as social reformers, Glenda Elizabeth

Gilmore, *Gender and Jim Crow: Women and the Politics of White Supremacy in North Carolina, 1869–1920* (1996); and on the racial conservatism of social progressives, Elizabeth Lasch-Quinn, *Black Neighbors: Race and the Limits of Reform in the American Settlement-House Movement* (1993). The revival of black protest is vigorously described in Stephen R. Fox, *The Guardian of Boston: William Monroe Trotter* (1971), and David Levering Lewis, *W. E. B. Du Bois: Biography of a Race, 1868–1919* (1993).

Progressivism and National Politics

National progressivism is best approached through its leading figures. John Milton Cooper, *The Warrior and the Priest* (1983), is a provocative joint biography of Roosevelt and Wilson that emphasizes their shared worldview. Lewis S. Gould, *The Presidency of Theodore Roosevelt* (1991), provides a useful synthesis. "Theodore Roosevelt: Icon of the American Century" at <http://www.npg.si.edu/exh/roosevelt/maver.htm> presents pictures from the National Portrait Gallery, a biographical narrative, and information on Roosevelt's family and friends. Aspects of national progressive politics can be followed in James Penick, *Progressive Politics and Conservation: The Ballinger-Pinchot Affair* (1968); James Holt, *Congressional Insurgents and the Party System* (1969); and David Sarasohn, *The Party of Reform: The Democrats in the Progressive Era* (1989). "The Evolution of the Conservation Movement" at <http://memory.loc.gov/ammem/amrvhtml/conspref.html> offers a timeline and archive of materials on the movement's development from 1850 to 1920. Naomi Lamoreaux, *The Great Merger Movement in American Business, 1895–1904* (1985), offers a sophisticated modern analysis of trust activity; Thomas K. McCraw, ed., *Regulation in Perspective* (1981), contains valuable interpretive essays on the problems of trust regulation; and James Livingston, *Origins of the Federal Reserve System: Money, Class, and Corporate Capitalism, 1890–1913* (1986), treats banking reform. A comprehensive rethinking of the progressive struggle to fashion a regulatory policy for big business is offered in Martin J. Sklar, *The Corporate Reconstruction of American Capitalism, 1890–1916: The Market, the Law, and Politics* (1988).

Chapter 21: An Emerging World Power, 1877–1914

Two useful surveys of late-nineteenth-century diplomatic history are Charles S. Campbell, *The Transformation of American Foreign Relations, 1865–1900* (1976), and Walter LaFeber, *The American Search for Opportunity, 1865–1913* (vol. II, *The Cambridge History of American Foreign Relations*, 1993). Invaluable as a historiographical guide is Robert L. Beisner, *From the Old Diplomacy to the New, 1865–1900* (2nd ed., 1986).

The Roots of Expansion

Standard works on the preexpansionist era are David M. Pletcher, *The Awkward Years: American Foreign Relations under Garfield and Arthur* (1963), and Milton Plesur, *America's Outward Thrust: Approaches to American Foreign Affairs, 1865–1890* (1971). Walter La Feber's highly influential *The New Empire, 1860–1898* (1963) places economic interest—especially the need for overseas markets—at the center of schol-

arly debate over the sources of American expansionism. A robust counterpoint is Fareed Zakaria, *From Wealth to Power* (1998), which asks why the United States was so slow (compared to other imperial nations) to translate its economic power into international muscle. On American business overseas the definitive work is Myra Wilkins, *The Emergence of the Multinational Enterprise: American Business Abroad from the Colonial Era to 1914* (1970). Other important books dealing with aspects of American expansionism are David Healy, *U.S. Expansionism: The Imperialist Urge in the 1890s* (1970); Robert Seager, *Alfred Thayer Mahan* (1977); Michael Hunt, *Ideology and U.S. Foreign Policy* (1987); Mark R. Shulman, *Navalism and the Emergence of American Sea Power, 1882–1893* (1995); and Kenneth J. Hagan, *This People's Navy: The Making of American Seapower* (1991). Emily S. Rosenberg, *Spreading the American Dream: American Economic and Cultural Expansionism* (1982), and Matthew Fry Jacobson, *Barbarian Virtues: The United States Encounters Foreign Peoples at Home and Abroad* (2000), explore the home roots of expansionism.

An American Empire

On the war with Spain, the liveliest narrative is still Frank Freidel, *A Splendid Little War* (1958). For fuller treatments, see John Offner, *An Unwanted War: The Diplomacy of the United States and Spain over Cuba, 1895–1898* (1988); David S. Trask, *The War with Spain in 1898* (1981); Ivan Musicant, *Empire by Default* (1998); and Lewis Gould, *The Spanish-American War and President McKinley* (1982), which emphasizes McKinley's strong leadership. Ernest R. May, *Imperial Democracy: The Emergence of America as a Great Power* (1961), exemplifies the earlier view that McKinley was a weak figure driven to war by jingoistic pressures. David Nasaw, *The Chief: The Life of William Randolph Hearst* (2000), is a fine new biography of the prime exponent of jingoism. The Library of Congress maintains an excellent Web site, "The Spanish-American War," at <http://lcweb.loc.gov/rr/hispanic/1898/> with separate sections on the war in Cuba, the Philippines, Puerto Rico, and Spain. On the Philippines, see Richard E. Welch, *Response to Imperialism: The United States and the Philippine-American War, 1898–1903* (1979), and, for the subsequent history, Peter Stanley, *A Nation in the Making: The Philippines and the United States, 1899–1921* (1974). Robert L. Beisner, *Twelve against Empire: The Anti-Imperialists, 1898–1900* (1968) remains the best book on that subject. "Anti-Imperialism in the United States" at <http://www.boondocksnet.com/ai/index.html> includes an extensive collection of documents, political cartoons, maps, and photographs from the period.

Onto the World Stage

On the European context a useful introduction can be found in the early chapters of Felix Gilbert, *The End of the European Era, 1890 to the Present* (4th ed., 1991). For a stimulating interpretation see L. C. B. Seaman, *From Vienna to Versailles* (1955). On American relations with Britain the standard work is Bradford Perkins, *The Great Rapprochement: England and the United States, 1895–1914* (1968). On Roosevelt's diplomacy, the starting point remains Howard K. Beale, *Theodore Roosevelt and the Rise of America to World Power* (1956). There are keen insights into the diplomatic views of both Roosevelt and Wilson in John Milton Cooper, *The Warrior and the Priest* (1983). On the thrust into the Caribbean, see Walter La Feber, *The Panama Canal* (1979); Richard Lael, *Arrogant Diplomacy: U.S. Policy toward Colombia, 1903–1922* (1987); David Healy, *Drive to Hegemony: The United States in the Caribbean, 1898–1917* (1988); and Thomas D. Schoonover, *The United States in Central America, 1860–1911* (1991). America's Asian involvements are treated in Thomas J. McCormick, *China Market: America's Quest for Informal Empire, 1893–1901* (1967); Michael H. Hunt, *The Making of a Special Relationship: The United States and China to 1914* (1983); and Akira Iriye, *Pacific Estrangement: Japanese and American Expansion, 1897–1911* (1972). On the Mexican involvement, see John S. D. Eisenhower, *Intervention! The United States and the Mexican Revolution* (1993). There is a lively and critical analysis of Wilson's misguided policies in Robert E. Quirk, *An Affair of Honor: Woodrow Wilson and the Occupation of Veracruz* (1962). The revolution as experienced by the Mexicans is brilliantly depicted in John Womack, *Zapata and the Mexican Revolution* (1968). The standard work on the American peace movement is Roland Marchand, *The American Peace Movement and Social Reform, 1898–1918* (1973).

Chapter 22: War and the American State, 1914–1920

Ronald Schaffer, *America in the Great War: The Rise of the War Welfare State* (1991), and David M. Kennedy, *Over Here: The First World War and American Society* (1980), provide comprehensive overviews of the period. See also Meirion Harries and Susie Harries, *The Last Days of Innocence: America at War, 1917–1918* (1997). The Public Broadcasting Service's "The Great War and the Shaping of the Twentieth Century" at <http://www.pbs.org/greatwar/index.html> is a companion to the documentary series. Its rich offerings, which emphasize the European context of the war, include bibliographies and maps. "World War I Documents Archive" at <http://www.lib.byu.edu/~rdh/wwi> provides extensive primary documents as well as a series of World War I links. On the links between the Progressive Era and the war, see Neil A. Wynn, *From Progressivism to Prosperity: World War I and American Society* (1986); John A. Thompson, *Reformers and War* (1987); and Robert M. Crunden, *Ministers of Reform* (1982). Ellis W. Hawley, *The Great War and the Search for a Modern Order, 1917–1933* (1979), stresses the continuities between the war years and the 1920s.

The Great War, 1914–1918

On America's entry into World War I, see John Coogan, *The End to Neutrality* (1981); Ross Gregory, *The Origins of American Intervention in the First World War* (1971); and Thomas A. Bailey and Paul Ryan, *The Lusitania Disaster* (1975). Studies of Wilson include August Hecksher, *Woodrow Wilson* (1991); Kendrick Clements, *The Presidency of Woodrow Wilson* (1992); Robert Ferrell, *Woodrow Wilson and World War I* (1985); and John Milton Cooper Jr., *The Warrior and the Priest: Woodrow Wilson and Theodore Roosevelt* (1983). See also David Steigerwald, *Wilsonian Idealism in America* (1994).

For American participation in the war, Russell Weigley, *The American Way of War* (1973), and Edward M. Coffman, *The*

War to End All Wars (1968), provide useful introductions. They can be supplemented by David F. Trask, *The AEF and Coalition War-Making, 1917–1918* (1993); and A. E. Barbeau and Florette Henri, *The Unknown Soldiers: Black Troops in World War I* (1974). "The Diary of Bugler Benjamin Edgar Cruzan," Battery F, 341st Field Artillery, 89th Division, 3rd Army, in which an ordinary soldier poignantly discusses his battle experiences, friendships, and the peace negotiations, is provided at <http://www.kancoll.org/articles/cruzan/c_diary2.htm>. The Library of Congress Web site, "American Leaders Speak: Recordings from World War I and the 1920 Election," available at <http://memory.loc.gov/ammem/nfhtml/>, offers voice recordings of John J. Pershing and other key figures of the World War I era. John Whiteclay Chambers II, *To Raise an Army* (1987), covers the draft. Allan Brandt, *No Magic Bullet* (1985), discusses anti-venereal-disease campaigns, and Mary E. Odem, *Delinquent Daughters* (1995), looks at attempts to control sexuality during the war years. Paul Chapman, *Schools as Sorters* (1988), describes the intelligence-testing movement.

War on the Home Front

Robert D. Cuff, *The War Industries Board: Business-Government Relations during World War I* (1973), provides an excellent case study of mobilization for war. See also Stephen Skowronek, *Building a New American State: The Expansion of National Administrative Capacities, 1877–1920* (1982). Valerie Jean Conner, *The National War Labor Board* (1983), and Melvyn Dubofsky, *The State and Labor in Modern America* (1994), cover federal policies toward labor. Jordan Schwarz, *The Speculator* (1981), is an insightful biography of Bernard Baruch.

Maurine Greenwald, *Women, War, and Work* (1980), and Barbara Steinson, *American Women's Activism in World War I* (1982), provide good overviews of women's wartime experiences. Ellen Carol DuBois, *Harriet Stanton Blatch and the Winning of Woman's Suffrage* (1997), and Christine A. Lunardini, *From Equal Suffrage to Equal Rights: Alice Paul and the National Woman's Party, 1910–1928* (1986), cover the final stages of the woman suffrage campaign. On the peace movement, see C. Roland Marchand, *The American Peace Movement and Social Reform, 1898–1918* (1973); Charles Chatfield, *For Peace and Justice: Pacifism in America, 1914–1941* (1971); and Charles DeBenedetti, *Origins of the Modern Peace Movement* (1978).

Efforts to promote national unity are covered in Stephen Vaughan, *Holding Fast the Inner Lines: Democracy, Nationalism, and the CPI* (1980). For George Creel's story, see his *How We Advertised America* (1920) and *Rebel at Large* (1947). On free speech, see Richard Polenberg, *Fighting Faiths: The Abrams Case, the Supreme Court, and Free Speech* (1987). For the experiences of Mexican Americans, see David C. Gutierrez, *Walls and Mirrors: Mexican Americans, Mexican Immigrants, and the Politics of Ethnicity* (1995), and George Sanchez, *Becoming Mexican American* (1993).

An Unsettled Peace, 1919–1920

On Wilson's diplomacy, see Thomas Knock, *To End All Wars: Woodrow Wilson and the Quest for a New World Order* (1992); Lloyd Ambrosius, *Woodrow Wilson and the American Diplomatic*

Tradition (1987); Arthur Walworth, *Wilson and the Peacemakers* (1986); and N. Gordon Levin Jr., *Woodrow Wilson and World Politics* (1968). For more on Versailles and the League of Nations, see Ralph A. Stone, *The Irreconcilables: The Fight against the League of Nations* (1970), and Arno J. Mayer, *Politics and Diplomacy of Peacemaking: Containment and Counter-Revolution at Versailles* (1967). See also William Widenor, *Henry Cabot Lodge and the Search for an American Foreign Policy* (1980), and Ronald Steel, *Walter Lippmann and the American Century* (1980). On American intervention in Russia, see David Foglesong, *America's Secret War against Bolshevism: U.S. Intervention in the Russian Civil War, 1917–1920* (1995); John L. Gaddis, *Russia, the Soviet Union, and the United States* (1978); and Peter Filene, *Americans and the Soviet Experiment, 1917–1933* (1967).

Robert K. Murray, *The Red Scare* (1955), summarizes the antiradicalism of the postwar period. See also John Higham, *Strangers in the Land* (1955); Burl Noggle, *Into the Twenties* (1974); and William D. Miller, *Pretty Bubbles in the Air: America in 1919* (1991). David Brody, *Labor in Crisis* (1965), describes the steel strike of 1919. On race relations, see Joe William Trotter Jr., ed., *The Great Migration in Historical Perspective* (1991); James R. Grossman, *Land of Hope: Chicago, Black Southerners, and the Great Migration* (1989); William M. Tuttle Jr., *Race Riot: Chicago in the Red Summer of 1919* (1970); Robert V. Haynes, *A Night of Violence: The Houston Riot of 1917* (1976); and Elliot M. Rudwick, *Race Riot at East St. Louis, July 2, 1917* (1964). For conflicting interpretations of the Sacco-Vanzetti case and the two men's innocence, see William Young and David E. Kaiser, *Postmortem: New Evidence in the Case of Sacco and Vanzetti* (1985), and Frances Russel, *Sacco and Vanzetti: The Case Resolved* (1986). On the anarchist context, see Paul Avrich, *Sacco and Vanzetti* (1996).

Chapter 23: Modern Times, the 1920s

General overviews of the 1920s are provided by Lynn Dumenil, *Modern Temper* (1995); William Leuchtenburg, *The Perils of Prosperity* (2nd ed., 1995); and Ann Douglas, *Terrible Honesty: Mongrel Manhattan in the 1920s* (1995). Robert S. Lynd and Helen Merrell Lynd, *Middletown: A Study in Modern American Culture* (1929), remains a superb study of American life in the 1920s. The Library of Congress's "American Memory Collection, Prosperity and Thrift: The Coolidge Era and the Consumer Economy, 1921–1929" at <http://memory.loc.gov/ammem/coolhtml/coolhome.html> is an extensive site with original documents, film footage, and scholarly insights on a variety of topics dealing with the 1920s.

Business-Government Partnership of the 1920s

Discussion of corporate developments can be found in Alfred Chandler, *The Visible Hand* (1977), and Robert Himmelberg, *The Origins of the National Recovery Administration: Business, Government, and the Trade Association Ideal, 1921–1933* (1976). On labor developments, see Irving Bernstein, *The Lean Years* (1960); David Brody, *Workers in Industrial America* (1980); and David Montgomery, *The Fall of the House of Labor* (1987).

The domestic and international aspects of the economy are treated in Jim Potter, *The American Economy between the Wars* (1974), and Emily Rosenberg, *Spreading the American Dream* (1982). Interpretations of foreign policy include Akira Iriye, *The Globalizing of America, 1913–1945* (1993); Warren Cohen, *Empire without Tears* (1987); William Appleman Williams, *The Tragedy of American Diplomacy* (1962); and Walter La Feber, *Inevitable Revolutions* (1983).

General introductions to politics in the 1920s can be found in David Burner, *The Politics of Provincialism* (1967); Robert Murray, *The Politics of Normalcy* (1973); and Alan Dawley, *Struggles for Justice* (1991). Biographies of the decade's major political figures include Donald McCoy, *Calvin Coolidge* (1967); David Burner, *Herbert Hoover* (1979); and Paula Elder, *Governor Alfred E. Smith: The Politician as Reformer* (1983). On women in politics, see Nancy Cott, *The Grounding of Modern Feminism* (1987); Elisabeth Israels Perry, *Belle Moskowitz* (1987); Robyn Muncy, *Creating a Female Dominion of Reform, 1890–1935* (1994); and Molly Ladd-Taylor, *Mother-Work: Women, Child Welfare and the State, 1890–1930* (1994). The State University of New York at Binghamton's page on "Women and Social Movements in the United States, 1775–2000" at <http://womhist.binghamton.edu/> is especially rich on the 1920s, with material on conflicts between African American and white women activists, women in the peace movement, and women's participation in partisan politics.

A New National Culture

David Nasaw, *Going Out: The Rise and Fall of Public Amusements* (1993), introduces the emerging mass culture. On movies, see Steven J. Ross, *Working-Class Hollywood: Silent Film and the Shaping of Class in America* (1998); Robert Sklar, *Movie-Made America*, (2nd ed., 1987); Larry May, *Screening Out the Past* (1980). Calliope Film Resources offers "The Classic Blues and the Women Who Sang Them" as a background piece to a commercially available documentary (*Wild Women Don't Have the Blues*). The site at <http://www.calliope.org/blues/blues1.html> provides a brief history of 1920s women blues singers that includes song lyrics, advertising posters, and photographs. Material on Clara Bow can be found in David Stenn, *Clara Bow, Runnin' Wild* (1988). Erik Barnouw, *A Tower in Babel* (1966), and Susan Douglas, *Inventing American Broadcasting* (1987), discuss radio. See also Melvin Patrick Ely, *The Adventures of Amos 'n' Andy: A Social History of an American Phenomenon* (1991). On advertising, see Roland Marchand, *Advertising the American Dream* (1985), and T. J. Jackson Lears, *Fables of Abundance* (1994). Paula Fass, *The Damned and the Beautiful* (1977), and Beth L. Bailey, *From Front Porch to Back Seat* (1988), cover youth, and Susan Strasser, *Never Done* (1982), and Ruth Schwartz Cowan, *More Work for Mother* (1983), discuss the lives of white middle-class women. Lizabeth Cohen, *Making a New Deal: Industrial Workers in Chicago, 1919–1939* (1990), suggests how working-class communities adapted mass culture for their purposes. Joan Shelley Rubin describes the middle class in *The Making of Middlebrow Culture* (1992).

The impact of the automobile on modern American life is amply documented by James Flink, *The Car Culture* (1975) and *The Automobile Age* (1988); on women and the automobile, see Virginia Scharff, *Taking the Wheel* (1991). For sports, see Allen Guttmann, *A Whole New Ball Game* (1988); Harvey Green, *Fit for America* (1986); and Susan Cahn, *Coming on Strong: Gender and Sexuality in Twentieth-Century Women's*

Sport (1994). The Negro Leagues are covered in Robert W. Peterson, *Only the Ball Was White* (1970), and Donn Rogosin, *Invisible Men* (1985).

Dissenting Values and Cultural Conflict

Paul Carter, *Another Part of the Twenties* (1977), outlines the decade's deeply felt cultural controversies. Background on rural and urban life is provided by Don Kirschner, *City and Country: Rural Responses to Urbanization in the 1920s* (1970); Zane Miller, *The Urbanization of America* (1973); and Jon Teaford, *The Twentieth-Century American City* (1986). John Higham, *Strangers in the Land* (1955), describes immigration restriction and nativism. Richard K. Tucker, *The Dragon and the Cross* (1991), and Leonard Moore, *Citizen Klansmen* (1991), cover the Klan's rise and fall, and Kathleen M. Blee, *Women of the Klan* (1991), and Nancy MacLean, *Behind the Mask of Chivalry* (1994), offer a provocative discussion of racism and gender in the 1920s. George M. Marsden, *Fundamentalism and American Culture* (1980), and William G. McLoughlin, *Fundamentalism in American Culture* (1983), cover religion; Edward J. Larson, *Summer of the Gods* (1997), treats the Scopes trial. Douglas O. Linder of the University of Missouri-Kansas City maintains a "Famous Trials" Web site at <http://www.law.umkc.edu/faculty/projects/ftrials/scopes/scopes.htm> that offers photos, cartoons, biographies of the participants, and firsthand accounts of the Scopes trial. On intellectual development, see Robert Crunden, *Body and Soul: The Making of American Modernism: Art, Music and Letters in the Jazz Age, 1919–1926* (2000); Roderick Nash, *The Nervous Generation: American Thought, 1917–1930* (1969); and Daniel Singal, ed., *Modernist Culture in America* (1991). Virginia Sanchez Korrol, *From Colonia to Community* (1983), covers the history of Puerto Ricans in New York City. On the Harlem Renaissance, see George Hutchinson, *The Harlem Renaissance in Black and White* (1995); David Levering Lewis, *When Harlem Was in Vogue* (1981); Nathan Huggins, *Harlem Renaissance* (1971); and Cheryl A. Wall, *Women of the Harlem Renaissance* (1995). For jazz and blues, see Burton Peretti, *The Creation of Jazz* (1992), Daphne Duval Harrison, *Black Pearls: Blues Queens of the 1920s* (1990); and Angela Y. Davis, *Blues Legacies and Black Feminism* (1998). Judith Stein, *The World of Marcus Garvey* (1985), describes the reformer. On Prohibition, see Andrew Sinclair, *Prohibition: The Era of Excess* (1962), and Norman Clark, *Deliver Us from Evil* (1976). The 1928 election is covered in Oscar Handlin, *Al Smith and His America* (1958); Kristi Andersen, *The Creation of a Democratic Majority, 1928–1936* (1979); and Allan J. Lichtman's quantitative study, *Prejudice and the Old Politics* (1979).

Chapter 24: The Great Depression

Useful overviews of the Great Depression are T. H. Watkins, *The Great Depression: America in the 1930s* (1993); John A. Garraty, *The Great Depression* (1987); and Robert S. McElvaine, *The Great Depression, 1929–1941* (1984).

The Coming of the Great Depression

Historians and economists continue to debate the causes of the Great Depression. See John Kenneth Galbraith, *The Great Crash* (1954); Milton Friedman and Anna Schwartz, *The Great Contraction, 1929–1933* (1965); Charles Kindleberger, *The World in Depression* (1974); and Michael Bernstein, *The Great Depression: Delayed Recovery and Economic Change in America, 1929–1939* (1988). Irving Bernstein, *The Lean Years* (1960), offers a compelling portrait of hard times during the Hoover years.

Hard Times

A wealth of material brings the voices of the 1930s to life. The Federal Writers' Project, *These Are Our Lives* (1939); Tom Terrill and Jerrold Hirsch, eds., *Such as Us: Southern Voices of the Thirties* (1978); and Ann Banks, ed., *First-Person America* (1980), all draw on oral histories collected by the Works Progress Administration during the 1930s. See also Robert S. McElvaine, ed., *Down and Out in the Great Depression* (1983). Evocative secondary sources include Studs Terkel, *Hard Times: An Oral History of the Great Depression* (1970), and Caroline Bird, *The Invisible Scar* (1966).

Descriptions of family life in the 1930s include Robert and Helen Lynd, *Middletown in Transition* (1937); Mirra Komarovsky, *The Unemployed Man and His Family* (1940); and Roger Angell, *The Family Encounters the Depression* (1936). Russell Baker's autobiography, *Growing Up* (1982), provides an often humorous description of family life in the 1930s. Glen H. Elder Jr., *Children of the Great Depression* (1974), and John A. Clausen, *American Lives: Looking Back at the Children of the Great Depression* (1993), consider the long-term effects. For more on youth, see Maxine Davis, *The Lost Generation* (1936); and John Modell, *Into One's Own: From Youth to Adulthood, 1920–1975* (1989).

Frederick Lewis Allen, *Since Yesterday* (1939), provides an impressionistic overview of popular culture in the 1930s. See also the essays in Lawrence W. Levine, *The Unpredictable Past* (1993), and Michael Denning, *Cultural Front: The Laboring of American Culture in the Twentieth Century* (1996). Much valuable material can be found on the University of Utrecht's "American Culture in the 1930s" site at <http://www.let.uu.nl/ams/xroads/1930link.htm>, which provides an invaluable list of "Internet Resources on the 1930s." Specific studies of movies and Hollywood include Andrew Bergman, *We're in the Money* (1971); Molly Haskell, *From Reverence to Rape: The Treatment of Women in the Movies* (2nd ed., 1987); and Thomas Schatz, *The Genius of the System: Hollywood Film Making in the Studio Era* (1988). On radio, see Arthur Frank Wertheim, *Radio Comedy* (1979). The University of Virginia's "America in the 1930s" is a comprehensive site. See especially "On the Air," which offers audio clips of *Amos 'n' Andy* and other series at <http://xroads.virginia.edu/~1930s/home_1.html>. Much valuable material can be found on the University of Utrecht's "American Culture in the 1930s" site at <http://www.let.uu.nl/ams/xroads/1930proj.htm>, which in turn points to other sites dealing with literature, film, and other aspects of American culture during the depression.

Material on women in the 1930s can be found in Susan Ware, *Holding Their Own* (1982); Winifred Wandersee, *Women's Work and Family Values, 1920–1940* (1981); and Lois Scharf, *To Work and to Wed* (1981). For the special dimensions of white rural women's lives, see Margaret Hagood, *Mothers of the South* (1939). Jeane Westin, *Making Do: How Women*

Survived the '30s (1976), is a lively account drawn from interviews. The birth control movement is surveyed in Linda Gordon, *Woman's Body, Woman's Right* (2nd ed., 1990); Estelle Freedman and John D'Emilio, *Intimate Matters: A History of Sexuality in America* (1988); and Ellen Chesler, *Woman of Valor: Margaret Sanger and the Birth Control Movement in America* (1992).

Harder Times

Developments in the black community during the 1930s are covered in Cheryl Lyn Greenberg, *"Or Does It Explode?" Harlem in the Great Depression* (1991); Jervis Anderson, *This Was Harlem, 1900–1950* (1982); and Robert Weisbrot, *Father Divine and the Struggle for Racial Equality* (1983). James Goodman, *Stories of Scottsboro* (1994), and Dan T. Carter, *Scottsboro* (1969), discuss that case. Donald Grubbs, *Cry from Cotton* (1971), tells the story of the Southern Tenant Farmers Union. Robin D. G. Kelley, *Hammer and Hoe* (1990), is an excellent account of Alabama communists during the Great Depression. Donald Worster, *Dust Bowl* (1979), evokes the plains during the "Dirty Thirties." James N. Gregory, *American Exodus: The Dust Bowl Migration and Okie Culture in California* (1989), treats the experiences of migrants and their impact on California culture and the economy. The Library of Congress's American Memory collection has extensive material on the depression, including a multimedia presentation, "Voices from the Dust Bowl: The Charles L. Todd and Robert Sonkin Migrant Worker Collection, 1940–41" at <http://lcweb2.loc.gov/ammem/afctshtml/tshome.html>. See also Kevin Starr, *Endangered Dreams: The Great Depression in California* (1996).

On the experiences of Mexican Americans during the 1930s, see Mario T. Garcia, *Mexican Americans: Leadership, Ideology, and Identity, 1930–1960* (1989), and *Memories of Chicano History: The Life and Narrative of Bert Corona* (1994). George J. Sanchez, *Becoming Mexican American* (1993), examines Chicano Los Angeles from 1900 to 1945; and David Gutierrez, *Walls and Mirrors* (1995), looks at Mexican immigration and the politics of ethnicity. See also Richard A. Garcia, *The Rise of the Mexican-American Middle Class* (1990). For Mexican American women's lives in the twentieth century, see Vicki Ruiz's overview, *From Out of the Shadows* (1998), as well as her *Cannery Women, Cannery Lives* (1987), and Patricia Zavella, *Women's Work and Chicano Families* (1987). On Asian Americans, see Judy Yung, *Unbound Feet: A Social History of Chinese Women in San Francisco* (1995) and Ronald Takaki, *Strangers from a Different Shore: A History of Asian Americans* (1989).

Herbert Hoover and the Great Depression

Hoover's response to the depression is chronicled in Alfred Romasco, *The Poverty of Abundance* (1965), and Jordan Schwartz, *The Interregnum of Despair* (1970). Eliot Rosen, *Hoover, Roosevelt, and the Brain Trust* (1977), treats the transition between the two administrations, as does Frank Freidel, *Launching the New Deal* (1973). On the 1932 election and the beginnings of the New Deal coalition, see David Burner, *The Politics of Provincialism* (1967); Samuel Lubell *The Future of American Politics* (1952); and John Allswang, *The New Deal in American Politics* (1978).

Chapter 25: The New Deal, 1933–1939

Comprehensive introductions to the New Deal include Robert S. McElvaine, *The Great Depression* (1984); William E. Leuchtenburg, *Franklin D. Roosevelt and the New Deal* (1963); John A. Garraty, *The Great Depression* (1987); Roger Biles, *A New Deal for the American People* (1991); and Harvard Sitkoff, ed., *Fifty Years Later: The New Deal Evaluated* (1985). On the appeal of Roosevelt and his fireside chats, see Lawrence Levine and Cornelia Levine, *The People and the President: America's Conversation with FDR* (2002).

The New Deal Takes Over, 1933–1935

The New Deal has inspired a voluminous bibliography. Frank Freidel, *Launching the New Deal* (1973), covers the first hundred days in detail. Monographs include Bernard Bellush, *The Failure of the NRA* (1975); Thomas K. McCraw, *TVA and the Power Fight* (1970); John Salmond, *The Civilian Conservation Corps* (1967); Roy Lubove, *The Struggle for Social Security* (1968); Mark Leff, *The Limits of Symbolic Reform: The New Deal and Taxation, 1933–1939* (1984); and Bonnie Fox Schwartz, *The Civilian Works Administration, 1933–1934* (1984). Ellis Hawley, *The New Deal and the Problem of Monopoly* (1966), provides a stimulating account of economic policy. Claire Bond Potter, *War on Crime* (1998), analyzes the Federal Bureau of Investigation and state building in the 1930s. Agricultural developments are covered in Theodore Saloutos, *The American Farmer and the New Deal* (1982); and Sidney Baldwin, *Poverty and Politics: The Rise and Decline of the Farm Security Administration* (1968). Alan Brinkley, *Voices of Protest* (1982), covers the Coughlin and Long movements.

The Second New Deal, 1935–1938

Roosevelt's second term has drawn far less attention than has the 1933–1936 period. James MacGregor Burns, *Roosevelt: The Lion and the Fox* (1956), provides an overview, as does Barry Karl, *The Uneasy State* (1983). Alan Brinkley, *The End of Reform* (1995), discusses the New Deal and liberalism between 1937 and 1945. The growing opposition to the New Deal is treated in Clyde P. Weed, *The Nemesis of Reform: The Republican Party during the New Deal* (1994), and James T. Patterson, *Congressional Conservatism and the New Deal* (1967).

The New Deal's Impact on Society

Katie Louchheim, ed., *The Making of the New Deal: The Insiders Speak* (1983), provides an engaging introduction to some of the men and women who shaped the New Deal. "The New Deal Network," sponsored by the Franklin and Eleanor Roosevelt Institute and the Institute for Learning Technologies, has an impressive site at <http://newdeal.feri.org/index.htm> with extensive images, features such as "Work-Study-Live: The

Resident Youth Centers of the NYA," and links to other New Deal sites. On women in the New Deal, see Susan Ware, *Beyond Suffrage* (1981). Blanche Cook, *Eleanor Roosevelt* (1991), takes the story to 1933; see also Lois Scharf, *Eleanor Roosevelt* (1987). Also of interest is Frances Perkins's memoir, *The Roosevelt I Knew* (1946).

On minorities and the New Deal, see Harvard Sitkoff, *A New Deal for Blacks* (1978); John B. Kirby, *Black Americans in the Roosevelt Era* (1980); Robert Zangrando, *The NAACP Crusade against Lynching, 1909–1950* (1980); and Nancy J. Weiss, *Farewell to the Party of Lincoln* (1983). For material on Mary McLeod Bethune, see Darline Clark Hine, ed., *Black Women in America: An Historical Encyclopedia* (1993). George J. Sanchez, *Becoming Mexican American: Ethnicity, Culture and Identity in Chicano Los Angeles, 1900–1945* (1993), and David G. Gutierrez, *Walls and Mirrors: Mexican Americans, Mexican Immigrants, and the Politics of Ethnicity* (1995), describe the politicization of Mexican Americans in the 1930s.

Irving Bernstein, *The Turbulent Years* (1970) and *A Caring Society: The New Deal, the Worker, and the Great Depression* (1985), chronicle the story of the labor movement through 1941 in compelling detail. Additional studies include Ronald Schatz, *The Electrical Workers* (1983); Bruce Nelson, *Workers on the Waterfront* (1988); and Lizabeth Cohen, *Making a New Deal: Industrial Workers in Chicago, 1919–1939* (1990). Steven Fraser, *Labor Will Rule* (1991), is a fine biography of CIO leader Sidney Hillman. A number of Web sites offer resources for local and state history. An excellent example is the Michigan State History Museum's "The Great Depression," with material on the Flint sit-down strike and New Deal relief programs at <http://www.sos.state.mi.us/history/museum/explore/museums/hismus/hismus.html>. For women and the labor movement, see Annelise Orleck, *Common Sense and a Little Fire* (1995).

On Indian policy, see Donald Parman, *Navajos and the New Deal* (1976); Laurence Hauptman, *The Iroquois and the New Deal* (1981); and Laurence C. Kelly, *The Assault on Assimilation: John Collier and the Origins of Indian Policy Reform* (1983). For rural electrification, see D. Clayton Brown, *Electricity for Rural America* (1980).

The various New Deal programs have found historians in Jerry Mangione, *The Dream and the Deal: The Federal Writers' Project, 1935–1943* (1972); Richard McKinzie, *The New Deal for Artists* (1973); and Jane DeHart Mathews, *The Federal Theater, 1935–1939* (1967). The Library of Congress page on the "Federal Theater Project 1933–1939" at <http://memory.loc.gov/ammem/fedtp/fthome.html> offers scripts, still photographs, costumes, and production materials for several plays put on by the Federal Theater Project. See also the library's excellent posting of over 55,000 photographs from the Farm Security Administration and Office of War Information Collection at <http://memory.loc.gov/ammem/fsowhome.html>. Marlene Park and Gerald Markowitz, *Democratic Vistas* (1984), survey New Deal murals and art, and Barbara Melosh, *Engendering Culture* (1991), looks at New Deal public art and theater. General studies of cultural expression include William Stott, *Documentary Expression and Thirties America* (1973), and Richard Pells, *Radical Visions and American Dreams* (1973). The creation of the New Deal's welfare system is treated in James T. Patterson, *America's Struggle against Poverty* (1981), which carries the story through 1980.

See also Michael Katz, *In the Shadow of the Poorhouse: A Social History of Welfare in America* (1986). Linda Gordon, *Pitied but Not Entitled: Single Mothers and the History of Welfare* (1994), assesses the impact of gender on welfare. For the enduring impact of Franklin Roosevelt on the political system, see William Leuchtenburg, *In the Shadow of FDR* (1983).

Chapter 26: The World at War, 1939–1945

John Morton Blum, *V Was for Victory* (1976); William O'Neill, *A Democracy at War* (1993); and Michael C. C. Adams, *The Best War Ever* (1994), offer good introductions to American politics and culture during the war years. A valuable collection of articles is found in Lewis A. Erenberg and Susan E. Hirsch, eds., *The War in American Culture* (1996). Studs Terkel, *"The Good War"* (1984), offers a powerful and provocative oral history of the war. John Keegan, *The Second World War* (1990), offers the best one-volume account of the battlefront aspects.

The Road to War

Depression and wartime diplomacy are covered in Robert Dallek, *Franklin D. Roosevelt and American Foreign Policy, 1932–1945* (1979), and Akira Iriye, *The Globalizing of America, 1913–1945* (1993). On American isolationism, see Wayne Cole, *Roosevelt and the Isolationists, 1932–1945* (1983). Warren T. Kimball, *The Most Unsordid Act* (1969), describes the lend-lease controversy of 1939–1941, whereas Kimball's *The Juggler: Franklin Roosevelt as Wartime Statesman* (1991), provides an overview of Roosevelt's leadership. Roberta Wohlstetter, *Pearl Harbor* (1962); Herbert Feis, *The Road to Pearl Harbor* (1950); and Gordon W. Prange, *At Dawn We Slept* (1981), describe the events that led to American entry into the war.

Organizing for Victory

George Flynn, *The Mess in Washington* (1979), and Harold G. Vatter, *The U.S. Economy in World War II* (1985), discuss America's economic mobilization. Mark S. Foster, *Henry J. Kaiser: Builder in the Modern American West* (1989), and Stephen B. Adams, *Mr. Kaiser Goes to Washington: The Rise of a Government Entrepreneur* (1997), are comprehensive accounts of Kaiser's career. Alan Winkler, *The Politics of Propaganda* (1978), covers the Office of War Information. On labor's role during war, see George Lipsitz, *Rainbow at Midnight: Labor and Culture in the 1940s* (1994); and Nelson Lichtenstein, *Labor's War at Home: The CIO in World War II* (1982). The National Archives Administration at <http://www.archives.gov/exhibit_hall/index.html?page=2> has two World War II sites. "A People at War" offers a number of documents, including a letter about the Navajo Code Talkers. "Powers of Persuasion: Poster Art from World War II" contains thirty-three color posters and a sound file of the song "Any Bonds Today." For more on politics in wartime, see James McGregor Burns, *Roosevelt: The Soldier of Freedom* (1970); Doris Kearns Goodwin, *No Ordinary Time* (1994); and Alan Brinkley, *The End of Reform* (1995).

Women's roles in wartime are covered by Susan Hartmann, *The Home Front and Beyond* (1982); Karen Anderson, *Wartime*

Women (1980); D'Ann Campbell, *Women at War with America* (1984); Ruth Milkman, *Gender at Work* (1987); and Sherna B. Gluck, *Rosie the Riveter Revisited: Women, the War, and Social Change* (1987). Judy Barrett Litoff and David C. Smith, *We're in This War, Too* (1994), includes letters from American women in uniform, and Leisa D. Meyer, *Creating GI Jane* (1996), discusses the Women's Army Corps. The Library of Congress at <http://lcweb.loc.gov/exhibits/wcf/wcf0001.html> has an online exhibit, "Women Come to the Front: Journalists, Photographers, and Broadcasters during World War II," that features articles, biographies, and photographs of eight women who covered the war. See also "Rosie Pictures: Select Images Relating to American Women Workers during World War II" at <http://lcweb.loc.gov/rr/print/126_rosi.html>.

Life on the Home Front

William M. Tuttle Jr., *"Daddy's Gone to War"* (1993), describes World War II from the perspective of the nation's children. Alan Clive, *State of War* (1979), provides a case study of Michigan during the war; Marilynn S. Johnson, *The Second Gold Rush* (1993), describes Oakland, California, and the East Bay. See also Gerald D. Nash, *The American West Transformed: The Impact of the Second World War* (1985). The Rutgers Oral History Archive of World War II at <http://fas-history.rutgers.edu/oralhistory/orlhom.htm> offers over 100 oral histories that cover not just the interviewees' war experiences but their life histories as well, providing valuable insights into community life in depression and wartime New Jersey. Clayton R. Koppes and Gregory D. Black, *Hollywood Goes to War* (1987), and Thomas Doherty, *Projections of War* (1993), cover the film industry. On racial tensions and the war, see Ronald Takaki, *Double Victory: A Multicultural History of America in World War II* (2001). The experience of black Americans is treated in Albert Russell Buchanan, *Black Americans in World War II* (1977), and Neil Wynn, *The Afro-American and the Second World War* (1975). On racial tensions, see Dominic Capeci Jr., *Race Relations in Wartime Detroit* (1984), and Mauricio Mazan, *The Zoot Suit Riots* (1984). Richard Dalfiume, *Desegregation of the U.S. Armed Forces* (1969), covers black soldiers in the military, and Phillip McGuire, *Taps for a Jim Crow Army* (1993), offers a collection of letters from black soldiers. Alan Berube, *Coming Out under Fire* (1990), is an oral history of gay men and lesbians in the military; see also John D'Emilio, *Sexual Politics, Sexual Communities* (1983), for the impact of the war on gay Americans. Maurice Isserman, *Which Side Were You On?* (1982), analyzes the American Communist Party during the war. Two compelling accounts of Japanese relocation are Audre Girdner and Anne Loftus, *The Great Betrayal* (1969), and Roger Daniels, *Prisoners without Trial: Japanese-Americans in World War II* (1993). See also John Tateishi, ed., *And Justice for All: An Oral History of the Japanese-American Detention Camps* (1984); Peter Irons, *Justice at War: The Story of the Japanese-American Internment Cases* (1983); and Page Smith, *Democracy on Trial: The Japanese-American Evacuation and Relocation in World War II* (1995). There are many Web sites on Japanese internment. The University of Washington provides a particularly interesting one at <http://www.lib.washington.edu/exhibits/harmony/default.htm> on the experiences of the Seattle Japanese American community's incarceration at the Puyallup Assembly Center; it includes letters, photographs, and other documents.

Fighting and Winning the War

Extensive material chronicles the American military experience during World War II. Williamson Murray and Allan R. Millett, *A War to Be Won: Fighting the Second World War* (2000); Gerald Linderman, *The World within War: America's Combat Experience in World War 2* (1999); and Russell F. Weigley, *The American Way of War* (1973), provide overviews. Ronald Schaffer, *Wings of Judgement: American Bombing in World War II* (1985), and Bradley F. Smith, *The Shadow Warriors: OSS and the Origins of the CIA* (1983), are more specialized. Stephen Ambrose, *D-Day, June 6, 1944* (1994) and *Citizen Soldiers* (1997), describe the end of the fighting in Europe. David S. Wyman, *The Abandonment of the Jews* (1984), describes the lack of American response to the Holocaust from 1941 to 1945. On East Asia, see John W. Dower, *War without Mercy: Race and Power in the Pacific War* (1986); Ronald H. Spector, *Eagle against the Sun: The American War with Japan* (1984); and John Toland, *Rising Sun: The Decline and Fall of the Japanese Empire* (1970).

American diplomacy and the strategy of the Grand Alliance are surveyed in Lloyd Gardner, *Spheres of Influence* (1993). The relationship between the wartime conferences and the onset of the cold war is treated in Walter La Feber, *America, Russia, and the Cold War* (8th ed., 1996), and Stephen Ambrose and Douglas Brinkley, *Rise to Globalism* (8th ed., 1997). Richard Rhodes, *The Making of the Atomic Bomb* (1987), and Martin Sherwin, *A World Destroyed* (1975), provide compelling accounts of the development of the bomb. See also Gar Alperovitz, *The Decision to Use the Atomic Bomb* (1995); Ronald Takaki, *Hiroshima: Why America Dropped the Atomic Bomb* (1995); and Robert Jay Lifton and Greg Mitchell, *Hiroshima in America: Fifty Years of Denial* (1995).

Chapter 27: Cold War America, 1945–1960

General works on the politics and diplomacy of the cold war era include James T. Patterson, *Grand Expectations: The United States, 1945–1974* (1997); William Chafe, *The Unfinished Journey* (4th ed., 1999), and Paul Boyer, *Promises to Keep* (1995). The Woodrow Wilson International Center for Scholars has established the "Cold War International History Project" at <http://cwihp.si.edu/default.htm>, an exceptionally rich Web site offering documents on the cold war, including materials from former communist-bloc countries.

The Cold War Abroad

The best overviews of the cold war are Walter La Feber, *America, Russia, and the Cold War, 1945–1990* (8th ed., 1997); Thomas G. Paterson, *On Every Front: The Making and Unmaking of the Cold War* (rev. ed., 1992); and Stephen Ambrose and Douglas Brinkley, *Rise to Globalism* (8th ed., 1997). Melvyn P. Leffler presents a masterful and exhaustive synthesis of Truman's foreign policy in *A Preponderance of Power* (1992). For critical views of American aims, see H. W. Brands, *The Devil We Knew* (1993), and Richard Ned Lebow and Janice Gross Stein, *We All Lost the Cold War* (1994). John Lewis

Gaddis blames the cold war on both the United States and the Soviet Union in *Strategies of Containment* (1982), although his more recent works, *The Long Peace* (1987) and *The United States and the End of the Cold War* (1992), are more sympathetic to American policymaking. For international perspectives on the cold war, see Melvyn P. Leffler and David S. Painter, eds., *Origins of the Cold War: An International History* (1994), and Thomas J. McCormick, *America's Half-Century* (1989). Specialized studies include Ernest R. May, ed., *American Cold War Strategy: Interpreting NSC-68* (1993); Laurence S. Kaplan, *The United States and NATO* (1984); Michael Hogan, *The Marshall Plan* (1987); and Richard Freeland, *The Truman Doctrine and the Origins of McCarthyism* (1972).

McGeorge Bundy, *Danger and Survival* (1989); Martin J. Sherwin, *A World Destroyed* (1975); and Gar Alperovitz, *Atomic Diplomacy* (2nd ed., 1994), cover the impact of atomic weapons on American policy. For developments in Asia, see Akira Iriye, *The Cold War in Asia* (1974); William Borden, *The Pacific Alliance* (1984); Warren I. Cohen, *America's Response to China* (2nd ed., 1980); and Michael Schaller, *The United States and China in the Twentieth Century* (1979) and *The American Occupation of Japan* (1985).

There is an abundance of scholarship on the Korean War, including William Stueck, *The Korean War: An International History* (1995); Clay Blair, *The Forgotten War* (1988); Max Hastings, *The Korean War* (1987); Callum McDonald, *Korea: The War before Vietnam* (1987); Burton Kaufman, *The Korean War* (1986); and Rosemary Foot, *The Wrong War* (1985). Especially influential are the two volumes of *The Origins of the Korean War* by Bruce Cumings: *Liberation and the Emergence of Separate Regions, 1945–1947* (1981) and *The Roaring of the Cataract, 1947–1950* (1990).

On Eisenhower's foreign policy, see Robert A. Divine, *Eisenhower and the Cold War* (1981). On American involvement in the Middle East, see Jarmo Oikarinen, *The Middle East in the American Question for World Order* (1999), and Michael Stoff, *Oil, War, and American Security* (1980). On Latin America, see Stephen Rabe, *Eisenhower and Latin America: The Foreign Policy of Anticommunism* (1988).

The Cold War at Home

Harry Truman, *Memoirs* (1952–1962), tells Truman's story in characteristically pointed language; see also Merle Miller's oral history, *Plain Speaking* (1980); David McCullough, *Truman* (1992), offers a generally sympathetic biography; Alonzo Hamby presents a more mixed view in *Man of the People: A Life of Harry S. Truman* (1995). The Truman Presidential Museum and Library provides a searchable collection of images and documents regarding the Truman presidency at <http://www.trumanlibrary.org/>. This collection is organized into categories such as the origins of the Truman Doctrine, the Berlin airlift, the desegregation of the armed forces, and the 1948 presidential campaign. Users can also browse through the president's correspondence. General accounts of the Truman presidency can be found in Robert J. Donovan, *Tumultuous Years: The Presidency of Harry S. Truman, 1949–1953* (1982); Donald R. McCoy, *The Presidency of Harry S. Truman* (1984); and William Pemberton, *Harry S. Truman* (1989). Critical perspectives are presented in Barton J. Bern-

stein, ed., *Politics and Policies of the Truman Administration* (1970). On Eisenhower's presidency, see Fred I. Greenstein, *The Hidden-Hand Presidency* (1982); Stephen Ambrose, *Eisenhower the President* (1984); Herbert S. Parmet, *Eisenhower and the American Crusades* (1972); and Charles C. Alexander, *Holding the Line* (1975).

The literature on McCarthyism is voluminous. Recent works include Richard Gid Powers, *Not without Honor* (1996); Richard Fried, *Nightmare in Red: The McCarthy Era in Perspective* (1990); and Stephen J. Whitfield, *The Culture of the Cold War* (1991). David Caute, *The Great Fear* (1978), provides a detailed account, which can be supplemented by Victor Navasky, *Naming Names* (1980), and Athan Theoharis, *Spying on Americans* (1978). The Center for the Study of the Pacific Northwest's site, "The Cold War and Red Scare in Washington State" at <http://www.washington.edu/uwired/outreach/cspn/curcan/main.html> provides detailed information on how the Great Fear operated in one state. Its bibliography includes books, documents, and videos. Two useful biographies are Thomas C. Reeves, *The Life and Times of Joe McCarthy* (1982), and David Oshinsky, *A Conspiracy So Immense* (1983).

The Emergence of Civil Rights as a National Issue

For the importance of the cold war for race relations, see Mary L. Dudziak, *Cold War Civil Rights: Race and the Image of American Democracy* (2000). Robert F. Burk, *The Eisenhower Administration and Black Civil Rights* (1984), looks at what the administration did and did not do. Richard Kluger, *Simple Justice* (1975), and Mark Tushnet, *The NAACP's Legal Strategy against Segregated Education* (1987), analyze the Brown decision and its context. Pete Daniels, *Lost Revolutions: The South in the 1950s* (2000), offers valuable insights about the emergence of the civil rights movement and the white response. Taylor Branch, *Parting the Waters: America in the King Years, 1954–1963* (1988), provides a good account of King's early years.

The Impact of the Cold War

For the impact of the cold war on American culture, see Tom Engelhardt, *The End of Victory Culture: Cold War America and the Disillusioning of a Generation* (1998) and Richard M. Fried, *The Russians are Coming, The Russians are Coming! Pageantry and Patriotism in Cold War America* (1999). On Americans' response to the bomb, see Paul Boyer, *By the Bomb's Early Light* (1985), and Allan M. Winkler, *Life Under a Cloud* (1993). Howard Ball, *Justice Downwind* (1986), covers nuclear testing in the 1950s. On the military-industrial complex, see Gregory Michael Hooks, *Forging the Military-Industrial Complex* (1991).

Chapter 28: The Affluent Society and the Liberal Consensus, 1945–1965

General introductions to postwar society include Paul Boyer, *Promises to Keep* (1995); James T. Patterson, *Grand Expectations: The United States, 1945–1974* (1996); and David Halberstam, *The Fifties* (1993).

The Affluent Society

For overviews of the economic changes of the postwar period, see David P. Calleo, *The Imperious Economy* (1982). Herman P. Miller, *Rich Man, Poor Man* (1971), and Gabriel Kolko, *Wealth and Power in America* (1962), discuss inequality in income distribution. Michael Harrington, *The Other America* (1962), documents the persistence of poverty in the postwar era.

Kenneth Jackson, *Crabgrass Frontier* (1985), provides an overview of suburban development. Herbert Gans, *The Levittowners* (1967), and Bennett M. Berger, *Working-Class Suburb* (1960), are sociological studies of suburbia written by contemporaries. On postwar development in the South and West, see Carl Abbott, *The Metropolitan Frontier: Cities in the Modern American West* (1993); Numan V. Bartley, *The New South, 1945–1980* (1995); and Richard Bernard and Bradley Rice, eds., *Sunbelt Cities* (1983).

Books that highlight the social and cultural history of the 1950s include Larry May, ed., *Recasting America* (1989), and Douglas T. Miller and Marion Nowak, *The Fifties* (1977). "Literary Kicks: The Beat Generation" at <http://www.charm.net/~brooklyn/LitKicks.html> is an independent site created by New York writer Levi Asher devoted to the literature of the Beat generation. The site includes writings by Jack Kerouac, Allen Ginsberg, Neil Cassidy, and others; material on Beats, music, religion, and film; an extensive bibliography; biographical information; and photographs. For popular culture, George Lipsitz, *Time Passages* (1991), surveys postwar television, music, film, and popular culture, and his *Rainbow at Midnight* (2nd ed., 1994) looks at working-class culture and rock 'n' roll. Other treatments of the mass media include James L. Baughman, *The Republic of Mass Culture* (1992); Peter Biskind, *Seeing Is Believing* (1983); and Larry May, *The Big Tomorrow: Hollywood and the Politics of the American Way* (2000). Vance Packard's influential unmasking of the advertising industry, *The Hidden Persuaders* (1957), can be supplemented by Stephen Fox, *The Mirror Makers* (1984).

Richard Easterlin, *American Baby Boom in Historical Perspective* (1962), analyzes the demographic changes, as does Landon Y. Jones, *Great Expectations* (1980). Elaine May's *Homeward Bound* (1988) is the classic introduction to postwar family life, providing a historical corollary to Betty Friedan's *Feminine Mystique* (1963). Recent revisionist work challenging this view can be found in Joanne Meyerowitz, ed., *Not June Cleaver* (1994) and Daniel Horowitz, *Betty Friedan and the Making of the Feminine Mystique* (1998).

Youth culture is the subject of William Graeber's *Coming of Age in Buffalo* (1990). James Gilbert, *A Cycle of Outrage* (1986), looks at juvenile delinquency in the 1950s. Peter Guralnick, *Last Train to Memphis* (1994), is the definitive biography of Elvis Presley's early years. Discussions of cultural dissent in the 1950s can be found in Bruce Cook, *The Beat Generation* (1971), and Dan Wakefield, *New York in the Fifties* (1992).

The Other America

Reed Ueda, *Postwar Immigrant America* (1994), examines new trends in immigration since 1945. Jacqueline Jones compares black and white urban migrants in *The Dispossessed* (1992). Thomas Sugrue, *Origins of the Urban Crisis* (1996), analyzes the economic decline and racial antagonism that plagued postwar Detroit. Donald Fixico, *Termination and Relocation* (1986), looks at federal Indian policy from 1945 to 1970.

Jon C. Teaford, *Rough Road to Renaissance* (1990); John Mollenkopf, *The Contested City* (1983); and Kenneth Fox, *Metropolitan America* (1985), offer the most complete accounts of postwar urban development.

John F. Kennedy and the Politics of Expectation

The literature on the Kennedy years is voluminous. Among the best general accounts are Richard Reeves, *President Kennedy: Profile of Power* (1993); James Giglio, *The Presidency of JFK* (1991); David Burner, *JFK and a New Generation* (1988); and Jim F. Heath, *Decade of Disillusionment: The Kennedy-Johnson Years* (1975). Critical views appear in Seymour Hersh, *The Dark Side of Camelot* (1997); and David Halberstam, *The Best and the Brightest* (1972). The John F. Kennedy Library and Museum's site at <http://www.cs.umb.edu/jfklibrary/> provides a large collection of records from Kennedy's presidency. The Reference Desk area contains frequently requested information, including transcripts and recordings of JFK's speeches, a database of his executive orders, and a number of other resources.

On foreign policy in the Kennedy years, see Michael Beschloss, *The Crisis Years: Kennedy and Khrushchev, 1960–1963* (1990), and Thomas Paterson, *Kennedy's Quest for Victory* (1989). Ernest R. May and Philip D. Zelikow, eds., *The Kennedy Tapes: Inside the White House during the Cuban Missile Crisis* (1997), provide verbatim accounts of the Cuban missile crisis. The Avalon Project at the Yale Law School's site, "Foreign Relations of the United States: 1961–1963 Cuban Missile Crisis and Aftermath" at <http://www.yale.edu/lawweb/avalon/diplomacy/forrel/cuba/cubamenu.htm> contains almost 300 official documents related to the crisis, including State Department memoranda, records of telephone conversations, transcripts of conversations in the White House, and CIA reports. Secondary treatments include James Nathan, *The Cuban Missile Crisis Revisited* (1992), and Thomas Paterson, *Contesting Castro* (1994). Gerald Posner, *Case Closed* (1993), provides the most definitive treatment of the Kennedy assassination.

The best overviews of the postwar civil rights movement are Robert Weisbrot, *Freedom Bound* (1990); Harvard Sitkoff, *The Struggle for Black Equality* (2nd ed., 1993); and Clayborne Carson et al., *The Eyes on the Prize Civil Rights Reader* (1991). On the relationship between foreign policy and civil rights, see Mary L. Dudziak, *Cold War Civil Rights: Race and the Image of Democracy* (2000). Histories of the major civil rights organizations include Carson's study of SNCC, *In Struggle* (1981), and August Meier and Elliot Rudwick, *CORE* (1973). Doug McAdam, *Freedom Summer* (1988), describes the experiences of northern volunteers during Freedom Summer and Henry Hampton and Steve Fayer, *Voices of Freedom* (1990) is an oral history of the movement.

Local accounts of grassroots organizing include William H. Chafe's superb study of Greensboro, North Carolina, *Civilities and Civil Rights* (1980), and two recent studies of Mississippi: John Dittmer, *Local People* (1994), and Charles M. Payne, *I've Got the Light of Freedom* (1995). The role of women in the civil rights movement is examined in Vicki L. Crawford et al., *Women in the Civil Rights Movement: Trailblazers and*

Torchbearers, 1941–1965 (1990). Martin Luther King Jr. told his own story in *Why We Can't Wait* (1964). His biographers include David Garrow, *Bearing the Cross* (1986), and Taylor Branch, *Parting the Waters* (1988) and *Pillar of Fire* (1998).

Lyndon B. Johnson and the Great Society

Lyndon Johnson's account of his presidency can be found in *The Vantage Point* (1971). Doris Kearns Goodwin, *Lyndon Johnson and the American Dream* (1976), and Merle Miller, *Lyndon: An Oral Biography* (1980), are based on extensive conversations with LBJ. Robert A. Caro focuses on Johnson's early career in *The Path to Power* (1982) and *Means of Ascent* (1989); Robert Dallek offers his own exhaustive account in *Lone Star Rising* (1991) and *Flawed Giant* (1998). Irwin Unger, *The Best of Intentions: The Triumph and Failure of the Great Society under Kennedy, Johnson, and Nixon* (1996) offers a critical overview of that ambitious program.

Chapter 29: War Abroad and at Home: The Vietnam Era, 1961–1975

Among the best general accounts of the Vietnam War are George Herring, *America's Longest War* (3rd ed., 1996); Stanley Karnow, *Vietnam: A History* (rev. ed., 1991); and Marilyn Young, *The Vietnam Wars, 1945–1990* (1991). Guenter Lewy offers a controversial defense of American involvement in *America in Vietnam* (1978). A useful Vietnam site is edited by Professor Vincent Ferraro of Mount Holyoke College and includes state papers and official correspondence from 1941 to the fall of Saigon, <http://www.mtholyoke.edu/acad/intrel/vietnam.htm>.

Into the Quagmire, 1945–1968

The origins of American involvement in Vietnam are covered in Loren Baritz, *Backfire: A History of How American Culture Led Us into Vietnam* (1985); Larry Berman, *Planning a Tragedy* (1982); H. R. McMaster, *Dereliction of Duty: Johnson, McNamara, the Joint Chiefs of Staff, and the Lies That Led to Vietnam* (1998); Lloyd Gardner, *Approaching Vietnam* (1988); David Halberstam, *The Making of a Quagmire* (rev. ed., 1988); and Brian VanDeMark, *Into the Quagmire* (1991). A fascinating insight into Vietnam policymaking in the 1960s can be found in Neil Sheehan, *The Pentagon Papers* (1971). Secretary of Defense Robert McNamara offers an insider's view and belated apologia in *In Retrospect* (1995).

For a sense of what the war felt like to the soldiers who fought it, see Mark Baker, *Nam* (1982); Philip Caputo, *Rumor of War* (1977); Michael Herr, *Dispatches* (1977); and Tim O'Brien, *If I Die in a Combat Zone* (1973). Wallace Terry, *Bloods* (1984), surveys the experiences of black veterans, and Keith Walker, *A Piece of My Heart* (1985), introduces the often forgotten stories of the women who served in Vietnam. Christian G. Appy offers a class analysis of the Vietnam experience in *Working-Class War* (1993). Neil Sheehan surveys the entire Vietnam experience through the life of career soldier John Paul Vann in *A Bright and Shining Lie* (1988).

The Cold War Consensus Unravels

There are a growing number of survey works on the 1960s, including David Steigerwald, *The Sixties and the End of Modern America* (1995); Terry Anderson, *The Movement and the Sixties* (1994); David Farber, *The Age of Great Dreams: America in the 1960s* (1994); Todd Gitlin, *The Sixties: Years of Hope, Days of Rage* (1987); and Maurice Isserman and Michael Kazin, *America Divided: The Civil War of the 1960s* (2000). A valuable anthology is Alexander Bloom and Wini Breines, eds., *Takin' It to the Streets* (2nd ed., 2002). "The Sixties Project," which is hosted by the University of Virginia at Charlottesville, offers personal narratives, special exhibits, and a bibliography of articles published in "Vietnam Generation" at <http://lists.village.virginia.edu/sixties/>.

The student activism of the 1960s is the subject of dozens of eyewitness accounts and scholarly works. See Nathan Glazer, *Remembering the Answers* (1970); and Philip Slater, *The Pursuit of Loneliness* (1970). On student revolt see W. J. Rorabaugh, *Berkeley at War* (1989); Kirkpatrick Sale, *SDS* (1973); Wini Breines, *Community and Organization in the New Left, 1962–1968* (1982); and James Miller, *Democracy Is in the Streets* (1987). The University of California Library's site, "Free Speech Movement Digital Archive: Student Protest-U.C. Berkeley" at <http://bancroft.berkeley.edu/FSM/>, offers newsletters, oral histories, student newspaper accounts, legal defense material, and audio recordings, as well as good links to related sites. The definitive book on the antiwar movement is Charles DeBenedetti, with Charles Chatfield, *An American Ordeal* (1990).

Morris Dickstein, *Gates of Eden* (1977), is an excellent account of cultural developments in the 1960s. Other sources include Roger Kimball, *The Long March: How the Cultural Revolution of the 1960s Changed America* (2000); Theodore Roszak, *The Making of a Counter-Culture* (1969); and Charles Reich, *The Greening of America* (1970). Gerald Howard, ed., *The Sixties* (1982), is a good anthology of the decade's art, politics, and culture. Philip Norman, *Shout! The Beatles in Their Generation* (1981), and Jon Weiner, *Come Together: John Lennon in His Times* (1984), cover developments in popular music.

Major texts of the black power movement include Stokely Carmichael and Charles Hamilton, *Black Power* (1967); James Baldwin, *The Fire Next Time* (1963); and Eldridge Cleaver, *Soul on Ice* (1968). *The Autobiography of Malcolm X* (cowritten with Alex Haley, 1966) has become a black literary classic; it can be supplemented by Michael Eric Dyson, *Making Malcolm: The Myth and Meaning of Malcolm X* (1995). William L. Van Deburg, *New Day in Babylon* (1992), provides a general historical account of the black-power movement.

Report of the National Advisory Commission on Civil Disorders (1968) analyzes the decade's major race riots. See also Joe R. Feagin and Harlan Hahn, *Ghetto Revolts* (1973), and Robert Fogelson, *Violence as Protest* (1971). Sidney Fine's book on the Detroit riot, *Violence in the Model City* (1989), provides the most thorough historical treatment of race rioting in this period.

Carlos Muñoz Jr., *Youth, Identity and Power: The Chicano Movement* (1989), and Juan Gomez-Quiñones, *Chicano Politics* (1990), examine the rise of the Chicano movement in the 1960s. Peter Matthiessen, *In the Spirit of Crazy Horse* (1983), chronicles the American Indian Movement's ongoing conflict with the FBI and the federal government. Historians at the University of Michigan maintain "A Study and Timeline of the Lakota Nation" at <http://www-personal.umich.edu/~jamarcus/new/>, which includes material on the American Indian Movement, the occupation of Wounded Knee in 1973, and the confrontation at the Bureau of Indian Affairs office in 1972. Martin Duberman, *Stonewall* (1993), looks at the birth of the gay movement in the late 1960s.

General histories of women's activism in the 1960s include Cynthia Harrison, *On Account of Sex: The Politics of Women's Issues, 1945–1968* (1988), and Susan M. Hartmann, *From Margin to Mainstream: American Women and Politics since 1960* (1989). The revival of feminism is examined in Blanche Linden-Ward and Carol Hurd Green, *Changing the Future: American Women in the 1960s* (1992); Jo Freeman, *The Politics of Women's Liberation* (1975), and Judith Hole and Ellen Levine, *The Rebirth of Feminism* (1971). Sara Evans, *Personal Politics* (1979), traces the roots of feminism in the civil rights movement and the New Left.

The Long Road Home, 1968–1975

The Tet offensive is the subject of Don Oberdoffer's *Tet! The Turning Point in the Vietnam War* (1971). The domestic events of 1968 are covered in David Caute, *The Year of the Barricades* (1968), and David Farber, *Chicago '68* (1988). Norman Mailer provides a contemporary view of the national political conventions in *Miami and the Siege of Chicago* (1968). William C. Berman, *America's Right Turn* (2nd ed., 1998), chronicles the rightward shift in politics. Kevin Phillips, *The Emerging Republican Majority* (1969), and Richard Scammon and Ben J. Wattenberg, *The Real Majority* (1970), describe the voters Richard Nixon tried to reach. Dan Carter, *The Politics of Rage* (1996), examines the political career of George Wallace.

William Bundy, *The Tangled Web* (1998), and Robert S. Litwak, *Détente and the Nixon Doctrine* (1984), are overviews of Nixon's foreign policy. On his Vietnam policy, see the general works on Vietnam listed above as well as the highly critical study by William Shawcross, *Sideshow: Kissinger, Nixon, and the Destruction of Cambodia* (1979). An account of the My Lai massacre can be found in Seymour Hersh, *Cover-Up* (1972). Robert Jay Lifton, *Home from the War* (1973); Paul Starr, *The Discarded Army* (1973); and Lawrence Baskir and William A. Strauss, *Chance and Circumstance* (1978), discuss the problems of returning Vietnam veterans.

Chapter 30: The Lean Years, 1969–1980

Bruce J. Schulman, *The Seventies: The Great Shift in American Culture, Society, and Politics* (2001), provides a provocative overview of the political and cultural issues of the 1970s. For a popular history of the period, see Peter N. Carroll's *It Seemed Like Nothing Happened* (1982).

The Nixon Years

Herbert Parmet's *Richard Nixon and His America* (1990) and Stephen Ambrose's three-volume *Nixon* (1987, 1991) are two of many biographies of a complex political leader. Kim McQuaid, *The Anxious Years: America in the Vietnam-Watergate Era* (1989), is an overview of the Nixon era. See also Garry Wills, *Nixon Agonistes* (rev. ed., 1990), and Nixon's own recollections in *RN: The Memoirs of Richard Nixon* (1978). On Nixon's economic policies, see Allen J. Matusow, *Nixon's Economy: Booms, Busts, Dollars, and Votes* (1998). On the Warren Court, see Morton J. Horwitz, *The Warren Court and the Pursuit of Justice: A Critical Issue* (1998).

Stanley Kutler, *The Wars of Watergate* (1990); Anthony Lukas, *Nightmare: The Underside of the Nixon Years* (1976); and Theodore H. White, *Breach of Faith* (1975), are comprehensive accounts of the Watergate scandal. For the Watergate scandal, a useful Web site is the National Archives and Record Administration's "Watergate Trial Tapes and Transcripts" at <http://www.archives.gov/nixon/tapes/tapes.html>, which provides transcripts of the infamous tapes as well as other useful links to archival holdings concerning Richard Nixon's presidency. Also of interest are the books by the *Washington Post* journalists who broke the story, Carl Bernstein and Bob Woodward: *All the President's Men* (1974) and *The Final Days* (1976). Stanley Kutler, *Abuse of Power: The New Nixon Tapes* (1997), is a collection of transcripts from the White House tapes relating to Watergate and other Nixon-era scandals.

An Economy of Diminished Expectations

Barry Commoner, *The Poverty of Power* (1976), and Robert Heilbroner, *An Inquiry into the Human Prospect* (1974), cogently assess the origins of the energy crisis and the prospects for the future. See also Lester C. Thurow, *The Zero-Sum Society* (1980), and Robert Stobaugh and Daniel Yergin, *Energy Future* (1980). Daniel Yergin, *The Prize* (1991), and John M. Blair, *The Control of Oil* (1976), treat OPEC developments.

General introductions to the economic developments of the decade are Barry Bluestone and Bennett Harrison, *The Deindustrialization of America* (1982); Richard J. Barnet and Ronald E. Muller, *Global Reach* (1974); Richard J. Barnet, *The Lean Years* (1980); John P. Hoerr, *And the Wolf Finally Came: The Decline of the Steel Industry* (1988); and Robert Calleo, *The Imperious Economy* (1982).

Reform and Reaction in the 1970s

Tom Wolfe gave the decade its name in "The Me Decade and the Third Great Awakening," *New York Magazine* (August 23, 1976). Influential books include Christopher Lasch, *The Culture of Narcissism* (1978), and Gail Sheehy, *Passages* (1976).

For a general overview of the environmental movement, see Samuel P. Hays, *Beauty, Health, and Permanence: Environmental Politics in the United States, 1955–1985* (1987). Roderick Nash provides a history of environmental ethics in *The Rights of Nature* (1989). Books that were influential in shaping public awareness of ecological issues include Rachel Carson, *Silent Spring* (1962); Paul R. Ehrlich, *The Population Bomb* (1968); Frances Moore Lappé, *Diet for a Small Planet* (1971); and Philip Slater, *Earthwalk* (1974). Lois Marie Gibbs describes her experience with the Love Canal crisis in *Love Canal: My Story* (1982). Charles McCarry chronicles Ralph Nader's crusade for consumer protection in *Citizen Nader* (1972).

On women and feminism in the 1970s, see Alice Echols, *Daring to Be Bad* (1989); Susan M. Hartmann, *From Margin to Mainstream: American Women and Politics since 1960*

(1989); and Winifred D. Wandersee, *On the Move: American Women in the 1970s* (1988). "Documents from the Women's Liberation Movement," culled from the Duke University Special Collections Library, emphasizes the women's movement of the late 1960s and early 1970s. This searchable site at <http://scriptorium.lib.duke.edu/wlm/> includes books, pamphlets, and other written materials on categories that include theoretical writings, reproductive health, women of color, and women's work and roles. Donald G. Mathews and Jane S. De Hart analyze the struggle over the ERA in *Sex, Gender, and the Politics of ERA* (1990), and Carol Felsenthal examines the life of the ERA opponent Phyllis Schlafly in *The Sweetheart of the Silent Majority* (1981). David Garrow, *Liberty and Sexuality: The Right to Privacy and the Making of Roe v. Wade* (1994), is an in-depth examination of the 1973 abortion decision. On the public abortion debate, see Faye Ginsberg, *Contested Lives* (1989), and Kristen Luker, *Abortion and the Politics of Motherhood* (1984). The Oyez Project at Northwestern University at <http://oyez.nwu.edu/> is an invaluable resource for over 1,000 Supreme Court cases, with audio transcripts, voting records, and summaries. For this period, see, for example, its materials on *Roe v. Wade, Bakke v. University of California,* and *Griswold v. Connecticut.*

Leigh W. Rutledge surveys the gay and lesbian movement in *The Gay Decades: From Stonewall to the Present* (1992). Thomas Byrne Edsall with Mary D. Edsall, *Chain Reaction: The Impact of Race, Rights and Taxes on American Politics* (1991), examines some of the divisive social issues of the 1970s. J. Anthony Lukas, *Common Ground* (1985), tells the story of the Boston busing crisis through the biographies of three families. Paul Moreno, *From Direct Action to Affirmative Action* (1997); Robert J. Weiss, *We Want Jobs* (1997); and Lydia Chavez, *The Color Blind* (1998), treat the controversial topic of affirmative action.

Alan Crawford, *Thunder on the Right* (1980), and Jerome L. Himmelstein, *To the Right: The Transformation of American Conservatism* (1990) survey the new conservatism. John Woodridge, *The Evangelicals* (1975), analyzes the rise of evangelical religion, and Quentin J. Schultze looks at evangelicals' use of the media in *Televangelism and American Culture* (1991). On the political role of the Christian right, see Michael Liensch, *Redeeming America: Piety and Politics in the New Christian Right* (1993).

Politics in the Wake of Watergate

John R. Greene examines the Ford administration in *The Presidency of Gerald R. Ford* (1995), as do James Cannon, *Time and Chance: Gerald Ford's Appointment with History* (1993), and Richard Reeves, *A Ford, Not a Lincoln* (1975).

Peter G. Bourne, *Jimmy Carter* (1997), is a comprehensive biography. Generally unfavorable portraits of the Carter presidency are found in Burton Kaufman, *The Presidency of James Earl Carter Jr.* (1993); Robert Shogan, *Promises to Keep* (1977); and Haynes Johnson, *In the Absence of Power* (1980). See also Gary M. Fink, ed., *The Carter Presidency: Policy Choices in the Post–New Deal Era* (1998); Erwin Hargrove, *Jimmy Carter as President* (1989); Charles Jones, *The Trusteeship Presidency* (1988); and Jimmy Carter's presidential memoirs, *Keeping Faith* (rev. ed., 1995). James Fallows, *National Defense* (1981),

provides an incisive overview of defense developments. See also A. Glenn Mower Jr., *Human Rights and American Foreign Policy: The Carter and Reagan Experiences* (1987). Gary Sick, *All Fall Down: America's Tragic Encounter with Iran* (1986), provides an account of the Iranian hostage crisis, and Jack Germond, *Blue Smoke and Mirrors* (1981), examines the presidential election of 1980.

Chapter 31: A New Domestic and World Order, 1981–2001

Few historians have turned their attention to the period after 1980, leaving the field to journalists, economists, and political scientists. The Bureau of the Census offers a fine introduction to the period in its *Statistical Abstract of the United States* (117th ed., 1997). Essays on important issues are available in the *Congressional Quarterly Researcher.*

The Reagan-Bush Years, 1981–1993

Haynes Johnson, *Sleepwalking through History* (1991), provides an excellent overview of America in the Reagan years. See also Michael Rogin, *Ronald Reagan: The Movie* (1987); Lou Cannon, *President Reagan: A Role of a Lifetime* (1991); Michael Schaller, *Reckoning with Reagan: America and Its President in the 1980s* (1992); and Peggy Noonan, *What I Saw at the Revolution* (1990).

On Reaganomics, George Gilder's *Wealth and Poverty* (1981) represents the views held by many in the Reagan administration, but David Stockman's memoir, *The Triumph of Politics* (1986), is more revealing. See also Benjamin Friedman, *Day of Reckoning: The Consequences of American Economic Policy under Reagan and After* (1988).

On the Bush administration, see James A. Baker, *The Politics of Diplomacy* (1995), and Stephen R. Graubard, *Mr. Bush's War: Adventures in the Politics of Illusion* (1992). "The Gulf War" at <http://www.pbs.org/wgbh/pages/frontline/gulf/> is an online documentary treatment of the Gulf War conflict. A companion to the Gulf War documentary produced by the PBS series *Frontline*, the site includes maps, a chronology, interviews with decision makers and soldiers from the various sides of the conflict, audio clips, and a section on weapons and technology. On politics, see E. J. Dionne, *Why Americans Hate Politics* (1992); William Greider, *Who Will Tell the People?* (1992); and Kevin Phillips, *The Politics of Rich and Poor: Wealth and the American Electorate in the Reagan Aftermath* (1990).

Foreign Relations under Reagan and Bush

For foreign policy, Stephen Ambrose and Douglas Brinkley, *Rise to Globalism* (8th ed., 1997), provide a comprehensive overview of the Reagan and Bush years. The Iran-Contra scandal is covered in Jane Hunter et al., *The Iran-Contra Connection* (1987). Good introductions to U.S. foreign relations with Central and South America include Walter La Feber, *Inevitable Revolutions* (1984), and Thomas Carothers, *In the Name of Democracy: U.S. Policy toward Latin America in the Reagan Years* (1991).

The emergence of a new world order has provoked commentary from economists, journalists, and historians, including

Paul Kennedy, *The Rise and Fall of the Great Powers* (1987); Joseph Nye, *Bound to Lead: The Changing Nature of American Power* (1990); Robert Kuttner, *The End of Laissez Faire* (1991); and Henry R. Nau, *The Myth of America's Decline* (1990). See also Michael Beschloss and Strobe Talbott, *At the Highest Levels: The Inside Story of the End of the Cold War* (1994), and Michael J. Hogan, ed., *The End of the Cold War: Its Meanings and Implications* (1992).

Uncertain Times: Economic and Social Trends, 1980–2000

Paul Krugman, *Peddling Prosperity: Economic Sense and Nonsense in the Age of Diminished Expectations* (1994), and Jeffrey Madrick, *The End of Affluence* (1995), provide overviews of economic trends since the 1970s. Lester C. Thurow offers an insightful analysis of the world economic changes accompanying the collapse of communism in *The Future of Capitalism* (1996). For overviews of U.S. competitiveness in the global marketplace, see Daniel Yergin and Joseph Stanislaw, *The Commanding Heights* (1998); Hedrick Smith, *Rethinking America* (1995). Books that address the growing inequality in American life include William J. Wilson, *The Truly Disadvantaged* (1987); Nicholas Lemann, *The Promised Land* (1989); and Andrew Hacker, *Two Nations: Black and White, Separate, Hostile, Unequal* (1992).

On women, work, and families, see Hilda Scott, *Working Your Way to the Bottom: The Feminization of Poverty* (1985), and Arlie Hochschild, *The Second Shift: Working Parents and the Revolution at Home* (1989). For feminism and its critics, see Susan Faludi, *Backlash: The Undeclared War on American Women* (1991). Toni Morrison, ed., *Race-ing Justice, En-Gendering Power* (1992), covers the Clarence Thomas–Anita Hill hearings.

David Reimers, *Still the Golden Door* (2nd ed., 1992), covers immigration policy in the postwar period. Roberto Suro, *Strangers among Us* (1998), shows how Latino immigration is transforming America. Ronald Takaki, *Strangers from a Different Shore* (1989), covers Asian Americans. On race and politics in California since 1978, see Peter Schrag, *Paradise Lost* (1998).

Randy Shilts, *And the Band Played On: Politics, People, and the AIDS Epidemic* (1987), is a controversial critique of inaction in the early years of the AIDS epidemic. Allan Bloom, *The Closing of the American Mind* (1987), and E. D. Hirsch Jr., *Cultural Literacy* (1988), deal with issues of curriculum, learning, and literacy. Lawrence W. Levine, *The Opening of the American Mind* (1996), challenges many of their assumptions. For differing views on affirmative action, see Stephen L. Carter, *Reflections of an Affirmative Action Baby* (1991), and Gertrude Ezorsky, *Racism and Justice: The Case for Affirmative Action* (1991). Gregg Easterbrook provides a general overview of the environment in *A Moment on the Earth* (1995). Daniel Yergin, *The Prize* (1991), chronicles how oil dominates modern life, with both economic and environmental consequences. The Gallup

Organization has been conducting public opinion surveys since 1935. Its site at <http://www.gallup.com> provides access to recent polls on politics, family, religion, crime, and lifestyle. This searchable site is an invaluable guide to contemporary American opinion. The United States Census Bureau's Web page at <http://www.census.gov/population/www/index.html> offers a rich variety of data—on health insurance, racial and ethnic composition, poverty, work environment, and marriage and family—providing insight into the major demographic changes transforming American society.

For the story of Bill Gates and Microsoft, see Steven Manes, *Gates* (1993), and James Wallace, *Hard Drive* (1992). Also of interest is Joshua Quittner and Michelle Slatalla, *Speeding the Net: The Inside Story of Netscape and How It Challenged Microsoft* (1998). For biotechnology, see Robert Cook-Deegan, *The Gene Wars* (1994); Arthur Kornberg, *The Golden Helix: Inside Biotech Ventures* (1996); and Eric S. Grace, *Biotechnology Unzipped* (1997).

Restructuring the Domestic Order: Public Life, 1992–2001

For an excellent overview of the Clinton administration's first year, see Elizabeth Drew, *Finding His Voice* (1994). Other sources include Joe Klein, *The Natural: The Misunderstood Presidency of Bill Clinton* (2002), and Roger Morris, *Partners in Power: The Clintons and Their America* (1996). Jurist, the Law Professors' Network, provides a "Guide to Impeachment and Censure Materials Online" at <http://jurist.law.pitt.edu/impeach.htm>, which offers extensive links to materials on the constitutional issues raised by impeachment and on public opinion polls, documents, and analysis specific to the Clinton impeachment. Richard Holbrooke, *To End a War* (1998), provides a compelling insider's account of the Dayton peace talks on Bosnia. William Greider, *Fortress America* (1998), examines the American military in the post–cold war era. On the Republican agenda, see Newt Gingrich, *To Renew America* (1995). See also Dan Balz and Ronald Brownstein, *Storming the Gates: Protest Politics and the Republican Revival* (1996), and Ralph Reed, *Active Faith: How Christians Are Changing the Soul of American Politics* (1996). On the 2000 election, see Alan M. Dershowitz, *Supreme Injustice: How the High Court Hijacked Election 2000*, and Bruce Akerman, ed., *Bush v. Gore: The Question of Legitimacy* (2002).

"The September 11 Digital Archive" at <http://911digitalarchive.org/> is cosponsored by the American Social History Project at the City University of New York Graduate Center and the Center for History and New Media at George Mason University. The site is part of an ongoing project to collect and preserve firsthand accounts of Americans' responses to the terrorist attack of September 11, 2001. The site includes oral histories, video and still images, and a valuable guide to Web sites on the topic.

Chapter 15
Voices from Abroad: David Macrae, "The Devastated South." From *America through British Eyes* by Allan Nevins, editor. Copyright © 1968 by Allan Nevins. Reprinted by permission of Peter Smith Publisher, Inc.

American Voices: Jourdon Anderson, "Relishing Freedom." From pp. 4–6 in *Looking for America*, Second Edition, Volume 1, by Stanley I. Kutler. Copyright © 1979, 1976 by Stanley I. Kutler. Used by permission of W. W. Norton & Company, Inc.

Chapter 16
American Voices: Ida Lindgren, "Swedish Emigrant in Frontier Kansas." From *Letters from the Promised Land: Swedes in America, 1840–1914* by H. Arnold Barton, editor. Copyright © 1975 by H. Arnold Barton. Reprinted by permission of the University of Minnesota Press.

Fig. 16.1. "Freight Rates for Transporting Nebraska Crops." Adapted from data on p. 352 in *The Nation Transformed* by Sigmund Diamond, editor. Reprinted by permission of George Braziller, Inc.

Chapter 18
Fig. 18.2. "Distributions of Weekly Wages for Black and White Workers in Virginia, 1907." Adapted from p. 184 in *Old South, New South: Revolutions in the Southern Economy since the Civil War* by Gavin Wright. Copyright © 1986 by Gavin Wright. Reprinted by permission of Basic Books, a division of Perseus Books Group.

Chapter 19
Voices from Abroad: José Martí, "Coney Island, 1881." Excerpt from *The America of José Martí: Selected Writings* by José Martí, and translated by Juan de Onis. Copyright © 1954 by Juan de Onis. Reprinted by permission.

Chapter 20
American Voices: Charles Edward Russell, "Muckraking." From *Bare Hands and Stone Walls* by Charles Edward Russell. Copyright © 1933 by Charles Scribner's Sons. Copyright © renewed 1961 by Charles Edward Russell. Reprinted by permission of Scribner, an imprint of Simon & Schuster Adult Publishing Group.

American Voices: Dr. Alice Hamilton, "Tracking Down Lead Poisoning." From *Exploring the Dangerous Trades: The Autobiography of Alice Hamilton* by Alice Hamilton. Copyright © 1943 by Alice Hamilton. Reprinted by permission of Little, Brown and Company.

Voices from Abroad: James Bryce, "Business Is King." Excerpt from pp. 384–87 in *America through British Eyes* by Allan Nevins, editor. Copyright © 1968 by Allan Nevins. Reprinted by permission of Peter Smith Publisher, Inc.

Fig. 20.1: "Growth in Federal Employees." From p. 41 in *The Federal Government Service*, edited by W. S. Sayre. The American Assembly, Prentice-Hall, Englewood Cliffs, NJ.

Chapter 21
American Voices: George W. Prioleau, "Black Soldiers in a White Man's War." Excerpt from *Smoked Yankees and the Struggle for Empire, 1898–1902* by Willard B. Gatewood. Copyright © 1987 by the Board of Trustees of the University of Arkansas. Reprinted by permission of the University of Arkansas Press.

Voices from Abroad: Jean Hess, Émile Zola, Ruben Dario. Excerpts from *The Anti-Imperialist Reader: A Documentary History of Anti-Imperialism in the United States,* volume 1, edited by Philip S. Foner and Robert C. Winchester. Copyright © 1984 by Holmes and Meier Publishers, Inc. Reproduced with the permission of the publisher. From *Major Problems in American Foreign Relations*, 2 volumes, by Thomas G. Paterson and Dennis Merrill, eds., and from *Selected Poems of Ruben Dario*, translated by Lysander Kemp. Copyright © 1965; renewed 1993 by Lysander Kemp. Reprinted by permission of the University of Texas Press.

Chapter 24
Song lyrics from *Duck Soup*. Four lines from "Freedom Hymn" written by Burt Kalmar and Harry Ruby and sung by Groucho Marx in the movie *Duck Soup*. Copyright © 1933 by Famous Music Corporation. Reprinted with permission.

American Voices: Larry Van Dusen, "A Working-Class Family Encounters the Great Depression." From *Hard Times* by Studs Terkel. Copyright 1986 by Studs Terkel. Reprinted by permission of Donadio & Olson, Inc.

Chapter 27

Voices from Abroad: Mary Agnes Hamilton, "Breadlines and Beggars." Excerpt from pp. 443–44 in *America through British Eyes* by Allan Nevins, editor. Copyright © 1968 by Allan Nevins. Reprinted by permission of Peter Smith Publisher, Inc.

Chapter 25
American Voices: Joe Marcus, "A New Deal Activist." From *Hard Times* by Studs Terkel. Copyright 1986 by Studs Terkel. Reprinted by permission of Donadio & Olson, Inc.

American Voices: Susana Archuleta, "A Chicana Youth Gets New Deal Work." From "But I Remember Susana Archuleta" in *Las Mujeres: Conversations from a Hispanic Community* by Nan Elsasser, Kyle MacKenzie, and Yvonne Tixier y Vigil. Copyright © 1980 by The Feminist Press at The City University of New York. Reprinted by permission of the publisher.

Chapter 26
American Voices: Monica Sone, "Japanese Relocation." Excerpt from pp. 176–78 in *Nisei Daughter* by Monica Sone. Copyright 1953; renewed 1981 by Monica Sone. Reprinted by permission of Little, Brown and Company.

A note about the index: Names of individuals appear in boldface; biographical dates are included for major historical figures. Letters in parentheses following pages refer to: *(f)* figures, including charts and graphs; *(i)* illustrations, including photographs and artifacts; *(m)* maps; and *(t)* tables.

American vs. European, 546
amusements in, 566–569
in art and literature, 570
decaying inner, 820, 825, 829–830,
847, 914, 924
Democratic Party and, 667, 718,
732, 762
flapper in, 678
gay communities in, 894
Great Depression protests in, 717
growth of, 544–545, 545(m), 571,
819(m)
high culture in, 569–571
immigrants in, 543, 543(i),
557, 920
industrialization and, 457
Korean immigrants in, 920(i)
Ku Klux Klan in, 684, 685(m)
liberalism in, 668
life in, 556–571
lighting of, 547–548
mass media and, 677
Mexican Americans in, 711
move to suburbs from, 815, 817
1928 election and, 692
1932 election and, 718
political machines in, 667
population growth and, 543
population shift to, 681, 681(m),
724, 825, 828–830
poverty in, 924
private/public, 548–549
Prohibition in, 688
riots in, 660, 660(i), 764, 849,
861–862, 862(m), 867, 869,
877, 924
skyscrapers in, 547
sprawl of, 821
Summer of Love (1967) in, 860
in Sun Belt, 818
ten largest U.S., 544(t)
transportation in, 546–547,
546(i), 571
urban development and, 841(t), 842
urban renewal and, 829–830, 880
voting districts and, 881
Citizens Clearinghouse for Hazardous
Waste, 891
Civil Aeronautics Act (1938), 682
Civil Defense Agency, 783(i), 807(i)
Civilian Conservation Corps (CCC),
724, 730(m), 731(t)
environment and, 741
Mexican Americans and, 739
Native Americans and, 740
WWII and, 761
civil liberties, 801(i), 946–947
civil rights
conservative opposition to, 846, 925
Eisenhower and, 805
federal government and, 816

Fourteenth Amendment and,
435–437, 438(t), 519, 525, 529
Fifteenth Amendment and,
438–439, 438(t), 525, 529–530,
530(i), 589–591
for homosexuals, 864–865, 867, 877
JFK and, 830, 840
LBJ and, 840–842, 847
legislation on, 841(t)
for Mexican Americans, 863, 877
for Native Americans, 863–864, 877
New Deal and, 735, 746
in 1970s, 905
1972 election and, 881
1980 election and, 903
Nixon and, 880
nonviolent protest and, 805
Truman and, 804
for women, 864–867, 877
WWII and, 750, 760–761, 760(i),
765–767, 777
Civil Rights Act (1866), 431, 435–436,
438(t)
Civil Rights Act (1964), 840, 841(t)
Title IX and, 889
women and, 866
Civil Rights Bill (1870), 449
Civil Rights Commission, National, 804
civil rights movement, 836–839,
836(m), 838(i), 842(i), 847, 856,
860–867, 935, 939
African Americans and, 804, 806,
856, 860–863, 862(m), 877
anticommunism and, 800
cold war and, 784, 797–798, 804,
806–807
conflicts within, 839
federal government and, 813, 838
Freedom Summer and, 857, 866
Harlem Renaissance and, 691
in 1970s, 894
school busing and, 869
sit-ins and, 836–837
television and, 838, 842
violence against, 839
WWII and, 761
Civil Service Commission, 516
civil service reform, 449, 516–517
Civil War (1861–1865)
financing of, 537
Reconstruction and, 429–430, 451
religion and, 452
roles of France and Britain in, 604
warships of, 610–611
Civil Works Administration (CWA),
725–726, 731(t)
Native Americans and, 740
women and, 735
Clark, Champ, 597(i)
Clarke, Edward H., 555
class. *See* social structure

class-action suits, 889
Clayton Antitrust Act (1914), 599
Clean Air Act (1970), 889
Clemenceau, Georges, 658
Clemens, Samuel. *See* Twain, Mark
Cleveland, Grover (1837–1908), 592
election of 1884 and, 518, 523
election of 1888 and, 515(i)
as president (1885–1889;
1893–1897), 516–518, 516(i),
520, 520(i), 535, 538, 605,
612–613
Pullman boycott and, 510–511, 538
as reformer, 518
The Cliff-Dwellers (Fuller), 570
Clifford, Clark, 798(m)
Clinton, Bill (William Jefferson; 1946–)
approval rating of, 932
balanced budget and, 931(i)
big government and, 930
first term of, 928
gays in the military and, 928
impeachment of, 931–932, 937, 948
Kyoto Treaty and, 927
scandals in administration of,
930–932, 934
welfare system and, 779, 779(i)
Clinton, Hilary Rodham, 929, 929(i)
coal mining, 487, 487(m), 489, 497,
513, 587
breaker boys and, 501(i)
decline of (1920s), 668
strikes and, 599
Coast Guard, 947
women in, 758
Cody, William F. (Buffalo Bill), 461
biographical information, 462–463,
463(i)
Cohan, George M., 643
Cohen, Lizabeth, 673
Colbert, Claudette, 762
Colby, William, 874
cold war, 452, 783–813, 871–872, 948
affluent society and, 815
in Afghanistan, 941
arms race in, 834
assessment of, 939
beginning of, 790
Berlin Wall and, 833
civil rights movement and, 784,
797–798, 804, 806–807
Cuba in, 833, 834(m)
domino effect and, 850, 855
economy and, 847
end of, 907, 912, 932(m), 937
in Europe, 788, 788(m)
impact of, 807–812
Iran and, 902
JFK and, 847
in Middle East, 796–797
nuclear test ban treaties and, 834